Dictionary
of the
Middle Ages

AMERICAN COUNCIL OF LEARNED SOCIETIES

The American Council of Learned Societies, organized in 1919 for the purpose of advancing the study of the humanities and of the humanistic aspects of the social sciences, is a nonprofit federation comprising forty-five national scholarly groups. The Council represents the humanities in the United States in the International Union of Academies, provides fellowships and grants-in-aid, supports research-and-planning conferences and symposia, and sponsors special projects and scholarly publications.

MEMBER ORGANIZATIONS
AMERICAN PHILOSOPHICAL SOCIETY, 1743
AMERICAN ACADEMY OF ARTS AND SCIENCES, 1780
AMERICAN ANTIQUARIAN SOCIETY, 1812
AMERICAN ORIENTAL SOCIETY, 1842
AMERICAN NUMISMATIC SOCIETY, 1858
AMERICAN PHILOLOGICAL ASSOCIATION, 1869
ARCHAEOLOGICAL INSTITUTE OF AMERICA, 1879
SOCIETY OF BIBLICAL LITERATURE, 1880
MODERN LANGUAGE ASSOCIATION OF AMERICA, 1883
AMERICAN HISTORICAL ASSOCIATION, 1884
AMERICAN ECONOMIC ASSOCIATION, 1885
AMERICAN FOLKLORE SOCIETY, 1888
AMERICAN DIALECT SOCIETY, 1889
AMERICAN PSYCHOLOGICAL ASSOCIATION, 1892
ASSOCIATION OF AMERICAN LAW SCHOOLS, 1900
AMERICAN PHILOSOPHICAL ASSOCIATION, 1901
AMERICAN ANTHROPOLOGICAL ASSOCIATION, 1902
AMERICAN POLITICAL SCIENCE ASSOCIATION, 1903
BIBLIOGRAPHICAL SOCIETY OF AMERICA, 1904
ASSOCIATION OF AMERICAN GEOGRAPHERS, 1904
HISPANIC SOCIETY OF AMERICA, 1904
AMERICAN SOCIOLOGICAL ASSOCIATION, 1905
AMERICAN SOCIETY OF INTERNATIONAL LAW, 1906
ORGANIZATION OF AMERICAN HISTORIANS, 1907
AMERICAN ACADEMY OF RELIGION, 1909
COLLEGE ART ASSOCIATION OF AMERICA, 1912
HISTORY OF SCIENCE SOCIETY, 1924
LINGUISTIC SOCIETY OF AMERICA, 1924
MEDIAEVAL ACADEMY OF AMERICA, 1925
AMERICAN MUSICOLOGICAL SOCIETY, 1934
SOCIETY OF ARCHITECTURAL HISTORIANS, 1940
ECONOMIC HISTORY ASSOCIATION, 1940
ASSOCIATION FOR ASIAN STUDIES, 1941
AMERICAN SOCIETY FOR AESTHETICS, 1942
AMERICAN ASSOCIATION FOR THE ADVANCEMENT OF SLAVIC STUDIES, 1948
METAPHYSICAL SOCIETY OF AMERICA, 1950
AMERICAN STUDIES ASSOCIATION, 1950
RENAISSANCE SOCIETY OF AMERICA, 1954
SOCIETY FOR ETHNOMUSICOLOGY, 1955
AMERICAN SOCIETY FOR LEGAL HISTORY, 1956
AMERICAN SOCIETY FOR THEATRE RESEARCH, 1956
SOCIETY FOR THE HISTORY OF TECHNOLOGY, 1958
AMERICAN COMPARATIVE LITERATURE ASSOCIATION, 1960
AMERICAN SOCIETY FOR EIGHTEENTH-CENTURY STUDIES, 1969
ASSOCIATION FOR JEWISH STUDIES, 1969

The Temptation of Christ on the Mountain. Panel painting by Duccio di Buoninsegna, leading Sienese artist of the early *trecento*. COPYRIGHT THE FRICK COLLECTION, NEW YORK

Dictionary of the Middle Ages

JOSEPH R. STRAYER, *EDITOR IN CHIEF*

Volume 12

THADDEUS LEGEND—ZWART^cNOC^c

CHARLES SCRIBNER'S SONS • NEW YORK

Copyright © 1989 American Council of Learned Societies

Library of Congress Cataloging in Publication Data
Main entry under title:

Dictionary of the Middle Ages.

Includes bibliographies and index.
1. Middle Ages—Dictionaries.   I. Strayer,
Joseph Reese, 1904–1987

D114.D5	1982	909.07		82-5904
ISBN 0-684-16760-3 (v. 1)			ISBN 0-684-18169-X (v. 7)	
ISBN 0-684-17022-1 (v. 2)			ISBN 0-684-18274-2 (v. 8)	
ISBN 0-684-17023-X (v. 3)			ISBN 0-684-18275-0 (v. 9)	
ISBN 0-684-17024-8 (v. 4)			ISBN 0-684-18276-9 (v. 10)	
ISBN 0-684-18161-4 (v. 5)			ISBN 0-684-18277-7 (v. 11)	
ISBN 0-684-18168-1 (v. 6)			ISBN 0-684-18278-5 (v. 12)	

Published simultaneously in Canada
by Collier Macmillan Canada, Inc.
Copyright under the Berne convention.

1 3 5 7 9 11 13 15 17 19   Q/C   20 18 16 14 12 10 8 6 4 2

PRINTED IN THE UNITED STATES OF AMERICA.

The *Dictionary of the Middle Ages* has been produced with
support from the National Endowment for the Humanities.

The paper in this book meets the guidelines for
permanence and durability of the Committee on
Production Guidelines for Book Longevity of the
Council on Library Resources.

Maps prepared by Patricia A. Rodriguez and Sylvia Lehrman.

Editorial Board

Advisory Committee

Editorial Staff

Contributors to Volume 12

MARILYN McCORD ADAMS
University of California,
Los Angeles
UNIVERSALS

F. R. P. AKEHURST
University of Minnesota
TROUBADOUR, TROUVÈRE

JAMES W. ALEXANDER
University of Georgia
WALES: MARCHER LORDS

MICHAEL ALTSCHUL
Case Western Reserve
University
WILLIAM MARSHAL

GEORGE R. ANDERSON
Brown University
WANDERING JEW LEGEND

THEODORE M. ANDERSSON
Stanford University
ÞIÐREKS SAGA:
VǪLSUNGA SAGA

MICHAEL ANGOLD
University of Edinburgh
THEODORE I LASKARIS;
THEODORE II LASKARIS

CHARLES M. ATKINSON
Ohio State University
TROPES TO THE ORDINARY OF
THE MASS

SUSAN M. BABBITT
American Philosophical Society
VILLEHARDOUIN, GEOFFROI DE;
WILLIAM OF TYRE

JERE L. BACHARACH
University of Washington
TULUNIDS

JULIE O. BADIEE
WAQ-WAQ ISLANDS

TERENCE BAILEY
Talbot College, University of
Western Ontario
TONES, MUSICAL

REBECCA A. BALTZER
University of Texas at Austin
WOLFENBÜTTEL, HELMSTEDT
MS 628

FRANK G. BANTA
Indiana University
WERNHER DER GARTENÆRE

JOHN W. BARKER
University of Wisconsin, Madison
THESSALONIKI; ZEALOTS

CARL F. BARNES, JR.
Oakland University,
Rochester, Michigan
THOMAS DE CORMONT; TOWER;
TRIBUNE; TRICLINIUM; VÉZELAY,
CHURCH OF LA MADELEINE;
VILLARD DE HONNECOURT;
WHEEL OF FORTUNE; WHEEL
WINDOW; WILLIAM OF
VOLPIANO; WYSBECK, JOHN;
YEVELE, HENRY

ROBERT BEDROSIAN
TᶜOVMA MECOPᶜECᶜI; VARDAN
AREWELCᶜI; ZAKᶜARIDS

JOHN BEELER
University of North Carolina
WARFARE, WESTERN EUROPEAN

JEANETTE M. A. BEER
Purdue University
VEGETIUS

JOHN F. BENTON
California Institute of
Technology
TROTA AND TROTULA

ROSALIND KENT BERLOW
TRADE, REGULATION OF;
WINE AND WINEMAKING

CAROL MANSON BIER
The Textile Museum,
Washington, D.C.
ZANDANĪJĪ

IRENE A. BIERMAN
University of California,
Los Angeles
ṬIRĀZ

SOLOMON A. BIRNBAUM
YIDDISH

GHAZI E. BISHEH
Jordan Archaeological Museum
ZAMZAM

DALE L. BISHOP
Interchurch Center, New York
VIDĒVDĀD; YAŠTS; ZURVANISM

RENATE BLUMENFELD-
KOSINSKI
Columbia University
TROY STORY

PATRICIA J. BOEHNE
Eastern College
TURMEDA, ANSELM

CLIFFORD E. BOSWORTH
University of Manchester
TRANSOXIANA;
YAᶜQŪB IBN LAYTH

MARY BOYCE
ZOROASTRIANISM

CLEO LELAND BOYD
YORK RITE

MARJORIE NICE BOYER
York College,
City University of New York
TRAVEL AND TRANSPORT,
WESTERN EUROPEAN;
VEHICLES, EUROPEAN

CONTRIBUTORS TO VOLUME 12

LEONARD E. BOYLE
*Pontifical Institute of Mediaeval
Studies, Toronto*
VACARIUS

KATHLEEN J. BRAHNEY
*Michigan Technological
University*
THIBAUT DE CHAMPAGNE

YURI BREGEL
Indiana University
TIMURIDS; ULUGH BEG

MICHAEL BRETT
University of London
WARFARE, ISLAMIC; ZIRIDS

STEPHEN F. BROWN
Boston College
THEOLOGY, SCHOOLS OF

ROBERT BROWNING
THEODORA I, EMPRESS;
TRANSLATION AND TRANSLATORS,
BYZANTINE; UNIVERSITIES,
BYZANTINE

LESLIE BRUBAKER
*Wheaton College,
Norton, Massachusetts*
THEODORE; TRIBELON;
TRIPTYCH; TRULLA; VELLUM;
VISITATION; VOLTO SANTO;
WESTWORK; WOLVINUS

JAMES A. BRUNDAGE
*University of Wisconsin,
Milwaukee*
TITHES; USURY

ANTHONY A. M. BRYER
University of Birmingham
TREBIZOND, EMPIRE OF

RICHARD W. BULLIET
Columbia University
TRAVEL AND TRANSPORT, ISLAMIC;
VEHICLES, ISLAMIC; VIZIER

CHARLES S. F. BURNETT
Warburg Institute
TRANSLATION AND TRANSLATORS,
WESTERN EUROPEAN

ROBERT I. BURNS, S.J.
*University of California,
Los Angeles*
VALENCIA

ALLEN CABANISS
University of Mississippi
THEGANUS

ROBERT G. CALKINS
Cornell University
TRÈS RICHES HEURES

DANIEL CALLAM
*St. Thomas More College,
University of Saskatchewan*
TRANSLATION OF BISHOPS;
TRANSLATION OF SAINTS

AVERIL CAMERON
Kings College, London
THEOPHYLAKTOS SIMOKATTES;
ZOSIMUS

DEREK C. CARR
University of British Columbia
VILLENA, ENRIQUE DE

EAMON R. CARROLL
Loyola University
VIRGIN MARY IN
THEOLOGY AND POPULAR
DEVOTION

JAMES E. CATHEY
*University of Massachusetts,
Amherst*
ULLR

A. C. CAWLEY
University of Leeds
TOWNELEY PLAYS

FRED A. CAZEL, JR.
University of Connecticut
WALTER, HUBERT

YVES CHARTIER
University of Ottawa
WILLIAM OF HIRSAU

FREDRIC L. CHEYETTE
Dartmouth College
TOULOUSE; VILLAGES:
SETTLEMENT

MARLENE CIKLAMINI
*Rutgers University,
New Brunswick*
VALLA-LJÓTS SAGA

WANDA CIŻEWSKI
Marquette University
WILLIAM OF CONCHES;
WILLIAM OF MOERBEKE

JEROME W. CLINTON
Princeton University
ᶜUMAR KHAYYĀM

ROSEMARY N. COMBRIDGE
*Queen Mary College, University
of London*
ULRICH VON ZAZIKHOVEN

LAWRENCE I. CONRAD
*The Wellcome Institute for the
History of Medicine*
UMAYYADS; WALĪD I IBN ᶜABD
AL-MALIK, AL-; WĀQIDĪ,
ABU ᶜABD ALLĀH MUḤAMMAD
IBN ᶜUMAR AL-; WĀSIṬ; YAᶜQŪBĪ,
AL-; YARMUK; YAZĪD I IBN
MUᶜĀWIYA

JOHN J. CONTRENI
Purdue University
THEODULF OF ORLÉANS;
WALAFRID STRABO

GLYNNIS M. CROPP
Massey University, New Zealand
TORNADA; VIDAS

SLOBODAN ĆURČIĆ
Princeton University
VITA OF KOTOR

MICHAEL T. DAVIS
Mount Holyoke College
TRADITIO CLAVIUM; TRADITIO
LEGIS; VERNICLE; VOTIVE CROWN

LUCY DER MANUELIAN
TIGRAN HONENCᶜ; TᶜOROS
ROSLIN; TᶜOROS TARŌNECᶜI;
TRDAT; VAHKA CASTLE;
XAČᶜKᶜAR; ZWARTᶜNOCᶜ

WACHTANG Z. DJOBADZE
*California State University,
Los Angeles*
TSROMI; URBNISI; WARDZIA;
XAXULI

JERRILYNN D. DODDS
Columbia University
VISIGOTHIC ART

CHARLES DOHERTY
University College, Dublin
ULSTER

JOHN E. DOTSON
*Southern Illinois University at
Carbondale*
TRADE, WESTERN EUROPEAN

KATHERINE FISCHER DREW
Rice University
THEODORIC THE OSTROGOTH;
VANDALS; VISIGOTHS

CONTRIBUTORS TO VOLUME 12

LAWRENCE M. EARP
University of Wisconsin, Madison
VITRY, PHILIPPE DE

MARCIA J. EPSTEIN
University of Calgary
VERS; VIRELAI

JOHN H. ERICKSON
St. Vladimir's Orthodox Theological Seminary
THEODORE BALSAMON;
THEODORE OF STUDIOS

ROBERT FALCK
University of Toronto
VIDERUNT OMNES

ANN E. FARKAS
Brooklyn College
USHAKOV, SIMON; YAROSLAVL

S. C. FERRUOLO
Stanford University
VITAL OF BLOIS; WALTER OF CHÂTILLON

EDWARD G. FICHTNER
Brooklyn College
ULRICH FÜETRER

RICHARD S. FIELD
Yale University Art Gallery
WOODCUT

JOHN V. A. FINE, JR.
University of Michigan
TOMISLAV; TVRTKO I; TVRTKO II

RUTH H. FIRESTONE
University of Missouri
WOLFDIETRICH; WUNDERER, DER

JERE FLECK
University of Maryland
VAFÞRÚÐNISMÁL

CLIVE FOSS
University of Massachusetts, Boston
URBANISM, BYZANTINE

ROBERTA FRANK
Centre for Medieval Studies, University of Toronto
ÞJÓÐÓLFR ÓR HVÍNI; ÚLFR UGGASON

JOHN B. FREED
Illinois State University
TRANSLATION OF EMPIRE;

WITTELSBACH FAMILY; WORMS, CONCORDAT OF

WALTER FRÖHLICH
THEODORIC OF FREIBERG

EDWARD FRUEH
Columbia University
THEODOFRID OF CORBIE;
USUARD; WALO OF AUTUN;
WIBERT OF TOUL

ASTRIK L. GABRIEL
University of Notre Dame
UNIVERSITIES

KARI ELLEN GADE
Indiana University
YNGLINGATAL

STEPHEN GARDNER
University of California, Santa Barbara
THORNTON, JOHN; TIERCERON;
VERTUE, ROBERT AND WILLIAM;
WALSINGHAM, ALAN OF;
WASTELL, JOHN; WESTMINSTER
ABBEY; WIBERT OF CANTERBURY;
WILLIAM OF SENS; WINCHCOMBE,
RICHARD

NINA G. GARSOÏAN
Columbia University
TRADE, ARMENIAN; TRDAT III
(IV) THE GREAT, ST.; VARDAN
MAMIKONEAN, ST.

ADELHEID M. GEALT
Indiana University
TORRITI, JACOPO; TRAINI,
FRANCESCO; TRECENTO ART;
UCCELLO, PAOLO; UGOLINO DA
SIENA; VANNI, ANDREA; VANNI,
LIPPO

BRUCE E. GELSINGER
VIKING NAVIGATION

HENRI GIBAUD
VULGATE

OWEN GINGERICH
Smithsonian Astrophysical Observatory
TOLEDAN TABLES

DOROTHY F. GLASS
State University of New York at Buffalo
VASSALLETTUS; WILIGELMO DA
MODENA

THOMAS F. GLICK
Boston University
TOLEDO; UMAYYADS OF
CÓRDOBA

GEOFFREY B. GNEUHS
VINCENT FERRER, ST.

PETER B. GOLDEN
Rutgers University, Newark
TOGHRIL-BEG; TURKOMANS;
UZUN ḤASAN; VOLGA BULGARS

DAVID GOLDFRANK
Georgetown University
VLADIMIR-SUZDAL

JANET E. GORMLEY
The Queen's University of Belfast
UBERTINO OF CASALE

OLEG GRABAR
Harvard University
ZĀWĪYA; ZIYADA

JAMES A. GRAHAM-CAMPBELL
University College, London
URNES STYLE;
VIKING ART

JUDITH GRANT
University of Auckland
VIE SEINT EDMUND LE REI, LA

GORDON K. GREENE
Wilfrid Laurier University
TRECENTO MUSIC

KAAREN GRIMSTAD
University of Minnesota
VǪLUNDARKVIÐA

SAMUEL GRUBER
Columbia University
URBANISM, WESTERN EUROPEAN

MINNETTE
GRUNMANN-GAUDET
University of Western Ontario
TUROLDUS

GREGORY G. GUZMAN
Bradley University
VINCENT OF BEAUVAIS

WILLIAM LIPPINCOTT
HANAWAY, JR.
University of Pennsylvania
VĪS U RĀMĪN;
XWADĀY NĀMAG

xi

CONTRIBUTORS TO VOLUME 12

NATHALIE HANLET
*Thiofrid of Echternach;
Waldrammus; Warnerius of
Basel; Wigbodus*

JOSEPH HARRIS
Harvard University
Þǽttir; Þrymskviða

AHMAD YUSIF al-HASSAN
Tools, Agricultural:
Islamic

EINAR HAUGEN
Harvard University
Vinland Sagas

EDWARD R. HAYMES
Cleveland State University
Virginal

HARRY C. HAZEL III
Gonzaga University
William of Auvergne

HUBERT HEINEN
University of Texas at Austin
Ulrich von Singenberg;
Ulrich von Winterstetten;
Wartburgkrieg

JOHN BELL HENNEMAN
Princeton University
Valois Dynasty

MICHAEL HERREN
York University
Virgil the Grammarian;
Vulgar Latin

ROBERT H. HEWSEN
Glassboro State College
Urmia, Lake; Van, Lake;
Vanand; Vaspurakan; Xlatᶜ

BENNETT D. HILL
St. Anselm's Abbey
Vital of Savigny, St.;
Whitby, Synod of;
William of Wykeham;
Wulfstan of Worcester, St.;
Wulfstan of York

MICHAEL J. HODDER
Wool

RICHARD C. HOFFMANN
University of York, Ontario
Tools, Agricultural:
European; Villages:
Community

KENNETH G. HOLUM
University of Maryland
Theodosius II the
Calligrapher

JOHN HOWE
Texas Tech University
Translation of Saints

ANNE HUDSON
Lady Margaret Hall, Oxford
Wyclif, John

ANDREW HUGHES
University of Toronto
Tonary; Tones, Reading and
Dialogue; Troper; Variatio

PENELOPE HUGHES
Waits

SHAUN F. D. HUGHES
Purdue University
Vǫluspá

MAHMOOD IBRAHIM
Birzeit University
ᶜUmar I ibn al-Khaṭṭāb

W. T. H. JACKSON
Columbia University
Theodore of Canterbury, St.;
Ulrich von Türheim;
Verecundus of Junca;
Visitatio Sepulchri; Vitae
Patrum; Walther von Speier;
Wichram of St. Gall

FRANK RAINER JACOBY
Brandeis University
Ysengrimus

PETER JEFFERY
University of Delaware
Tropes to the Proper of the
Mass

ALEXANDRA F. JOHNSTON
Records of Early English Drama
York Plays

GEORGE FENWICK JONES
University of Maryland
Walther von der Vogelweide;
Wittenwiler, Heinrich

JENNIFER E. JONES
Transfiguration; Tree of Life;
Trinity, Old Testament;
Twelve Great Feasts; Virtues
and Vices

PETER A. JORGENSEN
University of Georgia
Vilmundar Saga Viðutan

WALTER EMIL KAEGI, JR.
University of Chicago
Themes; Varangian Guard;
Warfare, Byzantine

RICHARD W. KAEUPER
University of Rochester
Treason; Trespass

WILLIAM E. KAPELLE
Brandeis University
Thegn

ALEXANDER P. KAZHDAN
*Dumbarton Oaks Research
Center*
Theodore Prodromos;
Theophanes Confessor;
Theophanes Continuatus;
Zonaras, John

HANS-ERICH KELLER
Ohio State University
Wace

THOMAS KERTH
*State University of New York at
Stony Brook*
Tristan, Legend of

HERBERT L. KESSLER
The Johns Hopkins University
Utrecht Psalter

DAVID N. KLAUSNER
University of Toronto
Urien Rheged; Welsh
Literature

DENNIS M. KRATZ
University of Texas at Dallas
Waltharius

HENRY KRATZ
University of Tennessee
Wolfram von Eschenbach

B. KREKIĆ
*University of California,
Los Angeles*
Varna

ANGELIKI E. LAIOU
Harvard University
Trade, Byzantine

IAN LANCASHIRE
*University of Toronto at
Mississauga*
Wynkyn de Worde

CONTRIBUTORS TO VOLUME 12

RICHARD LANDES
University of Pittsburgh
YEAR 1000, THE

TRAUGOTT LAWLER
Yale University
TREVISA, JOHN

JOHN LE PATOUREL
University of Leeds
WILLIAM I OF ENGLAND

ROBERT E. LERNER
Northwestern University
THIETMAR VON MERSEBURG;
VIGILIUS, POPE; WIDUKIND
OF CORVEY

JOHN LINDOW
*University of California,
Berkeley*
THOR; VALHALLA; VALKYRIE;
VANIR

FRANCES RANDALL LIPP
Colorado State University
WILLIAM IX OF AQUITAINE

ALICE CORNELIA LOFTIN
Virginia Polytechnic Institute
VISIONS

F. DONALD LOGAN
*Emmanuel College,
Boston*
VIKINGS

LARS LÖNNROTH
Göteborgs Universitet
TRÓJUMANNA SAGA

JAMES F. LYDON
University of Dublin
WALES: HISTORY

BRYCE LYON
Brown University
VERMANDOIS; YPRES

WILLIAM MacBAIN
University of Maryland
VIE DE STE. CATHERINE
D'ALEXANDRIE

MICHAEL McCORMICK
The Johns Hopkins University
VOLUMEN; WALTER OF
MAURETANIA; WATERMARKS;
WAX TABLETS; WIBALD OF
STAVELOT; WRITING MATERIALS,
WESTERN EUROPEAN

WILLIAM C. McDONALD
University of Virginia
WILDE ALEXANDER, DER

CATHERINE A. McKENNA
*Queens College, City University
of New York*
WELSH LITERATURE: POETRY

DAVID R. McLINTOCK
University of London
VOCABULARIUS SANCTI GALLI;
WESSOBRUNNER GEBET

WILFERD MADELUNG
The Oriental Institute, Oxford
ZAYDIS

GEORGE P. MAJESKA
University of Maryland
THEOPHANES THE GREEK;
VENETS; VLADIMIR, ST.;
VLADIMIR MONOMAKH;
VLADIMIR VIRGIN; YAROSLAV
THE WISE

KRIKOR H. MAKSOUDIAN
THADDEUS LEGEND; TᶜOVMA
ARCRUNI; VARDAPET

FRANK A. C. MANTELLO
Catholic University of America
TREVET, NICHOLAS

RALPH W. MATHISEN
University of South Carolina
VENANTIUS FORTUNATUS;
VICTORINUS

GUY MERMIER
University of Michigan
TRISTAN, ROMAN DE

BRIAN MERRILEES
University of Toronto
URBAIN LE COURTOIS; VIE
D'EDOUARD LE CONFESSEUR, LA;
VIE DE ST. AUBAN; VIE DE ST.
GILLES; VIE DE ST. LAURENT; VIE
DE ST. THOMAS BECKET; VIE DE
STE. MARGUERITE; VIE DE STE.
MODWENNE; VOYAGE DE ST.
BRENDAN, LE; WALDEF, L'ESTOIRE
DE; WALTER OF BIBBESWORTH;
WIGMORE ABBEY, CHRONICLE
OF; WILLIAM OF BRIANE

JOHN MEYENDORFF
*St. Vladimir's Orthodox
Theological Seminary*
THEODOSIUS OF THE CAVES, ST.;
THEOTOKOS

WALTER L. MOORE
Florida State University
VIA MODERNA

THERESA MORITZ
WILLIAM OF ST. THIERRY

MICHAEL MORONY
*University of California,
Los Angeles*
ᶜUMAR II IBN ᶜABD AL-ᶜAZĪZ

JOHN MUENDEL
Lakeland College
WATERWORKS

SANDRA NADDAFF
Harvard University
THOUSAND AND
ONE NIGHTS

JOHN W. NESBITT
*Dumbarton Oaks Research
Center*
WEIGHTS AND MEASURES,
BYZANTINE

FRANCIS OAKLEY
Williams College
ZABARELLA, FRANCESCO

DONNCHADH Ó CORRÁIN
University College, Cork
UÍ NÉILL

KENAN B. OSBORNE
*Franciscan School of Theology,
Berkeley, California*
TRINITARIAN DOCTRINE

ROGER OUSTERHOUT
University of Illinois
THEODORE METOCHITES

HERMANN PÁLSSON
University of Edinburgh
ÞÁTTR AF RAGNARS SONUM;
ÞORSTEINS SAGA VÍKINGSSONAR;
ÞORSTEINS ÞÁTTR BÆJARMAGNS;
YNGVARS SAGA VÍÐFÖRLA

ANGELO PAREDI
*Biblioteca Ambrosiana,
Milan*
TUSCANY; VISCONTI

KENNETH PENNINGTON
Syracuse University
VINCENTIUS HISPANUS

CAROL TALBERT PETERS
VITALE DA BOLOGNA

CONTRIBUTORS TO VOLUME 12

EDWARD PETERS
University of Pennsylvania
TORTURE

ALEJANDRO ENRIQUE
PLANCHART
*University of California,
Santa Barbara*
TRENT CODICES; WINCHESTER
TROPER

JAMES F. POAG
Washington University
ULRICH VON ESCHENBACH

JANET M. POPE
*University of California,
Santa Barbara*
WITENAGEMOT

JAMES M. POWELL
Syracuse University
WILLIAM OF APULIA

DAVID S. POWERS
Cornell University
WAQF

CHARLES M. RADDING
Loyola University
WERGILD

MARY LYNN RAMPOLLA
WILLIAM OF MALMESBURY

KATHRYN L. REYERSON
University of Minnesota
URBANISM, WESTERN EUROPEAN

ROGER E. REYNOLDS
*Pontifical Institute of Mediaeval
Studies, Toronto*
VESTMENTS; YORK TRACTATES

EARL JEFFREY RICHARDS
University of North Carolina
UNICORN

BENJAMIN Z. RICHLER
*Institute for Microfilmed Hebrew
Manuscripts, Jerusalem*
TRANSLATION AND TRANSLATORS,
JEWISH

BRYNLEY ROBERTS
National Library of Wales
WELSH LITERATURE: PROSE
WELSH LITERATURE: RELIGIOUS

ELAINE GOLDEN ROBISON
THOMAS OF HALES

LINDA C. ROSE
THEODORET OF CYR;
THEOPHANO, EMPRESS; THOMAS
THE SLAV; VICAR; YAHYA OF
ANTIOCH; ZACHARIAS OF
MYTILENE; ZENO THE ISAURIAN

MIRIAM ROSEN
WĀSIṬĪ, YAḤYĀ IBN MAḤMŪD
AL-

CHARLES STANLEY ROSS
Purdue University
VERGIL IN THE MIDDLE AGES

GUIDO RUGGIERO
University of Connecticut
VENICE

JAMES R. RUSSELL
Columbia University
WUZURG FRAMADĀR; XUSRŌ I
ANŌŠARWĀN; XUSRŌ II ABARWĒZ

JEFFREY BURTON RUSSELL
*University of California,
Santa Barbara*
WITCHCRAFT, EUROPEAN

ELIAS N. SAAD
TIMBUKTU

PETER SACCIO
Dartmouth College
WARS OF THE ROSES

GEORGE SALIBA
Columbia University
TRANSLATION AND TRANSLATORS,
ISLAMIC

ANTONIO SÁNCHEZ
ROMERALO
University of California, Davis
VILLANCICOS

ERNEST H. SANDERS
Columbia University
WORCESTER POLYPHONY

PAULA SANDERS
Rice University
YEMEN

BARBARA NELSON SARGENT-
BAUR
University of Pittsburgh
VILLON, FRANÇOIS

PAUL SCHACH
University of Nebraska
ÞÓRÐAR SAGA HREÐU;
VÁPNFIRÐINGA SAGA;

VÁTNSDŒLA SAGA;
VÍGA-GLÚMS SAGA;
VÍGLUNDAR SAGA

NICOLAS SCHIDLOVSKY
TROPARION

ELEANOR SEARLE
*California Institute of
Technology*
WALTER OF HENLEY

EDWARD A. SEGAL
WILLIAM OF JUMIÈGES;
WILLIAM OF POITIERS

LON R. SHELBY
*Southern Illinois University at
Carbondale*
ULRICH VON ENSINGEN

LARRY SILVER
Northwestern University
THEODORIC, MASTER;
VISCHER, PETER (THE ELDER);
WITTINGAU MASTER;
WITZ, KONRAD;
WOLGEMUT, MICHAEL

BARRIE SINGLETON
THIRSK, JOHN; TOREL, WILLIAM;
TORRIGIANO, PIETRO;
WALTER OF COLCHESTER;
WILLIAM OF WINCHESTER;
WILLIAM THE ENGLISHMAN;
WYNFORD, WILLIAM

JAMES SNYDER
Bryn Mawr College
WEYDEN, ROGIER VAN DER

HAYM SOLOVEITCHIK
Yeshiva University
USURY, JEWISH LAW

ROBERT SOMERVILLE
Columbia University
THOMAS À KEMPIS;
URBAN II, POPE

PRISCILLA P. SOUCEK
New York University
THULUTH; YĀM

SVAT SOUCEK
ULJAYTU KHUDABĀNDA

RUTH STEINER
*Catholic University of
America*
VENI CREATOR SPIRITUS

CONTRIBUTORS TO VOLUME 12

CHARLES L. STINGER
State University of New York at Buffalo
TRAVERSARI, AMBROGIO

MELVIN STORM
Emporia State University
TINTAGEL; TINTERN; TRIVIUM

JOSEPH R. STRAYER
Princeton University
WILLIAM OF CHAMPEAUX

RONALD G. SUNY
University of Michigan
WAXTANG I GURGASLANI

SANDRA CANDEE SUSMAN
TINO DI CAMAINO

WIM SWAAN
WERVE, CLAUS DE

R. N. SWANSON
University of Birmingham
TWO SWORDS, DOCTRINE OF

JAMES ROSS SWEENEY
Pennsylvania State University
VLACHS; VLAD ŢEPEŞ;
WALACHIA/MOLDAVIA

JOSEPH SZÖVÉRFFY
TUOTILO; WIPO OF BURGUNDY

ALICE-MARY M. TALBOT
THEODORA THE MACEDONIAN,
EMPRESS; ZOË THE MACEDONIAN

PETRUS W. TAX
University of North Carolina
WERNHER VON ELMENDORF;
WILLIAM VON EBERSBERG

MICHAEL D. TAYLOR
University of Houston
TREE OF JESSE; UGOLINO DI
VIERI

ROBERT TAYLOR
Victoria College, University of Toronto
TROBAIRITZ

J. WESLEY THOMAS
University of Kentucky
TRISTRANT; ULRICH VON
LIECHTENSTEIN; WIRNT VON
GRAFENBERG; WIZLAW III VON
RÜGEN

M. A. TOLMACHEVA
Washington State University
ZANJ

PETER TOPPING
Dumbarton Oaks Research Center
WILLIAM OF CHAMPLITTE

WARREN T. TREADGOLD
Hillsdale College
THEODORA II, EMPRESS

RALPH V. TURNER
Florida State University
WESTMINSTER, STATUTES OF

A. L. UDOVITCH
Princeton University
TRADE, ISLAMIC; URBANISM,
ISLAMIC

ANNE HAGOPIAN VAN BUREN
Tufts University
VRELANT, WILLEM;
WAUQUELIN, JEAN

ARJO VANDERJAGT
Filosofisch Instituut, Groningen
THIERRY OF CHARTRES

EVELYN BIRGE VITZ
New York University
VIE DES ANCIENS PÈRES, LA;
VIE DE ST. ALEXIS

F. W. VON KRIES
University of Massachusetts, Amherst
THOMASIN VON ZERCLAERE;
WINSBECKE; WOLFGER VON ERLA

STEPHEN L. WAILES
Indiana University
UNIBOS; WEINSCHWELG, DER;
WIRT, DER

WILLIAM A. WALLACE
Catholic University of America
THOMISM AND ITS OPPONENTS

TERRENCE WALZ
American Research Center in Egypt
WRITING MATERIALS, ISLAMIC

SETH WARD
University of Haifa
USURY, ISLAMIC LAW

SUZANNE FONAY WEMPLE
Barnard College
WOMEN'S RELIGIOUS ORDERS

LYNN WHITE, JR.
University of California, Los Angeles
THEOPHILUS

GREGORY WHITTINGTON
New York University
TRACERY; TRANSENNA; TRANSEPT;
TREFOIL; TRIFORIUM;
TRIUMPHAL ARCH; TRUMEAU;
TYMPANUM; VAULT; VOUSSOIR

JOHN WILLIAMS
University of Pittsburgh
VIMARA

JOSEPH WILSON
Rice University
WENDS

KLAUS WOLLENWEBER
Memorial University of Newfoundland
ZAHN, DER

CHARLES T. WOOD
Dartmouth College
TUDOR, OWEN

FRANK E. WOZNIAK
University of New Mexico
TMUTARAKAN, KHANATE OF

RONALD EDWARD ZUPKO
Marquette University
VIRGATE; WEIGHTS AND
MEASURES, WESTERN EUROPEAN

XV

Dictionary
of the
Middle Ages

Dictionary of the Middle Ages

THADDEUS LEGEND—ZWARTᶜNOCᶜ

THADDEUS LEGEND. Armenian sources since the fifth century have claimed St. Thaddeus as the one who introduced Christianity to Armenia, although the kingdom was not formally converted until about 314. It is not clear whether this tradition derives from the second-century pseudepigraphical *Doctrine of Addai* (or *Legend of Edessa*) or from an independent source. The fifth-century historian Pᶜawstos Buzand refers to him as "apostle" and mentions his martyrdom by a King Sanatruk of Armenia in the first or early second century. He also calls the see of the bishop of Armenia "throne of the Apostle Thaddeus" in three different contexts. Later Armenian historians were uncertain whether this Thaddeus was to be identified with the Apostle Jude Thaddeus or with some other of the seventy-two disciples of Christ.

According to the fifth-century Armenian *Life* of Thaddeus, the apostle converted Sanatruk's daughter Sanduxt and was martyred in the district of Artaz. The present-day monastery of St. Tᶜadei Vankᶜin in northwestern Iran is said to have been founded by Thaddeus and to be the site of his grave.

BIBLIOGRAPHY
Malachia Ormanian, *The Church of Armenia* (1955).

KRIKOR H. MAKSOUDIAN

[See also **Armenian Saints; Pᶜawstos Buzand.**]

ÞÆTTIR (sing., *þáttr*) are short narratives in Old Norse–Icelandic prose. The word itself has been thoroughly studied by Lindow (1978a). There are West Germanic cognates and reflexes in the modern Scandinavian languages. The standard etymology relates the word to, for example, Latin *texere* (to weave). The etymological meaning "a strand, a loop" is attested, though sparsely, in Old Icelandic and persists to the present day; metaphorical uses of the etymological sense are to be found from the tenth century on. The meaning "part," a generalization from the etymological sense, is attested in skaldic poetry from the tenth century and remains in modern Icelandic. In this sense the word was used in manuscripts to indicate a part of some larger whole; since the parts so indicated were often short stories of (more or less) independent origin and transmission, the word came to be used as a technical term for the independent short narrative. The earliest instances of this usage seem, however, to be no earlier than the fourteenth century. The earlier stages of semantic development antedate the introduction of writing and extensive Latin influence (*partes, digressiones,* and similar words), and in laws the term is of native Icelandic growth.

The short narratives we call *þættir* were also called *saga, frásǫgn, sǫgn* (all: story, tale), *hlutr* (item), *capitulum* (chapter), and so forth, in the manuscripts of the medieval period, or the stories were headed "concerning . . ." or lack an introduction. While there may be significant patterns of usage still to be pointed out, recent studies have concluded that there was no truly technical usage in this area in the medieval period; Icelandic scribes, like those of other medieval lands, were not concerned to make close distinctions in analysis of prose genres. Our traditional genre-system (*Íslendinga sǫgur, konunga sǫgur,* and others) is in the main a modern convenience but, insofar as it reflects medieval usage and a natural taxonomy, may also be congruent with an unexpressed medieval ("ethnic") system. However, modern usage in the area of the short narrative is relatively unsettled. Some scholars object to the use of modern terms such as "short story," and it is true that (modern) Icelandic terms (for instance *Íslendinga sǫgur*) do

1

have the advantage of providing material for technical terms that are relatively free of possibly false prior associations; by the same token they communicate less than metaphorical labels such as "novella" (Harris 1975a).

One special use of the term *þáttr* must be clarified. The nineteenth-century scholar A. U. Bååth launched a theory of the birth of the family sagas whereby preexisting oral short stories, *þættir*, were united by an overriding theme (fate) into sagas, and W. H. Vogt extended the theory to include a still more primitive, quite unformed kind of anecdote, which Vogt exemplified in the *frásagnir* of *Landnámabók*. Andersson (1964) has traced the demise of Bååth's "*þáttr* theory," and Gimmler has argued convincingly that the surviving texts we call *þættir* are stylistically incompatible with the sagas that were supposed to have been generated in this way. The "*þáttr* theory" has little to do with the extant texts we call *þættir*. These have been estimated at over one hundred (Lange), but the criteria for inclusion are too doubtful to allow any precision in such an estimate. In general *þættir* are shorter than sagas (though some *þættir* are longer than some sagas); beyond that a definition of the *þættir* very quickly becomes characterization of one group of texts.

Thus a survey of the field as conventionally defined should replace a formal characterization of the *þáttr* in general. Lange found three groups that corresponded in little to the *Íslendinga sǫgur, fornaldar sǫgur,* and *konunga sǫgur* and a fourth group of "skáld *þættir*," corresponding perhaps to the subgroup of family sagas now known as *skálda sǫgur*. Harris (1969) classified about seventy *þættir* in nine groups, of which three coincide with those of Lange; Joseph arranged about seventy-five titles in four categories that resemble those of Lange, and Bjarni Guðnason's two groups correspond roughly to categories 1 and 3 below. The taxonomic principles employed have varied; the following survey, based partly on narrative structure, will recognize and exemplify seven groups, but many "miscellaneous" *þættir* will remain without a pigeonhole.

(1) The best-known and, from a literary point of view, the finest group of *þættir* comprises at least thirty-one stories that tell of the changing relations of an Icelander with a Norwegian king or ruling jarl. Harris characterized these "king and Icelander *þættir*" as a generic group according to "outer form," especially narrative structure (1969, 1972), and according to "inner form," especially "theme"

and "ethos" (1969, 1976). The group's common narrative structure comprised six moments: *Introduction*; the Icelandic hero's *Journey In* to Norway; his *Alienation* from the king (through a killing or some lesser offense); a *Reconciliation* with the king (often predicated on a task, a poem, intervention of friends, or a trial); his return to Iceland in a *Journey Out* (often with marks of the king's affection); and a *Conclusion*. About half the corpus of the thirty-one *þættir* showed a fairly straightforward realization of this pattern, and several common types of variation were recognizable. Twenty-six of these stories seemed to have certain common denominators of theme: seventeen having "humanistic" and nine "religious" themes; by a still more general measure, that of weltanschauung, these short forms seemed to embody a high-medieval "comic" ethos by comparison to the heroic and tragic ethos of the longer sagas (1976, see also Faulkes). The titles of a few typical examples are: *Auðunar þáttr vestfirzka, Brands þáttr ǫrva, Gísls þáttr Illugasonar, Hrafns þáttr Hrútfirðings, Sneglu-Halla þáttr, Þorgríms þáttr Hallssonar, Þorsteins þáttr forvitna, Þorsteins þáttr skelks.*

(2) A second fairly well-defined group, set in Norway or the western islands, comprises as its central narrative event a moment of conflict or opposition between Christianity and paganism: "conversion *þættir*." Examples are *Rǫgnvalds þáttr ok Rauðs, Þáttr Eindriða illbreiðs, Vǫlsa þáttr, Sveins þáttr ok Finns,* and *Helga þáttr ok Úlfs*; similar but set in Iceland are *Svaða þáttr ok Arnórs kerlingarnefs* and *Þorhalls þáttr knapps.* A closely related subgroup focuses the conflict of Christianity and paganism on a Norwegian king's contact with the heroic past in *Norna-Gests þáttr, Tóka þáttr, Sǫrla þáttr,* and somewhat differently in *Albani þáttr ok Sunnifu.* A degree less realistic than group 1, the tone of these stories lies between the *fornaldar sǫgur* (or *fornaldarsögur*) and the *Íslendinga sǫgur*; Harris (1980) attempted to relate the narrative paradigm to notions implicit in Christian historiography.

(3) A small group of *þættir* take place in Iceland and closely resemble, in parvo, the family saga with its feud structure (Andersson 1967). Here we may place *Gunnars þáttr Þiðrandabana, Hrómundar þáttr halta, Þorsteins þáttr stangarhǫggs, Bolla þáttr,* and *Qlkofra þáttr,* a satirical analogue (and perhaps source) of *Bandamanna saga.* Joseph has argued that the paucity of these "feud *þættir*" is

evidence in favor of the Bååthian theory: very few short stories about feuds were *not* inflated to or incorporated in family sagas.

(4) Four brief anecdotes surrounding skaldic verses lack pertinence to the larger context of the king's saga in which they are preserved, and they are traditionally considered *þættir: Einars þáttr Skúlasonar, Jǫkuls þáttr Bárðarsonar, Mána þáttr Íslendings,* and *Þórarins þáttr stuttfeldar.* More developed than the "incidents" that seem to have accompanied individual skaldic verses (Wood), these four show some resemblance to our group 1.

(5) Similarly, some short narratives set in Iceland were constructed around the motif of a dream. *Kumblbúa þáttr, Bergbúa þáttr, Draumr Þorsteins Síðu-Hallssonar,* and *Stjǫrnu-Odds draumr* all report verses spoken by creatures in a dream. *Rauð-úlfs þáttr,* though set in Norway, and *Þiðranda þáttr ok Þórhalls* are perhaps to be considered more complex developments of this group, though both share some features with groups 1 and 2.

(6) At least two well-known þættir, *Helga þáttr Þórissonar* and *Þorsteins þáttr bœjarmagns,* can be considered analogues of the European medieval "journeys to the Other World" found in romances and, particularly, in Breton lays; both stories are set in Norway and share the tone and many motifs of the *fornaldar sǫgur.*

(7) *Orms þáttr Stórólfssonar* and *Þorsteins þáttr uxafóts* are full but short "biographies" comparable to *fornaldar sǫgur* such as *Ǫrvar-Odds saga.* The scene of the action, which specializes in troll-killings, is mainly Norway.

If the etymological sense of *þáttr* offers a false scent for literary research, the independence of these stories does constitute a genuine central problem. The majority are preserved as episodes embodied in much larger "host" sagas; yet their independence is widely assumed and referred to in writings on the saga literature. The most convincing evidence for this consensus stems from the history of textual transmission. Some *þættir* exist only in an independent form; in our group 1 this is true only of *Þorsteins þáttr Austfirðings,* which was probably composed late and escaped the notice of compilers of late versions of the saga of the appropriate king. In group 3, however, *Gunnars þáttr Þiðrandabana* and *Ǫlkofra þáttr* are both transmitted independently (and called "saga"). Four of the "dream þættir" of group 5 are transmitted independently together from an early period (details in Íslenzk fornrit [ÍF] 11: CX), but in general anthologies of

þættir seem to appear only in the fifteenth century and later (Lönnroth 1964; Gimmler, 15–16). In the significant case of *Stúfs þáttr blinda* there is a fuller independent version and a clipped redaction adapted to fit into a king's saga; B. M. Ólsen has shown that the independent version is more original, and the same conclusion may be drawn for the similar case of *Gull-Ásu-Þórðar þáttr.*

The next most reliable test depends on discrepancies between included *þættir* in two "host" manuscripts. *Morkinskinna* collects the sagas of the Norwegian kings from about 1035 to 1157; the manuscript, dated about 1280, is based on a lost "oldest Morkinskinna" from about 1220–1230. A stretch of text from this "oldest Morkinskinna" was copied into the huge *Flateyjarbók* manuscript (original part about 1387–1394) as a "younger addition" (before 1486/1487), but some *þættir* present in the extant *Morkinskinna* are missing in *Flatey-jarbók*'s copy of the "oldest Morkinskinna." Scholars conclude that the stories were interpolated into the manuscript tradition of *Morkinskinna* between 1220/1230 and 1280. Another manuscript that incorporated a version of *Morkinskinna* was *Hulda* (with its sister manuscript *Hrokkinskinna*), and similar (not identical) conclusions can be drawn from the position and presence of *þættir* in this manuscript group (Gimmler, Louis-Jensen).

Another class of evidence can be derived from style and language. *Hreiðars þáttr heimska* is an example of a story that manifests a number of forms much more archaic than those of its "host" *Morkinskinna,* and in *Ívars þáttr Ingimundarsonar* a preclassical stylistic trait (an *ek*-narrator) clashes with the style of *Morkinskinna.* There are also contradictions of fact and conception noticeable within *Morkinskinna* (between individual *þættir* and between a given *þáttr* and the main saga), especially in the attitude toward King Haraldr harðráði, that strongly suggest independent origins (Indrebø).

Finally one can point to the evidence (although much vaguer) of literary structure, especially the closed forms and shared narrative patterns, among *þættir*; but such patterns are not the exclusive criterion of a genre and may be shared with true "episodes" (Lönnroth 1975; Harris 1975a).

All in all, some caution seems in order: in general the texts we now call *þættir* come from independent origins and are preserved to us thanks to their having been incorporated into larger works; but some were conceived from the beginning as pendants to larger works (for instance, *Bolla þáttr* to *Laxdœla saga, Brandkrossa þáttr* to *Droplaugarsona saga*), and each of the over 100 texts has its own history. Gimmler rightly emphasizes the problematic nature of a large number of "borderline cases," *þáttr*-like episodes for which solid evidence of independent origin is lacking.

The oral life of the *þættir* or the stories they embody presents inconclusive dating possibilities similar to those of the sagas. Written forms are dated from the first quarter of the thirteenth century, and *þættir* apparently continued to be written through the fourteenth and fifteenth centuries. However, many are not datable with any precision. A few examples will illustrate dating. Some *þættir* (for instance, *Ívars þáttr Ingimundarsonar, Gull-Ásu-Þórðar þáttr, Stúfs þáttr blinda,* and *Þorvarðar þáttr krákunefs*) that must have been in the "oldest Morkinskinna," yet for reasons such as style and language are considered to have had an independent origin, must date from before 1220. Of the group that was interpolated into *Morkinskinna* in the mid thirteenth century, some may have been written then, but others may be much older; for example, the language of *Hreiðars þáttr* has been dated to the early thirteenth century or about 1210–1220; *Brands þáttr ǫrva* is assigned to the early thirteenth century; and *Þorsteins þáttr sǫgufróða* (better known as *Íslendings þáttr sǫgufróða*) may be from the first quarter of the thirteenth century. On the basis of its literary relations *Gunnars þáttr Þiðrandabana* has been placed in the first quarter of the thirteenth century. *Þorsteins þáttr stangarhǫggs* gives a genealogy that includes such mid-thirteenth-century figures as Snorri Sturluson (*d.* 1241); other considerations suggested to its editor a date before 1269, and we can say with relative confidence that the story was written about 1240–1269 (ÍF 11: XXXIII). *Þorleifs þáttr jarlsskalds* is placed toward the end of the thirteenth century or in the first part of the fourteenth on the evidence of literary relations (ÍF 9: CI), while the same considerations, together with more general ones of style, have suggested some time in the fifteenth century for *Jǫkuls þáttr Búasonar* (ÍF 14: XXII).

All the attributions of authorship represent literary-historical circumstantial evidence, and none approach certainty. *Qgmundar þáttr dytts ok Gunnars helmings* and *Þorvalds þáttr tasalda* are among the *þættir* that have been thought to have originated with the lost work of the monk Gunn-

laugr Leifsson (*d.* 1218/1219?), but a more recent assessment dates the former to the period between about 1240 and the beginning of the fourteenth and the latter to the thirteenth century or beginning of the fourteenth (ÍF 9: LXIII, LXVI). *Helga þáttr ok Úlfs* has been attributed on very general grounds to one of the scribes of *Flateyjarbók,* the priest Magnús Þorhallson (about 1390), by Sigurður Nordal and Finnbogi Guðmundsson (ÍF 34: CXXXVIII–CXXXIX). *Auðunar þáttr vestfirzka* ends with a reference in the past tense to a Þorsteinn Gyðuson who drowned in 1190, apparently providing a terminus a quo for the written story; in perhaps the most interesting authorship attribution in *þáttr* scholarship, Guðni Jónsson dated the story to 1190–1220 and assigned it to Snorri Sturluson, a relative of Þorsteinn Gyðuson, and there are some supporting arguments of value (ÍF 6: CVII).

The sources of the *þættir* are as varied as their dates and almost as indeterminate, to judge by the relatively small number that have been thoroughly studied. A few, such as *Bolla þáttr,* are clearly predicated upon a family saga; but in less obvious instances of reference to or knowledge of a saga, we confront the classic questions of oral or written source in studies of the saga literature. *Þorvalds þáttr tasalda* and *Qgmundar þáttr dytts* seem to show some influence from the written *Víga-Glúms saga* (ÍF 9: LVI; Harris 1975b), and the second part of this *þáttr* (on Gunnarr helmingr) preserves very old information about the cult of Freyr. *Vǫlsa þáttr* is a Christian satire on paganism that might date from the fourteenth century, but its verses preserve some very old ritual formulas, and the portrait of a phallic cult contains genuine ancient features (Heusler). Some *þættir* are based partly on skaldic verses; for example, *Sneglu-Halla þáttr*'s rambling narrative seems largely a series of anecdotes surrounding Halli's stanzas. *Norna-Gests þáttr* used a source similar to a part of the *Poetic Edda,* and *Tóka þáttr* gives the impression of being a politically inspired imitation of *Norna-Gests þáttr.* General characteristics of the *þættir* as short, predominantly nontragic narrative have led to some speculations about generic relations with the folktale (Lindow 1978b, Harris 1976, 1980), but more concrete results have been obtained in the study of individual *þættir* in relation to tale types and motifs: *Auðunar þáttr* and *Hreiðars þáttr,* for example, are rich in such relations (Lindow 1978b); *Þorsteins þáttr Austfirðings* seems to embody an international popular tale (Harris 1979); and *Hróa þáttr* is clearly a Scandinavian transformation of a European popular tale (Strömbäck).

In most cases where sources have been established with some probability we must marvel at the ability of Icelandic writers to assimilate and remold. *Ǫgmundar þáttr dytts*, for example, combines story material of very different types to a remarkable unity; the international narrative of *Þorsteins þáttr Austfirðings* is assimilated, though not so gracefully, to a native paradigm, and the author worked in a verse that apparently was originally unrelated (Harris 1975b, 1979). In *Rǫgnvalds þáttr ok Rauðs* we may recognize material borrowed from the saga histories of Norway, genuine information about pagan worship, typical Christian ideas about sin and about paganism, motifs of international folklore, and an international narrative motif possibly borrowed from a Celtic source, all worked into a generic frame with similarities to other Norse tales (Harris 1980).

Despite connections with folklore, the *þættir* participate in the predominantly historical character of Old Norse saga literature and in the problems raised by such a wide-ranging historical literature. The realistic stories of group 1 cluster mostly about the reigns of Ólaf Tryggvason (995–1000), Ólaf Haraldsson (1015–1030), Magnús Ólafsson (1035–1047), and Harald Hardråde (1046–1066) and are thus set in a slightly more modern period than the family sagas (mostly 930–1030). Some of the events reported will have been based on reliable family traditions, and to some extent they may reflect the kinds of personalities and situations that actually prevailed in the period of their setting; in a larger sense, however, their "historicity" seems to be that of historical fictions that project contemporary, thirteenth-century problems, especially the relationship of Norwegian royal authority and Icelandic independence, onto the past. Group 2, set in the conversion period around 1000, makes more room for the marvelous while still aspiring to psychological realism; here the reporting of real events is subordinated to a definitely Christian view of history in terms of conversion and salvation. Group 3 possesses the same kinds of "historicity" as the large-scale family sagas, while the relatively recent anecdotes of group 4, because of their attachment to verse, may be fairly trustworthy indications of real events. All these stories, even including the increasingly fantastic *þættir* of groups 5–7, have some "historical" significance as social and religious reflections of Icelandic medieval culture, but

the evaluation of their view of history, their literary interpretation, and the stylistic analysis of *þáttr* narrative (despite good beginnings in Gimmler) are still in their infancy.

BIBLIOGRAPHY

Bibliographies. Islandica, 1 (1908, repr. 1966), 3 (1910, repr. 1966), 5 (1912, repr. 1966), 24 (1935, repr. 1966), 26 (1937), 38 (1957); *Bibliography of Old Norse-Icelandic Studies* (1964–); *MLA International Bibliography* (1921–); "Bibliography of Scandinavian Philology," in *Acta philologica scandinavica* (1926–, appears irregularly).

Texts. Anthony Faulkes, ed., *Two Icelandic Stories* (1968); Edwin Gardiner, ed., *Fornar smásögur úr Noregs konunga sögum* (1949); Guðni Jónsson, ed., *Íslendinga Þættir* (1945), *Fornaldar sögur Norðurlanda*, 4 vols. (1950), and *Íslendinga sögur*, 13 vols. (1953); Þorleifur Jónsson, ed., *Fjörutíu Íslendinga-þættir* (1904); Wolf H. Wolf-Rottkay, ed., *Altnordisch-isländisches Lesebuch* (1967). See also *Íslenzk fornrit* (ÍF), a series of critical editions of Old Icelandic prose works (1933–, appears irregularly).

English translations. Nora Kershaw Chadwick, ed. and trans., *Stories and Ballads of the Far Past* (1921); Gwyn Jones, trans., *Eirik the Red and Other Icelandic Sagas* (1961, repr. 1966); Henry Goddard Leach, ed., *A Pageant of Old Scandinavia* (1946, repr. 1968); Hermann Pálsson, trans., *Hrafnkel's Saga and Other Icelandic Stories* (1971); idem and Paul Edwards, trans., *Gautrek's Saga and Other Medieval Tales* (1968); John Sephton, trans., *The Saga of King Olaf Tryggvason Who Reigned Over Norway* A.D. 995 to A.D. 1000 (1895); Jacqueline Simpson, trans., *The Northmen Talk: A Choice of Tales from Iceland* (1965); Guðbrandur Vigfússon and Frederick York Powell, trans., *Origines Islandicae* (1905, repr. 1976). See also Donald Fry, *Norse Sagas Translated into English* (1980) and listing of translations of individual *þættir* in *Islandica* bibliographies.

General Studies. Theodore M. Andersson, "Splitting the Saga," in *Scandinavian Studies,* 47 (1975); Heinrich Gimmler, "Die Thættir der Morkinskinna: Ein Beitrag zur Überlieferungsproblematik und zur Typologie der altnordischen Kurzerzählung" (diss., Frankfurt am Main, 1976); Bjarni Guðnason, "Þættir," in *Kulturhistorisk leksikon for nordisk middelalder,* XX (1976); Joseph Harris, "The King and the Icelander: A Study in the Short Narrative Forms of Old Icelandic Prose" (diss., Harvard, 1969), "Genre and Narrative Structure in Some Íslendinga Þættir," in *Scandinavian Studies,* 44 (1972), "Genre in the Saga Literature: A Squib," ibid., 47 (1975), and "Theme and Genre in Some Íslendinga Þættir," ibid., 48 (1976); Herbert S. Joseph, "The Þáttr and the Theory of Saga Origins," in *Arkiv för nordisk filologi,* 87 (1972); Wolfgang Lange, "Einige Bemerkungen zur altnordischen

Novelle," in *Zeitschrift für deutsches Altertum*, **88** (1957); John Lindow, "Old Icelandic *Þáttr*: Early Usage and Semantic History," in *Scripta islandica*, **29** (1978a); Lars Lönnroth, "Tesen om de två kulturerna: Kritiska studier i den isländska sagaskrivningens sociala förutsättningar," *ibid.*, **15** (1964), esp. 19–21, "The Concept of Genre in Saga Literature," in *Scandinavian Studies*, **47** (1975), and *Njáls Saga: A Critical Introduction* (1976), 68–76 and index *s.v.* "episode"; Jonna Louis-Jensen, *Kongesagastudier Kompilationen: Hulda-Hrokkinskinna* (1977).

"*Þáttr theory*" and "*frásagnir*." Theodore M. Andersson, *The Problem of Icelandic Saga Origins* (1964); A. U. Bååth, *Studier öfver kompositionen i några isländska ättasagor* (1885); Anna C. Kersbergen, "Frásagnir in de Laxdoela Saga," in *Neophilologus*, **19** (1934); Walter Heinrich Vogt, "Die frásagnir der Landnámabók: Ein Beitrag zur Vorgeschichte der isländischen Saga," in *Zeitschrift für deutsches Altertum*, **58** (1921).

Selected studies of individual þættir. The most important literary-historical work on individual *þættir* is found in the introductions to the editions in ÍF (above), esp. vols. 3–11, 14, and 24; See also Bo Almqvist, "Den fulaste foten: Folkligt och litterärt i en Snorrianekdot," in *Scripta islandica*, **17** (1966); Theodore M. Andersson, *The Icelandic Family Saga: An Analysis* (1967), (on *Þorsteins þáttr*); J. Bing, "Sunnivalegenden," in *(Norsk) Historisk tidsskrift*, 5th ser., **5** (1924), 533–545; A. L. Binns, "The Story of Þorsteinn Uxafót," in *Saga-Book of the Viking Society*, **14** (1953–1957); Marlene Ciklamini, "The Literary Perspective on Gísl Illugason's Quest for Blood Revenge," in *Scandinavian Studies*, **38** (1966); Stefán Einarsson, "Æfintýraatvik í Auðunar þætti vestfirzka," in *Skírnir*, **113** (1939); Bjarne Fidjestøl, "Tåtten om Harald Hardråde og fiskaren Þorgils," in *Maal og minne* (1971); Joseph Harris, "Christian Form and Christian Meaning in *Halldórs þáttr I*," in *Harvard English Studies*, **5** (1974), "*Qgmundar þáttr dytts ok Gunnars helmings*: Unity and Literary Relations," in *Arkiv för nordisk filologi*, **90** (1975b), "The King in Disguise: An International Popular Tale in Two Old Icelandic Adaptations," in *Arkiv för nordisk filologi*, **94** (1979) (on *Þorsteins þáttr Austfirðings*), and "Folktale and Thattr: the Case of *Rognvald and Raud*," in *Folklore Forum*, **13** (1980); Andreas Heusler, "Die Geschichte von Völsi," in *Zeitschrift des Vereins für Volkskunde* (1903), 24–39; Gillian Fellows Jensen, ed., *Hemings þáttr Áslakssonar*, Editiones Arnamagnaeanae, ser. B, III (1962); J. Lindow, "*Hreiðars þáttr heimska* and AT 326: An Old Icelandic Novella and an International Folktale," in *Arv*, **34** (1978b); Magnus Olsen, "En skjemtehistorie av Harald Hardraade," in *Maal og minne*, (1953) 1–22; Björn M. Ólsen, ed., *Stúfs saga . . .* , (1912); Friedrich Panzer, "Zur Erzählung von Nornagest," in P. Marker and W. Stammler, ed., *Vom Werden des deutschen Geistes: Festgabe Gustav Ehrismann . . .* , (1925), 27–34; Dag

Strömbäck, "En orientalisk saga i fornnordisk dräkt," in *Donum Grapeanum: Festskrift tillägnad överbibliotekarien Anders Grape på sextiofemårsdagen, den 7 mars 1945* (Uppsala, 1945), 408–444 (repr. in *Folklore och filologi* [Skrifter utg. av Gustav Adolfs Akademien för Folklivsforskningen], **48** [1970]); Arnold R. Taylor, "Auðunn and the Bear," *Saga-Book of the Viking Society*, **13** (1947–1948), 78–96; Ole Widding, "Dating *Rauðúlfs þáttr*," in *Mediaeval Scandinavia*, **1** (1968).

Miscellaneous relevant works. Gustav Indrebø, "Harald Hardraade i Morkinskinna," in *Festskrift til Finnur Jónsson* (1928), 173–280; Wolfgang Mohr, "Wandel des Menschenbildes in der mittelalterlichen Dichtung," in *Wirkendes Wort*, 1. Sonderheft (1952), 37–48 (rpt. *Wirkendes Wort: Sammelband II* [1963]); W. H. Vogt, "Wandel im altnordischen Menschentum," in *Preussisches Jahrbuch*, (1923), 315–322; Cecil Wood, "A Skaldic Note," in *Neophilologus*, **44** (1960).

JOSEPH HARRIS

[See also **Bandamanna Saga; Droplaugarsona Saga; Family Sagas, Icelandic; Fornaldarsögur; Helga Þáttr Þórissonar; Laxdæla Saga; Norna-gests Þáttr; Norse Kings' Sagas; Þorsteins Þáttr Bæjarmagns; Viga-Glúms Saga.**]

THANE. See Thegn.

ÞÁTTR. See Þaettir.

ÞÁTTR AF RAGNARS SONUM (The tale of the sons of Ragnarr) was composed in Iceland late in the thirteenth century and survives in a single vellum manuscript, *Hauksbók*, which was written shortly after 1300 by Haukr Erlendsson (*d.* 1334). It is a mixture of fact and fantasy: the leading characters are historical personages belonging to the ninth century and some of the narrative relates to actual events of that period, but as the author was more of a storyteller than a historian, choosing to follow the literary conventions of his time, the tale taken as a whole must be regarded as a piece of fiction.

The first part of the *þáttr*, describing the life and death of the Viking leader Ragnarr loðbrók and his sons' revenge, is a summary of *Ragnars saga loðbrókar*, to which the *þáttr* explicitly refers. However, there are several significant discrepancies between these two accounts, showing clearly that *Ragnars saga* in its present form can hardly have been the source of the *þáttr*. To solve the problem, scholars have therefore postulated a thirteenth-century version, now lost, of *Ragnars saga,* serving as the model for both.

But *Ragnars saga* was not the only work used by the author. Describing the killing of King Ella (that is, the South Saxon Ælle) of Northumbria, he quotes from the *Knútsdrápa* of the eleventh-century court poet Sighvatr Þórðarson. The way in which the author refers to the natural sons of Ragnarr, Ívarr and Ubbe, whom he calls Yngvarr and Hústó (apparently a scribal error for Hubbo), suggests that he may have known a Latin source. Certain genealogical details in this section derive from *Skjǫldunga saga.*

The second part of the *þáttr* deals with the progeny of Sigurðr ormr-í-auga (the snake-in-the-eye), one of Ragnarr's famous sons. Like his brothers, Sigurðr is described as a powerful war leader. He marries King Ella's daughter and is supposedly the founder of the royal houses of Denmark and Norway. The principal source for this genealogy appears to have been *Hálfdanar saga svarta* in Snorri Sturluson's *Heimskringla.*

The *Þáttr af Ragnars sonum* is a well-told tale, in which the story unfolds with clarity and passion. The calculating cruelty of Ivarr beinlausi (the Boneless), who had neither lust nor love but plenty of shrewdness and ruthlessness, does not arouse the reader's admiration, but it shows the author's narrative skill in handling an unsympathetic character performing a crucial function in the revenge pattern. The ambitions and ideals of Viking life in the ninth century are plausibly described, even though the author is guilty of an occasional anachronism, as for example when he makes Ragnarr's second wife take with her 1,500 knights when she leads a military campaign to Sweden to seek revenge for the deaths of her stepsons.

One of the principal aims of the tale was evidently to preserve early Scandinavian legends and to link them with the history of the kings of Norway. From that point of view it serves a similar purpose as *Af Upplendinga konungum,* also preserved in *Hauksbók.*

BIBLIOGRAPHY

The text is in Finnur Jónsson, ed., *Hauksbók* (1892–1896), xcl–xciii, 458–467; and Guðni Jónsson, ed., *Fornaldarsögur Norðurlanda,* I (1950), 289–303. See also Allen Mawer, "Ragnar lothbrók and His Sons," in *Saga-Book of the Viking Society,* **6** (1909/1910); A. H. Smith, "The Sons of Ragnar lothbrók," *ibid.,* **11** (1935); Jan de Vries, "Die Entwicklung der Saga von den Lodbrokssöhnen in den historischen Quellen," in *Arkiv för nordisk filologi,* **44** (1928).

HERMANN PÁLSSON

[See also **Fornaldarsögur; Ragnars Saga Loðbrókar; Skjǫldunga Saga.**]

THEATER. See **Drama.**

THEGANUS (*d. ca.* 848). A Frank of noble origin, he was *chorepiscopus* (rural bishop) of the diocese of Treves. The date and place of his birth are not known, but the date of his death is recorded as 20 March. Although the year is not given, it was about 848, for he appears in a document of 15 May 847. Very little information about his life is available.

Walafrid Strabo expressed admiration for Theganus' powerful oratory, sharpness in preaching and correction, and bitterness toward the arrogance of prelates of humble origin. Walafrid admired his teaching, manners, songs, sayings, and spirit, crediting him with knowledge of classical literature (he mentions Cicero, Livy, Cato, Plato, and Sappho). But Walafrid was also aware of and awed by Theganus' huge bodily frame. So tall and big, so gigantesque, was Theganus that Walafrid wrote that he felt like a very little mouse in the bishop's presence.

Except for a verse letter to Bishop Hatto (whom he called "duke and consul"), Theganus has left only his life of Emperor Louis I the Pious. Although the biography breaks off at the year 835 or 836, there is a fragment that carries it on through 837 or 838. It is, therefore, the latter date to which one should ascribe publication.

Theganus knew and used Einhard's *Vita Caroli Magni* as well as annals of the time. In fact much of the writing is more annalistic than biographical. The book gives evidence of some knowledge of Pope Gregory the Great's *Pastoral Care,* the canons of the apostles, Vergil's *Eclogues* and *Aeneid,* Ovid, and Homer, but above all of Scripture, both canonical and deuterocanonical. Theganus recorded the traditional descent of Louis the Pious from Arnulf through Ansegis, Pepin, Charles Martel, Pepin the Short, and Charlemagne; as well as his maternal ancestry from Gotefrid through Huoching, Nebi, Imma, and Hildegard. Theganus also recounted Louis' self-coronation in his father's presence; the presumed (inaccurate) illegitimacy of King Bernard of Italy, Louis' nephew; the murder of Gerberga, sister of Bernard of Barcelona; and the curious note that emissaries of Louis the German communicated with Emperor Louis by signs instead of words.

The physical description of Emperor Louis is conventional and no doubt derived from Einhard's portrayal of Charlemagne, but there are other characteristics mentioned that indicate real perception; for example, the indication that Louis rejected the old heroic heathen songs that his father loved. There is also the peculiarly apt remark depicting Louis as one who never laughed or smiled, not even when musicians and actors, buffoons and mimes, flute players and guitarists strolled through the banquet hall entertaining on high festivals; not even when all the guests were roaring with laughter at the grotesquerie.

Walafrid Strabo edited Theganus' book as he did Einhard's, divided it into fifty-eight chapters, and provided an introduction. But the book was seldom used in the Middle Ages. Only the annals of Lobbes and Flodoard's account of the church in Rheims employed it. It has survived to the present in very few manuscripts.

BIBLIOGRAPHY

Max Manitius, *Geschichte der lateinischen Literatur des Mittelalters*, I (1911), 653–655; *Monumenta Germaniae historica: Scriptores*, II (1829; repr. 1963), 585–604; Reinhold Rau, ed., *Fontes ad historiam regni Francorum aevi Karolini illustrandam*, I (1956), 213–253.

ALLEN CABANISS

[See also **Einhard; Flodoard of Rheims; Walafrid Strabo.**]

THEGN (thane) originally meant "servant" in Anglo-Saxon, but it came to replace *gesith* as the term for "noble." It is doubtful if this change in words reflected any social difference. As early as the sixth century, Anglo-Saxon society contained an elaborate set of gradations. The *gesith* was a noble warrior, and he was distinguished from lesser freemen by a higher wergild and the ability to swear stronger oaths. Members of this class probably held land, at least as members of a family; but many of them depended on the kings for maintenance either as household warriors or as landed retainers. The kings were supported by an elaborate system of royal tribute consisting of food renders and works that lay upon the land, and they rewarded their warriors by loaning them the right to receive the tribute from particular villages. Once a *gesith* had loanland, he still served the king as a warrior, and he probably also had ministerial responsibilities for overseeing the delivery of the tribute. He could also now marry and have a family. When he died, the land returned to the king.

This type of quasi-ministerial thegnage survived in parts of Northumberland and eastern Scotland as late as the twelfth century, but in the south the nature of the institution changed. In the late eighth century, kings began to give thegns hereditary possession of loanland. Such grants were called bookland, and they ended a king's right to receive the old tribute from the booked land. Thanks to such grants, the thegnage became a landed nobility over the course of the ninth and tenth centuries. It is not clear why kings made such grants, but the grants did not end royal rights entirely because the kings imposed new or reformulated burdens on the land and the obligation to serve in the army and repair bridges and fortifications.

By the years of West Saxon hegemony, the thegnage constituted the territorial aristocracy of the Anglo-Saxon kingdom. The status was hereditary, but it was not a closed caste: a combination of wealth and service to the king could boost a freeman into the thegnage. The thegns were still warriors and served in the army as mounted infantry. They were also responsible for providing the king with set numbers of men for the army and public works; these obligations were based on the amount of land they owned. On the other hand, much of a thegn's interest must have been absorbed by his lands and in local affairs. At least the more important thegns had rights of jurisdiction over their lands and a range of responsibilities in the shires and hundreds.

Many questions about this social group cannot be answered satisfactorily until the social evolution of the Anglo-Saxons is better known. In the early period, we have no idea how extensive the family land of the *gesiths* was; and even as late as the eleventh century, it is impossible to draw the contours of the thegnage because of the absence of information revealing the distribution of land among them. This problem is compounded by obscurity about the rules of inheritance in both periods. Finally, important lords still loaned out land to lesser thegns in the eleventh century, and scholars are deeply divided over whether these medial thegns were old-fashioned ministerial thegns or vassals in all but name.

BIBLIOGRAPHY

H. P. R. Finberg, ed., *The Agrarian History of England and Wales*, I, pt. 2, *A.D. 42–1042* (1972), 436–525; Eric John, *Land Tenure in Early England* (1960); William E. Kapelle, *The Norman Conquest of the North* (1979), chap. 3; Henry R. Loyn, *Anglo-Saxon England and the Norman Conquest* (1962), chap. 5; Peter Sawyer, "1066–1086: A Tenurial Revolution?" in *idem*, ed., *Domesday Book: A Reassessment* (1985); Frank M. Stenton, *Anglo-Saxon England*, 3rd ed. (1971).

WILLIAM E. KAPELLE

[See also **Chivalry; Class Structure, Western; England: Anglo-Saxon; Feudalism; Fief; Knights and Knight Service; Nobility and Nobles; Tenure of Land: Western European; Wergild.**]

THEMES (Byzantine Greek: *themata*; sing., *thema*). The term was first used in a military sense to designate Byzantine armies and subsequently also the districts of their respective military corps. The origin of the word is obscure and controversial. The prevailing explanation is that it referred to a notarial entry or notation for an army unit. An alternative explanation holds that it referred to emplacements of soldiers. Neither is entirely convincing, however. It is also not certain when the term began to be used—perhaps not until well into the eighth century.

Most probably, the themes were not the sudden creation of any one emperor or military reformer. There is no evidence to show that the formation of the themes was originally part of any comprehensive social and economic restructuring of the Byzantine Empire. Rather, the themes took their form gradually in a process that accelerated in response to the Arab conquests, invasions, and raids of the seventh century. Explicit documentation for their assumption of political responsibility for administration of a specific district appears only in the early decades of the eighth century.

The themes evolved in part from the military commands of the sixth century. Their number did not remain static but changed as the original themes were subdivided and as new themes were created in recently conquered territory. Thus, the two largest themes, the Anatolikon and the Armeniakon, originated in the respective commands of the *magister militum* for the Orient and the *magister militum* for Armenia, while the Thracian theme originated in the army of the *magister militum* for Thrace. The Opsikion theme began as the *obsequium*, an elite branch of the imperial army. It is possible that Thrakesion was another of the original themes. The commanders of these large armies all held the rank of *strategos* (general), with the exception of the Opsikion, which was headed by a count. The origins of the Kibyrrhaeot theme are controversial, but it and its predecessor, the Carabisiani, may have originated in the special naval command of the sixth-century quaestor Justiniani Exercitus.

The original large themes were army corps that coexisted with the older civilian administrative structure of the late Roman provinces. (The latter disappeared only in the eighth century.) During the emergencies of the seventh century the commanders of the thematic armies acquired extraordinary powers and responsibilities. It appears that they dispersed mounted soldiers to hold various localities. The commanders of the themes gradually assumed responsibility for civil as well as military affairs in the specific territory assigned to their themes, a process that lacks detailed documentation. Probably the majority of thematic soldiers were not kept mobilized throughout the year but were permitted to disperse, especially during the winter months if there did not seem to be any active military threat. The thematic armies constituted the core of the empire's effective manpower, although the elite mobile guard of tagmata in and near Constantinople was another major striking force, probably well developed by the second half of the eighth century. Thematic armies were fundamentally indigenous armies recruited from local Greek or Armenian sources; occasionally some foreigners, such as refugee soldiers, prisoners, and deserters, were incorporated.

The Asian themes were more powerful than the European ones. There is no explicit explanation in the sources for the causes of the subdivision of the original, large themes of Asia Minor, but many scholars have assumed that it resulted from imperial efforts to improve internal security by denying too much power to any one theme commander. In fact, the propensity of themes to engage in military revolts had no direct connection with the size of thematic armies and the size of the theme's territorial jurisdiction. Themes tended to revolt in response to unpopular governmental policies and decisions and, in particular, when they were allowed to concentrate forces near Constantinople on some pretext. Theme armies developed their own unit loyalties, and consequently there were some rivalries among themes. Unanimity of thematic armies in domestic conflicts was rare.

No reliable Byzantine statistics exist concerning the total number of Byzantine soldiers in thematic units at any time, and the Arab geographers' estimates of an aggregate strength of 70,000 or even much more seem exaggerated. The fullest evidence on the themes exists for the middle of the tenth century, when their total number in Asia Minor and Europe had increased to twenty-seven. This was during the reign of Emperor Constantine VII Porphyrogenitos, who wrote a treatise on the themes.

In the ninth and tenth centuries, soldiers' portions provided the means of support for many thematic soldiers, although the origins and degree of universality of the institution cannot be determined. There is no evidence to prove any initial linkage between the creation of the themes and the creation of soldiers' portions.

The mature themes of the tenth century were under the supreme authority of the *strategos,* who was appointed by, and removable at the will of, the emperor. In turn, the *strategos* had a group of subordinate military officers, *tourmarch*s, who directed the *tourmai,* or largest thematic subunits. However, the financial and logistical affairs of the theme were the responsibility of the *protonotarios* (first notary), who reported to the treasury in Constantinople and thus served as a source of information and as a potential check on dangerously ambitious or corrupt *strategoi.* It was the *chartoularios* of the theme who kept the muster list of thematic soldiers.

Fragmentation of the themes intensified by the beginning of the last quarter of the tenth century: a large number (90) of territorially modest thematic jurisdictions appeared. By the eleventh century it was common for themes to be commanded by a *dux* (duke) or *kritēs* (judge, especially for the smallest units). Moreover, the relative importance of thematic armies declined, as did the quality of their military personnel, equipment, and level of readiness. Governmental mistrust and neglect also greatly contributed to the decline of the thematic armies, while special units of foreign mercenaries became the best fighting forces of the Byzantine army. By the time of the Turkish invasions (middle and late eleventh century), the themes were no longer militarily very effective. These invasions finally eliminated what remained of the thematic armies, although the themes themselves, usually commanded by a *dux,* nominally survived as basic administrative units in the twelfth and thirteenth centuries.

Any evaluation of the military efficiency of the themes must acknowledge that they provided the troops who preserved and for a time even expanded the empire's frontiers in the Balkans and in Asia. At the height of the Arab offensives in the late seventh and the eighth centuries, the thematic armies could not win decisive battles in the field and instead usually relied upon passive strategies. They were unable to prevent much of the devastation of Asia Minor by the Arabs and of the Balkans by the Bulgars. They did, however, provide sufficient resistance to enable the Byzantine government to continue to exercise control when the temporary invaders returned to their own lands. Whatever the difficulties of the thematic armies, it is true that they did not strain the empire's finances as much as had the expensive Late Roman armies. They owed part of their success to their enemies' internal conflicts, as well as to their careful utilization of the heritage of Greco-Roman tactics, strategy, and drill.

BIBLIOGRAPHY

John Haldon, *Recruitment and Conscription in the Byzantine Army, c. 550–950* (1979); Walter E. Kaegi, *Byzantine Military Unrest, 471–843* (1981), "Heraklios and the Arabs," in *Greek Orthodox Theological Review,* 27 (1982), and "Two Studies in the Continuity of Late Roman and Byzantine Military Institutions," in *Byzantinische Forschungen,* 8 (1982); Johannes Karayannopulos, *Die Enthstehung der byzantinischen Themenordnung* (1959); Ralph-Johannes Lilie, "Die zweihundertjährige Reform," in *Byzantinoslavica,* 45 (1984); Nicholas Oikonomidès, *Les listes des préséances byzantines des IXᵉ et XIᵉ siècles* (1972); Agostino Pertusi, "La formation des thèmes byzantins," in *Berichte zum XI. Internationalen Byzantinisten-Kongress* (1958).

WALTER EMIL KAEGI, JR.

[See also **Anatolikon, Theme of; Armeniakon, Theme of; Byzantine Empire: History; Cavalry, Byzantine; Con-**

Empress Theodora and her retinue. Mosaic in the apse of S. Vitale, Ravenna, *ca.* 547. FOTO MARBURG/ART RESOURCE

stantine VII Porphyrogenitos; Dux; Islam, Conquests of; Magister Militum; Opsikion, Theme of; Roman Empire, Late; Seljuks of Rum; Soldiers' Portions; Strategos; Stratiotai; Tagmata; Warfare, Byzantine.]

BIBLIOGRAPHY

Max Manitius, *Geschichte der lateinischen Literatur des Mittelalters*, I (1911).

EDWARD FRUEH

[See also **Sex Aetates Mundi.**]

THEODERIC. See **Theodoric the Ostrogoth.**

THEODOFRID OF CORBIE, a monk who in 657 became abbot of the newly founded Corbie. In 681 he became a bishop, perhaps at Amiens. He was probably the author of a poem on the six ages of the world and its beginning, the *Versus de sex aetatibus et mundi principio.*

THEODORA I, EMPRESS (495/500—548), consort of Byzantine emperor Justinian I. Theodora was the daughter of a keeper of animals for the amphitheater, employed by the Green circus faction. Her stepfather obtained a similar post with the Blue faction, with which Theodora long maintained a connection. She performed on stage in sketches and mimes, often scurrilous, for which she had great talent, and enjoyed the sexual freedom customary among the theatrical demimonde. Hop-

11

ing to break out of her milieu, she accompanied a government official to Cyrenaica, but soon left him and slowly made her way back to Constantinople via Alexandria and Antioch. On her journey she made contact with leading members of the Monophysite wing of the church. Returning to Constantinople, she soon formed a liaison with Justinian, nephew and right-hand man of the emperor Justin I. Marriage between them was resolutely opposed by Justinian's aunt, the empress Euphemia, and was in any case forbidden by Roman law. On the death of Euphemia in 524 Justin granted Theodora the rank of patrician and amended the law regarding marriage between senators and theatrical persons. Justinian and Theodora were married in 525. In April 527 Justinian was proclaimed coemperor and, on 1 August, succeeded his uncle.

Theodora was intelligent, witty, impulsive, and decisive in situations where her husband was hesitant. Loyal in support of her friends, she was ruthless in the persecution of her enemies. She played a more public and political role than did the consorts of previous emperors, and is often named in state documents, in inscriptions on churches or public buildings, and in the oath of allegiance taken by officials. Popes addressed letters jointly to Justinian I and Theodora, and foreign ambassadors waited upon her. The problem is how independent her policy was. Hostile witnesses at the time attributed to her an authority as great as or greater than that of Justinian. The truth is probably that, although Theodora was never a mere cipher and, where her friends or her foes were concerned, she could pursue a personal policy, she generally acted in concert with Justinian, even where they appeared to follow different lines.

In 532 when Justinian's throne was shaken by a popular uprising, the Nika Revolt, Theodora dissuaded him from fleeing the capital and insisted upon the execution of the usurper Hypatius, an aristocrat and nephew of the former emperor Anastasius I. Anxious to retain control of the succession should Justinian die, she was hostile to Justinian's cousin Germanus and cool toward his great general Belisarios. Her protégés were often advanced to high office, for example, Peter Barsymes as praetorian prefect and Narses as commander in Italy. But her enmity did not always bring about the downfall of her foes.

Theodora corresponded with foreign potentates and gave secret instructions to Byzantine ambassadors. The most notorious case is that of the Ostro-

gothic princess Amalasuntha, to whom Justinian promised his protection while Theodora allegedly encouraged her assassination. It is not unlikely that in this as in other instances Theodora was the instrument of Justinian's unofficial diplomacy. The clearest example of the apparent opposition by Theodora to Justinian's policy is in church matters. Theodora was influential in the appointment of Monophysites to leading positions early in Justinian's reign and gave encouragement and protection to Monophysite clerics after persecution recommenced in 535. But there is much evidence of connivance, and it is likely that both Justinian and Theodora were primarily eager to attain church unity.

A lavish builder of churches, orphanages, and public buildings, she was buried in the church of the Holy Apostles, which she had had rebuilt (*ca.* 536–550) after its destruction by fire in 532 (now the site of the Mosque of the Conqueror, the Fātih).

Theodora is described as a slim, pale brunette. There is a contemporary mosaic portrait in S. Vitale, Ravenna, and a contemporary bust in Milan. Other alleged portraits are of doubtful authenticity.

BIBLIOGRAPHY

Antony C. Bridge, *Theodora: Portrait in a Byzantine Landscape* (1978); Robert Browning, *Justinian and Theodora*, 2nd ed. (1987); Charles Diehl, *Théodora, impératrice de Byzance*, 3rd ed. (1904), and *Figures byzantines*, 1ᵉ sér., 5th ed. (1912), 51–75, repr. in his *Impératrices de Byzance* (1959), 37–57; Berthold Rubin, *Das Zeitalter Justinians*, I (1960), 98–121.

ROBERT BROWNING

[See also **Belisarios; Byzantine History (330–1025); Demes; Early Christian Art; Justinian I; Monophysitism; Ravenna.**]

THEODORA II, EMPRESS (*ca.* 815–*ca.* 867). Married to the emperor Theophilos in 830, at his death in 842 she became regent for their infant son Michael III (r. 842–867). Her regency was a time of peace and prosperity, with the government largely conducted by the logothete of the dromos Theoktistos. In 843 she and Theoktistos held a council that restored the veneration of icons (on the first Sunday in Lent, since then commemorated as the Sunday of Orthodoxy by the Eastern church). On 20 November 855, encouraged by Theodora's brother Bardas, Michael III took power into his own hands by having Theoktistos assassinated. Theodora was relegated to a convent in 858.

BIBLIOGRAPHY

J. B. Bury, *A History of the Eastern Roman Empire* (1912), 143–161, detailed but somewhat outdated; Jean Gouillard, "Le synodikon de l'orthodoxie: Édition et commentaire," in *Centre de recherche d'histoire et civilisation byzantines: Travaux et mémoires,* 2 (1967), a full and recent treatment of the restoration of icons; P. Karlin-Hayter, "Études sur les deux histoires du règne de Michel III," in *Byzantion,* 41 (1971), a study of the main sources for the regency; George Ostrogorsky, *History of the Byzantine State,* Joan Hussey, trans. (1957, rev. ed. 1969), 217–223; Warren T. Treadgold, *The Byzantine State Finances in the Eighth and Ninth Centuries* (1982), for a discussion of Theodora's domestic policies, and *The Byzantine Revival, 780–842* (1988), for Theodora's career up to 842.

WARREN T. TREADGOLD

[See also **Bardas Caesar; Byzantine Church; Byzantine Empire: History; Michael III, Emperor; Photios.**]

THEODORA THE MACEDONIAN, EMPRESS (981?–1056), Byzantine ruler. The youngest daughter of Constantine VIII (*d.* 1028) and Helena, Theodora ruled briefly with her sister Zoë from April to June 1042, when Zoë married Constantine IX Monomachos (*r.* 1042–1055). Upon the latter's death in 1055, the seventy-four-year-old Theodora, the last survivor of the Macedonian dynasty, refused to take a male consort and ruled alone for nineteen months until her death.

BIBLIOGRAPHY

Georgius Cedrenus, *Historia,* Immanuel Bekker, ed., II (1839), 485–487, 537–542, 556, 610–612; Michael Psellos, *Chronographie,* Émile Renauld, ed. and trans., I (1926), 106–127, and II (1928), 72–82, and *The Chronographia of Michael Psellus,* E. R. A. Sewter, trans. (1953), 102–121, 195–205.

ALICE-MARY M. TALBOT

[See also **Byzantine Empire: History (1025–1204); Constantine IX Monomachos; Macedonians; Psellos, Michael; Zoë the Macedonian.**]

THEODORE OF CANTERBURY, ST. (*ca.* 602–690). Theodore of Tarsus, archbishop of Canterbury from 669 to 690, a Greek of Tarsus in Cilicia, was educated in Athens, ordained in Rome, and in 668 sent by Pope Vitalian to take over the archbishopric. At the synod of Hertford (673) he completely reorganized the still-chaotic English church by setting up manageable dioceses directly dependent on Canterbury. With the help of his African friend Hadrian he set up a school in Canterbury where Greek, astronomy, and mathematics could be studied and which provided an excellent library. This and other schools, such as that at Wearmouth, where Bede studied, made English culture the most flourishing in Western Europe.

BIBLIOGRAPHY

Charles W. Previté-Orton, *Shorter Cambridge Medieval History,* I (1952), 178f.; Max Manitius, *Geschichte der lateinischen Literatur des Mittelalters,* I (1911).

W. T. H. JACKSON

[See also **Canterbury.**]

THEODORE I LASKARIS (*ca.* 1174–1221), founder of the Empire of Nicaea. In 1199 he married Anna, the daughter of the Byzantine emperor Alexios III Angelos (1195–1203). After his father-in-law was overthrown in 1203 he escaped to Asia Minor, where he laid the foundations of the Empire of Nicaea. He was proclaimed emperor, probably in August 1204. Theodore "was swift in battle, quick of temper, and extremely generous"; on no occasion was his bravery more apparent than at the Battle of Antioch in 1211, where he killed the Turkish sultan in single combat, thus turning a certain defeat into victory. He was succeeded by his son-in-law, John III Vatatzes.

BIBLIOGRAPHY

Demetrios I. Polemis, *The Doukai: A Contribution to Byzantine Prosopography* (1968), 139.

MICHAEL ANGOLD

[See also **Byzantine Empire: History; Crusades and Crusader States; John III Vatatzes; Nicaea, Empire of.**]

THEODORE II LASKARIS (1221–1258), Nicaean emperor, the son of John III Vatatzes (*r.* 1221–1254). Theodore was born in November 1221, apparently at the very hour his father ascended the Nicaean throne. His father took great pains over his education, appointing the best scholars of the day, Nikephoros Blemmydes and George Akropolites, as his tutors. In 1235 Theodore married Helena, the daughter of the Bulgarian tsar, John Asen II (1218–1241). They had four daughters and one son, John IV Laskaris, born in 1250.

Theodore II Laskaris set great store by the concept of the "philosopher-king" and produced a number of philosophical and theological treatises (although they display little originality). He was also a hymn writer and a patron of church music. His letters, which have survived, are masterpieces of Byzantine letter writing, amusing and irreverent, and occasionally moving, as in his description of the ruins of ancient Pergamum. He nevertheless emerges from his letters as a violent, quick-tempered, and sarcastic man with a talent for coining wounding nicknames.

Even before he came to the throne in 1254, his relations with the court aristocracy were cool. They deteriorated still further once he tried to assert the traditional Byzantine concept of the autocratic emperor. He wanted to reduce the power of the aristocracy by raising up men of humble origins to the chief positions in the state, and he dealt ruthlessly with those he suspected of plotting against him. In the closing year of his reign a pathologically suspicious nature was aggravated by increasingly serious bouts of epilepsy, which led to his death. He was then succeeded by his son as emperor of Nicaea.

In his short reign, Theodore II Laskaris showed himself to be a ruler of great energy. His main achievement was to hold his father's conquests in the southern Balkans in the face of a Bulgarian invasion. He waged a resolute winter campaign in 1254–1255.

BIBLIOGRAPHY

C. Astrue, "La tradition manuscrite des oeuvres oratoires profanes de Théodore II Lascaris," in *Travaux et mémoires,* **1** (1965); J. Dräseke, "Theodoros Laskaris," in *Byzantinische Zeitschrift,* **3** (1894); Nicolaus Festa, ed., *Theodori Ducae Lascaris Epistolae CCXVII* (1898); Eurydice Lappa-Zizicas, "Un traité inédit de Théodore II Lascaris," in *Actes du VIe congrès international des études byzantines,* I (1950); Ioannes Papadopoulos, *Théodore II Lascaris: Empereur de Nicée* (1908); Demetrios I. Polemis, *The Doukai: A Contribution to Byzantine Prosopography* (1968), 109–111,

MICHAEL ANGOLD

[See also **Bulgaria; John Asen II; John III Vatatzes; Nicaea, Empire of.**]

THEODORE (*fl.* 1230's), one of three apparently Greek artists who frescoed the Church of the Ascension at Mileševo in Serbia for King Vladislav I (1234–1236) in painted imitation of mosaic. The frescoes display a renewed sense of volume and mass that presage the paintings at Sopoćani and, ultimately, Palaiologan murals.

Another Theodore, surnamed Apsuedes, painted the Enkleistra of St. Neophytos near Paphos on Cyprus in 1183.

BIBLIOGRAPHY

Gabriel Millet and Anton Frolow, *La peinture du moyen âge en Yougoslavie* (1954), pls. 63–83.

LESLIE BRUBAKER

[See also **Serbian Art and Architecture.**]

THEODORE BALSAMON (*ca.* 1130/1140–1195), Byzantine canonist, was a career ecclesiastic of the church of Constantinople. He served as nomophylax, or head of the imperial law school, and chartophylax, or chief legal adviser to the patriarch, before becoming titular patriarch of Antioch (between 1185 and 1191). His chief work, a commentary on the *Nomocanon in Fourteen Titles,* was undertaken at the request of emperor and patriarch in order to determine precisely the canon law then in force. Balsamon frequently cites recent patriarchal and imperial decisions, often verbatim, making the work a valuable source for the historian. He also wrote monographs on various canonical issues, and responses to a series of questions addressed by the patriarch of Alexandria to the permanent synod at Constantinople.

BIBLIOGRAPHY

Editions. *Patrologia graeca,* CXIX (1864), 904–909, 1,162–1,224; CXXXVII–CXXXVIII (1864); and K. Rhallēs and M. Potlēs, *Syntagma tōn theiōn kai hierōn kanonōn,* I–V (1852–1859).

Studies. Hans Georg Beck, *Kirche und theologische Literatur im byzantinischen Reich* (1959), 657–658; Gerardus Petrus Stevens, *De Theodoro Balsamone: Analysis operum ac mentis iuridicae* (1969).

JOHN H. ERICKSON

[See also **Nomocanon.**]

The Angel at the Sepulcher. Fresco by Theodore from the Church of the Ascension, Mileševo, *ca.* 1236. REPRODUCED FROM OTO BIHALJI-MERIN, ED., *ART TREASURES OF YUGOSLAVIYA.* © 1973 IZDAVAČKI ZAVOD YUGOSLAVIYA, BEOGRAD

THEODORE METOCHITES (1270–1332), perhaps the greatest proponent of the so-called Palaiologan renaissance in Byzantium. He is today best remembered for his restoration and decoration of the Chora monastery (Kariye Djami) in Constantinople. He held several important positions in the government of Andronikos II, including grand logothete (1321–1328), and he amassed great wealth. But he was deposed in the revolution of 1328. Virtually all of his prolific scholarly output has been preserved, including *Commentaries on Aristotle, Introduction to Astronomy, Miscellaneous Essays, Orations,* and *Poems.*

BIBLIOGRAPHY

Ihor Ševčenko, "Theodore Metochites, the Chora, and the Intellectual Trends of His Times," in Paul Underwood, ed., *The Kariye Djami,* IV (1975).

ROBERT OUSTERHOUT

[See also **Byzantine Art (843–1453); Byzantine Literature; Kariye Djami; Palaiologoi.**]

THEODORE OF STUDIOS (759–826), Byzantine monastic reformer and theologian. Born into a prominent and pious Constantinopolitan family, Theodore and his brother Joseph entered monastic life about 780 under the direction of their maternal uncle Plato, abbot of Saccudium near Mt. Olympus in Bithynia. Ordained a priest in 787, Theodore succeeded Plato as abbot on the latter's retirement in 794. He opposed Emperor Constantine VI's adulterous second marriage in 795 and withdrew from communion with Patriarch Tarasius, who had tolerated it. As a consequence he was exiled in 797, and his monastic community was dispersed. Recalled later the same year, after Constantine was overthrown by his mother, Irene, he returned briefly to Saccudium, but in 799 the threat of Saracen raids led him to move with the greater part of his community to the dormant monastery of Studios in Constantinople, which he reformed on a strict cenobitic pattern. The "moechian" or "adultery" controversy broke out anew in 806, when the new patriarch, Nikephoros, reinstated the priest who had blessed Constantine VI's adulterous marriage.

Theodore's vehement protest resulted in a second period of exile (809–811).

The accession of Emperor Leo V in 813 brought a revival of iconoclasm and with it a third and particularly harsh exile for Theodore. After Leo's assassination in 820, Theodore was recalled by the new emperor, Michael II, but not permitted to reside in the capital. Theodore died in this state of semi-exile, but in 844, after the restoration of orthodoxy, his remains, along with those of his brother Joseph, were brought back to Constantinople with high honors. Theodore's writings include two series of catechetical discourses intended for the spiritual guidance of his monks; several dogmatic treatises against the iconoclasts; diverse homilies and panegyrics; many hymns, particularly for the Lenten season; and roughly 550 letters, which provide an invaluable picture of his age.

BIBLIOGRAPHY

Sources. Giuseppe Cozza-Luzi, ed., *Patrum nova bibliotheca,* VIII (1871), pt. 1, 1–244, for letters and fragments, IX (1888), pt. 1, 1–318, for "Short Catechesis," and pt. 2, 1–217, for "Long Catechesis"; *Patrologia graeca,* XCIX (1860), for dogmatic works and letters; Jean Baptiste Pitra, *Analecta sacra spicelegio solesmensi,* I (1876), 336–380, for poetry.

Studies. Hans Georg Beck, *Kirche und theologische Literatur im byzantinischen Reich* (1959), 491–495; Alice Gardner, *Theodore of Studium: His Life and Times* (1905, repr. 1974); Patrick Henry III, "Theodore of Studios: Byzantine Churchman" (diss., Yale Univ., 1968).

JOHN H. ERICKSON

[See also **Byzantine Empire: History (330–1025); Iconoclasm; Irene, Empress; Leo V the Armenian, Emperor; Monasticism, Byzantine; Nikephoros, Patriarch; Studios Monastery.**]

THEODORE OF TARSUS. See **Theodore of Canterbury, St.**

THEODORE PRODROMOS (*ca.* 1100–after 1162, perhaps 1170's), a Byzantine poet. He was a court poet of the dowager empress Irene Doukaina and, from the 1130's, of John II Komnenos. After John's death his position deteriorated, and he sought a dwelling place in a church institution, although he continued to write occasional poems praising the new emperor, Manuel I, and his generals.

Besides poems dedicated to various events of court life that are very important sources for twelfth-century Byzantine history, he left an erotic romance, *Rodanthe and Dosikles,* rhetorical works (especially the epitaph of Stephen Skylitzes, the metropolitan of Trebizond), letters, humorous scenes, and scholarly treatises. His identity with Ptochoprodromos, the author of four satirical poems in the vernacular (on a man under his wife's thumb and on monastic life, for example) has been questioned by S. Papadimitriu, who also denied Prodromos' authorship of the so-called poems of Mangana. Hörandner, although inclined to reject the first hypothesis, accepts the latter suggestion and opposes Pseudo-Prodromos of Mangana to the genuine Prodromos.

Prodromos, a contemporary of the Komnenian dynasty, contributed greatly to the creation of the new ethical ideal of the noble warrior and emphasized the military deeds of emperors and their kin rather than their piety and connection with God—traditional topics of previous panegyrics. He was able to present human feelings such as love and sympathy with suffering, and confer on his heroes human qualities, including weakness. The author's personality is present throughout his works, and he even regards imperial victories as a means for him to walk confidently throughout the vast territory of the now safe empire. His soft irony extends also to his own person: Prodromos describes laughingly his terrible appearance after an illness or his unhappy visit to a dentist who, being a dwarf, caused the poet such pain that he imagined him a giant.

Prodromos was very popular with his contemporaries. His friend Michael Italikos, for example, once met a monk who knew the entire oeuvre of Prodromos by heart. His works found imitators from the twelfth century on, and he was praised by contemporaries, especially by his follower Niketas Eugenianos.

BIBLIOGRAPHY

Wolfram Hörandner, *Theodoros Prodromos: Historische Gedichte* (1974); Athanasios Kambylis, *Prodromea* (1984); Alexander P. Kazhdan and Simon Franklin, *Studies on Byzantine Literature of the Eleventh and Twelfth Centuries* (1984), 87–114.

ALEXANDER P. KAZHDAN

[See also **Byzantine Literature; John II Komnenos; Manuel I Komnenos.**]

THEODORET OF CYR (*ca.* 393—457/458), bishop of Cyr, was one of the leaders of the theological school of Antioch. He was posthumously condemned for his Nestorian views by the so-called Council of the Three Chapters (Second Council of Constantinople) in 553. Theodoret was the author of a number of exegetical works as well as of the *Historia religiosa,* a series of biographies of Syrian holy men, which contains material on economic and social history as well as on the development of the early ascetic tradition. His major work, written while he was in exile in 449–450, was a continuation of Eusebius' *Ecclesiastical History* covering the period from 325 to 428. In this history he uses many of the same sources as Sozomen and Socrates Scholasticus, although his religious views sometimes put his objectivity in doubt.

BIBLIOGRAPHY

P. Canivet, "Theodoret of Cyr," in *New Catholic Encyclopedia,* XIV (1967); F. Dölger, "Byzantine Literature," in *Cambridge Medieval History,* IV, pt. 2 (1967).

LINDA C. ROSE

[See also **Byzantine Literature; Councils (Ecumenical, 325–787); Nestorianism; Socrates Scholasticus; Sozomen.**]

THEODORIC, MASTER (*fl.* mid fourteenth century), Czech painter and probably chief designer of 129 panels in the Chapel of the Holy Cross in Karlstein Castle. The castle, consecrated 9 February 1365, was where Emperor Charles IV kept imperial and Bohemian relics and treasures. The artist's name in Latin, "Magister Theodoricus, pictor noster et familiaris," is documented in a 1367 charter of Charles IV, and he is registered by 1348 as *primus* magister in the Prague painters' brotherhood. His is noted for dominant, massive, compact figures in bright colors.

BIBLIOGRAPHY

Erich Bachmann, ed., *Gothic Art in Bohemia* (1977), 48–49; Antonín Friedl, *Magister Theodoricus* (1956); Antonín Matějček and Jaroslav Pešina, *Czech Gothic Painting, 1350–1450* (1950), 51–53; Jaroslav Pešina,

St. Jerome. Panel painting by Master Theodoric from Karlstein Castle, mid 14th century. NATIONAL GALLERY, PRAGUE.

"Meister Theodorich," in Anton Legner, ed., *Die Parler und der Schöne Stil, 1350–1400* (1978); Alfred Stange, *Deutsche Malerei der Gotik,* II (1936), 34–43.

LARRY SILVER

[See also **Fresco Painting; Gothic Art: Painting and Manuscript Illumination.**]

THEODORIC OF FREIBERG (**Theodoricus Teutonicus de Vriberg, Dietrich von Freiberg**) (*ca.* 1240—1318/1320), Dominican theologian and philosopher. Little is known about Theodoric's life. There is no evidence about his place of birth or about his family. (A suggested noble descent from the barons of Freiberg in Saxony cannot be substantiated.) He is thought to have read philosophy and theology at the Dominican study center at Cologne between 1260 and 1270. In 1271 he is recorded as having been lector of the community of Freiberg. From 1272 to 1274 he resumed his studies at the University of Paris. He was lector of the Dominican community of Trier (Treverensis) in 1280/1281 and returned to Paris, where he remained until 1293, studying the *sententiae,* the opinions of the doctors of the church on theological questions.

On 3 September 1293 Theodoric was elected provincial of the German Dominican province. He held this office and that of vicar general until May 1296. In 1296/1297 he once more returned to Paris and acquired the degree of *magister theologiae.* After Albertus Magnus he was the second thirteenth-century German to gain this degree. From then on he is thought to have taught at Paris as *magister actu regens* (university professor), holding the chair reserved for non-French teachers. During the following decade he appears to have written the majority of his philosophical and theological works.

Records give evidence of his administrative activities within the order. In 1303 he took part in the provincial chapter at Koblenz. It elected him to the office of definitor. Then he was a member of the general Dominican chapter in Toulouse in May 1304 and the general chapter of Piacenza in June 1310, where he was appointed vicar of the German chapter of the Dominican order. He succeeded Johannes von Lichtenberg in this office and held it until a new provincial was elected. There are no further records of his life.

Theodoric wrote a great number of works on natural science, philosophy, logic, and theology. The first complete edition of Theodoric's works, published from 1977 to 1985, lists twenty-four tracts, a small number of *quaestiones,* and four letters. It is not possible to date these writings precisely. On the basis of internal evidence, however, a relative chronology of Theodoric's writings can be established. A first group comprises about thirteen tracts, which appear to have been written during his lecture period at Paris from 1297 to 1304. A second group of later date consists of about eight tracts, which seem to have been composed after the general chapter at Piacenza in 1310.

Research based on the first edition of the complete works has displayed Theodoric as a most original thinker who emancipated himself from the ways of thinking of his predecessors and immediate contemporaries. According to Flasch's preface to the edition of Theodoric's works, the best introduction to his philosophy is the trilogy *De tribus difficilibus quaestionibus,* comprising *De visione beatifica, De animatione caeli,* and *De accidentibus.* Analyzing the traditional concept of consciousness, Theodoric transformed the terms of *ens* and *esse, substantia* and *ratio,* and *deus* and *creator* to suit his new concept of consciousness. Theodoric's reform of metaphysics, which was in essence anti-Aristotelian, led to a new meaning of the concept of category and the individual problems of categorial analysis. These writings show him to be a philosopher who set out to answer the difficult problems of the last decades of the thirteenth century, and thus came into collision with Scholastic philosophy, and in particular with Thomas Aquinas, whom the Dominicans wanted to institute as the sole teacher of the order. Relying more on experiment than on traditional authorities, even Aristotle, and being fully aware of St. Thomas' reasoning, Theodoric's writings present a detailed anti-Thomistic metaphysic on all important issues. Contrary to Thomas he denies a real distinction between *existentia* and *essentia.* It is, however, not the difference on individual issues that separates Theodoric from Thomas but the difference in their spiritual foundations. Theodoric is convinced that the idea of an eternal creation of the world does not constitute a contradiction. His concept of the world is determined by the Neoplatonic quadruple concept of divine unity, spiritual nature, souls, and bodies. His concepts of being and nature, substance and relations, and God and soul were put into a new context and thus changed important ideas of Greek and Christian tradition. Theodoric fundamentally influenced the philosophy and theology of the late medieval period and helped to define the concepts of modern science and German mysticism.

BIBLIOGRAPHY

Source. Theodorici opera omnia, edited under the direction of Kurt Flasch, 4 vols. (1977–1985).

Studies. Willehad Eckert, "Dietrich von Freiberg," in *Lexikon für Theologie und Kirche,* III (1959); B. Mojsisch, "Dietrich von Freiberg," in *Lexikon des Mittelalters,* III (1986); Loris Sturlese, "Dietrich von Freiberg," in *Die deutsche Literatur des Mittelalters: Verfasserlexikon,* II (1980), and *Dokumente und Forschungen zu Leben und Werk Dietrichs von Freiberg* (1984); William A. Wallace, "Dietrich von Freiberg," in *Dictionary of Scientific Biography,* IV (1971).

WALTER FRÖHLICH

[See also **Albertus Magnus; Optics, Western European; Philosophy and Theology, Western European: Late Medieval; Physics.**]

THEODORIC THE OSTROGOTH (*b. ca.* 454/ 455), king of the Ostrogoths from 471 to 526. The son of Thiudmir, Theodoric was born into the royal Amal family while the Ostrogoths were living in Pannonia as federates of the Eastern Roman Empire. From 461 to 470 he lived at the court of Emperor Leo I in Constantinople as a hostage for his people, learning much about Roman ways but not, apparently, learning to write. Between 471 and 481 he contested the leadership of the Ostrogoths with Theodoric (Theodoric Strabo), son of Triarius. Upon the death of his rival in 481, Theodoric the Ostrogoth united all the Goths. He led his people to Italy in 488–489, defeated Odoacer, and was recognized as patrician of the Eastern Empire commissioned to rule Italy.

The early years of Theodoric's reign were very successful. He maintained much of the Roman administrative system and civil service, tolerated Jews and Catholics (he rebuilt some Catholic churches even though he was an Arian), and enforced separate but equal justice for both Goths and Romans. The last years of his reign were marred by his fear of treason, probably caused by the increasing resistance of Catholic Romans to Arian rule. The executions of Boethius (*d.* between 524 and 526) and his father-in-law, the aged senator Symmachus (*d. ca.* 525/526), belong to this period.

During Theodoric's lifetime the Ostrogoths formed a strong state, exercising considerable influence over the other barbarians in the West. The kingdom weakened rapidly after his death and shortly thereafter was conquered by the Byzantine armies of Justinian.

BIBLIOGRAPHY

Thomas S. Burns, *The Ostrogoths: Kingship and Society* (1980); Wilhelm Ensslin, *Theoderich der Grosse* (1959); Gottardo Garollo, *Teoderico re dei Goti e degl'Italiani* (1879); Ludwig M. Hartmann, *Geschichte Italiens im Mittelalter,* I (1897); Thomas Hodgkin, *Theodoric the Goth* (1891, repr. 1980), *The Ostrogothic Invasion* (1896, repr. 1967), and, as trans., *The Letters of Cassiodorus* (1886); James J. O'Donnell, *Cassiodorus* (1979); Herwig Wolfram, *Geschichte der Goten* (1979).

KATHERINE FISCHER DREW

[See also **Boethius, Anicius Manlius Severinus; Byzantine History (330–1025); Cassiodorus Senator, Flavius Magnus Aurelius; Odoacer; Ostrogoths; Roman Empire, Late.**]

THEODOSIAN CODE. See **Codex Theodosianus.**

THEODOSIOPOLIS. See **Karin (Karnoy K^całak^c).**

THEODOSIUS OF THE CAVES, ST. (*d.* 1074), founder of cenobitic monasticism at the Pecherskaya Lavra (Monastery of the Caves) in Kiev. A disciple of St. Anthony, who had brought to Russia the monastic traditions of Mount Athos, Theodosius first lived alone in a cave, following his teacher's example. Later, however, he became the abbot of an organized community, which adopted the rule of the large Constantinopolitan monastery of Studios. As abbot, he committed his community to social work and took part, in the name of Christian justice, in the political events of his time. Several of his sermons are preserved. Monks of his monastery composed the first Russian chronicle and numerous lives of saints, which were collected in a *Paterikon* (*Pechersky Paterik*).

JOHN MEYENDORFF

[See also **Athos, Mount; Paterikon; Pecherskaya Lavra; Theodore of Studios.**]

THEODOSIUS II THE CALLIGRAPHER, EMPEROR (401–450), an Eastern Roman (early Byzantine) emperor from 402, when but an infant, until his death. While he reigned in Constantinople, the Eastern Empire prospered despite Hun wars and christological controversies, governed by capable ministers and by the emperor's energetic sister Pulcheria Augusta (399–453), who ruled jointly with her brother. Scrupulous, ascetic, and bookish, Theodosius devoted himself meanwhile to scholarship and manuscripts—hence the later sobriquet "calligrapher."

BIBLIOGRAPHY

John B. Bury, *History of the Later Roman Empire,* I (1923), 212–235; Kenneth G. Holum, *Theodosian Empresses: Women and Imperial Dominion in Late Antiquity* (1982); Adolf Lippold, "Theodosius II," in Paulys, *Realenzyclopädie der klassischen Altertumswissenschaft,* suppl. XIII (1973), 961–1,044.

KENNETH G. HOLUM

[See also **Byzantine History; Codex Theodosianus; Constantinople.**]

THEODULF OF ORLÉANS (*ca.* 760–821), a Visigoth who came to the court of Charlemagne near the end of the eighth century and joined a very influential group of scholars who advised the king. Awarded several abbacies, Theodulf served as bishop of Orléans until 817, when his political activities led Louis I the Pious to depose him and send him into exile. He remained in exile until his death.

Theodulf was one of the most prolific and original scholars of the early Carolingian period. He prepared a scholarly edition of the Bible and wrote several important theological treatises. As an ecclesiastical administrator he was responsible for a series of statutes intended to guide Christian life in his diocese. His poetry is remarkable for its technical proficiency, as an important source for Carolingian cultural history, and as a vehicle for Theodulf's biting satire. Some of the poems reflect a deep appreciation for art, which is also apparent in the church of St. Germigny-des-Prés, built under his direction, and in the decoration of the Bibles produced in his scriptorium.

BIBLIOGRAPHY

Franz Brunhölzl, *Geschichte der lateinischen Literatur des Mittelalters,* I (1975), 288–299, 549–550; Elisabeth Dahlhaus-Berg, *Nova antiquitas et antiqua novitas: Typologische Exegese und isidorianisches Geschichtsbild bei Theodulf von Orléans* (1975); Paul Meyvaert, "The Authorship of the *Libri Carolini:* Observations Prompted by a Recent Book," in *Revue bénédictine,* 89 (1979); Thomas F. X. Noble, "Some Observations of the Deposition of Archbishop Theodulf of Orleans in 817," in *Journal of the Rocky Mountain Medieval and Renaissance Association,* 2 (1981).

JOHN J. CONTRENI

[See also **Bible; Carolingian Latin Poetry; Carolingians; Charlemagne; Contraception, European; Latin Literature; Pre-Romanesque Architecture.**]

THEOLOGY. See Philosophy and Theology.

THEOLOGY, SCHOOLS OF. In the early Scholastic period, from 1080 to 1230, the term "school of theology" indicates a group of central thinkers who were surrounded by a number of authors sharing some distinctive traits or ideas. Some of these followers seemed to be in touch with the personal teaching of their master. Others corrected their master's positions after they were condemned, or provided explanations for issues that were not correctly interpreted. Some used the master's writings as the basis of their own teaching, simply interpreting the fundamental text with their own marginal notations. The connection between these masters and their followers is not always clearly defined; some even seem to be following two or more masters. But the influence of these masters carries on through their own works or those of their followers into the more famous treatises by the teachers of the late Scholastic period.

Anselm of Canterbury (1033–1109), for example, had a group of authors closely connected to him (certainly Anselm of Laon stands out), yet he does not seem to have gathered about him a clearly defined group of disciples. Yves Lefèvre would add to the list of Anselm of Canterbury's "school" Honorius Augustodunensis (1075/1080–*ca.* 1156), whom he considers the author of the *Elucidarium* (Clarification). Lefèvre, the latest editor of the *Elucidarium,* sees Honorius following the definitions concerning divinity represented by the *Monologion* of Anselm and referring to Anselm when he mentions "the subtlety of Masters" in the preface of the *Elucidarium.* Honorius, furthermore, seems to derive his ideas on the impossibility of ransoming from the devil, the sin of Adam, the necessary satisfaction for that sin, and the interpretation of the Incarnation and Redemption from Anselm's *Cur Deus homo* (Why did God become man?). Yet, argues Lefèvre, Honorius seems to know these not from a study of Anselm's writings; rather his tone shows closer contact with Anselm personally. The placing of Honorius in the school of Anselm, however, has been questioned by a long list of scholars, most recently by Robert D. Crouse.

The school of Anselm of Laon (*ca.* 1050–1117) is somewhat better established, including a number of well-known personalities such as Radulphus of Laon, Abelard, and perhaps Gilbert of Poitiers (also associated with the school of Chartres), although the latter two were even more famous for having their own schools. Adam of the Little Bridge (even he had a famous pupil, Godfrey of St. Victor) among his many writings has left a substantial letter he addressed "to his master Anselm" (Bruges, Bibliothèque de la ville, cod. lat. 536, ff. 89v–94v). Alberic of Rheims, with the help of other members of Anselm's school, challenged Abelard at the Council of Soissons in 1121 and even had him condemned there. This group, which claimed to represent Anselm's teaching, could never assimilate the positions of Abelard into its school and continued to resist them until Abelard was condemned at Sens in 1140. Lesser-known figures in the school were Gilbert the Universal, John of Tours, and Robert of Bosco (one of the defenders of Gilbert of Poitiers in 1248), who spent "seven years at the feet of Master Anselm." Finally, we should add to the rolls of Anselm's school the name of Archbishop Hugh of Rouen, whose most famous work, *Contra haereticos,* written about 1150, is considered one of the first Scholastic treatises on the church.

Certainly the most vilified member of Anselm of Laon's school is more famous for his own. Peter Abelard (*ca.* 1079–*ca.* 1142) had a short-lived but flourishing school. A number of works by his students reveal this fact. The brief and unpolished *Sententiae Florianenses* present us with some of Abelard's teachings before Walter of Mortagne, one of Peter's first critics and a student of Anselm of Laon and Alberic of Rheims, wrote to him, and before the rising tide of opposition caused him to revise some of his opinions. The *Sententiae* of Hermann are a more thorough and comprehensive presentation of Abelard's teachings and even preserve alternations in Abelard's positions due to criticism. The *Sententiae Parisienses I* are more scholastic in character, revealing the set format: *quaeritur, solutio, opponitur,* and *responsio.* The *Commentary on the Epistles of St. Paul,* found in a Cambridge manuscript and written just before St. Bernard's death in 1153, called Abelard "The Philosopher," and this Abelardian commentary gives evidence that "The Philosopher" lectured on all of Paul's epistles and not just on the *Epistle to the Romans* (whose exposition by Abelard himself survives).

Many other works by students illustrate Abelard's theology, but perhaps they should be separated somewhat from the foregoing since they also show a marked connection with the competing school of Hugh of St. Victor. In them the two traditions are juxtaposed and evaluated. These include the *Sententiae Parisienses II,* the *Ysagoge in theologiam,* the *Sententiae* of Roland Bandinelli (Pope Alexander III), the *Sententiae* of Omnebene (*d.* 1185), and an abbreviation of the *Commentary on the Romans.* Robert of Melun (*d.* 1167), Abelard's successor at the School of Arts in Paris, shows a strong dependence on Peter on many points in his *Quaestiones de divina pagina* and *Sententiae,* but

he also manifests an undeniable independence. Certain links to Abelard likewise show themselves in Robert's disciples, John of Cornwall, John of Salisbury (*d.* 1180), and Robert Pullen (*d.* 1146).

The "orthodox mystic" Hugh of St. Victor (*d.* 1141) had greater influence than even Abelard on theology in the twelfth and thirteenth centuries. Most famous for his *De sacramentis christianae fidei,* Hugh found strong followers in the unknown author of the *Summa sententiarum,* who frequently attacked Abelard, and in Clarenbaud of Arras (*d.* 1170), one of the great opponents of the school of Gilbert of Poitiers.

Gilbert of Poitiers (*ca.* 1075–1154), with his commentaries on the *Opuscula sacra* of Boethius and on Scripture, influenced, in an almost pure form, the *Commentary on St. Paul* (Paris, Bibliothèque Nationale, cod. lat. 686), the anonymous *Sententiae divinitatis,* and some collections of *Quaestiones.* The most famous names associated with Gilbert's school, though mixed with many non-Porretan influences, were Radulphus Ardens (last half of the twelfth century), Master Martin (end of the twelfth century), Simon of Tournai (*d.* 1201), Alan of Lille (*d. ca.* 1203), Guy d'Orchelles (early thirteenth century), and Pope Innocent III (*d.* 1216).

Peter Lombard (*ca.* 1100–1160), through his *Sentences,* could lay claim to a "school" of commentators on his work all the way up to the time of Melanchthon. He is known also for his glosses on the psalms (*Glossa in Psalmos*) and on the *Epistles of St. Paul* (*Glossa in Epistolas beati Pauli*), but it is the *Sentences* that drew early glosses in the margins of his text from Peter Comestor (*d.* 1178), Paganus, Chancellor Odo, Maurice of Sully, John of Tours, and a great number of anonymous commentators. Lombard's most famous disciples were Peter Comestor, who wrote the *Historia scholastica,* and the chancellor Peter of Poitiers (*d.* 1205).

Odo of Ourscamp or Soissons (*d.* 1171) claims to have heard Peter Abelard lecturing on the power of God and indicates his own disagreement with Peter's position. Odo himself seems to have been the head of an important school, since numerous collections of *quaestiones,* many belonging personally to him, are found in the manuscript libraries of a dozen European cities.

Andrew of St. Victor (*d.* 1175) dedicated himself to the study of Scripture in its literal sense and applied his method to much of the Old Testament. He had a very strong influence on the exegetical works and the *Summa de sacramentis* of Peter the Chanter (*d.* 1197), Robert of Courson (*d.* 1219), and Stephen Langton, archbishop of Canterbury (*d.* 1228).

William of Auxerre (*d.* 1237) brings us to the threshold of the golden age of Scholasticism. The *Summa aurea,* his most famous work, was abbreviated by Herbert of Auxerre and by Master Ardengus, and it influenced the early Dominican school of Hugh of St. Cher, Roland of Cremona, and John of Treviso. A scribe of John's *Summa in theologia* merely summarizes the prologue declarations of the Dominican follower of William when he writes: "Here ends the short and useful *Summa in theologia* which John of Treviso of the Order of Preachers composed, and in which he most especially imitates Master William of Auxerre and follows the opinions of others."

Artur M. Landgraf provides a long list of authors whose works have not yet been found. They are, however, the teachers whose names and citations fill the margins of theological works we possess from this period: Maurice of Sully, Achard, John of Tours, Gerard Puella, Gerard of Brussels, Gerard of Douai, Ivo of Chartres (to whom many works are attributed besides the *Commentary on the Psalms,* which survives in whole or part in four Parisian manuscripts), William of St. Bertin, Frowin of Engleberg, Peter of Corbeil, and Master Alardus. The lacunae suggested by this list underscore the provisional character of the history of this early period of Scholasticism and the tentative lines of the sketch we possess of its schools.

BIBLIOGRAPHY

Editions are cited in the articles on individual theologians. See also Marie-Dominique Chenu, *Nature, Man, and Society in the Twelfth Century,* Jerome Taylor and Lester K. Little, trans. (1968); Gillian R. Evans, *Old Arts and New Theology* (1980); Artur M. Landgraf, *Einführung in die Geschichte der theologischen Literatur der Frühscholastik* (1948); David Edward Luscombe, *The School of Peter Abelard* (1969); John Marenbon, *Early Medieval Philosophy (450–1150)* (1983); Jaroslav Pelikan, *The Christian Tradition,* III, *The Growth of Medieval Theology (600–1300)* (1978).

Stephen F. Brown

[See also **Aristotle in the Middle Ages; Plato in the Middle Ages; Philosophy and Theology, Western European; Quaestiones; Scholasticism, Scholastic Method; Schools, Cathedral; Universities;** and individual philosophers and theologians.]

THEOPHANES CONFESSOR (Homologetes) (*ca.* 760–12 March 818 on the island of Samothrace), a Byzantine chronicler. Born as the son of a general (*strategos*), he took the monastic habit at the age of eighteen and settled in a monastic foundation of his father's on Sigriane (southern coast of Propontis); later he founded a monastery on the island of Kalonymos and then came back to Sigriane, to the monastery of Megas Agros. A fervent worshiper of icons, he was exiled by the Emperor Leo V. There exists under his name a chronicle, the *Chronographia,* which was compiled between 811 and 814. It encompasses the period from Diocletian to the second year of Michael I's reign (285–813) and is a continuation of the chronicle by George Synkellos (*d.* 810/811). Recently, Cyril Mango proposed that Synkellos rather than Theophanes had written the *Chronographia.* Whether or not Theophanes is the author of this book, it remains a very important source, particularly for the eighth century, for both Byzantium and the neighboring territories, despite the author's hatred of the Iconoclasts, which led to many distortions of the events described. His social predilections are reflected in his characterization of Nikephoros I, whose economic and financial policy Theophanes tried to debunk: the son of a general had contempt for the representative of the bureaucracy whose reign ended in the military catastrophe of 811. Theophanes created a new type of historical writing. He consciously eliminated any hint of the author's evaluation of events and tried to create the illusion of complete objectivity. His language is consistently simple; his discussion of events is based on a chronological rather than topical order; and he appears to regard the simplest fact as a marvel revealing God's hidden will. Saints rather than emperors are the heroes of his narration; even a general, Belisarios, finds more sympathy than his lord, Justinian I. Among emperors, only Constantine the Great, the founder of the Christian empire, is a paradigmatic figure, with whom no later emperor can compete. Until the eleventh century the *Chronographia* was regarded as an exemplary historical work (see the preamble to John Skylitzes' chronicle). It was translated into Latin by Anastasius the Bibliothecarius. Theophanes is a saint of the Orthodox church.

BIBLIOGRAPHY

Sources. Theophanes Confessor, *Chronographia,* C. de Boor, ed., 2 vols. (1883–1885, repr. 1963). English translations are by A. Santoro (1982) and H. Turtledove (1982).

Studies. I. Čičurov, "Mesto 'Chronografii' Feofana v rannevizantiiskoi istoriografičeskoi tradicii (IV–načalo IX v.)," in *Drevneišie gosudarstva na territorii SSSR* (1983), 5–146; Herbert Hunger, *Die hochsprachliche profane Literatur der Byzantiner*, I (1978), 334–339; Cyril Mango, "Who Wrote the Chronicle of Theophanes?" in *Zbornik radova Vizanto-loškog instituta*, 18 (1978), 9–17. See also J. N. Ljubarskii, "Feofan Ispovednik i istocniki ego 'Chronografii,'" in *Vizantiiškii Vremennik*, 45 (1984), 72–86.

ALEXANDER P. KAZHDAN

[See also **Anastasius Bibliothecarius; Historiography, Byzantine.**]

THEOPHANES CONTINUATUS, or the "Continuators of Theophanes," a conventional name for a Byzantine historical compilation covering the period 813–961. It is preserved in an eleventh-century manuscript (Vaticanus 167) and consists of four different parts. The first part of *Theophanes continuatus* embraces the reigns of Leo V, Michael II, Theophilos, and Michael III. The second part is the life of Basil I, written either by Constantine VII Porphyrogenitos or by someone in his immediate milieu. Both of these parts coincide in their content with the work of Genesios, but the problem of their relationship remains unclear. The third part is dedicated to the reigns of Leo VI, Alexander, young Constantine VII, and Romanos I and presents one of the versions of Symeon the Logothete's chronicle. The last part describes the independent rule of Constantine VII and of his son Romanos II (until the conquest of Crete), but it is interrupted in the middle of a sentence. This portion was written by a contemporary, who might have been identified with Theodoros Daphnopates, though this has not been proved.

BIBLIOGRAPHY

Immanuel Bekker, ed., *Theophanes continuatus* (1838); Herbert Hunger, *Die hochsprachliche profane Literatur der Byzantiner*, I (1978), 339–343; Ihor Ševčenko, "Storia letteraria," in *La civiltà bizantina dal IX al' XI secolo*, II (1978), 89–127.

ALEXANDER P. KAZHDAN

[See also **Basil I the Macedonian, Emperor; Constantine VII Porphyrogenitos; Genesios, Joseph; Historiography, Byzantine; Michael III, Emperor; Symeon the Logothete.**]

The Transfiguration. Icon by Theophanes the Greek from the cathedral of the Transfiguration, Pereslavl, early 15th century. © 1981 ARNOLDO MONDADORI EDITORE AND MLADINSKA KNJIGA

THEOPHANES THE GREEK (Feofan Grek) (*b. ca.* 1340) was a Byzantine artist who came from Constantinople to Russia around 1370. After working in Novgorod (a number of his frescoes are preserved in the Transfiguration Church there), he moved in the 1390's to Moscow, where he painted several churches before collaborating with Andrei Rublev and Prokhor of Gorodets in decorating the Moscow Kremlin's Annunciation Cathedral (1405). A number of his icons can still be seen there. Theophanes brought to Russia the graceful, almost classical, treatment of the human figure and the carefully highlighted and delicately shaded palette of Palaiologan Byzantine painting.

BIBLIOGRAPHY

Igor E. Grabar, *Feofan Grek* (1922); George Heard Hamilton, *The Art and Architecture of Russia* (1954, 2nd ed. 1975); Viktor N. Lazarev, *Feofan Grek i ego shkola* (1961), trans. into German as *Theophanes der Grieche und seine Schule* (1968), and *Iskusstvo Novgoroda* (1947).

GEORGE P. MAJESKA

[See also **Byzantine Art; Prokhor of Gorodets; Rublev, Andrei; Russian Art.**]

THEOPHANO, EMPRESS (*d*. after 976), one of the most famous of the Byzantine empresses. Theophano, the daughter of a publican, was the wife of Romanos II and the mother of Basil II. She was a woman of great beauty, but the stories told about her indicate that her character left something to be desired. She had Romanos' five sisters forcibly put in convents, and she is accused of helping to poison Constantine VII and of murdering Romanos. It has also been alleged that she murdered her lover John Tzimiskes. When Romanos died in 963, she became regent and married Nikephoros II Phokas, who became basileus along with her two young sons. She and John Tzimiskes plotted Nikephoros' death, and John was proclaimed emperor, but the patriarch refused to crown him until John had punished his own accomplices in the murder of Nikephoros. John exiled Theophano to a convent, but she escaped. She was caught and exiled to Armenia, where she remained until 976, when her sons became the rulers, but she took no further part in state affairs.

BIBLIOGRAPHY

George Ostrogorsky, *History of the Byzantine State*, Joan Hussey, trans., rev. ed. (1969).

LINDA C. ROSE

[See also **Anna; Basil II "Killer of Bulgars"; Basileus; John I Tzimiskes; Nikephoros II Phokas; Romanos II.**]

THEOPHILUS (*fl.* late eleventh–early twelfth centuries) is the pseudonym of a German Benedictine who, possibly about 1126, wrote *De diversis artibus,* the best medieval treatise on techniques of the fine arts. He was probably Roger of Helmarshausen, a monk famous for his metalwork.

Theophilus was thoroughly versed not only in all the fine arts but also in the latest developments of Benedictine theology and spirituality. He was a

cosmopolitan in art matters, interested in Byzantine and Islamic crafts, and aware of Russian niello at a time when that technique was only beginning to be used in Russia itself.

Having withdrawn from the world into an abbey, Theophilus was not concerned with secular arts like shipbuilding or making armor. Yet his scope was great: he describes in detail the making of everything needed to assist the liturgical praise of God, from the altar's chalice to the stained glass windows to the organ pipes and bells for the towers. Much that is novel in technology emerges: the first oil pigments; the earliest description of a wiredrawing plate; a new formula for potassium glass that made it cheaper; the first description of the tin-plating of iron by immersion; the earliest general application to machine design of flywheels to equalize speed of rotation. The middle of the twelfth century witnessed great efforts to codify and clarify knowledge: the works of Gratian, Peter Lombard, Hugh of St. Victor, and Peter Comestor are examples. Theophilus' handbook for the monastic craftsman belongs in this company.

BIBLIOGRAPHY

Sources. De diversis artibus, C. R. Dodwell, ed. and trans. (1961); *On Divers Arts,* John G. Hawthorne and Cyril S. Smith, eds. and trans. (1963).

Studies. John Van Engen, "Theophilus Presbyter and Rupert of Deutz: The Manual Arts and Benedictine Theology in the Early Twelfth Century," in *Viator,* 11 (1980); Lynn White, Jr., "Theophilus Redivivus," in *Technology and Culture,* 5 (1964).

LYNN WHITE, JR.

[See also **Bells; Bronze and Brass; Émail Brun; Enamel; Glass, Western European; Gratian; Hugh of St. Victor; Metalsmiths, Gold and Silver; Metalworkers; Peter Comestor; Peter Lombard; Roger of Helmarshausen; Technology, Treatises on; Technology, Western.**]

THEOPHYLAKTOS SIMOKATTES (*d.* after 640), Byzantine historian and prefect and imperial secretary under Heraklios (*r.* 610–641), author of a history of the reign of Maurice (582–602), a dialogue on physics, and a collection of rhetorical letters. His *Histories* is the last of the early Byzantine classicizing histories and the most elaborate in terms of literary style and composition. It is prefaced with an elaborate dialogue between History and Philosophy, written in an affected classicizing style that refers to the restoration of learning in Constantinople under the patriarch Sergios (whose protégé he was) and the liberation of the historian himself under the new regime of Heraklios. Last of the successors of Procopius and Agathias, Theophylaktos went further in incorporating Christian material into classicizing history, yet outdid his predecessors in stylistic affectation.

The eight-volume *Histories* constitutes a rehabilitation of the reputation of Maurice, but Theophylaktos was not an eyewitness, having been born in Egypt, nor did he possess the practical military and political experience of Procopius. Since he rarely names his sources—he drew on eyewitness accounts, archives, and ambassadorial testimony available to him in his post as prefect—and the works of the chief authors he uses (Menander Protector and John of Epiphaneia) survive only in fragments, it is not easy to distinguish the value of his contribution. He tends to be vague on chronological matters, but in general his work is important as the major surviving source for the period.

To a modern reader Theophylaktos is memorable perhaps chiefly for his extraordinarily precious style, which derives from the rhetorical ambition that led him to compose letters. He resorts to clumsy periphrases in order to avoid modernisms and will deliberately change a quotation from a classical author in order to achieve a rhythmical clausula. Photios' opinion was that he carried stylistic ambitions too far and laid himself open to the charge of puerile excess. However, despite these affectations, he often wrote about Christian matters and showed himself to be an orthodox and patriotic Christian. Thus his classicism is very different from that of Procopius.

The *Quaestiones physicae* is a work of Theophylaktos' youth, a series of questions and answers on natural curiosities. Like the *Histories,* it is presented in an affected and elaborate literary style. He also wrote eighty-four highly rhetorical letters on moral, rustic, and erotic themes that are attributed to various personages with names drawn from the bucolic and comedy genres. These two works explain and illustrate many of the tendencies so obvious in Theophylaktos' historical work, which tend to be those most alien to modern readers.

BIBLIOGRAPHY

Sources. Epistolographi Graeci, Rudolf Hercher, ed. (1873); *Historiae,* Carl de Boor, ed. (1887, rev. ed. by Peter Wirth 1972); *Quaestiones naturali,* Lidia Massa Positano, ed. (1953).

Studies. N. H. Baynes, "The Literary Construction of the History of Theophylactus Simocatta," in *Xenia: Hommage international à l'Université nationale de Grèce* (1912); Paul Lemerle, *Le premier humanisme byzantin* (1971), 78–79; Theodor Nissen, "Das Prooemium zu Theophylakts Historien und die Sophistik," in *Byzantinisch-neugriechische jahrbucher,* 15 (1938); Zinaida Vladimirovna Udalcova, "K voprosy o mirovozzrenie vizantijskogo istorika VI v. Feofilakta Simokatty," in *Zbornik radova Vizantoloskog instituta,* 11 (1968), "Le monde vu par les historiens byzantins du IVe au VIIe siècle," in *Byzantinoslavica,* 33 (1972), and *Idejno-politicheskaya borba v ranney Vizantii* (1974); Otto Veh, *Untersuchungen zu dem byzantinischen Historiker Theophylaktos Simokattes* (1957).

AVERIL CAMERON

[See also **Agathias; Historiography, Byzantine; Maurice, Emperor; Menander Protector; Procopius.**]

THEOTOKOS (Greek, "the one who bore God"), a title designating the Virgin Mary. Used frequently by several Christian authors of the fourth century—for example, Alexander of Alexandria (*d.* 328), Gregory of Nazianzus (*d. ca.* 390), and Gregory of Nyssa (*d. ca.* 394)—the term became controversial in 428, when Nestorius, in sermons preached following his consecration as patriarch of Constantinople, declared it to be inappropriate. A devotee of the Antiochene christological doctrine held by Theodore of Mopsuestia, Nestorius found it impossible for a created human person to be "mother of God," since, according to the Council of Nicaea (325), the incarnate Son of God was eternally preexisting. Mary, therefore, gave birth not to God but to the man Jesus, with whom the Son of God was united as one person (*prosōpon*). Thus, the teaching of Nestorius implied the doctrine of the "two sons": in Jesus Christ the Son of God was united to the son of Mary, but the two remained distinct. *Prosōpon,* the term used to designate this union, could be interpreted as face or countenance and did not necessarily imply real personal unity of the two natures of Christ.

The writings of Cyril of Alexandria, directed against Nestorius, strongly affirm the absolute unity of subject in Christ, this subject being the Son of God or the incarnate Word of God. Consequently, no other person than this "Only Begotten Son" was born of Mary. *Theotokos* thus became a fundamental christological affirmation, endorsed by the Council of Ephesus (431), at which Nestorius was condemned, and reaffirmed by the Council of Chalcedon (451). In Byzantine Orthodoxy it became the main and most widely used title of Mary and was the only truly dogmatic definition of her dignity. Its confirmation by ecumenical councils led to the widespread development of Marian piety in the Christian East.

BIBLIOGRAPHY
Aloys Grillmeier, *Christ in Christian Tradition*, John Bowden, trans., I (1965, 2nd rev. ed. 1975); John Meyendorff, *Christ in Eastern Christian Thought*, 2nd ed. (1975).

JOHN MEYENDORFF

[See also **Christology; Church Fathers; Councils (Ecumenical, 325–787); Cyril of Alexandria, St.; Heresies, Byzantine; Nestorianism; Nestorius; Philosophy and Theology, Byzantine; Virgin Mary.**]

THESSALONIKI (**Thessalonica**), the leading city of nothern Greece, was founded in 316 B.C. by King Cassander of Macedonia, who named it for his bride, Thessaloníkē, sister of Alexander the Great. The Romans respected its vigorous municipal life and made it the provincial capital and major city on the Via Egnatia, the great military highway across the Balkans. It was a thriving metropolis when, about A.D. 50, the Apostle Paul preached there.

Under the Tetrarchy, Thessaloniki was the residence of Emperor Galerius (293–311), who adorned it richly, as the remains of his palace, triumphal arch, and mausoleum still attest. Galerius' persecution of Christians included the martyrdom in 303 of a young soldier-convert, Demetrius, who was soon recognized as the city's patron saint and traditional protector.

Seat of an imperial mint and base for Balkan military operations, Thessaloniki was favored by Theodosius the Great (r. 379–395), who had built the still-surviving city walls. A riot by the populace against his German garrison in 390 provoked his notorious massacre of some 7,000 Thessalonians in their hippodrome in retaliation.

The city's strategic importance was heightened in ensuing epochs of barbarian penetrations into the Balkans, especially during seventh-century in-undations by the Slavs. It withstood a series of fierce sieges, and by 688 Emperor Justinian II had restored its safety. Thereafter, its prosperity grew and it became a principal point of contact between Byzantium and the Slavs. From Thessaloniki came Constantine/Cyril and Methodios, the great ninth-century missionaries to the Slavs. Its annual October fair, linked to the feast of St. Demetrius, reflected its natural domination of Balkan commerce.

Thessaloniki's general peace and prosperity were jolted by occasional disasters. In the summer of 904 an Arab pirate fleet stormed and sacked it. The city also suffered from Bulgarian raids during the reign of King Symeon (893–927). In 1185 it was taken by the Normans, who sacked and occupied it brutally during a short-lived expedition.

After the Fourth Crusade shattered the Byzantine Empire (1204), Thessaloniki became the capital of a major Latin kingdom of Thessalonica under Boniface of Montferrat, who was killed in a Bulgarian ambush (1207). Latin rule in Thessaloniki ended in 1224, when Theodore Angelos, Byzantine despot of Epiros, seized it and made it capital of his ephemeral empire. Reincorporated into the restored Byzantine Empire of the Palaiologoi, Thessaloniki resumed its great political and commercial role, even rivaling Constantinople as the latter's prosperity was diverted by Italian mercantile interests. But political and economic strains bred social discontent, which produced an era of violent social strife and the establishment of a breakaway regime under the Zealots (1342–1350).

In the latter fourteenth century the city faced the advancing Turks, who seem to have subjected it to tributary status at times. Eventually, in 1423, too weak to maintain it, the Byzantines ceded it to the Venetians. The latter's brief regime ended when the Turks took it by storm in 1430. Sultan Murad II (1421–1451) was fond of it and made it the Ottoman capital during his reign. In the late fifteenth century began the influx of Jews, first Sephardic and then Ashkenazic, which colored the city's character under the Turks and down to its incorporation into the kingdom of Greece, on the feast of St. Demetrius, 26 October 1912.

BIBLIOGRAPHY
Firmin O'Sullivan, *The Egnatian Way* (1972); N. Papahadjis, *Monuments of Thessalonike*, William Sanford, trans., 2nd ed. (1962); Oreste Tafrali, *Thessalonique au quatorzième siècle* (1913), *Topographie de Thessalonique* (1913), and *Thessalonique dès origines au*

quatorzième siècle (1919); Apostolos E. Vacalopoulos, *A History of Thessaloniki,* T. F. Carney, trans. (1972), and *History of Macedonia, 1354–1833,* Peter Megann, trans. (1973).

JOHN W. BARKER

[See also **Ambrose, St.; Boniface of Montferrat; Byzantine History (1204–1453); Cyril and Methodios, Sts.; Epiros, Despotate of; Fairs; Jews in Europe; Murad II; Nicaea, Empire of; Zealots.**]

THIBAUT DE CHAMPAGNE (1201–1253). Called *roi de Navarre* in manuscript collections, Thibaut is considered the master of the northern French courtly lyric at its apogee (1225–1250). Author of thirty-six *chansons d'amour,* fourteen *jeux partis,* several *pastourelles, serventois,* crusade songs, and a *lai lyrique,* Thibaut stresses the paradoxical nature of love's suffering and the poet-persona's steadfastness toward the *dame.* Unique among trouvère lyrics of his time is Thibaut's use of sustained metaphors—that of the pelican, the unicorn, and the prison of love. Musically, Thibaut's lyrics may be considered among the finest of his generation.

BIBLIOGRAPHY

Source. Axel Wallensköld, ed., *Les chansons de Thibaut de Champagne* (1925, repr. 1968).

Studies. Kathleen J. Brahney, "The Poetry of Thibaut de Champagne: A Thematic Study" (diss., Michigan State University, 1976); Martha Rowe Dolly and Raymond J. Cormier, "*Aimer, souvenir, souffrir:* Les chansons d'amour de Thibaut de Champagne," in *Romania,* 99 (1978); G. Lavis and M. Stasse, *Les chansons de Thibaut de Champagne: Concordances et index* (1981).

KATHLEEN J. BRAHNEY

[See also **French Literature: Lyric; Jeu Parti; Pastourelle; Troubadour, Trouvère.**]

THIERRY OF CHARTRES (*fl.* first half of twelfth century), philosopher and theologian. First mentioned as *scolarum magister* at Chartres in 1121, Thierry that same year took part in the Council of Soissons, which condemned Peter Abelard. He was a fiery adversary of the Cornificians, who disregarded literary good form. Subsequently Thierry taught at Paris, where one of his students in rhetoric and logic was John of Salisbury. In 1141 he

succeeded Gilbert of Poitiers as chancellor at Chartres, assisting in 1148 at the Council of Rheims, which examined Gilbert's views on the Trinity. Thierry died between 1150 and 1155.

Thierry wrote commentaries on Cicero and Boethius, but his fame is based on two other works. In his *Heptateuchon* he argues that the seven liberal arts are the only instruments by which wisdom can be attained; especially important is the trivium. Thierry attempts a synthesis of Genesis and Plato's *Timaeus* (in Calcidius' version) in the *Tractatus de sex dierum operibus.*

He has been called a pantheist because of his ultrarealism. Two things stand out in his *Tractatus:* he gives the first mechanistic interpretation of movement (impetus theory), and he attempts to prove the existence of God and the necessity of the Trinity through arithmetical proofs (*probationes arithmeticae*).

BIBLIOGRAPHY

Sources. Paul Thomas, "Un commentaire au moyen âge sur la rhétorique de Cicéron," in *Mélanges Graux* (1884), includes excerpts; the complete text of Thierry's commentary is in Brussels, Bibliothèque royale Albert Iᵉʳ, MS 10057. Niklaus M. Häring, ed., *Commentaries on Boethius by Thierry of Chartres and His School* (1971), which also includes his *Tractatus de sex dierum operibus;* Wilhelm Jansen, ed., *Der Kommentar des Clarenboldis von Arras zu Boethius De Trinitate* (1926); Jules A. Clerval has published parts of the *Heptateuchon* in his *L'enseignement des arts libéraux à Chartres et à Paris dans la première moitié du XIIᵉ siècle, d'après l'Heptateuchon de Thierry de Chartres* (1889).

Studies. Jules A. Clerval, "Les écoles de Chartres au moyen âge du Vᵉ au XVIᵉ siècle," in *Mémoires de la Société archéologique d'Eure-et-Loir,* 11 (1895); Édouard Jeauneau, "Quelques aspects du platonisme de Thierry de Chartres," in *Congrès de Tours et Poitiers* (Association G. Budé): *Acts* (1954), and "Simples notes sur la cosmogonie de Thierry de Chartres," in *Sophia,* 23 (1955); Enzo Maccagnolo, *Rerum universitas: Saggio sulla filosofia di Teodorico di Chartres* (1976).

ARJO VANDERJAGT

[See also **Abelard, Peter; Arts, Seven Liberal; Gilbert of Poitiers; John of Salisbury; Philosophy and Theology, Western European; Plato in the Middle Ages; Trivium.**]

THIETMAR VON MERSEBURG (975–1018), author of a chronicle that is the most important surviving historical source for the reigns of Otto III and Henry II of Germany. Born of the highest Saxon nobility (his father was count of Walbeck and his mother a member of the family of the counts of Stade, distantly related to the Ottonians), Thietmar was destined from youth for a career in the highest echelons of the German church. He was educated in the imperial nunnery of Quedlinburg and then in the cathedral school of Magdeburg. When he was ordained as priest in 1004 the emperor Henry II honored him with the gift of a sumptuous vestment. As protégé of the archbishop of Magdeburg, Thietmar became bishop of Merseburg in 1009. Since the bishopric of Merseburg had been founded in 968 but dissolved in 981 and reestablished only in 1004, Thietmar's major goal as bishop was to win back all of Merseburg's old extent and properties. In this, however, he was not overly successful, being far better remembered for his work as a historian.

Thietmar ostensibly wrote his chronicle to praise the history of Merseburg, but in fact it more resembles a history of Germany from the early tenth century until his own time. It consists of eight books: the first four deal with the reigns of Henry I, Otto I, Otto II, and Otto III, respectively; the last four all treat the reign of Henry II, breaking off with events of 1018, the year Thietmar died. Thietmar's chronicle makes for difficult reading because it is full of digressions and is thoroughly lacking in continuity. Thietmar recognized this himself when he made excuses for being like a traveler who takes a winding road rather than a straight one. His work is also freighted with pretentious use of Greek words and numerous quotations and turns of phrase from classical Latin writers. Nonetheless it is a very valuable source because of the quality and range of its information. Although Thietmar drew on earlier histories for his earlier books, for the reigns of Otto III and Henry II he relied primarily on his own observations and oral reports from leading actors, including the emperor Henry II, who often stayed with him at Merseburg. Thus the chronicle is extremely well informed. It is also very honest: Thietmar always tells us where he stands and is not afraid to offer criticism, sometimes even of his heroes.

In addition, Thietmar was a man of many interests. He presented observations on the Hungarians, Danes, Anglo-Saxons, and above all the Slavic tribes who were neighbors to the Germans. He understood the Slavs' language, translated their given names, and described their customs. His work

is also full of reports about dreams, miracles, and the edifying deaths of pious men, making it in this respect a repository of popular beliefs worthy of comparison with the chronicle of Gregory of Tours. Not the least interesting parts of Thietmar's chronicle are occasional autobiographical remarks, such as his reference to his short stature and his face made comic by a broken nose and a boil on his left cheek, or his statement that when he was nineteen his mother was willing to offer him as a hostage to Viking pirates in exchange for his uncle. For all these reasons Thietmar's chronicle is rewarding to the political, the cultural, and the psychological historian alike.

BIBLIOGRAPHY
Sources. Thietmari Merseburgensis episcopi Chronicon, Robert Holtzmann, ed., in Monumenta Germaniae historica: Scriptores, n.s. IX (1935, repr. 1955); Thietmar von Merseburg: Chronik, Werner Trillmilch, trans. (1957).
Studies. Karl Langosch, "Thietmar von Merseburg," in Die deutsche Literatur des Mittelalters: Verfasserlexikon, Wolfgang Stammler, ed., IV (1953), 433–442; Annerose Schneider, "Thietmar von Merseburg über kirchliche, politische und ständische Fragen seiner Zeit," in Archiv für Kulturgeschichte, 44 (1962).

ROBERT E. LERNER

[See also **Germany: 843–1137; Otto III, Emperor.**]

THIOFRID OF ECHTERNACH (*d.* 1110), a Benedictine monk appointed abbot of Echternach in 1083, is renowned for his reforms of monastic conditions. He wrote lives of several pre-Carolingian saints—*Vita Liutwini* (*ca.* 1078), *Vita sanctae Irminae*, *Vita Bassini*, and *Vita Willibrordi*—and a collection of epitaphs for saints.

BIBLIOGRAPHY
Sources. Flores epitaphii sanctorum, in Patrologia latina, CLVII (1854), 297–404; Vita Bassini, in Acta sanctorum, March, I, 315–320; Vita sanctae Irminiae, in Monumenta Germaniae historica: Scriptores, XXIII (1874), 48–50; Vita Liutwini, Willibrord Lampen, ed. (1936); Vita Willibrordi, in Acta sanctorum, November, III, 459–500.
Studies. Willibrord Lampen, Thiofrid von Echternach

(1920); Ernst Winheller, *Die Lebensbeschreibungen der vorkarolingischen Bischöfe von Trier* (1935).

NATHALIE HANLET

[See also **Benedictines; Hagiography; Reform, Idea of.**]

THIRSK, JOHN (*d.* 1452), was the master mason of Westminster Abbey from 1420 until his death. Although work on the new nave was slack, in 1439 he started the spectacular, raised Henry V chantry chapel, reached by stair turrets. The idea for this arrangement goes back to Henry's will of 1415. Perhaps slightly earlier Thirsk began the high altar screen separating the sanctuary from Edward the Confessor's chapel. That was finished in 1440/1441. He also built the great east window of St. Margaret's, Westminster, for which he was paid in 1422/1423. In 1449 he became master mason of Windsor Castle. His original name appears to have been Crowche. Thirsk in Yorkshire is presumably where he originated.

BIBLIOGRAPHY

John Harvey, *English Medieval Architects* (1954), 262; W. St. John Hope, "The Funeral, Monument, and Chantry Chapel of King Henry V," in *Archaeologia*, 65 (1913–1914).

BARRIE SINGLETON

[See also **Henry V of England; Masons and Builders; Westminster Abbey.**]

ÞIÐREKS SAGA is a compendium of German heroic tales preserved in a thirteenth-century Norse translation. Since the German original or originals are lost, they can only be a subject of speculation. As a result, *Þiðreks saga* has sometimes been treated as a work of Norse literature, but it is more likely a relatively faithful translation of a German book with minor concessions to the Norse versions of the same stories familiar to the Norwegian translator. It is therefore no more Norse than the Norwegian reworkings of Chrétien's romances or the French chanson de geste material in *Karlamagnús saga*.

Þiðrekr is the Norse form of Dietrich, a figure in German heroic legend whose historical prototype is

Chantry chapel of Henry V in Westminster Abbey. Begun by John Thirsk, 1439. ROYAL COMMISSION ON THE HISTORICAL MONUMENTS OF ENGLAND

Theodoric the Great, Ostrogothic king of Italy from 493 to 526. The legend that grew up around the person of Dietrich in the early Middle Ages centered on the story of his defeat by Ermanaric (German: Ermrich; *Þiðreks saga*: Erminrekr), his exile at the court of Attila, and his eventual reconquest of Italy. This story is entirely fanciful and has no foundation in the historical facts of Theodoric the Great's Ostrogothic kingdom. The fullest German account of the legend is contained in *Das Buch von Bern* from the middle of the thirteenth century, but the story is much older and can be glimpsed as the background of the *Hildebrandslied,* which is extant in a manuscript from *ca.* 830.

Though Dietrich's exile and return are the kernel of the story, *Þiðreks saga* organizes a number of other unconnected or loosely connected stories around this central plot. The more important heroic figures included in this manner are Hildibrandr (cast as Þiðrekr's foster father), the chieftain Heimir (of whom little is known, but who is referred to in *Widsith* and *Beowulf*), Attila (Etzel in the *Nibelungenlied*), Velent (Wayland Smith, referred to in the Old English *Waldere* and the protagonist of the Old Norse heroic lay *Vǫlundarkviða*), Velent's son Viðga (referred to by Jordanes about 550 in the form Vidigoia), Sigurðr and Gunnarr (abundantly documented in the *Edda, Vǫlsunga saga,* and the *Nibelungenlied*), and Valtari (well known from the Old English *Waldere* fragments and the Latin recasting of a German heroic tale in *Waltharius*). Other lesser figures are known from the Middle High German Dietrich epics of the thirteenth century, for instance Ekka and Fasold (*Eckenlied*), Þéttleifr (German: Dietleib), and Ömlungr (German: Amelung). In addition to these heroic tales, *Þiðreks saga* includes a few bridal quest stories in the style of twelfth-century German minstrel epic, such as *König Rother,* the plot of which reappears as Ósantrix's wooing of Oda, daughter of King Milias of Hunland. Other tales of love and abduction attach to Samson and Hildisvið, Herburt and Hildr, Valtari and Hildigunnr, Apollonius and Herborg, and Íron and Bolfriana.

This heterogeneous material obviously confronted the author with a difficult problem in composition. A first perusal is likely to convince most readers that the problem remains unsolved and that the book is a loose conglomerate of stories without focus, but a closer reading reveals the operation of an organizing principle. In general the author's plan is to introduce the heroes one at a time, with information on their family background and rise to eminence, and to explain how they came to join Þiðrekr's circle. The completion of this circle of heroes is marked by a festive banquet at Þiðrekr's court. The narrative then turns to a series of romantic interludes accounting for the marriages of Ömlungr to Fallborg, Þiðrekr to Guðilinda, Fasold and Þéttleifr to Guðilinda's sisters, Valtari to Hildigunnr, and Viðga to Bolfriana. What follows is the core of the Dietrich legend: his exile, his adventures with his host Attila, and his victory over Erminrekr at Gronsport, preparing the way for his eventual return to Italy after several more intervening adventures, chiefly the death of Sigurðr and the fall of the Burgundians (told in fuller form in the *Nibelungenlied*). But already during the victorious battle at Gronsport Þiðrekr's retinue begins to dwindle ominously with the fall of the heroes Vildifer, Valtari, Nauðungr, Ortvin, Hjálprekr, Erpr, Þether, and Úlfráðr. In the remainder of the book Þiðrekr's vindication and reinstatement in his ancestral realm are overshadowed by the gradual falling away of his retinue as the remaining heroes succumb one

after the other: Sigurðr, Fasold and Þéttleifr, Gunnarr and Högni, Roðingeirr, Hildibrandr, Heraðr, Herniðr, Attila, and finally Heimir. Stripped of his chief glory, Þiðrekr himself disappears on a mysterious black horse.

The narrative is thus organized in terms of the life cycle: ancestry, birth, youthful adventure, mature prowess, marriage, and death. This cycle is experienced by a series of magnificent heroes who gather around the greatest hero of all, Þiðrekr. Þiðrekr is the quintessence of high adventure and leadership, and his fate (exile, loss of friends, and ultimate disappearance) seems to signal the futility of even the greatest endeavors. *Þiðreks saga* thus describes a rising line of accomplishment culminating in the creation of a society of heroes, but then plunging on a downward course of declining fortunes ending in death. The theme of vanity is reminiscent of the medieval Alexander legend, and the creation of an ideal warrior community recalls the Arthurian cycle.

Any attempt to isolate a structure requires close analysis, but the actual reading of *Þiðreks saga* is as confusing as the reading of the extended thirteenth-century prose romances. The life-cycle principle is nonetheless clear from the gathering of the marriages in a single sequence and from the division of Sigurðr's story, which is told sequentially in the *Nibelungenlied* and *Vǫlsunga saga,* into discrete units on his birth, early adventures and marriage, and death. These discrete segments are then inserted into the equivalent larger sections of the narrative. It therefore seems clear that the author breaks up the inherited stories in order to accommodate them to an overall structural scheme. This segmentation produces a complicated interweaving of narrative throughout the text.

If there is a plan underlying the total composition of *Þiðreks saga*, we must ask whether the plan was executed in Germany or Norway. The preface informs us that "this saga is composed according to the account ["telling"] of Germans and to some extent from their poems." The phrasing of this passage has led to the supposition that German tales and poems were gathered from German storytellers in either Norway or Germany and harmonized by a saga writer in Norway, but there is evidence that the section on the fall of the Burgundians ("Niflunga saga") was written in the north German city of Soest. Since the whole saga is organized according to a single premeditated plan, it is perhaps simplest to suppose that if part of that plan was carried out in Soest, all of it was executed by the same hand in the same place. We would otherwise need to ascribe extraordinary editorial powers to a Norwegian working from a combination of written and oral German sources. Once the book was completed in Soest, it was presumably brought to Norway and translated there.

The nature of the materials from which the book in Soest was assembled is even harder to assess. It seems clear that the section known as "Niflunga saga" was taken over from a written south German poem ("Ältere Not") that was also the source of the second part of the *Nibelungenlied,* but the south or north German provenance of other sections is disputed. Whatever the precise derivations of the various tales are, there is general agreement that much of the narrative is specifically north German and sheds valuable light on the popular literature of this otherwise sparsely documented region.

The dating of *Þiðreks saga* is uncertain. During the reign of King Hákon Hákonarson in Norway (1217–1263) a number of French works were translated into Norwegian, and it is tempting to place *Þiðreks saga* in this context. One chapter of *Þiðreks saga* was borrowed into *Vǫlsunga saga,* but the dating of this text is also uncertain and the possibility of a late interpolation cannot be excluded. In the absence of hard evidence, we must content ourselves with a rough guess that *Þiðreks saga* in its present form was set down sometime in the first half of the thirteenth century.

Scholarly attention has focused particularly on those portions which tell the story of Sigurðr and the fall of the Burgundians ("Niflunga saga"). This interest is dictated by the close affinities between the text of *Þiðreks saga* and the narrative of the *Nibelungenlied.* Since "Niflunga saga" is based primarily on the source of the second part of the *Nibelungenlied, Þiðreks saga* has special importance in illuminating the sources of the most famous medieval German epic.

The text of *Þiðreks saga* is preserved in a Norwegian parchment from *ca.* 1300 (*Mb*), two transcripts of lost Icelandic parchments made in the seventeenth century (*A* and *B*), and a Swedish translation, *Didrikskrönikan,* composed *ca.* 1460. *Didrikskrönikan* appears to be translated from Mb, but the exact relationship between *Mb* and *A* and *B,* and the roles of the five scribes of *Mb* (in which a single episode mysteriously appears twice in different forms), are particularly knotty textual problems.

BIBLIOGRAPHY

The standard editions are *Þiðreks saga af Bern,* Henrik Bertelsen, ed., 2 vols. (1905–1911), and (for the Swedish version) *Sagan om Didrik af Bern,* Gunnar O. Hyltén-Cavallius, ed. (1850–1854). There is a modern German translation by Fine Erichsen, *Die Geschichte Thidreks von Bern* (1967), and an English translation by Edward R. Haymes, *The Saga of Thidrek af Bern (Thidrekssaga af Bern),* (1988).

For the older bibliography see Halldór Hermannsson, "Bibliography of the Mythical-Heroic Sagas," in *Islandica,* 5 (1912), 54–60, and "The Sagas of the Kings (Konunga sögur) and the Mythical-Heroic Sagas (Fornaldar sögur): Two Bibliographical Supplements," in *Islandica,* 26 (1937), 68–71. On the manuscript problems see Heinrich Hempel, "Die Handschriftenverhältnisse der Thidrikssaga," in *Beiträge zur Geschichte der deutschen Sprache und Literatur,* 48 (1924), and Bengt Henning, *Didrikskrönikan: Handskriftsrelationer, översättningsteknik och stildrag* (1970), with bibliography, 22–23. For the occurrence of personal names in *Þiðreks saga* elsewhere in Germanic heroic literature see George T. Gillespie, *A Catalogue of Persons Named in German Heroic Literature (700–1600), Including Named Animals and Objects and Ethnic Names* (1973). On other names see William J. Paff, *The Geographical and Ethnic Names in the Þiðriks Saga: A Study in Germanic Heroic Legend* (1959), and Assar Janzén, "Names in the *Þiðriks saga,*" in *Journal of English and Germanic Philology,* 61 (1962).

On the Dietrich legend in general see Georges Zink, *Les légendes héroîques de Dietrich et d'Ermrich dans les littératures germaniques* (1950), and Joachim Heinzle, *Mittelhochdeutsche Dietrichepik: Untersuchungen zur Tradierungsweise, Überlieferungskritik und Gattungsgeschichte später Heldendichtung* (1978). The only systematic comparison of *Þiðreks saga* to the German legendary materials is W. E. D. Stephens' unpublished London M.A. thesis, "An Examination of the Sources of the Thidrikssaga" (1937). Stephens rightly emphasizes that the narrative of *Þiðreks saga* is strictly German.

See also Theodore M. Andersson, "An Interpretation of *Þiðreks saga,*" in John Lindow, Lars Lönnroth, and Gerd Wolfgang Weber, eds., *Structure and Meaning in Old Norse Literature* (1986); Thomas Klein, "Zur Þiðreks saga," in *Arbeiten zur Skandinavistik. 6. Arbeitstagung der Skandinavisten des deutschen Sprachgebietes: 26.9–1.10.1983 in Bonn,* Heinrich Beck, ed. (1985); Edith Marold, "Dietrich als Sinnbild der Superbia," *ibid.*

THEODORE M. ANDERSSON

[See also **Buch von Bern, Das; Eckenlied; Hildebrandslied; König Rothen; Nibelungenlied; Volsunga Saga; Volundarkviða; Waltharius.**]

ÞJÓÐÓLFR ÓR HVINI (or Þjóðólfr inn hvínverski, after a district in West-Agder, Norway) was a late-ninth-century skaldic poet and the author of *Haustlǫng* (*ca.* 900) and *Ynglingatal.*

Haustlǫng, like Bragi's *Ragnarsdrápa,* describes pictures painted and possibly carved on a shield. Þjóðólfr says that he received the splendidly colored shield from a certain Þorleifr, who is usually identified with Þorleifr the Wise, the man who advised Ulfljótr when the latter adapted the Norwegian Gulathing law for the Icelandic republic (*ca.* 927–930).

The twenty extant stanzas of the poem are preserved in manuscripts of *Snorra Edda.* Snorri twice gives its title as *Haustlǫng,* a name probably meaning "autumn long." The significance of the title is not clear: perhaps the poem was composed in the course of one autumn or winter, or perhaps the word was prominent in a lost strophe or refrain. Thirteen stanzas of *Haustlǫng* treat the myth of Iðunn and Þjazi; seven narrate Thor's battle with Hrungnir. Both stories portray gods carrying out bold exploits against the monsters of Giantland. The poem is a *drápa,* with one twice-repeated refrain found among the extant fragments. The meter is *dróttkvætt,* fully developed but not as strictly regulated as it was to become in the verse of later skalds. Þjóðólfr's kennings are numerous, complicated, and often puzzling, partly because of our limited knowledge of Norse mythology. Þjóðólfr, for example, never names directly the ox on which the gods dine but, instead, paraphrases it as "hay-reindeer," "yoke-bear," "whale of the rope [?]," and "horse of the fertility goddess [?]."

The myths are narrated with more color and detail than the artist who painted the shield could have provided. There is even some dialogue. Þjóðólfr's first story tells how the giant Þjazi in eagle form seized most of the gods' ox roast. An angry Loki hit the eagle with a pole; the pole stuck, Loki stuck, and Þjazi flew off to Giantland with Loki dangling behind. Loki managed to save his life by procuring for the giants what they most desired: the goddess Iðunn. Without her medicine, however, the gods see themselves grow old and gray. Loki, now threatened with death by the gods, flies in falcon shape to the giants, retrieves Iðunn (in nut shape), and returns home, with Þjazi (in eagle shape) in fast but vain pursuit.

The second myth tells of Thor's journey to the giant Hrungnir and their single combat, a battle that ends abruptly when Thor's hammer strikes the giant's head. Thor's drive through space with his team of goats is vividly described, beginning with stanza 14, 5–8:

> Ók at ísarnleiki
> Jarðar sunr, en dunði,
> móðr svall Meila blóða,
> mána vegr und hánum.

Earth's [the goddess's] son [Thor] drove to the iron-play [battle], and the moon's path [sky] resounded under him; anger swelled in Meili's brother [Thor].

Most frequently in Old Norse, the idea that *poema loquens pictura . . . debet esse* took the form of a shield poem in *dróttkvætt*; of these, *Ragnarsdrápa* is probably the oldest and *Haustlǫng* the best preserved. Helmut Rosenfeld has suggested that this genre is related to the shield descriptions in Homer and Hesiod and should be seen against a background of cult, the use of votive shields in pagan religious practice. Anne Holtsmark has urged that *Haustlǫng* be regarded as ritual drama, a cultic portrayal of the forces of fertility triumphant.

BIBLIOGRAPHY

The text of *Haustlǫng* is in Finnur Jónsson, *Den norsk-islandske skjaldedigtning* ([1908] 1912–1915), IA, 16–20; IB, 14–18; Ernst A. Kock, *Den norsk-isländska skaldediktningen,* I (1946), 9–12. The bibliography is in Lee M. Hollander, *A Bibliography of Skaldic Studies* (1958).

Studies. Anne Holtsmark, "Myten om Idun og Tjatse i Tjodolvs *Haustlǫng,*" in *Arkiv för nordisk filologi,* **64** (1949); Hallvard Lie, "'Natur' og 'unatur' i skaldekunsten," av Norske videnskaps-akademi i Oslo, II. Hist.-filos. Klasse, *Avhandlinger* (1957), esp. 78–79; Edith Marold, *Kenningkunst: Ein Beitrag zu einer Poetik der Skaldendichtung* (1983), esp. 153–210; Hellmut Rosenfeld, "Nordische Schilddichtung und mittelalterliche Wappendichtung," in *Zeitschrift für deutsche Philologie,* **61** (1936).

ROBERTA FRANK

[See also **Bragi Boddason the Old; Kenning; Loki; Snorra Edda; Thor; Ynglingatal.**]

THOMAS. See **Tristan, Roman de.**

THOMAS À BECKET. See **Becket, Thomas, Saint.**

THOMAS À KEMPIS (1379/1380—1471), author of spiritual and devotional works. The younger of two sons of a blacksmith and a schoolmistress, he was born at Kempen in the Rhineland. His surname was Hemerken (or Hammerken), which means "little hammer," and the designation "à Kempis" derives from his place of birth. Thomas' earliest education was at Kempen, but from 1393, for five or six years, he studied at Deventer. Here he fell under the influence of the Brethren of the Common Life and particularly of Florens Radewijns, the successor to Geert Groote, who had founded the Brethren. Although he actually lived for a time with a group of Brethren, rather than formally joining this order Thomas entered, in 1399, the house of regular canons at Mt. St. Agnes (near Zwolle), where his older brother John had just become prior.

It is unclear why, but Thomas' period of probation in this community lasted for eight years. He was professed only in 1407 and then ordained a priest between 26 July 1413 and 24 July 1414. With only brief exceptions, Thomas spent his entire adult life at Mt. St. Agnes. Little is known of his activity there, apart from his writings and transcriptions of manuscripts (including a copy of the Bible), although it is known that he twice served as subprior (in 1425 and again in 1448), and probably also as master of novices for an extended period. Having lived for more than ninety years, Thomas à Kempis died at Zwolle.

Thomas was a prolific writer of devotional, homiletical, and hagiographical works and also prepared a chronicle of his monastery that constitutes one of the chief sources for his life. He is a prime representative of the late medieval Devotio Moderna because of the practical spiritual advice contained in his undoubtedly genuine works and because he often has been deemed to be the author of the famous *Imitation of Christ*. Aside from the possibility that he composed that treatise, Thomas' numerous and all-too-little-known writings include *Concerning the Three Tabernacles* (considerations on poverty, humility, and patience); *Concerning the Faithful Stewart* (offering advice to a contemplative in charge of a monastery's possessions); *Soliloquy of the Soul* (a collection of many practical counsels for leading the soul to grace); two mystical treatises, *The Little Garden of Roses* and *The Valley of Lilies*, often printed together with the *Imitation of Christ*; a series of thirty *Sermons for Novices* (intended for those entering the community at Mt. St. Agnes); and *Lives* of both Groote and

Radewijns. As a collection, these and the entire corpus of Thomas' works are marvelous exemplifications of the spirit of the Brethren of the Common Life and especially of the tradition of this group fostered by the school associated with the house of regular canons at Windesheim, founded in 1386 by followers of Groote and Radewijns.

BIBLIOGRAPHY

The critical edition of Thomas' works is in M. Josef Pohl, ed., *Opera omnia,* 7 vols. (1910–1922). See also J. Mercier, "Thomas à Kempis," in *Dictionnaire de théologie catholique,* XV (1946), with a list of Thomas' works. For the controversy about the *De imitatione* see Tiburzio Lupo, "Nuovi codici Gerseniani del 'De imitatione Christi,'" in *Aevum,* 53 (1979); F. Chatillon, "Aux origines de l'imitation de Jésus-Christ," in *Revue du moyen âge latin,* **25–34** (1969–1978).

ROBERT SOMERVILLE

[See also **Brethren of the Common Life; Devotio Moderna; Groote, Geert; Mysticism, Christian.**]

THOMAS AQUINAS. See **Aquinas, St. Thomas.**

THOMAS DE CORMONT was master architect of Amiens Cathedral from about 1235 to about 1240, when he was succeeded by his son, Regnault. What Thomas built at Amiens is unknown. One tradition credits him with the eastern part of the transept and the lower portions of the choir. A more recent view attributes the west facade (begun in 1236) to him. It has also been suggested that Thomas was architect of the Ste. Chapelle in Paris.

BIBLIOGRAPHY

Amédée Boinet, *La cathédrale d'Amiens* (1926, 5th rev. ed. 1959); Georges Durand, *Monographie de l'église Notre-Dame, cathédrale d'Amiens,* 2 vols. (1901–1903); Alain Erlande-Brandenburg, "Le septième Colloque international de la Société française d'archéologie: La façade de la cathédrale d'Amiens," in *Bulletin monumental,* 135 (1977).

CARL F. BARNES, JR.

[See also **Amiens Cathedral; Architect, Status of; Gothic Architecture; Masons and Builders.**]

THOMAS OF CANTIMPRÉ (Brabantinus, van Bellinghen) (*ca.* 1201–*ca.* 1270/1272), encyclopedist and hagiographer, born probably at Leeuw-St.-Pierre, near Brussels. After schooling at Liège in 1217 he became a canon regular of St. Augustine at the monastery of Cantimpré (near Cambrai). In 1232 he changed his allegiance to the Dominicans at Louvain, who sent him to Cologne. There he studied under Albertus Magnus. After 1237 he studied for a time at the priory of St. Jacques in Paris. Thomas was probably a member of the commission that tried to settle the question of multiple benefices in France; he also took an active part in condemning Jewish literature. He returned to Louvain around 1240 to teach as lector, becoming subprior about 1246.

Thomas wrote a number of saints' lives. His fame, however, rests on two other works: the *Liber de natura rerum* (*ca.* 1245) and the *Bonum universale de apibus* (1256–1261).

In the thirteenth century Isidore of Seville's *Etymologiae* had lost its practical use as a book of general reference. Thomas is one of the three important encyclopedists of the thirteenth century, the others being Bartolomeus Anglicus (*De proprietatibus rerum, ca.* 1240) and Vincent of Beauvais (*Speculum maius, ca.* 1245–*ca.* 1260). Between 1228 and 1244 Thomas collected material discovered by scholars in the tenth, eleventh, and thirteenth centuries in Hebrew, Greek, Latin, and Arabic sources. He writes that for fifteen years he journeyed throughout France, Germany, and England in order to copy and summarize works for his *De natura rerum,* apparently sometimes translating from the Greek into Latin. He says in book 14 that he translated a book on precious stones—a subject that seems to have fascinated the medievals: *Cethel aut veterum Judeorum Physiologorum de lapidibus sententiae,* which is in fact the famous *Kiranides.*

The *De natura rerum* helped make available information, especially from pagan and Oriental sources, that was forbidden reading under the Dominican constitutions of 1228. As such it played a part in forming the ideas of Albertus Magnus and Thomas Aquinas of the possibilities of natural knowledge without a theological foundation. Schools and universities, partly through the influence of this kind of work, became more than theological institutes. Thomas' book is divided into seven sections: books 1–3 on man; books 4–9 on animals; books 10–12 on plants; book 13 on water; books 14–15 on precious stones and the

seven metals; books 16–18 on astronomy, astrology, and meteorology; book 19 on the universe and the four elements (a second edition adds a book 20 on planetary motion). Thomas' work was utilized by Vincent of Beauvais for his *Speculum maius* and by Albertus Magnus; it is often ascribed to the latter. *De natura rerum* was translated and adapted into Dutch (1269) and into German (1350 and 1472), and plundered for later encyclopedias.

Thomas' *Bonum universale de apibus* proved to be even more popular. He intends his work to be a guide to monastic life, and his bee analogy elaborates on the ninth book of *De natura rerum*; this is almost a topos: classical authors and the church fathers use the analogy between bees and human society frequently. Thomas' particular analogy is clear from the subdivision of his work: part 1 discusses the analogy between the "king" of bees and the *praelati,* who govern their people; part 2 continues with a comparison of the ordinary worker bees and the *subditi,* who are governed. Many of his analogies seem farfetched, and Thomas appears to realize this when he says, "And let me tell you too . . . ." His exempla, however, are not intended to be strictly ordered and connected to his main subject. They serve, rather, much as they serve a preacher, to goad men to do good and to keep from evil by means of practical, everyday stories, which have a greater effect than discussions on difficult problems of moral philosophy. For modern scholars the collection of exempla is important because of the bits of historical information that can be gleaned from them. The *Bonum universale* was circulated widely and translated into Dutch, German, and French.

BIBLIOGRAPHY

Sources. There is no complete edition of the Latin text of *Liber de natura rerum,* but there are extracts in Jean Baptiste Pitra, ed., *Specilegium Solesmense,* 4 vols. (1852–1858), III; a partial edition of book 3 in Alfons Hilka, *Liber de monstrosis hominibus orientis* (1911); and a partial edition of book 1 in Christoph Ferckel, *Die Gynäkologie des Thomas von Brabant* (1912). A Dutch translation and adaptation is Jakob van Maerlant, *Der naturen bloeme,* J. H. Bormans, ed. (1857). A German version is *Das Buch der Natur von Konrad von Megenberg,* Franz Pfeiffer, ed. (1861).

His saints' lives are book 3 of Jacques de Vitry, *Vita Mariae Oigniacensis,* in *Acta sanctorum,* June, V (1867); *Vita piae Lutgardis,* in *Acta sanctorum,* June, IV (1867); *Vita sanctae Christinae mirabilis,* in *Acta sanctorum,* July, V (1868); *Vita Margarete de Ypris,* in G. G.

Meersseman, "Les Frères Prêcheurs et le mouvement dévot en Flandre au XIIIᵉ siècle," in *Archivum Fratrum Praedicatorum,* **18** (1948).

There is a Latin edition of *Bonum universale de apibus* by George Colvener (1597, 1605, 1627); it was translated into Dutch, German, and French. A listing of translations can be found in Axters (see below) and H. de Vocht, *Biographie nationale de Belgique,* **25** (1932), 28–34.

Studies. Pauline Aiken, "The Animal History of Albertus Magnus and Thomas of Cantimpré," in *Specluum,* **22** (1947); St. G. Axters, "Bijdragen tot en bibliographie van de nederlandssche dominikaansche vroomheid I," in *Ons geestelijk erf,* **6** (1932) 15–24; Elie Berger, *Thomas Cantipratensis Bonum universale de apibus* (1895); Franciscus Hyacinthus Choquetius, *Sancti Belgii ordinis Praedicatorum* (1618), 88–101; William Hinnebusch, *The History of the Dominican Order* (1965–); Alexander Kaufmann, *Thomas von Chantimpré* (1899); Hermann Stadler, "Albertus Magnus, Thomas von Cantimpré und Vincenz von Beauvais," in *Natur und Kultur,* **4** (1906); Lynn Thorndike, *A History of Magic and Experimental Science,* II (1923), 372–400, with a list of manuscripts; J. F. J. van Tol, "Enkele opmerkingen in verband met *De naturis rerum* van Thomas van Cantimpré," in *Vereeniging tot het bevorderen van de beoefening der wetenschap onder de Katholieken in Nederland,* **31** (1939); Wouter Antonie van der Vet, *Het biënboec van Thomas van Cantimpré en zijn exempelen* (1902); G. J. J. Walstra, "Thomas de Cantimpré, *De naturis rerum:* État de la question," in *Vivarium,* **5** (1967) and **6** (1968).

ARJO VANDERJAGT

[See also **Alchemy; Bestiary; Biology; Dominicans; Encyclopedias and Dictionaries, European; Fachschrifttum; Jacques de Vitry.**]

THOMAS OF HALES (*fl.* 1250), thought to be a native of Gloucestershire, was a Franciscan author of Latin sermons, saints' lives, and scholastic disputations. He is remembered today for "A Luve Ron," which Rosemary Woolf calls "one of the small number of outstanding poems amongst the Middle English lyrics." Thomas addresses himself to a nun who, he says, desired that he compose a love song for her. In response to this request he warns of the vanity of worldly love and lyrically extols Christ as the only everlasting lover.

BIBLIOGRAPHY

Charles L. Kingsford, "Hales, Thomas," in *Dictionary of National Biography,* VIII (1890); Richard Morris, ed., *An Old English Miscellany* (1872), 93–99; John E. Wells, *A Manual of the Writings in Middle English, 1050–1400* (1916), 529–530, 852; Rosemary Woolf, *The English Religious Lyric in the Middle Ages* (1968), 60–63.

ELAINE GOLDEN ROBISON

[See also **Latin Literature; Middle English Literature: Lyric.**]

THÓMAS SAGA ERKIBYSKUPS, the common name for several Old Norse–Icelandic sagas about St. Thomas Becket of Canterbury (*d.* 1170). Soon after his canonization in 1173 the cult of St. Thomas became popular in Scandinavia and Iceland, and there is ample liturgical and iconographic evidence of this in all the countries. Only in Iceland and Norway, however, did this popularity result in major contributions to the vernacular hagiographic literature.

The oldest *Thómas saga* (1), now lost except for traces of it in later works, was a translation of the vita by Robert of Cricklade (*ca.* 1173), also lost but known as the source of an Anglo-Norman poem by Beneit, a monk of St. Albans. The translation was made about 1200, probably by the Icelandic priest Bergr Gunnsteinsson (*d. ca.* 1230), and it was in turn to be among the sources of versions 2–4, discussed below. The remaining texts are best divided into two almost complete sagas (versions 1 and 2) and two fragmentary texts (3 and 4). Questions of authorship and chronology must be left partly unanswered.

A very early extant saga (1) dating from the second half of the thirteenth century translates the so-called *Quadrilogus,* a Latin composition of material from the lives of St. Thomas by John of Salisbury, Alan of Tewkesbury, Herbert of Bosham, and William of Canterbury, and from a *passio* by Benedict of Peterborough. The translator-author is not known. There are reasons to believe that he was an Icelandic priest, Jón Holt (*d.* 1302), whose name has also been connected with versions (2) and (3), although the manuscript evidence has been used to argue for Norwegian provenance. Whatever its origin, it must have been a welcome addition to the already vast hagiographic repertoire in Old Norse prose.

An Icelandic saga (2) from the first half of the fourteenth century is found in the codex called

Tómasskinna after the saga (Copenhagen, Royal Library, Gks. 1008 fol.) and in some medieval fragments. Its author made use of the *Quadrilogus* translation (1) and a recension of the lost *Thómas saga,* supplemented with information from *Speculum historiale* by Vincent of Beauvais (*d.* 1264). Who the author is has been much disputed. Two well-known Icelandic priests and bookmen, Bergr Sokkason (*d.* 1350) and Arngrímr Brandsson (*d.* 1361 or 1362), have been suggested, as has Jón Holt.

The fragmentary sagas are found in fourteenth-century manuscripts. One of them (3) represents an expanded recension of the lost translation of Robert of Cricklade's work with additional material from John of Salisbury and Benedict of Peterborough. It is certainly older than version (2), whose author made use of a second edition of this recension. Again Jón Holt has been suggested as the author. The last saga to be mentioned here (4) is a brief and defective fourteenth-century text from a legendary (Stockholm, Royal Library, MS Perg. fol. nr. 2). It ultimately goes back to Robert of Cricklade and seems to represent the original, otherwise lost, Icelandic tradition very closely.

BIBLIOGRAPHY

Sources. Heilagra manna sögur, II, Carl R. Unger, ed. (1877), version 4; *Lives of Saints: Perg. Fol. Nr. 2 in the Royal Library Stockholm,* Peter G. Foote, ed. (1962), version 4; *Thomas saga erkibyskups,* Carl R. Unger, ed. (1869), versions 1–3; *Thómas saga erkibyskups: A Life of Archbishop Thomas Becket, in Icelandic, with English Translation, Notes, and Glossary,* I–II, Eiríkr Magnússon, ed. (1875–1883), versions 2–3; *Thomasskinna. Gl. Kgl. Saml. 1008 Fol., in the Royal Library, Copenhagen,* Agnete Loth, ed. (1964), version 2.

Studies. Hans Bekker-Nielsen, "Thómas saga erkibiskups," in *Kulturhistorisk leksikon for nordisk middelalder,* XVIII (1974); Peter G. Foote, "On the Fragmentary Text Concerning St. Thomas Becket in Stock. Perg. Fol. Nr. 2," in *Saga-Book,* **15** (1957–1961); Stefán Karlsson, "Icelandic Lives of Thomas à Becket: Questions of Authorship," in *Proceedings of the First International Saga Conference,* University of Edinburgh, 1971, Peter Foote *et al.,* ed. (1973); Ole Widding, Hans Bekker-Nielsen, and L. K. Shook, "The Lives of the Saints in Old Norse Prose: A Handlist," in *Mediaeval Studies,* **25** (1963).

HANS BEKKER-NIELSEN

[See also **Becket, Thomas, Saint; John of Salisbury; Saga; Vincent of Beauvais.**]

THOMAS THE SLAV (*d.* 823), as his name indicates, was probably of Slavic origin (although he came from Asia Minor). His importance in Byzantine history derives from his role as the leader of a ninth-century rebellion against the Byzantine Empire that lasted for several years. Putting down this revolt severely strained the resources of the empire. The conflicting accounts of the sources regarding Thomas often obscure rather than clarify what we know of him.

Thomas seems to have spent a considerable number of years living among the Arabs, and it has been suggested that he fled from the Byzantine Empire after having been involved with the wife of his patron. It is also unclear whether he was, as some sources claim, a friend and supporter of Emperor Leo V and, as a result, an enemy of Leo's successor, Michael II. What no sources dispute, however, is that his rebellion received widespread support from a large variety of groups throughout the empire.

Thomas claimed to be Constantine VI, the emperor who had been illegally deposed. Although this claim lent his enterprise at least a pretense of legitimacy, there is no evidence whatever that he really was Constantine. He gathered a great deal of support in his native area of Asia Minor: the sources tell us that he had the backing of Arabs, Persians, Armenians, Iberians, and other Caucasians. The revolt spread across the whole of Asia Minor, and Thomas attracted to his side all of the Asian themes with the exception of Opsikion and Armeniakon, which remained loyal to Emperor Michael II. That Thomas had the support of the Abbasid caliphs is reflected in the fact that he was crowned emperor of the Byzantine Empire in the Muslim city of Antioch by the patriarch of the city.

In addition to the varied ethnic support that Thomas achieved, he had the backing of the thematic fleet and of a number of the imperial tax collectors who financed his rebellion. His movement also seems to have had some religious and social overtones as well: Thomas apparently posed as a supporter of the iconodules against the iconoclastic emperor Michael II, and he also posed as a champion of the poor, who felt especially burdened by taxation and arbitrary imperial governors. With all of these disparate elements held together in what can only have been an uneasy alliance, Thomas marched across Asia Minor with a considerable army, crossed into Thrace with the help of the thematic fleet, added more support in Thrace, and finally laid siege to Constantinople in December 821.

Thomas' siege of the Byzantine capital lasted for over a year, but it ultimately failed, due in no small part to the assistance that Michael II received from the Bulgar khan Omurtag. The emperor had retained the support of the imperial (as opposed to the thematic) fleet, which destroyed Thomas' ships. In the spring of 823, Thomas was forced to raise the siege and flee, and his revolt collapsed. He himself was hunted down, tortured, and executed.

The real importance of Thomas' rebellion lay in his managing for several years to hold out against the emperor at Constantinople and to mount a serious threat against him. The effort required to defeat Thomas undermined the strength of the Byzantine Empire, and the decimation of the thematic fleet for its support of the rebellion may have contributed to the loss of Crete to the Arabs in 827 and possibly to the loss of Sicily to them as well.

BIBLIOGRAPHY

Paul Lemerle, "Thomas le Slave," in *Travaux et mémoires,* **1** (1965).

LINDA C. ROSE

[See also **Bulgaria; Byzantine Empire: History (330–1025).**]

THOMASIN VON ZERCLAERE (de Cerclaria) (*ca.* 1185–*ca.* 1259), canon regular at Aquileia, then the administrative seat of the patriarchate of Aquileia (now in the province of Friuli in Italy). He is known as the author of the first substantial didactic poem in German literature, *Der welsche Gast* (The foreign guest of the German tongue). It is his only extant work; another is lost but mentioned in book 1 of *Welsche Gast* as "buoch von der hoefscheit" (Book of courtesy). It was most likely written in Provençal.

Details of Thomasin's life can be derived from his work. He seems to have been at Aquileia when Wolfger von Erla became patriarch of Aquileia in 1204 and to have accompanied the patriarch to the coronation of Otto IV in Rome (4 October 1209) and to the Fourth Lateran Council (November 1215), events that left a clear imprint on his work. He was a native of Friuli (perhaps of Cividale), where the names of other family members occur in documents.

The composition of *Welsche Gast* was begun in the fall of 1215 and was completed in roughly ten months, as the author states at the beginning of book 9. Since Thomasin did not write in his native tongue, this is a remarkable feat. The *Welsche Gast* consists of a prose summary, prologue, ten books of text, and an epilogue; except for the summary, it is written in four-stressed couplets. Between the individual books and after the prologue there are transitional formulas, usually consisting of two distinct couplets. The total length of the poem is 15,406 lines, provided the summary is divided into 610 lines. Heinrich Rückert's edition (1852) has only 14,742 verses, counted as 14,752 as the result of two errors. (He also printed the summary, as well as some lines missing in the Codex Palatinus Germanicus 389, in the critical apparatus, without numbering them.) Of particular importance are 120 text illustrations that occur as an intrinsic part of *Welsche Gast* and that constitute the first pictorial cycle in a secular work in German literature. They agree in choice and spirit so much with the work that it is now assumed that the author himself had a hand in their conception and arrangement.

The summary (610 lines) is written in the first person and closely follows the arguments of the poem, also marking subdivisions (*liunt, liumt*). In the prologue (140 verses) the author names himself (685), gives his place of origin "von Friule" (681), and asks the reader's indulgence for possible linguistic mistakes, hoping that "tiutsche lant" (697), the *hûsfrowe* (698), will receive the work favorably. Book 1 (1,552 verses) begins with a discussion of modes of practical behavior and of learning processes. The quality of social life is viewed as dependent on the exemplary nature of the ruler in book 2 (854 verses). He is expected to be a mirror in which the individual may see himself.

The nature of constancy and inconstancy is considered. In book 3 (1,616 verses) the causes of human inconstancy are analyzed, while in book 4 (1,544 verses) the nature of constancy (*staete*) and its relation to virtue are emphasized. The effect of vice and virtue on human destiny are described and related to education in book 5 (1,106 verses). The situation of virtuous man in life is elaborated through the allegory of the Battle of Virtues and Vices in book 6 (1,684 verses), while book 7 (1,378 verses) considers the nature of body and soul and of the cognitive processes. Thomasin shows how understanding guides man to a good and virtuous life, whereas vice and sin have a blinding quality. The Seven Liberal Arts are related to learning.

The theme of book 8 (2,372 verses) is lack of moderation (*unmâze*) and its effect on human conduct in history and in the author's own time. It contains, as an admitted digression, a critique of Walther von der Vogelweide's criticism of Pope Innocent III and addresses Frederick II and the German princes, urging them to support a crusade to the Holy Land. Book 9 (1,340 verses) begins with a dialogue between the author and his tiring pen in which much biographical data is revealed. The book itself is devoted to a consideration of justice (*reht*) and its proper administration, which is presented as the outstanding social virtue. Book 10 (1,188 verses) considers the nature of generosity (*milte*) and its effect on human relationships. Since *milte* never gives that which is earned, but more than that, from a spirit of liberality, it beautifies human relationships. Thomasin views this spirit as *richer muot*. It is the crowning manifestation of virtue, as well as being dependent on virtue. In the epilogue (122 verses, which are formally part of it), the author names and addresses his book and sends it as a messenger (*bote*) into the world, to seek all who might benefit from it. Evil people are to be shunned, since they are incapable of acquiring good sense.

Welsche Gast is transmitted in twenty-four manuscripts dating from before 1500, of which only *W* (Wolfenbüttel, MS 37.19 Aug. 2°) is a copy of another existing manuscript (Munich, cgm 571). Recently an additional leaf with fifty-eight verses of text and illustrations, number 32 of the fragment *Ma* (Berlin, MS germ., fol. 757), has been found. Thus *Ma* can now be listed as an illustrated manuscript.

BIBLIOGRAPHY

Sources. Thomasin von Zerclaere der Welsche Gast, F. W. von Kries, ed., 4 vols., (1984–1985), I: *Einleitung, Überlieferung, Text, die Varianten des Prosavorworts* (1984), II: *Die Varianten der Hss. GFAD, der Büdinger und Sibiuer Fragmente* (1984), III: *Die Varianten der Redaktion S*** (1984), IV: *Die Illustrationen des Welschen Gasts: Kommentar mit Analyse der Bildinhalte, Schriftbandtexte, Verzeichnisse, Namenregister, Bibliographie* (1985). Another source is *Der wälsche Gast des Thomasin von Zirclaria*, Heinrich Rückert, ed. (1852, repr. with introduction and index by Friedrich Neumann 1965).

Studies. Bruno Boesch, *Lehrhafte Literatur* (1977); Klaus Grubmüller, "Eine weitere Handschrift von Tho-
masins 'Welschem Gast'," in *Zeitschrift für deutsches Altertum*, **97** (1968); Friedrich W. von Kries, *Textkritische Studien zum Welschen Gast Thomasins von Zerclaere* (1967), and "Zur Überlieferung des 'Welschen Gasts' Thomasins von Zerclaere," in *Zeitschrift für deutsches Altertum*, **113** (1984); Adolf von Oechelhäuser, *Der Bilderkreis zum Wälschen Gaste des Thomasin von Zerclaere* (1890); Friedrich Ranke, *Sprache und Stil im Wälschen Gast des Thomasin von Circlaria* (1908, repr. 1970); Catherine T. Rapp, *Burgher and Peasant in the Works of Thomasin von Zirklaria . . .* (1936); Dieter Richter, "Zur Überlieferung von Thomasins 'Welschem Gast,'" in *Zeitschrift für deutsches Altertum*, **96** (1977); Daniel Rocher, "Thomasin von Zerclaere, Innocent III, et Latran IV; ou, La véritable influence de l'actualité sur le *Wälscher Gast*," in *Le moyen âge*, **79** (1973), and *Thomasin von Zerclaere: Der Wälsche Gast (1215–1216)* (1977); Ernst J. F. Ruff, *'Der wälsche Gast' des Thomasin von Zerclaere: Untersuchungen zu Gehalt und Bedeutung einer mhd. Morallehre* (1982); Manfred Scholz, "Die 'Hûsvrouwe' und ihr Gast. Zu Thomasin von Zerclaere und seinem Puplikum," in Rose B. Schäfer-Maulbetsch, Manfred G. Scholz, and Günther Schweikle, eds., *Festschrift für Kurt Herbert Halbach . . .* (1972); Hans Teske, *Thomasin von Zerclaere. Der Mann und sein Werk* (1933); *Der Welsche Gast des Thomasîn von Zerclaere: Codex Palatinus Germanicus 389 der Universitätsbibliothek Heidelberg*, introduction to Thomasin's poetic work by Friedrich Neumann, the manuscript and its illustrations by Ewald Vetter (1974); Ursula Winter and Heinz Stǎnescu, "Ein neuentdecktes Fragment aus dem Welschen Gast des Thomasin von Zerclaere," in *Beiträge zur Geschichte der deutschen Sprache und Literatur* (Halle), **97** (1976).

F. W. VON KRIES

[See also **Frederick II; Innocent III, Pope; Middle High German Literature; Walther von der Vogelweide**.]

THOMISM AND ITS OPPONENTS.

Thomism (pronounced with a long *o* and sounding like "tome-ism") is the name given to the teachings of St. Thomas Aquinas (1224–1274), somewhat as the term Kantianism is applied to the teachings of Immanuel Kant. Like other "-isms," the word could indicate the entire body of writings authored by Aquinas, but it more usually refers to the main ideas that underlie his works or to the mentality that seems to characterize them. Because Aquinas' ideas have been taken up and developed by scores of thinkers throughout the centuries, a slightly more nuanced usage applies the term to what others have made of his thought in their attempts to understand it, interpret it, and develop it in contexts quite different from those of the mid thirteenth century. In this more refined sense, St. Thomas was not himself a Thomist (nor was Kant a Kantian), whereas his committed disciples and followers, such as Thomas Sutton (d. ca. 1315), John Capreolus (d. 1444), and Tomasso de Vio Cajetan (d. 1534), were so known in their day, and the label has consistently been applied to Jacques Maritain and Étienne Gilson in our own.

Just as Thomism has a variety of referents, so its "opponents" can be taken in various ways. During his lifetime Aquinas engaged in controversies and polemics with other philosophers and theologians, and at his death a number of his teachings were opposed by ecclesiastical authorities. The school he founded soon differentiated itself from other schools or movements, being generally supported by members of the Dominican order, to which he belonged, and just as actively combated by secular masters and by members of other religious orders, particularly Franciscans and Augustinians. Two of the more prominent Franciscans to oppose Thomistic teachings were John Duns Scotus and William of Ockham. Their systems, called Scotism and Ockhamism, respectively, were regarded throughout the later Middle Ages as opposed to Thomism in the sense of being alternative formulations of philosophical and theological thought.

Such being the case, in what follows an attempt will be made to supplement the account given of Thomistic teachings in the article on Aquinas by detailing some key points on which he was opposed in his lifetime and shortly after his death, then by tracing the growth of the movement known as Thomism throughout the Middle Ages, and concluding with some schematic characterizations of the movement that may serve to distinguish it from competing systems of thought.

ST. THOMAS AND HIS ADVERSARIES

St. Thomas was a prolific teacher and writer, as was his mentor St. Albert the Great; he was also an innovator who attempted to bring the pagan Aristotle into centers of learning long dominated by the Bible and Judeo-Christian thought. In addition, he was a mendicant friar, a member of a new type of religious order that relinquished the security of the monastery so as to evangelize the towns and universities then forming all over Europe. It was as a mendicant that Thomas met his first opposition at the University of Paris. Sent there by his order, and

appointed to the faculty along with the Franciscan Bonaventure by Pope Alexander IV in 1256, he encountered strong opposition from the secular masters of the university, led by William of St. Amour. William composed a vehement attack on the mendicants entitled De periculis novissimis temporum (On the latest perils of the times) that elicited replies both from Bonaventure and from Thomas. Later, when at Paris for a second professorship (1269–1272), Aquinas was attacked by William's followers, Gerard of Abbeville and Nicholas of Lisieux, and in turn responded to them. His three opuscula emanating from this controversy show him defending the friars against traditionalists who believed that religious should remain in their monasteries and not engage in teaching, preaching, or the care of souls.

Among the disputes raging at Paris during Aquinas' second professorship was one originating among the philosophers there concerning Aristotle's teaching on the human intellect. Siger of Brabant, a secular cleric who followed Averroës (Ibn Rushd) in his reading of Aristotle, held that there is only one intellect for all mankind—a view that questioned the reasonableness of the church's stand on personal immortality. On 10 December 1270 Étienne Tempier, bishop of Paris, condemned thirteen propositions in the writings of Siger and his followers. Earlier that same year (1270), Aquinas had written his important treatise on the unity of the intellect (De unitate intellectus); manuscript copies show that it was directed against Siger. The treatise bears witness to Aquinas' own mastery of Aristotle's text, to his enthusiasm for it, but to his rejection of the unorthodox interpretations being placed on it in the arts faculty of Paris by the Latin Averroists.

Bonaventure, to be sure, was as much behind the 1270 condemnation as was Aquinas. Notwithstanding their earlier collaboration in the controversy on the role of mendicants, however, tension began to develop between them on the matter of using Aristotelian philosophy in the elaboration of Christian theology. Bonaventure and his Franciscan confreres generally favored an older Augustinian approach, where faith took precedence over reason and where rational arguments, such as those advanced by the Latin Averroists, were increasingly seen as suspect. Probably at Bonaventure's instigation the Franciscan John Peckham attacked Aquinas on an issue that typified the differences between them, the problem of creation in time versus the eternity of the world. The Greek Aristotle had no concept of creation and saw the world as eternal, whereas the Bible and the Fourth Lateran Council clearly taught its creation at the beginning of time. To safeguard the church's position Peckham attempted to demonstrate the fact of temporal creation, whereas Aquinas, in what seemed to concede too much to the Aristotelian arguments, held that this fact was actually indemonstrable and could only be accepted on faith. Thomas' *De aeternitate mundi contra murmurantes* (On the eternity of the world against the murmurers—the "murmurers" being the Franciscans) is a masterful polemical treatise, but unfortunately it alienated him from this powerful group within the medieval church. Indeed, it set up an opposition between Dominicans and Franciscans that would be perpetuated in disputation after disputation and ultimately would bring about the disintegration of Scholastic theology.

A more serious problem, from the theological point of view, was Aquinas' strong advocacy of man's unity as set forth in his teaching on the unicity of the substantial form in the human being. The difficulty concerns a technical point in hylomorphic theory, namely, whether the intellective soul is the unique substantial form united to primary matter, or whether other substantial forms (such as a *forma corporeitatis*, or form of bodiness) are also present in the human composite. Franciscans were for the most part pluralists: they held that more than one substantial form had to be posited in man to resolve such theological problems as whether Christ, living and dead, was the same man, and whether Christ's body was one and the same on the cross and in the grave. Aquinas rejected that view and offered his own resolution of the theological difficulties. As he viewed it, to hold that man is a body by one form, living by another, an animal by a third, and a human by yet a fourth (the intellective soul) would be to destroy his essential unity. The argument was buttressed by strong psychological evidence and metaphysical principles based on Aristotle, but it failed to please many theologians. Aquinas' Christology allowed that the Lord, living and dead, was identically (*simpliciter*) the same man, but that the Lord's body, being made human by his intellective soul, remained the same only in a qualified way (*secundum quid*) after the separation of the soul from the body. This and similar stands caused his orthodoxy to be impugned at Paris and at other centers of theological study.

CONDEMNATIONS AND *CORRECTORIA*

Aquinas died, shortly after his second Paris professorship, on 7 March 1274. Exactly three years later, on 7 March 1277, in what was more than a mere coincidence, Tempier again issued a condemnation of the pagan Aristotle and those who followed his thought. This time some 16 of the 219 proscribed theses bore directly on St. Thomas' teachings. Eleven days later the Dominican archbishop of Canterbury, Robert Kilwardby, proclaimed a similar condemnation, going even further than Tempier by explicitly forbidding anyone to teach that the vegetative, sensitive, intellective principles are one simple form or to hold that a living body and a dead body are not bodies in the same sense. There could be no doubt that Thomas, and not Siger or other Latin Averroists, was the target of Kilwardby's action. To make matters worse, Peckham himself succeeded Kilwardby as archbishop of Canterbury and on 29 October 1284 renewed all of the latter's prohibitions. For Peckham this was no matter of scholastic hairsplitting: in his estimation Aquinas' teachings called into question a number of articles of the faith, particularly those bearing on the Incarnation, the Eucharist, and the resurrection of the body.

Even prior to Peckham's action, the Franciscans were concerned lest Thomas' teachings seduce members of their own order. On the heels of Kilwardby's condemnation, in 1278 the English Franciscan William de la Mare wrote a *Correctorium fratris Thomae* (Correctory of Brother Thomas) wherein he set out the errors he detected in Aquinas' writings. And in 1282 the Franciscan general chapter of Strassburg forbade the reading of St. Thomas's *Summa theologiae,* even by professors within the order, unless they studied William's *Correctorium* along with it.

Defenders of the Angelic Doctor, as Aquinas was called, were not lacking. The Dominican Giles of Lessines replied to Kilwardby with a detailed refutation of the archbishop's opinions entitled *De unitate formae* (On the unity of form), written in July of 1278. Three months earlier, the Augustinian Egidius Colonna (Giles of Rome) also came to Aquinas' defense with his treatise *Contra gradus et pluralitates formarum* (Against degrees and pluralities of forms). And the Dominican archbishop of Corinth, Peter of Conflans, appealed to Kilwardby to refrain from censuring Thomas' theological views, which he found perfectly sound and defensible.

At this stage a series of five works appeared under the general rubric *Correctoria corruptorii Thomae* (Correctories of the corruptor of Thomas), all directed against William's *Correctorium* and attempting to show that its author has a superficial grasp of Aquinas' doctrine. Had William properly understood it, they argued, he would have seen that it was in no way contrary to the Scriptures, the fathers of the church, or sound philosophy. Three of the *correctoria* came from Oxford Dominicans who, being under Kilwardby's prohibition, circulated their corrections anonymously. Recent scholarship has identified the first (*ca.* 1282) as the work of Richard Knapwell, revised in a fuller redaction by Thomas Sutton, the second (*ca.* 1283) as coming from the pen of Robert of Orford, and the third (1284–1286) as the initiative of William of Macclesfeld. The remaining two *correctoria* originated with Dominicans on the Continent: John of Paris wrote the first of these around 1293, and Rambert of Bologna the second, before he left Paris in 1299 to return to his homeland.

The *correctoria* give evidence of a Thomistic school forming around Aquinas' teaching, and the friars who composed them were among the first identifiable Thomists, men who claimed to understand Thomas' thought and defend it against his adversaries. Apart from such followers at Oxford and Paris, there were other Dominicans in Italy, particularly at Rome and Naples, who took up his cause. During his Italian sojourns Aquinas had consistently been a favorite in the curia of various popes (Alexander IV, Urban IV, and Clement IV), and it is interesting to note that the papacy never questioned his theological views. So orthodox did he appear to Pope John XXII that the pontiff canonized Thomas on 18 July 1323, less than fifty years after the condemnations of 1277. Meanwhile, at Paris, the Dominican John of Naples was teaching Thomism in the university by 1316, and finally, two years after the canonization a new bishop there, Étienne Bourret, revoked all of Tempier's censures that touched in any way "the teaching of Blessed Thomas."

MEDIEVAL THOMISTS (TO 1500)

Aquinas left no immediate successors among the Dominicans at Paris, mainly because his teaching in the theology faculty there precluded his having them as students of philosophy, in which his most distinctive views were developed. This meant that the early Thomists, even those who lived with him

at the Dominican priory of St. Jacques, had to absorb his thought by studying his Aristotelian commentaries and seeing how their teachings were used to develop a systematic theology. Friars from England and elsewhere on the Continent had studied in this way at Paris, and they formed the nucleus around which a Thomistic school gradually developed.

Among the English friars, William of Hothum might be called the first Thomist; he became the provincial of England in 1282 after studying at Paris and used every device at his command to protect those at Oxford writing the *correctoria* and to disseminate their works. Richard Knapwell unfortunately was a casualty to that dispute; excommunicated by Peckham, he was sent by Hothum to Rome to plead his case on privilege of exemption, only to be silenced there by a newly elected Franciscan pope, Nicholas IV. Thomas Sutton was more successful in his efforts. By training a philosopher, he completed two of Aquinas' unfinished commentaries on Aristotle and survived the *correctoria* dispute to defend Thomistic teachings against those of Duns Scotus and Henry of Ghent. His contemporary, William of Macclesfeld, developed into a controversialist of note and also combatted Henry, along with another secular master, Godfrey of Fontaines. He was assisted in these efforts by Robert of Orford, who likewise engaged Henry and Godfrey. The Dominican historian and humanist Nicholas Trevet propagated Thomism in his theological writings, as did his young contemporary Thomas Waleys. After 1320, however, nominalism began to make serious inroads among English Dominicans, with the result that Robert Holkot, for example, could be called a Thomist in but the weakest sense. Thomas of Claxton was unique among them in subscribing completely to Aquinas' doctrine in his *Sentence* commentary written around 1400.

In France, apart from John of Paris, who achieved fame in developing Thomistic views on the separation of church and state, the early Thomists included Bernard of Trille and Giles of Lessines, both Dominicans, and the secular master Peter of Auvergne. Another Dominican, Bernard of Auvergne, became the opponent of Henry of Ghent and Godfrey of Fontaines when they attained stature at Paris. But the best-known French Dominican in this genre was Hervaeus Natalis (Harvey Nedellec), whose *Defensio doctrinae fratris Thomae* (Defense of the teaching of Brother Thomas), written between 1303 and 1312, not only propagated Aquinas' doctrines but indirectly promoted his canonization. Less appreciated but having a better grasp of Thomas' thought was another French Dominican, William of Peter of Godin. Petrus Paludanus (Peter of La Palu) should also be mentioned along with William; although an enthusiastic follower of Thomas, he seems not to have had a profound understanding of his teachings. Finally, early in the fifteenth century, the most famous Dominican of the French school, John Capreolus, wrote an elaborate commentary on the *Sentences* entitled *Defensiones theologiae divi Thomae* (Defenses of the theology of St. Thomas). This work ably undertook to refute Scotus and the nominalists and earned for him the title *princeps Thomistarum,* "first among the Thomists."

German Dominicans did not propagate Thomism as strongly as the English and the French, possibly because of the attraction of Albert the Great and the Albertist school. The earlier followers of Thomas included John of Sterngassen, Nicholas of Strassburg, and John of Lichtenberg. Somewhat later Henry of Lübeck defended Thomistic teachings on individuation and on the real distinction in creatures between essence and existence at the University of Paris. In the mid fifteenth century, at Cologne, the secular masters Henry of Gorkum and John Tinctor lectured on the *Summa theologiae,* and later in the century the Dominicans John Versor and Gerhard of Elton achieved distinction as productive Thomists. At about the same time, in Budapest, the Dominican Petrus Nigri (Schwarz) wrote a voluminous *Clypeus Thomistarum* (Shield of Thomists), which defended Aquinas' doctrines against his various attackers.

In Italy, strong interest continued to be manifested in Thomistic teachings and their propagation. Rambert of Bologna and John of Naples have already been mentioned; to these Dominicans should be added Hannibaldus de Hannibaldis, Thomas' successor in the professorship at Paris, and Bartholomew of Lucca, one of his biographers. Remigio de' Girolami seems to have been the source of the Thomistic theology displayed in Dante's *Divina commedia.* In the fifteenth century, Antoninus of Florence wrote a *Summa theologiae moralis,* which extended Thomas' moral teachings into new areas. And at Bologna, Peter of Bergamo prepared a complete index of Aquinas' works in his *Tabula aurea* (Golden table), and taught Tommaso de Vio Cajetan, Dominic of Flanders, and Girolamo

Savonarola—all famous in their own right. Cajetan was largely responsible for the revival of Thomistic studies, sometimes called "Second Thomism," associated with the Council of Trent and the counterreformation; Dominic of Flanders wrote an influential *Summa divinae philosophiae* (Sum of divine philosophy); and Savonarola prepared a manual of apologetics, *Triumphus crucis* (Triumph of the cross), patterned on Aquinas' *Summa contra gentiles.*

To these many other names could be added, such as that of Juan de Torquemada, Spanish Dominican and later cardinal, who played an important role defending papal authority against the conciliarists in the fifteenth century. The full flowering of Iberian Thomism was not to occur until the next century, however, when the Dominicans Francisco de Vitoria, Domingo de Soto, Melchior Cano, and Domingo Báñez achieved fame (along with many scholars in the newly founded Jesuit Order), in the movement known as "Second Scholasticism." But leading up to them, throughout the High and late Middle Ages, a marked development of Thomistic doctrine had continued throughout Europe, and it is this movement that is known as medieval Thomism.

THOMISM AND COMPETING SCHOOLS

What were some of the issues that characterized the Thomistic school throughout this period, and how did they differ from those of competing schools? Being at root a progressive form of Aristotelianism, Thomism can be differentiated philosophically from many other schools on the basis of its distinctive interpretations of Aristotle. Such a characterization may be found in the article "Aristotle in the Middle Ages," where the teachings of Thomistic Aristotelianism are set off from those of the Augustinian, Scotistic, Nominalist (or Ockhamist), and Averroist varieties. To supplement this account, some areas in systematic theology may be pointed out where Thomists took issue with their contemporaries while remaining faithful to Aquinas' inspiration and attempting to develop his doctrine.

Like all Scholastic theologians, Thomists remain convinced that beyond the order of nature there is another order of reality, that of the supernatural, which would never be known to man unless God had revealed it to him. The fact of revelation, as contained in the Bible and in the teachings of the church, is what makes theology possible; accepted on faith, revealed truth can be integrated with the truths of reason and can provide man access to the hidden life of God. The distinctive note in Thomism is its confidence in unaided reason's ability to understand nature, to be complemented by faith so as to see how grace perfects nature, and thus to promote a harmonious relationship between the two sources of theology: faith and reason. Of man's two spiritual faculties, intellect and will, Thomists see intellect as the superior power of the soul; it is this power that explains man's rationality, and even the freedom of his will, since his will stands in subordination to his reason but is not dominated by it in a necessitating way. And just as intellect is superior to will in man, so it is in God. Obviously God's powers are different from man's, but they stand in analogous relationship to his, and on this basis Thomists concede a priority to God's intellect over his will in working out the various problems that arise in Scholastic theology. As opposed to them, most Franciscans—of the earlier Augustinian variety like Bonaventure or of the Scotist and Ockhamist schools—rank the will over the intellect in both God and man, and on this account come to different theological conclusions.

Usually there is no question of Catholic orthodoxy involved in the different positions, since they relate more to rational elaboration than to the content of faith and revelation, although partisans of Scotism and Thomism, for example, would occasionally label their opponents "heretics" throughout the course of history. But one matter on which there was a doctrinal difference is that of the Immaculate Conception, namely, the teaching that Mary was conceived in the womb of her mother without original sin. St. Thomas denied this teaching on the basis that it detracted from Christ's dignity as the savior of all men; in his view, Mary contracted the sin of Adam but was cleansed from it before the birth through the foreseen merits of her divine son. Duns Scotus, on the other hand, taught that she was actually preserved from original sin from the moment of her conception—a doctrine that was solemnly defined for Roman Catholics in 1854 by Pope Pius IX.

More typical of the differences between Thomism and Scotism are their respective teachings on the motive of the Incarnation, on the ability of human actions to merit eternal life, and on the nature of beatitude in heaven. With regard to the Incarnation, that is, the teaching that Christ, the Second Person of the Trinity, took on flesh and truly became man, Thomists and Scotists differ in their explanation of its motive, or as to why it came about. For St. Thomas the primary motive of the Incarnation was the Redemption of fallen mankind, and therefore if Adam had not sinned (his *felix culpa*, or "happy fault") God would never have become man. For Duns Scotus, on the other hand, God's love for man was the basic motive for the Incarnation and so Adam's sin was not its necessary condition. Similarly, Thomists decide issues relating to merit, that is, as to how human actions can be deserving of the reward of eternal life, on the basis of considerations of justice, whereas Scotists do so from those of charity. Again, for Thomists eternal life consists in seeing God face to face, since the fullness of happiness flows from this vision; thus for them the essence of happiness consists in an intellectual vision. For Scotists this takes too much away from love and charity; they see happiness as essentially an act of the will. In each instance the difference of theological conclusion is rooted in either an intellectualist or a voluntarist preference, and these preferences have characterized Dominicans and Franciscans, respectively, throughout their histories.

Ockhamists depart more radically from Thomists than do Scotists, but again differences may be highlighted in terms of voluntarist as opposed to intellectualist tendencies. Ockham placed great emphasis on the divine will as the supreme consideration operative throughout his theology and philosophy; whatever God can will without contradiction became for him the sole limit to be placed on God's omnipotence. Such a view had significant consequences for his understanding of the universe. Whereas both Thomists and Scotists saw the world as having an intrinsic intelligibility, Ockham saw it as radically contingent, dependent at every moment on the divine will, so much so that even the natures of things would be subject to change at God's whim. He extended this line of thought into the area of morality. Previous thinkers had identified the good on the basis of objective and rational norms; instead, Ockham based it subjectively on God's will. Sin was not for him intrinsically evil; rather its essential character consisted in doing something prohibited by God. It is easy to see, even from this brief sketch, how faith assumed much more importance for Ockham than it did for Aquinas, and how the role of reason came to be displaced by the nominalists from the high place it held within the Thomistic synthesis.

Compared to Thomism, Scotism had a somewhat uneven history, since its chief advocates came from within the Franciscan order and were drawn alternatively to the older views of Bonaventure and to the newer ones of Ockham. At Oxford, where Duns Scotus had taught, his principal followers were William of Alnwick and Robert Cowton. His doctrines proved more influential at the University of Paris, for he had studied and taught there also, and found disciples in Antonius Andreas, James of Ascoli, and Francis of Meyronnes. The last is usually credited with systematizing Scotism as an intellectual movement within Scholasticism. Other influential Scotists were John of Bassolis and Hugh of Newcastle. Francis of Marchia is especially worthy of mention for his advocacy of a theory of impetus, which played an important part in the development of medieval science. Otherwise Scotism languished during the fifteenth century, only to take on new life in the sixteenth, when printed editions of Duns Scotus' works became available and he was endorsed as their favored doctor by most branches of the Franciscan order.

The *via moderna* of Ockham, which soon blossomed into the broader movement known as nominalism, emerged as one of the strongest currents of thought in the late Middle Ages. In England, Adam Wodam (Wodeham) was an Ockhamist, and the same could be said of the Dominican Robert Holkot, though he himself claimed allegiance to St. Thomas. At Merton College, where logic and natural philosophy flourished along nominalist lines, the principal thinkers were Thomas Bradwardine, William Heytesbury, and Richard Swineshead—all important for their studies of motion. At Paris Jean Buridan carried on their tradition, and propagated it even more widely through those he influenced: Nicole Oresme, Albert of Saxony, and Marsilius of Inghen. Other leading nominalists included the Augustinian Gregory of Rimini as well as Peter D'Ailly, John Gerson, and Gabriel Biel. Support for the conciliar movement came from within their ranks, and they are generally credited with supplying a type of ecumenical theology that proved congenial to the Protestant Reformers.

The foregoing is a broad sketch of the Scholastic movement known as Thomism and the way it related to comparable movements in the High and late Middle Ages. With the Counter-Reformation, and particularly with the rise of the Jesuits in the sixteenth and seventeenth centuries, other movements came into existence and various labels have been applied to them, such as Suarezianism, Molinism, and Bañezianism. They are all named after their proponents—Francisco Suárez, Luis de Molina, and Domingo Báñez, respectively—although each is intelligible as a development within Thomism when the latter is broadly conceived. Suárez and Molina, Jesuits both, incorporated Scotistic and nominalist strains in their thought, whereas Báñez, a Dominican, combatted them for their departures from the original teachings of St. Thomas. Most of the disputes center on reconciling human freedom with divine grace and predestination, and explaining how all these can be preserved while safeguarding God's omniscience and the universal causality he exerts in the affairs of men.

Apart from its role in Second Scholasticism, Thomism entered a third phase of development during the late nineteenth and twentieth centuries in the movement known as Neo-Thomism or the Thomistic Revival. Great impetus for this revival came from Pope Leo XIII, whose encyclical *Aeterni Patris* of 4 August 1879 called for a return to the thought of St. Thomas as a means of solving contemporary problems. This papal endorsement stimulated much historical research as well as the preparation of critical texts, and generally has contributed to the growth of interest in medieval studies during the past century. Thomists who played a prominent part in the resulting renewal include Maurice de Wulf, Pierre Mandonnet, Marie Dominique Chenu, Fernand van Steenberghen, Jacques Maritain, and Étienne Gilson.

BIBLIOGRAPHY

Index Thomisticus (1974–) is a computer-based concordance of all the Latin terms and expressions in Aquinas' works. Extensive bibliographies of studies relating to Thomism down to 1965 may be found in the *Bulletin thomiste* (1923–1965); in 1966 this series was replaced by an annual publication, *Rassegna di letteratura tomistica*. Additional bibliographical surveys include Vernon J. Bourke, *Thomistic Bibliography, 1920–1940* (1945); Terry L. Miethe and Vernon J. Bourke, *Thomistic Bibliography, 1940–1978* (1980); and Paul Wyser, *Der Thomismus* (1951).

The definitive history of Thomism has yet to be written. Pioneer studies include Karl Werner, *Thomas von Aquino*, III, *Geschichte des Thomismus* (1859); and Martin Grabmann, *Mittelalterliches Geistesleben*, 3 vols. (1926–1956). The best survey in English is Frederick J. Roensch, *Early Thomistic School* (1964). Fuller details are given in William A. Hinnebusch, *The Early English Friars Preachers* (1951); Daniel A. Callus, *The Condem-*

nation of St. Thomas at Oxford, 2nd ed. (1955); and Fernand van Steenberghen, *Thomas Aquinas and Radical Aristotelianism* (1980).

More synthetic works that attempt to characterize the nature of Thomism as a system of thought include the following: Cornelio Fabro, *Breve introduzione al tomismo* (1960) and *Tomismo e pensiero moderno* (1969); Carlo Giacon, *Le grandi tesi del tomismo,* 2nd ed. (1948); Étienne Gilson, *The Spirit of Thomism* (1964); Paul Grenet, *Thomism: An Introduction,* James F. Ross, trans. (1967); Gallus M. Manser, *Das Wesen des Thomismus,* 3rd ed. (1949); Norbert del Prado, *De veritate fundamentali philosophiae christianae* (1911); Antonin G. Sertillanges, *Foundations of Thomistic Philosophy,* Godfrey Anstruther, trans. (1931).

WILLIAM A. WALLACE

[See also **Aquinas, St. Thomas; Aristotle in the Middle Ages; Augustinian Friars; Bonaventure, St.; Dominicans; Duns Scotus, John; Franciscans; Kilwardby, Richard; Nominalism; Ockham, William of; Peckham, John; Philosophy and Theology, Western European; Scholasticism, Scholastic Method; Siger of Brabant; Via Moderna.**]

THOR (Old Norse: Þórr) is a major god of Scandinavian mythology. His salient feature is his strength (*Snorra Edda, Gylfaginning,* chap. 11): he lives at Þrúðvangar (strength-fields) or Þrúðheimr (strength-home); his sons are Magni (strong) and Móði (brave), and his daughter Þrúðr (strength). Thor himself is the son of Odin and Earth, a lineage suggesting the union of the sky father and earth mother in other mythologies, producing a major god. His wife is Sif (kinship), known for her golden hair.

Thor makes explicit his mythological function in *Hárbarðsljóð* 23: "I was to the east and I killed giants, evil women who went to the mountain; great would be the family of giants, if they all lived; there would be hardly a man under Midgard." In other words, Thor protects men and the gods by battling and killing the forces of chaos. Most of the myths in which he figures feature this aspect of Thor.

Thor's greatest opponent is the Midgard serpent, Loki's son and the brother of Hel and the Fenris wolf. Poets during the Viking age knew of the encounter between Thor and the serpent, and artists apparently portrayed the story in carving on a stone in Altuna (Sweden) and a cross at Gosforth (Cumberland, England). These carvings stress the moment when Thor has fished up the serpent on his hook, not the outcome of the battle, and the skalds stress the same moment. They offer conflicting accounts of the outcome: Úlfr Uggason's *Húsdrápa* has Thor kill the serpent (str. 6), but Bragi Boddason's *Ragnarsdrápa* has Thor's companion, a giant, cut the line before Thor can kill the serpent (str. 19). The Eddic poem *Hymiskviða,* which tells the story in greater detail, seems to agree that Thor killed the serpent, but the strophe in question (24) is missing a long line. *Vǫluspá* has Thor meet the serpent at Ragnarǫk; each kills the other. *Snorra Edda* follows *Vǫluspá* in this and therefore allows the serpent to escape from Thor's hook (*Gylfaginning,* chap. 47).

Another encounter was that between Thor and the giant Hrungnir, told by the skald Þjóðólfr ór Hvini (Norway) in his *Haustlǫng* and at length in *Snorra Edda* (*Skáldskaparmál,* chap. 25). Their battle was important because Hrungnir was the strongest of all the giants and because it took the form of a duel and therefore had legal implications. Thor's second, Þjálfi, tricked Hrungnir by warning him of the god's attack from below, and when the giant put his shield on the ground and stood on it he was unable to protect himself from Thor's hammer and was killed. However, a portion of the giant's weapon, a hone, was lodged permanently in Thor's forehead, perhaps indicating the delicate balance of power between gods and giants. Þjálfi killed Hrungnir's companion, a clay giant with the heart of a mare. Dumézil has suggested that here there is a reflection of initiation ritual.

Other victims of Thor include the giants Geirrøðr and his daughters (Eilífr Goðrúnarson, *Þórsdrápa; Snorra Edda, Skáldskaparmál,* chap 27), Hymir (*Hymiskviða; Snorra Edda, Gylfaginning,* chap. 32), and Þrymr (*Þrymskviða*). Against Geirrøðr Thor must fight without his weapons and obtains new accoutrements (a belt of strength, iron gloves, and a staff) from the giantess Gríðr. From Hymir and Þrymr, Thor recovers objects of cultural importance: from Hymir a kettle in which the gods can brew beer for banquets and from Þrymr Thor's hammer, Mjǫllnir, which the giant had stolen. Thus, to a certain extent Thor plays the role of a culture hero.

The jocular tone of *Þrymskviða* (Thor dresses as Freyja, making an unlikely "bride" for the giant), echoed in other poems, finds its closest parallel in Snorri's ironic account of Thor's journey to the giant Útgarða-Loki (*Snorra Edda, Gylfaginning,*

45

chaps. 26–31). The giant tricks Thor and his companions, Loki and Þjálfi, in various tests: Thor attempts to empty a drinking horn attached to the sea, to lift a cat (actually the Midgard serpent), and to wrestle with an old woman (actually old age). Although he fails in these tasks, his acts involve creation (he drinks the sea down to low tide) and near victories over the serpent and mortality, and hence are mythically significant.

The Eddic poem *Alvíssmál* describes how Thor questions a dwarf, suitor to Thor's daughter, on the names of things among various mythological races, until the sun rises and bursts the dwarf. The suggestion of Thor's cunning is belied by *Hárbarðsljóð*, where Odin outwits Thor in a verbal duel.

The cult of Thor was widespread, particularly during the waning decades of paganism, when he seems to have focused opposition to Christ. Two skalds, Vetrliði Sumarliðason and Þorbjǫrn dísarskáld, celebrated the god with odes in the second person, cataloging the giants he killed. Poems of this sort to any other god are unknown. Runic inscriptions call on Thor to preserve the rest of the dead, or simply to hallow the runes—ordinarily Odin's province—and archaeologists have unearthed many amulets interpreted as miniature hammers of Thor, used to ward off evil. Men seem to have trusted Thor, for his name figures as the first component of many personal names and place-names. These are interpreted to indicate the growth and spread of the cult during the end of the Viking age. By then Thor had acquired aspects of both sovereignty and fertility and seems to have replaced Odin and Freyr as the chief Norse god. Vikings also brought the cult to England, Normandy, and perhaps also to the East. The Baltic Perkunas, Varangian Perun, and Lapp Horagalles appear to be related. The historical sources contain many references to worship of Thor and to Christ's and the missionaries' gradual ascendancy over him. By the late Middle Ages Thor had become a common troll in legendary sagas.

The closest parallel to Thor is the Indic god Indra, who shares Thor's strength, red beard, and enormous appetite. Indra's weapon, perhaps a bolt of lightning, was the work of a special craftsman; Sindri, a great craftsman among the dwarfs, fashioned Mjǫllnir, and the name *Þórr* meant "thunderer." Indra's great opponent was the dragon Vṛtra, whom he slew and thereby released the waters. This recalls the Midgard serpent and perhaps also the kettle Thor acquired from Hymir after hooking the serpent. Given these similarities, and others to such figures as Herakles, it seems probable that Thor derives from an Indo-European heroic god who protected men and gods by battling the forces of chaos.

BIBLIOGRAPHY

Among the handbooks see first Jan de Vries, *Altgermanische Religionsgeschichte,* 3rd ed. (1970), II, 107–153; E. O. G. Turville-Petre, *Myth and Religion of the North: The Religion of Ancient Scandinavia* (1964), 75–105; Åke V. Ström, "Germanische Religion," in *idem* and Haralds Biezais, *Germanische und baltische Religion,* (1975), 86–87, 103–104, 134–140; E. F. Halvorsen, "Þórr," in *Kulturhistorisk leksikon för nordisk middelalder,* XX (1976), 391–395. Also important are Helge Ljungberg, *Tor: Undersökningar i indoeuropeisk och nordisk religionshistoria* (1947); and F. R. Schröder, "Thor, Indra, Herakles," in *Zeitschrift für deutsche Philologie,* 76 (1957). Margaret Clunies Ross, "An Interpretation of the Myth of Thor's Encounter with Geirrøðr and His Daughters," in *Speculum Norroenum: Norse Studies in Memory of Gabriel Turville-Petre* (1981), offers a modern, psychologically oriented interpretation.

JOHN LINDOW

[See also **Æsir; Eddic Poetry; Fenris Wolf; Loki; Odin; Ragnarok; Scandinavian Mythology;** and individual authors and works.]

THORNTON, JOHN (*fl.* early fifteenth century), a master glazier, perhaps trained in Coventry. His masterpiece is the Great East Window of York Minster (1405–1408). This and his other work in the city revolutionized the famous York school of stained glass painting. He is also thought to have created the east window of Great Malvern Priory.

BIBLIOGRAPHY

John A. Knowles, "John Thornton of Coventry and the Great East Window in York Minster," in *Notes and Queries,* 12th ser., 7 (1920), and "John Thornton of Coventry and the East Window of Great Malvern Priory," in *Antiquaries Journal,* 39 (1959); Joan C. Lancaster, "John Thornton of Coventry, Glazier," in *Birmingham Archaeological Society Transactions,* 74 (1956).

STEPHEN GARDNER

[See also **Glass, Stained.**]

ÞORSTEINS SAGA VÍKINGSSONAR

Great East Window of York Minster by John Thornton, 1405–1408. PHOTO: WIM SWAAN

ÞORSTEINS SAGA VÍKINGSSONAR (The story of Þorsteinn Víkingsson), whose title hero is presented as the father of the eponymous hero of *Friðþjófs saga frækna,* was probably written around 1300; it survives in several manuscripts dating from the fifteenth century. It is essentially a Viking romance, the main emphasis being on the hero's exploits and adventures.

After a genealogical introduction, accounting for the ancestry of the Norwegian hero, who is said to be descended from giants and elves, the narrative proceeds to describe the fabulous exploits of his father, Víkingr, whose name is an indication of what kind of a man he is. Víkingr fights a duel with a particularly unpleasant Indian prince called Hárekr járnhauss (Iron skull) to save a Swedish princess, whom Hárekr wants for a wife, from a fate worse than death. After killing Hárekr, suffering temporary leprosy inflicted on him by Hárekr's malign system, joining King Njörfi of Opland in Norway in a pact of blood brotherhood, and disposing of Hárekr's monstrous brother, Víkingr becomes an earl under King Njörfi.

The blood brothers have nine sons each,

ÞORSTEINS ÞÁTTR BÆJARMAGNS

Þorsteinn being the foremost of Víkingr's sons and Jökull of Njörfi's. When the boys grow up, the friendship between Víkingr and Njörfi is severely tested, but they never fail to observe the exacting terms of their blood brotherhood. One day at a rough ball game, Jökull insults Þórir Víkingsson, who retaliates by killing one of Jökull's brothers. The incident leads to an extended and violent feud between the sets of brothers, though their fathers remain the best of friends. In the course of the conflict all the young men are killed, except Jökull and Þorsteinn, who are eventually reconciled. The pervasive tension is therefore not only between the two opposing sides, but also between father and son. As one would expect, the title hero shows constant courage and moderation, while his antagonist is impetuous and so unscrupulous that he even resorts to such ungentlemanly tricks as enlisting the help of sorcerers.

The story is rich in motifs recurring elsewhere in the *fornaldarsögur.* Lappish sorcerers; outlawed evildoers; a princess transformed into a giantess and later restored to her human form; two suitors seeking the hand of a desirable girl; Viking expeditions to Orkney, Saxony, and the Baltic; a helpful dwarf; and magic weather: these and other familiar features are essential ingredients in a tale of this kind.

Of all Þorsteinn's formidable adversaries, there are none more redoubtable than the parricide Ófi and his brother Ötunfaxi, who has fought and won ninety battles and eighty duels and whom no weapon can bite. It is only by using a knife provided by the helpful dwarf that Þorsteinn can finally dispose of Ötunfaxi.

BIBLIOGRAPHY
The text is in Guðni Jónsson, ed., *Fornaldarsögur Norðurlanda,* III (1950); the translation is in Rasmus B. Anderson and Jón Bjarnason, trans., *Viking Tales of the North* (1877).

HERMANN PÁLSSON

[See also **Fornaldarsögur.**]

ÞORSTEINS ÞÁTTR BÆJARMAGNS (The story of Þorsteinn Mansion-might) was composed in Iceland, probably in the fourteenth century. It survives on three vellum manuscripts (one of them a single leaf) written in the following century. Set in the reign of King Olaf Tryggvason of Norway (995–1000), who plays a significant role in the story, it describes the fantastic adventures of one of his retainers, Þorsteinn, who was "the biggest man in Norway, so big that in the whole country there was hardly a door he could walk through without some difficulty, and since he seemed a bit overdeveloped for most houses he got the name of Þorsteinn *bæjarmagn* [that is, Mansion-might]" (Pálsson and Edwards' translation).

Þorsteinn's first adventure takes him to *Undirheimar* (the underworld), which he reaches through a mysterious mound in a forest, and there he steals some treasures that he later gives to King Olaf. Next he rescues the child of a dwarf, who rewards him with four magical objects: a shirt that prevents the wearer from getting tired at swimming or being wounded by weapons, a ring ensuring that he will never be short of money, a black flint of invisibility, and a triangular pebble that produces a hailstorm, sunshine, and sparkling flames, depending on which side it is pricked.

On another trip, Þorsteinn comes to a strange country where he joins the enigmatic Goðmundr of Glæsisvellir, who is on his way to *Risaland* (Giantland). In the eyes of Goðmundr, Þorsteinn is so small that he calls him *bæjarbarn* (Mansion-midget). The formidable Geirröðr of Giantland, to whom the god Thor pays a visit in a tale told by Snorri Sturluson in the *Prose Edda* (*Skáldskaparmál*, chap. 27) and who figures also in Saxo Grammaticus' *Gesta Danorum*, gives a magnificent feast where he puts Goðmundr and his men to one test after another, including a ball game with a flaming seal's head, a wrestling bout, and a deadly drinking contest. With Þorsteinn's help, however, they are unscathed by the ordeal, and Geirröðr is killed by Þorsteinn on the last day of the feast.

On his way back from Giantland, Þorsteinn encounters the monstrous Agði, who goes blind at the sight of Þorsteinn's ship and later retires into a burial mound. Þorsteinn marries Agði's daughter, who becomes a Christian. The wedding takes place in Norway and during the festivities the living-dead Agði forces his way into the bridal chamber. It is only with King Olaf's help that the ghastly gatecrasher can be disposed of: the king "came and thumped Agði's head with a gold-trimmed staff, hammering him right into the ground."

On a later visit to the mysterious realm of Glæsisvellir, Goðmundr gives Þorsteinn control of the district of Grundir, which he rules for a while,

although Agði keeps coming back from the dead and destroying the old home. "One night Þorsteinn got out of bed and saw Agði wandering about, but Agði didn't dare go through any of the gates as there was a cross on every one of them. So Þorsteinn went over to his mound. It was open so he went inside. . . . Then Agði came into the mound, and Þorsteinn ran past him and put a cross in the doorway. The mound closed up, and since then nothing has been seen of Agði." Eventually Þorsteinn goes back to Norway and takes over his own possessions.

BIBLIOGRAPHY
The edited text is in Guðni Jónsson, ed., *Fornaldarsögur Norðurlanda*, IV (1954). Translations are in Hermann Pálsson and Paul Edwards, trans., *Gautrek's Saga and Other Medieval Tales* (1968); and Jacqueline Simpson, trans., *The Northmen Talk: A Choice of Tales from Iceland* (1965).
See also Marlene Ciklamini, "Journeys to the Giant-Kingdom," in *Scandinavian Studies,* **60** (1968); and Jacqueline Simpson, "Otherworld Adventures in an Icelandic Saga," in *Folklore,* 77 (1966).

HERMANN PÁLSSON

[See also **Fornaldarsögur; Saxo Grammaticus; Skáldskaparmál.**]

ÞÓRÐAR SAGA HREÐU (The story of Þórðr Tumult), which was probably composed shortly after the death of Bishop Egill Eyjólfsson (1341), is the least fantastic of the late sagas of Icelanders, despite the fact that it is virtually pure fiction. Although several of the characters bear the names of historical persons, most of them are not known from historical sources or from older sagas. The story seems to be based on local tales about buildings erected by Þórðr Þórðarson and on themes common to saga literature. Verbal and thematic echoes from older sagas, especially from *Njáls saga,* are loud and clear. In its present form *Þórðar saga* is a revision of an older work and is preserved in several vellums from the fifteenth century and in numerous later paper transcripts, many of which remain to be studied.

Banished from Norway for the slaying of King Sigurðr slefa, son of Queen Gunnhildr, Þórðr and his brothers, together with their sister Sigríðr, settle in the Miðfjörðr district in northern Iceland. Here hostility develops between Þórðr and the district chieftain, Miðfjarðar-Skeggi, who envies Þórðr because of his general popularity and especially because of the admiration of his son Eiðr for Þórðr, who has saved his life following a boat accident and who makes Eiðr his foster son. Hostility erupts when Þórðr slays Skeggi's nephew Ormr for trying to seduce Sigríðr, who is engaged to Ormr's brother Ásbjörn. The remainder of the saga consists of a monotonous series of stereotyped clashes between Þórðr and various kinsmen he is forced to kill in self-defense.

Bloodshed between Þórðr and Skeggi is repeatedly averted through the timely intervention of Eiðr, who eventually brings about a reconciliation between the two clans. The generation-gap theme, which is central to the story, is more consistently employed here than in any other saga, with the possible exception of *Eyrbyggja saga*. Aside from this theme, which seems not to have been especially relevant at the time of composition, the main purpose of the author probably was to create a story in the manner of the *Íslendingasögur* (family sagas) for the purpose of entertainment.

BIBLIOGRAPHY

The text is in Johannes Halldórsson, ed., *Kjalnesinga saga . . .* (1959, Islenzsk fornrit, XIV), and Guðni Jonsson, ed., *Islendinga sögur*, VI (1946). See also Paul Schach, "Some Observations on the Generation-Gap Theme in the Icelandic Sagas," in Harald Scholler, ed., *The Epic in Medieval Society: Aesthetic and Moral Values* (1977), and *Icelandic Sagas* (1984), 156–157.

PAUL SCHACH

[See also **Eyrbyggja Saga; Family Sagas, Icelandic; Njáls Saga.**]

THOUSAND AND ONE NIGHTS (also called *The Arabian Nights' Entertainment*; Arabic: *Alf layla wa-layla*), the most famous work of Arabic narrative literature. Of uncertain date and origin, it is a collection of tales from various times and places that is instigated and largely defined by the frame story of Shahrazad, the wise young woman who nightly tells her stories to King Shahriyar in order to prevent him from executing her the following morning. Within this frame, which opens and closes the work, are embedded numerous stories of differing narrative genres and styles.

In the course of its long and uncertain history, the *1001 Nights* has assumed multiple literary disguises. From its perhaps spurious Persian origins, recalled by the tenth-century Arab historian al-Masᶜūdī, to its early-eighteenth-century incarnation in Antoine Galland's famous translation as *Les mille et une nuits: Contes arabes traduits en français*, from its Grub Street dubbing as the *Arabian Nights' Entertainment* to its appearance as a complete printed Arabic text in 1835, the *1001 Nights* has followed a course that curiously resembles the long and winding route traveled by the hero of one of its most extended cycles, Qamar al-Zamān. The result is an unusually long and complicated literary and textual history. One cannot, for example, definitely locate the origins of the work that we call the *1001 Nights;* indeed, one cannot accurately speak of the definitive text of the *1001 Nights,* for there is no known single, original source from which it derives. One is instead confronted with a multiplicity of texts, none of which are in complete agreement linguistically, structurally, or semantically, and all of which have been awarded the title of the *1001 Nights*.

This textual multiplicity is to some extent a corollary to the problem of origins, an issue that has long provoked scholars of the *Nights*. Whether or not the work, which for the Western world has become the major touchstone of Arabic narrative literature, is, in its origins, of Arab provenance has been open to debate since the nineteenth century. In the earliest known extended reference to the *Nights*, al-Masᶜūdī indicated the Persian roots of the collection, and Joseph von Hammer, following Masᶜūdī's lead, in 1827 inaugurated a debate between himself and the leading French Orientalist, Silvestre de Sacy, who contended that the work was uniquely Arab in character and probably of Egyptian origin. Such an issue cannot, of course, be completely resolved, given the folkloric elements of the work and its initial status as an oral composition. What seems clear, however, is that the *Nights* developed progressively and absorbed in the course of its development various geographically and culturally determined narrative elements. The frame-story structure, for example, is very commonly found in Indian story collections; while the names of most of the characters in the frame story—Shahrazad, Dunyazad (Dīnāzād), and Shahriyar, in particular—are certainly Persian. The setting, characters, and incidents of many of the Hārūn al-Rashīd stories, however, are clearly located in medieval Baghdad. It is, then, most correct to think of the *1001 Nights* as a layered work, a work in which one can determine three primary narrative strata: the Persian, the Baghdadian, and the Egyptian, all of which are finally filtered through the frame story and translated, linguistically and culturally, into Arabic.

This heterogeneity is one of the central textual characteristics of the *1001 Nights* and extends to the kinds of stories that are included within the boundaries of Shahrazad's frame story. The individual works that make up the *1001 Nights* are not limited to fairy tales about jinn and magic lanterns, as Western readers are tempted to suppose, but rather include a variety of narrative styles and genres. Short exemplary tales like *The Tale of King Sinbad and the Falcon* contrast with complicated narrative cycles that are generated and prolonged by the act of storytelling itself, such as *The Porter and the Three Ladies of Baghdad;* while novels of chivalry stand alongside historical anecdote.

In his introduction to the German translation, Enno Littman has defined six narrative categories into which the works that make up the *1001 Nights* can be separated: (1) fairy tales (for example, ᶜAlā al-Dīnᵓ, ᶜAlī Bābā); (2) romances and novels (for example, ᶜUmar ibn al-Nuᶜmān, ᶜAjīb and Gharīb, ᶜAlī al-Zaybaq); (3) ancient Arabian legends (for example, *The City of Brass, The Pious Prince*); (4) didactic stories, fables, and parables (for example, *Sinbad the Wise, Tawaddud*); (5) humorous tales (for example, *Khalifa the Fisherman, Abū al-Ḥasan or the Sleeper Awakened*); and (6) anecdotes (for example, the various stories about Abū Nuwās, *The Princess and the Monkey*). In addition to these narrative categories, one should also note the presence of well over 1,000 poems that are interpolated throughout most of the works in the *1001 Nights.* Such generic variety speaks tellingly of the compositional flexibility of the *1001 Nights,* of the work's ability, thanks largely to its frame-story structure, to accommodate multiple literary forms. It also suggests the organic developmental character of the *Nights* in its earlier stages and the consequent absence of a canon of stories that defines the *1001 Nights.* Any story that could be contained within the borders determined by the frame story could be incorporated into the work, until its definitive written form was established in the late eighteenth century.

The Arabic editions of the text and its various translations reflect this diversity. The earliest extant textual evidence of the *1001 Nights* is a manuscript fragment dating from the ninth century; and although there are occasional references to the work in other texts, notably in al-Masᶜūdī's *Murūj al-Dhahab* (947) and Ibn al-Nadīm's *al-Fihrist* (987), the first extended text of the *Nights* is the fifteenth-century Egyptian manuscript that Galland used for his translation. This manuscript originally contained approximately 200 nights and was composed of four volumes, three of which are extant. It provides the basis for the edition edited by Muhsin Mahdi, which is the first to present the text in its linguistically and stylistically unadulterated form.

There are, at present, three basic editions of the *1001 Nights*; scholars have determined that the Breslau edition (1825–1843) edited by Maximilian Habicht was based on a spurious Tunisian manuscript. The oldest edition is the so-called Calcutta I edition, which appeared in 1814 and 1818. The text contains only the first 200 nights as well as the apparently independent story of *Sinbad the Sailor*. The subsequent editions of Bulaq (1835) and Calcutta II (1839–1842) are both complete and are based on a late-eighteenth-century Egyptian recension of the text. The Bulaq text in particular has over the years acquired the status of a Vulgate, although it bears a strong resemblance to the Calcutta II text in its larger outlines. All three editions have significantly improved the style and idiom of the manuscripts in an effort to make what is essentially a popular work into a literary one. Each of the editions opens with exactly the same five narrative cycles (*The Merchant and the Jinnee, The Fisherman and the Jinnee, The Porter and the Three Ladies of Baghdad, The Three Apples,* and *The Hunchback*), thereby suggesting a narrative core or a standard recension that, by the late eighteenth century, had come to be associated specifically with the *Nights.* Interestingly, none of the editions includes the stories for which the *1001 Nights* is best known in the Western world, most notably ᶜAlāᵓ al-Dīn and the Wonderful Lamp and ᶜAlī Bābā and the Forty Thieves.

It is one of the curious facts of literary history that the *1001 Nights* has never achieved the powerful literary standing in the canon of Arabic literature that it has in the Western world, in large part because of its popular status. It is, instead, the Western translations that have made it, in the words of one of its nineteenth-century translators (John Payne), "the most famous work of narrative fiction in existence." Indeed, nothing speaks as tellingly of the characteristic organic, almost protean aspect of the work as its literary history as a translated text, for it is in translated guise that the *1001 Nights* best shows its ability to accommodate on a narrative, stylistic, and linguistic level and still maintain its titled identity.

Nothing demonstrates this adaptability as well as the history of Antoine Galland's *Les mille et une nuits: Contes arabes traduits en français* (1704–1717), which launched the *1001 Nights* in Europe. Galland's efforts began with the translation of the independent text of *Sinbad the Sailor*. Upon learning that this cycle was part of a larger collection of tales known as the *1001 Nights*, however, he sent to Syria for the above-noted fifteenth-century manuscript of the work. The tales translated, he turned to certain manuscripts of isolated tales and then to an oral source, Ḥannā, a Syrian Maronite who had accompanied the traveler Paul Lucas to Paris. It was Ḥannā who supplied the material for the remaining *Nights*, either relating orally the stories that Galland abstracted in his journal or providing transcripts that Galland then translated directly. It was this polymorphous text that became the *1001 Nights* in Europe and initiated the vogue of the Oriental tale.

Galland's translation provided the basis for the anonymously translated *Arabian Nights' Entertainment*, which had probably appeared in England by 1713, but it was not until the nineteenth century that the noteworthy English translations of the *1001 Nights* appeared. Edward W. Lane's rendition (1839–1841) was, unlike Galland's earlier work, reasonably accurate and equipped with scholarly notes but offered only those stories which Lane judged appropriate for the contemporary reading public. Sir Richard Burton's *Thousand Nights and a Night* (1885), which relied heavily on the work of John Payne (1882–1884), was, in contrast to Lane's translation, all-inclusive (Burton even published six volumes of *Supplemental Nights* in addition to the original 1,001 in 1886–1888) and heavily annotated. All of these nineteenth-century translations, including the turn-of-the-century French translation of J. C. Mardrus (1899–1904), served as mouthpieces for the translators' own concerns and interests and deftly manipulated the *Nights'* capacity for improvisation. The two major twentieth-century translations, of Enno Littmann in German (1921–1928) and Francesco Gabrielli in Italian (1949), however, adhered insofar as possible in translation to the work's own inherent voice.

There is perhaps no more eloquent testimony to the power and vitality of the *1001 Nights* than its intertextual infiltration of subsequent literature. From Tawfīq al-Ḥakīm's *Scheherazade* to Edgar Allan Poe's "The Thousand-and-Second Tale of Scheherazade" and Théophile Gautier's "Mille et deuxième nuits," from Hugo von Hofmannsthal's "Märchen der 672. Nacht" to William Butler Yeats's "The Gift of Harun al-Rashid" and John Barth's "Dunyazadiad," the *1001 Nights* has served as an important generative literary source. It is hardly surprising then that, as the closing frame story tells us, long after Shahrazad and her king have died and their palace has fallen in ruins, the illuminated text of the *1001 Nights*, which has been written in gold ink, remains.

BIBLIOGRAPHY

Sources. The Alif Laila; or, Book of the Thousand Nights and One Night, W. H. Macnaghten, ed., 4 vols. (1839–1842); *The Arabian Nights Entertainments, in the Original Arabic*, Shuekh Uhmud bin Moohummud Shirwanee ul Yumunee, ed., 2 vols. (1814–1818); *The Thousand and One Nights*, Muhsin Mahdi, ed., 2 vols. (1984); Richard F. Burton, trans., *A Plain and Literal Translation of the Arabian Nights' Entertainments*, 16 vols. (1885–1886); Francesco Gabrielli, trans., *Le mille et una notte*, 4 vols. (1949); Antoine Galland, trans., *Les mille et une nuits: Contes arabes*, 3 vols. (1811); *Kitāb alf laylah wa-laylah*, ʿAbd al-Raḥmān al-Ṣafaṭī al-Sharqāwī, ed., 2 vols. (1835); Edward W. Lane, trans., *The Thousand and One Nights*, 3 vols. (1839–1841); Enno Littmann, trans., *Die Erzählungen aus den Tausend und ein Nächten*, 6 vols. (1921–1928); J. C. Mardrus, trans., *Le livre des mille nuits et une nuit*, 16 vols. (1899–1904); John Payne, trans., *The Book of the Thousand Nights and One Night*, 9 vols. (1882–1884).

Studies. Nabia Abbott, "A Ninth-century Fragment of the 'Thousand Nights': New Light on the Early History of the *Arabian Nights*," in *Journal of Near Eastern Studies*, 8 (1949); Muhsin Jassim Ali, "The *Arabian Nights* in Eighteenth-century English Criticism," in *Muslim World*, 67 (1977); Jamaleddine Bencheikh, "Premières propositions pour une théorie d'un schéma générateur: Essai d'analyse du texte narratif dans un conte des *1001 Nuits*," in *Théories/Analyses: Études arabes travaux Vincennes*, 1 (1981); Rachid Bencheneb, "Les Mille et une nuits et le théâtre arabe au XXᵉ siècle," in *Studia islamica*, 45 (1977); J. Jermain Bodine, "Magic Carpet to Islam: Duncan Black Macdonald and the Arabian Nights," in *Muslim World*, 67 (1977); Duncan Brockway, "The Macdonald Collection of Arabian Nights: A Bibliography," in *Muslim World*, 61 (1971), 63 (1973), and 64 (1974); V. Chauvin, *Bibliographie des ouvrages arabes ou relatifs aux arabes*, IV (1900); Enver Dehoï, *L'érotisme des Mille et une nuits* (1961); Rina

Drory, "'Ali Baba and the Forty Thieves': An Attempt at a Model for the Narrative Structure of the Reward-and-Punishment Fairy Tale," in *Patterns in Oral Literature,* Heda Jason and Dimitri Segal, eds. (1977). F. Rafail Farag, "The Arabian Nights: A Mirror of Islamic Culture in the Middle Ages," in *Arabica,* 23 (1976); Mia Gerhardt, *The Art of Story-telling: A Literary Study of the Thousand and One Nights* (1963); Claudine Gerresch, "Un récit des Mille et une nuits: Tawaddud, petite encyclopédie de l'Islam mediévale," in *Bulletin de l'Institut Fondamental de l'Afrique Noire,* 35 (1973); Ferial Ghazoul, *The Arabian Nights: A Structural Analysis* (1980); Claude Hagège, "Traitement du sens et fidélité dans l'adaptation classique: sur le texte arabe des *Mille et une nuits* et la traduction de Galland," in *Arabica,* 27 (1980); Andras Hamori, *On the Art of Medieval Arabic Literature* (1974) and "Notes on Two Love Stories from the *Thousand and One Nights,*" in *Studia islamica,* 43 (1976); Rida Hawari, "Antoine Galland's Translation of the *Arabian Nights,*" in *Revue de la litterature comparée,* 54 (1980); James Keyser, *"1001 Nights*: A Famous Etiquette Book," in *Edebiyat,* 3 (1978); C. Knipp, "The *Arabian Nights* in England: Galland's Translation and Its Successors," in *Journal of Arabic Literature,* 5 (1974); Enno Littmann, "Alf layla wa-layla," in *Encyclopaedia of Islam,* 2nd ed. (1960); Duncan Black Macdonald, "Maximilian Habicht and His Recension of the Thousand and One Nights," "Lost MSS. of the *Arabian Nights* and a Projected Edition of That of Galland," and "The Earlier History of the Arabian Nights," in *Journal of the Royal Asiatic Society* (1909, 1911, 1924), "From the Arabian Nights to Spirit," in *The Moslem World,* 9 (1919), and "A Bibliographical and Literary Study of the First Appearance of the *Arabian Nights* in Europe," in *Library Quarterly,* 2 (1932).

Muhsin Mahdi, "Maẓāhir al-Riwāyah wa-al-Mushāfaha fī Usūl 'Alf Laylah wa-Laylah," in *Revue de l'institut des manuscrits arabes,* 20 (1974); André Miquel, *Un conte des Mille et une nuits: Ajib et Gharib* (1977), "Dossier d'un conte des *Mille et une nuits,*" and "Mille nuits, plus une," in *Critique,* 36 (1980), and *Sept contes des Mille et une nuits* (1981); Peter D. Molan, "Maᶜrūf the Cobbler: The Mythic Structure of an Arabian Nights Tale," in *Edebiyat,* 3 (1978), and "Sinbad the Sailor: A Commentary on the Ethics of Violence," in *Journal of the American Oriental Society,* 98 (1978); Fatma Moussa-Mahmoud, "A Manuscript Translation of the *Arabian Nights* in the Beckford Papers," in *Journal of Arabic Literature,* 7 (1976); Tzvetan Todorov, "Les hommes-récits," in his *Poétique de la prose* (1971); Jennifer R. Walters, "Michel Butor and *The Thousand and One Nights,*" in *Neophilologus,* 59 (1975).

SANDRA NADDAFF

[See also **Arabic Literature, Prose; Hārūn al-Rashīd; Masᶜūdī, al-; Nadim, Ibn al-.**]

THREE CHAPTERS, COUNCIL OF. See **Byzantine Church.**

THRENOS. See **Lamentation.**

ÞRYMSKVIÐA (The lay of Þrym) is one of the best-known mythological poems of the *Elder (Poetic) Edda,* since its charming story, humorous style, and relatively unproblematic text have led to a long history of translation and commentary. In a mixture of narrative and dialogue, the poem tells how Thor awakens to find that his hammer, Mjǫllnir, on which the gods rely for protection against the giants, has been stolen. Thor and Loki borrow Freyja's feather-coat, and Loki, who acts as Thor's helper here as Þjálfi does in other mythological texts, flies to Giantland as a scout. He discovers that the giant Þrym has stolen the hammer and hidden it under the earth; Þrym will return it only in exchange for marriage to Freyja. Loki returns, but Freyja indignantly refuses to marry the giant. The gods take counsel; Heimdallr suggests that Thor in disguise substitute for Freyja, and the figure of the red-bearded thunder god attired as a bride is the central comic moment of the poem. Loki volunteers to accompany him as a bridesmaid, and the firmament trembles as Thor's chariot conveys the two "ladies" to the impatient groom. Þrym is complaisantly wealthy, but he has long felt the lack of Freyja; now, however, he is shocked by his bride's prodigious appetite and repelled by her fiery eyes. But the quick-witted Loki intervenes to save the day with flattering excuses, and at last Þrym produces the hammer to hallow the bride and lays it on her lap—his last act. For with a laugh Thor takes up the hammer and crushes Þrym and his household, including a minor character, the giant's aged sister.

Opinions about the date of *Þrymskviða* have ranged from the ninth century to the mid thirteenth, and different scholars have evaluated the same evidence—that of style, language, and literary relations—in very different ways. The formulaic style is repetitive and almost numerically symmetrical. De Vries and many successors interpreted this style as influenced by the ballad genre, and in fact the poem is the source of a late medieval Icelandic *rímur* poem and of Scandinavian ballads. The language has been judged old or else the work of a skillful archaizer; but the placement of the prefix-substitute of/um is faultless, and de Vries's dismissal of this criterion seems mistaken. There is likewise no consensus on the assessment of the poem's literary relations. For example, de Vries notes borrowings from at least five poems, while Sveinsson and Neckel focus on several loans from Þrymskviða in other works. Since Þrymskviða is not summarized in Snorri's Prose Edda and Þrym is mentioned only in late þulur, Hallberg concluded that Snorri had himself written the poem; Magerøy and Kvillerud also believe it to be late, if not by Snorri. However, Sveinsson's discussion dating the poem to the heathen period is the most satisfactory. The myth itself has also been attacked as late, but the extensive parallels in Estonian and Lappish folktale and myth seem to speak against this. In 1933 de Vries thought the myth a late confection, but by 1956 he viewed it as probably genuine. Instrumental in this change of heart were Dumézil's Indo-European parallels, and Schröder has provided a grand synthesis of the Eastern analogues and reconstructed the evolution of the old myth down to its perhaps-late extant poetic vehicle.

BIBLIOGRAPHY

Editions. Gustav Neckel, ed., *Edda: Die Lieder des Codex Regius nebst verwandten Denkmälern,* 4th ed. rev. by Hans Kuhn, I, *Text* (1962); Jón Helgason, ed., *Eddadigte,* II, *Gudedigte,* 2nd rev. ed. (1952); Eric V. Gordon, *An Introduction to Old Norse,* 2nd ed. rev. by Arnold R. Taylor (1957).

Translations. Henry Adams Bellows, trans., *The Poetic Edda* (1923, repr. 1957, 1969); Lee M. Hollander, ed. and trans., *The Poetic Edda,* 2nd rev. ed. (1962); Patricia Terry, trans., *Poems of the Vikings: The Elder Edda* (1969); Paul B. Taylor and Wystan H. Auden, trans., *The Elder Edda: A Selection,* with notes by P. H. Salus (1969).

Commentaries. Friedrich Detter and Richard Heinzel, *Sæmundar Edda mit einem Anhang,* II, *Anmerkungen* (1903); Barend Sijmons [Symons] and Hugo Gering, *Die Lieder der Edda,* II, *Kommentary* (1927), 309–326.

Studies. Sophus Bugge and Moltke Moe, *Torsvisen i sin norske form udgivet med en afhandling om dens oprindelse og forhold til de andre nordiske former* (1897); Georges Dumézil, *Le festin d'immoralité: Étude de mythologie comparée indo-européenne* (1924), 21–26, 51–60, 100, 135, 174–175, 204–206; Peter Hallberg, "Om Þrymskviða," in *Arkiv för nordisk filologi,* 69 (1954); Erik Harding, "Om några forna verbalprefix i Þrymskviða, företrädda av ersättningspartikeln *of (um),*" *ibid.,* 73 (1959); Wolfgang Krause, "Vingþórr," in *Zeit-schrift für deutsches Altertum,* 64 (1927); Reinert Kvillerud, "Några anmärkningar till Þrymskviða," in *Arkiv för nordisk filologi,* 80 (1965); O. Loorits, "Das Märchen vom gestohlenen Donnerinstrument bei den Esten," in *Sitzungsberichte der gelehrten Estnischen Gesellschaft,* 1930 (1932); Hallvard Magerøy, "Þrymkviða," in *Edda,* 58 (1958); Uku Masing, "Die Entstehung des Märchens vom gestohlenen Donnerinstrument (Aarne-Thompson 1148B)," in *Zeitschrift für deutsches Altertum,* 81 (1944); Wolfgang Mohr, "Thor in Fluss: Zur Form der altnordischen Überlieferung," in *Beiträge zur Geschichte der deutschen Sprache und Literatur,* 64 (1940); Birger Nerman, *The Poetic Edda in the Light of Archaeology* (1931), 25–28; Axel Olrik, "Tordenguden og hans dreng," in *Danske studier* (1905); Bertha S. Phillpotts, *The Elder Edda and Ancient Scandinavian Drama* (1920), 62–73, 133–136; Gerd Enno Rieger, "Þrk. 20 við scolom aca tvau," in *Skandinavistik,* 5 (1975); Franz Rolf Schröder, "Thors Hammerholung," in *Beiträge zur Geschichte der deutschen Sprache und Literatur,* 87 (1965); Samuel Singer, "Die Grundlagen der Thrymskvidha," in *Neophilologus,* 17 (1932); Alfred Vestlund, "Åskgudens hammare förlorad: Ett bidrag till nordisk ritforskning," in *Edda,* 11 (1919); Jan de Vries, "Over de dateering der Þrymskviða," in *Tijdschrift voor Nederlandse Taal en Letterkunde,* 47 (1928), *The Problem of Loki* (1933), and *Altgermanische Religionsgeschichte,* 2nd ed., II (1957), 144.

JOSEPH HARRIS

[See also **Eddic Poetry; Heimdallr; Loki; Scandinavian Mythology; Thor.**]

THULUTH, the name of an Arabic script characterized by its rounded letter forms. Literary sources suggest it was in use as early as the ninth century, but examples from that period have not been identified. Later authors use the term to designate a script with deeply curved terminals that was widely used in architectural epigraphy after the eleventh century.

BIBLIOGRAPHY

Nabia Abbott, "Arabic Paleography," in *Ars islamica,* 8 (1941); Adolf Grohmann, *Arabische Paläographie,* II (1971), 233–238.

PRISCILLA P. SOUCEK

[See also **Calligraphy, Islamic; Paleography, Arabic and Persian;** and illustration overleaf.]

TIERCERON, a subsidiary vaulting rib that appeared first in mid-thirteenth-century England. The rib originates from the main springing points of the vault but does not reach the central boss. Intersecting instead with the longitudinal or transverse ridge ribs, the tierceron creates a starlike pattern much favored in late medieval Germany and England.

BIBLIOGRAPHY

Jean Bony, *The English Decorated Style: Gothic Architecture Transformed, 1250–1350* (1979), 44; John Fleming, Hugh Honour, and Nikolaus Pevsner, *The Penguin Dictionary of Architecture* (1966), 232; Robert Willis, "On the Construction of the Vaults of the Middle Ages," in *Transactions of the Royal Institute of British Architects,* **1** (1842).

STEPHEN GARDNER

[See also **Boss; Gothic, Decorated (with illustration); Rib; Vault.**]

TIFLIS. See **Tbilisi.**

TIGRAN HONENC^c (*fl.* early thirteenth century). The wealthy Armenian merchant Tigran Honenc^c commissioned a church dedicated to St. Gregory the Illuminator in the capital of Ani (in present-day Turkey) in honor of the Zak^carid princes, according to the building inscription, dated 1215. The donor enumerated precious objects and a long list of diverse properties (vineyards, mills, warehouses, hostels) as his endowment.

The church of Tigran Honenc^c (also known as the church of St. Grigor Lusaworič^c) is one of the most richly decorated Armenian churches, with blind arcades, animal reliefs, and ornamental motifs on the exterior and frescoes on the interior. A rectangular hall church, it is cruciform in plan, with a central cupola resting on four engaged piers.

BIBLIOGRAPHY

Architettura medievale armena: Roma-Palazzo Venezia, 10–30 giugno 1968 (1968), 121; Marie Brosset, *Les ruines d'Ani,* I (1860), 147; Paolo Cuneo, *L'architettura della scuola regionale di Ani nell'Armenia medievale* (1977); Sirarpie Der Nersessian, *Armenian Art,* Sheila Bourne and Angela O'Shea, trans. (1978), 163–166; V. Harut^cyunian, *Monuments d'Armenie* (1975), 185–187; Harry F. B. Lynch, *Armenia: Travels and Studies,* I (1901, repr. 1965), 374–375; Josef Strzygowski, *Die Baukunst der Armenier und Europa,* 2 vols. (1918); T^coros T^coramanyan, *Nyut^cer haykakan čartarapetut^cyan patmut^cyan,* 2 vols. (1942–1948).

LUCY DER MANUELIAN

[See also **Ani, Monuments of; Armenian Art; Church, Types of (with illustration); Gregory the Illuminator, St.**]

TIMBUKTU. The fabled city of Timbuktu is today a small town of some 10,000 inhabitants in the central region of the Republic of Mali in West Africa. In the sixteenth century the population of the city reached 50,000 inhabitants. At that time it was the major terminus for the trade routes which crossed the Sahara from North Africa to West Africa. The subsequent decline of the city, much like its earlier growth, was slow and protracted. In its period of decline Timbuktu became the subject of an unusual lore of mystery and enigma. This stems, in part, from the account of Leo Africanus, who, in the early sixteenth century, had confused Timbuktu with Gao as the capital of Askia Muḥam-

Ivory panel with Arabic inscription in thuluth: "Night and day have mixed in the enjoyment of it."
Egyptian, 14th century. THE WALTERS ART GALLERY, BALTIMORE

mad, the celebrated ruler of the Songhai empire. In much of its history, including the Songhai period, Timbuktu was typically an autonomous city whose administration developed upon a self-perpetuating elite of Muslim scholars and jurists.

The local chronicles date the origins of the town to around 1100, when it served as a center of commercial exchange between the agricultural populations of the Middle Niger Delta—so called because south of Timbuktu the area is seasonally transformed into an immense shallow lake—and the pastoralists of the southern Sahara. The earliest settlers are reputed to have been Masūfa Tuareg of the Maghsharen branch who traded with Soninke merchants from "Wagadu," the people of the medieval kingdom or empire of Ghana. In its first two centuries of existence Timbuktu was not mentioned by any of the external Arabic geographical sources. However, in 1353 the city was visited by the famous Muslim traveler Ibn Baṭṭūta, who has left us the earliest extant account of Timbuktu. By that time the empire of Ghana had declined and was succeeded by the far-flung empire of Mali, of which Timbuktu formed a part. In this period Timbuktu was competing successfully with the city of Walata, further west, as the main terminus for trans-Saharan trade. In the meantime, a vast network of local trade routes, largely opened by the mercantile Wangara, came to link trans-Saharan commerce to various parts of West Africa, particularly through the influence of the city of Djenné (Jenné) in the core region of the Middle Niger Delta.

The period of the Songhai empire (ca. 1470–1591) was a golden age for Timbuktu. Following an interval of upheaval, when the Timbuktu scholars opposed the authority of Sunni ʿAli (r. 1464–1492), the illustrious monarch Askia Muḥammad established a decentralized order of imperial relationships that secured exceptional prestige, along with autonomy, for both Timbuktu and Djenné. Under the circumstances, the merchant classes of Timbuktu enjoyed unparalleled prosperity, largely owing to the lucrative commerce in salt, which was seasonally brought from mines in the central Sahara, and the exchange of salt for gold dust from further south. Another, more constant factor in the commercial wealth of Timbuktu was the exchange of cattle for grain between the pastoralists of the Sahara and the agriculturalists of the Niger Bend area. The import of textiles and other valued commodities through the trans-Saharan trade stimulated spectacular growth at Timbuktu

(and also at Gao, besides Djenné) during the Songhai period. It was also in this period that Muslim learning—largely in the jurisprudential tradition—had a great influence on the western Sudan. Timbuktu came to be seen locally as a prestigious "city of scholars." Jurists like Aḥmad Bāba—a prolific author of numerous extant works—achieved fame far beyond West Africa. This period of prosperity was abruptly brought to an end by the conquest of the Songhai empire in 1591 by Morocco.

The Moroccan conquest of the Songhai empire was quite as limited in its influence on West Africa as the European mercantile expansion to the coasts of West Africa. At that time the logistics of trans-Saharan commerce were beginning to succumb, in any case, to the maritime trade of the Atlantic. Nevertheless, the Moroccan conquest dealt a blow to the imperial Sudanic tradition, which was represented by the sequence of three empires, namely Ghana, Mali, and Songhai. Although Timbuktu became the capital of the Moroccan Ruma state, thereby continuing to prosper to an extent at the expense of Gao and Djenné, the whole network of trans-Saharan commerce entered into a phase of protracted decline from the seventeenth century onward. It is interesting that the chronicles of the seventeenth century harked back with nostalgia to the earlier Songhai period. It is also significant that the tradition of administration and leadership by scholars regained the initiative by the eighteenth century. The period of the well-known jihads in West Africa in the nineteenth century allowed Timbuktu to experience an additional period of prosperity—this time under the auspices of the caliphate of Ḥamdullahi (modeled upon the Songhai empire) prior to the French expansion and the conquest of the city by the French in 1894.

The growth and decline of Timbuktu parallel the fortunes of trans-Saharan commerce. However, there are unique features in the history of Timbuktu—and particularly its social composition and leadership—that cannot be correlated solely to its commercial character. One is an unusual level of ethnic and linguistic diversity. Besides Tuareg and Soninke, the earliest settlers, Timbuktu attracted Wangara, Malinke, and Sanḥāja settlers, and Arabs and Berbers from North Africa, during the period of the empire of Mali. Two other groups of settlers that came to exert great influence on the city were the Songhai, by far the most influential group culturally and linguistically, and the Fulanis. Despite the ethnic and linguistic variety of these groups and others, the city was able to establish a personality of its own, along with an unmistakable power of collective action. The unifying factor appears to have come about as the result of the early growth of Muslim learning and common subscription to Arabic literacy and learning in the jurisprudential tradition. It seems that the entire male free citizenry enjoyed one level of literacy or another, while leadership and authority devolved for the most part upon the learned scholars and jurists. Indeed, Timbuktu may typically be seen as a commercial city whose "upper bourgeois" classes gave leadership and authority to the learned scholars in their ranks. Given the close link between Muslim scholasticism and religious learning, the case of Timbuktu is of considerable interest to the study of medieval and postmedieval urbanism, particularly in the sub-Saharan African context. An elaborate hierarchy of learned status—from mere literacy at the base to erudition at the pinnacle—supplemented the factors of wealth, prestigious descent, and affiliation as determinants of influence and prerogative. Elements of this picture still characterized Timbuktu at the end of the nineteenth century, when authority was shared by a semicorporate *jamāᶜa* (collective leadership) at the time of the French conquest. It is rare to find a case where the scholastic ideal (even the Platonic ideal) exerted such a remarkable influence over several centuries in the history of a city.

BIBLIOGRAPHY

The local chronicles of Timbuktu are all in Arabic. The most important sources are the anonymous *Tedzkiret en-nisian . . . es-Soudan,* Octave Houdas, trans. (1901); Maḥmūd K't, *Tarikh el-Fettech,* A. Delafosse and Octave Houdas, trans. (1913, repr. 1964); Qāsim ibn Sulaimān, *Dhikr al-Wafayāt* (Paris, Bibliothèque Nationale, MS 5259, fols. 24v–34r); ᶜAbd al-Rahmān al-Saᶜdi, *Tarikh es-Soudan,* Octave Houdas, trans. (1898–1900, repr. 1964).

Parts of Heinrich Barth, *Travels and Discoveries in North and Central Africa,* 5 vols. (1857–1858), are important for illustrating the traditional precolonial society of Timbuktu. Horace Miner, *The Primitive City of Timbuctoo* (1953), discusses the ethnography of Timbuktu in the present century. The most complete historical study is Elias Saad, *Social History of Timbuktu* (1983). Also significant is Sékéné Modi Cissoko, *Tombouctou et l'empire Songhay* (1975). On the subsequent Moroccan Ruma period, Michel Abitbol, *Tombouctou et les Arma* (1979), is a useful profile of the Ruma dynasty. General material may also be found in John S. Trimingham, *A History of Islam in West Africa* (1962, 1970), and in J. F. A. Ajayi and Michael Crowder, eds., *History of West Africa,* 2 vols., 2nd ed. (1976). Translations of the external medieval Arabic sources are found in Nehemiah Levtzion and J. F. P. Hopkins, *Corpus of Early Arabic Sources* (1981). Although no excavations have been conducted at Timbuktu, recent findings from Djenné have appeared in Susan K. and Roderick J. McIntosh, *Prehistoric Investigations in the Region of Jenne, Mali* (1980) which call for reexamination of the origins of mercantilism in the Middle Niger Delta, including Timbuktu.

ELIAS N. SAAD

[See also **Baṭṭūṭa, Ibn; Mali; Trade, Islamic.**]

TĪMŪR. See **Tamerlane; Timurids.**

TIMURIDS, a dynasty founded by Tīmūr-i Lenk (literally, "Timur the Lame"; in European corrupted form "Tamerlane") that ruled in Central Asia and Iran from 1405 to 1507. After the death of Tīmūr in February 1405, a period of dynastic strife followed. The order of succession to the throne was not firmly established. Two elder sons of Tīmūr, Jahāngīr and ᶜUmar Shaykh, died before their father. At the death of Tīmūr, a great part of the empire was governed by two younger sons, Mīrānshāh and Shāhrukh (r. 1409–1447), who were holding as their appanages, respectively, western and eastern Iran. Neither of them, however, was considered by Tīmūr as his heir. It was apparently Jahāngīr's son Muḥammad Sulṭān who was destined for this position after 1399, but he too died before Tīmūr in 1403. Tīmūr then appointed as his heir another son of Jahāngīr, Pīr Muḥammad. Upon Tīmūr's death, however, none of his descendants and army commanders recognized the authority of Pīr Muḥammad. Instead, a majority of the army recognized as sovereign another of Tīmūr's grandsons, Khalīl Sulṭān, son of Mīrānshāh, who took possession of Samarkand, Tīmūr's capital, and ruled Transoxiana for four years. His authority was never recognized in other regions of the empire (though he is traditionally considered the first supreme ruler among the Timurids), and in his own possessions he had to fight rebellious emirs. The youngest son of Tīmūr, Shāhrukh, acting from his capital, Herat, succeeded, due to skillful diplomacy and military pressure, in replacing Khalīl Sulṭān with his own son Ulugh Beg in 1409. Khalīl Sulṭān was given the district of Rey (Rayy) as his appanage, where he ruled until his death in 1411. Gradually Shāhrukh reestablished the unity of the empire under himself. His authority was extended to the western provinces of Iran by 1414, after the war between Shāhrukh and ᶜUmar Shaykh's son Iskandar Sulṭān, the ruler of Fārs. The descendants of other sons of Tīmūr were deposed one by one and replaced in their appanages by the sons of Shāhrukh. The last representative of the Timurid branch descending from Jahāngīr, a grandson named Muḥammad Jahāngīr, ruled Ḥiṣār as Shāhrukh's vassal until his death in 1433.

The Timurid state under Shāhrukh and his successors was much smaller than the empire of Tīmūr. Territories conquered by Tīmūr in Anatolia and the Fertile Crescent were lost with Tīmūr's death; Azerbaijan and Iraq were lost to the Turkoman dynasty of the Qara Qoyunlu in 1408–1410. It would be erroneous, however, to claim, as has often been done, that the whole empire of Tīmūr "had fallen asunder" after his death. The core of the empire—most of Iran and Central Asia, with their considerable resources—remained intact under the Timurids, and their state was one of the most powerful in the entire Islamic world in the fifteenth century.

Under Shāhrukh the state enjoyed a long period of relative political stability and economic prosperity. Occasional separatist movements in western Iran were usually promptly suppressed. The most trouble to Shāhrukh was caused by the Qara Qoyunlu. He made several attempts to crush them and to regain Azerbaijan, and three times (1419–1421, 1429, and 1434) he led his troops to the west. Although Shāhrukh was victorious in all these campaigns, these victories resulted, at best, only in nominal recognition of the Timurid suzerainty by the Qara Qoyunlu. The northern regions of the Timurid state, in Central Asia, were from time to time (especially in the 1430's and 1440's) raided by the nomadic Uzbeks, who in 1435 even seized the northern part of Khwarizm; in the northeast the Moghuls from Semirechie and Kashgaria raided Farghāna and other border regions. In general, however, the northern borders remained stable, though the Timurids were on the defensive there throughout their rule.

It was apparently under Shāhrukh that the central and provincial administration of the empire was stabilized and assumed the shape that existed till the end of the dynasty. Most of the provinces were settled as fiefs (soyurghal, literally "grant") on the Timurid princes and military commanders and sometimes (as in Sīstān) on hereditary local rulers, who governed their possessions quite autonomously as long as they could ensure law and order and recognized the head of the dynasty as their sovereign. The names of both a Timurid prince ruling an appanage and his sovereign, the supreme ruler, were mentioned in the Friday sermon and on silver coins struck in the provinces. The central government usually retained some financial and administrative control over the soyurghals, and sometimes they could be taken away or transferred to other persons. Some soyurghals, however, were granted "for eternity," that is, they became hereditary possessions, and were combined with fiscal and administrative immunity. In the long run, the system of distributing the provinces as autonomously ruled soyurghals strengthened local particularism at the expense of the central government and was a source of internal political tensions in the Timurid state.

The death of Shāhrukh in 1447 was followed by several years of interdynastic wars. After some struggle, Ulugh Beg succeeded his father in Herat in 1448 but could not secure the rest of Khorāsān, where he met with the resistance of his two nephews Abu 'l-Qāsim Bābur and ᶜAlāʾ al-Dawla, sons of a younger brother of Ulugh Beg, Baysunghur. After two years' fight with these rivals as well as with his own rebellious emirs and his son ᶜAbd al-Laṭīf, Ulugh Beg was deposed and killed in 1449. The empire remained divided for another nine years. Transoxiana was ruled for six months by Ulugh Beg's son ᶜAbd al-Laṭīf and, after the latter's murder in 1450, by Ulugh Beg's nephew ᶜAbd Allāh. In 1451 ᶜAbd Allāh was overthrown and killed, with the help of the nomadic Uzbeks of Abu 'l-Khayr Khan, by a grandson of Mīrānshāh, Abū Saᶜīd, who remained master of Transoxiana, while Khorāsān was held by Abu 'l-Qāsim Bābur, with the Amu Darya as the border between the two states. At the end of 1458, one and a half years after the death of Bābur, Abū Saᶜīd seized Herat and became master of Khorāsān and the head of the dynasty, having for the second time reunited all Timurid possessions. Fārs and Kermān, lost to the Qara Qoyunlu during the disturbances following the death of Shāhrukh, could not be regained, and Transoxiana was subject to the frequent raids of the Uzbeks. In 1468 Abū Saᶜīd set off for a campaign against the Aq Qoyunlu in Azerbaijan, where he was defeated, taken prisoner, and in early 1469 executed.

The strongest among the adversaries of Abū Saʿīd within the Timurid clan was Sulṭān Ḥusayn Bayqarā (a great-grandson of ʿUmar Shaykh), who until then was living the life of a freebooter. He immediately took advantage of the fall of his rival and took possession of Herat in March 1469. The two sons of Abū Saʿīd, Sulṭān Aḥmad and Sulṭān Maḥmūd, remained in Transoxiana, not recognizing the authority of Sulṭān Ḥusayn. Thus, after 1469 the Timurid empire became finally divided between two branches of the dynasty: the descendants of Mīrānshāh in Transoxiana, ruling in Samarkand, and the descendants of ʿUmar Shaykh in Khorāsān, ruling in Herat. The border between the two Timurid states ran mainly along the Amu Darya, with the province of Khwarizm belonging to the Timurids of Khorāsān.

The last third of the fifteenth century was a period of relative peace and prosperity for both states, especially that of Khorāsān. It was brought to an end by the invasion of the nomadic Uzbeks, under Shaybānī Khan, from the steppes in the north. In 1500 Transoxiana was conquered by Shaybānī Khan, and the last Timurid ruler of Samarkand, Sulṭān ʿAlī, son of Sulṭān Maḥmūd, was killed. In 1505 Shaybānī Khan conquered Khwarizm, and in 1507 he conquered Herat, shortly after the death of Sulṭān Ḥusayn. The surviving members of the Timurid dynasty fled to Turkey and India. Ẓahīr al-Dīn Bābur, a grandson of Abū Saʿīd, after two unsuccessful attempts to reestablish the authority of his dynasty in Transoxiana, retreated to Kabul, from which he set out in 1526 to conquer Delhi and found the Indian dynasty known in the West as the Great Moghuls. A cousin of Bāber and his descendants ruled in Badakhshān, as vassals of the Great Moghuls, until the conquest of this province by the Uzbeks in 1584. After the fall of the Timurids, Central Asia was finally divided from Iran, where the Safawids came to power.

The Timurid period had great importance for the political, social, and cultural history of Central Asia and Iran. The Turkic tribes brought to these regions by the Mongol invasion remained the basis of the military power of the Timurids. Especially important were four tribes collectively described as the Chaghatais, to one of which, the Barlas, the dynasty itself belonged. Tribal nobility held the highest positions at the court and in the administration,

and the Chaghatais formed the bulk of the army. It is to the strength of this tribal element that the persistence of nomadic political tradition in the Timurid state can be attributed. During the same period, the Chaghatai Turks were gradually being integrated into the sedentary Iranian culture. As a result of this process, the Timurid political system combined steppe and Islamic traditions. At first, according to the steppe conception of sovereignty, members of the Chinggisid house were considered the exclusive bearers of royal charisma, having the right to the supreme title of khan. Therefore, Tīmūr did not adopt this title but was content with the more modest Turkic title beg (or parallel Arabic emir) and enthroned puppet khans of Chinggisid origin. He also stressed his kinship ties with the line of Chinggis (attested by his genealogy) and took two wives from the Chinggisids, which gave him the honorary title *küregen* (Persianized *gūrgān*: "[khan's] son-in-law"). Some of his descendants also had Chinggisid wives and bore the title *küregen* (Mīrānshāh, Ulugh Beg, Abū Saʿīd), and the Timurid dynasty was often called Gūrgānīya by Islamic writers. But already Shāhrukh ceased to enthrone puppet khans (they still remained in Samarkand under Ulugh Beg) and adopted the title of sultan, which symbolized the fact that he was also embracing the Islamic state tradition. All later Timurids were also styled sultans; at the same time the newly invented title *mīrzā* (contracted form, from *amīrzāda,* "emir's son") was usually added to their names. Nevertheless, the division of the empire into a number of autonomously ruled appanages among the princes of the Timurid clan—which continued till the end of the Timurid period and included also the redistribution of the appanages between the branches of the clan following interdynastic wars—reflected the traditional nomadic practice attested in all Central Asian states founded by steppe dynasties.

Other aspects of the social, political, and cultural life of the Timurid period were also characterized by a dichotomy between the nomadic Turko-Mongol elements and heathen steppe tradition and the sedentary Iranian elements and Islamic tradition. The state apparatus was divided into two main branches; one, dealing with the affairs of the army and, respectively, the Turkic population, and another, dealing with the civil administration and, respectively, the Iranian population. It seems that during the Timurid period the civil bureaucracy formed mainly from the members of old Iranian

58

urban aristocratic families gained in influence. This coincided with the decline of the Chaghatai tribes, which were gradually becoming sedentary and losing their military prowess, while their chiefs, becoming big landlords in their *soyurghal*s, were more interested in their landed property than in warfare. Military failures of the Timurids in the second half of their reign were probably a result of this erosion of the Chaghatai nomadic element.

The weakening of the nomads was paralleled by the flourishing of urban culture, brought about by expanding international and internal trade and relative political stability. Most of the Timurids, both supreme and provincial rulers, patronized literature, art, and science, especially Ulugh Beg, his brother Baysunghur, and Sulṭān Ḥusayn Bayqarā. This period, indeed, was the last brilliant period in the history of Islamic culture in Central Asia and Iran. These two regions under the Timurid rule were, however, culturally different. Central Asia, in the first half of the fifteenth century, excelled mainly in architecture and the exact sciences, astronomy and mathematics (due to the personal interests of Ulugh Beg); and in the second half of the fifteenth century there was a stagnation and even cultural decline. Khorāsān exceeded Central Asia in its cultural achievements, especially in literature and the arts, during the whole Timurid period. This cultural activity reached its highest point in Herat at the court of Ḥusayn Bayqarā, with such figures as the poets ʿAbd al-Raḥmān Jāmī and Mīr ʿAlī Shīr Nawāʾi, the historians Mīrkhwānd and Khwāndamīr, the miniature-painter Bihzād, and many others. An important part of the cultural life under the Timurids was the emergence of a new Turkic literary language, commonly known as Chaghatai, as well as a literature, which, due to the works of Nawāʾī could compete with Persian literature as a means of literary expression for Central Asian Turks.

In religious life, the Timurid period witnessed the emergence and spread of the Sufi order of the Naqshbandiyya. In Transoxiana it became a dominant political force in the second half of the fifteenth century, due to the activity of Khoja ʿUbayd Allāh Aḥrār and his disciples, and it is to their militant orthodoxy that the cultural decline of Transoxiana is often ascribed.

BIBLIOGRAPHY

No comprehensive monograph on the Timurids exists. The best general surveys are by H. R. Roemer, in *The Cambridge History of Iran*, VI: *The Timurid and Safavid Periods* (1986), 42–146, and Roemer's "Timurlular," in *Islam Ansiklopedisi* (in Turkish), XII (1974), 346–370, with an extensive bibliography. See also Vasily V. Barthold, *Four Studies on the History of Central Asia*, Vladimir Minorsky and T. Minorsky, trans., II: *Ulughbeg* (1958), III: *Mir ʿAli-Shir* (1962), 1–72.

On Persian historiography of the Timurids, see Charles Ambrose Storey, *Persian Literature: A Bio-bibliographical Survey*, 3 vols. (1927–1984), vols. I–II translated into Russian and revised, with additions and corrections, by Yuri Bregel (1972), II, pt. 1, 339–393, pt. 2, 787–849; on Persian biographical works related to the Timurid period, see Storey, *ibid.*, II, pt. 1 (1958).

On Timurid literature, see Jean Deny, ed., *Philologiae Turcicae Fundamenta*, II (1964), 304–361; and Jan Rypka, *History of Iranian Literature* (1968), 279–290. On art, see Basil Gray, ed., *The Arts of the Book in Central Asia, 14th–16th Centuries* (1979); Bernard O'Kane, *Timurid Architecture in Khurasan* (Islamic Art and Architecture, III) (1987); Arthur Upham Pope and Phillis Ackerman, eds., *A Survey of Persian Art* (1964), III–VI, VIII–XIII; Ivan V. Stchoukine, *Les peintures des manuscrits tîmûrides* (1954).

The best detailed description of cultural life under the Timurids is found in Aleksandr Nikolaevich Boldyrev, "Ocherki iz zhizni geratskogo obshchestva na rubezhe XV–XVI vv.," in *Trudy Otdela Vostoka Gosudarstvennogo Ermitazha*, **4** (1947).

A genealogical tree of the Timurids is provided by Eduard Karl Max von Zambaur, *Manuel de généalogie et de chronologie pour l'histoire de l'Islam* (1927, repr. 1976).

YURI BREGEL

[See also **Afghanistan; Aq Qoyunlu; Azerbaijan; Iran, History; Qara Qoyunlu; Samarkand; Tamerlane; Transoxiana; Turkomans; Ulugh Beg.**]

TINO DI CAMAINO (*ca.* 1280–*ca.* 1337), sculptor. Born in Siena, he was the son of the architect and sculptor Camaino di Crescentino di Diotisalvi. He was probably engaged as an assistant in the workshop of Giovanni Pisano in Siena before 1311. His secure works are: in Pisa, a baptismal font (1311), the tomb of Emperor Henry VII in the cathedral (February to July 1315), and a signed statue of the Madonna and Child (*ca.* 1316/1317); in Siena, the tomb of Cardinal Riccardo Petroni in the cathedral (January to June 1318); in Florence, the tomb of Archbishop Antonio degli Orso in the

Tomb of Archbishop Antonio degli Orsi in Florence Cathedral. Marble carving by Tino di Camaino, 1321. ALINARI/ART RESOURCE

cathedral (February to July/August 1321); in Naples, the tombs of Queen Mary of Hungary in S. Maria Donna Regina (December 1325/January 1326 to May 1326), Mathilde of Hainault (lost, 1331), Duke Charles of Calabria in S. Chiara (1 September 1332 to 31 August 1333), and Mary of Valois in S. Chiara (begun after 31 August 1333).

BIBLIOGRAPHY

Enzo Carli, *Sculture del duomo di Siena (Giovanni Pisano, Tino di Camaino, Giovanni d'Agostino)* (1941); Raffaello Causa, "Preciazione relative alla scultura del' 300 a Napoli," in *Sculture lignee nella Campania* (1950), 63–73; Gert Kreytenberg, "Tino di Camainos Grabmäler in Florenz," in *Städel-Jahrbuch,* n.s. 7 (1979); John W. Pope-Hennessy, *Italian Gothic Sculpture* (1955, 2nd ed. 1972, repr. 1985), 15–18, 183–186; Sandra Candee Susman, "Tino di Camaino, His Workshop and Followers: A Problem of Connoisseurship" (diss., Univ. of Chicago, 1976); Wilhelm R. Valentiner, *Tino di Camaino: A Sienese Sculptor of the Fourteenth Century* (1935).

SANDRA CANDEE SUSMAN

[See also **Agostino, Giovanni d'; Pisa Cathedral; Pisano, Giovanni; Trecento Art.**]

TINTAGEL, a village on the north Cornish coast near Camelford. Castle ruins stand on rocky cliffs nearby, held by legend to have been the birthplace of King Arthur. Divided into a mainland and an "island" site, the latter actually a peninsula, the castle was first built in the mid twelfth century by Reginald, earl of Cornwall. Most of the visible remains date from the thirteenth century. The peninsula also contains monastery ruins dating from pre-Saxon times, the most archaeologically rich Celtic monastic site in Britain. In the village itself the Old Post Office provides a fine example of a fourteenth-century manor house.

BIBLIOGRAPHY

Leonard Elliott-Binns, *Medieval Cornwall* (1955); F. E. Halliday, *A History of Cornwall* (1959); Nikolaus Pevsner, *Cornwall* (1951, 2nd ed. 1970); C. A. R. Radford, *Ministry of Works Guide* (1950) and "The Celtic Monastery in Britain," in *Archaeologia Cambrensis,* 3 (1962); Geoffrey Webb, *Architecture in Britain: The Middle Ages* (1956, 2nd ed. 1965), 7. For a general discussion of the archaeological study of British medieval sites, see Helen Clarke, *The Archaeology of Medieval England* (1984).

MELVIN STORM

[See also **Arthurian Literature; Matter of Britain.**]

TINTERN, a village in southeast Wales on the river Wye, noted for its famous abbey ruins. Tintern Abbey was founded in 1131 by Walter de Clare and colonized by Cistercian monks from Normandy, but the extensive ruins now visible date mainly from major rebuilding and expansion during the thirteenth and fourteenth centuries. The abbey's prosperity reached its height during the early fourteenth century, but following the Black Death in mid century it began to decline. After the abbey's dissolution in 1536 and the stripping of the roofs for lead, the buildings began to suffer the decay that continued until early in this century. During the

ṬIRĀZ

Ṭirāz of undyed linen with golden-tan silk. Egyptian textile of the Fatimid period (10th–12th centuries) with Kufic script inscription. TEXTILE MUSEUM, WASHINGTON, D.C.

Tudor era the village itself gained fame for its metal industry.

BIBLIOGRAPHY

D. E. Craster, *Tintern Abbey* (1963); Edward Foord, *Hereford and Tintern* (1925); F. A. Gasquet, *The Great Abbeys of England* (1903).

MELVIN STORM

[See also **Cistercian Order.**]

ṬIRĀZ. All textiles inscribed with the factory name and date of weaving are called *ṭirāz*. A Persian term meaning embroidery, *ṭirāz* was first applied to textiles with embroidered inscriptions, then to the factories that made them, and finally to inscribed textiles in general, regardless of how the inscription was fabricated.

A typical *ṭirāz* inscription might read, "In the name of God, the Compassionate, the Merciful, what was ordered to be made by the caliph," followed by the caliph's name, titles, and salutory phrases as well as the factory (*ṭirāz*), the city, and the date. The *ṭirāz* protocol formula first appeared in the Umayyad period (A.D. 661–750) and was later augmented, especially by the Fatimids (A.D. 969–1171). The inscription was first a caliphal prerogative, a sign of sovereign control linked politically with having one's name inscribed on coins and read in the khutbah. In time, the vizier's name was added, and sometimes the name of the heir apparent. In time, also, local governors altered the protocol formula to indicate greater independence.

This protocol was always inscribed on the out-put of the state-owned factories, called variously *ṭirāz al-khaṣṣa* (royal) and *ṭirāz al-ᶜāmma* (public), depending on who had access to them. But weaving textiles was not a state monopoly: privately owned workshops also produced inscribed textiles, sometimes including parts of the protocol and sometimes simply with wished blessings, but not displaying the *ṭirāz al-khaṣṣa* or *ṭirāz al-ᶜāmma* mark of state ownership. Regardless of factory origin or political content, all inscribed textiles are commonly called *ṭirāz*.

Medieval writers record that through the tenth century, during the Abbasid caliphate, the main public display of such inscriptions was on the kiswa, or Kaaba covering. The Kaaba, at Mecca, is the most important Muslim sanctuary and provided a place for a highly visible sovereign mark. During the Fatimid caliphate, however, more elaborate inscriptions, in terms of both aesthetic merit of presentation and length of political message, were displayed as insignia marking the various ranks in the hierarchy of the administration. The Fatimids distributed *ṭirāz* garments to their court and lavishly displayed inscribed silks and brocades, using the *ṭirāz* inscription to assert their legitimacy, which was often under attack.

So strongly did the Fatimids establish the link of royal display of the Arabic-inscribed band with royal power and magnificence that even the coronation robe and alb worn by the Holy Roman emperors from the time of Frederick II (r. 1220–1250) displayed such inscriptions with parallel content. Unfortunately, extant *ṭirāz* textiles, mainly linen with woven inscriptions in silk, do not match the medieval text descriptions of luxury silks; brocades; ornate, heavy gold inscriptions; and jeweled *ṭirāz*.

With the fall of the Fatimids in 1171, the political relationship of ruler to state-owned factories, the ostentatious display, and therefore the Mediterranean fashion for the inscribed bands, gradually disappeared in the Muslim world. Given the prominence of writing in Islamic society, the use of script on textiles did not diminish, however. Short phrases in repeat patterns appeared for a time on brocades and other textiles. But the inscribed band that is the essence of what is called *ṭirāz* soon disappeared.

BIBLIOGRAPHY

Irene A. Bierman, "From Politics to Art: The Fatimid Uses of *Ṭirāz* Fabrics" (diss., Univ. of Chicago, 1980); Lisa Golombek and Veronika Gervers, "*Tiraz* Fabrics in the Royal Ontario Museum," in *Studies in Textile History in Memory of Harold B. Burnham,* Veronika Gervers, ed. (1977), 82–125; Adolf Grohmann, "*Ṭirāz,*" in *Encyclopaedia of Islam,* lst ed., (1934); Ibn Khaldūn, *The Muqaddimah,* Franz Rosenthal, trans., II (1958, 2nd ed. 1967), 65–67; Ernst Kühnel, *Catalogue of Dated Tiraz* (1952); Robert B. Serjeant, "Materials for a History of Islamic Textiles Up to the Mongol Conquest," in *Ars islamica,* **9–16** (1942–1951), repr. as *Islamic Textiles: Material for a History Up to the Mongol Conquest* (1972).

IRENE A. BIERMAN

[See also **Costume, Islamic; Dībāj; Khilᶜa; Kiswa; Mulḥam; Sumptuary Laws, Islamic; Textiles, Islamic.**]

TIRO, PROSPER. See **Prosper of Aquitaine.**

TITHES. The tithe, a 10 percent tax levied by the church on most kinds of income, was the most important single element in medieval taxation. Tithes not only provided basic support for the clergy and the church, but were also vital to relief of the poor and many kinds of public functions in medieval society. In addition, rights to collect and use tithes became the focus of important controversies in theology and canon law.

HISTORICAL DEVELOPMENT

The history of tithes is deeply rooted in Judeo-Christian tradition. The Old Testament contains numerous references to tithes, which the ancient Hebrews levied primarily on agricultural products. The Torah treats the tithe as an obligation owed to God, but its earthly beneficiaries were primarily his ministers, who had the right to receive these revenues in compensation for the religious services that they performed. Portions of the tithes were also available for the poor and disadvantaged, while part of the income could also be allocated to government officials. Those who failed to pay their full share of the assessment were described as robbing God and were threatened with divine retribution for their misconduct.

New Testament treatments of the tithe breathe a different spirit. Although they imply that the payment of the tithe remains a religious duty, the Gospel passages that deal with tithing treat it as a formal obligation, secondary in importance to justice, mercy, and faith, and associate tithe payment with the formalistic observances of the Pharisees. While St. Paul did not specifically identify tithing as a practice of the Christian congregations with which he corresponded, he did emphasize the duty of Christians to support those who proclaimed the Gospel and to alleviate the distress of poor members of the Christian community.

Very little is known about tithe payments in the early Christian centuries or about the disappearance of tithing in the Eastern Empire. So far as can be determined from the scanty evidence, tithes were treated as moral obligations from the fourth century on. From the sixth century, the church in the West began to impose spiritual sanctions upon those who failed to pay their tithes. Secular authorities gradually intervened to compel tithe payment, perhaps as early as the reign of Pepin III; the practice was mandated in the Capitulary of Herstal by Charlemagne in 779. From this point on secular authorities often assisted the clergy by penalizing failure to pay the tithe.

By the early ninth century there is evidence that the clergy faced trouble in keeping control over tithe income and that laymen were beginning to appropriate tithes for secular purposes. The increasing volume of complaints about such practices during the late ninth century and the tenth century indicates that lay rulers frequently forced churches to donate tithe revenue to secular authorities, or else collected the tithes and disposed of them as ordinary revenues for their own use.

In addition, monasteries had begun to appropriate parishes and to keep their tithe income for monastic purposes. Sometimes monasteries, moreover, built parish churches of their own, and tithes from these augmented other monastic revenues. By the early ninth century a great many monasteries had come to depend upon the tithes from their parishes as an essential part of their income.

Thus by the eleventh century the tithes paid to parish churches were often no longer available for the parish's needs. By that point most parishes, and their tithes, were in the hands either of monks or of lay proprietors.

Eleventh-century church reformers saw control of the tithe as a critical issue in their program to reorganize the Western church. All tithe income, they maintained, should be used strictly for ecclesiastical purposes and rightfully belonged to the clergy. In 1050, Pope Leo IX forbade laymen to keep any tithes. Pope Alexander II (1061–1073) declared that those who refused to pay tithes were unworthy of being called Christians. At a council in 1078 Pope Gregory VII described lay possession of tithes as sacrilegious, meriting eternal damnation.

Despite the efforts of popes, councils, and synods to recover control of all tithe income, realistic reformers finally concluded that they would have to settle for a partial return of tithe revenues to local parishes. This compromise solution was adopted in 1215 by the Fourth Lateran Council (c. 32). The compromise was not successful everywhere. While it was almost universally accepted in northern Italy, it was only partially enforced elsewhere. Even so, the measure assured the parish clergy a minimum revenue, together with some independence from lay control. It also met with general approval among the lay authorities, who saw it as alleviating the financial needs of the clergy while leaving much of the tithe revenues in their own hands. After 1215, tithes largely ceased to be primarily ecclesiastical revenues and became a type of property that both laymen and clerics might own.

In the later Middle Ages the collection of tithes became increasingly difficult and complex. Many laymen and monks controlled tithes, and friars sometimes advised their hearers to give the money that they would have paid as tithes to charitable causes—including the friars themselves. Many Italian communes during the later Middle Ages substituted salary payments to their clergy for the traditional tithes; the clergy thus became in effect paid servants of the commune, rather than subsisting on their own tax income, and thus became to a degree dependent upon the municipality.

TITHE DOCTRINE AND ADMINISTRATION

The development of the Western church's doctrines concerning tithes was based on the premise that every Christian had an obligation to pay a tenth of his or her income to support the church and its ministers. Caesarius of Arles described tithe payment as indispensable to salvation, a message that later authorities reiterated frequently and urgently. But if everyone was obliged to pay, who was entitled to receive the yield of the tithe? Two schemes for dividing tithe revenues gained currency in the early Middle Ages. The so-called Roman system divided tithe income into four parts, one each for the bishop, the parish clergy, maintenance of church buildings, and relief of the poor. The competing Spanish system divided the income into three parts: for the benefit of the bishop, the clergy, and the church fabric. Acceptance of one plan or the other varied in different regions and periods. Gratian's *Decretum* reported both plans, without expressing a clear preference. The allocation of tithe revenues was probably never rigorously enforced, but represented an approximation for administrative guidance rather than a minutely binding regulation.

Despite differences of opinion concerning the ways in which tithe income should be apportioned, church authorities agreed that control of the tithe should never be vested in lay hands; rather, bishops had the right to determine how tithe revenues would be applied to the church's needs. The Pseudo-Isidorian decretals enunciated strongly worded policy statements on this issue, and these found their way into canon law. Gratian asserted that bishops and clergy ought to be supported by tithes and should not be dependent on secular sources of income. The Third Lateran Council (1179; c. 14) condemned the transfer of tithes from one layman to another.

Opinions varied as to the juridical nature of tithe rights. While some insisted that priests and bishops were only the conservators of tithes, which they collected and dispensed on behalf of the community, others maintained that tithe revenues, like other income, constituted a species of property that the owner could sell, assign, mortgage, or give away to whomever he pleased. Gerhoh of Reichersberg, although prepared to concede that tithes were property, asserted that they were inalienable and that their ecclesiastical recipients had no legal or moral right to dispose of them.

Practice clearly ran against those who claimed that tithes were inalienable property. In reality tithes were often donated or traded by those who controlled them. Tithes were especially popular gifts from laymen to monasteries, and monks gladly received them. From the donor's viewpoint, giving the tithes of a parish to a monastery was a bargain, since he or she was simply transferring an ecclesiastical income from one ecclesiastical recipient to another and lost only the fraction of the tithe income that he or she had previously kept. From the monastery's vantage point, the receipt of tithes increased income without entailing any significant expenditure, since the parish clergy often remained responsible for conducting services, maintaining church buildings, and supporting poor relief. The parish clergy and parishioners bore the costs of these transfers: the secular clergy lost a major source of revenue while remaining responsible for the outlays formerly supported by that revenue. The gap between parish income and expenditures had ultimately to be filled by the parishioners, who had to devote additional resources, beyond the tithes that they continued to pay, to maintain the parish and its clergy. Even so, by the late twelfth century a large fraction of all tithes in Western Europe had been diverted from secular churches to monastic communities or lay proprietors.

Canon lawyers and theologians maintained that the donor owed tithe payments to the church in which he or she was baptized and in which he or she received the other sacraments. But difficulties arose over the tithe claims of new parishes carved out of older ones in order to accommodate population growth or shifts in settlement patterns. In theory the church sought to protect the tithe rights of the older parish and required that members of the new unit continue their tithe payments to the old parish, while supporting the new one with additional contributions. Practice differed from theory, however, and in actuality new parishes usually claimed the tithes of their members at the expense of the old parish. Often the result was litigation in the church courts over the tithe payments. The great bulk of this litigation was between members of the clergy, very often between monks and secular clerics.

The faithful owed tithes on all types of income. Formally there were three divisions of the tithe obligation: the predial tithe referred to payment of one-tenth of the harvest from annual crops, mainly cereals, but also vegetables, fruit, and other products of the soil. The personal tithe was a 10 percent levy on the revenue from an individual's occupation; thus the income from a trade or craft and commercial income of all kinds, including even the earnings of a prostitute, came under this heading. Mixed tithes were levied on the produce of animal husbandry—meat, milk, eggs, wool, hides, leather,

and the like—as well as the game taken by a hunter or the catch of a fisherman. This predial tithe was sometimes called the greater tithe, while personal and mixed tithes were classified as lesser tithes. The net effect, in any case, was that virtually no income escaped liability for the tax.

The significance of these distinctions arose from differences in determining the tax base. All tithes were in principle levied on gross income. The payer was not allowed to deduct expenses or other taxes when calculating the income on which predial tithes were due. In levying personal tithes, however, the payer had the right to exclude necessary expenses, such as the cost of raw materials, from his tax base. There was also a difference in due date for the various kinds of tithe. Predial and mixed tithes were due when the income was realized—when the harvest was gathered, or the animal slaughtered, for example—while personal tithes could be paid at the end of the year.

Tithes might be collected directly by the parish priest or other recipient, who appeared in the fields or the barn or at the winepress or other appropriate place at harvest time to claim his portion of the produce. Many priests and other tithe holders, however, found it convenient to delegate the collection of tithes to a "tithe farmer," who acted as an agent in the collection process and claimed a portion of what he collected as remuneration. Tithe farmers also acted as commission agents: they sold the grain, meat, wool, and other products that they collected and remitted the proceeds to the owner of the tithe rights. Individuals who owed tithes sometimes also arranged to pay in cash rather than in kind.

The obligation to pay tithes fell universally upon all Christians in medieval Europe, regardless of location or occupation—even pirates in the North Sea paid tithes from the spoils that they took. In 1215 the Fourth Lateran Council (c. 67) extended the tithe obligation beyond the Christian community and required Jews to pay tithes as well, but only on property acquired from Christian owners.

There was remarkably little overt resistance to the tithe, and direct refusals to pay tithes are quite uncommon. Where substantial resistance occurred, as it did, for example, in late medieval London, the issues seem to have centered on the procedures for assessment and collection, rather than on the tithe obligation itself. Heretical groups, such as the Cathars, often refused to pay; indeed refusal to pay tithes was a reliable symptom of heretical beliefs. The most stubborn resistance to tithes commonly came from new converts to Christianity, who often found the tithe obligation an unwelcome consequence of baptism.

If open resistance to tithes was rare, however, covert resistance through tithe fraud and cheating was far more common. Peasants almost routinely hid a few sheaves of wheat or concealed a few bunches of grapes from the tithe collectors. Other tithe evaders sought to conceal their full income from the collectors by resorting to leasehold arrangements that enabled them to disclaim responsibility for tithing on part of the income that they in fact received. Those who paid substantial personal and mixed tithes frequently sought to pad their expense deductions when calculating tithe liabilities.

The few who refused to pay the tithe and the many who evaded their full obligation through tithe frauds were subject to severe penalties. Failure to pay the full tithe on all earnings carried with it the penalty of excommunication. Parish priests had ample incentive to heed the admonitions of bishops, synods, and other authorities to instruct their flocks carefully on tithing and to excommunicate tithe cheats during church services on major feast days. And if the fear of excommunication was not enough to restrain tithe fraud, popular writings and sermon literature were full of cautionary tales about military disasters, crop failures, plagues of locusts, and other catastrophes caused by God's wrath at those who failed to comply fully, promptly, and voluntarily with their tithe obligations.

A few Christians, notably lepers, enjoyed exemptions from tithe payments. Although early medieval monasteries normally paid tithes like everyone else, it became increasingly common during the twelfth century for new monasteries to receive exemptions from tithe obligations, or else to acquire the privilege of retaining their own tithes for distribution and use as they saw fit. By the end of the twelfth century such grants had been gradually withdrawn or restricted, and only the Cistercians, the Carthusians, and the military orders thereafter enjoyed freedom from tithes. Other monasteries, however, continued to have tithe exemptions on income from noval lands, that is lands newly put to agricultural use, as a result of clearing forests, draining marshes, or reclaiming land from the sea. Tithe exemptions on noval lands thus constituted a positive incentive for land reclamation and the expansion of the agricultural base upon which the medieval economy heavily depended.

CONCLUSION

Throughout the Middle Ages tithes played an important role in economic life. As the principal source of revenues for many public or quasi-public activities during much of the Middle Ages, tithes not only subsidized the spiritual and pastoral work of the church, but also supported a wide variety of activities that modern societies usually regard as secular responsibilities, including public welfare and education. In part because of continuing needs for revenue for these purposes, tithes continued to be collected, in many areas well into modern times, often with the active assistance of the state.

BIBLIOGRAPHY

Although there is no general history of the medieval tithe system, a number of more specialized works include overviews of tithe principles and practices. Especially helpful are Catherine E. Boyd, "The Beginnings of the Ecclesiastical Tithe in Italy," in *Speculum*, **21** (1946), and *Tithes and Parishes in Medieval Italy* (1952); Giles Constable, *Monastic Tithes from Their Origins to the Twelfth Century* (1964). On the relationship of tithes to the medieval economy as a whole, see John T. Gilchrist, *The Church and Economic Activity in the Middle Ages* (1969). Medieval tithes have been most systematically studied in France, especially in two books by Paul Viard, *Histoire de la dîme ecclésiastique principalement en France jusqu'au Décret de Gratien* (1909) and *Histoire de la dîme ecclésiastique dans le royaume de France aux XIIe et XIIIe siècles* (1912). For the late medieval and early modern periods, see also Emmanuel Le Roy Ladurie and Joseph Goy, *Tithe and Agrarian History from the Fourteenth to the Nineteenth Centuries* (1982).

The beginning of public enforcement of tithe obligations has been studied by Ulrich Stutz, "Das karolingische Zehntgebot," in *Zeitschrift der Savigny-Stiftung für Rechtsgeschichte*, Germanistische Abteilung, **29** (1908). Resistance to tithes is treated by Giles Constable in *Journal of Ecclesiastical History*, **13** (1962); while the relationship of tithe revenues to poor relief is treated by Brian Tierney, *Medieval Poor Law* (1959). On medieval theories about the relationship of tithes to other economic institutions see also John W. Baldwin, "The Medieval Theories of the Just Price," in *Transactions of the American Philosophical Society*, n.s. **49** (1959), pt. 4.

JAMES A. BRUNDAGE

[See also **Alexander II, Pope; Caesarius of Arles, St.; Capitulary; Carolingians and the Carolingian Empire; Church, Latin: Organization; Commune; Councils, Western; Gerhoh of Reichersberg; Gratian; Gregory VII, Pope; Hospitals and Poor Relief, Western European; Law, Canon; Leo IX, Pope; Papal States; Parish; Reclamation of Land; Simony; Taxation, Church.**]

TMUTARAKAN, KHANATE OF, a medieval Russian principality on the northeastern coast of the Black Sea. The first firm date for a Russian presence at Tmutarakan comes from the *Russian Primary Chronicle* for 988, when Vladimir I gave Tmutarakan to his son, Mstislav. How the Russians gained control of the city is not known.

In 1024, from his base at Tmutarakan, Mstislav put forward his claim to the much-disputed throne of his recently deceased father. Mstislav seized Chernigov in 1025 and forced his brother Yaroslav to reach a settlement in 1026 by which they divided Kievan Russia. As prince of Chernigov, Mstislav retained suzerainty over Tmutarakan. The next forty years at Tmutarakan are undocumented.

In 1064 a dispossessed prince, Rostislav, expelled the ruling prince, Gleb, from Tmutarakan, only to be compelled to withdraw himself upon the arrival of Gleb's father, Svyatoslav, from Chernigov (1065). Political intrigue cut short Svyatoslav's intervention, and Rostislav recovered Tmutarakan. Rostislav's subsequent efforts to expand his influence into the Crimea caused the Byzantine governor of Chersonesus (modern Kherson) to have Rostislav poisoned in 1066. Svyatoslav's son, Roman, was prince of Tmutarakan by 1069.

Tmutarakan was again drawn into the Kievan civil wars at the end of the 1070's. First Boris (1077) and then Oleg (1078) fled to Tmutarakan from their uncles Izyaslav and Vsevolod. With the aid of Roman, who was the ruler at Tmutarakan, Boris and Oleg made an abortive attempt against their uncles in 1078, as a result of which Boris died in battle, Roman was murdered, and Oleg was sent into a Byzantine exile (1079). Two years later Ratibor, Vsevolod's lieutenant, was driven from the city by still another pair of dispossessed princes, David and Volodor. These two latest holders of the khanate were driven out in 1083 by Oleg, who returned from exile.

As an apparent client of Emperor Alexios I Komnenos, who had helped to restore him to Tmutarakan, Oleg seems over the next ten years to have pushed the frontiers of the khanate to include Khazaria (interior Crimea), the Kerch and Taman peninsulas, and the east coast of the Black Sea (Zichia). In 1094 Oleg intervened in the Kievan civil wars only to be defeated and forced to retire to Tmutarakan two years later. By the terms of the general peace at Lyubech (1097), Oleg seems to have received Tmutarakan as his portion.

Sometime between 1097 and 1118, Tmutarakan passed under Byzantine domination, and the khanate of Tmutarakan ceased to exist.

BIBLIOGRAPHY
Source. Russian Primary Chronicle: Laurentian Text, Samuel H. Cross and Olgerd P. Sherbowitz-Wetzer, trans. and eds. (1953).
Studies. G. G. Litavrin, "À propos de Tmutorokan," in *Byzantion,* 35 (1965); Jonathan Shepard, "Another New England? Anglo-Saxon Settlement on the Black Sea," in *Byzantine Studies,* 1 (1974); A. V. Soloviev, "Domination byzantine ou russe au nord de la mer noire a l'époque des Comnenes," in *Akten des Internationalen Byzantinistenkongresses* (1960); George Vernadsky, *Kievan Russia* (1948).

FRANK E. WOZNIAK

[See also **Alexios I Komnenos; Kievan Rus; Vladimir, St.; Yaroslav the Wise.**]

TOGHRIL-BEG (early 990's–1063), a grandson of Seljuk, was, together with his brother Chaghrı-Beg, most responsible for the creation of the Seljuk state. The Seljuks, a prominent clan among recently Islamicized Oghuz Turks, enmeshed themselves in the troubled politics of Ghaznavid-Qarakhanid and intra-Qarakhanid rivalries. Following a setback in 1026 that resulted in the withdrawal of one Seljuk group to Khorāsān, Toghrıl and Chaghrı, leading the remaining group, shifted to the Khwārizmshāh state (1034). Menaced here by an old family foe, the Yabghu of Jand (the nominal leader of the Oghuz), they fled to central Khorāsān about 1035–1036. Desperate, they took the region, playing upon—to good advantage—the hostility between the Ghaznavid government and the wealthy towns. Merv, Nıshapur, and Herat submitted to them about 1037–1038. Mas⁢ud of Ghazna's attempt to crush them ended in a disastrous rout of Ghaznavid forces at Dandānqān in 1040.

Toghrıl and Chaghrı, following traditional Turkic practice, divided their realm for administrative purposes while maintaining its political unity. Toghrıl had the western part as his area of expansion. In the course of the 1040's he extended his authority to much of Iran and began to harry Transcaucasia. In 1055 he entered Baghdad as the "liberator" of the Sunni Abbasid caliphate from the Shiites. The titles and honors bestowed on (or extorted by) him legitimized his position. He was now sultan and "king of the East and West." His new, exalted status did not sit well with some of his kinsmen and tribesmen. The revolt of the Turkomans in 1059, tied to Fatimid-inspired Shiite conspiracies, was undoubtedly connected to these developments. Having suppressed the uprising, the aged Toghrıl forced the caliph to grant him his daughter in marriage. After Toghrıl's death, his successor, Alp Arslan, established a more correct and less intimate relationship with the caliphate.

BIBLIOGRAPHY

Sources. ᶜIzz al-Din Ibn al-Athīr, *Ibn-el-athiri chronicon,* Carl J. Tornberg, ed., IX–XI, (1851–1876); Bar Hebraeus, *The Chronography of Gregory Abu'l-Faraj,* Ernest A. W. Budge, trans., I (1932); Abū Fazal Muḥammad ibn Ḥusayn Bayhaqī, *Tarīkh-i Masᶜūdī,* Qasim Ghanī and ᶜAli A. Fayyāẓ, eds. (1945), trans. into Russian by A. K. Arends as *Abu-l-Fazl Baihaki: Istoriia Masᶜuda (1030–1041),* 2nd rev. ed. (1969), with English summary; Sadral-Din al-Ḥusaynī, *Akhbār al-dawlah al-Saljūqīyah,* Muḥammad Iqbāl, ed. (1933), trans. into Turkish by Necati Lügal as *Ahbār üd-devlet is-Selçukıyye* (1943); Tarīkh-i Mir Khwānd, *Rawzat al-ṣafāᶜ,* Riẓā Khān, ed., IV (1854), trans. into English by F. F. Arbuthnot and E. Rehatsek as *The Rauzat-us-safa; or, Garden of Purity,* 2 vols. (1891–1894); Muḥammad Rāwandī, *The Rāḥat aṣ-ṣudūr va āyat us-surūr,* Muḥammad Iqbāl, ed. (1921); Zahīr al-Dīn Nīshābūrī, *Seljuq-nāma* (1953).

Studies. Sergei G. Agadzhanov, *Ocherki istorii oguzov i turkmen Srednei Azii IX-XIII vv.* (1969); Vasily V. Bart'old, *Turkestan Down to the Mongol Invasion,* V. Minorsky, trans., 3rd rev. ed. (1968, repr. 1977); Clifford E. Bosworth, *The Ghaznavids* (1963); Claude Cahen, "Le Malik-nâmeh et l'histoire des origines seljukides," in *Oriens,* 2 (1949); Mehmed A. Köymen, *Selçuklu devri Türk tarihi* (1963).

PETER B. GOLDEN

[See also **Alp Arslan; Ghaznavids; Qarakhanids; Seljuks.**]

TOLEDAN TABLES, the most abundant form of astronomical tables surviving from the Middle Ages. Although these tables have been linked with the eleventh-century Spanish-Islamic astronomer al-Zarqālī (Arzachel), and although he is undoubtedly the author of some of them, others are copied ·from al-Battānī and al-Khwārīzmī, and it is not actually certain that the compilation should be attributed to him. The collection includes tables for converting from one calendar system to another; for finding certain trigonometric quantities; for establishing solar, lunar, and planetary positions;

and for calculating retrogressions, conjunctions, and eclipses; plus a short list of stars and astrological tables of houses.

A fundamental difference between the Toledan Tables, the earlier Handy Tables of Ptolemy, and the later, thirteenth-century Alfonsine Tables concerns the treatment of the celestial coordinate system. Ptolemy provided for a steady precessional motion of 1° per Egyptian year of the stars against the coordinate framework defined by the spring equinoctial point. By the eleventh century the Ptolemaic system was seriously out of adjustment, so the Toledan Tables specify the slow movement of the coordinate system by a cyclical or back-and-forth motion according to the so-called trepidation theory of Thābit ibn Qurra. By the thirteenth century Thābit's theory had also proved inadequate, and it was replaced by a combination precession-trepidation scheme in the Alfonsines.

The Toledan Tables took as their base the planetary positions at the time of the hegira; in the Latin West the tables were christianized by converting the base positions to the time of the Incarnation. Such tables made in Marseilles, Toulouse, and Novara are essentially adaptations of the earlier Toledan form.

BIBLIOGRAPHY

Owen Gingerich and Barbara Welther, "The Accuracy of the Toledan Tables," in Yasukatsu Maeyama and Walter Gabriel Saltzer, eds., *Prismata* (1977), 151–163; Gerald J. Toomer, "A Survey of the Toledan Tables," in *Osiris,* 15 (1968), esp. 1–74.

OWEN GINGERICH

[See also **Alfonsine Tables; Astrology/Astronomy, Islamic; Astronomy; Calendars and Reckoning of Time; Ptolemaic Astronomy.**]

TOLEDO, Spanish city located on the Tagus River seventy-one kilometers (forty-four miles) south of Madrid. Known in Arabic as Ṭulaiṭula, Islamic Toledo was a stronghold of formerly Christian converts to Islam (*muwalladūn*) who rose repeatedly in defiance of the ruling Umayyad dynasty. The most celebrated rebellion was that against al-Ḥakam I in 797, which ended with the "Day of the Ditch" (787), when the general (ᶜAmrūs ibn Yūsuf) to the prince ᶜAbd al-Raḥmān, emir of Córdoba, invited the disaffected leaders to a banquet and had their heads severed one by one.

From the late 1020's until the conquest of the city in 1085 by Alfonso VI of Castile, Toledo was ruled by the independent Dhu'l-Nūnid dynasty. Under al-Maʾmūn (r. 1043–1075), the city reached its greatest extent under Muslim rule (43 acres/106 hectares) as well as its highest population (37,000). Al-Maʾmūn accentuated the verdant nature of the city, described by Arab geographers as being filled with gardens irrigated by hydraulic wheels (norias). One of al-Maʾmūn's gardens was called the "Salon of the Noria," and this monarch employed the horticulturalists Ibn Baṣṣāl and Ibn Wāfid, whose agronomical treatises reflect their experience as royal gardeners.

At the moment of the Christian reconquest in 1085, Toledo was practically the only city in Islamic Spain that still held a large minority of Christians (Mozarabs). Alfonso VI entrusted the governance of the newly conquered city to a Mozarab notable, Sisnando Davidiz, but in succeeding years the Mozarab residents lost control of the urban administration to Castilian nobles and burghers, to whom they also lost out in the competition for estates and properties abandoned by fleeing Muslims. Those who acquired such properties became the new urban aristocracy.

Since Toledo had been capital of the Visigothic kingdom and, at the same time, the primary see of the Spanish church, its recapture from the Muslims held considerable symbolic importance. Alfonso VI used the symbol to declare himself "emperor of all the Spains," and in the fourteenth and fifteenth centuries the town's representatives in the Castilian cortes repeatedly strove to declare their precedence over the representatives of Burgos and Valladolid, two old Castilian cities that also regarded themselves as capitals.

Christian Toledo boasted a large and flourishing Jewish community whose palpable symbols are the two synagogues of S. María la Blanca (possibly dating to the late twelfth century) and El Tránsito, built by Peter the Cruel's adviser Samuel ha-Levi around 1357. There were two Jewish quarters, the Lesser, which was destroyed in the pogrom of 1391, and the Greater, which survived until the expulsion of the Jews in 1492. The quarters were defended by two so-called Jews' Castles, towers that also contained bakers' ovens and butchers' stalls.

Toledo's fame as a seat of learning antedated the Christian reconquest. Al-Maʾmūn was the patron of the astronomer al-Zarqāl, the author of the Toledan astronomical tables, which were reworked by the court astronomers of Alfonso X of Castile in 1252–1262. The glory of Alfonso's "school of translators" (which perhaps exaggerates the primacy of Toledo in the translation movement) resulted from the presence there of substantial groups of Mozarabs, Jews, and Muslims, as well as from that monarch's love of learning. As a result of this long tradition, medieval Toledo became synonymous with science and learning, particularly that of Eastern origin.

BIBLIOGRAPHY

On Islamic Toledo, see Leopoldo Torres Balbás, *Ciudades hispanomusulmanas*, 2nd ed., I (1985), 143–149; Évariste Lévi-Provençal, ed., *La péninsule ibérique au moyen âge d'après le Kitāb ar-Rawḍ al-Miʿṭar . . . d'ibn ʿAbd al-Munʿim al-Ḥimyarī* (1938), 157–162. On the Reconquest and the Mozarab problem, see Reyna Pastor de Togneri, "Problèmes d'assimilation d'une minorité: Les Mozarabes de Tolède (de 1085 à la fin du XIIIᵉ siècle)," in *Annales: Économies, sociétés, civilisations*, 25 (1970), and *Del Islam al Cristianismo: En las fronteras de dos formaciones económico-sociales, Toledo, siglos XI–XIII* (1975). On the Jewish community of Toledo in the later Middle Ages, see the essays in *Simposio "Toledo Judáico,"* 2 vols. (1973).

THOMAS F. GLICK

[See also **Alfonso X; Castile; Córdoba; Islam, Conquests of; Jews in Muslim Spain; Spain, Christian-Muslim Relations; Translation and Translators; Umayyads.**]

TOLEDO, MARTÍNEZ DE. See **Martínez de Toledo, Alfonso.**

TOME OF LEO. See **Leo I, Pope.**

TOMISLAV (*fl. ca.* 910–928), the greatest of medieval Croatia's rulers, acquired the throne of Dalmatian Croatia between 910 and 914. He probably directly succeeded Mutimir, who most likely was his father.

The Hungarians, who had moved into present-day Hungary in the 890's, were raiding central Europe and the Balkans. They threatened the states in the area. The chiefs of Pannonian Croatia, who were still under Frankish suzerainty, sought aid against the Hungarians from Tomislav. He defeated the Hungarians and established a lasting border between the Hungarians and Croatians along the Drava River. In so doing he took over all Pannonian Croatia and added it to his own state, thereby eliminating all Frankish overlordship over Pannonian Croatia and uniting the two Croatias for the first time. His territory was divided into three main regions: (1) his original Dalmatian lands extending from modern Rijeka to the Cetina River, which probably stretched inland into northwest Bosnia as far as the Vrbas River; (2) a semiautonomous *banovina* of Lika, Krbava, and Gacko; (3) a second semiautonomous *banovina* of Slavonia (between the Sava and Drava rivers).

Byzantium, fighting a major war with Symeon of Bulgaria, sent an embassy to Tomislav in about 923. An alliance was concluded between Croatia and Byzantium, and Tomislav received the Byzantine court title of proconsul. In 924 Tomislav granted asylum to Zaharije, the pro-Byzantine ruler of Serbia, who had been driven from his state by Symeon. This act plus his Byzantine alliance made Tomislav seem a danger to Symeon, who, in 926, launched a major attack on Croatia that Tomislav handily defeated, destroying a good portion of the Bulgarian attacking forces in the process. This success demonstrated that Tomislav had created an extremely powerful Croatian army. Constantine Porphyrogenitos, probably with exaggeration, claims that Tomislav was able to field 160,000 troops. Tomislav seems to have been crowned king about 925. It is not known when or by whom he was crowned. Our only evidence that he was in fact crowned is a letter, whose authenticity has been questioned, allegedly written in 925 by Pope John X calling him king.

Tomislav supported two major church councils at Split. The first, in 925, created a rational hierarchy for Dalmatia (Croatian and Byzantine) by subordinating all Dalmatia to the archbishop of Split. The second council, in 928, reaffirmed this decision, abolished the see of Nin (whose bishop objected to Nin's subordination to Split), and most probably also subjected the rest of the Croatian state (the Pannonian part) to Split as well. Tomislav probably died in 928, though Farlati, whose information is frequently questionable, has him live on until 940. Constantine Porphyrogenitos and Farlati each give totally different lists of rulers after To-

mislav, just as both give differing lists of his predecessors and different dates for his accession.

BIBLIOGRAPHY
John V. A. Fine, Jr., *The Early Medieval Balkans* (1983).

JOHN V. A. FINE, JR.

[See also **Bulgaria; Constantine VII Porphyrogenitos; Croatia; Dalmatia; Hungary; Serbia; Symeon of Bulgaria.**]

TONARY (*tonale, tonarium*). The Tonary was the musical handbook used, for practical purposes, to regulate liturgical chant and to describe the modal system, the modes or *toni,* in which chant was sung. This title was first used in the late tenth century, earlier forms of the book having been identified merely by their incipits. Thus one of the earliest tracts, a late-eighth-century work by Regino of Prüm, begins *Incipiunt octo toni.* In addition, until about the tenth century the tracts dealt only with the modal system as it applied to melodic plainchant, excluding psalmody and the coordination of psalms with melodic chants. Gradually, however, the central core of modal theory was accompanied by sections dealing with music in general, especially defining what music was, and with practical rules for psalms and antiphons. As the books expanded with this additional material, they were more likely to be independent volumes; indeed, later Tonaries are sometimes but a small part of treatises on music and musical styles in general. Tonaries containing only the core material needed for the services are often bound into the appropriate liturgical volume as a separate section.

Carolingian Tonaries originated in the musically productive areas around Metz. They use the Greek or Byzantine modal terminology that was current, identifying four modal groups as *Protus, Deuterus, Tritus,* and *Tetrardus,* each group subdivided into a higher and a lower range called "authentic" and "plagal." These terms are first explained in the important Tonary of Metz and in the Tonary of Aurelian of Réôme (*ca.* 850). As the center of musical importance shifted from the Carolingian empire to Aquitaine, the naming and numbering of modes changed. The eight modes were now numbered with Arabic numerals. They sometimes used other Greek names corresponding to the authentic ranges of the four groups mentioned above (*Dorian, Phrygian, Lydian, Mixolydian:* modes 1, 3, 5, 7). To these names the prefix *Hypo-* is added to name the plagal modes (2, 4, 6, 8). The terms "authentic" and "plagal" are retained.

As for the description of the modal characteristics themselves, up to the twelfth century this was done largely by referring to Byzantine intonation formulas, represented by melismas associated with special syllables such as NOEANE and NOEAGIS. These esoteric "words" and formulas were later replaced by paradigmatic melismas called *neumae* or pneumes (the terms "jubilus" and "melodia" are closely related in concept). These model melismas were supposed to represent, to demonstrate, and to include the characteristic melodic features of each mode. In many cases, these melismas were actually model chants, complete with texts constructed for the purpose and drawn from the New Testament. Thus, the model chants for modes 1 and 8, respectively, had the texts *Primum querite regnum Dei* (Matt. 6:33) and *Octo sunt beatitudines* (Matt. 5:3–11, where each verse begins with the word *Beati*).

From about the tenth century, and first appearing in the treatiselike Tonary *Commemoratio brevis,* psalmody was included. Henceforth, illustrations or descriptions of the psalm tones (and sometimes reading and other tones) were included, and rules for coordinating the antiphon and psalm were explained. In simple terms, the mode of the antiphon determined which of the eight psalm tones would be used. The intonation and reciting tone of the psalm tone were invariable and needed only to be listed: the termination of the psalm tone, however, was variable according to how the antiphon chant began. The termination was known as the differentia or EVOVAE (from the words in the Doxology at the end of every psalm: sEcUlOrUm AmEn): the opening notes of the antiphon were called the *variatio(n).* Of the several differentiae assigned, one was chosen in order to make a smooth transition to the *variatio.*

In the Tonary described below, some modes have nine differentiae: mode 8 has five, of which the first is used for thirty-nine different *variationes,* and the second for eighteen. The coordination can therefore become extremely complex. To eliminate the necessity to refer to the Tonary in every case, the liturgical books tended in the later Middle Ages to include the information that was necessary along with each chant. Thus, after each antiphon, the

psalm differentia was written down, perhaps also with its intonation and reciting tone. This coordination applied mostly to the combination of antiphons and psalms in the hours of the Divine Office, and also to certain Mass chants such as the introit (and, when they had psalm verses, to the offertory and communion chants also). But, in addition, other psalmodic material could be included. In particular, the verses of responsories, which were originally like psalm tones, may form a part of a Tonary. Miscellaneous material, such as the tones for Te Deum, tones for benedictions, reading tones, and other generally useful information, sometimes occurs.

A model late medieval Tonary is that of the Sarum use in England. Since for every mode it includes a chant drawn from the Office of Thomas of Canterbury, it must have been compiled after the 1170's. Although for Sarum use, it has universal pretensions: *et hoc non solum in ecclesia sarum usitatum est, verum eciam in universali ecclesia.* This Tonary is organized logically and carefully, progressing from the general to the detail. It has eight large sections, each devoted to one of the modes. Each section begins with a verbal description of the mode, with examples mentioned by textual incipit, distinguishing where necessary between Mass practice and Office practice, and between ordinary antiphons and psalms and Gospel antiphons and psalms such as the Magnificat and Benedictus. It states on which pitches the antiphons normally begin and names possible transpositions of the mode. The number of differentiae, neumae, and tones for the invitatory is stated, and a verbal description of the psalm tone is given.

Within each section devoted to a mode is a subsection dealing with each differentia in turn. Within each subsection, the number of *variationes* is stated, and each *variatio* is then described in words and with musical examples. At the end of each subsection is the *Amen* (that is, the EVOVAE) with the musical formula of the differentia above it.

There follow musical examples showing the normal psalm tone and the slightly more elaborate tones for the Gospel antiphons, then the neuma (with the old *Primum querite* texts underneath) and the invitatory tone(s) (mode 4, for example, has several invitatory tones, for different liturgical seasons), then the tone for the responsory verse (identified by the Doxology text that, like the verse, is sung to that tone). The *variationes* and differentiae for introits follow, and the introit psalm tone is given a little later. Separating them are the short alleluia melismas appended to various chants during Easter time (why they appear in this particular position is not clear).

Under mode 8, the peregrinus tone is included. This is a very special tone involving two different reciting notes and used for Psalm 113 (114), *In exitu Israel*. In this case the whole psalm tone is given in full for each verse.

Tonaries for the ecclesiastical orders have their own special characteristics. The Cistercian Tonary is particularly noteworthy, based on and implementing the chant reforms instituted by Bernard of Clairvaux in the early twelfth century. The thirteenth-century Dominican Tonary is strongly influenced by this Tonary.

By the sixteenth century, Tonaries had become manuals for the theory of music rather than practical books for use in the choir. The increasing appearance of the necessary information within the liturgical books themselves undoubtedly had a good deal to do with the demise of the Tonary as a practical book.

BIBLIOGRAPHY
Aurelian of Réôme (ca. 843): The Discipline of Music, Joseph Ponte, trans. (1968); Terence Bailey, *The Intonation Formulas of Western Chant* (1974), and, as ed. and trans., *Commemoratio brevis: De tonis et psalmis modulandis* (1979); Walter Howard Frere, ed., *The Use of Sarum*, 2 vols. (1898–1901, repr. 1969), II, Appendix, i–lxxiv; Lawrence Gushee, ed., *Aureliani reomensis Musica disciplina* (1975); Michel Huglo, *Les tonaires* (1971); Walter Lipphardt, ed., *Der karolingische Tonar von Metz* (1965).

ANDREW HUGHES

[See also **Antiphon; Aurelian of Réôme; Differentia; Divine Office; Evovae; Gregorian Chant; Jubilus; Melisma; Mode; Neuma; Noeannoe; Psalm Tones; Psalter; Regino of Prum; Sarum Chant; Sarum Use; Variatio.**]

TONES, MUSICAL (*toni, tonoi, Töne*). "Tone" had various meanings in the Middle Ages:

1. The most important reference was to the liturgical recitation formulas used in the Mass and Office for prayers, for protracted readings (such as psalms and canticles), and for the selected verses associated with certain responsories and antiphons. Some of these formulas—those for longer readings especially—are very simple, little more than recita-

tion on one note; other tones are more complicated, but more or less systematic in application.

2. "Tones" might also refer, more narrowly, to the reciting notes of such formulas.

3. In Germany, tones were the models, comprising both verse form and melody, upon which new songs were based (especially the Meisterlieder) from the fourteenth century onward. *Töne* were often named for the subject or the opening of the poem for which they were originally composed or best known ("In dem Ton: Ich stund an einem Morgen"). And frequently they were named for the author and the character of the melody ("Walther von der Vogelweide: Feiner Ton").

4. "Tones" sometimes referred to melodies in general (tunes).

5. "Tone" (*tonus, tonos*) was frequently used as the equivalent of "mode" (*modus, echos*), one of the eight classifications of Latin and Byzantine ecclesiastical chant. Such a usage is always an indication of the influence of classical music theory and is technically and historically more correct if the modes are conceived in the narrow terms of scale structures and relative pitch levels.

6. "Tones" refer also to the seven possible conjunct arrangements, or species, of the five tones and two semitones of the diatonic scale. The species were theoretical concepts drawn from the writings of classical Greek and Latin authors. These abstractions had virtually no practical application in medieval music.

7. The term referred to the steps of the musical scale.

8. Finally, a tone (*tonus*)—the modern term is "whole tone" or "major second"—is the larger of the two intervals employed in the diatonic scale.

BIBLIOGRAPHY
Horst Brunner, "Ton," in *New Grove Dictionary of Music and Musicians*, XIX (1980).

TERENCE BAILEY

[See also **Mode; Psalm Tone.**]

TONES, READING AND DIALOGUE. Solo versicles and choral responses occur throughout the liturgy. The liturgical greeting *Dominus vobiscum* and the response *Et cum spiritu tuo* are the best known. All these little dialogues are sung (or intoned or recited) to repeated pitches with a simple terminating formula such as a falling interval. Reading tones, among which we can include tones for lessons, prayers, and chapters, are similar, although sung entirely by a soloist until the final response of *Amen* or *Deo gratias;* each sentence is sung to the tone, with an appropriate formula to mark the punctuation. Sentences that are questions are sometimes sung on a pitch lower than the surrounding sentences, so that the formula can rise at the end.

Important readings such as Gospels, Prefaces, and the Canon have more elaborate tones and formulas. In the Passions of Holy Week the words of Christ, the Evangelist, and other speakers are distinguished by different reciting pitches and perhaps by different singers. The Lamentations of Holy Week have the most elaborate and distinctive tones of all, so that they can often be assigned to particular liturgical uses. The other tones, being so simple, are more or less indistinguishable across all European uses, although little work has been done to see whether identifying variants can be isolated.

BIBLIOGRAPHY

Willi Apel, *Gregorian Chant* (1958), 203–208; Andrew Hughes, *Medieval Manuscripts for Man and Office* (1982).

ANDREW HUGHES

[See also **Benedictions; Divine Office; Gregorian Chant; Music, Liturgical; Psalm Tones; Responsory.**]

TOOLS, AGRICULTURAL: EUROPEAN. Implements of agricultural production were used by most medieval people to obtain food and fibers for their own survival and that of the nonagricultural minority. Knowing the tool kit of a medieval farming group illuminates its daily life; changes in farm equipment relate to and help explain concomitant developments in the broader medieval economy. Generally speaking, the earlier medieval centuries saw basic experimentation with implement design but a rather stable and weak working tool kit. After about 1000 people used more, accepted new, and perfected old implements, but wholly unprecedented introductions ceased. The tool kit established by the end of the Middle Ages thus included ancient prototypes, early medieval innovations, and later medieval modifications of both. The following essay looks briefly at sources of knowledge about medieval agricultural tools, focuses on the function and design of important implement groups, and summarizes aspects of the overall evolution of medieval farmers' equipment.

SOURCES OF KNOWLEDGE

Information about medieval farm tools is remarkably hard to get. The literate minority had too little interest in, and too superficial acquaintance with, the objects they saw in the hands of the illiterates who worked. Thus the history of medieval implements must be pieced together from scraps of unintentionally preserved materials of three major kinds: written texts, pictures, and archaeological finds. All demand critical awareness before use.

Medieval written documents offer no technical description of an agricultural implement. Most, including the agricultural manuals from Al-Andalus, thirteenth-century England, and late medieval Italy, take tools as given. Even if they advise, it is more often a counsel of perfection for landowners or a crib from a classical Roman writer than a description of current peasant practice. Inventories of equipment are technically imprecise and suffer, as do all written records, from disjunction between changes in vocabulary and changes in the tools themselves. Thus modern scholars debate whether in certain early medieval texts *carruca* means "cart," as it had meant to the Romans, or "plow," as it did to later medieval writers, and whether authors' variations between *aratrum* and *carruca* reflect two different tools or just a learned and a popular name for one.

Artistic representations might seem to solve such problems: the object is what is shown. But because medieval artists commonly copied from prototypes of standard scenes, the tools they portrayed may have had no relationship to those in use when and where they worked. Nor were artists technologists or even necessarily good observers. Plows depicted in some late-fifteenth-century woodcuts, for instance, cannot have functioned. To add to the difficulty, early representations are rare, and no scholar has yet compiled a complete or even very full systematic collection of pictures showing any important medieval tool.

Archaeology offers recovered remnants of the implement itself or traces of its use. Most collections, however, and especially those for medieval western and Mediterranean Europe, are still meager and unsystematic. Interpretation is complicated by what survives and is datable. Although most medieval tools were of wood and changes in the wooden parts of, for example, plows and scythes have considerable importance, wood decomposes rapidly in most European environments. In addition, only organic remains like wood can be given an absolute dating by measurement of radioactive carbon. Furthermore, metal objects may move downward in the soil to distort even the relative chronology of stratigraphy. Thus, any serious tool study must draw cautiously on a variety of evidence and indicate the nature and limits of its inferential findings. Gaps in the available data and differences in the critical tests that scholars apply to their sources cause some differences of opinion on the evolution of medieval implements. Yet the available evidence does sustain some consensus on the history of those tools with which medieval agriculturalists worked through their annual cycles of productive labor.

PLOWS

The process of agricultural production normally starts with tillage, the preparation of the soil for seed. Most medieval agriculturalists did this with some kind of traction plow, a device that was dragged through the soil surface to break it up. Such tools had an ancient Middle Eastern origin and were known throughout Europe long before the medieval period. Members of this implement family can, and in medieval Europe did, differ widely in their design and operation. Most belonged to one of two major groupings, the ard (Latin: *aratrum*; French: *araire*; Italian: *aratro*; German: *Haken* or *Arl*; Danish: *ard*; Slavic: *ralo*; Lithuanian: *arklas*; Old Irish: *arathar*) or the plow (Latin: *carruca*; French: *charrue*; Italian: *piove*; German: *Pflug*; Danish: *plov*; Swedish: *plog*; Slavic: *plug*; Lithuanian: *pliugas*). The schematic illustration helps clarify features and variants of each.

The ard, sometimes called "scratch plow" in English, is defined by its symmetrical design and function. Its sole working part, the share, is a symmetrical blade or point of wood or iron that is pushed horizontally through the soil to crumble it. Ard design varies among frame types in which the beam, a combined stilt-sole, or the sole is the dominant element or in which the components are joined in a more rugged four-sided frame. (More elaborate classifications of ard and plow forms are often employed by ethnologists. However, the ad-

dition of wheels or even a coulter or simple moldboard or moldstroker to push the broken soil aside does not alter the fundamental character given an ard by its share.) This light and shallow-working machine is especially well suited for thin, light, and friable soils. Its action effectively disrupts the capillary flow of water to the surface and thus reduces evaporation in semiarid conditions like those of the Middle East and Mediterranean. Being maneuverable, the ard has further advantages for use in stony ground or newly cleared fields full of stumps and roots. But because it crumbles the soil only in the direct line of its advance, a full working of the soil surface demands a second plowing at right angles to the first, so that, all else being equal, users of the ard prefer to work approximately square units. Its shallow action necessitates periodic hand-digging of fields in permanent cultivation.

The plow, in contrast, has a distinct function because of its definitively asymmetrical design and action. Its three working parts—the vertical iron blade or coulter, the normally asymmetrical iron share, and the wooden extension or moldboard running back and out from one side of the share—together cut, lift, and invert a slice of soil. It plows a furrow from which the soil is removed and deposited upside down on the moldboard side of the plow. Wheels are not, therefore, a definitive element of the plow. On some soils they ease its use, but on sticky soils a wheelless swing plow can perform more handily. Nor is weight a distinguishing feature. A light foot or single-wheel plow turns well-worked or sandy soils with considerably less draft power, although it takes a skilled plowman to use it. The turnwrest or one-way plow demonstrates the importance of operational rather than just design asymmetry in the functional distinction between plow and ard. This implement has a symmetrical share and means to move both coulter and moldboard from one side to the other. With it the plowman can turn a furrow in the same direction with respect to the field irrespective of the direction in which he plows, a useful procedure on sloping land. Fixed-moldboard plows always throw the same way, usually to the right. Thus the right side of the plow is the "furrow side" and the left the "land side" (from the unbroken soil there). All plows in the illustration are shown from the land side.

Because the plow has the strength and design to lift and turn the soil, it is well suited to handle deep, heavy, and firm ground. The plowman can, but

SOME MEDIEVAL TRACTION PLOW TYPES

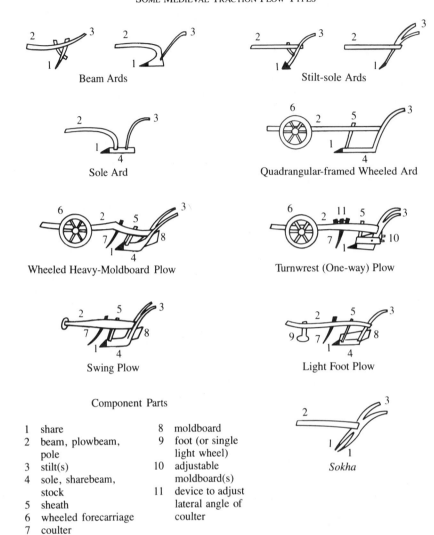

Beam Ards

Stilt-sole Ards

Sole Ard

Quadrangular-framed Wheeled Ard

Wheeled Heavy-Moldboard Plow

Turnwrest (One-way) Plow

Swing Plow

Light Foot Plow

Component Parts

1   share
2   beam, plowbeam, pole
3   stilt(s)
4   sole, sharebeam, stock
5   sheath
6   wheeled forecarriage
7   coulter

8   moldboard
9   foot (or single light wheel)
10 adjustable moldboard(s)
11 device to adjust lateral angle of coulter

Sokha

need not, turn all the furrows toward the center to produce a slightly domed field, the "ridge-and-furrow," which improves drainage in wet conditions. In the humid climate of transalpine Europe, the deep turning action of the plow brings minerals that have been leached downward by rainwater back to the surface, where they are accessible to the shallow roots of young grasses. It is, however, argued that some sole ards, especially if equipped with projections called ears (*aures*) or groundwrests and held at an angle by the plowman, turn a furrow, too. But this tilting action cannot be performed if the implement has wheels and a coulter, and it is the coulter and iron share that give the plow its special ability to cut through thick grassy or weedy sod, such as might be present in brushy

waste, natural grasslands, or old grain fields. All this size and strength mean that the more robust forms of the plow need considerable draft power and lack maneuverability. The plowmen thus preferred to work in long narrow strips that minimize the need to turn the machine.

Two less common but still significant sorts of traction plow known in medieval Europe have design features that conform poorly to the ard-plow dichotomy. The ristle knife or ristle plow is a coulter mounted independently on a beam (which is often wheeled). It goes before another implement to break heavy turf. Such a device was perhaps known to the first-century Roman author Pliny the Elder and occurred under various names from the Bay of Biscay north into Atlantic Europe, across Scandinavia to the eastern Baltic, and in the eastern Alps. The *sokha*, with distinctive paired shares and share beams, was the characteristic tillage implement of medieval northeastern Europe, from the Baltic to the Urals north of the fiftieth parallel. *Sokha* designs varied widely. Broad shares with shoulders or wings on horizontal soles could break and turn grassy turf. Narrow, near-vertical soles bounced up to clear rather than jam into stones and roots in forest clearings. Northern Russian peasants probably developed the *sokha* in the forest zone of European Russia before the twelfth century and carried it with them as they colonized the boreal forest thereafter.

Most medieval cultivators used the plow or ard. The latter was ancient. Before and during the Roman period a sole or quadrangular-framed ard dominated the Mediterranean basin and the western continent; other types occurred in northern and eastern Europe. Use of light iron shares was common, though not total, before the start of the Christian era. By the eleventh century, contemporary illustrations still confirm the prevalence of sole ards all along the Mediterranean and a tendency for this or another sturdy type to supplant older stilt-sole ards in eastern Europe north of the Alps. Throughout western and central Europe, however, the ard was, during and soon after the first millennium, largely supplanted by the plow. To describe and date this early medieval diffusion of the plow is, perhaps, the principal and most vexing problem in the history of medieval implements. A clear distinction must be drawn between the invention of components and their combination into a new tool, on the one hand, and the spread of this tool to general use, on the other.

At and beyond the frontiers of imperial Rome fleeting traces occur, between the first and fifth centuries, of northern peasants modifying their ards. Disputes about whether coulters reached Britain from northern Gaul before or with the Romans do not affect the considerable archaeological evidence that this device was being used there, in the Rhineland, and on both sides of the middle Danube. In the first century Pliny the Elder noted with some surprise that somewhere in what is now eastern Switzerland people put "little wheels" (*rotulae*) on what were surely ards, and by the fifth century this novelty had spread into Gaul and Pannonia.

Archaeological traces of turned furrows have been detected from barbarian settlements along the North Sea coast and from late Roman Britain, although scholars cannot agree whether these indicate use of a moldboard or tilting of an eared ard. Whether the slight asymmetry detected in certain shares recovered from the sites of late Roman date in Britain, Pannonia, Illyria, and the western Ukraine is to be attributed to poor workmanship, differential wear, or design is likewise a matter of debate. The linguistic root of the term "plow" in Germanic and Slavic is of unknown origin, but the development of indigenous terms for its parts and its use in both language groups argues that these peoples were familiar with the tool by about the fifth or sixth century. Thus it seems certain that the plow had non-Roman origins, whether in the damp coastal grasslands of the North Sea coast, as some would have it, or along the northern slopes of the eastern Alps or Carpathians, as others believe. By the time of Roman political collapse in the West, the components were available and the complete tool present in places, but it had not been widely adopted or become central to any agricultural production system. Some kind of fairly light ard was likely still normal.

Ambiguous references and scholarly inferences —but few hard data—argue for the slow spread of the plow during the second half of the first millennium. The weight of informed opinion is that the cost of its iron parts and its larger team combined with the lack of major positive inducements to limit severely the adoption of this tool by peasant cultivators. Many may have heard of it, but few could or would afford it. On the Continent, Germanic law codes of the sixth through eighth centuries occasionally employ the term *carruca* or *plovum* in contexts implying some distinction between these objects and an *aratrum*. Whether this meant more than the presence or absence of wheels is dubious.

Contemporary records of the Anglo-Saxons likewise fail to affirm that these people brought with them from the Continent to Britain any markedly advanced new tool. The eighth-century Exeter Book "plow riddle" lists no moldboard among the parts but does seem to describe the turning of a furrow. Even the surge of documentation of rural affairs associated with the Carolingian renaissance of the late eighth and ninth centuries fails to specify the special reality denoted by *carruca* and, in its stress on hand labor and its inventorying of meager tools and little expensive iron, implies the continued rarity of a more powerful tillage implement even on the best-managed estates of northern Gaul.

A moldboard plow shown in the Luttrell Psalter, 1340. British Museum, Add. MS 42130, fol. 170. BY COURTESY OF THE TRUSTEES OF THE BRITISH LIBRARY

About the same time, however, small but clearly asymmetric shares were being used alongside symmetric ones by Slavic peoples in Great Moravia and in the Elbe-Saale region. A little later the Anglo-Saxons discontinued use of their old word for a tillage implement, *sulh,* in favor of one based on the Vikings' *plógr.* Did that mean a simultaneous change in the object? By the later tenth and early eleventh centuries good archaeological remains of ground turned into genuine furrows occur in Cornwall, Wales, and Denmark, while three Anglo-Saxon illuminated manuscripts display tools clearly possessing coulters and wheels, and something enough like a moldboard to provoke scholarly controversy.

By—and many scholars would say during—the eleventh and twelfth centuries the plow came into general use in western and central Europe north of the Alps, probably spreading in association with the expansion of farmland into areas of heavy soils and with an increased availability of lower-priced iron. Manuscript illuminations of this period offer the first incontrovertible evidence of the moldboard,

and by the thirteenth century specimens susceptible to radiocarbon dating survive, joined in some regions by good finds of asymmetrical shares. In northern France, the Low Countries, England, Denmark, parts of Norway, western Germany, the eastern Alps, and perhaps Catalonia and Galicia the adoption process was well under way before 1100. The next century saw use of the plow expand considerably among western Slavic groups and along the middle Danube; peasants in western and southern Sweden adopted it then, too. In and after the thirteenth century the plow became a normal implement of tillage in much of east-central and eastern Europe. In all such areas and in the same relative sequence the plow then came to be recognized as the dominant element in the agricultural system, giving its name to standard arable holdings, assessments, and even superior status groups among the peasantry. The plow was, therefore, closely associated with what might be thought of as typical medieval agrarian civilization. Yet this perception should not be exaggerated.

In the High and later Middle Ages major techni-

76

cal changes in traction plows ceased. Instead, European peasants selected and modified their implements to fit local conditions and needs. Various typologically advanced and primitive designs were distributed across the medieval countryside, often appearing side by side to perform different tasks. A wheeled heavy plow descended from the quadrangular ard dominated vast areas of England, northern and central France, central Europe, and southern Scandinavia. Its form changed only superficially, although more iron reinforcements were likely added. A lighter variety of wheeled plow survived, too. One pulled by a single donkey or mule appears in the Bayeux Tapestry of about 1077, and roughly similar indigenous types were only partly replaced by ones with larger shares in Poland and Bohemia during the fourteenth century. A curved rather than straight moldboard first appears in an early-fifteenth-century French manuscript illumination, but generally this more efficient form was not widely used until the eighteenth century.

More important were the variant forms of plow that appeared in northwestern Europe and elsewhere from the thirteenth century on. About that time in English illustrations wheeled plows are gradually supplanted by swing plows, as is also the case in records from some small areas of northern France. Under the name *pluzica* the swing plow is also known from later medieval Masovia and as *perticarium* from some sections of central Italy. A late-thirteenth-century illustration from Brabant first displays an indubitable turnwrest plow, a form that spread only slowly in that general area during the later Middle Ages and was likely reinvented independently in the Carpathians in the sixteenth century. Light plows with a single foot occurred in England and the Low Countries, where they became especially popular on sandy soils after being fitted with a single wheel sometime in the fifteenth century. Another variant was common in Norway and western Sweden.

And still the ard remained in use. South of a line along the Alps and across France from north of Forez and Lyonnais through the middle of Bresse, plows occurred only in rare humid territories. The whole of the Mediterranean basin and its peninsulas employed various traditional local forms of the ard, sometimes without an iron share. And to the north of the great plow zone, in northern Norway and Sweden, Finland, and Estonia, the older implement retained an equivalent monopoly. Even in the lands of the plow it survived. Poorer

peasants in the Paris area still worked with ards around 1300. Others kept it for specialized use on light soils, to work manure into the field, to break clods left by the plow, or to stir the surface of old fields before sowing the new crop. The advent of the dominant plow, then, had placed a more potent and more varied kit of tools for tillage in the hands of medieval peasants.

HORSES AND HARROWS

Some of the strength and capacity of the plow arose from a roughly contemporary diffusion of improved draft teams and traction harnesses. Before and during the early Middle Ages, agricultural draft power was provided exclusively by oxen, most often four in number, harnessed with a shoulder yoke of ancient design. Use of the horse as a draft animal was not possible because a yoke chokes a pulling horse. Between the ninth and eleventh centuries the European West obtained and/or invented gear to use with horses: iron shoes, a rigid collar, shafts and traces, and a flexible coupling called the whiffletree. Subsequently the stronger and faster, but more expensive, horse was adopted, first for harrowing, then for plowing, by peasants in many of the better-off areas of the West. By the late thirteenth century draft horse teams were the norm in France, Picardy, Flanders, Lorraine, and parts of England and Germany. In the stereotypical northern Russian plowing scene or illustration one horse drew the *sokha*. Still, by and after 1500, oxen remained common even in the horse-oriented farming regions and quite unchallenged in the Nordic and the Mediterranean lands. Only minor local changes in their yokes had occurred.

The speed of the horse had its earliest and most widespread agricultural application in drawing the harrow, an implement that was dragged over the plowed field to break up clods and level the furrows. Roman farmers had known this tool, both as a light bundle of thorn branches or a hurdle and as a heavy wooden frame with teeth, though they used the latter mainly to tear out weeds. A harrow beam with oak teeth from North Holland has also been radiocarbon-dated to the third century. Harrows were, then, a universal element in medieval agricultural tool kits; both Roman forms are known throughout the period. European peasants seem, however, generally to have adopted the more elaborate and expensive frame harrow only during and after the eleventh century, and then gradually to have perfected its design. The original rectangular

Wheeled plow and harrow shown in Bibliothèque Royale de Belgique MS 11201-2, fol. 241 (1372). BIBLIO-THÈQUE ROYALE ALBERT I

shape was modified to the handier trapezoid in many regions during the later Middle Ages, but the still better triangle was confined to northern France from the thirteenth until the sixteenth century. In the same period harrows of the better-off slowly acquired iron teeth, especially in heavy-soil areas, where this was most advantageous. Medieval Europeans developed or popularized a new use for the tool, harrowing immediately after sowing to cover the seed more quickly than with a plow or hand rakes. Toothed roller harrows and smooth rollers, both known to Roman and Andalusian agronomists, had little importance in pre-sixteenth-century Latin Europe.

HAND DIGGING TOOLS

The size, development, and frequent mention in the records of the animal-powered tillage devices, the traction plow and harrow, should not obscure the considerable and lasting importance of hand digging tools in medieval agriculture. Then, as now, two basic types may be distinguished: mattocks and hoes, which have the blade hafted perpendicular to its width and are used with a striking motion, and

spades and digging forks, which are hafted parallel to the width of the blade and are worked by pressing them into the ground and then lifting. The breaking action of the first type seems to have had more value for the harder soil of semiarid regions, while the cutting action of the second is especially applicable to tough, heavy, and wet soils.

Designs of both types display considerable long-term stability from at least the Roman Iron Age into the modern period. The broad-bladed Roman mattock (*ligo*) recurs in its short-handled form as the Andalusian *misha*, well recorded in Visigothic illuminations and later agronomists' writings, and in northern pictures datable from the eleventh to the sixteenth century. The three-pronged iron digging fork, developed in the north and represented by archaeological finds of late Roman date from northeastern Gaul, is replicated in a late-thirteenth-century *Sachsenspiegel* manuscript from Dresden and in a series of fifteenth- and sixteenth-century Flemish illuminations. Even the Roman names for some such tools survive almost unchanged in modern Romance languages.

Known designs display wide functional variety

at all times: hoes straight and toothed; mattocks wide and narrow; spades flat, round, and pointed; handles long and short; with hand grips and without. The striking tools commonly needed an iron head unless they were reserved for very light work, but spades did not. Roman spades had iron blades, but iron-shod wood ones seem to have been the norm in the north then and on through the Middle Ages. They are commonly pictured, and the shoes are often found by archaeologists. Clay sticks less to wooden than to iron blades, but late medieval evidence suggests an increase in the frequency of wholly metal ones.

Medieval uses of hand tillage implements differed between those agricultural systems in which they played a primary role and those in which they served a more secondary or occasional one. The former were present, especially outside the plow zone, in the Mediterranean and in the far north and west.

For practitioners of an intensive Mediterranean agriculture, mattocks and hoes were the key to deep digging and regular stirring of the soil surface to keep weeds down and reduce evaporation. Andalusian agronomists of the eleventh to thirteenth centuries urged regular application of the *misha* for this purpose, and like practices were common on small, hilly fields in late medieval Dauphiné. Tuscan leases specify frequent deep digging with the spade (*vangatura*). In Atlantic and northern Europe, local forms of wooden and metal spades of extreme antiquity served to cut peat for fuel and to work turf and sod to raise crops.

In those regions where the plow became central to field farming, hand tools still had their uses. People worked gardens and vineyards with them throughout the Middle Ages. Hand labor with spade, mattock, and hoe to break clods and remove weeds in the field was heavily emphasized in Carolingian and early English lists of servile obligations. Calendars and labors of the months also commonly depict newly cleared land being dug with these tools.

HARVEST TOOLS

What tillage began and nature provided, harvest completed. Medieval agriculturalists used another array of tools to gather the crops for men and beasts. In the grain-growing that was at the center of medieval rural life, what started with the plow came at last to the sickle, the "emblem" of the cereal harvest.

Use of a one-handed curved blade to cut grain went back in Europe to the Neolithic era. Metal blades and a design balanced to the hand had pre-Roman origins. The Romans so widely diffused the balanced sickle that unbalanced forms were by 1000 abandoned even in northern Scandinavia and central Russia. All Western European languages name this tool from a Latin root, and, like the Romans, medieval Europeans possessed a full range of variations on the basic form: blade size, curvature, set, handle length, and smooth or serrated edges. A toothed sickle suited the normal medieval reaping procedure quite well. The sheaf of grain was grasped in the left hand and cut with a sawing stroke toward the reaper with the right. The serrated type thus seems to have gained in popularity through much of the medieval period. For speed, cleaner grain, less work hauling sheaves, and more stubble pasture, medieval reapers grasped and cut near the top of the stalks. Some medieval and considerable early modern evidence from areas as far apart as Scotland and Kiev shows that reaping, especially with the toothed sickle, was often a task of women. The sickle remained unchallenged in the grain harvest until the last centuries of the Middle Ages.

Other ways to harvest grain occurred where speed and reduction of labor costs had high priority. Gallo-Roman Gaul had known large comblike devices fixed to a wheeled hopper pushed by an ox and tended by one or two men. Useful on large, flat fields belonging to well-capitalized enterprises, they left no medieval successors. But during the later Middle Ages two alternative harvesting arrangements began to spread in opposition to the traditional sickle.

In early-fourteenth-century Flanders there appeared the *hak et pique* (also *pik, zicht, Sichte,* or *sape*), a kind of long-handled sickle or short curved scythe held in the right hand to cut grain that was secured with a hook held in the left. The work went faster and was easier, so fewer reapers were required. Introduced in the harvest of lentils, the *hak et pique* soon spread to cereals and, by the late fifteenth century, was used in areas of lowland northern Europe from England to the eastern Baltic.

Equally labor-saving and eventually of much broader diffusion was the adaptation of the grass-cutting scythe for grain. This, too, may have begun in the Low Countries, where scythes equipped with a half-circle of light wood on the handle above the blade (ancestor of the cradle) are depicted in fifteenth-century manuscripts. By that time use of the scythe for grain was already spreading in England and northern France. An independent center of diffusion is suggested by documentation of the practice in Poland and Hungary before 1500. But many regions had still not accepted it in the eighteenth century. Use of the scythe was encouraged by the need for straw litter to replace branches increasingly barred to peasants by forest-conscious landowners and by the saving speed with which it could reap dangerously overripe or wet crops. It coped poorly, however, with rough or rocky land and short, weedy, or beaten-down crops. Its use was combatted where customary rights to the stubble remained important, and, most seriously, it wasted some grain the sickle did not. Thus, in all known cases, the scythe was introduced for the cheaper spring grains, oats and barley, and only later trusted with the more valuable rye and wheat. Its adoption meant, moreover, a wholly different work routine and organization. The scythe was a man's tool.

No matter how it was cut, the grain had to be separated from the straw and chaff. In the Mediterranean world medieval peasants normally continued the Roman practice of treading the sheaves on a specially hardened outdoor threshing floor, using the hooves of oxen or a heavy wooden sledge. Outdoor threshing was unsuited to the damper conditions of northern Europe; in that area it is known only from Muscovy, where it was done on the dry, frozen ground in winter. The Roman alternative was to beat the sheaves with a long, curved, and flattened stick. The worker had to swing hard and bend low to achieve contact. This labor was much reduced by the invention of the jointed flail, probably in Gaul around 300. With the working end, the swipple or swingle, joined to a handle by a flexible leather coupling, the worker could employ a steady circular motion. One of the most important early medieval technical innovations, the flail spread across England, northern Italy, and central and eastern Europe, reaching the Russian lands by the twelfth century. There and elsewhere the flail was still traditionally a man's tool. Muscovite women threshed by beating the sheaves against a horizontal beam to obtain long, unbroken straw for thatching, weaving, and plaiting. Finally the threshed grain was cleaned by shaking and tossing in the wind with a basket or light wooden shovel, a method unchanged from antiquity.

The scythe slowly accepted in the grain harvest from the later Middle Ages on had a much older origin and traditional use as the grass-cutting tool par excellence. Its large, crescent-shaped blade was mounted at a right or acute angle to the handle and was swung in a curve to obtain a shearing or slicing action from the friction of the stems against the blade. Both a short and a long scythe were inherited by medieval Europeans after pre-Roman and Roman evolution. The short scythe, with a handle about the length of a man's arm and a blade perhaps half that, served as a generalized tool for cutting fodder. Local design variants fit traditions of one- or two-handed use. From the Atlantic to Muscovy this tool tended during later medieval centuries to give way to a large sickle or the long scythe. The long form came to "represent" large-scale haying with its large blade and man-sized handle (snath, sned), straight or curved. The latter shape achieved a working balance not possible with the former until the addition of separate hand grips in the twelfth century. A balanced design with hand grips permitted the mower to swing his body with outstretched arms and thus to gain a longer stroke that carried the cut out of the swath.

Various regional modifications of snath and grips, plus a general tendency toward a more acute hafting angle, perfected the tool during the later Middle Ages. Forms developed in Hainault and by immigrants to Vorarlberg from the Valais are well-documented examples. Such changes likely were preconditions for the subsequent use of the scythe for grain. The scythe required smooth, stone-free ground for best results, and the mower carried a fine-grained whetstone or a small anvil and hammer to maintain a keen cutting edge.

OTHER TOOLS

Blades, rakes, and shears. Few other tools used by most medieval farmers changed at all between Roman and modern times, though functional and regional variants are innumerable. Farmers cut woody vegetation, whether for forage or to train vines and fruit trees, with a single-edged curved or hooked blade. The originally Bronze Age design is manifest in medieval specimens and/or illustrations from Greenland to Russia to the Mediterranean. Large and long-handled, this tool was a billhook; small and short, a pruning knife. Shapes and uses of rakes, pitchforks, and scoop-bladed shovels endured over the same millennial span, passing without change from at least occasionally metal versions in Rome and Al-Andalus through entirely wooden medieval European forms, to a hesitant return to iron heads or blades in the fourteenth and fifteenth centuries. Herdsmen guarded their flocks with traditional staffs and clipped wool with one-piece, spring-bladed shears, the basic Iron Age pattern of which did not change when pivoting scissors appeared in the Roman Mediterranean during the first century B.C. and in northern Europe during the sixth or seventh century.

Ox carts, wheelbarrows, and butter churns. Early medieval peasants used rough two-wheeled ox carts of Celtic or Roman prototype; their fifteenth- or even eighteenth-century descendants modified these carts only to fit the newer horse harness and to gain strength from a little more iron. How regularly medieval farmers used larger four-wheeled wagons is, however, a poorly studied issue; they were certainly rare on British farms before the sixteenth century. Peasants did, however, quickly adopt the twelfth-century European invention of the wheelbarrow, which often occurs in farm inventories from the thirteenth century on. And in the fourteenth century French and Flemish stock raisers began to churn butter in a closed, coopered wooden vessel with a vertical dasher in place of an open bowl and paddle.

IRRIGATION

Not many medieval agriculturalists used irrigation. Those who did so in Christian Europe normally used the balanced bucket or swape brought from the Middle East by the Romans. Though it is shown in later medieval art from as far north as Germany, its diffusion is not well known.

To Muslim Al-Andalus, Arab immigrants had brought the hydraulic wheel or *nāᶜūra* (noria), the technical basis for the development of intensive year-round agriculture in a semiarid climate. The form commonly employed by individual peasants derived from Syrian prototypes. Entirely wooden, its more than 200 parts could be built and maintained by the farmer himself, perhaps with the help of the local carpenter. A donkey on a long shaft walked in circles to turn a horizontal lantern wheel geared to a vertical wheel that rolled an endless chain of pots lifting water from a deep well. The machine spread to Christian Spain, as the *sènia*, but no further into Europe at this time.

MATERIALS

Wood. In farm, village, and field, the Middle Ages was an age of wood. Throughout the period this material was employed wherever the special strength of metal was not essential to a tool's function. Carolingian property inventories and instructions to estate managers mention almost no iron; when used, it was so conserved that archaeologists cannot tell whether some tenth-century blades were for ards or hoes. Even much later, of fifty known illustrations of spades in thirteenth- through seventeenth-century Muscovite sources, thirty-two spades are all wood, fourteen are iron-rimmed, and only four are iron.

Iron. It is against this background that, in western Europe at least, key developments in the agricultural tool kit were associated with sudden surges in the use of iron. The halting diffusion of the plow before about 1000 was less due to peasant ignorance of the implement than to the shortage and expense of metal for its share and coulter. The eleventh- and twelfth-century generalization of this tool and of the harrow was closely associated with improvements in metallurgy that raised the supply and lowered the relative cost of iron. In the fourteenth and fifteenth centuries further progress of iron down the social scale began to place more metal reinforcement or protection on existing tools. Nearly all archaeological and iconographic evidence of iron rakes, spades, forks, and buckets postdates 1250. By the sixteenth and seventeenth centuries the plow of lowland Scots farmers not only bore an iron share and coulter but also had an iron-bound coulter mortise and iron surfaces on the sheath, moldboard, and sole.

PRODUCTION OF TOOLS

In the early centuries the peasant made nearly all the tools he needed himself. An Eddic poem of about the year 1000 expects a freeborn Norse yeoman's son to learn plow and cart production, and the same lack of alternative surely faced Carolingian peasants. Smiths were scarce, and so were their products. Detectable change begins with the plow. As early as about 1000 the Anglo-Saxon schoolmaster Aelfric portrayed the carpenter and smith as its builders. The diffusion of the plow on the Continent was linked with a proliferation of professional metalworkers serving nonaristocratic circles. A guild of sharemakers appeared at Metz in the twelfth century, only to be supplanted by village blacksmiths in the next. By the fourteenth century wheelwrights made plows to local specifications in Mecklenburg and England.

Further moves toward still broader market relationships began before 1500. In Styria, smiths specializing in the production of scythe blades for external sale formed a distinct and well-known craft, as did wheelwrights in forested areas in England. An ironmonger at Riez in fifteenth-century Provence stocked ready-made horseshoes, plowshares, and other tools for his predominantly peasant customers.

TOOLS AS CAPITAL

Both stability and change in medieval agricultural implements thus were related closely and bilaterally to constants and growth in the larger medieval economy and society. Neither scythe smith nor ironmonger could sell if peasants were unable to buy. Over the long run tools became more common, more refined, and a more valuable factor in the production process.

The poverty of early medieval farming capital is starkly shown by the inventory of tools on Charlemagne's estate at Annapes in Artois: two iron-tipped spades, two scythes, two sickles, and "wooden tools adequate for requirements." Compare this with the capital embodied in implements on the lord's farm at Bonnières, not far away, in 1315: eight long and eight short pitchforks, five iron two-pronged forks, five iron-tipped shovels, four spades, one mattock, one billhook, and two harrows. By the sixteenth century, agricultural writers from lands as far apart as England and Silesia were recommending—and real farm inventories were listing—one or more iron-reinforced plows, iron-toothed harrows, carts, wagons, hoes, spades, shovels, two or three sorts of forks, rakes, sickles, scythes, flails, and more.

Scholars perhaps too obsessed with the spread of the plow have suggested that, on northern French peasant farms during the years from 1050 to 1200, the value of the capital equipment first surpassed that of the land itself. This likely goes too far, for true quantitative data are wholly nonexistent; and as late as the seventeenth century, implements on Dutch farms did not exceed a tenth of the farmer's wealth. Still, an increase in plows and other tools did represent a comparatively massive growth in agricultural investment.

Who supplied this investment? Mostly the peasants themselves, though driven and encouraged, perhaps, by demanding lords. However, Carolingian landlords had shown no interest in technical improvement, and the same low rate of investment is demonstrable for closely managed thirteenth-century English estates. The larger, freer, or otherwise better-off peasants bore the burden. This meant a growing differentiation visible throughout Europe between well-to-do and well-equipped peasants and their poorer neighbors, and between rich rural regions and poor. In the fourteenth century French Midi, ards were as weak and iron was as rare as in Carolingian times.

BIBLIOGRAPHY

Major recent works and significant discussions of medieval tools are listed below; general economic histories are not included. For full bibliographic coverage of studies appearing since 1960, see Museum Rerum Rusticarum Hungariae, ed., *Bibliographia historiae rerum rusticarum internationalis* (1964 and following volumes).

Individual works include Iván Balassa, *Az eke és a szántás története Magyar-országon* (1973), "Die Verbreitung der Kehrpflüge in Europa," in *In memoriam Antonio Jorge Dias*, II (1974), and, as editor, *Getreidebau in Ost- und Mitteleuropa* (1972); Ulrich Bentzien, *Haken und Pflug* (1969); Lucie Bolens, *Les méthodes culturales au moyen-âge d'après les traités d'agronomie andalous* (1974) and *Agronomes andalous du moyen âge* (1981); B. Bratanič, "On the Antiquity of the One-sided Plough in Europe, Especially Among the Slavic Peoples," in *Laos*, 2 (1952); Alexey V. Chernetsov, "On the Origin and Early Development of the East-European Plough and the Russian Sokha," in *Tools and Tillage*, 2 (1972/1975); Georges Duby, *Rural Economy and Country Life in the Medieval West*, Cynthia Postan, trans. (1968), 16–22, 88–112, *The Early Growth of the European Economy*, Howard B. Clarke, trans. (1974), 13–17, 189–199, and, as editor with others, *Histoire de la France rurale*, I–II (1975); Alexander Fenton, "The Plough-Song: A Scottish Source for Medieval Plough History," in *Tools and Tillage*, 1 (1968/1971), and "Sickle, Scythe, and Reaping Machine: Innovation Patterns in Scotland," in *Ethnologia Europaea*, 7 (1973/1974); H. P. R. Finberg, ed., *The Agrarian History of England and Wales*, I, pt. 2: *A.D. 43–1042* (1972), 73–107 and *passim*; George E. Fussell, *Farming Technique from Prehistoric to Modern Times* (1966), 20–84, and "Ploughs and Ploughing Before 1800," in *Agricultural History*, 40 (1966).

Alan Gailey and Alexander Fenton, eds., *The Spade in Northern and Atlantic Europe* (1970); Bertrand Gille, "Recherches sur les instruments du labour au moyen âge," in *Bibliothéque de l'École des chartes*, 120 (1962); Thomas F. Glick, *Islamic and Christian Spain in the Early Middle Ages* (1979), 51–103, 217–247.

André G. Haudricourt and Mariel J.-B. Delamarre, *L'homme et la charrue à travers le monde* (1955), a classic example of the ethnographic approach; Karl Hielscher, "Fragen zu den Arbeitsgeräten der Bauern im

Mittelalter," in *Zeitschrift für Agrargeschichte und Agrarsoziologie*, **17** (1969); John Geraint Jenkins, *The English Farm Wagon*, 2nd ed. (1972); Ragnar Jirlow, *Die Geschichte des schwedischen Pfluges*, R. Justh, trans. (1970); E. M. Jope, "Agricultural Implements," in Charles Singer *et al.*, eds., *A History of Technology*, II (1956); Heinz Knothe, "Slawische Pflugfunde westlich der Oder," in *Tools and Tillage*, **2** (1972/1975), and "Historische Pfluggrenzen im westslawischen Bereich," in *Berichte über den II: Internationalen Kongress für Slawische Archäologie*, II (1973); Albert C. Leighton, *Transport and Communication in Early Medieval Europe A.D. 500–1100* (1972), 60–124; Grith Lerche, "The Ploughs of Medieval Denmark," in *Tools and Tillage*, **1** (1968/1971), and "The Radio-carbon Dated Ploughing Implements," *ibid.* and **2** (1972/1975); London Museum, *Medieval Catalogue* (1940, repr. 1954, 1967), 123–126, 153–157; A. T. Lucas, "Irish Ploughing Practices," in *Tools and Tillage*, **2** (1972/1975); W. Mitzka, "Pflügen und seine Wortgeographie," in *Zeitschrift für Agrargeschichte und Agrarsoziologie*, **6** (1958); Per Noe, "Pre-medieval Plough Marks in Viborg," in *Tools and Tillage*, **3** (1976/1979), "pre-medieval" here meaning Viking Age.

Charles Parain, "The Evolution of Agricultural Technique," in Michael M. Postan, ed., *Cambridge Economic History of Europe*, I: *The Agrarian Life of the Middle Ages*, 2nd ed., rev. (1966); F. G. Payne, "The Plough in Ancient Britain," in *Archaeological Journal*, **104** (1947), and "The British Plough: Some Stages in Its Development," in *Agricultural History Review*, **5** (1957); Zofia Podwínska, *Technika uprawy roli w Polsce średniowiecznej* (1962); František Šach, "Proposal for the Classification of Preindustrial Tilling Implements," in *Tools and Tillage*, **1** (1968/1971), containing an elaborate formal and functional typology; Bernard Slicher van Bath, "The Influence of Economic Conditions on the Development of Agricultural Tools and Machines in History," in J. L. Meij, ed., *Mechanization in Agriculture* (1960), and *The Agrarian History of Western Europe, A.D. 500–1850*, Olive Ordish, trans. (1963), 54–72, 170–188; Robert E. Smith, *The Origins of Farming in Russia* (1959) and *Peasant Farming in Muscovy* (1977), 7–54; Axel Steensberg, "North-west European Plough-types of Prehistoric Times and the Middle Ages," in *Acta archaeologica*, **7** (1936), still the most comprehensive survey of iconographic evidence, and *Ancient Harvesting Implements*, W. E. Calvert, trans. (1943); Bernard Wailes, "Plow and Population in Temperate Europe," in Brian Spooner, ed., *Population Growth: Anthropological Implications* (1972), an important critical review of the archaeological and other evidence; K. D. White, *Agricultural Implements of the Roman World* (1967) and *Farm Equipment of the Roman World* (1975); Lynn White, Jr., *Medieval Technology and Social Change* (1962), chap. 2 (see criticisms of this work in reviews by David Herlihy, in *Agricultural History*, **37** [1963], and R. H. Hilton and P. H. Sawyer, in *Past & Present*, **24** [1963]); David M. Wilson, "Anglo-Saxon Rural Economy: A Survey of the Archaeological Evidence and a Suggestion," in *The Agricultural History Review*, **10** (1962).

RICHARD C. HOFFMANN

[See also **Agriculture and Nutrition; Animals, Draft; Bayeux Tapestry; Capitulary; Estate Management; Forests, European; Guilds and Métiers; Irrigation; Law, German: Early Codes; Metallurgy; Nā^cūra; Reclamation of Land; Steelmaking; Surveying; Village Life.**]

TOOLS, AGRICULTURAL: ISLAMIC. When speaking about Islamic agricultural tools we are discussing the practices of Islamic Mediterranean agriculture, as well as of Iraq and Iran, during the Middle Ages. Over the centuries, and with the intimate knowledge of the soil and of the climatic conditions, there developed in these lands special techniques of plowing, harvesting, and threshing.

PLOWS

The Mediterranean plow cuts furrows to moderate depths that suited the hard, dry soil, the lack of humidity, and the hot, dry climate. The plow had a steel share (*sikka*). The size of the share depended on soil conditions. More kinds of soil were cultivated in Islamic times than had been the custom in antiquity, and the Arabic books on agriculture give instructions on the full exploitation of each type of soil. They stress the necessity of cultivating in such a way as to preserve the maximum amount of moisture in the soil. Even from nonagricultural works such as that of al-Maqrīzī we learn that very shallow plowing was needed in highlands for growing crops such as lentils, whereas in rich, irrigated lowlands special types of heavy plows known as *muqalqalāt* were used. Such heavy plows were necessary on sugarcane plantations. To draw the plows, oxen, horses, donkeys, and camels were used. Oxen were most common. The animals were used either singly or in pairs.

There were various types of plow construction. Ibn Sīda (*d.* 1066) gives more than twenty-five technical terms for the various parts of the plow. It would be useful to reconstruct some of these medieval plows, but we can gain a fair idea of the Islamic plow from studying the ones that currently exist in various countries. In Iran alone at least five different types are found. Despite the complexity of

Plowing with a small steel share. Islamic miniature of the Herat school, *ca.* 1483. THE METROPOLITAN MUSEUM OF ART, FLETCHER FUND, 1963 (63.210.49)

technical terms in Ibn Sīda, one can distinguish the main parts. The iron plowshare (*sikka*) was fitted to the stock (*dojr*). The draft pole (*silb*) transmitted the pull of the draft team to the stock. The plowman held the stilt (*dastaq, miqwam*) and pressed downward to engage the share in the soil. The yoke (*nīr*) rested on the shoulders of the draft animals and was connected to the draft pole. The pair of oxen was called *faddān*. Sometimes *al-faddān* was the whole setup, animals and equipment. The plows described above, which were suited to Mediterranean conditions, did not have the wheels or moldboards that were a feature of the heavy plows used in heavy, sticky, and clayey soils.

HARROWS AND DIGGING TOOLS

Hand tools were used for digging the land where the plow was not necessary or where it was difficult to use, mostly in orchards and vegetable fields. The pointed mattock (*mi^cwal*) was sometimes used to break up the soil. Spades (*mishāt*; plural, *masāhī*) of various shapes also were used extensively. The

different shapes were developed to meet various soil conditions.

Some land was prepared for agriculture by removing all rocks and stones. A type of pickax known as the *mi^cdan* or *sāqūr* was used in this operation. Tools for leveling land were either hand- or animal-powered. One device that was used to level the land was the *jārūf,* an ox-drawn implement.

Ibn Sīda speaks of harrows of various types. These were usually beams with projecting teeth that engaged the soil. One such harrow was the *mijarr,* which had a hole at each end and one rope passing through each hole. On the top side of the beam were two holes in which a bent hoop was fixed, and in the middle of the beam was a handle. The *mijarr* was drawn by two oxen. Another harrow was the *māliq*. Ibn Sīda says, "It is a broad wooden board drawn by oxen. It is weighed down to make level the furrows left by the share of the plow and thus bury the seeds."

Besides plowing and harrowing, agricultural operations included the division of the plowed soil into beds or basins suitable for irrigation. Several tools for digging and earth moving, such as the *jarrāfa,* were used to divide the soil and to raise the borders of these beds. The *jarrāfa* may have been similar to the *jārūf* of Ibn al-Bassāl (Cassianus Bassus). Another tool was the *mijnab,* a board similar to the harrow but without teeth. The sharp lower edge was used to raise the earth on channel sides.

While plants were in the early stages of growth, the soil was weeded and hoed frequently. The hoe known as *mi^czaqah* or *ṭūriyya* was used. Ibn al-Bassāl refers frequently to a hoeing tool used in Muslim Spain known as *minqash* (plural, *manāqish*). He says that *manāqish* are "hooklike, similar in shape to the sickles that are used in reaping crops, but they are stronger and larger." Rakes also were used. One type was the *musht,* one purpose of which was to comb the soil and to cover the seeds.

HARVESTING TOOLS

The prevailing harvesting implement was the balanced sickle (*minjal*), in which the blade was bent back near the handle and then curved forward. The grain stems were mostly cut near the base, and the reaping was done from a squatting position. The shape of the sickle enabled grain to be cut with less strain on the wrist. The *minjal* was the toothed sickle, while the smooth sickle was called the *mikhlab*.

The scythe was not used in Islamic regions. In Islamic agriculture, crops were reaped after maturing in the dry condition. The sickle was best suited for this purpose.

Heavy tools similar in shape to the sickle were used for cutting branches or trunks of trees. These were known as *miᶜḍad*. Palms and other trees were also cut by a *burt*. Another cutting implement was the *muqbila,* an ax. The same term also was applied to a knife.

Shears and scissors were used to harvest flowers, as is described by Ibn al Baṣṣāl. Several other cutting tools are listed by Ibn Sīda and other primary sources.

THRESHING AND WINNOWING

The simplest threshing method was to beat the harvested crop with a wooden flail (*midaqq*). This technique was confined to special crops or to areas where the threshing operation was undertaken on a very small scale. For larger operations, threshing was usually undertaken on a special threshing ground called the *baydar* (plural, *bayādir*), on the edge of a village. Wheat sheaves were laid in circular heaps that could be three feet high and twenty to thirty feet across. One method of threshing was by the treading of oxen or other draft animals. This method was more often used only as a preparatory operation to break the straw and to flatten the heaps. Another method was to use the threshing sled or board (*lawḥ*), a heavy, thick board (it could be two-and-a-half by six feet) studded underneath with flint stones. It was slightly curved upward on the front end. The board was dragged over the threshing floor by animals. It was an efficient device and had been used since pre-Islamic times in the Near East.

The third method was the threshing wheel or wain (*nawraj* or *ḥaylān*). One design is described by Ibn Sīda: "This is a machine made of wood with two pulleys lined with toothed iron. When the pulleys turn on the hay, they cut it. The two toothed pulleys are mounted on the two ends of a huge beam. A man sits on the beam to give weight. The machine is pulled by an ox." The version that is still used in some Islamic villages consists of two thick beams or skids held together by two cross beams. Between the skids are placed two axles, each fitted with a set of toothed disks. The machine is pulled by a draft animal, with a driver seated on top.

Winnowing, the blowing away of chaff from grain after completion of the threshing operation, was accomplished by a peasant who threw the threshed wheat into the air, using a wooden winnowing fork (*midhrā*). The wind carried the chaff away while the grain fell to the ground.

Before the grain was carried from the threshing floor, it was sifted with a coarse sieve (*ghirbāl*) to separate it from the unthreshed ears and straw. A finer sieve removed heavy impurities and stalk knots. The grain itself was handled by shovels (*rafsh, mijraf,* or *miqhafah*).

RICE HUSKING

Another main crop was rice, which needs husking before it is ready for consumption. Ibn al Baṣṣal describes one method. Rice was placed in leather bags and was pounded with oak mallets (*daq-qāqah*). Pebbles of rock salt might be pounded with the rice to speed up the husking operation. The pounded rice was then sieved. The husked rice passed through the sieve. The unhusked grains remained on top and were pounded again.

Al-Bīrūnī mentions that water-driven trip-hammers were used for beating and crushing operations in paper mills and in gold-ore crushing. They also were used until recently in Iran to husk rice. It remains to be investigated whether these types of mills go back to al-Bīrūnī's day.

TOOLS FOR GRAFTING FRUIT TREES

Arabic books of agriculture (*al-filāḥa*) contain chapters on the art and science of grafting fruit trees. Grafting is a surgical operation that requires special tools. Ibn al-Baṣṣal devoted two chapters to grafting from which we can gain an insight into the nature of such tools.

In one method, special knives of good-quality steel, similar to those used to cut into the hooves of horses, were used to make central deep cuts in tree branches. After the cut was made, a tool called a *minqār* was inserted. This was a steel chisel that was wedged to open the cut so that the grafted element could be positioned. When the wedge was removed, the grafted elements were fitted tightly together.

In another method the grafted element was inserted under the bark of the tree. A special sharp tool was used to cut the bark. It was made in different sizes to suit the thicknesses of the various tree barks.

QUALITY OF METAL TOOLS

The *muḥtasib* was a high municipal officer who assumed important duties, one of which was to control the quality of manufactured goods and to prevent cheating and adulteration. Several manuals were written for his guidance. One such manual was the *Maᶜālim al-qurba* of Ibn al-Ukhuwwa. It contains a chapter on the control of coppersmiths and blacksmiths. On the control of the latter it says: "Blacksmiths must not hammer out knives, scissors, pincers and similar tools from soft iron, which is of no use for the purpose. Some assure the purchaser that it is steel—which is fraudulent." Then he warns against offering for sale used nails that have been straightened to look as if they are newly forged. The same warning applies to spades, plowshares, and all kinds of ironware. "Anyone who practices this illegality must be rebuked and defamed publicly. If this action is repeated, he should be banished from among the Muslim community."

BIBLIOGRAPHY

Jawad Ali, *Tārīkh al-Aᶜrab qabl al-Islām* (1971), VII; Ibn Baṣṣāl, *Libro de agricultura,* José Millás Vallicrosa and Mohamed Aziman, eds. and trans. (1955); al-Bīrūnī, *Kitāb al-jamāhir fī maᶜrifat al-jawāhir,* F. Krenkow, ed. (1936); Thomas F. Glick, *Islamic and Christian Spain in the Early Middle Ages* (1979); Marshall G. S. Hodgson, *The Venture of Islam,* II (1974); Ibn Manẓūr, *Lisān al-Aᶜrab,* VI (1955), 90, X (1955), 100, and XI (1955), 196; al-Maqrīzī, *Kitāb al-mawāᶜiẓ wa'l-iᶜtibār,* I (1853); Adam Mez, *The Renaissance of Islam,* II (1957); Hassanein Rabie, "Some Technical Aspects of Agriculture in Medieval Egypt," in Abraham L. Udovitch, ed., *The Islamic Middle East, 700–1900* (1981); Ibn Sīda, *Kitāb al-mukhaṣṣaṣ,* X (1965) and XI (1965); Charles Singer *et al.,* eds., *A History of Technology,* II (1956); Ibn al-Ukhuwwa, *Maᶜalim al-qurba,* Reuben Levy, ed. (1938), with English abstract; Gaston Wiet, "Le monde musulman, VIIᵉ–XIIIᵉ siècles," in *Les origines de la civilisation technique* (1962), repr. in *History of Mankind,* III: *The Great Medieval Civilizations* (1975); Hans E. Wulff, *The Traditional Crafts of Persia* (1966), chap. 5.

AHMAD YUSIF AL-HASSAN

[See also **Agriculture and Nutrition, II: The Mediterranean Region,** and **V: The Islamic World; Animals, Draft; Fruits and Nuts; Irrigation; Mills; Muḥtasib; Nāᶜūra.**]

TORCHES. See Lighting Devices.

TOREL, WILLIAM (*fl.* 1290's), a London goldsmith who produced the first life-size bronze effigies in England in the early 1290's. Two of them, King Henry III and Queen Eleanor of Castile, survive in Westminster Abbey. The third, Queen Eleanor, at Lincoln Cathedral, is known from drawings. The unusual thickness of the metal testifies to the experimental and innovative character of the undertaking. Torel probably had more experience making smaller objects.

Queen Eleanor of Castile. Bronze tomb effigy by William Torel, early 1290's. Westminster Abbey, London. ROYAL COMMISSION ON THE HISTORICAL MONUMENTS OF ENGLAND

BIBLIOGRAPHY
Howard M. Colvin, *The History of the King's Works,* I (1963), 479–482; Lawrence Stone, *Sculpture in Britain: The Middle Ages,* 2nd ed. (1972), 142–143.

BARRIE SINGLETON

[See also **Bronze and Brass; Gothic Art: Sculpture; Westminster Abbey.**]

TORNADA. At the end of an Old Provençal lyric there may be one or more *tornadas,* or half-strophes, in which the rhymes and meter of the last lines of the final strophe are reproduced. The tornada thus serves as epilogue; poet's signature; dedication to a day, patron, or friend; instructions to a jongleur; or, as in the partimen, an appeal to judges.

BIBLIOGRAPHY
Dictionnaire des lettres françaises: Le moyen âge (1964); Roger Dragonetti, *La technique poétique des trouvères dans la chanson courtoise* (1960), esp. 304–305; István Frank, *Répertoire métrique de la poésie des troubadours,* I (1953); Albert Jeanroy, *La poésie lyrique des troubadours,* II (1934), 93.

GLYNNIS M. CROPP

[See also **Partimen; Provençal Literature.**]

T^COROS ROSLIN (active 1256–1268), master of the patriarchal scriptorium at Hṙomklay, was the foremost painter in the golden age of manuscript illumination in Cilician Armenia. Illustrator, and sometimes scribe, of seven manuscripts (five at the Armenian patriarchate, Jerusalem), with three others attributed on the basis of style, he introduced original and dramatic elements into the traditional compositions of the Gospel story, as, for example, in a Gospel containing scenes from daily life (1262; Baltimore, Walters Art Gallery, MS 539). The lively and expressive interpretations, harmonious compositions, elegant drawing, and brilliant colors make T^coros Roslin's extensive narrative cycles of the Gospel among the finest illuminations of the medieval world.

BIBLIOGRAPHY
Sirarpie Der Nersessian, *Manuscrits arméniens illustrés des XIIe, XIIIe, et XIVe siècles de la Bibliothèque des Pères Mekhitharistes de Venise,* I (1937), 86–165 *passim,*

The Crossing of the Red Sea. Miniature by T^coros Roslin, 1266. Jerusalem, Armenian Patriarchate, MS 2027, fol. 4v. FROM SIRARPIE DER NERSESSIAN, *ARMENIAN ART* © 1977, 1978 THAMES AND HUDSON

Armenian Manuscripts in the Freer Gallery of Art (1963), 25–35 *passim,* 40–46, 49–90 *passim, The Armenians* (1970), 150–152, *Armenian Manuscripts in the Walters Art Gallery* (1973), 10–30, and *Armenian Art,* Sheila Bourne and Angela O'Shea, trans. (1978), 133–144, 160, 224, 233; Mesrop Janashian, *Armenian Miniature Paintings of the Monastic Library at San Lazzaro* (1966), 11–12; Bezalel Narkiss, ed., *Armenian Art Treasures of Jerusalem* (1979), 47–62.

LUCY DER MANUELIAN

[See also **Armenian Art (with illustration); Cilician Kingdom; Hṙomklay.**]

T^COROS TARŌNEC^CI (T^coros of Tarōn) (active 1307–1346), a priest and artist, was the most prominent manuscript painter of Armenia in the fourteenth century. Born in Tarōn, he worked first in Cilician Armenia, then in Armenia proper at the monastery of Glajor, where he became the leading scribe and favorite painter of the scholar-abbot Esayi Nčᶜecᶜi (*Esayi Nčᶜecᶜi Bible*, 1318; Erevan, Matenadaran MS 206). His miniatures synthesize the iconography and style of painting in Armenia proper with ornamental compositions derived from Cilician art; they were among the first in Armenia to include Western themes. Twenty-two manuscripts, mainly Gospels, are attributed to him, several of which are at the Matenadaran in Erevan.

Matthew portrait from a Gospel MS by TᶜOros Tarōnecᶜi, 1321. Jerusalem, Armenian Patriarchate, MS 2360, fol. 18v. PHOTO: DAVID HARRIS

BIBLIOGRAPHY

Sirarpie Der Nersessian, *Manuscrits arméniens illustrés des XIIᵉ, XIIIᵉ, et XIVᵉ siècles de la Bibliothèque des Pères Mekhitharistes de Venise*, I (1937), 110–112, 115–117, 119–122, 132–137, *The Armenians* (1970), 151–152, 154, *Études byzantines et arméniennes*, I (1973), 519–700, and *Armenian Art*, Sheila Bourne and Angela O'Shea, trans. (1978), 220, 223–225; Bezalel Narkiss, ed., *Armenian Art Treasures of Jerusalem* (1979), 75–76; Avedis K. Sanjian, *A Catalogue of Medieval Armenian Manuscripts in the United States* (1976), 29, 83–85.

LUCY DER MANUELIAN

[See also **Armenian Art; Glajor** (with illustration).]

TORRIGIANO, PIETRO (1472–1528), Florentine sculptor who worked in England from 1511 to 1518. He is best known for his work on the tombs of Lady Margaret Beaufort, the mother of Henry VII (contracted in 1511), and King Henry VII and his queen, Elizabeth of York (carved 1512–1518), all found in Westminster Abbey. The bases of these tombs were the first pure examples of Italian Renaissance art executed in England. The Gothic architectural detail around Lady Beaufort's effigy was probably stipulated in a drawing supplied to Pietro Torrigiano. The superb effigies far surpassed any previous English work but failed to lay the basis for a new national style. The sculptor died in Seville, Spain, apparently in disgrace, according to Vasari.

Tomb of Henry VII in Westminster Abbey. Marble and gilt bronze carving by Pietro Torrigiano, 1512–1518. ROYAL COMMISSION ON THE HISTORICAL MONUMENTS OF ENGLAND

BIBLIOGRAPHY
F. Grossmann, "Holbein, Torrigiano, and Some Portraits of Dean Colet," in *Journal of the Warburg and Courtauld Institutes*, **13** (1950); Margaret Whinney, *Sculpture in Britain, 1530 to 1830* (1964), 4–5.

BARRIE SINGLETON

TORRITI, JACOPO (*fl.* end of the thirteenth century), Roman painter and mosaicist. His principal surviving works include the signed apse mosaics of S. John Lateran dated about 1291 and the mosaics depicting the Coronation of the Virgin of about 1295 or 1296 in S. Maria Maggiore, Rome, one of the earliest-known representations of this subject. On the basis of style, the half-length figures of Christ, the Virgin, St. John the Baptist, and St. Francis (in fresco) in the second vault of the transept of the upper church of S. Francesco in Assisi are attributed to him. Torriti's style developed out of a Byzantine heritage that contributed to his monumental, impersonal, and hieratic interpretation of the deity.

BIBLIOGRAPHY
Gertrude Coor-Achenbach, "The Earliest Italian Representation of the Coronation of the Virgin," in *Burlington Magazine*, **99** (1957), 328–330; Heinrich Karpp, *Die frühchristlichen und mittelalterlichen Mosaiken in Santa Maria Maggiore zu Rom* (1966); Walter F. Oakeshott, *The Mosaics of Rome from the Third to the Fourteenth Centuries* (1967).

ADELHEID M. GEALT

[See also **Assisi, San Francesco; Mosaic and Mosaic Making.**]

TORTURE. The term "torture" has two meanings, a vague and general one that changes with the intentions of the individuals who use it, and a specific meaning that is rooted in legal history. The first meaning is often used casually of many instances of personal assault in medieval Europe, from extralegal forms of interrogation to outright sadism. Its history is part of the general history of human cruelty. The second meaning can be traced more narrowly.

Judicial torture was recognized in Roman law, from a very early date in the case of slaves and, under the empire, in cases of treason. By the sixth

Coronation of the Virgin (*ca.* 1295/1296) and Dormition (*ca.* 1305). Mosaic by Jacopo Torriti in S. Maria Maggiore, Rome, *ca.* 1295/1296 and *ca.* 1305. ALINARI/ART RESOURCE

century the *Digest* of Justinian contained a section devoted to judicial torture (*Digest* 48, 18), and interrogation by the infliction of physical torment appears to have been extended routinely to the *humiliores*, that is, to those free citizens not ranked as *honestiores*. The Germanic legal systems that replaced Roman law in Western Europe after the sixth century made no provision for the torture of free persons (although some evidence exists that the Visigoths may have employed it in order to determine whether an accused should be sent to the ordeal). Not until the twelfth century did torture reappear in European legal practice, along with the spread of inquisitorial procedure and its new standards of proof.

According to the standards of proof increasingly accepted in late-twelfth-century courts, convictions in capital crimes could be obtained only by the testimony of two eyewitnesses or by the confession of the accused. If there was sufficient evidence, the accused might be legally tortured in order to secure confession to a crime that he seemed likely to have committed. Torture seems to have been revived in secular courts and only at the end of the twelfth century to have been discussed in legal literature. Torture was accepted in inquisitorial investigations and heresy trials from the mid thirteenth century. It was routinely employed as an incident of legal procedure in most of the criminal courts of Western Europe, with the exception of England and Scandinavia. In these areas, since the trial jury could convict on much slighter evidence, torture was not needed. Torture certainly began to be employed in England during the sixteenth century, although not in common-law courts.

The forms of judicial torture were generally restricted to the strappado (the distension of joints, nerves, and muscles by dropping a person suspended on a rope), the rack, fire applied to the soles of the feet, and slow suffocation by the forced ingestion of water. Although legal literature contained many restrictions on its application, it appears that torture was often carelessly performed and caused even more suffering than it was designed to. The use of torture in the sixteenth and seventeenth centuries was essentially a continuation of the principles and methods of its application in the twelfth and thirteenth centuries.

BIBLIOGRAPHY
Piero Fiorelli, *La tortura giudiziaria nel diritto comune,* 2 vols. (1953–1954); John H. Langbein, *Torture and the Law of Proof* (1977); Edward Peters, *Torture* (1985).

EDWARD PETERS

[See also **Châtelet; Inquest, Canonical and French; Inquisition; Jail Delivery; Law (various articles); Ordeals.**]

TOSAFOT. See **Talmud, Exegesis and Study of.**

TOULOUSE. The city of Toulouse is located in southwest France on the right bank of the Garonne River, near an outcropping of rock that since prehistory provided a ford and thus a route from the Mediterranean to Aquitaine and the Atlantic. Probably of Celtic origin, the city was Roman from the second century B.C. From that period little remains except the grid plan. The Roman wall (late third to early fourth century) enclosed nearly 90 hectares (225 acres) and included substantial open space. This became the medieval *cité.*

Thinly populated before 1000, it began to grow by 1050. Privileges similar to those of bastides were granted to attract settlers to various quarters within the walls. By 1150 suburbs had been built across the river at the head of the newly completed bridge (St. Cyprien) and around the monastery of St. Sernin, north of the *cité* (the bourg). A wall enclosing both the bourg and *cité* was constructed around 1140. The population numbered perhaps 35,000 early in the fourteenth century. Devastated by the plague and by war (especially during 1374–1384), the population dropped to about 24,000 in 1398 and 22,500 in 1405. The medieval city was destroyed in 1463 by a fire that raged for two weeks.

The major monuments to survive were the monastery of la Daurade (called *deaurata* for its gold mosaics), of Visigothic or Frankish construction, the oldest church in France dedicated to the Virgin (razed 1802–1817); the monastic church of St. Sernin, first built in the fifth century and rebuilt in the eleventh; the Gothic masterpiece of the Dominican convent; and the cathedral (part eleventh, part thirteenth century).

Political, economic, and social developments. The Visigoths conquered Toulouse in 413. There Theodoric I established his court, and under Euric (466–484) the city enjoyed a golden age. After the Battle of Vouillé (507), Toulouse was captured by the Franks. In the seventh century, as Merovingian power was shredded by fratricidal wars, it became the seat of virtually independent dukes. Spared by the Berbers, who besieged it in 721, it was turned into a center of Carolingian defense against Islam, especially under Count William, the conqueror of the Spanish March, whom medieval bards turned into the "William of Orange" of their epic poems. In 849 Charles the Bald named Frédol count of Toulouse, Pallars, Ribegorza, Rodez, and Limoges as a reward for his betrayal of Pepin II. From his brother, Raymond I, descended the "Raymondins," who kept the title of count of Toulouse until 1249.

When, from the late eleventh century on, the counts of Toulouse shifted their major political interest to the valley of the Rhône and Provence and then acquired Tripoli during the First Crusade, the city reaped political privileges in return for money and military support. For Count Raymond V (1184–

1194), Toulouse was not even an administrative center, and after the Gregorian reform the bishop had lost all political power within its walls. The citizens had their "common council" by 1152. By 1176 that council's membership represented quarters of the city. Between 1189 and 1208 it became virtually independent of the count. Toulouse formed a city-state, like those of Italy, using its militia to subject villages and lords for nearly twenty-five miles (40 km) around to its control and its levies. As a symbol of that independence, the municipal government built a palace for itself (1190–1204).

Toulouse was not a major economic center. By 1200 its merchants appeared in Catalonia and Navarre and at the fairs of Champagne, but many of its inhabitants remained half artisans and half peasants; cows, goats, and pigs roamed the streets, and vineyards, orchards, and gardens could be seen within its walls. Its most significant "export" was probably pilgrimage service; St. Sernin, with its estates from Périgord to Navarre, was the city's primary financial power. Although its role in the wine trade increased in the thirteenth century and both its financial connections with England and its armor and leather industries developed, Toulouse's strength remained that of a political center.

During its decades of independence, deep fissures appeared in the city's society, exacerbated by the Cathar heresy. Armed factions gathered; the bourg set itself against the *cité*; and during the Albigensian Crusade inhabitants marched off to support both sides. As a result of the crusade, Toulouse passed to Alphonse of Poitiers in 1251 and then, in 1271, into the royal domain, becoming a major administrative center for the monarchy in the south. Its university, founded in 1229 to combat heresy, quickly became noted for its law school. In 1317 the bishopric became an archbishopric. A *parlement* functioned briefly in the city around 1300; it became permanent in 1443.

The counts of Toulouse. The counts of Toulouse lost all their lands in 872 when Bernard I was killed by Bernard Plantevelue of Auvergne. Bernard's younger brother Odo recovered only Toulouse and Rouergue after 885. On his death, the two counties were divided between his sons and remained so until the death of Berta, the last of the Rouergue line, around 1065. By 924 the family was claiming supremacy over all of Septimania and for a few years over the duchy of Aquitaine as well. The house of Poitou recovered the latter, but William

Taillefer (961–1037) extended the Raymondins' interests to the Rhône by marrying the heiress to part of Provence.

The brothers William IV and Raymond IV of St. Gilles confirmed these Mediterranean interests when together they conquered Rouergue from Berta's husband, the count of Auvergne, and Raymond then took the title marquis of Provence (1088) and invented the title duke of Narbonne. Raymond was one of the leaders of the First Crusade and ended his life as count of Tripoli. From Raymond IV to the Albigensian Crusade the story of the house is one of nearly continuous warfare against the counts of Barcelona (later kings of Aragon) for hegemony over the lands between the Pyrenees and the Alps. At one time or another this combat attracted the armed intervention of the dukes of Aquitaine (William IX, 1098, 1112–1120; Louis VII and Henry II, both in the name of Eleanor, 1141, 1159; Richard I, 1196), Pisa, Genoa, and the emperor Frederick Barbarossa (as suzerain in Provence), as well as all the aristocratic houses from Béarn to Nice. The spread of heresy through this region also attracted the intervention first of the Cistercians, then of Pope Innocent III, and finally of the crusaders the pope called down upon them.

The storm began when Raymond VI was accused in 1208 of plotting the death of Peter of Castelnau, the papal legate. Raymond adroitly reconciled himself with the church and deflected the crusade against the Trencavel viscounts. But in 1211 Simon de Montfort turned his army against Raymond. Toulouse was besieged. The city successfully resisted, but the defeat of the count and King Pedro of Aragon at Muret in 1213 allowed Simon finally to enter. In 1215 the Fourth Lateran Council made Simon count of Toulouse, took Avignon and the Comtat Venaissin for the papacy, and left the other Provençal lands to the future Raymond VII. But Raymond VI and his son returned, favored by revolts at Toulouse, Avignon, and elsewhere. Only when King Louis VIII took the leadership of the crusade in 1226 was the fate of the Raymondins settled. The Treaty of Paris (1229) provided for the marriage of Raymond VII's daughter Jeanne to Alphonse of Poitiers, giving suzerainty over lower Languedoc and the expected inheritance of Toulouse to the Capetians. The church again acquired the Comtat Venaissin. Raymond VII spent the rest of his life at war in Provence attempting to undo the Treaty of Paris. When his attempts to remarry and produce a male heir failed, he finally took the cross. He died in 1249.

BIBLIOGRAPHY

Charles Higounet, "Un grand chapitre de l'histoire du XIIe siècle: La rivalité des maisons de Toulouse et de Barcelone pour la prépondérance méridionale," in *Mélanges d'histoire du moyen âge dédiés à la mémoire de Louis Halphen* (1951); Walther Keinast, *Der Herzogstitel in Frankreich und Deutschland* (1968), chap. 7 and bibliography; Émile-G. Leonard, *Catalogue des actes des comtes de Toulouse*, III (1932); Jean-Pierre Poly, *La Provence et la société féodale, 879–1166* (1976), 318–359; Philippe Wolff, *Histoire de Toulouse* (1961), bibliography.

FREDRIC L. CHEYETTE

[See also **Albigensians; Aragon, Crown of (1137–1479); Cathars; Inquisition; Languedoc; St. Sernin, Toulouse; Urbanism, Western European.**]

TOURNAMENTS. See **Games and Pastimes.**

TOURS, BATTLE OF. See **Poitiers, Battle of.**

T^cOVMA ARCRUNI (*fl.* 852–904), Armenian historian of the early tenth century who is the author of the history of the feudal Arcruni (Artsruni) family. The early-fourteenth-century colophon appended to the end of the *History* refers to the author as *vardapet*, a title given to doctors of the church. The title of the *History* identifies him as T^covma and indicates his Arcruni origin. T^covma claims to be an eyewitness to the murder of the Arab emir Yūsuf in 852. The last event recorded in the *History* took place in 904. In the introduction of the *History* we are told that Prince Grigor Derenik of Vaspurakan (847–887) commissioned T^covma to write the present work. In chapters 6 and 11 of book I, Prince Gagik, son of Grigor Derenik, is singled out as the patron of the book. The author presumably began his undertaking during the reign of Grigor Derenik and completed it during that of Prince Gagik.

The work is divided into three books, of which the first is for the most part based on Movsēs Xorenac^ci's *History* and traces the origin of the Arcruni to the progeny of the Assyrian king Senek^cerim. The first five chapters of the second book contain a garbled medley of historically unreliable information about the period from the mid fifth to the early ninth century. Book III, which is about the ninth century and the early years of the tenth, is the most valuable section of the work. The author's scope is narrow and restricted mostly to the events concerning the Arcruni. The *History* has reached us in an incomplete form, with a section missing at the end. Instead, the work of an anonymous tenth-century writer, also incomplete, covering the period from the 880's to the 930's, has been appended. The patron of this anonymous author is also Gagik Arcruni, who is always referred to as king. A final section, which is the work of a second anonymous author, and a colophon at the end bring the narrative down to the fourteenth century. The *History* of T^covma and the additions of the anonymous authors, which deal with the Arab, Seljuk, and Mongol periods of domination, are valuable sources for the historian of the Middle East.

BIBLIOGRAPHY

Thomas Artsruni, *History of the House of the Arts-runik^c*, Robert W. Thomson, trans. (1985).

KRIKOR H. MAKSOUDIAN

[See also **Arcrunis; Armenia: History of; Armenian Literature; Gagik/Xač^cik-Gagik; Movsēs Xorenac^ci; Vardapet.**]

T^cOVMA MECOP^cEC^cI (**Thomas of Medzoph**) (1378–1446). Information about this fifteenth-century Armenian author is found in T^covma's own *History,* in the *Life of T^covma Mecop^cec^ci,* written by his student, Kirakos Banasēr (the "philologist"), and in a number of fifteenth-century colophons. T^covma was born in 1378 in the district of Aɫiovit, north of Lake Van. He received his early education at the monastery of Mecop^c, north of Arčeš, but the invasions of Tamerlane and the attacks of Turkoman bands obliged him to move from place to place, frequently fleeing for his life. In 1395 he went to Suxara (Xaṙabasta) monastery in southern historical Armenia, where he studied with some noted Armenian scholars. In 1406, together with twelve classmates, he went to one of the most important seats of learning in Armenia, the monastery of Tat^cew in Siwnik^c, eastern Armenia. After a residence of only two years there, Tᶜovma, his classmates, and their renowned teacher Grigor Tatᶜewacᶜi were forced to flee to Mecopᶜ monastery to escape the Qara Qoyunlu ("black sheep") Turkomans. After Tᶜovma received the dignity of vardapet (doctor of the church) in Erevan, eastern Armenia, he returned to Mecopᶜ, where he engaged in teaching and literary activity. However, between 1421 and 1437 southern Armenia once again became a theater of warfare between Turkomans, Mongols, and Kurds. In 1430 Tᶜovma fled for his life to the island of Lim in Lake Van. In 1436 he and his students fled to Xlatᶜ, Arčeš, and Arckē. Tᶜovma Mecopᶜecᶜi was one of the major protagonists involved in transferring the Armenian *katholikosate* from Sīs in Cilicia back to Ējmiacin in 1441. After the realization of his dream, Tᶜovma returned to his beloved Mecopᶜ, where he died three years later, in 1446.

The *History of Tamerlane and His Successors,* although the major source for Armenia in the late fourteenth and early fifteenth centuries, is, nonetheless, a rather defective production. Written for the most part from memory, the work contains historical inaccuracies and jumps episodically back and forth from one decade to another. The *History* commences with the devastations wreaked on Siwnikᶜ by the northern Tatars in 1386. Tamerlane's invasions of 1387, 1388, 1395, 1401, and 1402 on numerous districts of eastern and western Armenia and Georgia are described with the immediacy of a terrified eyewitness. The account is even more detailed for the first three decades of the fifteenth century.

BIBLIOGRAPHY

The noncritical Armenian edition of Tᶜovma's history is *Patmutᶜiwn Lank-Tᶜamuray ew yaǰordacᶜ iwrocᶜ arareal Tᶜovma vardapeti Mecobecᶜwoy* (1860). The English translation is Tᶜovma Metsobetsᶜi's *History of Tamerlane and His Successors,* Robert Bedrosian, trans. (1987). The hagiographical Life of Tᶜovma Mecopᶜecᶜi was published twice in Armenian and is available in a Russian translation, *Pamiatniki armianskoi agiografii* (Monuments of Armenian hagiography), Kᶜ. S. Ter-Davtyan, trans. and ed. (1973), 157–163. Tᶜovma's other surviving work exists only in Armenian (*Tᶜovma Mecopᶜecᶜu Yišatakarane* [Tᶜovma Mecopᶜecᶜi's colophon]), K. Kostanean, ed. (1892). The classical Armenian text of Tᶜovma's *History* was published in French by Felix Nève, *Exposé des guerres de Tamerlan et de Schah-Rokh dans l'Asie occidentale* (1861). A commentary by Nève is "Étude sur Thomas de Medzoph," in *Journal asiatique,* 5th ser., 6 (1855).

For a supplementary bibliography and information, see Robert Bedrosian, "The Turco-Mongol Invasions and the Lords of Armenia in the 13th–14th Centuries" (diss., Columbia Univ., 1979), 42–46.

ROBERT BEDROSIAN

[See also **Armenia: History of; Armenian Literature; Qara Qoyunlu; Tamerlane; Tatᶜew; Turkomans.**]

TOWER, a vertical construction of masonry or timberwork or a combination of both, either freestanding or incorporated into a large architectural complex such as a church or fortifications. Medieval towers were used for a variety of purposes, including defense, lighting, and the housing of bells. They were polygonal, rectangular, round, or square in plan.

CARL F. BARNES, JR.

[See also **Bells; Bulgarian Art and Architecture; Castles and Fortifications; Construction: Building Materials; Wastell, John** (with illustration).]

TOWN. See **Urbanism.**

TOWNELEY PLAYS constitute one of the four extant cycles of English medieval biblical plays, the others being those of York, Chester, and N-town. There are thirty-two plays in the cycle, nine of which are incomplete owing to the loss of leaves from the manuscript. They range from the Creation to the Judgment in the manner of an English Corpus Christi play, dramatizing the human story from its beginning to its end and pivoting on Christ as the savior of mankind.

The manuscript (now in the Huntington Library, San Marino, Calif., MS HM 1) dates from the fifteenth century, possibly from the 1480's, and is named after the Towneley family, which owned it for several centuries. Several of the plays are associated with Wakefield (in West Yorkshire) and its craft guilds. The name "Wakefield" is written in red as a part of the title of the first play (Creation) and the third (Noah). There are names of places in Wakefield or its neighborhood mentioned in the second play (Murder of Abel) and the two Shepherds' plays. Also, there are names of craft guilds added in sixteenth-century hands to five plays. Although this evidence is limited, it seems safe to infer that the cycle as a whole is the Corpus Christi play performed during the fifteenth and sixteenth centuries by the guilds of Wakefield. Indeed, it is likely to be the Corpus Christi play referred to in the Wakefield Burgess Court records of 1556 and 1559/1560.

It is not known how the Wakefield plays were staged. They may have been performed "in one fixed locality, on a multiple stage, and in the round" (in the words of Martial Rose), that is, in the manner of some of the N-town plays. They may have been staged processionally on pageant wagons at several stations in turn, as at Chester and York. Or they may have been performed in each of these ways at different periods of Wakefield's history. The Wakefield record for 1556 refers to "pagyauntes": "Item a payne is sett that everye crafte and occupacion doo bringe furthe theire pagyauntes of Corpus Christi daye as hathe bene heretofore used. . . . Item a payne is sett that everye player be redy in his pagyaunt at setled tyme before 5 of ye clocke in ye mornynge." The second of these references points to the use of pageant wagons, perhaps for processional staging, perhaps for taking part in the Corpus Christi procession before the play itself was performed in a fixed locality.

It is uncertain when the cycle was put together or where all the pageants came from. But two things stand out: the influence of the York cycle and the contributions made by the Wakefield Master. The pervasive influence of York has been explained by Marie C. Lyle as due to the borrowing of the entire York cycle by Wakefield before 1390, after which each cycle was considerably revised and underwent many changes not found in the other. Her case for the original identity of the York and Towneley cycles has not met with general acceptance. For example, Arnold Williams believes Towneley "to be a patchwork, put together rather late (*ca.* 1420), and not representing any long local tradition at Wakefield." Most scholars would agree with Grace Frank that the parent-cycle theory is both too simple and too sweeping and would prefer "to speak of Towneley's borrowings from York . . . and to posit the original identity of individual plays . . . rather than the identity of the cycles themselves." As far as individual plays are concerned, it was pointed out by Lucy Toulmin Smith, the editor of

the York plays (1885), that five Towneley plays (Exodus, Christ and the Doctors, Resurrection, Harrowing of Hell, and Judgment) are similar to their extant York counterparts. To these five plays may be added ninety-eight lines common to the Towneley Scourging and the York play of Christ led up to Calvary. No one would now seriously challenge the hypothesis that these plays and lines in the Towneley cycle were borrowed (with changes and later revisions) from York originals.

Many of the contributions of the Wakefield Master, which were probably made before 1450, are unmistakable. Five complete plays (Noah, the two Shepherds' plays, Herod the Great, and the Buffeting), written in a distinctive stanza, are certainly his; and the same stanza and verbal mastery, the same satiric vision and powerful dramatic sense, can be seen in parts of the Murder of Abel and several other plays. This remarkable author has undoubtedly strengthened some of the major themes of the cycle. Because of him the conflict between the city of men and the city of God is dramatized with greater intensity, and the prophecies of Christ's coming (linking the Old and New Testament plays) receive added emphasis.

John Gardner is convinced that "however many poets may have helped to write the cycle, they worked according to one writer's plan," a plan laid down by the Wakefield Master. He supports this conviction by examining not only the familiar features of the Master's technique ("the characteristic stanza, the randy language, the social criticism") but other less obvious features of this writer's work, such as "the thematic use of verbal repetition, the ironic use of scriptural typology, the consistent manipulation of patterns of imagery (especially satanic imagery), and the oddly modern cutting of transitional devices." These characteristics, he maintains, are found in a sufficient number of plays in the cycle, apart from those plays generally accepted as written or revised by the Wakefield Master, to suggest strongly "the work of some controlling intelligence."

Whatever the uncertainties of Gardner's thesis may be, he is undoubtedly right to insist that the theme of heavenly-earthly conflict, in all its manifestations, is a special concern of the Wakefield playwright. This theme does not always manifest itself in a direct conflict between God and the devil. It more often broadens out into a conflict between earthly representatives of the *civitas Dei* and *civitas terrena*. Thus Cain in the Murder of Abel play is not the devil, but he is certainly the devil's man as well as a type of the Jews who allegedly killed Christ; and he is opposed to Abel, a human being who is also a type of Christ. In this way the use of typology enables the Christian dialectic of good and evil to be dramatized in human terms.

BIBLIOGRAPHY

A[rthur] C. Cawley, *The Wakefield Pageants in the Towneley Cycle* (1958), and, with Jean Forrester and John Goodchild, "References to the Corpus Christi Play in the Wakefield Burgess Court Rolls: The Originals Rediscovered," in *Leeds Studies in English,* **19** (1988); Hardin Craig, *English Religious Drama of the Middle Ages* (1955), 214–218; George England and Alfred W. Pollard, eds., *The Towneley Plays* (1897); Jean Forrester and A. C. Cawley, "The Corpus Christi Play of Wakefield: A New Look at the Wakefield Burgess Court Records," in *Leeds Studies in English,* 7 (1974), an article that points out the uncertain source of a number of items added by J. W. Walker to the 1556 Wakefield Burgess Court record (these doubtful items include the reference to "pagyaunt" quoted above); Grace Frank, "On the Relation Between the York and Towneley Plays," in *PMLA,* **44** (1929); John Gardner, *The Construction of the Wakefield Cycle* (1974); Marie C. Lyle, *The Original Identity of the York and Towneley Cycles* (1919); Martial Rose, ed., *The Wakefield Mystery Plays* (1961), 26, a modernized version for performance; Martin Stevens, "The Missing Parts of the Towneley Cycle," in *Speculum,* **45** (1970), and "The Manuscript of the Towneley Plays: Its History and Editions," in *Papers of the Bibliographical Society of America,* **67** (1973); *The Towneley Cycle: A Facsimile of Huntington MS HM 1,* with introduction by A. C. Cawley and Martin Stevens (1976); J[ohn] W. Walker, *Wakefield: Its History and People,* 2 vols., 2nd ed. (1939); Arnold Williams, *The Characterization of Pilate in the Towneley Plays* (1950), 72; Rosemary Woolf, *The English Mystery Plays* (1972), 54–76, 310.

A. C. CAWLEY

[See also **Chester Plays; Corpus Christi, Feast of; Drama, Western European; Mystery Plays; N-Town Plays; Second Shepherds' Play; York Plays.**]

TRACERY, in Gothic architecture, the ornamental patterns of branching mullions and ribwork in the upper part of a window. The term itself seems not to predate the seventeenth century, the medieval designation being "forms" or "form pieces." There are two principal types of tracery, both of which appeared in the late twelfth or early thirteenth century.

Plate tracery is the simpler and somewhat earlier type. It consists of a solid stone spandrel or plate set in the window head above the lights; it is pierced by simple openings (circles, quatrefoils, and so on). In round or rose windows (Laon, Chartres), the resemblance to a plate is readily apparent. Plate tracery was eventually superseded by bar tracery, which uses much less stone and allows greater freedom of design. Bar tracery is composed of intersecting ribs or bars that branch out from the mullions of the window to create decorative patterns in the window head. All the various types of tracery except plate are bar traceries.

Geometrical tracery (thirteenth century), characteristic of High Gothic architecture in France, consists of lobed circles or foils set above lancet lights. Kentish tracery is a geometrical type found mainly in Kent, with barbs projecting between the foils. In Y-tracery the window mullion branches out in the form of a Y. Intersecting tracery (thirteenth–fourteenth centuries) uses multiple Y-shaped mullions that overlap to form an intersecting grid. In reticulated tracery (thirteenth–fourteenth centuries), circles drawn out into ogee shapes are arranged in horizontal rows to form a netlike pattern. Curvilinear tracery (also called flowing or undulating tracery; fourteenth century) is typical of the English Decorated style and uses elaborate patterns of compound or ogee curves. A related form in France is called Flamboyant tracery (fourteenth–fifteenth centuries) because the compound curves describe flamelike patterns. Panel tracery (fifteenth century) typifies the Perpendicular style in England, with straight-sided tracery panels repeated in rows between the window mullions and above the lights. It is also called Perpendicular or rectilinear tracery.

Tracery patterns are used to categorize the phases of Gothic architecture, and the student should refer to the architectural literature for more detailed information.

While tracery had its origins in window design, its forms became nearly universal in Gothic art and architecture. The word is also used to describe similar ornament when applied to walls, vaults, doors, screens, panels, manuscript illumination, and the full range of the decorative arts.

BIBLIOGRAPHY

Jean Bony, *The English Decorated Style: Gothic Architecture Transformed, 1250–1350* (1979), in which the importance of the adoption of traceried windows for

St. Étienne of Sens, rose window of south transept showing tracery in the Flamboyant style, 1490.
PHOTO: WIM SWAAN

English Gothic architecture is stressed. See also Peter Draper's review of this book in *Art Bulletin,* **64** (1982), 330–332. See also Martin S. Briggs, *Concise Encyclopedia of Architecture* (1959), 344; John Fleming, Hugh Honour, and Nikolaus Pevsner, *The Penguin Dictionary of Architecture,* 2nd ed. (1972); Paul Frankl, *Gothic Architecture* (1962), esp. 175–179; Roland Sanfaçon, *L'architecture flamboyante en France* (1971), 16, *passim.*

GREGORY WHITTINGTON

[See also **Glass, Stained; Gothic Architecture; Gothic, Decorated; Gothic, Flamboyant; Gothic, Perpendicular; Lancet Window; Mullion.**]

TRADE, ARMENIAN. The geographical position of Armenia athwart the east-west land routes linking the Mediterranean basin by way of Asia Minor to the Iranian and Muslim worlds as far as Central Asia and eventually the Far East guaranteed the importance of its commercial role as long as these routes preserved their international character. As early as the Hellenistic period, the southern Armenian province of Sophenē prospered from its proximity to the cities of northern Syria and Mesopotamia. The major transit route from the Persian capital of Ecbatana to the cities of the east coast of the Black Sea probably passed through the Armenian capital of Artašat (Artaxata) in the valley of the Araks. Both the discovery of numerous coin hoards and the foundation of a number of cities in Greater Armenia and Sophenē attest the prosperity of the region, which remained the main transit area between Iran and the Black Sea coast from the second century B.C. until the end of the sixth century A.D.

Despite a temporary setback in the chaotic period of the third century and the Persian king's sack of the Armenian cities between A.D. 364 and 367, when much of their population was deported to Iran, according to the Armenian historian Pᶜawstos Buzand, Armenia soon regained its commercial importance. According to the late-fourth-century map known as the *Tabula Peutingeriana*, Artašat was the junction point of a massive network of roads, minutely studied by Hakob Manandian, that ran west to Satala and Asia Minor, south toward Tigranakerta (Miyāfārqin), north to Sebastopolis (Dioskurias) on the east coast of the Black Sea, and eastward to Ecbatana. According to an edict of 408–409 preserved in the *Code* of Justinian (IV.63.4) and reconfirmed by the Byzantine-Persian treaty of 562, Artašat was designated, with Nisibis and Callinicum, as one of the three authorized transit points for trade with Sasanian Persia at which special finance officials, the *comites commercium,* supervised the customs.

Justinian's historian, Procopius, praised the favorable location of the new Armenian capital of Dwin with its populous surrounding villages where "merchants conduct their business [and bring merchandise] from India and the neighboring regions of Iberia and from practically all the nations of Persia and some of those under Roman sway" (*Persian War*, II.25.1–3). Local goods, such as grain, wine, dyes, and horses, for which Armenia had been famous since antiquity, formed part of this commercial activity, but the main item was unquestionably the all-important silk from the Far East, required by the luxury industries supplying the Byzantine court, over whose transit the Sasanians preserved an absolute monopoly until 552, despite various imperial attempts to circumvent it. The lists of Byzantine and Persian weights and measures drawn up by the Armenian scholar Anania Širakacᶜi in the second half of the seventh century are clear indications of the international character of Armenian trade.

This early commercial development was under-mined by the break in the Persian silk monopoly when cocoons were finally smuggled into the Byzantine Empire. A far more serious blow was dealt by the Arab invasions of the mid seventh century. Endemic warfare between Byzantium and the Arabs resulting in the closing of the overland routes, the increasingly heavy taxation imposed by the caliphate after the census of 724–725, and the shift of Muslim trade east or south to the Mediterranean basin, all contributed to the stagnation and decline of Armenian commerce in the later seventh and eighth centuries. The northern cities of Georgia and Azerbaijan, such as Tbilisi (Tiflis) and Bardhaᶜa (Partaw), continued to prosper from the trade with the Khazars and the Slavs beyond the Caucasus, but the great Armenian cities Dwin and Karin (called "Qaliqalā" by the Arabs) in the west, Naxčawan in the Araks Valley, and Arčēš on the northern shore of Lake Van became Arab military garrisons rather than commercial centers.

This regression, however, proved temporary. Armenia's favorable geography once again contributed to a rapid revival, aided by the return of greater political stability and the reopening of the overland routes in the second half of the ninth century. The period of the Bagratid kingdom (late ninth to mid eleventh centuries) was one of great prosperity resulting from a brilliant commercial and industrial expansion extolled by both native Armenian historians and Arab geographers such as Ibn Ḥawqal, al-Iṣṭakrī, and al-Muqaddasī. The main east-west highway now linked Dwin with the coastal city of Trebizond (whose annual fair was attended by Armenian and Caucasian merchants), by way of the new cities of Ani, Kars, and Arcn (near Karin). Kars was also the junction for a northern branch highway connecting it to the eastern Black Sea ports by way of the Iberian city of Artanuč. A second route, primarily through the southern lands of the Muslim emirates around Lake Van rather than through the lands of the Armenian Bagratids, linked Persian Azerbaijan with Syria, Mesopotamia, and Asia Minor from Ardebīl, by way of Marāgha, Xoy, Berkri, Arčēš, Xlatᶜ, Bitlis (Bałēš), and Miyyafarqin to Amida (Diyarbakir). Here, too, a northern branch ran from the junction point at Arčēš on Lake Van to Manazkert, Karin, Erzincan, and Sebaste (Sivas). Still other routes linked Dwin and Bardhaᶜa, where they intersected with roads to Tbilisi, Ardebīl, and Derbent. Indeed, a Bagratid *Itinerary* from the late tenth century goes so far as to include the distances from Dwin to Constantinople, Rome, Damascus, Jerusalem, the Persian Gulf, and Alexandria.

The revival of commerce contributed to the growth of cities and towns, most of which lay along the highways. Contemporary sources speak of forty-five cities and twenty-three additional urban settlements. Many of these "cities" were little more than small towns, but the main ones, such as Kars, Arcn, and particularly the capital, Ani (whose walls had to be rebuilt a generation after it became the Bagratid capital, in order to triple its area), were major urban centers with public buildings, palaces, churches, baths, inns, bazaars, and paved streets as well as water and sewage systems. Archaeological excavations, more reliable than the inflated figures proposed by historians, support the hypothesis of a population of 50,000–100,000 at Ani, far greater than that of contemporary Western cities. Although still military in character and dominated by their citadels, the Armenian cities of the Bagratid period were again economic centers as well. The excavations of Dwin and Ani have shown extensive workshop districts testifying to a considerable artisan and merchant population. The commercial importance of Arcn was so great that it even dispensed with the walls that protected other cities.

The growth of native industries was reflected in the types of goods exported, which tended to be local in the Bagratid period, in contrast with the transit character of much of the earlier trade. Food, timber, and mineral products were still important: timber from the slopes of Ararat, salted fish (particularly the prized *tirrix* of Lake Van), wine, nuts, metals and minerals (silver from Sper, copper, lead, red and yellow arsenic, mercury, copper sulfate, borax), vegetable and mineral dyes, salt from the mines of Kulp, and natron from Lake Van for the bakeries of Iraq. Horses, mules, and rare white falcons from the snow belt were also exported. Nevertheless, manufactured goods clearly dominated the market, and the marginal illuminations of Armenian manuscripts amply illustrate the multiplicity of local crafts. Corroborative archaeological excavations have brought to light the workshops of potters, blacksmiths, armorers, goldsmiths, tanners, and weavers. The decorated ceramics and glassware of Dwin were famous. But the greatest demand, according to Arab sources, was for choice textiles: cushions, covers, curtains, rugs, multicolored flowered silks called *bosjun,* and, above all, the famous "Armenian goods" (*asnaf al-armani*), dyed red with the local *qirmiz* (English: kermes) and embroi-

dered with silks or gold, which were the specialty of Artašat. According to the geographer Ibn Ḥawqal, these "do not have their equals in any part of the world." An index of the enormous economic growth, resulting from the twin expansion of commerce and the local industries feeding it, is provided by the widespread building activity of the period and its artistic brilliance, of which Ani, the "city of one thousand and one churches," is perhaps the best example.

The Byzantine annexation of Armenia in the mid eleventh century, followed almost immediately by the Seljuk invasions, put a violent end to the prosperity of the Bagratid era. The great cities were sacked and building activity came to a standstill from about 1061 until 1150. The economy followed the political shift southward to Cilicia, which flourished in the twelfth and thirteenth centuries on the trade of the Italian maritime cities with the Levant and subsequently with the Far East. The Seljuk era in Greater Armenia is insufficiently known and presents numerous problems. Some local economic life must have survived, since the larger cities continued to thrive despite the absence of much international trade. This is particularly true at Ani, bought by the Shaddadids in 1072, but also at Xlat^c under the Shāh-armen, Kars, and Karin. The full strength of this vitality did not, however, manifest itself until the subsequent period.

Stimulated yet again by relative peace under the Zakarid viceroys of the Georgian crown early in the thirteenth century, but most of all by the resumption of the transit trade to the East passing through Ani from the newly created empire of Trebizond and the Genoese and Venetian Black Sea trading posts, the Armenian economy grew rapidly. The appearance of Armenian merchant settlements as far away as Georgia, the Crimea, and the middle Volga, as well as renewed building activity, bear witness to the return of prosperity. The enormous wealth of such Armenian merchants as Tigran Honenc^c, whose lengthy 1215 Ani inscription records the ownership of entire villages as well as hostelries, baths, mills, private houses, barns, oil presses, and gardens, or Master Umek, who bought Getik for 40,000 gold ducats, has led Joseph Orbeli to the conclusion that the Zakarid period marked the economic apogee of Armenia, although his enthusiasm is not fully shared by Manandian.

Briefly checked by the destructive invasions of the Khwārizmshāhs (1225–1231) and the Mongols

(1236–1244), Armenian commerce expanded still further in the first century of Mongol domination (*ca.* 1236–1335). The failure of the Mongols to control Syria, and the active Black Sea trade of the Italian cities, which spread to the Caspian in search of the silks from Ghilan, increased the importance of the northern transit route through Armenia. The main highway linking the thriving Cilician seaport of Āyās on the Mediterranean with Tabrīz, the new commercial center of the Mongol Ilkhanids, and thence to India, and the silk route to the Far East are described by the early-fourteenth-century Florentine merchant Francesco Pegolotti, who lists all the stops from Āyās, through Caesarea (Kayseri), Sebaste, Erzincan, Karin (where the silk route intersected the route from Trebizond), Bagawan, and Xoy, to Tabrīz. Its central portion is identical to the route described almost a millennium earlier by the *Tabula Peutingeriana.* A secondary route from Trebizond and Asia Minor, known to Marco Polo and the fourteenth-century Muslim writer Ḥamdallāh al-Qazwīnī, ran through southern Armenia by way of Karin, Xnus, Manazkert, Arčēš, Xoy, and Marand. The contemporary Armenian historian Kirakos of Ganjak observed that caravans traveled under the protection of special Mongol charters. Their travels took them increasingly far afield: grave inscriptions, Catalan maps, and the account of the thirteenth-century Franciscan monk William of Rubruck record Armenian artisans and settlements deep in Central Asia. The wealth of Umek's son Čar and of Sahmetin, who in 1261 built a summer palace at Mren at a cost of 40,000 gold ducats, matched that of the preceding generation.

The early Mongol period, however, proved to be the Indian summer of the economic prosperity of Armenia. As has been observed by most scholars, the increasingly oppressive Mongol taxation gradually brought ruin to the country. Also, the hub of international trade shifted from the Armenian cities to Tabrīz and nearby Sultaniya, far to the southeast. Even the highway detailed by Pegolotti already bypassed the northern cities of Kars and Ani, although it still crossed central Armenia. The southern portion of the country still thrived, and both Marco Polo and the fourteenth-century Arab traveler Ibn Baṭṭuta praised the textiles, metalwork, and wealth of Erzincan and Karin, but by the mid fourteenth century an irreversible decline had set in, accelerated by the chaos following the Ilkhanid collapse in 1335, which endangered the overland routes. Repeated attempts were made by the Italian

cities to revive trade with the East, the mint at Ani struck gold coins as late as the fifteenth century, and the southern Armenian route to Tabrīz briefly regained its importance; but the increasing anarchy, aggravated by the raids of Tamerlane in the late fourteenth and the early fifteenth centuries and the endemic warfare of the Turkoman dynasties, hastened the final economic collapse. Armenian merchants were constrained to abandon their homeland and settle in the Crimea, Eastern Europe, or other colonies. By the end of the fifteenth century, the total alteration in the geographic pattern of trade brought about by the discovery of the sea routes to the East ended once and for all the value of the overland highways, and with them the participation of Greater Armenia in international trade.

BIBLIOGRAPHY

The two main itineraries are in *Itineraria romana: Römische Reisewege an der Hand der Tabula Peutingeriana,* Konrad Miller, ed. (1916, repr. 1964); Francesco Balducci Pegolotti, *La pratica della mercatura,* Allan Evans, ed. (1936, repr. 1970). For most of the references to Armenian commerce in Armenian and Arabic sources, see Hakob A. Manandian, *The Trade and Cities of Armenia in Relation to Ancient World Trade,* Nina G. Garsoïan, trans. (1965). See also Babken N. Arhakᶜelyan, *Kᶜaghakᶜnerě ew arᶜhestnerě Hayastanum IX–XIII darerum,* 2 vols. (1958–1964); Marius Canard, "Les împots en nature de l'Arménie à l'époque ᶜabbâside," in *Revue des études arméniennes,* n.s. 8 (1971); Wilhelm von Heyd, *Histoire du commerce du Levant au moyen âge,* 2 vols. (1885–1886, repr. 1959), esp. II, 73–134; Joseph Laurent, *L'Arménie entre Byzance et l'Islam depuis la conquête arabe jusqu'en 886* (1919), rev. ed., Marius Canard, ed. (1980); Aram Ter Ghewondyan, "Les împots en nature en Arménie à l'époque arabe," in *Revue des études arméniennes,* n.s. 11 (1975–1976), and *The Arab Emirates in Bagratid Armenia,* Nina G. Garsoïan, trans. (1976).

NINA G. GARSOÏAN

[See also **Albania (Caucasian); Anania Širakacᶜi; Ani in Širak; Araks River; Arčēš; Arcn; Armenia; Artašat; Āyās; Bagratids; Bardhaᶜa; Berkri; Cilician Kingdom; Derbent; Dyes and Dyeing; Erzincan; Exploration; Georgia; Ilkhanids; Karin (Karnoy Kᶜałakᶜ); Kars; Khazars; Khwārizmshāhs; Kirakos of Ganjak; Manazkert; Mongol Empire; Muqaddasī, al-; Naxčawan; Nisibis; Pᶜawstos Buzand; Procopius; Qirmiz; Sasanian History; Sebaste; Seljuks; Shaddadids; Silk; Slavs; Tabula Peutingeriana; Tbilisi; Tigran Honencᶜ; Travel and Transport, Islamic; Trebizond; Van, Lake; Xlatᶜ; Zakarids.**]

TRADE, BYZANTINE. Trade was an important component of the Byzantine economy, although in fact agriculture was the primary economic activity. During the latter part of the twentieth century, historians stressed noneconomic mechanisms for the distribution of products in the ancient and medieval economies. Nevertheless, although such mechanisms were indeed present, trade existed throughout the Byzantine period at the local, regional, and international levels. Its extent, form, and significance varied with political circumstances and with the development of the economy as a whole.

EARLY PERIOD THROUGH
SIXTH CENTURY

Commercial activity through the mid sixth century followed the patterns and techniques inherited from the Roman Empire. International, long-distance trade was quite active, although it catered to a limited market. The east-west axis of travel continued to be the most important in terms of that trade, which carried the spices, pearls, precious stones, and silks of the Far and Middle East to the Byzantine Empire and further west, to Italy and other western provinces. The Byzantine merchant traveled east to frontier posts to pick up these commodities and bring them into the Mediterranean world. Sometimes the Byzantines even traveled to the places of production of these commodities, according to the monk and former merchant Cosmas Indicopleustes.

The internal trade of the Byzantine Empire was, in some ways, more important in the early period, for the empire functioned as a great trading complex, with a common currency and low internal duties (2 or 2.5 percent). Among the factors inhibiting commercial activity, however, were the difficulties of transportation and state interference, particularly in the provisioning of Constantinople and in the needs of the army, which were partly met by levies in kind. The government controlled the transporting of Egyptian grain to Constantinople by using the *navicularii* (shipowners), who were bound to at least partial state service. This undoubtedly curtailed the activities of the private merchant, as did the imposition by Justinian I (*r.* 527–565) of a de facto state monopoly in silk manufacturing. Furthermore, the state produced arms in its own factories. Nevertheless, internal trade did exist, at the local level in the form of exchanges between villages in fairs, as also between the towns and the surrounding countryside, and even over fairly long distances. The major eastern cities manufactured luxury items, which were sent to the rest of the empire: for example, papyrus and high-quality glass produced in Alexandria, and silk cloth and jewelry produced in Beirut and Tyre. The market for such products was relatively small, restricted to the wealthy, who could afford them. Merchants, in this period, were a diversified group, which included wholesale traders, along with merchants of limited means and petty traders. For some, trade was a lucrative profession. The *Pratum spirituale* (Spiritual meadow), composed around 600, mentions a rich Alexandrian family that had its wealth invested in ships and gold, a significant sum, even though much smaller than the wealth of the great landlords. The majority of merchants, however, were people of modest means and social status.

SEVENTH CENTURY

The military and political crises of the seventh century were attended by grave economic changes that affected the economy of exchange (that is, trade) as well as the agricultural system of the empire. A general decline in population, due to plagues and man-made catastrophes, had inevitable economic consequences. So did the loss of the rich eastern provinces to the Arabs: Constantinople felt the effects of the loss of Egypt immediately, for the free issues of bread, which had begun on the day of the inauguration of the city (11 May 330), came to an end during the reign of Heraklios (610–641). From this time on, the policy of the Byzantine emperors was to maintain a low price for bread rather than to restore its free issue. The population of Constantinople declined. Many cities shrank until they were simply small fortified military posts. Only a few, such as Constantinople, Thessaloniki, and Ephesus, continued as centers of trade and manufacturing. The Byzantine economy and society became heavily agricultural.

The invasions and insecurity affected internal and international trade differently. Internal trade appears to have suffered more, partly because the great manufacturing centers of the East had been lost and partly because travel by land had become extremely unsafe, especially in the Balkans. Furthermore, the restructuring of agrarian society that occurred in the seventh century tended toward self-sufficiency and did not favor the accumulation of large, marketable surpluses in the hands of individuals. The internal market became much more restricted than it had been in the earlier period. The low level of internal exchange may be reflected in the fact that very few copper coins survive from this period. Nevertheless, even under these conditions trade never stopped entirely. The *Miracles of St. Artemius,* written shortly after 659, mentions a number of merchants, among them a man from Chios. There is evidence of trade between Thessaloniki and the Macedonian hinterland. Fairs are attested in, among other places, Cyprus, Thessaloniki, and Ephesus; in 787, the annual fair of Ephesus was yielding at least 100 pounds of gold in duties.

Long-distance trade also continued to some extent in the seventh century and afterward, despite the great difficulties created by the general economic decline, the Arab invasions and conquests, and the eventual disruption of the sea routes by Muslim pirates. In the early seventh century, the Life of St. John the Almsgiver, patriarch of Alexandria, mentions the exchange of Egyptian wheat for English tin; the Sutton Hoo burial treasure includes Byzantine silver plate; the Life of St. Gregory the Decapolite shows the saint traveling by merchantman, around 820, from Ephesus to Proconessus (the present-day island of Marmara), and then also by sea from Thessaloniki to Italy and back.

Indeed, it has been argued that the seventh century saw significant advances in two areas. The first was the power and wealth of the seaman-merchant, who seems to have profited from the relative accessibility of sea travel, compared to the difficulties of land routes. (The Rhodian Sea Law, which regulated the activities of merchants and sailors and which determined the contracts that may have been the origin of the later Italian *commenda,* probably dates from this period.) The second development is that of the silk industry, which grew significantly in the course of the seventh century, using raw silk produced within the Byzantine Empire. The manufacturing of silk cloth was so extensive that in 768 Constantine V paid a ransom of 2,500 silk robes to recover prisoners taken by Slavic pirates—although admittedly in this instance we are dealing with an example of noneconomic distribution of commodities.

EIGHTH THROUGH TENTH CENTURIES

The Arab conquests meant a reorientation of the economic life of the empire toward Constantinople and the Black Sea area, which now became a Greek sea. In the eighth and ninth centuries the provisioning of Constantinople—a most important element in internal exchange—was done from Thrace, the Black Sea coast, and Asia Minor; even long-distance trade with the east was diverted toward the Black Sea coast. Constantinople became the principal entrepôt of the eastern trade; it also became an important center of manufacturing, especially of silk cloth and luxury products.

Information concerning Byzantine commerce in the tenth century, a pivotal period, is biased, for it primarily concerns Constantinople. It may be observed in general that this was a period of population increase and prosperity in the Byzantine Empire, but that the economy was still preponderantly rural and based to a considerable extent on self-sufficiency. Still, some evidence, including legal provisions regarding fairs (996), shows that there were markets in the countryside that drew merchants both from the immediate vicinity and from more distant areas. The situation is clearer with regard to Constantinople. Here, traders came from various parts of the world to sell their merchandise and buy the products of Byzantine manufacturing. Among others, there were Syrians, carrying silks and spices; Russians, who brought slaves, furs, and honey; Bulgarians, carrying linen cloth; and Italians. They traded in Constantinople under conditions strictly controlled by the state. They had to stay at specially designated places; they could remain for only three months; and their clients were the members of particular guilds who came together to inspect and buy the merchandise, presumably so that they would not engage in competition that would raise prices. Furthermore, the export of Byzantine commodities was strictly controlled, especially that of silk cloth of the best quality, which for the Byzantines had both a political and a ceremonial function.

In the course of the late ninth and the tenth century, trade with Italy became more important, both because of renewed Byzantine influence in the area and because of the development of an Italian market, with which are connected the activities of such commercial cities as Amalfi and Venice. Both of these had political ties with Byzantium, a factor of some importance in their history. The Amalfitan merchants were the first to acquire trade privileges and a colony in Constantinople in the tenth century; they would be supplanted by the Venetians in the eleventh.

In terms of internal trade, the *Book of the*

Prefect is a valuable source, particularly for the trade of Constantinople. Compiled for the most part during the reign of Leo VI (886–912), the *Book of the Prefect* shows a large variety of trades, some essential for the provisioning of the city (butchers, bakers, grocers), some connected with silk manufacturing and trade, as well as professions that provided services crucial for the orderly conduct of trade, for example, bankers and notaries. The government, through the prefect and his officials, regulated commerce in Constantinople, defined the scope of the activities of each guild, and controlled the price of important commodities, especially bread.

The attitude of the Byzantine aristocracy toward trade has been contrasted unfavorably to that of the ruling class of cities like Venice. It is true that, at least until the eleventh century, the aristocracy had a stated disdain toward the merchants. On the other hand, it must be remembered that merchants and shipmasters grew rich in the ninth and tenth centuries; that the empress Theodora II, the restorer of the icons, owned great trading ships; and that the Byzantine aristocracy was quite willing to participate in Constantinopolitan commercial activity by renting real estate to merchants.

GROWTH OF CITIES:
ELEVENTH AND TWELFTH CENTURIES

In the late tenth century, and more rapidly in the eleventh, the rural character that Byzantine society had acquired in the seventh century became less pronounced, as cities grew and developed. The circulation of money increased, and so did commercial activity, both internally and internationally. The merchants and artisans became important groups in urban society. In the eleventh century the Senate became open to members of the merchant group, and in the same period political instability gave rise to urban riots in which artisans and merchants played an active role. With the accession of the Komnenoi to the throne in 1081, the merchants declined in political importance and were, once again, excluded from the Senate.

Commerce, however, remained highly developed in the Komnenian period, and the activities of Byzantine merchants extended both within the empire and outside it. Constantinople continued to function as a major outlet for long-distance trade, as well as a center for the exchange of merchandise from all parts of the empire. The twelfth-century Jewish traveler Benjamin of Tudela could compare

the city only to Baghdad. According to Benjamin, Constantinople drew merchants from Syria, Persia, Egypt, Russia, the Balkans, Spain, and Italy; they exchanged spices, the luxury products of Byzantine manufacturers (silk cloth, objets d'art), products of local industries (cheaper cloth), and agricultural products from all parts of the Byzantine Empire. In other words, Constantinople functioned as the center of a sphere of trade relations involving not only Italy, the East, and Egypt, but also Russia and other northern lands, as well as the Turkish part of Asia Minor.

Provincial cities were also rich and populous in this period, especially in the European provinces of the empire. Thessaloniki was the second most important commercial center, where, according to a twelfth-century source, a multitude of traders went to exchange their products during the fair of the feast of St. Demetrios. The source mentions merchants from the Byzantine Empire, from Bulgaria and the Danubian lands, from Italy, Spain, and France. The major product exchanged seems to have been cloth of various kinds; other commodities from the Black Sea and Egypt were also traded. The cities of Thebes (center of silk production until it was sacked by the Normans in 1147), Corinth (center of glass manufacturing until the late twelfth century), Almyros, Sparta, and even Athens reached their highest level of medieval development in the twelfth century. All of these cities functioned as markets for the agricultural products of the countryside: olive oil, wine, cotton, and wheat were collected and then exported, usually to Constantinople, Italy, or Alexandria, by Byzantine or, increasingly, Italian merchants. Smaller towns (Janina, Kastoria, Zagora) were centers of local trade.

The increased commercial activity in the twelfth century was due in part to the fact that Western Europe was becoming an important market and that the activities of its merchants were quickening the economic life of the entire eastern Mediterranean basin. To some extent, Byzantine merchants profited from these developments. We find them in various commercial centers, in the eastern and western Mediterranean: in Barcelona, Béziers, Montpellier, Alexandria, Cairo, and Damietta. They actively participated in long-distance trade as well as in the internal trade of the Byzantine Empire. But, although some merchants and bankers had become rich, their political power as a group was limited by an aristocracy whose wealth was based on agriculture and land. Merchants often led or participated in riots; the most important such riot was in 1182, when the artisans and merchants of Constantinople rose against the Western merchants, whose activities were threatening the wealth of the Byzantines.

INFLUENCE OF WESTERN MERCHANTS

The period of the Komnenoi saw, along with an upsurge in the urban economy, the economic penetration of Western merchants into the Byzantine system of exchange; it was a development that would eventually bring the eastern Mediterranean under the economic domination of Venice and Genoa. But that result was not yet apparent in the late eleventh and twelfth centuries, when Komnenian emperors began to give first to the Venetians and then to the Pisans and Genoese the commercial privileges that made their trading activities easier and less costly. The first important privileges were granted to Venice in 1082, in exchange for the help the Venetian fleet had given to Alexios I against the Normans. The most important clause gave Venetian merchants the right to trade freely in Constantinople and many provincial cities, with the exception of Crete, Cyprus, and the Black Sea area. The Black Sea coasts were kept under Byzantine control because of their importance for the provisioning of Constantinople, and Crete because of its important strategic position and the fact that it was a stepping-stone to Egypt; possibly the emperor wanted to protect Byzantine trade with Alexandria. It is more difficult to speculate on the reasons for the exclusion of Cyprus. The Venetian traders were also relieved of the *kommerkion*, the 10 percent ad valorem tax on merchandise that was paid by all other merchants, Byzantine and foreign. This clause was extended in 1126 to cover Byzantine merchants in their transactions with Venetians. These privileges came at a time when Venice was experiencing a growing population and economy, and much facilitated its further commercial expansion.

Similar privileges were granted to Pisa (1111) and Genoa (1155); the merchants of both these cities were less favored than the Venetians, since they still paid a *kommerkion* of 4 percent, but they were more favored than their Byzantine counterparts. After 1082 the Byzantine emperors were more or less forced by political circumstances (the need for Italian naval support) and the fear of attack by the Italian fleets to grant these privileges. By the late twelfth century, the Venetians had extended their activities to cover the internal trade of the empire, perhaps even the local trade centered in the small provincial towns.

Emperors of the Komnenian dynasty, who ruled 1081 to 1185, and the Angeloi dynasty, who succeeded them (1185–1204), made spasmodic efforts to rescind the privileges granted to Western merchants, but their policy could not be sustained. Many Westerners resided in the Byzantine cities: 10,000, 20,000, and 30,000 Venetians are variously attested in Constantinople before their expulsion in 1171; even without the Venetians the attested number of Westerners in Constantinople in 1180 was 60,000, well over 10 percent of the population. They dealt in agricultural products, silks, and spices. Byzantine merchants began to be slowly supplanted by Western merchants in the markets of Alexandria.

In reaction to the growing Western presence, Manuel I Komnenos expelled all Venetians from the Byzantine territories in 1171; eleven years later, mobs in Constantinople massacred large numbers of Westerners and burned or confiscated their property. The political results of the economic penetration of Western traders into the Byzantine economy were increasing hostility and an increasing need for the West to establish secure commercial outposts in the Byzantine Empire. Venice was able to achieve this aim through her participation in the Fourth Crusade and the capture of Constantinople in 1204.

LATE PERIOD TO 1453

With the Fourth Crusade, the conditions affecting Byzantine trade changed. Venice acquired a preponderant position in the Byzantine economy of exchange. The Byzantine rulers of the splinter state of Epiros made treaties with the Venetians, while the other major Byzantine state, the empire of Nicaea, moved toward self-sufficiency, maintaining trade relations primarily with the Seljuks. In the course of the thirteenth century the importance of Constantinople as an entrepôt increased considerably; the formation of a large Mongol state and the existence of the so-called *Pax mongolica* made the northern trade routes much safer to merchants than the southern routes. When the Byzantines recaptured Constantinople in 1261 the city was a very active commercial center and remained so even after the collapse of the *Pax mongolica* (*ca.* 1340), indeed until the early fifteenth century.

Despite the reestablishment of the Byzantine Empire with its capital at Constantinople, the economy of exchange continued to be dominated by Italian merchants, especially those of Venice and Genoa who, by the early fourteenth century, had more or less divided the Aegean into spheres of economic influence. Because they controlled the markets, communications, and, to some degree, finances, the Italian merchants dominated long-distance trade and the trade with Western Europe. Byzantine and Greek merchants continued to exist, both in Constantinople and in the provinces, those controlled by the Byzantines and those ruled by Westerners, but their activities were severely circumscribed.

In the Palaiologan period (1258–1453), we encounter for the first time the visible participation of Byzantine aristocrats in trade and banking. Most of the traders, however, were men of small or moderate means, including sailors. For the most part, Byzantine merchants were involved in retail trade, both for the internal market and as an integral part of the larger trade that the Italians controlled. This phenomenon is particularly true after 1350, for until that time it is possible to find Byzantine merchants whose activities were more extensive and varied, and whose interests clashed with those of the Italian merchants.

The Byzantine lands exported to the West mostly raw materials and agricultural products. Wheat continued to be exported to Genoa even in the late fourteenth century, at a time when it was scarce in Constantinople. In return, the Byzantines imported from Italy increasingly large quantities of cloth, as well as soap and arms. Native Byzantine industries seem to have disappeared in the process.

The visible predominance of Italian merchants in this period led an older school of historians to the mistaken assumption that Byzantine merchants had disappeared. While this is far from being so, Byzantine merchants did function under circumstances that they did not control; and this economic dependence is evident also in the political sphere, where the merchants did not act to preserve or extend class interests, except possibly during the civil war of 1341–1347. As for the Italian merchants, their preponderance is well established with imperial privileges issued at various times from 1267 on. Western merchants received exemptions from customs and other duties and the right to establish colonies in the capital and other cities. The abandonment of state interference in economic matters, which had traditionally characterized the Byzantine economy, is evident in these grants, which, until the

1320's, tried to safeguard some of the rights of the state and its subjects but by the early fifteenth century only reflected the virtually complete capitulation of the Byzantine state.

BIBLIOGRAPHY

Hélène Antoniadis-Bibicou, *Recherches sur les douanes à Byzance* (1963); Michel Balard, *La romanie génoise* (1978); A. E. R. Boak, "The Book of the Prefect," in *Journal of Economic and Business History*, 1 (1929); Silvano Borsari, "Per la storia del commercio veneziano col mondo bizantino nel XLI secolo," in *Rivista storica Italiana*, 88 (1976); George I. Brătianu, *Études byzantines d'histoire économique et sociale* (1938); Gerald W. Day, "Manuel and the Genoese: A Reappraisal of Byzantine Commercial Policy in the Late Twelfth Century," in *Journal of Economic History*, 37 (1977); M. F. Hendy, "Byzantium, 1081–1204: An Economic Reappraisal," in *Transactions of the Royal Historical Society*, 5th ser., 20 (1970), and *Studies in the Byzantine Monetary Economy, c. 300–1450* (1985); Wilhelm von Heyd, *Histoire du commerce du Levant au moyen âge*, 2 vols. (1885–1886, repr. 1959); A. H. M. Jones, *The Later Roman Empire* (1964); Angeliki E. Laiou-Thomadakis, "The Byzantine Economy in the Mediterranean Trade System: Thirteenth–Fifteenth Centuries," in *Dumbarton Oaks Papers*, 34 (1980); Paul Lemerle, *Cinq études sur le XIe siècle* (1977).

Ralph-Johannes Lilie, *Handel und Politik* (1984); Robert S. Lopez, "Silk Industry in the Byzantine Empire," in *Speculum*, 20 (1945), and "The Role of Trade in the Economic Readjustment of Byzantium in the Seventh Century," in *Dumbarton Oaks Papers*, 13 (1959); Nicolas Oikonomidès, "Quelques boutiques de Constantinople au Xe siècle: Prix, loyers, imposition (*Cod. Patmiacus 171*)," in *Dumbarton Oaks Papers*, 26 (1972), *Hommes d'affaires grecs et latins à Constantinople (XIIIe–XVe siècles)* (1979), and "Silk Trade and Production in Byzantium from the Sixth to the Ninth Century: The Seals of Kammerkiarioi," in *Dumbarton Oaks Papers*, 40 (1986); Jean Rougé, *Recherches sur l'organisation du commerce maritime en Méditerranée sous l'empire romain* (1966); Nicolas Svoronos, "Société et organisation intérieure dans l'empire byzantin au XIe siècle: Les principaux problèmes," in his *Études sur l'organisation intérieure, la société, et l'économie de l'empire byzantin* (1973); Speros Vryonis, Jr., "Byzantine Demokratia and the Guilds in the Eleventh Century," in his *Byzantium: Its Internal History and Relations with the Muslim World* (1971).

ANGELIKI E. LAIOU

[See also **Agriculture and Nutrition; Alexandria; Alexios I Komnenos; Angelos; Benjamin of Tudela; Beirut; Byzantine Empire; Commenda; Constantine V; Constantinople; Cosmas Indicopleustes; Cyprus, Kingdom of;**

TRADE, ISLAMIC. Long-distance international trade had a long and venerable history in the Middle East even before the advent of Islam. From antiquity, the urban civilization of the Middle East was a natural locus for trade. Towns and urban settlements inevitably gave birth to trade, commerce, and exchange. The biblical caravan merchants who rescued Joseph from the pit into which his jealous brothers had flung him testify to the antiquity of long-distance overland trade in western Asia, just as King Solomon's romance with the Queen of Sheba testifies to an ancient tradition of seaborne commerce. Not only was western Asia in and of itself a place of trade, it also served in ancient times (as it was destined to do again in medieval and premodern times) as a bridge and transit point for Eastern goods and merchants destined for Mediterranean markets and for merchandise and traders going from the West to the East. It thus served as both market and entrepôt.

TRADE AND THE NEW ISLAMIC ORDER

The rise and fall of empires may have affected the security of the trade routes: the ease with which goods were transported and exchanged across long distances. By the time Islam appeared on the scene in West Asia and North Africa, however, long-distance trade was a firmly established feature of the area's economic and cultural life. Thus, the new Islamic rulers of the Middle East and North Africa fell heir to a long and developed tradition of commerce, replete with institutions and instruments for its accomplishment. Furthermore, some of the groups from the Arabian Peninsula were not entirely ignorant of long-distance trade or without some firsthand, direct experience in its pursuit. While their culture was essentially that of Bedouin tribesmen, some of the leading figures of early Islam, including the Prophet himself and some of his closest companions, had knowledge of and

experience in the caravan trade that traversed the Arabian Peninsula linking the ports and incense-producing areas of southern Arabia to the markets of Byzantium, Syria, and Egypt. This trade, however, was not nearly as extensive as some scholars have recently claimed, and Mecca's international commercial importance in the early seventh century has been much exaggerated.

While the new Islamic order of the late seventh and early eighth centuries did not invent trade, the rearrangement of political, cultural, and economic boundaries resulted in a tremendous expansion of commerce within the domain controlled by Islam. First, the new order tied together under one political jurisdiction a number of areas that were very diverse ecologically, climatically, and thus economically. Within little more than a century of its appearance, the world of Islam extended from the Atlantic shores of Spain and Morocco across North Africa and southwestern Asia into northern India and Central Asia. Never before in history had such a vast and varied area of the globe come under one political and military jurisdiction. And, even after the political unity of this empire dissolved, it remained for most of the Middle Ages, from the point of view of commercial and economic exchange, a single cultural unit.

This diversity was a powerful impetus to exchange within the Islamic domain, an impetus further strengthened in the first century or so of the Islamic era by the infusion into the economy of large amounts of gold and silver as a result of the dethesaurization of precious objects taken as booty by the victorious Arab conquerors. The richness and prolific variety of this exchange are revealed in a mid-ninth-century Arabic treatise entitled *The Investigation of Commerce* that describes and enumerates merchandise available on the markets of Baghdad and Iraq, then the centers of the Islamic caliphate. A very partial list includes panther skins, rubies, ebony, and coconuts from India; silk, paper, peacock feathers, female slaves, eunuchs, and marble workers from China; felt and black hawks from North Africa; donkeys, papyrus, and fine cloth from Egypt; and musk, sugar cane, and furs from Khwarizm in Central Asia. These exotic luxury products were supplemented by a wide choice of textiles and objects that were affordable for a cross section of city dwellers.

Baghdad in the ninth and tenth centuries was the center of a great empire, and the richness of its markets as reflected in the *The Investigation of*

Commerce could certainly not be duplicated throughout the Islamic realm. On a less spectacular scale, and in sharp contrast to early medieval Europe, the numerous cities and towns in the domain of Islam were the crossroads for local, regional, and international trade. This was in part due to the existence of a number of structural and cultural features in Islamic society throughout the Middle Ages that provided an underpinning for the vigorous pursuit of commerce.

First among these factors was precisely the existence of a vigorous urban life. In sharp contrast to early medieval Europe, the map of the medieval Islamic world, from Morocco in the West to the borders of China in the East, was dotted with cities and towns. They may have varied in size and in importance and complexity, but all invariably contained a marketplace and some level of craft activity. Such was the importance of cities in medieval Islam that, as Claude Cahen has contended, "unlike medieval Western Europe, the whole of civilization was found in the town; it was only there that administration, law, religion and culture existed." The inordinate concentration of political, administrative, and religious personnel and services in cities and towns inevitably created a demand for goods and services that only commerce could satisfy.

COMMERCIAL ARRANGEMENTS

From the earliest times, Islamic law and the customary practice prevalent in the Islamic world provided merchants and traders with the commercial techniques to structure and facilitate trade and exchange. Long before they existed in the West, merchants in the Islamic world had at their disposal accepted legal mechanisms for extending credit and for transferring and exchanging currencies over long distances. So, for example, the *suftaja,* or letter of credit, allowed a merchant to advance or transfer a sum of money to a business associate at some distant place with the full confidence that the transfer would be expeditiously accomplished. The tenth-century geographer and merchant Ibn Ḥawqal reports that he himself saw a letter of credit for the huge sum of 40,000 dinars in the Saharan oasis of Sijilmasa. The business documents of the Cairo genizah contain numerous examples of such *suftajas,* usually for much more modest sums, and they confirm that these instruments of credit were always scrupulously and strictly honored. In addition, there was extensive use of promissory notes, called *ṣakk* in Arabic, which were probably func-

tionally and etymologically the origins of our modern checks.

Medieval long-distance trade, whether it traversed international boundaries or moved within the vast expanse of the Islamic domain, required substantial investments of capital to cover the cost of acquiring goods at distant points and of transporting them and caring for them until they could be profitably disposed of. Given the means of transport and communication available to medieval merchants, any commercial enterprise, in order to succeed, necessarily involved the collaboration of many people. They were also subject to grave risks, both natural and man-made. Islamic law, which in this regard largely reflected commercial practice, provided traders with a wide array of possibilities for dealing with these problems. By means of a variety of flexible partnership arrangements, merchants were able to pool their capital to finance commercial enterprises; they were able to join together their time and energy for profitable trade, and, through these same partnerships, they were able to reduce risks and losses by distributing the burden among several parties.

One of the most versatile and important of such joint ventures was an arrangement that later became known in medieval Europe as the *commenda.* This was an agreement in which an investor entrusted capital or merchandise to an agent-manager who was to trade with it and then return to the investor the principal and a previously agreed share of the profits. For his labor the agent received the remaining share of the profits. In the event of an unsuccessful business venture, the financial loss was borne exclusively by the investor; the agent lost only the time and effort that he expended. The *commenda* (Arabic: *qirāḍ, muḍāraba*) blended the advantages of a loan with those of a partnership. As in a partnership, profits and risks were shared by both parties, the investor risking capital, the agent his time and effort. As in a loan, the *commenda* entailed no liability for the investor beyond the sum of money handed over to the agent, and when it accrued, the profit corresponded to the interest on a loan. The last point is especially important in view of the very strict prohibition in Islamic law against any explicit form of usury. On the whole, this ban was observed during most of the Middle Ages, but did not inhibit investment in trade because of the many licit ways one could obtain a good return on one's money through various accepted forms of commercial association.

Trade in the Islamic domain was also nurtured by a generally positive religious attitude toward commerce and toward the honest pursuit of profit. The prophet Muḥammad himself was a merchant by profession, as were some of his most distinguished Meccan followers. The Koran commends honest trading, as do numerous traditions attributed to the Prophet and his companions. The Prophet is quoted as declaring: "Seeking one's livelihood is a duty incumbent on every Muslim, as is the seeking of knowledge." A merchant who dies while traveling in the pursuit of trade is, according to one tradition, assured a place in paradise on the same level as a martyr who gives his life for the cause of Islam. The profit motive, that is, profit as the ultimate goal of any commercial endeavor, was not only approved by Islamic religious scholars, but was often made the criterion by which commercial conduct was judged. Any arrangement that enhanced the chances for profitability and did not violate any religious prohibition was accepted and considered licit.

MEDITERRANEAN TRADE

The extent and nature of trade between the Islamic world and Western Europe in the first centuries following the Islamic conquests have been the subjects of very important speculation and controversy in the historiography of medieval Europe. More than a half century ago, the distinguished medievalist Henri Pirenne enunciated his famous thesis that attributed the true beginning of the European Middle Ages to the consequences of the advent of Islam in the Mediterranean region. In his famous phrase, "Without Mohammed, Charlemagne is inconceivable." According to Pirenne's thesis, it was the shattering of the cultural and religious unity of the Mediterranean in the late seventh century by the spread of Islam on its eastern and southern shores that constituted the death knell of the Roman world. This development was, in his view, primarily a result of the near-total interruption of economic and commercial contact between the Middle East and Western Europe for at least two centuries, an interruption that forced Europe to shift its economic and cultural gaze away from the south toward the north, thus giving rise to new cultural, social, and political institutions—those of medieval Europe. While echoes of the lively historical debate provoked by the Pirenne thesis are still audible to this day, a certain consensus has been achieved. There is no question that commercial

contact between the Islamic Middle East and Western Europe seriously declined during the seventh through ninth centuries, but it did not entirely cease. Furthermore, long-term demographic and other trends were responsible for this decline. The Islamic states placed no political or other barriers in the way of commercial exchange between the two shores of the Mediterranean.

Until the early eleventh century, the preeminent commercial center of the Islamic world was located in Baghdad. Overland and maritime trade routes linked the markets of Iraq and Persia with the products of almost the entire civilized world—with India, China, and Malaysia in the Far East, with Central Asia and the Volga area to the north, with East Africa, Egypt, North Africa, and Byzantium to the south and west. In the early eleventh century, disturbances in the East and the commercial expansion of Western Europe combined to shift the commercial center of the Islamic domain to the southern and eastern Mediterranean, most particularly Egypt. It is also for this period and region that our documentation becomes much more abundant, thanks to the business records of Mediterranean and Indian Ocean merchants preserved among the documents of the Cairo genizah. The renewed trade between Europe and the Islamic areas of the Mediterranean that began in the eleventh century endured and continued to grow until the end of the Middle Ages.

During the eleventh and twelfth centuries, Egypt's chief indigenous export was flax and linen, commodities eagerly sought by European and North African merchants who frequented the markets of Cairo and Alexandria. Egypt also served, as it continued to do until the sixteenth century, as the transit market for Eastern spices (most notably, pepper) and other Oriental products. From the West, Egypt imported (and frequently reexported) silk from Spain and Sicily, textiles from various points around the Mediterranean, olive oil from Tunisia, and metals (iron, copper, lead, tin, and mercury) from Spain and other European countries. These commodities, of course, represent only the most important items of exchange, and were supplemented by a long list of exotic and less exotic (even ordinary) items. In the later Middle Ages, woods and metals figured very prominently in Egyptian imports, as did young male slaves to supply the Mamluk system of Egypt. European textiles also became more and more important as import items. In return, European merchants sought to acquire increasing quantities of Eastern spices.

The structure of trade in the Islamic world, nurtured by both a continuing internal demand and a growing demand from Europe and elsewhere, remained in place until the end of the Middle Ages and beyond. Even after the discovery of America and after the maritime discoveries of the late fifteenth century that gave Western Europe direct access to the markets of the Far East, the commercial activity within the Islamic domain continued virtually unabated. Given the worldwide expansion of trade, however, the markets of Islam were reduced to a kind of sideshow.

BIBLIOGRAPHY

Eliyahu Ashtor, *A Social and Economic History of the Near East in the Middle Ages* (1976); Claude Cahen, "Economy, Society, Institutions," in *Cambridge History of the Middle East,* II (1970), 511–538; Michael A. Cook, ed., *Studies in the Economic History of the Middle East* (1970); S. D. Goitein, *A Mediterranean Society,* I, *Economic Foundations* (1967), "Mediterranean Trade Preceding the Crusades: Some Facts and Problems," in *Diogenes,* 59 (1967), and, as compiler and translator, *Letters of Medieval Jewish Traders* (1973); Robert S. Lopez, "The Trade of Medieval Europe: The South," in *Cambridge Economic History of Europe,* II (1952), 257–354; *idem* and Irving W. Raymond, eds. and trans., *Medieval Trade in the Islamic World: Illustrative Documents Translated with Introductions and Notes* (1955, repr. 1961); Henri Pirenne, *Mohammed and Charlemagne,* Bernard Miall, trans. (1939, repr. 1963); A. L. Udovitch, *Partnership and Profit in Medieval Islam* (1970) and, as editor, *The Islamic Middle East, 700–1900: Studies in Economic and Social History* (1981).

A. L. UDOVITCH

[See also **Baghdad; Banking, Islamic; Cairo; Cairo Genizah; Commenda; Fairs; Furs, Fur Trade; Islam, Conquests of; Mamluk Dynasty; Mints and Money, Islamic; Roads in the Islamic World; Şinf; Slavery, Slave Trade; Taxation, Islamic; Travel and Transport, Islamic; Urbanism, Islamic; Usury, Islamic Law.**]

TRADE, WESTERN EUROPEAN. The trade of Western Europe in the Middle Ages was, on the large scale, divided into two great "trading spheres," each centered on an inland sea, and each with its own special characteristics. The trade of northern Europe centered on the Baltic and North seas and the river systems that empty into them.

Southern European trade looked to the Mediterranean as its great highway. In general terms the northern trade was characterized by bulk goods, such as foodstuffs and other basics, with few luxury goods of any importance. The trade of the south, while it included a large and active trade in bulk goods, took its characteristic "flavor" and much of its vigor from the carriage of Eastern luxury wares. These trading spheres overlapped in Flanders and Champagne, where merchants from all over Europe met at the great international fairs of the High Middle Ages, and later at the markets of Bruges and Antwerp.

There is also a fundamental chronological division of medieval trade that is as important as its geographical division. From the late Roman period until the end of the first millennium, trade was minimal and, as a general trend, in decline. Then, around the end of the tenth century, Western Europe began a period of sustained economic growth that was to last for 300 years.

The decline of the Roman Empire in the West was economic as well as political. The well-developed trading networks that existed within the empire began to crumble even before any significant barbarian incursions. The hold of Rome on the Western imagination has been such over the centuries that it is easy to forget that the magnificent life in marble halls was lived by only a very few. The typical denizen of the Roman Empire was not a toga-draped senator but a peasant living on the verge of starvation. Even in Rome itself the vast majority of the population was underemployed and living on the dole.

The largest-scale movement of goods within the empire was the regular shipment of grain from Egypt to Rome, but it is doubtful whether we should consider this to be trade at all, since it was organized by the government, paid for by tribute from all over the empire, and distributed to the emperor's clients, the Roman mob. The remaining movement of goods seems to have gone largely to support the army (again this was essentially a government activity) and to provide luxuries for the elite.

The civil wars of the third century A.D. had a disastrous effect on the fragile Roman economy. Diocletian's Edict on Maximum Prices, issued in 301, is dramatic evidence of the inflation and increasing government rigidity that the previous century's disturbances had brought about. This decline was accelerated in the West as the empire broke up into many kingdoms. It was increasingly impossible for the declining economy to support the refined and expensive tastes of the elite. In general, the standard of living of the upper classes continued to fall until after 900, despite occasional periods of amelioration. The standard of living of the majority of the population, the peasants, could not have fallen as much, since most of them were living only at a subsistence level even while the empire prospered. Still, their lot could not have been a happy one as the upper classes struggled to maintain their standard of living. This overall decline in the economy brought with it a reduction in the already small exchange of goods, both in the total amount of goods moved and in the distances over which they were transported.

EARLY MIDDLE AGES

Henri Pirenne's description of Western Europe in the ninth century as "a civilization which had retrogressed to the purely agricultural stage; which no longer needed commerce, credit, and regular exchange for the maintenance of the social fabric" became the central issue in a debate that has dominated discussions of the early medieval economy throughout most of the twentieth century. The "Pirenne thesis," simply stated, argued that commerce between East and West continued, though the center shifted eastward, until the rise of Islam broke the essential connections in the seventh century. Then, after the middle of the tenth century, commercial contacts were renewed through the Mediterranean and Baltic seas. In this view the Western European economy was dependent on the East, and through a kind of "contagion" theory of economic development it was assumed that once economic connections were opened, they spread and grew. The cause of the economic revival of Western Europe was seen as the obverse of the cause of its decline: the reestablishment of contact with areas where commerce had continued unbroken.

Two fundamental criticisms of this picture of the early medieval economy can be made. First, there was a good deal of decline before 700 that Pirenne minimized. Second, many of the details of the cutting of trade by Muslim expansion have been modified. It now seems clear that, just as the trade of the Roman Empire was not as extensive nor as rich as is often popularly imagined, so also there never was a time when trade disappeared entirely or when the economy of Western Europe "reverted completely to barter."

Studies of the early medieval economies that were prompted by Pirenne's seminal work have shown that trade, even long-distance trade between East and West, never entirely disappeared, though it did become exceedingly tenuous. Though undoubtedly the volume of commerce declined precipitously from an already small Roman base, there was, even in the eighth and ninth centuries, always some exchange. Even the costly fabrics and spices of the East continued to find their way west. In the tenth century Gerbert of Aurillac found Eastern silks and spices readily available in the markets of Italy. Still, there is no doubt that trade in the Carolingian period was pitifully small when compared to that of the Roman Empire, which Charlemagne wished to emulate.

As the standard of living declined in the West it remained relatively higher in the East, so that the goods and commodities that the West was able to provide were not particularly attractive in Byzantine and Islamic markets. Slaves, certain raw materials, such as timber, leather, grain, and salt, and a few cheap goods were sufficient to bring only a trickle of the coveted Eastern luxuries to the Germanic kingdoms. Trade within Western Europe itself also declined as local economies approached a degree of uniformity that made any substantial exchange of goods pointless. The growth of trade in Western Europe from the late tenth century on should be seen as the development of an underdeveloped area, rather than as the revival of a lost Roman economy.

Still, several forces were at work to maintain at least a minimal level of trade, even in the worst of times in the ninth century. First, necessity dictated that some goods be moved. Salt, the only effective preservative known and a highly prized condiment, was available in only a few places and was thus the object of a considerable commerce. Both archaeology and documentary sources attest to a trade in quernstones, which were necessary to grind grain into flour and for which really suitable stone was available in only a few geological formations. In the Merovingian period there was an important center of quernstone production in the Eifel Mountains that sent stones as far away as northern England. There is also evidence of trade in grain and other foodstuffs.

A second motivation, and one that produced a commerce whose historical visibility is out of all proportion to its size, was the demand of the elite political and religious leaders (a very small proportion of the population) for prestigious luxuries either for themselves, to underscore their rank in society, or to give to one another as suitably impressive gifts. The variety of these luxuries was much greater, even if the quantity in circulation was much smaller, than that of the more utilitarian goods. In the luxury category were precious metals, both as coin and plate; fine textiles (silks and fine woolens); fierce hunting dogs and spirited horses; falcons; strong, sharp swords; earthenware pots of striking design and elaborate decoration; glassware and window panes; wines; and spices. There were also stunning individual items, such as the elephant given to Charlemagne by Hārūn al-Rashīd or the small seventh-century statue of Buddha from northern India which was found at Helgö in Sweden.

The considerable traffic in human beings was also important. Slaves were the only product of Western Europe in great demand in the sophisticated markets of the East.

In the West, the establishment of the Frankish kingdom in the fifth century brought a shift toward the north in the demand for luxury goods. The heart of Frankish government was in the northern part of what had been Gaul, and the courts established there inevitably drew a large proportion of the luxury trade.

Most prominent among the merchants of the Frankish era were the inhabitants of Frisia, which lay along the North Sea coast of Europe. The Frisians engaged in a trade that linked the Frankish lands, Scandinavia, and Britain from the seventh to the ninth centuries. These coastal inhabitants were primarily farmers and fishermen whose familiarity with the seas and whose central location fitted them admirably for the role of part-time merchants. The scant and loosely organized commerce of the period could not support many full-time traders.

In the ninth century the Scandinavians burst on the European scene, opening the last period of barbarian invasions. The destruction wrought by Viking raids is well fixed in the popular imagination; their role as traders is less well known. The Vikings displaced the Frisians in the trade of the North Sea and the Rhine Valley and established a trading sphere of their own in the Baltic area that reached down the Russian rivers as far as Byzantium and Persia. They offered furs from Finland and Russia and slaves captured in their many raids. Indeed, slaves may well have been the staple item in Viking trade. Their greed for slaves undoubtedly contributed to the fear that their raids inspired. The

Viking center at Hedeby in southeastern Jutland was well situated for access to both the Baltic and the North Sea. In many ways the trade of the Vikings foreshadowed that of the later medieval Hansa.

In an age when the scale of trade was very small and the merchant's occupation was only part-time, buyers and sellers commonly gathered in convenient locations at prearranged times to exchange goods. These fairs soon became regular features of the medieval economic landscape. Regional fairs existed all over Europe, but a few became centers for the wholesale exchange of goods from distant lands. By the end of the eleventh century fairs located close to one another were being organized into "cycles" that spread the trading activities of the region in an orderly way through the year. One of the earliest of such cycles of fairs was organized in Flanders in the twelfth century. As the Flemish cities developed into permanent centers of exchange this fair cycle was abandoned. The best-known and most important of the medieval fair cycles was held in Champagne, a cycle of six fairs held in various towns on a rotating basis throughout the year. Carefully cultivated by the enlightened policies and good government of the counts of Champagne, these fairs were a crucial international market from the twelfth until the fourteenth century, when changing trade patterns and chronic warfare brought about their end.

RISE OF ITALIAN MERCHANTS

Throughout the Middle Ages luxury trade was certainly smaller in terms of tons of goods moved, and quite possibly in terms of gross value, but this was the trade that fired the imagination, then and now. Trade in exotic goods such as pepper and semiluxuries such as fine woolen cloth provided the greatest margins of profit and involved the elites of Western European society. These goods moved along a broad path that ran from the eastern shores of the Mediterranean through Italy to the mouths of the Rhine. In the early centuries of the Middle Ages this trade was largely in the hands of inhabitants of the Eastern lands: Greeks, Jews, and Syrians. Gradually the Italians were able to make the advantages of their central position felt. At first those Italian cities that were at least nominally a part of the Byzantine Empire were able to use this connection to replace the Easterners in the carrying trade. As the Byzantine navy declined in power, its chief base in the Adriatic, Ravenna, also declined and was replaced by Venice as an independent outpost of the Eastern Empire. Farther south on the Italian peninsula Amalfi, Gaeta, and Bari also prospered.

The Venetians exported slaves, timber, salt, iron, and fish from the lands at the head of the Adriatic in return for spices from the East. At the same time they built up a prosperous regional trade with the Po Valley. The trade of the southern cities was more complex. The agricultural products that were the chief wealth of southern Italy did not find so ready a market in Byzantium that they could be directly traded for expensive manufactured goods and Eastern spices. Instead they were shipped to North Africa, where they could be sold for gold from still further south or exchanged for wax or oil. These African goods were then shipped to Constantinople to be exchanged for the spices and other luxuries that the elites of the West demanded.

Toward the end of the tenth century Pisa and Genoa began to mount a counteroffensive against the Muslims who had occupied the islands of the western Mediterranean and had even established bases in southern France and Italy. Pisa was the leader in this alliance, Genoa very much the junior partner. Gradually Corsica and Sardinia were brought under their control. Until the Norman conquest of southern Italy and Sicily opened the entire sea to them (1072–1091), the two cities were confined to the western basin of the Mediterranean; they were less prosperous and less powerful than Amalfi and the other cities of Byzantine Italy. By the end of the eleventh century the northern Italian maritime cities—Pisa, Genoa, and Venice—were poised to assume the leading role in late medieval commerce that is so closely associated with their names.

It has been usual to attribute the dominance of the Italian cities in the Levantine trade of the late Middle Ages to the crusades, which brought them bases and trading posts in *Oltremare* (as they called the lands of the crusading states) and, in the Fourth Crusade, broke the power of the Byzantine Empire. The military power projected by the early crusades may well have accelerated the rise of the Italian cities to maritime dominance of the Mediterranean routes, but it should not be regarded as the sole factor in their success. The Italian maritime cities were on their way to establishing their leadership in Mediterranean trade before the crusading movement began. Venice, already strong and only nominally Byzantine, was granted important commercial privileges that gave its citizens an advantage over all other inhabitants of the empire in return for

helping to repel the Norman invasion of Dalmatia (1081–1085). When this crisis passed the Venetians were able consistently to cajole or bully the Byzantine emperors to renew their privileges. As Pisan and Genoese ships began to appear in the eastern Mediterranean it was already clear that the competition for domination of the Mediterranean was among the Italian cities.

By the beginning of the thirteenth century Italy was the leading commercial center of Western Europe, and Venice, Genoa, and Pisa were its most important trading cities.

Although Pisa and Genoa had been the most active in supporting the crusading armies along the coast of *Oltremare,* the Venetians reaped the greatest rewards as a result of the one crusade in which they did play a crucial role—the fourth. After the Fourth Crusade, Venice acquired an extensive chain of bases from the eastern shores of the Adriatic to the Golden Horn. Genoa and Pisa, early allies, fell into conflict in the twelfth and thirteenth centuries, and by 1284 the Genoese had prevailed, supplanting Pisa as the chief rival of Venice.

The main Venetian trade routes had their eastern termini in Constantinople, the ports of *Oltremare,* and Alexandria. Goods from these ports were shipped to Venice and from there went up the Po to markets in Lombardy or over the Alpine passes to the Rhône and into France. By the twelfth century, though, the Venetians began to encounter heavy competition from the Genoese and Pisans, who were more favorably placed geographically in relation to the French markets. By the early thirteenth century Venice had begun to develop Germany as an important hinterland. Linens, fustians, iron, and copper came to Venice from Germany for shipment to the east, while Greek wines and Egyptian cotton found their way back north.

Genoese merchants did not have as great a presence in Greece as the Venetians, though they did have a colony at Pera, across the Golden Horn from Constantinople. The Genoese presence was strongest in Cyprus, at Āyās (Lajazzo) in Cilicia, and, in the latter half of the thirteenth century, around the Black Sea. Although luxury goods were important to the Genoese (their colonies in the Black Sea area were important termini for caravans from the Orient), on the whole bulk commodities such as grain and alum made up the greater part of their cargoes. Grain from the Black Sea coasts and alum from the mines at Phocaea and Chios were a mainstay of Genoese trade, and they developed very large ships to handle these cheap, bulky cargoes efficiently.

By the middle of the thirteenth century the Genoese and Venetians had come into conflict. They fought four major wars before the end of the fourteenth century. In the end Venice dominated the lucrative luxury trade of the East and the Genoese shifted their attentions to bulk goods and to the western Mediterranean, where the markets of Spain and southern France proved very profitable for them. The ports of southern France gave the Genoese access to the Rhône Valley and thence to all of northern France.

The inland cities of Italy, such as Milan and Florence, did not develop as early as the maritime cities. Milan, centrally located in Lombardy near the water routes of the Po and the central and western Alpine passes, became a leading industrial and commercial center. Its large population, supported by the rich agriculture of the Lombard plain, provided a major market that underpinned the several fairs held there each year. Milan was a center for almost every kind of manufacture (it was especially known for cloth and arms), so that much of its trade was in goods that the city itself produced. In Tuscany, both Pisa and Lucca were originally ahead of Florence in economic development. The Arno, unlike the Po, is only rarely navigable as far upstream as Florence; Pisa, usually hostile to the Florentines, dominated its mouth. Thus, the Florentines were forced to seek their outlets to foreign markets through Ancona and Genoa. Not until the defeat of Pisa in 1406 did Florence have direct access to the sea. Specialization in high-quality woolen cloth, whether by finishing Flemish cloth or by manufacture from English and Spanish wool, gave Florentine industry a product that could bear high transportation costs.

COMMERCIAL TECHNIQUES

The feature that most distinguishes medieval trade from commerce in the modern age is its venturing nature. In modern wholesale trade, goods are not usually manufactured or acquired until a relatively certain market is assured, whether through actual orders or through sophisticated market research techniques. The medieval merchant had no such assurances when he acquired goods for sale. Merchandise was bought and transported in the hope, presumably based on experience, that it could be sold later at a profit.

For most of the Middle Ages it was necessary for a merchant to accompany his goods as they traveled from point of origin to market. This requirement necessarily limited the size of ventures as well as their duration. By about 1300 the Italians, especially, had perfected techniques of capital mobilization and of bookkeeping that enabled a talented, hardworking, and lucky entrepreneur to build and keep under control a large business organization. Traveling merchants were replaced at the upper end of the economic spectrum by resident merchants like the famous merchant of Prato, Francesco Datini. Established in one location for extended periods, they operated through networks of partnerships held together by correspondence. This system eventually came to dominate both the northern and southern trading spheres, although the Hansa merchants did not reach such sophisticated levels of management as did the Italians, who used advanced tools like double-entry bookkeeping.

THE LOW COUNTRIES AND THE HANSEATIC LEAGUE

The Low Countries were a center of trade second only to northern Italy. This area was filled with small- to middle-sized cities that were very active in the manufacture of high-quality woolen cloth. By the thirteenth century Bruges and Ghent were busy ports where Italian merchants came to buy cloth and to sell goods that the prosperous Flemings needed or desired. The *Zibaldone da Canal*, a fourteenth-century Venetian merchant's notebook, contains a list of forty-eight kinds of cloth that were imported into Venice. Twenty-eight of these are identified by place-names from northwest France and Flanders, reflecting the extent to which this area dominated cloth manufacture in the High Middle Ages. By the fifteenth century, commercial leadership in the Low Countries had shifted from Bruges to Antwerp, and the area had become the center of interregional trade. Here the two great trading spheres of north and south came together.

In the north, as the Viking raids subsided, the Scandinavians failed to keep pace with developing commercial techniques and were pushed out of the northern markets by the Germans. In the twelfth century a string of towns was established along the southern shore of the Baltic Sea, of which Lübeck was the most important. As they came to dominate the trade of the Baltic Sea, merchants from these towns followed the routes that the Vikings had opened eastward into Russia. They also established trading posts in Bruges and London in much the same way merchants from the south of Germany became established in their *Fondaco dei Tedeschi* (German warehouse) at Venice in the early thirteenth century. Throughout the thirteenth century the military conversion to Christianity of Prussia, Lithuania, and Livonia carried Germans and German trade northeastward along the Baltic coast. In order to regularize the exploitation of the new markets created by the foundation of German towns in these areas, the Hanseatic League was formed.

A loose organization of the German merchants who made Visby on the island of Gotland the center of their activities had existed from the twelfth century. It was, however, insufficiently strong to really protect the interests of those merchants. Several early leagues, or Hanse, were established in the thirteenth century in an attempt to provide more effective organization. But not until a league of Rhineland cities centering on Cologne joined with the Baltic ports in 1369 did the Hanseatic League as we usually think of it really come into existence.

The axis of Hanseatic trade ran from Reval in Estonia to London. The Baltic area at first exported forest products such as timber, pitch, honey, wax, and furs. Later, grain, especially rye, from Poland and Lithuania became more and more important, not reaching its peak until the seventeenth century. From France and the Low Countries, and through them from Italy, came luxury goods and Oriental spices for the elite.

The most important Baltic import, however, was not a luxury, but salt. The rise of Lübeck to dominance of the Hanseatic cities was at least partly due to salt from nearby Lüneburg that was traded eastward, where it was exchanged for the agricultural and forest products of Poland and Russia. It was also used to preserve the herring of the Skanör fish fairs and cod from Norway. Control of the salt, so necessary if the fish were to be shipped any distance, allowed the Germans early on to dominate the Scandinavian fish markets. These salted fish were shipped south to urban markets as far away as England and France and even northern Italy. The demand for salted fish was fueled by late-winter meat shortages and the religious requirements of the Lenten fast. As the trading networks of the German Hansa cities throve the demand for salt increased. Since it could be produced much more cheaply and efficiently by the solar evaporation of seawater in the southern parts of Western Europe, by the fourteenth century "bay salt" from the French coast along the Bay of Biscay—or more precisely, the Bay of Bourgneuf—became a major item in the return cargoes of Hanseatic ships.

TRANSPORTATION

The paths of medieval commerce can be determined in a general way, and any historical atlas or textbook dealing with the Middle Ages will have a map of "medieval trade routes" depicting a network of sea and land routes linking the major centers of trade. Roman roads survived into the medieval period, and, at some times and in some areas, there were laws requiring that they be maintained. They were, however, of less importance than is often imagined. The existence of paved roads, even in a state of disrepair, exerts a powerful attraction to the modern mind, accustomed as we are to automobile travel and its requirements. But the Roman roads were designed for marching legions of infantry, not for the pack animals and carts of merchants. The most useful feature of the Roman roads to the Middle Ages would have been the bridges that carried them over water obstacles. Yet the bridges were the first features to disintegrate with neglect, and, despite laws, orders, and exhortations to the contrary, the evidence is that they were not generally kept up. And, of course, in the areas of Western Europe outside the boundaries of the empire there never had been any roads. For the most part, unimproved tracks barely distinguishable from the surrounding countryside sufficed. These cowpaths—and many of them no doubt were literally that—wandered from place to place providing a great number of alternative routes.

Often politics were the deciding factor in determining which path trade would take at any particular time. Tolls were numerous. Landowners, both great and petty, often viewed the movement of merchants as a golden opportunity for gain. Charges were levied merely for the right to pass through the owner's holdings, without any connection to improvement or maintenance of a road or other aids to transportation. If costs became too great, or banditry too much of a threat, then traffic would seek alternative routes.

Transportation on land was by mule train or ox-drawn cart; on water by boat, ship, or barge. Much less effort is required to move a load on the almost frictionless surface of water than to move the same load overland. Less effort translated im-

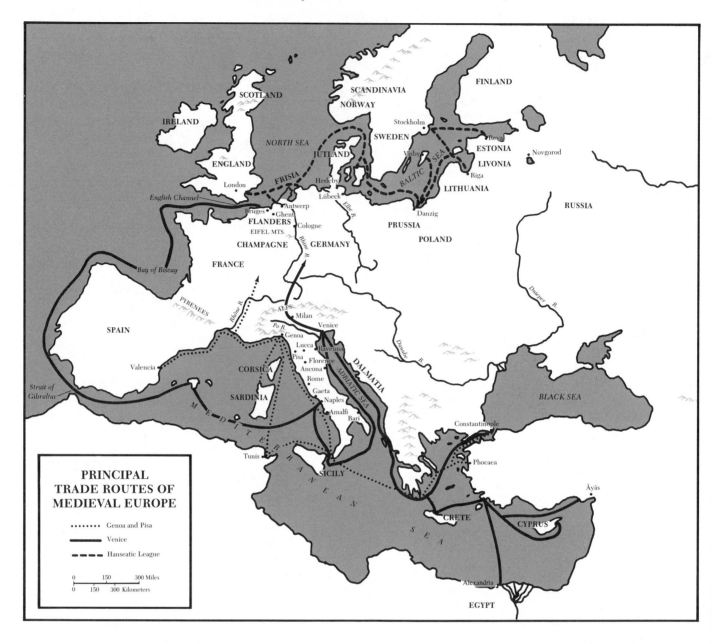

**PRINCIPAL
TRADE ROUTES OF
MEDIEVAL EUROPE**

········· Genoa and Pisa

————— Venice

- - - - - Hanseatic League

| 0 | 150 | 300 Miles |
| 0 | 150 | 300 Kilometers |

mediately into fewer men to pay and animals to feed and, therefore, less expense. For this reason rivers or sea routes were preferred whenever they were available. Rivers were the great highways of medieval commerce, and great rivers such as the Rhine, the Rhône, and the Po were very important commercial arteries. Wherever possible the inland routes followed rivers. If the rivers were swift, they could at least be used when going downstream. The smaller expense of water transportation even justified the enormous effort of building canals in many places. The Po Valley of northern Italy was an area

where the extensive canal network was especially well developed.

Since transportation by water was by far the least expensive way to move goods of all kinds, it is not surprising that the most successful trading centers of the Middle Ages were well situated in relation to water routes. This goes far to explain the success of the Italian cities of Venice and Genoa. The greatest water highway of them all was the Mediterranean Sea and its various connected basins and arms. A mere glance at a map of Europe shows that these two cities are located at the farthest northern extent of the Mediterranean sea routes. From Venice the Po is readily at hand, as well as several lesser rivers, and a relatively short overland haul (the expense of which luxury goods from the East could bear) would cross the easy passes in the eastern Alps to the Danube and even to the Rhine. Genoa did not have immediate access to an important river, but it was not far by sea from the mouth of the Rhône. The Genoese could also reach the Po Valley and the Alpine passes beyond via a relatively easy passage across the Apennines. In the late thirteenth century it was a Genoese merchant, Benedetto Zaccaria, who demonstrated the practicality of the route through Gibraltar to England and the Low Countries, though it was, in the end, the Venetians who exploited it the most thoroughly. Italy as a whole profited from its central position to build its role as the dominant middleman in the medieval economy.

LATE MIDDLE AGES

The population crisis of the fourteenth century, brought on by the Black Death and compounded by the enlarged scope and destructiveness of warfare, had predictable effects on trade toward the end of the Middle Ages. There may or may not have been a decline in the medieval economy that would justify speaking of the "depression of the Renaissance"; European-wide statistics that would allow a definitive answer in that controversy simply do not exist. It does, however, seem likely that the scope of trade was diminished. On the very simplest level, the size of the market was diminished and did not begin to recover until the late fifteenth century. There also appears to have been a greater disparity between rich and poor, so that while the few could, and did, spend large sums on ostentation, the market for ordinary goods was smaller in both relative and absolute terms.

The decline in urban populations often meant a contraction in the trade in bulk goods. For example, the northern Italian cities had imported large quantities of grain, sometimes over great distances. After the mid-fourteenth-century plagues most of them could feed themselves with the production of their own countrysides.

The commerce in Oriental luxuries, which by the end of the fourteenth century was dominated by Venice, was not interrupted by Turkish conquests in the fifteenth century any more than it had been stopped by the irruption of Islam in the seventh, nor was the opening of the route around

Africa by the Portuguese more than a temporary setback.

The Genoese suffered far more in the fifteenth century. Their politics became ever more chaotic. They lost Phocaea, the source of alum, which had been such an important element in their trade, and the Florentines became exporters of alum from the papal mines at Tolfa.

The Low Countries suffered in the late Middle Ages from the multiple blows of the Hundred Years War, silting harbors, and changing tastes. The last was probably the most disastrous. The fine woolen cloths that had been the backbone of the Flemish economy faced increased competition from linen and silk.

The evidence as we currently understand it strongly suggests that as the Middle Ages came to an end there was a considerable economic dislocation. Fernand Braudel has suggested that there is a kind of long-term rhythm to the European economy, a secular trend, which reached a crisis about 1350 and continued to decline until the beginning of the sixteenth century. The exact pattern of this crisis is as yet unclear; it may never be entirely plain, but it appears that the story of the trade of Western Europe in the Middle Ages ends as it began, with a tale of decline.

BIBLIOGRAPHY

John N. L. Baker, *Medieval Trade Routes* (1938); Egil Bakka, "Scandinavian Trade Relations with the Continent and the British Isles in Pre-Viking Times," in *Early Medieval Studies*, 3 (1971); A. R. Bridbury, "The Dark Ages," in *Economic History Review*, 22 (1969); *Cambridge Economic History of Europe*, 2nd ed., II (1952) and III (1963); Armand O. Citarella, "Patterns in Medieval Trade: The Commerce of Amalfi Before the Crusades," in *Journal of Economic History*, 28 (1968); Philippe Dollinger, *The German Hansa*, D. S. Ault and S. H. Steinberg, trans. and eds. (1970); Alfons Dopsch, *The Economic and Social Foundations of European Civilization*, M. G. Beard and Nadine Marshall, trans. (1937); Georges Duby, *The Early Growth of the European Economy*, Howard B. Clarke, trans. (1974); G. C. Dunning, "Trade Relations Between England and the Continent in the Late Anglo-Saxon Period," in Donald B. Harden, ed., *Dark-Age Britain* (1956); Moses I. Finley, *The Ancient Economy* (1973); Peter Garnsey, "Grain for Rome," in Peter Garnsey, Keith Hopkins, and C. R. Whittaker, eds., *Trade in the Ancient Economy* (1983); Jacques Heers, *Gênes au XVe siècle* (1961); Wilhelm von Heyd, *Histoire du commerce du Levant au moyen âge*, 2 vols. (1885–1886, repr. 1959); Richard Hodges, *Dark Age Economics* (1982).

Dirk Jellema, "Frisian Trade in the Dark Ages," in *Speculum*, 30 (1955); Frederic C. Lane, *Andrea Barbarigo, Merchant of Venice* (1944), *Venice and History* (1966), and *Venice: A Maritime Republic* (1973); Archibald R. Lewis, *Naval Power and Trade in the Mediterranean, A.D. 500–1100* (1951) and *The Northern Seas: Shipping and Commerce in Northern Europe, A.D. 300–1100* (1958); Archibald R. Lewis and Timothy J. Runyan, *European Naval and Maritime History, 300–1500* (1985); Robert S. Lopez, *The Commercial Revolution of the Middle Ages, 950–1350* (1971, repr. 1976) and *Su e giù per la storia di Genova* (1975); Robert S. Lopez and Irving W. Raymond, eds. and trans., *Medieval Trade in the Mediterranean World* (1955); Gino Luzzatto, *An Economic History of Italy from the Fall of the Roman Empire to the Beginning of the Sixteenth Century*, Philip Jones, trans. (1961); Harry A. Miskimin, *The Economy of Early Renaissance Europe, 1300–1460* (1969); Iris Origo, *The Merchant of Prato: Francesco di Marco Datini* (1957); Henri Pirenne, *Economic and Social History of Medieval Europe*, I. E. Clegg, trans. (1937); Norman J. G. Pounds, *An Economic History of Medieval Europe* (1974).

Gerhard Rösch, *Venedig und das Reich: Handels- und verkehrspolitische Beziehungen in der deutschen Kaiserzeit* (1982); Mikhail I. Rostovtzeff, *The Social and Economic History of the Roman Empire*, 2nd ed. (1957); Jeremy A. Sabloff and C. C. Lamberg-Karlovsky, eds., *Ancient Civilization and Trade* (1975); Adolf Schaube, *Handelsgeschichte der romanischen Völker des Mittelmeergebiets bis zum Ende der Kreuzzüge* (1906); Wolfgang von Stromer, "Nuremberg in the International Economics of the Middle Ages," in *Business History Review*, 44 (1970); Fernand Vercauteren, "The Circulation of Merchants in Western Europe from the 6th to the 10th Century: Economic and Cultural Aspects," in Sylvia L. Thrupp, ed., *Early Medieval Society* (1967); C. R. Whittaker, "Late Roman Trade and Traders," in Peter Garnsey, Keith Hopkins, and C. R. Whittaker, eds., *Trade in the Ancient Economy* (1983).

JOHN E. DOTSON

[See also **Accounting; Banking, European; Barbarians, Invasions of; Bruges; Champagne, County; Charlemagne; Constantinople; Crusades and Crusader States; Exploration; Fairs; Fairs of Champagne; Flanders and the Low Countries; Florence; Furs, Fur Trade; Genoa; Ghent; Glass, Western European; Gotland; Hanseatic League; Hārūn al-Rashīd; Hedeby; Islam, Conquests of; Italy, Byzantine Areas of; Italy, Rise of Towns in; Law, French: In South; Lübeck; Markets, European; Metalsmiths, Gold and Silver; Milan; Mints and Money; Navigation; Normans and Normandy; Pera-Galata; Pisa; Pottery; Ravenna; Roads and Bridges; Roman Egypt, Late; Roman Empire, Late; Salt Trade; Ships and Shipbuilding; Slavery, Slave Trade; Textiles; Travel and Transport; Venice; Vikings; Wine; Wool.**]

TRADE, WESTERN EUROPEAN: REGULATION OF. European trade regulations over the thousand-year period of the Middle Ages were varied and sometimes intricate. In Western Europe in the tenth century, for example, there was very little trade. This is in sharp contrast to the highly regulated economy in the Byzantine Empire or the bustling bazaars in the Islamic world. Furthermore, conditions in Western Europe in the tenth century give no hint of the sophisticated commercial society of the later Middle Ages.

In Western Europe, many different levels of authority were involved in regulating trade. Some forms of regulation, such as the standardization of money, weights, and measures, were recognized as sovereign rights. During the disorders of the early Middle Ages, however, these rights were often delegated to or usurped by local powers. Their history in the later Middle Ages is one of recovery of control by revitalized central powers. These central powers were also increasingly active in regulating other areas of trade, granting privileges to individual foreign merchants, entering into treaties providing for reciprocal rights, and otherwise encouraging economic development within their territory.

Local authorities were more effective in regulating the everyday operations of the marketplace. Enlightened territorial lords as well as municipal governments recognized the benefits to be realized from commercial exchange. Private groups of merchants and tradesmen, such as guilds, were also active in regulating the production and sale of goods.

The church played an important role in the regulation of trade. This role was highly complex and has therefore often been misunderstood. The church was a source of doctrine that influenced business practice. It was also an actor of major importance in both economic and political matters. As a wealthy institution that served both as producer and consumer of goods and as a focal point for social activities, the church served as a catalyst for the recovery of European economic life, providing means and occasion for the exchange of goods as well as of ideas.

In general, the regulation of trade in the Middle

Ages in Western Europe attempted to establish controls over the quantity and quality of goods available in the marketplace and to encourage the development of commercial activity. In the process it created many of the concepts of orderly but competitive markets, fair trade, standardization, and truth in labeling that underpin the modern commercial world, and that are taken for granted today.

FROM ITINERANT MERCHANTS
TO SEDENTARY MARKETS

Until the eleventh century, almost all local commerce was conducted in the local marketplace. This was usually nothing more than an open space where crowds might gather, possibly adjacent to a parish church. A cemetery might be the site of a local market, providing not only open space but also hallowed ground where lawless elements, who might not hesitate to plunder the goods of an itinerant peddler if they met him en route, might think twice before defying a higher judge. With the recovery of economic life in the eleventh century, the value of land surrounding cemeteries increased substantially.

The open spaces that served as marketplaces were furnished with stalls and benches, which merchants could rent from the local lord, who controlled the market. In the course of time, the lord might construct halls to provide shelter for those doing business in the marketplace. The rental of places in the market proved to be a lucrative source of income for the local lord, who could also profit from duties on incoming merchandise, fees on the use of his weights and measures, and fines levied on litigants in his court. He might also require that retailers be licensed, as were the butchers of St. Ives in Huntingdonshire, site of an important fair in England. Most local markets never developed any further. They served the needs of local commerce by attracting buyers and sellers within a radius of one day's travel to and from the market. In time, local merchants tended to conduct business more and more from their own homes, although foreign merchants were often restricted to trading in the marketplace.

Meanwhile, the more successful markets began to attract merchants from greater distances, particularly on important feast days. In the course of the twelfth century, some of these came to be organized into the great cycles of fairs that were spaced out over the year, providing a quasi-permanent market

in the areas to which international merchants flocked. The great cycles of fairs served as transitional institutions that bridged the gap between the largely self-sufficient agrarian society that existed around the year 800 and the complex commercial economy of the later Middle Ages.

By stimulating international trade, the fairs precipitated their own demise. As the volume of trade increased, it eventually became sufficient to support the activities of sedentary merchants, who acted through agents and factors in the major commercial centers of Western Europe.

Merchants faced considerable danger in traveling to and from the fairs or other centers of international trade. The attitude of the lord of the territory through which the merchants traveled varied tremendously from place to place and from time to time. During the Carolingian period, international merchants were often granted personal privileges, including exemptions from customs and tolls, to encourage their activities. In the eleventh century, the proclamation of the Truce of God stimulated trade by threatening anathemas to those who violated the peace by preying on travelers on certain days of the week.

As the routes became more frequently traveled, enlightened rulers, such as the late-twelfth and early-thirteenth-century counts of Champagne, granted safe-conducts to international merchants traveling in their territories. These contributed significantly to the success of many fairs, as they did for the fairs of Champagne. The depredations of the robber barons in the Rhineland during the later Middle Ages, however, seriously discouraged the commerce in that area.

Merchant guilds organized armed convoys for the mutual protection of their members on long-distance journeys, and guild regulations often stipulated the arms that guild members were expected to bear. In the later Middle Ages, the services of professional carters enabled international merchants to avoid the rigors of the trip by shipping goods to associates, agents, or factors.

Privileges were sometimes granted to merchants in return for services. During the crusades, the Venetians received extensive privileges in the Kingdom of Jerusalem in return for their military aid, including the right to have their own church, baths, and oven; freedom from taxation; and the right to be judged by their own laws in cases involving only Venetians. Later, Florentine merchants were granted rights by the kings of Naples to export grain from southern Italy in return for loans to the Neapolitan crown. In 1311, the Florentine exports amounted to around 45,000 tons of grain. Even in 1329, a year of famine, the Florentines were permitted to export wheat from Apulia despite the threat of local riots.

The granting of generous privileges to foreign merchants in exchange for services to the crown, however, created a potentially dangerous situation for them as well. Their privileged position was often deeply resented by the local populace. Moreover, what can be given can also be taken away. In the fourteenth century, Italian merchants received extensive trading privileges in England in return for loans to the crown. Thought safe, such loans proved to be as risky as any other. Edward III defaulted on his loans in 1341, resulting in the bankruptcy of the great banking houses of the Peruzzi in 1343 and the Bardi in 1346, which provoked a chain reaction in the industry from which the Florentine economy never completely recovered.

The central government sometimes intervened against the interests of foreign merchants in order to protect local interests. In 1277, Philip III of France prohibited the exportation of wool and wheat and other grains from the country. In 1303, Pisa prohibited the importation of semifinished woolens in order to protect the local industry.

Foreign merchants in a city were often restricted in their housing to a particular quarter or building. Restrictions were also placed on their conduct of business. They might, for instance, be required to trade in the marketplace, where they could be more easily supervised, rather than at their residences or in the port of embarkation.

WEIGHTS, MEASURES, AND PRICES

The maintenance of standards of weights and measures was one of the regalian rights of sovereignty. The early Carolingian rulers reformed the weights and measures being used in lands under their control, and were concerned with maintaining uniform standards. In subsequent periods, however, the authority to supervise standards was often granted to local potentates or usurped, so that by the eleventh century there were enormous variations in standards from one community to the next. For instance, the bushel, which was the basic measure used for dry products throughout France, varied not only from place to place but, within the same locale, from one item to the next: the bushel of wheat differed from that of oats, wood, or salt.

Communities were zealous in upholding their local standards. Local authorities required that merchants use the local weights and measures and sometimes placed authenticated measures in a public place, such as the door of the town hall, where they could be consulted to confirm the accuracy of the weights being used in the transactions.

Heavy penalties were imposed on those who used other measures. The laws of Frederick II of Sicily (d. 1250) imposed a fine of one pound of gold on anyone using false weights and measures. If the perpetrator was unable to pay, he was to be publicly flogged, with the weight or measure hung around his neck. His hand was to be amputated for a second offense, and he was to be hung for a third. The town of Châtillon, in Burgundy, imposed a fine of sixty-five sous *tournois* on the seller if the measures were too small; if they were too large, he was fined only five sous. The merchant might also suffer confiscation of his goods. In 1275, when a canvas dealer at the fair of St. Ives was found to have used a false measure, not only were his goods seized but also those of three other canvas dealers with whom he shared a booth at the fair.

Authorities were also concerned about prices. The just price, for medieval merchants and traders in Western Europe, was the price established by the community as a whole, through the unfettered conduct of business in the marketplace. If one wished to find out what the just price was, one would go to the marketplace and find out what was being paid for a given commodity. Under certain circumstances, such as times of famine, the proper authorities, in their capacity as representatives of the community as a whole, could intervene on behalf of the community to set prices.

In England, the Assize of Measures in 1196 established a national system of measures. The various assizes of bread controlled the cost of bread by regulating the weight of loaves of various grains according to the price of the grain from which they were made. The higher the cost of the grain, the smaller the loaf of bread. The price for the loaf of bread remained the same. The weight of each type of loaf was established locally each year on the basis of the price of each type of grain, subject to change if there were significant fluctuations in the price of grain.

The individual, however, was forbidden to take any action that would affect the market price for his own personal profit. Laws prohibiting forestalling (preventing commodities from reaching the market), engrossing (attempting to corner the market), and regrating (buying in quantity in the market for resale in the surrounding countryside at exorbitant prices) were very common. As long as a merchant did nothing to manipulate the price, he was justified in accepting whatever people were willing to pay.

St. Thomas Aquinas discussed the dilemma faced by a merchant who arrived with a shipload of grain in a town that was experiencing a famine. The merchant knew that just one day out there were two other ships loaded with grain headed for this port. Must he reveal that information to his potential customers? No, said St. Thomas. As long as the merchant had done nothing to impede the other ships' arrival, he was justified in charging whatever the price was in the marketplace. It might, however, be charitable on his part to reveal the information.

Guilds often attempted to regulate the prices their members charged. Municipal governments were often controlled by the guilds, so it is not surprising that the laws against practices that interfered with the freedom of trade were not invoked to control the guilds. They were, however, used to punish journeymen's associations that went on strike for higher wages and better working conditions, on the grounds that such actions were in restraint of trade. The tensions between masters and journeymen were particularly intense in Flanders with the decline of the Flemish textile industry in the late Middle Ages and as the journeymen sank into the ranks of the impoverished.

QUALITY CONTROLS

The guilds played a major role in regulating the quality of manufactured goods. Guild regulations often included standards of workmanship, and by the end of the Middle Ages an applicant for membership in a guild was often required to demonstrate that he was capable of meeting those standards by submitting a sample of his work (his masterpiece). Regulation of conditions in the workshop, such as the almost universal prohibition against work by candlelight, would sometimes affect the quality of goods. The regulations might also specify the quality of the raw materials to be used or prohibit such practices as mixing poor-quality materials with good, or re-using old materials.

Manufactured goods were often marked to show the workshop from which they came. The mark of a particular master came to be recognized and to command a better price than that of another. The marks were often recorded in the records of the guilds, and the value of a known trademark was recognized by the fact that, when a master retired from business, his mark could be sold.

In the early stages of the recovery of the economy in the twelfth and thirteenth centuries, when there was plenty of opportunity for all, the guild regulations were by and large beneficial. As the economy began to contract in the later Middle Ages, and as guild members became more and more concerned with protecting their own interests and way of life, the guilds were often in opposition to economic innovation and protective of vested interests.

It was more difficult to control the quality of agricultural products than that of manufactured goods. Wine, perhaps more than most other agricultural commodities, offered ample opportunities for nefarious practices. The medical writer Arnald of Villanova (d. 1311) reported that "some wine dealers cheat people when they taste the wines. They make bitter and sour wines appear sweet by persuading the wine tasters to eat first licorice or nuts or old salty cheese or dishes that have been well cooked with spices." He recommended that customers taste in the morning, after rinsing out their mouths and eating a few bites of bread dipped in water, "for whoever tries out a wine on a quite empty or on a quite full stomach will find his mouth and his tasting spoiled." Other techniques were used to mask sourness or weakness. The wines might be heated to produce a fuller, more pleasurable taste, a practice that only hastened their spoilage.

Numerous regulations dealt with the adulteration of wines. The consuls of Toulouse, for example, issued regulations against the addition of such noxious substances as clay, salt, brazil, alum, calomel, and lime. Watered wine was also a very common problem, and, since new wines were generally more expensive than old, the mixture of old wines with new was sometimes prohibited except for the purpose of replenishing barrels for the loss due to evaporation. The statutes of the wine merchants of Paris forbade any mixing or blending of wines and barred the storage of any substance, such as the dregs of wine or putrified wine, that might be used to fool the public.

In Paris the taverner was required to grant access to his cellar to anyone who wished to observe him drawing the wine from the barrels, on pain of a fine of £4 *parisis* for each violation, one of which went to the accuser. In Oxford, complaints of university scholars in 1293 that local taverns were selling putrid wines led to a royal inquiry and ultimately to royal regulation of standards and prices. London taverners could not even store Rhenish and other white wines or sweet and dry wines in the same cellar.

The penalties for infractions of these regulations were very severe. The statutes of Liège of 1317 threatened those who adulterated wines with excommunication, confiscation, or three years' banishment, in addition to fines. The authorities in England in 1364 were inclined to let the punishment fit the crime when John Penrose, taverner of the City of London, was convicted of selling unwholesome wine. He not only lost the right to trade as a vintner but was also sentenced to drink a draft of his own brew and to have it poured over his head. The loss of reputation might be sufficient to impose serious penalties on the miscreant. An important London merchant of the fifteenth century who was charged with defrauding a customer found that he was unable to sell his wines in the city and was forced to accept a lower price than his competitors accepted from out-of-town customers.

Authorities were also concerned with proper labeling of goods. The 1607 statutes of the wine brokers of Beaune undoubtedly reflected medieval practices when they warned their members, "Let them not mark any wines with the mark of the town which are not good and worthy of the mark, on pain of being immediately removed from office." This concern for the accurate identification of the place of origin of wines was very common. The twelfth-century customs of St. Omer, for example, included a provision requiring the proper identification of wines by origin. In Bergerac in 1322 Renaud V, seigneur of Pons, restricted the use of the place-name to wines produced in that area, and four years later a distinctive mark was introduced. By the late Middle Ages each town had a distinctive method of binding the wine barrels, further helping to identify place of origin.

The proper identification of the place of origin was of concern to the authorities in the areas in which the wines were marketed as well as in the areas in which they were produced. In 1332, Bishop Adolph of Liège justified his regulation of wine sales as a response to popular complaints about the uncertainty of the provenance of some of the wines offered for sale. In Paris, since wines were taxed

from the fourteenth century on according to their place of origin, officials had an added incentive to ensure proper identification. The rewards for mislabeled wines were still sufficient to tempt unscrupulous dealers. There is a record in Burgundy of a case in 1475 in which a merchant was found guilty of having bound sixty barrels of wine of Tournus in the manner of the wines of Beaune.

THE IMPLEMENTATION OF REGULATIONS

International merchants—venturing into strange and often hostile environments—needed some protection against the arbitrariness of local authorities as well as the expeditious resolution of disputes and, occasionally, assistance in enforcing contracts. In addition, foreign merchants and their goods might be seized by local authorities as a reprisal for misdeeds committed by other citizens of their homeland. It was therefore in their interest to see to it that their homeland cooperated with the distant communities in enforcing obligations and judgments against the appropriate parties.

The Magna Carta granted protection to the persons and goods of foreign merchants who were in England at the time of the outbreak of hostilities with their homeland, as long as English merchants were safe in their country, and the Statute of Westminster of 1275 forbade the distraint of a foreign merchant for a debt that was not his. International treaties frequently included reciprocal agreements to this effect.

Commercial disputes could always be heard in the local courts, be they seignorial, municipal, or guild courts, but such litigation was often protracted and involved procedures with which the foreign merchant was unfamiliar, in an environment in which he would be viewed with suspicion, if not outright hostility. Foreign merchants required more expeditious, equitable, and informal proceedings. Special merchant courts, such as the Pie Powder courts of England (so called because of the dusty feet of the travelers, the *pieds poudrés*), developed at fairs and markets to serve these needs. The merchant courts were presided over by merchant judges who dispensed a kind of common law for merchants, based on internationally recognized commercial practice and heavily laced with considerations of equity. Merchant courts might also hear claims originating elsewhere, when appropriate. For example, a party might be able to sue at one fair for debts payable at another. Many of the basic principles of modern commercial law were hammered out in these courts, such as the distinctions between real property and chattels, the acceptance of the use of documents to create obligations and transfer property, the introduction of the notion of implied warranties, and the creation of the law of trademarks and patents.

The wholesale buyer was often a stranger to the area of production and could not be expected to be familiar with local commercial practices, weights, and measures, or even the local dialect in which business was conducted. On the other hand, the local citizen needed protection against the unscrupulous practices of foreign merchants who were there one day, gone the next. By the late Middle Ages a variety of officials were on hand to watch out for the consumer's interests, including brokers, town criers, binders, and keepers of weights and measures.

Brokers played an important role in serving as middlemen for the wholesale merchant and also as regulatory agents because of the requirements imposed on them by their professional associations. Sometimes the connection was explicit. At the fairs of St. Ives, a number of brokers served at the same time as fair officials, responsible for maintaining standard measures of canvas.

Brokerage came to be a ubiquitous commercial practice in Western Europe in the late Middle Ages; brokers were active in the commerce of wood, cloth, grain, and virtually every other commodity for which there was a large international market. The earliest reference to a broker occurs in the Genoese records of Giovanni Scriba in 1154. By the thirteenth century brokers were to be found in every important town involved in international commerce. Once again, some of the best examples come from the wine trade.

The use of brokerage in wine sales is attested in a letter of 1319 from King Philip V of France, in which he cites wine brokers as being in the first rank of professions concerned with provisioning the city of Paris. The king stipulated payment for the service at the rate of twelve deniers per barrel of wine, six for the broker and six for himself.

The institution of brokerage combined both public and private functions. On the one hand the broker was to serve the merchant by whom he was paid. On the other he was to supervise foreign merchants and protect local interests. His remuneration was normally paid by the buyer at a specified rate per unit, and he was not to accept other forms of remuneration. The statutes of Liège of 1332, for example, forbade him to accept any presents or gifts. The presence of a wine broker was required in Liège whenever wines belonging to foreign merchants were tasted in the cellars of the town.

The method of appointing brokers varied from place to place and from time to time. Until 1468 the brokers of Dijon were appointed by the municipal government for one-year terms shortly after the election of the mayor, which took place in June. After that date the office was normally farmed out. By then there were five or six brokers each year who served under the supervision of one of the aldermen. The broker had to be a local citizen and was often prohibited from participating in a related line of work, such as commerce or cooperage. The statutes of Liège also forbade the host of a merchant from serving as his broker, although this practice was common elsewhere.

Criers were employed to advertise the wines for sale, where they might be found, and their price. A thirteenth-century ordinance from Toulouse quoted one such cry: "Go to the cellar of Raimond or William for the good wine of Caraman or Lanta or Verfeil or Balma." Criers were forbidden to announce the wines as originating anywhere but in the place of their growth. The criers of Paris were required to take an oath to be on the lookout for good measures and to report bad ones if they should find any. Taverners found guilty of using bad measures were fined.

The crier could enter any tavern and cry its wine as long as the tavern had retail wines for sale and did not already have a crier. If the crier found people drinking in the tavern, he would ask them what price they paid and advertise that price, whether the taverner wanted him to or not. The taverner could not refuse his services; if the taverner did not permit him to enter the house, the crier could advertise the wines at the rates charged by the king. If the taverner claimed that he did not have wines for sale, he was required to take an oath to that effect. The crier was thus a supervisor of the retail trade, investigating not only the place of origin of the wines offered for sale but also the price charged and measures used by local taverners.

A crier of Paris in the late thirteenth century received four deniers a day from the tavern and was prohibited by his oath from accepting more. He had to pay one denier for each day he held office to the Brotherhood of the Merchants of Paris. This was due even if he did not have a tavern to cry, except for Sundays, days of sickness, or days on which he was on pilgrimage. He was expected to cry the wines twice a day except during Lent, on Sundays and Fridays, during Christmas week, and on the eve of major feasts, when he cried only once a day. On Good Friday or on the day of the death of the king, the queen, or one of their children, he was not required to cry at all. If the king put his own wines up for sale, all other sales were to cease and all of the criers were to advertise the wines of the king, "morning and evening, at the crossroads of Paris."

Other officials protected the buyer against misrepresentation and the use of false weights and measures. Goods were wrapped in special outer cloths, tied with ropes, and sealed by officials to prevent adulteration of the product. Even so, such bundles were not above suspicion. Special wardens accompanied the Flemish wool merchants to the English fairs in the mid thirteenth century. Guild regulations required each merchant to submit his cloths to the wardens for inspection before offering them for sale, to prevent the use of false seals that would enable dealers of inferior goods to misrepresent their wares.

Since each community had a distinctive method of binding its wine barrels, towns in wine-producing areas sometimes appointed an official binder. One is mentioned in Dijon in 1468, but in view of the concern for proper labeling of barrels the office probably originated much earlier. Official measurers were also appointed to see that the size of the barrels conformed to the standard. The measurer was entrusted with the official measure, a bar of metal like a yardstick. Wine barrels that conformed to the regulations were marked with his official mark, and fines were imposed for those that were not. In Dijon in the fifteenth century there were three measurers, who were named to office in the beginning of November, soon after the new wines came on the market, and who served one-year terms. They normally worked in pairs, unless the sale involved less than three barrels of wine.

Other commodities and manufactured goods likewise came under the regulatory control of the central or royal government. In England, for example, after the Assize of Cloth in 1196, all woolen cloths were to have a standard width of about two yards. Each city, town, or county was required to appoint four to six men to enforce its provisions. Penalties were established for infractions. The impact of royal control in England, however, was a long-drawn-out process and was not without opposition. In the mid thirteenth century, Henry III attempted to apply the provisions of the assize to foreign cloths as well. The Flemish merchants made a formal protest in 1254 because they were unaccustomed to such standardization. In the end, the attempt to regulate foreigners was apparently abandoned.

There was also opposition from local authorities to royal control. The records of the fairs of St. Ives reveal a dispute in 1291 between a representative of the crown and the officers of the fair over who should appoint the supervisor of the measures. In the end, the authority of the local lord to appoint the supervisor was upheld, as long as he enforced the royal regulations.

BIBLIOGRAPHY
David Abulafia, "Southern Italy and the Florentine Economy, 1265–1370," in *Economic History Review,* 2nd ser., **34** (1981); Howard L. Adelson, *Medieval Commerce* (1962); John W. Baldwin, "The Medieval Merchant Before the Bar of Canon Law," in *Papers of the Michigan Academy of Science, Arts, and Letters,* **44** (1959); Rosalind Kent Berlow, "The Development of Business Techniques Used at the Fairs of Champagne," in *Studies in Medieval and Renaissance History,* **8** (1971); and "The 'Disloyal' Grape: The Agrarian Crisis of Late Fourteenth-century Burgundy," in *Agricultural History,* **56** (1982); Harold J. Berman, "Mercantile Law," in his *Law and Revolution* (1983); Étienne Boileau, *Le livre des métiers,* René de Lespinasse and François Bonnardot, eds. (1879); E. Boutaric, "Des poids et mesures au quatorzième siècle," in *Revue des sociétés savantes des départements,* 2nd ser., **3** (1860); Kenneth S. Cahn, "The Roman and Frankish Roots of the Just Price of Medieval Canon Law," in *Studies in Medieval and Renaissance History,* **6** (1969); Eleanora M. Carus-Wilson, *Medieval Merchant Venturers* (1954); J. Délissey and L. Perriaux, "Les courtiers gourmets de la ville de Beaune," in *Annales de Bourgogne,* **34** (1962); François L. Ganshof, *Histoire des relations internationales,* I, *Le moyen âge* (1953); John T. Gilchrist, *The Church and Economic Activity in the Middle Ages* (1969); David Herlihy, Robert S. Lopez, and Vsevolod Slessarev, eds., *Economy, Society, and Government in Medieval Italy* (1969); J. A. van Houtte, "Les courtiers au moyen âge: Origine et caractéristiques d'une institution commerciale en Europe occidentale," in *Revue historique de droit français et étranges,* 4th ser., **15** (1936).

Maryanne Kowaleski, "The Commercial Dominance of a Medieval Provincial Oligarchy: Exeter in the Late Fourteenth Century," in *Mediaeval Studies,* **46** (1984); Robert S. Lopez and Irving W. Raymond, trans. and eds., *Medieval Trade in the Mediterranean World* (1955); Michel Mollat, *Le commerce maritime normand à la fin du moyen âge* (1952); Ellen Wedemeyer Moore, *The*

Fairs of Medieval England (1985); Iris Origo, *The Merchant of Prato: Francesco di Marco Datini* (1957); Norman J. G. Pounds, *An Economic History of Medieval Europe* (1974); John H. Pryor, "The Origins of the *Commenda* Contract," in *Speculum*, **52** (1977), and "Mediterranean Commerce in the Middle Ages: A Voyage Under Contract of *Commenda*," in *Viator*, **14** (1983); Yves Renouard, *Les hommes d'affaires italiens du moyen âge* (1949, new ed. 1968) and *Études d'histoire médiévale*, 2 vols. (1968); Kathryn L. Reyerson, "Commercial Fraud in the Middle Ages: The Case of the Dissembling Pepperer," in *Journal of Medieval History*, **8** (1982); Raymond de Roover, "The Concept of the Just Price: Theory and Economic Policy," in *Journal of Economic History*, **18** (1958), and "The Organization of Trade," in *Cambridge Economic History of Europe*, III (1963); Alan S. C. Ross, "The Assize of Bread," in *Economic History Review*, 2nd ser., **9** (1956); Frank I. Schechter, *The Historical Foundations of the Law Relating to Trademarks* (1925); Sylvia L. Thrupp, *The Merchant Class of Medieval London, 1300–1500* (1948); Philippe Wolff, *Commerces et marchands de Toulouse (vers 1350–vers 1450)* (1954).

ROSALIND KENT BERLOW

[See also **Arnald of Villanova; Banking, European; Champagne, County; Fairs; Fairs of Champagne; Food Trades; Guilds and Métiers; Hanseatic League; Markets; Roads and Bridges; Travel and Transport; Urbanism; Usury; Weights and Measures; Wine Trade.**]

Traditio clavium, depicted in a miniature from the Evangeliary of Henry II. Munich Bayerische Staatsbibliothek, cod. lat. 4452, fol. 152v., *ca.* 1007–1014. FOTO MARBURG / ART RESOURCE

TRADITIO CLAVIUM (delivery of the keys), based on Matthew 16:19, represents Christ's bestowal of the keys of heaven on St. Peter. It thus symbolizes his preeminence over the other apostles and, by extension, the primacy of the bishop of Rome. In medieval versions of the scene, as in the apse of S. Costanza, Rome, or the Pericopes of Henry II, Peter receives one or two keys with veiled hands and while standing. The *traditio clavium* is often combined with the *traditio legis*.

BIBLIOGRAPHY

Johannes Kollwitz, "Christus als Lehrer und die Gesetzübergabe an Petrus in der konstantinischen Kunst Roms," in *Römische Quartalschrift*, **44** (1936); Joachim Poeschke, "Schlüsselübergabe an Petrus," in *Lexikon der christlichen Ikonographie*, IV (1972); Louis Réau, *Iconographie de l'art chrétien*, II, pt. 2 (1957), 313–315.

MICHAEL T. DAVIS

[See also **Iconography; Orcagna, Andrea (with illustration); Traditio Legis.**]

TRADITIO LEGIS (delivery of the laws), the depiction of Christ giving the law in the form of a scroll to Peter as Paul stands to the left in an attitude of acclamation. It was probably created in the fourth century for the apse decoration of St. Peter's, Rome. Although this theme underscores the primacy of Peter, it is fundamentally eschatological, for Christ appears as the majestic risen Lord of the Second Coming. In representations of the *traditio legis* from the sixth century on, Christ is often shown seated between Peter and Paul, thus echoing royal law-giving ceremonies.

BIBLIOGRAPHY

Yves Christe, "Apocalypse et 'Traditio Legis,'" in *Römische Quartalschrift*, **71** (1976); Cäcilia Davis-Weyer, "Das Traditio-Legis-Bild und seine Nachfolge," in *Münchner Jahrbuch der bildenden Kunst*, 3rd ser., **12** (1961); Christa Ihm, *Die Programme der christlichen Apsismalerei vom vierten Jahrhundert bis zur Mitte des achten Jahrhunderts* (1960); Walter N. Schumacher,

Traditio legis, depicted in the apse mosaic of S. Constanza, Rome, 4th century. ALINARI / ART RESOURCE

"Dominus legem dat," in *Römische Quartalschrift,* 54 (1959), and "Traditio Legis," in *Lexikon der christlichen Ikonographie,* IV (1972).

MICHAEL T. DAVIS

[See also **Early Christian Art; Iconography.**]

TRAILBASTON. See **Oyer and Terminer, Trailbaston.**

TRAINI, FRANCESCO (*fl. ca.* 1321–*ca.* 1350/ 1375), Pisan painter. Little is known about this important master. Between 1344 and 1345, a Francesco Traini was paid for an altarpiece depicting St. Dominic for the church of S. Caterina in Pisa. Now in the Museo Civico in Pisa, it is the key to his style and the basis for the attribution of frescoes in the Pisa Camposanto. *The Triumph of Death, The Last Judgment,* and *Hell* are among the greatest frescoes to survive from the trecento, and if Traini was their author he ranks among the principal painters of the period.

Lacking documentation, scholars have proposed dating these frescoes anywhere from the 1320's to the 1350's. This dispute over their chronology makes their role in the so-called "Black Death" style unclear. Damaged during World War II, they were detached and partly restored, and their sinopie (underdrawings) have been extensively studied. They and the frescoes reveal a master of consummate draughtsmanship and a skillful and imaginative narrator. His style is likely based on the works of Simone Martini and the Lorenzetti brothers. The animation, sprightly proportions, and supple gestures of the figures in frescoes finds no real counterpart in other mid-trecento Florentine painting. It is very likely that they inspired the Florentine painter Antonio Veneziano, who provided frescoes for the Camposanto between 1384 and 1386.

BIBLIOGRAPHY

Enzo Carli, *Pittura pisana del trecento: La seconda metà del secolo* (1961); Millard Meiss, "The Problem of

The Triumph of Death. Fresco in the Pisa Camposanto, attributed to Francesco Traini, mid trecento.
ALINARI / ART RESOURCE

Francesco Traini," in *Art Bulletin*, **15** (1933), and *Painting in Florence and Siena After the Black Death* (1951); Joseph Polzer, "Observations on Known Paintings and a New Altar Piece by Francesco Traini," in *Pantheon*, **29** (1971).

ADELHEID M. GEALT

[See also **Fresco Painting; Lorenzetti, Ambrogio; Lorenzetti, Pietro; Simone Martini; Sinopia; Trecento Art.**]

TRANSCAUCASIA. See **Caucasia.**

TRANSENNA, in early Christian architecture, a lattice or openwork screen of wood, stone, or metal enclosing a shrine, from the Latin word meaning net or latticework. The term is sometimes applied, by extension, to any chapel railing, chancel barrier, or other screen or enclosure, even when these are solid.

BIBLIOGRAPHY
Martin S. Briggs, *Concise Encyclopaedia of Architecture* (1959), 344, for brief definition and illustrations; Kenneth John Conant, *Carolingian and Romanesque Architecture, 800 to 1200* (1959, 4th rev. ed. 1978), esp. 45, for a brief discussion of late Spanish Visigothic examples.

GREGORY WHITTINGTON

[See also **Screen; Screen, Chancel.**]

TRANSEPT, the transverse portion of a cruciform church, perpendicular to the main axis; also, each of the two arms of this cross axis (the north and south transepts). The transept generally crosses between the nave and chancel but is sometimes at the west end of the nave. In English Gothic cathedrals, the transepts are usually doubled, with a secondary transept to the east of the main crossing.

BIBLIOGRAPHY
Richard Krautheimer, *Early Christian and Byzantine Architecture* (1965), esp. 363, for a brief definition of each of the various transept types.

GREGORY WHITTINGTON

[See also **Basilica; Chancel; Church, Types of; Gothic Architecture; Nave; Romanesque Architecture.**]

TRANSFIGURATION. The vision of Christ in glory during his earthly life is referred to as the Transfiguration, one of the Twelve Great Feasts of the Eastern church (see Matt. 17:1–13, Mark 9:2–13, and Luke 9:28–36). After returning from their first missionary journey, Christ took Peter, James, and John up onto the mountain to pray. There they witnessed Christ transfigured in a radiant vision flanked by the prophets Moses and Elijah. Peter offered to build three shrines on that site, but a voice from the clouds intervened and said: "This is my son, hear him" (Luke 9:34–36). Tradition holds that the vision occurred on Mount Tabor, although a few scholars have suggested Mount Hermon or the Mount of Olives.

The feast of the Transfiguration, originating in the Eastern church, is celebrated on 6 August. Originally this was a local and unofficial feast, but it was widely celebrated by the eleventh century. In the Western church, the feast was introduced in 1457, when Calixtus III required its celebration to commemorate a victory over the Turks at Belgrade on 6 August 1456.

In Christian iconography, the Transfiguration is represented as early as the fifth century in the chapel mosaics of Hosios David, Thessaloniki, and had become a convention by the sixth century. Christ is typically depicted standing on a mountain, flanked by Moses and Elijah. The apostles may be prostrate at his feet. This type is common until the sixteenth century. For an illustration see "Theophanes the Greek" in this volume. Another type, such as Raphael's Transfiguration in the Vatican, shows the Savior floating in the air.

BIBLIOGRAPHY

Ormonde M. Dalton, *Byzantine Art and Architecture* (1911); André Grabar, *Christian Iconography: A Study of Its Origins* (1968); Frederick Hartt, *History of Italian Renaissance Art* (1969).

JENNIFER E. JONES

[See also **Early Christian Art; Iconography; Twelve Great Feasts.**]

TRANSLATION AND TRANSLATORS, BYZANTINE. As a result of its multilingual character and numerous contacts with foreign communities—Christian, Muslim, and pagan—the translation of scientific, religious, philosophical, and literary texts played a part in the political and cultural life of the Byzantine Empire. The role and importance of such translations varied with the changing internal and external circumstances.

EARLY BYZANTINE PERIOD (330–641)

Before the Arab conquests of the seventh century the Byzantine Empire was a polyethnic and multicultural society. Partly due to the needs of the Christian church, new literary languages developed, particularly in Egypt, Syria, and Armenia. There was much translation from Greek into these languages, not only of religious works but also

scientific, medical, and philosophical texts for practical or educational use. Literature in the narrow sense, including poetry, rhetoric, and history, generally failed to cross the language barrier, although an epitome of Homer seems to have been translated into Syriac.

Syriac and Coptic translations began to appear in the fourth century and Armenian in the fifth. Almost all of these translations are unpretentious, word-for-word renderings, particularly the Armenian works. The translators were mainly clergymen and teachers. There was naturally less translation from these languages into Greek. But some Syriac religious works were translated, particularly those of Ephraem Syrus (fourth century), Isaac of Antioch (fifth century), and Isaac of Ninevah (sixth century).

Greek and Latin were the dominant languages of the early Byzantine Empire, and there was much official translation in both directions, for example, of the proceedings of church councils. Some works of the Greek church fathers, particularly John Chrysostom, were translated into Latin at an early date. Latin versions of Aristotle's logical works were made by Boethius and others. Cassiodorus' monastery at Vivarium was a center of translation which aimed to preserve the Greek cultural heritage in the West.

Translations of legal texts were a special case. Justinian's *Corpus iuris* was translated into Greek for teaching purposes in Constantinople in the late sixth century, whereas the Latin versions of his Greek enactments were official texts prepared for use in reconquered Africa and Italy. Latin literature was not much translated into Greek. Eutropius' epitome of Roman history, however, was thrice translated.

MIDDLE BYZANTINE PERIOD
(641–1204)

Byzantine society at this time was closer to being exclusively Greek-speaking, and its culture more self-contained than in the earlier period. There was consequently much less translation into or out of Greek. The *Dialogues* of Gregory the Great were translated into Greek by the Calabrian Greek pope Zacharias (741–752), and the work became widely known in the Byzantine world. There was some translation from Arabic beginning in the eleventh century. Symeon Seth in Constantinople translated the collection of fables *Kalīla wa Dimnah* (second half of the eleventh century), and both he and

Constantine of Rhegium in Italy translated Arabic medical works. Both translators were natives of bilingual areas. Georgian monasteries on Mount Athos and elsewhere were centers of translation of philosophical, scientific, and religious texts. Translation into Armenian continued both before and after the subjugation of Armenia by the Byzantines. The translation of the liturgy, the Scriptures, and selections from the Greek church fathers into Old Slavonic by Cyril (d. 869) and Methodios (d. 885) and their pupils and followers laid the foundations of Christian culture among the Slavonic peoples.

LATE BYZANTINE PERIOD (1204–1453)

During these years Byzantine society became more open to external influences, particularly from the Latin West, because of the Latin conquest of 1204, the continuing occupation by Western powers of much former Byzantine territory, and the negotiations and polemics between the Greek and Latin churches. Knowledge of Latin became less rare at Constantinople. Maximos Planudes (1255–1305) translated works by Augustine and Boethius, as well as those of Cicero, Ovid, and other classical Latin authors. The late fourteenth century saw the translation of most of Thomas Aquinas and of works by Anselm of Canterbury and others by Demetrios Kydones and his circle. An anonymous translation of Augustine's *City of God* belongs to the same period. There was much translation of Latin theology and philosophy in the fifteenth century.

In addition to the translations of Latin works, Old French and Italian verse romances were translated or adapted into vernacular Greek, including the *Roman de Troie* of Benoît de Ste. Maure. Also, in both Constantinople and Trebizond, medical, astronomical, and other scientific works were translated from Arabic and Persian.

Until the last days of the empire, the Byzantine political and cultural elite remained largely monoglot, and there was no organized study of foreign languages. Partly for this reason the Byzantine state maintained a staff of diplomatic interpreters, recruited from the numerous bilingual populations of the empire. These individuals were stationed both in the capital and in the frontier provinces. Interpreters were attached to each unit of the Varangian guard. Arabic interpreters were particularly important, but there were also interpreters for Armenian, Georgian, Latin, Slavonic, Khazar, and other languages spoken throughout the continually shrinking Byzantine world, until the final dissolution at the hands of the Ottomans in 1453.

BIBLIOGRAPHY

Berthold Altaner, "Beiträge zur Geschichte der altlateinischen Übersetzungen von Väterschriften," in *Historisches Jahrbuch*, 61 (1941); Anton Baumstark, *Die christlichen Literaturen des Orients* (1911) and *Geschichte der syrischen Literatur* (1922); Pierre Courcelle, *Late Latin Writers and Their Greek Sources*, Harry E. Wedeck, trans. (1969); Deno J. Geanakoplos, *Interaction of the Sibling Byzantine and Western Cultures in the Middle Ages and Italian Renaissance (330–1600)* (1976); Michael Rackl, "Die griechischen Augustinusübersetzungen," in *Miscellanea Francesco Ehrle*, I (1924); Steven Runciman, "Byzantine Linguists," in Iōannēs T. Kakridēs, ed., *Prosphora eis Stilpōna P. Kyriakidēn* (1953); Wolfgang O. Schmitt, "Lateinische Literatur in Byzanz: Die Übersetzungen des Maximos Planudes und die moderne Forschung," in *Jahrbuch der österreichischen byzantinischen Gesellschaft*, 17 (1968); Michael Tarchnisvili, *Geschichte der kirchlichen georgischen Literatur* (1955); Hiranth Thorossian, *Histoire de la littérature arménienne* (1951).

ROBERT BROWNING

[See also **Aristotle in the Middle Ages; Boethius, Anicius Manlius Severinus; Byzantine Literature; Cassiodorus; Classical Literary Studies; Demetrios Kydones; Greek Language, Byzantine; Ovid in the Middle Ages.**]

TRANSLATION AND TRANSLATORS, ISLAMIC. The sources that discuss the rise of science and philosophy in Islam—traditionally called "foreign sciences"—almost unanimously agree that these "rational" sciences came into being as a result of the direct translations of earlier Greek, Syriac, Indian, and Pahlavi sources. From *al-Fihrist* of Ibn al-Nadīm (ca. 987) to the *Muqaddima* of Ibn Khaldūn (1377), there also seems to be a general agreement among the same sources that these translations were executed by foreigners to Arabic, and mostly by foreigners to Islam itself. According to *al-Fihrist*, the bulk of the translators were Syriac-speaking Christians who lived mostly in Mesopotamia and Damascus.

HISTORICAL BACKGROUND

The beginnings of this translation activity are far from being settled. The sources either preserve a legendary account of the undertaking of these translations, such as their being initiated by the dream of the caliph al-Maʾmūn (813–833), or remain silent about the whole question. Only Ibn al-Nadīm attempted to place the whole movement within the general historical perspective of Islamic civilization and tried to interpret it as a natural, gradual movement motivated by intellectual, political, and economic conditions. He stated, for example, that the first translations "from one language to another"—probably meaning a systematic organized activity—that took place in Islamic times was patronized by the Umayyad prince Khālid ibn Yazīd (*d.* 704/708), who was interested mainly in medicine, astrology, and alchemy. These early translations are mentioned in the same context as the translations of the *dīwān*s of Iraq and Damascus, the first from Pahlavi to Arabic and the latter from Greek to Arabic. The term *dīwān* itself is ambiguous here; from the scanty evidence supplied by Ibn al-Nadīm in connection with the *dīwān*s of Iraq, it seems to have included more than the administrative documents that the term commonly denotes. From the account of Ibn al-Nadīm, one can surmise that the *dīwān* must have included at least some elementary arithmetical operations. But it is not at all certain whether these *dīwān* translations included any other scientific material of any sophistication.

The dates that Ibn al-Nadīm assigns to the translations of the *dīwān*s of Iraq and Damascus supposedly coincided with the reigns of al-Ḥajjāj in Iraq for the first (694–714), and ʿAbd al-Malik (685–705) or his son Hishām ibn ʿAbd al-Malik (724–743) for the second. This means that some translation activities may have taken place during the first half of the eighth century, the time when coincidentally paper was introduced into the Muslim empire as a result of contact with China by way of Central Asia.

This translation activity seems to have been uninterruptedly continued under the early Abbasids, who came to power after a bloody revolution in 750. The second caliph of this dynasty, al-Manṣūr (754–775), is said to have patronized the first major translation of scientific texts from Sanskrit (for example, the *Mahasiddhanta* [*Sindhind*]) sometime during the 770's. This same caliph is also supposed to have obtained a copy of Euclid's *Elements* from Byzantium and, according to Ibn Khaldūn, he was the first to have it translated into Arabic. The Sanskrit translations have survived only in secondary quotations, while that of the *Elements* seems to have disappeared. The earliest translation of the *Elements* that has survived was completed by al-Ḥajjāj ibn Maṭar during the reign of the fifth Abbasid caliph, the famous Hārūn al-Rashīd (786–809), and was reviewed by the same translator under the reign of Hārūn's son al-Maʾmūn. Other translations of the *Almagest* and some medical Indian texts were also completed during the reign of Hārūn al-Rashīd.

It was al-Maʾmūn who finally saw to it that the flourishing translation activity was systematized, financed, and institutionalized by creating for it an endowment that came to be known as Bayt al-Ḥikma (House of Wisdom), which was supposed to guarantee its perpetuation. Under this caliph, for example, both translations of the *Almagest* and the *Elements* were completely reworked, supposedly to improve them in both language and content. It is not clear, however, how much the surviving translations ascribed to Isḥāq ibn Ḥunayn (*d.* 910) and Thābit ibn Qurra (*d.* 901) owe to these "Maʾmūnī" translations, as they came to be called by the later sources, to allow one to confirm this statement. But the one copy of the *Almagest* that was definitely reworded by al-Ḥajjāj ibn Maṭar during the Maʾmūn period (Leiden Oriental MS 680) speaks highly of the quality and the scientific control of the text to substantiate the claim made above.

The sources are not clear about the fate of al-Maʾmūn's Bayt al-Ḥikma. From all appearances, it probably survived the death of its patron in 833 by only a few years and was soon dissolved. From then on, translations were patronized mainly by wealthy individuals who did not necessarily muster political power. The most famous of these individuals are the three brothers who are collectively known as the Banū Mūsā. They also contributed their own scientific production to the works that they commissioned for translation. Other patrons are also known from the only surviving detailed account of the translations of the medical works of Galen of about A.D. 150, and naturally included physicians in this case.

Viewed as a whole, the most important feature of this translation activity, which seems to have started toward the beginning of the eighth century, is that by the middle of the ninth century most of the major scientific works of India, Persia, and Greece were available in Arabic. In particular, the Greek philosophical and scientific corpus was almost totally completed during the first half of the ninth century. A good number of those Greek texts survive only in their Arabic translations. And when the twelfth-century Latin translators were introduced to the Greek scientific tradition, they either found it only in Arabic or found Arabic translations to be superior to the extant Greek manuscripts, giving rise to the general impression in the Latin West that the Arabic translations constituted a veritable storehouse of the wisdom of classical antiquity.

CIRCUMSTANCES AND LANGUAGE OF TRANSLATIONS

It was stated above that most translations were officially patronized at first, and only in the latter part of the ninth century did they become widespread and patronized by individuals who were not necessarily in official political positions. The quality of these translations were also varied insofar as they were produced by several translators who sometimes worked individually and sometimes in teams. In general, by the middle of the ninth century the entire translation movement was not at all subject to any official restrictions on language and content, and one has to assume that it continued as a natural response to a need that must have existed during the latter part of ninth-century Baghdad. In this effort, the Greek tradition was singled out for intensive, systematic treatment, whereas very little, if anything at all, was still being sought from the Indian and the Pahlavi traditions during the ninth century. All this led to the Arabization of most of the scientific and philosophical texts of Greek antiquity.

It is also important to note that about the same time, when the Greek texts were being translated, original Arabic scientific and philosophical works were being produced. The names of Muḥammad ibn Mūsā al-Khwārizmī (*fl.* 830), Yaᶜqūb ibn Isḥāq al-Kindī (*d.* 870), and Thābit ibn Qurra attest to the vitality of this original Arabic production.

It had been thought for some time that the Greek literary corpus, such as the *Iliad* and Greek drama (as opposed to the scientific and philosophical texts), had been on the whole excluded from this activity. Late-twentieth-century research in literary Arabic, however, has begun to change this picture slightly, for there is some evidence now that at least a few sections of Homer's *Iliad* may indeed have been translated into Arabic sometime during the ninth century. Nevertheless, the nature of the evidence uncovered so far, and its scantiness, still reinforce the point that the main Arabic interest in the Greek tradition was in the philosophical and scientific writings. Similar observations could be made about the medieval Latin translation movement from Arabic.

Finally, when one considers the quality of translations into Arabic, two important questions have to be raised. These are mainly in regard to the adequacy of Arabic as a language on the conceptual level to express the ideas of the original language from which the translations were being made, and whether the texts were available to the translators in their original language rather than in an intermediary language, such as Pahlavi (in the case of the Sanskrit texts) and Syriac (in the case of Greek). A text known only through an intermediary language would be considerably less reliable than one available in the original. In the case of the Arabic translations from Greek, the question of the intermediary language is especially significant, for Syriac has long been held to have been the first recipient of the Greek corpus, and only later did Arabic gain direct access to Greek. This is further complicated by the fact that most Arabic translators (if not all) either knew Syriac as a mother tongue or were well versed in it as a liturgical language, for they were mostly Christians who used Syriac for liturgical purposes, even if they did not speak it at home. One is also further hindered in evaluating the role of Syriac in the translation of the Greek tradition because most of the Syriac scientific sources mentioned in the secondary Arabic sources as having been used by the Arabic translators are themselves lost and hence are not available to scholars for in-depth studies and comparative work. The Syriac manuscripts still available do not unfortunately go much beyond the few treatises of the logical parts of the Aristotelian corpus; next to nothing remains of the Galenic or Hippocratic medical material of which the secondary sources speak in clear terms. Thus from the nineteenth century on, all modern studies on the subject remain mainly speculative, lacking the necessary proof to substantiate the role of Syriac as an intermediary language. And even if one were to engage in such speculations, it would be hard to assert that there had been an intermediary Syriac translation of the sophisticated Greek scientific or philosophical texts, such as Euclid's *Elements,* Ptolemy's *Almagest,* Diaphantus' *Arithmetica,* or the non-logical works of Aristotle.

Therefore, the conclusion reached by Lucien Leclerc in 1876 was still true in the late twentieth century, namely, that although the Arabic translators may have used Syriac translations of Greek medical works as intermediary texts, those translators owe nothing to Syriac at least as far as the mathematical sciences are concerned. The scanty evidence of the existence of a Syriac *Almagest* or a Syriac copy of the *Elements* that has come to light since Leclerc's time is not substantial enough to warrant a revision of his conclusion. In fact, a close study of the surviving astronomical works of Severus Sebokht (*d.* 666), for example, and of Bar Hebraeus (*d.* 1286) gives the impression that the first did not use the *Almagest* in either Greek or Syriac, and the second knew of the *Almagest* only through the Arabic sources, as his arabized terminology clearly shows. Furthermore, it is highly improbable that these two Syriac scientists would have avoided using a Syriac copy of the *Almagest*, for example, had one existed.

As for the adequacy of Arabic for the translation of Greek sources, it is important to remember that every translation is essentially an interpretation, and as such Arabic exhibited great flexibility in developing its own scientific and philosophical terminology. From a close study of the sources, for example, one is struck by the vitality of the creative production of scientific works that was taking place simultaneously with the translation activity. The two processes were so intertwined that it is hard to determine whether the terminology of the translators was influencing that of the original writers or vice versa.

TRANSLATORS

The list of translators from the various languages into Arabic that was supplied by Ibn al-Nadīm in *al-Fihrist* included more than sixty names; some of them were mentioned as a family of translators, as in the case of "the family of Nawbakht." Although more than forty of these translators worked on the translations of the Greek sources, only a handful was responsible for the bulk of the work. One, Ḥunayn ibn Isḥāq (*d.* 873), is supposed to have translated more than one hundred medical texts of the Galenic corpus alone. We are certain he also translated other works, for some of them have survived in his translation. This same translator's work will be studied below at greater length, for he has left us the only detailed account of the conditions and methods of translation that prevailed in his time.

The sources that speak of Ḥunayn's life and works as well as his own writing on translation also mention the names of other translators associated

with him, including his own son Isḥāq ibn Ḥunayn and his nephew Ḥubaysh. From the description of the method of operation, it looks as if Ḥunayn did not work entirely alone; it may very well be that the prolific production with which he is credited was actually done under his supervision and general editorship rather than by him alone.

Ḥunayn's son Isḥāq (*d.* 910) became an equally famous translator in his own right, not as much for his prolificness as for his work on the major scientific Greek texts, for example, the *Almagest* and the *Elements*. According to the surviving sources themselves, both texts were corrected (*iṣlāḥ*) by Thābit ibn Qurra. In two surviving copies of translations of the *Almagest* the introduction reads thus: "The Great Book, known as *Almajisṭī*, translated from Greek into Arabic by Isḥāq b. Ḥunayn b. Isḥāq the physician and corrected [*ṣaḥḥaḥahu*] by Thābit b. Qurra for Abū Ṣaqr Ismāᶜīl b. Bulbul. Everything that is included in this book, or in any part of it or its marginalia by way of explanation, abridgment, elucidation, demonstration, simplification, clarification, rectification, annotation, emendation, and correction is due to Thābit b. Qurra al-Ḥarrānī." The extensive cooperation between Isḥāq and Thābit in this work is readily apparent, in a relationship that seems to have been typical of the works of these two men.

Isḥāq ibn Ḥunayn is also responsible for the translation of several Aristotelian works. But here too, his work was sometimes also edited by other people—such as his joint work with al-Ḥasan ibn Ṣuwār—which leads one to conclude either that these specialized works were translated by teams of translators or that Isḥāq's technical competence in the subject matter required some improvement. In all likelihood it was due to the latter, for most sources are in agreement about Isḥāq's eloquence in Arabic (*faṣīḥ*), hence giving no reason to doubt his linguistic abilities. But from the evidence of the works that he himself had composed rather than translated, one may conclude that he might not have been as competent in the technicalities of mathematics or philosophy. What is clear, however, is that the surviving translations credited to Isḥāq tend to use Arabic technical terminology rather than transliterated Greek as in the case of most Syriac sources and the works of other translators, a fact that could possibly be explained by the team work and *iṣlāḥ*.

A contemporary of Isḥāq ibn Ḥunayn, by the name of Qusṭā ibn Lūqā al-Baᶜalbakkī (*d.* 912), a

Greek who lived in Baalbek in modern Lebanon (hence al-Baᶜalbakkī), was also engaged in the translation of Greek technical texts. He is credited with translating a variety of books, including Diaphantus' *Arithmetica*, Theophrastus' *Meteorologica*, Hero's *Mechanica*, and some of the works of Galen and Hippocrates.

Finally, Thābit ibn Qurra, perhaps more than any other translator, was an original scientist in his own right. Some of his works on mathematics, astronomy, mechanics, and medicine have survived and attest to his sophistication and command of the Greek technical sources. In addition to his collaboration with Isḥāq and others, he contributed to the translation movement with his own translations, chief among them his rendition of Nichomachus' *Arithmetic*.

These are only a few of the many translators who must have worked in ninth-century Baghdad. That there were so many people engaged in translating is a clear indication of the vitality of the intellectual life in Baghdad at the time. There is also some evidence that these translators were handsomely rewarded for their services. Banū Mūsā, for example, who were scientists themselves, patronized three of the above-mentioned translators at a cost of 500 dinars per month. Even divided among the three, this sum would still have been an impressive amount by the standards of ninth-century Baghdad.

METHODS OF TRANSLATION

The detailed account by Ḥunayn ibn Isḥāq of the works of Galen that had been translated into Arabic not only informs us about the transmission history of these works, but allows us to observe some of the actual mechanics of the translations in which Ḥunayn was involved. And although we know from another secondary source that Ḥunayn had his own method concerning the technique of translation, we can still assume that Ḥunayn's account regarding Galen's works is more or less representative of the conditions and methods of translation that prevailed at the time. Before analyzing this account, a word about his technique of translation.

We are told by the fourteenth-century biographer al-Ṣafadī (*d.* 1365) that Ḥunayn had his own method of translation—which Ṣafadī preferred—in contradistinction to that of Yūḥannā ibn al-Biṭrīq and others. Whereas Yūḥannā and his followers tried to match each Greek word with an equivalent Arabic word, progressing one word at a time,

Ḥunayn and his school considered whole sentences; only after ascertaining their meaning in Greek would they render them into Arabic, without attempting to retain the order of the original words.

The fact that Ḥunayn was conscious of the method and circumstances of his work is clearly illustrated by his reference to what could be called his criteria of translations in the account referred to above. In the introduction of that missive, Ḥunayn asserts that one has to ask three questions in connection with any translated work: (1) for whom was the translation done (because the patron of the translation plays a decisive role in its quality and style); (2) the age of the translator, which is one way of determining his experience; and (3) the number of copies upon which the translation is based, for the more copies one has the better the original text can be controlled.

The fact that the patron plays an important role in determining the quality of the translation is best illustrated in Ḥunayn's own case when he says that he "sought the clearest language" when he translated for a patron "who constantly required it" and who obviously knew the subject matter very well. In another case, Ḥunayn says that he translated a book in very concise terms, for the patron concerned was of extremely sharp mind. That patron apparently added his own commentary to the text, thus creating a variant version of it.

As for the age of the translator, Ḥunayn refers to it in several places by saying that such and such a translation was bad because he or someone else, like Sergius of Rasᶜainā, completed it when still young and inexperienced. Ḥunayn says of his translation of Galen's *Natural Faculties,* for example, that he had translated it badly when he was still a teenager "about seventeen years of age" from "a Greek copy with many lacunae," but "corrected it later when" he "had come of age." That, he says, "accounts for the variants that one may find in the copies of this book." In many other instances, Ḥunayn tells us that such and such a book was not translated or was translated badly because he had only one Greek manuscript from which to work. Every time he acquired other manuscripts, he went back and corrected his translation.

The importance of determining a dependable original text before one begins to translate cannot be emphasized enough, for at various times Ḥunayn seems to have gone through a process to produce what we now identify as a critical edition of the original Greek text. In one instance, he says that

131

once he acquired more Greek manuscripts of the text in question he "collated them with one another until one correct copy was obtained." At another time, he says that he could not verify the first six chapters of a book, for he "had only one copy of them, which also had many mistakes." He later managed to obtain another copy, which he "collated with the first and corrected it as much as possible," and he "was still hoping to find a third." As part of his editing procedure, he sometimes found himself passing judgment on the contents of a book in terms of whether there had been interpolations by other authors. On the book dealing with fever cycles, he says that "one may find another chapter attributed to Galen in this part, but it is not his." And in the case of the book on *Drugs,* he says that "a chapter has been added to it on the same subject attributed to Galen" and that it was not Galen's but rather "that of Philagrios."

But seeking additional manuscripts, collating them, and authenticating their contents is not always an easy task. At times, Ḥunayn traveled as far as Aleppo and Alexandria because he had heard of the existence of another copy of a book, only to find out that the rumor was not true.

Despite his cautious approach to translation, Ḥunayn, the author, does not restrain himself from adding new material, either fresh compositions or commentaries, to a book when he feels confidently in control of its subject matter. In one instance, he added a chapter "apologizing for Galen on account of what he had said in the seventh chapter of his book" on the opinions of Hippocrates and Plato. In another instance, he says that he had "added explanations to the difficult parts" of the Hippocratic oath that he had translated. And in yet another case, he says that he "added an incomplete brief explanation" of the Hippocratic text *On Airs, Waters, and Places* and "added another brief explanation" to Galen's commentary on Hippocrates' *Nutriment.*

Once an original text had been established, the translation of that text itself could take several years to be completed. At times one feels that the process was a continuous one and had no determined end. In the case of the book on *Natural Faculties,* Ḥunayn says that he "first translated it from a Greek copy that had many mistakes." Then, when he improved the original text, he "checked it again and found several errors" that he "corrected." Then, after he had "matured further," he "checked it another time and corrected it."

Even after working on a book for a long time, one might still find that a patron did not like the style of the end product and would ask that it be changed. In one case, Ḥunayn "had recently translated (a book) for Bakhtīshū" in his "usual habit of translation, which was the most erudite [*afḍal*], most eloquent [*ablagh*], and closest to Greek without doing any injustice to Syriac"—the language into which it was translated in this case. Then he says that the patron asked him "to change the translation into a more lucid, simple and more common language"—which he did.

With all this activity, it is only natural that Ḥunayn could not actually complete all the translations that he undertook. In one case he explicitly says that he gave a book "to a man from Edessa by the name of Thomas who translated what had remained," and that Ḥunayn only "checked it, corrected it, and added to it the first part."

He at times felt that the texts could be improved and their benefit generalized further if they were cast in a different style. The book *On Treatment of Diseases* (Galen's commentary on a work by Hippocrates) had been translated completely when he found out that he could do better by "summarizing its contents in the style of question and answer." He did the same, this time in Syriac, to Galen's commentary on the *Epidemics.* In still another instance he says, "I translated it into Syriac and made a compendium for it." Then Ḥubaysh translated it into Arabic.

Finally, one must admit that not every book could be translated. For example, Galen's book on the *Words of Hippocrates* "is in one chapter. His purpose in it is to explain the obsolete words used by Hippocrates in all of his works. The book is useful only to those who read Greek. Others who read languages other than Greek do not need it, nor could it be translated in the first place." He, however, had a copy of it in his own library.

Although other translators may have operated differently, it is reasonable to assume that such standards and problems were more or less common in ninth-century Baghdad, and other translators had to resort to their own means to complete the translation. Qusṭā ibn Lūqā, for example, in his translation of Hero's *Mechanica,* had to make a decision about a lacuna in the original manuscript that could not have been too different from the decisions Ḥunayn would have had to make under similar circumstances. At one point Qusṭā says: "In this place there is a lacuna in the Greek text.

The text was written by guessing that it should be so."

It is unfortunate that we do not have more treatises by medieval translators in which they discuss their own translations, for, as we have seen from Ḥunayn's missive, one gains a much better appreciation of the task of translating and can better understand that what one takes to be a translation has to be viewed against the background of all these issues. It is still remarkable that someone like Ḥunayn could overcome these problems and translate almost the whole Greek medical corpus into Syriac and Arabic. It is more remarkable still that within a period of about fifty years the translators of Baghdad and Damascus managed to produce first-rate translations of most of the wisdom of antiquity, be it Indian, Persian, or Greek.

BIBLIOGRAPHY

Anton Baumstark, *Geschichte der syrischen Literatur* (1922); Gotthelf Bergsträsser, ed. and trans., *Ḥunain ibn Isḥāq über die syrischen und arabischen Galen-Übersetzungen* (1925), for Ḥunayn's missive to ʿAlī ibn Yaḥyā; Ibn al-Nadīm, *Kitab al-Fihrist*, Riza Tajaddud, ed. (1971), and *The Fihrist*, Bayard Dodge, trans. (1970), 571ff., to be used cautiously; Lucien Leclerc, *Histoire de la médecine arabe* (1876), outdated but still useful for problems of transmission; Carlo Nallino, *ʿIlm al-Falak* (1911) and *Raccolta de scriti editi et inediti* (1944), for translation of astronomical works into Arabic; David Pingree, "The Greek Influence on Early Islamic Mathematical Astronomy," in *Journal of the American Oriental Society*, 93 (1973), and "ʿIlm al-Hayʾa," in *Encyclopaedia of Islam*, new ed., III (1971); Franz Rosenthal, *The Classical Heritage in Islam* (1975), 17ff.; Moritz Steinschneider, *Die arabischen Übersetzungen aus dem griechischen* (1960); Richard Walzer, *Greek into Arabic: Essays on Islamic Philosophy* (1962).

GEORGE SALIBA

[See also **Archimedes in the Middle Ages; Aristotle in the Middle Ages; Astrology/Astronomy, Islamic; Clocks and Reckoning of Time; Mathematics; Medicine, History of; Nadīm, Ibn al-; Philosophy and Theology, Islamic; Plato in the Middle Ages; Science, Islamic.**]

TRANSLATION AND TRANSLATORS, JEWISH.

Jews performed a twofold function in translation in the Middle Ages: they translated works into Hebrew for the benefit of their coreligionists, and they translated or collaborated in translating books, mainly from the Arabic, into Latin or the vernacular for the benefit of Christian scholars.

The importance of Jewish translations in Western cultural history cannot be exaggerated. Translations into Hebrew made available texts, methods, and instruments to the Jewish scholar, physician, and scientist before they were known to Christian scholars. In turn, the Jews transmitted these ideas and discoveries to the West. Hebrew translations preserved Arabic texts that were subsequently lost in the original. For example, Māshāʾallāh's *Book on Eclipses* is known only through the Hebrew and Latin translations.

TRANSLATIONS INTO HEBREW

Jews living within the Christian realm wrote their scholarly works almost exclusively in Hebrew, a language that was understood, it seems, not only by scholars but by most laymen also. In the East after the Muslim conquest, however, Arabic gradually replaced Hebrew and Aramaic as the chief literary language and was used by Jews not only for philosophical or scientific discourses but even for the most esoteric works on ritual law, talmudic commentaries, and mysticism. Judeo-Arabic culture flourished in the Orient and in Muslim Spain, especially from the ninth to the twelfth century. It is only toward the end of that era that the first translations into Hebrew appeared. The earliest translations from Arabic into Hebrew were Karaite writings translated by Tobias ben Moses of Jerusalem toward the middle of the eleventh century in Constantinople and Isaac ben Reuben of Barcelona's translation of Hay Gaon's treatise on laws of purchase made in 1078, some fifty years after the author's death.

The proliferation of translations into Hebrew began in the twelfth century. Abraham ibn Ezra, a Spanish scholar traveling through northern Europe and Italy, translated a number of grammatical and astrological works. Abraham bar Ḥiyya of Barcelona incorporated Arabic scientific contributions into his Hebrew works. It was the Jewish emigration from turbulent Muslim Spain to southern France and Italy, combined with the cultural awakening in Western Europe, however, that opened the way for the proliferation of Jewish translating activities in the following two centuries.

At this time, Judah ibn Tibbon, the patriarch of a dynasty of Hebrew translators in Languedoc (southern France), emerged. Known as the "father of Jewish translators," he translated (at the request of a Provençal scholar) Baḥya ibn Paquda's *Farāʾid al-Qulūb* under the title *Ḥovot ha-Levavot* (Duties of the heart) in 1161. He continued translating classical Jewish ethical and philosophical treatises, including Saadiah Gaon's *Kitāb al-Amānāt wa-al-Iʿtiqādāt,* Judah Halevi's *Kuzari,* and Solomon ibn Gabirol's *Kitāb Iṣlāḥ al-Akhlāq,* as well as works on Hebrew grammar.

Judah's son Samuel (*ca.* 1160–*ca.* 1230), a disciple of another translator, Joseph Kimḥi, was one of the most prolific of the Hebrew translators. Samuel was a contemporary and admirer of Maimonides, whose Hebrew code of Jewish law, *Mishneh Torah,* so excited the Jewish scholars of Western Europe that they were eager to read his controversial philosophic and exegetical works written in Arabic. Hence Samuel undertook with the author's encouragement to translate Maimonides' *Dalālat al-Ḥāʾirīn* (Guide of the perplexed) and continued translating other works by the master as well as works on philosophy and medicine by various Arabic authors. Judah al-Ḥarizi, a Spaniard who lived for a while in southern France and the Middle East and who was a contemporary of Samuel, made a new, less literal translation of Maimonides' *Guide,* but it failed to supersede its predecessor. He also translated part of Maimonides' commentary on the Mishnah, previously translated by Samuel, and other works by Galen, ʿAli ibn Riḍwān, and al-Ḥarīrī.

Samuel ibn Tibbon's son Moses (1240–1283) and son-in-law Jacob Anatoli (1194–1285) continued the family tradition. Moses translated a few additional works by Maimonides but concentrated mainly on philosophical works, mostly by Averroës (Ibn Rushd), and on various medical and astronomical works by Arab writers. These reflected the cultural tastes of Western Europe in the thirteenth century, common in this case to both Jews and Christians. Jacob Anatoli emigrated to Naples, in Italy, where he translated several philosophical works of Averroës as well as Ptolemy's *Almagest* and other astronomical works from Arabic. Jacob ben Maʿhir, a nephew of Moses who lived at the end of the thirteenth century, translated mainly scientific works, including Euclid's *Elements,* and also wrote a few original astronomical treatises in Hebrew.

Thirteenth-century translators from Arabic active in other parts of Europe included Nathan ha-Meati (Italy?), who translated medical works, including the entire *Canon* of Avicenna (Ibn Sīnā),

and Zeraḥia ben Isaac ben Shealiel Gracian (Spain), who translated both philosophical and medical works.

In the thirteenth century the first Hebrew translations from Latin appeared. Solomon ben Moses Melgueuil of Provence (*ca.* 1250) translated a number of treatises, including *De somno et vigilia,* attributed to Aristotle, and works by Averroës, Avicenna, and Matthias Platearius, from Latin. His contemporary Berakhiah ha-Nakdan compiled a Hebrew adaptation of Adelard of Bath's *Quaestiones naturales.* In Italy, Samuel ben Jacob of Capua and Hillel ben Samuel of Verona also translated from Latin.

In the fourteenth century Jewish scholars were active in translating both from Arabic and from Latin. Most of the translations from Arabic were made by Jews from Spain and Provence, the most prolific of them being Kalonymus ben Kalonymus, known as Maestro Calo, who translated over twenty-five mathematical, astronomical, medical, and philosophical works by al-Fārābī, Averroës, Ptolemy, Euclid, and others. Samuel ben Judah ben Meshullam, another Provençal scholar, translated more than ten works on similar subjects, many of them by Averroës. Translations from Latin, mostly of medical and Christian scholastic works, were made by many Spanish, Italian, and Provençal Jewish scholars. Jews often earned their livelihood as physicians throughout Europe, although they were rarely admitted to Christian medical schools. They were often, therefore, self-taught, learning their art through apprenticeship and from books; for this reason it is not surprising that so many medical books were translated into Hebrew, both from Arabic and later from Latin.

More surprising perhaps was the interest generated by the Christian Scholastics. Judah Romano of Italy (mid fourteenth century) translated about twenty short treatises by Thomas Aquinas, Egidius, Albertus Magnus, Boethius, and others. Later, in fifteenth-century Spain, Elijah Habillo translated other works by Thomas and Ockham. By then few European Jews could read Arabic and only a small number of translations from Arabic were made. Translations from Latin continued to be produced in Italy and Spain and to a lesser degree in southern France, but no single figure emerged to dominate this literary activity.

The earliest Jewish translators often faced technical difficulties because they lacked suitable Hebrew equivalents for scientific and philosophical terms. To overcome this problem they often used new word forms modeled on the Arabic, or they simply adopted the Arabic terms in lieu of Hebrew equivalents. This process enriched the Hebrew language and made it possible for later authors to write original scientific works in Hebrew. Most of the early translations endeavored to remain as faithful as possible to the original text. This sometimes led to a rather awkward style and, in imitating Arabic sentence structure and word order, to violations of Hebrew syntax. Occasionally the translator lacked sufficient mastery of the Arabic language or of the subject matter in the work being translated, resulting in an obscure or unreliable translation. Many translators, not satisfied with existing translations, undertook to produce new versions. Thus, Judah al-Ḥarizi, accusing Samuel ibn Tibbon of having written an obscure translation of Maimonides' *Guide,* proceeded to compose his own translation. Al-Ḥarizi's version, however, was accused of being even less faithful to the original, and it failed to supersede Ibn Tibbon's work. Many other works are extant in two, three, or more translations. One book of Avicenna's *Canon* was translated at least five times, probably within a period of one hundred years.

TRANSLATIONS INTO LATIN
AND THE VERNACULAR

In addition to providing translations into Hebrew, Jews functioned as intermediaries in the translation of works from Arabic into Latin or into the vernacular and later as translators directly from Arabic and Hebrew. At the beginning of the twelfth century Latin scholars from the north made their way to Spain in order to acquaint themselves with Arabic scholarship. In all probability many of them turned to Jews for assistance in translating from Hebrew into Latin. One striking example is Rabbi Abraham bar Ḥiyya of Barcelona, also called Savasorda. In addition to writing original works in Hebrew into which he incorporated Arabic science, he collaborated with Plato of Tivoli to produce a large number of scientific translations in the 1130's. Among the works translated by the two are books on astronomy, astrology, and mathematics, such as *De horarum electionibus* by al-Imrami, al-Battānī's *De motu stellarum,* and a version of Bar Ḥiyya's own geometrical treatise *Liber embadorum.* Avendauth, at one time thought to have been a convert and identified by some scholars with John Hispanus, and now generally believed to be the

philosopher and historian Abraham ibn Daud (*ca.* 1110–1180), collaborated with Dominicus Gundisalvis in translating Avicenna's *De anima,* Avendauth having translated the work from Arabic into Spanish for Gundisalvis, who then translated it into Latin.

Some Jews, many of them converts, translated directly from Arabic into Latin. Petrus Alphonsi, believed to have been the Spanish Jew Moses ha-Sefaradi of Huesca, wrote a book on astronomy that incorporates Arabic learning, and he may have translated or adapted al-Khwārizmī's work on astronomy, a translation attributed by some sources to Adelard of Bath. It is possible that Adelard and Alphonso collaborated in the preparation of one of the versions of al-Khwārizmī's work. Abraham ibn Ezra, who translated from Arabic and wrote original astronomical and astrological works in Hebrew, wrote in England in 1160 a Latin work on the astrolabe, which may have been translated from the Hebrew. One of his works, *Reshit Ḥokhmah,* was translated into French in 1273 by a Jew named Hagin.

In the thirteenth century Jews were prominently associated with a number of intellectual projects based on Arab and Greek sources. Frederick II in Sicily (1194–1250) and his son Manfred (1232–1266) encouraged the translation of Arabic philosophy and science into both Latin and Hebrew. Frederick invited Jacob Anatoli to Sicily and seems to have encouraged other Jewish scholars and translators. Toward the end of the thirteenth century and at the beginning of the fourteenth, several Jewish translators remained active in the courts of the Angevin sovereigns. Ferragut (Faraj ben Solomon) translated several medical works by Rhazes (al-Rāzī) into Latin, among them *Liber continens;* Moses of Palermo was educated in Latin in order to translate for Charles of Anjou; and Kalonymus ben Kalonymus was engaged to translate Averröes' *Destructio destructionis.*

In Castile, King Alfonso X (1252–1284) encouraged the translation and adaptation of scientific works that he himself often revised or edited. The most remarkable work produced by Alfonso's academy was the Alfonsine Tables, lists of planetary movements written in Castilian. Among the Jews who participated in their preparation was Isaac ben Sid, who translated al-Battānī's astronomical work into Castilian, and Judah ben Moses Cohen, who translated an astrological work by Ali Abi 'l-Rihal. The *Libros del saber de astronomia,* an encyclopedia of astronomy produced under Alfonso, includes several works translated from Arabic by Jews.

In northern Italy a Jew, Bonacosa, translated Averroes' *Colliget* into Latin in 1265, and a convert, Jacob of Capua, collaborated in the translation of the *Taysīr* by Avenzoar (Abū Marwān ibn Zuhr) and translated Maimonides' work on hygiene and a book of Indian fables into Latin.

Jews appear on the intellectual scene again as transmitters of Hebrew, Greek, and Arabic culture toward the end of the fifteenth century. Elijah Delmedigo (*ca.* 1460–1497) of Padua, a teacher of Pico della Mirandola, translated various treatises by Averroes into Latin. Paulus Ricius (Ricci), a Jew of German origin, translated various cabalistic works into Latin. Abraham de Balmes (*d.* 1523), a physician to Cardinal Grimani, translated works by Avempace (Ibn Bājja), Averroes, Geminus, and others from Hebrew into Latin. The last of the medieval Jewish translators, the Spanish-born Jacob Mantino, studied in Bologna and Padua. He translated from Hebrew into Latin works by Maimonides, Gersonides, Avicenna, and Averroes, including the standard Latin edition of Averroes published soon after Mantino's death in 1553.

BIBLIOGRAPHY

Edwyn R. Bevan and Charles J. Singer, eds., *The Legacy of Israel* (1928), 202–245; José M. Millás y Vallicrosa, "Translations of Oriental Scientific Works," in Guy S. Métraux and François Crouzet, eds., *The Evolution of Science* (1963); David Romano, "La transmission des sciences arabes par les Juifs en Languedoc," in Édouard Privat, ed., *Juifs et Judaïsme de Languedoc* (1977); Moritz Steinschneider, *Die hebräischen Übersetzungen des Mittelalters und die Juden als Dolmetscher* (1893).

Benjamin Z. Richler

[See also **Abraham bar Ḥiyya; Abraham ben Meïr ibn Ezra; Alfonsine Tables; Arabic Numerals; Aristotle in the Middle Ages; Astronomy; Clocks and Reckoning of Time; Mathematics; Philosophy and Theology, Jewish: Islamic World; Plato in the Middle Ages; Science, Jewish.**]

TRANSLATION AND TRANSLATORS, WESTERN EUROPEAN. The Middle Ages was punctuated by bursts of translating activity in different areas at different times. As examples, one may cite the rediscovery of the classics in the Court School of Charlemagne; the translations of Latin works into Old English in the time of King Alfred (871–899); the translations of Latin works into Old Norse in Iceland in the thirteenth century; the translations from Greek into Latin made under Robert I (1309–1343), the Angevin king of Naples; and the translations of medical works into English made during the fourteenth and fifteenth centuries.

The attention of twentieth-century scholars has focused particularly on the reception of Greek and Arabic science and philosophy in the West. Translations were made from the Arabic in Spain, southern Italy, and the crusader states, with the peak of the activity coming in the twelfth century. The Latin West also had direct contacts with the living Byzantine Greek traditions in science, philosophy, and theology through Ravenna in the sixth century, through the Ottonian court in the ninth century, through Sicily and southern Italy from the eleventh to the fourteenth century, and through the Pisan and Venetian quarters in Constantinople itself in the twelfth century.

Bibliography concerning some of these translations is given below, at the end of this article, and the most important translators are given separate articles in this dictionary. This article seeks to draw some general conclusions about the role of the translator in the Middle Ages. It also seeks to respond to such questions as: What were his resources? What were his aims? What were his methods, that is, how did he tackle the task of translating? And what was his audience?

THE TRANSLATOR'S RESOURCES
AND TRAINING

Grammars. The translator may have been able to use his own resources as a bilingual speaker, but even so he would have had to learn or invent the appropriate technical terms in the receptor language. Others needed to learn their source language in order to become translators. In this they were hampered by a shortage of good textbooks. There was in fact little formal language training (beyond that of Latin) in schools and colleges in the Middle Ages. Latin grammars had achieved a didactic form from the sixth century for non-Romance speakers and served as models for grammars of other languages. Grammars for Greek and Provençal were written in Latin in the thirteenth century. The earliest Arabic grammar in Latin, however, was that made for the dialect of Granada by Pedro de Alcala around 1500.

Word lists, glosses, and lexicons. Word lists were more common. They ranged from St. Jerome's explanations of difficult Hebrew expressions to two substantial Arabic-Latin-Arabic glossaries of the twelfth century, a Hebrew-Italian glossary of the thirteenth century, and fragments of glosses to the lingua franca of the Mediterranean surviving in the Cairo genizah. Most of these glosses served particular aims, such as restoring the Roman rite to the Mozarabic church in Spain, aiding travelers to the Holy Land, or furthering missionary movements.

The glossaries that were read in the schoolroom, such as the list of words deriving from Greek in Eberhard of Béthune's *Grecismus* and Alexander Neckham's *Corrogationes Promethei,* were hopelessly ill-informed. The nearest we come to dictionaries of the kind that might have been composed to help with translating literary or scientific works are the Hebrew-Italian glossary of Moses of Salerno and a Greek-Latin lexicon that is now in the College of Arms in London (MS Arundel 9), which may have been used by Robert Grosseteste. There are also occasionally short lists of technical terms, with explanations, appended to translated texts.

Training. Formal teaching of foreign languages entered late into the schools and universities. Much has been made of the provisions of the Council of Vienne of 1311–1312, through which professorships were to be set up in Greek, Arabic, Hebrew, and Syriac in the universities of Paris, Oxford, Bologna, and Salamanca, and at the papal curia. These professorships, however, were designed specifically for training missionaries and arose out of the same impulse as the thirteenth-century *studia linguarum* of the friars, and there is little evidence that the injunctions of the council were fully carried out. The first appointment of a lecturer to teach Greek literature appears to have been made in Florence in 1360. (French was widely taught in English schools in the later Middle Ages, but remained an "extra" on the curriculum at Oxford University.)

As early as the twelfth century, Peter Abelard endorsed the study of Hebrew for the nuns of the Paraclete, and Roger Bacon in 1266–1267 brought to the pope's attention the importance of learning Hebrew, Greek, and Latin for the study of theology, and of learning Arabic for philosophy and the conversion of the infidels. Such pleas appear, how-

ever, to have had little effect. Lorenzo Minio-Paluello's statement that "Greek scholarship in the thirteenth century was not the product of a long tradition in well-organized schools, but the hard-won possession of isolated individuals," can be applied to all foreign languages during that period.

Translators were forced back onto their own initiatives. John of Salisbury found himself a Greek teacher. Robert Grosseteste invited Greek clerks to Lincoln, and probably learned his Greek from John Basingstoke, who wrote the earliest Greek grammar for Latin readers. The Sicilian translator of Ptolemy's *Almagest* (*ca.* 1160) applied himself to learning the language and reading some preliminary mathematical works before translating this magnum opus. Sometimes the name of the native speaker who helped the translator survives. He may have interpreted the text as well as attempted to teach the language.

Teachers and students. Several translators have the title *magister*—for instance, Hugo of Santalla; Magister "Johannes," a collaborator of Dominicus Gundissalinus; Hermann von Carinthia, also called *scholasticus*; and Gerard of Cremona, *dictus magister.* Although it appears from the title *magister* that these translators were teachers, there is no evidence that they actually taught their students how to translate. Rather, they taught the underlying subject matter that interested them. We know of several scholars who studied under Hermann and Gerard, for instance, but as far as we know none of them became translators themselves. The one example of a "second-generation" translator from Arabic into Latin is a certain "Ocreatus," who translated an Arabic multiplication table for his "master," the translator Adelard of Bath. In the case of Jewish translators, on the other hand, the skill of translating was often passed from one generation to another, as, for instance, in the Tibbonid and Kalonymus families.

Translators in other professions. Sometimes enlightened kings encouraged translating within their courts. Alfonso X, king of Castile and León from 1252 to 1284, employed some fifteen different translators to turn works from Arabic into Castilian. When their function is mentioned, however, they are described as notaries, scribes, envoys, or doctors, and not as translators. Charles V, king of France (1364–1380), had at least eight translators rendering works from Latin into French, but these were the leading intellectuals of his circle, including Nicole Oresme, the philosopher.

THE TRANSLATOR'S AIMS AND INTERESTS

At any point during the Middle Ages, to speak of a "professional translator" would be misleading. Bilingual speakers often found themselves employment as interpreters, and occasionally translators fulfilled this role. For example, Burgundio of Pisa assisted in the discussions between Western and Eastern clergy in Constantinople in 1136. Mention of payment to the translator is made in the case of Peter the Venerable of Cluny, who, in 1141, persuaded Hermann von Carinthia and Robert of Ketton "with a great sum of money" to translate several Islamic theological texts, including the Koran. But Hermann and Robert were not primarily translators. Robert was an archdeacon, and both were more interested in science, particularly mathematics and astronomy, than they were in the Arabic language. Even William of Moerbeke, who virtually single-handedly revised and completed the translations of Aristotle's works from the Greek in intervals in his active ecclesiastical career, considered himself primarily a philosopher, prevented from writing his own philosophical works by his other duties. An interest in the subject matter came before an interest in the language. Thus, the translators of medical works in the Middle Ages tended to be doctors, while those of works concerning the science of the stars were often astrologers.

The poverty of the Latins. The translations were made because of the "poverty" of the receiving culture in the fields in which the translators were interested. The phrase *Latinorum penuria* ("the poverty of the Latins") is repeated like a litany by translators from Greek and Arabic alike (for example, Alphanus of Salerno, Hugo Etherianus, and Gerard of Cremona) and is echoed by translators from Latin into the vernacular. Several translators describe their search for the rich treasuries of another language. Adelard of Bath, writing in the early years of the twelfth century, accounts for his journey from Tours to the Greek-speaking part of Italy with the words: "What French studies are ignorant of, studies from across the Alps will reveal; what you will not learn amongst the Latins, Greek eloquence will teach you." Gerard of Cremona went to Spain to search for the Arabic text of Ptolemy's *Almagest*.

The lure of the exotic. The mere fact that a work derived from (or was said to derive from) another language might add a touch of the exotic to that work. Many magical and popular scientific works have impressive pedigrees which trace their subject matter through several languages. The *Secret of Secrets*, a manual of statecraft and a regimen of health attributed to Aristotle, gives a story that is part true, part fantastic, but typical of the genre:

> John, son of Patricius, who translated this book, a most skilled and faithful interpreter of tongues, says: There was no repository or temple in which philosophers were wont to deposit their secret works which I did not visit, nor was there any highly qualified man whom I believed to have some knowledge about philosophical works whom I did not search out, until I came to the oracle of the Sun which Asclepius had constructed for himself. In this I found a certain hermit . . . whom I served diligently and beseeched piously that he might show me the secret writings of that oracle. This he freely granted, and, among the rest, I found the longed-for work, in search of which I had come to that place . . . and I translated it first from the Greek language into Chaldean, and then from Chaldean into Arabic.

Numerous works in Latin, and from Latin translated into the vernaculars, purported to be themselves translations of the writings of Hermes Trismegistus, al-Kindī, Plato, or Aristotle, so that their readers would be led to think that they were being initiated into ancient or Oriental wisdom.

THE TRANSLATOR'S METHODS AND THEORIES

A doctor or an astrologer, or even a storyteller, might extract the essence of a foreign work or works without providing a translation in the strict sense. Thus, a work on weather forecasting is said to have been "summarized from the writings of the Indians" and "edited" by Hermann von Carinthia. Petrus Alfonsi was the "composer" (*compositor*) of a book of exemplary tales, probably originally in Hebrew. Constantine the African's versions of Arabic medical texts are notoriously free. The pattern repeats itself in the case of Latin medical texts rendered into Middle English, such as the summaries of Latin treatises on phlebotomy mentioned by Linda Voigts. The *sensus* is more important than the *littera*.

Yet, the *sensus* itself was sometimes considered to have been betrayed. Stephen of Antioch made a new translation of the *Kāwil al-malikī* of ʿAlī ibn al-ʿAbbās because of what he regarded as the inadequacy of Constantine's version. A "Johannes" wrote a new translation (from Greek) of Aristotle's *Posterior Analytics* because he found Boethius' incomplete and James of Venice's defective (though he tacitly made use of the latter).

Western traditions of translating. The translator who took his task seriously, although he lacked both an institutional formation and, in all probability, a master to whom he might apprentice himself, could still follow a tradition. This tradition was established on the twin authority of the giants of biblical and philosophical translation respectively, St. Jerome (*ca.* 331–419/420) and Boethius (*ca.* 480–524/526).

In St. Jerome, the classical mode of translating, established by Cicero in his "De optimo genere oratorum" (14 and 23) and Horace in his "Ars poetica" (vv. 133–134), is modified, not so much for the sake of greater accuracy and scientific method as for spiritual reasons. Jerome explains, in his letter to Pammachius, that the accepted method is to render sense for sense and produce an elegant Latin, befitting the orator, and this is the method he would prefer to use himself. However, in translating Holy Scripture the very order of the words has a mystical significance and must be preserved in the translation.

Boethius, apparently aware of Jerome's strictures, goes a stage further. He applies the *verbum de verbo* method to philosophical works, too. He apologizes for being, in so doing, a mere "faithful interpreter" (Horace's term) of the text, rather than a composer of elegant Latin. His words, at the beginning of his second commentary on the *Isagoge* of Porphyry, were to become the classical expression of medieval translation theory:

> I fear that I shall commit the fault of the faithful interpreter when I render each word by a word corresponding to it. The reason for this approach is that, in the writings in which knowledge of the subject matter is sought, it is not the charm of limpid speech but the unsullied truth that has to be expressed. Therefore I feel I have been most useful if, in composing books of philosophy in the Latin language, through the integrity of a completely full translation, not a single letter of the Greek is found missing.

This passage is alluded to by John Scottus Eriugena in the preface to his translation of Pseudo-Dionysius the Areopagite's *De caelesti hierarchia.* That the *verbum de verbo* method of translation was identified with the name of Boethius is suggested by a passage in the preface to the translation of Abū Maᶜshar's *Introductorium maius* (*al-Madkhal al-Kabīs*), in which Hermann von Carin-

thia records some words of advice given to him by his collaborator, Robert of Ketton: "Although, dear Hermann, neither you, according to your custom, nor any other well-advised interpreter of a foreign language, should in any way depart from the precept of Boethius in translating things, nevertheless it seems that a course at variance with Boethius' should at times be followed."

A twelfth-century commentator on Boethius' *De arithmetica* (MS Bern 633, fol. 21ᵛ, col. a) writes that "there are three kinds of translating. The first is when only the substance (*materia*) is transmitted; the second is when the substance is transmitted and the sense of the words (*sensus*) is preserved; the third gives the substance and the sense and is a word-for-word (*verbum ex verbo*) translation." The third method, the commentator adds, is the most difficult.

Roger Bacon, in the chapter on the study of foreign languages in his *Opus tertium*, refers to St. Jerome's letter to Pammachius and cites Boethius as the only translator who knew both the source and receptor languages. Even Jerome does not escape Bacon's stringent criticism.

Burgundio of Pisa, the translator of several theological works from Greek into Latin in the mid twelfth century, gives the most detailed history of the *verbum ex verbo* method of translating from antiquity to his day in the prologue to his translation of the commentary of St. John Chrysostom on the Gospel of John. Burgundio repeats the words of St. Jerome and cites as examples of *verbum ex verbo* translation the Septuagint, the Vulgate, and Calcidius' translation of Plato's *Timaeus,* among other works.

The *verbum ex verbo* method appears to have been the norm in the great period of translating philosophical and scientific works from Greek and Arabic. The extent to which it could be applied depended partly on the nature of the source language, partly on the scrupulousness of the translator.

Burgundio, in the preface referred to above, states that he has decided to translate *verbum ex verbo* but is obliged to fill in deficiencies in Latin by representing a Greek word with a Latin periphrasis of two or three words, or by replacing what would result in a barbaric expression in Latin with a correct and appropriate turn of phrase. His contemporary, Henricus Aristippus, in the preface to his translation from Greek of Plato's *Meno,* adheres to a literal translation because he fears that "if he allowed his small intelligence to alter the strict sense, he would introduce alien meanings."

The translations from Greek of Aristotle's philosophical works in the twelfth and thirteenth centuries are so closely literal that anonymous translators can be differentiated from each other on the basis of the different Latin words they use for the same Greek terms. (Lorenzo Minio-Paluello has isolated on this basis at least eight different translators, most of them anonymous, from the twelfth century alone.) In many instances a Latin translation has given modern scholars a better reading of the original Greek text than the existing Greek manuscripts, which are often later and freer with their source than the Latin.

Arabic, because it is not an Indo-European language, is less amenable than Greek to a word-for-word translation into Latin. Hugo of Santalla (*fl.* 1145) gives a graphic picture of the difficulties facing an Arabic-Latin translator:

> Often the translator gasps under the strain of the difficulties. He sees some strange word that resists being translated correctly because of either the variety of diacritical marks on the letters, or the lack of marks—often, too, because of the incompatible differences of languages in all of which the significance of the roots is different. Then he simply guesses what the word means, lest he may seem to have left out a word, or to be more stupid than he already is.

John of Seville, otherwise notorious for his rendering of Arabic into a Latin that follows Semitic rather than Romance syntax, apologizes in the preface to his translation of Pseudo-Aristotle's *Regimen sanitatis* for not completely following the letter, but, in certain cases, following the sense instead. Hermann von Carinthia complains about the prolixity of the Arabic language and abbreviates his original texts considerably.

It is the translators from Arabic into Latin who received the severest censure from Roger Bacon in his chapter on the study of foreign languages. He writes that "there are others who translated an almost unending series of works into Latin, like Gerard of Cremona, Michael Scot, Alfred the Englishman, Hermann the German . . . ; these had the presumption to translate innumerable works but knew neither sciences nor languages, not even Latin."

This censure is unjust. In Arabic-Latin translations, however, one can often make a distinction between an interpreter—who, to a greater or lesser extent, explains the source text—and the translator, who produces the Latin version. Thus, Gerard of Cremona is said to have "latinized" Ptolemy's *Almagest,* while a certain Mozarab called Ghalib was "interpreting it" ("Galippo mixtarabe interpretante Almagesti latinavit"). It has been assumed that the interpreter translated the Arabic text into a vernacular Romance language, which was then latinized, and this assumption is borne out by, for example, the translations of Alfred of Sareshel, which retain several Spanish words. However, the text established by Simone van Riet for a passage in the preface to the translation of Ibn Sīnā's *De anima* concerning the method used by the translators, suggests that a Jew called Avendauth was pronouncing (*proferente*) the Arabic words one at a time as they were spoken by the people (*vulgariter*), while the Christian archdeacon, Dominicus Gundissalinus, who presumably spoke Arabic but did not read the language, wrote down the Latin equivalent to each of these words as he heard them. None of these methods, of course, would be as good as a direct translation from the Greek text if that were available, as was noted by the anonymous twelfth-century translator of Ptolemy's *Optics.*

THE TRANSLATOR'S AUDIENCE

The public for which translations were made was as various as the subjects of the translations and the languages into which they were made. Translations of philosophical and scientific works from Greek and Arabic into Latin were most frequently meant for a university readership or for the use of specialists in particular fields. The translation of works from Latin into various vernaculars suggests that literacy was spreading beyond the precincts of the schoolroom and the church. For example, the adaptations of Adelard of Bath's treatise on falconry into Old French and Provençal in the thirteenth century suggest that the nobility was reading these works. Linda Voigts describes how one medical work was "Englished" for a barber-surgeon.

The spread of the influence of a scientific work geographically and through the various strata of a society can be assessed from its translation history. The medical aphorisms of Ibn Māsawayh were translated from Arabic into Latin in the twelfth century, and by the fifteenth century had been translated (at least in part) into Scottish Gaelic. Extracts from the *Rosa medicinae anglicana* of

John of Gaddesden (d. 1361) were translated into Irish in the Yellow Book of Lecan in 1390.

Several popular traditions of divination, magic, medicine, and cosmology can be traced to translations, often those made from Arabic in the twelfth century. The main audience for translations, however, was in the schoolroom. The staple diet of quadrivial university education in the West was the works of Aristotle, Euclid, Ptolemy, Hippocrates, Galen, Ibn Sīnā, and al-Rāzī, and commentaries and other works derivative from these. All these authors were studied in Latin translations until the time of the Renaissance and the humanist revival of the classics in their original languages.

CONCLUSION

Medieval translations were much disparaged in the Renaissance. Representative of this criticism is Leonardo Bruni's opinion of William of Moerbeke's translation of Aristotle's *Nicomachean Ethics*, expressed in the preface to his own translation of about 1417. He accuses the earlier translation of being barbarous, and hardly Latin at all, of being both too literal and too inaccurate, and of containing too many untranslated Greek words. He advocates, here and in his tract "On the Right Way of Translating" (*ca.* 1420), a concern for literary style in translating. Yet Bruni's criticism is unjust. The best of the translators of the Middle Ages had evolved a methodology that befitted the materials with which they were working, and they were truly masters of their craft.

BIBLIOGRAPHY

Commentators on translating, in chronological order. Cicero, "De optimo genere oratorum," in his *De inventione, De optimo genere oratorum, Topica*, Harry M. Hubbell, trans. (1949); St. Jerome, Epistula 57, "Ad Pammachium de optimo genere interpretandi," in Isidorus Hilberg, ed., *Sancti Eusebii Hieronymi epistulae*, I (1910), 503–526 (the text is also in G. J. M. Bartelink, *Liber de optimo genere interpretandi [Epistula 57]: Ein Kommentar* [1980]); Boethius, *In isagogen Porphyrii commenta*, Georgius Schepss and Samuel Brandt, eds. (1906); Burgundio of Pisa, preface to the translation of St. John Chrysostom's commentary on the Gospel of John, in Peter Classen, *Burgundio von Pisa* (1974); Roger Bacon, *Opus tertium*, c. 25 ("De linguis seu de utilitate grammaticae"), in J. S. Brewer, ed., *Fr. Rogeri Bacon opera quaedam hactenus inedita*, I (1859), 88–95; Leonardo Bruni, "Praefatio in libros Ethicorum Aristotelis" and "De interpretatione recta," partial editions by Hans Baron in *Leonardo Bruni Aretino: humanistisch-philosophische Schriften* (1928), 75–96.

For further examples see the prefaces to translations edited by Haskins in his *Studies* and the relevant volumes of *Aristoteles latinus,* listed below.

Catalogs of translations. Marie-Thérèse d'Alverny, "Avicenna latinus," in *Archives d'histoire doctrinale et littéraire du moyen âge*, **28–37, 39** (1961–1970, 1972); Francis J. Carmody, *Arabic Astronomical and Astrological Sciences in Latin Translation: A Critical Bibliography* (1956); Alistair C. Crombie, *Medieval and Early Modern Science*, I (1959), 37–47 (a table of translations from Greek and Arabic, with translators and dates); Léopold Delisle, "Traductions faites pour Charles V," in his *Le cabinet des manuscrits de la Bibliothèque Impériale*, I (1868); G. Hardarson and S. Snaevarr, *Heimspekirit á íslandi fram til 1900* (1982); Pearl Kibre, "Hippocrates latinus," in *Traditio*, **31–38** (1975–1982); Paul O. Kristeller, F. Edward Cranz, and Virginia Brown, eds., *Catalogus translationum et commentariorum: Mediaeval and Renaissance Latin Translations and Commentaries,* in progress (1960–); Georgius Lacombe *et al.*, eds., *Aristoteles latinus: Codices*, 2 vols. (1939–1955), with Laurentius Minio-Paluello, ed., *Supplementa altera* (1961); J. T. Muckle, "Greek Works Translated Directly into Latin Before 1350," in *Mediaeval Studies*, **4** (1942) and **5** (1943); Moritz Steinschneider, *Die hebraeischen Übersetzungen des Mittelalters und die Juden als Dolmetscher* (1893, repr. 1956) and "Die europäischen Übersetzungen aus dem Arabischen bis Mitte des 17. Jahrhunderts," in *Sitzungsberichte der kaiserlichen Akademie der Wissenschaften* (Vienna), phil.-hist. Klasse, **149** (1904) and **151** (1905) (repr. 1956); Lynn Thorndike and Pearl Kibre, *A Catalogue of Incipits of Mediaeval Scientific Writings in Latin*, 2nd ed. (1963); Franz J. Worstbrock, *Deutsche Antikerezeption, 1450–1550*, pt. 1: *Verzeichnis der deutschen Übersetzungen antiker Autoren, mit einer Bibliographie der Übersetzer* (1976).

Studies. Marie-Thérèse d'Alverny, "Translations and Translators," in Robert L. Benson and Giles Constable, eds., *Renaissance and Renewal in the Twelfth Century* (1982); Bernhard Bischoff, "The Study of Foreign Languages in the Middle Ages," in his *Mittelalterliche Studien*, II (1967), 227–245; Georg Bossong, *Probleme der Übersetzung wissenschaftlicher Werke aus dem Arabischen in das Altspanische zur Zeit Alfons des Weisen* (1979); Sebastian Brock, "Aspects of Translation Technique in Antiquity," in *Greek, Roman, and Byzantine Studies*, **20** (1979); Charles S. F. Burnett, "Some Comments on the Translating of Works from Arabic into Latin in the Mid-Twelfth Century," in Albert Zimmermann *et al.*, eds., *Orientalische Kultur und europäisches Mittelalter* (1985), 161–171; D. A. Callus, ed., *Robert Grosseteste, Scholar and Bishop* (1955), 36–68; Charles Homer Haskins, *Studies in the History of Mediaeval Science* (1924, 2nd ed. 1927); M. R. James, "A Graeco-

Latin Lexicon of the Thirteenth Century," in *Mélanges offerts à M. Émile Chatelain* (1920), 396–411; Paul Kunitzsch, *Glossar der arabischen Fachausdrücke in der mittelalterlichen europäischen Astrolabliteratur* (1982); David C. Lindberg, "The Transmission of Greek and Arabic Learning to the West," in his *Science in the Middle Ages,* (1978), 52–90; José María Millás y Vallicrosa, *Las traducciones orientales en los manuscritos de la Biblioteca catedral de Toledo* (1942); Lorenzo Minio-Paluello, *Opuscula: The Latin Aristotle* (1972); Alastair J. Minnis, ed., *The Medieval Boethius: Studies in the Vernacular Translations of De Consolatione Philosophiae* (1988); John E. Murdoch, "Euclides Graeco-Latinus: A Hitherto Unknown Medieval Latin Translation of the *Elements* Made Directly from the Greek," in *Harvard Studies in Classical Philology,* **71** (1967); Maura Power, *An Irish Astronomical Tract* (1914); Evelyn S. Procter, *Alfonso X of Castile, Patron of Literature and Learning* (1951); Charles Samaran, "Pierre Bersuire," in *Histoire littéraire de la France,* **39** (1962), 259–450; W. Schwarz, "The Meaning of *Fidus interpres* in Medieval Translation," in *Journal of Theological Studies,* **45** (1944), 73–78; Simone Van Riet, *Avicenna latinus, Liber de anima seu Sextus de naturalibus I–II–III* (1972), 91–105; Juan Vernet Ginés, *La cultura hispano-árabe en oriente y occidente* (1978); Linda E. Voigts, "Editing Middle English Texts," in Trevor H. Levere, ed., *Editing Texts in the History of Science and Medicine* (1982), 39–68, and "Medical Prose," in A. S. G. Edwards, ed., *Middle English Prose: A Critical Guide to Major Authors and Genres* (1984); Robert O. Weiss, "The Translators from Greek of the Angevin Court of Naples," in *Rinascimento,* **1** (1950), 195–226.

CHARLES S. F. BURNETT

[See also **Adelard of Bath; Alexander Romances; Alfonso X; Alfred the Great and Translations; Alphanus of Salerno; Archimedes in the Middle Ages; Aristotle in the Middle Ages; Astrology/Astronomy; Bacon, Roger; Bible, French; Bible, Old and Middle English; Boethius, Anicius Manlius Severinus; Bruni, Leonardo; Burgundio of Pisa; Cairo Genizah; Classical Literary Studies; Constantine the African; French Literature: Translations; Geoffrey of Monmouth; Grosseteste, Robert; Gerard of Cremona; Herman the German; Hermann von Carinthia; Hilduin of St. Denis; Jerome, St.; John Scottus Eriugena; Livres de Jostice et de Plet, Li; Lo Codi; Lull, Ramon; Mandeville's Travels; Mathematics; Matter of Britain, Matter of France, Matter of Rome; Medicine, History of; Michael Scot; Missions and Missionaries, Christian; Optics, Western European; Oresme, Nicole; Peter the Venerable; Pierre de Fontaines; Philosophy and Theology, Western European; Plato in the Middle Ages; Pseudo-Dionysius the Areopagite; Ptolemaic Astronomy; Spanish Literature: Bible Translations; Spanish Literature: Translations; Textbooks; William of Moerbeke.]**

TRANSLATION OF BISHOPS (from the past participle of *transferre,* "to transfer"). A bishop is "translated" when he is moved from one diocese to another. The early church disapproved of translations and passed laws against them because the relationship between a bishop and his church was thought to be as close and as indissoluble as that of marriage. Translations continued, nevertheless, because the importance, the prestige, and the wealth of major sees required and attracted management by the most able clerics. With the imperial patronage of Christianity in the fourth century came an additional reason for bishops to move: their activity in the civil and judicial functioning of the empire. Because of this, episcopal appointments and translations became more and more the emperors' prerogative, particularly in the Eastern church. As a result, translations of bishops were very common, and the old rules against them fell into desuetude. As Christianity moved north from Constantinople, the intimate relationship between church and state continued. In the Slavic nations the appointment of bishops depended ultimately on both the Byzantine emperor and local rulers, and translations continued to be a normal part of church life.

In the West the rule against a bishop's changing his see was at first more strictly observed. The number of translations increased with the rise of the Frankish kingdoms and royal control of church affairs. Because the reception of a bishopric had become a sign of royal favor, a reward for some service performed, or a source of revenue to the state treasury, bishops who had some such claim upon the king could expect to move to a more important see. Occasional synodal objections were without effect.

During the investiture controversies of the eleventh and twelfth centuries, the popes tried to gain control of episcopal appointments. But their objections to bishops changing their sees were not so much against translation in itself as against an independent exercise of civil authority in church matters. Translations were universally accepted because, in the words of Thomas Becket (*d.* 1170), they served both the general profit of the kingdom and the church's need as long as they were approved by the archbishop, the pope, and the king. There were frequent translations into the papacy itself, especially during the Avignon period (1309–1377). Like many other bishops, these popes often arrived at their position after a series of translations.

The Council of Constance (1414–1418) passed a

decree concerning translations. Except for a grave reason, no bishop was to be moved against his will because a fear of being translated might weaken his enforcement of the church's rights. Even this moderate decree remained only a pious wish.

BIBLIOGRAPHY

R. G. Davies, "Thomas Arundel as Archbishop of Canterbury," in *Journal of Ecclesiastical History,* **24** (1973), describes the career of a fourteenth-century bishop who rose to the see of Canterbury in a series of translations; Pius Gams, *Series episcoporum ecclesiae catholicae* (1873–1886, repr. 1957), a list of bishops in union with Rome from the earliest times until the nineteenth century, with their translations indicated; A. Hamilton Thompson, *The English Clergy and Their Organization in the Later Middle Ages* (1947), esp. chap. 1, "The Episcopate," including information about the translation of bishops.

DANIEL CALLAM

[See also **Church, Latin: Organization; Investiture and Investiture Conflict.**]

TRANSLATION OF EMPIRE. Although it is commonly believed that the theory of the transfer of dominion from one world empire to another had its origins in such biblical passages as Daniel 2:21, these texts referred to the overthrow of individual kings or changes in dynasties. The theory originated, instead, among such Roman historians as Sallust, whose views were adopted by Christian writers, such as Eusebius of Caesarea. The formula *imperium* or *regnum transferre* entered the Bible from Roman historiography through Jerome's translation. While ancient authors had used the phrase for events that occurred outside of Roman history, medieval scholars applied it to events that took place within the time span of the Roman world monarchy, most notably Charlemagne's imperial coronation.

Since Daniel's vision of four world empires appeared to indicate that the Roman Empire would survive until the appearance of the Antichrist, most medieval writers before 1100 viewed Charlemagne's coronation as a revival either of the unified Roman Empire that had existed before Diocletian or of the Western Empire of late antiquity. The latter interpretation had the advantage of also explaining the continued existence of the Byzantine

Empire. The permanent union of the imperial dignity with the German crown after 962, growing anti-Greek feelings, and the belief in the unity of Christendom made the dualism implicit in this interpretation unacceptable by the twelfth century. It was replaced by the view that the rule of a united Roman Empire had been transferred in 800 from the Greeks to the Franks and/or Germans (those writers who did not perceive the Franks as Germans argued that a second translation had occurred in 962). The transfer could be attributed to Charlemagne's acclamation by the Roman people, Charlemagne's God-given virtues and victories, or Charlemagne's coronation by the pope.

The latter curial theory of the *translatio imperii* seems to have originated during Alexander III's battle against Frederick I Barbarossa in the 1160's and was employed by Innocent III to justify his intervention in the disputed German election of 1198. Innocent's letter to Duke Berthold of Zähringen, which declared that the German princes had obtained the right to elect the future emperor when the apostolic see had transferred the Roman Empire from the Greeks to the Germans in the person of Charlemagne, entered canon law as the decretal *Venerabilem.* Implicit in this curial interpretation was the threat that the pope could also deprive the princes of their electoral rights and the Germans of their imperial dignity.

The curial theory lost its political significance after the electors declared at Rhens in 1338 that the German king exercised his imperial authority from the moment of his election, but the theory survived among both Catholic and Protestant historians, especially in Germany, until the seventeenth century. A number of factors contributed to its gradual abandonment: the humanists' study of Roman history; the discovery of nations that had never been ruled by Rome; the papacy's quiet renunciation of its claims to immediate authority in temporal matters; and Calvin's exegesis of Daniel's vision of four world empires as having been fulfilled by the time of the Incarnation.

BIBLIOGRAPHY

Werner Goez, *Translatio imperii: Ein Beitrag zur Geschichte des Geschichtsdenkens und der politischen Theorien im Mittelalter und in der frühen Neuzeit* (1958). The text of Innocent's letter to Berthold of Zähringen is in *Regestum Innocentii III Papae super negotio Romani imperii,* Friedrich Kempf, ed. (1947), 166–175.

JOHN B. FREED

Procession possibly showing the relics of St. Stephen being transported to Constantinople and received by the empress in 421. Byzantine ivory plaque, 6th century, TRIER, CATHEDRAL TREASURY

[See also **Alexander III, Pope; Charlemagne; Elections, Royal; Eusebius of Caesarea; Frederick I Barbarossa; Germany: Idea of Empire; Holy Roman Empire; Innocent III, Pope; Investiture and Investiture Conflict; Jerome, St.; Papacy, Origins and Development of; Roman Empire, Late.**]

TRANSLATION OF SAINTS, the solemn carrying of saints' relics to altars where they will have final resting places. Translations may be within a church or local or long-distance. Related ceremonies include inventions of the saints (the discoveries of their relics) and elevations (the raising of their bodies to more exalted resting places). In the early Middle Ages such rituals had the effect of canonization. Hagiographers recorded these events and their attendant miracles in literary genres bearing the same names: *translatio, inventio,* and *elevatio.*

Translation customs developed gradually. At first Christians, observing the Roman prohibitions against disturbing bodily remains, left the ancient cities to journey to suburban cemeteries to venerate the corporeal relics of martyrs. Such relics began to come to Christians from the mid fourth century onward, when the Eastern Roman emperors translated them to converted temple sites and to Constantinople. From the fourth century, translations

and dismemberments of the bodies of saints were common in the Greek church. When Constantinople was dedicated as the new Eastern capital in 330, relics were required to assure the protection of God and the prestige of the city. Accordingly, in 356–357 the relics of Sts. Andrew, Luke, and Timothy were carried to the "New Rome."

Although in the West the popes, at least through the time of Gregory the Great (*d.* 604), discouraged the division and physical translation of saints' bodies, nevertheless churches gladly accepted relics evacuated from devastated areas. Ambrose did not hesitate to translate Gervais and Protais, and a relic trade did exist, known from occasional criticism of abuses.

Merovingian saints' lives frequently conclude with attached *elevationes* because these witness the official acclamation of the saints. The elaborate translation rituals described in Merovingian liturgical handbooks suggest the ancient ceremonies for the arrival (*adventus*) of an emperor.

From the eighth through the eleventh century, the West transported and dismembered holy bodies with a zeal that surpassed the East, where interest had shifted to icons. The great Carolingian monasteries, especially those in recently christianized areas, sought new relics of holy patrons for their altars. The cemeteries of Rome were now opened to relic hunters thanks to popular pressure and to the

144

Carolingian/papal alliance. Although Charlemagne attempted to control the resulting flood of translations, his legislation had little effect in later years, when monks and their saints fled Viking invaders, French collectors found holy bodies in Spain, and Otto the Great looted the tombs of Italy. In this era *translationes* became independent literary works read liturgically for special feasts: the narrative patterns even include accounts of relic thefts, following Einhard's *Translatio et miracula SS. Marcellini et Petri* (*ca.* 830).

An elaborate procedure was followed when relics were to be translated, whether to another city or merely to a more splendid shrine. Permission of the king was required for the former. The solemn procession and installation were preceded by a vigil and fasting and accompanied by special rites that have continued to this day in ceremonies of consecrating an altar or church. Miracles were profuse along the route. The date of translation often became a new feast, such as that of Thomas Becket (*d.* 1170) on 7 July 1220.

In later centuries the significance of translations declined, despite the importation of Eastern relics by crusaders, the accumulation of large private relic collections, and the popularity of elevations, ostentations, and relic peregrinations. The official need for elaborate relic ceremonial was weakened by the secularization of governmental and judicial processes. Elevations lost much of their meaning when the Fourth Lateran Council (1215) established canonization as a papal prerogative.

BIBLIOGRAPHY

A comprehensive treatment of translations is Martin Heinzelmann, *Translationsberichte und andere Quellen des Reliquienkultes* (1979). See also Peter Brown, *The Cult of the Saints: Its Rise and Function in Latin Christianity* (1981); Patrick J. Geary, *"Furta Sacra": Thefts of Relics in the Central Middle Ages* (1978); Kenneth G. Holum and Gary Vikan, "The Trier Ivory, *Adventus* Ceremonial, and the Relics of St. Stephen," in *Dumbarton Oaks Papers*, 33 (1979); John M. McCulloh, "From Antiquity to the Middle Ages: Continuity and Change in Papal Relic Policy from the 6th to the 8th Century," in Ernst Dassmann and K. Suso Frank, eds., *Pietas: Festschrift für Bernhard Kötting* (1980); O. F. A. Meinardus, "An Examination of the Traditions Pertaining to the Relics of St. Mark," in *Orientalia christiana periodica*, 36 (1970); Pierre Riché, "Translation de reliques à l'époque carolingienne," in *Le moyen âge*, 82 (1976); Gerd Tellenbach, "Zur Translation einer Reliquie des Heiligen Laurentius von Rom nach Lüttich im elften Jahrhundert," in *Storiografia e storia: Studi in onore di Eugenio Duprè Theseider*, II (1974).

DANIEL CALLAM
JOHN HOWE

[See also **Einhard; Hagiography; Martyrdom; Martyrology; Relics; Reliquary.**]

TRANSOXIANA, the lands beyond the Oxus River (or Amu Darya) (Arabic: *Mā warāʾ al-Nahr,* "the land that lies beyond the river"), now substantially the Uzbek, Tadzhik, and Kirghiz SSR's. The term was always a vague one, and in Islamic times might have included the more northerly kingdom of Khwarizm (ancient Chorasmia) on the lower reaches of the Oxus. The borders of Transoxiana ended where the political control of Islam ended, which meant, until the eleventh century, the valley of the Jaxartes (Syr Darya). Beyond lay the steppes of Siberia, into which Islam only gradually penetrated over a period of centuries against such indigenous beliefs as shamanistic animism and an admixture of older faiths such as Christianity and Buddhism. This expansion of Islam was checked only by the advance of Muscovite Russia across Siberia to the Pacific in the seventeenth century.

Arab troops first crossed the Oxus in 674 under the general ʿUbayd Allāh ibn Ziyād, and advanced to Bukhara. The Iranian princes of this region of Soghdia (Sogdiana; Arabic: *al-Sughd*), between the Oxus and the Jaxartes, fought a tenacious battle against the invaders, with help from the western Turks of the steppes and from the distant Chinese Empire, which claimed a vague suzerainty over Central Asia. With the final defeat of a Chinese army near Talas and Tashkent in 751, Arab control of the region became reasonably firm. The Islamization of the region now proceeded, slowly and unevenly. From the lands of the Samanids (819–1005), Islamic evangelism was carried into the surrounding steppes, leading to the conversion of Turkic tribes there, including the Oghuz, which around the year 1000 burst into the Islamic world and established the powerful Great Seljuk sultanate (1038–1194).

Further waves of steppe peoples now found that Transoxiana provided an easy corridor into the rich, plunder-laden lands of the Middle East. Hence, it was through Transoxiana that the Mongols burst in the thirteenth century, and Tam-

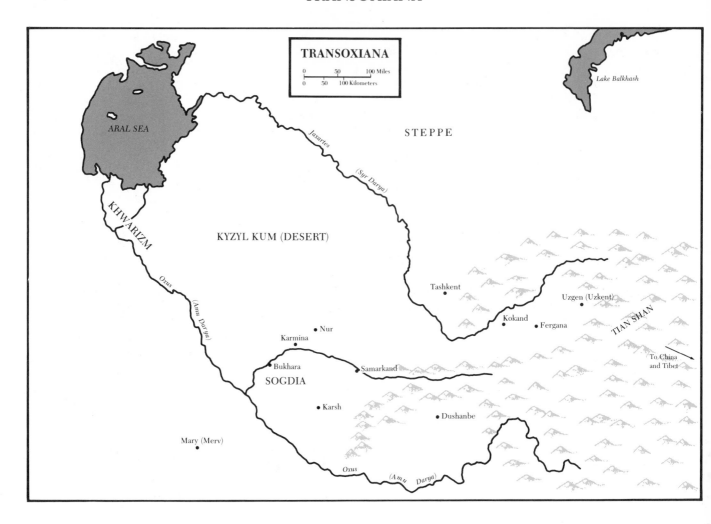

TRANSOXIANA

0   50   100 Miles
0   50   100 Kilometers

ARAL SEA

Lake Balkhash

STEPPE

KHWĀRIZM

Jaxartes

(Syr Darya)

KYZYL KUM (DESERT)

Oxus

(Amu Darya)

Tashkent

Uzgen (Uzkent)

Kokand

Fergana

TIAN SHAN

Nur

Karmina

Samarkand

To China
and Tibet

Bukhara

SOGDIA

Karsh

Dushanbe

Mary (Merv)

Oxus   (Amu   Darya)

erlane (Tīmūr) in the late fourteenth century. It was not until the advent of firearms to the region, in the sixteenth century, that the settled peoples were able, through their superior firepower, to turn the tables on the nomadic horsemen from Central Asia.

Economically and commercially, Transoxiana was especially important for the medieval caliphate in that it was through this region that large numbers of Turkic slaves, supremely valued as soldiers, came into the Middle East, together with such products of the steppes and forests of Siberia as hides, honey, wax, and, above all, luxury furs. Even Chinese porcelain made the long and hazardous land journey through Central Asia to the caliphal lands. Furthermore, the manufacture of paper seems to have been introduced to the Islamic world from China via Central Asia in the eighth century. The trade through Siberia and southern Russia led to the circulation of Islamic silver coins in large quantities in Russia, Scandinavia, and northern Europe between the ninth and eleventh centuries.

BIBLIOGRAPHY
Vasily V. Barthold, *Four Studies on the History of Central Asia,* 3 vols., Vladimir Minorsky and T. Minorsky, trans. (1956–), and *Turkestan Down to the Mongol Invasion,* T. Minorsky, trans., 4th ed. (1977); Emil Bretschneider, *Medieval Researches from Eastern Asiatic Sources,* 2 vols. (1888); Hamilton A. R. Gibb, *The Arab Conquests in Central Asia* (1923, repr. 1970); René Grousset, *The Empire of the Steppes,* Naomi Walford, trans. (1970); Gavin Hambly, ed., *Central Asia* (1969); Francis H. Skrine and Edward D. Ross, *The Heart of Asia* (1899, repr. 1973).

CLIFFORD E. BOSWORTH

[See also **Bukhara; Furs, Fur Trade; Iran; Islam, Conquests of; Khazars; Khwārizmshāhs; Mongol Empire; Qarakhanids; Samanids; Samarkand; Seljuks; Slavery, Slave Trade; Tamerlane; Timurids; Turkomans.**]

TRANSVERSE ARCH. See **Arch.**

TRAVEL AND TRANSPORT, ISLAMIC. Freedom of movement is one of the hallmarks of medieval Islamic civilization. Geographers, chroniclers, travel diarists, and religious writers provide ample and continuous testimony to the importance of travel for the middle and upper strata of society. The exposure of other social groups to travelers and foreign commodities was also influential in shaping the culture.

Reasons for travel were numerous, some of them applying simultaneously to the same individual. Long-distance trade was well established from the very beginning of Islam, and was encouraged by religious attitudes developed within the strongly commercial environment of Mecca. Islam regarded a journey to perform the pilgrimage rites at Mecca as a duty incumbent upon every capable Muslim at least once in a lifetime. And from the eleventh century on, there was increasing interest in pious visitations and pilgrimages to myriad other shrines and holy tombs throughout the Islamic world. Trade and pilgrimage could be combined without religious objection, and several years might be spent making the pilgrimage to Mecca from some distant location.

A third travel objective was commonly combined with these two: the search for religious knowledge, particularly in the form of traditional lore (*ḥadīth*) concerning the prophet Muḥammad. Indeed, some of the sayings of the Prophet explicitly enjoined such travels in quest of knowledge. But more important as an inspiration was the educational stricture, which prevailed through the eleventh century, that valid learning was dependent upon direct oral transmission. A *ḥadīth* relating the words or deeds of the Prophet might be read in a book; but for an aspiring scholar to learn it himself in a fashion that would permit him in later life to transmit it to students of his own, it was necessary for him to sit at the feet of a scholar who could recite it to him orally just as that scholar had once heard it from his teacher. This requirement of an unbroken chain of oral transmission (*isnād*) going back to the Prophet, regarded as the best possible guarantee of authenticity in this vital area of religious knowledge, made it necessary for the industrious scholar to spend months or years traveling from city to city to collect additional lore.

Virtually every scholar of significance traveled extensively at some point in his life, but no simple itinerary can be gleaned from an examination of their wanderings because the search for *ḥadīth* was not governed by a set curriculum. Lore about the Prophet might be found almost anywhere, although major cities like Baghdad, Mecca, Nishapur, and Damascus naturally had the highest concentrations of active teachers. Consequently, there was nothing remarkable about a Spanish Muslim studying in eastern Iran, an eastern Iranian studying in Yemen, a Yemeni studying in Cairo, or an Egyptian studying in Spain.

Other important motivations for travel were nomadic migrations, military campaigns, flight from war or economic distress, and population transfers by government fiat. These categories of movement are not travel in the strictest sense, but they occurred often and fulfilled much the same social and economic function by facilitating an extensive intermixture of peoples and cultures over the broad geographic area of medieval Islam. One form of military travel, the journey to a frontier area to fight against non-Muslims, deserves special note because it was frequently inspired by an individual's religious zeal and could dovetail with the other forms of religiously sanctioned travel.

The impression of a society in which long-distance travel is comparatively commonplace is further reinforced by the infrequency of historical evidence regarding political barriers to travel, even between hostile states, or efforts by governments to control the movements of their subjects. A standard indicator of the strength and prosperity of an Islamic state is the remark that the routes were so secure that travelers could move wherever they wished without molestation. Strong governments are praised for measures to improve facilities for travelers along the routes, such as wells, bridges, and caravansaries. Unhindered travel appears to have been a goal of medieval Islamic government.

Yet travel remained a difficult, exhausting, and expensive activity. Coastal areas and riverine cities that could be reached by water transport were comparatively easy to travel to, but most of the medieval Islamic world depended upon overland connections, which were more arduous, though not necessarily more risky, since shipwreck or pirate attack was as common a peril as banditry. Since wheeled transportation had disappeared from the Middle East almost entirely over the several centuries immediately prior to the rise of Islam, overland transportation was primarily by foot, riding animal, or pack animal. Horses were the special mounts of the military; the ordinary traveling population made do with donkeys, mules, and camels, the latter sometimes being fitted with litters for women or the infirm. Journeying was most commonly by caravan or large traveling party for reasons of security. Daily stages of roughly twenty miles made any trip of a hundred miles or more a major enterprise, and serious travelers normally planned on being absent from their home city for months or years, or forever. The post relay system used by strong governments was several times faster but was not available to ordinary travelers and merchants.

Because of the high cost of overland transport—a bulky commodity like grain roughly doubled in price when shipped a distance of 100 miles—travelers counted upon finding their provisions at intermediate stopping points; in this way small towns and villages that lay on or near trade routes benefited from contact with travelers and involvement in their commerce. Thus the economic characteristics of the transportation system reinforced the overall impact of travelers as agents for disseminating information and ideas throughout the Islamic world. This dissemination, in turn, assisted greatly in the formation of a comparatively uniform pattern of social, religious, and economic institutions that, like the use of Arabic as a lingua franca, softened the hardships of travel and helped the student, merchant, and pilgrim to find a familiar and comfortable reception at the end of a long journey.

BIBLIOGRAPHY

Richard W. Bulliet, "A Quantitative Approach to Medieval Muslim Biographical Dictionaries," in *Journal of the Economic and Social History of the Orient,* 13 (1970), and *The Camel and the Wheel* (1975); Solomon D. Goitein, *A Mediterranean Society,* I, *Economic Foundations* (1967), chap. 4, and *Letters of Medieval Jewish Traders* (1973), chap. 8; André Miquel, *La géographie humaine du monde musulman jusqu'au milieu du 11ᵉ siècle,* I (1967), chap. 4.

RICHARD W. BULLIET

[See also **Animals, Draft; Fairs; Geography and Cartography, Islamic; Ghāzī; Ḥadīth; Jihad; Mecca; Pilgrimage, Islamic; Postal and Intelligence Services, Islamic; Trade, Islamic.**]

TRAVEL AND TRANSPORT, WESTERN EUROPEAN. The Middle Ages presents a paradox with regard to travel. On the one hand, it was the period in which serfs were forbidden to leave the land on which they had been born and in which *stabilitas* (remaining in the same monastery continuously) was considered a prime virtue of a monk. On the other, the medieval period was the great age of pilgrimages; the universal church drew the clergy and faithful to Rome; and rulers and nobles necessarily led an itinerant life. Some of these contradictions can be explained by considering the Middle Ages first in its early period and then in its later development. The Middle Ages inherited a low volume of travel and transport from the end of the Roman period, and disorder and invasions discouraged circulation until the end of the first millennium. Thereafter, travel and transport expanded and reached a much higher level by the end of the Middle Ages than had existed in ancient times.

THE LEGACY OF ROME

A noteworthy benefit of the Roman Empire was easy communication. From the eastern Mediterranean all the way to Britain travel was safe, and it was smoothed by a magnificent network of roads, the remains of which are still to be seen in various parts of Europe. The facility of communication contributed to the early spread of Christianity, and during the first two centuries A.D. a substantial interchange of goods among different parts of the empire had promoted prosperity. By the fourth century, however, there had begun the decline in travel and transportation that was to characterize the early Middle Ages. For example, cultivators were forbidden to leave their farms, and trade became more and more local. In the fifth century, when there was a Visigothic kingdom in southern Gaul, Sidonius Apollinaris (*ca.* 431/432–487/488), prefect of Rome and then bishop of Clermont and a member of a great Gallo-Roman family, wrote to friends and acquaintances, chiding them for staying in the country and devoting themselves to increasing production on their farms. In the Roman tradition, Sidonius called such rustic activities dirty, as well as lazy, for the proper residence of a man of birth was in town and his true vocation was the imperial service. Sidonius' letters show that the Roman roads were being repaired and that the imperial post, the *cursus publicus,* was still in operation, as it was a century later, when Venantius Fortunatus traveled in Gaul. (Use of the post was restricted to government officials, messengers, and those summoned on imperial business.) Sidonius, when prefect of Rome, wrote that the use of the imperial horses and riverboats made the journey thither quick and easy. The route was adequately provided with rest houses, ferries, and bridges.

Travel was more difficult for private persons. Sidonius fulsomely thanked a visitor for having come to him despite the length of the stages, the shortness of the days in winter, the scarcity of provisions, the cramped space of the rest houses, and the state of the roads covered with snow or sloughs of mud. Sidonius valued the amenities while traveling. When leaving town on a hot day for a remote spot in the country, he sent his servants ahead to pitch a tent eighteen miles away in a wooded spot by a cool spring, so that the midday meal would be enjoyable.

In the fifth and sixth centuries travel in Gaul was unsafe. Both Sidonius and Gregory of Tours mention the activities of brigands. Kidnapping of free men and women to be sold as slaves still occurred even in Carolingian times. The battles and skirmishes of the Burgundians and the Franks meant that the timing of journeys had to be carefully calculated. It is true that Sidonius in the fifth century traveled all over southern Gaul, and Fortunatus in the sixth, coming from Italy, visited towns from Trier to Toulouse. It is probable that in Sidonius' period, and also under the Merovingians, men of rank ordinarily traveled with armed retainers. Sidonius, in encouraging his friend Eutropius to enter public service, mentioned among his qualifications the possession of "horses, armor, raiment, money, and servants."

There was no government provision for the delivery of personal letters. Sidonius, like Petrarch 900 years later, relied on travelers going in the direction of his correspondents. He complained of searching everywhere for someone traveling to the destination of his missives. Sometimes his couriers were clerics journeying on church business, but one, named Amantius, frequently employed, went regularly to the port of Marseilles to make purchases for patrons in Auvergne.

Travel and transportation sometimes declined and sometimes revived under the Merovingians and Carolingians, but evidently the volume was never large. In decline during most of the sixth century, the port of Marseilles revived at the end of the century and in the early seventh. Gregory of Tours mentions the importation of oil into Marseilles, evidently for purposes of lighting. In the seventh century the monks of St. Denis near Paris were granted the means by King Dagobert I to buy six wagonloads of oil a year out of the revenues of the Marseilles customs office. In 661 the abbey of Corbie was being provisioned with oil and spices brought to the Rhône delta. Trade routes seem to have extended up the Rhône and Saône rivers, and also along the Seine and the Meuse, the Moselle, and the Rhine. In the Merovingian period merchants were to a very large extent Orientals: Greeks, Syrians, and Jews. Perhaps this is not surprising. In Rome there had been no social prestige in being in business but much in owning land. The land itself was ostensibly valued not for its income but rather for the status associated with it. Sidonius, writing in the fifth century on behalf of a friend wishing to recover an estate that had belonged to his ancestors, carefully explained that the sole motive was filial piety, certainly not a desire to increase his fortune!

Travel was curtailed under the Merovingians as their governmental activity declined. This meant a decrease in the volume of travel and in the ease with which officials moved about compared with the period of the Roman Empire. Imperial bureaucrats had used the post, but the Merovingians let it go out of use. Instead of the relays of horses, the rest houses, the ferries of late Roman times, Merovingian officials traveling on the king's service relied on certain persons obligated to provide them with food, lodging, and the means of transportation. The volume of travel by royal officials (as opposed to the king's household) remained small in the early Middle Ages.

TRAVEL FOR RELIGIOUS PURPOSES
FROM LATE ANTIQUITY
TO THE CAROLINGIAN PERIOD

Western Europe in the Middle Ages experienced a great growth in travel for purposes of religion. Christianity encouraged greater circulation compared with ancient religions. Paganism had seen pious journeys to the oracles of Greece at Delphi and elsewhere, but state (as opposed to mystery) religions did not engage in missionary activity, and pagan worship was organized locally, so there was no need of priestly journeys for purposes of consultation. In contrast, Christianity in the Middle Ages motivated journeys for all these reasons: pilgrimages, conversion of the heathen, and ecclesiastical administration.

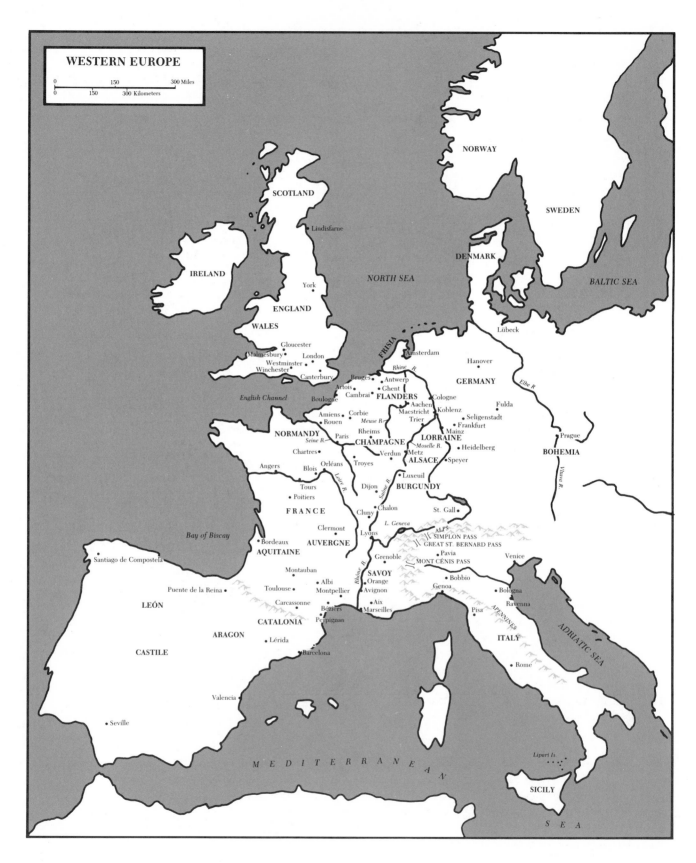

WESTERN EUROPE

0   150   300 Miles
0   150   300 Kilometers

NORWAY

SWEDEN

SCOTLAND

• Lindisfarne

DENMARK

NORTH SEA

BALTIC SEA

IRELAND

York •

ENGLAND

WALES

Lübeck •

Gloucester •

Malmesbury •   London •

Westminster

Winchester •   Canterbury •

Amsterdam

Hanover •

Rhine R.

GERMANY

Elbe R.

FRISIA

Bruges •   Antwerp •

Artois •   • Ghent

Cologne •

Fulda •

English Channel

Boulogne   Cambrai •   FLANDERS

Aachen •

Seligenstadt •

Prague •

Amiens •   • Corbie

Maestricht •   Koblenz

• Frankfurt

Rouen •   Meuse R.   Trier •

Mainz

NORMANDY   Seine R.   Paris •   Rheims •

LORRAINE

Heidelberg •

BOHEMIA

Chartres •   CHAMPAGNE

Moselle R.

Vltava R.

Orléans •   Verdun •   Metz •

• Speyer

Angers •   Blois •   Troyes •   ALSACE

Loire R.   • Luxeuil

Tours •   Dijon •   BURGUNDY

• Poitiers   Seine R.

St. Gall •

FRANCE   Chalon •

Cluny •

L. Geneva   ALPS

Clermont •   Lyons •

SIMPLON PASS

Bay of Biscay   AUVERGNE

GREAT ST. BERNARD PASS

• Bordeaux   Grenoble •   Pavia •   Venice •

AQUITAINE   MONT CÉNIS PASS

Santiago de Compostela •   Rhône R.   SAVOY

Montauban •   • Orange   Bobbio •

Puente de la Reina •   Albi •   Avignon •   Genoa •   • Bologna

LEÓN   Toulouse •   Montpellier   • Aix   Ravenna •

Carcassonne •   Marseilles •   Pisa •   APENNINES

Béziers •

CATALONIA   Perpignan •   ITALY   ADRIATIC SEA

ARAGON   • Lérida

CASTILE   Barcelona •

Rome •

Valencia •

MEDITERRANEAN

• Seville

Lipari Is.

SICILY

SEA

150

Pilgrims. In many ways, pilgrimages satisfied the needs of the medieval Christian: the respect for ritual, the veneration of relics, and the conviction that spiritual benefits could be derived merely from approaching the remains, possessions, or earthly scene of the life of a saint. Many a sinner, burdened by the past, believed that his or her sins were blotted out by a pilgrimage to the distant shrine of a martyr or saint.

In the fourth century there were journeys to Jerusalem to visit the scenes of the Lord's passion, but there also began to be pilgrimages to shrines in Western Europe. In the fifth century Sidonius mentioned a local pilgrimage, and in the sixth Fortunatus, cured of an eye disease, traveled from Italy into Gaul and gave thanks at the shrine of St. Martin of Tours, to whom he attributed his recovery. Gregory of Tours gives numerous instances of the sick being brought from a distance to be cured by St. Martin.

There were many pilgrimages to Rome. The early guidebooks list the churches and relics to be seen. A guidebook from the early ninth century, extant at the monastery of Einsiedeln, notes alternative itineraries that allow the pilgrim to see all the churches of that great reliquary, Rome. As early as the seventh century English pilgrims began to arrive in Rome. King Alfred the Great of Wessex (*r.* 871–899) as a boy made the pilgrimage to Rome with his father, and King Cnut was there in 1027.

Missionaries. Missionary activities involved extensive journeys in Gaul, Germany, and the British Isles at the end of the sixth and in the seventh and eighth centuries. We have some details on the journey of the monk Augustine and his companions (probably as many as forty persons), sent by Gregory the Great to convert the Anglo-Saxons. On 23 July 596 the pope wrote letters thanking the abbot of Lérins, the bishop of Aix, and the governor of Provence at Marseilles for extending assistance to the missionaries. After their sojourn in what is now southern France, they set out again for England, which they reached after a leisurely journey of some nine months across Gaul. Augustine and his group saw Theodoric of Burgundy and his grandmother, Brunhilde, perhaps at Chalon-sur-Saône or Orléans; Theodobert of Austrasia at Rheims or Metz; and Chothar II, probably at Paris. The missionaries seem to have gone up the Rhône and Saône river valleys and along the Loire, then north to Boulogne to take ship for Richborough in England. Probably they journeyed through France by riverboat, be-

cause much use seems to have been made of waterways by travelers in the sixth century. Augustine proceeded to Canterbury, for King Ethelbert of Kent had a Christian wife. The conversion of the Anglo-Saxons made progress slowly, and the northern part of the British Isles was christianized by Celtic missionaries from Ireland and Scotland.

The Irish were some of the greatest travelers of the early Middle Ages—or perhaps "wanderers" would be more apt. In contradistinction to the ideal of *stabilitas* was the desire for exile for reasons of asceticism, the longing to be a perpetual pilgrim for the love of Christ. (Also, it should be noted that sometimes a pilgrimage was simply an excuse to escape the monotony of life in the cloister.) Conversion had put Ireland in touch with southern and southwestern Gaul in the fifth century, at a time when schools still flourished there. Irish learning acquired a great reputation, as did Celtic monasticism. Bede speaks of English nobles and lesser men going to Ireland "either for the grace of sacred learning or a more austere life." The Irish were dedicated missionaries and promoters of monasticism in the seventh century. They founded monasteries at Luxeuil in France, Bobbio in Italy, St. Gall in Switzerland, Lindisfarne in Scotland, and Malmesbury in England. For their part the Anglo-Saxons founded the convents of Jarrow and Wearmouth, which became famous centers of learning. The Celts did not follow the Roman form of Christianity, but the English church to a very large extent did. It was the pope who commissioned Boniface, an English Benedictine monk and archbishop, and accredited him to Charles Martel for the conversion of Germany with the help of English monks and nuns. He organized new bishoprics in Germany and founded the monastery of Fulda. Boniface can be called a great traveler, for in addition to his journeys in Germany he visited Rome.

Because the monks of the British Isles were famous for their learning, they were welcome at monasteries, in episcopal households, and at royal courts. For example, Alcuin, a monk of York, was invited by Charlemagne to come to his court, head the palace school, and take a leading role in the reformation of church liturgy, the procurement of authentic copies of ancient works, and the improvement of the script. These objectives entailed numerous trips to Rome and also within the kingdom of the Franks. The Monk of St. Gall tells us that two Irishmen, coming to Gaul with a shipload of merchants, stood in the fair and cried that they had wisdom to sell. Charlemagne, hearing of their wares, invited them to his court, made one a teacher at a school, and sent the other to a monastery in Pavia. The most famous of the Irish exiles was John Scottus Eriugena, who settled at the court of Charles the Bald in the ninth century.

Church administrators. Religious reasons for travel included ecclesiastical administration and politics as well as pilgrimages. To signify an archbishop's metropolitan authority over his province, he was supposed to receive the pallium, and the usual way was for the archbishop to make the journey to the pope to be invested with it. In the Middle Ages the popes themselves were mobile: prior to the eighth century their political orientation had been eastward, toward Constantinople; in the eighth century it changed, and popes began traveling north and northwest from Rome as their political orientation shifted to Western Europe. In 753/754 Pope Stephen II crossed the Alps to beg protection from Pepin against the Lombards. For centuries afterward, popes continued to travel in Western Europe, especially Italy and France.

Well before Charlemagne's time pilgrimages attracted many. All classes undertook pilgrimages. In the sixth, seventh, and eighth centuries they were especially popular with Irish and Anglo-Saxon monks, some of whom for religious reasons wandered continually. Nevertheless, from an early period there were criticisms of pilgrimages, especially for monks and nuns after the Rule of St. Benedict of Nursia (*fl.* first half of sixth century) became increasingly popular and in the West supplanted the Rule of Pachomius, which had been the inspiration for Irish monasticism. St. Benedict introduced stability as one of the vows of the monk. The biographer of St. Ansgar (*d.* 865) felt obliged to defend the actions of his hero, who disobeyed his abbot and left the monastery of Corbie to become a missionary to the inhabitants of Denmark and Sweden.

OTHER TRAVELERS
IN THE CAROLINGIAN PERIOD

Religion was not the only motive for travel in Carolingian times. There were crowds of vagrants on the roads, so many that Charlemagne's capitularies admonish masters to keep their poor dependents at work so as to eliminate homeless folk. Charlemagne was generous in alms to these people, as were the aristocracy and ecclesiastics. Some of these wanderers were minstrels, who spread the news and influenced the reputations of warriors, heroes, and kings. Other travelers, fugitives from the rigors of serfdom, evidently had sufficient hope for a better life elsewhere to induce them to run away from their tenancies. Yet there were threats of highwaymen and slave traders who kidnapped travelers on lonely stretches of road.

Merchants and carriers. There seems to have been something of a revival of trade in the late eighth and early ninth centuries. Slaves were one of the chief exports, especially by the merchants of Verdun, who transshipped their human merchandise from the Slav and Avar regions, sometimes to Spain and sometimes to the East. Carolingian weapons, jewels, and coins have been found in Denmark. Frisian cloth was traded, as was salt from the Bay of Bourgneuf and the lagoons of the Adriatic. Paris trafficked in grain and in the wines of the Île-de-France, Burgundy, and Champagne.

Among the travelers escorting goods were the tenants of the great abbeys. One of their obligations was to transport the products of their convent. Thus in the Carolingian period the tenants of St. Germain-des-Prés acted as carriers to Angers, Blois, Orléans, Troyes, and Quentovic (in Frisia, at the mouth of the Canche in Flanders). At the end of the eighth century these men were exempt from tolls at Amiens, at the Frisian town of Duurstede (on the Meuse delta), and at Maestricht, which shows how far serfs, legally forbidden to quit their tenancies, traveled in the service of the abbeys. Charlemagne's capitulary *De villis* provided for the cartage of produce from the royal estates to wherever the royal household happened to be. The cartage to market of goods produced on their estates was not the only transportation necessary for the abbeys, which purchased articles from abroad. For example, the abbeys of St. Wandrille and Ferrières-en-Gâtinais obtained their monks' cloth from Artois and Frisia. Rivers were very important as trade routes, and there seem to have been numbers of boats on the French rivers and in southern Germany. Quentovic and Duurstede had extensive contacts with England, and Venice had important trade with the East.

Artists and architects. In addition to learned men there were other specialists who traveled to the court of Charlemagne. Artists from Byzantium and from Italy were invited to decorate manuscripts and to work on the palace at Aachen. The plan of Charlemagne's palace chapel there reveals a debt to S. Vitale in Ravenna and also to Constantinople.

Roman ruins provided stone, and columns and mosaics were brought from Ravenna.

Carolingian administrators. Carolingian government, too, required a certain amount of travel. Every year the king of the Franks ordered his notable men to meet with him in an assembly. The functions of government were very limited, but the professional judges, or *scabini,* and the royal commissioners, or *missi dominici,* traveled about the kingdom to enforce the law. The paucity of government officials was a contributing factor to the mobility of the Carolingian monarch, as it had been to that of the Merovingians and was to be to that of later medieval kings. Throughout the Middle Ages government was personal. It depended on the character of the ruler. It was essential for the king to show himself to his people to gain their loyalty and, in an age when the development of government was rudimentary, personally to oversee its operations in various parts of the realm. Charlemagne spent most of his reign traveling and fighting; only in his later years did he settle down, more or less, at Aachen and build an official residence there.

THREATS TO TRAVELERS

Throughout the early Middle Ages trade and transport tended to increase whenever there was protection adequate to allow travelers to hope to reach their destinations in safety. However, in the ninth and tenth centuries travel in Western Europe was shattered by incursions of Muslims, Vikings, and Magyars. In 867, Pope Nicholas I, deeply involved in controversy with the Byzantine emperor, would have preferred to call a council at Rome of all the archbishops, but the "evils of the time" made a meeting impossible. The Muslims took Sicily, sacked Rome and Marseilles, and settled in southern France at a fortified post. Their depredations were so severe that Genoa and Marseilles were almost abandoned, and land routes between Italy and France were cut. The marauders ambushed merchants and pilgrims in the Alps, but in 972 they were a little too successful when they captured and held for ransom the abbot of Cluny on his way back from Italy. Indignation at this outrage was such that an expedition was organized to take the bandits' citadel. The Muslims were expelled not only from France but, by the beginning of the eleventh century, also from mainland Italy.

The Vikings were much more of a menace than the Muslims. The Northmen managed to sack Seville, but their main successes took place farther north, where centralization of the government was ineffective. The Vikings permanently ruined the Frankish ports of Quentovic and Duurstede in Frisia; devastated towns and villages in Ireland, England, and France; and plundered all the important monasteries in France and the British Isles. The ruin of the monasteries meant a decline in learning, and as soon as King Alfred (r. 871–899) had defeated the Northmen, he turned his attention to the revival of learning. He collected a band of scholars, apparently with difficulty, for only two were native Englishmen; the others came from northern France, northern Germany, and Wales.

At the same time the Magyars raided Germany, Italy, and France, avoiding the towns and plundering the countryside. Only after the middle of the tenth century were the invaders of Europe permanently repulsed, and only then could travel and transport revive. There was a significant increase in travel at the end of the tenth and beginning of the eleventh century, despite the breakdown of central authority in the Carolingian Empire, a state of affairs that the early Capetians only slowly began to rectify.

ECONOMIC REVIVAL

Many of the reasons for travel already in existence in the early Middle Ages continued into the later Middle Ages, notably church administration, pilgrimages, and the peripatetic life of rulers and nobles. However, around the year 1000 a series of developments occurred that promoted travel and transportation. One of these was a great increase in trade and in industrial production.

In Roman times the commercial and industrial part of the empire had been in the East, while the West was largely agricultural, and this situation continued during the first half of the Middle Ages. Through the tenth century, towns were chiefly administrative centers. In general, people, money, food, and security were in short supply in the West, with a consequent low volume of travel and transportation.

By the beginning of the second millennium there had been the introduction of new crops, an increase in population and in the acreage devoted to agriculture, and an augmentation of food surpluses that allowed some members of the community, hitherto involved in food production, to specialize in other pursuits. In the High Middle Ages whole regions could, and did, begin to import food and to devote their energies to other things—for example, Flanders, which became famous for textiles. Merchants chiefly engaged in the luxury trade gave the impetus for the foundation of towns, which were to be such an important feature of the later period. Beginning in the eleventh, but reaching its full scope only in the twelfth and thirteenth centuries, the development of towns greatly increased travel for commercial purposes.

RELIGIOUS TRAVEL: TENTH THROUGH FIFTEENTH CENTURIES

The religious reforms and intensification of the spiritual life in the tenth, and even more in the eleventh, century meant an increase in travel because of a tightening in organization and an augmentation in the centralization of the church. The pope alone had authority over the convents of the order of Cluny, founded in 909. Earlier it had been usual for the local bishop to control the monasteries of his diocese, each of which was independent of every other. Cluny, however, was the center of an order with dependent monasteries, entailing a continual coming and going among them for purposes of consultation and inspection. The men who introduced the new monasticism into England had spent some time in continental houses: St. Dunstan, later archbishop of Canterbury (d. 988), was at Ghent, which had been reformed from Grogne and Gorze in Lorraine, and Oswald (d. 992), later bishop of Worcester and archbishop of York, at Fleury, which had been revitalized under the influence of Cluny.

Veneration of relics. The increased spirituality of the tenth and eleventh centuries augmented popular veneration of relics, artifacts that had experienced an astounding proliferation in the eighth and ninth centuries. They were so valuable that false relics were manufactured, and both authentic and spurious ones were stolen. Einhard contrived the surreptitious removal from Rome of the bones of the martyrs St. Marcellinus and St. Peter; so far from being embarrassed by the means of acquisition, he wrote an account of the translation of the relics to his abbey of Seligenstadt and recounted the miracles performed there.

Toward the middle of the eleventh century something new was added in the history of relics. In addition to being paraded in the locality, they were taken on tour to distant provinces and countries for the purpose of collecting alms, or recovering possessions appropriated by the nobles, or to aid in battle. These journeys were especially likely to be undertaken when it was a question of rebuilding a convent or cathedral. It is surprising that the monks and canons were willing to risk on the road their precious saints' bones (relics were still being stolen in the early twelfth century) and their silver reliquaries decorated with statuettes, valuable enough to attract the covetousness of the impious.

The peregrinations of these relics in the period must demonstrate that travel was reasonably safe (at least for religious purposes); that the roads in the summertime, the usual season for these journeys, were passable; and that there was enough money in circulation to make alms collection worthwhile. The practice of taking relics on tour originated in northern France, Flanders, and adjacent parts of the Holy Roman Empire about 1050; the custom spread in the twelfth century to England and Aragon, and it continued until about 1550. Sometimes the collectors went far afield, the French visiting England and, in the fourteenth century, Rome.

Travel to Rome. Another portent of things to come was the revival of the imperial pretensions of Rome, where Charlemagne had been crowned. Emperor Otto I and his successors also were crowned in Rome, and they rescued the papacy from domination by the Roman aristocracy. The renewed view of Rome as an imperial capital is reflected in a tenth-century guidebook that placed the Capitol in Rome at the top of the list of the Seven Wonders of the World and expected visitors to admire and appreciate ancient Roman monuments as well as relics and churches.

Rome continued to attract many pilgrims; in the early tenth century a duke of Aquitaine made an annual pilgrimage to the Eternal City. Towards the end of the tenth century, however, Rome began to experience competition from Santiago de Compostela in northwestern Spain, reputed to possess the bones of St. James the Great, and around 1000 the duke of Aquitaine habitually spent Easter either at Rome or at Santiago.

The investiture conflict and the reform movement greatly increased the administrative powers of the Roman curia, and therefore the amount of travel to and from Rome. Papal legates journeyed all over Christendom, enforcing ecclesiastical regulations. At the same time disagreements over jurisdiction or titles to property, which formerly would have been settled locally, were now decided in Rome. This meant a steady stream of visitors to the

154

Eternal City. For example, a jurisdictional dispute in 1092–1093 brought Lambert de Guines, bishop of Arras, to Rome. Because the count of Flanders was indignant that the diocese of Arras had recently been transferred from the archdiocese of Cambrai to that of Rheims, the archbishop of Rheims dispatched the new bishop to Rome to be consecrated by the pope. The urgency of the matter caused the bishop and his party (five men plus servants, perhaps twelve people in all) to set out in the worst season for traveling—just before Christmas. Leaving Rheims 24 December 1092, the party stopped at the monastery of Toussaint-en-l'Isle, where the bishop took part in celebrating the ritual of the Nativity. Thence the party hurried to Troyes (a distance of 49 miles [79 km] traveled in one day) but quickly left it as unsafe because of the hostility between Philip I of France and the count of Flanders. The bishop and his companions spent several days at the monastery of Molesme before taking up again what the scribe calls "the labor and difficulty of the roads." They rested two days at Dijon and visited Cluny before reaching the Rhône. Presumably they planned to descend the river, which was very commonly done by travelers in the period, but we are told that the floods of the Rhône were so violent that they were delayed for six days. The party reached Rome on 19 February 1093, after a journey of fifty-seven days. On the way back the weather was much more favorable for journeying because the party left Rome after Easter. The travelers took ship to Pisa and thence to Genoa. They crossed France by the same route as before, and the bishop was able to officiate in his cathedral at Pentecost, after a journey of thirty-seven days.

There seem to have been no great alarms on this journey to Rome in 1092–1093, but there were serious dangers for travelers in this period in northern France and in Flanders. After having gone all the way to Rome and back in safety, Lambert de Guines was captured on his way to the Council of Clermont in 1095. He was accompanied by his archdeacon, two abbots, and eight other ecclesiastics, and perhaps as many servants. As they left Provins, all these clergy, with the exception of the abbot of St. Vaast, were seized by a robber-knight. The abbot informed the bishop of Provins, brother of the miscreant, who repented and threw himself at the feet of Bishop Lambert de Guines. All were released and proceeded to Clermont after a delay of three days. Also, as bishop of Arras, Lambert de

Guines had occasion to complain to the countess of Flanders that people of his diocese had made pilgrimages to Rome in safety, only to be held for ransom on their return to her land, by the provost of Bapaume.

Pilgrimages. After the year 1000 the Middle Ages saw a vast acceleration in a category of travel that went back to the fourth century: the pilgrimage. The abbots of the reformed houses in Lorraine, Burgundy, Flanders, and Normandy organized pilgrimages in the eleventh century, and the bishops and lay lords who believed in the new piety actively supported the monks. It is not surprising that the founder of Cluny should have been an ardent pilgrim. The vast sweep of social classes involved in pilgrimages is shown by the persons who went on the First Crusade—from the rootless and "masterless" men and women who followed Peter the Hermit, living off the land and committing depredations all the way to Constantinople, to the sons of kings and nobles who organized their own expeditions. The pilgrims' motives seem to have been as diverse as their origins. To practice asceticism, to obtain spiritual benefits, to gain favors from the saints, and to expiate misdeeds are reasons amply attested; but there is also some evidence for pilgrimages as an escape from monotony, difficulties, or dangers at home, or even as a ticket to adventure that would satisfy curiosity about the world or as a release from customary inhibitions imposed by one's usual environment.

Pilgrimages were considered an especially efficacious means of imploring divine favor in the second half of the Middle Ages. In 1304, Mahaut, countess of Artois and Burgundy, sent a proxy on a pilgrimage to Santiago de Compostela when her daughter was ill. If one had promised to accomplish a pilgrimage and could not do so, it was acceptable to donate to a good cause the sum that would have been spent on the journey. For example, at the end of the fourteenth century money intended to fulfill a vow to visit Santiago de Compostela was instead donated to rebuilding an arch of the bridge at Romans. Many wills provided a sum of money for some individual to make a journey to a shrine, particularly Santiago de Compostela, for the benefit of the soul of the deceased.

Some travelers were involuntary pilgrims, condemned by a civil or ecclesiastical court to make an expiatory journey to a far-off shrine as a penalty for having committed crimes. In the twelfth century a robber on the lands of St. Germain-des-Prés, a dependent of the abbey, promised to make a pilgrimage to the Holy Land with his wife and never to return. Usually, however, such pilgrims were required to return, bringing with them a certificate from the shrine. In most cases the journey was to be performed barefoot, in penitential clothing, without resting more than one night in any one place. If the crime had been extremely serious, the penitent wore chains about his neck. After arriving at the destination, he or she performed certain rituals of humiliation and repentance, and received a receipt from the presiding priest. Then he returned home.

The Inquisition in southern France was especially active in condemning heretics to make pilgrimages. It recognized four major shrines—Rome, Santiago de Compostela, St. Thomas of Canterbury, and the Three Kings of Cologne—and nineteen minor ones, all located in present-day France. From what is now Belgium, beginning in the thirteenth century, courts sent criminals on expiatory pilgrimages to Avignon and elsewhere in southern France, but these were not the only destinations. In Flanders in 1319 a man condemned for beating a woman was sentenced to make penitential pilgrimages to both St. Gilles-en-Provence and St. Andrews in Scotland. Mandatory pilgrimages were still being used as a form of punishment for criminals in the fourteenth and fifteenth centuries, but less often. By this time there was a regular scale of fines that could be paid as a substitute for performing the required journey to a holy shrine. Criminals were not the only involuntary pilgrims. By the Treaty of Athis in 1305 between Philip the Fair and the Flemish, 3,000 citizens of Bruges, to expiate the massacre of the French soldiers at Bruges, were required to make pilgrimages: 1,000 beyond the seas and 2,000 to various sanctuaries. Subsequently, it was necessary to commute the pilgrimages to fines.

If pilgrimages could be a form of penance, they could also be a pleasure. The circumstances under which the journey was performed made all the difference. Not until the end of the fourteenth century is there clear evidence that pilgrims were actually enjoying the trip. Certainly Chaucer's pilgrims were on holiday, although they were making the journey to seek the intercession of St. Thomas. They traveled on horseback and spent the night at a comfortable inn. Various pilgrim guidebooks from the fifteenth century offer a more mundane and practical view of pilgrimages, for example *Information for Pilgrims unto the Holy Land,* printed by

Wynkyn de Worde in 1498, and the account of Friar Felix Fabri.

As there was a great variety in the social status of pilgrims, so was there in the style in which they traveled. It is a mistake to assume that every pilgrim's costume included a broad-brimmed hat, a great mantle, a purse, a sack, and a staff, or to suppose that all of them made their journeys on foot. Joinville does indeed recount that the abbot of Cheminon gave him his purse and staff, and that after visiting local shrines he left, barefoot and in his shirt, to join St. Louis's first crusade in 1248. Within a few miles, however, Joinville soon rejoined his troops and journeyed in a manner befitting his rank. In the thirteenth century Eudes Rigaud, archbishop of Rouen, undertook more than one pilgrimage, but apparently only one on foot. It was from Paris to Chartres, a distance of 60 miles (just over 96 km) in hopes of being cured of a fever. In 1394 the duchess of Burgundy made a short pilgrimage on foot, although there were more than 200 horses in the company. These were exceptional cases, in which the unusual act of walking represented a form of penance. A merchant of Montauban, Barthélemy Bomis, made the pilgrimage to Rome to take advantage of the great pardon afforded by the jubilee of 1350. (The jubilee, first proclaimed by the pope in 1300, was a year in which special indulgences were earned by pilgrims going to Rome.) The whole party was on horseback, including the farrier who went along to look after the horses. The party bought him a horse.

There were fluctuations in the popularity of shrines. In Merovingian and Carolingian times St. Martin of Tours had been a foremost shrine, but it was later eclipsed by Rome, St. Thomas of Canterbury, and Santiago de Compostela. There was a very effective effort to promote Santiago de Compostela. A pilgrim's guide to that shrine, written about 1139, gave four routes across France, chosen to enable the traveler to see a maximum number of holy relics. One crossed southern France via St. Gilles, Montpellier, and Toulouse; another went via Orléans, Tours, Poitiers, Saintes, and Bordeaux. Of the other two, one went by way of Conques, with the shrine of Ste. Foy, and the other by way of Vézélay and St. Léonard-en-Limousin (highly recommended by the guide). All these itineraries joined at Puente de la Reina, from which a single route led to Santiago de Compostela.

There were confraternities of Santiago de Compostela, whose members promised to make a pilgrimage to Santiago themselves and who supported hospices in numerous cities for the purpose of aiding pilgrims. For example, there was such a confraternity at Paris in the twelfth century with hospices there and at St. Quentin, Amiens, and Nîmes. Its members promised to make the pilgrimage to Santiago but were allowed to commute their vow for a money payment.

Pilgrimages continued to be very popular during much of the fifteenth century. There were such crowds of pilgrims that in 1400, at the time of the jubilee, the royal council of France forbade the king's subjects to make the journey to Rome for fear that the pilgrims might be so numerous as to deprive the kingdom of its defenses against its enemies and also drain the finances of the land. Further disadvantages were that the money would be spent in the territories of the antipope (such was the council's statement), and in any case the journey would be dangerous for the pilgrims, since it would be among enemies.

Despite their vogue, pilgrimages had been under attack from the beginning, and in the fifteenth century their volume was about to experience a precipitous decline. Pilgrimages were a part of the growth of ritual during the second half of the Middle Ages, a period that, however, also witnessed the flowering of mysticism. As this spiritual movement dispensed with the outward forms of religion, so it also saw no point in travel for pious ends. Thomas à Kempis' devotional work the *Imitation of Christ* stated that those who go on many pilgrimages are seldom or never saved. From this opinion it is only a short step to the criticism of Erasmus, to the disapproval of the Reformation, and to the seventeenth-century classification of pilgrims as vagabonds.

TRANSPORT AND TRADE-RELATED TRAVEL

Before the industrial development of the Middle Ages, the goods transported were chiefly agricultural produce, although they included such necessities as salt and such luxuries as fine wool cloth. Despite the disorder and bad roads of the ninth and tenth centuries there was considerable movement of bulky goods over substantial distances. The great abbeys of the Carolingian period, including Prüm (southwest of Cologne) in the Rhenish province, St. Rémi of Rheims, and St. Germain-des-Prés, required their tenants to transport the surplus from

their lands to points where it could be sold. From Prüm it was taken to Cologne, Coblenz, Metz, Verdun, and Frankfurt am Main. From the lands of St. Germain-des-Prés it was carted to Quentovic and Orléans, Angers, and Troyes. The produce chiefly consisted of wine, and St. Germain-des-Prés was involved in the international wine trade. Grain, too, was transported to various locations. In May, tenants of the abbey of St. Germain-des-Prés were required to bring many small beams and sawed boards to the abbey in Paris, where there was a strong demand—since Paris was built mostly of wood at the time.

Because of the rudimentary development of fairs, it was worthwhile in the ninth and tenth centuries for Flemish abbeys, such as the abbey of St. Bertin at St. Omer (and also for the chapter there), to own vineyards in northern France and along the Rhine to supply wine for the Mass and also for consumption by the monks. Transportation was furnished by corvée of the tenants. By the twelfth century there was a flowering of fairs and markets, and St. Omer developed into a great market for wine. Accordingly, it no longer paid for St. Bertin to insist on corvées, and in the thirteenth century the vineyards were farmed out.

By the twelfth century there had been an expansion of the quantity and variety of goods sold. When Flanders began to specialize in producing textiles, it imported not only raw material (wool) from England, but also foodstuffs, especially grain. The agricultural boom in England from the mid twelfth to the mid thirteenth century was based on the transportation of produce to industrial centers. Other bulky goods, such as wine, continued to be transported over considerable distances.

Beginning in the eleventh century, transportation was to an increasing extent carried on by merchants, whose commercial activity stimulated the revival of towns in northern Europe. Many of these men spent the greater part of the year traveling from fair to fair, buying where goods were cheap and selling where they were dear. There were numerous fairs in the medieval period in Western Europe; the most famous and important were the fairs of Champagne, which flourished from the last quarter of the twelfth century through about 1280, and declined into insignificance in the early fourteenth century. The counts of Champagne addressed one of the great problems of medieval travel and transport—that of safety. They declared that merchants traveling to the fairs were protected by the "safe conduct of the fairs," and the counts were able to obtain the cooperation of the dukes of Burgundy and the kings of France to guarantee the safety of merchants traveling to the fairs across their dominions.

Rotating among four towns, the fairs of Champagne covered almost the entire year and attracted merchants not only from Flanders, northern France, and Italy, but also from Montauban, Toulouse, Lérida, Barcelona, Cologne, Lübeck, and St. Gall. The success of the fairs was facilitated by the location of Champagne on important land routes between northern and southern Europe, because by this time (unlike late Roman times) the French road network was centered on Paris, only a short distance from Provins, one of the fair towns. There were routes from the north via Bapaume and Crépy-en-Valois to Paris or, more directly, by way of Rheims. Across Burgundy a route led via the Col-de-Jougne to the Simplon or the Great St. Bernard Pass; or it was possible, after crossing a considerable stretch of land, to descend the Saône to Lyons, where the traveler could take the road to Lake Geneva or across Savoy to Mont Cénis. It was also possible to descend the Rhône to Avignon and then go to Marseilles, or to turn west along the southern route toward Montpellier or Spain. It is important to note that the traffic passing to and from the fairs of Champagne was essentially overland commerce, and that the Seine or Saône-Rhône route served only a limited number of merchants and was used for only part of the journey.

The chief product from northern Europe at the fairs of Champagne was cloth, which was bought either to be used in southern France or Italy or to be exported to the East. The Italians provided alum, woad and other plants for dyes, leather, and spices, especially pepper. Before the decline of the fairs there was a tendency for merchants to become less mobile and to transfer both the travel and the transportation connected with their business into the hands of specialists. By the middle of the thirteenth century, buyers were signing contracts with professional carriers to transport goods between the fairs and southern France or Italy. Some of the agreements of the 1290's specified that the cloths involved should be transported on packhorses, not in carts. Other specialists at the fairs included weekly couriers from Italy who delivered letters and news to business agents. The fairs became not only places where goods were bought and sold but also places where accounts were settled.

The Italians, who had dominated the fairs of Champagne, established local branches of their firms in Barcelona, France, Flanders, and England, and through their business techniques dominated international trade. They were papal collectors, and amassed and forwarded to Rome vast sums from various parts of Christendom.

The Germans actively traded with Italy, and in northern Germany the Hanseatic League achieved a monopoly and dominated trade in the Baltic region. The Flemish ceased to travel abroad to promote and export their products, but French merchants traveled extensively in the fourteenth and fifteenth centuries. When Jean, duke of Berry, reduced the number of consuls of Riom from eight to four, he gave as a reason the fact that the consuls were for the most part merchants attending to their goods and were frequently out of town.

Provincials were unable to take full advantage of the newest business techniques, which allowed the Italians to do much of their business by correspondence. To purchase a letter of exchange for its consuls at Paris, the town of Albi in 1369 was obliged to send to Montpellier, where one was to be had.

As far as transportation is concerned, neither water nor land routes can be said to have dominated the scene. In France there was an association of merchants frequenting the Loire, and the hanse of Paris possessed important privileges relative to transit on the Seine. The Loire, Rhône, Moselle, Meuse, and Rhine were much used for transportation. In the mid fourteenth century, papal agents ceased purchasing the wine of St. Pourçain-sur-Sioule, almost 109 miles (about 175 km) from Chalon-sur-Saône, to which point it was carted, then put on a boat for Avignon. Transportation doubled the price of St. Pourçain wines, while the carriage of the wines of Beaune, about 16 miles (26 km) from a stream, raised the price only by half.

The establishment of an all-water route via the Mediterranean and Atlantic from Italy to the Low Countries did not mean the abandonment of the land routes across the Alps to France and to Germany, and thence to the Low Countries and England. There is considerable evidence that travelers preferred to journey on land in France, unless the entire journey could be accomplished by water—as, say, between points on the Loire or, during the residence of the popes at Avignon, from Lyons by way of the Rhône to that city. Long after there were ships sailing between England and Italy, many

Englishmen still preferred the "Dutch way" across Germany and the Alps.

PERIPATETIC ROYALTY

German kings and emperors. That characteristic phenomenon of the early Middle Ages—the frequent travel of medieval kings—continued unabated in the later Middle Ages. The kings and great nobles were continually on the road.

The German kings from the time of Otto I (936–973) were always traveling. They preferred to celebrate the great feasts of the liturgical year at certain agreed-on places, but their schedules were perpetually altered by their political objectives. The Salian kings (1024–1125) possessed a necropolis at Speyer, but neither they nor later rulers of the Holy Roman Empire had a fixed capital. The problem of shelter restricted their travels for the most part to those sections of the kingdom where the rulers themselves possessed domains or to places where lodging for the royal suite was furnished by abbeys. Rarely did the rulers appear north of a line drawn from the Lippe River through the Teutoburgerwald to Hannover. They also were seldom in the East.

English kings. The same pattern of mobility was prevalent in England and France. William the Conqueror, having made good his claim to the English throne, did not have a single seat of government but held his court at three different cities. He wore his crown during Easter at Winchester, during Whitsuntide at Westminster, and during midwinter at Gloucester. In the next century Walter Map's description of Henry II says, "He was always traveling about on intolerable daily journeys which seemed twice the normal length, and he was merciless in this to his household which followed him." It should not be forgotten that, after the conquest of England and before the loss of most of their possessions on the Continent, the English kings spent much—and in some cases all—of their time away from England and on the Continent.

French kings. Some idea of the frequency of French rulers' journeys may be gained from noting that in 1319 Philip V changed his place of abode eighty-one times, in 1321 Charles IV moved from one place to another on sixty-three occasions, and in 1329 Philip VI changed his resting place eighty-one times.

Various reasons have been suggested for the perpetual travels of medieval rulers. One factor was the necessity of showing themselves to their people to gain their loyalty; also, visits allowed inspection of the government of the realm. Beyond the political objectives there were other reasons for the journeys of the great. Travel allowed kings to indulge in a favorite sport—hunting—and mobility contributed to the proper utilization of the produce of manors. In the thirteenth century Walter of Henley advised the countess of Lincoln, as soon as her crops were harvested, to plan her sojourns for the year at the different manors, staying longer at the larger ones and a shorter time at the smaller. As far as the kings of France are concerned, by the later Middle Ages consumption of produce seems to have had little to do with determining their itinerary. The efficiency of food distribution may be illustrated by the fast service that supplied Paris with saltwater fish during Lent. There is good evidence that kings and lords led a life of continual moving because they preferred to do so. No other explanation can account for a mode of life that, in the case of the dukes of Burgundy in the late fourteenth century, involved a change of abode every two or three days, or for the fact that Jean, duke of Berry, spent half his days on the road.

ITINERANT ADMINISTRATORS, LEGISLATORS, AND JUSTICES

The medieval king was the head of the government, and members of his household were the officials. When the king traveled, so did the government. Even the archives journeyed with the royal household, in special barrels on packhorses. This was true in France up to 1194, when King Richard the Lionhearted captured the archives after a battle, and it was the case in Germany into the thirteenth century. Anyone having business with the court had first to determine where it was, and then follow the king on his itinerary until the affair was settled. There were many complaints about this method of running the government. Peter of Blois complained of the quality of life with the court of Henry II—the miserable food and drink, poor lodgings, danger of disease, and the lack of rest, because the king constantly, on the spur of the moment, altered the itinerary. Article 17 of the Magna Carta provided that the Court of Common Pleas should not follow the king but be held at a fixed place. Nevertheless, the use of traveling royal justices had a long history, from the time of William the Conqueror, during the reign of Henry II, and even into the fourteenth century.

In France town officials delegated to negotiate on taxes sometimes had to journey much farther than originally planned, and sometimes failed to find the king altogether. In the course of the thirteenth and fourteenth centuries, several departments of the government, such as the treasury, came to reside permanently in Paris rather than to follow the peregrinations of the court.

Increasing centralization in England and France meant that more and more civil servants in the provinces received orders (frequently by special messenger) from the central government and also traveled to Westminster or Paris to report or to deliver taxes collected by them. In France more and more cases were appealed to the parlement of Paris; for example, the town of Albi had to send consuls to the capital to represent the municipality in a lawsuit against the chapter. Travels to promote municipal interests and privileges absorbed a great deal of the time and energies of town officials in the fourteenth and fifteenth centuries in France. In England the development of parliament, and in France of the estates, especially regional estates, meant journeys not only for the great, lay and ecclesiastical, but also for the middle class, representing the towns. In the fourteenth century neither the Commons in England nor the Third Estate in France seems to have been enthusiastic about the trouble, hazards, and expense of attending these meetings.

Improvements in organization and centralization of lay governments were paralleled by the papal monarchy. More and more cases that had been settled in local courts were forwarded to the Roman curia, whether it was in Italy or in Avignon. Avignon was removed from the local political feuds in Italy and also more centrally located, so that most of Christendom found it more convenient. As much as five weeks of travel were saved in going to Avignon rather than to Rome. At this time there was an increasing emphasis on church finance. Papal visitations frequently consisted only in the collector's announcing to all the abbeys of a particular region that on such and such a day or days he would be at some specified point to receive visitation fees. Also, since a great many benefices were now distributed by the pope, large numbers of would-be officeholders converged on the curia. The papal diplomatic efforts, church government, and speedy couriers all augmented the volume of travel.

JOURNEYING ARTISTS, ARTISANS, WRITERS, AND SCHOLARS

In addition to pilgrims, merchants, couriers, carriers, and government and ecclesiastical officials, there were other categories of travelers: students, minstrels, artists, artisans, and laborers. In England masons journeyed from one place to another to work on the king's buildings, and there is much evidence in France of workmen leaving their native town or village in search of work. In Flanders a good many agricultural workers left to colonize eastern Europe, and during the growth of towns runaway serfs found them a haven. After the Black Death, people from the countryside moved into the towns to replenish the diminished population.

Minstrels and jongleurs were almost necessarily travelers, and artists very frequently so. Jongleurs were in demand at feasts and celebrations, and the search for patronage preoccupied many writers—one has only to think of Froissart's travels. The movements of rulers and nobles influenced the journeys of artists and architects. Shortly after Emperor Henry VI exiled Tancred's widow and daughter from Sicily and sent them to enforced residence in the abbey of Hohenburg in Alsace, there was completed, about 1200, the magnificently illustrated manuscript of the abbess Herrad, the *Hortus deliciarum*. Obviously a Sicilian model book had been used in preparing the illustrations. There are other German manuscript paintings of the period that are also based on Sicilian sources. It is certainly probable that the ladies brought with them either the actual model book or the artist who prepared it. Byzantine influence appears at about the same time in English illustrations, probably because there was so much travel between Sicily and England. For example, Adelard of Bath and John of Salisbury spent some time in Sicily. Even when it can be established that ideas traveled, it is sometimes difficult to prove that artists did as well. Perhaps the medium of transmission was manuscripts. It is known that French architects worked in England, Germany, and Hungary at the height of the vogue for French Gothic. And in the fifteenth century we know that French artists, such as Jean Fouquet, were going to Italy to study.

The movements of many troubadours are well documented between the middle of the twelfth and the middle of the thirteenth century. They were of all classes, from a duke to the son of a baker, and included clerics, merchants, and sons of lesser nobles. Although patronized by aristocrats in southern France, the troubadours found more ample support in Spain. Raimon de Miraval praised the joie de vivre and liberality of the Catalans, qualities he considered dead in his native region of Carcassonne. The kings of Aragon, Castile, and León were patrons of many troubadours, but before the end of the twelfth century troubadours were already going to Italy, first to Boniface of Montferrat and then to the Malespina and Este families. The troubadour Peire Vidal was at the court of Castile in 1187, then in the Holy Land with the Third Crusade, and in Italy in 1193–1196. In 1198 he went to Hungary, doubtless to accompany a daughter of Alfonso II of Aragon, who married the king of Hungary. Next he was in Spain and afterward at Genoa.

Minstrels traveled not only for patronage but also to learn. In the fourteenth century the dukes of Burgundy sent their minstrels to the schools of Germany. There was a definite connection between clerks and jongleurs. Uc de St. Circ, from near Rocamadour, was sent to Montpellier to learn to be a clerk, but what he learned there were songs, verses, *sirventes*, and the deeds of men and women of merit. He wound up a roving career as a troubadour in Italy sometime after 1253, at about the age of sixty. The *Carmina burana*, with its celebration of wandering scholars known as goliards, is well known. In the thirteenth century four French synods insisted that clerks should not be jongleurs, goliards, or buffoons. Nevertheless, in France and in Germany, goliards are mentioned in the fourteenth century, and they had the reputation of being vagabonds.

The travels of clerks and students were extensive. As far back as the tenth century Richer of St. Remi had journeyed from Rheims to study at Chartres, and Gerbert of Aurillac (later Pope Silvester II) went to Spain for the same reason. In the course of the eleventh and twelfth centuries, scholars from northern Europe went to Spain, Sicily, and southern Italy to learn Greek science from Arabic and Greek manuscripts. There was a great increase in the number of students who were willing to travel from place to place to sit at the feet of famous masters. In the early twelfth century many students were attracted to Paris by Abelard's lectures, and the Diet of Roncaglia (1158) referred to all the students wandering for the sake of knowledge.

The universities of Bologna and Paris were international institutions and attracted teachers and students from all over Europe. In its greatest period the most famous professors at the University of Paris were foreigners—English (Alexander of Hales, Roger Bacon), German (Albertus Magnus), Italian (St. Bonaventure, Thomas Aquinas), Scottish (John Duns Scotus), and Flemish (Siger of Brabant). Of the nations into which the students were organized, the Picard included the Low Countries, and the English nation in 1331 had students from the Holy Roman Empire, Hungary, Bohemia, Poland, Sweden, Denmark, Norway, Scotland, Ireland, and England. About this time the English for the most part abandoned the University of Paris.

Early in the fourteenth century there was a decline in the number of students at the University of Paris. Part of the reason was the foundation of other universities in France and Germany: Avignon in 1303, Orléans in 1309, Cahors in 1332, Grenoble in 1339, Perpignan in 1350, Orange in 1365, and, in the Holy Roman Empire, Prague in 1348 and Heidelberg in 1385. Another reason was that the Hundred Years War (1337–1453) hindered students from traveling in France. There were few Germans at Orléans, although at one time so much German was heard in the streets that one might have thought oneself in Germany.

Although the Treaty of Brétigny (1360) provided that students should not be molested while traveling in France, the temper of the times was against considering English students as clerics rather than as Englishmen. In 1417 the English students at the University of Toulouse were expelled from the town. Feeling against the English ran sufficiently high at this time for the name of the English nation at the University of Paris to be changed to German. In the fifteenth century the University of Paris tended to attract, first of all, students from northern France and the Holy Roman Empire, Scandinavia, and Scotland, while the Aragonese and Catalans preferred the University of Toulouse. The University of Paris had its own messengers to carry mail for its members and proctors sent to the Roman curia to protect its interests and procure benefices for its members.

In the last two centuries of the Middle Ages there was less travel to the Roman curia. The English parliament passed the statutes of Provisors (1351) and of Praemunire (1353), limiting papal provision to English sees and appeals from English courts to Rome. The Great Schism (1378–1417) made it more difficult to obtain papal benefices, as did the Pragmatic Sanction of Bourges (1438) and the Diet of Mainz (1439). By these measures many of the rights of papacy over the clergy and ecclesiastical revenues were conveyed to temporal rulers.

At this time there was a change in the attitude toward indigent students. From the early Middle Ages charity had been considered a good deed that contributed toward one's salvation. Largess has been called the queen of the medieval virtues. Who received the charity was less important than the act of giving. In the fourteenth century a favorite legacy was to found a small hospital, an overnight shelter for the indigent, for students, and for pilgrims. Nevertheless, in England in the fourteenth century wandering students were obliged to have testimonial papers on pain of being considered beggars and clapped into jail.

PLEASURE IN TRAVEL

Toward the end of the Middle Ages, criticism of travel increased and wandering students, pilgrims, and vagabonds fell into disfavor. There were also fewer reasons for travel. Merchants now had local agents resident in distant cities and were able to supervise their activities and communicate with them through the new commercial devices, such as double-entry bookkeeping, letters of credit, and bills of exchange. Church administrative matters, such as lawsuits and appointments, were often settled regionally in England, France, and Germany. In the fifteenth century in France civil lawsuits no longer required long, expensive journeys to Paris, partly because regional courts were set up and partly because citizens of some towns and cities and members of some universities acquired the privilege of always being sued locally. It has been stated that the failure of the estates-general to wrest power from the French king was partially due to the reluctance of town representatives to brave the inconvenience and expense of travel.

Other segments of the population continued to travel for a variety of reasons. Knights, who had long sought out tourneys and distant wars for the sake of their reputations and to advance their fortunes, continued to do so. There were others who traveled for the pleasure it gave them.

Travel literature. One of the earliest records (apart from fictional accounts) of pleasure in travel is connected with Petrarch's ascent of Mt. Ventoux in 1336. He states that he went to the mountaintop only from a desire to see the famous height. He rejected several companions because of their *frigida incuriositas* (their cold lack of curiosity), but he took along a copy of St. Augustine's works and made allegorical comparisons between climbing the mountain and his moral progress in life. In contrast, we find a personal reaction to nature from Michault Taillement, poet and *valet de chambre* of the duke of Burgundy, who traveled through the Jura Mountains in 1430 only because he had been sent there by his master. He recorded his impressions of the horrifying nature of the enormous rocks and noisy cascades. Another personal reaction is recorded by a tourist on a sightseeing tour, Antoine de la Sale, author of *Petit Jehan de Saintré,* who climbed to the crater of a volcano in the Lipari Islands in 1407. "Counsels of mad youth [*folle jeunesse*] made us go," he explained. The same excuse could not have been valid in 1420, when he investigated the enchanted grotto of a sybil located in the Apennines. Perhaps the most appropriate excuse for travel and travel literature, however, is that of the herald Gilles Le Bouvier in his *Le livre de la description des pays* from the mid fifteenth century:

> Because many people of divers nations and countries delight and take pleasure, as I have done in times past, in seeing the world and the various things therein, and also because many wish to know without going there, and others wish to see, go, and travel, I have begun this little book.

BIBLIOGRAPHY

Source. Sidonius Apollinaris, *Poems and Letters,* 2 vols., W. B. Anderson, trans. (1936–1965).

Studies. P. M. Bechtum, *Beweggründe und Bedeutung des Vagantentums in der lateinischen Kirche des Mittelalters* (1941); A. S. Cook, "Augustine's Journey from Rome to Richborough," in *Speculum,* **1** (1926); Donald R. Howard, *Writers and Pilgrims: Medieval Pilgrim Narratives and Their Posterity* (1980); Jean A. A. J. Jusserand, *English Wayfaring Life in the Middle Ages (Fourteenth Century),* Lucy Toulmin Smith, trans. (rev. ed. 1930); Albert C. Leighton, *Transport and Communication in Early Medieval Europe, A.D. 500–1100* (1972); Federigo Melis, *I trasporti et le communicazioni mel medioevo* (1984); George B. Parks, *The English Traveler to Italy, I: The Middle Ages* (1954); Henri Pirenne, *Medieval Cities,* Frank D. Halsey, trans. (1948); Grace Stretton, "The Travelling Household in the Middle Ages," in *The Journal of the British Archaeological Association,* n.s. 40 (1934); Jonathan Sumption, *Pilgrimage: An Image of Mediaeval Religion* (1975); Helen J. Waddell, *The Wandering Scholars* (1927, repr. 1955), revised as *Songs of the Wandering Scholars,* Felicitas Corrigan, ed. (1982).

MARJORIE NICE BOYER

[See also **Carolingians and the Carolingian Empire; Corvée; Crusades and Crusader States; Fairs; Household, Chamber, and Wardrobe; Mandeville's Travels; Markets; Missi Dominici; Missions and Missionaries; Papacy, Origins and Development of; Penance and Penitentals; Pilgrimage; Pilgrims' Guide; Pragmatic Sanction of Bourges; Relics; Roads and Bridges; Rome; Santiago de Compostela; Slavery, Slave Trade; Vehicles.**]

TRAVERSARI, AMBROGIO (1386–1439), was a Florentine monk, humanist, and churchman whose career was devoted to the revival of the Latin and Greek church fathers. He was the earliest and most prolific of the Italian humanists engaged in patristic studies, and his interest in Christian antiquity set important precedents for the work of such later Christian humanists as Erasmus.

Born in Portico, a village in the Romagna, Traversari went to Florence in 1400 and entered the Camaldolese monastery of S. Maria degli Angeli. There, without a teacher, he learned Greek. This accomplishment, and his cultivation of classical studies, brought him into contact with the Florentine patrician and bibliophile Niccolò de' Niccoli (d. 1437), who remained a lifelong friend. Through Niccoli's influence Traversari became familiar with all the leading Italian humanists of the day, and during the 1420's his cell at the Angeli was the setting for an informal humanist academy that included Cosimo de' Medici, the future ruler of Florence. Niccoli's indefatigable efforts and prodigal spending enabled Traversari to acquire the rare and ancient codices on which his patristic scholarship was based.

Humanism was a critical intellectual influence on Traversari's patristic studies. Philology and textual criticism formed the core of his scholarship, and rhetorical values largely determined his choice of patristic authors and subjects. It was John Chrysostom's eloquence, for instance, that led Traversari to translate so many of this Greek Father's sermons and treatises, and he was similarly drawn to the persuasive power of Basil the Great (d. 379) and Gregory of Nazianzus (d. 389/390). Moreover, Traversari was convinced that contemporary religious problems had little to do with formal theology, marked as this was by scholastic "aridities" and "quibbles." Rather, the main issue was the promotion of piety—to generate the impulse for Christians to enact in their lives the philosophy of Christ—and in this, he believed, the Fathers clearly were morally superior to the Scholastics. It is revealing, too, that the main audience to which Traversari addressed his some two dozen patristic translations was made up of other humanists. His concern for his stature in the humanist movement is indicated further by his determination to collect, revise, and formally "publish" his correspondence, which is among the most voluminous of the quattrocento (fifteenth-century) humanists.

Traversari's career took an abrupt turn in 1431, when he became general of the Camaldolese order. For the next three years he journeyed ceaselessly through northern Italy, making reform visitations to the monasteries of his order. Just as in his patristic scholarship he sought the resuscitation of the ancient wisdom and authority of the church fathers, so in this work of monastic reform he was determined to make the monasteries under his charge reflect the pristine sanctity of the early church. In this, however, long-entrenched patterns of ecclesiastical and secular privilege made his efforts largely unsuccessful.

This entrance into the wider public life of the church was followed in 1435 by Traversari's appointment as papal legate to the Council of Basel. There, arguing from patristic authority and the historical precedent of the early Christian centuries, he sought to uphold papal authority against conciliarist challenges.

Traversari's last and most important public role came during the Council of Ferrara-Florence (1438–1439). There his knowledge of Greek and extensive patristic learning proved instrumental to the theological exchanges between Greek Orthodox and Roman Catholic prelates, and to the resultant temporary ending of the centuries-long schism between Eastern and Western Christianity.

BIBLIOGRAPHY

Traversari's correspondence is collected in Laurentius Mehus, ed., *Ambrosii Traversarii generalis camaldulensium . . . latinae epistolae*, 2 vols. (1759, repr. 1968).

A book-length study of Traversari is Charles L. Stinger, *Humanism and the Church Fathers: Ambrogio Traversari (1386–1439) and Christian Antiquity in the Italian Renaissance* (1977), containing bibliographical references to other relevant sources and secondary literature.

See also Deno John Geanakoplos, *Interaction of the "Sibling" Byzantine and Western Cultures in the Middle Ages and Italian Renaissance (330–1600)* (1976).

CHARLES L. STINGER

[See also **Basil the Great; Camaldolese, Order of; Church Fathers; Councils, Western (1311–1449); Gregory of Nazianzus, St.; Reform, Idea of.**]

TRDAT III (IV) THE GREAT, ST. (*ca.* 280–*ca.* 330), Arsacid king of Greater Armenia from about 298, at the time of the Christianization of the country. The Armenian tradition set out in the so-called Agatᶜangełos cycle gives a straightforward account of his career. Carried to the Roman Empire as an infant after his father's murder, he served in the imperial army, impressed the ruler by his prowess, and was restored to his throne. There, he began by persecuting St. Gregory the Illuminator and the Christians, was punished by being transformed into a wild boar, repented after his sister's divine visions, and collaborated with St. Gregory in destroying all the pagan shrines in Armenia and in imposing baptism on the Armenians. Finally, he made a visit to "Rome," where he was welcomed by the pope.

Recent scholarship has shown that this account owes much to an epic tradition and that the historical events and chronology are far more complicated. The evidence of contemporary Sasanian inscriptions must be reconciled with classical and Armenian historical sources: considerable confusion between Armenian rulers bearing the same name seems to have occurred, and political divisions within Greater Armenia have been obscured. The most probable recent reconstruction dates Trdat's birth about 280, his escape to the empire in 287, and his return to a Greater Armenia reunited under Roman aegis after the Peace of Nisibis in 298. Following the policy of his patron, Diocletian, Trdat then carried on a persecution of Christians within his realm until the beginning of a new era of toleration in the empire after 313, which permitted the consecration of an Armenian patriarch at Caesarea, capital of the province of Cappadocia, in the following year. The length of Trdat's reign can be reconstructed as thirty-two years, thus giving 330 as the probable year of his death.

BIBLIOGRAPHY

Manuk Abeghian, *Istoriia drevnearmianskoĭ literatury*, new ed. (1975), 33–35, 42–45; Paul Ananian, "La data e le circostanze della consecrazione di S. Gregorio Illuminatore," in *Le muséon*, **74** (1961), 43–73, 317–360; Nina G. Garsoïan, "The Iranian Substratum of the Agatᶜangełos Cycle," in Nina G. Garsoïan, Thomas F. Mathews, and Robert W. Thomson, eds., *East of Byzantium: Syria and Armenia in the Formative Period* (1982); Robert W. Thomson, ed. and trans., *Agathangelos: History of the Armenians* (1976); Cyril Toumanoff, "The Third-century Armenian Arsacids: A Chronological and Genealogical Commentary," in *Revue des études arméniennes*, n.s. 6 (1969), and *Manuel de généalogie et de chronologie pour l'histoire de la Caucasie chrétienne* (1976), 76, 516.

NINA G. GARSOÏAN

[See also **Agatᶜangełos; Armenia: History of; Arsacids/Aršakuni, Armenian; Gregory the Illuminator, St.**]

Interior of Ani Cathedral, designed by Trdat, 989–1010. DR. ARMEN HAGHNAZARIAN, RESEARCH ON ARMENIAN ARCHITECTURE, AACHEN

TRDAT (*fl.* 989–1035), the brilliant Armenian palace architect of Ani, is noted for his masterpiece, Ani Cathedral (989–1010), with its pointed arches, clustered piers, and soaring verticality, and for his reconstruction (989–994) of the dome of Hagia Sophia in Constantinople.

Trdat also constructed the church at Argina (ca. 985–990) for Kat^cołikos Xač^cik I Aršaruni and, for King Gagik I, the massive church of St. Grigor Lusaworič^c (completed 1000, now collapsed), a copy of the seventh-century Armenian church of Zwart^cnoc^c. Others attributed to him are St. P^crkič^c at Ani (1035), two churches at Sanahin (966) and Hałbat (976–991), monasteries, and Ani's walls and towers (977–989).

BIBLIOGRAPHY

Sirarpie Der Nersessian, *The Armenians* (1969) and *Armenian Art* (1978); William Emerson and Robert L. Van Nice, "Hagia Sophia: The Construction of the Second Dome and Its Later Repairs," in *Archaeology,* 4 (1951); Varaztad Harouthiounian and Morous Hasrathian, *Monuments of Armenia* (1975), 125–129; Richard Krautheimer, *Early Christian and Byzantine Architecture* (1975), 219, 346, 348; Josef Strzygowski, *Die Baukunst der Armenier und Europa,* II (1918).

Lucy Der Manuelian

[See also **Ani, Monuments of; Armenian Art; Gagik I; Hagia Sophia; Hałbat; Sanahin; Zwart^cnoc^c.**]

TREASON. The history of treason in medieval English law and politics serves almost as a mirror to the growth of the early English state. The emerging power of kingship is evident in the very existence of a concept of treason, with all of the attendant horrors of the sentence carried out upon traitors. The development of a "constitutional" side, however, though less pronounced, is evident in the restrictions that came to circumscribe royal power and in the compromises regarding definitions and procedures that the crown was willing to accept, even in the laws that struck down those whom the king considered his worst enemies.

In the early Middle Ages treason was not distinct from felony and still retained its feudal sense of breach of faith between vassal and lord, which led to escheat. Rebellion against the king was not treason according to the customs of early feudal states. Once the formal defiance (*diffidatio*) was proclaimed, a good, open fight with the king was a vassal's right, often exercised. There were, however, certain offenses that had long been considered treasonable and that usually led to a death sentence.

The list included compassing or imagining the king's death, sedition (without fair warning) by the vassal or by others at his instigation, and affording aid to the kings' enemies. The origin of these treasons in violation of the feudal bond is apparent and reminds us that a king was feudal dominus as well as rex.

But by the reign of Edward I (1272–1307), the power of kingship had built impressively on feudal foundations and was transcending feudalism in the development of the state. Moreover, the royal power was finding suitable theoretical expressions in revived ideas borrowed by crown lawyers from the classical Roman law. To the personal, feudal notions of treason, the lawyers could add a refined sense of outrage for offenses against the public authority vested in the king, at a time when the practical capacity of that authority had been greatly augmented. Thus it is not surprising that the imperious Edward I and his advisers wrote an important first chapter in the history of high treason as they sought to deal with the Welsh and Scots, who stubbornly resisted conquest by English arms. It suited Edward's purposes to treat these enemies as traitorous rebels. By the end of the reign more than a score of important political opponents of the crown had been executed for treason, the charge generally including the levying of war against the king. In the trial of the Welsh leader David ap Gruffudd (1282), broken feudal obligations were still a prominent feature in the accusation; less of this feudal element appeared a few years later in the trial of Rhys ap Maredudd (1292). The Scottish war seems to have crystallized Edward's views. In 1305 William Wallace, who was accused (among much else) of waging war against the king with banners displayed (the sign of a state of war), was hanged, disemboweled, and decapitated; his entrails were burned and his body quartered. (David ap Gruffudd had suffered a similar fate.)

Horrendous though these punishments were, the legal procedure itself might have seemed ominous to a perceptive observer. The crown was groping its way toward a procedure of conviction by notoriety. In 1292 the lord Rhys was termed a manifest rebel; in 1306 sixteen Scots were convicted by the king's record (an official statement), that is, appeal or indictment and verdict were all rolled into one, with the idea of public ill-fame serving as a cloak to mask the novelty.

Edward II, in one of the most troubled medieval reigns (1307–1327), applied this procedure to his domestic enemies. In 1318 Gilbert de Middleton was convicted by record before justices of King's Bench on charges including waging war against the king with banners displayed; he was executed with all of the frightful refinements used against David ap Gruffudd and William Wallace. In 1322 Thomas of Lancaster was similarly charged with warring against the king with banners displayed. He was convicted by the king's record, although the sentence of drawing and hanging was mitigated in his case to beheading. In the following year Andrew Harclay was convicted by king's record in an even more summary procedure. But this technique should not be thought exclusively a royalist weapon. Edward II's enemies were quick to use it against their hated foes at the king's side. Royal favorites like Hugh le Despenser the elder and the younger, already outlawed, were convicted in parliament by the record of the barons and a king under baronial control. Particularly important was the charge of accroaching (that is, usurping) the royal power to themselves. This charge had been used before by the crown (as in Edward I's accusations against Nicholas de Segrave in 1305), but under Edward II the king was the target of the action rather than the initiator, since it was his advisers who were accused. In fact, accusations of lèse-majesté were proving to be a double-edged sword; if the king could punish offenses against his public authority, powerful subjects could strike at his "evil councillors" on similar charges. The reigns of the first two Edwards had thus brought significant developments in the concept of treason. Open war against the king in his own realm was likely to lead to treason charges and, in a tense political setting, favorites whom the king could no longer protect might find themselves accused of accroaching royal power. Trial might take place before any of a number of courts, but the outcome would likely be predictable, for conviction was usually secured by record.

These tendencies would be greatly altered in the reign of Edward III (1327–1377). Though the young king convicted Roger Mortimer by notoriety in 1330, Mortimer's heir was able to have this conviction quashed in 1354. From then on ill-fame might serve as an indictment, but was not, as before, tantamount to conviction. Summary conviction by the king's record did survive and was used, especially in the reigns of Richard II and Edward IV, but only in cases brought on the charge of fighting the king in open war. Similarly, summary conviction for treasonable military acts would

outlast the Middle Ages in the form of martial law. Accroaching the royal power, however, was in the time of Edward III potentially a more serious issue than conviction by record. It was then being used not as a weapon of magnate opposition, but as a tool in a campaign for law and order.

Whatever concern Edward III felt for public order, his need for parliamentary taxes to finance the French war forced him to listen attentively to the growing chorus of complaint over the state of the peace in his own realm. He may thus have decided to use a very broad definition of accroaching the royal power, including attacks on royal officers and judges, as one element in a law-and-order campaign. The danger, soon perceived by the politically important segments of society, was that such use of the charge of accroaching would greatly broaden a definition of treason. This political sensitivity on the part of lords and commons could only be augmented, for the lords, by an economic consideration. Lords were well aware that treason convictions against any of their tenants eliminated the chance of forfeitures; traitors' possessions went to the king at once and in perpetuity, but felons' possessions went to the lord after the king had enjoyed their use for a year and a day.

Moreover, the extension of the definition of treason was not limited to accroaching. Early in Edward's reign his judges treated some cases of riding armed to rob, slay, or capture as if they were treason. It seems that the judges wanted to aggravate the accusation against certain offenders, imposing frightening and impressive death sentences in the hope of deterring the lawlessness that was a cause of great public outcry. But again the concern for public order did not outweigh the concern of those lords with prospects of forfeitures and perhaps with a penchant themselves for riding forth armed to rob and slay.

These potential expansions of the concept of treason and the concern they aroused form the background to the great statute of treasons of 1352. But to posit some bitter conflict between king and lords over treason would be incorrect. Edward III seems to have accepted readily the narrow definition that would reduce his own chance of forfeitures for treason; undoubtedly the larger goal of war taxation voted by a less discontented parliamentary commons seemed a greater good. In any case, since the king made no later attempt to return to the situation before 1352, and since his relations with the magnates and commons were relatively cordial (until the troubled last years of his reign), the 1352 statute was given a chance to become, in Bellamy's words, "hallowed by time."

Two types of treason were clearly distinguished. Petty treason meant the slaying of a master by a servant, of a husband by a wife, or of a prelate by a lesser cleric. These offenses were treated essentially as felonies. High treason involved crimes against the king's person or regality. Specifically, this included compassing or imagining the king's death, or the death of his wife or heir; the violation of his wife or eldest daughter or the wife of his eldest son; or the slaying of the chancellor, treasurer, justices of either bench, eyre justices, assize justices, or any other justices with oyer and terminer powers, if these justices were slain while in their places performing their offices. Counterfeiting money or the king's seal, or bringing false money into the realm, were likewise classed as high treason. In doubtful cases the judges were to delay giving judgment until the issue was considered before the king in parliament and declared treason or felony.

Read only for its details, the statute at first seems unlikely to merit Sir Edward Coke's accolade that it stands second in importance only to Magna Carta. But in context one can at least appreciate Coke's sense of the role the statute played in medieval law and politics. Several significant trends of the early fourteenth century were ended. Summary conviction on the king's word, as we have seen, largely disappeared. The crown thus tacitly condemned some of the trials carried out under Edward II, for the statute insisted that for a man to be found guilty of treason "he must be provably attainted of open fact by men of his own condition" (Bellamy). Moreover, the amorphous charge of accroaching the royal power, which seemed on the way to entering any definition of high treason, was excluded, and disappeared by the mid fifteenth century. In the Good Parliament of 1376, for example, Richard Lyons was accused of misprision (that is, official misconduct), not of accroaching the royal power. An extension of treason via accroaching would have created an intolerable situation in which mere intimacy with the king might lead to the most severe penalties and forfeitures known to the law. In general, the statute by its very conservative nature ended a long period in which the meaning of treason seemed to be growing into a vaguely despotic conception, unwelcome to the parliamentary commons, who provided the pressure that secured the statute.

Yet the reign of Richard II in particular would show that the 1352 statute had by no means settled all the issues of definition nor precluded the possibility of further royal expansion. During the 1381 rising, for example, local juries labeled as treason whatever seemed to them to rank as treason when they presented their indictments: murder of men loyal to the crown; destruction of houses owned by loyalists; destruction of royal records or buildings; providing assistance to rebels. The rising demonstrated that the crown had no clear judicial policy on popular rebellion; but by the fifteenth century the 1352 statute was stretched to cover popular insurrection, since it could lead to the king's death. This clause, in fact, proved to be a great expansion joint in the statute and was used by the crown lawyers in a way analogous to the use made by the U.S. federal government in the nineteenth century of its right to regulate interstate commerce. Few cases that the crown wanted to prosecute could not be fitted into the clause against compassing the king's death. Any issue that caused the king such concern that his health was affected jeopardized his life and thus was subject to the 1352 statute. The lawyers could even argue that any offense that caused the people to withdraw their love for the king thereby caused worry, which endangered his health and life.

More spectacular than such sophistry was the attempt of Richard II to extend the law of treason to match his sense of the royal prerogative. His famous questions to the judges in 1387 show how far he might push the prerogative in the area of treason; in fact, he considered all attempts by act or by words to thwart his prerogative as treason. He tried some charges of levying war against the king by summary procedure based on the king's record in the Court of Chivalry. During his reign, in a manner reminiscent of the troubles of Edward II, the king and the magnate opposition to the king used similar tactics. In 1388 the Lords Appellant obtained convictions of four royal favorites whom they appealed (accused) of treason in parliament after the lords had, using the 1352 statute, declared their crimes to be treason. The convictions were grounded in notoriety. When Richard II struck back at the Lords Appellant in 1397–1398, he, too, used parliamentary appeals of treason. But after the king was deposed in 1399, a commons petition successfully barred all future appeals of treason.

Despite the very troubled character of fifteenth-century English political life, the scope of treason was not generally a major issue pitting king against great lords. Most kings seem to have been satisfied with the existing definition. The various fifteenth-century statutes which modified or supplemented that definition were much less important than the original statute of 1352. In fact the role of parliament in treason proceedings was in general reduced; in most questionable cases the judges relied on a broad interpretation of the clause of the 1352 statute regarding compassing or imagining the king's death rather than the procedural device, also provided by the statute, of submitting doubtful cases before the king in parliament. Parliamentary declarations of treason survived into the fifteenth century only as one necessary but rather formal element in the act of attainder, and such declarations were nearly always in line with the 1352 statute. Only with the Tudor period did parliament vigorously legislate on the subject of treason, passing sixty-eight treason statutes between 1485 and 1603. Writing in the early twentieth century, W. S. Holdsworth could proclaim the 1352 statute "still the foundation of the law of treason"; the trial of the Irish nationalist Roger Casement in 1916 turned on the interpretation of clauses in this statute.

Throughout the late Middle Ages most treason trials were conducted by a process not very different from that used for ordinary felony or trespass cases. As Bellamy has said, "From the prisoner's viewpoint the only noticeable difference in being tried for treason was that he could not plead benefit of clergy and, if found guilty, he was dragged to the gallows behind a horse." The accused heard the indictment against him (though he was not given a copy of it), and if he pleaded innocent his case went before a *petit* (trial) jury. He could challenge up to thirty-five prospective jurors. This scene might be enacted in any of a number of courts, for the crown made no deliberate attempt to bring all treason cases before one particular court. Trials were conducted by King's Bench, special commissions, the steward of the household, chancery, council, the Court of Chivalry, and parliament. But most treason cases across the fifteenth century and on into the Tudor era were heard by oyer and terminer justices. From the mid fifteenth century an increasing number of indictments was drawn up by crown lawyers after asking questions of jurors or examining suspects. A grand jury, shown the list of charges, stated if the bill were true or not. If true, the case went to a petit jury. Though the procedure

might be similar to that for accused felons, the likelihood of conviction was much greater. The crown clearly pressured jurors by all means at its disposal, and there is some evidence that jurors on occasion found their task distasteful. But in overview the law of treason appears moderate to most historians and seems to have been carried out in nearly all cases in accordance with the legal procedures then accepted.

BIBLIOGRAPHY
J. G. Bellamy, *The Law of Treason in England in the Later Middle Ages* (1970) and *The Tudor Law of Treason* (1979); James V. Capua, "The Early History of Martial Law in England," in *Cambridge Law Journal*, **36** (1977); William S. Holdsworth, *A History of English Law*, II, III, 3rd ed. (1923); Maurice Keen, "Treason Trials Under the Law of Arms," in *Transactions of the Royal Historical Society*, 5th ser., **12** (1962).

RICHARD W. KAEUPER

[See also **Assize; Assize, English; Edward I, II, III of England; Escheat, Escheator; Felony; Impeachment and Attainder; Jury; Justices of the King's Bench; Law, English Common; Law, Procedure of; Oyer and Terminer; Trailbaston; Richard II.**]

TREBIZOND, EMPIRE OF, one of the Greek states formed after the capture of Constantinople by the army of the Fourth Crusade in 1204. It was founded by the grand *komnenos* Alexios I as a vehicle for his bid for Constantinople, but Seljuk Turk and Nicaean Greek campaigns in 1210–1214 put an end to his hopes for the Byzantine throne. Trebizond therefore became a sort of empire in exile until 1282, when John II (1282–1297) abandoned his pretensions to Byzantium in exchange for marriage to a daughter of Emperor Michael VIII Palaiologos (1259–1282), who had taken Constantinople in 1261. Henceforth, rulers of Trebizond styled themselves "emperor and autocrat," not "of the Romans" (Byzantines), but "of all the East, the Iberians [perhaps Georgians of Soteriopolis], and the lands beyond [perhaps the Crimea], the grand *komnenos*" (more of a title than a family name).

Administratively, the grand *komnenoi* inherited the old Byzantine theme (military province) organization of Chaldia, with its *banda* (military parishes) and *allelengyon* (communal tax), comprising a ninth-century local defense system that they maintained in working order until 1461. But they

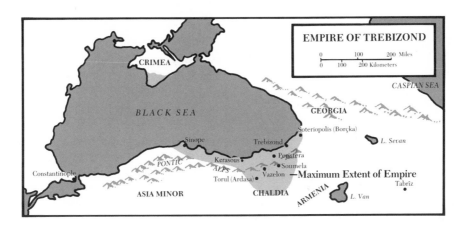

were also alert to governmental and legal developments in contemporary Constantinople and maintained in miniature the full panoply of a Byzantine court, with over 150 officers, where the power of Chaldian warlords was legitimized by Greek titles. In its fourteenth-century civil wars and Orthodox religious controversies Trebizond mirrored events in Constantinople. But while the grand *komnenoi* maintained good relations with the Palaiologoi after 1282, they were more concerned for their survival, making alliances with local Mongol, Georgian, and Turkoman (especially Aq Qoyunlu [white sheep]) neighbors. They intermarried with Muslim dynasties without compromising the essentially Byzantine character of the empire's culture, to such effect that Trebizond outlived Constantinople and was not surrendered to the Ottomans by the last grand *komnenos,* David, until 1461.

Often treated as an exotic appendix to late Byzantine history, the Empire of Trebizond was in fact the political surfacing of something much more substantial: a Pontic regionalism with distinct social, economic, and geographical characteristics that long preceded, and survived, the pocket empire itself. This separatist, but nevertheless Byzantine, culture had formidable continuity, and the cult of its patron saint, Eugenios, gave Trebizond an identity.

The Pontic Alps long shielded the Greeks of the coast from Arab and Turkish attack, and the Chaldian theme, which linked Trebizond with its hinterland, became virtually independent of Constantinople by 1075.

Three factors encouraged the flourishing of the empire in 1204–1461.

First was the Pontic coastland. A dense Greek population of smallholders and transhumants (perhaps 250,000 after the Black Death) tilled the steep, fertile valleys north of the Pontic Alps and grazed their flocks on the high pastures. They exported wine, olive oil, hazelnuts, and alum. The lands of the great families of the coast were expropriated by Grand *Komnenos* Alexios III (1349–1390) after the civil wars, which enabled him to endow monasteries such as Soumela, Vazelon, and Peristera, and allowed them to nurture a lively Byzantine culture. Among Trebizond's scholars, two attended the Council of Ferrara-Florence (1438–1439): Cardinal Bessarion (*ca.* 1403–1472) and George Amoiroutzes (*d.* 1475), the empire's last grand treasurer, who went on to serve Sultan Mehmed II.

Second was the Chaldian hinterland. Ruling clans such as the Gabras, Kabazites, and Tzanichites controlled the passes (essential to traders and invaders), castles such as Torul (Ardasa), and ranches of Chaldia south of the Pontic Alps. The eastern forests were dominated by Hemşinli (Armenian) and Laz (west Georgian) chieftains as far as Soteriopolis. All usually cooperated with the coastal government and outlived it: the Ottomans did not suppress Torul and Soteriopolis until 1479.

Third was commerce. The empire's prosperity coincided with the late-thirteenth-century opening of the Trebizond-Tabriz route, which linked Genoese and Venetian traders (such as Marco Polo) with the Mongol markets of Central Asia through Chaldia. For two centuries Trebizond was for Europeans the port of Persia. The grand *komnenoi* taxed the transit trade, which was stimulated by their own silver coinage (asper), introduced by Manuel I the Fortunate (1238–1263). The grand *komnenoi* therefore had to balance their relations with Italian merchants, rulers of Tabriz, and local Turkoman emirs.

169

BIBLIOGRAPHY

Anthony A. M. Bryer, *The Empire of Trebizond and the Pontos* (1980), *Peoples and Settlement in Anatolia and the Caucasus, 800–1900* (1988), and, with David Winfield, *The Byzantine Monuments and Topography of the Pontos*, 2 vols. (1985); Chrysanthos, Metropolitan of Trebizond, *Istorias tis ekklisias Trapezountos* (1933); William Miller, *Trebizond: The Last Greek Empire* (1926, repr. 1968).

ANTHONY A. M. BRYER

[See also **Alexios I of Trebizond; Aq Qoyunlu; Bessarion; Byzantine Empire: History; Crusades and Crusader States; Epiros, Despotate of; Latin Empire of Constantinople; Nicaea, Empire of; Palaiologoi.**]

TŘEBOŇ, MASTER OF. See **Wittingau, Master of.**

TRECENTO ART. The last decades of the dugento (thirteenth century) and the first years of the trecento (fourteenth century) saw a dramatic transformation of artistic expression in Italy. Changes in religious thought, a revival of urban life, thriving economic conditions, and the growth of a strong middle class contributed to a gradual acceptance of the value of life and the pleasures of the material world. Such powerful thinkers as St. Francis of Assisi (*d.* 1226) brought the individual closer to the deity, emphasized God's benevolence, and rejoiced in the beauties of physical creation. Increased personal and collective wealth contributed to a resurgence of building and artistic production. Citizens joined innumerable monastic, fraternal, civic, charitable, and guild organizations that actively commissioned artists to decorate their buildings and churches. Art remained primarily an expression of religious thinking, just as human activity was principally measured against religious criteria.

But the new conceptions of God and man produced a change in the way religious images were wrought. Christ and the Virgin were represented with greater naturalism than in previous centuries. Aspects of Christ and Mary's earthly life were explored in detail, so that the art of narration took on a new and growing significance. Man drew closer to God through the medium of art.

TUSCAN ART TO 1348

Pisa. The most important early developments took place in Tuscany, with Pisa taking the lead. Her sculptors are notable for their narrative power and inventiveness, and for the broad dissemination of their influence. Giovanni Pisano (*ca.* 1250–*ca.* 1314), son of Nicola Pisano (*fl.* 1258–1280), carried on his father's development toward a classically inspired conception of the human form. Sculpture was principally an architectural embellishment, but through Giovanni it took on a narrative and emotional power that distinguished it from mere decoration. Between 1285 and 1297, Giovanni served the opera of Siena Cathedral, most likely designing the facade and carving the fourteen figures of prophets and wise men and women whose animated intensity enabled them to dominate their setting in a new and dramatic way.

Called to Pisa, where he worked between 1297 and 1310, Giovanni signed and dated his pulpit (noted for its new unity of action, narration, and composition) for S. Andrea in Pistoia, in 1301. Between 1302 and 1311 he carved a pulpit for Pisa Cathedral (illustrated at "Pisano") and, most likely, sculpted the *Madonna and Child* in the lunette above the baptistry entrance as well as another full-length *Madonna and Child* for the Arena Chapel, Padua. Among his last works is the ruined tomb of Margaret of Luxembourg (*ca.* 1311; Genoa, Palazzo Bianco). Remarkable for its departure from traditional funerary form, it depicts Margaret awakened by angels to confront her Redeemer. Brilliantly infusing a sense of the temporal with the eternal, it remains among the most profound expressions of human aspiration.

From the fertile Pisano shop sprang a number of important sculptors whose activities spanned most of Italy. Arnolfo di Cambio (*fl. ca.* 1265–1302) is credited with the full-length figure of Charles of Anjou (*ca.* 1277; Rome, Capitoline Museum) and with a fountain in Perugia. Two signed ciboria in Rome, one at S. Paolo Fuori le Mura and the other at S. Cecilia, dated 1285 and 1293, respectively, and the tomb of Cardinal de Braye (*d.* 1282) found in S. Domenico, Orvieto, are among Arnolfo's chief works. Characterized by their monumental conception of human form based on architectonic principles of balancing mass and weight, Arnolfo's work probably also includes the massive figures of the Madonna and Child that decorated the facade of the cathedral of Florence until the sixteenth century. Arnolfo most likely designed the

Fragment from the tomb of Margaret of Luxembourg. Marble sculpture by Giovanni Pisano, *ca.* 1311.
MUSEUM OF S. AGOSTINO, GENOA

facade, incorporating these imposing figures, which were compatible with—but not overpowered by—their architectural surroundings. These impressive forms helped establish the Florentine tradition for monumental, heroic art that survived well into the cinquecento (sixteenth century).

Tino da Camaino (*ca.* 1285–*ca.* 1327) was the most notable Sienese follower of Giovanni Pisano. First recorded as the *capomaestro* (head master) for the cathedral of Pisa, Tino contracted in 1315 to sculpt the now fragmented tomb of Emperor Henry VII. In 1318 came the tomb of Cardinal Petroni, now reconstructed in the cathedral of Siena. Between 1321 and 1323 Tino worked in Florence, where he produced the tombs of Gastone della Torre in S. Croce and Antonio Orso, bishop of Florence, in the cathedral. Called to Naples in 1323, Tino was active there, as evidenced by the tombs of Mary of Hungary in S. Maria Donna Regina, Charles of Calabria in S. Chiara, and Mary of Valois, also in S. Chiari. Inspired by Arnolfo and Giovanni, Tino infused his figures with a lyrical grace and brooding melancholy that are also derived from the work of painters, in particular the Lorenzetti brothers and Giotto. He borrowed figure types and gestures from both sources as well, as a comparison between Orso and Giotto's Arena Chapel *Flagellation* demonstrates.

Lorenzo Maitani (born in Siena in 1330), pupil of Giovanni Pisano, was *capomaestro* for Orvieto Cathedral by 1310 until his death. There, he probably designed the lower facade and played a major part in the execution of the extant reliefs—Genesis, Tree of Jesse, Old Testament Prophecies, the Life of Christ, and the Last Judgment—that cover the four piers. These scenes are based on Giovanni Pisano's expressive, linear, and almost abstract late style. (See illustrations at "Maitani.")

Andrea Pisano (*ca.* 1295–*ca.* 1348), who probably trained in Pisa, is noted for the execution of the first pair of bronze doors for the Florentine Baptistery from about 1330 to 1336. Andrea's work balanced realism within the constraints of decorative function. His episodes from the Life of John the Baptist are all set within a quadrilobe form. Each narrative is simply stated and conforms to the overall decorative intent, with a high degree of technical mastery and compositional inventiveness. (See illustration at "Pisano.")

Florence. Florence had no native school of sculptors but produced a remarkable tradition of painters. Foremost among them was Giotto di Bondone

Madonna. Panel painting by Giotto, *ca*. 1305. Formerly Church of Ognissanti (All Saints), now Uffizi, Florence. ALINARI / ART RESOURCE

(*ca*. 1267–1337). Where he trained is unknown, but by 1310 his fame had spread throughout Italy, bringing commissions from Rome, Naples, and Padua. He might have known the work of Pietro Cavallini in Rome and no doubt knew Ceni di Pepi (Cimabue) in Florence as well as the sculpture of Giovanni Pisano and Arnolfo di Cambio. Giotto's earliest works far outstrip his predecessors' in breadth of conception and innovation. The *Crucifix* (Florence, S. Maria Novella) is an unprecedented interpretation of a convincing human form suspended on the cross, while his *Madonna* (*ca*. 1305; Florence, Uffizi) is a spatially cohesive, psychologically accessible, yet powerfully imposing interpretation of a devotional image.

Giotto's greatest masterpiece, the Arena (Scrovegni) Chapel frescoes in Padua, dates from roughly the same time and remains unsurpassed as a consummate wall decoration and brilliantly conceived narrative and composition. Forty-one individual pictures illustrate the Life of the Virgin and the Life of Christ in a heroic yet profoundly human interpretation of the sacred texts. Giotto's late career is visible in the partially damaged frescoes of the Bardi and Peruzzi chapels of S. Croce, dating from the 1330's. Here the artist used greater restraint, broader brushwork, subdued color, and more subtle, less concentrated narrative to illustrate the lives of St. Francis and John the Baptist.

Giotto's contribution, if any, to the frescoes illustrating the Life of St. Francis in the church of St. Francis at Assisi is in dispute—the styles are too varied to have a common origin. Between 1334 and 1337 Giotto served as *capomaestro* for the cathedral of Florence, and he designed its campanile. His impact was felt in all subsequent Florentine and Italian painting, but Siena, Florence's neighbor, developed an idiom that was original and remarkably independent.

Siena. The great Sienese tradition began with Duccio di Buoninsegna (*ca*. 1255/1260–*ca*. 1318). No frescoes by him are known, but several exquisite panels—the *Crevole Madonna*, the *Madonna of the Franciscans* (about 1280) and the *Rucellai Madonna*, commissioned for S. Maria Novella in 1285—reveal his early development of a delicate, sumptuous world, more refined and more elevated than the sturdy, heroic milieu of Florentine art. His most ambitious and magnificent surviving work is the large *Maestà* painted between 1308 and 1311 for the high altar of Siena Cathedral and now in the cathedral museum (Museo dell'Opera del Duomo; illustrated at "Duccio"). The Virgin, represented as the Queen of Heaven surrounded by a court of saints and apostles, is unequaled for the graceful and subtle combinations of color and line. The real and the ideal blend in a dazzling, unearthly vision that would dominate Sienese sensibility for several centuries. On the back of the *Maestà* Duccio executed a large cycle of Christ's life, full of anecdotal flavor and richness of detail in scenes constructed with deliberate spatial ambiguities to enhance the tension between the real and the fictive.

Duccio's most profound impact was on Simone Martini (1280's–1344), whose earliest known work, the *Maestà* fresco for the council chamber in the Palazzo Pubblico, Siena (1315), is based on Duccio's model. Simone's figural conception absorbed much natural observation, adding dimensionality and believability to his forms, but they remain idealized, resplendent, supremely beautiful,

Maestà. Fresco by Simone Martini in the Council Chamber of the Palazzo Pubblico, Siena, 1315.
ALINARI / ART RESOURCE

opulently dressed, and elegant beings. Few documents fix Simone's career, but around 1330 he may have painted the brilliantly colored frescoes depicting the Life of St. Martin in S. Francesco at Assisi. In 1333 Simone signed and dated his unparalleled achievement, the *Annunciation* (with wings by Lippo Memmi; Florence, Uffizi; illustration at "Annunciation"), a fully developed fusion of flat, ornate linearity and volumetric renderings of form —anticipating the future developments of Tuscan painting for the rest of the century. Copied no less than sixteen times, this panel and Simone's *St. Louis of Toulouse Crowning Robert of Anjou* (1317) are watersheds for the history of trecento painting, blending a love for traditional decorative effect with the new understanding of the human form evolved by Giotto and subsequent generations. Simone's late career brought him in 1340 to Avignon, where only fragments remain of his work.

The Sienese Pietro Lorenzetti (*fl. ca.* 1315–1348), unlike Simone, sought a cohesion rather than a formal tension in his work, as is evident in

his earliest dated panel, the polyptych of the *Virgin and Saints* (1320; Arezzo, Pieve di S. Maria). Inspired by Duccio, Giovanni Pisano, and Giotto, Pietro charted an independent course, based on the spatially cohesive and monumental forms of Giotto's art and the emotional expressiveness of the Sienese tradition. Pietro's *Madonna,* part of the Carmelite Altarpiece and dated 1329, is based on Giotto's Ognissanti *Madonna,* but is far moodier and more introspective, expressing a brooding passion. Pietro's involvement in the undated, undocumented frescoes of the Life of Christ in S. Francesco, Assisi, is problematic, but certain scenes— the *Entombment* and the *Deposition*—are his undisputed masterpieces, revealing an unparalleled emotional intensity and dramatic richness. Pietro's imagination reinterpreted these episodes in a startingly gripping way, taking the art of narration to new levels of personal interpretation. Pietro's experimentation with conceptions of space and his overcoming of old spatial restrictions is characteristic of Pietro's art, and nowhere are old restrictions

173

Birth of the Virgin. Triptych by Pietro Lorenzetti, 1335/1342. Formerly Siena Cathedral, now Museo dell'Opera del Duomo, Siena. ALINARI/ART RESOURCE

exceptionally distinct variants—one almost spectral, the other soberly monumental. But Ambrogio's contribution to trecento art is best known in his fresco cycles painted between 1336 and 1339 depicting the effects of good and bad government, in Siena's Palazzo Pubblico. (See illustration at "Lorenzetti.") These are the earliest known full-fledged landscapes in European art. Based on a skilled use of paint and incisive, sympathetic observation of nature that characterized all of his work, they are among the most famous paintings from the trecento. In 1342, Ambrogio painted his *Presentation to the Temple,* which served as a model for generations of painters throughout Europe. It, like Pietro's *Birth of the Virgin,* is exceptional for its convincing space, animated figures, and richness of narrative—all this a full century before the Renaissance.

Sienese painting had a considerable impact on the rest of Italian art. In Florence, where artists shaped their styles on Giotto's model, Sienese influences were also felt. Taddeo Gaddi (*ca.* 1300–*ca.*

less inhibiting than in the *Birth of the Virgin* (Siena, Museo dell'Opera del Duomo). Documented as having been painted between 1335 and 1342, it is the earliest example of tripartite panels used to depict a single cohesive space. Together with Simone's *Annunciation,* it reveals a Sienese interest in narration that extends to the altarpiece—formerly limited to devotional, iconic images.

Ambrogio Lorenzetti (*fl. ca.* 1317–1348) was Pietro's brother and artistic equal. Like Pietro, he was most likely trained by Duccio and also developed a highly inventive, imaginative vocabulary. His earliest dated work, the *Madonna and Child* (1319; church of Sant'Angelo a Vico l'Abate), is based on a dugento model but already reveals his probing natural observation and a sophisticated understanding of pictorial form. Numerous half-length Madonnas—*Madonna del Latte, Rapolano Madonna, Madonna and Child with Sts. Dorothy and Mary Magdalen*—demonstrate Ambrogio's ability to reinvent consistently a traditional image. His *Maestàs* (Massa Marittima, Palazzo Preco; Siena, S. Agostino; Monte Siepi, S. Galgano) are in turn three independent original interpretations of another image type. *Annunciations* in Monte Siepi, S. Agostino, and the Siena Pinacoteca (1344) are

Madonna del Latte. Panel painting by Ambrogio Lorenzetti, 1320/1348. Church of S. Francesco, Siena. ALINARI/ART RESOURCE

174

1366), active in Giotto's shop for twenty-four years, is best known for his fresco cycle depicting the Life of the Virgin (*ca.* 1332–1338; Florence, Baroncelli Chapel, S. Croce). Based on Giotto's form, the cycle's lively anecdotal quality and fanciful architecture are derived from the Lorenzettis and Simone Martini. Maso di Banco (*fl. ca.* 1325–1350), one of Giotto's most genial followers, was equally inspired by Sienese painting. His principal surviving works—the *Life of St. Sylvester* (*ca.* 1336; Florence, Bardi di Vernio Chapel, S. Croce), two *Coronation of the Virgin* frescoes (at Florence in S. Croce, and at Assisi in S. Francesco, respectively), and two half-length Madonnas (Florence, S. Spirito; Berlin-Dahlem, Staatliche Museen)—are, in their sensuality and subtle melancholy, inspired by the work of Simone Martini and the Lorenzettis.

Bernardo Daddi (*ca.* 1290–*ca.* 1348), perhaps the most prolific and popular Florentine painter of his generation, adopted both Sienese image types—the half-length Madonna and the portable triptych—and incorporated a Sienese decorative element into his rather stocky, sweet-faced Madonnas.

TUSCAN ART AFTER THE BLACK DEATH

Florence. Daddi's career and those of many other painters ended in 1348 as a result of the Black Death, which decimated Italy. New generations of painters working in different styles emerged. Their art has often been seen as a reaction to the plague. Such a causal relationship between art and history is, however, difficult to prove. Much of the stylistic impulse for the art of Andrea Orcagna (*fl.* 1330–1368) and Nardo di Cione (*fl. ca.* 1343–1365/1366) in Florence has its origins with Simone Martini. Nardo di Cione's most important surviving work is the *Last Judgment* fresco cycle of about 1354–1357 that surrounds Orcagna's signed and dated (1357) altarpiece, *Christ in Majesty with Saints* (both Florence, Strozzi Chapel, S. Maria Novella; both illustrated in volume 9). This latter work depicts Christ presenting the keys to St. Peter and a book of Scriptures to St. Dominic. Spatially ambiguous, depicting a stern and relentless Christ, full of blazing, sharply keyed colors, Orcagna's panel is worlds away from the soft, sensuous, placid beings that people Nardo's *Last Judgment* fresco.

Orcagna's style in this altarpiece is in some measure due to the iconography. Still, in Florence, the current style of painting shifted in emphasis to the figure set against gold grounds or surrounded by elaborately brocaded floor planes and backdrops, rather than placed within an architectural framework of enveloping thrones. This spatial ambiguity, first stated by Duccio and Simone Martini, found favor among Florentine painters, such as Niccolò di Tommaso, Jacopo di Cione, Andrea di Firenze, Niccolò di Pietro Gerini, and Giovanni del Biondo, who gradually eliminated any sense of volume in the figures and created gaudy, multicolored images based on repetitious and non-illusionistic formulas. A taste for balance gave way to strict symmetry, and only toward the end of the century, in the late works of Agnolo Gaddi, Spinello Aretino, and Antonio Veneziano, was there a return to an interest in space, volume, and a more natural interpretation of form.

Siena. Sienese painters, principally Barna di Siena (best known for his fresco cycle in the Collegiata, San Gimignano), Lippo Memmi, Bartolo di Fredi, Paolo di Giovanni Fei, and Taddeo di Bartolo, explored and refined the rich tradition established by their ancestors. All developed a general tendency toward intensified emotion, violent narration, the dazzling effect of rich colors, and elaborately textured gold grounds. Sienese influence extended in many directions. Pisa's greatest mid-century fresco cycle—the *Triumph of Death* (illustrated on page 125), often attributed to Francesco Traini (*fl.* 1321–1363) —is dependent on Simone Martini and Ambrogio Lorenzetti. Sienese painters worked as far south as Orvieto and as far north as Venice, where their influence blended with the local tradition established by Paolo Veneziano (*fl.* 1333–1358; *d. ca.* 1367).

ART IN NORTHERN ITALY

In Padua, two notable masters, Guariento di Arpo (*fl. ca.* 1338–1370) and Altichiero (*fl. ca.* 1330–1395), can be called two of Giotto's most gifted followers. Altichiero's genius survives mainly in the frescoes in the Chapel of S. Felice, documented as having been executed in the 1370's, and the Oratory of S. Giorgio in the Santo, documented in 1384, both in the basilica of S. Antonio, Paduci. Using Giotto's models, Altichiero deepened space, added a sense of atmosphere, and incorporated a portraitlike realism to his figures into his brilliantly ordered compositions. Altichiero anticipated by nearly fifty years the development of space and volume in fifteenth-century Florentine art—notably in the work of Masaccio.

The Crucifixion. Fresco by Altichiero in the Oratory of S. Giorgio, Padua, 1379. ALINARI / ART RESOURCE

LATE TRECENTO SCULPTURE

Documents indicate that sculptural activity flourished in the second half of the trecento, but little survives. Nino Pisano (*fl.* 1348–1368), who succeeded his father as Orvieto's *capomaestro,* produced a series of languorous Madonnas, among them the *Virgin and Child* in S. Maria Novella, Florence. Orcagna was responsible for the magnificent tabernacle (1359; Florence, Or San Michele), carved with scenes of the life of the Virgin, made to enshrine the miracle-working image by Bernardo Daddi (replacing a lost original). Orcagna's most notable successor was Giovanni d'Ambrogio (*fl.* 1366–1418), who based his figures of the Virtues (1386–1387; Florence, Loggia dei Lanzi) on designs by Agnolo Gaddi (*fl. ca.* 1369–d. 1396).

CONCLUSION

Trecento art can be characterized as the constant reinterpretation of the past by successive generations of artists. Motivated by a deep respect for the meaning and power of older images, an awareness of modernity, and a need for self-expression, artists reshaped and adapted older ideas and forms in a wide variety of ways. The 1330's saw a gradual shift in emphasis on decorative effects. The large simple shapes of early trecento altarpieces gave way to gaudy, compartmentalized triptychs and polyptychs, replete with predellas, wings, and pinnacles, and embellished with carved and gilded frames. In Florence especially, mural painters were caught up in the trend for decoration and tended to reduce the space in their frescoes to achieve an overall ornamental quality. Sculptors also kept their figural conceptions within the bounds of ornament, so that figures and actions harmonized with a superimposed design as well as with the intended narrative message.

Each decade brought changes, and in each instance the past was the fertile source of inspiration. In the 1380's and 1390's, Florentine painters began to reexplore Giotto's monumental, heroic figure style in a manner sometimes called the Giottesque Revival. While not abandoning their love of linearity, pattern, and symmetry, many Florentine artists reintroduced a sense of volume and specificity of character into their work. A notable change is seen in the late works of Agnolo Gaddi and Spinello Aretino. Their subtle fusion of decoration with illusion (whose ultimate origins lie with Simone Martini and Nardo di Cione) found its most exquisite expression in the art of Lorenzo Monaco and scores of his followers in the quattrocento, as well as in the early Lorenzo Ghiberti.

In a sense, the Florentines turned rather more slowly toward naturalism than did artists elsewhere. Altichiero's precocious contributions were completed in the early 1380's, and his achievements were unequalled in Florence. Antonio Veneziano, the most gifted exponent of spatial and figural unity working in Florence during the 1380's and 1390's, was most likely trained outside Florence. Vasari's patriotic assessment of Florentine artistic preeminence still guides most of today's scholarly research in trecento art, so it will take future generations of scholars to identify further the importance of the non-Florentine artists for later developments in Italian painting and sculpture.

BIBLIOGRAPHY
Frederick Antal, *Florentine Painting and Its Social Background* (1948, repr. 1975); Bernard Berenson, *Italian Pictures of the Renaissance: Central Italian and North Italian Schools,* 3 vols. (1968), *Italian Pictures of the Renaissance: Florentine School,* 2 vols. (1963), and *Italian Pictures of the Renaissance: Venetian School,* 2

vols. (1957); Ferdinando Bologna, *Early Italian Painting* (1964) and *I pittori alla corte angionina di Napoli, 1266–1414* (1969); Gene Brucker, *The Society of Renaissance Florence* (1971); Enzo Carli, *Pittura medievale pisana* (1958); Cennino Cennini, *The Craftsman's Handbook,* Daniel V. Thompson, Jr., trans. (1933); Bruce Cole, *Giotto and Florentine Painting, 1280–1375* (1976) and *Sienese Painting from Its Origins to the Fifteenth Century* (1980); Dominic E. Colnaghi, *A Dictionary of Florentine Painters from the 13th to the 17th Centuries* (1928); Joseph A. Crowe and G. B. Cavalcaselle, *A New History of Painting in Italy* (1864, 2nd ed. 1908); George H. Edgell, *A History of Sienese Painting* (1932); Richard Fremantle, *Florentine Gothic Painters* (1975); Edward B. Garrison, *Italian Romanesque Panel Painting: An Illustrated Index* (1949); Helmut Hager, *Die Anfänge des italienischen Altarbildes* (1962); George Kaftal, *Iconography of the Saints in Tuscan Painting* (1952); John Larner, *Culture and Society in Italy, 1290–1420* (1971); Raimond van Marle, *The Development of the Italian Schools of Painting,* 19 vols. (1923–1938); Millard Meiss, *Painting in Florence and Siena After the Black Death,* (1951, repr. 1964); Ottavio Morisani, *Pittura del trecento in Napoli* (1947); Robert Oertel, *Early Italian Painting to 1400* (1966); Richard Offner, *Corpus of Florentine Painting,* 18 vols. (1930–), and *Studies in Florentine Painting* (1927); Walter and Elisabeth Paatz, *Die Kirchen von Florenz,* 6 vols. (1940–1954); John Pope-Hennessy, *Italian Gothic Sculpture* (1955, 2nd ed. 1972); Giulia Sinibaldi and Giulia Brunetti, *Pittura italiana del duecento e trecento* (1943); Alistair Smart, *The Assisi Problem and the Art of Giotto* (1971); James H. Stubblebine, *Duccio di Buoninsegna and His School,* 2 vols. (1979); Henry Thode, *Franz von Assisi und die Anfänge der Kunst der Renaissance in Italien* (1885, 4th ed. 1934); Evelyn Sandberg Vavalà, *La croce dipinta italiana e l'iconografia della Passione* (1929) and *Sienese Studies* (1953); Adolfo Venturi, *Storia dell'arte italiana,* 11 vols. in 23 (1901–1940, repr. 1967), with index, 2 vols. (1975); Carlo Volpe, *La pittura riminese del trecento* (1965); John White, *Art and Architecture in Italy, 1250–1400* (1966) and *Duccio: Tuscan Art and the Medieval Workshop* (1979).

ADELHEID M. GEALT

[See also **Arena Chapel; Assisi, San Francesco; Dugento Art; Fresco Painting; Gothic Art; Maestà; Panel Painting;** entries on individual artists, most with illustrations.]

TRECENTO MUSIC, the term used to refer to the Italian music of the fourteenth century and, more particularly, to the polyphonic repertoire. The term "trecento," literally meaning "three hundreds," is employed with specific reference to the century from 1300 to 1399. French music of the same period is referred to as a new art (*ars nova*) because a musical style and notational practice different from that of the thirteenth century (*ars antiqua*) emerged around 1310–1320. In Italy there are no polyphonic antecedents as obvious as those in France. Kurt von Fischer has shown in his essay published in 1961, however, that trecento polyphony had distinct roots in an indigenous repertoire of solo song with improvised instrumental accompaniment.

The poetic repertoire of the troubadours, which reached its zenith prior to 1300, provided French composers with a wealth of sophisticated texts for musical settings. Italian was accepted as a suitable language for lyric verse only after Dante (1265–1321) and his contemporaries elevated it to the so-called *dolce stil nuovo* (sweet new style). The forms of troubadour poetry were well known and imitated to a limited extent in Italy. A distinctly Italian spirit was cultivated, however, by a host of gifted poets such as Petrarch (1304–1374). Three Italian musical forms resulted from the collaboration of poets and composers: ballata, madrigal, and caccia. The madrigal is unique to Italy. The ballata, rather than being akin to the French ballade, is similar in form to the virelai, and the caccia employs compositional principles like those of the French chace.

MUSICAL NOTATION

The notational practice of trecento music differed from that in use elsewhere and gave a distinctive style to the music composed. Note shapes were the same as those employed throughout Europe, but the use of the dot (*punctus divisionis*) differed. In Italy it signified primarily a unit of rhythmic measure equivalent to a breve (*brevis*), like the present-day bar line. Thus, the groupings of notes between these dots, be they semibreves or minims, determined the value of the notes. No absolute value could be inferred for any note shape; its value depended on the context. Combinations of groupings, in three separate divisions, were given names signifying the time signature or mensuration being used; letters as an abbreviation of the grouping employed were included in the manuscript as a guide to performers. In any one composition, several mensurations were often used in the musical sections of one part and between voices.

The concept of perfect and imperfect (triple and duple) time, found also in the French notational practice, is obvious in the first division. The French employed a circle for perfect, a semicircle for imperfect, and proportional signs that appear as fractions to indicate the four subsets in the second division. The groupings of the third division are almost totally exclusive to the Italian notation and involve very small note values performed at a rapid pace. The syncopations across the bar line that are common in the French *ars nova* do not become a feature of this notation; instead, rapid patter figures in vocal works and elaborate ornamental figures of the earliest keyboard intabulations or interpolations of chansons (Faenza Codex, Faenza, Biblioteca Communale, MS 117) are cultivated within the bar-line concept of the Italian notation.

Toward the end of the fourteenth century there was sufficient interchange among French and Italian musicians, partly because of the papal court at Avignon, that both notational practices fused to create the very complex *ars subtilior* rhythmic subtleties. In order to inform performers of the rules to be applied to a particular composition, Italian composers of the mixed notational style added the letter *g* (*gallica*) to indicate the application of French rules.

MUSICAL FORMS

The primary interest of composers and performers of the trecento focused on polyphonic music with secular poetry. There are, however, a few settings of sacred hymns, sequences, and processional songs in conductus, or note-against-note style. Sung by trained singers during religious services or processions, these musical settings display little of the subtle nuances of the secular works. Usually with two composed parts only, that is, with no preexisting tenor part, and with each part declaiming the text simultaneously, these compositions suited the paraliturgical purposes for which they were written. Musical elaboration was sufficiently simple not to obscure the texts.

The three secular forms mentioned above received the most attention and have been recorded in extant manuscripts in sufficient numbers to justify individual attention.

Madrigal. The trecento madrigal must not be confused or equated with the sixteenth-century musical composition of the same name. Although poetry by prominent literary figures such as Petrarch is employed in the trecento as well as in the late Renaissance madrigal, the musical practice and form differ considerably. The designation "madrigal" apparently derived from *matricale,* meaning the vernacular or mother tongue. In its early stages a variety of line lengths and stanzas made up its form. The basic pattern, however, consisted of a group of three-line stanzas, or *terzetti,* followed by a one- or two-line ritornello. By midcentury a more or less standard form had evolved: all lines were of eleven syllables, two or three *terzetti,* a two-line ritornello, and a consistent rhyme scheme throughout. Musical settings of these texts consisted of two sections of music usually in different mensurations or meters. The first section was repeated by performers for each *terzetto;* the second section was then used for the ritornello. Composers gave each

Trecento Musical Notation

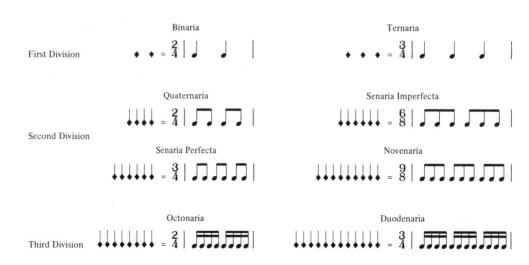

178

of the three lines of the first *terzetto* a unique setting, concluding with a strong cadence and rest; thus the first musical section had three subsections. In the second musical section one phrase could be used for the two poetic lines, or each line of text could be set separately. If the two main sections of music are represented by *a* and *b,* and the subsections by more letters, the musical form of a typical madrigal is as follows:

	Terzetto I	Terzetto II	(Terzetto III)	Ritornello
Two main sections:	*a*	*a*	*(a)*	*b*
Subsections:	*a b c*	*a b c*	*(a b c)*	*d d* or *d e*

The style of the polyphony usually consisted of two active upper voices, each singing the text, and a slower-moving untexted tenor performed on an instrument.

Ballata. The ballata of the early trecento was monophonic (one-voice) rather than polyphonic. Originating as a song for dancing, the ballata retained a character less sophisticated than the madrigal even when given polyphonic settings.

The poetic form consisted of an opening refrain section (*ripresa*), followed by a stanza of two or more lines, the *piedi* (feet), and a concluding section called *volta* (turning). The terms gain further meaning when the musical setting is observed. The opening *ripresa* is a repeated section of music and text. Different music was composed for the two *piedi;* the *volta* lines are sung to the opening music of the *ripresa,* thus justifying the idea of "turning." Any number of stanzas, or *piedi* and *volte,* could be employed. The musical form is therefore *A b b a A b b a A* . . . (the capital letter *A* signifying the repeated *ripresa*). In actual practice, the *ripresa, A,* was not likely to be repeated by performers between the verses of the *piedi* and the *volta* section.

The rhyme scheme of the poetic lines varied considerably. Nevertheless, a usual plan in a twelve-line ballata was *A B B A* (*ripresa*) *c d c d* (*piedi*) *d e e a* (*volta*); this scheme would then be repeated for further verses. Capital letters signify repeated verse lines of the *ripresa.* Notice particularly that the *volta* partakes of the *piedi* rhyme in its first line and of the *ripresa* in its fourth line. Another usual feature of a poem of this length was to employ seven-syllable lines consistently.

Caccia. Both the Italian term *caccia* and the French *chace* signify chasing, and this has been taken to mean the hunt. Though many of the French poems depict hunting scenes, the Italian caccia is much less tied to this subject. It is more

likely that the term refers to the musical structure: the voices written as a canon, thus chasing one another. Whereas a typical chace was a three-part vocal canon, the caccia employed only two canonic voices over a noncanonic, untexted tenor. A further feature of the caccia is its usual division into two sections, the last, shorter section serving as a repeated ritornello, which may or may not be canonic.

Programmatic effects were common in the text. The poet often composed words with onomatopoeic sounds depicting bird calls or other sounds of the country, as well as using dialogue. Musical settings of the poems occasionally contain words in otherwise untexted instrumental parts, instructing performers to make exclamatory cries for dramatic effect.

Sacred music. Even though many of the trecento composers were priests or monks, their main preoccupation, as can be reconstructed from the extant manuscripts today, was with the secular forms. Motets are rare in the trecento Italian polyphonic manuscripts. Some scholars have suggested that this form was actively cultivated in Italy as well as in France, but the existing repertoire from Italy has very few motets. Settings of movements of the Mass, invariably in an unexploratory two-voice style, are found added to the manuscripts as incidental material. Liturgical music remained, therefore, restricted in Italy to the monophonic chant tradition primarily. As new saints were created, and special religious feast days were inaugurated, the chant repertoire was augmented in particular localities by unknown composers.

COMPOSERS

Several trecento composers are identified with particular compositions in the manuscripts; the majority of pieces, however, are anonymous. Biographical details are often sketchy. In any case, they fall beyond the scope of this account.

The first composers to gain prominence were active at the northern courts of the Visconti family in Milan and the Scaligieri family in Verona and Padua. The Rossi Codex, which contains the earliest trecento repertoire, includes works by Jacopo da Bologna (Jacobus of Bologna), Giovanni da Cascia (Johannes de Florentia), and Maestro Piero. Three other composers who were centered in Florence were Gherardello da Firenze, Lorenzo Masini (Lorenzo da Firenze), and Donato da Cascia (Donatus de Florentia).

The most celebrated and prolific composer of the trecento was Francesco Landini, represented now by 152 polyphonic compositions, all but 12 of them ballate. In spite of his having been afflicted with blindness in childhood, he became a master performer on several instruments, most notably the organ. His tombstone and his portrait in the Squarcialupi Codex depict him with a portative organ in his arms. Though Landini lived until 1397, he did not participate in the mixing of the French and Italian styles, a practice that was common at the end of the century in the compositional movement in southern French courts.

Two other composers during the latter part of the century are noteworthy for having developed a new forward-looking style. Mateo da Perugia (Matteo of Perugia, *d. ca.* 1418) and the Belgian-born Johannes Ciconia (*d.* 1411) aimed for a musical style quite contrary to the rhythmically elaborate *ars subtilior* movement. The compositions they produced have a more unified texture, a less angular melodic line, and a much simpler rhythmic style. The general effect found in these compositions is typical of much of the secular music of the following century.

OTHER COUNTRIES

The term trecento, as explained previously, is used in musicological circles to refer specifically to the music of fourteenth-century Italy, just as *ars nova* refers to the French music of the same period. Nevertheless, since the term trecento also refers generically to the century regardless of country, mention should be made here of the music of other countries.

Spain. The only regions of Spain that contributed significantly to the musical repertoire of the trecento were Aragon and Catalonia. The courts of this northern area had close ties to France and were, in fact, major employers of the musicians of France and Italy. No unique Spanish music of any major significance is extant.

England. During the fourteenth century in Britain, a very interesting style of music developed. There appear to have been few exchanges of theoretical treatises or compositions between Britain and the Continent, or, if there were, the composers in each area remained uninterested in each other's artistic production. The style, which is now called "English discant," has sonorities akin to a much later time. Intervals of thirds and sixths were prominent, and melodies had a smoother flow than those preferred in France and Italy. Though far fewer compositions from Britain have survived, a greater proportion of them are in four and five parts than is evident in continental compositions. Composers in Britain preferred the conductus to the motet and started the development of a new form, the carol (*carole*), which became an important element in fifteenth-century British music.

Germany. In Germany the minnesong (*minnesang*) tradition of the thirteenth century continued, though with less vigor, remaining a solo-song repertoire. A few German composers, such as Oswald von Wolkenstein, traveled to French and Italian courts gathering pieces of the polyphonic repertoire. Back in Germany, they often made contrafacta arrangements by using the French music and inserting German minnesong poetry or, as was the case with Oswald von Wolkenstein, poetry newly written for the purpose.

MUSICAL INSTRUMENTS

A wide variety of instruments were used by musicians to accompany voice parts or to perform vocal compositions on the instruments alone. Some music for dancing is extant, but it is usually a solo part around which improvisation apparently occurred. No exact reference is made in the manuscript sources regarding which instrument was to play a certain part. The range of the instruments and the range of the written musical part is a partial guide. We do know, however, that trumpets and horns were almost exclusively the provenance of the nobility and were used during state processionals or in battle. The quieter instruments, such as those of the string family called *vielles* (fiddles), psaltery, harp, and lute, were regularly employed to double the voices, or to play accompanying parts at indoor banquets. The more boisterous wind instruments included the shawms, which are an early version of the double-reed family of oboes and bassoons, and the sackbuts (*sacqueboutes*), which are akin to the modern trombone. These were usually employed in outdoor performances.

Organs of various sizes were common both in churches and also in the chambers where the secular repertoire was performed. In the latter case, the small portative organ became a regular member of the ensemble. Flutes and recorders not unlike those presently in use were regularly included in ensemble groups. Drums of various kinds and sizes were common as well.

CONCLUSION

The fourteenth century was a very lively time musically, particularly in Italy, France, and Britain. Various wealthy families patronized, even competed for, the finest performers and composers, and thereby created an environment in which musical composition was treated as a serious and highly skilled art form, and musical performance was developed to a very high level of achievement. The intricate rhythmic subtleties of the late fourteenth century are as complex as any music written since that time.

It is important to observe that many of the compositions that involved both music and poetry were produced by one gifted person. Poetry and music were perceived by many artists to be one unified art form, and this sense of unity created much of the vitality of the music of the trecento.

BIBLIOGRAPHY

Armen Carapetyan, "The Codex Faenza, Biblioteca Comunale, 177 [*Fa*]: A Facsimile Edition," in *Musica disciplina*, **13** (1959) (published separately by the American Institute of Musicology as *Musicological Studies and Documents*, X [1962]); Gaetano Cesari, *La cappella musicale del Duomo di Milano*, pt. 1: Fabio Fano, *Le origini e il primo maestro di cappella: Matteo da Perugia* (1956); Suzanne Clercx, *Johannes Ciconia: Un musicien liégeois et son temps (vers 1335–1411)*, 2 vols. (1960); Kurt von Fischer, *Studien zur italienischen Musik des Trecento and frühen Quattrocento* (1956), "Zur Entwicklung der italienischen Trecento-notation," in *Archiv für Musikwissenschaft,* **16** (1959), and "On the Technique, Origin, and Evolution of Italian Trecento Music," in *The Musical Quarterly*, **47** (1961); Ursula Günther, "The 14th-century Motet and Its Development," in *Musica disciplina*, **12** (1958), and "Das Manuskript Modena, Biblioteca Estense α M.5.24 (*olim* lat. 568)," in *Musica disciplina*, **24** (1970); Richard H. Hoppin, *Medieval Music* (1978); Karl K. Klein, ed., *Die Lieder Oswalds von Wolkenstein* (1962, rev. ed. 1975); Ivana Pelnar, "Neu entdeckte Ars-nova-sätze bei Oswald von Wolkenstein," in *Die Musikforschung*, **32** (1979); Nino Pirrotta, "Per l'origine e la storia della 'caccia' e del 'madrigale' trecentesco," in *Rivista musicale italiana*, **48** (1946), and *The Music of Fourteenth-century Italy* (1964); Dragan Plamenac, *Keyboard Music of the Late Middle Ages in Codex Faenza 117* (1972). *Polyphonic Music of the Fourteenth Century* (1956–1989) is a twenty-four volume series containing all the extant polyphonic music of the trecento. The editors include Margaret Bent, Kurt von Fischer, Alberto Gallo, Gordon K. Greene, Anne Hallmark, Frank Ll. Harrison, Peter Lefferts, Thomas Marrocco, Ernest Sanders, and Leo Schrade. Another useful series is the Convegno internazionale sull'ars nova musicale del trecento italiano, published every four years by the Centro di studi sull'ars nova italiana del trecento, in Certaldo.

GORDON K. GREENE

[See also **Ars Antiqua; Ars Nova; Ars Subtilior; Ballata; Caccia; Carols, Middle English; Conductus; Contrafactum; Dance; Dante Alighieri; Faenza Codex; Italian Literature: Lyric Poetry; Jacobus of Bologna; Landini, Francesco; Madrigal; Motet; Musical Instruments, European; Musical Notation, Western; Oswald von Wolkenstein; Virelai.**]

TREE OF JESSE, an image that typically consists of Jesse (the father of King David) reclining and a vine or tree springing from his side or loins to embrace

Tree of Jesse depicted in the Psalter of Queen Ingeburge of Denmark, early 13th century. Chantilly, Musée Condé, MS 9 (1695), fol. 15v. GIRAUDON, PARIS

Christ's ancestors and culminate in the Virgin and her Son (Is. 11:1–2; Matt. 1:1–17). Kings, prophets, sibyls, and even prophetic or Gospel illustrations may be incorporated. It appears to have been invented in the twelfth century in the West.

BIBLIOGRAPHY

Lexikon der christlichen Ikonographie, Engelbert Kirschbaum, ed., IV (1972), 549–558 (with ample bibliography); Charles Little, "An Ivory Tree of Jesse from Bamberg," in *Pantheon,* 33 (1975); Émile Mâle, *Religious Art in France: The Twelfth Century,* Harry Bober, ed., Marthiel Mathews, trans. (1978), 171–177; Gertrud Schiller, *Iconography of Christian Art,* 2 vols., Janet Seligman, trans. (1971), I, 15–22; Michael D. Taylor, "The Prophetic Scenes in the Tree of Jesse at Orvieto," in *Art Bulletin,* 54 (1972), and "A Historiated Tree of Jesse," in *Dumbarton Oaks Papers,* 34 (1981); Arthur Watson, *The Early Iconography of the Tree of Jesse* (1934).

MICHAEL D. TAYLOR

[See also **Iconography.**]

TREE OF LIFE, a Judeo-Christian symbol of salvation and immortality. The Tree of Life existed in the mythopoeic traditions of several Oriental cultures, such as Sumeria, Babylonia, Persia, and Assyria, as an illustration of the transience of human life.

Genesis 2:9 related that God planted two special trees among those in the Garden of Eden: the Tree of Knowledge of good and evil and the Tree of Life. In Christian symbolism the cross can be viewed as the true Tree of Life, and the tree in the Garden of Eden as a prefiguration of it. In Christian iconography, Christ is sometimes depicted as being crucified on the Tree of Life (called the "living cross"). This cross, composed of living branches, appeared in the sixth century and was prevalent until the fourteenth century. (For an example see "Pacino di Bonaguida.")

New Testament references to the Tree of Life are Revelation 2:7 and 22:1–2.

BIBLIOGRAPHY

Ormonde M. Dalton, *Byzantine Art and Archaeology* (1911, new ed. 1961); André Grabar, *Christian Iconography: A Study of Its Origins* (1968); Gertrud Schiller, *Iconography of Christian Art,* 2 vols., Janet Seligman, trans. (1971).

JENNIFER E. JONES

[See also **Cross, Forms of.**]

Tree of Jesse and Tree of the Cross. Miniature from the *Speculum humanae salvationis,* German, *ca.* 1340–1350. KREMSMÜNSTER MONASTERY LIBRARY

TREFOIL, an opening or ornamental frame in the shape of three radiating leaves or petals, used in Gothic tracery. It is composed of three lobes or foils arranged circularly. The points of intersection of these three segments of circles point inward and are called cusps.

GREGORY WHITTINGTON

[See also **Gothic Architecture; Quatrefoil, Tracery.**]

TREFOLOGION. See **Paterikon.**

TRENT CODICES, seven fifteenth-century music manuscripts: Trent, Museo Provinciale d'Arte (Raccolta Museo Nazionale), manuscripts 87–92/1374–1379 [TR 87–92], and Biblioteca Capitolare, manuscript 93 (olim B.L.) [TR 93].

TR 87–92 were discovered in the Biblioteca Capitolare by Franz Haberl, who reported them in his 1885 study on Guillaume Du Fay (earlier, corrupted form: Dufay). They were loaned to the Vienna Hofbibliothek in 1891 and returned to Italy in 1918. TR 93 was discovered by Rudolf Ficker in 1920. A thematic catalog of TR 87–92 appears in *Denkmäler der Tonkunst in Österreich (DTÖ)*, 14–15, and one of TR 93 appears in *DTÖ* 61. The codices have approximately the same dimensions, almost 9 by 12 inches (about 20 by 30 cm), and are written on paper in white mensural notation.

The earliest, TR 87 and TR 92, were copied between 1435 and 1450. TR 87 (23 fascicles, 265 folios) has six sections: (I) Fascicles 1–2 (1r–24v) may have been two independent fascicles (2 has its own signature foliation) but were added as a unit to TR 87. (II) Fascicles 3–13 (25r–124v) are a continuous manuscript with signature foliations on the rectos of the first half of each fascicle—the signature order was disturbed in binding (original order: 5, 11, 13, 6, 7, 10, 3, 9, 8, 4), but pieces copied across the joints make restoration of the original order impossible. (III) Fascicle 14 (155r–166v) was an independent gathering to which the scribe signed his name, Puntschucherh, on folio 161v. (IV) Fascicles 15–17 (167r–196v) were apparently bound blank, a later hand adding a Mass on folios 197v–175r. (V) Fascicles 18–19 (197r–218v) were begun as a motet collection, but the writing stops on folio 200v. (VI) Fascicles 20–23 (219r–265v) are an independent manuscript with nine pieces by an otherwise unknown composer, H. Battre.

TR 92 (22 fascicles, 264 folios) has three sections: (I) fascicles 1–12 (1r–144v) form a continuous manuscript containing composite Masses (each preceded by an introit) and many additions in sundry hands; (II) fascicles 13–20 (145r–239v) are a random collection of sacred and secular works in several hands; (III) fascicles 21–23 (240r–264v) are blank. Guido Adler (*DTÖ* 14–15) suggests that Puntschucherh's hand appears in TR 92, and Charles Hamm (1981) states that some fascicles of TR 87 and TR 92 were interchanged in binding. Neither view is tenable, but it is possible that TR 87 and TR 92 were copied in part from common models. TR 87, like TR 92-II, is a random collection of sacred and secular works, but some fascicles show clear signs of organization; TR 87:6 has

sequences, and TR 87:12 began as a chansonnier. The music in both manuscripts ranges from the 1390's to 1436, and most works date from 1400 to 1430. English music of Leonel Power and John Dunstable's generation is prominent, as are Guillaume Dufay, Gilles Binchois, and composers in the papal and imperial chapels. The repertory reflects the musical exchanges of the conciliar age, and the paper points to north Italy or Savoy. Many of these sections apparently reached Trent separately in the 1450's.

TR 93 (33 fascicles, 382 folios) was copied in northern Italy in the 1450's. Originally thought to be a copy of TR 90, it was shown by Margaret Bent to be its model. It is a manuscript in two sections:

(I) Fascicles 1–30 (1r–355v) are a liturgical collection following a plan that separates the pieces by category: it has Introits (1r–94v) with some interpolations, Kyries (95r–125v), Glorias (126v–210r), Sequences (201v–234v) with some interpolations, Credos (236v–297r), and Sanctus of Sanctus-Agnus pairs (295v–255r).

(II) Fascicles 31–33 (356r–382v) have textless works (some recognizable as Mass sections or secular songs), Mass sections, and hymns. TR 93 has few composers' names, but many works can be attributed through concordances. The repertory ranges from about 1400 to 1450. It is a central source for the *cantus firmus* Mass after Dunstable and transmits several important English Masses. These appear to be incomplete because the scribe eliminated the troped Kyries and missed some of the Sanctuses and Agnuses as well.

TR 88–90 were copied under Johannes Wiser, who signed TR 90 (465v). He was rector of the cathedral school in Trent (1459–1465) and chaplain (1470–1486) to Bishop Johann Hinderbach (r. 1465–1486). His scribal work probably predates 1470. The earliest of his codices is TR 90 (39 fascicles, 465 folios), a manuscript that can be divided into two sections: (I) Fascicles 1–24 (1r–182r), a copy of TR 93-I in which Wiser added some works but eliminated all original interpolations and the sequences. TR 90 shows later revisions in his hand—he modernized some details of the music and made other changes that indicate he had access to independent sources for the repertory of TR 93. These sources are reflected in (II) TR 90-II, fascicles 24–39 (182v–465v), a random collection of Masses, vespers music, motets, and songs. Masses in TR 90-II are copied as cycles, and one or two works complete cycles that are excerpted in TR 93. The repertory of TR 90-II is slightly later than that of TR 93. A chanson (463v) has a Latin contrafact in honor of Bishop Georg II (d. 1465), suggesting that TR 90 was compiled prior to 1465.

TR 88 (35 fascicles, 422 folios) is a manuscript with no apparent plan. It has Mass cycles, a collection of Mass propers (113v–220r, 351v–359r), vespers music, motets, and songs. Some of it seems to be a continuation of TR 90-II, as it has some of the troped Kyries, Sanctuses, and Agnuses left out of TR 93 and TR 90-I. The repertory ranges from about 1440 to 1460, including English and continental *cantus firmus* Masses. Dufay, Cornago, Johannes Ockeghem, Domarto, and Faugues are represented. A piece in honor of Georg II (336v–337r) indicates a date prior to 1465.

TR 89 (36 fascicles, 425 folios) is even more random than TR 88. Twenty-four fascicles (1–7, 10, 14, 18, 22–35) have Mass cycles; six (8–13) have Magnificat antiphons. There are also hymns, Magnificats, Mass propers, and secular songs. It may well be that TR 89 was a series of quasi-independent fascicles later bound together. The repertory ranges from about 1440 to 1465. Dufay, Ockeghem, Antoine Busnois, and Johannes Martini are represented. A poem in honor of Hinderbach (199r) points to a date after 1465 for the compilation.

TR 91 (22 fascicles, 259 folios) is a miscellaneous source in various hands and may have been put together from independent fascicles. Eighteen of them transmit Masses (1–3, 5–7, 9–16, 19–22); the others contain vespers music (17–18) and a random collection of motets and Mass propers (fascicle 4). The repertory ranges from about 1460 to 1475. Busnois, Martini, and Loyset Compère are represented, but composers of Dufay's generation are largely absent. The manuscript probably dates from after 1470.

Though often inaccurate and problematic, these codices are crucial sources for fifteenth-century music. Only in the late twentieth century did they begin to receive the study they deserved.

BIBLIOGRAPHY

Guido Adler *et al.*, eds., *Sechs [Sieben] Trienter Codices*, in *Denkmäler der Tonkunst in Österreich*, 14–15, 22, 28, 53, 61, 76, 120 (1900–1970); Margaret Bent, "Some Criteria for Establishing Relationships Between Sources of Late-Medieval Polyphony," in Iain Fenlon, ed., *Music in Medieval and Early Modern Europe: Patronage, Sources, and Texts* (1981), and, as ed., *Fifteenth-century Liturgical Music*, II, *Four Anonymous English Masses* (1979); Rudolf Bockholdt, "Notizen zur Handschrift Trient '93' und zu Dufays frühen Messensätzen," in *Acta musicologica*, 33 (1961); *Codex Tridentinus 87[–93]*, 7 vols. (1959–1970); Hellmut Federhofer, "Trienter Codices," in Friedrich Blume, ed., *Die Musik in Geschichte und Gegenwart*, XIII (1966); Laurence Feininger, ed., *Monumenta polyphoniae liturgicae sanctae ecclesiae Romanae*, 2nd ser., I (1947); Rudolf Ficker, "Die frühen Messenkompositionen der Trienter Codices," in *Studien zur Musikwissenschaft*, 11 (1924); Rebecca L. Gerber, "The Manuscript Trent, Castello del Buonconsiglio 88: A Study of Fifteenth-century Manuscript Transmission and Repertory" (diss., Univ. of California at Santa Barbara, 1984); Robert E. Gerken, "The Polyphonic Cycles of the Proper of the Mass in the Trent Codex 88 and Jena Choirbooks 30 and 35," 3 vols. (diss., Indiana Univ., 1969); Ronald L. Gottlieb, "The Cyclic Masses of Trent Codex 89," 2 vols. (diss., Univ. of California at Berkeley, 1958); Franz X. Haberl, *Wilhelm du Fay* (1885); Charles Hamm, "A Group of Anonymous English Pieces in Trent 87," in *Music and Letters*, 41 (1960), "Manuscript Structure in the Dufay Era," in *Acta musicologica*, 34 (1962), and "Sources, MS, §IX,2," in Stanley Sadie, ed., *The New Grove Dictionary of Music and Musicians*, XVIII (1981); Masakata Kanazawa, "Polyphonic Music for Vespers in the Fifteenth Century," 2 vols. (diss., Harvard, 1966); Edward Kovarik, "Mid-fifteenth-century Polyphonic Elaborations of the Plainchant *Ordinarium Missae*," 2 vols. (diss., Harvard, 1973); Walther Lipphardt, *Die Geschichte der mehrstimmigen proprium Missae* (1950); Richard Loyan, ed., *Canons in the Trent Codices* (1967); Renato Lunelli, "La patria dei codici musicali tridentini," in *Note d'archivio per la storia musicale*, 4 (1927); Nino Pirrotta and Danilo Curti, eds., *I codici musicali tridentini a cento anni della loro riscoperta: Atti del convegno musicale Laurence Feininger* (1986); Gary Spilsted, "Toward the Genesis of the Trent Codices: New Directions and New Findings," in *Studies in Music from the University of Western Ontario*, 1 (1976); Hans Tischler, "A Three-part Rondellus in Trent MS 87," in *Journal of the American Musicological Society*, 24 (1971); Tom R. Ward, "The Structure of the Manuscript Trent 92-I," in *Musica disciplina*, 29 (1975); Richard J. White, "The Battre Section of Trent Codex 87," 2 vols. (diss., Indiana Univ., 1975); Peter Wright, "On the Origins of Trent 87$_1$ and 92$_2$," in *Early Music History*, 6 (1986).

ALEJANDRO ENRIQUE PLANCHART

[See also **Agnus Dei (Music); Chansonnier; Codex; Codicology, Western European; Folio; Gloria; Introit; Kyrie; Motet; Motet Manuscripts; Sanctus; Sequence, Late.**]

TRÈS ANCIEN COUTUMIER. See **Custumals of Normandy.**

TRÈS RICHES HEURES, a lavish book of hours (Chantilly, Musée Condé) begun for Jean, duke of Berry, by the Limbourg brothers about 1413 but unfinished at his death in 1416. It was completed by Jean Colombe for Charles I, duke of Savoy, about 1485. It contains the most innovative of the Limbourgs' miniatures and represents the height of the International Gothic style in France.

BIBLIOGRAPHY

Jean Longnon and Raymond Cazelles, *The Très Riches Heures of Jean, Duke of Berry,* Victoria Benedict, trans. (1969); Millard Meiss, *French Painting in the Time of Jean de Berry: The Limbourgs and Their Contemporaries,* 2 vols. (1974), I, 143–224, II, pls. 538–597, 643–644.

ROBERT G. CALKINS

[See also **Book of Hours; Colombe, Jean; Gothic, International Style; Gothic Art: Painting and Manuscript Illumination; Jean, Duke of Berry; Limbourg Brothers (with illustration); Manuscript Illumination: Western European (with illustration).**]

TRESPASS. It is hardly surprising that the complex story of the emergence and role of trespass ("that fertile mother of actions," as Frederic W. Maitland termed it) in English law has occasioned much controversy. But the arguments of Alan Harding, developing the view of Maitland that trespass was derived from the appeal of felony, and placing trespass in a broad political and social context, seem compelling.

In the twelfth century an Englishman who thought himself wronged could allege breach of the king's peace as the passport bringing his case into the royal courts. He often charged that his opponent had acted *vi et armis* (by force and arms), and the defendant would correspondingly deny *vim et injuriam* (force and injury). The early action seems to have merged what would later be the differentiated actions of appeal and complaint, criminal and civil process, categories of felony and trespass. But especially with the legal revolution of Henry II, distinct civil writs and remedies appeared, and the same king established public machinery for the presentment of major crimes. Thus the old, single, undifferentiated action, which might simultaneously involve private criminal accusation and recovery of damages, became an anomaly. What was to be done about breaches of the king's peace short of felony, and how were victims to obtain satisfaction?

The action of trespass developed across the thirteenth century in answer to these questions. A plaintiff might bring an appeal against the defendant in the shire court but omit the formal charge of felony, thus eliminating the chance that he might have to hazard trial by battle. When the king's justices in eyre arrived, he might not prosecute his appeal (especially if he had failed to omit the "words of felony") or his case might be thrown out of court because it did not charge felony yet was technically an appeal. A fine paid to the crown could be a price he would willingly risk, for the case would be prosecuted by the crown even if the plaintiff defaulted. Some plaintiffs were able to begin by formal appeal and then reduce the charge to a less formal complaint (*querela*) before the king's justices. The advantage of beginning by an appeal was that it secured the attachment (arrest) of the defendant.

By the mid thirteenth century a writ to initiate trespass actions was available. The model of this original writ (one initiating legal action) seems to have been an earlier (*ca.* 1220) judicial writ (a writ issued by a judge in the course of litigation) for the arrest of the defendant in cases involving breach of peace. Trespass actions begun by writ soon became stereotyped as "civil" trespasses. By 1278, actions for damages in excess of forty shillings could be brought in royal courts even if the trespass charge did not include the use of force. Writs were issued "on the case" (alleging the particular circumstances of the plaintiff's claim—slander, nuisance, negligence, and so on), not because of a formal allegation of force. From trespass on the case most of the modern Anglo-American torts derived. Trespass "on the case" and trespass *vi et armis* were never completely assimilated.

The great mid-thirteenth-century expansion of trespass jurisdiction, however, was based on charges involving deeds done *vi et armis et contra pacem domini regis* (by force and arms and against the king's peace). The volume of business coming before the eyre justices and special commissioners (such as oyer and terminer justices) "represented the appearance in the king's courts of a whole range of petty injuries and of a class of plaintiff below that mainly interested in land-ownership and franchises" (Harding). By allowing and even encouraging trespass actions in the royal courts, the crown acquired vast new judicial territory and a new social layer of plaintiffs seeking the king's justice. Thus, the development of trespass is a chapter in the history of the English state as well as of English law.

BIBLIOGRAPHY

Morris S. Arnold, *Select Cases of Trespass from the King's Courts, 1307–1399,* I (1985); John H. Baker, *Introduction to English Legal History* (1971); John S. Beckerman, "The Forty-Shilling Jurisdictional Limitation in Medieval English Personal Actions," in Dafydd Jenkins, ed., *Legal History Studies 1972* (1975); Alan Harding, "Plaints and Bills in the History of English Law, Mainly in the Period 1250–1330," *ibid.,* and "The Origins of Trespass, Tort, and Misdemeanour," in his *The Roll of the Shropshire Eyre of 1256* (Selden Society, XCVI) (1980), xxxii–lviii; Frederic W. Maitland, *The Forms of Action at Common Law,* A. H. Chaytor and W. J. Whittaker, eds. (originally published in a collection titled *Equity,* 1909) (repr. 1962); S. F. C. Milsom, "Trespass from Henry III to Edward III," in *Law Quarterly Review,* 74 (1958).

RICHARD W. KAEUPER

[See also **England: 1216–1485; Felony; Henry II of England; Justices, Itinerant; Law, English Common; Oyer and Terminer.**]

TREVET, NICHOLAS (*ca.* 1258—after 1334), English Dominican scholar, exegete, commentator, and chronicler. A son of Sir Thomas Trevet (an itinerant justice), he joined the Order of Preachers and was at its Oxford priory by November 1297. A papal letter mentions him as lector at the London convent of the order in September 1324. Of his career between these two dates we know that he was a regent master in the Oxford schools from about 1303 until 1307, and again from 1314 to 1315, and that he traveled to Italy and spent time at the Dominican *studium generale* in Paris. That he lived until at least 1334 is evident from his statement in his Anglo-Norman *Cronicles* that John XXII (1316–1334) was pope for nineteen years. Trevet read widely, acquiring an encyclopedic learning and a reputation as a polymath. He produced some thirty works in a number of fields. The popularity evidenced by the extraordinary number of manuscripts containing writings attributed to

him was largely a reflection of the extent to which his talents as a commentator on biblical, patristic, and classical texts were admired and valued. He would draw upon his familiarity with previous commentators to supply a patchwork of appropriate quotations, or, in the case of most of his nonbiblical commentaries, he would adopt a rigidly pragmatic expository style, paraphrasing his text and pausing to discuss various grammatical and rhetorical forms, historical and technical matters, and so forth.

In 1307 his commentaries on Genesis (subsequently revised and dedicated to John XXII) and Exodus were approved by the Dominican general chapter; another, on Leviticus, was submitted shortly thereafter to Aymeric, his master general. Expositions of the remaining two books of the Pentateuch and of the Paralipomenon were also apparently completed, as was one of the psalter for John of Bristol, Trevet's prior provincial, a copy of which was ordered for the papal library. He also applied his expository skills to Augustine's *City of God,* the Augustinian Rule, and Boethius' *Consolation of Philosophy,* his commentary on which enjoyed an exceptionally wide circulation. Three expositions of classical writers are extant, the first such commentaries to have survived. John XXII commissioned one on Livy's Roman history; the Dominican cardinal, Nicholas of Prato, requested another on the *Tragedies* of Seneca; and to John of Lenham, Edward II's confessor, Trevet dedicated (*ca.* 1314) an exposition of the elder Seneca's *Declamations.*

Toward the end of his life he turned to the compilation of three historical works, indulging what much of his expository writing suggests was a strong predilection for historiography. The well-known *Annales* begins with the events immediately prior to Stephen's accession and ends with a valuable contemporary narrative of Edward I's reign. A universal chronicle in Latin, called *Historia* in some manuscripts and dedicated to Hugh of Angoulême, papal nuncio and archdeacon of Canterbury, covers the period from the Creation to Christ's birth. The Anglo-Norman *Cronicles,* probably Trevet's last work, is a summary of world history from the Creation to the 1330's written for Princess Mary of Woodstock, a daughter of Edward I, and containing the story of Constance exploited later by Chaucer for the Man of Law's Tale. Among other extant works of Trevet are *Quodlibeta, Quaestiones disputatae,* a pair of "scientific" *opuscula*

(*De computo Hebraeorum* and *Canones coniunctionum, oppositionum, et eclipsium solis et lunae*), and a treatise on the Mass dedicated to John Droxford, bishop of Bath and Wells.

BIBLIOGRAPHY
Ruth J. Dean, "Nicholas Trevet: A Study of His Life and Works, with Special Reference to His Anglo-Norman Chronicle" (diss., Oxford, 1938) and "Nicholas Trevet, Historian," in J. J. G. Alexander and M. T. Gibson, eds., *Medieval Learning and Literature* (1976); A. B. Emden, *A Biographical Register of the University of Oxford to A.D. 1500*, III (1959); W. Goffart, "The Subdivisions of Trevet's *Chronicles* in Bodleian Library MS Fairfax 10," in *Scriptorium*, **36** (1982); T. Kaeppeli, *Scriptores Ordinis Praedicatorum medii aevi*, III (1980), 187–196; Paul O. Kristeller and F. Edward Cranz, *Catalogus Translationum et Commentariorum: Mediaeval and Renaissance Latin Translations and Commentaries*, II (1971), 341–342, and III (1976), 446–448; F. A. C. Mantello, "The Editions of Nicholas Trevet's *Annales sex regum Angliae*," in *Revue d'histoire des textes*, **10** (1980).

FRANK A. C. MANTELLO

[See also **Chronicles; Dominicans; England: 1216–1485; Exegesis, Latin; Historiography, Western European; Oxford University**.]

TREVISA, JOHN (*ca.* 1340–1402), translator, was born in Cornwall, studied and apparently taught at Oxford in the 1360's and 1370's, later worked there intermittently, and served at least from 1390 as vicar of Berkeley and chaplain to Thomas, the fourth Lord Berkeley. Perhaps excepting the makers of the Wyclif Bible (of whom he may have been one), he is the major translator of medieval England. He translated two massive and important books, Ranulf Higden's universal history *Polychronicon* (1387) and Bartholomaeus Anglicus' encyclopedia *De proprietatibus rerum* (1398), and four lesser ones: the Gospel of Nicodemus, *Dialogus inter militem et clericum*, Richard Fitz-Ralph's *Defensio curatorum*, and Egidius Colonna's *De regimine principum*. His translations—generally clear and often pungent—established English as a fit vehicle for handling philosophical and scientific material.

BIBLIOGRAPHY
Sources. *Polychronicon Ranulfi Higden monachi Cestrensis*, Churchill Babington and Joseph R. Lumby,

eds., 9 vols. (1865–1886); *Dialogus inter militem et clericum, Richard FitzRalph's Sermon: "Defensio curatorum"* . . . *by John Trevisa* . . . , Aaron J. Perry, ed. (1925); "The Gospel of Nicodemus . . . ,'" Hack Chin Kim, ed. (diss., Univ. of Washington, 1964); "The English *Polychronicon*: A Text of John Trevisa's Translation of Higden's *Polychronicon*, Based on Huntington MS. 28651," Richard A. Seeger, ed. (diss., Univ. of Washington, 1974); *On the Properties of Things: John Trevisa's Translation of Bartholomaeus Anglicus "De proprietatibus rerum,"* M. C. Seymour *et al.*, eds., 2 vols. (1975).

Studies. David C. Fowler, "John Trevisa and the English Bible," in *Modern Philology*, **58** (1960), "New Light on John Trevisa," in *Traditio*, **18** (1962), "John Trevisa: Scholar and Translator," in *Transactions of the Bristol and Gloucester Archaeological Society*, **89** (1970), and "More About John Trevisa," in *Modern Language Quarterly*, **32** (1971); Sven L. Fristedt, *The Wycliffe Bible*, pt. 3: *Relationships of Trevisa and the Spanish Medieval Bibles* (1973).

TRAUGOTT LAWLER

[See also **Bible, Old and Middle English; Chronicles; Egidius Colonna; Encyclopedias and Dictionaries; Higden, Ranulf; Translation and Translators**.]

TRIBELON (from the Greek for "three curtains"), a triple arcade, especially that arcade inserted between the narthex and the nave of a church, which was often fitted with three curtains between the columns. The church of the Virgin Acheiropoietos in Thessaloniki (450–470) retains a well-preserved example.

BIBLIOGRAPHY
Jean Ebersolt, Henri Saladin, and M. Le Tourneau, *Les églises de Salonique* (1916); Anastasios K. Orlandos, *Hē Basilikē xylostegos tēs mesogeiakēs lekanēs* (1950–1959). For a discussion and definition see Richard Krautheimer, *Early Christian and Byzantine Architecture* (1965), esp. 74, 363.

LESLIE BRUBAKER

[See also **Narthex** (with illustration).]

TRIBUNE, a term designating: (1) a platform projecting from a wall, supported by arches, columns, or piers, frequently containing an organ or used by musicans; and (2) a vaulted or roofed gallery above the aisle of a basilican church, as deep as the aisle

Tribune (2) in north transept wall of Noyon Cathedral, *ca.* 1185. FOTO MARBURG/ART RESOURCE

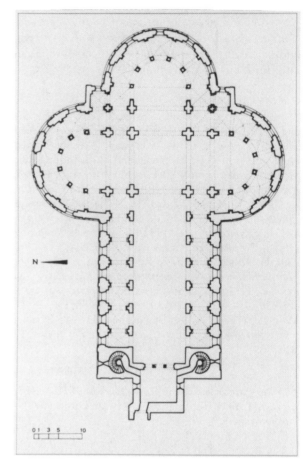

Triclinium plan of St. Maria im Kapitol, Cologne. FROM HANS ERICH KUBACH, *ROMANESQUE ARCHITECTURE.* © 1975 ELECTA EDITRICE, MILAN

below and relatively taller than a triforium. Vaulted tribunes provide structural stability to the construction (for instance, at Noyon Cathedral, France).

CARL F. BARNES, JR.

[See also **Aachen, Palace Chapel; Basilica; Organ (for illustration); Romanesque Architecture.**]

Antiquity and the Early Middle Ages," in *Art Bulletin,* 44 (1962).

CARL F. BARNES, JR.

[See also **Apse; Choir Church, Types of; Tetraconch.**]

TRICLINIUM, a plan composed of three identical or nearly identical apses set tangentially to one another so as to form a trilobe with one side open. Derived from Roman dining furniture arrangements, the triclinium plan (also called a triconch) was employed in medieval palaces and was the basis of the choir plan of many medieval churches, such as St. Maria im Kapitol at Cologne.

BIBLIOGRAPHY

Irving Lavin, "The House of the Lord: Aspects of the Role of Palace Triclinia in the Architecture of Late

TRIFORIUM, in Gothic churches, a shallow wall passage above the main arcades and below the clerestory, opening onto the nave, choir, or transepts through arches and functioning as a service passage for the vaults of the side aisles. Originally applied only to the Norman wall passage at Canterbury Cathedral with its triple-arched openings (hence the name), "triforium" has become a general term; it is frequently misapplied to a gallery or tribune.

GREGORY WHITTINGTON

[See also **Clerestory (with illustration); Gallery; Tribune.**]

TRINITARIAN DOCTRINE. Medieval Christian scholars inherited the basic foundations of Trinitarian doctrine from the apostolic and patristic periods of Christian history. The main developments may be outlined as follows:

(1) The doctrine of the Trinity was historically developed through theological efforts to affirm and understand the full divinity of Jesus Christ. This christological base is vital to any comprehension of Trinitarian doctrine.

(2) At the councils of Nicaea (325), Ephesus (431), and Chalcedon (451), the full divinity of Jesus was affirmed; at the First Council of Constantinople (381) the full divinity of the Holy Spirit was affirmed as Catholic faith. These four councils were held in highest esteem throughout the Middle Ages and were often compared to the four Gospels themselves.

(3) Early christological heresies, such as Docetism, Arianism, and Sabellianism, as well as heresies denying the divinity of the Holy Spirit, such as Macedonianism, defended in one way or another the unicity of God, which, they claimed, disallowed either the incarnation of God in Jesus or a divinity of the Holy Spirit. The orthodox theologians of these early centuries countered with a doctrine of God that affirmed the unicity of God but allowed for an incarnation of God and a sending of the Spirit. This doctrine of God was the doctrine of the Trinity.

(4) Throughout these discussions, certain terms came into technical theological usage—hypostasis (*persona*), physis (*natura*), hypokeimenon (*substantia*), ousia (*essentia*)—but no definition of these terms had been either agreed on or developed. Only after 500 did such terms find technical definition.

(5) Pastorally, the Christian community found that the late Old Testament understanding of God, namely a God who is totally other, did not lend itself to an incarnate God. Likewise, when the early Christians moved out to the Greek world, the doctrine of God as found in the Stoics and in Middle Platonism was one of total spirit. Connection with matter was the opposite of the divine. Thus, neither the Jewish doctrine of God nor that of the major Greek philosophers lent any assistance to a Christian view of God, which involved at its very core an incarnation of the divine. The subsequent development of a Christian doctrine of God was the doctrine of a Trinitarian God, which allowed for the incarnate Jesus as well as creation in time and not an eternity of creation.

(6) Two theological patterns had been established for Trinitarian thought prior to 500—the psychological approach of Augustine on the one hand and the *perichoresis* approach of the Cappadocians, especially Basil the Great, on the other. Augustine, for his part, stressed that the Logos was the full expression of the Father, in a way similar to thought being the expression of a thinker. The mutual love between the Logos (thought) and the Father (thinker) was the Holy Spirit. Basil insisted on a clarification of terms that the Synod of Alexandria in 362, under Athanasius' presidency, had left unclarified. Basil allowed only one ousia and three hypostases in God. The ousia and the hypostases mutually coexist or co-dwell in each other, which in Greek was termed *perichoresis*.

Other issues beyond these six points contributed to this early legacy of Trinitarian thought, but these six issues were the major building blocks that the medieval scholar inherited.

From 500 to 1500 theological discussion on the Trinity seems to have developed around four different emphases. None of these emphases are self-contained, and individual authors often touched on all of them. Nonetheless, most medieval authors employed one or another of them in a predominant way. Likewise, during these 1,000 years there are approximately fifty authors who treated the Trinity in a prolonged and serious way; beyond these authors there were many others who commented on the Trinity, but in a secondary way. Thus, the medieval literature is broad and varied. The four emphases might be expressed as follows: (1) the Trinity explained against the background of heresy; (2) the Trinity explained as God *ad intra* (God related internally so that the terminus of his action remains within the cause; for example, thinking remains immanent in the human mind); (3) the Trinity in creation and history, that is, *ad extra* (God related externally so that the terminus of an action is produced outside the cause; for example, parents begetting a child); (4) the ability to know the Trinity by natural reason alone, not by revelation.

THE TRINITY AGAINST THE BACKGROUND OF HERESY

Medieval writing on the Trinity at times was occasioned by various heresies. In the period closest to 500, the heresies of Arianism and Sabellianism dominate. Fulgentius of Ruspe (*d.* 527) in his *Liber de Trinitate ad Felicem* specifically has these two heresies in mind: "Let Sabellius hear we are. Let him hear three, and may he believe that there are three persons. . . . Let Arius, however, hear *one,* and let him not state that the Son is of a different nature." The *Filioque* is mentioned without hesitation; for Fulgentius this is a given. *Filioque* became a technical term in Western Trinitarian theology. It indicated that the Spirit proceeds from both the Father and the Son. The Eastern Trinitarian theology rejected this, stressing that the Spirit proceeds from the Father alone. The Eastern theologians felt that this latter approach better preserved the full divinity of the Spirit. Fulgentius' treatise is basically Augustinian, and due to the pressure of the Scythian monks the term "persona" was interpreted in strict Chalcedonian fashion. Throughout the Middle Ages this volume on the Trinity was held in high regard and was used as a model for other treatises on the Trinity.

The *Quicumque* or Athanasian Creed (as it was called from the thirteenth century on) begins to appear around the same time as Fulgentius. The anti-heretical tone is muted, particularly as regards Sabellianism, but Arianism, not in its classical form but in its Germanic form, found among the early Goths and Vandals, is clearly confronted.

In this early medieval period we find the Trinity mentioned specifically as the cornerstone of the Christian faith in many sermons and letters by authors such as Columbanus (*d.* 615), Boniface V (*d. ca.* 625), King Dagobert I (*d.* 639), Eligius, bishop of Noyon (*d.* 660) (at least in homilies attributed to him), Damian of Pavia (*d.* 715), and Boniface, archbishop of Mainz (*d.* 754).

In the sixth century, Spain had witnessed an orthodox defense of the Trinity against the Priscillians. Martin of Braga (*d.* 579/580) had written a letter, *De trina mersione,* defending the traditional Augustinian approach. In a similar vein are the works of Leander of Seville (*d.* 600) and Isidore of Seville (*d.* 633). Isidore also brought an Augustinian approach to his presidency at the Fourth Council of Toledo, which developed a Trinitarian and christological creed. Echoes of this approach can also be found in Ildephonsus of Toledo (*d.* 667), Taion of Saragossa (*d. ca.* 683), and Julianus of Toledo (*d. ca.* 690).

Various local councils during this early medieval period formulated a statement on the Trinity: Lateran (649), Fourth Council of Toledo (638), Ninth Council of Toledo (675), and the Fourteenth (684), Fifteenth (688), and Sixteenth (693) councils of Toledo. These last three focused on the different Trinitarian views of Julian, bishop of Toledo, and Benedict II, bishop of Rome.

A far different heresy forms the background for Alcuin of York (*d.* 804) in his *Liber Alcuini contra haeresim Felicis.* This Felix was the bishop of Urgel, friend of Bishop Elipando of Toledo. Together with Megestius, Egila, and many others in northern Spain and southern Gaul, these men advanced a form of adoptionism in the eighth century. Felix became the main writer for the group, and Alcuin, under the aegis of Charlemagne, became the main defender of both orthodox Christology and orthodox Trinitarian doctrine. Remarkably, Alcuin employed citations not only from the Latin fathers but also from the Greek fathers (which he found in the so-called *Acta concilii ephesini*). Alcuin's method was to cite patristic text after patristic text. By doing this, Alcuin indicated that Felix did not stand in the mainstream of theological thought; indeed, he ran counter to it and was therefore heretical. Such a method offers little room for original thinking on the Trinity, and consequently this florilegium of Alcuin remains primarily a witness to traditional Trinitarian statements.

Against this same heresy and under the leadership of Paulinus of Aquileia (*d.* 802), the Council of Friuli, near Venice, restated traditional Trinitarian doctrine against any form of Gallic adoptionism and at the same time expressed belief in the *Filioque.* Agobard of Lyons (*d.* 840) fought against the same Gallic adoptionism, while Theodoluph of Orléans (*d.* 821) and his group of French monks in Jerusalem spoke out for the *Filioque.*

The controversy with Photios over the *Filioque* occasioned several Western treatises on the Trinity. Ratramnus of Corbie (*d.* 868) wrote *Contra Graecorum opposita,* a volume that appeared on the eve of his death. For that period of history, the task that Pope Nicholas I had asked for, and that, through Hincmar of Rheims and Odo of Beauvais, had been entrusted to Ratramnus, was monumental, for it required a thorough substantiation of the *Filioque* by painstaking research in numerous monastic libraries ferreting out statements from both Latin and Greek fathers. Ratramnus' study centered largely on the Latin fathers, but occasionally he mentioned one or another of the Greek fathers. Hrabanus Maurus (*d.* 856) was also co-opted into this substantiation of the *Filioque.* Anselm (*d.* 1109) in his *De processione Spiritus Sancti contra Graecos,* in connection with Urban II's efforts at union, likewise focused his treatment of the Trinity on the controversial *Filioque*. Paschasius Radbertus (*d.* 865) and Hincmar of Rhiems (*d.* 882), two very influential Western ecclesiastics, expressed in writing their adherence to the *Filioque* as well.

Guitmund of Aversa (*d.* 1095) and Peter Damian (*d.* 1072) helped form a bridge from this polemical presentation of the Trinity to a truly theological investigation of the Trinity. While still somewhat defensive and traditional, these two authors began, even at this early medieval stage, to move, though only slightly, to a more metaphysical approach to Trinitarian theology.

Roscelin of Compiègne (*d. ca.* 1125) was charged with an early form of nominalism. He seems to have maintained that the three persons are separate entities and only morally united to God's essence through the divine will and power. Anselm responded strongly to Roscellin in *De fide Trinitatis et de incarnatione Verbi,* in which he cites Roscelin's view: "If, he says, in God the three persons are only one thing and not three things, each one separate from the other, like three angels or three souls, so that, indeed, they are one in will and power, the Father and Spirit, consequently, become incarnate together with the Son." Peter Abelard (*d.* 1142) was also accused of perpetuating the errors of Roscelin, not only by William of St. Thierry and Bernard of Clairvaux, but also in the *Capitula haeresum Petri Abaelardi,* written by scholars of the school of Laon, with, perhaps, a final section by Walter of Mortagne (*d.* 1174).

At the Council of Verona in 1184, under Lucius III, a number of heretical movements were roundly condemned; among the more noteworthy were Neomanicheism, various expressions of anticlericalism, and groups who were influenced either by Judaism or by Islam, which denied the Trinity through an overemphasis on the unicity of God. At this council the teaching on the Trinity was worded polemically against these groups.

In 1208 Innocent III imposed a formula of faith on Durandus of Huesca, who had come under the influence of the Waldensians and to some extent the Albigensians. The Trinity, in these heretical views, was being undermined by a divine dualism: a God of the Old Testament and a God of the New Testament. This kind of thinking, however, peaked in the heretical teachings of Joachim of Fiore (*d.* 1202). At the Fourth Lateran Council in 1215, in a rare moment for a council, the bishops approved the teaching of Peter Lombard by name—usually no theologian is ever mentioned by name—and condemned the teaching of Joachim, specifically on the matter of the Trinity.

At the Second Council of Lyons in 1274, under the leadership of Pope Gregory X, a profession of faith was drawn up that the new Byzantine emperor, the Greek Michael VIII Palaiologos, was to endorse, containing a brief, traditional (Western) approach to the Trinity. Similarly, at the Council of Ferrara-Florence, under Eugenius IV, a decree for the Greek church was formulated in 1439, which included a statement on the procession of the Spirit: the Spirit proceeds "from the Father together with the Son . . . as from one principle and a single spiration." At the same council a decree for the Jacobites was formulated, in which the traditional Western teaching on the Trinity was likewise affirmed.

All these discussions and writings on the Trinity were occasioned by controversy and by the polemics surrounding various heresies. These works basically looked back to tradition and cited church fathers to defend their given stance. This amassing of such citations preserved many of these early texts, but the polemic approach did not occasion a great deal of creative thought as regards the Trinity. Only when the polemics were not in the forefront did the Middle Ages develop a more theological approach to the Trinity.

THE TRINITY IN A THEOLOGY *AD INTRA*
Although strongly motivated by a defense of the full divinity of Jesus and therefore of the Incarnation, theologians gradually came to understand that the Trinity could not be seen merely as functional (*ad extra*), but must be considered also as constitutive (*ad intra*) of the divine essence. If God is triune only with respect to creation or to an incarnation, then Trinity is not of the essence of God, since there could be a time when God did not create and therefore would not be essentially triune. Aristotle had understood that the unmoved mover could be the source of all movable beings, but only if this God from eternity had been a creating God: hence the eternity of matter. Because of their understanding of God's revelation in Genesis, the medieval scholars denied this eternity of created matter. How can one say that a creative God is the same as a noncreative God, when the act of creation comes from the divine essence itself? Is creation really a free, unnecessitated act of God, or is it a necessary act of God? For a certain number of medieval

scholars, the Trinity could not be seen simply as a way in which God operated, if and when God moved outside of himself; rather, there was need for the Christian doctrine of God to understand Trinity as the very essence of God and thereby provide the basis for the free and unnecessitated act of creation.

Boethius (d. 524), in many ways, began this emphasis on the divine essence, which culminated in the writings of John Duns Scotus. Boethius wrote two treatises that were important in this regard: *Liber quomodo Trinitas unus Deus ac non tres dii,* dedicated to his father-in-law, Symmachus, and *Utrum Pater et Filius et Spiritus Sanctus de divinitate substantialiter praedicentur?* dedicated to John the Deacon. In these works Boethius clearly moved speculation on the Trinity away from its ties to the Incarnation and away from polemics in general to a sophisticated philosophico-theological approach to the Trinity. Boethius dealt with such terms as substance and essence and the way in which these apply and do not apply to God, using Aristotle's categories without scruple. For Boethius, tritheism is rationally excluded; the unicity of God is maintained. Boethius was the first, in fact, to give us a definition of "person": the individual subsistence of a rational nature; and he presented the position that the three "persons" in God are to be understood in terms of Aristotle's category of relation. The first of his works was often cited by medieval scholars and served as a model for future speculation on the Trinity.

It was really not until the twelfth century that further significant developments in this approach were made. Roscelin of Compiègne was clearly influenced by Boethius' understanding of "person." Of more importance, though, was the work of Richard of St. Victor (d. 1173). In contrast to his predecessor, Hugh of St. Victor (d. 1141), who remained outspokenly Augustinian, Richard united Anselm's approach to God, the highest being of all (*summum omnium*), with the notion of the highest love (*summa charitas*). There is some dependence in this on Pseudo-Dionysius. Self-love, at its best, provides for an alter ego. Mutual love at its highest and most unselfish level requires yet a third object of love. The peak of highest love exists only in the ability to allow for a consort of love (*Praecipuum summae charitatis existit solumodo in posse pati consortium amoris*). Such a triune love presupposes unity. This love is neither private nor jealous but gladly invites others to share whatever is loved. In doing this, Richard developed a new philosophical

definition of person: the incommunicable subsistence of a rational nature (*incommunicabilis subsistentia naturae rationalis*). These views obviated a difficulty that Boethius' definition and program had unwittingly sponsored: namely, that there is an underlying subsistence beneath the "accidents" or "relations." For Richard this love essence can exist only in some form of plurality. Plurality does not subsist in some unity; rather, love unity is inconceivable except in and through plurality.

Peter Abelard, particularly in books III and IV of *Theologia christiana,* discusses the unicity of God and then explains why the Father is not his own Son and the Son is not his own Father, and similarly as regards the Holy Spirit. Abelard is clearly and solidly speculating on the Trinity *ad intra.* His volume is an original work on the triune God, and its fundamental inspiration is Christian. Tritheism is excluded; the persons are distinguished because of their properties; the property or individuating aspect of the Father is to be self-proceeding; the Father proceeds from no other reality than his own self. The Son's property or individuating aspect is to come from the Father alone, begotten eternally, not created, not made, not proceeding. The technical theological term is "begotten." The Holy Spirit's property or individuating aspect is to proceed from both the Father and the Son, not created, not made, not begotten, but proceeding. In this way Abelard, relying heavily on Boethius, distinguishes each person of the Trinity.

Abelard, as is known, ran into opposition, especially from William of St. Thierry (d. 1148) and Bernard of Clairvaux (d. 1153). However, many of his ideas were continued by Peter Lombard (d. 1164). The Quarracchi editors indicate that he is "the catholic Abelard, filled with the spirit of Hugh." Peter Lombard was not the first to construct a summa. Already, Anselm of Laon, Robert Pullus, and others had done this. But Lombard, basing himself heavily on Abelard and Hugh of St. Victor, developed the major medieval textbook: the *Sentences.* The very first section of this book begins with the Trinity. There is no effort to establish the existence of God first and only then move to the Trinity; rather, the Trinity is God, and immediately he treats of God *ad intra,* which includes his study of the Trinity. Augustine is cited more than 1,000 times; Hilary and Ambrose come next with about 100 citations each. His approach to the Trinity, then, is Augustinian, with reliance on Hugh of St. Victor. There is nothing polemical in his treatment;

he uses philosophical terms as though they were fully acceptable. The work of God *ad extra* reveals to us the *ad intra* God, the Trinity, but his method is not to go from creation to the Trinity. Instead, following Augustine, he utilizes the psychological model of God's inner Trinitarian life. His major problem, however, is the threeness of the persons. To come to grips with this problem, Lombard employs the conventional pattern of "relation." Here, Lombard retreats from the psychological approach of Augustine (a position that the followers of Lombard almost abandon) and unites relation to property. Essence, person, relation, and property are more sharply defined, but not in any profoundly original way. Still, for the next 300 years, Lombard's work established the ground plan for theological thought, including that concerning the Trinity. Lombard, in this matter of the Trinity, is conservative in the best sense of the term, but also hesitant to move too far beyond the givens of traditional theology.

Peter Lombard had a number of immediate followers who continued his line of thought, not only on the Trinity, but also on most points in his theology: Magister Bandini (twelfth century), who compiled a condensed version of the *Sentences;* Peter of Poitiers (*d.* 1205), one of his own students; Gandulph of Bologna, who was both a canonist and a theologian of the twelfth century and who at times sided with Lombard but at times went his own way; William of Auxerre (*d.* 1231), who wrote the *Summa aurea,* which was extremely popular and quite dependent on Lombard. Robert Kilwardby (*d.* 1279), a Dominican, relied on Lombard and preceded Thomas Aquinas in his Augustinian approach to theology. Although none of these authors provided any creative material on Trinitarian thought, they are important, since they witness to the influence of Peter Lombard's thought, including his thought on the Trinity.

Gilbert of Poitiers (*d.* 1154) was a strong academic figure from the school of Chartres; he died as the bishop of Poitiers. If Abelard, his contemporary, might be seen as the dialectician in twelfth-century theology, Gilbert was its metaphysician. Some of his remarks on the Trinity made at a diocesan synod at Poitiers in 1146 were brought to the pope, Eugenius III. As a result, a consistory was convened at Paris in 1147, and another at Rheims in 1148. In these sessions, Bernard of Clairvaux accused him of dividing the divine essence, that is, of distinguishing *Deus* from *divinitas,* and of dividing the divine

properties, for example, *Pater* from *paternitas,* and so on. Gilbert defended his positions in a quite subtle and philosophical way, and the consistory found Gilbert to be orthodox. Bernard of Clairvaux remained dissatisfied and held a small council, denouncing Gilbert's teaching on the Trinity, but the results of this council were never accepted by Eugenius III.

A key person at the University of Paris was Alexander of Hales (*d.* 1245). He was highly instrumental in introducing Lombard's *Sentences* as a textbook into the university system. His own *Summa theologica,* after a small section on theology as a science, takes up the issue of the knowledge of God here on earth, *De cognitione Dei in via.* Almost immediately the question arises whether human reason of itself might come to know the Trinity. Alexander denies this possibility, since the Trinity is, on the one hand, the highest *esse* of everything, while on the other hand the mind, because of original sin, is too weak to penetrate the mystery of being. Nonetheless, as Alexander develops the question of the eternity of God, the relationship of creation and Trinity is noted. The same is found in his treatment of the goodness of God. Although Alexander remains, to some degree, faithful to Augustine, it is clear that Boethius and above all Richard of St. Victor are fundamental to his Trinitarian teaching. Alexander's exemplarism sets the stage for that of Bonaventure. His reliance on Richard of St. Victor prepares the way for Bonaventure's more thoroughgoing Greek-inspired Trinitarian teaching. Alexander advances the understanding of a doctrine of Trinity *ad intra* in his careful analysis of the difference between unity and plurality. Again, when discussing the number in the Trinity, the communication of a being is explained through a communication by nature, the generation of the Son, and a communication by will, the procession of the Spirit. Here again, the principle—goodness is diffusive of itself: *bonum est sui diffusivum,* which Alexander clearly adopts from Richard of St. Victor—plays an essential role for the Trinity *ad intra.* Alexander establishes the Franciscan approach to the Trinity, which is elaborated throughout the next two centuries.

Alexander's student, Bonaventure (*d.* 1274), though generally associated with Augustinian thought, does not, surprising to say, follow Augustine in his teaching on the Trinity. Rather, he follows the direction of the Greek fathers. God is understood as the primordial mystery of love, "a mystery of infinite productivity, and this productivity is elaborated in the form of Trinitarian doctrine" (Hayes). The Father is emphasized in his primacy, since from him the other two divine persons emanate. An infinite, immanent, emanating God, namely Trinity, is of the essence of God, God's very unicity, and thereby is the ultimate context for a free and unnecessitated creation and a free and unnecessitated incarnation. Bonaventure, in many ways, moves between the medieval emphases on a metaphysical study of God *ad intra* and a functional study of God *ad extra*. Bonaventure's approach to the Trinity provides a solid insight into the dilemma: If God is immovable and eternal, how can He create? How can He become incarnate? Bonaventure sees that the very essence of Christianity is endangered unless some basis between God in His very essence and God in His works *ad extra* can be established. For Bonaventure the key is the insight into the Trinity that Richard of St. Victor and Alexander developed and that likewise rests on the *perichoresis* teaching of the Greek fathers.

One can trace the influence of Alexander and/or Bonaventure on Eudes Rigaud (*d.* 1275) and John of Rupella (*d.* 1245), both students of Alexander; William de la Mare, who in the thirteenth century indicated sharply the division between the Franciscan and Dominican approach; Nicholas of Occham, thirteenth century; Roger Marston (*d.* 1303); John Peckham (*d.* 1292); and Ramon Lull (*d.* 1315/1316). In all of these scholars, God the Father is ultimately presented with the property of the inability to be born, *innascibilitas;* the goodness of God is seen as the source of self-communication; the Son is generated by nature, *ex natura*; and the Spirit proceeds by way of God's will, *voluntas Dei*.

In an even more penetrating way, John Duns Scotus (*d.* 1308) teaches that the Trinity is the only possible way God could be. He capitalizes on Anselm's correction of the understanding of will. At the time of Anselm, will was generally described in a way that included the capacity to sin and was therefore excluded from God. Anselm, in a rather revolutionary definition, spoke of will as pure perfection: as the power to maintain rectitude for its own sake (*potestas servandi rectitudinem propter seipsum*), with justice as the rectitude of the will maintained for its own sake (*rectitudo voluntatis proper se servata*). In this definition, the will is therefore eminently predicated of God. It is on this understanding of the will that Duns Scotus deepens the thought of Hugh of St. Victor: God is the perfect lover; "the perfect lover wishes the beloved to be loved" (Wolter). For Duns Scotus this perfection of love is infinitely free in God, and it is this ultimate and absolute freedom that lies at the very base of Duns Scotus' understanding of God. Still, such infinite and absolute freedom has an aspect of necessity, a necessity that comes not from deficiency but from perfection: a firmness in action belongs to perfection. Therefore necessity does not take it away but rather posits what belongs to perfection if there is to be freedom (*firmitas in agendo est perfectionis; igitur necessitas in ea non tollit sed magis ponit illud quod est perfectionis; si est libertas*). God, in absolute freedom, can only be Trinity. Absolute freedom involves an unjealously shared love. Because of this absolute freedom involving shared love, Duns Scotus will go on to base both the free and unnecessitated act of creation and that of the incarnation. The Abelardian question whether God could have created otherwise than he did, a question repeatedly affirmed by the medieval scholars, is continued by Duns Scotus, who upholds the absolute freedom and power of God, *potentia Dei absoluta*. Through the determined power of God, *potentia Dei ordinata*, however, God created only this present world, in which there is a free, unnecessitated incarnation. The divine persons in Duns Scotus are, as with most medieval scholars, relations or modes of being of the divine essence. However, Duns Scotus teaches that as relations they are not really distinct from the divine essence, nor are they only logically distinct from the essence and from each other. Utilizing the notion of formal distinction, a distinction midway between real and logical, Duns Scotus is able to maintain the full reality of these personal relations on the one hand and the unity of God on the other. For Duns Scotus, then, perfect unity implies both incommunicability (*incommunicabilitas*) and communicability (*communicabilitas*). He clearly bases his approach on Bonaventure.

Duns Scotus had a strong medieval following. Peter Aureoli (*d.* 1322), Peter John Olivi (*d.* 1298), and William of Occham (*d.* 1240) stand out in the period immediately after Scotus' death, but even at the Council of Trent almost one-half of the conciliar theologians were Scotists, which witnesses to his rather dominating influence in the latter part of the Middle Ages.

Albertus Magnus (*d.* 1280) was another major figure at the University of Paris, utilizing in a most creative way Aristotelian notions as he explained the Christian faith. Still, in his teaching on the Trinity he remained rigidly close to Augustine. It is indeed remarkable that his colleague Bonaventure, who more often than not was the follower of Augustine, took a non-Augustinian route as regards the Trinity, while Albertus, who often moved beyond Augustine, remained carefully traditional to the psychological interpretation of the Trinity developed by Augustine. The Father knows Himself in the Son and therefore the Son is the Word of truth; the Spirit is the mutual love between Father and Son. The good, as a metaphysical concept, is secondary to the true. However, Albertus is not totally clear as regards the procession of the Spirit in his attempt to explain the difference between generation and spiration. Albertus formulated the five properties of the divine relations: as regards the Father, (1) innascibility, (2) active generation; as regards Father and Son, (3) active spiration; as regards the Son alone, (4) passive generation; as regards the Spirit alone, (5) passive spiration. This way of speaking, in Counter-Reformation Catholic theology, came into common usage. Albertus remained with Boethius' definition of person rather than that of Richard of St. Victor. In the works of God *ad extra,* the material world has certain vestiges of the Trinity, but in a most imperfect way; only the human soul is an image of the triune God, through memory, intelligence, and will. However, Albertus does not have a theology of exemplarism such as that of Alexander, Bonaventure, and Duns Scotus.

Thomas Aquinas (*d.* 1274), yet another major figure at the University of Paris, followed Albertus' approach to the Trinity, and accordingly remained very close to Augustine. Thomas stressed more than any other preceding theologian the revelatory aspect of Trinitarian thought. He clearly distinguishes between a knowledge of God that one can have by way of reason, and a knowledge of the Trinity that one can have only by way of revelation. By emphasizing the distinction between a basis of similitude, *ratio similitudinis,* which is the differentiation between Father and Son, and the tendency to what is willed, *inclinatio in rem volitam,* which is the differentiation between Father and Son on the one hand (*Filioque*) and the Spirit on the other, Thomas rather clearly indicated the difference between generation and procession or spiration. The core of Thomas' Trinitarian doctrine lies in his presentation of relation. These are real relations, not simply logical ones, although their reality in

God cannot be other than the very reality or essence of God. The difficulties that Gilbert of Poitiers and Joachim of Fiore had had to face on this matter of properties and relations vis-à-vis the divine essence were strong incentives for Thomas not to make a real distinction between essence and relation. Only among themselves are the relations clearly and really distinct. Thomas, however, does not develop anything like the formal distinction, and as a result Thomas called the relations subsistent. They are not really distinct from the divine essence. Thomas, like Albert, preferred Boethius' definition of person over that of Richard of St. Victor. In his presentation, Thomas in many ways developed metaphysically Augustine's Trinitarian thought to its maximum, but this also meant, in Leo Scheff-czyk's view, that he brought no new ideas to Trinitarian theology.

The immediate followers of Thomas were numerous: Ulrich of Strassburg (*d.* 1277) and Godfrey of Fontaines (*d. ca.* 1306) were both quite influential. Perhaps, though, Meister Eckhart (*d. ca.* 1328) can be seen as the one who completes the Thomistic synthesis, even though he does so by using Neoplatonic and mystical thought patterns. With Eckhart the Trinity becomes much more integrated into Christian spiritual life. A century later Nicholas of Cusa (*d.* 1464) builds on the Neoplatonic base of Eckhart, although not on his spirituality.

These medieval authors who developed a study of the Trinity *ad intra* provided a creative and profound approach to this aspect of Christian thought. Nevertheless, a study of the Trinity *ad intra* alone becomes not only abstract but unrealistic. The medieval counterpart to this *ad intra* Trinity was the equally creative and profound medieval discussion of the Trinity *ad extra.*

THE TRINITY IN CREATION AND HISTORY

Not since Augustine's *City of God* had the Christian world seen another panoramic theological treatise until the work of Rupert of Deutz (*d.* 1129), *De sancta Trinitate et operibus eius.* This work is a monumental undertaking, in which the author finds vestiges of the Trinity throughout creation and history. If God creates the world, and this God is Trinitarian, the reflection of a Trinitarian God must be seen in the works *ad extra.* Rupert began this approach to the Trinity for the medieval world, and this emphasis continued on through the doctrine of divine exemplarism. Rupert's work is divided into three parts, corresponding to the "proper" work of each person in the Trinity: God the Father, revealed in the seven days of creation; God the Son, revealed in the seven ages of the world, that is, from the fall of Adam and Eve to his own passion and death; God the Spirit, revealed through the pouring out of his seven gifts, from the Incarnation to the Last Judgment. Rupert accomplished this by a running commentary on the one recognized authority of his time, the Bible. However, Rupert lacked the ability to rewrite *ad intra* Trinitarian doctrine itself. He stayed with the manifestations *ad extra,* with only a brief and quite traditional discussion on the Trinity *ad intra.* His work is a summa of salvation history, reaching down to his own times. The work was the largest of its kind, requiring a division into six parts in its manuscript tradition. Very few monasteries preserved all the manuscripts needed for a single copy of this work, but "in numbers alone, with over two hundred fifty extant copies of his works, Rupert far surpassed Benedictine contemporaries" (Van Engen). Still, Bernard of Clairvaux and Hugh of St. Victor outstripped Rupert at least in manuscript influence.

Throughout the Middle Ages a number of scholars continued, though in a much more modest vein, the approach of Rupert: Hugh of Amiens (*d.* 1164), Gerhoh of Reichersberg (*d.* 1169), Anselm of Havelberg (*d.* 1158), and Adam of Dryburg (*d.* early thirteenth century). All approached the Trinity from the *ad extra* emphasis. Joachim of Fiore was an even more influential representative of this approach to the Trinity, but Joachim became involved in an antichurch position, which proved his undoing.

Above all, the Franciscan theologians, with their strong teaching on exemplarism, developed the *ad extra* approach to Trinitarian thought. The significance of this entire approach to the Trinity is based on the search for a theological foundation that allows the eternal and infinite God to be both creator and incarnator. Again and again, the theologians of the Middle Ages addressed the issue of a God who at one time had not created and at another time was creator. Was there a change in God? If so, how can God be perfect? The basis for the power to create must, then, at least ontologically, antedate the act of creation itself. In the very essence of God there must be a basis, a *ratio,* for creation. If the doctrine of God is narrowly based on the oneness of God and the otherness or transcendence of God, God cannot be presented as a God who creates. Moreover, if God is so transcendent and so unified, a true incarnation is impossible. Jesus therefore would not be truly God and truly human (Council of Chalcedon), and the very basis of Christianity would be undermined. A Trinitarian view of the Godhead has multiplicity in its very nature, however, and so allows for an incarnation. In these aspects of God's works *ad extra* the approach of Rupert, Hugh of St. Victor, Alexander, Bonaventure, and Duns Scotus is fully justified; indeed, if this approach is not taken, the doctrine of the Trinity becomes abstract and theologically meaningless. The issue is not a functional Trinity over against an essential Trinity; rather, the issue, which these authors faced, was far more profound: there could be nothing at all *ad extra* unless there was an *ad intra* divine basis for multiplicity.

THE TRINITY AND NATURAL REASON

If the creator of the world is essentially a Trinitarian God, many medieval theologians consequently raised the question about the natural knowability of the Trinity. By and large their answer was negative. Albertus Magnus, in many ways, summarizes this thinking: first, human knowledge recognizes that an indivisible nature cannot be the numerical suppositum (substance or substratum) for a plurality; second, the mystery of the Trinity is in itself ineffable, *mirabilis,* and as a result no human reason can attain to it; third, because the likeness of God in the creature is imperfect, it is deficient in its ability to represent, *deficit in repraesentando*—God cannot therefore be perceived by natural reason. Alexander of Hales, we saw, indicated that original sin had so clouded the human mind that it is unable to attain the very depth of being: the Trinity. Robert Grosseteste (*d.* 1253) holds this same position, although he notes that without the corrupt body, the human mind would have some knowledge of the Trinity. This is affirmed because of Grosseteste's understanding of light. John Peckham (*d.* 1292) in *Super magistrum sententiarum* speaks about the differentiation of God's essence and the three persons in such a way that he lays the foundation for Duns Scotus' formal distinction between Divine Person and Divine Essence. Since for Peckham there is no eternal creation, there must be a pluralism, which is not merely logical, and not tritheistically real, and yet is the basis for God's creation. Richard of Middleton (Richardus de Mediavilla, *d.* early fourteenth century) sees a correlation between the Divine Persons as relative properties added to the essence of God and the soul's potencies and the way they are added to the essence of the soul. The divine persons are interdependent, in a way similar to the potencies of the soul and their interdependence. The persons of the Trinity are not identical; the soul's potencies (will, memory, and so forth) are also not identical. Richard of Middleton, like John Peckham, argued for some sort of intermediate formal distinction between the Divine Essence and the Divine Persons. In similar vein, Duns Scotus sees in the potencies of the human soul a vestige of the Trinity. All of these were respectable efforts by Christian scholars to probe by using human reason ever more deeply into the mystery of the Trinity *ad intra*. All of these Oxford scholars were in the Franciscan tradition of exemplarism: a reflection of the Trinity *ad extra*. This *ad extra* vestige occasioned the study of the limits of human reason vis-à-vis the Trinity.

When the *ad extra* basis was not clearly seen, then more radical questions began to arise: Is the Trinity contrary to right reason? Is the attempt to combine one and three illogical? In the late fifteenth and early sixteenth centuries there arose a fairly widespread movement of anti-Trinitarians, who denied the Trinity for a variety of reasons: Conrad of Gassen, Ludwig Hetzer, J. Kautz of Worms, Claudius of Savoy, J. Campanus, D. Noris of Delft, Miguel Serveto, Bernardino Ochino, Matteo Garibaldo, George Blandrata, Francesco Stancaro. The number of these anti-Trinitarians alone is significant, but of even greater significance is the question: Why did this anti-Trinitarian theology arise? The roots of this anti-Trinitarian movement lie primarily in those earlier medieval discussions of the Trinity, which had severed themselves from the question of the Trinity *ad extra* in creation and incarnation. A theological discussion of the Trinity that does not take into consideration, in some way or another, either incarnation or creation is doomed to failure. When the very occasion for a discussion of the Trinity was lost sight of, teaching on the Trinity became inexorably abstract, and the argument moved from its christological and cosmological base to a very narrow logical base: How do the one (unity) and the three (plurality) combine to form a single essence? Is this not totally irrational? The anti-Trinitarians of the sixteenth century certainly thought so. Moreover, another factor entered into this anti-Trinitarian rootage: namely, the influence of medieval Jewish and Islamic thought on

some scholars. This influence emphasized a monistic understanding of God, which could not possibly allow an incarnation. In many ways this was a reversion to the position Christians found themselves in when they attempted to explain the divinity of Jesus against the background of either the Jewish doctrine of God prevalent in the first century or the Stoic and middle Platonic doctrine of God in the Greek world of the first four centuries. Both of these doctrines so emphasized the otherness of God that an incarnation was virtually impossible, and creation either was not metaphysically thought out (the Jewish approach in Genesis) or was maintained only by a correlative teaching of the eternity of matter. This issue of creation, of course, remained for the late medieval and early Reformation scholar a difficult one, since creation seemed to imply a change in God. To obviate this problem, the possibility of the eternity of matter tended to be an ever-recurring explanation, with the claim that this was the better interpretation of Aristotelianism itself.

CONCLUSION

These four emphases were the framework for the medieval teaching on the Trinity. None of them was exclusive, and most writers touched on all of them. Still, most medieval scholars tended to centralize their Trinitarian thought on one or the other. The Christian world has not seen since this medieval period another age in which so much creative and profound theological thought on the Trinity has taken place. Subsequent thought on the Trinity remained fully indebted to the insights of these remarkable medieval scholars.

BIBLIOGRAPHY
Sources. Peter Abelard, "Theologia christiana," in Eloi M. Buytaert, ed., *Petri Abaelardi opera theologica*, II (1969); Albertus Magnus, *Commentarium in libros IV sententiarum* (1893); Alcuin of York, "De fide sanctae et individuae Trinitatis" and "Liber contra haeresin Felicis," in *Patrologia latina*, CI (1851), 9–58, 87–120; Alexander of Hales, *Summa theologica*, I (1924); Anselm of Canterbury, "Liber de fide Trinitatis et de incarnatione verbi," in *Patrologia latina*, CLVIII (1853), 259–283; Thomas Aquinas, *Summa theologiae prima pars* (1941); Augustine, *De Trinitate*, W. J. Mountain, ed. (1968); Basil the Great, *Letters*, 2 vols., Agnes C. Way, trans. (1951–1958); Boethius, *The Theological Tractates and The Consolation of Philosophy*, H. F. Stewart and E. K. Rand, ed. and trans. (1918, rev. ed. 1973); Bonaventure, *Commentaria in IV libros sententiarum*, I (1934); Fulgentius of Ruspe, "Liber de Trinitate ad

Felicem," in *S. Fulgentii episcopi Ruspensis opera* (1968), 633–646; Robert Grosseteste, *Super libros posteriorum analyticorum Aristotelis*, Richard C. Dales, ed. (1963); Robert Kilwardby, *Quaestiones in librum primum Sententiarum*, Elisabeth Gössmann, ed. (1986); Martin of Braga, *De trina mersione* (1969); Ratramnus of Corby, "Contra graecorum opposita," in *Patrologia latina*, CXXI (1852), 223–346; Richard of St. Victor, "De Trinitate," *ibid.*, CXCVI (1855), 887–992; Rupert of Deutz, *De Sancta Trinitate et operibus eius*, Hrabanus Haacke, ed. (1971–1972); William of Auxerre, *Summa aurea*, I (1980); William of Ockham, *Scriptum in librum primum sententiarum* (1977).

Studies. Gary B. Blumenshine, ed. *Liber Alcuini contra haeresim Felicis* (1980); Jean-Paul Bouhot, *Ratramne de Corbie* (1976); John H. van Engen, *Rupert of Deutz* (1983); Jean Gribomont, ed., *Les oeuvres du Saint-Esprit par Rupert de Deutz* (1967–); Zachary Hayes, *The Hidden Center: Spirituality and Speculative Christology in St. Bonaventure* (1981); G. Hibbert, "Mystery and Metaphysics in the Trinitarian Theology of St. Thomas," in *The Irish Theological Quarterly*, 31 (1964); Damian McElrath, *Franciscan Christology* (1980); A. Michel, "Trinité," in *Dictionnaire de théologie catholique*, XV, pt. 2 (1950); Leo Scheffczyk, "Lehramtliche Formulierungen und Dogmengeschichte der Trinität," in *Mysterium salutis*, 2 (1967); Dorothea E. Sharp, *Franciscan Philosophy at Oxford in the Thirteenth Century* (1930); Allan B. Wolter, *Duns Scotus on the Will and Morality* (1986).

KENAN B. OSBORNE

[See also **Adoptionism; Arianism; Christology; Church, Early; Councils (Ecumenical, 325–787); Councils, Western; Docetism; Filioque; Heresies, Western European; Nominalism; Philosophy and Theology, Western; Pseudo-Dionysius the Areopagite**; and individual authors.]

TRINITY, OLD TESTAMENT. The concept of the Trinity, that one God exists in three persons equally as one substance, is the central dogma of Christian theology. The term "Trinity," or *trias*, was first used by Theophilus of Antioch (*ca.* 180) to refer to Christ, God, and the Holy Spirit of the New Testament. The use of "Trinity" has no scriptural foundation but is used to designate the doctrine. The concept of the Trinity is foreshadowed in the Old Testament in the theophanic character of the visions of Abraham and Isaiah. The apparition of the three mysterious men to Abraham (Genesis 18) was generally accepted by Christian theologians as a manifestation of the Trinity. In medieval iconog-

raphy, especially in the Byzantine Empire, Abraham's vision commonly represented the Trinity in pictorial cycles. Other Trinitarian motifs found in the Old Testament are the threefold Sanctus of the vision of Isaiah (Isa. 6:3) and the frequent mention of God, his Wisdom, and his Spirit.

BIBLIOGRAPHY

Ormonde M. Dalton, *Byzantine Art and Archaeology* (1911, new ed. 1961), 650, 652, 670; André Grabar, *Christian Iconography* (1968), 114–117.

JENNIFER E. JONES

[See also **Church, Early; Iconography; Rublev, Andrei (with illustration); Trinitarian Doctrine; Ushakov, Simon (with illustration)**.]

TRIPTYCH (from the Greek for "threefold"), in antiquity, a set of three writing tablets hinged or tied together. Throughout the Middle Ages, painters, sculptors, ivory carvers, and metalworkers made triptychs ranging in size from small carved ivory, wooden, or metal devotional objects to larger, more permanently fixed altarpieces. The triptych consists of three panels, generally fastened or hinged together, usually with the two lateral leaves narrower than the central panel so that they could be folded over to protect the central field. The exterior faces of these leaves often received decoration as well.

Examples include several tenth-century Byzantine triptychs carved in ivory, at Dumbarton Oaks in Washington, D.C.; a Flemish metal, enamel, and jeweled triptych from Stavelot Abbey, dating from the mid twelfth century, that functions as a reliquary for fragments from the True Cross and contains mounted in its central field two small gold Byzantine triptychs of the eleventh century (New York, Pierpont Morgan Library; shown at "Romanesque Art"); the Flemish painter Robert Campin's *Merode Altarpiece* of 1425–1430 at the Cloisters (New York, Metropolitan Museum); and the large (approximately 8 feet/2.4 meters high) *Nativity Altarpiece*, also by a Flemish master, Hugo Van der Goes, at the Uffizi in Florence (*ca.* 1476).

BIBLIOGRAPHY

Donald L. Ehresmann, "Some Observations on the Role of Liturgy in the Early Winged Altarpiece," in *Art Bulletin*, 64 (1982), with bibliography; Kurt Weitzmann,

Abraham welcoming three celestial visitors ("Old Testament Trinity"). Mid-4th-century mosaic in S. Maria Maggiore, Rome. ALINARI / ART RESOURCE

Catalogue of the Byzantine and Early Mediaeval Antiquities in the Dumbarton Oaks Collection, III (1972), 58–72.

LESLIE BRUBAKER

[See also **Altarpiece; Byzantine Minor Arts (with illustration); Campin, Robert; Diptych; Flemish Painting; Goes, Hugo Van Der (with illustration); Gothic Art: Painting; Gothic Art: Sculpture; Polyptych; Retable; Trecento Art (with illustration).**]

TRISTAN, LEGEND OF. The Tristan legend recounts the love of Tristan for Isolde, the wife of his uncle, King Mark. Standard features include Tristan's slaying of the Irish warrior Morholt, his winning of Isolde for Mark, the inadvertent drinking of the love potion, exposure by enemies at court, banishment in the forest, and the death of the lovers.

Scholars agree that the legend is of Celtic origin and identify the protagonist with Drest or Drust (r.

ca. 780), the son of the Pictish king Talorcan (Talorc). No direct evidence of the contents of this earliest stage of the legend survives, but Gertrude Schoepperle has demonstrated that an episode very similar to Tristan's battle with Morholt in an Irish saga (*The Wooing of Emer*) reflects an interpolation of the tale of Drust into that of the Ulster hero Cú Chulainn. Thus, it is probable that the Celtic tale of Drust contained only this episode.

The name appears in the Welsh tradition as Drystan or Trystan, son of Tallwch, where Drystan, perhaps under the influence of the Irish *Pursuit of Diarmaid and Grainne*, becomes the lover of Essyllt, wife of his uncle, King March. It is probably during this period (ninth to twelfth centuries) that many of the standard motifs of the legend were added: the love affair itself, the nephew-uncle relationship, the localization of the court at Tintagel in Cornwall, the episode of the harp and the rote, the forest exile, the barrier between the sleeping lovers, and the splashing water. The Welsh version probably ended with the death of the lovers immediately after the forest exile. This period also marks the crucial merging of the Drystan and Arthurian

King Mark bans Tristan and Isolt from the court. Miniature from a 13th-century manuscript of Gottfried von Strassburg's *Tristan*. Munich, Staatsbibliothek, Cod. germ. 51, fol. 90. FOTO MARBURG / ART RESOURCE

spheres, as can be seen from the appearance of the names of the three principals among Arthur's courtiers in other Welsh texts.

The primary medieval versions of the legend—those of Béroul, Thomas of Brittany (or Britain), Eilhart von Oberge, and Gottfried von Strassburg—descend from a lost French source (*ca.* 1150) commonly termed the *Estoire*. Very little is known about this work, including the identity of its author or, in fact, whether it was actually a unified romance or an orally transmitted core, the details of which could be substantially modified by a particular performer.

Several candidates have emerged as the possible author of the *Estoire*. In his *Roman de Renart* (*ca.* between 1175 and 1205), Pierre de Saint-Cloud noted a version of the Tristan legend, now lost, by La Chievre, whose identity remains unclear. Thomas names as his sole source a certain Bréri, who has often been linked to Bledhericus, a Welsh *fabulator famosus* mentioned by Gerald of Wales, and to the *conteur* Bleheris, who at some time between 1100 and 1140 recited Arthurian tales at the court of the count of Poitou, either William IX (*d.* 1127) or his son William X (*d.* 1137). Advocates of Bleheris as the compiler of the *Estoire* emphasize particularly the connection of the court of Poitou with the continental dissemination of the *matière de Bretagne* in the person of Chrétien de Troyes, whose sometime patroness was Marie de Champagne, granddaughter of William X. In his *Cligés* (*ca.* 1176), Chrétien lists among his compositions a work "du roi Marc et d'Iseut la Blonde," also now lost. Although few scholars accept the possibility that Chrétien is the author of the *Estoire*, this thesis does find the occasional champion.

Reconstructions of the *Estoire* have been made by Schoepperle, Bédier, Ranke, and Golther, all of whom differ to some extent on the details; however, it seems certain that the *Estoire* incorporated major expansions in the narrative: the death of the lovers after the forest exile is postponed by Tristan's banishment and his marriage to Isolde of the White Hands, and his biography is supplemented by the tragic love story of his parents. Because these narrative accretions have parallels in Breton folktales, many believe that they document the migration of the legend from Wales to Brittany. Thomas and Gottfried locate Tristan's birthplace in Brittany, not in Lyoness, meaning Scottish Lothian, whereas Béroul uses "Loenoi." Similarly, the change in the name of Tristan's father from Tallwch to Rivalen may have been influenced by the existence of a historical Tristan, son of Rivalon (or Rivelon), who was lord of Vitré from 1030 to 1045 and quarreled with the duke of Brittany.

The most important contribution of the *Estoire* is the unification of the previously episodic plot material into a narrative whole. This is accomplished by replacing the magic spells that bind the lovers in earlier versions with a love potion that controls them utterly, both creating continuity in their series of sexual encounters and at the same time mitigating the moral responsibility for their infidelity.

Scholars traditionally divide the written texts based on the *Estoire* into two groups, the *version commune* (Eilhart, Béroul) and the *version courtoise* (Thomas, Gottfried), although this distinction is more apparent than real. Except for Eilhart's version, which is preserved in three manuscripts from the fifteenth century, no complete version of these texts survives. The two groups are distinguished primarily through their treatment of the potion and the problems that arise from it. In Eilhart (German, *ca.* 1170–1190) and Béroul (Anglo-Norman, *ca.* 1170–1190), the effects of the potion, which diminish after a specified time, are seen as a disruptive force in the ordered courtly world. Neither author is much concerned with the inner lives of his characters or with the ethical nature of their dilemma; rather, they emphasize the cleverness of the lovers in evading detection. The vigor and directness of the narration probably preserve to a great degree the tone of the *Estoire.*

The *version courtoise* is the achievement of the Anglo-Norman Thomas of Brittany (*ca.* 1150–1170), who refined the source material to conform to the (literary) ideals of chivalry and courtly love. This version served as the source for Gottfried's German text (*ca.* 1210), which ends abruptly during Tristan's courtship of the second Isolde (of the White Hands) and overlaps with the surviving Thomas fragments by only a few lines. The absolute power of love is the central theme of the courtly *Tristan:* the effects of the potion are permanent. The narration is frequently interrupted by authorial excursuses that probe the nature of true love.

Both authors are concerned with consistency and probability in the plot material and reject those traditional episodes that seem illogical or that conflict with courtly sensibilities. In Gottfried's work, which has been termed one of the greatest achievements of medieval literature, the "Tristan love" assumes a mystical quality characterized by overt religious symbolism, as seen particularly in the description of the grotto of love.

Contemporary efforts to complete Gottfried's unfinished text were made by Ulrich von Türheim (*ca.* 1230–1235) and Heinrich von Freiberg (*ca.* 1290), although both follow Eilhart's version. Eilhart was also the source for a Czech translation made between 1250 and 1350 and for a German chapbook printed in 1484. Thomas' text inspired the Old Norse prose saga by the monk Robert, *Tristrams saga ok Ísöndar* (1226) and the anonymous English *Sir Tristrem* (*ca.* 1300) and Italian *Tavola ritonda* (*ca.* 1325–1350). Other treatments include: Marie de France's *Lai du chievrefeuil* (*ca.* 1165); the Bern and Oxford versions of the *Folie Tristan* (*ca.* 1170); the anonymous German *Tristan als Mönch* (*ca.* 1250); the prose *Roman de Tristan de Léonois* compiled by Luce del Gast (or Gaut) and Hélie de Boron (*ca.* 1250–

1350); the anonymous Italian *Tristano Riccardiano* (*ca.* 1272–1300); Sir Thomas Malory's *Le Morte Darthur* (1470); and the Spanish *El cuento de Tristán de Leonís* (*ca.* 1400) and "Herido Está Don Tristán" (fifteenth century).

Among postmedieval treatments of the legend are: Pierre Sala, *Tristan* (*ca.* 1525–1529), anonymous, *I due Tristani* (1534), Hans Sachs, *Herr Tristrant mit der schönen königin Isalden* (1553), Matthew Arnold, *Tristram and Iseult* (1852), Richard Wagner, *Tristan und Isolde* (1859), Alfred Tennyson, "The Last Tournament," in *Idylls of the King* (1871), Algernon Charles Swinburne, *Tristram of Lyonesse* (1882), Joseph Bédier, *Le roman de Tristan et Iseut* (1900), Thomas Mann, *Tristan* (1903), Thomas Hardy, *The Famous Tragedy of the Queen of Cornwall* (1923), E. A. Robinson, *Tristram* (1927), John Masefield, *Tristan and Isolt* (1927), E. R. Reynolds, *Tristram and Iseut* (1930), Florence M. Pomeroy, *Tristan and Iseult: An Epic Poem in Twelve Books* (1958), Ruth Schirmer, *Tristan* (1969), and Rosemary Sutcliff, *Tristan and Iseut* (1971).

BIBLIOGRAPHY

A good source for Thomas' version is *Le roman de Tristan par Thomas,* Joseph Bédier, ed., 2 vols. (1902–1905, repr. 1968). Roger S. Loomis, ed., *Arthurian Literature in the Middle Ages* (1959, repr. 1969), includes valuable essays by Helaine Newstead, Eugène Vinaver, and Frederick Whitehead. Also important is the journal *Tristania* (1975–).

Major studies on the development of the Tristan legend include: Sigmund Eisner, *The Tristan Legend: A Study in Sources* (1969); Joan M. Ferrante, *The Conflict of Love and Honor: The Medieval Tristan Legend in France, Germany, and Italy* (1973); Wolfgang Golther, *Tristan und Isolde in den Dictungen des Mittelalters und der neuen Zeit* (1907); Bodo Mergell, *Tristan und Isolde: Ursprung und Entwicklung der Tristansage des Mittelalters* (1949); Friedrich Ranke, *Tristan und Isold* (1925); Gertrude Schoepperle [Loomis], *Tristan and Isolt: A Study of the Sources of the Romance,* 2 vols., 2nd ed. (1960); Franz R. Schröder, "Die Tristansage und das persische Epos 'Wîs und Râmîn,'" in *Germanisch-Romanische Monatsschrift,* n.s. 11 (1961).

THOMAS KERTH

[See also **Anglo-Norman Literature; Arthurian Literature; Chrétien de Troyes; Courtly Love; Folies Tristan; French Literature: To 1200; German Literature: Romance; Gottfried von Strassburg; Heinrich von Freiburg; Marie de Champagne; Marie de France; Ulrich von Türheim.**]

TRISTAN, ROMAN DE. The Tristan legend is among the most famous of the Middle Ages and perhaps second in importance only to that of King Arthur. It is among the earliest Celtic legends exploited by the French poets. The earliest—now lost—version of the Tristan legend in Old French, known as the *Estoire*, has been dated by Joseph Bédier about 1154 and by other scholars between 1150 and 1160. Its surviving texts are listed below:

(1) The *Tristan* of the Anglo-Norman Thomas of Brittany, also called the *version courtoise*, composed after 1150 and probably around 1170. It is said to follow closely the early lost version called *version commune*, but it also has as sources Wace's *Brut*, the *Disciplina clericalis*, and (perhaps) Chrétien's *Cligés*. Thomas' poem has 3,130 lines and exists in five manuscripts, all of them fragmentary. Thomas' version, composed of eight fragments, is considered more courtly than Béroul's, in the sense that it fully endorses the principles of *fin' amors*. The lovers' flight into the Morois forest is not an exile but the triumph of love. In contrast with Béroul's version, Thomas deals in vast monologues with the problems of courtly ideology, love, and passion. The trials of love are willingly accepted and freely assumed by Thomas' lovers. The larger part of Thomas' poem deals with Tristan's marriage to Iseult of the White Hands and ends with the pathetic death of the lovers. With Thomas, the magic potion's effect lasts through the lovers' death, while Béroul sets a time limit for the potion's power. Thomas' version was probably the source of Gottfried von Strassburg's *Tristan and Isolt*, written about 1210. Thomas may also have influenced two other texts: the Middle English version, *Sir Tristrem* (probably dating from the last decade of the thirteenth century) and the Old Norse saga of Friar Robert, *Tristrams saga ok Ísöndar* (1226). In addition, there is little doubt that the author of the *Prose Tristan* (1215–1235) knew both Thomas' and Béroul's works. The Oxford *Folie Tristan* is based on the work of Thomas.

(2) Béroul's *Tristran* (this is the spelling of the unique manuscript), also called the *version commune*, one of the oldest written in the *oïl* dialect. We know very little about Béroul, but it is safe to assume that he was a continental Norman who wrote his *Tristran* between about 1170 and about 1190 in an Anglo-Norman dialect close to that of Amiens. Like the text of Thomas, Béroul's version is fragmentary; only 4,485 octosyllabic lines have

been preserved. The work, which draws from mythical Celtic and Pictish elements, may have had as its main source a lost derivative of the first lost version of the legend. Béroul's tone is less elevated, less courtly, than Thomas', but it is more human and more moving throughout. Béroul's fragment begins with the meeting of the lovers under a tree while King Marc is spying upon them from above; the story ends with the public justification of Yseut in front of Marc and King Arthur and with the revenge of Tristran upon the evil barons who plotted against the lovers. Béroul's version has a close German parallel, the Middle High German version of Eilhart von Oberge. It also influenced the author of the Berne *Folie Tristan* and the French *Prose Tristan*.

(3) *Folie Tristan*, the Oxford version of which was written by an Anglo-Norman author near the end of the twelfth century. It is closely related to Thomas' version. It tells how Tristan managed to see Yseut during his exile by disguising himself as a madman. The Berne version, probably written by a Norman poet, runs to 572 lines (as opposed to the 998 lines of the Oxford version). It was written at the beginning of the thirteenth century and is closely related to Béroul's version. It tells of Tristan's ruse to see Yseut during his banishment from King Mark's court.

(4) The *Lai du chievrefuil* (Lai of the honeysuckle) by Marie de France, a poetess writing in England during the latter half of the twelfth century. It is an episode drawn from Tristan's first exile and tells how he let the queen know of his presence as she was riding through the forest where he was hidden. The honeysuckle wrapped around the hazel branch and tightly attached to it was the secret message that the two lovers could not be separated any more than the branch and the honeysuckle.

(5) The prose *Tristan* (known in the medieval era as *Le roman de Tristan de Léonois*) of the thirteenth century. It is an elaboration of the Vulgate cycle in which the story of Tristan is linked with the Grail theme and the Lancelot-Guinevere story. The *Prose Tristan* rapidly superseded the earlier poetical versions. In fact, it is the main source of the Italian *Tavola ritonda* (fourteenth century), of the German "Volksbuch" *Die Histori von Herren Tristan und der schoenen Iso den von Irlande*, of the Spanish *Libro del esforçado cavallero Don Tristan de Leonis*, of the Danish *En meget smuk Historie om den aedle og tappre Tristran*, and of the Russian *Trishchan i Izhotta*. Finally, we should not forget

the influence of the prose *Tristan* on Malory's *Le Morte Darthur* (1469–1470, published 1485).

(6) The short episode (lines 453–662) called *Donnei des amanz* (A dispute between lovers). It was composed near the end of the twelfth century.

(7) The episode (lines 3,309–4,832) of the *Tristan menestrel* in Gerbert de Montreuil's continuation of Chrétien's *Perceval*.

(8) The lost poem of Chrétien de Troyes.

BIBLIOGRAPHY

Sources. Joseph Bédier, ed., *Le roman de Tristan par Thomas*, 2 vols. (1902–1905, repr. 1968); Béroul, *Tristran and Yseut*, Old French text with English translation, Guy Mermier, trans. (1987); Renée L. Curtis, ed., *Le roman de Tristan en prose*, 2 vols. (1963–1976); Alfred Ewert, ed., *The Romance of Tristan by Béroul*, 2 vols. (1939, repr. 1971); Gerbert de Montreuil, *La continuation de Perceval*, 3 vols., Mary Williams and Marguerite Oswald, eds. (1922–1975); Ernest Hoepffner, ed., *La folie Tristan de Berne* (1934, 2nd ed. 1949) and *La folie Tristan d'Oxford* (1939, 2nd ed. 1943); Bartina Wind, ed., *Les fragments du Tristan de Thomas*, 2nd ed. (1960).

Studies. Renée L. Curtis, "The Problems of the Authorship of the Prose Tristan," in *Romania*, 79 (1958); Jean Frappier, "Structure et sens du Tristan: Version commune, version courtoise," in *Cahiers de civilisation médiévale*, 6 (1963); Pierre Jonin, *Les personnages féminins dans les romans français de Tristan au XII*[e] *siècle* (1958); Jean Marx, "La naissance de l'amour de Tristan et Iseut dans les formes les plus anciennes de la légende," in *Romance Philogy*, 9 (1955); Gertrude Schoepperle [Loomis], *Tristan and Isolt: A Study of the Sources of the Romance*, 2 vols., 2nd ed. (1960).

A valuable compilation, particularly for the essays by Helaine Newstead and Eugène Vinaver, is Roger S. Loomis, ed., *Arthurian Literature in the Middle Ages* (1959, repr. 1969).

GUY MERMIER

[See also **Anglo-Norman Literature; Arthurian Literature; Brut, The; Chrétien de Troyes; Courtly Love; Disciplina Clericalis; Folies Tristan; French Literature: To 1200; Gerbert de Montreuil; German Literature: Romance; Gottfried von Strassburg; Malory, Sir Thomas; Marie de France; Wace.**]

TRISTRAMS SAGA OK ÍSÖNDAR (Saga of Tristram and Ísönd) is a Norwegian prose translation of the *Tristan* of Thomas of Brittany (*fl.* 1150–1170), a translation made in 1226 at the request of King Håkon Håkonsson by a certain Friar Robert. The work has been preserved in three fragments of one vellum and one fragment of a second vellum from about 1450 and in three complete or almost complete paper transcripts from 1688–1728. The manuscripts are all Icelandic. Friar Robert is also believed to have translated *Elis saga ok Rosamundu* (*Elie de St. Gille*) and the *Strengleikar* or *Ljóðabók* (the *Lais* of Marie de France) and possibly several other French works. From his command of the language it is almost certain that Robert was a Norwegian.

The importance of *Tristrams saga* for Tristan research consists in the fact that it is the only complete member of the Thomas branch (*version courtoise*) of the Tristan story and the only translation of Thomas' work in existence. As far as can be determined, the translation is correct except for a few individual words. The translator added only a prayer by Ísönd in the final chapter, but he omitted numerous long discursive monologues and dialogues, especially those dealing with love as a general phenomenon or personal affliction, as well as the intrusions of Thomas. He attempted to reproduce the effect of rhyme and rhythm through the use of alliteration, pairs of synonyms, and other rhetorical devices. Although somewhat pompous at the beginning, the style gradually becomes increasingly more limpid and flexible.

Tristrams saga was followed by a veritable flood of Norwegian translations of romances and other foreign works, some of the originals of which are no longer extant. Preserved almost entirely in Icelandic manuscripts, these *riddarasögur* (sagas about knights) inspired many Icelandic imitations. *Tristrams saga* has exerted a persistent and pervasive influence on medieval Icelandic literature. Derived from *Tristrams saga* are the poignantly beautiful Icelandic ballad *Tristrams kvæði* (*ca.* 1400), the rustic *Saga af Tristram ok Ýsodd* (*ca.* 1450), and several *Märchen*. *Tristrams saga* also influenced later *Islendingasögur* (sagas of Icelanders), notably *Grettis saga*.

BIBLIOGRAPHY

Sources. "The Icelandic Saga of Tristan and Isolt," Joyce Hill, trans., in her *The Tristan Legend: Texts from Northern and Eastern Europe in Modern English Translation* (1977); *Saga af Tristram og Ísönd*, in *Riddarasögur*, Bjarni Vilhjálmsson, ed., I (1949); *The Saga of Tristram and Ísönd*, Paul Schach, trans. (1973).

Studies. Álfrún Gunnlaugsdóttir, *Tristán en el norte* (1978); Henry Goddard Leach, *Angevin Britain and Scandinavia* (1921); Paul Schach, "Tristan and Isolde in

Scandinavian Ballad and Folktale," in *Scandinavian Studies*, **36** (1964), "The Style and Structure of *Tristrams Saga*," in *Scandinavian Studies: Essays Presented to Dr. Henry Goddard Leach*, Carl F. Bayerschmidt and Erik J. Friis, eds. (1965), "Some Observations on the Influence of *Tristrams saga ok Ísöndar* on Old Icelandic Literature," in *Old Norse Literature and Mythology: A Symposium*, Edgar C. Polomé, ed. (1969), and "Some Observations on the Translations of Brother Róbert," in *Les relations littéraires franco-scandinaves au moyen âge* (1975); Margaret Schlauch, *Romance in Iceland* (1934).

PAUL SCHACH

[See also **Elis Saga ok Rosamundu; Grettis Saga Ásmundarsonar; Lai, Lay; Marie de France; Riddarasögur; Strengleikar.**]

TRISTRANT, a verse romance by the German poet Eilhart (Eylhart, Eilardus de Oberge). Composed between 1170 and 1190, *Tristrant* gives the earliest complete account of the love story of Tristan and Isolde and is the version that, according to many scholars, most closely resembles the lost original. The work is extant in fragments of three early manuscripts; in three later, complete ones; a Czech translation; and a chapbook. In one of the later manuscripts a part of Eilhart's version of the Tristan legend fills out the unfinished portion of that of Gottfried von Strassburg; the Czech translation is also a complete work that uses the redactions of Gottfried and Heinrich von Freiberg as well as that of Eilhart. The earlier fragments are from the end of the twelfth or the beginning of the thirteenth century; the others are of the fifteenth century, although presumably based on thirteenth-century sources. All are corrupted to the extent that it is impossible to reproduce the exact language of the first *Tristrant*, but there is close agreement with regard to plot, style, and general spirit. One can therefore gain a reliable acquaintance with this romance, even though minor details have been altered.

Little is known of the poet who refers to himself in a late *Tristrant* manuscript as "von Hobergin her Eylhart." He is generally assumed to be the "Eilardus de Oberge" whose name appears as a witness to ten documents (1189–1207) indicating that he was a vassal of Duke Henry the Lion. This assumption has some support from the fact that the manuscripts contain traces of a Low German like that spoken at the court of Braunschweig and at

Oberg, about 10 miles (16 km) to the west. As narrator, the poet reveals a little of his personality but nothing of his life, and no other medieval work mentions him. Eilhart's source was doubtless a French romance, either the original Tristan version or a close redaction of it, which perhaps was brought to Braunschweig by Mathilde, the daughter of Eleanor of Aquitaine, when she became the duke's second wife. Another possibility is that the poet accompanied Henry to England when he was banished by Emperor Frederick I and learned the story there.

Because of the rapid development of German narrative verse during the last quarter of the twelfth century, an assessment of Eilhart's position in literary history depends to a considerable extent on the date of composition of his romance. If it was written in the 1170's—which, all things considered, is most likely—he was an innovator in style, language, and manners, as well as in subject matter. If he wrote after 1185 (the approximate date of Heinrich von Veldeke's *Eneide*), he was outside the mainstream, presenting material that was new to Germany in archaic dress. In either case, however, Eilhart's *Tristrant* is a major representative of a legend that has lent itself to greatly differing poetic treatments.

Eilhart's work presents a classic tale of the hero's struggle against fate, always emphasizing the desperate, though sometimes comic, situation of a strong and resourceful man confronted by enigmatic forces that seem bent on his destruction. The theme of Tristrant and his destiny is developed by means of a variety of devices: the repeated use of irrational elements to direct the action; frequent references to luck, chance, and fate; the exploitation of highly paradoxical and ironical situations; and the employment of quite unlikely, but still possible, coincidence. The two chief instruments of fate are the sea and the love potion, which are also used as symbols: the sea as the outer, the potion as the inner, necessity that determines the hero's life. The question as to the nature of his destiny—whether malignant, benevolent, or indifferent—is never answered, but at the end is a hint that it is at least meaningful.

Structurally *Tristrant* is a model of symmetry. Like many Arthurian romances, it consists of five parts held together by a series of parallel situations and events. Eilhart pairs parts 1 and 5 (the Rivalin-Blankeflur and Kehenis-Gariole episodes), 2 and 4 (the journeys to Ireland and Cornwall respectively), and the first and second halves of part 3 (the sojourns at Mark of Cornwall's court and in the wilderness), so that the later adventures are somewhat like a mirror image of the earlier ones. Certain pervasive motifs also contribute to the structural unity of the work and, since they reveal aspects of the nature of fate, reinforce the thematic unity as well. The chief motifs are the journey, joy-grief, the substitute, the hunt, and death, all of which are developed in distinct and consistent patterns.

The narrative style is generally informal and casual, sometimes repetitive, often deficient in explanatory material, and rather careless with respect to details. There is little attempt to motivate or interpret the action. Several stylistic devices are handled with skill: the intentionally restricted point of view, the use of epithets (which, unlike those of most medieval narrative verse, are always appropriate to the individual and his immediate condition), and a spotlighting technique with which the author focuses on the primary actors and actions. Over one-third of *Tristrant* consists of dialogue, distinguished by a pronounced tendency to pass without warning from indirect to direct discourse and by the staccato quality of the latter. Rapid exchanges, with the conversation shifting back and forth with each verse and sometimes with each half verse, are perhaps Eilhart's most distinctive stylistic feature. His language is simple and unadorned, with few foreign words, similes, or poetic exaggerations. Lightly ironic humor pervades the work, leaving only a few consistently serious scenes.

Tristrant soon became well known: traces of several episodes appear in subsequent narratives, and its hero and heroine are mentioned in many medieval works. As one might expect, Eilhart's romance influenced the *Tristan und Isolt* (*ca.* 1210) of Gottfried von Strassburg and, to a greater extent, the continuations of the latter's incomplete work by Ulrich von Türheim and Heinrich von Freiberg. *Tristrant* also inspired medieval art, especially certain fourteenth-century tapestries and some of the murals at Runkelstein Castle in the South Tyrol.

During most of the period since the first printing of the chapbook in 1484 the German public knew the Tristan story only through the successive editions of this variant, for Eilhart's verse treatment, together with the other Tristan narratives, had faded into obscurity. When they were rediscovered toward the end of the eighteenth century, it was Gottfried's version that made Germany familiar with the medieval love story.

BIBLIOGRAPHY

Ulrich Bamborschke, ed., *Das altčechische Tristan-Epos*, 2 vols. (1968–1969); Alois Brandstetter, ed., *Tristrant und Isalde: Prosaroman* (1966); Danielle Buschinger, ed. and trans., *Tristrant* (1976); Hadumod Bussmann, ed., *Tristrant* (1969); J. W. Thomas, trans., *Eilhart von Oberge's "Tristrant"* (1978).

J. WESLEY THOMAS

[See also **German Literature: Romance; Gottfried von Strassburg; Heinrich von Freiberg; Heinrich von Veldeke; Ulrich von Türheim.**]

TRIUMPHAL ARCH, in Roman architecture, a decorative building type erected in honor of a military victory or triumph and consisting of a single freestanding archway (Arch of Titus, Rome) or of a large central archway flanked by two smaller side arches (Arch of Constantine, Rome). In early Christian basilicas and later churches of similar plan, the term is applied to the end wall of the nave with its great arch that frames the apse or chancel. This area, like the apse itself, is often enriched with decoration, as in the mosaic *arcus triumphalis* of S. Maria Maggiore in Rome. The term is sometimes applied as well to classicizing arched wall tombs of the Renaissance (Leonardo Bruni's tomb, S. Croce, Florence). In all cases the association is with triumph, whether military, ecclesiastical, or humanistic.

GREGORY WHITTINGTON

[See also **Arch; Basilica;** and illustration overleaf.]

TRIVIUM, the part of the medieval seven liberal arts that preceded the quadrivium in the curriculum and was composed of grammar, rhetoric, and dialectic. It was thus the basis of the secular side of the medieval school curriculum. The term itself does not appear before the ninth century, although the catalog of arts that it embodies, along with the quadrivium, has its roots in ancient Greece.

In the fourth century B.C., Isocrates developed the system of arts studies that was to remain standard through antiquity. In the system of Isocrates, the liberal arts were a preparation for the study of philosophy. The general outlines of this system survived antipathy to classical learning in the early church and entered the Christian Middle

Triumphal arch in S. Maria Maggiore, Rome. 4th century. ALINARI / ART RESOURCE

Ages as the seven-part structure defined in Martianus Capella's *Marriage of Philology and Mercury* (fifth century).

The Christians of Alexandria viewed the trivium and the other arts as preparatory to philosophy; they in turn saw philosophy as preparatory to theology. The Middle Ages, however, came commonly to view the arts as themselves comprising the whole of philosophy and hence serving as the "handmaidens" of theology.

Grammar, primarily the practical study of Latin, included literature as well as language. Teachers used such grammar texts as those of Priscian and Donatus and drew literature from classical Latin prose and poetry as well as from the Bible and patristic theologians.

The study of rhetoric involved considerations more practical then theoretical and included within its purview the study of law during the early Middle Ages, although this ceased with the rise of universities and separate law faculties. Students of rhetoric were instructed in the composition both of prose and of poetry, with special attention given, particularly after the tenth century, to the writing of letters.

The third branch of the trivium, dialectic, was essentially the study of formal logic.

In theory, the trivium was to be taught to all who came to school, with the quadrivium taught only to the best students. Often, in practice, however, the curricula of individual schools were more limited, even with respect to the trivium itself, with the result that the only universally studied subject was grammar (hence the designation "grammar school").

During the twelfth century and following, with the rise of the universities, the study of grammar gave way to the increasing dominance of dialectic,

206

a trend particularly in evidence in northern Europe. Some scholars pursued even the study of grammar using solely the methods of the logician and ignoring the evidence provided by literary texts. The preeminence of dialectic in the north was to contribute to the development of the scholastic theology of Paris, while, on the other hand, the preservation in Italy of grammatical and rhetorical studies, the latter including law, would contribute to the rise of legal studies at Bologna and, ultimately, to the development of the humanistic studies of the Renaissance.

BIBLIOGRAPHY

Ernst Robert Curtius, *European Literature and the Latin Middle Ages,* Willard R. Trask, trans. (1953), 36–61; Richard W. Hunt, *The History of Grammar in the Middle Ages* (1980); Paul O. Kristeller, *Renaissance Thought and Its Sources,* Michael Mooney, ed. (1979); Max L. W. Laistner, *Thought and Letters in Western Europe: A.D. 500 to 900* (1931); Richard McKeon, "Rhetoric in the Middle Ages," in *Speculum,* 17 (1942); Henri-Irénée Marrou, *A History of Education in Antiquity,* George Lamb, trans. (1956); Louis J. Paetow, *The Arts Course at Medieval Universities with Special Reference to Grammar and Rhetoric* (1910); Pio Rajna, "Le denominazioni *trivium* e *quadrivium*," in *Studi medievali,* n.s., I (1928); William Harris Stahl *et al., Martianus Capella and the Seven Liberal Arts,* 2 vols. (1971–1977).

MELVIN STORM

[See also **Alcuin of York; Arts, Seven Liberal; Classical Literary Studies; Dialectic; Dictamen; Grammar; Latin Language; Law, Schools of; Martianus Capella; Medicine, Schools of; Notker Teutonicus; Philosophy and Theology, Western European; Priscian; Quadrivium; Rhetoric, Western European; Schools, Grammar; Textbooks; Universities; Vergil in the Middle Ages.**]

TROBAIRITZ. Among the some twenty nobly born women troubadours who composed lyric *cansos* and *tensos* in southern France during the twelfth and thirteenth centuries, the best known are Azalais de Porcairagues, Castelloza, and the Comtessa de Dia. Their songs reflect the viewpoint of the lady, or *domna,* in the courtly love relationship, their tone being more forthright and sensual than the more ritualized and more abstract expression of the male troubadours.

BIBLIOGRAPHY

Meg Bogin, *The Women Troubadours* (1976); Oskar Schultz-Gora, *Die provenzalischen Dichterinnen* (1888).

ROBERT TAYLOR

[See also **Canso; Comtessa de Dia; Courtly Love; Provençal Literature; Tenso; Troubadour, Trouvère.**]

TRÓJUMANNA SAGA is a Norse saga version of the legend of Troy, based mainly on Dares Phrygius' *De excidio Troiae* plus some material from Ovid and other Latin authors. Three different redactions of the saga have been preserved in several manuscripts, of which the earliest are from the beginning of the fourteenth century. The original translation of Dares' Latin text was made either in Iceland or in Norway, probably before 1250. Around 1300 it was interpolated with passages from the so-called *Ilias latina,* Vergil's *Aeneid,* and other works. In the manuscripts it is often preserved together with *Breta sǫgur,* a translation of Geoffrey of Monmouth's *Historia regum Britanniae,* to which it forms an introduction. Both works seem to represent attempts to use the saga form to expound chivalric ideals and classical learning in accordance with the educational policy of the Norwegian court in the thirteenth century. *Trójumanna saga* may have had some influence on later Icelandic saga literature, especially through its "literary portraits" and treatment of pagan mythology.

BIBLIOGRAPHY

Sources. Jonna Louis-Jensen, ed., *Trójumanna saga* (1963) and *Trójumanna saga: The Dares Phrygius Version* (1981).

Studies. Wilhelm Greif, *Die mittelalterlichen Bearbeitungen der Trojanersage* (1886); Jonna Louis-Jensen, "Trójumanna saga," in *Kulturhistorisk leksikon for nordisk middelalder fra vikingetid til reformationstid,* XVIII (1974); Lars Lönnroth, "Porträtt, skepp och namn i *Trójumanna saga*—ett textkritiskt bidrag," in *Acta philologica scandinavica,* 27 (1965); Frank G. Nelson, "The Date, Sources, and Analogues of *Trójumanna Saga*" (diss., Univ. of California at Berkeley, 1937).

LARS LÖNNROTH

[See also **Breta Sǫgur; Geoffrey of Monmouth; Norway; Troy Story.**]

TROPARION (*pl.* troparia), the most general term for hymnographic texts of the Byzantine Orthodox church. In a narrow sense "troparion" usually applies to certain text categories, as, for example, the texts related to the feast of the day or the strophes in the odes of a *kanōn*. Limited analogies can be drawn between the use of troparia in the East, and the tropes and antiphons of Western chant.

BIBLIOGRAPHY

Heinrich Husmann, "Hymnus und Troparion," in *Jahrbuch des Staatlichen Instituts für Musikforschung Preussischer Kulturbesitz* (1971), 7–86; L. Petit, "Antiphone dans la liturgie grecque," *Dictionnaire d'archéologie chrétienne*, I, pt. 2 (1907), 2,301–2,303; Oliver Strunk, "Tropus and Troparion," in his *Essays on Music in the Byzantine World* (1977), 268–276; Egon Wellesz, *A History of Byzantine Music and Hymnography,* 2nd ed. (1961, repr. 1963).

NICOLAS SCHIDLOVSKY

[See also **Hymns, Byzantine; Kanōn; Liturgy, Byzantine Church; Music, Byzantine.**]

TROPER. Tropers contain tropes. Tropes are additions to liturgical texts, made for particular institutions and associated with different liturgical genres. As a consequence they often appear in the manuscripts wherever it is convenient to include them. Many manuscripts or sections of manuscripts, however, contain little or nothing but tropes, with or without the genre to which they are attached. These books may be called tropers. A book containing only tropes was dependent on a separate book containing the parent chants. Most tropers date from the tenth to twelfth centuries, during the heyday of troping. Because sequences continued to be used and written, sequentiaries may date from later in the Middle Ages.

Normally, tropers are organized in a convenient, practical way, following the order of the church year or the order of the liturgical items to which the tropes belong. The manuscript Paris, Bibliothèque Nationale, lat. 903 is an important early troper, published in facsimile in Paléographie Musicale no. 13. It begins as a Gradual with some tropes included and continues with a section containing only tropes for the Proper of the Mass; the next section has the Ordinary of the Mass arranged as usual in groups of Kyries, Glorias, and so on, troped as

necessary; a section with sequences follows. Well-known tropers come from Aquitaine (in a set of several manuscripts, now in the Bibliothèque Nationale, some of which contain polyphony), from Nonantola, and from Anglo-Saxon England. Perhaps the most famous are the two Winchester Tropers, dating from the very late tenth century. Apart from polyphonic settings and sequences, they contain tropes for all the items of Proper and Ordinary of the Mass, and often the parent chant is included, at least in incipit.

Like these two books, many tropers are very small, the page size being about that of a postcard. This is a clear indication that performance of tropes was by a soloist. Many tropers probably belonged to individual singers, and contained their personal repertory.

BIBLIOGRAPHY

Facsimiles of the Aquitainian tropers are *Paris, Bibliothèque nationale, fonds latin 1139, 3719, and 3549*; and *London, British Library, add. 36881.* All are in the series Facsimiles of Mediaeval Manuscripts, Institute of Mediaeval Music, Ottawa (1986/1987–). Another facsimile is Giuseppe Vecchi, ed., *Troparium, sequentiarium Nonantulanum (Cod. Casanat. 1741)* (1955).

Studies include Jacques Chailley, "Les anciens tropaires et séquentiaires de Saint-Martial de Limoges (Xᵉ–XIᵉ siècles)," in *Études grégoriennes,* **2** (1957); Heinrich Husmann, ed., *Tropen- und Sequenzenhandschriften* (1964), with inventories and bibliographies; Alejandro Planchart, *The Repertory of Tropes at Winchester,* 2 vols. (1977).

ANDREW HUGHES

[See also **St. Martial School; Sequence (Prosa); Tropes to the Ordinary of the Mass; Tropes to the Proper of the Mass; Winchester Troper.**]

TROPES TO THE ORDINARY OF THE MASS. In manuscript sources dating from the tenth into the sixteenth century, various items of the Ordinary and the Proper of the Mass appear together with additional texts and music. The most common designation for these additions is tropus (from the Greek *tropos,* "turn" or "figure"), usually in the plural, tropi. Other terms, such as versus, laudes, preces, verbae, prosae, and prosulae, are also found.

Faced with the variety of medieval designations for these additions, modern scholars have found it

TROPES TO THE ORDINARY OF THE MASS

Sanctus with Tropes and Prosula

Trope: Gloriosa dies adest, qua surrexit praepotens ex mortuis; omnes dicite, eia: *Sanctus,*

Trope: Idem Deus conditor hominum factus est redemptor die ista: laudem dicite, eia: *Sanctus,*

Trope: Iam "Gloria in excelsis" cantant sancta agmina; hymnum dicite, eia: *Sanctus,*

Dominus Deus Sabaoth. Pleni sunt caeli et terra gloria tua. Osanna in

excelsis. Benedictus qui venit in nomine Domini. Osanna **[Prosula:]** Dulcis est

cantica melliflua, Nimisque laudabilia organica. Trine une, deprecemur omnes in

hac aula, Suscipe cum agmina Angelorum carmina. Dicat nunc: *Osanna in excelsis.*

That glorious day is here, on which our Lord arose from the dead; let all say "Eia!" *Holy,* The same God, the founder of the human race, has been made its redeemer on this day; say His praise, "Eia!" *Holy,* Now the holy host sings "Glory to God in the highest"; say the hymn "Eia!" *Holy, Lord God almighty. Heaven and earth are full of your glory. Hosanna in the highest. Blessed is he who comes in the name of the Lord. Hosanna.* Very sweet is the mellifluous song, as are praises sung with instruments. With three in one, let everyone in this hall pray, "Hear our songs with the host of angels, which should now say '*Hosanna in the highest.*'"

NOTE: Sanctus text is in italics. Dotted lines (· · ·) signify the trope melodies; dashed lines (– – –) signify the Sanctus melody, including final hosanna with prosula. *Source*: AH, vol. XLVII, pp. 304, 343.

difficult to establish a consistent terminology for describing them. Some (for instance, Handschin and Hoppin) have chosen to group all additions to the standard liturgical repertoire under the generic term "trope," qualifying this further according to whether the addition is textual, musical, or both. Others (for instance, Evans, Crocker, and the present author) have chosen to follow the relatively consistent usage of the St. Martial manuscripts (tenth–twelfth centuries), distinguishing between the term "trope," a newly composed text with music added to an established liturgical chant, and "prosula," a text added to a preexistent melisma (melody).

Examples of both trope and prosula are among the additions to the Ordinary of the Mass in the Middle Ages. These additions include the following: (1) tropes to the Kyrie, Gloria, Sanctus, Agnus Dei, and Ite missa est (tropes for the Credo are extremely rare) and (2) prosulae for the Kyrie, the Hosanna melisma of the Sanctus, and the Regnum melisma of the Gloria trope *Regnum tuum solidum.*

The various procedures displayed in these additions to the Ordinary are most clearly represented in the tropes and prosulae to the Sanctus. Trope phrases (text and music) introduce and are interpolated between the phrases of the Sanctus, expanding its meaning and, in this case, relating it to a given feast. A similar function is served by the prosula text underlaid to the melody for *Osanna* [hosanna] *in excelsis.* (It should be noted that the great majority of texts for tropes and prosulae to the Ordinary are not limited to a single feast of the liturgical year.) In performance, the choir would sing the Sanctus in alternation with a soloist singing the tropes. The Hosanna melisma would probably be vocalized by the choir on the final "a" of "hosanna," while the soloist(s) would sing the prosula in melodic unison with the choir. The assonance created between prosula and melisma by the "a" ending of each phrase of the prosula (a characteristic of many early prosulae) would be especially effective in performance, articulating each textual and musical phrase and imparting a sense of cohesiveness to the whole.

One of the most problematic aspects of tropes to the Ordinary results from the fact that the Ordinary chants are relatively later than the chants of the Proper. Unlike the chants of the Proper, those of the Ordinary appear together with their tropes in the earliest musical sources to contain them. Many of these chants are delivered only with tropes. The problem is complicated by the fact that chants for the Ordinary continued to be composed throughout the Middle Ages. In many instances, therefore, the "original chant" may have been composed at or about the same time as its tropes or prosulae, and any distinction made between the chant and its additions may be purely arbitrary. The best example of this problem is the Kyrie, but it pertains to other Ordinary chants as well. This question and others have helped to make tropes to the Ordinary a particularly vital topic for research in recent years.

BIBLIOGRAPHY

Sources. Editions of texts are *Tropi graduales: Tropen des missale im Mittelalter*, I: *Tropen zum Ordinarium Missae*, in *Analecta hymnica medii aevi*, XLVII (1905, repr. 1961), the standard collection of texts for tropes and prosulae to the Ordinary, the chief drawback being that it includes only poetic or quasipoetic texts, thereby excluding many of the earliest tropes and prosulae, which are in prose; *Corpus troporum* [CT], Ritva Jonsson *et al.*, eds. (1975–)—see especially Gunilla Iversen, ed., *Tropes de l'Agnus Dei* (1980).

Facsimile editions include the series Paléographie Musicale (1889–), especially no. 15, *Benevento, Biblioteca Capitolare, MS VI.34* (1937, repr. 1971), and no. 18, *Rome, Biblioteca Angelica, MS 123* (1969); Giuseppe Vecchi, ed., *Troparium, sequentiarium Nonantulanum: Cod. Casanat. 1741* (1955).

Studies. Willi Apel, *Gregorian Chant* (1958, 3rd ed. 1966), 429–442; Charles M. Atkinson, "The Earliest Settings of the Agnus Dei and Its Tropes" (diss., Univ. of North Carolina, 1975) and "The Earliest Agnus Dei Melody and Its Tropes," in *Journal of the American Musicological Society*, 30 (1977); David A. Bjork, "The Kyrie Repertory in Aquitanian Manuscripts of the Tenth and Eleventh Centuries" (diss., Univ. of California at Berkeley, 1976) and "The Kyrie Trope," in *Journal of the American Musicological Society*, 33 (1980); Richard L. Crocker, "The Troping Hypothesis," in *The Musical Quarterly*, 52 (1966); Jacques Handschin, "Trope, Sequence, and Conductus," in *The New Oxford History of Music*, II (1954); Richard H. Hoppin, *Medieval Music* (1978), 130–156; Heinrich Husmann, *Tropen- und Sequenzenhandschriften* (1964), a catalog of trope manuscripts; Ritva Jonsson, "Amalaire de Metz et les tropes du Kyrie eleison," in O. S. Due, H. Friis Johansen, and B. Dalsgaard, eds., *Classica et mediaevalia: Francisco Blatt septuagenario dedicata* (1973); Margaretha Landwehr-Melnicki, *Das einstimmige Kyrie des lateinischen Mittelalters* (1955, repr. 1968), 80–85, primarily a catalog of melodies for the Kyrie; Eva Odelman, "Comment a-t-on appelé les tropes?" in *Cahiers de civilisation médiévale*, 18 (1975); Alejandro Enrique Planchart, *The Repertory of Tropes at Winchester*, 2 vols. (1977); Klaus Rönnau, *Die Tropen zum Gloria in excelsis Deo. Unter besonderer Berücksichtigung des Repertoires der St. Martial Handschriften* (1967); Martin Schildbach, *Das einstimmige Agnus Dei und seine handschriftliche Überlieferung vom 10. bis zum 16. Jahrhundert* (1967), 65–67, a catalog of melodies for the Agnus Dei; Bruno Stäblein, "Die Unterlegung von Texten unter Melismen: Tropus, Sequenz und andere Formen," in Jan LaRue, ed., *International Musicological Society: Report of the Eighth Congress, New York, 1961*, I (1961), especially useful for its discussion of the Kyrie and its prosulae, and "Tropus," in Friedrich Blume, ed., *Die Musik in Geschichte und Gegenwart*, XIII (1966); Peter Josef Thannabaur, *Das einstimmige Sanctus der römischen Messe in der handschriftlichen Überlieferung des 11. bis 16. Jahrhunderts* (1962), 88–98, a catalog of melodies for the Sanctus, with an excellent treatment of tropes and prosulae associated with the chant.

CHARLES M. ATKINSON

[See also **Agnus Chant; Agnus Dei (Music); Ars Poetica; Benedicamus Domine; Gloria; Hymns, Latin; Ite Chant; Kyrie; Mass, Liturgy of the; Melisma; St. Martial School; Sanctus.**]

TROPES TO THE PROPER OF THE MASS.

Though some modern writers use "trope" as an all-embracing term for every type of musical or textual addition to the Gregorian chant repertoire, medieval sources distinguish different genres, including (1) the sequentia (continuation), a wordless melody that served as a virtuosic expansion of the jubilus melody at the end of the alleluia; (2) the prosa (prose), a text set to a sequentia melody; (3) the prosula (little prose) or verba (words), a shorter text written to fit a textless melisma or melody in an offertory, alleluia, gradual, tract, or sequentia; (4) the farsa (stuffing), an interpolation of music and text into a cantillated reading from the Bible, which provided a kind of commentary; (5) the tropus, a composition of new music and text that formed an introduction to or interpolation into an introit, offertory, or communion chant. The interchangeable sections were often called versus, which term also referred to other types of medieval poetry.

SEQUENTIA

Rhapsodic, wordless singing was an ancient Christian practice; medieval alleluia chants appear to preserve a distant memory of this in the jubilus, a long melisma on the last syllable of the word alleluia, which was sung both before and after the psalm verse that stood at the center of the piece. In

Ambrosian and Mozarabic chant, the second alleluia had a much longer and more elaborate jubilus, while in Gregorian chant the same jubilus was sung both times (see Ex. 1). When Gregorian chant was imported into the Carolingian Empire, however, the Frankish singers seem to have retained the practice of the other Latin liturgies by substituting a longer melisma for the second jubilus. Many of the early sequentia melodies, however, exhibit confusing traits that have never been fully explained. Though each has the word alleluia written at the beginning, many have no discernible relationship to any known Gregorian alleluia. All the sequentiae are given names, some of which indicate the corresponding alleluia while others, such as *Planctus cygni* (The swan's lament), do not. Many of the melodies are made longer by frequent internal repetitions of certain melodic phrases, which is also a feature of some Ambrosian and Mozarabic melodies. Yet the notation of some sequentiae suggests that they had once had words. Perhaps what began as a jubilus substitute had already emerged as an independent genre.

PROSA

In the preface to his *Liber hymnorum* (*ca.* 884), Notker Balbulus, the first great author of prosae, said that he wrote them to fit the textless sequentia melodies, imitating a novelty he learned from a wandering monk. But it was not long before the *sequentia cum prosa* came to be thought of as a unit, called prosa or prose in the Romance languages, and sequentia or sequence/sequenz in English and German. The fact that some early sequentia melodies were notated as though they had words (that is, with few ligatures and many single notes) suggests that the merger of music and text began very early. The final result was a complete change in the form of the texts, which, as the name "prosa" indicates, were originally written in measured prose designed to fit the sequentia. By the twelfth century new, poetic texts were being written by such poets as Adam of St. Victor, the most important author of the new type. Many of the most famous examples of the prosa belong to this later type, including *Verbum bonum et suave; Veni, Sancte Spiritus; Lauda Sion; Stabat Mater*; and *Dies irae*.

PROSULA

The prosula, like the early prosa, was a new text added to an older melody; but while the prosa was designed to fit an entire sequentia, the prosula was fitted only to certain phrases of a sequentia, or to melismatic sections of other kinds of chants. One of the oldest and best-known is the prosula *Psalle modulamina* (early ninth century), designed to fit the melody of *Alleluia Christus resurgens*, as shown in Example 1. While a prosa could have been written to fit a sequentia replacing the notes over the last syllable of alleluia, this prosula is fitted to the entire piece. Thus, where the original alleluia had long melismatic sections, with many notes set to a single syllable, the prosula supplies a new syllable to almost every note. A sign of the author's skill was his ability to match syllables of the prosula text with syllables of the original chant text, as in *Psalle/Alle, Christus, resur-*, and so on.

FARSA

The farsae or farses have received the least study of all the genres. They were usually interpolated into the Epistle reading at Mass, and their melodies offered some contrast to the repetitious reading tones used for the biblical text. There are some examples of French farsae, vernacular translations of the Latin Epistle. In at least one case, Epistle farsae appear to be based on a preexistent chant of another genre.

TROPUS

The tropus or trope is the most complex type, in which new words and music are inserted freely at several points in the original chant. Example 2 gives the text of the Christmas introit *Puer natus* with a set of tropes taken from an eleventh-century manuscript. The introit text (based on Isa. 9:6 and Psalm 97 [98]) is shown in italics. It should be remembered that there was considerable variety regarding the length and number of versus and the place in the chant at which they were inserted. Both the original introit and the tropes were meant to be sung, each to its own distinctive melody. In Example 2 it should be noted that the trope texts fill out the original chant text, for instance, "*A child is born to us* whom the prophets long ago foretold." Just before the psalm *Cantate domino* is a command addressed to the leader of the choir, "say, Sir, 'eia,'" reminding him that it was his task to begin the psalm. Such reminders to individual singers and interrelationships between trope and original text are thoroughly typical of the repertoire. *Eia* was a common exclamation in most types of medieval music.

The extraordinary variety among the different

TROPES TO THE PROPER OF THE MASS

Example 1

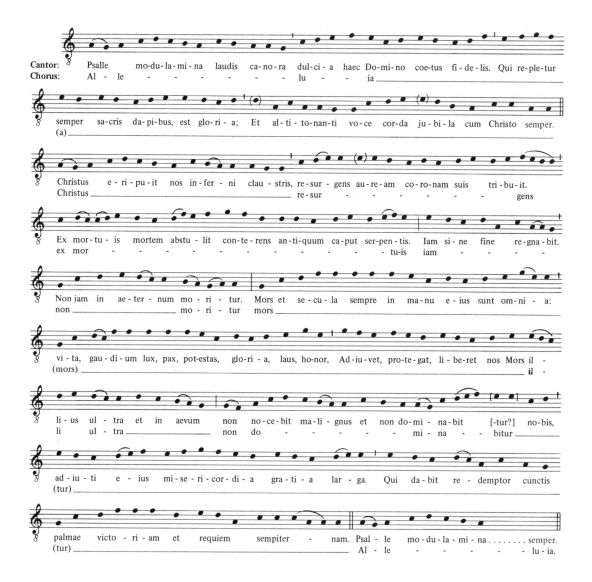

Translation of alleluia: Alleluia. Christ, being raised from the dead, will never die again, death has no more power over him. Alleluia. (Rom. 6:9)

Translation of prosula: Sing to the lord these harmonious, sweet melodies of praise. The faithful assembly, which is always satisfied by the sacred feasts, is in glory, and with a voice thundering from on high, O hearts, jubilate with Christ always. Christ has delivered us from the bonds of hell; rising he gave a golden crown to his own. He has carried away death from the dead, trampling the ancient head of the serpent. Now he will reign without end, now he will not die forever. Death and all ages are always in his hand: life, joy, light, peace, power, glory, praise, honor; may he help, protect, deliver us. His death will no longer harm him forever, and the evil one will not dominate us, helped by his mercy and abundant favor, the redeemer who will give to all palms of victory and eternal rest. Sing to the Lord these harmonious, sweet melodies of praise . . . with Christ always.

Alleluia with prosula. After J. Smits van Waesberghe, "Zur ursprünglichen Vortragsweise," p. 155. Munich, Bayerische Staatsbibliothek, 9543, fol. 199v. CORPUS TROPORUM, II.1, pp. 28–29

Example 2

Gaudeamus hodie quia deus descendit de celis et propter nos in terris *Puer natus est nobis,*
Quem prophete diu uaticinati sunt *et filius datus est nobis*
Hunc a patre iam nouimus aduenisse in mundum *cuius imperium super humerum ejus*
Potestas et regnum in manu eius *et vocabitur nomen eius*
Admirabilis consiliarius, deus fortis, princeps pacis, *magni consilii angelus.*
Cantate domino canticum nouum, "eia," dic domne, "eia," *Cantate domino canticum novum quia mirabilia fecit.*
Glorietur pater cum filio suo unigenito *Gloria patri et filio et spiritui sancto, sicut erat in principio, et nunc,*
  et semper, et in saecula saeculorum. Amen.

Let us rejoice today, because God has descended from heaven and for our sake on Earth *A child is born to us* whom the prophets long ago foretold *and a son is given to us.* We have known that now he has come from the Father into the world, *upon his shoulder dominion rests,* power and royal authority are in his hand, *and his name will be called* wonderful counselor, mighty god, prince of peace, *angel of good counsel.* Sing to the Lord a new song, "eia," say Sir, "eia." *Sing to the Lord a new song for he has done wonders.* Let the Father be glorified with his only-begotten Son, *Glory be to the Father and to the Son and to the Holy Spirit, as it was in the beginning, is now, and ever shall be. Amen.*

Introit with tropes. After Paris, Bibliothèque Nationale, fonds latin MS 887, fols. 9v–10r. CORPUS TROPORUM, I.1, p. 319

---

genres that modern writers lump together as tropes is a major attraction to scholars; for once the basic Gregorian chant repertoire was completed, these pieces offered a major new arena for medieval creativity.

BIBLIOGRAPHY

General. Manuscript tropers and prosers are cataloged in Heinrich Husmann, *Tropen- und Sequenzenhandschriften* (1964). For facsimiles and editions of specific manuscripts see Andrew Hughes, *Medieval Music: The Sixth Liberal Art,* rev. ed. (1980), 103–104, with further bibliography on 104–110, 278–279. Many trope texts are now being published in the series *Corpus troporum* (1976–). An older edition is Clemens Blume, ed., *Tropen zum Proprium Missarum,* in *Analecta hymnica medii aevi,* 49 (1906).

Sequentia. Henry Marriott Bannister, *Anglo-French Sequelae,* Anselm Hughes, ed. (1934, repr. 1966); Klaus Heinrich Kohrs, *Die aparallelen Sequenzen: Repertoire, liturgische Ordnung, musikalischer Stil* (1978).

Prosa. Richard Crocker, *The Early Medieval Sequence* (1977); Margot E. Fassler, "Who Was Adam of St. Victor? The Evidence of the Sequence Manuscripts," in *Journal of the American Musicological Society,* 37 (1984); Wolfram von den Steinen, *Notker der Dichter und seine geistige Welt,* 2 vols. (1948); Kees Vellekoop, *Dies irae dies illa: Studien zur Frühgeschichte einer Sequenz* (1978).

Many prosa texts have been edited in the following collections: *Analecta hymnica medii aevi,* 7–10, 34, 37, 39, 40, 42, 44, 53–55 (1886–1922); for an index see Max Lütolf, ed., *Analecta hymnica medii aevi: Register,* 3 vols. (1978); and Eugène Misset and W. H. James

Weale, eds., *Thesauris hymnologicis hactenus editis supplementum amplissimum . . . ,* 2 vols. (1888–1892).

Prosula. Olof Marcuson, "Comment a-t-on chanté les prosules?" in *Revue de musicologie,* 65 (1970); Joseph Smits van Waesberghe, "Zur ursprünglichen Vortragsweise der Prosulen, Sequenzen und Organa," in *Diapason: De omnibus. Ausgewählte Aufsätze von Joseph Smits van Waesberghe, Festgabe zu seinem 75. Geburtstag* (1976); Ruth Steiner, "Prosula," in *The New Grove Dictionary of Music and Musicians* (1980), XV.

Farsa. Michel Huglo, "Farse," *ibid.,* VI.

Tropus. Ruth Steiner, "Trope," *ibid.,* XIX; Günther Weiss, *Introitus-Tropen,* I: *Das Repertoire der südfranzösischen Tropare des 10. und 11. Jahrhunderts,* in *Monumenta monodica medii aevi,* III (1970).

PETER JEFFERY

[See also **Adam of St. Victor; Ambrosian Chant; Farcing; Gradual; Gregorian Chant; Introit; Jubilus; Mass, Liturgy of the; Melisma; Notker Balbulus; Offertory; Sequence (Prosa); Sequence, Late.**]

TROTA AND TROTULA. Trota is the name of a woman physician who practiced at Salerno in the twelfth century; *Trotula* is the name given in the Middle Ages to a collection of treatises dealing with women's medicine and beauty care, and apparently by extension to their supposed author.

Almost nothing is known of Trota except that she wrote a handbook of general medical care, or *Practica.* This work was excerpted in a Salernitan compendium called *De aegritudinum curatione,* which was formerly preserved in the Codex Salernitanus in Breslau (the modern Wrocław). The Codex Salernitanus is now apparently lost. Excerpts also appear in another Salernitan collection made around 1200 and now in Madrid.

Compared to the academic medicine of most Salernitan authors, that advocated by Trota seems to have been the medicine of an empirical practitioner with little interest in theory. For instance, though Salernitan physicians normally recommended bleeding for such disorders as excessive menstruation, Trota did not prescribe phlebotomy for any gynecological condition. In her own day she achieved a reputation equivalent to that of a master.

Trota's *Practica* dropped from attention and was apparently not copied in the later Middle Ages. Instead, three treatises that first appeared in manuscript about 1200 circulated under the name of Trotula, which seems to have been a diminutive or adjectival form of Trota. There is, however, no compelling evidence to show that she wrote any of them. The most common, beginning *Cum auctor,* was often known as the *Trotula maior;* it concentrates on gynecology and obstetrics. A second treatise, beginning *Ut de curis,* deals largely with women's medicine but also gives some advice on cosmetics and beauty aids. A third, called *De ornatu,* deals, as its name suggests, with cosmetics and care of the body. These latter two treatises were often combined as the *Trotula minor.* In other manuscripts all three texts were run together without a break. More than 100 manuscripts containing one or more of these treatises have been identified, making them the most popular gynecological texts of the later Middle Ages.

One or more of the three texts were translated into Latin verse and into Irish, English, French (both verse and prose), German, Flemish, and Catalan.

In 1544 a physician from Hagenau named Georg Kraut rearranged the material from the three treatises attributed to Trotula and published it at Strassburg as one unified work, which he called *De passionibus mulierum* (On the diseases of women). This factitious work was pirated by Paulus Manutius of the Aldine Press in 1547 and was then frequently reprinted throughout the sixteenth and seventeenth centuries and as late as 1778.

Unlike Trota's *Practica,* the three treatises attributed to Trotula recommend remedies and practices similar to those of male Salernitan physicians who followed Constantine the African. It seems likely that all three of these texts were written by men, and in one case it is clear, for *De ornatu* in its original form as a separate treatise has a prologue in which a male writer declares that he compiled the work because women had often asked him for advice. Nevertheless, their popularity in the Middle Ages was enhanced because they were thought to be by a woman, and such authors as Rutebeuf and Chaucer heralded the name of Trotula. In modern times controversy over the identity of Trotula and the authenticity of the writings attributed to her has been intense.

BIBLIOGRAPHY

For material from the *Practica* of Trota, see Konrad Hiersemann, *Die Abschnitte aus der Practica des Trottus in der Salernitanischen Sammelschrift "De aegritudinum curatione"* (1922); Madrid, Biblioteca de la Universidad, Complutense MS. 119 (formerly 116-Z-31), fols. 40v–44v.

On Trotula and the texts attributed to her, see John F. Benton, "Trotula, Women's Problems, and the Professionalization of Medicine in the Middle Ages," in *Bulletin of the History of Medicine,* 59 (1985), which reviews the earlier literature. Most of Kraut's frequently printed reworking of the Latin text has been translated into English by Elizabeth Mason-Hohl as *The Diseases of Women, by Trotula of Salerno* (1940).

JOHN F. BENTON

[See also **Constantine the African; Hildegard of Bingen, St.; Medicine, History of; Medicine, Schools of.**]

TROUBADOUR, TROUVÈRE. Both troubadours and trouvères were composers of lyric songs in strophic form. The former composed in Old Occitan (Old Provençal), while the latter used Old French. Their songs were destined to be sung, but there is not much information about the conditions of public performance. Usually the same person composed both words and music; but the composers were not usually the performers (jongleurs). The most typical and productive period for the troubadours was about 1150–1200, while the most illustrious of the trouvères belong to the thirteenth century. The songs of both groups of poet-composers have been preserved in various manuscripts (chansonniers), most of which are now in public libraries such as the Bibliothèque Nationale in Paris, the Vatican Library, and the Bodleian. Many of the songs have been published (even several times) in critical editions of the various poets and in anthologies, often with facing-page translations into various modern languages.

While there is a strong resemblance between the two corpora of songs, they may conveniently be treated separately.

THE TROUBADOURS

The main characteristics of the troubadour song are already discernible in the poems of William VII, count of Poitiers, who was also Duke William IX of Aquitaine (r. 1086–1127). He is the earliest troubadour whose poems have survived, and he may actually have been the first.

The other poets from the first half of the twelfth century are sometimes seen as a second generation following William: Jaufré Rudel, Cercamon, Marcabru, and Bernart Marti are the principal poets of this group. They are followed in the second half of the twelfth century by many other poets, including most of the practitioners of the Old Occitan love song: Raimbaut d'Aurenga, Bernart de Ventadorn, Peire d'Alvernha, Giraut de Bornelh, Peire Vidal, Peirol, and, closer to the end of the century, Arnaut Daniel, Folquet de Marseilles, Raimbaut de Vaqueiras, and the Monk of Montaudon. Of those who wrote during or after the Albigensian Crusade (1209–1229), to be noted are Aimeric de Péguilhan, Peire Cardenal, Aimeric de Belenoi, Guilhem de Montanhagol and Guiraut Riquier in Occitania itself, and several poets of Italian origin who used Old Occitan as their poetic medium: Lanfranco Cigala, Bonifacio Calvo, and Sordello. In Catalonia, several poets, such as Guilhem de Berguedan and Cerveri de Girona, chose Occitan as their poetic language. Patrons of the poets included the great nobles of the Midi: the counts of Toulouse, Count Barral of Marseilles, and Viscountess Ermengarde of Narbonne. Foreign patrons included Boniface of Montferrat in Italy, Alfonso II and Pedro II of Aragon, and Eleanor of Aquitaine, who, on becoming successively queen of France and queen of England, took Occitan poets and poetry into the courts of those countries. A few poems by women survive, and the names of several poetesses, such as the Comtessa de Dia and Castelloza, are known to us.

The form of troubadour poems varies remarkably little from the earliest productions to the latest. Composed of short lines, predominantly seven, eight, or ten syllables long, the songs rarely exceed sixty lines in length. Each song is made up of stanzas, the favorite length of which is eight lines, and each stanza either reproduces an unvarying rhyme scheme such as *a b a b c c d d* or diverges in regular ways from the rhyme matrix of the first stanza. In many poems the sounds of the rhymes (and not merely their order) are repeated from stanza to stanza (*coblas unissonans*). Thus, in a poem having six eight-line stanzas with the rhyme scheme *a b a b c d d c*, the poet would need twelve words with the rhyme sound of *a*, twelve with the sound of *b*, and so on. Sometimes the sound of the rhyme was changed after every second stanza (*coblas doblas*). One or two short stanzas or envois (*tornadas*), reproducing the rhyme scheme and sounds of about the second half of the last full stanza, often closed the poem.

Perhaps because of the great similarity of form among the stanzas, their order was subject to change, and the manuscript tradition is rarely unanimous about the order of the stanzas except the first and the *tornada*. However, various devices, perhaps mnemonic, such as the repetition of a word from the last line of one stanza in the first line of the next stanza (*coblas capfinidas*) could be used to fix the order of stanzas. In some poems the same refrain word appears in each stanza at the same place in the stanza or at a predictably changing place. The culmination of these tendencies is found in the sestina of Arnaut Daniel, where the words ending the lines of the first six-line stanza appear in a different but predictable order at the ends of the lines of each succeeding stanza. The lines do not rhyme with each other within the stanza. The troubadours do mix lines of unequal length in a stanza; they use both masculine and feminine rhymes, although their alternation is not de rigueur; and they do use recurring interior rhymes that make it hard to decide just how the division into lines is to be made.

The often used vocabulary of the troubadours reflects their preoccupations. By far the commonest noun is *amor*, followed by *cor(s)*, *domna*, *joy*, *pretz*, and *Dieu*. The meanings of all these words are not completely clear. *Cor(s)*, for example, might mean "heart" or "body," suggesting sentimental or physical love, respectively. *Joy* can also suggest sentimental or physical pleasure, and the correct interpretation of this word has probably been debated more than that of any other in the troubadour vocabulary. *Pretz*, difficult to translate into English, seems to suggest "perceived worth, reputation," while its counterpart, *valor*, suggests more the "intrinsic (even if unperceived) worth" of a person. Other important and frequently occurring words include *merce, mal, ben,* and *semblan.* Other nouns whose referents are sometimes held to be central to *fin'amors* (*mesura, cortesia, joven*) are actually rather rare. However, the frequently used vocabulary of troubadour songs is so pervasive and so cohesive that the central issues of the poetry are always expressed in much the same terms. Each word in the vocabulary implies all the others and is definable only in terms of all the others.

The great mass of the troubadours' songs use a vocabulary of a remarkable homogeneity; some poets, however, cultivate a style using rare words, especially at the rhyme (*trobar ric*). In the works of a few poets, this formal tendency is accompanied by deliberate hermeticism (*trobar clus*) that makes it likely that at least some of their poems were not readily understood even by their contemporaries. Most poets, however, composed in the easy, transparent style (*trobar leu* or *trobar plan*). A few remarks and arguments within the poetic corpus show that the choice of style was deliberate and was discussed by the poets themselves.

Occitan poetry was meant to be sung, and the troubadour who composed the text usually composed the melody as well. The manuscripts containing the approximately 250 extant melodies indicate (except in a very few cases) only the pitch of the notes and not their rhythm. The ambiguous notation of the melodies has allowed some scholars to insist that the songs were sung according to one or another of the rhythmic modes, and in some modern editions the songs are transcribed according to this principle. Other scholars claim that the performance of the songs was more like a free declamation, where the units were not feet or bars but whole lines. Since Old Occitan was most likely not word-stressed (like modern English or German) but group-stressed (like modern French), the modal theory requires the performer to stress rhythmically many unstressed syllables and not to stress certain stressed syllables. The declamatory theory seemingly contradicts fewer of the observed facts as contained in the manuscripts. The debate between the theories is not, however, by any means ended.

The poet was expected to compose a new melody for each song, but the melodies are not sophisticated and are even quite conventional, presenting less interest to musicologists than the texts do to literary scholars.

A metrical analysis of the surviving corpus of troubadour poems (2,542 pieces, according to István Frank) suggests the prevalence of certain patterns. Thus a listener hearing a poem for the first time could probably have expected (1) that the rhyme scheme, and probably the rhyme sounds, of the first stanza of eight lines would be repeated in the succeeding four or five stanzas of the song (which would end predictably with a *tornada*), and (2) that the meanings of the words would be pretty clear. The song would have a new melody, whose structure would follow fairly closely the metrical structure of the words.

The listener would also have some expectations about the subject of the song. Almost the only subject of the *canso* (song), the dominant genre of the extant corpus, is (courtly) love. While there are topoi in the Occitan lyric, such as the mention of the season of the year or of the poet's intention to write a song in the first stanza, and some sort of apostrophe and the use of an identifiable proper name or a pseudonym (*senhal*) in the *tornada*, the poet is generally free to develop his material at will. The *cansos* of the troubadours are written in the first-person singular, for the poet is himself the lover and his poem ostensibly presents his own situation and feelings. Although critics have sometimes remarked on the sincerity of tone of certain troubadours, it is generally impossible to determine whether a given song was really based on the poet's current experience. Rather, the similarity of the situations and attitudes depicted tends to suggest that the *canso* is a stylized genre and not a sincere expression of a particular individual's emotions, although those emotions may well have been felt, at some time, by any or all of the poets. Attempts to write biographies of the poets by arranging their extant poems in some coherent order are as unsatisfactory today as they were in the thirteenth-century biographies (*vidas*) of the poets.

Written many years after most of the poets had died, the *vidas* rely mostly on evidence in the poems themselves. They are not considered authoritative by modern scholars, although it is admitted that they may also have been based partly on biographical material passed down orally by contemporaries. Today the *vidas* are studied more as examples of early short narratives than as background material for the troubadours.

A troubadour *canso* presents the poet's feelings at a given moment rather than relating a change through time. A temporal perspective is introduced by the poet's consideration of how he reached his present position and how he foresees the future. The whole discussion centers on the relationship between the poet-lover and his lady (*domna*). Typically this relationship begins with the poet's unreciprocated passion for some lady he has seen. Indeed, she is at first unaware of his passion. This (for the poet) painful emotion is the subject of many poems; it is said to be all-absorbing, powerful, ineluctable, and controlling. But the poet does not seek to rid himself of his pain (*mal, dolor*), for he knows it can be turned to joy (*joy*) if the lady comes to reciprocate his feelings and actions. He therefore resolves to try to win her love by bringing his case before her. The poet's *joy* is sometimes referred to in physical, erotic terms.

The desirable qualities that the poet attributes to himself are those of the good feudal vassal: fidelity, uncomplaining service, long-suffering and exclusive devotion. Apart from this principal metaphor of the poet/lover as feudal vassal, the *canso* is poor in images (metaphors and similes). While the lady is loved (at least at first) for her physical beauty, the lover's claims to her love are all moral qualities. He hopes for success in the future, although nothing assures him of it; and he fears that any past success or encouragement may be illusory. It is very clearly the lady who is in control of the situation: the poet is not in a position to demand anything. He has no rights; his progress does not depend on himself. Like a sinner seeking grace, he cannot earn his reward. He can only hope for it and request it; if it comes at all, it will only be through an act of pity (*merce*) on the lady's part. It is this subordination of the lover to his all-powerful *domna* that constitutes the great originality of *fin'amors* as expounded in the troubadour lyrics and that is subsequently an element of all manifestations of what is sometimes called "courtly love."

A great many troubadour songs discuss the early stages of the love relationship and often do not progress beyond it. Some, however, suggest that the lady may eventually reward or at least encourage her suppliant lover. From the status of unknown admirer, he may proceed to become an authorized suitor or even a successful lover (*drut*). Variations in the content of the poems of individual troubadours depend on their attitude toward their lady, their progress toward *joy*, their degree of hope or despair. The poet may be typically or successively timid, hopeful, despairing, ironical, or (rarely) presumptuous. He may even leave or threaten to leave one lady for another, return to an abandoned lady

with bowed head. Or he may attempt moral blackmail, claiming that he is dying of love—surely the lady would not want his death on her conscience. The marital status of the lady is not made clear. Although it is often assumed that she is married, a husband is rarely mentioned. The lover's real enemies, called the *lauzengiers,* are his rivals or other persons interested in preventing his success by influencing his lady against him or by revealing his love to all.

In tone, many troubadour poems are argumentative. They try to persuade, to make a case for the poet/lover. While the poems do address the lady directly in the "you" form, most of the textual material discusses her in the third person: since the lady's identity is kept secret, the poet cannot address her publicly. Thus, even if she is referred to in the third person, the lady is an intended listener. The poet speaks to others only in order to elicit sympathy for his plight or to offer them an example of the poet's art. Occasionally the poet curses the *lauzengiers.*

There is a variation on the model of the *domna* as suzerain and the poet as vassal, with the lady's love (or her body?) as a kind of fief. The poets sometimes see *Amor* (feminine in Old Occitan and Old French) as suzerain (lady), to whom the poet is a vassal. In this case, the lady represents the fief. The presentation of Amor personified as a powerful suzerain anticipates the allegorical narratives of the thirteenth century and also allows the poet to hold someone other than the perfect lady responsible for his misery.

It has been asserted that troubadour poems all sound alike—the subject matter *is* rather predictable. However, the audience—refined, restricted, and knowledgeable—was alert and responsive to subtle variations in expression. The form of the *canso*, then, was as an invention within set rules known to and respected by both poet and audience. The medieval listener's (and also the modern reader's) enjoyment and appreciation of the songs, therefore, requires a familiarity with the style and content of the poems—a kind of apprenticeship.

The other genres of troubadour poetry are distinguished from the *canso* by their form, by their subject matter, or by both. The *sirventes* has the same form as the *canso* but treats subjects other than love, such as praise, political or moral comment, and personal attacks on others. A subgenre of the *sirventes* is the *planh*, a lament for a dead lord. In the genre of the *tenso*, two or more authors debate a topic, often a point of courtly casuistry, usually in successive stanzas. The *partimen* is similar to the *tenso*. The subject for debate is presented as a kind of challenge in the first stanza. The second author then chooses the side he prefers to defend, leaving the other side to the challenger. Again the subject was often love. A formal "anti-*canso*" exists in the *descort*, in which the succeeding stanzas use a different metrical system or even a different language, supposedly to express the author's bewilderment in love. Of a more popular type are the *pastourelle*, the *alba*, and the various dance songs. In the first of these a knight attempts to seduce a shepherdess; in the second, the dawn song, the lovers regret that they must part at daybreak; and in the dance song (*balada, dansa*) a refrain appears after each stanza, and the subject is often an unhappy marriage (*chanson de malmariée*).

For many years the most debated topic in troubadour studies was that of its origins. Various theories were proposed: the *canso* was seen as inspired by classical models, by medieval Latin poetry, by indigenous popular poetry, and by the *zajal* of Muslim Spain. Most scholars today adopt a cautiously eclectic explanation of the origin of Occitan lyric poetry, and the debate over origins has been replaced by an exploration of the aesthetic principles of the *canso* and of the relationship of the text to the accompanying melody. Of more interest than the possible origins of troubadour songs is the way that the texts and melodies were imitated in other countries: in Catalonia, Castile, Galicia-Portugal, northern France, Italy, Sicily, and even Germany and England. In addition, the notion of *fin'amors*, with its potential dynamism, was soon exploited, especially in northern France, in the *roman courtois* and later in the allegorical tradition leading to the *Roman de la Rose*. The echoes of *fin'amors* may still be heard in many of the songs composed today.

THE TROUVÈRES

More studies have been devoted to the troubadours than to the trouvères, the northern French poets of the twelfth and thirteenth centuries, perhaps because the latter are seen as the imitators and followers of the former. What is true of the troubadours, therefore, may also be said of the trouvères. Nevertheless there are distinctions: the trouvères composed in Old French, and their social institutions were somewhat different from those of their southern neighbors. Consequently, some minor but very real differences between the two corpora existed already from the first. Furthermore, the poetic traditions developed separately, especially in the thirteenth century.

Among the first to compose songs on the model of the *canso* in Old French was Chrétien de Troyes, better known for his Arthurian romances. He was soon joined by such poets as Gace Brulé, Blondel de Nesle, the Châtelain de Coucy, and Conon de Béthune in the twelfth century, and Thibaut IV, count of Champagne (king of Navarre from 1234), Guiot of Dijon, and Gautier d'Épinal in the early thirteenth century. By that time certain poets had formed *confréries* or *puys* (poetic guilds) that held competitions. The best-known of these is the Puy d'Arras, among whose members were Audefroy le Bastart, Guillasume le Vinier, Andrieu Contredit, and Adam de la Halle. Such a *confrérie* was not formed in Occitania until the fourteenth century, after the end of the troubadour period.

The trouvères wrote chansons as the troubadours had written *cansos*, as well as examples of the *serventois*, *tenson*, and *jeu-parti*. In these aristocratic genres they followed their Occitan models closely. For the reader who knows the troubadour *corpus*, the trouvère chansons sound quite familiar. Certain differences nonetheless appear.

In form the Old French chanson is more rarely *unissonans* than is the *canso*, and the use of a refrain becomes more and more frequent as the thirteenth century progresses. The repetition of certain lines eventually leads to the creation of fixed forms such as the rondeau and the virelai. The Old French vocabulary differed from the Old Occitan. Some of the cognate terms, for instance, may designate different notions in the two languages (as in the case of the words *senhor/seigneur*, since feudalism in northern France was not what it was in Occitania). And certain words whose sonorities allow their exploitation in pairs in Old Occitan (such as *sai e lai*) do not invite such exploitation in Old French (*ci et là*). A systematic comparison of the two poetic languages remains to be made. The troubadour hermetic *trobar clus* is not much imitated in the northern lyric.

The chanson accentuates the misery of the lover and the influence of the *losengiers*, who are likened to bad poets and bad lovers (bad because insincere). The trouvères invent more, and more personal, comparisons than do the troubadours. The physical nature of the poet's hoped-for reward is hardly ever mentioned, and the lover seems much more subjugated and servile than in the *canso*.

In the less aristocratic genres, the Old French lyric is not dependent on Occitan models, and exhibits several genres totally lacking in the Midi. In particular may be noted the numerous songs in which the lyric "I" voice is that of a woman (*chanson de malmariée*) and the more frequent occurrence of narrative in the poems. In northern France there is a greater corpus of parodic or burlesque songs (*sottes chansons*) and nonsense songs (*fatrasies*). In the popular genres the poems are more frequently anonymous.

BIBLIOGRAPHY

Selected anthologies. Emmanuèle Baumgartner and Françoise Ferrand, *Poèmes d'amour des XIIe et XIIIe siècles* (1983); Pierre Bec, ed. and trans., *Anthologie des troubadours* (1979); Frederick Goldin, ed. and trans., *Lyrics of the Troubadours and Trouvères* (1973); Raymond T. Hill and Thomas G. Bergin, *Anthology of the Provençal Troubadours*, 2 vols., 2nd ed. (1973); Alan R. Press, *Anthology of Troubadour Lyric Poetry* (1971); Samuel N. Rosenberg and Hans Tischler, *Chanter m'estuet: Songs of the Trouvères* (1981).

Studies. Pierre Bec, *La lyrique française au moyen âge XIIe–XIIIe siècles*, 2 vols. (1977–1978); Frank M. Chambers, *An Introduction to Old Provençal Versification* (1985); Glynis M. Cropp, *Le vocabulaire courtois des troubadours de l'époque classique* (1975); Roger Dragonetti, *La technique poétique des trouvères dans la chanson courtoise* (1960, repr. 1979); István Frank, *Répertoire métrique de la poésie des troubadours*, 2 vols. (1953–1957, repr. 1971); Alfred Jeanroy, *La poésie lyrique des troubadours*, 2 vols. (1934, repr. 1 vol. 1973); Moshé Lazar, *Amour courtois et "fin'amors" dans la littérature du XIIe siècle* (1964); Robert A. Taylor, *La littérature occitane du moyen âge: Bibliographie sélective et critique* (1977); Hendrik Van der Werf, *The Chansons of the Troubadours and Trouvères: A Study of the Melodies and Their Relation to the Poems* (1972); idem and Gerald A. Bond, *The Extant Troubadour Melodies* (1984); Paul Zumthor, *Essai de poétique médiévale* (1972).

F. R. P. AKEHURST

[See also **Adam de la Halle; Alba; Anglo-Norman Literature; Arnaut Daniel; Bernart de Ventadorn; Blondel de Nesle; Canso; Cercamon; Chansonnier; Chansons de Malmarieé; Chrétien de Troyes; Châtelain de Coucy; Comtessa de Dia; Conon de Béthune; Courtly Love; Descort; Envoi; Folquet de Marseilles; French Language; French Literature; Gace Brulé; Giraut de Bornelh; Guiraut Riquier; Jaufré Rudel; Jeu-Parti; Joglar/Jongleur; Marcabru; Partimen; Pastourelle; Peire Cardenal;**

The death of Hector. Miniature from a manuscript of Benoît de Sainte-Maure's *Roman de Troie*, 1264. COLLECTION OF 'HUIS BERGH' AT 'S-HEERENBERG, NETHERLANDS.

Peire d'Alvernha; Peire Vidal; Provençal Language; Provençal Literature; Raimbaut d'Aurenga; Raimbaut de Vaqueiras; Rondeau; Sirventes; Thibaut de Champagne; Tornada; Trobairitz; Vidas; Virelai; William IX of Aquitaine.]

TROY STORY. The story of Troy, one of the most enduring subject matters in world literature, enjoyed great popularity in the Middle Ages. One of the earliest medieval texts dealing with the destruction of Troy is the eleventh-century *De excidio Troiae*, written in Latin by Bernard of Fleury. Another well-known text is the *Ylias* (*ca.* 1152) of Simon Chèvre de Or, or Aurea Capra.

But the Trojan story became most widely known through the work of Benoît de Sainte-Maure. He was a clerk from the region around Tours who worked at the court of King Henry II of England, to whose wife, Eleanor of Aquitaine, he dedicated his

Roman de Troie. Written in Old French around 1165, this work comprises more than 30,000 octosyllabic verses and is thus the longest of the romances of this period. These romances, all written probably in the 1150's and 1160's, deal with classical subjects such as the Seven Against Thebes or the Story of Aeneas and are based on Latin authors (the *Roman de Thèbes* derives from Statius' *Thebaid*, the *Roman d'Enéas* from Vergil's *Aeneid*).

Benoît's *Roman de Troie* has as its principal sources two texts by the late classical authors Dares and Dictys. Dating from the fifth and fourth centuries A.D. respectively, their works were, in the Middle Ages, believed to be eyewitness accounts of the events at Troy. Dares in his *De excidio Troiae historia* claims to have fought on the Greek side, whereas Dictys in his *Ephemeris belli Troiani* presents himself as an observer in Troy. According to Benoît they fought by day and wrote at night! Homer's *Iliad* was not used as a source: for Benoît it was discredited by the simple fact that Homer lived centuries after the destruction of Troy and would thus have been incapable of writing the truth about the events. It should be added that Benoît knew no Greek and had no direct access to Homer's work. Benoît also used other Latin sources, such as Ovid's *Metamorphoses,* Hygin's *Fabulae,* and Servius' commentary on Vergil.

Benoît's romance, unlike Homer's *Iliad,* gives a chronological account of all the events surrounding the fall of Troy. He begins with the expedition of the Argonauts and ends with the death of Ulysses many years after the destruction of Troy.

The prologue of the *Roman de Troie* is highly interesting; it reveals the writer's philosophy concerning his task, an expression of what might be called twelfth-century humanism. The importance of learning from the ancients is stressed as well as the role of the medieval poet in the transmission of this learning. In order to illustrate the way by which ancient knowledge has reached France Benoît invents a story in which the geographical transmission of the text (Greece–Rome–France) is paralleled by the linguistic transformations from Greek to Latin to Old French.

The story proper begins with Jason and his quest for the Golden Fleece. Medea aids him in this enterprise, and their love is described in detail. Monologues and dialogues provide some psychological insight into the lovers' minds. Medea's vengeance for Jason's eventual treachery, however, is given scant treatment ("n'en dirai plus," says Benoît [v. 2043], and thus shows that at all times he has the right to be selective).

The first destruction of Troy (Ylion) is presented as a direct result of the refusal of Laomedon (who is at that time king of Troy) to let Jason and the Argonauts land on his territory. During this first fall of Troy, Priam's sister Esiona is abducted to Greece. Priam founds a new Troy, and one of his first actions is to try to recover Esiona. A diplomatic mission to Greece ends with the rape of Helen.

The Greeks quickly assemble a gigantic army and under the leadership of Agamemnon lay siege to Troy. All the great heroes and heroines are portrayed at the beginning of the war: Agamemnon, Menelaus, Achilles, Patroclus, the two Aiases (Ajaxes), Ulysses, Diomedes, and many others on the Greek side, as well as Priam, Hector, Deiphobos, Troilus, Paris, Aeneas, Hecuba, Cassandra, and others on the Trojan side.

There follows the long treatment of the many battles and ruses which finally lead to the fall of Troy. We then follow several of the Greek heroes on their journeys home and witness Ulysses' death, caused by his (and Circe's) son, Telegonus.

In the course of the story, Benoît dazzles his audience with his knowledge of history, cosmology, and geography (he maps out the entire world in order to locate the realm of the Amazons). He also takes pleasure in describing marvelous works of art such as the "Chambre de Beautés," where Hector's embalmed body is displayed. The love episodes also play an important role, and much attention is given to the sentiments of Medea and Jason, Troilus and Briseis, Diomedes and the same Briseis (episodes invented by Benoît), and Achilles and Polyxena.

Benoît's interest in psychology becomes apparent here. He insists on the purely human motives determining the actions in his romance. The role of the gods, all-important in the Greek tradition, is of little significance here.

As in the other romances of antiquity, the framework of the action is medieval. Such appurtenances as clothes, arms and armor, buildings, titles (there are priests and bishops in the romance), and so on, are clearly contemporary to Benoît. The council and battle scenes also reflect twelfth-century conventions.

Benoît's work was extremely successful. An extraordinarily large number of manuscripts (twenty-seven complete manuscripts and eleven fragments) have survived to this day, a sign that the text was very popular and hence recopied many times. Benoît was one of the first authors writing in French to popularize the idea of Trojan origins. The first mention of French Trojan origins goes back to Fredegarius' seventh-century Latin chronicle, but in later centuries most European nations laid claim to Trojan ancestors, often in order to legitimize new dynasties. Vernacular texts recounted both the fall of Troy and the destinies of Trojan survivors (such as Aeneas, in the twelfth-century translation of Vergil's *Aeneid,* the *Roman d'Enéas*) and their progeny (such as Aeneas' great-grandson Brutus, the supposed ancestor of the Britons, in Wace's *Roman de Brut* [1155]). Modeled on Aeneas' founding of Rome, many of these popular stories on antique subjects became parts of European foundation myths.

Benoît's *Roman de Troie,* one of the most detailed and entertaining of these texts, therefore gave rise to many reworkings and translations. In the thirteenth century Benoît's verse romance was transformed into prose and integrated into a universal history, which covered the periods from the creation of earth to Caesar. By the end of the thirteenth century Benoît's romance was translated into Latin by Guido delle Colonne as the *Historia destructionis Troiae.* This text in turn became very influential. It was translated several times into Italian (for example, by Filippo Ceffi in 1324) and into Spanish (for example, the *Crónica troyana* of Pero López de Ayala). A mystery play by Jacques Milet (*La destruction de Troye la Grant*) and Raoul Lefevre's *Recueil des Troyennes histoires* (translated into English by William Caxton about 1474), both dating from the fifteenth century, were also based on Guido's text. John Lydgate as well as Boccaccio were inspired by Guido's *Historia,* and via Chaucer (*Troilus and Criseyde, ca.* 1385) it reached Shakespeare (*Troilus and Cressida,* 1602).

Of the Middle High German versions of Benoît's romance the earliest is that of Herbort von Fritzlar at the beginning of the thirteenth century. It was followed by Konrad von Würzburg's immense compilation of over 40,000 verses left incomplete by his death in 1287 and the 30,000 verses of the Pseudo-Wolfram von Eschenbach (end of the fourteenth/beginning of the fifteenth century). A prose redaction, derived from Konrad, was written by Heinrich von Braunschweig, and another prose version appears in the *World Chronicle* by Rudolf von Ems (*d.* 1254).

Other medieval versions of the Troy story derive not from Benoît's text but directly from Dares. Near the end of the twelfth century Joseph of Exeter wrote his *De bello trojano,* and Albert von Stade completed his *Troilus* in 1249. Translators of Dares' text into Old French include the anonymous author of the *Histoire ancienne jusqu'à César* (1208–1213), Jean de Flixecourt (1262), and Jofroi de Waterford (1270–1300).

A Nordic version of Dares can be found in the *Trójumanna saga* (shortly before 1263).

It is impossible to list in this space all medieval versions of the Troy story. Extensive lists appear in Wilhelm Greif's work and Léopold Constans' edition of Benoît's *Roman de Troie,* VI (1912).

BIBLIOGRAPHY

The text of Benoît's work, with notes and commentary, appears in Léopold Constans, ed., *Le roman de Troie,* 6 vols. (1904–1912, repr. 1968). Studies include C. David Benson, *The History of Troy in Middle English Literature* (1980); Hermann Dunger, *Die Sage vom trojanischen Kriege in den Bearbeitungen des Mittelalters und ihren antiken Quellen* (1869); Edmond Faral, *Recherches sur les sources latines des contes et romans courtois du Moyen Age* (1913); Wilhelm Greif, *Die mittelalterlichen Bearbeitungen der Trojanersage* (1886); Nathaniel E. Griffin, *Dares and Dictys: An Introduction to the Study of Medieval Versions of the Troy Story* (1907); Rudolf Witte, *Der Einfluss von Benoîts "Roman de Troie" auf die altfranzösische Literatur* (1904); B. Woledge, "La légende de Troie et les débuts de la prose française," in *Mélanges . . . Mario Roques,* II (1953), 313–324.

RENATE BLUMENFELD-KOSINSKI

[See also **Benoît de Sainte-Maure; Boccaccio, Giovanni; Chaucer, Geoffrey; Epic, Latin; French Literature; German Literature: Romance; Herbort von Fritzlar; Konrad von Würzburg; Latin Literature; Lydgate, John; Matter of Britain, France, Rome; Spanish Literature: Troy Story; Trójumanna Saga; Vergil in the Middle Ages.**]

TRUCE OF GOD. See **Peace of God.**

TRULLA (Latin, "ladle"; Greek: *chernibon*), a shallow bowl with an elongated handle, derived from a Roman implement found in both secular and sacred contexts. In Christian usage a trulla was paired with a ewer to create a set for handwashing during the Eucharistic rite. The Riha paten of about

577 at Dumbarton Oaks (Washington, D.C.) depicts in relief such a set below the Communion of the Apostles; similar sets also appear in pagan contexts, as illustrated in the Vergilius Romanus (Rome, Vat. lat. 3867, fol. 100v.) of about 500.

BIBLIOGRAPHY
Marlia Mundell Mango, *Silver from Early Byzantium* (1986), 104–107, 165–170.

LESLIE BRUBAKER

[See also **Altar—Altar Apparatus; Paten.**]

TRULLO, COUNCIL OF. See **Councils (Ecumenical).**

TRUMEAU, a stone mullion or pier dividing a doorway into two bays, and serving as a central support for the lintel and tympanum of an arched portal. Trumeaus first appear in Romanesque architecture and are often richly carved (see illustration in vol. 10, p. 497). In Gothic portals the trumeau may be furnished with a projecting base for a statue of the Virgin and Child, Christ, or a saint.

GREGORY WHITTINGTON

[See also **Gothic Architecture; Gothic Art: Sculpture; Romanesque Architecture; Romanesque Art; Tympanum.**]

TSROMI (C^cromi). A stone church dedicated to all saints, located in the Georgian province K^cart^cli. It was built by Stephanos II, who was bestowed with the Byzantine title of hypatos (consul) by the emperor Heraklios shortly after 626, when Byzantine armies took Tbilisi.

Tsromi belongs to the "cross-in-square" type, where the dome is not supported by the lateral walls as in Djvari, but by four freestanding piers in the center of the church. On the west side above the narthex it has a gallery for the accommodation of women. Similar to Syrian and Armenian churches, the semicircular apse does not project but is contained within the rectangular plan of the church. It is emphasized by two triangular niches placed on either side between the apse and the pastophories. The church is somewhat enlivened by sculptures of

stylized plant motifs. The conch (half-dome) is decorated with mosaics depicting two apostles flanking the central figure of Christ, who holds an open scroll with an inscription (John 11:25) alluding to the Resurrection, the only known example of its kind in early Christian apse programs.

BIBLIOGRAPHY
Adriano Alpago-Novello *et al., Art and Architecture in Medieval Georgia* (1982); Georgi Chubinashvili, *Georgische Baukunst*, II (1934); Rusudan Mepisashvili and Vakhtang Tsintsadze, *Arts of Ancient Georgia* (1979).

WACHTANG DJOBADZE

[See also **Church, types of; Georgian Art and Architecture; Pastophory.**]

TUATH. See **Irish Society.**

TUDESCHIS, NICHOLAUS DE. See **Nicolaus de Tudeschis.**

TUDOR ARCH. See **Arch.**

TUDOR, OWEN (Owen ap Meredith ap Tider) (*ca.* 1400–1461), the grandfather of Henry VII, is usually considered the founder of the Tudor dynasty, largely because he was the first of that name to become intimately involved in the affairs of England—and of its royal house.

Owen was probably born at Snowdon, but the details of his life are often lost in a haze of legend and scholarly controversy. As a cousin of Owen Glendower, the Welsh foe of Henry IV, he must have found it difficult to enter royal circles, but enter he did, probably in 1420 as a member of Sir Walter Hungerford's retinue in France. After Henry V died in 1422, Owen came to the favorable attention of his widow, Catherine of Valois, who made him a clerk of her wardrobe. Their relationship blossomed and ultimately resulted in at least four children, two of whom—Edmund and Jasper—are well known to history. Although no marriage ever took place publicly, there is little reason to doubt one's existence: Henry VI never challenged the legitimacy of the offspring, and in 1452 he made his half-brothers Edmund and Jasper earls of Richmond and Pembroke, respectively, an unlikely honor for bastards. For many years, it was thought that a long-lost act of 1427/1428 had prohibited such a marriage. The statute was rediscovered and published in the 1970's, however, making it clear that what was required was merely the king's consent.

After Catherine's death in 1437, Owen experienced varied fortunes. Imprisoned that summer on an uncertain charge, he escaped to northern Wales and was subsequently restored to grace. Thereafter the recipient of various gifts from the king, he proved a loyal Lancastrian, though surely not of a stature to warrant his ultimate fate. The earl of March, soon to become Edward IV, had him beheaded at Hereford immediately after the Lancastrian defeat at Mortimer's Cross in February 1461.

BIBLIOGRAPHY

Sydney Anglo, "The *British History* in Early Tudor Propaganda," in *Bulletin of the John Rylands Library,* **44** (1961); S. B. Chrimes, *Henry VII* (1972), 3–12, 325–326; Ralph A. Griffiths, "Queen Katherine of Valois and a Missing Statute of the Realm," in *Law Quarterly Review,* **93** (1977), *The Reign of King Henry VI* (1981), and *idem* and Roger S. Thomas, *The Making of the Tudor Dynasty* (1985); Thomas Artemus Jones, "Owen Tudor's Marriage," in *Bulletin of the Board of Celtic Studies,* **11** (1943).

CHARLES T. WOOD

[See also **England: 1216–1485; Henry V of England; Henry VI of England; Prophecy, Political: Middle English; Wars of the Roses; Wales.**]

TUGHRIL-BEG. See **Toghrıl-Beg.**

TULUNIDS. The Tulunid dynasty governed Egypt and most of Syria as semi-independent rulers under the overlordship of the Abbasid caliphate between 868 and 905. The first Muslim rulers to make Egypt their power base, the Tulunids managed to limit the tribute they paid to the caliph and kept the bulk of their revenues for local development, most notably a new administrative center near Al-Fusṭāṭ. Eco-

nomic activity in Egypt increased dramatically under the Tulunids, and later Egyptian Arab historians called the Tulunid era a golden age.

Aḥmad ibn Ṭūlūn, the founder of the dynasty, was born in 835 in Samarra, Iraq. The son of a Turkish military slave in the service of the caliph, he received the military training normal for his class, but he also studied theology. After his father died, his mother married the Turkish general Bākbāk. In 868 the Abbasid caliph al-Muᶜtazz (866–869) appointed Bākbāk governor of Egypt. Bākbāk, following a policy established by previous governors, appointed another to act in his place: his stepson Aḥmad ibn Ṭūlūn. The founder of the Tulunid dynasty entered Al-Fusṭāṭ (Cairo), the capital of Egypt, on 15 September 868.

Although Tulunid rule is dated from 868, Aḥmad was technically not governor until 872 nor did he have control over all of Egypt in 868. A critical turning point came when a revolt by the governor of Palestine in 871 was put down by the governor of Syria, Amājūr. At this time, the caliph also called on Ibn Ṭūlūn's aid, and the ruler of Egypt used this pretext to gain access to the Egyptian treasury and to raise his own large army. Modeling his expanded corps on that of Abbasid Iraq, Ibn Ṭūlūn increased the number of his military slaves, particularly Turks for the cavalry and Sub-Saharan Africans for the infantry. Some sources write of a slave army of 24,000 cavalry and 40,000 infantrymen, augmented by 7,000 free mercenaries.

A new administrative center, Al-Qaṭāᵓiᶜ, was built north of Al-Fusṭāṭ. The complex included a large mosque, a palace complex, barracks where troops were housed according to occupation and ethnic origin, and a parade ground. The architecture reflected artistic traditions found in Iraq. Other building activities by Ibn Ṭūlūn included an aqueduct and a hospital.

Aḥmad ibn Ṭūlūn's reputation is also based on his administrative reforms and his ability to increase significantly the tax revenues of Egypt. The most important source of revenue was agriculture. Ibn Ṭūlūn rebuilt the ancient Nilometer (a device for measuring the height of the annual Nile flood) on Rhoda Island outside Al-Fusṭāṭ, which was used to determine tax rates. It has been estimated that his annual income reached 4.3 million dinars. Two examples can illustrate the wealth available to Aḥmad ibn Ṭūlūn: it is estimated that he was annually sending in 2.1 million dinars, as well as other items, to the Abbasid caliphs before 875, when he significantly reduced the tribute; and when he died in 884 the treasury was said to have 10 million dinars. Another major source of income was the manufacture of textiles, especially *tiraz*. (These were honorific robes with inscribed bands that included the caliph's name; often they were embellished with gold and silver thread.)

Egyptian trade grew and economic exchanges with Byzantium continued regardless of political differences. The development of a naval base at Acre owed perhaps as much to Aḥmad ibn Ṭūlūn's economic policies as to his limited military adventures in Syria and southeastern Anatolia. Trade as well as diplomatic activities led to the creation of a department of correspondence (*dīwān al-rasāʾil*).

The political history of the reign of Aḥmad ibn Ṭūlūn is an extremely complex tale of power struggles centering on Samarra, the Abbasid capital. Often these intrigues pitted Aḥmad ibn Ṭūlūn against the caliph's brother, al-Muwaffaq, who exercised supreme power in fact. Fortunately for ibn Ṭūlūn, al-Muwaffaq was never able to turn his full energies or forces against Egypt because of a more serious problem, the Zanj revolt in southern Iraq.

In 878, with the death of the Syrian governor Amājūr, Ibn Ṭūlūn moved into Syria and southeastern Anatolia, establishing his own rule. He then had to return to Egypt to put down the revolt of his son ʿAbbās.

Around this time, Ibn Ṭūlūn began asserting publicly his own independence by adding his name to that of the caliph in the *tiraz* (879) and on the Egyptian coinage (880). He later ordered the name of al-Muwaffaq, the caliph's designated successor, to be cursed in the mosques under his control. The war of words and mutual threats continued between al-Muwaffaq and Aḥmad ibn Ṭūlūn until the latter died in Damascus on 10 May 884.

Khumārawayh, Ibn Ṭūlūn's son (and his designated heir as early as 882), became head of the family's holdings, but without the caliph's formal approval. Al-Muwaffaq, hoping to end Tulunid rule, moved to exploit the new ruler's inexperience. In February/March 885 a battle took place in southern Palestine between the Tulunid forces under Khumārawayh and Abbasid troops under the future caliph al-Muʿtaḍid (892–902). Although both commanders fled, the Tulunid forces eventually won. Khumārawayh reversed this early poor impression of his abilities and became an effective

general. He consolidated Tulunid control over Egypt, Syria, parts of Anatolia, and a few areas east of the Euphrates River.

In 886 Khumārawayh and al-Muwaffaq came to a mutual understanding. The Tulunids ended their slandering of al-Muwaffaq in the Friday sermons and acknowledged Abbasid sovereignty. The Tulunid family was granted the governorship of Egypt and Syria for thirty years. Khumārawayh had control over Friday sermons, the mints, the appointment of judges, and the land tax. The annual tribute is not listed in the sources, but, in an 892 agreement between Khumārawayh and the caliph al-Muʿtaḍid confirming the old treaty, an annual tribute of presumably 300,000 dinars is listed, plus 200,000 for each preceding year of Khumārawayh's rule. Territories east of the Euphrates were returned to Abbasid control.

Although some scholars focus on Khumārawayh's ability to hold such a large territory and to improve his image as a military leader, most writers—medieval and modern—have stressed his frivolous spending habits, mentioning, for example, his royal palace with its painted and carved human representations, his zoo, or his large pool of mercury. The wedding of his daughter Qaṭr al-Nadā to al-Muʿtaḍid was described in the medieval sources as extremely expensive. When Khumārawayh was murdered by one of his servants in 896, these same Arab sources claim that the treasury was empty.

The history of the Tulunids after Khumārawayh is a dreary record of family feuds, murders, civil wars, attacks by external forces, and the eventual capture of Tulunid lands by Abbasid forces in 905. Khumārawayh's son Jaysh was governor for nine months in 896 before he was murdered by the military. His younger brother Hārūn succeeded as governor (896–905), but by 897 there was civil war. In 902 a large Tulunid force sent to Syria to fight the Shiite Qarmatians deserted to the Abbasid army. The last Tulunid, Aḥmad's son Shaybān, governed for only twelve days before Al-Fusṭāṭ was captured by the Abbasid army under Muḥammad ibn Sulaymān in March 905.

The Abbasid general destroyed all of Aḥmad ibn Ṭūlūn's administrative center, Al-Qaṭāʾiʿ, except the mosque, which became the most important mosque of the Muslim community of Al-Fusṭāṭ. Even today it continues to symbolize the power, wealth, and sense of independence associated with Tulunid rule (see illustration at "Islamic Art and Architecture").

BIBLIOGRAPHY

Sources. Ibn al-Athīr, *al-Kāmil fī al-ta'rīkh* (1965–1966); al-Balawī, *Sīrat Aḥmad ibn Ṭūlūn*, M. Kurd ᶜAlī, ed. (1939); Ibn al-Dāya, *Al-Mukāfāh* (1914); Ibn Khallikān, *Wafāyat al-aᶜyān*, Muḥammad M. ᶜAbd al-Ḥamīd, ed. (1948); al-Kindī, *The Governors and Judges of Egypt*, Rhuvon Guest, ed. (1912); al-Maqrīzī, *al-Mawāᶜiz wa al-iᶜtibar fī dikr al-khiṭaṭ wa al-āthār* (ca. 1970); Ibn Saᶜīd, *Fragmente aus dem Mughrib*, K. Vollers, ed., in *Semitistische Studien*, I (1894), and *Kitāb al-Mughrib fī ḥula al-Maghrib*, Knut L. Tallquist, ed. (1899); al-Tabarī, *Ta'rīkh al-rusul wa al-mulūk*, M. J. de Goeje, ed. (n.d.); Ibn Taghrī Birdī, *al-Nujūm al-zāhirah fī mulūk Miṣr wa al-Qāhirah* (1929–1972); al-Yaᶜqūbī, *Historiae*, M. Th. Houtsma, ed. (1883).

Studies. Carl H. Becker, *Beiträge zur Geschichte Ägyptens unter dem Islam*, 2 vols. (1902–1903); Gladys Marie Frantz, "Saving and Investment in Medieval Egypt" (diss., Univ. of Michigan, 1978); H. A. R. Gibb, "Ṭūlūnids," in *Encyclopedia of Islam*, IV (1934); Oleg Grabar, *The Coinage of the Ṭūlūnids* (1957); U. Haarmann, "Khumārawayh," in *Encyclopaedia of Islam*, 2nd ed., V (1986); Zaky M. Hassan, *Les Tulunides* (1933) and "Aḥmad ibn Ṭūlūn," in *Encyclopaedia of Islam*, 2nd ed., I (1960); Sayyidah I. Kāshif and Ḥassan Aḥmad Maḥmūd, *Miṣr fī ᶜaṣr al-Tūlūniyyīn wa al-Ikhshīdiyyīn* (1960); Dominique Sourdel, *Le vizirat ᶜabbāside de 749 à 936*, 2 vols. (1959–1960); Gaston Wiet, *L'Égypte arabe* (1937).

JERE L. BACHARACH

[See also **Abbasids; Anatolia; Cairo; Caliphate; Dinar; Egypt, Islamic; Mints and Money, Islamic; Navies, Islamic; Samarra; Sects, Islamic; Syria; Ṭirāz; Trade, Islamic; Zanj.**]

TUOTILO (Tutilo) (*ca.* 850–913), a monk of St. Gall and a contemporary of Notker Balbulus. Tuotilo's fame as a musican, poet, and artist does not rest entirely on fact. Most importantly, although he was long thought to be the inventor of the trope as a new hymn form, this is no longer considered to be true. Still, he was perhaps the first romantic artist figure in the Middle Ages, and so we should not be surprised that his person has attracted migrating legends and anecdotes.

Our chief source for the Tuotilo legend is Ekkehard IV's *Casus sancti Galli* (History of St. Gall). Here Ekkehard collected not only historical facts but also oral traditions and legends about the monastery and its outstanding figures of the past. In Tuotilo's case, Ekkehard has clearly mixed fact and fiction to produce an exemplary portrait of an artist. Modern research, through a critical use of all the available evidence, has produced a somewhat clearer picture of the historical Tuotilo. This picture continues to emphasize his general significance as an artist.

Ekkehard, who wrote a century after Tuotilo's death, places Tuotilo in the circle of Ratpert and Notker Balbulus, an outstanding group of monks and poets toward the end of the ninth century. In addition to supplying details of Tuotilo's artistic career, Ekkehard also narrates anecdotes that give us a sense of his character. It seems that Tuotilo was a capable man of affairs as well as an artist. According to Ekkehard, he often acted as an agent for St. Gall in the outside world; he was an eloquent speaker and had a fluent command of at least two languages. He also seems to have possessed considerable personal courage. Ekkehard tells us that Tuotilo was once set upon by highwaymen, and that he chased them away.

Modern research supports Ekkehard's contention that Tuotilo was an outstanding artist and craftsman. He may also have been a capable builder. In St. Gall, Tuotilo is said to have worked on a cross made of gems and to have gilded the altar of the Virgin Mary and the pulpit. He seems to have been particularly good at ivory carving; charming pieces ascribed to him survive to this day.

Tuotilo's relationship to tropes rests on very uncertain ground, although it seems certain he must have composed some music in this form. Ekkehard provides us with a list of Tuotilo's tropes. One, *Viri Galilei,* is recorded in musical manuscripts with neumes, with no text added. There has been much confusion over another of his tropes, *Omnipotens genitor fons,* which is not identical with the one so popular in England. His *Hodie cantandus* and *Omnium virtutum gemmis* belong to the liturgy of the Christmas season; the text of *Hodie cantandus* points to the dramatic character of many early tropes. Two other tropes listed by Ekkehard are found in musical manuscripts: *Gaudete et cantate* and *Quoniam Dominus Jesus.*

For Léon Gautier, Tuotilo was the probable inventor of the trope. This theory was later proved wrong, and recently Richard Crocker has questioned the utility of viewing tropes as a uniform genre.

For some other scholars, such as Karl Young, Tuotilo was probably the poet of the most famous Easter trope, *Quem quaeritis,* which has commonly and praises him as an oustanding singer among the monks of St. Gall. It seems likely that Tuotilo's contribution to tropes was both as a poet and as a composer, and his originality may have been greater in the music than in the texts.

BIBLIOGRAPHY

Source. Ekkehard IV, *Casus sancti Galli,* Hans F. Haefele, ed. (1980), with German trans.

Studies. James M. Clark, *The Abbey of St. Gall as a Centre of Literature and Art* (1926); Richard L. Crocker, "The Troping Hypothesis," in *Musical Quarterly,* **52** (1966); Ernest T. De Wald, "Notes on the Two Tuotilo Ivories in St. Gall," in *Art Bulletin,* **15** (1933); Léon Gautier, *Histoire de la poésie liturgique au moyen âge,* I, *Les tropes* (1886), 33–39, 61–67; Osborne B. Hardison, Jr., *Christian Rite and Christian Drama in the Middle Ages* (1965); Karl Langosch, "Tutilo," in his *Die deutsche Literatur des Mittelalters: Verfasserlexikon,* IV (1953), 529–536, and "Tutilo (Nachtrag)," *ibid.,* V (1955), 1,095–1,098; Ernst G. Rüsch, *Tuotilo: Mönch und Künstler* (1953).

JOSEPH SZÖVÉRFFY

[See also **Drama, Liturgical; Ekkehard IV of St. Gall; Hymns, Latin; Music, Western European; Neumes; Notker Balbulus; Poetry, Liturgical; Ratpert of St. Gall; Tropes to the Proper of the Mass.**]

The Ascension. Carved ivory book cover attributed to Tuotilo, *ca.* 900. ST. GALLEN, STIFTSBIBLIOTHEK

been seen as the starting point for the development of medieval liturgical drama. The manuscript tradition and the age of *Quem quaeritis* rule out his authorship, and, more recently, O. B. Hardison has argued against the theory that *Quem quaeritis* was of seminal significance for the history of early medieval drama.

Ekkehard also says that Tuotilo taught singing,

TURKOMANS, an Oghuz Turkic nationality including 2,028,000 people in the USSR (1979) and some 2 million Turkoman speakers in Afghanistan, Iran, Turkey, Iraq, Syria, and Jordan. The ethnonym—*Türkmen* in Turkic—is derived from the tribal name *Türk.* It is mentioned as early as the eighth century in a Chinese source and became a fixture in Islamic historico-geographical literature in the tenth century. A Persian explanation of this term, *Turk-mānand*—"similar to a Turk"—an obvious popular etymology, probably points to the considerable Iranian admixture present among them.

Initially, "Turkoman" was a politico-religious term denoting a Turkic convert to Islam. Thus, al-Bīrūnī (*Kitāb al-jamāhir fī maᶜrifat al-jawāhir,* F. Krenkow, ed. [1936–1937], 205) notes that "when any Oghuz converts to Islam the Oghuz say 'he has become a *Turkmān.*'" These Turkomans were largely but not exclusively Oghuz; Qarluqs and other Turks also bore this name.

The massive Turkoman incursions into the Near and Middle East are associated with the Seljuks. In

1026 the Oghuz/Turkomans affiliated with Arslan Isrā'īl ibn Seljuq went to Khorāsān. Their depredations there led to their expulsion and scattering in Iran and Iraq. Thereafter they figured prominently in the murky politics of central and western Iran and "Persian Iraq." With the migration hither of the Seljuks and associated tribes, all of whom we may term Turkomans, they began to raid Transcaucasia, Mesopotamia, and Anatolia. The Seljuks were never able to fully control them. Thus, Alp Arslan was drawn into conflict with the Byzantines at Manazkert (Manzikert) in 1071 by the activities of ungovernable Turkoman bands. The Seljuks, hoping to rid themselves of these troublesome predators, encouraged their movement to the western borders. Here, as *ghāzīs*, they could direct their energies against the infidel. Nonetheless, tension between the Seljuks, increasingly representatives of traditional Islam and Near Eastern monarchic principles, and the more egalitarian Turkomans grew. The influx of Central Asian Turkomans into the Middle East, brought about by Qara Khitai expansion, exacerbated the problem. This discontent culminated in the seizure of the Seljuk sultan Sanjar (1118–1157) by the Turkomans in 1153 (he escaped in 1156).

In the decades preceding the Mongol conquests, Seljuk military men and Turkoman chieftains established their own domains as atabegs or begs. The Mongols pushed still more Turkomans into Iran and Anatolia. These new arrivals often came with urbanized or semi-sedentary elements and their own religious leaders. Their Islam, marked by heterodoxy, retained many shamanistic elements. The religious issue, combined with their shabby treatment by the government, fueled the revolt (1240–1241) of one of their spiritual leaders, Bābā Isḥāq, on the eve of the Mongol advance into Asia Minor.

The Mongol presence did little to hamper the further development of the Turkoman beyliks. Those on the frontier (*uj*), such as the Ottomans, given the role of the dervishes and *baba*s (popular preachers) in Turkoman society, fostered *ghāzī* traditions as well. Others, in the East, formed powerful tribal confederations such as the Qara Qoyunlu and Aq Qoyunlu, many of whose tribes were later associated with the Safavid and Qajar dynasties.

BIBLIOGRAPHY

Sources. Ebülgāzī Bahadir Han, *Shajara-yi Tarākimal Rodoslovnaya turkmen*, Andrei N. Kononov, ed. and Russian trans. (1958); Kitab-ı Dede Korkut, *Dede Korkut Kitabı*, Muharram Ergin, ed. (1964), Russian: *Kniga moego deda Korkuta*, V. V. Bartold, trans. (1962); Rashīd al-Dīn Ṭabīb Faẓlallāh, *Jāmi ͑at-tawārīkh*, I/1, Aleksandr A. Romaskevich, A. A. Khetagurov, Abdul-Kerim A. Ali-zade, eds. (1965), Russian: *Sbornik letopisei*, I/1 A. A. Khetagurov, trans. (1952), German: *Die Geschichte der Oğuzen der Rašīd ad-Dīn*, Karl Jahn, trans. (1969), Turkish: *Oğuz Destanı*, A. Zeki Velidī Togan, trans. (1972).

Studies. S. G. Agadzhanov, *Ocherki istorii oguzov i Turkmen Srednei Azii IX–XIII vv.* (1963); Vasily V. Bartold, *Four Studies on the History of Central Asia*, III, V. and T. Minorsky, trans. (1962), and *Turkestan Down to the Mongol Invasion*, T. Minorsky, trans., 3rd rev. ed. (1968, repr. 1977); Claude Cahen, "Notes pour l'histoire des Turcomans d'Asie Mineure," in *Journal asiatique*, 239 (1951), and *Pre-Ottoman Turkey*, J. Jones-Williams, trans. (1968); Dmitry E. Eremeev, *Ètnogenez turok* (1971); Peter B. Golden, "The Migrations of the Oğuz," in *Archivum Ottomanicum*, 4 (1972); Ahmed Fuad Köprülü, *Les origines de l'empire Ottoman* (1935); Faruk Sümer, *Oğuzlar* (1967); Ismail H. Uzunçarşılı, *Anadolu beylikleri ve Akkoyunlu Karakoyunlu devletleri*, 2nd ed. (1969); Speros Vryonis, *The Decline of Medieval Hellenism in Asia Minor and the Process of Islamization from the Eleventh Through the Fifteenth Century* (1971).

PETER B. GOLDEN

[See also **Alp Arslan; Anatolia; Aq Qoyunlu; Armenia, History of; Cavalry, Islamic; Ghāzī; Karamania; Ottomans; Qara Qoyunlu; Seljuks; Seljuks of Rum; Toghrıl-Beg; Warfare, Islamic.**]

TURKS, OTTOMAN. See Ottomans.

TURKS, SELJUK. See Seljuks.

TURMEDA, ANSELM (*ca.* 1352–after 1423), is one of the most colorful writers of medieval Catalan literature. A Mallorcan by birth, he was a contemporary of Bernat Metge. Turmeda's most important work, *La disputa de l'ase,* appeared in 1417–1418, about twenty years after Metge's *Lo somni.* At age twenty Turmeda became a Franciscan. He had studied physics and astronomy at Lleida (Lérida) and later studied theology in Paris and Bologna. About 1387, at the age of 35, he apostatized in Tunis and thereafter enjoyed a distinguished career as high functionary and adviser to the rulers of Tunis. Turmeda adopted the name Abdallah el Tarjumí. He continued to write in Catalan and maintain contact with his homeland. He received offers of safe conduct and papal pardon but did not accept them.

As a writer, Turmeda is usually referred to as a rationalist who is firmly within the Catalan tradition of realism. Some of his material is Oriental, but he also lies within the tradition of Ramon Lull. Despite his apostasy he retained awareness of contemporary political and social developments in Europe. His prophecies were widely circulated in Europe at the time of the Great Schism and the Compromise of Casp (1412). Modern critics have called him a precursor of modern skepticism because of his interest in anthropological investigation and minimizing of the afterlife. Other aspects of his writing indicate a picaresque spirit, a biting pessimism, even misanthropy. His intense realism, his doubts concerning resurrection for man and beast, and the foreign studies of his youth help to account for his Averroist label.

Turmeda's most important treatise is *La disputa de l'ase*, in which he debates an ass and seven insects in a dream. The principal topics are the nature of man, his intellective soul and natural wisdom, and immortality. A series of tales and reminiscences intended to illustrate the seven deadly sins are also included. Religious orders are sharply criticized via an examination of realities of the times. These tales are set in Italy and Catalonia. Concluding the work are a series of prophecies.

The critic Asín Palacios has shown that Turmeda made extensive use in this work of large sections of the twenty-first treatise and other passages of the *Encyclopedia of the Pure Brethren* (*Risā'il Ikhwān al-Ṣafā*). For his *Disputa de l'ase*, Turmeda's cultural symbiosis is shown by the author's own physical presence in the Oriental world of talking animals. The theological and social arguments based on the *Encyclopedia* are interrupted in order to digress on his own student experiences and tales of the seven deadly sins. The treatise concludes with a Christian tenet stressing revealed faith, and a Muslim argument stressing a more naturalistic knowledge of religion, in accord with the naturalistic observation set forth in the twenty-first treatise of the *Encyclopedia*. Turmeda adapted his *Disputa* based on arguments from the *Encyclopedia*. However, his structure, wit, and personal interjections are original.

The *Tuhfa* is Turmeda's Arabic autobiography and polemic against Christianity, particularly the divinity of Christ. It was written for his Muslim readers in Tunis and became well known throughout the Muslim world. It is still in print in Arabic. Turmeda's tomb is a place of veneration in Tunis.

Turmeda's unique fusion of two cultures stresses the value of Muslim theology and philosophy for the West and its enrichment in the thinking of a friar reared in Catalan monasticism. Turmeda himself, however, was neither submerged nor overwhelmed by these new influences, as witnessed by his textual interweaving of the beliefs of the *Encyclopedia of the Pure Brethren* with his own witty and skeptical personality and misanthropic creed.

Rather than a polemicist or apologist, Turmeda was an astute observer enriched by two cultures, balanced between two worlds. This contribution to Catalan realism is unique and represents a more modern literary concept than that of his predecessors.

BIBLIOGRAPHY
Sources. The following works of Turmeda, all originally in Catalan, are known:
Llibre de bons amonestaments, 1398. A book of Christian moral counsel, adapted from *Dottrina dello schiavo de Bari*. Used in Catalan schools until the early nineteenth century.
Cobles de la divisió del regne de Mallorques, 1398. A poem of political allegory, more elevated in style and poetic quality than the *Llibre*.
De les coses esdevenidores segons los profetes, 1405.
Altra ordinació o profecia, 1406.
La disputa de l'ase, 1417–1418. Followed by prophecies beginning "En nom de l'essència. . . ." No copy of the 1509 Barcelona edition remains. A French version in a 1544 Lyons edition was reprinted by R. Foulché-Delbosc in *Revue hispanique*, 24 (1911). It is available today in a Catalan translation by Marçal Olivar (1928). Olivar has also presented the *Cobles* and *Llibre de amonestaments* directly from Barcelona manuscripts in *Bernat Metge-Anselm Turmeda Obres Menors* (1927).
Tuhfat al-arib fi-l-radd ala ahl al-Salib, 1420, is his anti-Christian polemic for Muslims. *La Tuhfa*, Miguel de Espalza, ed. and trans. (1971), contains both the Arabic original and the Spanish translation.
The anonymous *Libre de tres* has been attributed by some scholars to Turmeda, based on similarities of some passages. They may, however, be borrowings.
Studies. Miguel Asín Palacios, "El original árabe de la *Disputa del asno contra Fr. Anselmo Turmeda*," in *Revista de filología española*, 1 (1914); Marcelino Menéndez y Pelayo, *Historia de los heterodoxos españoles*, I

(2nd rev. ed., 1941) and *Orígenes de la novela,* I (1956); Manuel Milà i Fontanals, *Obres completes,* III (1890), 163–164, 328–330; Martí Riquer, *Història de la literatura catalana,* II (1980); Josep (José) Romeu Figueras, *Literatura catalana antiga,* II (1961); Jordi Rubió i Balaguer, "Un text català de *La Profecía de l'Ase* de Fra Anselm Turmeda," in *Estudis universitaris catalans,* 7 (1913); Elvir Sans, "Fra Anselm Turmeda en 1402," in *Homenatge a Antoní Rubió i Lluch,* III (1936).

PATRICIA J. BOEHNE

[See also **Catalan Literature; Encyclopedias and Dictionaries, Arabic and Persian; Metge, Bernat.**]

TUROLDUS. A latinized version of a name common in England and Normandy between 1050 and 1150, the word Turoldus appears in the last verse of the Oxford *Roland,* which is considered to be the oldest French version: "Ci falt la geste que Turoldus declinet." Diverse interpretations of *falt, geste,* and *declinet* have led to much debate about Turoldus' role in the poem. Was he the author of the Oxford text, the author of a Latin or French source (written or oral), the scribe, or simply the performing minstrel?

BIBLIOGRAPHY

Joseph Bédier, *La Chanson de Roland commentée* (1927, repr. 1968), 31–40; Gerard J. Brault, *The Song of Roland: Analytical Edition,* I (1978), 340–341; Edmond Faral, *La Chanson de Roland* (1934, repr. 1942, 1948), 53–58; Rita Lejeune, "Turold dans la tapisserie de Bayeux," in *Mélanges . . . René Crozet,* I (1966), 419–425.

M. GRUNMANN-GAUDET

[See also **Roland, Song of.**]

TURPIN. See **Pseudo-Turpin.**

TUSCANY. Tuscany remained Roman until 489, when Theodoric led the Ostrogoths into Italy. Under Theodoric there were some ten years of peaceful cohabitation between Goths and the indigenous peoples. There followed the unhappy years of the Gothic War (535–553). In the year 542, the Gothic leader Totila won a splendid victory over the Byzantines at Mugello. In the summer of the year 552 Narses succeeded in crushing Totila's army. In Tuscany the only city that did not immediately surrender to the Byzantines was Lucca, which Narses captured only after a three-month siege. The Byzantines were hated for their rigorous tax system. The massive invasion of Lombardy in the year 569 met little resistance in Tuscany.

We know little about the situation in Tuscany in the Lombard period. In Tuscany, as in much of Italy, in the sixth and seventh centuries there was continuous devastation of the cities and rural areas. During the reign of Liutprand (712–744) the Tuscan cities were reborn; Lucca seems to have been the most eminent. Charlemagne's invasion of 773–774 ended Lombard rule in northern Italy. The Lombards held out in Lucca, Chiusi, and Città di Castello, so Charlemagne sent Frankish contingents to Florence and established Gudibrando as duke (784–791) in the city. Charlemagne spent Christmas 786 in Florence.

From about 810 the Bavarian Boniface, a follower of Charlemagne, governed Tuscany as duke-count from Lucca. His family controlled Tuscany for almost 150 years. In the year 817 Emperor Louis the Pious entrusted Boniface I with Corsica as well. His son Boniface II (r. 823–839) in the year 828 scattered a large consignment of Muslim pirates in Corsica and Sardinia and pursued them along the coast of Tunisia. He added Pisa, Pistoia, and Luni (La Spezia) to the Luccan region, dominating a large part of Tuscany, from the mountains of Lumigiana to the gates of Florence. His son Adalbert I (r. 845–898) became master of the Apennine Pass, which controls the communications between the north and Rome; he also became the lord of Vollenna and of Florence and was one of the most powerful men in Italy. Adalbert II the Rich (r. ca. 889–915), in the period of the dissolution of the Carolingian Empire, supported various pretenders to the crown of Italy, while his son Guido (r. 915–930) married Marozia from the Roman noble family of Cresentii, who had been a mistress of Pope Sergius III and exerted a great power in Roman papal politics.

During the Ottonian restoration, the rulers of Tuscany (now with the rank of marquess) aligned themselves with the imperial forces. Hugh of Tuscany (r. 961–1001), the "grand baron" remembered by Dante, especially ensured the faithfulness of Tuscany to the child emperor Otto III. During the long absences from Italy of Emperor Henry II (r. 1002–1024) the Tuscan cities were divided.

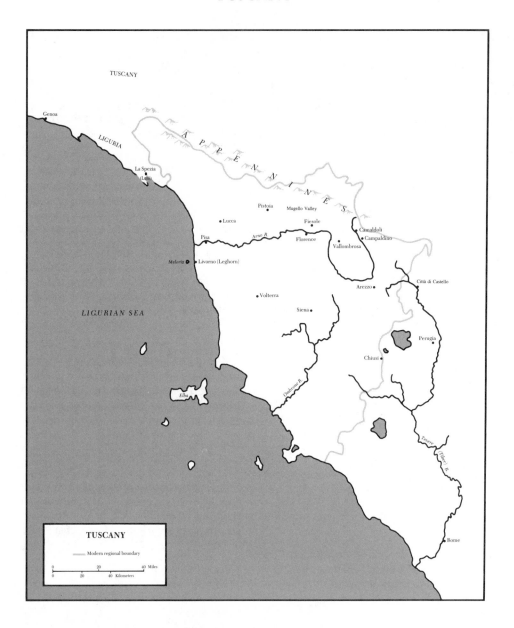

Some, like Lucca, sided with Arduin of Ivrea, who was elected king of the Lombards in 1002; others sided with the emperor. They also made war between themselves: Pisa fought Lucca and Florence fought Fiesole, while the Saracens pillaged the Tuscan coast. In this confused and uncertain situation Boniface, count of Canossa, already lord of the principal cities of Emilia, extended his dominion to Tuscany. In the year 1028 Emperor Conrad II (r. 1027–1039) officially gave to the count of Canossa the rule of Tuscany. In Tuscany during the general movement of church reform promoted by Pope Leo IX, St. Romuald established Camaldoli

in 1012 and St. John Gualberti founded Vallombrosa in 1038.

Boniface was killed by a conspiracy in 1052. His widow, Beatrice, succeeded him. She married Godfrey of Lorraine, head of the opposition to Emperor Henry III, who for revenge took Beatrice and her daughter Matilda to Germany as prisoners. As successor to her mother, Matilda, marquess of Tuscany, was always an implacable enemy of Emperor Henry IV. To break the resistance of her followers, the emperor made grand concessions to Lucca and to Pisa. But Florence remained faithful, and although Henry besieged it, the city turned back his assault (1082) and was then able to expand her preeminence over the surrounding countryside and affirm her autonomy.

After the death of Matilda in 1115, Florence found herself involved in the struggle between Lucca and Pisa. After Fiesole was destroyed (1125), Florence became a free community governed by her consuls. Other Tuscan communities now became independent: Pisa, Lucca, Siena, Pistoia, and Volterra. In the war of Frederick II against the Italian communities and the papacy, Ghibelline Pisa helped the emperor and defeated the Genoese fleet (1241). Ferocious quarrels between the various notable families upset the lives of the Florentines: Amidei and Uberti were Ghibellines, while the Buondelmonti and the Donati were Guelphs. To assure access to the sea for her commerce in the thirteenth century, Florence allied herself with Genoa against Pisa. When the Pisans were defeated at Meloria (1284), Florence insisted on exemptions and immunities for her trade. The Florentines fought Arezzo at Campaldino to liberate the roads to Rome (1289). Then they occupied Pistoia. New divisions arose in Florence between the Cerchi clan (Whites) and the Donati (Blacks). Amid the burdens caused by a lengthy and unsuccessful war against Lucca, the discontent of the people grew. The duke of Athens, Walter of Brienne, was brought in to end the quarrels and was acclaimed signore (1342–1343), but after eleven months was expelled. The government of the city fell into the hands of the guilds. In the summer of 1378 there was the uprising of the Ciompi (cloth workers). In spite of this turbulence, some middle-class Florentine families were able to assume a strong economic position and therefore accumulate political power. Toward the end of the fourteenth century, Florence opposed the expansion of Milan under the Visconti, who had gained control of Pisa, Siena, and Perugia. The Florentines occupied Arezzo in 1386 and conquered Pisa in 1406. They also acquired Livorno (Leghorn). The family of Cosimo de Medici (1389–1464), backed by the riches of his bank, prevailed over those of the other powerful Florentine families. Cosimo was exiled, but returned in triumph in 1434. Under his patronage Florence became the leading city in Italy for art and culture. The prestige and financial power of Florence was displayed when it played host in 1439 to the council that proclaimed the union of the Latin and Greek churches. The years in power of Lorenzo the Magnificent (1464–1492) were those of maximum splendor for the Florentine court. The conspiracy of the Pazzi (26 April 1478) against the Medici only served to reinforce their dominion because it gave them the reason to eliminate about 100 opponents.

In the tormenting events of the long war between Emperor Charles V and the kings of France, the Medici, several times expelled, always returned to power.

BIBLIOGRAPHY

Robert Davidsohn, *Geschichte von Florenz*, 4 vols. in 6 (1896–1927, repr. 1969), Italian trans. by Giovanni B. Klein, *Storia di Firenze*, 4 vols. in 8 (1956–1968); Antonio Falce, *La formazione della marca di Tuscia (sec. VII–IX)* (1930); Lorenzo Pignotti, *Storia della Toscana sino al principato*, 10 vols. (1815), English trans. by John Browning, *History of Tuscany Interspersed with Essays*, 4 vols. (1833); Fritz Schillmann, *Florenz und die Kultur Toskanas*, 2nd ed. (1938).

ANGELO PAREDI

[See also **Barbarians, Invasions of; Camaldolese, Order of; Ferrara-Florence, Council of; Florence; Guelphs and Ghibellines; Italy; John Gualberti, St.; Lombards, Kingdom of; Matilda of Tuscany; Medici; Pisa; Romuald of Ravenna, St.; Siena; Theodoric the Ostrogoth.**]

TUTILO. See **Tuotilo.**

TVRTKO I (1338–1391). Tvrtko, the son of Stjepan II Kotromanić's brother Vladislav and Jelena Šubić, was only fifteen when he succeeded his uncle in 1353 as ban of Bosnia. The state he inherited had little centralized administrative apparatus, and many aristocrats in outlying regions took advantage of Kotromanić's death to secede. The Hungarian king, Louis (Lajos) I (1342–1382), wooed these nobles, and some of the Hrvatinići of the Donji Kraji joined Louis. Just prior to Kotromanić's death, Louis had married Kotromanić's daughter; Louis demanded from Tvrtko the western Bosnian lands of Završje and the Krajina as her dowry. Tvrtko, then in a weak position, had to go to Hungary in 1357 and surrender these territories in exchange for his own confirmation as ruler of Bosnia and Usora, as vassal of the Hungarian king.

After this Tvrtko worked to obtain support from the nobles to his north. In 1363, with the aid of some of the Hrvatinići, he stopped two major Hungarian offensives against Bosnia. However, his struggle with the Bosnian nobility continued; in 1366 Tvrtko had to flee from Bosnia when various nobles rebelled and put his brother Vuk on the throne. Tvrtko made peace with Louis, and with Hungarian aid regained Bosnia in 1367. Re-established in power, he secured his position in the north. Then he became involved against Nikola Altomanović, a Serbian nobleman to his southeast, whose activities (and alliance with Sanko Miltenović, the leading nobleman of Bosnian Hum) threatened Bosnia's holdings in Hum. Tvrtko allied with the Hungarians, with the ban of Srem (Sirmium), Nicholas Garai (Gorjanski), who was a Hungarian vassal, and with the Serb Lazar Hrebeljanović, against Altomanović. The allies' victory enabled Tvrtko to annex in late 1373 the Upper Drina and Lim regions, giving him all Hum. In 1377, taking advantage of a local rebellion, he obtained Trebinje, Konavli, and Dračevica.

As a result of the acquisition of this Serbian territory and of the extinction in 1371 of the Nemanjić dynasty in Serbia, to which Tvrtko belonged as a descendant of King Dragutin's daughter, Tvrtko claimed the Serbian kingship. He was crowned king of Serbia and Bosnia in 1377 at the monastery of Mileševo on the recently conquered Lim. This title gave him no authority within Serbia itself. After Djuradj (George I) Balšić died in 1379, Tvrtko took over the Balšić holdings on the "Montenegrin" coast. Tvrtko continued his association with the Serbian prince Lazar and sent a contingent to the Battle of Kosovo (1389) that fought sufficiently well for Tvrtko to announce a Christian victory over the Turks. After Louis of Hungary died in 1382, a civil war followed for the Hungarian throne. In this Tvrtko sided with Charles (and subsequently Charles's son Ladislav) of Naples against Sigismund of Luxembourg. As a result Tvrtko presumably regained the lands lost to Hungary in 1357. He clearly made himself overlord between 1387 and 1389 over much of Croatia (south of Velebit) and Dalmatia (including Omiš, Split, Trogir, Šibenik, and even several islands). Kotor, which had been under Hungarian protection, became his in 1385. In 1390 Tvrtko added "Croatia and Dalmatia" to his title.

Tvrtko was Catholic, but he tolerated all three of Bosnia's religious confessions. In 1374 he married Dorothea, daughter of John Stracimir, the Bulgarian prince of Vidin. They had no surviving sons.

Upon his death in 1391 Tvrtko was succeeded by a cousin, Stefan Dabiša.

BIBLIOGRAPHY

V. Ćorović, *Kralj Tyrtko I Kotromanić* (1925); John V. A. Fine, Jr., *The Late Medieval Balkans* (1987).

JOHN V. A. FINE, JR.

[See also **Banus; Bosnia; Hungary; Lazar Hrebeljanovic.**]

TVRTKO II (*d.* 1443). An illegitimate son of Tvrtko I, Tvrtko II first ruled Bosnia (1404–1409) as a puppet of the nobility after Ostoja's overthrow. Sigismund of Hungary offered Ostoja support and defeated the Bosnians in a major battle that took place at Dobor in September 1408, bringing about the submission of Hrvoje, the leading Bosnian aristocrat, by early 1409. Ostoja's restoration duly followed. Tvrtko II was restored in 1420 after Ostoja's son Stefan Ostojić was overthrown. Tvrtko made peace with Hungary in 1426, provoking an Ottoman attack that forced him to accept Ottoman suzerainty. His relations with the Turks soon deteriorated, causing them to sponsor Radivoj, another son of Ostoja, as king. This brought Tvrtko back into the Hungarian camp in 1435, but he was compelled to reaffirm Ottoman suzerainty in 1437. Tvrtko had close relations with the Franciscans serving in Bosnia; he defended them against the order's attempts to reform them.

BIBLIOGRAPHY

John V. A. Fine, Jr., *The Late Medieval Balkans* (1987); P. Živković, *Tvrtko II Tvrtković* (1981).

JOHN V. A. FINE, JR.

[See also **Bosnia.**]

TWELVE GREAT FEASTS. Celebrated by the Eastern church, these feast days commemorate events in the lives of Christ and the Virgin. The feasts are: the Annunciation, the Nativity, the Presentation in the Temple, the Baptism, the Transfiguration, the Raising of Lazarus, the Entry into Jerusalem, the Crucifixion, the Anastasis, Pentecost, the Ascension, and the Dormition of the Virgin. In Byzantine art, the Twelve Great Feasts are often depicted together in mosaic or fresco cycles.

BIBLIOGRAPHY

Otto Demus, *Byzantine Mosaic Decoration* (1948); Ernst Diez and Otto Demus, *Byzantine Mosaics in Greece* (1931); David Talbot Rice, *Art of Byzantium* (1959).

JENNIFER E. JONES

[See also **Byzantine Art; Early Christian Art; Iconography; Liturgy, Byzantine Church; Virgin Mary;** and articles on individual feasts.]

TWO SWORDS, DOCTRINE OF. As it had developed by 1300, the doctrine of the two swords provided the most concise statement of the ideology of universal papal sovereignty. As vicar of Christ, and possessing plenitude of power, the pope was not only the wielder of the spiritual or ecclesiastical sword and thus the supreme authority in spiritual jurisdiction on earth, but also the possessor of the secular sword, the channel for the transmission of secular authority by commission or concession to the princes. Although unable to use the secular sword himself, except in extraordinary circumstances such as the government of the papal territories in central Italy, or (as was claimed) when the imperial throne was vacant, the pope was nevertheless seen as the ultimate repository under Christ of power in both church and state.

The construction of the doctrine of the two swords effectively took place in the two centuries after 1050. It reveals the way in which papal theorists could combine biblical exegesis, Roman law, forgery, and wishful thinking to create a coherent definition of papal power. Ultimately, the doctrine was rooted in the Bible. The number of swords was established in Luke 22:38. Their individual identifications as spiritual and material (later ecclesiastical and temporal) were provided by Eph. 6:17 and Rom. 13:4 (this last also being incorporated into a separate theory of royal power itself based on the sword image). For the purposes of the papal theory, the critical link resulting in the subjection of the material sword to ecclesiastical supervision was the incident related in the Gospel narratives (especially John 18:10–11) in which Peter, attempting to resist Christ's arrest at Gethsemane, draws his sword and strikes the high priest's servant. Christ's rebuke of Peter's action established the Petrine connection.

Initially, the image of two swords was little involved in the church-state dichotomy, merely providing an allegorical motif for other dualities, as when Alcuin (*d.* 804) used them to exemplify body and soul. But the exegetical tradition, seemingly derived from the early theologian Origen, provided a basis for future developments. The papalist theory itself seems to have evolved in three main stages. Initially the two swords were seen as the image of complementary coercive authorities, both having a spiritual purpose, but wielded independently by the ecclesiastical and secular powers. If the church (defined broadly, and not at this stage necessarily identified with the papacy) failed to secure submission by the errant to its authority through the use of spiritual penalties such as excommunication, it could request the assistance of the secular authorities, in accordance with their biblical obligations. This version of the theory lingered throughout the medieval period, with the church continuing to request the assistance of the secular arm in dealing with obdurate excommunicates and (later) heretics. During the eleventh century the theory seems to have changed slightly: the church gradually claimed authority in its own right to command and control the use of the secular arm, whether externally (as with crusades), or internally, against those whom it saw as a threat to its own peace and security. Within this version of the doctrine, the power of command was in time restricted to the papacy alone, where it remained as an element in theories of the crusade. Finally, in the twelfth and thirteenth centuries, this claim to command was itself transmuted into the notion that it was the church (increasingly identified as the papacy) that granted or at least legitimized the exercise of secular jurisdiction, principally but not necessarily through the ritual of coronation.

Predictably, a crucial stage in this transformation occurred during the investiture conflict, at the turn of the eleventh and twelfth centuries. The first known writer who explicitly used the two swords to represent the rival jurisdictions of church and state was Gottschalk of Aachen, when supporting Emperor Henry IV against Pope Gregory VII. (Earlier ascriptions of this first "political" use of the two-sword image to Peter Damian are apparently based on a work wrongly attributed to him.) Gottschalk used the two-sword analogy in terms based on the differentiation of spiritual and secular authority set forth by Pope Gelasius I (492–496) in his statement *Duo sunt quippe* (in the twelfth century incorporated into canon law as dist. 96, can. 10, of the *Decretum*). But his use of the motif suggests that it was already something of a commonplace in imperialist circles. With other writers of the period he was specifically responding to the activities of Gregory VII and his successors, who seemed to be replacing the doctrine of two swords with a doctrine of three swords, with the papacy commanding the use of an additional material sword on its own authority, rather than through the agency of the princes. The relative papal and secular uses of the sword image during this period, and through to the later years of the twelfth century, show signs of ambiguity and terminological confusion, under cover of which the later papalist ideology was able to evolve. Although the swords were frequently identified in traditional terms as representing aspects of coercive authority with spiritual purposes, the new political overtones were also present, developing when commentators misapplied or misunderstood statements of their predecessors and used them for their own purposes.

The supreme instance of such misunderstanding is provided in the case of what was to prove the classic formulation of the two-sword theory, produced by St. Bernard when addressing Pope Eugenius III in his tract *De consideratione* (4.3), written in 1151:

> Both the spiritual and material sword ... belong to the church, but the latter is drawn for the church and the former by it; one by the hand of the priest, the other by that of the soldier; but the latter surely is used at the bidding of the priest and by the order of the emperor.

The precise circumstances and implications of this statement remains uncertain, but in time it proved highly important. Considered in the light of contemporary developments concerning the image of the two swords, it fits perfectly into the traditional concept of complementary coercive spiritual authorities. However, looked at with the benefit of hindsight, it also provides a pithy summary of later papalist political doctrine. During the later twelfth century, it was the canonists who gradually incorporated the political interpretation of the two-sword motif into the overall mesh of papal hierocratic theory, integrating it with the Roman law concept of the plentitude of power of the highest authority, a power that the pope exercised as vicar of Christ and successor to St. Peter in the governance of a monolithic universal *ecclesia*. It was also integrated with the notions of papal secular authority based on the forged Donation of Constantine, a document that purported to be a constitutional grant of Constantine I by which he handed over to Pope Sylvester I imperial power and rulership of the West. Contemporary developments in coronation rituals (especially those for the empire), the construction of the theory of papal power to depose monarchs, and the transformation of the role of the prince (again, especially that of the emperor) from that of minister of God in his own right to one as minister of the church (and, as that, of a church itself increasingly subjected to papal centralization) further contributed to the idea that secular authority was a papal concession. At the end of the twelfth century, one of the most extreme statements of this hierocratic view was presented by the canonist Alanus Anglicus, and when this was incorporated into the *glossa ordinaria* to the *Liber extra* in the following century (gloss to X.4.17.7, *ad regem*) it became a commonplace of canonistic ideas. The extent to which the popes themselves, as opposed to their lawyers, actually accepted this extremist version of the two-sword theory is unclear. Innocent III (1198–1216) may in fact have been chary of it, despite his claims to extended papal jurisdiction by reason of sin (*ratione peccati*) and despite his use of the image of the biblical priest-king Melchisidek as part of the definition of papal status. The first explicit papal statement of the two-sword theory in its entirety appears only during the pontificate of Gregory IX (1227–1241), but thereafter it was fully incorporated into the papal ideological armory.

By 1300 the political version of the doctrine of the two swords was a traditional component of papal ideology and was duly included in Boniface VIII's high-sounding but hollow summary of papal theories, the bull *Unam sanctam* (1302). However, the doctrine was no more than a mental construct, essentially created by the canonists, on rather weak foundations. Theologians had been slower to adopt it, the first apparently being Robert Grosseteste in the thirteenth century, and they remained more receptive to the older idea of the two forms of coercive authority for spiritual purposes. When they were called on to defend the theory, there were frequently signs of insecurity in their arguments. Feudal and civilian (that is, Roman) lawyers generally ignored or challenged the papal claims, either retaining the concept of two autonomous authorities, or even wishing to subject the spiritual to the secular. Only when dealing with Germany and the empire—very much special cases—are there signs of acceptance of the papal theory by secular lawyers.

The papalist interpretation of the doctrine of the two swords was a neat summary of papal claims and of the doctrine of universal papal sovereignty. But this papal definition was only one of several possible interpretations of a vaguely formulated analogy. The other forms persisted throughout the later Middle Ages, along with indications of a challenge that questioned the whole methodological foundation for the doctrine. But until the Reformation the theory was not destroyed. It was only after the schisms of the sixteenth century that the doctrine of the two swords faced a concerted challenge aimed at its total destruction.

BIBLIOGRAPHY

Most works on the papacy and on medieval political thought deal with the doctrine of the two swords in some way, usually subsidiary to their main concerns. The following studies deal specifically with the doctrine, either as a whole, or with aspects of its development, and provide indications of further literature: Gerard E. Caspary, *Politics and Exegesis: Origen and the Two Swords* (1979); Hartmut Hoffman, "Die beiden Schwerter im hohen Mittelalter," in *Deutsches Archiv für Erforschung des Mittelalters,* 20 (1964); Elizabeth Kennan, "The *De consideratione* of St. Bernard of Clairvaux and the Papacy in the Mid Twelfth Century: A Review of Scholarship," in *Traditio,* 23 (1967); Joseph Lecler, "L'argument des deux glaives (Luc XXII, 38) dans les controverses politiques du moyen âge," in *Recherches de science religieuse,* 21 (1931), and 22 (1932); Wilhelm Levison, "Die mittelalterliche Lehre von den beiden Schwertern," in *Deutches Archiv für Erforschung des Mittelalters,* 9 (1952); Alfons M. Stickler, "Sacerdozio e regno nelle nuove ricerche attorno ai secoli XII e XIII nei decretisti e decretalisti fino alle decretali di Gregorio IX," in *Miscellanea historiae pontificiae,* 18 (1954). Stickler has been a prolific producer of considerations of the two-sword theory, the majority of which are mentioned in the notes to his article.

R. N. SWANSON

[See also **Bernard of Clairvaux, St.; Boniface VIII, Pope; Gelasius I, Pope; Gregory VII, Pope; Grosseteste, Robert; Investiture and Investiture Conflict; Kingship, Theories of; Papacy; Origin and Development of; Plenitudo Potestatis.**]

TYMPANUM (Latin, "drum," "panel"), in classical architecture, the triangular space enclosed by the horizontal and raking cornices of a pediment. In a medieval arched portal, the tympanum is that part above the lintel of the doorway and below the arch itself. Tympana are often adorned with sculpture; in the mid thirteenth century open or glazed tympana appear in France (Rheims).

GREGORY WHITTINGTON

[See also **Gothic Sculpture; Moissac, St. Pierre (with illustration); Romanesque Art (with illustration); Trumeau; Vézelay, Church of La Madeleine (with illustration).**]

UBERTINO OF CASALE (*ca.* 1259–after 1329), Franciscan mystic and controversialist renowned for his *Arbor vitae crucifixae Jesu* (The tree of the crucified life of Jesus) and for his defense of the Franciscan Spirituals against the Conventuals and the papal curia.

Ubertino was born at Casale, near Vercelli in northern Italy. He entered the Franciscan order in 1273. On completion of his novitiate he spent nine years at the *studium generale* in Paris, where the ardor that had characterized his earlier contemplative life was dampened by his concentration on study and lecturing. His dissatisfaction with the direction his life was taking was intensified on his return home to Italy as lector. Although his meetings with Angela of Foligno and John of Parma redirected him toward the contemplative life, it was in Peter John Olivi, whom he met in Florence in 1287, that Ubertino found his true spiritual and intellectual mentor. The two friends soon became the leaders of the Tuscan group of Franciscan Spirituals. The Spirituals held that the obligation to live modestly (the *usus pauper*) was fundamental to the true observance of the rule of St. Francis, while the Conventuals held that the use, if not the ownership, of property was acceptable.

In 1289 Ubertino became an itinerant preacher in Tuscany and Umbria. The oratorical skills he employed to castigate the Conventuals gained him a public following but also led to his superiors' sending him into retreat at Alverna in 1304, primarily because they saw as a thinly veiled attack on the papacy his exposition of the Joachimite doctrine of the *ecclesia carnalis* (*i.e.,* the belief that the present, carnal church of the second *status* of history would be subsumed into the fully contemplative life of the third and final *status*).

At Alverna he wrote his masterpiece, the *Arbor*

vitae crucifixae Jesu. This work draws its primary inspiration from the poverty of Christ, but there is also evident influence from the church fathers, St. Bernard, Joachim of Fiore, Olivi's own *Postilla in Apocalypsim,* the *Rotuli* of Fra Leone, the *Sacrum commercium,* the *Second Life* of St. Francis by Thomas of Celano, and the *Lignum vitae* of St. Bonaventure. The five books of the *Arbor vitae* are an amalgam of autobiography, scriptural exegesis, mystical reflections, scholastic reasoning, and apocalyptic commentary, including specific and vituperative denunciations of popes and Conventuals. Ubertino did not attack the institution of the papacy but individuals whom he saw as usurpers of the chair of Peter. He looked forward to an angelic pope and wrote, "I entirely withdraw all that the Holy Roman Church shall show to be untrue."

Returning to public life as chaplain to Cardinal Napoleone Orsini, Ubertino became the chief advocate of the Spiritual cause and staunchest defender of Olivi before Clement V, at the Council of Vienne in 1311–1312, and later before John XXII.

John XXII condemned the doctrine of the absolute poverty of Christ in his bull *Cum inter nonnullos* (in November 1323). Although, in 1322, Ubertino had abandoned the corollary doctrine of the necessity to renounce corporate as well as private possession, his steadfast adherence to the *usus pauper* and his loyalty to Olivi put his life in jeopardy, and following a summons for his arrest, he fled Avignon in September 1325, to a destiny shrouded in mystery. One recurring medieval tradition holds that he eventually met with a violent death.

Ubertino and the Spirituals attempted to maintain the Byzantine unity of grace and nature. Thomas Aquinas had influenced the trend of philosophical thought toward a dichotomy: the relative autonomy of the intellect led to the development of natural theology, and philosophy became distinct from revelation. Minister General Bonaventure had striven to maintain a balance between these two trends of thought within the Franciscan order, but after his death in 1274 the differences had reemerged. The Spirituals later turned increasingly to apocalyptic beliefs. Many found inspiration in Ubertino's *Arbor vitae* and his use of Joachim of Fiore to bestow on poverty the sanction of sacred history.

Ubertino's most abiding influence was on the Spirituals, on Dante's *Paradiso,* and on St. Bernardino of Siena (1380–1444). His desire for a com-

munity based on St. Francis' ideal of poverty was realized in the Brothers of the Strict Observance.

BIBLIOGRAPHY

Source. Ubertino da Casale, *Arbor vitae crucifixae Jesu* (1485). The 1961 reprint of this work has an introduction and bibliography by Charles T. Davis.

The *Prologus primus* of the first book of the *Arbor vitae* affords the fullest account of Ubertino's early life. The bibliography by Davis includes a full list of Ubertino's minor works.

Studies. Frédégand Callaey, *L'idéalisme franciscain spirituel au XIVe siècle: Étude sur Ubertin de Casale* (1911); Charles T. Davis, "Ubertino da Casale and His Conception of *altissima paupertas,*" in *Studi medievali,* 3rd ser., 22 (1981); Decima L. Douie, *The Nature and the Effect of the Heresy of the Fraticelli* (1932, repr. 1978), 120–152; P. Godefroy, "Ubertin de Casale," in *Dictionnaire de théologie catholique,* XV (1950), 2,021–2,034; E. G. Salter, "Ubertino da Casale," in P. Sabatier *et al.,* eds., *Franciscan Essays* (1912), 108–123.

JANET E. GORMLEY

[See also **Angela of Foligno; Bonaventure, St.; Clement V, Pope; Councils, Western; Franciscans; Joachim of Fiore; John XXII, Pope; Ockham, William of; Peter John Olivi.**]

UCCELLO, PAOLO (also called Paolo di Dono, 1397–1475), early Italian Renaissance painter. Most likely trained by Ghiberti, Uccello enrolled in the painters' guild Arte dei Medici e Speziale in 1415. No major early works survive. His earliest surviving work is the fresco monument to the fourteenth-century mercenary Sir John Hawkwood, dated 1436, in the cathedral of Florence. Although the dates of Uccello's two masterpieces are open to a variety of interpretations, he probably executed his major surviving mural, *The Flood and the Recession of the Flood* [or *Waters*], painted for the Chiostro Verde (Green cloister) of S. Maria Novella, Florence, about the mid 1440's. Similarly, three panels depicting the Battle of San Romano (now dispersed among the National Gallery, London; the Uffizi, Florence; and the Louvre, Paris) were probably done at roughly the same time for the Palazzo Medici, even though some scholars place these works as late as 1456. Whether they were remnants of bedroom furniture (*spaliere* or *cassoni,* for example) or some of the earliest known purely decorative paintings remains to be determined. Most sources identify them with the embel-

The Battle of San Romano. Panel painting by Paolo Uccello, 1440's. Now in National Gallery, London.
ANDERSON ROMA / ART RESOURCE

lishment of Lorenzo de' Medici's bedroom. However, just what that embellishment consisted of is no longer known.

In all of his work, Uccello displayed a virtuoso understanding of Brunelleschi's mathematical perspective; indeed, it is for his use of this technique that he is best known. But Uccello's perspective did not have the purpose of creating some idealized theoretical version of realistic space. Instead, his perspective, as his surviving work demonstrates, lies in the great tradition of decorative designs for walls and furniture in the form of painting or inlaid wood. He created deliberately fanciful, playful images, which used space and form to exaggerate perspective to draw the viewer's attention to the artist's skill in employing it. His visual games must have delighted the educated audience for which they were intended.

BIBLIOGRAPHY

John Pope-Hennessy, *Paolo Uccello,* 2nd ed. (1969).

ADELHEID M. GEALT

[See also **Brunelleschi, Filippo; Ghiberti, Lorenzo.**]

UGOLINO DA SIENA (Ugolino di Nerio) (*fl.* 1317–1327), Sienese painter. A follower of Duccio, Ugolino is best known for a signed polyptych, which originally formed the high altar of S. Croce, in Florence. The work is now dispersed in various museums in London, New York, Philadelphia, and Richmond (Surrey). Another polyptych is intact at the Clark Institute, Williamstown, Massachusetts (illustration overleaf).

BIBLIOGRAPHY

Bernard Berenson, *Italian Pictures of the Renaissance: Central and North Italian Schools,* 3 vols. (1968); Cesare Brandi, *Duccio* (1951); Bruce Cole, *Sienese Painting from Its Origin to the Fifteenth Century* (1980); Gertrude Coor-Achenbach, "Contributions to the Study of Ugolino di Nerio's Art," in *Art Bulletin,* 37 (1955); James H. Stubblebine, *Duccio di Buoninsegna and His School,* 2 vols. (1979); John White, *Art and Architecture in Italy, 1250–1400* (1966), 258, and *Duccio: Tuscan Art and the Medieval Workshop* (1979).

ADELHEID M. GEALT

[See also **Duccio di Buoninsegna; Trecento Art.**]

Virgin and Child with Sts. Francis, Andrew, Paul, Peter, Stephen, and Louis of Toulouse. Polyptych by Ugolino da Siena, *fl.* 1317–1327. STERLING AND FRANCINE CLARK ART INSTITUTE, WILLIAMSTOWN, MASS.

UGOLINO DI NERIO. See **Ugolino da Siena.**

UGOLINO DI VIERI (*fl.* 1329–1380/1385), Sienese goldsmith. Ugolino is famed for his translucent, basse-taille enamels, which approximate the modulations of contemporary painting by the Lorenzetti. The Reliquary of the Miraculous Corporal of Bolsena at Orvieto Cathedral (1337–1338) is his chief work; others are the Reliquary of St. Savinus, Orvieto, and a paten in Perugia.

BIBLIOGRAPHY

B. Bini, "Sono senesi gli smalti del bustoreliquiario di San Donato ad Arezzo," in *Antichità viva,* **18** (1979); Enzo Carli, *Il reliquiario del corporale ad Orvieto* (1964) and *Il Duomo di Orvieto* (1965), esp. 123–132; Guido di Dario, "Precisazioni su Ugolino di Vieri e soci," in *Napoli nobilissima,* **6** (1967); John White, *Art and Architecture in Italy, 1250–1400* (1966), 300–301.

MICHAEL D. TAYLOR

[See also **Enamel.**]

UÍ NÉILL, a dynasty of Irish kings and overkings. The origins of the Uí Néill are obscure. John V. Kelleher observes: "The Uí Néill emerge into history like a school of cuttlefish from a large ink-cloud of their own manufacture; and clouds and ink continued to be manufactured by them or for them throughout their long career." Scholars have differed sharply about their provenance. Eoin Mac Neill believed that they were Connachta (of the race of Conn, one of their legendary ancestors), that their stock gave their name to the province of Connacht, and that the Uí Néill (whose eponym was Niall Noígiallach, "of the nine hostages") were descendants of these expansive branches of the Connachta. Thomas F. O'Rahilly argued that the Uí Néill kingdoms of the midlands were founded by Goidels (the last Celtic invaders of Ireland) led by Tuathal Techtmar (one of the prehistoric and probably legendary ancestors of the Uí Néill), who landed at Brega (on the east coast) and pushed their way west, gained possession of Tara, and carved out a midland kingdom for themselves at the expense of the Laigin (Lagin) to the south and the Ulaid to the north. Expansive branches of the same dynasty made themselves masters of the province of Connacht, to which they gave their name, and in the early fifth century the sons of Niall divided among themselves the midland territories and the province of Ulster that they had newly conquered.

Francis Byrne, who feels that it is difficult,

Reliquary of the Miraculous Corporal of Bolsena at Orvieto Cathedral. Gold metalwork and basse-taille enamels by Ugolino di Vieri, 1337–1338. SCALA/ART RESOURCE

though not impossible, to reconstruct the early history of the Uí Néill, would argue from the later distribution of their kingdoms that the conquests of the Uí Néill began in Connacht and took two directions: north to Donegal and east through Leitrim and Longford to the midlands and Meath. In the north they encountered the powerful over-kingdom of the Ulaid, whose principal center, Emain Macha, near Armagh, fell to the sons of Niall in the middle of the fifth century and whose principal vassals, a medley of subordinate tribes called Airgialla (hostage givers), were overrun by the Uí Néill in the sixth and seventh centuries. In the midlands they conquered Mide, Brega, and

239

Tethbae; carved out a large kingdom at the expense of the Laigin and others; and established themselves as kings of Tara.

These conflicting views are all, to a degree, interpretations of traditional genealogy or story. The salient points of the teachings of the genealogists may be gleaned from the accompanying table, which represents the relationships as conceived perhaps in the middle of the seventh century. One can be sure that the Airgialla have no genealogical connection with the Uí Néill; their presence in the genealogy merely indicates that they were vassals of the Uí Néill. That the relationship should be represented in this manner is, I imagine, due to the influence of Armagh, which lay in Airgialla territory and was ruled by clerics of the Airgialla. The connections with the Connachta are also suspect. One cannot go beyond stating that in the middle of the seventh century the leading dynasties of the Connachta, rightly or wrongly (and in the case of

the Uí Briúin almost certainly wrongly), believed themselves to be kindred of the Uí Néill.

For the rest, the genealogical schema that represents some seven kingdoms of the Uí Néill as founded by seven eponymous brothers, all sons of the dynastic eponym, is far too neat and structured to be likely to be historical. The eighth son, Conall, who is an exception to this pattern, is an exception very probably because he is the great-grandfather of two Uí Néill dynasts who flourished in the sixth century—Colmán Már and Áed Sláne, eponymous ancestors of the two branches of the southern Uí Néill (Clann Cholmáin and Síl nÁeda Sláne) that were to dominate in the midlands in the seventh and eighth centuries. The sources appear to have undergone a major rewriting in the late seventh century, and possibly there were later rewritings, for the annals admit that the mid-seventh-century succession to the overkingship of the Uí Néill was a matter for doubt among historians. We can dimly

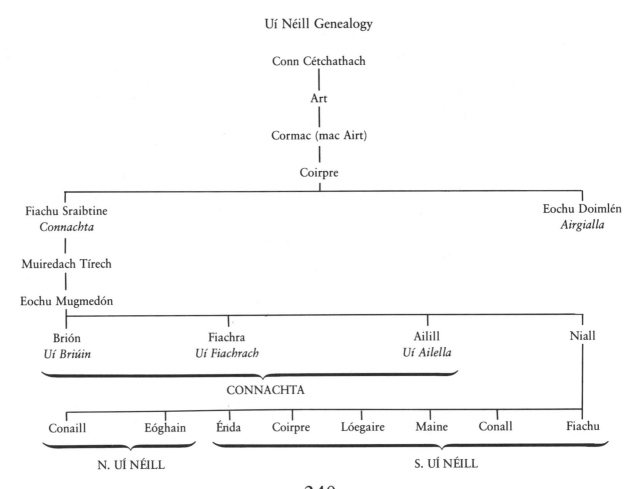

Uí Néill Genealogy

Conn Cétchathach

Art

Cormac (mac Airt)

Coirpre

Fiachu Sraibtine
Connachta

Eochu Doimlén
Airgialla

Muiredach Tírech

Eochu Mugmedón

Brión
Uí Briúin

Fiachra
Uí Fiachrach

Ailill
Uí Ailella

Niall

CONNACHTA

Conaill　　Eóghain　　Énda　　Coirpre　　Lóegaire　　Maine　　Conall　　Fiachu

N. UÍ NÉILL　　　　　　　　　S. UÍ NÉILL

240

discern behind the structured and syncopated gene-alogical story a much longer if more turbulent history.

It seems likely that Uí Néill expansion came in at least two separate waves, probably from Connacht. The kingdom of Coirpre, which was divided into three in the eighth century—Coirpre Droma Cliab in Sligo, Coirpre Gabra in Longford (Tethbae), and Coirpre Laigen in south Meath and Kildare—is likely to have been an early overkingdom stretching from Sligo to Longford and later, with the further expansion of the Uí Néill, to Meath and the borders of Leinster. Coirpre, the eponym, whom early lists recognize as overking of the Uí Néill, is expunged from later king lists and damned by the hagiographers as early as the end of the seventh century. Lóegaire has a similar distribution: some early genealogical materials state that the kingdom extended from Lough Erne to Slige Assail (between Tara and Lough Owel).

In addition, a number of subordinate peoples with whom the Uí Néill are closely associated and some of whose traditions the genealogists of the Uí Néill purloined for their patrons—Gailenga, Luigne, Cianachta, Corcu Trí—have a distribution pattern in the midlands, in north Connacht, and, to a lesser degree, in the north parallel to that of the Uí Néill. This tends to suggest that some of these peoples may be the remnants of older Connacht-midland overkingdoms founded by less fortunate fellow adventurers and associates of the Uí Néill in their first period of expansion. Some of the midland Uí Néill—Maine and Cinéal Fiachach in particu-lar—may be lineages of other origins who grafted themselves onto the Uí Néill stem—a common occurrence—when the Uí Néill had achieved polit-ical success. The story of the conquest of the Ulaid and the fall of Emain Macha sorts ill with the admission of the Uí Néill historians: that it was as a result of the Battle of Móin Dairi Lothair (dated in the annals to 562/563) that the northern Uí Néill broke out of their fastness in Donegal and began the drive east across Ulster that was to make them the most important power in the north by the eighth century.

From an early period the Uí Néill laid claim to the kingship of Tara, which their propagandists tended to regard as the kingship of Ireland. The origins of the kingship of Tara are shrouded in mist. It is generally considered to be a sacral or cultic kingship that was not confined to any one dynasty. The earliest Leinster material, which dates to the seventh century, claims that prehistoric kings of Leinster were kings of Tara; there are similar shadowy Munster claims; and in one of the seventh-century law tracts it is said that Congal Cáech (Cláen), overking of the Ulaid (627–637), had been king of Tara. Whatever its origins, the prestige of the kingship of Tara in early Christian times and before was enough to attract the conquering Uí Néill and lead them to make every effort to appro-priate the title for themselves. Toward the end of the seventh century that claim was fairly well established. Muirchú, the biographer of St. Patrick, paints Tara as the Irish Babylon, "then the capital of the realm of the Irish," and he describes Lóegaire as a "scion of the family that held the kingship of almost the entire island."

These claims are highly tendentious and prema-ture, but they do give one interpretation of the position and ambitions of the Uí Néill in the late seventh century. Adamnan, who is concerned above all with Christian concepts of kingship and a member of an Uí Néill lineage, has Columba de-scribe Diarmait mac Cerbaill, king of Tara, who is said to have died in 563, as *totius Scotiae regnato-rem a Deo ordinatum* (by God's authority ruler of all Ireland) and warn Diarmait's son, Áed Sláne (ancestor of Síl nÁeda Sláne), "ne tibi a Deo totius Euerniae regni praerogatiuam monarchiae prae-destinatam parricidali faciente peccato amittas" ("not to lose the prerogative of monarchy over the kingdom of all Ireland, predestined for you by God, by reason of the sin of parricide," *Vita Columbae*, I, 36). Adamnan's sympathies are clearly with his kinsmen; and it is no accident that Domnall mac Áedo, king of Tara, is described in his death notice in the Iona Chronicle (Annals of Ulster) in 642 as *rex Hiberniae*. He had, after all, defeated Congal Cáech in the Battle of Mag Roth in 637, ensured the dominance of the Uí Néill, and belonged to the same lineage as the abbots of Iona.

The views of the Uí Néill propagandists of the seventh century no doubt reflect the aims of the Uí Néill, and in the wake of continuing territorial aggrandizement they put forward the tendentious claim that the overkings of the Uí Néill were kings of Ireland and that the kingship of Tara was identical with the kingship of Ireland. Such was never the case in reality, but from the late seventh century until the rise of Brian Boru in the late tenth, the overking of the Uí Néill was usually the most powerful king in Ireland.

At a relatively early but uncertain date the

northern Uí Néill divided into two leading and frequently hostile segments, Cinéal Conaill and Cinéal Eóghain, named for their eponymous founders, Conaill and Eóghain (a third segment, Cinéal Énna, was of little importance). All the sources indicate that Cinéal Conaill was rather more powerful than Cinéal Eóghain down to the middle of the seventh century. The last of their kings to hold the overkingship of the Uí Néill was Flaithbertach mac Loingsig, who abdicated in 734. Cinéal Eóghain made every effort to exclude their kinsmen from the overkingship, and after the Battle of Cloitech (789) that exclusion became permanent. The expansion of Cinéal Eóghain south and east came slowly and painfully, and in the eighth and ninth centuries they brought the mid-Ulster kingdoms of Airgialla under their rule. The victory at Leth Cam (827) made their rule secure. From about 750 Armagh came increasingly under their control, and though it continued to be ruled by Airgialla families, these families became the dependents of Cinéal Eóghain.

Despite grandiose and largely propagandistic claims, the real establishment of Uí Néill power in the midlands was the work of Áed Sláne and his immediate successors. Their rivals and kinsmen, Clann Cholmáin, were late starters. They achieved overkingship of the Uí Néill only in 743; thereafter, with one exception (944–956), they ruthlessly excluded Síl nÁeda Sláne from the overkingship. The other branches of the Uí Néill in the midlands were excluded from the overkingship at a very early period and in some cases the historical record was amended accordingly. The development of two mature and mutually hostile segments of Síl nÁeda Sláne in the middle of the eighth century left the way open for Clann Cholmáin to dominate the midlands.

By the 740's the classic Uí Néill political structure had come into being following the consolidation of Cinéal Eóghain in the north and Clann Cholmáin in the midlands. Henceforth, the overkingship of the Uí Néill dynasty as a whole, usually called the kingship of Tara (and equated with the kingship of Ireland), alternated with regularity but not without friction between them. The claims of the Uí Néill did not, however, go unchallenged. In the early eighth century, Cathal mac Finguine, king of Munster (721–742), waged successful war against the Uí Néill, devastated Brega, and was remembered by the Munstermen as one of the greatest of their kings. It is likely that at a meeting at Terryglass in 737, Cathal and the king of the Uí Néill agreed to a delimitation of their spheres of influence that effectively excluded the Uí Néill from Munster.

In Feidlimid mac Crimthainn, the ascetic clericking of Munster, a shrewd politician in church as well as in state, the Uí Néill encountered a much more formidable enemy. Toward the end of the previous century the Uí Néill had made a number of devastating attacks on Munster, but Feidlimid, who ruled from 820 until his death in 847, turned the tables dramatically. He campaigned against the Uí Néill in 823 and 826, and forced Conchobar mac Donnchada, king of the Uí Néill, to a conference at the monastery of Birr, on the border of Munster and the Uí Néill lands. He fished in the troubled waters of Armagh ecclesiastical politics—now more than ever an Uí Néill monastery—and it is evident that he had wide territorial ambitions that may even have extended to establishing his authority over the Uí Néill. This he failed to do; the Uí Neill retained their hegemony and Máel Sechnaill, who succeeded to the kingship of the Uí Néill a year before the death of Feidlimid, was to be one of the greatest of their kings.

Máel Sechnaill belonged to Clann Cholmáin. Within a year of his accession, Feidlimid died and Munster fell to lesser men. By 851 Máel Sechnaill had crushed any local opposition to his rule and made himself master of the lands of the southern Uí Néill. He marched north against the Ulaid, and at a royal conference held at Armagh the king of the Ulaid acknowledged his supremacy. Between 854 and 858 Máel Sechnaill led a series of expeditions against Munster, devastated the province widely, and took the hostages of the province. Ironically, he found his most determined opponents among his own kinsmen, the northern Uí Néill; and though he led a great army of the forces of Leinster, Munster, Connacht, and southern Uí Néill into the north in 860, he was not successful and a desultory struggle continued until his death in 862. In his obituary the annalists entitle him *rí Érenn uile* (king of all Ireland), but his achievements were even more important historiographically than historically. Henceforth, the primacy of the Uí Néill "was universally accepted, at all events in theory" (as Daniel A. Binchy observes), and the understanding of the professional recorders of the past was increasingly brought into conformity with that doctrine.

The political reality was altogether more complex. From the death of Máel Sechnaill until the accession of Congalach Cnogba (of Knowth) in 944, and under the rule of such able kings as Áed Finnliath (*d.* 879), Flann Sinna (*d.* 916), Niall Glúndub (*d.* 919), and Donnchad Donn (*d.* 944), the Uí Néill were extremely powerful. Under Cormac mac Cuilennáin (902–908) Munster challenged their hegemony, but Cormac's attempt ended in failure and ultimately in the collapse of his own dynasty, the Eóganacht. However, the Uí Néill were soon to be wracked by a number of vicious dynastic struggles in which segments of the dynasty—Cinéal Conaill and Síl nÁeda Sláne—long absent from power struggled for the kingship. The reign of Domnall ua Néill (956–980) witnessed a fierce struggle between the northern and southern Uí Néill as Domnall attempted with great energy, and using novel military methods, to dominate the midlands and establish a kingship of Ireland based on firm territorial lordship and effective royal power. Though the annalist entitles him *ard-rí Érenn* (high king of Ireland) in his obituary, he had failed to realize his ambition. Three decades of dynastic strife had greatly weakened the Uí Néill; the kings of the provinces had grown powerful; and in Munster, Dál Cais had seized the kingship and ousted the Eóganacht, and were soon to do the same to the Uí Néill. Domnall's successor, Máel Sechnaill mac Domnail (*d.* 1022), was the last Uí Néill king of Tara in the old style.

Much changed in the wars of the great dynasties in the eleventh and twelfth centuries. The kings of Munster, Leinster, and Connacht dominated Ireland for periods, each pursuing the political prize of the kingship of Ireland with a new ruthlessness. In the course of these struggles the southern Uí Néill collapsed, and their territories were divided and redivided as spoils by the victors. The northern Uí Néill, now led by Meic Lochlainn, maintained themselves to greater effect, and though they enjoyed only one short period of overall dominance (1156–1166), they were frequently in a position to checkmate others.

In the period subsequent to the Norman invasion, the leading families of the northern Uí Néill maintained a precarious independence from the colony and later, on the ruins of the earldom of Ulster, built up some of the greatest Gaelic lordships of the Middle Ages. What remained of the kingdom of the southern Uí Néill was overrun by the Normans. Apart from a few families that survived as local lords, the leading dynasties disappeared from history.

BIBLIOGRAPHY

Daniel A. Binchy, "The Fair of Tailtiu and the Feast of Tara," in *Ériu,* 18 (1958), "The Passing of the Old Order," in Brian Ó Cuív, ed., *Proceedings of the International Congress of Celtic Studies 1959* (1962), and *Celtic and Anglo-Saxon Kingship* (1970); Francis J. Byrne, "The Ireland of St. Columba," in J. L. McCracken, ed., *Historical Studies,* V (1965), "Historical Note on Cnogba (Knowth)," in George Eogan, "Excavations at Knowth, Co. Meath, 1962–1965," in *Proceedings of the Royal Irish Academy,* 66, sec. C (1968), *The Rise of the Uí Néill and the High-Kingship of Ireland* (1970), and *Irish Kings and High-Kings* (1973); James Hogan, "The Irish Law of Kingship with Special Reference to Aileach and Cenél Eoghain," in *Proceedings of the Royal Irish Academy,* 40 (1932); John V. Kelleher, "Early Irish History and Pseudo-history," in *Studia hibernica,* 3 (1963); Eoin MacNeill, *Phases of Irish History* (1919, repr. 1970), *Celtic Ireland* (1921, repr. 1981), and *Saint Patrick* (1964); G. Mac Niocaill, *Ireland Before the Vikings* (1972); Gerard Murphy, "*Baile Chuind* and the Date of *Cín Dromma Snechtai,*" in *Ériu,* 18 (1958); Séamus Ó Ceallaigh, *Gleanings from Ulster History* (1951); Donnchadh Ó Corráin, *Ireland Before the Normans* (1972), "Nationality and Kingship in Pre-Norman Ireland," in T. W. Moody, ed., *Nationality and the Pursuit of National Independence* (1978), and "High-Kings, Vikings, and Other Kings," in *Irish Historical Studies,* 21 (1979); Thomas F. O'Rahilly, *Early Irish History and Mythology* (1946, repr. 1957); Paul Walsh, *Leaves of History* (1930), "Meath in the Book of Rights," in John Ryan, ed., *Féilsgríbhinn Eoin Mhic Néill* (1940), and "The Ua Maelechlainn Kings of Meath," in *Irish Ecclesiastical Record,* 57 (1941).

DONNCHADH Ó CORRÁIN

[See also **Adamnan, St.; Áed Sláne; Armagh; Cashel; Cinéal Eóghain; Connacht; Cormac Mac Airt; Cormac Mac Cuilennáin; Dál Cais; Eóganacht; Ireland; Leinster; Munster; Tara.**]

ʿULAMĀʾ (**Ulema**), scholars, and more specifically religious scholars, in the Islamic world who have been widely influential in Islamic history. They were the depositories of Islamic knowledge and, in their ubiquitousness, they were the interpreters of the Koran, compilers and authenticators of the *ḥadīth,* formulators of the *sharīʿa,* and state officials with civil and judicial responsibilities. They were theologians, lawyers, judges, legal consultants, witnesses, prayer leaders, preachers, and teachers. They were scribes, secretaries, emissaries, market inspectors, and tax collectors. The ʿ*ulamāʾ*

molded public opinion, mobilized masses, and defused protests. They legitimized the regime, sanctioned its taxes, and mobilized public support for it when the state was threatened. But just as they could support a regime, they could also bring it down. Thus, the ᶜulamāᵓ were the driving force behind the formation of Islamic consciousness, whether static and in favor of the status quo or dynamic and in favor of change.

With their pervasive role in the elaboration of the religious, political, legal, and economic institutions, the ᶜulamāᵓ never formed a distinct class. They were, however, part of the elite in their various walks of life. The ranks of the ᶜulamāᵓ promised the best opportunities for social and economic mobility, and thus their membership was continuously augmented by individuals from all sectors of society, from humble craftsmen to members of peasant or merchant families to sons of mamlūks.

The rise of religious education and the emergence of the ᶜulamāᵓ can be linked ultimately to the need of the early Islamic community to propagate its beliefs, as Muḥammad did when he instructed and sent his agents to the various parts of Arabia. But the spark was provided by the political controversy surrounding the death of the third caliph, ᶜUthmān, and the subsequent events of the "trials" (known to Western historians as the First Civil War, 656–661). Political stands were expressed through the theological debate regarding the nature of faith and works. This early schism became the impetus for the development of Islamic dogma as professed by the three main sects of Islam, the Sunna, the Shīᶜa, and the Khawārij.

The study of the Koran and the ḥadīth, as cornerstones of ᶜulamāᵓ education, was further necessitated by the more immediate need for a legal framework to regulate the vast cultural complex that came under the control of the Islamic state. This led to the eventual formation of several law schools, four of which are recognized as those of orthodox or Sunni Islam. The consolidation of the fourth school or rite of Sunni Islam, the Hanbalī, during the second half of the ninth century is illustrative of the role and the extent of their influence on the development of Islamic society. The rise of the Hanbalī school was at the expense of the Muᶜtazila, a religio-philosophical group that had strong connections to the Abbasid regime until 847 and to the merchant community. Of concern here was whether the Koran, as the word of God

and the primary source of law, was created or uncreated: temporal and subject to amendment or eternal and unchangeable.

Until then, the ᶜulamāᵓ had been able to establish a clear separation between the legislative and the executive branches in Islamic society; the ᶜulamāᵓ elaborated the law, and the state enforced it. Adoption of the doctrine of the createdness of the Koran could change this relationship and the Abbasid caliph al-Maᵓmūn (d. 833) enforced this Muᶜtazilite doctrine to the point of imposing a miḥna (religious inquisition) to assure that appointed qadis adhered to his position. But the more conservative, landed ᶜulamāᵓ, led by Aḥmad ibn Ḥanbal, won out. This failure at institutional transformation, in addition to other factors, contributed to the decline of the power of the caliph and of the institution of the caliphate.

With the rise of Sufism (Islamic mysticism), the ᶜulamāᵓ, especially the legally minded, were embroiled in yet another controversy, since the sharīᶜa (fundamental law revealed in the Koran) could regulate faith and works, as evidenced in the actions and social relations of the individual, but could not regulate the faith that springs from the inner self, which the mystics advocated. This dilemma was finally reconciled by the scholar and jurist al-Ghazālī (d. 1111); hence, mysticism became part of Sunni Islam, and many ᶜulamāᵓ became members, even leaders, of Sufi ṭarīqas. As a leading pro-establishment intellectual at Baghdad, al-Ghazālī also attacked Islamic philosophers who had been at pains to reconcile revelation with reason. His book Tahāfut al-falāsifa (Downfall [or incoherence] of the philosophers) prompted an equally strong response from the Spanish Muslim philosopher Ibn Rushd (Averroës) in the book Tahāfut al-Tahāfut (Downfall of the downfall [of al-Ghazālī's book]). Eventually, ecstatic, syncretic, and cultic tendencies crept back into orthodox Islam when, during the Mamluk period, they were popularized by Sufi dervishes, who introduced many irrational and alien concepts, thus providing bases for ᶜulamāᵓ across the ages to proclaim their reform movements.

The ᶜulamāᵓ also had a strong presence in the economy either through direct participation as merchants, craftsmen and professionals or through their legal profession. Hanafi scholars, for example, introduced legal tricks into the sharīᶜa largely to circumvent the Koranic ban on ribā (interest). The ᶜulamāᵓ validated and witnessed business transactions, sales, wills, transfers of property, inheritances, and marriages. They became guardians of minors and orphans and managed their wealth for them. They also came into control of charitable endowments (*awqāf*) and supervised the dispensing of their income to the recipients, whether individuals or such institutions as mosques, schools, or hospitals. As *muḥtasibs* (market inspectors), morals such as honesty, fair prices, proper weights and measures, quality, and good public behavior came under their jurisdiction also.

For all of their influence, the ᶜ*ulamāᵓ* did not have a formalized system of education until late in the eleventh century, when Baghdad and much of western Asia came under the domination of the Seljuks and when their vizier Niẓām al-Mulk (*fl.* 1063–1092) introduced the madrasa system. These were schools or colleges for the education and training of scholars to serve in the bureaucracy and to participate in the propagation of Sunni ideals and thus engage their Shiite counterparts who had been similarly trained in al-Azhar, founded earlier (969/970) by the Fatimids in Cairo. The establishment of the madrasa system concretized the alliance of the ᶜ*ulamāᵓ* with the ruling institution. This alliance was most evident during the Mamluk period when an alien, non-Arabic-speaking military elite dominated Egypt and Syria and thus had to depend on the ᶜ*ulamāᵓ* to fill the various posts and to act as the intermediaries between the rulers and the subject population. The preeminence of the ᶜ*ulamāᵓ* in the Muslim world continued until the advent of modern bureaucracies and secular educational systems in the nineteenth century.

BIBLIOGRAPHY

Hayyim J. Cohen, "The Economic Background and the Secular Occupations of Muslim Jurisprudents and Traditionalists in the Classical Period of Islam," in *Journal of the Economic and Social History of the Orient (JESHO)*, 13 (1970); Benjamin R. Foster, "Agoranomos and Muḥtasib," *ibid.*; Nikki Keddie, ed., *Scholars, Saints, and Sufis* (1972); Ira Lapidus, *Muslim Cities in the Later Middle Ages* (1967, repr. 1984), 107–115, 130–141, and, as editor, *Middle Eastern Cities* (1969); Afaf Lutfi al-Sayyid Marsot, "The Political and Economic Function of the ᶜ*Ulamāᵓ* in the Eighteenth Century," in *JESHO*, 16 (1973); W. Montgomery Watt, *The Formative Period of Islamic Thought* (1973).

MAHMOOD IBRAHIM

[See also **Azhar, al-; Caliphate; Damascus; Ḥadith; Hanbal, Aḥmad ibn Muḥammad ibn; Islamic Administration; Koran; Law, Islamic; Madrasa; Muḥtasib; Muᶜtazila, al-; Schools, Islamic.**]

ULEMA. See ᶜUlamāᵓ.

ÚLFR UGGASON (*fl.* late tenth century), Icelandic skald, composed *Húsdrápa* (House ode), in Old Norse *dróttkvætt*, probably around 985. The fourteen separate half-stanzas that have survived are preserved in manuscripts of *Snorra Edda*. Their fifty-six lines relate three mythological tales carved on the wainscoting of an Icelandic hall: the strange procession to Baldr's funeral pyre, the struggle between Heimdallr and Loki for possession of Freyja's necklace, and Thor's contest with the Midgard serpent. The last seems to have been a favorite subject of northern artists: it appears on Danish and Swedish stone carvings and is treated by the author of the Eddic *Hymiskviða*, by Bragi and his near contemporary Ǫlvir hnúfa, and by the tenth-century poet Eysteinn Valdason.

According to *Laxdœla saga* (chap. 29), Úlfr Uggason delivered his poem within the hall, at the wedding feast for the owner's daughter, and was handsomely rewarded. *Húsdrápa* is a picture poem in the tradition of Bragi's *Ragnarsdrápa* and Þjóðólfr's *Haustlǫng*. Thor's hammer—traditionally used to hallow the bride at weddings—is portrayed in *Húsdrápa*, as it must have appeared on the wainscoting: crushing the head of the Midgard serpent, threatening the skull of the giantess Hyrrokin, and consecrating a funeral pyre on which Baldr and Nanna lie dead.

The *drápa* has a one-line refrain—*Hlaut innan svá minnum*—the syntax and sense of which are obscure. The line may have formed part of a *klofastef* (a split refrain), a *stef* consisting of several lines, each inserted separately. The refrain as it stands seems to say, "[The hall] was thus adorned within with memorials." Beneath the several meanings of *minni* (memorials in the form of old-lore carvings, memorial toasts offered up to the gods at pagan banquets, or oral commemorations in general) lies a sense of the power of memory.

Úlfr's kennings are often complex and sometimes comic. His first stanza encloses a simple kenning for poetry (*Grímnis gjǫf* [Odin's gift]) with a second, far more elaborate one: *Hildar hjaldrgegnis geð-*

fjarðar ló (a billow from the mind fjord [breast] of the noise-champion of Hildr [Odin]). His sixth stanza refers to the head of the world serpent as *hlusta grunnr* (ground of ears), a kenning almost as extravagant as that for the same serpent's head in *Hymiskviða*: "too ugly high hill of the hair." The half-stanzas of *Húsdrápa* are intense, dramatic re-shapings of what the poet would have seen before him on the carved panels: the gleaming eyes of Thor and of the serpent, and the gods' burnished helmets and swords, all illuminated by the flickering flames of the hearth fire. The last descriptive stanza relates how the giantess Hyrrokin came rushing on her wolf-steed to launch Baldr's funeral ship:

> *Fullǫflug lét fjalla*
> *framm haf-Sleipni þramma*
> *Hildr; en Hropts of gildar*
> *hjalmelda mar felldu.*

The very powerful goddess of the fells [giantess] made the sea-Sleipnir [ship; Sleipnir was Odin's horse] thrust forward; and Hroptr's [Odin's] champions [berserks] of the helmet fires [swords] felled her horse [wolf].

Úlfr opens *Húsdrápa* with an image of poetry as a wave from Odin's breast; he ends stanza 14 with a consonant vision: "There the river comes to the sea."

BIBLIOGRAPHY

Editions are Finnur Jónsson, *Den norsk-islandske skjaldedigtning*, IA (1912), 136–139 (diplomatic text), and IB (1915), 128–130 (normalized text with Old Norse prose renditions translated into Danish); Ernst A. Kock, ed., *Den norsk-isländska skaldediktningen*, I (1946), 71–72. A useful study is Jan de Vries, *Altnordische Literaturgeschichte*, 2nd ed., I (1964), 206.

ROBERTA FRANK

[See also **Baldr; Dróttkvætt; Eddic Poetry; Heimdallr; Kenning; Laxdœla Saga; Midgard Serpent; Scandinavian Mythology; Skaldic Poetry; Snorra Edda; Thor.**]

ULJAYTU KHUDABĀNDA (Öljeitü, *b.* 1282; *r.* 1304–1316), the eighth Ilkhanid sultan to rule Iran and a fifth-generation descendant of Genghis Khan. Uljaytu (Mongolian, "Felicitous One") was the name he adopted on his accession to the throne; it usually preceded Khudabānda, Persian for "God's slave," a counterpart of the Arabic ᶜAbd Allāh and a name frequently used by converts to Islam. Uljaytu's names were symbolic of the religious climate of his time and society; his earliest names appear to have been the Central Asian words Bogha ("Bull") and Temür ("Iron"), for he was born at a time when shamanism and *yasa,* the Genghisid tribal law, were still predominant among the Mongols of Iran. Christianity had begun to spread among the ruling family, especially the women, however, and Uljaytu's mother, a Nestorian Christian, had him baptized as Nicholas. After a brief flirtation with Buddhism and upon conversion to Islam (possibly due to the influence of his wife), his personal name became Muḥammad, while another of his earlier names, Kharbānda (Persian, "Assherd," but possibly an adaptation of Mongolian, Ghurbanta, "Third" [son of Arghun]), changed to Khudabānda. Finally, upon his accession, in addition to Mongolian Uljaytu, he also adopted the Arabic *laqab*s (honorific surnames) Ghiyāth al-Dunya wa ᶜl-Dīn, so that his full name was Muḥammad Ghiyāth al-Dunya wa 'l-Dīn Uljaytu Khudabānda, or just Uljaytu Sultan.

Uljaytu, like Ghāzān before him, converted first to Sunnite Islam; the early coins of his reign thus bear the names of the four orthodox caliphs. His switch to Shiism was in part caused by his distaste for the mutual intolerance of the Hanafi and Shafii representatives of Sunnite Islam at the court. It appears that similar factors worked in favor of a trend toward Shiite Islam among the common people of his time as well. The Twelver Shīᶜa (Ithnā ᶜasharī) denomination was adopted, and henceforward Uljaytu's coins bore the names of the twelve imams.

In foreign relations Uljaytu's accession coincided with an impressive, although ultimately ineffective, attempt to recreate Mongol unity under the leadership of the Great Khan Temür in Peking, a unity reminiscent of the time of Genghis Khan and Great Khan Ögedey. One expression of this attempt was an embassy he received at Ujan that included envoys of Chabar and Qaydu, each a khan of a principal Inner Asian *ulus,* and somewhat later the envoys of Toqta, khan of the Golden Horde; another was a letter Uljaytu sent in 1305 to the French king Philip IV the Fair in which he stressed this reestablished unity. Despite his conversion to Islam, Uljaytu continued the friendly diplomatic contacts with Christian Europe so characteristic of his predecessors; he sent an embassy to France with letters to Pope Clement V, Philip IV, and Edward I of

England. The European leaders continued to hope for a definitive Mongol conversion to Christianity and the resulting alliance against Islam, and the embassy concealed from them the sultan's conversion to the latter religion. Geopolitical factors, however, continued to play a role; combined with the Shiite nature of Uljaytu's conversion, they led to occasional cooperation between him and the Byzantines: Uljaytu married Maria, sister of Andronikos II Palaiologos, the Byzantine emperor, and relieved some of the pressure on the emperor by combatting the Turkish princes of Anatolia. On the southwestern front, Uljaytu's failure to take the Syrian town of Rahba (1313) marked the end of the Ilkhanids' half-century-long contest with the Mamluks of Egypt. Closer to home, Uljaytu's attempt to conquer the province of Gilan brought little more than promise of tribute from the local princes and cost him his ablest commander, Qutlughshah.

Throughout the years of Uljaytu's rule, one of the two principal statesmen of Ilkhanid Iran was Rashīd al-Dīn; it was Uljaytu who encouraged him to, or perhaps even suggested that he, expand his historical work *Tārīkh-i Ghāzān*, a history of the Mongols, so as to make it a history of Eurasia: the famous *Jāmi ᶜal-tawārīkh* (Compendium of histories) was the result. Uljaytu established Sultaniye as the realm's capital, and built there a mausoleum (shown at "Islamic Art") that became his final resting place and one of the most brilliant monuments of Islamic architecture. He may have planned to transfer there the remains of the Shiite imams from Iraq. Uljaytu patronized other forms of Islamic art as well, best exemplified by an illuminated oversized thirty-volume Koran. He also took a keen interest in the geographical features of Iran, ordering a topographical survey that included measuring the roads and setting up milestones. The astronomical observatory at Maragheh continued to flourish under his support.

Uljaytu died on 17 December 1316, only thirty-five years old. His early death may have been hastened by excesses of diet and drinking characteristic of the Mongol elite. A tragic by-product of Uljaytu's sudden demise was Rashīd al-Dīn's execution under Abū Saᶜīd.

BIBLIOGRAPHY
Edward Granville Browne, *A Literary History of Persia,* III (1924, repr. 1964), 46–51; Henry Hoyle Howorth, *History of the Mongols,* III (1888, repr. 1965), 534–584; Bertold Spuler, *Die Mongolen in Iran,* 4th rev. ed. (1985), esp. 90–98. See also *Cambridge History of Iran,* V (1968), 397–406 and bibliography, esp. 691–694.

SVAT SOUCEK

[See also **Ghāzān (Khan), Maḥmūd; Golden Horde; Ilkhanids; Iran, History; Mongol Empire; Sects, Islamic; Shāfiᶜī, al-.**]

ULLR, one of the oldest of the North Germanic gods. Although the traditions concerning Ullr have been transmitted only in fragmentary form, it is possible to conclude on the basis of the alternation in form between Ullr and Ullinn, the evidence of place-names, and the literary allusions that are preserved that Ullr may once have been the dominant god among the Svear of central Sweden. The name is generally acknowledged to be cognate with the Gothic *wulþus* (magnificence), Old English *wuldor* (glory), and Latin *vultus* (expression, appearance). Ullr, formed like Óðr and Njǫrðr with the Indo-European suffix *-tu- (Proto-Germanic *wulð-), indicates an archaic stage of Old Norse, as does the further extension in *-in-, which yielded Ullinn, like Óðinn (Odin). Place-names that are compounds of Ullr with *vin* (meadow) or *akr* (field), again indicating great antiquity, are concentrated in Swedish Uppland with a later extension to the Norwegian Oplandene. But the sites themselves seem already to have been abandoned long before the arrival of Christianity and the written transmission of the literary-mythological traditions.

Ullr's dwelling was in Ydalir (yew dale) (*Grímnismál 5*). Snorri, in *Gylfaginning 31* and *Skáldskaparmál 14*, says that Ullr is unsurpassed as an archer and skier, and gives as other names for him *bogaáss* (bow god), *veiðiáss* (god of the hunt), and *ǫnduráss* (ski god). The yew was both the symbol of eternal fertility (compare the evergreen tree at the well by the heathen temple at Uppsala) and the best material for the making of bows. Ullr in his snowy setting has been viewed as the seasonal antipode to Freyr, the god of vernal fertility, or as the "original" fertility god, whose association with the yew symbolized a magic winter survival. Elgqvist sees a possible etymological connection with "well" and the proximity of place-names to springs as an indication that Ullr was originally the well itself, particularly the kind that remains open throughout the winter. He postulates that the association with the evergreen tree was primary, and the mythologem of Ullr as the hunter vanquishing the winter fastness with bow and skis secondary.

Some few hints of the nature of Ullr's cult are that oaths were to be sworn "on Ullr's ring" (*at hringi Ullar*), that a kenning for shield was "Ullr's keel" (*Ullar kjóll*), and that he was also known as "the shield god" (*skjaldaráss*). There were rings on shields, and Elgqvist points out that rings are found hewn in Upplandic stones. He notes in particular a quartzite gravestone located near Ulleråkers assembly place (*tingsplats*) and St. Erik's well in Uppsala.

If Ullr had a role in the warrior cult, his position must have been assumed by Odin when the latter became the predominant god of the north.

BIBLIOGRAPHY

Erik Elgqvist, *Ullvi och Ullinshov* (1955), 57–121; Anne Holtsmark, "Ullr," in *Kulturhistorisk leksikon for nordisk middelalder,* XIX (1975); Snorri Sturluson, *The Prose Edda,* Arthur G. Brodeur, trans. (1916), 41, 114; Edward O. G. Turville-Petre, *Myth and Religion of the North* (1964), 182–184; Jan de Vries, *Altgermanische Religionsgeschichte,* II, 2nd ed. (1957), 153–163.

JAMES E. CATHEY

[See also **Eddic Poetry; Grímnismál; Gylfaginning; Odin; Scandinavian Mythology.**]

ULRICH FÜETRER (*ca.* 1430–after 1496), Bavarian painter, poet, and historian. Born in Landshut (Lower Bavaria) of a reputable family, he probably attended the local Latin school and later may have been apprenticed to the painter Dietrich Zeiller, who was active there about 1440. In the later 1440's or early 1450's, Füetrer moved to Munich, possibly at the suggestion of Jakob Püterich von Reichertshausen (*ca.* 1400–1469), a ducal official and judge in Landshut in 1442, and a passionate reader and collector of epic poems of the twelfth and thirteenth centuries. Füetrer's name appears for the first time in Munich in 1453 in a record of payment for wax and dyes. Although he was an officer of the painters' guild at various times between 1459 and 1494, no painting by him has survived. In contemporary records, his name appears several times as a painter of frescoes in monasteries, castles, and public buildings in and near Munich; of these works, two series of coats of arms remain, one in the Munich Old City Hall (Altes Rathaus), the other over the gatehouse of the hunting lodge of Grünwald south of Munich. The last direct reference to him is from the year 1496; presumably he died shortly thereafter.

Between 1478 and 1481, Füetrer compiled his *Bayerische Chronik* (Bavarian chronicle); like all his written works, it was dedicated to his patron, Duke Albrecht IV of Bavaria (1465–1508). It was probably Püterich who introduced Füetrer at court; in his *Der Trojanerkrieg* (Trojan war), he refers to Püterich and to several other artists and poets in the circle around Albrecht. Füetrer's main literary work is the *Buch der Abenteuer* (Book of adventures), a reworking of earlier epic poems in three books, composed in the seven-line *Titurelstrophe.* Book I, containing about 3,000 strophes, retells the story of the Knights of the Grail as found in Albrecht von Scharfenberg's *Der jüngere Titurel* (Young Titurel), Wolfram von Eschenbach's *Parzival,* Heinrich von dem Türlin's *Diu Krone* (The crown), and the anonymous epic *Lohengrin.* This book also contains sections about Merlin and the Trojan War; it is possible that the latter was composed separately and then incorporated into the work at a later time. Book II, about 2,500 strophes in length, consists of seven independent "histories," each named for its main character: Wigoleis, Seifrid de Ardemont, Meleranz, Iban, Persibein, Poytislier, and Flordimar. Book III, about 5,700 strophes in length, is a verse rendering of Füetrer's earlier prose novel *Lanzelot.* The dating of these works is less certain than that of the *Bayerische Chronik,* but the available evidence indicates that the prose *Lanzelot* was written about 1467 and Book I of the *Buch der Abenteuer* between 1473 and 1478. Books II and III were composed after the completion of the *Chronik* in 1481—Book II by 1487 and Book III shortly thereafter.

Füetrer as poet and historian is a representative of the *Ritterrenaissance* (the renaissance of chivalry) of the later fifteenth century. In the *Buch der Abenteuer* he celebrates the deeds and ideals of knighthood that he found in his sources. His *Bayerische Chronik,* a history of the ducal house of Wittelsbach from earliest times, was consulted by such later historians as Aventinus and remains an important contribution to Bavarian historiography.

BIBLIOGRAPHY

Sources. Alice Carlson, ed., *Ulrich Füetrer und sein "Iban"* (1927); Edward G. Fichtner, ed., *Der Trojanerkrieg* (1968) and "A Knight's Progress: Ideal and Reality in Ulrich Füetrer's 'Poytislier,'" in *Monatshefte,* **74** (1982); Heribert A. Hilgers, ed., *Wigoleis* (1975); Kurt

Nyholm, ed., *Die Gralepen in Ulrich Füetrers Bearbeitung* (1964), which includes Book I of the *Book of Adventures*, exclusive of the *Trojan War*; Friedrich Panzer, ed., *"Merlin" und "Seifrid de Ardemont" von Albrecht von Scharfenberg in der Bearbeitung Ulrich Füetrers* (1902); Arthur Peter, ed., *Prosaroman von "Lanzelot"* (1885, repr. 1972); Reinhold Spiller, ed., *Bayerische Chronik* (1909, repr. 1969); Friederike Weber, *"Poytislier" aus dem "Buch der Abenteuer" von Ulrich Füetrer* (1960).

Studies. Edward G. Fichtner, "Umlaut in the Manuscripts of Füetrer's *Trojanerkrieg*," in *Journal of English and Germanic Philology*, 67 (1968); Wolfgang Harms, "Anagnorisis-Szenen des mittelalterlichen Romans und Ulrich Füetrers *Buch der Abenteuer*," in *Zeitschrift für deutsches Alterum*, 95 (1966), and "Zu Ulrich Füetrers Auffassung vom Erzählen und von der Historie," in *Zeitschrift für deutsche Philologie*, 93 (1974): Sonderheft "Spätmittelalterliche Epik"; Hans-Georg Maak, "Die nichthöfischen Stilelemente in Ulrich Füetrers *Abenteuerbuch*," in *Neuphilologische Mitteilungen*, 68 (1967), and "Das sprachlich-stilistische Vorbild von Ulrich Füetrers *Abenteuerbuch*," in *Zeitschrift für deutsche Philologie*, 93 (1974): Sonderheft "Spätmittelalterliche Epik"; Kurt Nyholm, "Das höfische Epos im Zeitalter des Humanismus," in *Neuphilologische Mitteilungen*, 66 (1965), and *Albrechts von Scharfenberg "Merlin"* (1967); Stephen L. Wailes, "Theme and Structure in Ulrich Füetrer's 'Poytislier,'" in *Modern Language Notes*, 92 (1977).

EDWARD G. FICHTNER

[See also **Albrecht von Scharfenberg; Arthurian Literature; German Literature; Gottfried von Strassburg; Heinrich von dem Türlin; Lohengrin; Middle High German Literature; Troy Story; Wolfram von Eschenbach.**]

ULRICH VON ENSINGEN (*d.* 1419), German master mason who was appointed *Baumeister* of Ulm Minster in 1392, *Werkmeister* of Strasbourg Cathedral in 1399, and *Baumeister* of the Frauenkirche in Esslingen in 1400. Thus he served simultaneously as architect for three of the most important German ecclesiastical projects of his time. His beautiful elevation drawing for the west tower and spire of Ulm has survived, although it was not executed by himself or later builders.

BIBLIOGRAPHY

Friedrich Carstanjen, *Ulrich von Ensingen* (1893); Otto Kletzl, "Das Frühwerk Ulrichs von Ensingen," in *Architectura*, 1 (1933).

LON R. SHELBY

[See also **Architect, Status of; Gothic Architecture; Masons and Builders; Strasbourg Cathedral.**]

ULRICH VON ESCHENBACH (Etzenbach) was born in north Bohemia, probably around the middle of the thirteenth century, a member of the German-speaking population there. Although the poet repeatedly refers to Wolfram von Eschenbach as his model, there is no evidence of familial relationship. Indeed his attitude toward his literary material would seem to indicate that Ulrich was not a member of the knightly class but rather a bourgeois. The evidence of his surviving works appears also to show that he had received a clerical education. He demonstrates a knowledge of Latin, theology, the Bible, and a wealth of religious writing, but it is not probable he was ordained a priest. Ulrich demonstrates that, in addition to his familiarity with churchly matters, he was quite well versed in secular literature. He knew the works not only of Wolfram but also of Hartmann von Aue, Gottfried von Strassburg, the minnesingers of the classical period, and many other epic and lyric poets as well. Although, according to his own testimony, he was not particularly well off, he did live for a period of time at the court in Prague and was personally acquainted with King Ottokar II himself. His works include the *Alexander, Wilhelm von Wenden*, and probably the *Herzog von Ernst D*.

References in Ulrich's *Alexander* to Ottokar II and Wenzel II of Bohemia lead to the conclusion that this work was composed between 1271 and 1286. The main source for the lengthy narrative poem was the Latin *Alexandreis* of Walter of Châtillon. Ulrich borrowed additional material from the prose romance *Historia de preliis* and augmented his treatment of individual scenes from his wide-ranging knowledge of German literary traditions (particularly Wolfram). The poet has in fact taken what was an essentially historical account of the world conqueror (his major Latin source) and re-formed it, combining it with the matter of romance so that love, adventure, fine sentiments, and medieval courtly etiquette come to play an important role. Ottokar II of Bohemia was fond of comparing himself with Alexander. Ulrich's classical hero bears Ottokar's escutcheon (the lion), and the poet's lengthy narrative (28,000 lines plus a 2,000-line addendum), with its historical and chivalric dimensions, is surely intended as a legitimation of the growing political and cultural ambitions of the court in Prague.

Wilhelm von Wenden (over 8,358 lines) was composed sometime after the completion of the *Alexander,* probably around 1290. Again the purpose of Ulrich's literary undertaking is praise of the royal house of Bohemia. The hero of the poem is presented as an ancestor of Wenzel (Wenceslaus) II, and the work's heroine is given the name Bene, a play on the German word *gut* and surely a reference to Guta, the daughter of Rudolf of Habsburg, whom Wenzel married in 1287. According to a prologue in one of the late manuscripts of the poem, Ulrich's source was transmitted to him by a Bohemian Dominican. The story material is similar to that which we find in the anonymous German work *Die Gute Frau* (*La bone dame*) and this thirteenth-century poem may have suggested the allusion in Ulrich's work to Wenzel's wife. The narrative belongs to a tradition represented by the St. Eustachius legend and the *Guillaume d'Angleterre* (the latter probably leaving its trace in the name of Ulrich's hero—Wilhelm). The basic narrative, whatever its precise source, was one not unfamiliar to medieval tradition. It is the story of a noble ruler and his wife who abandon their position in society because of a religious conversion and take up a life of pilgrimage and poverty. The couple are separated by circumstances from one another and from their twin sons, then ultimately reunited and reinstated in rule. And, just as in the *Alexander* history is seen through the prism of romance, so here in Ulrich's *Wilhelm* the sharp contours of Christian legend are softened by the values of courtly culture. Realistic details inserted into the work seem to constitute an argument for the necessity of the emerging territorial estate.

The *Herzog Ernst D,* which combines historical, chivalric, and fantastic elements, has also been attributed to Ulrich. This work is decidedly less successful than the other two, and it has recently been argued that certain political tendencies of the work would have been unthinkable at the court in Prague and that the work could not have been composed there.

BIBLIOGRAPHY

Sources. Friedrich von der Hagen, ed., *Herzog Ernst D,* in *Deutsche Gedichte des Mittelalters,* I (1808); Hans-Friedrich Rosenfeld, ed., *Wilhelm von Wenden* (1957); Wendelin Toischer, ed., *Alexander* (1888).

Studies. Hans-Joachim Behr, "Literatur und Politik am Böhmerhof, Ulrich von Etzenbach, *Herzog Ernst D* und der sogenannte 'Anhang' zum *Alexander,"* in *Zeitschrift für deutsche Philologie,* **96** (1977); Margot Hühne, *Die Alexanderepen Rudolfs von Ems und Ulrichs von Eschenbach* (1939); Rainer Kohlmayer, *Ulrichs von Etzenbach "Wilhelm von Wenden"* (1974); Käthe Leonhardt, *Quellengeschichtliche Untersuchungen zum Wilhelm von Wenden des Ulrich von Eschenbach* (1931); Hermann Meier, *Zum Reimgebrauch im Herzog Ernst D und bei Ulrich von Eschenbach* (1930); Hans Paul, *Ulrich von Eschenbach und seine Alexandreis* (1914); Hans-Friedrich Rosenfeld, "Zum Wilhelm von Wenden Ulrichs von Eschenbach," in *Neophilologus,* **12** (1927), *Herzog Ernst D und Ulrich von Eschenbach* (1929), "Zum Alexander-Anhang Ulrichs von Eschenbach," in *Zeitschrift für deutsches Altertum,* **68** (1931), and "Der Kreuzfahrtdichter und Ulrichs von Eschenbach Anhang zum Alexander," in *Zeitschrift für deutsche Philologie,* **56** (1931); D. J. A. Ross, "*Alexander* and Antilois the Dwarf King," in *Zeitschrift für deutsches Altertum,* **98** (1969).

JAMES F. POAG

[See also **Alexander Romances; Bohemia-Moravia; German Literature: Romance; Gottfried von Strassburg; Gute Frau, Die; Hartmann von Aue; Herzog Ernst; Middle High German Literature; Walter of Châtillon; Wolfram von Eschenbach.**]

ULRICH VON LIECHTENSTEIN (*ca.* 1198–*ca.* 1275), a prolific poet, was the author of fifty-seven minnesongs, a *Leich,* three long love letters in verse, a novel in eight-line stanzas, and a lengthy debate in rhymed couplets. A wealthy and influential Styrian knight, he played a significant role in the affairs of his native duchy, especially during the unsettled times of the interregnum that followed the death of Emperor Frederick II.

Ulrich's lyric poetry seems to have been composed when he was young, because the simplicity of most of the strophic patterns and rhyme schemes resembles the style of the early thirteenth century and because it has neither the broad humor nor the chatty didacticism that characterizes the later works. The songs employ the situations, motifs, symbols, and points of view of the established minnesong tradition, but, in spite of a lack of originality, their clarity, ease of expression, distinctness of theme, and carefree lightheartedness give them a special stamp and place them among the best of the postclassical period. The author has provided valuable information about the structure of different kinds of medieval lyric verse by classifying most of his own according to type: *sincwîse* (melody to be sung), *tanzwîse* (dance tune), *vrouwentanz* (ladies' dance), *reye* (a fast-moving group dance), *langiu wîse* (perhaps a through-composed tune), *ûzreise* (march), and *tagewîse* (dawn song). The majority of his songs are dance songs. The single *Leich* presents a regular pattern of versicles— *a b c d e f e b c d e f e g*—in which the first and the last are not paired and one occurs four times. All of Ulrich's melodies have been lost, but he says of the *Leich* that it had high notes and quick notes. His songs have been popular with translators, and English versions of some of them have appeared in many anthologies. Their chief models were probably the compositions of Reinmar von Hagenau and Walther von der Vogelweide.

The love letters, which the poet calls *büechlîn,* average nearly 400 lines in length. The predominant iambic tetrameter is frequently varied by the inclusion of trimeter lines, trochaic feet, feminine rhyme, triplet rhyme, and the omission of initial unstressed syllables, so that the effect is that of lyric, rather than of narrative, verse. The first two letters consist of dialogues, between the author and the letter itself and between the author and a personified Lady Love, respectively; the third addresses itself directly to the recipient. All are filled with extravagant praise of his lady love and assertions of complete devotion to her in the usual stylized language of the convention of courtly love. The literary value of the letters is less than that of the songs.

About 1255 the songs and the letters were incorporated into the novel *Frauendienst,* which poses as an autobiographical account of the service of two ladies. It is a humorous parody of the minnesong, with all its traditional conceits and motifs: the aloof lady, the messenger, the watchman, the languishing lover who performs knightly feats in his lady's honor and composes songs in her praise, and other standard elements. In the service of the first lady the hero—nominally disguised as Dame Venus, but playing the role of Lady Love—undertakes a journey from Venice to Bohemia, jousting with the local knights along the way. To serve the second lady he makes a similar jousting tour as King Arthur and thus adds the parody of the popular Arthurian romance to that of the minnesong. The overall humorous effect was increased for Ulrich's fellow Styrians by his use of many of them as actors in his

story. Verisimilitude is gained by several references to contemporary historical events.

Ulrich's last work, entitled *Der Frauen Buch,* purports to have been composed at the request of his lady love. It presents a dispute in 2,134 verses as to which sex was responsible for the prevailing low spirits of courtly society. At the end the author comes on the scene as a mediator and decides in favor of the lady, saying that the social malaise was caused by the decline in the faithful service of ladies. In a light, conversational tone the poem treats a conventional motif of courtly literature and witnesses to the medieval interest in forensic techniques and argumentation for its own sake. It has been taken too seriously by some scholars, who have assumed that the author was exposing and lamenting a real and widespread cultural decline.

Der Frauen Buch in no way compares with *Frauendienst,* which is one of the most original compositions of the medieval period. The *Frauendienst* is the first long work of German narrative fiction to be told in the first person, to have a specifically contemporary setting and cast, to maintain a consistently humorous tone, and to include lyric verse. Its uniqueness has led many historians of literature to believe, in spite of a large number of improbable and several impossible incidents, that the work really was autobiography. However, Ulrich did not need to look far to find literary inspiration for his innovations. Some of the songs of Neidhart von Reuental relate amusing episodes in the first person about the discomfiture of a knight with the author's name who seeks the favor of a rude country girl, three of Tannhäuser's songs are parodies on a courtly level of the concept of service of ladies, and two of his *Leiche* tell humorous love stories that begin like traditional minnesongs but unexpectedly turn out quite differently. The chief source for the new ideas, however, was Wolfram von Eschenbach's *Parzival,* to which Ulrich refers. Its narrator corresponds closely to that of *Frauendienst:* both are illiterate knights who compose verse but do not consider themselves professional poets, and each has a wife of whom he is very fond and a lady love whom he at last forsakes because of her unkindness and attacks with bitter songs. *Parzival* also refers to contemporary people and events and has a long, comic account of a knight's service of ladies: the Gawain story. Other similarities between the two works confirm Ulrich's debt to Wolfram without diminishing the former's accomplishments. For not only did he further develop what he had borrowed, but he transferred everything from an epic to a lyric framework, so that his novel—a parody of the courtly love lyric—is itself basically an expanded minnesong.

BIBLIOGRAPHY

A survey of the research on Ulrich up to 1968 and an extensive bibliography appear in J. W. Thomas, *Ulrich von Liechtenstein's "Service of Ladies"* (1969). Most of the subsequent scholarship falls into one of two groups, that which is primarily interested in the relationship between *Frauendienst* and mid-thirteenth-century society and that which treats strictly literary matters. The former includes: Timothy McFarland, "Ulrich von Lichtenstein and the Autobiographical Narrative Form," in Peter Ganz and Werner Schröder, eds., *Probleme mittelhochdeutscher Erzählformen: Marburger Colloqium 1969* (1972); Ursula Peters, *Frauendienst: Untersuchungen zu Ulrich von Lichtenstein und zum Wirklichkeitsgehalt der Minnedichtung* (1971); Klaus M. Schmidt, "Späthöfische Gesellschaftsstruktur und die Ideologie des Frauendienstes bei Ulrich von Lichtenstein," in *Zeitschrift für deutsche Philologie*, **94** (1975).

Recent studies that are chiefly concerned with literary problems include: Saul N. Brody, "The Comic Rejection of Courtly Love," in Joan M. Ferrante *et al.*, eds., *In Pursuit of Perfection: Courtly Love in Medieval Literature* (1975); Ingeborg Glier, "Diener zweier Herrinnen: Zu Ulrichs von Lichtenstein *Frauendienst*," in Harald Scholler, ed., *The Epic in Medieval Society: Aesthetic and Moral Values* (1977); J. W. Thomas, "*Parzival* as a Source for *Frauendienst*," in *Modern Language Notes*, **87** (1972), and "The Minnesong Structure of Ulrich von Liechtenstein's *Frauendienst*," in *Zeitschrift für deutsches Altertum und deutsche Literatur*, **102** (1973).

J. Wesley Thomas

[See also **Arthurian Literature; German Literature: Lyric; Gottfried von Strassburg; Hartmann von Aue; Middle High German Literature; Minnesingers; Neidhart "von Reuental"; Tannhäuser; Wolfram von Eschenbach.**]

ULRICH VON SINGENBERG (thirteenth century), minnesinger. Documents indicate that Ulrich, the author of some thirty songs (as many as 134 strophes), had not reached his majority in 1209, but that in the 1220's he was active as a seneschal (*Truchsess*) of St. Gall, an office his father held before and his son after him. One document associates him with Henry VII, the son of Frederick II, at Ulm in 1227. He names Walther von der Vogelweide as his master. His songs also betray the strong influence of Reinmar der Alte and probable acquaintance with some songs by Albrecht von Johansdorf and Neidhart "von Reuental." A love for etymological puns and elaborate internal rhyme links him to Gottfried von Neifen, but the affinities are general rather than specific.

Singenberg's variations on known models consistently lack the pithiness and flair of the originals, and scholars are generally agreed in decrying his epigonalism. Nevertheless, his songs are accomplished enough to suggest that their apparent diffusiveness is a response to a changed aesthetic and a new relationship between singer and audience rather than a demonstration of artistic impotence. In song 31, his parody of Walther's vowel song, he seems to address the question of originality versus tradition directly. He remarks in song 20 how his comfortable position in life differs from Walther's struggle for existence. In his case, according to Müller, obscurity in political and gnomic songs may reflect his independence of support from a patron.

Verbal linking of strophes, which gives many songs a greater unity than those of earlier singers, may be an accidental result of a love for repetition rather than conscious artistry. In several songs, however, comments on the process of composition are woven into the fabric of the song (especially in song 27). Ulrich both reflects and anticipates a tendency to introduce concrete, realistic details into idealistic song (for example, song 12) that is rare among his precursors but common in the thirteenth and subsequent centuries. He playfully reshapes and mixes traditions with abandon. Particularly felicitous examples of Ulrich's hybrids are the boasting song with an explicit revocation in the refrain and an implicit one in the lady's response (song 4), or the dawn song parody, which employs the compositional principles of song 4 but reverses its message to a lament on unrequited love implicitly revoked by the refrain and explicitly rejected by the lady (song 9).

BIBLIOGRAPHY

Karl Bartsch, ed., *Die schweizer Minnesänger* (1886, repr. 1964), xxvi–xliii, 12–58, 409–419; Helmut de Boor, *Die höfische Literatur: Vorbereitung, Blüte, Ausklang 1170–1250* (1953), 334–335; Ulrich Knoop, *Das mittelhochdeutsche Tagelied: Inhaltsanalyse und literarhistorische Untersuchungen* (1976); Ulrich Müller, *Untersuchungen zur politischen Lyrik des deutschen Mittelalters* (1974), 56–59, 103, 328 n. 1, 346–347, 488, and *passim*; Emil Ploss, "Walthers Spruch 28.1–10 und die

Parodie des Singenbergers," in *Beiträge zur Geschichte der deutschen Sprache und Literatur, Sonderheft,* **94** (1972); Max Schiendorfer, *Ulrich von Singenberg, Walther und Wolfram: Zur Parodie in der höfischen Literatur* (1983); Ludwig Wolff, "Ulrich von Singenberg," in Wolfgang Stammler and Karl Langosch, eds., *Die deutsche Literatur des Mittelalters: Verfasserlexikon,* IV (1953).

HUBERT HEINEN

[See also **German Literature: Lyric; Middle High German Literature; Minnesingers; Neidhart "von Reuental"; Reinmar der Alte; Walther von der Vogelweide.**]

ULRICH VON TÜRHEIM (*fl. ca.* 1230–1280), poet, apparently a member of an impoverished family of noblemen in the Augsburg region. The name is found in local documents from 1236 to 1286, but there is no proof that they refer to the poet. He does say in the *Rennewart* that he was told of its French source by Otto der Bogener, a wealthy bourgeois of the region, documented in 1246. Ulrich dedicated his *Tristan* to Otto von Winterstetten. And Rudolf von Ems, in the *Alexander* and *Willehalm,* praises Ulrich's work. A fragment of what is probably his earliest work, *Cliês* (*ca.* 1230), an adaptation of the *Cligès* of Chrétien de Troyes, is preserved.

In about 1235, Ulrich wrote his continuation of the *Tristan* of Gottfried von Strassburg. He begins with the wedding of Tristan and Isolde White Hands at Arundel and continues with the adventures of Tristan and her brother Kaedin, including the resumption of relations with Isolde the Fair at Mark's court. Kaedin is killed in the amorous pursuit of the wife of a neighboring knight, and Tristan himself is wounded by a poisoned spear. Only Isolde the Fair can cure him, but Isolde White Hands says that the sail of the ship sent to fetch her is black, a sign that she is not aboard, and Tristan dies. Isolde the Fair dies on his body, and King Mark, now convinced that the love potion was responsible for their conduct, has them buried together.

The continuation is based on Eilhart von Oberge and has little in common with Gottfried's poem. Its style is crude, and there is none of Gottfried's deep psychological insight. Nor is there any feeling for the effects of sexual love on the social order. In style and treatment this continuation is far inferior to that of Heinrich von Freiberg. It shows that the author did not understand his model and that he merely added adventures to bring the story to a conclusion.

Ulrich also completed the *Willehalm* of Wolfram von Eschenbach. His poem, of more than 36,400 lines, is more concerned with Willehalm's nephew by marriage, Rennewart, than with the hero of the title. It tells how Rennewart is converted to Christianity and marries Alise, daughter of King Loys (Louis) and niece of Willehalm. She dies giving birth to Malifer, who is kidnapped by heathens, fights for them, and later encounters his father in battle when Rennewart interrupts his retirement in a monastery to take up arms against the Saracens. Much of the later action is devoted to the adventures of Malifer, although there are numerous references to Willehalm's career as a hermit and monk and to his wife, Kyburg, who dies as a saint. Ulrich is more interested in the legendary and didactic features of the story than was his model, Wolfram, and conventional religion plays a greater role in his work. The poem, extant in thirty-two manuscripts, was clearly very popular, perhaps because it does not follow Wolfram in his attempts to understand the pagan ethos and to distinguish between pagan and Christian motivation. The two works of Ulrich are good examples of the desire of late-thirteenth-century poets to "finish" the works of the great masters even though the ability to understand the spirit in which they were written had gone forever.

BIBLIOGRAPHY

Gerhard Meissburger, *Tristan und Isold mit den weissen Händen: Die Auffassung der Minne, der Liebe und der Ehe bei Gottfried von Strassburg und Ulrich von Türheim* (1954); Ulrich von Türheim, *Willehalm,* Samuel Singer, ed. (1893), *Rennewart* (=*Willehalm*), Alfred Hübner, ed. (1938), and *Tristan,* Thomas Kerth, ed. (1979).

W. T. H. JACKSON

[See also **Arthurian Literature; Chrétien de Troyes; German Literature: Romance; Gottfried von Strassburg; Rudolf von Ems; Tristan Legend; Wolfram von Eschenbach.**]

ULRICH VON WINTERSTETTEN (*fl.* 1241–1280), minnesinger, known as Schenk (cupbearer) Ulrich von Winterstetten und Schmalenegg. He is attested in documents from 1241 to 1280. Scholars tend to assume that his songs were products of his youth, before he became the canon of Augsburg (by

1258). A few have even suggested that not he but, rather, a retainer of his father (attested in 1239) was the singer. Ulrich, however, may have continued to compose and sing his decidedly secular songs as a cleric. Silvia Ranawake feels some strophic forms betray familiarity with clerical Latin poetry. A cleric, Johann von Konstanz, jotted down several lines of Ulrich's second *Leich,* apparently from memory, to test his quill. There seem to be personal references in a few songs, though their significance is disputed.

Ulrich's *Tagelieder* are reminiscent of Wolfram von Eschenbach (and Otto von Botenlauben), and his courtly dialogue is similar to one by Walther von der Vogelweide. As a minnesinger whose five *Leiche* and forty songs reflect the formal complexity of Gottfried von Neifen, a familiarity with Neidhart, and some manner of relationship to Tannhäuser, he has been regarded (for example, by Helmut de Boor) as an epigone of epigones. Though Hugo Kuhn's ingenious rehabilitation of him comes close to damning with faint praise, Carl von Kraus's preference for his diversity over Neifen's pallor (which von Kraus abets with his atheteses) does more justice to his wit and subtle virtuosity.

Several of Ulrich's *Leiche* echo Italian dances, and Karl Bertau argues convincingly that they were intended to accompany dances at court, with animations of a fictitious set of characters and admonitions to an audience serving as performance cues. His songs largely lack such obtrusive signals of interaction with the audience. Though most of them have clever refrains and several of them parallel French (and especially Provençal) noncourtly forms often considered dances, the songs do not seem to have had the same function as the *Leiche.* Ranawake has suggested the Provençal influence may have come by way of Italy. Neifen was, and Ulrich may have been, associated with Frederick II (perhaps in Sicily).

BIBLIOGRAPHY

Karl H. Bertau, *Sängerverslyrik: Über Gestalt und Geschichtlichkeit mittelhochdeutscher Lyrik am Beispiel des Leichs* (1964); Helmut de Boor, *Die höfische Literatur: Vorbereitung, Blüte, Ausklang 1170–1250* (1953); Joachim Bumke, *Ministerialität und Ritterdichtung: Umrisse der Forschung* (1976); Carl von Kraus and Hugo Kuhn, eds., *Deutsche Liederdichter des 13. Jahrhunderts,* I (1951), 495–554, and II (1958), 558–597; Hugo Kuhn, *Minnesangs Wende,* 2nd ed. (1967); Silvia Ranawake, *Höfische Strophenkunst: Vergleichende Untersuchungen zur Formentypologie von Minnesang und Trouvèrelied* (1976); Olive Sayce, *The Medieval German Lyric, 1150–1300* (1982).

HUBERT HEINEN

[See also **German Literature: Lyric; Gottfried von Neifen; Middle High German Literature; Minnesingers; Neidhart "von Reuental"; Tannhäuser; Walther von der Vogelweide; Wolfram von Eschenbach.**]

ULRICH VON ZAZIKHOVEN (also Zatzikhoven) (*ca.* 1200), the author of *Lanzelet,* a Middle High German Arthurian romance in courtly couplets. Ulrich names himself in line 9,344 and is thought to be the "Uolricus de Cecinchovin" (Zezikon) who is described in a St. Gall document of 1214 as *plebanus Loumeissae* (probably parish priest of Lommis [in the Swiss canton of Thurgau]), and to whom the title *capellanus* immediately preceding the name has been thought to refer. Ulrich's lost (probably Anglo-Norman) source, which he claims to have followed faithfully, reached him through Hugh de Morville, a hostage (as we learn from Ulrich alone) for Richard the Lionhearted (lines 9,323–9,341), which gives a terminus post quem for *Lanzelet* of 1194 or possibly 1193. This hostage could have been (1) Hugh de Morville, the baron of Burgh-on-Sands who died in 1202; (2) the murderer of Thomas Becket, if he survived after 1176 and was not identical with 1; or (3) the subsequent bishop of Coutances (*d.* 1238). Ulrich may have used an intermediary Rhenish source either alongside or in place of the Romance original.

The relative chronology of *Lanzelet* and Hartmann von Aue's *Erek* is not known; either may be the earliest Arthurian romance in Middle High German, but most scholars regard *Lanzelet* as having been influenced by *Erek.* It has been claimed with varying degrees of cogency that Lanzelet was influenced by Hartmann, Gottfried, and especially Wolfram, and that Lanzelet influenced the *Nibelungenlied* and Wirnt von Grafenberg's *Wigalois;* in this question much depends on one's criteria for establishing influence.

Lanzelet is known from two intact manuscripts (W and P) and three sets of fragments (B, S, and G/Gk). Ulrich is mentioned by Rudolf von Ems, Jakob Püterich von Reichertshausen, and Ulrich Füetrer, and his *Lanzelet* probably by Heinrich von Freiberg; he is quoted on an illustration in the

Manesse manuscript (Heidelberg, Codex Palatinus 848).

The hero, Lanzelet, grows up nameless and unaware of his identity. After a series of knightly and amorous adventures he wins his queen, Iblis, whereupon he is told his name. He successfully champions Guinevere against Valerin, who claims her as his wife, and later helps Arthur rescue her from Valerin, who has abducted her. He and some other knights then rescue the knights Walwein and Erek, whom Arthur had reluctantly exchanged for the sorcerer Maldue's help with Guinevere's release. Arthur is Lanzelet's maternal uncle and there is no suggestion that Lanzelet is Guinevere's lover. The romance ends with Lanzelet's restoration to his father's realm as king and his assumption of sovereignty over the kingdoms Iblis has inherited from her father.

Ulrich's syntax is relatively straightforward. The late main verb in rhyme position is, as in Hartmann's *Erek,* not uncommon. His vocabulary is large and combines fashionable courtly expressions with traditional poetic diction. His rhymes are usually pure, but to achieve this he enlarges his choice of rhyme words by using alternative forms of a number of words (doublets).

Research on *Lanzelet* is inevitably affected by the loss of Ulrich's source(s) and by our ignorance of the relation of his Romance source to Chrétien de Troyes's *Chevalier de la charrette.* Critical interest in the poem has concentrated on structural, political, and generic aspects, as well as on the love theme and on the Arthurian team spirit that distinguishes *Lanzelet* from its better-known, more individualistic contemporaries.

BIBLIOGRAPHY

Sources. Lanzelet. Eine Erzählung, K. A. Hahn, ed. (1845), repr. with postscript and bibliography by F. Norman (1965); *Lanzelet,* Kenneth G. T. Webster, trans., rev. and enl. by Roger Sherman Loomis (1951), reviewed by M. O'C. Walshe in *Modern Language Review,* 48 (1953).

Studies. Karl Heinz Borck, "Lanzelets *adel,"* in *Festschrift für Siegfried Grosse zum 60. Geburtstag* (1984); Teresa Mary de Glinka-Janczewski, "Ulrich von Zatzikhoven's *Lanzelet:* A Critical Study" (M.A. thesis, Univ. of London, 1963); Markku Kantola, *Studien zur Reimsprache Ulrichs von Zazikhoven: Ein Beitrag zur Vorlagenfrage* (1982); John Margetts, "Eheliche Treue im 'Lanzelet' Ulrichs von Zatzikhoven," in *Festschrift für Siegfried Grosse zum 60. Geburtstag* (1984); Emil Öhmann, "Anklänge an Ulrichs von Zazikhoven Lanzelet in *Nibelungenlied, Nibelungenklage* und *Wigalois,"* in *Neuphilologische Mitteilungen,* 47 (1946); Jean-Marc Pastré, "*L'ornement difficile* et la datation du *Lanzelet* d'Ulrich von Zazikhoven," in Danielle Buschinger, ed., *Université de Picardie, Centre d'Études Médiévales, Actes du colloque des 14 et 15 Janvier 1984: Lancelot* (1984); René Pérennec, "*Le livre français de Lanzelet* dans l'adaptation d'Ulrich von Zatzikhoven," *ibid.;* Roland Rossbacher, "'Lanzelet': Artusritter, Königssohn und gewählter König. Ulrichs von Zatzikhoven politische Stellungnahme," in *Jahrbuch der Oswald von Wolkenstein Gesellschaft,* 3 (1984/1985); Ernst Trachsler, *Der Weg im mittelhochdeutschen Artusroman* (1979).

ROSEMARY N. COMBRIDGE

[See also **Arthurian Literature; German Literature: Romance; Hartmann von Aue; Middle High German Literature; Wolfram von Eschenbach.**]

ULSTER, northernmost state of early Celtic Ireland. The earliest contemporary information relating to Ulster comes from Ptolemy's map. The names relating to Ulster derive from information gathered by the Romans as a result of Agricola's military activity in northern Britain and Scotland in the 80's of the first century A.D. Rivers, tribes, and tribal capitals are mentioned. Of these, the *Voluntii* (**Uluti*) are the Ulaid (later Dál Fiatach in east Down) and *Isamnion* is Emain, or Navan Fort near Armagh.

The saga *Táin bó Cúailnge,* the glory of early Irish literature, depicts prehistoric Ulster with its capital at Emain Macha in confrontation with the forces of Connacht and Leinster. If this reflects a historical situation, it does so as a mere shadow. The boundaries of the ancient province of Ulster, originally as far south as the river Boyne, shrank during the early historic period, until by the twelfth century the province constituted an area approximating only to the two counties of Down and Antrim in the northeast.

It is very likely that there was a strong pre-Celtic element in the population, and this may be represented by the peoples in the northeast known as the Cruthin or Cruithni (*q*-Celtic form of the word *Pretani* as used by classical writers). But by the sixth and seventh centuries these peoples are Gaelic-speaking and material culture is everywhere the same. Although the Irish used the word *Cruthin* when referring to the Picts of Scotland, there is no connection between the two peoples in the historical period. The Dál Riata occupied the glens of

Antrim in the northeast and from the fifth century had begun to settle in Scotland. They eventually joined with the Picts to form the kingdom of Alba in the ninth century. This colonization caused the Gaelicization of Scotland, as did a similar settlement in the Isle of Man from southeast Ulster. This brought about a cultural province in the north Irish Sea area which was to last until the end of the Middle Ages.

Within Ulster the power of the Ulaid declined as the Uí Néill consolidated their position in county Donegal in the fifth and sixth centuries. They gradually conquered the Cruthin and Airgiallan tribes in counties Derry, Tyrone, and Fermanagh. By 827 in the Battle of Leth Cam the Uí Néill had become the dominant power in the north. During this period too, and largely under Uí Néill patronage, the church of Armagh grew to become the religious capital of Ireland. Its founder had been the humble British missionary Patrick, who had been active in the north, but by now the propaganda of Armagh had elevated him to the position of national apostle.

Despite their history of defeat and the continuous contraction of their territory, the Ulaid still regarded themselves as the rightful kings of the province. In 1004 they suffered yet another massive defeat by the Uí Néill king, Áed ua Néill, at their inauguration site of Craeb Tulcha. They survived into the twelfth century, when the kingship was held by the Mac Duinnshléibhe (Donleavy).

The coming of the Normans resulted in the conquest of Ulster by John de Courcy. In the thirteenth century the Mac Duinnshléibhe were kings of the "Irish of Ulster." By the end of the century they gave up the struggle and took service with Ua Domhnaill in Donegal. The Uí Néill could finally call themselves *rí Ulad* with the collapse of the earldom of Ulster. This was symbolized in 1381 by the feast held for the poets of Ireland by Niall Ua Néill at Emain Macha—the ancient but now grassgrown "capital" of Ulster.

BIBLIOGRAPHY

Francis John Byrne, "The Ireland of St. Columba," in *Historical Studies*, 5 (1965), and *Irish Kings and High-Kings* (1973, repr. 1987); T. E. McNeill, *Anglo-Norman Ulster* (1980); Gearóid Mac Niocaill, *Ireland Before the Vikings* (1972) S. O Ceallaig, *Gleanings from Ulster History* (1951); Donnchadh Ó Corráin, *Ireland Before the Normans* (1972), and "Historical Need and Literary Narrative," in *Proceedings of the Seventh International Congress of Celtic Studies at Oxford, July 1983*, D. Ellis Evans *et al.*, eds. (1986); Annette J. Otway-Ruthven, *A History of Medieval Ireland* (1968).

CHARLES DOHERTY

[See also **Armagh; Celtic Languages; Connacht; Dál Riata; Ireland; Leinster; Patrick, St.; Picts; Scotland; Táin bó Cúailnge; Uí Néill.**]

ULUGH-BEG (22 March 1394–27 October 1449), ruler of the Timurid dynasty in Central Asia (1409–1449), was the elder son of Shāhrukh and grandson of Tīmūr (Tamerlane). Named at birth Muḥammad Taraghay, he received the nickname Ulugh-Beg (literally, Great Prince), which was used instead of his proper name from early childhood. In 1409 he was installed by his father in Samarkand as the ruler of Transoxiana, under the guardianship of Emir Shāh Malik. In 1411 Shāh Malik was removed; Ulugh-Beg thereafter enjoyed full authority in his dominion, which included most territories of the Timurid state north of the Amu Darya. He remained an obedient vassal of his father, frequently going to Herat to give Shāhrukh an account of his actions and supplying army contingents for Shāhrukh's military campaigns. The interference of Shāhrukh in the internal affairs of Transoxiana under Ulugh-Beg seems to have been minimal, if any.

In international affairs the main concern of Ulugh-Beg was his relations with the northern nomadic neighbors: the Moghuls in Semirechie and eastern Turkistan, and the Uzbeks north of the Syr Darya. In 1416 he annexed Kashghar and left his governor there. Then he intervened in the internal strife in Moghulistan, supporting one of the contenders for the throne. His protégé, however, immediately began hostile action against Ulugh-Beg, who set off for Moghulistan in 1424 with a big army. The campaign was victorious but without lasting political results for Ulugh-Beg. Relations with the Moghuls remained mainly hostile; Ulugh-Beg lost Kashghar to them in the late 1420's or early 1430's, and the Moghuls often raided Farghānā and other border areas of Ulugh-Beg's possessions. Ulugh-Beg's military enterprises against the Uzbeks also ended in failure. He helped one of the Jochid princes, Baraq, to establish his authority in the steppe. Having achieved this, Baraq turned against his patron, and in 1427 Ulugh-Beg was utterly defeated by the Uzbeks near Sïghnaq, north of the Sir Darya. The defeat almost cost Ulugh-Beg his appanage, and from then until the death of Shāhrukh he never again participated personally in military campaigns. The Uzbeks raided the Timurid possessions in Central Asia no less frequently than the Moghuls.

Ulugh-Beg followed Turko-Mongol political traditions more than other descendants of Tīmūr (Tamerlane). Through his marriage to a Chinggisid princess, he had the honorary title *küregen* ([khan's] son-in-law), which he apparently appreciated. He kept puppet khans of Chinggisid origin in Samarkand (a custom that had been abandoned by the pious Shāhrukh), and royal decrees were published in their names. In court life and army affairs, Ulugh-Beg often adhered to heathen steppe customs and tried to imitate his grandfather, to the dismay of the representatives of Islamic orthodoxy. A number of stories have come down in the sources that make his actions appear inconsistent with Islamic religious law. At the same time, however, he showed his respect for the religious establishment, building mosques, madrasas, and mausoleums provided with rich endowments; some of them (in Samarkand, Bukhara, Shahrisabz, and Ghujduwān) have been preserved to the present day.

After the death of Shāhrukh in 1447, Ulugh-Beg began a struggle for his father's throne with his nephews in Khorāsān. He captured Herat in 1448, but rebellions of military commanders and an Uzbek raid against Samarkand and Bukhara forced him to return to Transoxiana at the end of that year. Ulugh-Beg's elder son, ʿAbd al-Laṭīf, rebelled against him in 1449, defeated him in battle, took possession of Samarkand, and had him killed on 27 October 1449.

In the history of the Islamic world, Ulugh-Beg is remembered less as a political figure than as a scholar. His main interest (probably acquired from Persian scholars brought by Tīmūr to Central Asia) was astronomy. He had an observatory built near Samarkand (in a seventeenth-century work the date of completion of construction is given as 1428–1429) and in it worked with several collaborators, among whom were the prominent astronomers and mathematicians Ghiyāth al-Dīn Jamshīd Kāshī, ʿAlī Qushchi, and Qaḍī-zāde-i Rūmī. The main result of their observations was Ulugh-Beg's astronomical tables, entitled *Zīj-i sulṭānī-yi Gūrgānī*, or *Zīj-i Ulugh-Beg*, and composed not earlier than 1437. The tables were very popular in the Islamic world and later in Europe, where they became known in the mid seventeenth century. It is supposed that the observatory of Ulugh-Beg influenced the first European observatories.

Ulugh-Beg, like other Timurids, patronized poetry—which, however, did not flourish at his court as it did at the court of Herat. A Persian work on the history of the Chinggisids, entitled *Ūlūs-i arbaʿa-yi Chingīzī*, is ascribed to Ulugh-Beg, but it apparently was merely commissioned by him; only its later abridged version, by an unknown author, entitled *Shajarat al-atrāk*, has survived.

BIBLIOGRAPHY

Vasily V. Barthold, *Four Studies on the History of Central Asia*, Vladimir Minorsky and T. Minorsky, trans., II: *Ulugh Beg* (1958), which includes references to primary sources—additional bibliography is in the Russian original, Vasily V. Barthold, *Sochinenia*, 2nd ed., II, pt. 2 (1964), 23–177; see also A. Sayili, *The Observatory in Islam* (1960), esp. 260–289. On the manuscripts, text editions, and translations of the astronomical work by Ulugh-Beg, see Charles A. Storey, *Persian Literature: A Bio-bibliographical Survey*, 3 vols. (1927–1984), II, pt. 1 (1958), 67–72; on *Ūlūs-i arbaʿa-yi Chingīzī*, Charles A. Storey, *Persidskaya literatura: Bio-bibliografichesky obzor*, translated into Russian and extensively revised by Yuri Bregel, II (1972), esp. 777–779. On the inscription on Ulugh-Beg's tomb at Samarkand, see *Epigrafika Vostoka*, II (1949), 47.

YURI BREGEL

[See also **Iran, History; Samarkand; Science, Islamic; Tamerlane; Timurids; Transoxiana; Turkomans.**]

ʿUMAR I IBN AL-KHAṬṬĀB (*ca.* 592–644), the second caliph (634–644) and the real founder of the Islamic state. An influential member of the clan of ʿAdī, a man of powerful presence, and a most eloquent speaker, he was the emissary of the Quraysh (Muḥammad's tribe) when they needed one. Before his conversion to Islam, ʿUmar vehemently opposed Muḥammad and regarded Islam as a divisive movement. His conversion marked a complete turnaround for the man and for the new faith. In fact, Muḥammad had been preaching privately when ʿUmar converted, and it was he who urged Muḥammad to profess his teachings publicly. ʿUmar, along with the first caliph, Abū Bakr, became Muḥammad's close adviser, his confidant, and the father-in-law of the Prophet.

About the forty-fifth person to join Islam, he was instrumental in introducing such legislation as the *hadd*, punishment for drinking wine, veiling of the Prophet's wives as ordained in a Koranic verse, night prayer during the month of Ramadan, and the prohibition of temporary marriage (practiced especially by merchants). He was in favor of free enterprise in the marketplace, as indicated by his stand against *ihtikar* (monopoly) and price fluctuations. He was the first to urge the collection of the Koran and it was he who inaugurated the Muslim calendar, to commence with the hegira (Muḥammad's move to Medina in 622). He instituted the verbal call to prayer, arguing for a human touch rather than the use of instruments as practiced by Christians and Jews. His superior qualities were demonstrated by Muḥammad's saying that if there were to be a prophet after him, it would be ᶜUmar. It is even said that no controversy was settled by the Koran that did not take ᶜUmar's opinion into account. A firm believer in Muḥammad, he refused to believe that the Prophet had died until he was soothed by the firm statements of Abū Bakr, elected first caliph under the initiative of ᶜUmar.

ᶜUmar, who participated in early Muslim battles against the Quraysh and even led a few raids himself, transformed the skirmishes initiated by his predecessor into full-fledged expansion and conquest. It was during his reign that Muslims conquered what became the core area of the Islamic state in the medieval period. The well-planned and organized expansion was waged simultaneously on three fronts: Iraq and the eastern front, Syria, and Egypt.

The Iraqi campaign, the earliest, was led by Khālid ibn al-Walīd before his transfer to Syria. A series of skirmishes during Abū Bakr's caliphate led to the subjugation of Al-Ḥīra, capital of the Sasanian client state of the Lakhmids, and a few other towns and oases. But the first encounter with an organized Sasanian army, soon after ᶜUmar took office as Abū Bakr's designate, resulted in a disastrous defeat for the Muslims at the Battle of the Bridge (634), due largely to their inability to deal with the elephants in the Sasanian vanguard. Alarmed by this reversal, ᶜUmar called for a general mobilization to the point of forced conscription. The newly formed army, led by Saᶜd ibn Abī Waqqāṣ, marched toward Iraq and joined the remnants of those who survived the Battle of the Bridge at Al-Qādisīya (Kadisiya). A regrouped Sasanian army led by Rustam met the Muslims in 636 or 637.

Although outnumbered, the Muslims won a decisive victory at Al-Qādisīya and the Sasanian troops were routed. The Muslims quickly took the Sasanian capital of Ctesiphon and thus consolidated their hold on the Sawād, the rich alluvial plains of Iraq. The Muslims continued to inflict further defeats on the Sasanians and to frustrate any hope of their recovery, especially after the battles at Jalula (637) and Nihavand (642), which saw the final collapse of the Sasanian regime. Most provinces of western Persia, such as Azerbaijan, Ahwaz, and Fārs, were incorporated into the Islamic domain during ᶜUmar's caliphate.

In Syria, the Muslims had been successfully engaging Byzantine troops and their Arab allies when ᶜUmar took office. By 636 the Byzantines had amassed a huge army, which moved toward southern Syria, forcing the Muslims to retreat and vacate some cities they had occupied, such as Ḥims (Emesa) and Damascus. The two forces, again with the Muslims outnumbered, met in 636 or 637 on the banks of the Yarmuk, a tributary of the Jordan, where another momentous victory was achieved by the Muslims. Heraklios, commanding his troops from Antioch, left the Syrian province to inaugurate its indelible arabization and islamization. Following this victory the Muslims split into several divisions to retake the cities they had vacated and to effect a regional pacification of Syria. Syrian cities submitted according to treaties based on the guarantee and protection of the inhabitants and their possessions, property, and places of worship in return for the payment of tribute and/or taxes. Terms of such treaties favored the merchant class, as the treaty with Baᶜlabakk would testify. ᶜUmar also allowed merchants from hostile areas to operate within the Islamic domain as long as they paid the required taxes.

Pacification of Syria was so thorough that even though much of the Muslim army perished during the plague of Amwas (639), Syria remained under the firm control of Medina. ᶜUmar himself appeared twice in Syria, once to receive the submission of Jerusalem (638) and again for a conference with his commanders held at Jabiya, the Muslims' base of operations in the Golan Heights. At this conference ᶜUmar discussed with his commanders such issues as distribution of booty, administrative divisions, and further military action.

The Egyptian campaign, led by ᶜAmr ibn al-ᶜĀṣ, began at the conclusion of the Jabiya conference. Without waiting for reinforcements from Medina,

ʿAmr crossed the Sinai near Al-ʿArīsh and headed straight to Pelusium, which he took with little resistance. Rather than crossing the Nile Delta for Alexandria at this point, the Muslims remained on the eastern side and marched south toward the top of the delta, where they besieged the fortress of Babylon. When additional troops arrived from Medina, the combined Muslim force stormed the fortress and occupied it (640). Amr's army then crossed the Nile and headed toward the well-fortified capital of the Egyptian province of Alexandria. With no major resistance to block their advance, the Muslims appeared before the walls of Alexandria and proceeded to lay siege to the city. By 643 the city submitted according to a treaty reached between the two sides. Once the capital was taken the Muslims easily acquired the allegiance of its dependencies, such as Barqa and the numerous oases in the Libyan desert.

The Arab/Islamic expansion was accompanied by a significant demographic transformation, not only in terms of population transfer but also in terms of urbanization on a scale unprecedented in the history of western Asia. This was accomplished by the establishment of new cities in the conquered territories. ʿUmar ordered the establishment of several cities, three of which went on to play a more significant role in Islamic history than others: Basra and Kufa in Iraq and Fusṭāṭ in Egypt.

Built to consolidate the conquest and to house the troops and their dependents, these cities became the provincial capitals from which the vast state was governed and controlled. They became the focal points for mobilization of additional troops as well as for the steady stream of non-Arab Muslims (*mawālī*) who were gradually integrated into a structure dominated by the mercantilist Arab/Islamic ruling class. These cities were built near already existing urban structures and were cosmopolitan right from the start in that they were not exclusively Arab or military. Basra, built near Al-Ubulla (Apollogos), grew to become the major port on the Persian Gulf, where the Arab/Islamic merchants were in contact with the major surplus-producing regions from China to East Africa. Fusṭāṭ, strategically located to control Upper and Lower Egypt, became the major commercial and administrative metropolis in northern Africa. Here ʿUmar commissioned his governor to excavate a defunct pharaonic canal that connected the Nile with the Red Sea. This canal, known as *Khalīj amīr al-muʾminīn,* became the major conduit for chan-

neling Egypt's surplus wealth, especially grain, to Arabia. Kufa, built near Al-Ḥīra, is the first of those cities to become the seat of the caliphate when ʿAlī ibn Abī Ṭālib, the fourth caliph, moved there in search of manpower and resources. Most Kufans remained loyal to ʿAlī and his descendants, and Kufa was where early Shiism was elaborated and where major Shīʿa revolts were declared.

ʿUmar introduced an administrative and fiscal structure for the developing Islamic state. The state was divided into provinces and each was governed by a military commander who was assisted by a fledgling bureaucracy of lesser officials. Administrative specialization was not yet clearly defined, as those governmental positions, including that of the caliph, were created in an ad hoc fashion with little specification of the nature and extent of the power of the caliph or his deputies. ʿUmar changed his cumbersome title of "successor of the successor of the Prophet" to the more general title of *amīr al-muʾminīn* (commander of the faithful). He also began the practice of assigning a salary for officials of the state, including the caliph. As the requirements of running a state became more complex, the caliph had no time to work in the marketplace to earn a living, as Abū Bakr had done. Along with a governor, ʿUmar appointed an imam to lead the prayers, a qadi to judge in disputes between the Muslims, and an official in control of *bayt al-māl* (the treasury). ʿUmar, frugal and extremely sensitive about the relationship of his officials to the swelling public wealth, maintained a tight grip on his officials to the point that he confiscated half of the officials' wealth upon dismissal, on the correct assumption that officials had easy access to the treasury and thus had an unfair economic advantage over others. ʿUmar's control of his governors and the respect he commanded from them is also revealed by the smooth and uneventful dismissal of the powerful Khālid ibn al-Walīd from the command of Syria even though he had just led the Muslims to victory at the Yarmuk River.

A registry system (*dīwān*) was initiated by ʿUmar to keep track of the troops and their dependents, for each fighter had an annual stipend graded according to the stage at which he joined the Islamic expansion; those who joined before Al-Qādisīya received a considerably higher sum than those who joined later. Dependents such as women and infants received a fixed stipend. Along with this, ʿUmar attempted to institute a new social hierarchy based on precedence and Islamic seniority: members of the Prophet's family received a higher stipend than others; those who joined Islam before the Battle of Badr (624) or the Truce of Ḥudaibīya (628) received a higher stipend than those who joined after the conquest of Mecca (630).

As for the tax structure, ᶜUmar argued against the division of the conquered lands and their inhabitants, those that had been taken by force, among the Muslim soldiers under the Koranic principle of *fay*ᵓ (distribution of booty). ᶜUmar declared that Sawād, for instance, was to be held in perpetuity (*waqf*) for the Muslims. The inhabitants were left free and in possession of their plots to become like sharecroppers with the state. The state collected its share of the produce and distributed it to the soldiers, thus creating a basic relationship between the soldiers and the state: they protected and expanded the frontiers of the state, and the state distributed the wealth. ᶜUmar ordered two of his officials to perform a cadastral survey of the Sawād to determine a graded tax on the land (*kharāj*), which was adjusted according to the crop, fertility of the land, and the method of its irrigation. Former crown lands and lands whose owners either perished or fled were declared *ṣawāfī*, state land to be under the discretion of the caliph. Land grants to individual Muslims were given out from this category. A graded poll tax (*jizya*) was also collected from able-bodied non-Muslims who accepted Islamic rule (dhimmis).

Another distinguishing characteristic of ᶜUmar's caliphate was his attempt to reach a compromise between the established elite, made up of former Meccan leaders and traditionally wealthy merchants, and the newly emerging segment of the ruling class, especially those who attained some measure of social and economic mobility as a result of their participation in the Islamic expansion and all the social, political, and economic activity that took place as a result. This is clear not only from his attempt to create a new hierarchy based on Islamic seniority, but also from his careful selection of governors who belonged to the latter group.

ᶜUmar tried to set precedents for the young state. He appointed at his deathbed an elective council (*shūrā*) made up of five prominent Meccan Muslims who were to select the successor from amongst themselves. Although this body was successful in its immediate task, it was not revived again. ᶜUmar died of wounds from an assassin's dagger on 3 November 644, leaving behind a well-established and organized state.

BIBLIOGRAPHY

Aḥmad ibn Yaḥyā al-Balādhurī, *The Origins of the Islamic State*, Philip K. Hitti, trans., 2 vols. (1916–1924); Alfred J. Butler, *The Arab Conquest of Egypt and the Last Thirty Years of Roman Dominion*, P. M. Fraser, ed., 2nd ed. (1978); Leone Caetani, *Annali dell'Islām*, III–IV (1910–1911); Daniel C. Dennett, *Conversion and the Poll Tax in Early Islam* (1950); Fred M. Donner, *The Early Islamic Conquests* (1981); ᶜAbd al-ᶜAzīz Dūrī, "Landlord and Peasant in Early Islam," in *Der Islam*, 56 (1979); Paul G. Forand, "The Status of the Land and Inhabitants of the Sawād During the First Two Centuries of Islam," in *Journal of the Economic and Social History of the Orient*, 14 (1971); Francesco Gabrieli, *Muhammad and the Conquests of Islam*, Virginia Luling and Rosamund Linell, trans. (1968); Donald R. Hill, *The Termination of Hostilities in the Early Arab Conquests, A.D. 634–656* (1971); Philip K. Hitti, *Makers of Arab History* (1968); Ibn ᶜAbd al-Ḥakam, *The History of the Conquest of Egypt, North Africa, and Spain*, Charles C. Torrey, ed. (1922); Muḥammad ibn Saᶜd, *Kitāb al-tabagat al-kabir*, Eduard Sachau *et al.*, eds., 9 vols. (1904–1940); Władysław Kubiak, *Al-Fusṭāt: Its Foundation and Early Urban Development* (1982); William Muir, *Annals of the Early Caliphate from the Death of Mahomet to the Omeyyad and Abbaside Dynasties A.H. XI–LXI (A.D. 632–680)* (1968); M. A. Shaban, *Islamic History, A.D. 600–750 (132 A.H.): A New Interpretation* (1971); al-Ṭabarī, *Taᵓrīkh al-rusul wa'l-mulūk*, Muḥammad Abū al-Faḍl Ibrāhīm, ed., III–IV (1962).

Mahmood Ibrahim

[See also **Abū Bakr; ᶜAlī ibn Abī Tālib; ᶜAmr ibn al-ᶜĀs; Arabia; Badr, Battle of; Cairo; Caliphate; Commander of the Faithful; Diplomacy, Islamic; Emir; Heraklios; Ḥīra, al-; Imam; Iraq; Islam, Conquests of; Islam, Religion; Islamic Administration; Khālid ibn al-Walīd; Koran; Kufa, al-; Lakhmids; Mecca; Medina; Muḥammad; Qadi; Quraysh; Sasanian History; Shīᶜa; Waqf; Yarmuk River.**]

ᶜUMAR II IBN ᶜABD AL-ᶜAZĪZ (682/683–720), Umayyad caliph, (717–720), was born in Medina. His father, ᶜAbd al-ᶜAzīz ibn Marwān, was governor of Egypt from 685 to 705, during which time ᶜUmar's uncle, ᶜAbd al-Malik, was commander of the faithful (*amīr al-muᵓminīn*). On his mother's side he was a descendant of ᶜUmar ibn al-Khaṭṭāb. When he was a boy his father sent him from Egypt to Medina to be educated, and he grew up in this center of piety and learning. When his father died in 704, his uncle, ᶜAbd al-Malik, brought him to Damascus and had him marry his daughter,

Fāṭima. In 706 the caliph al-Walīd ibn ᶜAbd al-Malik appointed him governor of the Hejaz, and ᶜUmar returned to Medina. He is said to have consulted ten pious authorities of Medina, who advised him in administrative matters. His most important achievement as governor was the rebuilding of the *masjid* of Muḥammad at Medina in 707. Syrian and Coptic workmen set the mosaics, and the lamps were hung with golden chains. Because many Iraqis escaped to the Hejaz to enjoy his milder rule, al-Ḥajjāj, the governor of Iraq, secured ᶜUmar's dismissal in 711/712.

When his cousin Sulaymān ibn ᶜAbd al-Malik died in 717 after nominating him as his successor, ᶜUmar became the commander of the faithful. He ruled for only two and one-half years, but his reign marked a turning point in the history of the Islamic empire because it came at the end of a brief period of spectacular conquest and at the beginning of serious internal social, economic, and political problems. ᶜUmar's administrative reforms, although not generally successful, were the first recognition of and attempt to deal with these problems. Although he had lived as luxuriously as any other prince, as a ruler he lived simply and frugally. He had the mosaic-decorated walls of the *masjid* of Damascus covered with tent-cloth and melted down the golden chains of the lamps because they distracted people from true devotion. He returned the property at Fadak to the descendants of ᶜAlī and stopped the practice of cursing ᶜAlī during public worship. Since he was genuinely pious himself and respected the scholars at Medina who were his teachers, they enhanced his reputation for posterity. He seems to have been regarded as the *mahdī* whose arrival was associated with the year 100 of the hegira.

The millennial drive for universal empire was replaced by the equally millennial concept of the universality of Islam. The unsuccessful siege of Constantinople from 716 to 718 was expensive. It strained the resources of the state and aggravated fiscal oppression. ᶜUmar lifted the siege and turned his attention to internal consolidation, stronger, more centralized and efficient government, and administrative uniformity by applying the same policies in all provinces. ᶜUmar's reforms involved increased central control and were intended to be applied over the entire empire. Innovations were put in terms of a "return" or "restoration" of earlier practices, especially those of ᶜUmar ibn al-Khaṭṭāb. He is said to have collected administra-

tive precedents (*sunna*) concerning taxes, the payment of blood money, and inheritance, and had copies sent to the provinces. He forbade his officials to engage in trade while in office because of the unfair advantage which that gave them. He abolished transit tolls and market taxes, built caravan stations along the road to Khorāsān, and proposed establishing a uniform system of weights and measures throughout the empire.

Together with his successors he is associated with the establishment of provincial finance officials (ᶜummāl; singular, āmil) as independent officers, appointed by the caliph, to collect taxes more efficiently and to act as a check on the independent authority of the governors. He supported the Marwānī assertion of divine destiny. In a letter against the Qadarīya he defended God's foreknowledge with arguments based on the Koran, declaring that its existence was evidence of God's foreknowledge, and that as such, it was determining, which seems to assume that the Koran was eternal. He opposed the position associated with Ḥasan al-Baṣrī that God only preordained good but not evil by saying that it would lead people to say that God didn't preordain good either. He argued that if people decided between good and evil according to their own will, God would have to share his power with a partner.

ᶜUmar also considered certain passages of the Koran (suras 7:157, 9:11, 34:28) to mean that Muḥammad's message was universal. He favored the conversion of Christians, Jews, and Zoroastrians to Islam but required peasants who converted to leave their land and houses, which then became the property of the Islamic community (*fay*ᵓ), and to move to the garrison cities to live with the Muslims, where they would pay the Islamic alms tax of *zakāt*. He also encouraged pastoral Arabs to sell their animals and settle in the garrison cities as soldiers by promising them the rewards of conquest. Peasants who fled from their land were obliged to pay only the tax on their land. Land abandoned by converts was to be cultivated by the remaining villagers, and if a peasant who converted stayed on his land, its ownership reverted to the village community. The point of these provisions was to allow conversion and to preserve the tax base at the same time. For the same reason ᶜUmar also prohibited the sale of land that was subject to the *kharāj* tax in Iraq to Muslims after 719 because such land became their private property, which reduced the tax base (since Muslims paid a lower rate), and, he claimed, resulted in the ruin of the land and the oppression of the peasants. He made land that was subject to the *kharāj* tax in Iraq the joint property of the Islamic community. He defined *jizya* as the tax that a farmer paid on his produce, an artisan on his earnings, and a merchant on his profit. Muslims were required to pay taxes on their own land. ʿUmar's fiscal reform allowed converts to pay the same taxes as Muslims in similar circumstances.

ʿUmar's policies are also associated with the emergence of dhimmi status for protected non-Muslims. Christian monks and clergy in Egypt were exempted from paying taxes, but *jizya* was imposed on others who refused to convert. Membership in dhimmi communities was officially disapproved, the payment of *jizya* was regarded as degrading, and non-Muslims were excluded from the administration and made subject to sumptuary laws.

The general effect of ʿUmar's fiscal reform was to decrease revenues and increase expenses. His governor of North Africa in 718 is said to have been so favorable to converts that all of the Berbers became Muslims, which ruined the finances of the province. To the objections of his *āmil* in Egypt that conversions would reduce revenues, ʿUmar made his famous retort that "God sent Muḥammad as a missionary, not as a tax collector." But, in fact, his fiscal reforms did not survive his death. He was succeeded by his cousin Yazīd ibn ʿAbd al-Malik.

BIBLIOGRAPHY

Josef van Ess, "ʿUmar II and His Epistle Against the Qadarīya," in *Abr-nahrain*, 12 (1971–1972); H. A. R. Gibb, "The Fiscal Rescript of ʿUmar II," in *Arabica*, 2 (1955); Ibn ʿAbd al-Ḥakam, *Sīrat ʿUmar ibn ʿAbd al-ʿAzīz* (1927, repr. 1964); Ibn Saʿd, *Kitāb al-Tabaqāt*, V (1869), 242–302; Ismāʿīl ibn ʿUmar ibn Kathir, *ʿUmar ibn ʿAbd al-ʿAzīz*, n.d. (196?).

MICHAEL MORONY

[See also **Alms Tax, Islamic; Caliphate; Commander of the Faithful; Ḥajjāj ibn Yūsuf al-Thaqafī, al-; Hejaz; Islamic Administration; Koran; Marwān, ʿAbd al-Malik ibn; Medina; Poll Tax, Islamic; Sunna; Taxation, Islamic; ʿUmar I ibn al-Khaṭṭāb; Walīd I ibn ʿAbd al-Malik, al-; Zoroastrianism.**]

ʿUMAR KHAYYĀM (Ghiyāth al-Dīn Abu'l-Fatḥ ʿUmar ibn Ibrāhīm al-Khayyāmī, 18 May 1048–4 December 1131). In his own day, ʿUmar Khayyām was widely known and respected for his contribu-

tions to astronomy and mathematics, but to subsequent generations he has come to be known principally as the author of quatrains (*rubāʿī*; pl., *rubāʿiyāt*) imbued with a melancholy skepticism.

The place of ʿUmar's birth was probably Nishapur, and it is generally assumed that it was there that he grew to manhood and was educated, although nothing is known with certainty of his early life.

ʿUmar lived in turbulent and uncertain times; the scholar could pursue his studies only with royal patronage, and then only with difficulty. He was fortunate that he first attracted the favor of the Quarakhanid ruler of Transoxiana, Shams al-Mulk Naṣr ibn Ibrahim, for whose chief qadi he composed his treat on algebra, the *Risāla*, and then of his rival, the Seljuk sultan Jalāl al-Dīn Malikshāh (r. 1072–1092), who became both his patron and his friend. ʿUmar spent some eighteen years in Malikshāh's service, mostly in Isfahan. During this time he supervised the preparation of a set of astronomical tables, played a leading part in the preparation of a new solar calendar—called Mālikī or Jalālī in honor of his patron—drew up plans for a major new observatory to be located at Isfahan, and composed several commissioned works on philosophical and theological subjects. With Malikshāh's death, ʿUmar lost both a patron and the patronage of the court; the observatory was never completed.

The corpus of ʿUmar's scientific work is small but of a very high order, and he enjoyed a substantial reputation as a scholar and scientist in his own day. Remarkably, there is no contemporary evidence for his skill as a poet. The quatrains that survived him and have given him—largely through the agency of Edward FitzGerald's 1859 translation—a vast international reputation are not cited or mentioned by any source from his own day. In all likelihood they were the casual productions of a scientist with a literary bent. The *rubāʿī*, while employed by professional poets, was also, like the Japanese haiku, a form in which every literate person with poetic aspirations composed. Such poems by nonprofessional poets circulated by word of mouth, and were recorded only in private albums, not gathered into a *dīwān*, the collected poems of a professional poet.

The earliest citations of ʿUmar's poems are found in a manuscript dated 1161, and the first mention of him as a poet was in 1176/1177. The first complete *rubāʿī* dates from 1209. After this, citations of his work become more common, and by the mid fourteenth century some sixty poems had appeared. A century later, when the first surviving collections of the entire body of his quatrains were made, the number of individual poems had grown to 158 in one manuscript and twice that in another. From that time until the commencement of efforts to prepare a scholarly, critical edition of his poetry in the nineteenth century, the number grew by leaps and bounds. By the end of the century there were some 1,200 quatrains ascribed to ᶜUmar Khayyām.

Understandably, the first question that the scholarly study of ᶜUmar has had to address has been that of ascertaining what was truly his work. Starting with the earliest poems as the standard of authenticity, several scholars have succeeded in paring the corpus down to roughly a hundred poems. While there is a large measure of overlap between these attempts, there is no consensus, nor, in the absence of a reliable manuscript from the poet's own time, is there likely to be one.

In Iran, ᶜUmar was accounted a minor poet skilled in the quatrain until the startling success of FitzGerald's translation forced a reevaluation of his work. Since then his reputation has grown to the point where he is read and cited with surprising frequency.

BIBLIOGRAPHY

The best brief survey of ᶜUmar's scientific contributions is that of B. A. Rosenfeld and A. P. Youschkevitch in the *Dictionary of Scientific Biography*, VII (1973). ᶜAlī Dashtī, *In Search of Omar Khayyam*, L. P. Elwell-Sutton, trans. (1971), provides a more discursive introduction to the poet's times and to his poetry. Parichehr Kasra, *The Rubāᶜīyāt of ᶜUmar Khayyām* (1975), gives the texts and literal translations of the earliest quatrains and provides a survey of Khayyām scholarship. The chapters by L. P. Elwell Sutton in *The Cambridge History of Iran*, IV (1975), on "The 'Rubāᶜī' in Early Persian Literature" and by J. A. Boyle, on "ᶜUmar Khayyām: Astronomer, Mathematician, and Poet," are informative and thorough.

JEROME W. CLINTON

[See also **Isfahan; Malikshāh; Nishapur; Seljuks.**]

UMAYYAD ART

UMAYYAD ART. The Umayyad period (661–750) saw Islamic art come of age. From their capital of Damascus, in Syria, the Umayyads ruled an empire that at its height stretched from France to

Wall mosaic from the Great Mosque of Damascus; 706. SONIA HALLIDAY PHOTOGRAPHS

the Indus, and they drew both workmen and artistic inspiration from many of these conquered provinces. Architecture—first religious, then secular—was their favored form of visual expression; the development of glazed pottery, book painting, carpets, and other distinctively Islamic minor arts lay in the future. Although some of the finest Umayyad mosques have either vanished (Medina) or been totally rebuilt (Aleppo and the Aqṣā mosque, in Jerusalem), two supreme masterpieces of religious architecture survive. The Dome of the Rock in Jerusalem (completed 691/692), an octagon with a double ambulatory encircling the much-venerated but still enigmatic rock on the Temple mound, used the Christian *martyrium* form to upstage the nearby church of the Holy Sepulcher. (See illustrations in volumes 4 and 6.) The Great Mosque of Damascus (705–715) boldly recasts the standard components of a Christian basilica to secure a new lateral emphasis in keeping with the needs of Islamic worship. Both monuments are of impressive size

Portals of Quṣayr al-Ḥayr West, 8th century. Now in the National Museum, Damascus. PHOTO: BLAIR/BLOOM

and are situated in perhaps the most public sites in their respective cities. Sumptuously decorated in marble and wall mosaics, they use lengthy Koranic inscriptions as a proselytizing device. These various features suggest that they were meant to symbolize the new faith that had taken over the formerly Christian strongholds of the Near East.

Umayyad secular architecture is dominated by the country establishments of the caliphs and their entourages. Their form combines two essentially unrelated building types of Roman origin: the *villa rustica* and the frontier fort. The latter model accounts for their dimensions, salient gateways, battlements, and corner towers; the former for, inter alia, the courtyard surrounded by a two-story portico giving onto luxury apartments and service quarters. Such residences, typified by Quṣayr al-Ḥayr West and Usais, were set amid intensively and extensively exploited agricultural land irrigated by dams, aqueducts, and canals, and were thus as much manor houses as pleasure pal-

aces. Much grander than these are a pair of palaces erected in the 740's by al-Walid II. Khirbat al-Mafjar, a loose agglomeration of palace, mosque, fountain court, bath hall, and other discrete units, draws its inspiration from models like Hadrian's Tivoli palace complex. Mshattā, on the other hand, a tightly regimented square design broadly reminiscent of Diocletian's palace at Split, has a more military and absolutist flavor. These palaces offer the most splendid decoration, especially in figural sculpture, in the entire canon of Umayyad secular art.

Umayyad art is essentially eclectic, experimental, and propagandist. Nurtured in the millennially hellenized soil of Syria, it grafted the classical heritage onto Islamic art, but also looked increasingly to the east—Mesopotamia, Iran, Central Asia, even India—for inspiration. The encounter of these mutually incompatible approaches to visual art and the limitless funds available for building projects combined to stimulate innovation. Media and themes alike were transposed and reshuffled in new combinations; familiar motifs took on new lineaments when unexpectedly magnified or miniaturized. The results could be brash and vulgar; but they were undeniably full of life and visually arresting. This surface excitement, expressed primarily in superabundant ornament, a feature destined to characterize Islamic art in general, should not, however, be allowed to obscure the serious political and religious intent of much Umayyad art. The religious buildings use epigraphy to refer to paradise or, like Umayyad coins, to express an anti-Christian polemic. The palaces frequently assert the absolute power of the caliph or his dominance over East and West. In both types of monument, ostentatious decoration proclaimed the fabulous wealth of the patron. Thus art was made to serve—in approved late antique fashion—the ends of political power and prestige.

BIBLIOGRAPHY

K. A. C. Creswell, *A Short Account of Early Muslim Architecture* (1958), 11–158, and *Early Muslim Architecture: Umayyads, A.D. 622–750*, 2nd ed., 2 vols. (1969); Oleg Grabar, *The Formation of Islamic Art* (1973); Ernst Emil Herzfeld, "Die Genesis der islamischen Kunst und das Mshatta-Problem," in *Der Islam*, **1** (1910); Ugo Monneret de Villard, *Introduzione allo studio dell'archeologia islamica* (1968); Katharina Otto-Dorn, *L'art de l'Islam*, J. P. Simon, trans. (1967), 19–65.

ROBERT HILLENBRAND

UMAYYADS

[See also **Aleppo; Almoravid Art; Caliphate; Calligraphy, Islamic; Damascus; Dome of the Rock; Islamic Art and Architecture; Medina; Mosque; Syria.**]

UMAYYADS, a clan of the Meccan-based Arab tribe of Quraysh and the founders of the first Muslim dynasty (661–750). Despite more than a century of intense scholarly study, the history of the Umayyads remains, for historiographical reasons, unclear in many respects. Systematic works of history were not yet being written through most of the Umayyad era. Reports on individual events or discussions of limited themes were circulated, in large part orally but to some extent in writing as well, and much of this material was heavily biased or fanciful. Polemical and tendentious accounts by the regime's enemies abounded; many reports were merely edifying or entertaining anecdotes; and points of limited or no foundation often expanded into detailed historical narratives elaborated for the purpose of arguing legal, doctrinal, or factional (that is, nonhistorical) issues.

Sustained historical writing was clearly emerging by the late Umayyad period, but historiographical difficulties were in fact compounded after the Abbasid revolution. Matters relating to the history of the fallen regime were, in the first instance, heavily colored by the hostility and biases of the victors. And when the old material was finally compiled and assessed, it was extremely difficult to determine the relative worth of the various accounts, not least of all because on many points there was serious contradiction and confusion, while on other matters nothing at all was known. The existence of enormous gaps, coupled with the fact that the Umayyad era was also the formative age of Islam, further led to the retrojection of large amounts of folkloric and didactic material into the tradition, and also to the filling of gaps with such arbitrary and often stereotyped amplifications as were necessary to produce an even and plausible narrative. The problem is thus not the lack of a coherent account of Umayyad history bearing the often-evoked "ring of truth," but rather the existence of multiple such accounts that pose major contradictions and, on many points, the possibility that none of them presents an accurate version of events. Further, the formulations of Iraq, the focus of

opposition to the Umayyads, are far better preserved than those of Syria, the Umayyad imperial center, and the non-Islamic sources are only occasionally helpful in assessing reports from the Islamic tradition. Historical reconstruction in such a situation quickly becomes arbitrary and speculative as greater detail is sought, and it is likely that even on some major points there has always been disagreement and confusion as to exactly what happened. The field of Umayyad history is thus highly controversial and likely to remain so.

THE FOUNDATIONS OF UMAYYAD POWER

The Umayyads rose to prominence as a result of socioeconomic and political developments in pre-Islamic Arabia. The clan played an important role in Arabian trade and by the mid sixth century was one of the most powerful families of Quraysh in Mecca. As commerce required cooperation with tribes controlling the territories through which caravans had to pass, the economic rise of the Umayyads was accompanied and conditioned by their increasing social and political influence. Led by Abū Sufyān ibn Ḥarb, the clan enjoyed a dominant position in Mecca by the time of the emergence of Islam, with wealth concentrated in commercial ventures and landholding, both of these giving them contacts and influence among the Arab tribes in Syria. Though apparently long opposed to the prophet Muḥammad, and hence at first discredited upon the Muslim occupation of Mecca (630), the Umayyads were too important to be excluded entirely. Indeed, the Muslim leadership seems to have been anxious to turn the Umayyads' influence to the advantage of Islam. Umayyad tribesmen participated in the early Arab conquests, and their chieftains, including Abū Sufyān, we are told, played important roles as military leaders.

Umayyad fortunes in the early caliphate centered on the rise of two of the clan's leading figures, Muʿāwiya ibn Abī Sufyān and ʿUthmān ibn ʿAffān. As the Arab conquest of Syria drew to a close in 639, a great plague carried off most of the Muslim leadership and left a void that allowed the emir Yazīd, a son of Abū Sufyān, to rise to overall command of Arab forces in Syria. When Yazīd also died late in the epidemic, command passed to his brother Muʿāwiya, an exceptionally able leader and diplomat who immediately began to consolidate his position and authority in the province, which he was to rule from Damascus as governor for the next eighteen years. He strengthened and broadened close relations with the Syrian tribes, particularly the great tribal confederacy of Quḍāʿa; carefully controlled immigration, settlement, and the distribution of lands and benefits; and occupied his warriors with further campaigns against Byzantium. All this gave him a firm and loyal power base founded on the Arab tribes.

Muʿāwiya's position was further enhanced with the elevation of his cousin ʿUthmān ibn ʿAffān to the caliphate in 644. ʿUthmān was appointed by a deliberative council (*shūrā*) of six Quraysh elders, and, as this council was dominated by traditional Arab mercantile interests, it naturally favored a contender from a clan committed to such interests (as the Umayyads certainly were). To more pious opinion, ʿUthmān was at least acceptable as one of the earliest converts to Islam and an elder companion of the Prophet. Such credentials led later tradition to distance him from the Umayyad dynasty, but ʿUthmān was in all but name its founder. As caliph he recognized the dangerous implications of the growing power of particularist forces and countered them with major steps toward centralization. He confirmed Muʿāwiya as governor of Syria and appointed Umayyad kinsmen to other important provincial posts. Such policies were later condemned as nepotistic, but they should rather be seen as efforts to establish orderly and effective government by relying on men experienced in administrative and fiscal affairs and tribal politics, and bound to the caliph by ties of personal loyalty. ʿUthmān also asserted the caliphate's authority over taxation, provincial revenues, and the distribution of stipends and lands, and in so doing undercut the power of tribal notables (*ashrāf*) and clans not allied with or tied to Umayyad interests. The trend toward centralization is also evident in his collection and codification of the Koran, a measure that provided a basis for spiritual unity.

The rise of Muʿāwiya and ʿUthmān marked the full recovery of the Umayyads from such setbacks as their traditionally dominant position had suffered in the earliest years of Islam. Muʿāwiya was firmly entrenched in Syria, and ʿUthmān's caliphate strengthened the Umayyads elsewhere as well. Indeed, it could be said that their position was so strong that when civil war cut short ʿUthmān's reign, the ultimate reassertion of Umayyad rule was the predictable result from the outset.

THE FIRST CIVIL WAR AND THE SUFYANIDS

Renewed conquests in North Africa and Khorāsān and Muʿāwiya's campaigns against Byzantium diverted attention from internal tensions for a time, but eventually ʿUthmān's policies provoked a mounting tide of discontent and finally open opposition. Resistance by provincial elements to what they saw as caliphal encroachments on their interests, resentment of the favored position of the Umayyads and their allies, disputes over land and revenue, tribal frictions within the provinces between the original conquerors and latecomers, and agitation in the name of Islam: all these were interrelated factors that eventually undermined the position of ʿUthmān, who ruled a vast and rapidly created empire that did not yet possess the minimal state structures required to cope effectively with such grave difficulties. Consultations with and support from his Umayyad kinsmen governing in the provinces failed to resolve the situation, and by 656 both Egypt and Iraq were in a state of near revolt. In the summer of that year contingents of Egyptian and Kufan warriors marched on Medina to advance their grievances. ʿUthmān was practically besieged in his own house, and in the course of negotiations some of the tribesmen rioted, broke into the caliph's house, and killed him.

The murder of ʿUthmān led to a period of great turmoil known as the *fitna* (tribulation or strife), commonly referred to by Western historians as the First Civil War (656–661). The only leader in Medina acceptable to the various opposition groups was the Prophet's cousin ʿAlī ibn Abī Ṭālib, who—so we are told—had already been an outspoken critic of ʿUthmān and, since the Prophet's death in 632, a caliphal candidate with a vocal circle of supporters, the *shīʿat ʿAlī* (faction of ʿAlī), later known simply as the Shīʿa. ʿAlī was soon proclaimed caliph by the provincial elements now in control of Medina, but he never enjoyed general support and some seem to have suspected him of complicity in ʿUthmān's death. Early Syrian tradition does not yet include ʿAlī among the caliphs, and it is likely that his position was never very strong. By contrast, the expulsion of ʿUthmān's governors in Egypt and Iraq had left Muʿāwiya as the only Umayyad with a firm base of support, and the disarray prevailing everywhere else after ʿUthmān's death made his position in Syria a strong one.

The First Civil War involved conflict on three

fronts, only one of which involved the Umayyads directly, but all of which played into Muᶜāwiya's hands. ᶜAlī almost immediately had to face a rebellion in Mecca by ᶜĀʾisha, once Muḥammad's favorite wife, and Ṭalḥa ibn ᶜUbayd Allāh and al-Zubayr ibn al-ᶜAwwām, two members of the *shūrā*. The revolt was crushed in the Battle of the Camel (656), but it obliged ᶜAlī to move his base of operations to Iraq, a hotbed of factional tensions, and at a crucial time diverted his efforts from the problem of Muᶜāwiya, who as a kinsman of ᶜUthmān refused to pay homage to ᶜAlī and demanded vengeance. This posed a second focus of conflict, for although Muᶜāwiya did not at first claim the caliphate, he promoted himself as "ruler of the Holy Land" (*malik al-arḍ al-muqaddasa*) and his strong position made him a grave threat to ᶜAlī. Negotiations between the two sides proved fruitless, and the armies finally clashed in the Battle of Ṣiffīn (657). No clear victor emerged, however, and the two sides agreed to further negotiations. This in turn opened a new sphere of conflict, for a large segment of ᶜAlī's forces rejected arbitration and deserted him when he refused to renew the fight. When these forces, the Kharijites (*khawārij*, "rebels" or "seceders"), went on to condemn ᶜAlī and to elect their own caliph, Ali attacked them at al-Nahrawān in Iraq (658) in what was apparently a virtual massacre. But this only further fragmented ᶜAlī's support and led to more defections.

In the meantime, forces loyal to Muᶜāwiya occupied Egypt, the Syrians gave him their pledge of homage (*bayᶜa*), and he successfully concluded a truce with Byzantium (highlighting his diplomatic skills) and organized a symbolically very important pilgrimage to Mecca. The arbitration between ᶜAlī and Muᶜāwiya soon proved a fiasco, however, and it was becoming clear that the triumph of Muᶜāwiya would mean order while continued support for ᶜAlī promised only prolonged confusion and disarray. ᶜAlī soon controlled no more than al-Kufa and in 661 was assassinated there by a Kharijite. The civil war ended with Muᶜāwiya's recognition as caliph by all the empire, but not with a solution to the problems that had provoked the crisis in the first place. The conflict was a resounding victory for the Sufyanid branch of the Umayyad clan, which in the persons of Muᶜāwiya, his son Yazīd, and his grandson Muᶜāwiya II was to rule for the next two decades.

As caliph, Muᶜāwiya pursued his former policies as governor of Syria on a grander scale, now aiming to establish a politically coherent imperium legitimately governed by his regime. Tribalism continued to be the dominant force in Arab sociopolitical life, and Muᶜāwiya, renowned for his skill in tribal politics and particularly for his *ḥilm* (a quality of prudent forbearance compounded with a keen eye for opportunity), presented himself as a traditional tribal chieftain, or *sayyid*. He curried the favor of the *ashrāf*, consulted with these tribal notables on imperial and provincial affairs in regular meetings of his *shūrā*, skillfully (and usually successfully) negotiated points of dispute with them, and in general tried to tie their interests to those of his regime. Such practices met with considerable success, and the Sufyanids enjoyed, in particular, the solid support in Syria of the confederacy of Quḍāᶜa. In the provinces the *ashrāf* dealt with their tribesmen much as the caliph dealt with the notables themselves, and the result was to create a complex hierarchy of loyalties that sustained the Sufyanid regime.

However, while it was true that the Sufyanids could not rule without the cooperation of the *ashrāf*, it was equally true that the tribal standing of individual notables was largely conditioned by their ability to gain benefits from the emir and caliph, and hence by the willingness of the regime to deal with them. Already in Sufyanid times, then, the Umayyads were able to pursue ᶜUthmān's centralizing policies in more authoritarian directions. Muᶜāwiya claimed not only legitimacy on traditional tribal grounds, as the champion of the wrongfully slain ᶜUthmān, but, more importantly, absolute authority as deputy of God (*khalīfat Allāh*), thus disavowing the principle of individual responsibility to clan and community that had justified his position in the struggle with ᶜAlī. Pronouncements by the caliph were of absolute legal authority and loyalty to him was demanded as a religious imperative. Active opposition, as had occurred in ᶜUthmān's day, was not tolerated; and, so long as the network of tribal loyalties held together, the Sufyanids were able to deal harshly with defiance from both Kharijites and sympathizers of the Shīᶜa.

The interplay of authoritarian principles and more egalitarian tribal ideals was highlighted by Muᶜāwiya's designation of his son Yazīd as his successor, a measure intended to preserve the intricate tribal balance that sustained Sufyanid rule. The succession of a son to a role previously played by his father was no novelty in tribal tradition, but for allegiance to the son to be demanded (rather than proffered by general accord), and while the father still lived, certainly was. Muᶜāwiya devoted great efforts, in customary tribal manner, to the planning, consultation, and persuasion required to win support for Yazīd's succession, but there was little doubt that coercion and force were available alternatives. Although a few notables in Medina withheld their approval, Yazīd's nomination was secured and he succeeded his father without incident upon Muᶜāwiya's death in 680, thus setting a precedent of dynastic succession.

The new order was manifest in both the capital and the provinces. With Muᶜāwiya's accession the caliphate shifted to Damascus, henceforth the administrative center for the entire Islamic world. A caliphal palace, al-Khaḍrāʾ (The Green [Dome]), was built and became the focus for an emerging Umayyad court life combining, on the one hand, elaborate ceremonies and imperial symbolism borrowed from Byzantine and Sasanian usage, and, on the other, the traditions of the Arab tribes, whose poets and spokesmen were a prominent feature. The functions of imperial government were delegated among various bureaucratic departments (dīwāns), and in these Christian officials continued in the important roles they had played since the days of Muᶜāwiya's governorship. Under Yazīd the caliphate also assumed a public works function, Damascus benefiting from a number of agricultural and water projects. In the provinces, authority was delegated to a small circle of trusted emirs, often from the tribe of Thaqīf, allies of Quraysh since pre-Islamic times. The emirs exercised full executive, military, and fiscal powers, supervised their own provincial bureaucracies, and reported directly to the caliph. Their provincial capitals, all new Arab creations, rapidly expanded from garrison camps to important cities on which the emirs lavished much attention in buildings and public works projects. The provincial centers also thrived as military staging points, for with the civil war at an end foreign expansion was resumed. Arab forces spread across North Africa and founded the garrison town of Qayrawān in 670, and armies in the East operated as far afield as Transoxiana. There were frequent raids into Byzantine Anatolia, and on two occasions (669, 674–680) Constantinople itself was attacked. Such operations expanded the domains of Islam, provided revenue for the treasury, and kept the tribal warriors occupied with booty-rich operations on the frontiers.

ᶜABD AL-MALIK AND THE SECOND CIVIL WAR

The greatest achievement of the Sufyanids, and primarily of Muᶜāwiya, was that, having inherited from their predecessors the means to conquer more than to govern, they devised a system that sustained the unity of their domains and laid the foundations for further institutional development. There were, however, serious weaknesses. The Umayyad-Quḍāᶜa hegemony rankled many Arab elements. Iraq, the economic heartland of the empire, resented what its notables saw as unfair exploitation and usurpation of their rights from Damascus; the Arabian ashrāf were dismayed by the declining influence of the Hejaz; and the indefinite extension of the Sufyanid system, implicit in Yazīd's succession, aroused misgivings even within Syria. Sufyanid politics addressed relations between the regime and the particularist interests of the provincial tribes, but offered no definitive solution to interclan quarrels. The Kharijites posed a continuing threat to order in the East; the tribally mixed town of al-Kufa became an increasingly difficult forum for anti-Umayyad and specifically pro-ᶜAlid sentiment; and newly converted Muslim "clients," the mawālī, were rapidly developing into a class resentful of their second-class status.

Though apparently outlandish in lifestyle, Yazīd was a capable military commander with broad tribal support. Shortly after his succession, however, al-Ḥusayn ibn ᶜAlī, the son of Muᶜāwiya's opponent in the First Civil War, and ᶜAbd Allāh ibn al-Zubayr refused to pay him homage and sought sanctuary from arrest in Mecca. Al-Ḥusayn soon thereafter received word of support in al-Kufa and set out for Iraq. His supporters there were crushed by the Umayyads, however, and, in an incident that would raise further cries against the regime, al-Ḥusayn and almost all of his small retinue were trapped and killed at Karbalāʾ (680). Yazīd sought to negotiate with Ibn al-Zubayr, but the situation in the Hejaz finally exploded in 683, when unrest in Medina swelled into a revolt calling for the deposition of Yazīd, driving Umayyad elements out of the town, and leading Ibn al-Zubayr's supporters in Mecca to hail him as caliph. An Umayyad army sent to deal with the trouble put down the Medinan revolt in the Battle of al-Ḥarra (683) and marched on and besieged Mecca. The outcome would probably have been an Umayyad victory and an end to the conflict, but during the siege Yazīd suddenly died.

The sudden hiatus in Sufyanid rule at the height of a political crisis encouraged dissident Arab elements to coalesce into a grouping capable of opposing the Umayyad-Quḍāᶜa hegemony. This realignment manifested itself in tribal terms, with the confederation of Qays, claiming to represent the "northern" tribes, confronting the "southern" coalition of Quḍāᶜa. As the Sufyanid system disintegrated, the new caliph, Muᶜāwiya II, was left with little support beyond the Quḍāᶜa strongholds in Syria, and the Umayyad army at Mecca even seems to have tried to negotiate terms for Ibn al-Zubayr's own succession. When the talks failed, the Umayyad forces abandoned the siege and hurried back to Syria, where Muᶜāwiya II died within months of his father. With the Sufyanid line offering no personality as a focus for unity, the enemies of the Umayyads almost everywhere capitalized on the mounting chaos: Ibn al-Zubayr was proclaimed caliph in most of the provinces; Kharijite rebellions were raised by the Najdīya in Arabia and the Azāriqa in Iraq and Iran; and in Syria the forces of Qays threw their support behind the Zubayrids and massed against the Umayyad regime, and even Quḍāᶜa seems to have wavered.

With their regime on the verge of collapse, the Umayyad notables and their allies met in a great council (684) at al-Jābiya, south of Damascus. Negotiations brought Quḍāᶜa back into the Umayyad fold, and the council elected as caliph Marwān I ibn al-Ḥakam, an able advisor to all of the Umayyad rulers before him, but himself not a Sufyanid. With the clan's unity restored, Marwān was able to defeat the Qays and other tribal rivals in a great battle at Marj Rāhiṭ, and so regain control of all Syria. He also reoccupied Egypt, and other campaigns were underway when the aged ruler died.

After Marj Rāhiṭ, Marwān had been able to win support for the succession of his son ᶜAbd al-Malik, whose succession began a new branch of the Umayyad dynasty, the Marwanids, that was to produce all of the remaining Umayyad caliphs. The new ruler faced a situation in which the civil war was rapidly degenerating into a general dissolution of order in which a broad range of Arab factions, Shiite and Kharijite groups, and even some of the mawālī participated, fighting each other as much as the Umayyads. That Ibn al-Zubayr's own position was precarious was demonstrated by Marwān's easy recovery of Egypt, and in 685 the same problem was highlighted in al-Kufa, where al-Mukhtār,

proclaiming himself the champion of the divinely guided (mahdī) Muḥammad ibn al-Ḥanafīya, revolted and seized most of northern Iraq and parts of Iran from the Zubayrids. Local conflicts flared up in many places, banditry and tribal brigandage swelled to catastrophic proportions, and plague epidemics broke out in both Syria and Iraq.

ᶜAbd al-Malik was for several years fully occupied with internal dissension in Syria and the possibility of war with Byzantium. In 689, however, the caliph concluded a truce with the Byzantines to secure the Syrian frontier and in 691–692 he advanced through northern Mesopotamia and retook Iraq, already exhausted by fighting between the supporters of Ibn al-Zubayr, al-Mukhtār (defeated and killed by the Zubayrids in 687), and the Kharijites. This left Ibn al-Zubayr isolated in the Hejaz, and ᶜAbd al-Malik sent one of his best commanders, al-Ḥajjāj ibn Yūsuf, to deal with him. Al-Ḥajjāj crushed the Kharijite revolt of the Najdīya, took Medina, and after a six-month siege captured Mecca. Ibn al-Zubayr was killed in the fighting, and with his death the Second Civil War formally ended (692).

Turmoil in the East, however, had still to be contained, and to this end ᶜAbd al-Malik transferred al-Ḥajjāj to al-Kufa in 694. The Azāriqa in Iran were crushed only after several years of intense fighting; there was unrest in Khorāsān in 697; and even within Umayyad ranks in Iraq there was trouble. The climax of these disturbances came in 700, when Iraqi ashrāf under the Ibn al-Ashᶜath rose in a rebellion, supported by many mawālī, posing a renewed threat to Umayyad rule until defeated by al-Ḥajjāj in 701. It was only in ᶜAbd al-Malik's last years that his empire was finally once again at peace, and even then calm in the East did not endure and was secured only through the heavy-handed rule of al-Ḥajjāj, who exercised enormous power and governed all of the eastern provinces until his death in 714.

Although the uprising of Ibn al-Zubayr proved in itself to be of only minor significance, the other conflicts that arose in the Second Civil War had consequences of the utmost importance. The Battle at Marj Rāhiṭ, in which many Qays notables died, irrevocably split the Arab tribes and left a legacy of factional animosity and recurring violence that widened the rift between Quḍāᶜa and Qays. Such factionalism spread to the provinces as well, and, combined with the opportunistic defection of the ashrāf during the crisis, it discredited the Sufyanid system of rule based on the cultivation and manipulation of Arab tribal relations. In addition, the conflict had revealed the shallow basis for legitimization that such a system provided among the Arabs at large, and even more so, among the swelling ranks of new non-Arab Muslim converts with no stake in the tribal system. Practically all of the empire had at one time or another repudiated the Umayyads, and the Islamically oriented propaganda of Kharijite groups and the Shīʿa had won significant support. The precise content of this propaganda is difficult to determine, but it is clear that social justice was seen to subsist in the promotion of Islam, and that in these terms the Umayyads were not regarded as possessing greater claims to legitimacy than other Arab clans.

ʿAbd al-Malik and his successors thus sought to consolidate the authority of their regime on firmer foundations. Dynastic succession, though still unpopular in many quarters, was recognized as the only means to ensure the smooth transfer of power, and elaborate steps, not always successful, were taken to regularize the system and to guarantee enforcement of the caliph's choice of successor. As a tribal family based in Syria, the Umayyads could not undercut the position of the Syrian *ashrāf,* but elsewhere they concentrated authority in the hands of a small circle of trusted professional officers (rather than protégés or tribal allies of the caliph) at the head of standing armies and ruling vast areas as their military commands. Most particularly, the troublesome East was long ruled as occupied territory by al-Ḥajjāj, based in the newly created town of Wāsiṭ and enforcing his will not by negotiation with the *ashrāf* but with a force of Syrian regulars. Administration at all levels became more specialized as more *dīwān*s were established, and a dense communications network (*barīd*) provided the governors and caliphs with rapid intelligence on all affairs.

At the same time, the Marwanids sought to promote the Islamic legitimacy of their regime. The claim to rule as God's deputies, chosen for the caliphate as the heirs of ʿUthmān, was further asserted, probably with the propaganda of the civil war in mind. Muḥammad was acknowledged as the founder of the faith and the source of the legitimacy of the caliphate itself; but the Umayyads claimed to rule by hereditary right and derived their authority not from the Prophet, but directly from ʿUthmān, who had been raised to the office by God and wrongfully slain by his enemies. By virtue of their

victory in the civil war, they also claimed to be deliverers from error, dispensers of justice, and givers of divinely approved law—in sum, God's appointed orderers of the Muslim community (the *umma*), and, as such, entitled to demand absolute loyalty.

To be seen in light of these efforts is an important series of public initiatives undertaken by ʿAbd al-Malik and pursued by his successors. These measures are often described in terms of Arabization, but of equal importance was their Islamic dimension: the Umayyad view of the Arabism of their regime was inseparably bonded to their conception of Islam, and initiatives by the Umayyad caliph were, after all, executed in his capacity as deputy of God. In the Umayyad bureaucracy, Arabic replaced the previous languages of administration (Greek in Syria, Pahlavi in Iran, and Coptic and Greek in Egypt). Effected over a long period across the empire, the change aimed to centralize the machinery of government along Arab lines; but while there was probably no dramatic change in personnel, Arabic was the language of Islam and in the long term those who stood to benefit were Muslims, whether Arabs or new Arabic-speaking converts. ʿAbd al-Malik's reign also saw the introduction of new distinctly Islamic coinage replacing Byzantine and Sasanian iconophile motifs with Arabic inscriptions, primarily Koranic phrases stressing the might and strict monotheistic viewpoint of Islam. In this era the building projects of the caliphs began to include major Islamic monuments, the first being the spectacular Dome of the Rock, erected by ʿAbd al-Malik on the Temple Mount in Jerusalem.

THE APOGEE OF THE UMAYYAD ERA

ʿAbd al-Malik was succeeded by his sons al-Walīd I (705–715) and Sulaymān (715–717), his nephew ʿUmar II ibn ʿAbd al-ʿAzīz (717–720), and then two more sons, Yazīd II (720–724) and Hishām (724–743). This era marked the climax of the Umayyad caliphate and was signaled by a vigorous revival of the conquests. In the West, Umayyad troops in North Africa reached the Atlantic; in 711 they crossed the Strait of Gibraltar and by 714 the Visigoths of Spain had been conquered. Much is made in modern Western scholarship of Charles Martel's defeat of the Arabs near Poitiers (732), but the momentum of conquest may already have been spent in Spain, and further efforts were hampered not so much by European resistance as by recurrent Berber unrest in North Africa, culminating in the revolt of Maysara al-Maṭgharī in 740. In the Near East, Constantinople was besieged for the third time (716–718) in a bitter campaign that ended in Umayyad defeat. Further east, however, the regime enjoyed great success. Ṭabaristān was subdued, major inroads were made into Transoxiana and Farghāna, and forays in Central Asia reached the frontiers of China before expansion on this front stalled in fighting with the Türgesh Turkic tribes in the caliphate of Hishām. To the south, Arab forces crossed Baluchistan, captured the port of Daybul in 711, and penetrated up the Indus Valley to Multan.

On the economic scene, the pattern of subsistence agriculture in villages clustered around small-to-medium-sized towns came increasingly to be dominated by a market economy characterized by the growth of large cities thriving on trade. This development was stimulated by the disappearance of internal frontiers as the Umayyad Empire expanded, by the large-scale movement of persons and goods associated with Arab migration and the conquests, by the enormously lucrative commercial opportunities involved in supplying armies and disposing of revenues collected in kind, and by the stability of the new Umayyad coinage. Movement toward the formation of a distinct merchant class was underway, and the resulting urban growth was rapid and profound. Al-Fusṭāṭ (later Cairo) and Basra, for example, grew from ephemeral garrisons of tents and huts in the 640's to the greatest cities and cultural centers of Egypt and Iraq a century later.

Military expansion and economic growth brought vast revenues to the Umayyad treasury and likewise enriched a new class of wealthy Arab notables, and it was at this time that there emerged a pattern of ambitious internal development. Canals and irrigation systems were repaired and extended, and large tracts of unexploited land were reclaimed and either devoted to agriculture or developed into personal estates. Roads and way stations were built and steps were taken to improve rural security and stamp out banditry, charitable services for the poor and disabled were established, and in at least one instance quarantine and support facilities were set up for lepers. The most renowned Umayyad programs, however, were the building projects of al-Walīd and Hishām. The former erected the great Umayyad mosque in Damascus (*ca.* 711), and in other cities in the provinces congrega-

tional mosques were rebuilt or enlarged. Palaces and residences were founded in the Syrian countryside, and most of the impressive sites surviving today are to be assigned to one or the other of these caliphs.

This era also marked an important stage in the rise of Islamic literary culture and scholarship. The Marwanids were generous patrons of poets and displayed interest in a variety of subjects, especially fields relevant to arguments over the legitimacy of the Umayyad regime. History, for example, was the battleground for the controversy over the killing of ʿUthmān. And in emerging theological discussions the Umayyads had a vested interest in promoting the views of the Murjiʾa, which stressed faith over works and argued that the latter (including deeds of caliphs) could be judged only by God on the Resurrection Day. The Qadarīya, on the other hand, were opposed for their insistence on personal accountability before both God and the community of believers. Imperial patronage was thus problematic: the main centers of Islamic culture in fact stood largely outside such circles, and the studies characteristic of the intellectual and cultural development of Islam were often pursued with greatest vigor in the foci of opposition to the Umayyads. Philology, literary prose, law, Koranic exegesis, and *ḥadīth* were all fields that, although not ignored in Syria, were most prominently represented by scholars in Medina, Basra, and al-Kufa.

Such developments were all manifestations of a broader trend. While the Sufyanid regime essentially comprised a continuation of the old Byzantine and Sasanian order under Arab auspices, the Marwanid branch of the Umayyads presided over the emergence of a distinctly Islamic culture and political system. This transformation involved not only elements of efflorescence, however, but also serious social tensions between partisans of the old order and those whose interests lay in the promotion of the new. These tensions focused on the problems of Arab factionalism and Islamization.

In the wake of the Second Civil War the tribal tensions exacerbated by Marj Rāhiṭ crystallized more clearly in factions within the Umayyad armies. Beyond Syria such groupings also emerged in Iraq, where Basran alignments split along new lines to bring the "northern" grouping of Muḍar into confrontation with Yemen, a "southern" grouping that in fact comprised a confederation of Azd, a tribe recently swelled to large numbers in Basra, and Rabīʿa, a formerly "northern" faction seeking allies against its rival Muḍar. These factions were never sharply defined in their tribal composition or objectives, and should be seen as fluid military groupings anxious to preserve and promote their own interests as opposed to the Umayyad regime and other factions. Indeed, underlying the factional tensions and shifting lines of cleavage was the enormously disruptive factor of the gradual disintegration of the traditional norms and patterns of Arab tribalism. At the social level, contingents from different tribes intermingled and intermarried in the provinces, eventually established roots there, and came to regard these regions as their homes. The local interests thus engendered tended to displace former tribal interests and to disrupt old loyalties and ties. This trend was further reinforced in the economic sphere, where widening discrepancies in wealth and living standards between those who enjoyed high stipends or income from landholdings (especially notables and early comers) and the majority, who received lower stipends or nothing at all, often placed members of the same tribe at cross purposes.

These developments had serious destabilizing effects, and, once established in Iraq, army factionalism quickly spread to the frontier territories that it ruled. It was in Khorāsān, governed from Basra, that major problems first arose. In 698 al-Ḥajjāj gave the governorship of Khorāsān to al-Muhallab ibn Abī Ṣufra, a general from the tribe of Azd who had distinguished himself against the Azāriqa. Al-Muhallab used his office to promote the interests of his own family within Azd and also of the Yemenite faction generally, and when he died in 702 his son Yazīd continued these policies. After an erratic two-decade official career interrupted by several sojourns in prison or in hiding, Yazīd raised a rebellion in Basra that gained the support of Azd and the other Yemenites and soon engulfed Wāsiṭ, al-Kufa, and southern Iran. In 720, however, Yazīd fell in battle and the remnants of the fleeing family were eventually either killed or captured. Reflecting the complexities noted above, the revolt did not adhere strictly to tribal cleavages and had significant Muḍarī support, while even some elements within Azd opposed it. Nevertheless, it seriously exacerbated factional tensions, for the fall of the al-Muhallab family (both father and son soon rose to the status of folk heroes in Basra) was seen as an ignominious "southern" defeat, while the "northerners" not only dominated the army that had defeated and killed Yazīd but also subsequently

won most of the key provincial appointments in the East. Though efforts were made to reduce tensions between the factions, they were largely unsuccessful and the problem continued to worsen.

Closely linked to the problem of factionalism was the equally important issue of Islamization. In earliest Islamic times the Arab conquerors comprised a tiny minority ruling a vast population of non-Muslims. Although Islam was open to all, the faith was generally seen as an Arab one and conversion was neither expected nor encouraged. The two sides were to a significant extent isolated from one another, but this was never absolute and the isolation probably began to break down almost immediately. There had always been a non-Arab presence in Arab armies, and new garrison towns and other urban centers proved to be foci for the diffusion of both Arabic and Islam. Non-Muslim functionaries dominated the rudimentary provincial administrations of the early caliphate, for example, and played major roles in the imperial bureaucracy once the caliphate moved from Medina to Damascus. The indigenous population also found lucrative opportunities in the vigorous trade, commerce, and exchange activities of the Arab centers. In the agrarian hinterlands the weakening of the old feudal structures, the massive redistribution of land and wealth resulting from the conquests, and the relatively greater mobility of the peasantry tended to fragment village societies and render them more amenable to external influences. All of these circumstances were highly favorable to the spread of both Arabic and Islam.

The diffusion of the language and faith of the Arabs posed certain problems. Arabization in time helped to blur the already ambiguous and largely amorphous distinction between Arab and non-Arab, and so further promoted the development of local interests at the expense of those of the tribe. Islamization, though closely linked to Arabization, had major social and economic repercussions of its own. Although details are extremely difficult to sort out, it is clear that in general taxation and social status were more favorable for the Muslim than for the non-Muslim, thus posing a distinct material incentive for conversion (which is not to say, however, that crass opportunism accounts for the phenomenon of Islamization). But while no Islamic regime could oppose the spread of the faith, large-scale Islamization posed a grave dilemma. To grant the new converts, the *mawālī*, the favorable tax status due to Muslims would result in a sharp decline in the tax base and render it impossible for provinces to collect the level of revenues owed to the state. But refusal to grant the *mawālī* the rights enjoyed by Arab Muslims provoked social unrest and protests of injustice and played into the hands of Kharijite and Shiite groups already agitating against Umayyad rule.

All of these difficulties were symptomatic of the dramatic shift from a sociopolitical order in which the crucial distinction was between Arab and non-Arab, to one in which it lay between Muslim and non-Muslim. The society produced by the spread of Arabic and Islam and the rise of interests transcending those of the tribe and including both Arabs and *mawālī* was increasingly drawn to ideals of Islamic identity and Muslim equality. The factionalism and Syrian hegemonism of the Marwanid era, as well as the old order's now archaic abuses and inequalities in personal status, land tenure, and taxation, stood in ever sharper contrast to these values and challenged the regime to implement reforms. The name of ᶜUmar II ibn ᶜAbd al-ᶜAzīz dominates accounts of efforts to deal with this problem; and although it is unlikely that he alone appreciated and sought to resolve it, the measures taken in his brief reign are known in fuller detail and were clearly of importance. Commitment to remote and costly military expeditions was sharply curtailed, and the disastrous siege of Constantinople was lifted in 718. Sweeping reforms regularized fiscal, land, and taxation policies, discrimination against the *mawālī* was abolished, and efforts were made to come to terms with the Kharijites and the Shiites. It is impossible to determine the extent to which these reforms were implemented, for ᶜUmar II lived to rule for only two years and problems quickly resurfaced as his successor, Yazīd II, undid almost all that he had tried to accomplish.

THE COLLAPSE OF THE UMAYYAD REGIME

The caliphate of Hishām is best remembered for his building projects and campaigns against the Turkic tribes on the eastern frontier, but in fact internal opposition was also becoming a matter of great importance. The Shiites in al-Kufa rebelled on several occasions, a Kharijite revolt among North African Berbers twice defeated Hishām's armies, and even in Damascus the agitation of the Qadarīya was sufficiently serious to result in the execution of its leader, a certain Ghaylān al-Dimashqī. The greatest difficulties, however, arose in Khorāsān. Here, far from Syria and Iraq, Shiite groups were prominent, and the civilian Muslim population seems to have shared sentiments of resentment over unfair taxation, domination from Syria, and discrimination against the *mawālī*, and in general over rule by a regime of highly suspect Islamic credentials. From a more positive viewpoint, the intermingling of Arab settlers and local *mawālī* had produced a population with their own highly developed local interests. Indeed, this had reached the point where a rebellion led by al-Ḥārith ibn Surayj (734) was able to unite Muḍarī and Yemenite Arabs and the *mawālī* in opposition to the Umayyads in Transoxiana and Khorāsān, and for a time even allied with the non-Muslim Türgesh. In such an environment the missionaries of the Hāshimīya, an ᶜAlid movement in al-Kufa calling for an Islamic order restoring justice and bringing to power a member of the Prophet's family, found a favorable reception. The Umayyad authorities arrested and often executed the missionaries it detected, but the movement continued to grow.

The chain of events that brought down the Umayyads began not in Khorāsān, however, but in Syria. During Hishām's long reign other members of the Umayyad house became heavily involved in the factional politics of the Syrian forces, probably with dissension over the succession in mind. When Hishām died (743), the contender who moved fastest to consolidate his position was the heir-apparent al-Walīd II ibn Yazīd. Already linked by blood ties to responsibility for the humiliations suffered by the Yemenite faction in connection with the governorship of al-Ḥajjāj and the revolt of Yazīd ibn al-Muhallab, al-Walīd II soon proved to be a harsh and imprudent ruler committed to the partisan interests of the Qays. Within a year the Yemenites revolted, seized Damascus, killed al-Walīd in a rural retreat, and installed Yazīd III ibn al-Walīd in his place. The new caliph immediately promised sweeping fiscal, military, and social reforms, but was of course obligated to the Yemenites who had brought him to power and in any case died after only a few months on the throne (September 744), before his programs could be implemented.

Yazīd was succeeded by his brother Ibrāhīm, but the latter enjoyed little support and was soon challenged by a formidable rival, Marwān ibn Muḥammad, governor of al-Jazīra (in northern Mesopotamia), Armenia, and Azerbaijan. A superb general and leader of a seasoned army of mostly Qaysī troops, Marwān consolidated his position after the death of al-Walīd II and now marched into Syria, calling for the restitution of the rights of the murdered caliph's two sons and gathering Qaysī tribal support as he advanced. A battle ended in a victory for Marwān; and when it also resulted in the murder of al-Walīd's sons, then held captive in Damascus, Marwān marched on to occupy the capital and have himself proclaimed caliph (December 744).

As Syria had proven itself hopelessly riven by factional tensions, Marwān soon decided to transfer his capital to Ḥarrān in northeast Syria, where he had a strong Qaysī base of support. This and other measures provoked a Yemenite revolt, paralleled, as in earlier civil wars, by the repudiation of the regime elsewhere. Anti-Umayyad elements had already seized al-Kufa and southwest Iran in 744, Kharijite forces took al-Kufa themselves in 745 and advanced north through Iraq and the Jazīra, other Kharijite elements raised a rebellion in Arabia in 746, and Egypt was wracked by army mutinies and peasant revolts. Marwān's veterans were able to cope with most of these uprisings, but the disorder prevented the caliph from dealing with a new crisis, this time in Khorāsān. Inflamed by the Qays-Yemen strife in Syria, Muḍar-Yemen tensions in the East soon developed into a violent conflict. By this time the Hāshimīya had gained much support in the area of Merv, where the Arab settlers were primarily of Azd and other Yemenite tribes, and the movement was now under the control of the capable Abū Muslim. Seizing the opportunity afforded by Umayyad disarray, Abū Muslim raised a rebellion in the countryside around Merv. When the Umayyad factions both appealed to him for support against the other, the Yemenite character of Abū Muslim's immediate base of support led him to take their side. The Qaysīs were driven out of Merv (748), and the Yemenites soon found themselves caught up in a movement aimed not just against the Qays in Khorāsān, but against Umayyad rule in general. The rebellion gained momentum as it moved westward, the urban centers of Iran fell one after another, and Umayyad forces were defeated in several major battles. Iraq was invaded in 749, al-Kufa fell in September, and in November the Abbasid Abu 'l-ʿAbbās was proclaimed caliph there. Probably hindered by massive plague epidemics in Syria and Iraq in 749, Marwān finally marshaled his own forces for battle, but suffered a complete defeat at the Great Zāb River near Mosul in January 750. His army scattered and the last Umayyad caliph fled through Syria to Egypt, where he was captured and killed several months later.

One family member escaped to Spain and founded a new regime there, but in general the demise of Marwān marked the ruin of his family as well. Umayyad princes of the Marwanid line were hunted down and massacred in a number of incidents, the tombs of the Umayyad caliphs (except for that of ʿUmar II) were violated and desecrated, and, at Wāsiṭ, the last Umayyad garrison surrendered with guarantees of clemency, only for the commander and all of his Muḍarī troops to be slaughtered.

In the two earlier civil wars the Umayyads had emerged victorious because they had been able to maintain Syria as a strong and united base during struggles in which the alternative to the unity and order upheld by the Umayyad regime, for all its imperfections, seemed to be anarchy and the dissolution of the empire. But by late Umayyad times all this had changed. The Umayyad military in the provinces was split by factionalism and eventually even the ruling house in its imperial center succumbed to the temptation to choose sides for the sake of immediate gains. At the same time, major social changes and the process of Islamization made it possible to endow a more universalist Islamic program with coherent focus and form. Once the Hāshimīya demonstrated its military viability and its commitment to order and unity, the Umayyads were abandoned on all sides—even the cities of Syria closed their gates on the fleeing Marwān. The demise of the regime stands as a stark testament to the tremendous changes that had transpired since the days of Muʿāwiya and ʿAbd al-Malik. But while its effort to maintain political unity under its own auspices had failed, surely of far greater importance was its achievement in nurturing Islam as a world religious and cultural order and endowing it with its distinctive Arab coloring.

BIBLIOGRAPHY

Still a classic and indispensable account is Julius Wellhausen, *The Arab Kingdom and Its Fall,* Margaret Graham Weir, trans. (1927, repr. 1963). The best introduction to the history of the Umayyads and the problems involved in the study of this period is Gerald R. Hawting, *The First Dynasty of Islam: The Umayyad Caliphate A.D. 661–750* (1986). See also Nabīh ʿAqil, *Khilāfat Banī Umayya* (1972); Patricia Crone, *Slaves on Horses: The Evolution of the Islamic Polity* (1980); Fred M. Donner, "The Formation of the Islamic State," in *Journal of the American Oriental Society,* **106** (1986); H. A. R.

Gibb, *Studies in the Civilization of Islam*, Stanford J. Shaw and William R. Polk, eds. (1962); Marshall G. S. Hodgson, *The Venture of Islam: Conscience and History in a World Civilization*, I (1974); Tilman Nagel, *Staat und Glaubensgemeinschaft im Islam*, I (1981); Albrecht Noth, "Früher Islam," in *Geschichte der arabischen Welt*, Ulrich Haarmann, ed. (1987), 73–100; M. A. Shaban, *Islamic History: A New Interpretation*, I (1971).

On more specialized points, see *Cambridge History of Arabic Literature*, I, *Arabic Literature to the End of the Umayyad Period*, A. F. L. Beeston *et al.*, eds. (1983); Michael Cook, *Early Muslim Dogma* (1981); Patricia Crone and Martin Hinds, *God's Caliph: Religious Authority in the First Centuries of Islam* (1986); Daniel C. Dennett, *Conversion and the Poll Tax in Early Islam* (1950); A. A. Duri, *The Historical Formation of the Arab Nation: A Study in Identity and Consciousness*, Lawrence I. Conrad, trans. (1987); Gerhard Endress, *Einführung in die islamische Geschichte* (1982); Ziaul Haque, *Landlord and Peasant in Early Islam* (1977); Henri Lammens, *Études sur le siècle des Omayyades* (1930); *Studies on the First Century of Islamic Society*, G. H. A. Juynboll, ed. (1982); W. Montgomery Watt, *Islamic Philosophy and Theology* (1962) and *Islamic Political Thought* (1968); Julius Wellhausen, *The Religio-political Factions in Early Islam*, R. C. Ostle, ed., R. C. Ostle and S. M. Walter, trans. (1975).

LAWRENCE I. CONRAD

[See also **Abbasids; ʿAbd Allāh ibn al-Zubayr; Abū Sufyān; ʿĀʾisha; Alids; ʿAlī ibn Abī Ṭālib; Arabia; Basra; Cairo; Caliphate; Constantinople; Damascus; Diplomacy, Islamic; Dome of the Rock; Farghānā; Ḥajjāj ibn Yūsuf al-Thaqafī, al-; Hejaz; Hishām ibn ʿAbd al-Malik; Ḥusayn ibn ʿAlī, al-; Iraq; Islam, Conquests of; Islamic Administration; Islamic Art and Architecture; Kufa, al-; Marj Rāhiṭ; Marwān, ʿAbd al-Malik ibn; Marwān I ibn al-Ḥakam; Marwān II ibn Muḥammad; Medina; Muʿāwiya; Poitiers, Battle of; Quraysh; Sects, Islamic; Shīʿa; Syria; Transoxiana; ʿUmar II ibn ʿAbd al-Azīz; Walīd I ibn ʿAbd al-Malik, al-; Wāsiṭ; Yazīd I ibn Muʿāwiya.]**

UMAYYADS OF CÓRDOBA, Arab dynasty of Syrian origin that ruled Spain from 756 until the early eleventh century. The founder of the dynasty was the Umayyad prince ʿAbd al-Raḥmān ibn Muʿāwiya I (born near Damascus in 731), who survived the slaughter of most of his family in the Abbasid revolution of 750. In search of a throne promised him by an oracle, the young prince made his way to Morocco, where he was received by the Nafza Berbers, the tribe of his mother. Umayyad clients in southern Spain welcomed him there in August 755 and, after the failure of an attempt to form an alliance with the governor, Yūsuf al-Fihrī, ʿAbd al-Raḥmān captured Seville in March 756 and entered Córdoba in May, when he was proclaimed emir.

The political history of ʿAbd al-Raḥmān's long reign (756–788), as well as that of his successors until the early tenth century, was characterized by the continuous tribal infighting that typifies segmentary tribal societies, whereby political stability is predicated upon a process of the constant testing of strength among continually shifting tribal and ethnic coalitions. Thus, much of the emir's attention was devoted to the pacification of rebellious tribes of generally pro-Abbasid sympathies. ʿAbd al-Raḥmān I declared Islamic Spain, called *al-Andalus* in Arabic, independent of the Abbasid caliphate.

An early rebellion in 763 in the south of Portugal, led by the Yemeni Arab al-ʿAlāʾ ibn Mugīth, ended with the embalmed heads of the rebel chiefs being sent to Qayrawān wrapped in the black flag of the Abbasids—a notorious incident said to have caused the Abbasid caliph to exclaim, in reference to ʿAbd al-Raḥmān I, "Praise be to God that He has placed the sea between that devil and me!" The most serious challenge to his rule, nevertheless, was the Berber uprising led by the mystic Shakya ibn ʿAbd al-Waḥīd (768–776). Another rebellion, led by the governor of Saragossa, Sulaymān ibn Yaqzan, which began around 767/768 in a climate of overt pro-Abbasid conspiracy, led to the disastrous intervention and defeat of Frankish troops under Charlemagne in 778, an episode that terminated with the Basque attack on the Frankish rearguard at Roncesvalles, of which the *Song of Roland* is a literary account.

ʿAbd al-Raḥmān I ruled through a small circle of military and civil administrators, most of whom were either his relatives or clients of his family who had migrated to Spain upon hearing of his success. Indeed, the emir considered it a great achievement to have reunited his clan in Spain. He directed construction of the oldest portion of the mosque of Córdoba, as well as a summer palace, al-Ruṣāfa, modeled after one of the same name built by his grandfather in Syria.

ʿAbd al-Raḥmān I was succeeded by his son Hishām I (*r.* 788–796) in a climate of open rebellion, both by two disgruntled brothers and by Yemeni Arabs in the region of Tortosa. The rest of his reign, however, was marked by internal calm, giving the emir ample time and resources to mount summer campaigns against Bermudo I and Alfonso II of Asturias, whose capital of Oviedo was sacked in 794. A pious Muslim, Hishām encouraged the study of Islamic law, particularly that of the Malikite school that became established in al-Andalus during his reign and that of his successor.

Hishām I was succeeded by his second son, al-Ḥakam I (r. 796–822). The early years of his reign were troubled by rebellions of *muwalladūn* (indigenous converts to Islam) in Toledo and Saragossa. In Córdoba itself, resistance was centered in a suburb called Secunda, where in 805 seventy-two notables conspired against the emir and were crucified. This rebellion led to the formation of a strong palace guard under the leadership of the Christian count Rabīᶜ. Resentful of Rabīᶜ's power and bridling against newly instituted taxes, a more popular revolt, including many *muwalladūn*, broke out in Secunda in 818. Al-Ḥakam crucified most of the leaders and exiled as many as 20,000 dissidents to Morocco. He was succeeded by his son, ᶜAbd al-Raḥmān II (r. 822–852), who had been responsible for the pacification of Toledo.

ᶜAbd al-Raḥmān II found himself at the head of a nominally pacified kingdom but with numerous elements of the population disaffected by his father's policy of harsh repression. He won the support of the urban masses, particularly those of Córdoba, and of the religious leadership by crucifying the despised Rabīᶜ. He then faced a Berber-*muwallad* coalition that rose against him in the Mérida region beginning in 828, with the active support of Alfonso II of Asturias. ᶜAbd al-Raḥmān II continued the practice of directing summer raids against the Asturians, during the reigns of both Alfonso II and his successor Ramiro I. Later in his reign, ᶜAbd al-Raḥmān II concentrated on quelling revolts by *muwallad* dissidents in Saragossa and sent a column to fight the Franks near Narbonne in 850.

Under the rule of ᶜAbd al-Raḥmān II, al-Andalus acquired the status of an independent state in the eyes of the Islamic world. There was no longer any active fear of retribution from the Abbasids. Indeed when, in 840, a delegation sent by the Byzantine emperor Theophilus arrived in Córdoba, seeking the emir's aid in containing the pro-Abbasid Aghlabid rulers of Tunisia and Sicily, ᶜAbd al-Raḥmān II responded courteously and dispatched his own ambassador, the poet Yahya al-Gazal, to Constantinople, but felt no need to join in any military

adventures. Somewhat paradoxically, ᶜAbd al-Raḥmān II admired Abbasid governmental institutions and strove to remodel his own administration along Eastern lines. As a result, all power, both civil and religious, came to be concentrated in the person of the emir. He instituted royal textile and coinage monopolies and established a fixed hierarchy of public offices, which entailed the reorganization of the state treasury from which all officials were paid. The annual income of the emirate reached 1 million dinars, and court life under ᶜAbd al-Raḥmān II was notably opulent, as Eastern tastes and styles (associated with the court singer Ziryāb, himself a former servant of the Abbasids) were introduced. In keeping with Eastern norms of governance, the emir rarely appeared in public, preferring to remain in his palace and to entrust the administration of the court to a corps of eunuchs.

ᶜAbd al-Raḥmān II was succeeded by his son Muḥammad I (r. 852–886), who perfected and extended the administrative techniques introduced by his father. He introduced the office of *ḥājib* (chamberlain), a kind of prime minister who also led the summer military raids against Asturias, and entrusted high court offices to a small coterie of aristocratic Arab families from Córdoba. A good diplomat, Muḥammad I secured peaceful relations with the Rustamid dynasty in North Africa, with Charles the Bald, and with the *muwallad* Banū Qasī family, which ruled independenly in Tudela. Hostility against the Asturian kingdom, however, was particularly marked, and mercenaries were introduced into the raiding parties. The Asturians, under Ordoño I, contributed a strong contingent of troops to aid a Toledan rebellion in 854, but the emir's army prevailed, inflicting heavy casualties.

Near the end of Muḥammad's reign, in 879, a *muwallad* from the mountains of Málaga named ᶜUmar ibn Ḥafṣūn began a revolt that was to harass the Umayyads for nearly fifty years. When Muḥammad was succeeded in 886 by his son al-Mundhir, Ibn Ḥafṣūn called for open revolt against the Arab dynasty that, he alleged, had humiliated *muwalladūn* and treated them like slaves. Al-Mundhir set out to punish the rebels in the spring of 788, besieging Ibn Ḥafṣūn at the latter's fortress at Bobastro, where the emir fell sick and died.

Al-Mundhir, about whom little is recorded apart from his struggle with ᶜUmar ibn Ḥafṣūn, was succeeded by his brother ᶜAbd Allāh (r. 888–912), who, in 891, was able to force the rebels into retreat without gaining any lasting advantage over them.

276

ᶜAbd Allāh, according to some reports, was implicated in the death of his brother and, after attaining power, eliminated several of his remaining brothers. He was a pious Muslim but narrow of vision and apparently dominated by the religious leaders (*faqīhs*) of Córdoba. He faced continual and serious rebellions by *muwalladūn,* not only from Ibn Ḥafṣūn, but also from Ibn al-Jilliqī ("son of the Galician"), who ruled as an independent prince in Mérida, and from the Banū Qasī (children of the Qasī) of Saragossa, who may have formed an alliance with Ibn Ḥafṣūn in 898. The apparent breakdown of the Umayyad state during this period seems related to the increasing pace of the indigenous populations's conversion to Islam, making them a majority among competing Muslim groups.

ᶜAbd Allāh was succeeded by his grandson ᶜAbd al-Raḥmān III (*r.* 912/913–961), the greatest Umayyad ruler, who recaptured most of the territory held by ᶜUmar ibn Ḥafṣūn in 913, ending for all practical purposes this long-lived rebellion. In other campaigns during the first two decades of his reign, he also returned to Umayyad control the chronically rebellious regions of Mérida and Toledo. His foreign policy was to apply constant pressure against the Christian kingdoms of northern Spain and to counter Fatimid designs in North Africa both by strengthening his naval defenses and through a diplomatic offensive intended to enhance the independence of Berber chieftains there. In 927 ᶜAbd al-Raḥmān III captured Melilla, at the eastern end of the Rif mountains in Morocco, to serve as an advanced defensive base; four years later he established a similar outpost at Ceuta. From these two bases he was able to establish a kind of Umayyad protectorate over much of northern and central Morocco.

In 929 ᶜAbd al-Raḥmān III took the symbolically significant step of proclaiming himself caliph, an act that reinforced the political independence of al-Andalus from the Fatimids as well as from the Abbasids and stressed the legitimacy of Umayyad pretensions to leadership in the Islamic world. He sought to embody the majesty and power of the newly proclaimed caliphate in a palace-city, Madīnat al-Zahrāʾ, which he began to build, at enormous expense, outside Córdoba in 936. The caliph took up residence in the new court complex around 945 and began to transfer government bureaus there from Córdoba. When he died in 961, ᶜAbd al-Raḥmān III left a pacified realm, but one in which all power had become concentrated in his own hands, with civil authority delegated through slaves, and with military power falling increasingly into the hands of Berber mercenaries who had been recruited to bolster the Umayyads' military efforts on the Christian frontier.

ᶜAbd al-Raḥmān's son al-Ḥakam II (*r.* 961–976) was a pious and learned man (his library was said to have been the best in Europe) who continued his father's policies. He ruled through slaves and accentuated the recruitment of North African Berbers into the army. Al-Ḥakam's hegemony in the peninsula was absolute, and he received a constant stream of diplomatic embassies from the Christian rulers who hoped both to secure the advantage against their rivals and to stave off punitive expeditions from the Umayyads. The contemporary accounts probably exaggerate the obsequiousness of the dethroned Ordoño IV of León, who begged the caliph to help him recover his throne from Sancho I. An alliance among the Christian kingdoms obliged al-Ḥakam to lead personally a military foray in the summer of 963. In 973, he took action on his southern flank, sending his chamberlain Ghālib to retake Ceuta, which had been captured by Idrīsid forces.

Al-Ḥakam's death initiated a dynastic crisis, inasmuch as his son and heir, Hishām II, was a boy of ten and unable to contain the power struggle that erupted between the principal slaves of his father, on the one hand, and Hishām's own staff, on the other. The latter was headed by Muḥammad ibn Abī ᶜĀmir, called al-Manṣūr (the feared Almanzor of the Christian chronicles). Al-Manṣūr became vizier of the new caliph, whom he virtually imprisoned at Madīnat al-Zahrāʾ, and by 981 he had eliminated all of his rivals for power. In the same year, he took up residence in a new administrative city to the east of Córdoba called Madīnat al-Ẓāhira.

Throughout the last decade of the tenth century, al-Manṣūr waged constant campaigns against the Christian kingdoms, the most famous being a raid against Santiago de Compostela in the summer of 997, during which his soldiers razed the basilica to the ground and removed its bells to Córdoba. Al-Manṣūr died in Medinaceli in Castile at the end of his campaign in 1002. His military successes had been owing to his reorganization of the Umayyad army, whereby he replaced tribal units with mixed contingents and added thousands of mercenaries, mainly Berbers, to the regular army. Many of these Berbers had been defeated by Umayyad forces in

North Africa, as al-Manṣūr had taken advantage of civil strife to extend direct rule in Morocco as far south as Fēs. He ruled from Córdoba as a dictator, having won the allegiance of the religious class with such flamboyant measures as the burning of volumes from al-Ḥakam II's library.

Al-Manṣūr was succeeded as chamberlain by his son ʿAbd al-Malik al-Muẓaffar, who maintained a unified and peaceful realm until 1008, when he died, apparently murdered by his brother ʿAbd al-Raḥmān Sanchuelo, who maneuvered the weak Hishām II into naming him heir to the caliphal crown. Elements of the Córdoban aristocracy then conspired to replace both Hishām and his chamberlain with a grandson of ʿAbd al-Raḥman III named Muḥammad II ibn Hishām (Muḥammad al-Mahdi), who ordered the destruction of Madīnat al-Zāhira in February 1009. A confused period followed, during which a son of ʿAbd al-Raḥmān III, Sulaymān al-Mustaʿīn, wrested the throne from Muḥammad II. The latter won it back only to be assassinated in July of 1010 and replaced by Hishām II, who ruled again as the puppet of al-Manṣūr's general, the slave Wāḍiḥ. Hishām reigned nominally until 1013, when he was apparently murdered on the orders of Sulaymān, who returned to power for three years. After an interregnum, during which power passed into the hands of the Arab Hammudids, another Umayyad, ʿAbd al-Raḥman IV, was proclaimed caliph in April 1018, only to be assassinated soon after. Power then alternated between Hammudids and a number of Umayyad puppets. The last of these, Hishām III al-Muʿtadd, reigned from 1027 to 1031, when the caliphate was finally abolished, although it had long since ceased to have any political meaning.

The fall of the caliphate of Córdoba and its subsequent dismemberment into a number of "party kingdoms" (ṭaʾifa or taifas) ruled by Arab, Berber, or slave (mamlūk) potentates were the inevitable result of a decisive shift in the ethnic balance of power. The Umayyads had been able to rule, in the eighth and ninth centuries, by playing off warring Arab, Berber, and Muwallad factions against one another and by securing enough unity among Muslims to dominate the Christian indigenous majority. In the tenth century, the muwalladūn had become the majority, and the Umayyads found it expedient to entrust their military affairs increasingly to newly introduced, powerful contingents of Berbers who, by the end of the century, had become difficult to control. The Islamization of the country rendered obsolete the civil-military apparatus typical of a garrison state that had been appropriate when most of the subjects were non-Muslim. The emergence of the party kingdoms, therefore, represented a political adjustment to a new ethnic equilibrium, characterized by regional political units that were ruled by whatever group happened to be most powerful.

BIBLIOGRAPHY

The standard political history of the Umayyads of Córdoba, which is followed here, is Évariste Lévi-Provençal, *Histoire de l'Espagne musulmane,* 3 vols. (1950–1953, 2nd ed. 1967), which was revised and translated by Emilio García Gómez as *España musulmana hasta la caída del califato de Córdoba (711–1031 de J. C.),* in Ramón Menéndez Pidal *et al.,* eds., *Historia de España,* IV, 2nd ed. (1957). On the social background of Umayyad politics, see Pierre Guichard, *Al-Andalus: Estructura antropológica de una sociedad islámica en occidente,* Nico Ancochea, trans. (1976); and Thomas F. Glick, *Islamic and Christian Spain in the Early Middle Ages* (1979).

THOMAS F. GLICK

[See also **Abbasids; Asturias-León; Berbers; Caliphate; Córdoba; Hispano-Mauresque Art; Manṣūr, Ibn Abī ʿĀmir al-; Qayrawān, al-; Spain, Muslim Kingdoms of; Umayyads.**]

UNCTION OF THE SICK is the Christian practice of praying for the seriously ill and anointing them with oil in the name of the Lord, as directed in James 5:14–16. During the first millennium of Christian history, references to it are mainly in the lives of the saints, which offer many accounts of miraculous healings following such unction. The prayer over the sick was in fact said over the oil (normally olive oil) when it was formally blessed prior to use. It was blessed by bishops or priests or certain saintly individuals to whom healing powers were attributed. After the death of wonder-working saints, oil was sometimes blessed by exposure to their relics. Once blessed, the oil could, in the early centuries, be applied by clerics or laypersons, or sufferers could rub it on themselves.

During the early Middle Ages, liturgical rites were composed for the more formal administration of unction by priests or presbyters. In the West, the Mozarabic liturgy of Spain had elaborate rites for the sick. Forms for blessing and applying oil are given in the Spanish priests' handbook, the *Liber ordinum*. The Ambrosian rite of northern Italy had its forms for a priest to bless oil and apply it, after laying his hands on the head of the sick with prayer. The Celtic rite provided a brief form for anointing before Holy Communion.

In the ancient Roman rite, laypeople brought containers of olive oil to church on Maundy Thursday, when the bishop blessed them during Mass. They took this oil home for family use. There was no formal rite for the clergy to anoint the sick. In the ninth century, when the Roman liturgy had been implanted in northern Europe, such a form was compiled by combining Roman prayers for the healing of the sick with prayers and chants from the Mozarabic unction rite. The priest was directed to apply the oil to different parts of the body of the sufferer and to lay hands on the head. During the following centuries, this Franco-Roman order for anointing the sick was often used for the dying or the hopelessly ill. Thus, "Extreme Unction" gradually came to be viewed, not as a means of healing, but as a spiritual preparation for death.

In the East the Byzantine rite provided an elaborate service of prayer and oil, still directed in the Orthodox euchologion. If circumstances permit, seven priests officiate. The oil is blessed and each priest anoints the sufferer after Bible readings and lengthy prayers. Outside the Byzantine or Great church, some other Oriental Christian communities have in the past utilized similar rites. In Nestorian tradition, pulverized relics of saints are mixed into the healing oil. At the popular level, Eastern as well as Western Christians have sometimes practiced simple nonliturgical unctions for therapeutic purposes, using oil obtained from lamps burning in the shrines of saints or from similar sources.

BIBLIOGRAPHY

Antoine Chavasse, *Étude sur l'onction des infirmes* (1942); H. Boone Porter, "The Origin of the Medieval Rite for Anointing the Sick or Dying," in *Journal of Theological Studies*, n.s. 7 (1956); Frederick W. Puller, *The Anointing of the Sick in Scripture and Tradition* (1904), the pioneering critical study; *Service Book of the Holy Orthodox-Catholic Apostolic Church*, Isabel F. Hapgood, trans., 3rd ed. (1956), 332–359.

H. Boone Porter

[See also **Death and Burial; Extreme Unction; Sacramentary.**]

UNIBOS. Preserved in a single manuscript (Brussels 8176), the story of "Unibos" (one ox) is told in Latin in 216 stanzas, each composed of four eight-syllable lines rhymed *a a b b*. The manuscript was written in the eleventh century, so the anonymous poem originated not later than 1100 and perhaps considerably earlier. Internal evidence suggests that it was composed in the northwestern part of the Holy Roman Empire, perhaps the Netherlands.

The following story is told: A farmer so poor that he has only one ox comes to be called "Unibos." When this ox dies, he skins it and carries the hide to market, where it brings a tiny sum, but on the way home he comes across a horde of silver coins. Back in his village the coins strike the attention of three authorities—the mayor, the priest, and the provost (administrator of a large estate)—and to disarm their suspicions Unibos claims to have received the huge sum for his ox hide. Driven by greed, all three slaughter their oxen and carry the skins to market, but are scorned when they demand huge prices and finally must pay the skins in fine for their attempted fraud. When they come to kill him, Unibos outwits them by drenching his wife with pig's blood, having her feign death, then apparently reviving her by playing a magic flute. Washed and dressed, she seems to the authorities younger and prettier than before, so they buy the flute and murder their wives, hoping to restore them to youth and loveliness. Failing to accomplish this, they are about to slay Unibos when they see his mare dropping silver coins rather than dung (he had inserted them appropriately a short time before); they buy the mare, but obtain only the natural product from her. Seizing Unibos, they seal him into a barrel in order to drown him. While they are celebrating in the tavern, Unibos persuades a swineherd to take his place, then returns to the village a few days later with the herd of swine, telling of a marvelous realm at the bottom of the sea where he obtained them. The three men, following his directions, leap into the ocean from a cliff and are drowned.

"Unibos" is the work of a talented poet. The verse is crisp and witty, the composition adroit. Reference in the second stanza to the currency of the tale "at the table of a great prince," and in the third stanza to a kind of mimic-dramatic declamation, offers interesting insights into social and aesthetic context. Although the victory of the abject farmer over his betters might suggest criticism of the feudal order, one must remember the drowning of the lowly swineherd, arranged by Unibos himself. The moral of the tale is that greed and lust make men stupid, and stupid men deserve what they get.

BIBLIOGRAPHY
Karl Langosch, *Waltharius, Ruodlieb, Märchenepen: Lateinische Epik des Mittelalters mit deutschen Versen* (1956), 252–305 (text with German trans.), 379–382 (notes and bibliography); Joachim Suchomski, *Delectatio" und "Utilitas." Ein Beitrag zum Verständnis mittelalterlicher komischer Literatur* (1975), 106–110.

STEPHEN L. WAILES

[See also **Latin Literature.**]

UNICORN. The legend of the unicorn occurs in all medieval cultures, with fabulous, medicinal, allegorical, programmatic, and decorative meanings. The unicorn (Greek: *monokeros*; Latin: *unicornis* or *rhinoceros*; Arabic: *karkaddan*; Old French: *licorne*; Middle High German: *einhorn* or *monizirus*) is first mentioned by Ctesias (*ca.* 400 B.C.), a Greek physician at the Persian court, who told of a savage wild ass with a horse's body, a goat's head, and a single, spiral horn. The legend of the unicorn owes its widespread diffusion not to numerous ancient reports (Aristotle, Aelian, Pliny) but to the *Physiologus* and to patristic commentary on passages in the Vulgate where *monokeros* (the Septuagint translation of the Hebrew *re'em*, wild ox or aurochs) is rendered by either *unicornis* or *rhinoceros*, whence the equivalence of these two beasts for Jerome, Tertullian, Gregory, and Bede. Latin patristic writers averred parallels between Christ born of the Virgin Mary and the unicorn, which could be captured only by a virgin.

Earlier Greek patristic commentators, in the wake of the First Council of Nicaea (325), interpreted the unicorn's single horn as a symbol of divine unity. Islamic remarks on the *karkaddan* appear almost exclusively in travelogues with reference either to medicinal or magical properties of the unicorn's horn, to its fierceness, or to the hunt. Islamic commentators assign no religious significance to the unicorn; their belief that the unicorn's horn could detect poison is mentioned in the writings of Hildegard of Bingen, Albertus Magnus, and

Pietro d'Abano. The tradition of assigning medicinal properties to the unicorn's horn, dating back to the Greek *Physiologus,* gained particular currency in the Latin West after the twelfth century. Medieval German writers speak of a jewel at the base of the horn with healing powers.

At this time in the West both the increasingly important vernacular bestiary tradition and the erotic exploitation of the legend—that the proud lover is tamed by his beloved just as the unicorn is captured by a virgin—somewhat eclipsed earlier patristic exegesis. Examples of the vernacular tradition are Guillaume le Clerc's *Bestiaire divin* (*ca.* 1210) and Brunetto Latini's *Li livres dou tresor* (1262–*ca.* 1265); erotic versions are found as early as the fifth century in the Syriac translation of the *Physiologus* and are evidenced in the thirteenth century both in *Minnedichtung* and in Richard de Fournival's *Bestiaire d'amour.* The extent of this secularization of the unicorn may be attested also in the presence of the unicorn in certain illustrated Hebrew codices, such as Ashkenazi bestiaries and fifteenth-century manuscripts of Issac ben Sahula's *Meshal ha-Kadmoni.*

Perhaps as a reaction to this growing secularization, some fifteenth-century interpreters viewed the hunt of the unicorn as an allegory of the Annunciation in the *hortus conclusus* (enclosed garden). This late tradition underscores the wealth and freedom of medieval interpretations and applications of the unicorn. No iconographical prototype from classical art influenced the depiction of the unicorn: a late-fourth-century Syrian church mosaic is the earliest representation thus far uncovered. In Islamic art the unicorn is primarily decorative. Illustrated *Physiologus* manuscripts concentrate on the hunt of the unicorn. Late medieval ivory caskets juxtapose programmatically the slaying of the unicorn with the tryst of Tristan and Isolde in the orchard. The fifteenth-century "Hunt of the Unicorn" tapestries at the Cloisters, New York, do not seem as programmatic as the "Dame à la licorne" tapestries at the Musée de Cluny, Paris, which, according to Alain Erlande-Brandenburg, depict a renunciation of the uncontrolled senses.

BIBLIOGRAPHY
Johann von Antoniewicz, "Ikonographisches zu Chrestien von Troyes," in *Romanische Forschungen,* 5 (1890); Maria-Teresa Canivet and Pierre Canivet, "La licorne dans les mosaïques de Ḥuarte-d'Apamène (Syrie, IVᵉ–Vᵉ siècles)," in *Byzantion,* 49 (1979); Jürgen Ein-

horn, *Spiritalis unicornis: Das Einhorn als Bedeutungsträger in Literatur und Kunst des Mittelalters* (1976); Alain Erlande-Brandenburg, *La dame à la licorne* (1978); Richard Ettinghausen, *The Unicorn* (1950); Margaret Freeman, *The Unicorn Tapestries* (1976); Leopold Kretzenbacher, *Mystische Einhornjagd: Deutsche und slawische Bild- und Wortzeugnisse zu einem geistlichen Sinnbild-Gefüge* (1978); Thérèse Metzger and Mendel Metzger, *Jewish Life in the Middle Ages: Illuminated Hebrew Manuscripts of the Thirteenth to the Sixteenth Centuries* (1982), 26–27; Odell Shepard, *The Lore of the Unicorn* (1930, repr. 1979); Liselotte Wehrhahn-Stauch, "Einhorn," in *Reallexikon zur deutschen Kunstgeschichte*, IV (1958).

EARL JEFFREY RICHARDS

[See also **Allegory; Allegory, French; Bestiaire d'Amour; Bestiary; German Literature: Allegory; Latini, Brunetto; Tristan, Legend of.**]

UNIVERSALS were the key issue in one of the great debates of medieval philosophy, the battle between nominalism and realism. The debate about universals focused on the ontological status of these sharable properties.

Followers of the Platonic tradition observed that many particular entities may share a feature, perhaps in varying degrees or imperfectly. They argued that there must be some exemplar of that feature which is that feature supremely and through itself (Augustine, *De Trinitate* VIII 3.6.9; Anselm, *Monologion*, cc. 1–3).

Medieval philosophers reacted to the Platonic tradition in various ways. The basic positions had already been outlined by the third-century philosopher Porphyry, in his introduction to Aristotle's *Categories*. Aristotle had grouped all men into a species called man and all animals into a genus called animal. The question then arose, for Porphyry, whether these categories of species and genus existed in the mind alone, or in reality as well; if in reality, whether that reality was corporeal or incorporeal; and if incorporeal, whether they existed separate from particular entities (Plato's position) or in particular entities (Aristotle's position).

It is not clear whether any medieval philosopher held that universals, or shared properties, had corporeal existence. Perhaps Abelard's teacher Roscelinus (*ca.* 1050–*ca.* 1125) did, if he held that genera and species were the spoken sounds corresponding to "animal" and "man."

Christian Platonists, such as Augustine around 400 and Anselm around 1100, maintained that shared properties did in fact exist outside the human mind, although they did not have any corporeal existence. They located this incorporeal existence in God's mind. The Platonist position has been called extreme realism.

The Aristotelian position, that universals exist only in the particulars where they are made manifest, has been called moderate realism. The moderate realist position was developed in a number of directions during the Middle Ages. Some philosophers held that, although universals never exist independently of particulars, the universals are nevertheless fully universal in the particulars. Peter Abelard attributed this position to William of Champeaux around 1100; Walter Burley held it in the fourteenth century. Other philosophers assigned a double mode of existence to universals such as genera and species, holding that they are fully universal only in the mind as general concepts ("animal," "man"), but that they also appear in a "contracted" form in the particular entity.

The problem of the universal in the particular entity was a theologically important issue affecting the nature of the Trinity and the nature of human individuality. Some philosophers, such as Thomas Aquinas, said that so far as its existence in reality was concerned, human nature was only particular and in no way common. Others, such as John Duns Scotus, insisted that human nature was at least potentially universal or common even insofar as it existed in a particular individual.

Peter Abelard in the twelfth century and William of Ockham in the fourteenth both denied that universals were anything other than names or concepts. Abelard held that the genus "animal" and the species "man" were the words "animal" and "man" together with their signification—that is, the concepts "animal" and "man." Ockham identified universals primarily with naturally significant names or concepts and secondarily with conventionally significant names. Commonly called nominalism, their position is less misleadingly dubbed conceptualism.

Although nominalism stirred considerable controversy when Ockham proposed it, the position became commonplace in the latter half of the fourteenth century and was held by Jean Buridan, Albert of Saxony, Pierre d'Ailly, Gregory of Rimini, and others.

BIBLIOGRAPHY

Sources. Peter Abelard, "Incipiunt glossae secundum magistrum Petrum Abaelardum super Porphyrium," Bernhard Geyer, ed., in *Beiträge zur Geschichte der Philosophie und Theologie des Mittelalters,* 21 (1933), 1–32; Anselm of Canterbury, *Monologion,* in Franciscus S. Schmitt, ed., *Opera omnia,* I (1946), 1–87; Thomas Aquinas, *De ente et essentia,* M.-D. Roland-Gosselin, ed. (1926); Augustine, *De Trinitate libri XV,* W. J. Mountain, ed., 2 vols. (1968); Walter Burley, *Super artem veterem Porphirii et Aristotelis* (1497, repr. 1967); John Duns Scotus, *Ordinatio: Liber secundus,* in his *Opera omnia,* VII, Carlo Balić, ed. (1973); William of Ockham, *Ordinatio,* I, 2, 4–7, in his *Opera theologica,* II, Stephanus Brown and Gedeon Gál, eds. (1970); John Wyclif, *Tractatus de universalibus,* Ivan J. Mueller, ed. (1985), and *On Universals,* Anthony Kenny, trans. (1985).

Studies. Marilyn McCord Adams, *William Ockham,* 2 vols. (1987); Rosa Padellaro De Angelis, *Conoscenza dell'individuale e conoscenza dell'universale nel XIII e XIV secolo* (1972); John Marenbon, *From the Circle of Alcuin to the School of Auxerre: Logic, Theology, and Philosophy in the Early Middle Ages* (1981); James A. Summers, *St. Thomas and the Universal* (1955); Martin M. Tweedale, *Abailard on Universals* (1976).

MARILYN MCCORD ADAMS

[See also **Abelard, Peter; Ailly, Pierre d'; Albert of Saxony; Anselm of Canterbury; Aquinas, St. Thomas; Aristotle in the Middle Ages; Augustine of Hippo, St.; Boethius; Buridan, Jean; Burley, Walter; Duns Scotus, John; Gregory of Rimini; Nominalism; Ockham, William of; Philosophy and Theology, Western European; Plato in the Middle Ages; Realism; Roscelinus; William of Champeaux.**]

UNIVERSITIES. The Latin term for university (*universitas*) first appeared in a classical Latin text of Cicero, meaning the whole of mankind (the human race). Throughout the early Middle Ages it was synonymous with college (*collegium*), society (*societas*), and body (*corpus*) of individuals. The word *universitas* in the terminology of legists in the twelfth century designated a group of people having juridical existence. It was frequently used to denote "collectivity." The term *universitas* to designate the entire body of masters and students organized into a society was used for the first time in 1221 by the corporation of Paris masters and students: *nos universitas magistrorum et scolarium* (the university of masters and students).

Another expression to denote university was *studium,* designating an institution of higher learning. In the *studium generale* or *studium universale* students were recruited from a wide area, and, in opposition to the *studium particulare,* it had the right to grant a license for teaching in any part of the world (*ius ubique docendi*).

ORIGINS

The conditions that favored the rise and establishment of universities in the thirteenth century already existed in the two previous centuries: (1) The communal movement, which arose when cities began attracting people from the country, favored the formation of autonomous corporations and guilds. This offered a model for scholars at the great centers of learning on how to become an organized corporation (*universitas*). (2) The existence of outstanding cathedral and canonical schools had created a nucleus for scholarship. (3) The appearance of new disciplines and school manuals preceded the emergence of new learning in the existing scholastic milieu. The translations of Adelard of Bath, Dominic of Gundisalvi, Gerard of Cremona, John of Seville, and others in Sicily and Spain; contact with the civilization of the Arab world; the discovery of the *Organon,* an ensemble of treatises on logic by Aristotle; and the revival of Roman law, together created a feverish desire for learning, which produced the same kinship among clerics that reigned among knights. The tenure of the seven liberal arts was broken and modern methods of dialectics appeared. The new species of learned men were called scholastics (*scholastici*). The quarrels of the Investiture Controversy necessitated the revival of Roman and canon law. Important canonical collections appeared, culminating in the *Decretum* published about 1140 by the Bolognese monk Gratian.

Privileges. With the emergence of the universities in Paris, Bologna, and Oxford, followed by Montpellier and Orleans, the university emerged as a third power, positioned between the papacy and the empire. Both the state and the church sought the support of this third power, which represented "wisdom." Both the papacy and the empire were ready to protect the new universities, particularly at two great centers of Christianity, Paris and Bologna.

The oldest privilege (*Authentica habita*), incorporated into the *Corpus iuris civilis,* was granted to scholars by Frederick Barbarossa at the Diet of Roncaglia in 1158. It exempted them from the jurisdiction of secular authorities (*privilegium fori*), except in criminal cases, and guaranteed safe conduct and protection to traveling students. A similar privilege was given by Philip Augustus in Paris in 1200, exempting scholars from the jurisdiction of secular authorities but making them subject to ecclesiastical tribunal. The provost of the city of Paris was forbidden to arrest or imprison a scholar and was directed to turn one who was accused of a crime over to the bishop of Paris or his official. The popes gave support, even against the bishop and chancellor, to the autonomous association of Paris masters.

On 13 April 1231 Gregory IX issued his *Parens scientiarum,* the quasi-foundation bull of the University of Paris, acknowledging the right of the university to suspend courses, confirming previously granted scholarly privileges, and ordering the chancellor to bestow licenses to teach theology and canon law only upon worthy candidates. He was forbidden to demand any remuneration for the licentiate. In Oxford, from the reign of Henry III (1216–1272) onward, it became customary for each monarch to guarantee the liberties, privileges, and immunities of the university, as granted by his predecessor.

To protect their privileges, the universities, particularly Paris, frequently used a new weapon: the cessation of courses. During the course of the Middle Ages, misjudging the patience of the royal power, the University of Paris abused this privilege, which was finally abolished by Louis XII in 1499, when the university became subject to the royal will. Another important privilege granted by the papacy to clerics studying at various *studia generalia* was the right to procure church benefices and to enjoy their incomes while studying at universities.

ARCHETYPES OF UNIVERSITIES: PARIS, BOLOGNA

The structural evolution of universities of later foundation depended on the model originally adopted following either the magisterial archetype of Paris or the student-university type of Bologna.

Paris. The Paris masters were already called an "honorable society" (*honestas societas*) around 1180 by Alexander Neckham. In the last quarter of the twelfth century this "society" had certain rules regarding the granting of the dignity of master to aspiring students. The chancellor, who had the right to grant the license for teaching, and the bishop initially opposed the autonomy of the new corporation. The papacy sided with the masters. In 1208–1209 Innocent III acknowledged the right of the "community of masters" to act as a corporation (*societatis in magistralibus*). By 1212–1213 the chancellor was instructed to license any candidate in theology, canon law, medicine, and arts presented under certain conditions by the masters. In 1215 the guild of masters and students obtained their own statutes, given by the papal legate Robert of Courson. From about 1222 to 1237 the corporation acquired the right to elect its own officers and proctors and, from 1245, its head, the rector. The seal, reserved for autonomous corporation, which had been broken by the papal legate in 1225, was granted in 1246.

An important feature of the Paris archetype was the dominant position of the faculty of arts, the foundation of the higher faculties—medicine, law, and theology. The masters of the faculty of arts were expected to be enrolled in higher faculties because "one should not grow old in arts." The faculty of arts considered itself mother (*mater et matrix*) of the higher faculties of theology (*sacratissima*), canon law (*consultissima*), and medicine (*saluberrima*).

The faculty of arts was divided into French, Picard, Norman, and English (later called English-German) "nations." These served as administrative, regional, and fraternal groups headed by proctors. The term "nation" was first mentioned in 1222 and the four nations in 1249. Each nation was subdivided into provinces. Students below the rank of master of arts could not be members of the nations. The feasts of their patron saints (St. Thomas of Canterbury and St. William, archbishop of Bourges, for the French; St. Nicholas and St. Firmin for the Picard; St. Roman for the Normans; St. Edmund [in the fifteenth century, Charlemagne] for the English-German nation) were celebrated with solemnities. The nations' finances were administered by a receptor elected for one year. By the end of the Middle Ages, with the loss of the international character of the University of Paris due to the absence of foreign students, particularly from the territory of the duke of Burgundy, the nations lost their original importance. This Paris archetype was followed with some modification by almost all the universities in northern Europe.

Bologna. By the second half of the twelfth century Bologna became the center of legal studies thanks to the presence of famous masters, among them Irnerius (*ca.* 1055–*ca.* 1130), Martinus, Bulgarus, Jacobus, and Hugo, advisers of Emperor Frederick Barbarossa, all legists and Gratian canonists. Prosperity was due to the teaching of Roman law, forbidden in Paris and in England by the bull *Super speculum* of Honorius III in 1219. Bologna also offered lectures on practical sciences such as the art of composition, aimed at training notaries and civil servants. The *ars notaria* was a discipline that formed a link between the liberal arts and law. Thanks to the protection guaranteed by *Authentica habita,* students ("pilgrims for the sake of study") converged on Bologna. From 1189 the commune of Bologna imposed an oath on the doctors that they would teach only in their city ("lest the university in our city grow smaller") and made the statutes of the commune binding on them. Foreign students did not enjoy legal security at Bologna, nor were they protected by the city. To protect themselves, around 1193 they formed their own organization (*universitas scholarium*) and very soon imposed their will on the doctors. By the middle of the thirteenth century two confederations existed, the cismontane (*universitas citramontanorum*) and ultramontane (*universitas ultramontanorum*), the first for students from the Italian peninsula and the second for students coming from outside Italy. These two confederations shaped Bologna into a student type of university. The students, however, were more mature and older than their counterparts at the faculty of arts in Paris, many of them having had adminsitrative experience. Therefore, their elected head, the rector, was well qualified to run the business of the university.

The students' power at Bologna resided in their economic bargaining force, because the doctors depended upon fees collected from the students, according to contractual agreement. Complaints against nonpaying students were very frequent. In the first quarter of the thirteenth century relations between the students and the commune of Bologna became strained because the latter repeatedly required oaths against any attempts to transfer to another city. Scholars dissatisfied with the policy of the commune opted for secession, which gave birth to the short-lived universities of Vicenza (1204), Arezzo (1215), and Vercelli (1228).

In 1219 Honorius decreed that no one could teach without a license granted by the archdeacon of Bologna, acting as the chancellor. Furthermore, he consented to the students' right of secession and opposed the oaths requested by the commune. In 1228 the foreign students were given the same privileges enjoyed by the citizen-students of Bologna. Around 1230 the *studium* of Bologna was firmly established, with papal and imperial privileges. The nations were headed by *conciliarii,* called proctors in the German nation, who together with the rectors governed the university. In 1265 the ultramontane university had thirteen nations: French, Spanish, Provençal, English, Picard, Burgundian, Poitevin-Gascon, Tourainian, Norman, Catalonian, Hungarian, Polish, and German. In 1291 Nicholas IV granted the "license to teach everywhere" (*ubique docendi*). In the second half of the thirteenth century the universities of arts and medicine emerged. They received official recognition in 1316, increasing the number of universities in Bologna to three. The faculty of theology was officially inaugurated in 1364, thanks to the efforts of Cardinal Albornoz, founder of the College of Spain in Bologna. During the middle of the fourteenth century salaried lectureships were established and all doctors were appointed by the commune. Bologna lacked the administrative and representative unity symbolized by the personality of the rector in Paris, who was entitled to speak in the name of the university. In the fifteenth century the autonomy of the corporation declined. In the sixteenth century the two student universities of law had only one rector.

OTHER SPONTANEOUS FOUNDATIONS

There are three types of universities according to manner of origin: (1) the spontaneous foundations, which grew out of already existing schools; (2) papal, imperial, communal, or joint foundations; and (3) the so-called paper universities, those with foundation charters but which never came into existence.

The universities of Paris and Bologna were not founded, but were spontaneous, like the University of Oxford. Oxford surfaced around 1208–1209, following a conflict between clerics and the townspeople. The first statutes were granted in 1214. The chancellor was appointed from among the doctors by the bishop of Lincoln. Though organized on the Paris model, the university was structurally close to Bologna. The making of statutes was thrust upon the great assembly (*congregatio magna*), the daily government was assigned to the small assembly (*congregatio minor*), while the "black assembly" of the liberal arts students (*congregatio nigra*), so called because of the dress they wore, deliberated separately.

Montpellier had schools of arts and medicine functioning as early as the twelfth century. William VIII, in 1181, assured the freedom of teaching to physicians desirous of opening a school. Under the jurisdiction of the bishop of Maguelone, licenses were granted by the chancellor appointed from the doctors. In 1220 the university of medicine received its statutes. Around 1230 the university of jurists, where later Petrarch studied civil law, came into existence. In 1289 Montpellier was officially raised to the rank of *studium generale* by Pope Nicholas IV.

Toulouse, the first university founded by a papal charter, was established in 1229 to eradicate the growing Albigensian heresy. The *ius ubique docendi* was given to its graduates by Gregory IX in 1233. Orléans was strengthened by the Paris secession of masters and students in 1229–1231 and was favored due to its teaching of civil law, which was prohibited in Paris. Officially recognized as a university in 1306 by a bull of Clement V, it declined in the fifteenth century. Angers emerged with the arrival of Paris students around 1229; it was confirmed as a *studium generale* in 1337.

FRANCE

The French provincial universities were a cross between the Paris and Bologna types, dominated by legal studies with moderate student participation in the government. Avignon was founded in 1303 by Boniface VIII, with faculties of arts, jurisprudence, and medicine. Cahors (1332) was founded by John XXII with the same privileges as Toulouse. Grenoble (1339) was created by Benedict XII at the request of Dauphin Humbert II. Its territory was disputed by the empire and France. It did not become active until the creation of the Parlement of Grenoble in 1453. Orange (1365), an imperial foundation by Charles IV, had a precarious existence.

During the fifteenth century more and more princes expressed a desire to found their own universities. Aix was established in 1409 by the count of Provence, with letters patent by Louis II, in 1413. It was endowed with a student-type university constitution. Statutes survive from 1420–1440; the archbishop of Aix acted as the first chancellor. Dôle (1422) was founded by a bull of Martin V at the petition of Philip the Good, duke of Burgundy. Degrees in theology were authorized by

Eugenius IV in 1437; the rector was elected by proctors and councillors. Poitiers (1431), politically an Armagnac university, was founded by Charles VII to counterbalance the political influence of Paris. A papal bull was given by Eugenius IV, with the same privileges as Toulouse. Caen (1432) was founded by the English during the Hundred Years War, under letters patent from Henry VI. A bull was granted by Eugenius IV (1437). It was modeled on Paris but without nations; the bishop of Bayeux was named the chancellor. The solemn inauguration with an English rector, Michael of Tregury, later archbishop of Dublin, took place in 1439.

Bordeaux (1441), the creation of the municipality, was founded by Eugenius IV upon the petition of the councillors of Henry VI of England; it was modeled on Toulouse. Valence (1452), founded by the dauphin (later Louis XI) to replace Grenoble as the university of the dauphiné, obtained a papal bull in 1459 from Pius II. The rector, as in Avignon and Aix, was called *primicerius*. It was a student type of university. Nantes (1460) was chartered by Pius II at the request of the duke of Brittany. The statutes followed the customs of Caen and Angers. Bourges (1464), instituted at the request of Charles, duke of Berry, and his brother Louis XI, and sanctioned by Pope Paul II, opened in 1467 with a strong German nation.

ITALY

Salerno, a proto-university noted for medical teaching in the twelfth century, never became an organized *studium*. At the beginning of the thirteenth century, Reggio (nell'Emilia) and Modena existed without confirmation. Vicenza owed its origin to the 1204 migration of students from Bologna, but shortly thereafter came to an end. Arezzo existed by 1215; its statutes date from 1255, but it declined shortly afterward. It was revived in 1338 by migrants from Bologna who left that city because of an interdict imposed there. A foundation brief was issued by Charles IV to the city where (he said) a *studium* had long existed. Padua (1222) was born due to the migration of students and masters from Bologna. It suffered from a secession to Vercelli in 1228, but nevertheless survived with two universities: ultramontane and cismontane. In 1346 its prerogatives were confirmed by Clement VI and a faculty of theology was authorized by Urban V in 1363. The *tractatores,* elected by students, were intermediaries between the *studium* and the commune. Venice later conferred upon the rector the right to wear a robe of purple and gold. Naples, founded by Frederick II in 1224, was the first university founded by imperial charter. Theology was taught there by the friars and St. Thomas lectured during 1272–1274.

Vercelli (1228) was established by students from Padua, but lost importance by the middle of the fourteenth century, when the short-lived Turin (1405) replaced it as the university for Piedmont. The University of the Roman Curia (1244–1245) was founded by Innocent IV and governed by a college of doctors. Oriental languages were taught there. Siena was founded in 1246, Charles IV renewed its privileges in 1357. Piacenza (1248) was created by Innocent IV with the privileges of Paris. In 1398 Gian Galeazzo Visconti, exercising his right as vicar of the empire, issued a new charter, but it declined after 1404–1412. The University of the City of Rome (*Studium urbis*) was founded by Boniface VIII in 1303. Having disappeared during the Great Schism, it was resuscitated in 1431 by Eugenius IV. Perugia (1308) was chartered by Clement V and reconfirmed in 1318 by John XXII; it received an imperial bull from Charles IV in 1355. Treviso (1318), chartered by Frederick of Austria, was a short-lived university. Pisa (1343) gained importance by the migration of students from Bologna following the interdict of Benedict XII imposed on Bologna in 1338. The Black Death of 1348 led to a decline of the university, but it was revived by Florence in 1473 thanks to Lorenzo de' Medici.

Florence (1349), confirmed by a bull of Clement VI, received imperial privileges from Charles IV in 1364. The Florentine commune forbade its students to study elsewhere, but some students went to Pisa in 1472, probably due to the high cost of lodging in Florence. Florence was the first to establish a chair of poetry, with Boccaccio as its first occupant (1373–1374). In Pavia at an early date important teachers lectured on Lombard law. It received a charter from Charles IV (1361) to teach jurisprudence, philosophy, medicine, and arts, and it had a papal bull given by Boniface IX in 1389. After 1400 it declined but regained its force and became the university of the population of Milan. Ferrara (1391), established by the bull of Boniface IX at the request of Albert of Este, obtained the privileges of Bologna and Paris. The hiring of Guarino of Verona (1436) enhanced the prosperity of the *studium*; in 1474 there were fifty-two teaching doctors there. Turin (1405), founded by Louis of Savoy,

count of Piedmont, was confirmed by the bull of Benedict XIII in 1405. The 1412 charter of Emperor Sigismund mentioned the teaching of theology there and John XXIII approved this in 1413. After the death of the founder in 1418 the university deteriorated, but it was reorganized by Duke Amadeo VIII. Catania (1434) was created by Alfonso the Magnificent, king of Aragon and Sicily, and a bull of Eugenius IV was issued in 1444.

At Italian universities the model of Bologna prevailed, with emphasis on legal studies and student participation in the government. Supervision by and interference from the communes frequently disrupted their independence. They were characterized by little ecclesiastical control, with laicization prevailing, and by their impressive buildings, which served as teaching quarters.

UNIVERSITIES IN SPAIN

Medieval Spanish universities were royal (*respectu regni*), and consequently national, foundations. Usually one *studium generale* was created in each kingdom, modeled after that of Bologna and closely connected with cathedral and chapter schools. The definition of the *studium generale* was given by the *Siete partidas,* issued in 1263.

Palencia (1208–1212), the oldest Spanish university in Castile, was founded by Alfonso VIII and showed the influence of the Paris magisterial type. St. Dominic studied there in 1184, but it ceased to exist by the middle of the thirteenth century. Valladolid (mid thirteenth century) was made a *studium generale* by Pope Clement VI in 1346, with the faculty of theology established in 1418 by Martin V. It was a student-type university, with election to salaried chairs decided by students. The whole body of doctors and students was called *claustrum.* Salamanca (1227–1228), a Bologna-type university, was founded by Alfonso IX of León. Privileges were granted by the second founder, Ferdinand III of Castile (1243). The statutes of 1411 were promulgated, and theological chairs established, by Pedro de Luna (Antipope Benedict XIII). Apparently women also studied here. Lérida (1300) was founded by James II of Aragon; Boniface VIII conferred the privileges enjoyed by Toulouse and students elected the rector. On the rector's advice the municipality's *prohombres* and *consiliarii* made nominations to the salaried chairs. Perpignan (1350) was founded by Pedro IV the Ceremonious, but its real existence began with a bull of Clement VII in 1379. The faculty of theology was confirmed in 1447 by Nicholas V.

Huesca (1354), founded by Pedro IV for his Aragonese subjects, was modeled on Lérida. Expenses for the *studium* were paid from taxes imposed on meat sold in the marketplace of Huesca. After its decline, Paul II renewed its privileges in 1464. Barcelona (1450) was jointly founded by Alfonso V and Nicholas V. Apparently some kind of medical university had been founded there in 1401. Saragossa (1474), a Paris-type magisterial university, was issued a bull by Sixtus IV. It was an institution of lesser importance. Palma (1483) was instituted by Ferdinand the Catholic with observance of the tradition of the doctrine of Ramon Lull. Sigüenza (1489) benefited from the generosity of Don Juan López de Medina and was supported by Cardinal Mendoza, who was the bishop of Sigüenza and the archbishop of Seville. In a college-convent three chairs (theology, canon law, and arts) were organized; it was sanctioned by Innocent VIII in 1489. Alcalá (1499) received a bull by Alexander VI for the College of San Ildefonso to grant degrees on the petition of Jiménez de Cisneros, archbishop of Toledo. It was inaugurated in 1508 with statutes published in 1510. Valencia (1500) was established by the Valencian pope, Alexander VI, as a *studium generale* for studies in theology, canon and civil law, medicine, liberal arts, Latin, and Greek.

PORTUGAL

Lisbon and Coimbra (1290) was issued a bull of foundation by Nicholas IV at the request of the abbot of Alcobaça, confirming the foundation by King Dinis. The bishop was authorized to grant the *ius ubique docendi* in all faculties except theology. Due to conflict with the citizens of Lisbon, the university was transferred to Coimbra in 1308–1309. The royal charter of 1309 shows the constitutional influence of Bologna and Salamanca. The royal prerogative was eminent, reserving the right of "protector" for the appointment of professors. Later the university "commuted" between Lisbon and Coimbra; finally, with the new foundation bull of 1380, it remained in Lisbon until 1537.

GERMANY

Princes played a considerable role in the establishment of German universities. The Great Schism also contributed to the emergence of important universities, with many Paris masters being forced to leave Paris because of their allegiance to the Roman pope.

Prague (1347–1348) was founded by Clement VI in 1347 at the request of Emperor Charles IV, who issued his own charters in 1348 as king of the Romans and king of Bohemia and in 1349 as king of the Romans and elected emperor in Eisenach. The constitution followed that of Paris, with Bolognese influence. The archbishop of Prague was the chancellor. A Bologna-style, separate jurist university was established in 1372. There were four nations (Bohemia, Poland, Bavaria, Saxony) headed by *consiliarii*. A quarrel between Germans and Czechs resulted in the royal decree of Kutná Hora in 1409, which bestowed upon the Czech nation ("true inheritors of this land") three votes and gave to the other three nations combined only one, thus nationalizing the university. The German subjects consequently left Prague and founded the University of Leipzig. Vienna was founded by Duke Rudolph IV of Austria on 12 March 1365 and received papal confirmation from Urban V on 18 June 1365. A faculty of theology was excluded. The first statutes (6 June 1366) followed the Paris model with four nations (Austria, Saxony, Bohemia, Hungary). Albert of Saxony, a Paris graduate, became the first rector. After the death of the founder on 27 July 1365 and the departure of Albert of Saxony in 1366, the university stagnated. It was revived by Duke Albert III after 1383 and reorganized thanks to Henry of Langenstein (*d.* 1397) and Henry of Oyta (*d.* 1397), distinguished theologians ousted from Paris during the Great Schism. The Albertine constitution (1384), the work of Henry of Langenstein, reduced the influence of the faculty of arts. Rectors were elected from any faculty. Urban VI granted the establishment of a faculty of theology in 1384. The statutes were given in 1385 for the entire university and in 1389 for the faculties. From 1377 until the end of the century 3,600 students were matriculated at Vienna. The Hussite troubles in Prague made Vienna a leading university in the fifteenth century.

Among the German universities, Heidelberg (1385) owed its origin to the consequences of the Great Schism, which caused the departure of noted German scholars from Paris. With a bull of foundation from Urban VI, Heidelberg received a charter issued by the palsgrave Rupert I (1386). Marsilius of Inghen from Paris became its first rector. The constitution is closer to the Paris type than those of Prague and Vienna. The provost of Worms became

Students at a lecture by Frater Henricus de Allemania. Miniature by Laurencius de Voltolina from a compendium of Aristotle, after 1350. BERLIN, STAATLICHE MUSEEN / BILDARCHIV PREUSSISCHER KULTURBESITZ

the chancellor; Conrad von Gelnhausen was the first. Cologne was the seat of an old Dominican *studium generale* where Albertus Magnus and St. Thomas taught in the thirteenth century. At the demand of the municipality this university was established by Urban VI on 21 May 1388 and opened the following year with a modified Parisian constitution but with no nations at all. Erfurt (opened 1392) was granted foundation bulls in 1379 by Clement VII and by Urban VI in 1389. It resembled a Parisian type of university with no nations but *consiliarii* from each faculty. The archbishop of Mainz was chancellor. Martin Luther was inscribed into the matricula in the summer semester of 1501 as "Martinus Ludher ex Mansfeldt"; he became master of arts in 1505 and doctor in 1512. Würzburg (1402) was originally an episcopal foundation; a bull of Boniface IX conferred the privileges of Bologna. Leipzig (1409) was founded by Frederick and William, landgraves of Thuringia, for students who left Prague after the edict of the Kutná Hora. A papal bull was given on 9 September 1409 by Alexander V. The bishop of Merseburg was named chancellor. The university was divided into four nations (Polish, Meissen, Saxon, and Bavarian) with *consiliarii* according to the Prague model.

Rostock (1419) was founded by John III and

Albert V, dukes of Mecklenburg, and by the town municipality (*consulatus et civium*), with a papal bull by Martin V. The constitution was modeled after Leipzig, with no nations but with a new official called a *promotor,* who supervised the observation of the statutes, with the bishop of Schwerin acting as chancellor. The faculty of theology was granted in 1432. The university was transferred to Greifswald in 1437, returned in 1443, and went to Lübeck for 1487–1488. In August 1488, it returned to Rostock. Trier (1454, 1473) was modeled on Cologne, with a bull of establishment given by Nicholas V in 1454; the actual opening took place in 1473. Through the efforts of Henry Rubenow, burgomaster and first rector, Calixtus III granted the bull to Greifswald (1456) within the territorial jurisdiction of the duke of Pomerania-Stettin. Freiburg im Breisgau was granted a papal bull by Calixtus III in 1455 at the request of Mechtildis, archduchess of Austria, conferring the power upon the bishop of Constance to erect a university. The ducal charter of Albrecht VI given in 1457 conferred the privileges of Paris, Vienna, and Heidelberg upon the university. The first matriculation actually began 27 April 1460. The earliest statutes of the faculty of arts are dated 1460–1490. A papal bull was issued by Pius II to Basel in 1459 at the request of the commune of Basel; it opened on

288

4 April 1460. The bishop of Basel acted as chancellor over this Bologna-and-Paris type of university with statutes influenced by Erfurt. Ingolstadt was founded by a bull of Pius II in 1459 at the request of Prince Louis, duke of Bavaria; it opened in 1472. The bishop of Eichstätt functioned as chancellor and the constitution was modeled on that of Vienna, but with no nations.

Mainz (1476) was founded by Sixtus IV at the petition of Archbishop Diether. The latter issued the first charter in 1477. The first rector was elected in 1478. Tübingen was issued a papal bull by Sixtus IV in 1476 at the request of Eberhard, count of Württemberg. The ducal charter and statutes were published in 1477. Gabriel Biel and Johann Reuchlin taught there and Philip Melanchthon and Johann Eck studied there. The foundation charter for Wittenberg (1502) was issued by Emperor Maximilian I at the request of Frederick the Wise, elector of Saxony, bestowing upon it the privileges enjoyed by the universities of Bologna, Siena, Padua, Pavia, Perugia, Paris, and Leipzig. The statutes date from 1508. Frankfurt an der Oder (1506) was granted an imperial bull by Maximilian I in 1500, but owes its foundation to Joachim I of Brandenburg and his brother Albrecht, with a papal bull from Julius II. The statutes were inspired by Leipzig. Conradus (Koch) Wimpina became the first rector.

THE LOW COUNTRIES

The bull of foundation was given to Louvain by Martin V on 9 December 1425 at the solicitation of John IV, duke of Brabant, supported by the commune and the collegiate chapter of St. Peter of Louvain. The charter authorized four faculties (arts, civil law, canon law, medicine). Thanks to the support of Philip the Good, duke of Burgundy, the faculty of theology was established by the bull of Eugenius IV in 1432. The enrollment declined in 1436–1446 and again in 1490–1491 due to political insecurity. In 1518 the Erasmian dream was realized and a college for the teaching of the Greek, Latin, and Hebrew languages (*Collegium trilingue*) was established, thanks to the 1517 will of Canon Jerome of Busleyden. The statutes of the university, drafted between 1446 and 1453, were modeled on those of Paris, Cologne, and Vienna. The faculty of arts was divided into four nations: Brabant, Walloon (Gallia), Flanders, and Holland. The chancellor was the provost of St. Peter's of Louvain. The bull of Eugenius IV (1443) stipulated that the nomination to professorial prebends was to be left to the burgomaster and counsuls of the city of Louvain.

POLAND AND HUNGARY

Kraków was established on 12 May 1364 by Casimir the Great, the last Piast on Poland's throne, following the model of a Bologna-type student university where rectors and professors were elected by students and law studies were given a prominent place. The subjects of the university enjoyed the same privileges as in Bologna and Padua, namely, indemnity from taxes. A bull of Urban V confirmed the foundation on 1 September 1364, but did not allow the establishment of a faculty of theology. After the death of the founder in 1370, the university came to an early end. The reorganization was assumed by Hedwig (Jadwiga), queen of Poland. On 11 January 1397 Boniface IX, at the request of the queen and King Władysław, granted the faculty of theology privileges similar to those of Paris. King Władysław thus became the founder of the Jagiellonian University with his charter of 26 July 1400 for *stabilimento studii generalis* (strengthening the university) following the German models of Prague, Leipzig, and others. By 1500 some 1,500 to 2,000 students attended the university, where mathematical and astrological studies were favored. Copernicus studied there from 1491 to 1494.

The city of Pécs (Fünfkirchen) on the crossroads to Italy was the richest among all the Hungarian bishoprics at the time of foundation of the university, with a long tradition of local clerics studying abroad. A papal bull of Urban V was issued on 1 September 1367. The upkeep of the university and payment of professors were left to the king. Galvano Bettini, a native of Bologna, taught canon law there from 1371 to 1373. Gregory IX, on 16 January 1376, exempted the doctors and students of the university from the obligation of residence for the term of five years. The faculty of civil and canon law was still functioning there around 1389–1404, but later declined, and must have been extinct by 1465. At the request of Emperor Sigismund, king of Hungary, Boniface IX created the university at Óbuda in 1395 and appointed Lucas Demetrius, provost of the collegiate chapter of St. Peter's, to be the first chancellor. It functioned until 1403, when an insurrection against Emperor Sigismund broke out and Benedict of Macra, a distinguished professor, was imprisoned. With a bull of John XXIII, it was revived on 1 August 1410 with faculties of theology, canon law, civil law, medicine, and arts enjoying the privileges of Paris, Bologna, Oxford, and Cologne. A sizable delegation of seven masters from Óbuda University attended the Council of Constance (1414–1418).

Pozsony (Pressburg; modern Bratislava) was authorized by Paul II in 1465 by a charter addressed to Johannes Vitéz, archbishop of Esztergom, the first chancellor of the university, and to the bishop of Pécs, Janus Pannonius. It followed the model of Bologna. Regiomontanus taught astronomy there from 1467 to 1471, together with Martin Bylica of Olkusz. It declined after the death of King Matthias Corvinus in 1490.

SCANDINAVIA

The actual founder of the university at Uppsala was Archbishop Jacob Ulvsson, a graduate of Rostock and Paris. The papal bull was issued by Sixtus IV on 27 February 1477, granting the privileges of Bologna. Secular confirmation came from the Swedish privy council on 2 July 1477, granting the privileges of Paris. No medieval statutes have been preserved. Notes on lectures followed by Olaus Johannis Guto, a native of the island of Gotland, at the university (ca. 1482–1486) show the German influence (Greifswald and Leipzig) in the curriculum of studies. The university ceased to exist sometime around 1531.

Petitioned by King Christian I, Sixtus IV issued a bull on 19 June 1475 authorizing the archbishop of Lund to erect a *studium generale* in any place selected by the king. In 1478 Copenhagen was chosen. The 1479 statutes followed the Cologne pattern. In 1497 John II forbade the Danes to frequent any other university (Uppsala excepted) unless they spent three years previously at Copenhagen. The university ceased to exist in 1530. It was revived by King Christian III in 1539 as a university of Protestant character.

ENGLAND

Cambridge emerged after the migration of Oxford scholars to Cambridge in 1209. It began to function regularly in 1231–1232. Papal recognition came on 14 June 1233 from Gregory IX. Constitutions or statutes were compiled around 1250. The statute of 17 March 1276 increased the power of regent masters, lessening that of the chancellor. A papal bull of confirmatory character was issued by John XXII at the request of Edward II in 1318. By the middle of the fifteenth century, Cambridge

became the rival of Oxford. It was very active during the schism.

SCOTLAND

Scottish universities were episcopal foundations sustained by their generosity. Teachers, mostly Paris graduates, initiated higher studies at St. Andrews around 1411–1412. It was formally established by Henry Wardlaw, bishop of St. Andrews, himself a Paris graduate, in 1412. It was confirmed by Benedict XIII in 1413, followed by a series of papal bulls. The constitution of the faculty of arts was influenced by Paris, although the university itself was modeled after Cologne. Its acts exist from 1413 to 1588. Glasgow was established by William Turnbull, bishop of Glasgow and former student at Louvain, and confirmed by Nicholas V in 1451 with the privileges of Bologna. The earlier statutes, now lost, were replaced by those of 1482–1483; the constitution was similar to that of St. Andrews, with details borrowed from Cologne. The bishop of Glasgow was called "rector-chancellor" with the same power as the rector of Bologna. He delegated jurisdiction to the rectors elected by the students of the four nations. James II of Scotland granted important privileges in 1453.

William of Elphinstone (1431–1514), bishop of Aberdeen and former student at Paris and Orléans, was responsible for the foundation of the University of Aberdeen. A bull was granted by Alexander VI in 1494/1495 and published in 1496/1497 in St. Machar's Cathedral. The royal charter of King James IV followed the same year. The constitution was influenced by that of the University of Orléans, with four nations as student organizations. The university actually came into existence around 1500 with the arrival of Hector Boece from Paris. Then it was fused with the College of St. Mary's in Nativity, later known as King's College, founded in 1505 by William of Elphinstone on the Paris model and confirmed by Pope Julius II in 1506.

PAPER UNIVERSITIES

Paper universities are those for which papal or imperial bulls were issued but which never came into existence. They included, in France: Gray (1291), by Pope Nicholas IV at the petition of Otto IV, count of Burgundy; and Pamiers (1295), by Pope Boniface VIII. In Italy: Verona (1339), with a bull of Benedict XII; Cividale del Friuli (1353), by Emperor Charles IV; Geneva (1365), with a bull of

Charles IV at the petition of Amadeus VI, count of Savoy; Lucca (1369), erected by Emperor Charles IV, with another bull in 1387 by Urban VI; Orvieto (1378), granted by Gregory XI in 1377, the actual bull was given by Urban VI; Fermo (1398), by Boniface IX, confirmed by Callixtus III in 1455, revived by the bull of Sixtus V in 1585; and Mantua (1433), with privileges given by Emperor Sigismund, confirmed by Emperor Frederick III. In Germany: Kulm (1366), with a bull of Urban VI at the petition of the Teutonic order; and Luneberg (1471), by Emperor Frederick III. In Spain: Calataydd (1415), in Aragon, with a bull by Benedict XIII; and Gerona (1446), by Alfonso V, came into existence by a bull of Paul V in 1605. In Ireland: Dublin (1312), a bull was issued by Clement V, but it remained a university in name only.

COLLEGES

Colleges in the twelfth and early thirteenth centuries were nothing more than endowed charitable institutions called hospices. The purpose of the founder was to provide board and lodging for poor students. A hall or hostel was a house rented by students. The *paedagogia*, where students lived together, directed by a master or *paedagogus* in their studies, appeared only during the fifteenth century. The earliest hospice in Paris was the Collège des Dix Huit (1180), followed by St. Thomas (*ca.* 1186), later (1247) called St. Nicholas of Louvre, the college of Constantinople (*ca.* 1204), the Good Children (Bons Enfants) of St. Honoré (1208–1209), and St. Victor (before 1248). The colleges later developed into autonomous communities where students and masters lived in an endowed building governed by statutes given by the founder and approved by ecclesiastical authorities; students engaged in learning and teaching under an elected official, variably called president, preses, warden, prior, principal, master, or grand master.

FRENCH COLLEGES

Paris was the true home of the collegiate system, which varied in nature. There were regional colleges founded for members of various French dioceses studying in Paris. There were colleges for the regular clergy, including Mathurins (before 1209), Val des Écoliers (*ca.* 1228), Dominicans (1229), Franciscans (*ca.* 1238), Bernardins (1246), Canons of Prémontré (1252), Benedictines Cluny (1260),

and St. Denis (since 1229, again *ca.* 1263). Finally, there were colleges established for foreign students: Dacia (1275), Uppsala (1285), Skara House (1292), House of Linköping (1317), Lombards (1334), and a college for German students (before 1345).

Among the seventeen or so thirteenth-century colleges, the Sorbonne (1252–1258), founded by Robert of Sorbonne, chaplain of St. Louis, was of European-wide importance. It was followed by the establishment of the colleges Du Trésorier (1268), D'Harcourt (1280), and Cholets (1295), among others. During the fourteenth century, thirty-seven or so colleges or halls opened in Paris, an average of one every other year during the first half of the century. Some of the most notable are: Lemoine (1302), where Buridan studied; Navarre (1304), a mixed college founded by Queen Joan of Navarre for twenty grammarians, thirty students in arts, and twenty theologians, where Pierre d'Ailly and Nicole Oresme were grand masters; Aicelins, later Montaigu (1314), a controversial college of strict discipline, in Erasmus' time called "Maison des Haricots"; Narbonne (1317) where Clement VI studied; du Plessis (1321); Ave Maria (1336); Lisieux (1336); Autun (1341); Dormans (Beauvais) (1370); Maître Gervais (1370), which funded two scholarships in mathematics; Dainville (1380); and Fortet (1391), where Calvin resided. About twelve colleges were established in the fifteenth century; Ste. Barbe (1460) and Coquerel (1463) were the most outstanding.

Though they were independent organizations, the university had statutory rights over the Paris colleges because their members belonged to the nations. After 1452 *reformatores,* or visitors, were elected to inspect the colleges and enforce discipline. As a general rule, from 1463 the students had to reside in colleges or *paedagogia.* Most of the French colleges were located on the Montagne Ste. Geneviève or around the rue du Fouarre.

Only a few colleges were founded at provincial French universities due to the higher income of students there. The most notable were, in Toulouse, St. Martial (1358), Maguelone (1363), and de Foix (1440); and in Montpellier, Brescia (1360) and the Twelve Physicians (Douze Médecins, 1369). Among those established in the fifteenth century were, at Poitiers, the College of Puygarreau, founded by Damoiselle de Puygarreau in 1478; at Caen, Collège du Boys (1491), founded by Pierre Cauchon; and, at Dôle, the Cluniac College of St. Jerome (1494) and the Cistercian College (1498).

ENGLISH COLLEGES

Early English colleges were not as exposed to adversities as those in Paris. In Oxford, between the thirteenth and fifteenth centuries, eleven "secular" colleges were established, among them seven founded by "religious" orders. Merton (1264) was a prototype of the English graduate college, known for its school of scientific speculation. It was followed by the foundation of University (1280) and Balliol College (1282). In the fourteenth century Exeter (1314–1316), Oriel (1324–1326), and Queen's (1341) were established along with the jewel of the English colleges, the New College (1379), a landmark in college architecture. Its founder, William of Wykeham, instituted a salaried system for tutors called *informatores*. Lincoln (1429), All Souls (1438), and Magdalen College (1479–1480) were the first to inaugurate endowed college lectureships open to all at the university.

The oldest college in Cambridge in the thirteenth century was Peterhouse, established by Hugh of Balsham, bishop of Ely, in 1284. In Cambridge, from the thirteenth through fifteenth centuries, some thirteen colleges were established, seven of them during the fourteenth century: Michaelhouse (1324); King's Hall (*ca.* 1317), whose fellows were appointed by the crown and supported by the royal exchequer; University or Clare Hall (1326); Pembroke (1347); Gonville (1349); Trinity Hall (1350); and Corpus Christi (1352). Foundations of the fifteenth century were: God's House (1441–1442) for grammar students (in 1505 it was absorbed by Christ's College); King's College (1441), founded by Henry VI with statutes copied from New College; Queen's College (1448); St. Catherine's (1475); and Jesus College (1497).

SCOTTISH COLLEGES

At the University of St. Andrews, the College of St. Salvator (1450) was established first, followed by St. Leonard (1512). At Aberdeen, the King's College (1505) resembled the German college type. The masters were prebendaries of a church. Hector Boece from the College of Montaigu in Paris became its first head.

SPANISH COLLEGES

Spanish colleges included the College of Oviedo (1386) at Salamanca, the Colegio Mayor de San Bartolomé (1401), with statutes revealing an Italian-type student university; and, in Lérida, St. Mary's (1372), the oldest college in Spain.

The college system did not blossom in Portugal.

ITALIAN COLLEGES

In Italy the colleges did not play as important a role in the life of the university as in the northern European universities. In Bologna, in addition to the colleges of Avignon (1267), Brescia (1326), and Reggio (1362), the most influential and carefully founded was the College of Spain, established in 1367 by Gil Albornoz, former archbishop of Toledo, for thirty students from Spain, with eight in theology, eighteen in law, and four in medicine. The original statutes of 1368–1369 were lost, but the revised statutes of 1375–1377 are extant. In Perugia, the Collegium Gregorianum (1362) harbored forty scholars. In Padua nine small colleges were established, the first in 1363. The largest was the Collegium Pratense (or Ravenna, 1394) with twenty students. In Siena the Sapienza (1404) was modeled on the College of Spain in Bologna. Turin had the Collegio Grassi or La Sapienza (1457) and another with no name, known as Collegium Scholarium, founded by Sixtus IV in 1482.

GERMAN COLLEGES

German colleges differed from French, English, Spanish, and Italian colleges. With few exceptions, they were founded initially for masters and furnished endowed professorships for the university, usually connected with cathedrals that provided the ecclesiastical prebends as salaries.

In Prague the Collegium Caroli, established by Charles IV, opened on 30 July 1366 for twelve masters of arts, among them a *biblicus,* who explained the Bible, and a *sententiarus,* lecturing on the *Sentences* of Peter Lombard, and other students in theology, all supported by prebends of the Royal Collegiate Chapel of All Saints. With an important library, it resembled Oxford more than the Paris model. Other foundations were the House of the Poor (Domus Pauperum, 1379); the College of King Wenceslaus IV (1381); and the College of Lithuania (1397) for theologians, founded by Queen Hedwig of Poland.

A Collegium Ducale (1384) in Vienna was established by Duke Albrecht (Albert) III for twelve masters of arts, one of them a bachelor in theology, and one or two doctors in theology. They received canonical prebends from the church of All Saints, also called St. Stephen's.

In Heidelberg the Collegium Jacobiticum (1389) was founded by Ruprecht (Rupert) I for Cistercians. The Collegium Artistarum (14 May 1390), founded by Conrad Gelnhausen, was confirmed by Ruprecht II the Older, and endowed further on 10 or 11 August 1390 and on 21 May 1391. The Collegium or Contubernium Dionysianum (1396), founded by Gerlach of Hamburg, was confirmed by Ruprecht II the Older and Ruprecht III the Younger for six poor students and six masters in arts.

In Cologne the Kronenbursa (1430) or Collegium Coronarum was founded by the will of Herman Dwerg of Herford in Westphalia, and by Johannes Vorburg of Alkmaar, for one rector and twelve students in theology, and civil or canon law for a five-year term. It began to function in 1439. The oldest surviving statutes were composed in 1497–1504. Beside a small college like Ruremundanum (1483) several bursas were erected, such as Bursa Montis (Montana) (1419/1420) by Henry of Gorkum and the Laurentius Bursa (Laurentiana) or *bursa florentissima* (1422) by Heimericus de Campo. Johannes Kuch, after leaving the Laurentius Bursa, founded the Kuckanerbursa (Kukana, 1450), which was later transferred to a house at the sign of the Three Crowns, thereafter called Bursa Trium Coronarum (or Tricoronatum). Of lesser importance was the Bursa Corneliana (1420), named after Cornelius Baldwin from Dordrecht, the successor of the founder, Johannes Custodis of Attendorn.

In Leipzig the masters of arts were housed in the Collegium Majus, with statutes promulgated in 1416, and in the Collegium Minor or Fürsten Collegium. The College of the Blessed Virgin (Beatae Mariae Virginis or Frauencolleg), founded in 1416 by Johannes Ottonis de Monsterberg, was confirmed by Landgrave Frederick in 1422 for five masters of arts from Silesia and one from Prussia. Its oldest surviving statutes date from 1445.

In Erfurt the Collegium Universitatis, after 1436 called Collegium Majus, existed since 1392, harboring eight masters of arts. The Collegium Amplonianum or Porta Coeli was founded by Amplonius Ratingk de Fago in 1412 and refounded in 1433 for fifteen members. The college possessed a magnificent library. Besides these two important institutions, several small bursas functioned: Bursa Pauperum, founded by Nicholas of Gleiwitz, canon of Breslau, was attached to the Collegium Majus in 1418; Zum Steinlauen or *ad Lapidem Leonis*; Nova Domus; Alba Rota; and Aedes Divi Georgii, called

Georgsbursa since 1466, where Martin Luther later lived.

In Greifswald, Duke Wratislaw IX instituted the Collegium Major in 1456 for six rectors of arts and 200 students of Arts, the Collegium Minor for four masters and 150 students, and a college for six jurists.

From the beginning of the foundation of the university in 1419, two colleges existed in Rostock. The Collegium Majus or Philosophicum, alternately called White College (*Album*) and College of Theologians and Masters of Arts (*Collegium theologorum et artistarum*), was established for eight masters: two theologians, three masters of arts and bachelors in theology, and three simple masters of arts. Four were appointed by the prince and four by the city. The Collegium Minus served the jurists. Besides these two colleges several bursas or *regentia* were founded: the Bursa Olavi, later called Norwegianorum, and the Red Lion (Domus Rubei Leonis) both existed in 1443; the Unicorn (Collegium Unicornis); the Gate of Heaven (Porta Coeli); Eaglsburg (Ars Aquilae), mentioned in 1500; and the Half Moon (Domus Mediae Lunae, 1472).

The Collegium Georgianum or Collegium Novum in Ingolstadt was established by George the Rich, the son of the founder of the university, in 1494 on the Paris model of one regent master and eleven poor students recommended by the delegates of eighteen cities, among them Landshut, Ingolstadt, Launingen, and Otting. They had to earn the title of master of arts within five years, and then continue at the faculty of theology. Eleven bursas also existed, the best-known being the Bursa Parisiensis (Pariserwurst) and Bursa Pavonis.

In Freiburg im Breisgau the first foundation, the Domus Carthusiana or College of St. Jerome (1485), was endowed by Conrad Arnolt of Schorndorf for six theologians. The oldest bursa established in Freiburg im Breisgau was the Pfauenbursa (Bursa ad Pavonem or Peacock Bursa), where Johannes Eck taught nominalism in 1460. In the Bursa Aquilae (Eagle's Bursa) realism was professed by 1484. Preparations for the foundation of the Collegium Sapientiae (At the sign of wisdom) go back to 1496, when the founder, Johannes Kerner, professor at the University of Freiburg im Breisgau, and since 1493 titular bishop of Augsburg, drew up his will, which he modified in 1497 and 1501. The statutes were sanctioned in 1505. Provisions were made for twelve students from all faculties, who were allowed to spend ten years for studying theology, seven for law, six for medicine, and four for philosophy. Their statute book is splendidly illustrated with eighty pleasing miniatures, giving a detailed account of medieval college life.

COLLEGES IN THE LOW COUNTRIES

Within 100 years of its foundation, the University of Louvain possessed seven colleges. Two were for theologians: the College of the Holy Spirit (1445), for seven students in theology, established by the Flemish knight Louis of Rijcke; and the College of Houterle (1510), founded by Henry of Houterle, *scholasticus* of St. Peter. Two were established for civil law: Winckele College (1475), founded by Jan van Winckele, notary; and the College of St. Ivo (1483), founded by Robert de Lacu (van de Poel), professor of law. One was for canon law: the College of St. Donatian (1484), founded by Antony Haneron, councillor of the duke of Burgundy. Two were for arts students: the College of Malines (1500), founded by Arnold Trot, beadle of the faculty of theology; and the College of Arras (1508), founded by Nicholas Ruter, bishop of Arras. The Collegium Trilingue, a college for the study of Hebrew, Greek, and Latin, was established around 1517. Besides colleges, Louvain possessed pedagogies (residential houses) where professors lived with students from the faculty of arts, teaching and acting as tutors. Four pedagogies gained fame: the Pig (Porcus, 1428); the Falcon (Falco, before 1434); the Castle (Castrum, 1458); and the Lily (Lilium, ca. 1490), which was established by the celebrated master Charles Virulus or Mennekens. The House of the Poor (Domus Pauperum, 1500) owes its origin to the famous theologian Johannes Standonck, who modeled it after the College of Montaigu in Paris.

COLLEGES IN POLAND AND HUNGARY

Colleges in Kraków, as in the German universities, were established for regent masters: the Collegium Majus or College of King Władysław Jagiełło (1400), for regents of higher faculties; the Collegium Minor (1449), for students of liberal arts; and the Collegium Canonistarum (1403), founded by Bishop Wysz for canon lawyers. Queen Jadwiga (Hedwig) labored in 1397 on the establishment of a college for students from Lithuania. Several bursas were also founded, among them Bursa or Contubernium Pauperum (1409–1410), founded by Johannes Isner; and the Bursa Jerusalem (1454), for 100 students, both noble and poor, established by

Zbigniew Oleśnicki. A donation for a Hungarian bursa, Bursa Hungarorum, by Nicholas Belonka, a Polish nobleman, is mentioned in 1452; his will was approved in 1457. The bursa flourished between 1493 and 1506. The German Bursa Alemannorum was active during 1487–1523.

PROGRAM OF STUDIES

Students who enrolled in universities sought the degrees of bachelor, licentiate, master, or doctor in any one or several of the four faculties of arts, medicine, law, and theology. In Paris the students registered under a master; in the universities of later foundation they immatriculated, which meant that their names were inscribed in a register called a matricula.

Arts. Youths, thirteen or fourteen years of age, enrolled into the faculty of arts. After having been instructed at the elementary level in the grammar of Donatus as grammarians or "donatists," they entered the faculty of arts, where they studied logic (from the *Summulae* of Peter of Spain) as *summulista* and later as *modista*. As *sophista*, students learned how to demolish the arguments of adversaries in *sophismata* disputations. Commenting on the *Disticha Catonis* and learning proverbs offered an opportunity to teach morals, reading excerpts from Roman poets to give instruction in classics, and studying Trojan history and *Aurora* (a versified Bible) supplied knowledge of history. Mathematics was taught in such manuals as *Algorismus* and *Computus*. *Algorismus* was a textbook used to learn the art of calculating and the principles of arithmetic. *Computus* calculations enabled the finding of the date of Easter. It was one of the disciplines of the quadrivium. Sometimes it was composed not only in Latin but in French verses. At the advanced level, students in the faculty of arts studied Priscian, speculative grammar, natural philosophical books, ethics, and metaphysics. The aim of the faculty of arts was to prepare students for higher faculties. Generally, the arts students had to follow courses for six "passive" years and practice (conducting disputations and disputes) for two "active" years. To become a bachelor of arts, the student had to pass three stages: (1) disputations before Christmas; (2) examinations before a jury composed of masters; and (3) disputations (*determinacio*) under the auspices of his master. Upon completion of these requirements he became a *determinans*. After performing the prescribed disputations he earned the title of bachelor of arts. The *subdeterminans* was a poor student who was allowed to carry out some of the requirements of disputations, replacing a rich student in return for payment. A bachelor was a sort of apprentice; therefore, he could teach only under the supervision of a master. Bachelors with degrees earned at a university other than Paris were admitted only after fulfilling certain conditions.

To obtain a license to teach, granted in the name of the pope by the chancellor either of Notre Dame (*en bas*) or of Ste. Geneviève (*en haut*) in Paris, one had to be twenty-one years of age and read the prescribed books on natural philosophy, astronomy, and ethics by Aristotle and Euclid. Once examined and accepted, the licentiate was not acknowledged master until he made his *inceptio* (in Bologna called *conventatio*). This was a solemn investiture of the licentiate into the fellowship of the masters, an occasion when he received the magisterial insignia, biretta and gloves, accompanied by accolade. He was required to deliver a formal lecture accompanied by a harangue in praise of his discipline. Once he was a master (*magister*), at approximately twenty-two years of age, a distinction was made between the regent master, who was actually teaching, and the nonregent, who was qualified but not lecturing, and was probably enrolled as a student in the higher faculty of law, medicine, or theology.

Theology. The student at the faculty of theology had to follow the lectures of a master for five to seven years. After justifying his scholarity, he became *cursorius biblicus,* a bachelor who was expected to deliver cursory lectures on the Bible for two years. He had to read one book of the Old Testament in his first year and one book of his choice from the New Testament the following year. Then he lectured on the *Sentences* of Peter Lombard, chapter by chapter, as *sententiarius* for two years, always under the jurisdiction of a master. After participating in various academic exercises, disputes, and sermons, usually for three months, he became *baccalaureus formatus* until the awarding of his licentiate, an exercise that occurred every two years. To become master of theology he had to participate in (1) the *Vesperiae* disputation, held on the evening of his magisterial promotion; (2) the *Aulica,* the disputation delivered in the bishop's hall the morning after the *doctorandus* received his magisterial insignia and his commendation by the promoting master (*magister aulandus*); and (3) following the two previous exercises, the *resumpta* or *resumptio,* delivered by the new master in his

school on the first school day (*legibilis*). He "resumed," or took up again, one of his disputed questions and clarified what had been left unexplained. No one could become master of theology before the age of thirty-five; it required at least twelve years of study.

Canon law. In the faculty of canon law, the *Decretum* of Gratian and the *Decretales* of Gregory IX were delivered in "ordinary" lectures. The *Liber sextus* of Boniface VIII, the *Clementines* of Clement V, and the *Extravagantes* of John XXII were taught in "extraordinary" lectures. Forty-eight months of study within six years or so were required before becoming bachelor and forty additional months for the licentiate.

Civil law. At the faculty of civil law, parts of Justinian's *Corpus juris civilis,* the *Digestum vetus,* and the first nine books of the *Codex* were taught in the morning as ordinary lectures. The *Infortiatum* and *Digestum novum* were extraordinary lectures given in the afternoon. The law text was divided into sections called *puncta,* and the teacher was obliged to reach the end of his analysis, the *punctum,* in a definite time period (*punctatio*). Until his fifth year, the student participated passively in civil law school. During the sixth year he gave lessons on *Corpus iuris civilis*; in the seventh he delivered ordinary lectures on the *Digestum vetus* and gave extraordinary lectures on the *Digestum novum,* in addition to repetitions and lectures on the *Institutes.* During the seventh and eighth years he could lecture on ordinary texts, conduct "repetitions" and "questions." Then he became *baccalareus in actu legens.* To obtain the degree of *laureatus* in Italy he had to pass an examination, called *tentamen in camera,* before a single doctor, then another, the *rigorosum,* before all the doctors and the archdeacon. Finally, he was assigned two passages (*puncta*) for analysis. If the votes were favorably presented by his doctor or promotor, he became a licentiate. Normally he would then proceed to the doctoral ceremony. The doctoral degree given in canon law was called *doctor decretorum*; in civil law, *doctor legum.* The degree in both laws was called *doctor utriusque iuris.*

Medicine. To become a bachelor in medicine at Paris the student had to study about thirty-six months if he was a master of arts and forty-eight months if he was not. After a general examination with all masters present and particular examinations before elected examiners, the candidate had to submit evidence by calling witnesses (who produced certificates) to prove his time spent at the university, his scholarity (*probatio temporis*). Ordinary and extraordinary lectures were offered, using a great variety of textbooks: among the many were the works of Constantine the African (*d. ca.* 1087); the *De urinis* of Theophilus (*fl.* seventh century); the *Viaticum* of Ibn al-Jazzār (*d.* 1004/1005); books of Isaac Israeli (*ca.* 855–*ca.* 955), offering commentaries on Galen and Hippocrates; the *Antidotarium* of Nicholas of Salerno (*ca.* twelfth century); and didactic poems called *Versus egidii* of Gilles of Corbeil (*fl.* 1190–1220). Among textbooks used at Montpellier during the thirteenth century was the *Lilium medicine* (1303–1305) of Bernard of Gordon, the *Chirurgia* of Henry of Mondeville (*ca.* 1260–*ca.* 1320), and that of Guy de Chauliac (*ca.* 1290–*ca.* 1367/1370). At Bologna, Roland of Parma (*fl. ca.* 1200) and William of Saliceto (*ca.* 1210–*ca.* 1280) excelled in surgery, preferring knife to cautery.

To obtain a licentiate in medicine, a degree conferred every two years, the students had to give four courses on the theory and practice of medicine, defend two theses, and obtain training in medicine, including dissection, before being promoted to *licentiatus* by the chancellor. To become a master in medicine, the candidate had to give a lecture upon receiving his doctoral bonnet. Three months after the *inceptio* the new master had to hold a disputation called *pastillaria,* when a festive meal was offered by the new master to his confreres. Paris lagged behind Montpellier and Bologna in teaching anatomy. In Bologna the first dissection took place around 1266–1275; in Paris it was first recorded in 1407. It became a regular part of the curriculum there by 1494.

TEACHING METHODS

The masters had two duties in their teaching, to give lectures (*lectiones*) and to conduct disputations (*disputationes*). *Lectio* was synonymous with teaching; the master commented on and interpreted a text, chapter by chapter (*expositio*), weaving his own thoughts into the commentary or *glossa*. He began his lectures in the early morning (*hora prima*), around 6:00 or 7:00, when the clergy recited the first hours of the Divine Office. He spoke until 9:00 (*hora tertia*). Ordinary lectures were given by the regent masters in the morning, extraordinary lectures by the bachelors in the afternoon. A law professor, before giving the literary exegesis of the text, explained the contents of the title, read glosses, repeated the case (*casus*), noted objections (*contrarietates*), stated the general rule called *brocarda,* then made distinctions and raised questions. The exposition of the text was accompanied by questions, followed by arguments, then references to authorities (*ad appositum*), and finally the solution. Lecture and commentary concluded with questions, later collected and transcribed.

Didactic disputations were known in the twelfth century and flourished during the Scholastic period. The master presided, selected a subject or topic to be disputed, and opened the discussion. Everyone present could raise an argument for (*pro*) or against (*contra*). Those in favor spoke first, then those objecting, in order of seniority. The public was therefore divided into *opponentes* and *respondentes*. After the last objection and answer the master gave his final exposition, proposing his solution, called *determinatio*, usually given the morning of the first school day (*legibilis*) following the dispute. All the participants were required to be present. Every master had to hold an ordinary or solemn disputation at least once a week (*disputatio ordinaria* or *solemnis*). At the faculty of arts disputations on logic were called *de sophismatibus* and held in the afternoon. At the faculty of theology, the *quolibet* or *quodlibet* was a disputation dealing with randomly chosen subjects on anything proposed, without restrictions. This was one of the principal magisterial acts, an occasion when social, economic, and ecclesiastical questions, contemporary events, and delicate problems (such as the condemnation of the Templars in 1311–1312) could be discussed and disputed, sometimes in two sessions. The masters reserved the right not to accept indiscreet or politically dangerous questions.

In the fourteenth century the bachelors in theology were required to hold one *quolibet* before being admitted to the licentiate. After the *quodlibetarius* finished his exercise, the bachelors and students present were occasionally allowed to ask amusing questions. In law schools in Italy questions had to be collected and transcribed in *grossa litera*; then the exemplar was handed over to the beadle for safekeeping. The questions collected were called *questiones disputatae de Quolibet, questiones determinatae,* or *questiones disputatae et determinatae.* In both lectures and disputations the search for truth was more important than rhetorical brilliance.

Repetitio originally meant reviewing the material that had been explained in the morning; later it became synonymous with disputations. According to the 1317–1347 Bologna statutes, *repetitio* of doctors started the first Monday after the feast of St. Luke (18 October), which was the first teaching day of the academic year. *Repetitio* should not be confused with *repetitores* (tutors), who helped young students at their domiciles to better understand material taught in schools. The *reportatio* (or *reportatura*) was when a question or commentary of the master was taken down in writing by a student present at the former's academic exercise. On certain occasions, particularly in Italy, public readings of newly written books took place at universities. The author was crowned with laurel and honored as *laureatus*.

ADMINISTRATION, ORGANIZATION, AND FINANCES OF UNIVERSITIES

The officers of the university. The first ranking officer of the university was the chancellor. In Paris he was appointed by the bishop; in Oxford he was elected by the masters, but confirmed by the bishop of Lincoln; in Prague the chancellor was the archbishop himself. It was up to the chancellor to grant degrees in the name of ecclesiastical authorities. In some universities in southern France, the head of the university was the *primicerius,* who sometimes discharged the duties of the chancellor. The rector was the highest dignitary within the university. In Paris he was elected by the intrants of the four nations; at the other universities he was chosen by different procedures. The title *magnificus* dates back to the fifteenth century only. The proctors in Paris were heads of the nations; in Bologna, heads of the German nation. They were invested with more power than the *consiliarii.* In English universities they were business managers, handling finances and supervising discipline. In Bologna the *consiliarii* were elected by the representatives of the nations. They governed together with the rector. In Paris the receptor of the nations, acting as treasurer, was elected for a year; in Bologna he was called *massarii.*

The key holders, *clavigerii,* were possessors of the keys to the chest of the university. To open it, all the *clavigerii* had to be present. The beadle was a kind of liaison officer between the masters and students. During solemn processions he carried a mace (*sceptrum, virga, baculus*), an ensign of authority of university officials (rector, proctor, and dean). In early times it was a wooden rod; in the fourteenth century it developed into an elaborate silver staff, with coat of arms and images of patron saints of universities employed as decorative motifs. The *nuntius,* or messenger, transacted the business of the university, assured contact with the parents, and dispersed to students or officers of the university money that had been sent by their parents or superiors. In Bologna beadles served as bankers and money changers for the subjects of the universities. The taxor determined the amount of rental fees the landlords were allowed to ask from the students. The *inrotulator* was responsible for the preparation of the rolls of petition for benefices to be sent to the papal curia. The *librarius* or *stationarius* was in charge of the diffusion of manuals and procured the exemplar (standard version) of the text from the authors. This exemplar consisted of several separated sheets, or *pecia,* a manuscript on parchment folded into quires consisting of four folios. These *peciae* were distributed to scribes who reproduced them from the original exemplar. Thus, several copyists were able to work on the very same exemplar. The *peciarius* assured the correctness and purity of the texts intended for schoolbooks. The *correctores peciarum,* correctors of the *pecia,* carried out the actual correction upon the original exemplar, preparing a kind of critical edition.

The dean was originally the oldest, most respected member of a faculty or nation. Later the higher faculties, medicine, law, and theology, were headed by deans. The faculty of arts had its dean generally from the second half of the fourteenth century. The apostolic conservators (*conservatores*) assured protection and respect for university privileges and presided over their "court of conservation." In Rostock a *promotor* and *superintendens* filled the role of public prosecutor and was entrusted with the enforcement of university statutes. In Bologna the notary (*notarius, tabellio*) recorded the events of the university. The *syndicus* was an advocate and lawyer, a sort of assessor to the rector. In Paris the *syndicus,* later called *promotor universitatis,* was an important permanent officer, a counsel. The heads of colleges were called preses, president, prior, warden, grand master, or magister. The *conventor* was the principal of bursas or student halls. In Cambridge, the master of glomery (*magister glomeriae*) was the superintendent of grammar schools and grammarians (*glomerelli*). The office of the *reformatores* in Bologna functioned through a board appointed by the city government or prince in control of the university. In Paris they were elected by the faculty of arts and in the fifteenth and sixteenth centuries made official visitations to the colleges. Their duty was to enforce the governing statutes and oversee and restore discipline.

The academic year. In Bologna the year began around the feast of St. Luke, 18 October, and ended between the middle of August and 7 September. In Paris it opened around the Exaltation of the Holy Cross (14 September), though real inauguration occurred on the feast of St. Rémy (1 October). The period from this date until around Easter was the *ordinarium magnum*; from Easter until the end of June, the *ordinarium parvum*, when ordinary lectures were delivered. In principle there was no official vacation in Paris, but academic activities slowed down between 29 June and 14 September.

Meeting places. The early universities did not possess buildings. Meetings were held in churches and convents. In Paris the church of St. Severin was preferred by the theologians, Sts. Cosmas and Damian by the arts students. St. Julien le Pauvre, along with the convent of the Mathurins and the chapter house of the Cistercians, was used by the general congregation of the entire university. In Bologna, ultramontanes met in the Benedictine church of St. Proclus, arts students in the Franciscan church, jurists in the sacristy of the Dominicans.

Academic dress. At the medieval university, there was no uniform academic dress, but the clerics had to wear a cape (*cappa*), preferably of black material. Fur was allowed in winter. A miniver hood was worn by the rectors and masters. The toga, a sort of cassock, was originally worn under the cape. In certain faculties the biretta was a distinctive sign of masters; it was sometimes replaced by the *pileum*, resembling a round cap. Some colleges specified the color of the dress worn by their members. In Queen's College, Oxford, blood-red or purple robes were donned in remembrance of the Passion of Christ. In Paris, the College of Navarre prescribed a livery of black; at Dormans (Beauvais), blue or violet. In the College of Montaigu, the poor students (nicknamed *capettes*) wore gray capes.

University libraries. The first university libraries emerged in the colleges. The Sorbonne compiled a list of its manuscripts in 1290; the catalogue of 1338 registered 1,722 volumes. Merton College in Oxford, from its foundation date (1264) until 1385, accumulated 569 volumes. In 1438 Heidelberg received an important library bequeathed by Prince Louis III.

College statutes, such as those of Ave Maria, Dormans (Beauvais), Navarre, and Fortet, contained detailed regulations concerning the management of libraries. The books were kept in chests (*cistae*) and usually were given out upon the deposit of a sufficient pledge.

Salaries of masters. In the early years of the university accepting remuneration for teaching was frowned upon. Knowledge was considered a gift from God that could not be sold. An intermediary solution suggested the possibility of accepting remuneration if the student offered it spontaneously (*sponte*) or willingly. The amount of payment was expected to be proportionate to the wealth of the donor and the rank of his master. In later periods a distinction was made between receiving payment as the "price of the goods" and the "price of the labor." It was clarified by the canonists that payment was requested not for selling truth and learning but for the labor for which the teacher was hired (*quasi operas suas locans*). The professors in Paris, Bologna, and Oxford collected their fees (*collecta*) directly from the students. In Italian universities the payment was regulated by a contract (*condotta*) between the students and masters, but students were frequently delinquent in their payments. Later the masters were appointed to salaried positions, receiving a fixed amount of payment from the commune or municipality.

In the Holy Roman Empire the masters were supported by a combination of ecclesiastical prebends and church revenues connected with cathedral and collegiate chapters. In Louvain the professors were presented to these benefices by the burghers of the city. The income of masters varied according to universities. In fifteenth-century Padua half of the masters received an annual salary of less than fifty florins, equivalent to that of an unskilled worker. In Louvain during the first part of the fifteenth century the average salary fluctuated between 150 and 200 florins. Financial support assured by the prince or commune later on led to the right of presentation to professional chairs similar to that of the *ius patronatus* prevailing in ecclesiastical appointments, a procedure that terminated the administrative independence of the once privileged university.

To obtain a benefice in higher faculties, petitions had to be sent to Rome with names written on a rotulus or roll. Presented collectively by the university, it had a much greater chance to be honored. From the first quarter of the fourteenth century Paris and Oxford prepared rolls to be dispatched to Rome. By the middle of the fifteenth century growing secular influence within universities ended the practice of petitioning collectively for benefices.

Financial obligations of the students. In order to satisfy payment for degrees and other extraordinary expenses, such as for the rector and beadle, the students were taxed according to their *bursa*, a unit based upon their weekly expenditures for food and lodging. They were divided into rich (*solventes*) or poor (*pauperes*). The latter had to swear that they were without means to support themselves (*juravit paupertatem*). In Paris, between 1425 and 1494, the poor accounted for about 18 percent; in Vienna between 1377 and 1413, 25 percent; and in Leipzig between 1409 and 1430, 19 percent. According to a 1471 Leipzig statute, someone was considered poor if he had less than ten florins. In Prague and Heidelberg the limit was twelve florins. It is evident that poor students were not excluded from medieval universities. Students in colleges were supported by their fellowship, assured by the founders or by royal or princely subventions.

The medieval university for students and masters was a real *alma mater* (dear mother), an institution that protected its sons, promoted their fame, acknowledged their merits, defended their reputations, and, after their death, in anniversary solemnities, with grateful affection, did not fail to recommend their scholastic memories to prosperity.

BIBLIOGRAPHY

Bibliographies. E. H. Cordeaux and D. H. Merry, *A Bibliography of Printed Works Relating to the University of Oxford* (1968); Astrik L. Gabriel, *Summary Bibliography of the History of the Universities of Great Britain and Ireland up to 1800, Covering Publications Between 1900 and 1968* (1974); Rafael Gibert *et al.*, *Bibliographie internationale de l'histoire des universités*, I, *Espagne, Louvain, Copenhague, Prague* (1973); Simonne Guenée, *Bibliographie de l'histoire des universités françaises des origines à la révolution*, 2 vols. (1978–1981).

General studies. John H. Baldwin and Richard A. Goldthwaite, eds., *Universities in Politics: Case Studies from the Late Middle Ages and Early Modern Period* (1972); Alan E. Bernstein, *Pierre d'Ailly and the Blanchard Affair* (1978); Vern L. Bullough, *The Development of Medicine as a Profession* (1966); Alan B. Cobban, *The Medieval Universities* (1975); Jean Dauvillier, "Origine et histoire des costumes universitaires français," in *Annales de la faculté de droit de Toulouse*, 6 (1958); Philippe Delhaye, "L'organisation scolaire au XIIᵉ siècle," in *Traditio*, 5 (1947); Peter A. Ford, "The Medieval Account Books of the Parisian College of Dainville," in *Manuscripta*, 9 (1965); Astrik L. Gabriel, "The College System in the Fourteenth-century Universities," in Francis Lee Utley, ed., *The Forward Movement of the Fourteenth Century* (1961), *Garlandia: Studies in the History of the Mediaeval University* (1969), and, as ed., *The Economic and Material Frame of the Mediaeval University* (1977); Franz Gall, *Die Insignien der Universität Wien* (1965); Herbert Grundmann, *Vom Ursprung der Universität im Mittelalter* (1957); Charles Homer Haskins, *The Rise of Universities* (1923); Stephen d'Irsay, *Histoire des universités françaises et étrangères dès origines à nos jours*, 2 vols. (1933–1935); Pearl Kibre, *The Nations in the Mediaeval Universities* (1948) and *Scholarly Privileges in the Middle Ages* (1962); Louis John Paetow, *The Arts Course at Medieval Universities, with Special Reference to Grammar and Rhetoric* (1910); Jacques Paquet, *Salaires et prébendes des professeurs de l'Université de Louvain au XVᵉ siècle* (1958); Gaines Post, "Alexander III, the *Licentia Docendi*, and the Rise of the Universities," in *Anniversary Essays in Mediaeval History by Students of Charles Homer Haskins* (1929); Hastings Rashdall, *The Universities of Europe in the Middle Ages*, F. M. Powicke and A. B. Emden, eds., 3 vols. (1936); Sven Stelling-Michaud, "L'histoire des universités au moyen âge et à la renaissance au cours des vingt-cinq dernières années," in *Rapports* (XIᵉ Congrès internationale des sciences historiques), I (1960); Lynn Thorndike, *University Records and Life in the Middle Ages* (1944); Donald E. R. Watt, "University Clerks and Rolls of Petitions for Benefices," in *Speculum*, 34 (1959).

France. Gray C. Boyce, *The English-German Nation in the University of Paris During the Middle Ages* (1927); P. Feret, *La faculté de théologie de Paris et ses docteurs les plus célèbres, moyen âge*, 4 vols. (1894–1897); Astrik L. Gabriel, *Student Life in Ave Maria College, Mediaeval Paris* (1955) and *Skara House at the Mediaeval University of Paris* (1960); Palémon Glorieux, *Aux origines de la Sorbonne*, I, *Robert de Sorbon* (1966); Marie Henriette Jullien de Pommerol, *Sources de l'histoire de l'Université d'Orléans* (1974); Richard H. Rouse, "The Early Library of the Sorbonne," in *Scriptorium*, 21 (1967), 42–71, 227–245; David Sanderlin, *The Mediaeval Statutes of the College of Autun at the University of Paris* (1971); Cyril Eugene Smith, *The University of Toulouse in the Middle Ages* (1958); *Les universités du Languedoc au XIIIᵉ siècle* (1970); Jacques Verger, ed., *Histoire des universités en France* (1986).

Italy. John M. Fletcher, "The Spanish College—Some Observations on Its Foundation and Early Statutes," in *Studia Albornotiana*, 12 (1972); Berthe M. Marti, ed., *The Spanish College at Bologna in the Fourteenth Century* (1966); Nancy G. Siraisi, *Arts and Sciences at Padua* (1973); Pietro Vaccari, *Storia della Università di Pavia*, 2nd ed. (1957); Armando F. Verde, *Lo studio fiorentino, 1473–1503*, 3 vols. (1973–1977).

Spain. Ajo G. y Sáinz de Zúñiga, *Historia de la universidades hispanicas*: I, *Medievao y renacimiento universitario* (1957).

Portugal. Artur Moreira de Sà, *Les origines de l'université portugaise et son évolution jusqu'en 1537* (1970).

Germany. Joseph Aschbach, *Geschichte der Wiener Universität,* 2 vols. (1865); Edgar Bonjour, *Die Universität Basel* (1971); Gray C. Boyce and William H. Dawson, *The University of Prague* (1938); Hansmartin Decker-Hauff *et al.,* eds., *Beiträge zur Geschichte der Universität Tübingen* (1977); Georg Kaufmann, *Die Geschichte der deutschen Universitäten,* 2 vols. (1888–1896); H. Ott and J. M. Fletcher, eds., *The Mediaeval Statutes of the Faculty of Arts of the University of Freiburg im Breisgau* (1964); Elisabeth Schnitzler, *Beiträge zur Geschichte der Universität Rostock im 15. Jahrhundert* (1979); Paul Uiblein, *Mittelalterliches Studium an der Wiener Artistenfakultät* (1987).

Poland and Hungary. Astrik L. Gabriel, *The Mediaeval Universities of Pécs and Pozsony* (1969); Oscar Halecki, "The Universities of the Polish-Lithuanian Commonwealth from the XIV to the XVII Century," in *Polish Review,* 5 (1960); Kazimierz Lepszy, *Jagiellonian University of Cracow: Past, Present, and Future* (1964).

Scandinavia. Sten Lindroth, *A History of Uppsala University, 1477–1977* (1976); Anders Piltz, *Studium Upsalense: Specimens of the Oldest Lecture Notes Taken in the Mediaeval University of Uppsala* (1977).

England. Alan B. Cobban, *The King's Hall Within the University of Cambridge in the Later Middle Ages* (1969), and "The Medieval Cambridge Colleges: A Quantitative Study of Higher Degrees to c. 1500," in *History of Education,* 9 (1980); Henry W. Carless Davis, *A History of Balliol College,* rev. by R. H. C. Davis and Richard Hunt and supplemented by Harold Hartley *et al.* (1963); Alfred B. Emden, *A Biographical Register of the University of Oxford to* A.D. *1500,* 3 vols. (1957–1959), and *A Biographical Register of the University of Cambridge to 1500* (1963); M. B. Hackett, *The Original Statutes of Cambridge University: The Text and Its History* (1970); J. R. L. Highfield, ed., *The Early Rolls of Merton College, Oxford* (1964); Gordon Leff, *Paris and Oxford Universities in the Thirteenth and Fourteenth Centuries* (1968, repr. 1975); Charles Edward Mallet, *A History of the University of Oxford,* I (1924); *Oxford Studies Presented to Daniel Callus* (1964); Heather E. Peek and Catherine P. Hall, *The Archives of the University of Cambridge* (1962); Frederick M. Powicke, *The Medieval Books of Merton College* (1931); Beryl Smalley, "Robert Bacon and the Early Dominican School at Oxford," in *Transactions of the Royal Historical Society,* 4th ser., **30** (1948); Henry P. Stokes, *Ceremonies of the University of Cambridge* (1927); James A. Weisheipl, "Curriculum of the Faculty of Arts at Oxford in the Early Fourteenth Century," in *Mediaeval Studies,* **26** (1964).

Scotland. Peter J. Anderson, *Studies in the History and Development of the University of Aberdeen* (1900); Ronald Gordon Cant, *The University of St. Andrews* (1946, rev. ed. 1970) and, with Francis C. Eeles, *The College of St. Salvator* (1950); Annie I. Dunlop, *Acta facultatis artium Universitatis Sanctiandree: 1413–1588* (1964); John Durkan and James Kirk, *The University of Glasgow, 1451–1577* (1977); Donald E. R. Watt, *A Biographical Dictionary of Scottish Graduates to* A.D. *1410* (1977).

A㎝ʀɪᴋ L. Gᴀʙʀɪᴇʟ

[See also **Adelard of Bath; Ailly, Pierre d'; Aristotle in the Middle Ages; Arts, Seven Liberal; Biel, Gabriel; Bologna, University of; Bulgarus; Bull, Papal; Cambridge, University of; Cato's Distichs; Charter; Commune; Constantine the African; Corpus Iuris Civilis; Courson (Courçon), Robert of; Decretum; Dialectic; Gerard of Cremona; Glossators; Hugolinus; Irnerius; Israeli, Isaac; Jacobus; Law, Canon; Law, Civil; Law, Schools of; Libraries; Lull, Ramon; Martinus Gosia; Mathematics; Medicine, History of; Medicine, Schools of; Oresme, Nicole; Oxford University; Paris, University of; Pecia; Peter Lombard; Philosophy and Theology, Western European; Quodlibet; Schism, Great; Scholasticism, Scholastic Method; Schools; Textbooks.**]

UNIVERSITIES, BYZANTINE. The medieval Greek world knew no autonomous and continuing institutions of higher education comparable to the universities of the later Middle Ages in Western Europe. But higher education, both general and professional, was provided by private teachers, by members of professional groups, and by officially appointed teachers paid by the state. Rome, Athens, and Alexandria were the main centers in the early period. In the fifth century they were overtaken by Constantinople, which from the seventh century on remained the sole center of higher study.

The principal social functions of higher education were the production of civil servants skilled in the use of language, the training of future ecclesiastical functionaries and dignitaries, the training of doctors and lawyers, and the conservation and transmission of a traditional culture. These were the considerations which led the Byzantine state, and sometimes also the church, to support, and sometimes to control, higher education.

From the foundation of Constantinople in 330 teachers were drawn to the new city, and there were sporadic measures of official supervision and support. In 425 Theodosius II established a clear distinction between private teachers and publicly appointed teachers, paid from imperial funds, teaching in the capital, and enjoying privileges and prestige. There were originally ten each for Greek and Latin grammar, five for Greek rhetoric, three for Latin rhetoric, two for law, and one for philosophy. A similar system continued, with varying degrees of official support, until the seventh century. Justinian (r. 527–565) reorganized the teaching of law, with four professors each in Constantinople and Beirut. There is evidence of officially appointed teachers of medicine in Constantinople and Alexandria. The closing of the Academy in Athens in 529 because of the provocatively pagan stance of its professors, and the conquest of Alexandria and Beirut by the Arabs in the mid seventh century, led to the concentration of all higher education in Constantinople. Youths from as far away as Armenia went to Constantinople to study, and then filled posts of influence as far afield as Merovingian Gaul and Visigothic Lusitania.

Continuing pressure from Arabs to the south and from Slavs, Avars, and Bulgars to the north led to a catastrophic economic decline and a radical transformation of Byzantine life, yet both general and specialized higher education continued to receive official support. The details are wrapped in later legend, but most of the time there was some provision for the teaching of grammar, rhetoric, philosophy, law, and medicine, though the level of such teaching may often have been low. It is likely, in view of the increasing role of religion in providing social cohesion, that the church played a part in the process of higher education.

The improving military, political, and economic situation of the empire in the ninth century was accompanied by a series of measures to improve the provision and quality of higher education. Theophilus (r. 829–842) founded a school at which one of the teachers was Constantine (Cyril), the future apostle of the Slavs.

In 863 chairs of grammar, rhetoric, and philosophy (including mathematics, astronomy, and music) were founded and provided with premises in the imperial palace. Basil I (r. 867–886) continued or revived this foundation. Constantine VII (r. 913–959) appointed many distinguished men to chairs, and his institution seems to have existed until late in the tenth century. In all this it is difficult to know whether we are dealing with a series of new foundations or with periodic revivals of a languishing institution. In any case provision for officially sponsored higher education was more or less continuous for about a century and a half. The teaching of law seems to have been left in the hands of the

legal profession with no public control or subvention. There was little support for education from Basil II (r. 976–1025), and the field was left to private teachers. In 1045 Constantine IX founded new schools of law and philosophy, in which the professor was supported by assistants and a library. This presupposes adequate arrangements for the teaching of the preliminary studies of grammar and rhetoric. How long these institutions survived after the accession of Alexios I (r. 1081–1118) is not clear. In any case the leading role in the provision of higher education began to be taken by the church, supported by imperial funds.

During the twelfth century the Patriarchal School, with its teachers of grammar, rhetoric, and Old and New Testaments, numbered among its teachers many of the leading men of letters, including Theodore Prodromos and Eustathios. Only at this period was there institutionalized teaching of theology in Byzantium. Manuel I (r. 1143–1180) established official posts for teachers of philosophy and medicine, which were sometimes held by clergymen in the course of their careers. The capture of Constantinople by the crusaders in 1204 ended all official patronage of higher education. The government in exile in Nicaea gave support to individual teachers. After the Byzantine restoration in 1261 attempts were made to provide more permanent institutions. Many of the old titles were revived. But in reality it was a question of spasmodic official support for this or that teacher, and the main weight of providing the higher education needed by late Byzantine society was borne by private teachers, who often combined teaching with some other profession or activity. Such a man was Maximos Planudes (1260–1310), diplomat and monk, noteworthy for his knowledge of Latin and his openness to Western culture. Another was the historian Nikephoros Gregoras (1290/1291–1360), who helped to revive the study of mathematics and astronomy. A third was Manuel Chrysoloras, diplomat and man of letters, who was invited to a chair in Florence in 1396 and largely determined the pattern of Greek studies of the early Italian humanists. In the fifteenth century many other Constantinopolitan teachers followed in his footsteps. The combination of centralized patronage, increasing impoverishment, and continuous warfare prevented the development of autonomous local corporations of teachers, such as became the nucleus of Western European universities.

Byzantine nonspecialist higher education followed a pattern established in Hellenistic times. It began with "grammar," that is, the study of literature, its techniques and values, based on the reading of classical poetry. The next stage was "rhetoric," the study and practice of the art of self-expression within the framework of a millenary literary tradition. This involved both the reading of classical prose and the study of the theory of rhetoric. The third stage, "philosophy," often amounted to no more than a superficial introduction to Aristotelian logic, but a good teacher might give his pupils much more. Eustatios' commentaries on Homer are an example of good teaching of grammar; the many surviving manuals and commentaries on ancient rhetoricians show what the rhetor taught; and the philosophical treatises of Michael Psellos and John Italos, as well as the Byzantine commentaries on Aristotle, introduce us to the lecture room of the philosopher.

The proportion of the population enjoying higher education was always infinitesimal. Yet those privileged few, as well as performing their role in their own society, conserved and developed the heritage of antiquity and eventually transmitted it to the world of the Renaissance.

BIBLIOGRAPHY

Robert Browning, "The Patriarchal School at Constantinople in the Twelfth Century," in *Byzantion*, 32–33 (1962–1963); A. D. E. Cameron, "The Last Days of the Academy at Athens," in *Proceedings of the Cambridge Philological Society*, 195 (1969); Friedrich Fuchs, *Die höheren Schulen von Konstantinopel im Mittelalter* (1926); Paul Lemerle, *Le premier humanisme byzantin* (1971); trans. by Helen Lindsay and Ann Moffatt as *Byzantine Humanism* (1986); Paul Speck, *Die kaiserliche Universität von Konstantinopel* (1974).

ROBERT BROWNING

[See also **Alexios I Komnenos; Aristotle in the Middle Ages; Basil I; Basil II; Byzantine History; Byzantine Literature; Constantine VII Porphyrogenitos; Constantine IX Monomachos; Constantinople; Cyril and Methodios, Sts.; Grammar; Islam, Conquests of; Italian Renaissance, Byzantine Influence on; John Italos; Justinian I; Manuel I Komnenos; Manuel Chrysoloras; Nikephoros Gregoras; Philosophy and Theology, Byzantine; Psellos, Michael; Quadrivium; Rhetoric: Byzantine; Theodore Prodromos; Theophilus; Trivium.**]

UNIVERSITIES, ISLAMIC. See Schools, Islamic.

URBAIN LE COURTOIS, a short anonymous Anglo-Norman poem of the thirteenth century containing advice from a father to his son about personal and public conduct. The text, which exists in several versions, is also known as the *Apprise de nurture.*

BIBLIOGRAPHY

In Frederic Spencer, "L'Apprise de nurture," in *Modern Language Notes,* 4 (1889), 101–106, is printed the text of Cambridge University Library, MS Gg.1.1; in Paul Meyer, "Urbain le Courtois," in *Romania,* 32 (1903), 68–73, is printed the text of Cambridge, Trinity College, MS 0.1.17.

BRIAN MERRILEES

[See also **Anglo-Norman Literature; Courtesy Books.**]

URBAN II, POPE (*r.* 1088–1099), reformer and preacher of the First Crusade, was born Odo, to a noble family, probably in Châtillon-sur-Marne (in the diocese of Soissons), about the year 1035. He was educated at Rheims, where he became a student of St. Bruno of Cologne, who later founded the Carthusian order. Bruno's influence on the young man was profound, and, as pope, Urban called Bruno to Italy to serve as an adviser.

The future Urban II became archdeacon at Rheims sometime between 1055 and 1060, but at an undetermined date left that city and entered the monastery of Cluny. He served as prior at Cluny from about 1070 until his appointment in 1079/1080 under Pope Gregory VII as cardinal-bishop of Ostia.

Late in the year 1084, at the darkest moment of Gregory VII's reign, the pope entrusted Urban with an important legation to Germany. Through this mission Urban was able to experience personally the political and ecclesiastical situation in the north. He convened a synod at Quedlinburg during Easter week (20–26 April) of 1085, where the ordinations and consecrations of all schismatic followers of the antipope Clement III were condemned. Ten years later, Urban again would address the ordination and consecration of schismatics in detailed rulings promulgated by the Council of Piacenza.

On 25 May 1085, Pope Gregory VII died at Salerno. Gregory's reign was followed by the brief pontificate of Abbot Desiderius of Monte Cassino as Pope Victor III. On his deathbed Victor recommended as his successor Urban, who was then chosen as Roman pontiff on 12 March 1088 at Terracina.

The pontificate of Urban II has too often been seen merely in light of the First Crusade, which was inaugurated at the Council of Clermont in November 1095. A more accurate appraisal of those years must place Urban's reign fully within the context of eleventh-century papal history and the concomitant movement for reform. It was Pope Urban II who brought the Gregorian party back from the low ebb it experienced around the time of Gregory's death. While struggling for and eventually gaining a diplomatic advantage over the antipope Clement III, Urban also succeeded in advancing the program of Gregory VII by repeated condemnations of clerical incontinence, simony, and lay investiture.

Urban's reign can be divided into two major segments. The first period extends from his election in 1088 and his brief residence in Rome in 1089, through the time of his stay in southern Italy, to the point of his return to Rome at the end of the year 1093. The second period encompasses the remainder of Urban's pontificate, from his return to Rome to the councils of Piacenza and Clermont in 1095 to his death in 1099.

During the first period of his reign, Urban worked primarily to outmaneuver the forces of Clement III, to secure his own acceptance at Rome, and to regain credibility for the Gregorian cause. The second segment of his reign was a time of increased activity in the area of church reform, marked especially by the renewal and amplification of the reform programs at the two great synods held during the year 1095, at Piacenza and Clermont.

Urban also held synods at Melfi in 1089, at Benevento in 1091, at Troia in 1093, at Tours and Nîmes in 1096, at the Lateran in Rome in 1097, at Bari in 1098, and at St. Peter's in Rome in 1099. The synod at Bari was especially concerned with relations between the Latin and Greek churches. At this synod, Anselm of Canterbury defended the Latin use of the *Filioque* clause in the creed.

The records for Urban's pontificate are sparse. It is clear, however, that no pope since Leo IX, nearly a half century earlier, had traveled so widely and been so visible throughout Latin Christendom. By the end of Urban's reign, the bleak prospects faced by the Gregorian party a decade earlier had been replaced with a revived reform movement under

papal control, as the fortunes of Emperor Henry IV and the antipope, Clement III, waned.

In the historical writing of the past half century or more, much has been made of the notion of a "Gregorian reform." Yet recent scholarship has shown that this idea, if taken specifically to mean a movement toward reform in which the program of Pope Gregory VII himself was recognized as dominant, had less currency in the eleventh and twelfth centuries than it has today. Texts from Gregory's pontificate do not predominate in the canon law books and the propaganda literature of the time. From the beginning of the twelfth century to the compilation of Gratian's *Decretum* (*ca.* 1141), Pope Urban II is far more prominent as a source in such literature than is Gregory VII. The investiture conflict, and the ensuing spectacular political struggle that erupted during Gregory's reign, often dominate modern treatments of the eleventh- and twelfth-century reform. Such an interpretation obscures the great contribution made by Urban II in restructuring the Gregorian reform, and in both advancing the reform and dealing with the political tensions which had been inherited from the time of Pope Gregory.

The preaching of the First Crusade by Pope Urban must be seen in the broader context of his pontificate. Urban had been concerned about relations with Byzantium during the early years of his reign. It is even possible that ambassadors from the Byzantine emperor Alexios I were permitted to deliver an appeal at the Council of Piacenza for Western troops to help battle the Turks. It was not until November 1095, however, after preparations during the previous months, that Urban made a formal public plea for warriors to march to Jerusalem to recover that city from Islamic control, and in the process of so doing to aid the Greeks.

It is very difficult to retrieve Urban's thoughts about this venture. From the available evidence, however, it seems that the Council of Clermont did legislate about the crusade as one of many features of the synod, but not as the council's sole or even most important consideration. It enacted regulations defining the indulgence applicable to those who undertook the journey and also stipulated that the property of participants should remain under the Peace of God during their absence. It is furthermore possible, although the evidence is unclear, that under Urban's leadership at Clermont decisions were made about the composition and leadership of the venture and also about the government of territory captured from the Muslims and the disposition of churches in such territory.

Urban died in Rome on 29 July 1099, without learning that the crusaders had captured Jerusalem two weeks before, on 15 July.

BIBLIOGRAPHY

Sources. Philipp Jaffé, *Regesta pontificum Romanorum,* I, 2nd ed. (1885), 657–701 (which must be supplemented by items available in the bibliographies of the works listed below); Robert Somerville, *The Councils of Urban II, I: Decreta Claromontensia* (1972).

Studies. Alfons Becker, *Papst Urban II.* (1964), is indispensable for Urban's life and his policies toward the major political entities in Latin Christendom. The expected second volume of this work will treat Urban's Oriental policy in detail.

See also Horst Fuhrmann, *Papst Urban II. und der Stand der Regular kanoniker* (1984); John T. Gilchrist, *Was There a Gregorian Reform Movement in the Eleventh Century?* (1970) and "The Reception of Pope Gregory VII into the Canon Law (1073–1141)," in *Zeitschrift der Savigny-Stiftung für Rechtsgeschichte: Kanonistische Abteilung,* 59 (1973); Francis J. Gossman, *Pope Urban II and Canon Law* (1960); Friedrich Kempf, "Urban II," in Friedrich Kempf *et al., The Church in the Age of Feudalism* (1969); Stephan Kuttner, "Brief Notes: Urban II and Gratian," in *Traditio,* 24 (1968), and "Urban II and the Doctrine of Interpretation: A Turning Point?" in *Studia Gratiana,* 15 (1972); Robert Somerville, "The Council of Clermont and the First Crusade," *ibid.,* 20 (1976).

ROBERT SOMERVILLE

[See also **Alexios I Komnenos; Bruno the Carthusian, St.; Celibacy; Clermont, Council of; Councils, Western; Crusades and Crusader States; Gerhoh of Reichersberg; Gregory VII, Pope; Henry IV of Germany; Investiture and Investiture Conflict; Law, Canon; Leo IX, Pope; Matilda of Tuscany; Nicolaitism; Papacy, Origins and Development of; Peace of God, Truce of God; Reform, Idea of; Seljuks of Rum; Simony; Tithes.**]

URBANISM, BYZANTINE. The history of the Byzantine city can be divided into two distinct periods: the late antique (284–610) and the Byzantine (610–1453). They are separated by the catastrophic invasions of the Persians and Arabs, which began in the seventh century. In the former period, urban life maintained much of the appearance and institutions of classical antiquity, whereas the city of the later age was fundamentally different. For ease of comparison, this discussion will treat only cities in Asia Minor and the Balkans, those areas that remained Byzantine throughout the Middle Ages.

The ancient Greco-Roman city, though much transformed, still flourished in the sixth century, although in many cases it had begun to decline. The great variety of late antique urbanism may be approached through specific examples, from which common elements will emerge.

Constantinople, the capital, was by far the greatest city of the age, built on such a scale that most of the other cities here discussed would fit within its walls with room to spare. The general plan is still clear despite its history of constant occupation and rebuilding, which has obliterated most of the late antique city. Constantinople stood on a peninsula shaped roughly like a triangle with its apex toward the east. Broad boulevards radiated from a square near the apex for some six miles (9.6 km) toward the land walls that isolated the peninsula from the mainland of Thrace. A golden milestone from which all distances in the empire were counted adorned the square, and near it were the great buildings that reflected the structure of the city and state: the senate house, the cathedral, the imperial palace, and the hippodrome.

The emperor and the church dominated the society; the senate, largely ornamental, represented a rich landowning aristocracy. The vast population had no formal political role in this absolutist state but could make its opinion known through acclamations and riots in the hippodrome, where chariot races attracted an avid and tumultuous following. The emperor had a box in the hippodrome, which he could enter directly from the palace to hear the voice of the people. In 532, much of the city center was destroyed in a riot of the highly organized racing fans. It was rebuilt by Justinian, whose church of Hagia Sophia, dedicated in 537, is the greatest monument of the age. The imperial palace, now largely destroyed, occupied the eastern point of the city. Outside its walls, churches, houses, and commercial districts clustered together around broad colonnaded streets lined with shops. Large squares punctuated the streets and served as centers of trade and manufacture. Most of this activity was carried out by individual artisans who both made and sold their products. Much is known of the churches of the capital, little of the rest. The western part of the city was largely occupied by cisterns and gardens and was probably never densely populated. The four-mile-long (6.4 km) rampart of the land walls was another marvel of the age, with its double row of towers rising to a height of sixty feet (about 18 m) and protected by a moat. Built in the early fifth century, the walls were never substantially improved and resisted assault for 1,000 years. The city may have had a population of 300,000; all estimates are highly speculative.

Constantinople was mostly a product of late antiquity. Newly built cities, like new districts of old cities, show similar regular planning, with colonnaded streets and broad squares. Notable among them, on a small scale, is Justiniana Prima, near the birthplace of Justinian. This regularity, however, was not typical of the majority of cities, which had grown organically for centuries. The many surviving urban remains in Asia Minor illustrate the transformation of urban life in late antiquity. In all of the examples to be considered, archaeology has made a substantial contribution to our knowledge.

Ephesus preserved Hellenistic regularity and Roman grandeur. It featured two main streets, lined with colonnades and paved with marble, which met below the theater in the center of the city. To the north was a gymnasium, the governor's palace, and the stadium, and to the west, a vast complex of gymnasium, baths, and exercise grounds. The Goths had left much of this in ruins, later covered with houses, some quite substantial. The shell of a vast market building nearby had been used to install the cathedral church of the Virgin and the palace of the bishop. The large open square of the marketplace adjoined the theater, with a temple converted into a church above it. To its south lay a Roman library, whose monumental facade had been made into a fountain. The main street, lined with closely packed apartments, baths, shops, fountains, and monuments, led from there to the civic center. The generous plans and lavish decoration in marble, mosaic, and fresco of the excavated apartments reveal an impressively high standard of living. The senate house, the city hall, another bath-gymnasium complex, and a monumental fountain, along with some ruined temples, surrounded the open square of the civic center. Then, beyond another bath and the city gates, stretched the vast necropolis. The ruins of one of the wonders of the ancient world, the temple of Artemis (Diana), stood a mile away. It was now used as a quarry, most notably for the basilica of St. John, which Justinian built on the supposed site of the Apostle's grave.

Ephesus reveals both continuity and transforma-

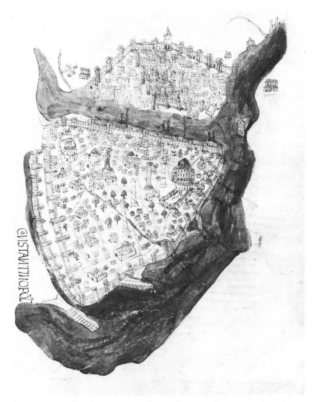

Constantinople. Map from the *Liber insularum archipelagi* (1420). PARIS, BIBLIOTHÈQUE NATIONALE, MS LAT. 4825, fol. 37v

tion. The plan of the ancient city was preserved, along with many of its monumental public buildings, which represented services available to the population. Some public buildings, however, were abandoned. Bazaars along the streets became prevalent as many of the regular open spaces came to be cluttered with poor construction. The Christianization of the city was especially notable: temples were ruined or put to new uses, and their place taken by churches, some built on an equally vast scale. Crosses were everywhere in evidence, as was color: colonnades were paved with mosaic, facades covered with fresco. Nominally, the city was governed by its senate, but this institution was in decline, and authority was wielded instead by the bishop and great landowners. In provincial capitals like Ephesus, the governor played a dominant role: not by accident were the streets lined with statues of former proconsuls.

Other cities presented a similar appearance. At Sardis, colonnaded streets, shops, and baths were built or maintained, temples were abandoned, and—a rare feature in the surviving record—an opulent synagogue was built near the center. At Aphrodisias, most of the Roman buildings, monumental structures of marble occupying a remarkably large proportion of the city, were preserved. Added to them were the palaces of governor and bishop; and the main temple was converted into the cathedral. Side, in Anatolia, featured broad, straight, colonnaded streets and the usual monumental buildings, but it was remarkable for the vast quarter devoted to the bishop's palace. In all these cases, a circuit of walls, a typical feature of the age, surrounded most or all of the area of the ancient city.

The examples cited have been of provincial capitals, which profited from the generosity of governor and archbishop. Old, disused buildings were usually sacrificed for the new building projects. To the same end, some of the neighboring and less important towns were plundered, so that the impressive picture of urban prosperity must be qualified. The general picture of wealth was not universal and not shared by all regions equally; some ancient cities were in decline. Such a place was Athens, as revealed by the excavations of its marketplace and civic center. The main buildings had succumbed to third-century invasions, and the ruins were used to build a new wall surrounding a small part of the ancient city. Although a surviving temple was converted into a church and a philosophical school of some size rose among the ruins, most of the central area was desolate in the sixth century. Some of it, however, had been converted to light industrial use, which may have given the place a modicum of self-sufficiency.

This dismal image of Athens may serve as introduction to the fate of the Byzantine city after the devastating invasions of the seventh century. Basically, many cities were destroyed and the rest so severely reduced that continuity with antiquity was largely broken and a new type of urban life emerged. In this, the dominant features were loss of autonomy, disappearance of most public services, and construction largely limited to churches and fortifications, in keeping with the needs of the age. Written sources reveal little of Byzantine medieval urbanism; it is here that archaeology makes its greatest contribution.

The two greatest cities, Constantinople and Thessaloniki, escaped the general devastation and preserved their ancient areas, but virtually nothing is known of the latter. The capital remained the greatest city of the world, but the little evidence available shows clearly that it was falling into ruin and becoming increasingly shabby. Some recovery began in the ninth century, and subsequently many churches and some palaces were constructed, but none on the scale or with the magnificence of late antiquity. The churches were mostly small; if their floor plans are placed side by side, they barely equal that of Hagia Sophia.

In Asia Minor and Greece the physical aspect of cities varied. Some still maintained their ancient areas, but most were reduced, some even to mere fortresses. The little that is known of the former, in cases like Smyrna, Attaleia, or Nicaea, suggests that they contained much empty space within their walls. Some of the others, however, are well known from excavations. At Ephesus, new walls were built in the Dark Ages (seventh to ninth centuries), leaving about half the area of the ancient city abandoned outside their circuit. The medieval town was of two parts: the city by the harbor, which was gradually abandoned, and the fortress on the hill around the church of St. John, which became the center. In the former, the only substantial construction was the rebuilding of the church of the Virgin on a much smaller scale. And the latter came to consist of a densely crowded assemblage of small houses and industrial installations over which towered the dilapidated cathedral.

Similar or even more extreme phenomena are evident in most of the other cities of western Asia Minor, once a rich and densely populated area. At Sardis virtually the whole area of the city was given up and the town retreated to its heavily fortified acropolis, whose walls were made of the ruins of the ancient city. Below, settlements like villages lay scattered among the ruins. Miletus and Aphrodisias took shelter within the walls of their massive ancient theaters, while at Magnesia on the Maeander the former marketplace was fortified to become the town. Other cases show varying degrees of reduction; in all, churches and fortifications are virtually the only new constructions. The churches are invariably minuscule compared with those of late antiquity, doubtless thus indicating a sharply reduced urban population. The walls are often large and substantial and are built in a great variety of styles. But they almost never display any sophistication in the art of war or represent any advance over ancient work. New towns of the age are rarely more than large fortresses.

In most cases, the period of severe decline was over by the tenth century, when some cities began to expand outside their walls. This phenomenon was more evident in Greece than Asia Minor, which was soon exposed to the attacks of the Turks. In other cases, such as Corinth, a revival is indicated by an increasing abundance and density of construction, almost all of it small and poor. In no case did the cities approach the size and wealth they had possessed in the sixth century.

In general, the medieval Byzantine city was small and poor, like its contemporaries in the West. Unlike them, however, it rarely developed any local autonomy. Under the militarized administration of the Dark Ages, the cities were ruled by their bishops and by subordinates of the provincial commander. Only in the latest period did any exhibit some independence, and then only when the central government was especially weak.

BIBLIOGRAPHY

Charalampos Bouras, "City and Village: Urban Design and Architecture," in *Jahrbuch der österreichischen Byzantinistik*, 31 (1981); Dietrich Claude, *Die byzantinische Stadt im 6. Jahrhundert* (1969); Clive Foss, *Byzantine and Turkish Sardis* (1976), "Archaeology and the 'Twenty Cities' of Byzantine Asia," in *American Journal of Archaeology*, 81 (1977), and *Ephesus After Antiquity* (1979); Arnold H. M. Jones, *The Greek City from Alexander to Justinian* (1940); Cyril Mango, *Byzantium: The Empire of New Rome* (1980); Homer Thompson, "Athenian Twilight: A.D. 267–600," in *Journal of Roman Studies*, 49 (1959).

CLIVE FOSS

[See also **Anatolia; Byzantine Empire; Constantinople; Early Christian and Byzantine Architecture; Ephesus; Hagia Sophia; Thessaloniki.**]

URBANISM, ISLAMIC. The world of medieval Islam was largely a world of cities. Within a century of the birth of Islam in the Arabian Peninsula in the early seventh century, the adherents of the new religion had extended their political and military hegemony from the borders of India and Central Asia in the east to the shores of the Atlantic and the foothills of the Pyrenees in the west. All of the Sasanian Empire and some of the fairest provinces of the Byzantine Empire now came (permanently as it turned out) under Islamic hegemony. While the desert and its oases were the setting of its birth, it was the cities and towns of the ancient world that became the setting of Islam's growth and maturity. From Mecca and Medina—which remained objects

of pilgrimage and holy cities for all Muslims—the centers of power, culture, and wealth moved to such urban sites as Damascus, Baghdad, and Samarkand, and to Cairo, Qayrawān, Fēs, and Córdoba. For dynastic and administrative reasons, many new cities were created during the early centuries of the Islamic era. The two great metropolises of the medieval Islamic world—and among the greatest cities of the early Middle Ages anywhere—Baghdad and Cairo, were founded in the Islamic era, the former in 762/763 and the latter in 969 (as a Fatimid extension of Al-Fustāt, founded 641). The same was true for many others, such as Qayrawān and Al-Mahdia in Tunisia; Fēs and Marrakech in Morocco; and Al-Kufa, Basra, and Gorgān in Iraq and Iran.

At a time when urban life in most of Christian Europe was at its nadir, cities in the Islamic world were flourishing. The question as to whether there was some feature of Islam that either required or encouraged its adherents to reside in cities cannot be answered unequivocally. Rather, what we can say is that the cities of the Middle East and North Africa which came under Islamic rule were affected by its religious and legal requirements, and that, in turn, early Islam was affected by the culture of urban life it encountered in the course of its expansion. This interaction gave rise to a great variety of urban forms that, in spite of their differences, exhibited a certain degree of similarity based on their shared system of religious, cultural, and social values.

Concentration of power and wealth. Riches and military and political power tend to gravitate toward urban centers. The advent of Islamic rule did not, with one major exception, entail any radical new prescriptions for city life. It gave rise, instead, to a number of gradual, organic modifications of preexisting urban forms and traditions, ultimately resulting in cities and towns that were recognizably "Islamic." The concentration of power and wealth in the cities was even greater than in preceding periods. Cities and towns were the seats of governmental and legal administration and of religious learning and education. Most importantly, the physical holders of power, the rulers and their military entourages, were almost exclusively located in their urban palaces and citadels. The surpluses of the agricultural hinterlands in the form of taxes flowed into their coffers and then out into the cities. This served as a powerful stimulus to the expansion of economic life, the growth of trade and urban

Mosque and marketplace, depicted in a Safavid miniature attributed to Mīrzā ʿAlī, mid 16th century. COURTESY OF THE FREER GALLERY OF ART, SMITHSONIAN INSTITUTION, WASHINGTON, D.C.

markets, and the development of crafts and industry, as well as to the flourishing of learning. Art and architecture were patronized and subsidized by the rulers and members of the urban elite. By the late eighth century the political unity of Islam began to fray at the edges. New autonomous dynasties frequently translated into new cities, or at least new regional capitals, with their own centers of administration and education, their own markets and mosques, palaces and citadels, and other types of monumental architecture; such was the case with Baghdad for the Abbasids, Cairo for the Fatimids, Fēs for the Idrisids, and Marrakech for the Almoravids. Thus, the first few centuries of the Islamic era witnessed the increased prominence of cities as centers of power and culture. In some cases this happened at the expense of smaller towns and villages. For example, archaeologists have found

that in Iraq, in the land behind Baghdad, many of the lesser, pre-Islamic urban settlements disappeared in the Islamic period.

Coastal cities. Most of the pre-Islamic cities of the Near East and North Africa continued their existence undisturbed into the Islamic era. Many, however, experienced significant changes in their political and economic roles. An examination of the distribution of Islamic cities in the Middle East during the Middle Ages reveals a striking fact. No major political or administrative center was located on the seacoast. Furthermore, even though there were numerous Islamic coastal towns of some economic and commercial importance, the major entrepôts of trade and economic life were invariably located some distance inland. On the Mediteranean coastline, which came under Islamic domination in the seventh and eighth centuries, Antioch and Caesarea gave way to Damascus and Ramle (the administrative, inland capital of Palestine); Alexandria yielded to Cairo; and Carthage to Qayrawān.

An ambivalence and wariness with regard to the sea characterized the medieval Muslim polities of the Mediterranean. The sea was a menacing frontier to the Muslim rules of the Middle East. This view of the sea remained a motif of Islamic political and military thinking throughout the Middle Ages. The threat of the sea to the medieval Islamic world of the Mediterranean did not derive from its unpredictable winds and storms, but was rather a "strategic" one. The sea was the one vulnerable frontier from which Islamic control of the lands bordering on the Mediterranean could be seriously threatened.

In the early years of Islam, according to Ibn Khaldūn, the caliph ʿUmar ibn al-Khaṭṭab recommended "that the Muslims be kept away from seafaring. No Arab traveled by sea save those who did so without ʿUmar's knowledge or they were punished by him for it." ʿUmar refused repeated requests of Muʿāwiya, his military commander in Syria, for permission to raid the Byzantine-held outposts on Cyprus, which, in the words attributed to Muʿāwiya, were so close to the Muslim-held Syrian coast that the Muslims could hear "the barking of the dogs of the Christians." Ibn Khaldūn attributes ʿUmar's policy to his recognition of the fact that "the Arabs were not skilled in navigation and seafaring," skills that their adversaries at that time, the Byzantines and European Christians, possessed to a high degree.

Even after the Muslims of the southern and

eastern coasts of the Mediterranean did indeed acquire many of the maritime skills of their predecessors and adversaries, this ambivalence toward the sea and naval activity persisted. Throughout the Middle Ages, the coastal towns of Syria, Palestine, and Egypt were regarded as frontier outposts. Tyre, Sidon, Ascalon (Palestine), Damietta (Dimyāṭ), and Alexandria are usually designated by the term *thaghr* (frontier fortress), the very term used to designate the march areas of raids and counter-raids on the shifting borders separating Islam from Christendom. Crete, Cyprus, Sicily, and other Mediterranean islands held by the Muslims were similarly called *ath-thughur al-jazarīya* (island frontier fortresses). Even such points as Alexandria and Damietta, where the Mediterranean coastline for hundreds of miles in either direction had been firmly under Muslim control for many centuries, the hostile and threatening area was perceived as beginning at land's end. The naval lifeline of the crusader presence in the Levant for almost two centuries reinforced Muslim wariness of the sea. The Mamluks of Egypt and Syria (*ca.* 1250–1517) embarked upon a systematic policy of destroying the fortifications of the cities and towns of the Syro-Palestinian coast, thereby denying any potential enemy a coastal foothold from which he might then penetrate inland and threaten the very foundations of their power. Ports and coastal towns of Egypt were not as severely affected by this policy as those on the Syrian coast.

Mosque and market. Historians of urban life often made comparisons between the symmetrical, broad thoroughfares and generous public spaces of classical cities and the narrow, winding streets and cramped quarters of their Islamic successors. As it turns out, this was a mistaken comparison. Medieval Islamic cities of the Middle East were the successors not of Hellenistic and Roman cities, but of the cities of late antiquity. By the seventh century, the neat grid patterns of many ancient cities had given way to much less regular forms, and various structures—both public and private—had encroached on their public plazas. While making his way from Jerusalem to Egypt, the mid-eleventh-century traveler Nāṣir-i-Khusraw noted the following: "I came to a town on the edge of the sea called Ascalon, which had a fine bazaar and cathedral mosque." The combination of mosque and marketplace was indeed the original hallmark of the Islamic city. These two institutions existed adjacent to each other in virtually all cities throughout the

Islamic domain, and together they constituted the main loci of public space within the city. Rendering to God what is God's and to Caesar what is Caesar's was not a concept that gained currency in Islam. Consequently, the distinction between religious and political space, as exemplified by the existence of a temple and an agora in Roman times, or a church and a marketplace in Christian times, did not carry over into the Islamic era.

Mosques not only inherited the religious role of the temples and churches that preceded, frequently at the identical locations, but also assumed, spatially, many of the political and cultural functions of previously discrete public places and structures. According to the Koran, the Muslims "were brothers through their religion." The basis of the early Islamic polity was the common faith: religion, community, and politics were closely intertwined. Thus, in addition to sites for congregational prayer, mosques turned into places of general public gathering where all sorts of communal and political concerns could be attended to. The earlier functions of the agora, that of public forum and meeting place, were now assumed by the mosque. As one authority noted, its very architecture proclaimed its purpose. Early mosques contained large, open inner courtyards, spacious enough to accommodate a considerable portion of a city's adult male population. In one case, that of Aleppo, the ancient agora was actually incorporated into the mosque's courtyard; in most other cases this incorporation, although symbolic and not physical, was no less real. The mosque became a center not only for religion and politics but also for all sorts of public functions. It served as a multifunction, all-purpose public building. Activities and events that in earlier ages transpired in the amphitheater, the agora, the hippodrome, and the gymnasium now had the undifferentiated space of the mosque as their setting. Worship, religious education, general administration, and public assembly all took place in mosques. The central, congregational mosques at which the community gathered for the weekly Friday noon prayer were supplemented by numerous neighborhood mosques that on a more limited scale reproduced many of the same activities. Only the largest and most populous cities boasted of more than one congregational mosque. In terms of urban life, the specific gravity of the mosque was indeed very high. In different times and different places other religious structures and spaces emerged on the urban landscape, such as the madrasa (religious college), the *muṣalla* (oratories usually located near cemeteries), and particularly the tombs and shrines of holy men, which became important centers of local pilgrimage and popular piety.

It was Aristotle's opinion that the public square and forum of the city should not be dirtied by merchandise and should not become a thoroughfare for craftsmen and workmen. The pre-Islamic cities of the Middle East appear to have heeded these views. In none do we find markets and manufacture located at the center of the city. The placement of the market at the very core of the city was an invention of Islamic urbanism. Markets shared with mosques the distinction of being the two recognized and accepted spaces for extrafamilial sociability. In Islamic towns, markets were always located around the central mosque. They were places of both manufacture and exchange. The fourteenth-century writer Ibn Baṭṭūṭa, whose travels took him from Morocco to China, observed that the structure of markets throughout the Muslim domain seemed to follow a similar pattern. First, the bazaar was organized according to trades and professions, with producers or retailers of the same merchandise occupying adjacent stalls and workshops, thus giving rise to a series of spatially defined submarkets such as the coppersmiths' market, the textile-sellers' market, the slipper-makers' market, and the like. Second, the location of the various markets with respect to the mosque frequently followed a hierarchical order. To quote Ibn Baṭṭūṭa: "Near the mosque as a religious center we will find the suppliers of the sanctuary, the market of the candle merchants, the dealers in incense and other perfumes. Near the mosque as an intellectual center we will find also the market of the booksellers, the market of the bookbinders, and, as its neighbor, the market of the leather merchants and the makers of slippers." All the baser occupations, such as tanning and dying, were located at the very edges of the market. The markets of most towns made special provisions in the form of warehouses, hostelries, and caravansaries to accommodate the merchants and merchandise involved in the flourishing international trade.

Like all markets, the market in the Islamic city was primarily a place for economic exchange; however, it was not just that. It was also the place of meeting and interaction for individuals from the different quarters of the city and for people of varying ethnic, religious, and geographic background. This amalgam of economic, social, and religious elements is reflected in the institution of the *muḥtasib,* the official assigned the task of overseeing the marketplace. This title is usually rendered in English as "market inspector." His duties, however, involved more than just supervising the honesty and harmony of the market's transactions. He was enjoined to "command the good and prevent the reprehensible," and his role can more aptly be described as a supervisor of public space and public morals. He was supposed not only to check the honest weights of the merchants and the sanitary care of foodstuffs but also to oversee the sober behavior and chaste comportment of all those who appeared in the public space of the market.

A separation between residential and commercial areas was a feature of most medieval Islamic cities. The residential areas were divided into quarters or neighborhoods, and these in turn were made up of coresidential family households. Privacy and security were the two major concerns in the topographical and architectural arrangement of these residential quarters. The social and religious values of the medieval Islamic world—values that were shared equally by its non-Muslim residents—recognized the right of each household to privacy within its own walls. Consequently, houses in medieval Muslim towns were oriented away from the streets and thoroughfares and turned inward toward their courtyards. Doors and windows were placed in a manner that maximally reduced the possibility of unwelcome visual intrusions into the intimacy of the family's life. The streets in the residential quarters were not intended to facilitate traffic. They were frequently narrow and winding, with very little open space. Restricting access to these quarters only to those who were familiar with their twists and turns served the needs of the residents by enhancing both their security and their privacy.

In observing medieval Islamic cities, any student of medieval European urbanism is bound to be struck by the absence in the Islamic context of well-articulated urban institutions. In contrast to the ancient city or to the Western communes of the later Middle Ages, Islamic cities possessed no special legal or corporate status. The town as such is not recognized in Islamic law. Nor can we identify any stable autonomous institutions for internal governance, such as guilds or municipal councils. On the whole, historians have made too much of these absences, for, as S. D. Goitein has pointed out, "the medieval Islamic city was a place where one lived, not a corporation to which one belonged." The ᶜulamāᵓ, or religious scholars, served as a cohesive force within the urban amalgam, as did the muḥtasib and a number of formal and informal groupings, including the extended families, the neighborhoods, local constabulary, and religious orders. And we can conclude by again citing Goitein:

> Despite their organizational weakness, however, the Islamic cities represented effective social realities. As seats of the government or its representatives they guaranteed relative security; as local markets or international emporiums they provided economic opportunities; and with their mosques and madrasas, their churches, synagogues, and schools, their bathhouses and other amenities, they contained all a man needed for leading a religious and cultured life.

BIBLIOGRAPHY
Robert M. Adams, *The Land Behind Baghdad* (1965); R. Brunschvig, "Urbanisme médiévale et droit musulman," in *Revue des études islamiques*, **15** (1947); Richard W. Bulliet, *The Patricians of Nishapur* (1972); Claude Cahen, "Mouvements populaires of autonomisme urbain dans l'Asie musulmane de môyen age," in *Arabica*, **5** (1958), **6** (1959); Solomon D. Goitein, *A Mediterranean Society: The Jewish Communities of the Arab World . . .*, IV: *Daily Life* (1983), 1–33, Oleg Grabar, "Cities and Citizens," in Bernard Lewis, ed., *The World of Islam* (1976), 89–116; David Herlihy, Harry A. Miskimin, and A. L. Udovitch, eds., *The Medieval City* (1977); Ibn al-Ukhuwah (Muḥammad ibn Muḥammad), *Maᶜālim al-qurba fī aḥkam al-ḥisba* [Manual of the market inspector], with a summary translation, Reuben Levy, trans. (1938); Hugh Kennedy, "From *Polis* to *Madina*: Urban Changes in Late Antique and Early Islamic Syria," in *Past and Present*, **106** (1985); Ira M. Lapidus, *Muslim Cities in the Later Middle Ages* (1967), and, as ed., *Middle Eastern Cities: A Symposium on Ancient, Islamic, and Contemporary Middle Eastern Urbanism* (1969); Jacob Lassner, *The Topography of Baghdad in the Early Middle Ages* (1970); Jean Sauvaget, *Alep* (1941); Samuel M. Stern, "The Constitution of the Islamic City," in Samuel M. Stern and Albert H. Hourani, eds., *The Islamic City* (1970), 25–50; Gustav E. von Grunebaum, "The Structure of the Muslim Town," in *Islam: Essays in the Nature and Growth of a Cultural Tradition* (1955), 141–158.

A. L. UDOVITCH

[See also **Agriculture and Nutrition: The Islamic World; Baghdad; Baṭṭūṭa, Ibn; Cairo; Córdoba; Damascus; Fēs; Islam, Conquests of; Islamic Administration; Islamic Art and Architecture; Khaldūn, Ibn; Madrasa; Marrakech; Mecca; Medina; Mosque; Muḥammad; Muḥtasib; Muṣalla; Pilgrimage, Islamic; Schools, Islamic; Ships and Shipbuilding, Mediterranean; Trade, Islamic; Travel and Transport, Islamic.**]

URBANISM, WESTERN EUROPEAN. By the time of the barbarian invasions of Europe in the fifth century, the late Roman towns of the West had begun a long decline and were shrunken considerably in size and in population. In addition, many were fortified. The fate of towns varied considerably in the age of the invasions, with urban life fading in the north, but persisting longer in the south. The Merovingian town belonged to the count and the bishop. By the Carolingian period the town had been emptied of much of its lay population, becoming essentially a clerical bastion. The ninth- and tenth-century invasions of Vikings, Saracens, and Magyars further damaged the fragile network of Western towns. From the late tenth and eleventh centuries, however, the West experienced an economic recovery, giving rise to a commercial revolution and an urban revival of impressive magnitude. Old Roman centers flourished anew, towns sprang up at propitious geographic locations, and by the twelfth century lords themselves were creating urban habitats. The twelfth and thirteenth centuries witnessed enormous demographic and economic expansion in towns. An urban patriciate emerged. Emancipation from the feudal power structure was achieved through various means; in the case of Italy, this period is aptly termed a communal age. An apogee of medieval urban development had been reached by the year 1300. Fourteenth-century crises—famines, plague, and war—devastated Western European towns, and it would only be with the demographic recovery of the later fifteenth century that many towns reestablished themselves in an era that was no longer feudal. But the lasting social, economic, and legal gains of medieval urbanism were not lost: the future of Europe belonged to the urban bourgeoisie.

THE EARLY MIDDLE AGES

One of the most dramatic instances of retrenchment and shrinkage that distinguishes the ancient world from the medieval is to be found in the medieval town. The civilizations of the Greeks and the Romans were essentially urban. The city was the site of authority, the center of administration, and the vehicle of export of ancient civilization. In contrast, the barbarians and their institutions were not, in general, associated with towns, although there certainly existed fortified enclosures, oppida, in Gaul and in Germany. The Germans had been in contact with Roman frontier towns, such as Cologne and Mainz along the Rhine and Regensburg and Budapest along the Danube, and there are reports of towns of Roman influence beyond these rivers about which we lack specific knowledge. Tacitus' remark that the Germans did not live in cities may be an overstatement, but it is founded in fact. When conquering England, the Anglo-Saxons thought towns such as London, York, and Canterbury the work of giants, and they settled outside them. In contrast, the Visigoths and Ostrogoths were more imbued with Roman urban values than were the Anglo-Saxons or, indeed, the Franks.

At Christmas 406, the Germans forced the *limes* (frontiers) of the Rhine near Mainz and crossed into Roman territory. In Gaul, northern Italy, and Spain there were reports of urban destruction such as the secondhand account given by St. Jerome. Devastation in towns of the West was profound. After the sack of Rome by Alaric the Visigoth in 410, there was some stabilization of the situation, and a modus vivendi developed between Romans and barbarians. From the end of the fifth century the Germans ceased to suppress the towns in the regions they occupied, but those towns that survived shrank further in size. In the Mediterranean areas—Italy, Spain, and southern France—towns showed considerable continuity, remaining administrative, intellectual, and financial centers.

Christianity had a profound influence on the topography of early medieval towns. After Constantine, Christian religious activities no longer needed secrecy. Churches were officially installed in towns, frequently in an old temple or on its site, in one of the large buildings of a forum, or in proximity to the urban walls. From the fourth century one finds emerging a cathedral complex made up of at least two distinct edifices, a church and a baptistery, and often three buildings, two sanctuaries, one large for important ceremonies, one small for funeral offices and again a baptistery. Whether two (the New and Old Testaments) or three (the Trinity), there was symbolic meaning behind this multiplication of structures. Close by was the episcopal palace. Additional oratories dedicated to saints were built within towns. One of the characteristics of the medieval town was the large number of urban parish churches. The cemeteries, outside along the main roads under the Romans, continued to multiply in the Merovingian suburbs. Other suburban occupants included the burgeoning monastic establishments.

The contrasts between towns of the Roman period and those of the early Middle Ages were profound. From a complex juridical vocabulary associated with towns in antiquity one passes in Merovingian times to a simplified system of classification. Three terms were used by the Merovingians to describe urban forms: civitas, castrum, and *vicus*. The civitas, now restricted to the town only, was a fortified episcopal town, the head of a diocese. According to the chronicler Fredegarius, King Rothar held that when one destroyed the wall of such a town, one had to change the appellation to *vicus*. This latter term designated an unfortified center of settlement above the level of a rural village or a rural estate. Until the tenth century, "castrum" signified every fortified locality that did not have the right of civitas. By the tenth century "castrum" had come to mean fortress per se.

Materially, little is known of the Merovingian town. Texts inform us that efforts were made at times to repair the walls. In many towns there existed in the fortifications a praetorium, or citadel residence of a military leader, a relic of Roman times. Crowding was frequent. In the late sixth century in his *History of the Franks*, Gregory of Tours noted as commonplace the fact that a house at Angers had three stories. Most domestic building was in wood; there was therefore a constant danger of fire. Gregory recounted the story of a woman who predicted a fire in Paris. In a dream she had seen a man coming from the basilica of St. Germain-des-Prés; he was holding a torch in his hand and setting fire to the merchants' houses, which sat side by side. Most public or civic edifices for the distraction of the populace in Roman times had disappeared, although arenas were occasionally used. Again, Gregory told of the repair of arenas in Paris and in Soissons. When the Merovingian king came to town, he often resided with the bishop or the count or in a suburban monastery, but rural palaces were preferred residences. The royal patrimony represented an important part of urban soil, inherited as it was from the Roman fisc or acquired through confiscations from the Gallo-Roman aristocracy. Urban and rural holdings of the church increased enormously in the seventh and eighth centuries. Communal or municipal property, by contrast, disappeared almost entirely, only to reappear in the eleventh century.

It is impossible to give any numerical estimate of Merovingian town populations. Often we are in ignorance of the surface area of towns so that even a basic maximum calculation based on town size is not feasible. It is probable that there was considerable population in the suburbs as well as inside the walls. A civitas might have several thousand inhabitants, a castrum several hundred. Ferdinand Lot suggested that Merovingian Paris had 2,000 people. Until the seventh century Syrians, Anatolians, and Jews continued to populate the towns, as we learn from the texts of Salvian, Gregory of Tours, and others. These Orientals were often engaged in long-distance commerce, at times as agents of the crown. Later, only the Jews remained, in degenerating conditions. Slaves were also a part of the Merovingian urban population. Generally, throughout the Merovingian era there was a trend toward greater homogenization of the population. What aristocratic elements remained now retreated to the countryside. The middle class diminished in size as artisanal activities developed a rural focus. On the other hand, the clergy grew in importance and in number, and until royal funds ran out in the seventh century military elements, especially garrisons of Franks in the frontier towns, formed a part of urban population.

The political role of the town was in progressive decline throughout the Merovingian period. The fifth century witnessed the creation of a new functionary, the *defensor civitatis,* who became for a time the leader of the town. Such officials were noted in Meaux in the sixth century and in Paris as late as the seventh. However, increasingly, in the absence of the Merovingian king, the count became the chief political official with military, judicial, and financial responsibilities. He was not, however, an urban magistrate. By the end of the Merovingian period both king and count had departed from the town, leaving power to the bishop. There was thus an abandonment of the link between public authority and the town. Now authority was to reside in the countryside, and a juridical distinction would develop between the town and the surrounding rural area.

With these trends, it is hardly surprising that the intellectual role of the town, that of educator under the Romans, underwent a decline. Municipal chairs of rhetoric and other disciplines persisted till the end of the fifth century in towns such as Clermont, Lyons, Vienna, and Autun, but in Gaul by the sixth century, educational functions were being transferred from the state to the church, as schools became associated with cathedrals and especially with monasteries. According to Pierre Riché, lay education, other than private tutoring, which was employed by certain senatorial families of the Midi until the mid seventh century, became a thing of the past. In Italy the Roman educational structures persisted longer. The town would experience a revival of educational functions in the eleventh and twelfth centuries, when one finds lay schools established in the shadow of cathedrals.

CAROLINGIAN TOWNS

There has been considerable historical debate about the place of the town in Carolingian civilization. Pirenne considered urban form of little importance for the Carolingians. The early Carolingians identified with rural Austrasian roots and had palaces such as those of Charles Martel at Quierzy, Verberie, Attigny, Jupille-sur-Meuse, Herstal, Meersen, and elsewhere. None of these localities had an urban quality about it. The Carolingians would cede the last urban palaces of their predecessors, the Merovingians, to the bishops. Worms alone was retained. When the Carolingian king came to town for ceremonial purposes, he invoked his hospitality rights and stayed with the bishop.

Charlemagne continued the rural traditions of the first Carolingians, holding assemblies in the country and receiving ambassadors in rural palaces. However, after his conquest of the Lombard kingdom in 774, he retained the former Lombard urban capital at Pavia and urban palaces in other towns, such as Verona. This contact with Italy may have encouraged a certain interest on Charlemagne's part in towns, first in Worms, where he made sixteen stays between the years 770 and 791, and then in Aachen, which became his principal residence from 784.

In Aachen, Charlemagne made an enormous effort to construct a monumental sort of town with a palace built in stone, whereas all the other Carolingian residences were of wood. Charlemagne took materials from Theodoric's palace in Ravenna and constructed his palatine chapel in octagonal form, copying the church of S. Vitale in Ravenna. His audience hall was modeled after the audience hall of the emperor Constantine at Trier, while his palace was an imitation of the pope's Lateran palace in Rome. Around these stone buildings

Charlemagne constructed fortifications with four gates, creating a distinctly urban impression. On the model of the Lombard capital of Pavia, he required the principal bishops of the realm to have residences at Aachen. From the time of his son Louis the Pious we have a record of the residences of merchants in the town. And the creation of a palace school restored the urban educational function.

Interest in towns continued briefly among later Carolingians. Louis the Pious legislated for the ensemble of towns within his kingdom regarding rights of hospitality and the maintenance of bridges and public buildings. In 832 a capitulary ordered a survey of public edifices, with the further order to repair them. These later Carolingian efforts were of ephemeral effect since by the second quarter of the ninth century the dismemberment of public authority had begun apace, counts were considering their offices hereditary, and royal authority was withdrawing from most towns except those within the direct domain of the sovereign.

The church had a further topographical influence on towns under the Carolingians. Grander churches were built. Carolingian canonical reform brought the construction of canonical cloisters around the cathedral. Schools and hospitals were also established. There developed a new animated cathedral quarter, which became the nucleus of the town. Ironically, in the ninth century, as the Viking invasions multiplied, bishops were opening up the old civitas area and tearing down walls. Some efforts at repair occurred between 850 and 860. Carolingian architects operated with some principles of urbanism at sites like Geneva, utilizing a rigorous gridiron plan adapted to the relatively simple needs of the time. Overall, however, the return to the town initiated by Charlemagne failed because it was linked to a political effort that did not endure.

INVASIONS OF THE NINTH AND TENTH CENTURIES

At the end of the Carolingian epoch a new period of crisis was in full swing. Europe was besieged by a second wave of invaders: Vikings, Saracens, and Magyars. Sadistic destruction is noted in the remaining texts, most of them written by clerics who described in detail the damage done to churches. These were often the first places to be attacked because they held treasures of gold and silver in the form of reliquary caskets, crosses, vessels, and other objects. Towns were burned, their suburbs ravaged. Rural populations took refuge inside urban fortifications, causing overcrowding, which made defense more difficult. The Vikings raided all along the coasts of France, the Low Countries, and England. Their longships gave them speed and enabled them to exploit the psychologically devastating element of surprise. They never drove up the Rhine, but they did reach such inland sites as Nevers on the Loire in central France and Tournus on the Saône, north of Lyons, the final but still vulnerable refuge of the monks of Noirmoutier with their relics of St. Philibert. Their saga of flight drove them from the island of Noirmoutier off the west coast of France on a futile sixty-year search for safety.

The potential for destruction on the part of all three sets of invaders was considerable, but, in the beginning at least, fortified towns could lock their gates and hold out for as long as supplies lasted. Military machines such as battering rams were necessary to take walled towns. Though at first the invaders lacked the knowledge of such military equipment, it was not long before the Vikings began to manufacture siege machinery. Except for Pavia, the Magyars rarely took towns, although they had a technique of launching burning projectiles over the walls. The Saracens paralyzed urban life and wreaked considerable destruction in Provence, in the Alps region, and in a large part of Italy. The relatively rich suburban life of Provence and Liguria disappeared.

In reaction to the threat, fortification and refortification took place in Western towns, but it was slow, hampered in the beginning by the continuing policy of using the old fortifications as a quarry. Finally in the 960's people began to fortify bridges, towns, and monasteries. Cambrai, Rheims, Paris, Troyes, and other places saw old walls restored and reinforced; by the end of the ninth century most towns were in a state of defense. Suburbs were fortified in about half the towns by additions to the old city walls or by new fortifications. In some cases, as at St. Quentin, the suburb survived the invasion shock, whereas the town did not. Recurrent raids caused enormous havoc in towns such as Poitiers.

The topographical layout of many towns was altered, with cathedral and monastic complexes generally simplified as a result. Burial restrictions for the interior of the fortifications and for the interior of churches were eliminated. Suburbs ceased to be the quarter of monks and cemeteries.

When they reappeared in the eleventh century, they were sites of economic activity and were inhabited by artisans and merchants. The old fortified civitas quarter remained essentially clerical, and the clergy retained its place as the most significant group of urban landowners. By and large, the second invasion era did not result in ruptures of urban continuity, except in a few important cases, such as the North Sea commercial centers of Duursted and Quentovic. The Viking invasions were even beneficial, since they forced the recirculation of precious metals that had been stocked in churches and monasteries.

The invasion era came to a close in the later tenth and early eleventh century. Many other factors were now also propitious for urban growth. A warmer climate and the spread of agricultural technology resulted in greater yields and a surplus that could support the more specialized nature of urban life. In the eleventh century Western Europe experienced the beginnings of a commercial revolution, which was closely linked to urban revival.

THE HIGH MIDDLE AGES

The commercial dynamism of the Italo-Byzantine towns, Venice, Amalfi, Gaeta, Naples, Bari, and Salerno—with their triangular trade linking southern Italy with North Africa and the Near East—was already well established by the late tenth century. Salt, glass, slaves, and agricultural products of southern Italy were exchanged in North Africa for gold, which was in turn used in the Near East to procure spices, silks, and other exotic products for sale in Italian markets. The *Honorantie civitatis Papie* records the influx of these items from the East. Rome was an important outlet for ceremonial cloths imported by Amalfi. Of the Italo-Byzantine towns, only Venice escaped the Norman conquest of southern Italy in the mid and late eleventh century. Venice continued to dominate Byzantine commerce, having in 1082 expanded the trading privileges first obtained in 992 from Byzantium.

The advent of the crusade era secured the fortune of Venice and of newcomers Genoa and Pisa, whose star had been rising in the late eleventh century. Acting as transporters of troops and supplies, these towns played a vital role in the victory of the Franks in the Holy Land and were amply rewarded with *fondachi* in the Syrian ports, providing them easy access to the products of the East. Antioch, Beirut, Laodicea (Al-Lādhiqiya), Gibelet, Tyre, Sidon, Acre, Jaffa, and Ascalon experienced Italian commercial colonization. French towns such as Marseilles, Montpellier, and Narbonne also established colonies in the Holy Land in the course of the twelfth century. Until the fall of Acre to the Turks in 1291, the European commercial presence along the seacoast of Syria and Palestine was significant. The islands of Cyprus and Rhodes assumed greater importance as commercial centers after the fall of Acre.

The crusade era opened the Mediterranean to European commerce, creating vital outlets for the products of the Western European cloth industry, first that of Flanders for luxury cloths, and then those of northern and southern France for cloths of lesser quality. The Flemish *drie steden* (three cities), Bruges, Ypres, and Ghent, developed thriving cloth industries in the twelfth century. By the late twelfth century the Champagne fair towns—Troyes, Provins, Lagny, and Bar-sur-Aube—were becoming centers of exchange of northern cloths for goods of the Mediterranean. In the thirteenth century an annual cycle of six fairs emerged in Champagne. Raw materials and armaments also proved much in demand as European exports, but by and large Europe ran a trade deficit, creating a drain of precious metals to the East.

Industrialization involving specialization of occupation and proto-capitalist infrastructure was a phenomenon of the urban history of the High Middle Ages. The medieval urban industry par excellence was the cloth industry. While the overall level of urbanization in Western Europe probably did not exceed 13 percent in the Middle Ages, in areas of northern Italy such as Tuscany, where there was a cloth-finishing industry (the Arte di Calimala in Florence) and, by the thirteenth century, a total cloth industry (the Arte della Lana in Florence), urbanization reached 30 percent. In Flanders, it reached 40 to 50 percent. Flemish towns became dependent on long-distance import of grains and other foodstuffs for their bustling industrial population.

Demographically, the European town expanded in the High Middle Ages. In and of themselves, medieval European towns were devourers of people, who could not reproduce themselves because of poor hygienic conditions. However, an influx of population from the overpopulated countryside provided the motor of urban demographic growth. Considerable evolution is evident in the topographic enlargement of towns. Pisa grew from 30 to 114 hectares (one hectare equals 2.47 acres) in the years 1150–1250; Bologna, from 23 to 114 hectares; and Florence, from 23 to 80. Population figures are difficult to obtain for most towns because statistical evidence is lacking. For some towns, however, evidence exists that can lead to widely differing estimates of population. The population of Paris, for example, has been estimated at from 80,000 on the low end to a high of over 200,000. Florence, Venice, and Milan had populations of upward of 100,000 by the year 1300. Flemish towns did not exceed 50,000. Towns such as Toulouse, Montpellier, and London (the latter was by far the largest town in the British Isles) had between 30,000 and 40,000. The medieval agglomeration of 5,000 or even 2,000, too, might be important and displayed characteristics that were clearly distinguishable from the rural habitat.

Town origins took many forms. Old Roman sites revived; propitious geographic features such as major crossroads or natural harbors became the loci of urban growth. Monasteries and castles acted as pre-urban nuclei. Lay and ecclesiastical lords founded towns for military, political, and fiscal motives. *Villes neuves* (new towns), *sauvetés* (sites of asylum or refuge), and *bastides* (fortified towns) abounded.

The population composition varied greatly from one town to another. A merchant patriciate made up of older noble elements and more recent mercantile achievers dominated the economic and political scene in Italy. Elsewhere, patrician lineages with strong commercial connections included few of older noble background. Monks and secular clergy continued to represent a significant, though numerically less dominant, segment of the population. Educated persons might also be numerous as towns assumed intellectual and cultural roles. In the course of the thirteenth century, urban schools were organized into universities of law, medicine, philosophy, theology, and the arts, contributing substantially to the educated personnel of towns, royal administration, and the church. To handle the complexities of business and administration, Italian towns contained hundreds of notaries: Bologna contained perhaps as many as 2,000; Florence and Padua, 600; and Milan, 1,500. Below the urban elite, tradespeople resided in considerable numbers. The food trades were an omnipresent element in medieval towns. Cloth-industry personnel might also be numerous, though revisionist studies of the composition of Italian urban population, in Lucca and Bologna, for example, suggest that the figures

of medieval contemporary historians, such as Giovanni Villani, are extremely inflated. Medieval towns often contained a fair number of agricultural workers. Finally, one must note the existence of a vagabond population of have-nots, the *nichils* of medieval tax records, whose numbers may have been dependent on the charitable and health facilities—monasteries and hospitals—available in a particular town.

It is with the High Middle Ages that studies of the medieval urban family become possible. By the eleventh century, agnatic lineage had triumphed among the nobility over the relatively equal influence of maternal and paternal lines of descent in the early Middle Ages, though in towns such as Ghent, among the urban bourgeoisie, maternal kinship was still of considerable importance. Dowry and inheritance practices varied considerably from region to region throughout Europe. The persistence of clans and their geographic grouping within towns characterized northern and southern Europe.

Professional organizations in the form of guilds or corporations grouped members of the same occupation or people of a common economic background. Children were apprenticed early to members of the urban trades and underwent lengthy training in their specialties. Women participated extensively in the urban economy of crafts and industry but rarely found their way to full membership in guilds. Urban women, like women in general, experienced the increasingly restrictive effects of bureaucratization and formalization of guilds, universities, and political administrations. By the mid thirteenth century, trades frequently adopted statutes dictating the nature and function of their occupations. Well before the formalization of professional ties, the association of individuals by occupational orientation had been common and often spawned political offshoots.

Politically, it was the elite merchant class, excluding women, that dominated urban government, always oligarchical in nature throughout the Middle Ages. In Italy, where urban autonomy was first to flourish, the mercantile sector, comprised of numerous noble elements, asserted formal independence of governance in the tenth and eleventh centuries. Consulates were formed, often with representation of groups within the elite. Pisa, Biandrate, Asti, Milan, Arezzo, and Genoa all preserve some reference to such an institution before the year 1100. Milan's communal government of 1130 consisted of ten *capitanei* (tenants-in-chief), seven *vavassores* (subvassals), and six citizen commoners. Urban political institutions were in flux in Milan and elsewhere for a time, with the number of consuls varying considerably. Small and large councils with a general assembly of all enfranchised citizens were also part of the governing structure. Many Italian towns emancipated themselves completely from the local lord's authority. The victory of the Lombard League of towns in the late-twelfth-century struggle against Emperor Frederick I Barbarossa (Legnano, 1176; Peace of Constance, 1183) assured Italian urban independence in the north.

Elsewhere in Europe bishops, lay nobles, and kings were at times the antagonists and at times the protagonists of the urban autonomy movement. At a minimum, freedom of personal status and release from the characteristic burdens of the manorial regime were assured. In its most advanced form, urban independence signaled fiscal, economic, judicial, and political autonomy. Louis VI, Louis VII, and Philip II granted many charters to towns of Capetian France. The success of this movement usually varied in inverse proportion to the power of the secular authority, particularly the king. Where there was a strong king, as in England, towns did not achieve true independence of governance. Similarly, with the reigns of Louis IX and Philip IV, French towns began to lose their autonomy.

Southern French consulates owed a great deal to the Italian model and appeared about fifty years after the first Italian examples. Fiscal, military, and economic prerogatives resided with the consular government. Whereas in theory justice remained in seigneurial hands, in practice it tended to be dominated by the consuls. In central France the prominent institution was the town of franchise or privilege, with less autonomy of operation than the consulate; model charters, such as those of Lorris-en-Gâtinais and of Beaumont-en-Argonne, influenced 80 and 500 towns, respectively. In northern France the communes—of which there were never many—enjoyed a relatively brief era of independent urban government. Generally they were established in a violent revolution before the king could assert his influence.

The late-eleventh-century communal movement in Germany coincided with that in France. Sworn association was initiated by the merchants, who opposed the local lord, often the bishop, as in Italy. The establishment of urban autonomy in some cases came after violence, as at Cambrai in 1076,

Cologne in 1074 and 1112, and Worms in 1073. In other cases, it resulted from peaceful measures, as at Freiburg im Breisgau in 1121 and Lübeck in 1159.

In Italy, Germany, Flanders, and, to a lesser degree, France the thirteenth century witnessed an internal power struggle in the towns, first between the old patriciate and the newcomers to economic fortune and later between these groups and the tradespeople. The political solution to urban turmoil often came in the form of more autocratic rule.

THE LATE MIDDLE AGES

The fourteenth and fifteenth centuries were for Western Europe an era of crisis: political, social, economic. Famine, plague, and war wracked town and countryside alike with death and destruction. Individual towns suffered in varying degrees from these troubles, but, overall, the great expansive trend of urban growth in the previous three centuries came to an end.

Towns, particularly those on the Continent, continued to field militias and to organize into leagues in the later Middle Ages. The victory of the Flemish urban militias over the flower of French chivalry at Courtrai in 1302 was followed by their devastating defeat at the hands of the French at Cassel in 1328. The Matins of Bruges in 1302, when French officials and urban patrician supporters of the French were massacred by tradespeople, reflected the kind of violent conflict that could erupt in towns. The urban upheavals surrounding the regime of Jacob van Artevelde in Ghent at mid century were echoed in revolts in the late 1350's against the demagoguery of Étienne Marcel, the provost of the Water Merchants in Paris. Revolts occurred periodically in southern French towns during the fourteenth century. In Germany bitter conflict separated the older patrician regimes from the craft guilds, which fought to gain admission to urban government. The Ciompi revolt in Florence in 1378 was only one example of late medieval Italian urban violence.

With the growing weakness of central government in Germany following the end of the Hohenstaufen dynasty, leagues such as the League of Rhenish Cities organized to preserve some political stability; they soon found themselves at odds with the aggrandizing territorial princes. In Italy, towns that had long been autonomous vis-à-vis any central power warred with one another as their signori leaders or, in the case of Florence, the more diversified but primarily oligarchic leadership, sought to expand their regional influence and bring smaller towns under their control.

The revival of hostilities with England at the opening of the Hundred Years War in 1337, after over a century of peace following the reconquests in western France by Philip Augustus, meant that France was again the battleground. A spate of refortification and enlargement of fortification was carried out in areas of the south of France where the mercenary companies marauded in the 1350's. Urban inhabitants went to new extremes to ensure their safety. The population of Montpellier manufactured an enormous wax devotional candle identical in length with the new suburban fortifications in order to supplement spiritually their physical defense against Duguesclin and his crew.

Another and perhaps more sinister development associated with war was the royal predilection for increased urban taxation. Demands made on towns for contributions to aid the French king's efforts in Flanders or against the English in France pepper the fourteenth and fifteenth centuries. Only St. Louis in an earlier era had been as exacting on towns around Paris, such as Beauvais, in the preparations for his crusades.

Internal urban violence and regional and "national" warfare occurred in an increasingly strained economic climate. Subsistence problems struck the urban setting by the early fourteenth century as the food needs of the European population overall outpaced the productivity of the agricultural economy. Some historians see a Malthusian crisis in the situation. Falling agricultural yields, the exhaustion of marginal lands that had been pressed into cultivation, and a deteriorating climate contributed to the difficulties. Municipal chronicles of the late thirteenth and the early fourteenth century contain a constant litany of natural disasters. People lived in fear of cold spells, storms, and, alternatively, long droughts, against which there was no defense. Agriculture enjoyed only limited technology and anything but hardy plants. Moreover, difficulties of transportation and ignorance of food preservation meant that surplus in one area could not be husbanded for future crises or shipped to areas already in need.

Prices fluctuated wildly in the late Middle Ages, especially in inland towns. The most volatile commodities were grains. At Toulouse from November 1374 to April 1375 grain prices rose 300 percent;

from November 1375 to August 1376 they declined by 500 percent. During the years 1360–1450, grain prices on an index of 100 ranged from 22 to 712. Industrial goods showed less variation: wax went from 76 to 125; pastel dye, from 50 to 140.

For towns dependent on imports of food, especially grain, from the immediate area and often from farther afield, the results were shortages and a rise in food prices, resulting in great hardship, malnutrition, and often starvation for the urban poor. For example, during the famine of 1316 the port of Bruges in Flanders could procure supplies from ports of the estuary much more easily than could the inland town of Ypres. From 1 May to 30 October 1316, there were more than 2,000 deaths in Bruges and 2,800 in Ypres (77 and 108 per week), representing respectively about 5.5 percent and 10 percent of the urban population. In a normal period the death rate of these towns was about fifteen to sixteen per week. In an era of crisis such as that of 1315–1317, the death toll could rise to between 150 and 190 a week.

A concomitant of the great famine of 1315–1317 was disease related to improper growing conditions, in this case excess moisture. Ergotism evolved from the overgrown grain of rye, which developed a fungus containing a lethal acid. It attacked the undernourished, burning them up with thirst. Another, gangrenous form manifested itself primarily in France, and a deadly nerve form struck Germany. People who ate sheep that had contracted anthrax themselves acquired this bacterial disease, which caused external ulcerating nodules or lesions in the lung. Because of the instability of the agricultural economy and the problems of productivity dating from the late thirteenth century, the urban populations were weakened in health and vulnerable to epidemics, the worst of which was still to come.

The Black Death reached Europe in late 1347, carried from the Near East by Genoese galleys escaping from the Turkish siege of Caffa on the Black Sea. The Turks, infected with the plague, had catapulted victims over the walls, thus infecting the urban population. The Genoese vessels landed first in Sicily, whence the plague spread along the trade routes to Genoa, Venice, and the south of France in 1348. In January 1348 it was reported at Marseilles, and by the spring of 1348 it had reached Paris. While continuing in areas already attacked, the plague struck London in fall 1348, Vienna in 1349, Strasbourg in 1349, the Low Countries in

1349, Ireland in 1349, Scandinavia in 1349–1350. The first siege of the plague was over by 1352. However, it would recur at intervals of ten or twenty years throughout the fourteenth and much of the fifteenth century. The last major outbreak of the plague in Western Europe occurred in the 1720's.

A demographic plateau, and indeed, a demographic downtrend, detected in some towns, such as Pistoia, in the early fourteenth century gave way with the onslaught of the plague to a dramatic population decline. From 31,220 in the area of Pistoia in 1244, the population dropped to 4,772 in 1427. The population of Toulouse went from about 30,000 in 1335 to about 8,000 in 1430. While most towns may never have been totally deserted in this era, ghost towns or villages can be counted in the hundreds in Germany and England. Some few towns escaped demographic decline and actually increased in size. Lübeck and other Hanseatic cities, such as Rostock, Dutch cities, and Milan in Italy were among those that experienced growth.

In social terms, case studies of towns, such as Albi, indicate that the urban social and economic structure was not radically altered in the plague era, despite major demographic losses. Women of the urban mercantile elite in the late Middle Ages experienced an increase in sex-segregated roles, which foreshadowed the capitalist society and economy of early modern Europe. While individual women such as Margery Kempe and whole urban groups such as the beguines exercised impressive self-determination and were undeniably visible, historians seem in basic agreement about the downturn in the status of women by the end of the Middle Ages.

CONCLUSION

The crisis of the fourteenth and fifteenth centuries left the urban landscape of Europe, forged by the urban revival of the High Middle Ages, diminished but otherwise essentially unchanged. At the end of the fifteenth century demographic and economic recovery was visible everywhere. Europe was embarking on the great age of discoveries, in which towns and their merchant inhabitants would be major participants, though now, except in Italy, in association with the early modern state. The urban Middle Ages left a permanent legacy in economy, society, and government for later centuries.

BIBLIOGRAPHY

Maurice Beresford, *New Towns in the Middle Ages: Town Plantation in England, Wales, and Gascony* (1967); Edith Ennen, *Frühgeschichte der europäischen Stadt* (1953); Eugen Ewig, "Residence et capitale pendant le haut moyen âge," in *Revue historique*, **230** (1963); André Gouron, "Diffusion des consulats méridionaux et expansion du droit romain aux XIIᵉ et XIIIᵉ siècles," in *Bibliothèque de l'École des chartes*, **121** (1963); Jacques Heers, *Family Clans in the Middle Ages: A Study of Political and Social Structures in Urban Areas*, Barry Herbert, trans. (1977); David Herlihy, *Pisa in the Early Renaissance: A Study of Urban Growth* (1958) and *Medieval and Renaissance Pistoia* (1967); idem and Christiane Klapisch-Zuber, *Les toscans et leurs familles* (1978); A. B. Hibbert, "The Origins of the Medieval Town Patriciate," in *Past and Present*, 3 (1953); Martha Howell, *Women, Production, and Patriarchy in Late Medieval Cities* (1986); Diane Owen Hughes, "Urban Growth and Family Structure in Medieval Genoa," in *Past and Present*, 66 (1975); John K. Hyde, *Padua in the Age of Dante* (1966); Jean Lestocquoy, *Les villes de Flandre et d'Italie sous le gouvernement des patriciens* (1952); Robert S. Lopez, *The Commercial Revolution of the Middle Ages* (1971) and "Of Towns and Trade," in Robert S. Hoyt, ed., *Life and Thought in the Early Middle Ages* (1967); Harry A. Miskimin, *The Economy of Early Renaissance Europe, 1300–1460* (1969); idem, David Herlihy, and A. L. Udovitch, eds., *The Medieval City* (1977); John H. Mundy, *Liberty and Political Power in Toulouse, 1050–1230* (1954) and, with Peter Riesenberg, *The Medieval Town* (1958); Lucien Musset, *Les invasions: Le second assaut contre l'Europe chrétienne, VIIᵉ–XIᵉ siècles*, 2nd ed. (1971), and *Les invasions: Les vagues germaniques* (1965), trans. as *The German Invasions* (1975); David Nicholas, "Medieval Urban Origins in Northern Continental Europe: State of Research and Some Tentative Conclusions," in *Studies in Medieval and Renaissance History* (Lincoln, Nebraska), 6 (1969), *Town and Countryside: Social, Economic, and Political Tensions in Fourteenth-century Flanders* (1971), and *The Domestic Life of a Medieval City* (1985); Charles Petit-Dutaillis, *Les communes françaises* (1947); Henri Pirenne, *Medieval Cities: Their Origins and the Revival of Trade*, Frank D. Halsey, trans. (1925); Hans Planitz, *Die deutsche Stadt im Mittelalter* (1965); Colin Platt, *The English Medieval Town* (1976); Johan Plesner, *L'émigration de la campagne à la ville libre de Florence au XIIIᵉ siècle* (1934); Susan Reynolds, *An Introduction to the History of English Medieval Towns* (1977); Fritz Rörig, *The Medieval Town* (1967); Josiah Cox Russell, *Late Ancient and Medieval Population* (1958) and *Medieval Regions and Their Cities* (1972); Carl Stephenson, *Borough and Town* (1933); Louis Stouff, *Arles à la fin du moyen âge*, 2 vols. (1986); Richard E. Sullivan, *Aix-la-Chapelle in the Age of Charlemagne* (1963); James Tait,

The Medieval English Borough (1936); Sylvia L. Thrupp, *The Merchant Class of Medieval London* (1948); Daniel Waley, *Mediaeval Orvieto* (1952) and *The Italian City Republics* (1969); Philippe Wolff, *Commerces et marchands de Toulouse (vers 1350–1450)* (1954).

KATHRYN L. REYERSON

[See also **Aldermen; Baptistery; Barbarians, Invasions of; Bastide; Beguines and Beghards; Black Death; Borough (England-Wales); Carolingians and the Carolingian Empire; Castles and Fortifications; Charter; Class Structure, Western; Commune; Constitutio de Feudis; Consuls, Consulate; Demography; Échevin; Fairs; Family, Western European; Famine in Western Europe; Food Trades; German Towns; Guilds and Métiers; Hanseatic League; Italy, Rise of Towns in; Lombard League; Markets, European; Mayor; Podesta; Schools, Cathedral; Schools, Grammar; Taxation; Trade, European; Universities;** and articles on individual cities.]

URBANISM, WESTERN EUROPEAN: ARCHITECTURAL ASPECTS

TOWNS IN THE EARLY MIDDLE AGES

Little is known of the physical layout of cities and towns before the year 1000. Recent archaeological excavations, however, have begun to provide evidence for some continuity of an urban tradition between the collapse of Roman administrative authority and the rise of merchant towns after the eleventh century.

Some Roman cities were occupied as administrative centers for local rulers—whether Byzantine, Merovingian, Lombard, or Carolingian. The Lombards preserved some degree of urbanism through their designation of thirty-five cities as duchies, among them Milan, Pavia, Cividale, Verona, Brescia, Spoleto, Benevento, Pistoia, and Lucca. Pavia, as residence of the Lombard king, especially flourished. Roman structures were maintained, and some new palaces and churches were erected by Lombard patrons. There is no evidence, however, that the Lombard rulers had an urban vision. They inherited fully developed, but badly maintained, ancient urban infrastructures, which they kept up as best they could when it served their purpose.

The collapse of towns was a gradual process of demographic decline, loss of function, and material impoverishment. In the marble-exporting town of Luni, poor wooden huts occupied the former civic center as late as the sixth century. In Verona and Brescia, which continued as occupied centers throughout the early Middle Ages, there was much less dense settlement, but certain building characteristics tied the site to the past—for instance, building houses along the old Roman street lines.

In many parts of Italy, and even more in other parts of the empire, urban sites were totally abandoned for up to several centuries. In Britain, dozens of towns and forts were left empty, only to be resettled during the Anglo-Saxon period, when walled enclosures provided ideal defenses. Sparse occupation sometimes continued for religious or political reasons on an older site, but the earlier urban activities and functions were lost. A church or a royal residence might serve, at best, to mark the spot for future resettlement and diversification of social and economic activity.

Mainz, for example, continued to be known as a civitas throughout the early Middle Ages and housed a bishop. It had, however, few other traditional urban characteristics. In the ninth century the town consisted of farms, vineyards, orchards, and small plots separated by country lanes. Large areas must have been without any buildings. So, too, appeared Rome. Large numbers of documents from the late Middle Ages mention fields, orchards, and vineyards; and maps and drawings from the sixteenth century show most of the area of the ancient city still under cultivation.

The most densely populated and most economically active settlements in Europe in the early Middle Ages were not in the old Roman world, but on the shores of the North Sea, where after the late seventh century there emerged specialized trading and industrial centers. These were mostly new settlements, though in Britain, London and York were established on Roman sites. The Anglo-Saxon trading centers situated on the coast or on rivers have names that include the element *wic* or *wih*, which likely referred specifically to the trading aspect of the place. Southampton, known as Hamwih, may have had its origins in the increased prosperity under Ine (*r.* 688–726). Specifically, it was probably due to the increasing importance of nearby Winchester as a royal and episcopal center. The two centers complemented each other, Hamwih concentrating on commercial and industrial activities, and having signs of a large population, while Winchester had the king, bishop, and private estates. Winchester, with its royal and ecclesiastical authorities, was called *urbs* and *civitas*. Hamwih was designated *mercimonium, villa, pagus, wih, wic,* and *tun.*

At Southampton, traces of settlement cover thirty-seven hectares (about ninety-two acres), with evidence of substantial long-distance trading activity in the form of imported pottery and glass, lava millstones, and coins. There is evidence for the working of bronze, iron, lead, and silver (including the minting of coins); the manufacture of pottery and textiles; and the production of wood, bone, and antler objects. A system of gravel roads ran parallel and at right angles to the riverbank and was repeatedly repaired until the abandonment of the site in the tenth century. The settlement does not seem to have been fortified. In a commercial sense Hamwih was an active urban place, and undoubtedly had one of the largest population concentrations in Britain at that time. It seems, though, to have lacked the civic, political, and religious institutions that would have given it a fuller urban life.

Other trading centers were even larger than Hamwih. Dorestad, near Utrecht in Holland, was situated at the junction of the Rhine and Lek rivers. In the course of two centuries it grew to cover an area of over 200 hectares (about 500 acres). As a trading center and port it was an important intermediary in the exchange of wine, pottery, glass, and grinding stones with less sophisticated northern kingdoms abundant in raw materials. Dorestad appears to have peaked between 780 and 830, when wooden merchant buildings stretched along the river banks, obscuring the native village that was the nucleus of the site. Plank walkways were built out into the river from the buildings to connect them directly with boats. Dorestad may have been the base of the Frisian traders who are frequently mentioned in early medieval sources.

Hamwih and *wics* like it, and the international entrepôts such as Dorestad, do not fit formally or politically into the mainstream of European town development. Their activities as trading centers where goods and customs from northern and southern Europe, as well as Asia, were exchanged did, however, lay a foundation for the more widespread mercantile activities of the eleventh century, which spurred the development of the independent town of the later Middle Ages.

TYPES OF TOWNS

The medieval town had many forms. Each was the result of unique circumstances that shaped it: history, geography, economy, and more. Yet, the many common elements of medieval towns that allow us to speak of a "medieval urbanism" at all reflect the realities of medieval society. These often outweighed distinctions in creating the urban environment of the Middle Ages.

Medieval towns essentially developed from four different beginnings: (1) those that continued on from antiquity, retaining their basic rectangular forms, or continued on ancient sites that never had grid plans; (2) those that grew up in the post-antique period naturally, without systematic planning, around castles, monasteries, or independent church structures; (3) those that grew up on a favorable location—a trading post or rest stop, a crossroads or a river ford; (4) those that were newly founded in their entirety.

Towns of Roman origin. From the third century on, the threat of invasion caused towns to build defensive walls, often greatly reducing their actual size to maximize defensive capability and minimize defensive costs. These new wall circuits, including the one built around Rome by Emperor Aurelian (r. 272–279), would define the limits of many European towns for centuries to come. Cities where episcopal sees had been established sometimes survived—though frequently they did not. In the Lombard duchies of Spoleto and Benevento, of some 100 bishoprics, only about one-tenth survived by 700.

When occupation continued, it was in the shadow of ancient remains. The old city forms survived because they were too difficult to remove. The ground level rose with the accumulation of rubble and organic debris. New buildings, even of the most temporary sort, used the ancient walls as foundations. Pathways often continued to follow the ancient streets, since these were the least obstructed passages. But as debris accumulated, the old streets narrowed and the straight streets curved. Dozens of towns, when demographic, economic, and political circumstances allowed them to revive, continued what was essentially the old Roman street network within the old Roman walls, but with many small adjustments.

Ancient public buildings remained in place, too big to move or destroy totally. Sometimes they were fortified, as in Rome, where by the twelfth century theaters, amphitheaters, and arches became urban castles, and the mausoleum of Emperor Hadrian became Castel Sant'Angelo, stronghold of the city and bridgehead at the surviving central Tiber crossing. The amphitheater of Nîmes actually became the city when it was fortified by the Visigoths. And at Arles, when the outer walls of the town were destroyed in the eighth century, the amphitheater was fortified and settled, and the arena became the town square.

During the early Middle Ages there were also new settlements founded by refugees from invasion and disease. Defensible sites were chosen on hilltops, where tightly packed villages closed to the outside were established; and on islands, where water acted as a protective barrier. The Orthodox Christians of Aquileia found refuge from the Lombards on the island of Grado, and Venice probably was founded at the same time.

Natural towns. Perhaps the most common type of medieval town development was the process of encirclement, in which some central element—such as a castle, church, or monastery—attracted settlers, who built close to the attracting building until it formed the core of an urban community. Encircled cores often later became the focal points of radial towns, especially when more than one road led to the center. Roads leading to the center were like the spokes of a wheel. When development reached a certain point along these spokes, a wall often was built that enclosed the inner core, the radiating roads, and the emptier spaces between the roads. These spaces could be slow to fill up because they were not directly connected with the center. In some towns inner ring roads opened these wedge-shaped areas for developing, but in many cases they remained lightly settled and under cultivation, while more intensive growth continued along the radial roads outside the protective wall.

The generative element of the linear, strip, or ribbon plan was a single street or road, along or around which the rest of the settlement grew. A major route—for trade or for pilgrimage—might spawn many such settlements. Starting as a rest stop, post stop, or ferry crossing, the site would then develop support communities. The focus of the settlement was always the central street, which might in time be widened to accommodate a market. Where the topography allowed, settlement often expanded on either side of the main route, or on one side if the road skirted a riverbank or seashore.

More complex variants of the linear town developed at crossroads, where growth along more than one axis was possible, thus forming a cross. The intersection often served as a market area that later could be developed into a more regular space.

When development of an intersection of perpendicular roads was more systematic, a series of cross axes in both directions could develop, creating a grid plan with dominant central streets.

PLANNED TOWNS

There were few newly planned towns in Europe before the twelfth century. Only in Anglo-Saxon England, where Alfred the Great and his successors created a network of fortified settlements as a defensive strategy against the Danish armies then occupying part of the country, was systematic town foundation undertaken.

After his victory over the Danes at Edington (878) Alfred set out to defend his kingdom of Wessex, and to establish a base for the reconquest of England, by securing thirty defended places, so spaced that no part of the kingdom was more than thirty kilometers (about twenty miles) from a fortified center. The forts established by Alfred varied greatly in size and in the number of men required for their defense. Ten sites can be called forts, and the remaining can be regarded as towns of simple physical and social organization. These include four resettled Roman walled towns (Winchester, Chichester, Bath, and Exeter), four new towns with rectangular perimeters on previously open sites (Wallingford, Wareham, Cricklade, and Oxford), and twelve new fortified settlements on promontory sites (including Lydford, Lyng, Malmesbury, and Shaftesbury).

The towns show traces of rectilinear street layouts, and in the larger places the grid was linked to the fortifications by a ring of streets just within the walls. This internal ring allowed rapid movement within the walls by the town's defenders. The regular layout of rectangular blocks within the ring suggests a policy of equal land distribution for settlers.

The largest of these settlements was Winchester. As the result of extensive excavations, our knowledge of the development of that town is considerable. It occupied the full area of 58.2 hectares (about 145 acres) within older Roman walls, with the southeastern area of the city forming a royal and ecclesiastical quarter containing cathedral, royal palace, and (from the late tenth century) bishop's palace. Street names of the late tenth and eleventh centuries indicate the concentration of economic activities within the town—Tannerestret (tanners' street), Flesmangerestret (butchers' street), Scowrtenestret (shoemakers' street), and Sildwortenestret

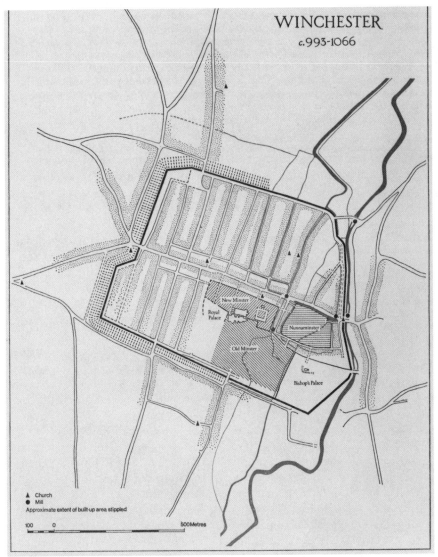

Plan of Winchester, *ca.* 993–1066. REPRODUCED FROM *WINCHESTER IN THE EARLY MIDDLE AGES.* © 1976 OXFORD UNIVERSITY PRESS

(shieldmakers' street). Similar town divisions existed in York, then a Viking center, around the same time.

The urban framework of tenth-century Winchester was the regular street layout that is still in use today. The main elements of this are a preexisting east-west thoroughfare (High Street); a single back street parallel to High Street on either side; a series of regularly spaced and parallel north-south streets at right angles to High Street; and an intramural or wall street running inside the entire circuit of the walls, linking the ends of High Street and the north-south streets. This layout diverges noticeably

from the Roman street pattern. Only High Street approximates the path of an earlier Roman street, and this is due to its role of funneling traffic between the gates in the town wall.

In the twelfth and thirteenth centuries, as a result of population increase and territorial expansion by militarily dominant states, a wave of town foundation swept Europe. The rise of regionalism, in which one central city or state expanded its power over a wide territory and established satellite towns reliant on the founding city, caused large numbers of new towns to be built in southwest France, England, Wales, northern Italy, and eastern Germany. Royal, noble, and communal patrons used the enticement of personal liberties to draw settlers to their new foundations. In return they expected greater control over the territory and increased tax revenues due to new commercial activity.

The most common plan for these towns was the orthogonal grid, especially for towns built on level sites; but the grid plan varied in the number of intersecting streets, the total number of blocks created, the size of the area laid out, the amount and location of open space left within the grid, and the relative importance of central axes. Medieval planners used the grid flexibly, often subordinating it to the natural contour of the site. This provided more comfort, was aesthetically more pleasing, and cost much less, for it meant less excavation and leveling of new streets. In most new towns the streets were laid out at the time of foundation, but buildings often were not erected until the fourteenth and fifteenth centuries, if at all. Few of these towns had the potential for becoming important independent centers. Lübeck and Leipzig, attached to older, well-sited centers, are exceptions.

Among the earliest of the new towns was Montauban in southwest France, founded by Alphonse-Jourain, count of Toulouse, in 1144 with settlers from the town of Montauriol who were eager to escape service to their lord. The new town, on the Tarn River, was walled and was laid out on an irregular grid that emanated from an open square in the center of town. Though a local effort, the creation of Montauban, ex novo, marks the beginning of an age of deliberate town planning in Europe on an extremely large scale. Close to 1,000 new towns were started across Europe during the following two centuries.

In France the new frontier towns were called bastides. The towns were small, often consisting only of the blocks that faced a central market square. Besides donating the land, the founder paid for the laying out and leveling of the streets and the square. He might also construct a mill, a bakehouse, and other facilities that would pay for themselves over time. If the town was successful, the founder could expect a good return from his investment, much more than if he had put the land under cultivation. The land was subdivided into plots, an arrangement that was facilitated if a grid plan was followed, and a plot was assigned to each settler, who was responsible for building his own house within a specified period of time. Towns founded for a specific military purpose were walled. Of the

nonmilitary, only those founded by a particularly strong or rich patron could expect such expensive protection. About a third of the new towns in France and England were fortified.

Aigues-Mortes and the *ville nueve* at Carcassonne, founded by St. Louis in the 1240's, and Montpazier, founded by Edward I of England in 1284–1285, represent the most sophisticated examples of this type. Other founders of bastides include Alphonse of Poitiers, who established at least thirty-nine separate towns in the mid 1200's, and Eustache de Beaumarchais, royal seneschal at Toulouse, who founded a number of large grid-plan bastides in the 1280's.

Bastides had plans that accommodated site peculiarities. One type, used for a hill site with a castle on the summit, was to have a single main street snake up the hill, often narrowing as it approached the top. Side streets branched off the main artery in a fishbone pattern, with more streets off the lower side than off the upper. The main square was at the bottom of the hill. A variation was used for towns, or town extensions, laid out on shoulder spurs. The main artery followed the ridge; the side streets branched off and ran down either side.

There were 172 new town foundations in medieval England after the Norman conquest, 84 in Wales, and 125 in English Gascony. The grid plan is a common layout of these foundations, though linear and radial towns also were laid out. The towns with grids can be divided into two classes: one with a total of nine or twelve squares, and one much larger and easily expandable on its long axis. The size of the grid often depended on the restrictions of the site. For the market, a block of the grid was sometimes left open, but markets were often set on the town's high street or along river quays.

The fullest account we have of the foundation of a new town in England is the creation of new Winchelsea by King Edward I. Special meetings of experts were called to "devise, order, and array" the new town before its creation. The old town, a port city, was being washed away by storms and shifting river currents, and the king was losing his tax revenues. Edward I chose a new site, on a hill, to refound the town. A grid plan was imposed, with streets intersecting at right angles to create thirty-nine blocks (quarters). The east-west streets were numbered: Prima Strata, Secunda Strata, Tertia Strata, and so on. The surveyor of the site, Henry le Waleys, was told, "You shall plan and give direc-

Carcassone, showing Visigothic walls of the 6th century. PHOTO: DANIEL PHILIPPE

tions for streets and lanes, and assign places suitable for a market and for two churches." A monastery for the White Friars was built over two quarters. Land for a cemetery also was included, as was a twelve-acre King's Green at the southeast corner of town. Wells were dug, and, beneath the houses built for merchants, vaulted cellars were excavated and built. The market space was along one of the main north-south streets near the center of town. Unlike many other new towns, an empty block of the grid was not left for commerce. At new Winchelsea, most mercantile activity probably took place on the quay below the town.

In Italy, more new towns were founded for defense than for income, and they were often sited at preexisting crossroads for strategic reasons, then fortified. A typical example is Castelfranco Veneto, founded in 1189 by Treviso as a stronghold against the Paduans. It is enclosed within square walls and has a strong east-west axis, onto which open two piazzas catercorner to each other, with a minor north-south axis that ends at the crossing. The other streets form concentric squares within the wall enclosure.

In Cittadella, built in 1210–1211 by the Paduans, the two axes of the crossing are essentially equal. They completely dominate the rest of the plan, which creates a checkerboard arrangement of rectangular blocks formed by a series of east-west and north-south streets of equal width that repeatedly intersect at right angles. This grid occurs within an overall circular plan defined by enclosing walls and a surrounding moat.

A large number of new towns were founded in Piedmont. Villanova d'Asti, for example, on the road from Turin to Asti, was founded in 1248 on a grid plan comprised of three north-south streets and five east-west streets, covering one-and-a-half hectares. It was doubled in size thirty years later, following the original plan. Also in 1248 the commune of Alba founded Cherasco. The plan was a grid covering thirty hectares divided into forty-eight rectangular blocks (six rows of eight). The two main axes were lined with porticoes.

In central and southern Italy royalty founded towns on a large scale. Frederick II founded L'Aquila in 1204, and in 1256 his son Manfred built Manfredonia with materials from nearby Si-

325

Town of Feurs in the Forez district. Miniature in the 14th-century *Armorial d'Auvergne*. PARIS, BIBLIOTHÈQUE NATIONALE, MS FR. 22297, fol. 449

ponto. The new town had a rigid checkerboard plan with the piazza the result of an empty block. In 1309, Charles II of Anjou founded Cittaducale, also using a grid plan.

ELEMENTS OF THE MEDIEVAL TOWN

Town walls and gates. One of the basic characteristics of all medieval towns is the defensive wall. In many early medieval towns, and in smaller settlements, wooden palisades or defenses of wood and earth were often used. This was particularly true in northern Europe, where wood was readily available. Whenever possible, however, towns built their walls of masonry. Stone or brick walls were structurally superior and offered greater protection. The walls loomed large, both physically and psychologically. In the early Middle Ages the walls and gates were the tallest urban structures. Church towers and private fortified towers did not generally surpass town walls in height before the eleventh century. In Verona the parapet of the wall was more

than 11 meters (almost 36 feet) from the ground. In Senlis, the walls would have seemed especially large because the area they enclosed was quite small: 6.33 hectares (almost 17 acres), within a wall circuit of only 850 meters (almost 2,789 feet).

Some towns never outgrew their ancient wall circuit. Florence, in contrast, built a larger wall circuit in the 1170's, and was building a third wall by the mid fourteenth century. Todi expanded its Roman wall in the 1240's to enclose its outlying *borghi*. In Paris, Philip II Augustus ordered a new wall built around the right bank of the city, and, anticipating greater expansion on the left bank, he had the large underpopulated area walled, beginning in 1210.

New town walls followed the ancient pattern of construction. They were tall, continuous structures, marked by frequent rectangular or semicircular towers, and less frequent gates that were defended by larger protruding towers. Until the advent of modern artillery changed warfare in the fifteenth century, town walls were remarkably similar in appearance from place to place throughout Europe. Walls usually followed the most economical route, enclosing the greatest amount of space with the least amount of construction and taking into account topographical features when they could be exploited for defense. Thus, the typical medieval town wall tended to be roughly circular. Curved walls also were preferred for defensive reasons, as they left fewer blind spots than walls that met at right angles.

Walls and gates served for defense, and made it easier to regulate goods and collect tariffs. In the sixth century Gregory of Tours described the still-standing thirty-foot-high wall of Dijon, with its thirty-three towers and four gates. Gregory could not understand why such a strong walled settlement was not then called a town. In the popular perception, it certainly was one.

Within the wall were the gates. Every city gate was in some way a triumphal arch. In his city gate at Capua, Emperor Frederick II (1194–1250) fully recognized this, and consciously imitated the triumphal arch form of ancient Rome (a example was visible at nearby Benevento). Heavily decorated gates were not, however, compatible with defense, so it was not until the fifteenth century that decorative classisizing gates became common in Italy. Ordinarily, medieval gates were sober, but for festive occasions they could be richly decorated with colorful tapestries and banners.

Open spaces. In the medieval town, open space was a valuable commodity. The need for freely accessible streets and squares was balanced by the increased need for space for the full variety of urban functions, both private and public. By the thirteenth century the struggle for space within the town was partially resolved through legislation.

Urban spaces were rarely planned for a specific purpose. Streets were processional routes, markets, front yards, and playgrounds, as well as carriers of foot, animal, and wheeled traffic. Squares served as markets, religious centers, courtrooms, meeting places, theaters, military muster grounds, and even as the sites of execution. By the late Middle Ages shortage of open space forced the definition and protection of spaces that still existed. Concurrently, efforts were made to embellish these spaces. Boundaries were more carefully arranged; buildings bordering the open spaces were made more uniform whenever possible; and decorative columns and fountains often were erected.

Important buildings usually bordered open spaces or were set off by open space. Cathedrals, especially, were frequently left free on several sides. This open space, known as a parvis, allowed large gatherings of people around the church for religious celebrations and for markets.

The disparate forms and buildings of central squares were unified by arcades, often with different kinds of vertical supports and arches of different widths. Public buildings, usually churches or town halls, had monumental stairways or protruding balconies that served as spatial accents.

Streets. Streets in medieval towns were primarily for pedestrian use. Wheeled traffic was usually restricted to the few wider streets—the arteries that traversed a town from end to end. In new towns there were many more wide streets. When the bishop of Worcester founded Stratford-on-Avon, he laid out new streets fifty feet (about fifteen meters) wide and made the main market street ninety feet (about twenty-seven meters) across.

Until the late Middle Ages, when officials were designated to keep streets and squares open for the public good, the tendency was for private individuals to encroach as much as possible on public space through building facades, balconies, and porticoes. Off the main commercial streets, a rule of thumb for building was often to leave only enough space for the passage of one heavily loaded donkey to pass.

By the thirteenth century, and even earlier in some parts of Italy, the ability to annex public space for private use was increasingly limited. Towns regulated the heights of towers and the heights and widths of balconies and other projections from buildings. Even the size and position of market stalls were regulated, as were the days and ways in which shop owners could display their wares on the street.

Until the thirteenth century, medieval streets were rarely, if ever, paved. One aspect of late medieval urbanism was the widespread paving of streets. In many towns, citizens were responsible for financing the pavements in front of their properties, up to a maximum width, and tolls on carts were sometimes applied to street improvement. Public funds were assigned, or private funds solicited, to pave areas around churches. Main streets in Paris were paved after 1184 by an order of Philip II Augustus when, as the chronicler Rigord reports, "the horse-drawn wagons crossing the Cité raised such a fetid smell from mud piled in the streets that opment of the college precincts altered the town plans.

Housing. The houses of the medieval town were extremely varied. The size, shape, plan, elevation, and building material differed greatly from region to region, and especially between the towns of northern Europe and those of the south. Because of the limited space within each town and the desirability, even necessity, for houses to front on a street, most house plots in the later Middle Ages were much narrower than they were deep. In Italian towns especially, the row or strip house, with divisions into vertical bays, developed. In both north and south the width of a house, typically five or six meters (sixteen to almost twenty feet), was due to the available size of wooden beams that rested on the structural walls (masonry in the south, wood in the north). A narrow door from the street, with stairs to upper floors, was on one side of the facade. The ground floor, used as a shop, workroom, or storage space, had its own wide entrance from the street that filled much of the lot

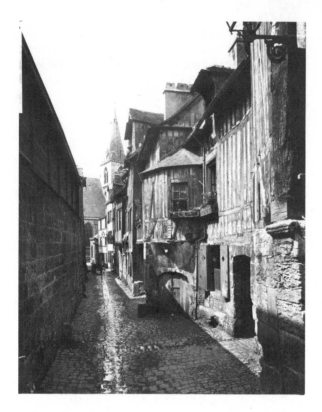

Late medieval street in Rouen (destroyed in World War II).
PHOTO: ROGER VIOLLET

the king could endure it no longer." Streets were first paved in Florence in 1237, and in Lübeck in 1310.

Covered walkways, or porticoes, lined the main streets of many European towns. They offered protection from rain in the north and from sun in the south, and everywhere provided additional space for shopkeepers to display their wares. In most medieval towns they took the form of arcades supported by columns or masonry piers. In Rome, however, where the classical tradition was strong and ancient materials were available, the intercolumniations were spanned by flat entablatures.

Medieval street plans were not eternally fixed. Though many changes took place after the fifteenth century—usually the closing of streets and the filling in of open spaces—routes were changed in the Middle Ages, too. This was most common when major building projects took over large lots in town. The building of churches, civic structures, market structures, university compounds, and monasteries affected the preexisting street pattern. In Oxford and Cambridge, for example, the devel-

The Effects of Good Government. Detail from the fresco by Ambrogio Lorenzetti showing shops and covered walkways, 1338–1339. Palazzo Pubblico, Siena. ALINARI/ART RESOURCE

frontage. This layout changed during the fifteenth century, when strictly residential palaces displaced commercial activity in many neighborhoods. The owner usually lived on the first floor above ground level. Depending on the size of the house, upper floors housed children, servants, apprentices, and storage space. Kitchens and open loggias were frequently placed at the top of the house to allow cooking smoke to escape and to lessen the risk of fire.

In northern Europe wood and half-timbering construction were favored. In England a traditional Saxon "hall" type of house was adapted to the long urban lots. The pitch of roofs was steep, with houses usually joined at the eaves. Stone construction was only for the very rich.

Religious buildings. Prominent in every medieval town were the churches. For the most part, towns grew around their cathedrals, which were often the buildings with the longest continuous history. Cathedral sites were venerated for specific historical associations, for the tombs of religious leaders they contained, and for the long devotional traditions that grew up around them. Even when new cathedrals were built, as was frequently the case from the twelfth century on, the site usually remained unchanged. Smaller churches were established in towns as they grew. Most neighborhoods had parish churches, sometimes financed and built by a leading family or by a craft group strong in the area. For the most part, parish churches were small and unpretentious, blending in with the housing around them but spatially set off by an open square in front.

Monasteries often established rival organizations to the cathedral chapter, and these were often expressed architecturally by the construction of large churches with tall towers in the center of town. The introduction of the urban monasteries of the preaching friars, from the thirteenth century on, altered the religious life of towns, creating new centers of devotional activity. The Franciscans and Dominicans, the largest of the new orders, built most lavishly. For their large complexes they often were forced to choose open tracts on the edge of town.

Public buildings. The most important public buildings of any town, aside from religious structures, were those erected to house the many activities of the civic government. Beginning in the early thirteenth century, as power in towns passed from bishops and nobles to more popular regimes, im-

pressive town halls were built. In Italy, these were generally situated near the cathedral and bishop's palace, which were usually close to the market square. In many towns civic and religious authorities were housed opposite each other across the public square.

Though the architecture of civic palaces varied from place to place, certain features were usually present. Some sort of outdoor meeting area, such as a large balcony or terrace, or an open loggia, was necessary, often in connection with the town square. Inside, the most important element was a large hall where public assemblies could gather. The most common arrangement would be to have a covered hall built over an open ground floor.

In northern towns public architecture developed differently, emulating the architecture of the great merchant organizations that were, in effect, rulers of many towns. The cloth house and other market buildings dominated public life in Lübeck and Bruges. In addition to these buildings for sales and meetings, warehouses and large workshops were numerous. As in Italian commercial port cities, they crowded along the waterfronts.

Commercial buildings. In Viking York, as early as the tenth century, street names such as Coppergate (woodworkers' street), and Skeldergate (shield-makers' street) suggest the existence of special industrial sections. In larger towns the grouping of similar crafts continued throughout the Middle Ages.

Medieval streets were lined with shops. Though each town had its business sections in the center, overall there was a great deal of integration of residential and commercial use, with families, often with apprentices, living in the upper stories of houses while craftsmen and merchants used the ground floors. The most exclusive shops lined the most frequented streets. In Florence the money changers and goldsmiths had shops on the Ponte Vecchio; in Paris they were located on the Grand Pont, along with the drapers. In Rome the goldsmiths and money changers were situated on the Via del Banchi, named after their stalls.

Neighborhoods. All but the smallest towns were divided into neighborhoods that existed as administrative or religious units or as family enclaves. These districts, quarters, or parishes frequently depended on a central open space—perhaps in front of a church or by a wall. Streets connecting houses clustered around such open spaces were often more like corridors of a large house. Though in the large cities of the late Middle Ages there were neighborhoods clearly differentiated by economic and social class, in most middle-sized towns there was a great mix of status within districts and along single streets. Often rich and poor lived side by side, sometimes in a patron-client relationship.

From the early Middle Ages, in commercial and pilgrimage towns separate districts existed for specific national groups. During the Carolingian period Rome had permanent neighborhoods of Saxons, Frisians, Lombards, and Greeks. The Milanese refugees from the Lombard invasion set up their own community in Genoa, and the Lombards initially separated themselves from native populations in the towns they occupied. Frisian traders had "colonies" in York, Mainz, and Worms from the eighth to the eleventh century; and Venetian, Genoese, and Pisan traders established themselves separately in towns around the Mediterranean in the following centuries. In England after the Conquest, the Normans built new "French streets" as well as fortified castles within older towns. Jews, who were often invited to cities to stimulate economic activity, were usually allowed to live where they pleased, though they tended to congregate together. The creation of ghettos began in Spain and Portugal in the late fourteenth century, from which time Jews were increasingly restricted throughout Europe. Walled ghettos in Germany and Italy are mostly the product of the fifteenth and sixteenth centuries.

The town outside the walls. Town life did not end at the walls. There was always a close relationship between town and countryside. In the early Middle Ages markets and other commercial activities concentrated outside city gates to avoid the tolls and taxes required by town officials. In France these semi-autonomous merchant communities were known as faubourgs until their incorporation into the cities by extension of the city walls and the extension of city rights to their residents. In the later centuries only specialized markets, such as animal markets, and the big seasonal fairs were left outside the walls.

The activity of commerce attracted more permanent service buildings, and, in part because the gates of the towns were shut at sunset, inns and hostels usually were built at the gate, as well. Inside the gate were commercial districts that depended on the transport of raw materials or finished products for their business. Materials could enter the town by the gate and reach their destination without being transported through the center.

Sanctuaries and monasteries were commonly situated outside the town. Cities of Roman origin—such as Rome, Toulouse, Rheims, and Verona—all had major churches outside the walls. During the Carolingian period royal palaces were associated with extramural monasteries. In most places it was not until the eleventh century that the decision was taken to move the see church within the town walls. In Rome, with its many extramural Christian catacombs, efforts were made from the ninth century on to remove martyrs' remains to safety within the walls. In the same century Leo IV had the *borgo* around St. Peter's walled, but only after the Saracens had sacked the district in 846. This new Leonine quarter became the true center of medieval Rome.

Hospitals and especially leprosariums were set outside the walls to isolate the sick. Many of these hospitals were near town gates to serve pilgrims and travelers. At Toulouse there were seven leprosariums and twelve hospitals by the mid thirteenth century. At least twelve of these charitable foundations were located outside the town, mostly near gates.

Slaughterhouses and tanneries, often kept out of the city by law because of their waste and stench, and mills and textile workshops, which required abundant water, also clustered outside the walls.

BIBLIOGRAPHY

Michael Ashton and James Bond, *The Landscape of Towns* (1976); Maurice W. Barley, ed., *The Plans and Topography of Medieval Towns in England and Wales* (1976); Maurice Beresford, *New Towns of the Middle Ages* (1967); Martin Biddle, "The Development of the Anglo-Saxon Town," in *Settimane di studio del Centro italiano di studi medioevo*, 21 (1974), and, as ed., *Winchester in the Early Middle Ages* (1976); Wolfgang Braunfels, *Mittelalterliche Stadtbaukunst in der Toskana* (1953); Donald Bullough, "Urban Change in Early Medieval Italy," in *Papers of the British School at Rome*, 34 (1966), and "Social and Economic Structure and Topography in the Early Medieval City," in *Settimane di studio del Centro italiano di studi medioevo*, 21 (1974); Norman F. Carver, Jr., *Italian Hilltowns* (1979); Virginia Wylie Egbert, *On the Bridges of Mediaeval Paris: A Record of Early Fourteenth-century Life* (1974); Joseph Gies and Frances Gies, *Life in a Medieval City* (1981); Enrico Guidoni, *Arte e urbanistica in Toscana, 1000–1315* (1970); Jeremy Haslam, ed., *Anglo-Saxon Towns in Southern England* (1984); Richard Hodges and David Whitehouse, *Mohammed, Charlemagne, and the Origins of Europe: Archaeology and the Pirenne Thesis* (1983); Spiro Kostof, *A History of Architecture: Settings and*

Rituals (1985); Richard Krautheimer, *Rome: Profile of a City, 312–1308* (1980).

Pierre Lavedan and Jeanne Hugueney, *L'urbanisme au moyen âge* (1974); Ernest Lauer, "The First Wall of the Rhenish Episcopal Cities," in *Speculum,* **6** (1931); Guido Mengozzi, *La città italiana nell'alto medio evo* (1931); Lewis Mumford, *The City in History* (1961); John H. Mundy, "Hospitals and Leprosaries in Twelfth- and Early-Thirteenth-century Toulouse," in John Mundy *et al.,* eds., *Essays in Medieval Life and Thought, Presented in Honor of Austin P. Evans* (1955); John Mundy and Peter Riesenberg, *The Medieval Town* (1958); Luigi Piccinato, *Urbanistica medievale* (1978); Henri Pirenne, *Medieval Cities: Their Origins and the Revival of Trade,* Frank D. Halsey, trans. (1925, repr. 1956); Colin Platt, *The English Medieval Town* (1976); Susan Reynolds, *An Introduction to the History of English Medieval Towns* (1977); Howard Saalman, *Medieval Cities* (1968); G. Schmiedt, "Città scomparse e città di nuova formazione in Italia," in *Settimane di studio del Centro italiano di studi medioevo,* **21** (1974); Paul Zucker, *Town and Square* (1959).

SAMUEL GRUBER

[See also **Aldermen; Alfred the Great; Bastide; Borough (England-Wales); Bruges; Catacombs; Communes; Consuls, Consulate; Echevin; Fairs; Florence; Guilds and Métiers; Hospitals and Poor Relief; Leprosy; Lombards, Kingdom of; London; Markets, European; Mayor; Milan; Paris; Podesta; Roads and Bridges; Rome; Trade; Villages: Community.**]

URBNISI, one of the most ancient cities in Georgia, is located in central Kᶜartᶜli. It is frequently mentioned in chronicles as having been well established and prosperous. Surrounded by fortified walls with projecting semicircular towers, it was an important center for trade in early medieval times and, as excavations conducted by Parmen Zakaraya revealed, contained numerous dwellings and commercial structures. Among the churches the most notable is a three-nave basilica (105 × 49 feet/ 32 × 15 meters) from the second half of the sixth century that was restored in the seventeenth century. The nave is three times as wide as the aisles. The arched barrel vault supported by cruciform piers is typical of early Christian basilicas in Georgia.

BIBLIOGRAPHY
Parmen Zakaraya, *Zodchestvo gorodishch Urbnisi* (1965).

WACHTANG DJOBADZE

[See also **Georgia: Geography; Georgian Art and Architecture.**]

URIEN RHEGED (*fl.* sixth century), son of Cynfarch, was the British ruler of the kingdom of Rheged. His dominions extended west from beyond the Solway Firth (considered the center of the kingdom) over much of modern Cumbria to include parts of northern Lancashire and Yorkshire. Historically, little is known of Urien outside of the brief notice in chapter 63 of the *Historia Brittonum,* attributed to Nennius, which lists the Bernician kings at the end of the century, including Hussa (585–592) and Theoderic (572–579):

> Against these, four kings fought: Urbgen (Urien), Riderchen (Rhydderch Hen), Guallauc (Gwallawg), and Morcant. Theoderic fought fiercely against Urbgen and his sons. During that time, sometimes the enemy, sometimes the Welsh held the upper hand, and he trapped them for three days and three nights on the island of Metcaud (Lindisfarne), but, during the expedition he was assassinated on the orders of Morcant out of jealousy because his military skill and leadership were greater than all other kings'.

A portrait of Urien's magnanimity, generosity, and military leadership is contained in the nine poems addressed to him and to his son Owain (later spellings: Ewen, Iwein, Yvain) by Taliesin, who is mentioned by Nennius (chap. 62) as having written at the same time. Urien's name appears frequently in early Welsh genealogies, and his life attracted a considerable admixture of semi-history and legend. The later saga poetry of Llywarch Hen, supposedly a cousin to Urien, deals largely with his death, and both Urien and Owain (especially under the spelling Yvain) figure prominently in Arthurian romances. Some ecclesiastical traditions also attach to Urien's name: St. Kentigern (*d.* 612) was traditionally his grandson; and a further clerical son wrote a life of St. Germanus of Auxerre. This may be the Rum (Rhun) son of Urien whom Nennius (chap. 63) equates with Paulinus, archbishop of York, who was responsible for the conversion of Edwin of Northumbria in 627.

BIBLIOGRAPHY
Nora K. Chadwick, *The British Heroic Age: The Welsh and the Men of the North* (1976), 80ff., 93f., 103–108, 112–124; Patrick J. Ford, intr. and trans., *The Poetry of Llywarch Hen* (1974); Kenneth H. Jackson, *The Gododdin: The Oldest Scottish Poem* (1969); John E. Lloyd, *A History of Wales,* I (1910, 3rd ed. 1939, repr. 1948), 162–166; Nennius, *British History and the Welsh*

Annals, John Morris, ed. and trans. (1980), 78–79; Taliesin, *The Poems of Taliesin,* Ifor Wiliams, ed., J. Caerwyn Williams, trans. (1968).

DAVID N. KLAUSNER

[See also **Arthurian Literature; Chrétien de Troyes; Historia Brittonum; Kentigern, St.; Nennius; Scotland: History; Strathclyde, Kingdom of; Taliesin; Wales: History; Wales: Marcher Lords; Welsh Literature.**]

URMIA, LAKE (Avestan: Chaechasta; Armenian: Kaputan Cov [blue lake]; Greek: Margiana, Martiana, or Ma[n]tiana; modern Persian: Urmia, then Reza'iyeh, and since 1979 Urmia again). The largest lake in the Middle East, Lake Urmia lies in northwestern Iran at an altitude of 4,183 feet (1,280 meters). It is 80 to 88 miles (128–141 kilometers) long by 23 to 36 miles (37–58 kilometers) broad, depending on the season, and covers an area of about 1,545 to 2,320 square miles (4,000–6,000 square kilometers), with an average depth of 16 feet (5 meters). A saline body, Lake Urmia is about three-fifths as salty as the Dead Sea, and only a few salt-tolerant plants live in its waters. It originally was much larger, for there is geological evidence that the towns of Urmia (Reza'iyeh), Tabrīz, and even Maragheh lay on its earlier shores. The lake contains many barren, rocky islands, the largest of which, Shahi, was the site of a castle where Hulagu and other Mongol rulers were buried. A mixed population of Armenians, Kurds, and Nestorian Christians once lived north and west of the lake; few but Kurds remain there today.

BIBLIOGRAPHY

Hermann Abich, "Untersuchung d. Wässer d. Caspisches Meeres, Urmia- und Wan-Sees," in *Memoires de l'Académie de St. Petersbourg, sciences-mathématiques,* 6th ser., **3** (1856); Sowren T. Eremyan, *Hayastaně ěst "Ašxarhac^oyc^"-i (Armenia according to the Geography)* (1963), 58 *s.v.* "Kaputan Cov"; R. T. Günther, "Contributions to the Geography of Lake Urmi and Its Neighborhood," in *Geographical Journal,* **14** (1899), and "Contribution to the Natural History of Lake Urmia," in *Journal of the Linnaean Society, Zoology,* **27** (1900); Nikolai V. Khanyakov, "Notices physiques et géographiques sur l'Azerbaidjan," in *Bulletin de la classe physique-mathématique de l'Académie de Russie,* **16** (1858); Ferdinand F. C. Lehmann-Haupt, *Armenien, einst und jetzt,* 2 vols. in 3 (1910–1931), I, chap. 6; Harry F. B. Lynch, *Armenia: Travels and Studies,* 2 vols. (1901, repr. 1965), II, 43, 469–470; Vladimir Minorsky,

"Urmiya," in *Encyclopaedia of Islam* (1934); *Nagel's Encyclopedia-Guide: Iran* (1978), 134–135.

ROBERT H. HEWSEN

[See also **Armenia, Geography; Astrology/Astronomy, Islamic; Tabrīz.**]

URNES STYLE. The Urnes style represents the final phase of Viking art and is named after the superb wood carvings on the church at Urnes in western Norway. It developed about 1040 from the Ringerike style and is composed of interlooping schemes of elegantly curving animals and snakes. It remained popular into the twelfth century, when it was superseded by European Romanesque art.

BIBLIOGRAPHY

Signe Horn Fuglesang, "Stylistic Groups in Late Viking and Early Romanesque Art," in *Acta ad archaeologiam et artium historiam pertinentia* (1981), 79–125; H. Shetelig, "Urnesgruppen," in *Foreningen til norske Fortidsmindesmærkers Bevaring, Aarsberetningen* (1909), 75–107; David M. Wilson and Ole Klindt-Jensen, *Viking Art* (1966, 2nd ed. 1980), 147–160.

JAMES A. GRAHAM-CAMPBELL

[See also **Celtic Art; Jellinge Style; Mammen Style; Ringerike Style; Viking Art.**]

USHAKOV, SIMON (1626–1686), the last great icon painter of medieval Russia. An extremely versatile artist, he was employed by the Muscovite court not only as a painter of icons and frescoes, but also as a designer of metalwork and a map maker. Obviously aware of European art, Ushakov tried to introduce Western ideas into his painting. His icons are thus a strange blend of conventional iconography and three dimensionality.

BIBLIOGRAPHY

George Heard Hamilton, *Art and Architecture of Russia* (1954, 2nd ed. 1975); Igor E. Grabar, ed., *Istoria russkogo iskusstva,* VI (n.d.), 425–454; Konrad Onasch, *Russian Icons,* I. Grafe, trans. (1977), 13–14.

ANN E. FARKAS

[See also **Russian Art.**]

Wood carving from a church door at Urnes, Norway, in the Urnes style, after 1050. RIKSANTIKVAREN, OSLO

Old Testament Trinity. Icon painting by Simon Ushakov, mid 17th century. LENINGRAD, STATE RUSSIAN MUSEUM/SOV-FOTO/PHOTO BY V. FEDOSEYEV

USK, THOMAS (*ca.* 1350–1388), scrivener and author of the *Testament of Love*. The son of David Usk, a cap maker, he was born in London, where he spent most of his life.

Usk was involved in the efforts of John Northampton and his associates in the nonvictualing trades to gain economic and political power in London. The opposing party, led by Nicholas Brembre, consisted of merchant capitalists of London, men who controlled the economic life of London and were engaged in victualing, foreign trade, and money lending. They tended to support King Richard II, who seemed most likely to continue their prerogatives and support their varied interests.

In October 1383 Northampton tried to secure reelection as mayor for a third term, but was defeated by Brembre. The agitation of Northampton's followers against Brembre developed into riots during January and February of 1384, which were suppressed by Brembre. Several of Northampton's supporters fled from London, including Usk, who was eventually found by Brembre's men and imprisoned in July 1384.

While in detention, Usk had a change of heart about Northampton's actions and his own part in them. In July of 1384 he wrote his "Appeal," a legal statement giving a detailed account of Northampton's actions against Brembre. The "Appeal" became a key document in August 1384, when North-

333

ampton appeared before the king to answer to the charge of treason. It is also of interest as one of the earliest datable examples of London English.

In the trials of August and September 1384, Northampton and several of his followers were sentenced to death, but that punishment was remitted at the urgent request of the queen. Usk was pardoned for his part in the disturbances, but he was a man marked for retribution by his former associates as one who had betrayed them. From September 1384 to March 1385 Usk was kept in safe custody by Brembre. This period of enforced leisure provided Usk occasion for writing the *Testament of Love*. He evidently had access to manuscripts and materials needed to put in literary form his explanation for having betrayed Northampton's party. He evidently sought to justify his actions; no doubt he also hoped to promote his own fortunes.

From the summer of 1385 until 1388, he enjoyed royal patronage, first by appointment as the king's sergeant-at-arms, and then, in September 1387, as undersheriff of Middlesex. Usk's good fortune soon turned to bad, however, when Thomas Woodstock, duke of Gloucester, led a group of nobles, who came to be known as the Lords Appellant, against the king. At the end of 1387, when the Lords Appellant gained power, Usk's alliance with the royalist party proved to be his undoing; he was arrested in late December 1387.

The trials of those arrested were held before the king in a session of parliament, later called the Merciless Parliament. Brembre was executed on 20 February 1388. Usk was tried on 3 March, but the trial was merely a matter of form. The Lords Appellant had decided to punish Usk, and he was without legal recourse or powerful friends. He was sentenced to be drawn, hanged, and beheaded. The sentence was carried out the next day in a particularly brutal fashion. After being drawn and hanged, he was cut down while still alive and beheaded with agonizing slowness; records show that it took nearly thirty strokes of the sword.

The events of 1383 and 1384 form the context of the *Testament*, a long prose work in three books, which describes Usk's involvement in London politics. Usk's account is not easy to follow because the references to events are oblique and the work is allegorical. The *Testament* can be summarized briefly as follows: An unnamed narrator portrays himself in prison, separated from "Margaret," whom he has served faithfully for seven years. When Love, in the form of a beautiful lady, appears

to offer him comfort and advice, he recounts in allegorical form his recent involvement in the "storm" of London politics. Love replies by adapting the advice of Lady Philosophy in the *Consolation of Philosophy* by Boethius; she urges him to despise earthly glory and the other goods of Fortune, and to devote himself to a life based on reason and the love of virtue. In addition, Love discourses on the relation of grace and free will and urges him to place his trust in the goodness and grace of the Margaret pearl, who is said to embody "grace, learning, or wisdom of God, or else holy Church."

In his design of the *Testament* as an allegorical vision of the consolation received from a wisdom figure by a man in prison, Usk evidently is comparing his situation to the famous unjust imprisonment of Boethius. In addition to Usk's adaptation of Boethius' *Consolation*, there is evidence that he knew Chaucer's translation of that text, *Boece*, as well. Usk also drew on Chaucer's *Troilus and Criseyde*, which he quotes; because Usk's text can be dated, his use of Chaucer's text provides the best evidence for the composition of the *Troilus* as before May 1385.

An unusual borrowing occurs at the end of book II and in much of book III of the *Testament*, where Usk draws directly and at length from a tract by St. Anselm of Canterbury (1033–1109), *De concordia praescientiae et praedestinationis et gratiae Dei cum libero arbitrio* (On the harmony of the foreknowledge, the predestination, and the grace of God with free choice, 1106–1107). Usk's understanding of this difficult text is imperfect, and he often misinterprets or mistranslates passages, but his work in these sections of the *Testament*, along with Chaucer's *Boece*, are the earliest sustained examples of philosophical prose in Middle English.

The *Testament* is an important example of late-fourteenth-century English prose, despite the fact that it is often hard to understand. It has some passages of descriptive power and is especially interesting in showing the sort of writing that a scrivener of London used in seeking clemency for his misdeeds: a love allegory drawing on Boethius and Anselm.

No manuscript of the work survives. It is available to us only in the edition of Chaucer's works issued by William Thynne in 1532. Thynne's attribution of the *Testament* to Chaucer persisted until the mid nineteenth century. Only in 1897 did Walter W. Skeat discover an acrostic in the text formed by the first letter of each chapter. When an erroneous shift of text made by Thynne in book III is corrected, the acrostic reads: MARGARET OF VIRTU HAVE MERCI ON THIN VSK.

BIBLIOGRAPHY

Sources. "The Appeal of Thomas Usk Against John Northampton," in Raymond W. Chambers and Marjorie Daunt, eds., *A Book of London English, 1384–1425* (1931 and later printings); *The Testament of Love,* in Walter W. Skeat, ed., *Chaucerian and Other Pieces* (1897 and later printings); and *Thomas Usk's Testament of Love,* John Leyerle, ed. (Toronto Medieval Texts and Translations, 1989).

Studies. Ramona Bressie, "The Date of Thomas Usk's *Testament of Love,*" in *Modern Philology,* **26** (1928), and "A Study of Thomas Usk's *Testament of Love* as Autobiography" (diss., Univ. of Chicago, 1928); George Sanderlin, "Usk's *Testament of Love* and St. Anselm," in *Speculum,* **17** (1942).

JOHN LEYERLE

[See also **Middle English Literature; Richard II.**]

USUARD (**Iswardus**) (*fl.* 838–875), Benedictine monk and martyrologist, active in St. Germain-des-Prés, Paris. While a monk, he began compiling a martyrology under the orders of Emperor Charles II. Usuard combined two types of martyrologies—a simple listing of names and feast days and information about each saint's life. His work became the model for later martyrologies.

BIBLIOGRAPHY

Source. Patrologia latina, CXXIII (1852), 453–992.

Studies. Jacques Dubois, ed. and trans., *Le martyrologie d'Usuard* (1965), which also contains a French translation of Usuard's work; Max Manitius, *Geschichte der lateinischen Literatur des Mittelalters,* I (1911), 361–362 n. 6.

EDWARD FRUEH

[See also **Martyrology.**]

USURY, in the vocabulary of medieval theologians and canonists, meant any return received or demanded on a loan in addition to the loaned property itself. Usury in this sense was both a sin, for which penance had to be done, and a canonical

crime, for which church courts might impose penalties. Usurers were required to restore their unlawful gains to the rightful owners, and church lawyers vigorously sought to detect schemes to evade the usury prohibition. Medieval usury rules had significant implications for the development of credit and finance systems.

Christian prohibitions of interest-taking on loans had historical roots in ancient Israel. The Torah forbade Jews to charge interest on loans to fellow Jews, although it allowed interest on loans to foreigners. This prohibition became the subject of voluminous rabbinical commentaries and formed a central part of the legal system of late ancient and medieval Jewry.

The Mosaic usury prohibition was apparently not a major concern of Jesus or his early followers, for the New Testament contains only a few scattered references to the matter.

The Romans, on the other hand, had no objections to charging interest on loans, and Roman businessmen did not often lend money or goods gratuitously. Although Roman lawyers insisted that a loan in the strict sense (*mutuum*) must be interest-free, this simply meant that arrangements about interest payments must be the subject of a separate contract (*stipulatio*) between borrower and lender. Roman law did impose limits on interest. The Law of the Twelve Tables set the limit at 100 percent per year; during the late Republic and the Empire this was reduced to 12 percent. Compound interest (*usurae usurarum, anatocismus*), on the other hand, was forbidden by law.

The Christian emperors made no abrupt break with past policies on charging interest. Constantine explicitly affirmed the validity of agreements that involved interest payments, provided that the rates did not exceed the legal maximum. Justinian reduced the maximum rates from 12 percent to 6 percent for business loans and 4 percent for nonbusiness purposes, but he allowed agricultural loan rates to run as high as 12.5 percent annually.

The first general restriction that the church placed on interest charges was an action by the Council of Nicaea (325) that forbade clerics to charge interest on loans. Any cleric who contravened this rule was to be deposed. Local councils adopted similar prohibitions, and the so-called Canons of the Apostles likewise forbade bishops and priests to charge interest when they lent money.

Patristic writers extended this ban on charging

interest to include the laity as well. St. Jerome maintained that laymen were as much obliged as clerics to forgo interest when they made loans to other Christians. The Christian dispensation, he argued, had generalized the Old Testament interest ban to include Christians. St. Ambrose contended that Christians did have the right to charge interest—but only on loans made to persons against whom they had a right to make war; all other interest charges by Christians were illicit, for, according to Ambrose, "You have no right to take interest, save from him whom you have a right to kill" (*De Tobia*, 15). St. Augustine declared that charging interest on loans, although the law allowed it, was no better than legalized robbery.

The earliest papal ban on the taking of interest by Christians occurred in a letter of Pope Leo I in 444. Leo's pronouncement was incorporated into canon law as a cornerstone of medieval usury legislation. Ecclesiastical sanctions against those who took interest were reinforced in the late eighth and ninth centuries by similar enactments in the capitularies of Charlemagne and his successors.

Medieval usury doctrine underwent only slight change between the fourth and the late eleventh century. Demand for credit in this period was relatively low, the economy was dominated by agriculture, and capitalism did not yet exist. Loans were normally for consumption purposes and came out of surplus money or property that was not in high demand for other purposes. In such a society the ban on interest on loans between coreligionists in small, mostly rural, communities made sense. The practice of the better-off making gratuitous loans to the needy could be seen as virtuous. The support of that practice would be desirable social policy.

But as the economy became more diversified and as towns and cities began to grow during the late eleventh and twelfth centuries, incentives to disregard the church's ban on interest charges multiplied and the rationale for the ban became less clear. Church authorities responded at the Second Lateran Council (1139) by reiterating the traditional prohibition. By the close of the twelfth century popular preachers, such as Fulk of Neuilly and Robert of Courson, were conducting full-fledged campaigns to denounce those who charged interest on loans and to encourage local councils and synods to renew the older sanctions against usury.

As the problem of interest charges became more acute owing to greater demand for loans and changes in the nature of business activity, canon lawyers became more exact in their treatment of the issue. Gratian's *Decretum* (*ca.* 1140) defined any loan repayment where the amount repaid exceeded the amount loaned as a usurious transaction. This definition excluded from the ban profits of contracts other than loans. Gratian also wished to prevent lenders from disguising loans as fictitious sales and exacting interest through other types of deceptive transactions. For this reason he broadened his definition of usury so that it included any return on a transaction that was greater than the original investment in it. Later canonists displayed juristic ingenuity in defining the distinction between interest on loans, which they forbade, and profits from ordinary business, which most canonists thought should be permitted. The basis of the distinction was the concept of ownership (*dominium*). When a creditor leased a house to a tenant, for example, ownership remained with the landlord and the rent that he received was compensation for the use of property that belonged to him. But when a creditor loaned money or some commodity, such as wheat, to a borrower, ownership of the loaned property passed from lender to borrower. In that case, if the borrower repaid not only the original sum of money or quantity of wheat, but also some additional money or some further quantity of wheat to the creditor, he was paying for the use of property that he owned. This, the canonists maintained, was unjust and contrary to law, for it amounted to a charge for the use of the borrower's own property. Their reasoning applied only to consumable property, such as money or grain or wine, but not to transactions involving non-fungibles, such as the lease of a house, where the use of the loaned property did not involve its consumption by the borrower.

Arguing on these lines, canonists maintained that usury in their sense of the term not only was prohibited by the Scriptures and the fathers of the church, but also ran contrary to natural law. Hence they held that Roman laws that allowed interest charges were invalid and that all interest on loans of consumables was forbidden, regardless of the interest rate. Nor did it matter, they added, how general the practice might be. Even if everyone charged interest on loans, these transactions would still be immoral and illegal. Further, it was irrelevant whether the lender was a cleric or a layperson: usury in the canonistic sense of the term was unacceptable for everyone.

Scholastic writers found further reasons, in addition to the juristic ones, to justify the ban on interest-taking. Some Scholastics argued that money is sterile: it does not reproduce itself, and therefore taking a return on a loan of money is unnatural. Later Scholastics, however, rejected the sterility argument. Other churchmen reasoned that charging interest on loans was a means of making money without working for it, so that the usurer made a profit even while he slept, and this, they contended, was immoral. Usury, they felt, was the most sordid and blameworthy type of commerce. Biblical commentators interpreted the Gospel episode in which Jesus drove the money changers and merchants out of the Temple (Matt. 21:12–13) as evidence that these views had divine approval. Moreover, usury was described as antisocial. If Christians were allowed to loan money at interest, the rich would abandon the hard work of agriculture; this would eventually cause great famines in which the poor would perish, because they would be so impoverished by their interest payments that they would be unable to buy scarce and costly food. Thus usury, they argued, not only was morally wrong, but would lead to social disaster.

During the twelfth and thirteenth centuries popes and councils enacted ever more rigorous penalties for those who took interest on loans. The practice was forbidden to both clerics and laymen and was prohibited even if the ultimate purpose was pious, as for example loans made to redeem prisoners from captivity. The mere intention of charging interest on a loan, whether fulfilled or not, violated the law. The Third Lateran Council (1179) declared that usurers were excommunicate, that if they died without repenting this sin they could not be buried in consecrated ground, and that churches must refuse any gifts from usurers. Numerous local councils reiterated these provisions, which were incorporated in a special title devoted to punishments for usury in the *Decretals* (1234) of Gregory IX. Clerics guilty of usury were to be suspended from their functions and deprived of ecclesiastical office. Usurers, whether clerics or laymen, were also classed as *infames* and thus were ineligible to hold public office or honors and to testify in court. Princes were commanded to expel usurers from their territories and never to readmit them. Landlords were forbidden to rent houses to persons engaged in the business of lending money for interest. Clerics who allowed usurers to be buried in sacred ground were held guilty of usury themselves.

Wills and testaments made by usurers were invalid, and the heirs of a usurer who died without making restitution were subject to the same penalties as the deceased. Either the usurer or his heir must return all ill-gotten gains to those who had paid the interest charges or to their heirs. No usurer could expect pardon until restitution was complete. Since it was not always possible to discover who the victims had been or where they were, the church might in such situations apply the restitution money to other pious causes, such as the defense of the Holy Land or the building of new churches. Judges were authorized to proceed against usurers ex officio without any complaint from the victims, and accused usurers were not allowed to delay proceedings against them by appealing on points of law to other courts.

The fate of the usurer, whether punished by the courts or not, was generally believed to be grim. Dante described in exquisite detail the tortures visited upon the souls of usurers in the seventh circle of hell.

The system of earthly penalties was less efficient than Dante's infernal counterpart. Pawnbrokers and petty moneylenders were hauled before the ecclesiastical courts in considerable numbers and forced to repay the interest they had received. At this level, the machinery for the repression of usury worked fairly smoothly. But enforcement was far less effective when it came to large-scale investors and major financial entrepreneurs, who took pains to disguise interest payments as something else. Church officials made strenuous efforts to make the system work and required those suspected of usury to turn their account books over to the authorities for inspection. But the ingenuity of accountants and legal advisers often outstripped the capacity of the auditors to discover covert interest charges.

One problem that faced those who attempted to enforce the usury prohibition was the difficulty of distinguishing interest payments from other illicit profits. Canon law not only banned usury but also forbade dishonest gain (*turpe lucrum*) from other commerce. Dishonest gain meant the profits from a transaction in which one bought goods at a low price in order to sell them later at a higher price. Dishonest gain meant in effect what we would describe as commodity speculation. If the buyer actually took delivery of the goods and transported them to another locality for sale, for example, his profits were not classed as dishonest gains. Even the buyer who bought more of a commodity than he needed for his own use and disposed of the surplus for a profit was not guilty of making dishonest gains. Since so much depended upon the intention of the parties, church authorities had considerable difficulty in monitoring business activity in order to enforce the prohibition of usury and dishonest gains.

Enforcement of these policies was further complicated by the exceptions that the law admitted to its own rules. Interest charged to an enemy against whom one had a right to make war was lawful, so that interest-bearing loans to Saracens and heretics were exempt from the ban. Nor did the law forbid debtors to give gifts to their creditors, an exception that provided ample opportunity for deceptive practices. Dowry transactions were also exempt from the anti-usury rules, so that a marriage settlement could be deposited with a merchant for investment and the profits divided between the merchant and the investor without violating the rules against usury. Other exceptions to the usury ban allowed creditors to receive compensation for the risks involved in investments, to take fair compensation for the opportunity costs of a gratuitous loan, and to impose penalties upon borrowers for late payment or nonfulfillment of other conditions of the loan. These exceptions could be manipulated by the unscrupulous to hide interest payments.

Other ways of evading the ban on interest charges occurred to medieval lawyers and their clients. One might enter into a fictitious sale, for example, in which one party pretends to sell a property to the other and then buys it back at a higher price, although in actuality the property never changed hands. This practice was denounced by Pope Alexander III and forbidden by several councils. Fictitious rental agreements were used in the same way, as well as credit sales, mortgages, and other devices. Try as they might, the church's enforcement agencies never fully matched the ingenuity of evaders. The ultimate sanction lay in the conscience of the lender, but the temptations of profit often proved stronger than the will to resist them. Medieval churchmen themselves were frequent patrons of the usurers whose activities they denounced, and ecclesiastical dignitaries routinely borrowed from Jews and Christians alike and just as routinely paid interest on their loans. Monasteries, cathedral chapters, bishops, cardinals, and the popes themselves were all involved in money-lending activities, usually as borrowers, more rarely as lenders. Credit financing of ecclesiastical activities was commonplace and the interest paid in these transactions was normally disguised.

The medieval campaign to repress usury hit hardest at pawnbrokers and petty moneylenders, while bankers and financiers in the higher reaches of society escaped largely unscathed. The church's very success in driving pawnbrokers out of business however, had the unintended result of making loans more difficult to obtain. This tightening of consumer credit, in turn, resulted in a general rise in the interest rates that the campaign sought to abolish. The usury prohibition, on the other hand, had little practical impact on commercial activity and did not seriously hamper the development of capitalism. By the fourteenth century legal exemptions had alleviated the rigors of the usury ban and ingenious lawyers stood ready to provide merchants with the means to profit from loans by finding ways around the usury law. After about 1350 there was a decline in prosecutions for usury and the church was in the process of modifying its usury policy so as to allow lenders to charge moderate interest rates without legal penalty. This was the result of changes both in general economic conditions and also in commercial practices.

The medieval church's anti-usury regulations represented the first systematic attempt in the West to formulate an economic theory. Religiously motivated, the theory rested upon the assumption that freely available consumer credit would result from the abolition of interest on loans. For three centuries the church struggled to make the theory work, but people stubbornly refused to act as the theory predicted that they would. Finally church authorities modified the theory and lifted the penalties against moderate interest charges, while continuing to condemn excessive interest as usury.

Although medieval usury theory lacked rigorous intellectual consistency and although it produced results that its framers never intended, it nonetheless represents a pioneering effort to construct a large-scale rational economic policy and to apply that policy to social problems through legal mechanisms. The authorities who attempted to implement the usury prohibition failed to secure the objectives that they sought. But they rightly perceived that economic policy is a moral issue, as well as an intellectual and practical concern, and they were correct in their assumption that the price of credit is a key factor in the operation of any economic system.

BIBLIOGRAPHY

Basic treatments of medieval usury doctrine and practice are John T. Noonan, Jr., *The Scholastic Analysis of Usury* (1957); John T. Gilchrist, *The Church and Economic Activity in the Middle Ages* (1969); and Terence P. McLaughlin, "The Teaching of the Canonists on Usury (XII, XIII, and XIV Centuries)," in *Mediaeval Studies*, **1** (1939) and **2** (1940). The role of the usury law in the context of medieval development of capitalist ideas is examined by John F. McGovern, "The Rise of New Economic Attitudes—Economic Humanism, Economic Nationalism—During the Later Middle Ages and the Renaissance, A.D. 1200–1500," in *Traditio*, **26** (1970). Other important treatments of medieval usury doctrines include Walter Taeuber, "Geld und Kredit im Dekret Gratians und bei den Dekretisten," in *Studia Gratiana*, **2** (1954); John W. Baldwin, *Masters, Princes, and Merchants: The Social Views of Peter the Chanter and His Circle*, 2 vols. (1970), and "Medieval Theories of the Just Price," in *Transactions of the American Philosophical Society*, n.s. **49** (1959).

On practical applications of usury doctrine and its bearing on economic realities see Fedor Schneider, "Das kirchliche Zinsverbot und die kuriale Praxis im 13. Jahrhundert," in *Festgabe . . . für Heinrich Finke* (1904); Jean Ibanès, *La doctrine de l'église et les réalités économiques au XIIIe siècle* (1967); Arwed Blomeyer, "Aus der Konzilienpraxis zum kanonischen Zinsverbot," in *Zeitschrift der Savigny-Stiftung für Rechtsgeschichte: Kanonistische Abteilung*, **66** (1980). For the practice of the English Courts Christian in dealing with usury cases see R. H. Helmholz, "Usury and the Medieval English Church Courts," in *Speculum*, **61** (1986).

JAMES A. BRUNDAGE

[See also **Alexander III, Pope; Banking, European; Banking, Jewish, in Europe; Councils, Western; Courson, Robert; Decretals; Gregory IX, Pope; Law, Canon; Leo I, Pope; Trade, European.**]

USURY, ISLAMIC LAW. The Arabic term *ribā*, literally "excess," is almost invariably translated as "usury," but *ribā* is far broader in scope than the English term suggests. Any excess whatsoever demanded in the repayment of a loan constituted, for medieval Muslim jurists, "usurious" interest. Exchanges of precious metals (including cash) or certain foodstuffs were also prohibited when the transactions involved unequal amounts of the same commodity, even if different in quality and exchanged on the spot. Loans with interest were nevertheless made, sometimes by means of legal fictions. The prohibition of *ribā* applied to all, including non-Muslims, but the latter were at times prominently engaged in such activities.

The Koran condemns *ribā* in loans with increasing sharpness, probably indicative of the increasing scope of the prohibition: "O ye who believe, devour not *ribā*, doubling and redoubling" (3:130). This refers to a Meccan practice whereby a debtor who could not meet his obligation on time was granted an extension, but the amount he owed was doubled. At the end of the extension period this process could be repeated.

Ribā is contrasted with alms: God abolishes profits based on *ribā*, while alms will be augmented with interest to the donor (2:276). The taking of interest by Jews is condemned (4:161). The prohibition of usury also appears as a stipulation in Muḥammad's treaty with the Christians of Najrān, who were later expelled for breaking this clause.

Still, no clear, comprehensive explication of the Koranic rules regarding *ribā* was ascribed to Muḥammad. According to an Islamic tradition, the last revelation was the prohibition of *ribā*, and Muḥammad died before interpreting it. This is problematic and rather unlikely, although it correlates well with the diversity of early Islamic practices.

A loan with *ribā* was typified as the sale of "one dinar for two"; Islamic jurisprudence extended this prohibition dramatically. Muḥammad was said to have prohibited any "sale of gold for gold, silver for silver, wheat for wheat, barley for barley, dates for dates, and salt for salt, except like for like, equal for equal, and hand to hand." This prohibition postdates that of interest on loans; some of Muḥammad's closest companions are said to have been ignorant of it until informed by others. Jurists tended to interpret the specified foodstuffs as referring to all foods, or foods sold by weight or measure. Items sold individually, such as hens or watermelons, are often mentioned as exceptions, as are nonfoods and slaves. *Ribā* was prohibited in exchanges of the standard monetary metals, gold and silver, whether in the form of bullion, coins, or objects composed of these metals or in which these metals were used as a significant part of an alloy. Thus exchanges must involve equal measures of gold if bullion is to be used to pay for minted dinars, or dinars to pay for a gold cup. *Ribā* was but rarely applied to exchanges involving metals not used in the major coinages.

The highly urbanized and mercantile society of medieval Islam could not have existed without loans, credit, and the costs of interest these normally entail. By the early tenth century, caliphs and viziers turned to merchants to advance huge sums, secured by letters of credit, financial income from the taxes of a province, or by a grant of government land. These bankers, known as *jahābidha* (singular, *jahbadh*), were usually paid a service charge, often in a different metal; the typical figure was one dirham per dinar.

The system of partnerships allowed for business loans to be construed as capital investment, generating profit, rather than as a loan generating *ribā*. Typically an "active partner" would receive what amounted to an interest-bearing loan from his partner(s) and conduct the operation of the business. In theory the labor and risk involved justified the increment in the return.

Despite all the above, there was still a need for legal fictions to effectuate interest-bearing loans while avoiding *ribā* on technical grounds. Two of the four major Orthodox law schools allowed the use of such stratagems, most of which involved the loan being converted into two separate transactions. A borrower would purchase an item from the lender on credit. The lender would then repurchase the item for a smaller amount of immediate cash. Sometimes a third person was involved, so that the cash and credit sales did not involve the same two parties. A slight variation was to sell a borrower, on credit, an item with a standard market value, charging him more than the usual price. He then obtained his cash on the open market. The borrower might sell something of value to the lender for cash and repurchase on credit; in this case the item was surety for the loan. Alternatively, a borrower might sell the lender real estate for a term, for ready cash. The rent or income from the property would serve as interest.

The prohibition of *ribā* applied to men and women, freemen and slaves, Muslims and non-Muslims. It was said to have been prohibited by all religions, and in fact the Islamic prohibitions show a great affinity for those of Jewish law. Only Abū Ḥanīfa permitted a Muslim to sell a non-Muslim "one dinar for two" outside Islamic lands. All forbade taking *ribā* from *dhimmī*s, that is, non-Muslims under Islamic protection. According to Islamic law, the prohibition of *rībā* in Islamic lands extended to the activities of non-Muslims, but in practice *dhimmī*s were rarely prevented from taking or granting interest if no Muslims were involved. However, a qadi should adjudicate a case of *ribā* according to Islamic law if it came before him. It was deemed especially improper for Muslims to pay interest to *dhimmī*s; this placed the latter in a position of superiority to Muslims.

Christians and Jews nevertheless played a prominent role as *jahābidha* and money changers. They were in fact allowed to serve in government positions only as bankers (and physicians) by a decree of al-Muqtadir in 908, and their prominence in these professions was noted by medieval historians and travelers. Non-Muslims also were highly represented in such trades as silver- and goldsmithing, at least in part because pious Muslims wished to avoid the possibility of *ribā*.

BIBLIOGRAPHY

Neşet Çağatay, "Ribā and Interest Concept and Banking in the Ottoman Empire," in *Studia islamica*, **32** (1970); Haim Hermann Cohn, "Usury," in *Encyclopaedia judaica*, XVI (1971); Walter J. Fischel, "Djahbadh," in *Encyclopaedia of Islam*, new ed., II (1965), and *Jews in the Economic and Political Life of Mediaeval Islam* (1937, repr. 1970); Mir Siadat Ali Khan, "Mohammadan Laws Against Usury and How They Are Evaded," in *Journal of Comparative Legislation and International Law*, 3rd ser., **12** (1929); Fazlur Rahman, "*Ribā* and Interest," in *Islamic Studies*, **3** (1964); Joseph Schacht, "Ribā," in *Encyclopaedia of Islam*, 1st ed., III (1936), "Bay^C," in *EI*, new ed., I (1960), and *An Introduction to Islamic Law* (1964); Abraham L. Udovitch, *Partnership and Profit in Medieval Islam* (1970) and "Theory and Practice of Islamic Law: Some Evidence from the Geniza," in *Studia islamica*, **32** (1970); Ibn al-Ukhuwwa, *The Ma^Cālim al-qurba fī aḥkām al-ḥisba*, Reuben Levy, ed. (1938).

SETH WARD

[See also **Abū Ḥanīfa al-Nu^Cmān ibn Thābit ibn Zūṭā; Banking, Islamic; Dinar; Islam, Religion; Jews in the Middle East; Koran; Law, Islamic; Muḥammad; Muqtadir, al-; Najrān; Qadi; Trade, Islamic; Waqf.**]

USURY, JEWISH LAW. Usury is defined in talmudic law as "wages for waiting," that is, money paid for deferred payment of a loan. Usury is viewed as a violation of the Pentateuchal injunction (Exod. 22:24; Lev. 25:37). Rabbinic law extended the range of this injunction to include forms of commodity loans and mortgages. The line distinguishing the Pentateuchal from the rabbinic injunction is not always clear, though the difference is far-reaching. While the courts will not enforce collection of interest on a loan that contravenes either a Pentateuchal or rabbinic injunction, restitution is enforced only if a Pentateuchal law has been breached.

The usury injunction covers five major areas: (1) money repaid at a later date, (2) commodities lent and repaid with increment at a later date, (3) deferred payments of purchase, if the price paid at the later date is higher than the one that obtained at the time of sale, (4) possessory mortgages, or antichresis, that is, the creditor takes possession of a house or field of the debtor for the period of the loan and resides there or utilizes his crop, without deducting the rent or produce from the principal, and (5) commenda, a silent partnership in which one person provides the capital, the other the initiative and labor.

Such restrictions posed serious obstacles to most forms of business enterprise or merchant and agricultural credit. Certain allowances are already to be found in the Talmud, and numerous (though not all) medieval commentators and jurists raised these allowances to normative status. Purchasing on credit was allowed with a price higher at the time of repayment than the one at the time of sale, on condition that no explicit statement was made at the time of sale that were it to be paid then the price would be lower—even though this was clearly understood. Some authorities ruled that symbolic deduction of rent or produce from the capital sufficed to allow possessory mortgages. Commendas were allowed if the active partner received symbolic wages.

The Pentateuchal injunction forbade interest between Jews but allowed the taking or paying of interest to a foreigner (nokhri). Both Christians and Muslims were viewed as "foreigners." Rabbinic law forbade such interest but made exceptions if no other means of subsistence was available. The frequent summary taxation and impositions coupled with the progressive exclusion of Jews from trade and commerce led Jacob ben Meir (Rabbenu Tam) to write: "We may allow taking interest from non-Jews because there is no end to the yoke and the burden king and nobles impose upon us. Everything we take is thus needed for subsistence. Moreover we are condemned to live in the midst of other nations and cannot earn our living in any other manner [except by moneylending.]"

As Jews in medieval Europe were engaged in moneylending, liquidity was essential, and replenishment of assets through direct borrowing was a major problem. The major exception developed by Rashi and simplified by Rabbenu Tam was the use of a Gentile straw man. A Jew would request a Gentile to serve as his intermediary in requesting a loan from another Jew. Legally two loans had taken place: the first from Jew to Gentile, the second from Gentile to Jew.

In Muslim countries Jews were not restricted to moneylending, and what lending took place elicited little comment. In Europe, however, Jewish moneylending was a frequent object of attack by Christian writers from the latter half of the twelfth century on. In modern times, some historians have averred that Jews entered this field not simply because of the pressure of circumstances, but also against the wishes of leading rabbinical authorities. There is no evidence for this claim. In Jewish law no special stigma attaches itself to the injunction against usury, just as none exists in Babylonian, Roman, Byzantine, or Muslim law. Indeed there was none in Western Europe until the latter half of the twelfth century. The intensely negative connotations that still attend the term "usury" are a unique creation of the High Middle Ages and the period of the Reformation.

BIBLIOGRAPHY

Immanuel Bernfeld, *Das Zinsverbot bei den Juden nach talmudisch-rabbinischem Recht* (1924); Boaz Cohen, *Jewish and Roman Law*, II (1966), 433–456; Haim H. Cohen, "Usury," in *Encyclopaedia judaica*, XVI (1972); Moses Hoffmann, *Der Geldhandel der deutschen Juden während des Mittelalters bis zum Jahre 1350* (1910); Gavin Langmuir, "The Jews and the Archives of Angevin England: Reflections on Medieval Anti-Semitism," in *Traditio*, 19 (1963); J. Marcuse, *Das biblisch-talmudische Zinsenrecht* (1895); J. J. Rabinowitz, "Some Remarks on the Evasion of Usury Laws in the Middle Ages," in *Harvard Theological Review*, 37 (1944); Haym Soloveitchik, "Pawnbroking: A Study in Ribbit and of the Halakah in Exile," in *Proceedings of the American Academy for Jewish Research*, 38–39 (1972); S. Stein, "The Development of the Jewish Law of Interest from the Biblical Period to the Expulsion from England," in *Historia judaica*, 18 (1955), and "Interest Taken by Jews from Gentiles," in *Journal of Semitic Studies*, 1 (1956); A. L. Udovitch, "At the Origins of the Western Commenda: Islam, Israel, Byzantium?" in *Speculum*, 37 (1962).

HAYM SOLOVEITCHIK

[See also **Banking, European; Banking, Jewish, in Europe; Commenda; Jacob ben Meir; Law, Jewish; Rashi (Rabbi Solomon ben Isaac).**]

Psalm 42 (43) in the Utrecht Psalter, showing Truth and the Psalmist (with lyre), 820's. UTRECHT, BIBLIOTHEEK DER RIJKSUNIVERSITEIT, COD. 32, fol. 25r

UTRECHT PSALTER. Probably produced during the 820's in the Benedictine abbey of Hautvillers near Rheims, the Utrecht Psalter (Universiteitsbibliotheek, cod. 32) is the masterpiece of Carolingian illustration and one of the most problematic works of medieval art. Written in rustic capitals and illustrated with lively pen drawings, the Utrecht Psalter is an overtly classicizing work. The imaginative piecing together of diverse ancient images is typically Carolingian. The manuscript influenced later ninth-century art (for example, the ivory reliefs on the throne of St. Peter, Vatican), and was copied several times in England, where it was located from about 1000.

BIBLIOGRAPHY

Vollständige Faksimile-Ausgabe im Originalformat der Handschrift 32, Utrecht-Psalter, aus dem Besitz der Bibliotheek der Rijksuniversiteit te Utrecht, 2 vols. (series: Codices selecti, LXXV) (1982–1984).

HERBERT L. KESSLER

[See also **Anglo-Saxon Art; Drawings and Model Books; Ivory Carving; Pre-Romanesque Art** (with illustration).]

UZUN ḤASAN (*r.* 1453–1478), ruler of the Aq Qoyunlu. His state ultimately included Azerbaijan, Armenia, much of eastern Georgia, Kurdistan, Iraq, and much of Iran. Its capital was Tabrīz.

Uzun (tall) Ḥasan rose to power amid domestic strife complicated by rivalry with the Qara Qoyunlu ruler, Jihānshāh. Each promoted his rival's domestic opponents. Having established his authority by 1457, Uzun Ḥasan expanded into Armenia and Kurdistan. The resultant conflict with the Ottomans initially centered on Trebizond (in 1458 Uzun Ḥasan had married Theodora Komnena, the niece of the last Komnenian ruler), which fell to the Ottomans in 1461. Uzun Ḥasan then shifted his attention eastward, defeating and killing Jihānshāh (1467). This brought about the appearance in 1468 of Jihānshāh's ally, the Timurid Abū Saʿīd. Uzun Ḥasan, somewhat daunted by the large and growing army of Abū Saʿīd that was advancing towards him, made repeated offers of peace and friendship. These overtures were haughtily rebuffed. However, Abū Saʿīd, a reckless and incautious commander, soon found himself trapped in his own winter camp. His army, weakened by desertions, was then defeated. He was captured and turned over in 1469 to his enemy, a rival Timurid, Yādgār Muḥammad, who had him killed.

As the master of territories from Khorāsān to Mesopotamia, Uzun Ḥasan was considered the only force capable of halting the Ottomans. Venice, in particular, had been exchanging embassies with him since 1463. Despite much diplomatic activity and the creation of a kind of alliance between Uzun Ḥasan and Venice, European aid (Venice did ship artillery and guns in 1473) never reached the Aq Qoyunlu in sufficient quantities to play a decisive role. Uzun Ḥasan again met the Ottoman forces in eastern Anatolia (he was trying to secure access through Qaramania to Mediterranean ports where the shipment of European guns awaited him), and after an initial success was defeated by Ottoman artillery at Bashkent in August 1473. Although no territorial losses resulted, Uzun Ḥasan's prestige had been badly shaken. Revolts by his son and brother followed.

Notwithstanding some attempts to centralize his government, Uzun Ḥasan was never able to create a unified polity out of a conglomeration of nomadic and semi-nomadic Turkomans, Arabs, Iranians, and Transcaucasians. After his death, family strife led to the collapse of his state. The Safavid shah Ismāᶜīl (whose mother was the daughter of Uzun Ḥasan and Theodora Komnena) ultimately took control over many of his tribes.

BIBLIOGRAPHY

Abū Bakr-i Ṭihrānī, *Kitāb-i Diyārbakriyya*, Necati Lugal and Faruk Sümer, eds., 2 vols. (1962–1964); Dzhafar Ibragimov, *Feodalnye gosudarstva na territorii Azerbaidzhana XV veka* (1962); Kᶜartᶜlis Tsᶜkhovreba, S. Qaukhchᶜ-ishvili, ed., II (1959), 341–342, 478–480, also in Russian (abridged), *Vakhushti Bagrationi: Istoriia tsarstva gruzinskogo*, N. T. Nakashidze, trans. (1976), 22–24; Gyula Moravcsik, *Byzantinoturcica*, 2nd ed., II (1958), 228–229 (Byzantine sources); Vladimir F. Minorsky, "Uzun Ḥasan," in *Encyclopaedia of Islam*, 1st ed., IV (1934); Avedis K. Sanjian, *Colophons of Armenian Manuscripts, 1301–1480* (1969); John E. Woods, *The Aqquyunlu: Clan, Confederation, Empire* (1976)

PETER B. GOLDEN

[See also **Aq Qoyunlu; Azerbaijan; Qara Qoyunlu; Tabrīz; Trebizond, Empire of.**]

VACARIUS (*ca.* 1115/1120–*ca.* 1205), Italian jurist and canonist. A graduate of Bologna about 1140, some four years later Vacarius went to England at the invitation of Archbishop Theobald of Canterbury to help him in his quarrel with the papal legate, Henry of Blois, bishop of Winchester. In the employment of Archbishop Roger of York before 1159, he became rector of Norwell in Yorkshire and a prebendary of Southwell, accompanied the archbishop to Normandy in 1171, and served as judge-delegate in England for various popes. In 1198 he was commissioned by Innocent III to preach the crusade in the diocese of York; he was still active as late as 1205.

Silenced by King Stephen before 1154 for his part in the propagation of Roman and church law, he went to Northampton to study theology and composed there *De assumpto homine*. He also wrote a *Summa de matrimonio* which is critical of Gratian and, before 1170, *Liber contra multiplices et varios errores,* which takes an Italian school-fellow to task for heretical views.

His chief claim to fame is his *Liber pauperum,* an epitome in nine books of the *Digest* and *Codex* of Justinian, which he put together about 1170 in order to introduce "poor students" of church law in England to the principles of Roman law. Although there is no proof that he ever taught at Oxford, his *Liber* was the textbook of Roman law in the fledgling school of canon law there around 1200, and exerted such an influence that its adherents were known as *pauperistae*. Sometime after the composition of the *Liber,* he also prepared a companion *Apparatus glossarum,* drawing on the teaching of the so-called four doctors of Bologna, Bulgarus, Martinus, Hugo, and Jacobus, all or some of whom had been his teachers. Because of the influence of the *Liber pauperum,* which lasted well into the thirteenth century, Vacarius is generally regarded as the founder of scientific legal studies in England.

BIBLIOGRAPHY

Leonard E. Boyle, "The Beginnings of Legal Studies at Oxford," in *Viator,* **14** (1983); Nicholas M. Haring, "The *Tractatus de Assumpto Homine* by Magister Vacarius," in *Mediaeval Studies,* **21** (1959); F. W. Maitland, "Magistri Vacarii *Summa de matrimonio*," in *Law Quarterly Review,* **13** (1897); Ilarino da Milano, *L'eresia di Ugo Speroni nella confutazione del maestro Vacario* (1945); Richard W. Southern, "Magister Vacarius and the Beginning of an English Academic Tradition," in *Medieval Learning and Literature: Essays Presented to Richard William Hunt,* J. J. G. Alexander and M. T. Gibson, eds. (1976); Peter Stein, "Vacarius and the Civil Law," in *Church and Government in the Middle Ages: Essays Presented to C. R. Cheney,* C. N. L. Brooke *et al.,* eds. (1976); Francis de Zulueta, ed., *The Liber Pauperum of Vacarius* (1927).

LEONARD E. BOYLE

[See also **Bologna, University of; Bulgarus; Gratian; Hugo; Jacobus; Justinian I; Law, Canon; Law, Civil; Law, Schools of; Martinus Gosia.**]

VAFÞRÚÐNISMÁL is a mythological poem of the *Poetic Edda*; it appears as the third item of the Codex Regius 2365 4°. The latter half (strophes 20/2 on) is included in Codex Arnamagnaeanus 748 4° and eight and a half strophes are cited in the *Snorra Edda*. The meter is regular *ljóðaháttr*, except in five strophes (38, an extra long line; 42 and 43, an extra short line; 27, a half-strophe; and 55, three half-strophes). From strophe 18 on the speaker (Odin or Vafþrúðnir) is noted in the margin of the Codex Regius.

The frame begins with a dialogue between Odin (Óðinn) and Frigg: Odin wishes to test Vafþrúðnir's fame as a wise giant. The god journeys to the giant's hall (5) and greets him with a challenge (6). Vafþrúðnir accepts and threatens Odin's life, should he prove the less knowledgeable (7). Odin, as usual, uses a cover name to conceal his identity (8). After some discussion of the contest Vafþrúðnir asks his first question (11); after only four answers he is satisfied and roles are switched (20). The god's first twelve questions are introduced by a numbering formula, later (from 44 on) a "Far have I traveled" formula is used. Vafþrúðnir succeeds in answering all of Odin's questions but the last (54), to which he must respond with an admission of defeat.

Vafþrúðnir's four questions elicit little more than some names and the size of the final battlefield. But Odin's begin with the cosmogony—here the Ymir variant (21)—and include a giant genealogy (28–35), Njǫrðr's origin (39), and the war games of the fallen heroes at Odin's hall (41). His second series of questions focuses on the eschatology: the survival of mankind through the *fimbul* winter, the second-generation sun and the latter-day gods (47–51), and the destruction of Fenrir by Víðarr (53). Snorri comments on much of this content in the concluding pages of the *Gylfaginning*—but the value of his additional information depends on our general assessment of his credibility.

Vafþrúðnismál is of particular interest for two reasons. First, the answers supply mythological data that (since the poem is generally considered one of the oldest examples of Eddic poetry) are of substantial value to the student of Germanic religion. Second, the poem appears to have provided the model for the "knowledge confrontation" with Odin, in particular when concluded with the "Odin's question." Since only Odin could know what he whispered in Baldr's ear, the use of this question means certain victory. At the same time, if one assumes that such contests forbid posing a question unless one knows the answer, "Odin's question" is an apotheosis—it identifies the questioner as Odin himself.

Vafþrúðnismál is obviously Snorri's model for the "knowledge confrontation" frame of *Gylfaginning*. Although he was familiar with the poem much as we know it, Snorri chose to truncate its structure by bringing the confrontation to a close after Gylfi's questions. On the other hand, in the *Gestumblindi* episode of *Hervarar saga* the posing of the "Odin's question" unmasks the god. The model of the "knowledge confrontation" has here forced structural changes on a variant of folktale type 922: the "abbot" must pose the riddles, not the king, so that the scene may culminate in the "Odin's question." A similar derailment may explain *vǫlva*'s recognition of Odin at the end of *Baldrs draumar*.

BIBLIOGRAPHY

A text edition is Gustav Neckel, ed., *Edda: Die Lieder des Codex regius nebst verwandten Denkmälern*, 3rd ed., rev. by Hans Kuhn, I (1962). Translations are *The Poetic Edda*, Henry Adams Bellows, trans. (repr. 1968); *The Poetic Edda*, Lee M. Hollander, trans. (repr. 1962).

Barend Sijmons and Hugo Gering provide a commentary in *Die Lieder der Edda*, II, *Kommentar* (1927). See also Halldor Hermannsson, "Bibliography of the Eddas," in *Islandica*, 13 (1920); the annual bibliographies (1927–1962) in *Arkiv för nordisk filologi* and *Acta philologica scandinavica*; Jóhann S. Hannesson, "Bibliography of the Eddas," in *Islandica*, 37 (1955); and *Bibliography of Old Norse-Icelandic Studies* (1963–).

JERE FLECK

[See also **Alvíssmál; Baldrs Draumar; Eddic Poetry; Hervarar Saga ok Heiðreks Konungs; Odin.**]

VAHKA CASTLE, near Feke in present-day Turkey, was one of the chief strongholds of the Cilician Kingdom of Armenia. The main seat of the Rubenid family, later the ruling dynasty of Cilicia, it was

Vahka Castle from the southwest. REPRODUCED FROM T. S. R. BOASE, ED., *THE CILICIAN KINGDOM OF ARMENIA.* © SCOTTISH ACADEMIC PRESS 1978

originally captured from the Byzantines around 1097/1098 by Constantine I, Ruben I's son. Recaptured by Emperor John II Komnenos in 1138, then regained from the Danishmendids around 1145 by the Cilician baron Leo I's younger son, Tᶜoros II, it remained in Armenian hands almost continuously until its eventual capture by the Mamluks. Of historical interest as military architecture because of siting, layout, and construction, Vahka has features in common with fortresses at Tumlu, Yilan, and Anavarza (Anazarba).

BIBLIOGRAPHY

Thomas S. R. Boase, ed., *The Cilician Kingdom of Armenia* (1978); Sirarpie Der Nersessian, *Études byzantines et arméniennes,* 2 vols. (1973), and *Armenian Art* (1978); J. G. Dunbar and W. W. M. Boal, "The Castle of Vahga," in *Anatolian Studies,* **14** (1964); John Thomson, "Castles in Cilicia," in *Geographical Magazine,* **23** (1951).

LUCY DER MANUELIAN

[See also **Cilician Kingdom; Danishmendids; John II Komnenos; Leo I/II of Armenia; Mamluk Dynasty; Ruben I; Rubenids.**]

VAKHTANG GURGASALI. See **Waχtang I Gurgaslani.**

VAŁARŠAPAT. See **Ējmiacin.**

VALDAMBRINO, FRANCESCO DI. See **Francesco di Valdambrino.**

VALENCIA. The Spanish Mediterranean coast, south of Tortosa and north of Murcia, was variously divided under the Romans, the Visigoths, Justinian's Byzantium, the Visigoths again, and Muslim dynasties. Today it constitutes the provinces of Castellón de la Plana, Valencia, and Alicante; these contemporary borders are transversed by some two dozen natural or historical zones (*comarcs*) that define the extraordinarily variegated landscape. Each *comarc* was the center of a network of towns and farms clustered around a main city or castle. The city of Valencia was preeminent, with Játiva a lesser rival south of the Júcar River, insular Alcira always important in the center, and the crusader-founded Castellón eventually the heart of the north.

The eastern region of Islamic Spain, called Sharq al-Andalus in Arabic, briefly conquered by the Cid in 1094 and recovered by the Almoravids in 1102, was a semi-autonomous province of the disintegrating Almohad empire, partly under the *wālī* Abū Zayd and partly under the rebel Zayyān, when James the Conqueror (1218–1276) took it by piecemeal crusade from 1232 to 1245. Since Roman law had elevated and transformed the powers of kingship, James established Valencia and the recently conquered Balearics as separate kingdoms within his Crown, or Realms, of Aragon, where they served to counterbalance his older dominions. Valencia received its own parliament, money, and law code, and a third of the itinerant king's presence.

The cartographer Willem Blaeu described Valencia in 1635 as "about sixty leagues long, and seventeen wide at its widest point," containing "four cities, sixty towns surrounded by walls, and a thousand villages . . . watered by thirty-five rivers, large and small, among which five are principal"; the city of Valencia stood at the mouth of the Guadalaviar (Turia) River. In James's day the region bristled with fifty major castles or walled towns, arranged for protection in depth. A series of intensely irrigated plains (*huertas*) dotted its coastal sectors, and bustling port cities linked it in trade with North Africa, the Balearics, and southern France. Its wealth and maritime orientation gave James's Crown of Aragon a new direction, away from the Provence and Languedoc holdings that the northern French were progressively absorbing and toward Mediterranean expansion. (Tunis was soon a client state; Sicily fell to James's successor, Peter II [Pere II in Catalonia, Pere I in Valencia, 1276–1285]; and Greece and Sardinia became building blocks in a widening "empire.")

Because the crusade had progressed more by maneuver and surrender than by pitched battle, Muslims remained the majority, a parallel society under their castellans, or councils of sheiks, with their own law, language, and religion. Only at Burriana and the city of Valencia did resistance last until the best terms left were expulsion. Emigration of the elite and removal of castellans and notables after revolts from the 1240's to the 1270's increasingly ruralized and isolated this majority. At the end of his life, James complained that only 30,000 Christians (or perhaps Christian households) had come to settle, whereas the defense of the frontier required a minimum of 100,000 settlers. The northern third of the kingdom balanced its sparse Muslim population with estates of magnates and military orders, and with Christian influx at such points as Burriana, Morella, and Peñíscola. The main Christian settlement was in the central region around the city of Valencia. The southern third long remained Muslim, with colonial enclaves especially at Alcira, Gandía, and Játiva, and scattered in the mountains. The settlement process under James is imperfectly mirrored in the kingdom's *Repartiment*, books of land division.

To this frontier of promise and easy change came settlers of the coastal region, especially from the progressive, mercantile Catalan counties. The more feudal, strock-raising, upland kingdom of Aragon, with its different language and laws, dominated much of Valencia's hinterlands. The tension arising from this dual settlement pattern created disequilibrium throughout the kingdom's history. A scattering of Hungarian, German, Italian, and especially Languedocian settlers can be discerned; probably few Mozarabs (arabized Christians) had survived to welcome their coreligionists. The characteristic holding was an irrigated small farm, with supplemental pieces of dry farming (olives, vines, cereals) or grazing land. Tenure was usually by "sharing" (*eixaric*): the landlord was entitled to a set rent, from a tenth to a third, and the farmer, who in effect owned his land, could alienate or sell it at will.

Within the many cities aristocrats and knights freely engaged in commerce, fusing with nouveaux riches patricians whose urban or rural investments made their life-style equivalent. A more modest class of merchants and craftsmen, together with a growing proletariat, balanced the notables. The crown kept most of the cities and a great amount of land; aristocratic and ecclesiastical elements domi-

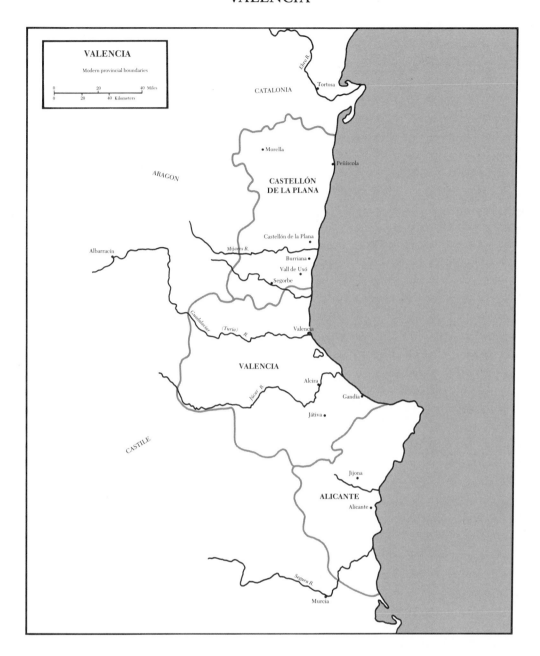

nated the rest, protected by feudal privileges. Thus the new kingdom was a balance of royal, feudal, and semi-autonomous communal jurisdictions and interests, of several genres of rural-against-urban patterns, of Aragonese versus Catalan cultures, of middling and aristocratic bourgeoisies, and of rival family factions among the affluent. Valencia was basically dominated by its communes, on the pattern that ran from Barcelona to Rome—a set of city-states under the comital dynasty; but whereas the Italian and southern French communes tended to marginalize and even dispense with their counts,

Valencia had its extensive area tightly held by a count-king who evolved more and more effectively into a real sovereign. The *Aureum opus* of Valencian royal privileges shows a high level of autonomy and republicanism and the "pactist" mentality of Mediterranean Spain. From 1410 these controlling attitudes declined, and under the Reyes Católicos (Ferdinand and Isabella) at the turn of the century, they collapsed.

James organized his new kingdom under his son as procurator or viceroy, with lieutenant-procurators directing two subordinate lieutenants (north and south of the Júcar River); later the kingdom was divided into three segments by the Uxó, Júcar, and Jijona rivers. The bailiff general was officer for regalian properties and revenues. Under him, one on each side of the Júcar, were two subordinate bailiffs, and under them, a complex of local bailiffs and tax farmers. The parliament (*corts*), convened for crises, evolved into a permanent mini-parliament (*generalitat*) from 1340. In its final form (1418–1419) there were thirty-two representatives, and a parliamentary palace (*palau*) was built in the city of Valencia in 1482. Each town had its elected executive board (*jurats*), a legislative council, a magistrate who acted as market and community inspector or consumer advocate (*mostassaf*), and a court, the justiciar (*justícia*). After 1330 there were separate justiciars for civil and criminal jurisdictions. Local custom was codified by settlement charters (*cartas pueblas*), by traditional town-district and regional charters imported from homeland cities (*furs, fueros*), and especially by the overarching *Furs de València,* promulgated as a municipal *Costums* in 1240, called the *Furs* in 1252 as it continued to spread in the kingdom, and proclaimed more universally by the kingdom-wide *corts* in 1261. A landmark in European legal history, the *Furs* was the first thoroughly romanized code of general application. In maritime law, the autonomous court and code of the *Consolat de mar* flourished from 1283.

There were three dioceses in the kingdom, under the metropolitan at Tarragona: Tortosa, in the north; Valencia, covering most of the remainder (becoming a metropolitan see itself in 1492), and Segorbe-Albarracín, an enclave between them. The Valencian see (and the town of Játiva) gave Europe its "good" (Borgia) pope Calixtus III (*d.* 1458), and both the "bad" Borgia Alexander VI (*d.* 1503) and his infamous son Cèsar. Valencia's most famous ecclesiastic was the visionary Dominican preacher and arbiter of the Great Schism, St. Vincent Ferrer (1350–1419). Preparatory and advanced schooling flourished from the mid thirteenth century; a formal university functioned briefly from 1245, though it is a common mistake among historians to view this date as abortive and to prefer the date 1500 (or 1493).

The city was exceptionally rich in religious orders from the beginning: military, mendicant, ransomer, hospitaler, and various groups of nuns. Europe's hospital movement was amply reflected, especially St. Vincent's double hospital and monas-

tery (1244, honoring the kingdom's patron, the Roman martyred here in 304) and Europe's first psychiatric hospital, the Casa dels Folls (also known as Hospital d'Ignoscents, 1409). The kingdom provided a bridge for Islamic-European interchange in medicine, particularly in the circles around the famous Arnald of Villanova (*ca.* 1240–1311), Muḥammad al-Shafrā (*fl.* 1300), Joan Gilabert Jofre (1363–1417) for psychiatric therapy, and Lluís Alcanyís (*fl.* 1475), a leader of medical reform.

Crown mechanizing of the celebrated Islamic paper industry at Játiva (perhaps *ca.* 1270) was significant in spreading the use of paper in Christendom; when printing came, the city of Valencia became Spain's publication center (the first Bible in a Romance language appeared here in 1478). The Islamic irrigation system, equally celebrated, was improved and expanded; the weekly water courts are widely misunderstood to be Islamic in origin. The Christians also continued the Muslims' traditional leather and ceramics crafts; Manises and Paterna plates won international fame. Textiles and shipbuilding were among the crafts that multiplied the capital's guilds to over 100. As an established slave market, Valencia began varying its wares, especially from the fifteenth century, with slaves from black Africa.

The kingdom had a lively political history of its own and simultaneously was involved in affairs affecting the entire Crown of Aragon. A mid-fourteenth-century social revolt turned into war between royalists and unionists (allied with nobles of Aragon); so bloody that Pope Clement VII had to intervene, it ended in a unionist defeat (1347–1348). The city's staunch help to Peter IV the Ceremonious against Peter I the Cruel of Castile won it the royal motto "Leal y Coronada" (Loyal and Crowned). Also during the fourteenth century the last circle of walls went up (1365), and the Black Death struck recurrently (a dozen plagues, from 1348 into the fifteenth century).

In the fifteenth century Valencia became the premier city of Spain, rivaling international emporia like Venice. Its population, 15,000 at the conquest and 40,000 in 1418, rose to 75,000 by 1483, out of the Valencian kingdom's 500,000 total. The financial and credit structure was crowned in 1407 with a royal-municipal bank (the Taula de Canvis); merchant operations led to construction of the magnificent Merchants' Exchange (Llotja, 1483–1498); civil and ecclesiastical buildings in Flamboyant Gothic style and private mansions transformed the capital. The crown established a branch of its central archives here in 1419. The aristocratic families earned an international reputation for hedonism, widening the gap between them and the moralistic lower classes. A life-style of tournaments, knight-errantry, factional disputes, and class struggle culminated in civil war that was ended by the Compromise of Caspe (1412).

The fifteenth century was Valencia's literary golden age, especially as the temporary removal of king and court from Barcelona to Naples accelerated Italian influences. An aristocratic current contended with a realistic-satirical bourgeois literary current. This was the age of the poets Ausiàs March (1397–1459), Jordi de S. Jordi (*ca.* 1395–1425), Joan Roís de Corella (1433/1443–1497), and the satirist of women Jaume Roig (1434–1478), as well as of the novelists Joanot Martorell (*ca.* 1413–1468) and Martí Joan de Galba (*d.* 1490), the religious writer Isabel de Villena (1430–1490), and the pioneer humanist Joan Lluís Vives (1492–1540). Poetry competitions brought together rival professionals: in 1474, forty from every class contended and printed the results. This was a brilliant culmination to a long tradition in Valencian (Catalan) literature, beginning almost with the conquest, earlier represented by the memoirist-historians Ramon Muntaner (1265–1336) and Bernat Desclot (probably Bernat Escrivá, *d.* 1288), as well as by the great Francesc Eiximenis (*ca.* 1326–1409), whose writings mirror both official and intimate Valencian life in the fourteenth century. An intense musical tradition culminated in the theoretical treatises of Guillem de Puig (also known as Guillem de Podio, *fl.* 1480); musical mystery plays, especially the famed *Misteri d'Elx,* survive largely in post-medieval form.

Amid the cultural triumphs, as Vincent Ferrer thundered his terrifying sermons and merchant fleets sailed to Flanders and the Levant, mobs sacked the Moorish quarter (1456), presaging a forced conversion (1522) and eventual expulsion (1609). The kingdom's Jews, invited to settle in large numbers previously, suffered the sacking of their quarters in 1391, a reflection of the wider pogroms in Spain that year. Anti-Semitic regulations multiplied in the following century until the Jews were expelled from all of Spain (1492). Near the turn of the century, the reign of Ferdinand the Catholic saw a political, social, and economic transition to new structures and ideology, with an

autocratic crown controlling urban administration, which led to the 1502 revolt, and drawing heavy financial support for the Italian wars and even for Columbus' voyage (especially through an adoptive Valencian, the converso Lluís de Santàngel). American gold soon cost Valencia its financial leadership. The Inquisition began activity in Valencia in 1484. Rural refeudalizing, urban strife, corruption, commerical crises, piracy and plague, the Moorish and Jewish tragedies, and the bitter social war of the brotherhoods (known as *germanias* in Catalan, 1519–1523), which pitted aristocratic landlords against the guild members and their allies, finally closed Valencia's medieval chapter.

BIBLIOGRAPHY
Long regionalized and somnolent, Valencian historiography was reborn in the late twentieth century; its pace and quality is accelerating as post-Franco sectional autonomy releases patriotism and polemic. Rich and relatively untapped archives make the kingdom a frontier for historians. A full bibliography on the organizational period of the kingdom, including archival orientation, can be found in my books and articles, especially in *Crusader Kingdom.*

The *Gran enciclopedia de la región valenciana,* 12 vols. (1973–1977), is a mine of information and graphics; the *Geografía general del reino de Valencia,* 5 vols. (1920–1927), is an indispensable supplement. Many significant monographs are in the series *Congreso de historia de la corona de Aragon,* nos. 1–12 (1909–1987); see also *Primer congreso de historia del país valenciano,* 3 vols. (1973–1974). Pertinent regional journals include *Anales del Centro de cultura valenciana* (city of Valencia), *Saitabí* and *Ligarzas* (University of Valencia), and especially *Boletín de la Sociedad castellonense de cultura* (Castellón de la Plana).

Other important works on Valencia include Lluís Alanyá, ed., *Aureum opus priuilegiorum ciuitatis et regni Valentie* ([1515] 1972); Ernest Belenguer Cebrià, *València en la crisi del segle XV* (1976); Robert I. Burns, *The Crusader Kingdom of Valencia,* 2 vols. (1967), *Islam Under the Crusaders* (1973), *Medieval Colonialism: Post-Crusade Exploitation of Islamic Valencia* (1975), "The Realms of Aragon: New Directions in Medieval History," in *Midwest Quarterly,* **18** (1977), *Moors and Crusaders in Mediterranean Spain* (1978), "Canon Law and the Reconquista," in *International Congress of Medieval Canon Law, V* (1980), "Piracy as an Islamic-Christian Interface in the Thirteenth Century," in *Viator,* **11** (1980), "Societies in Symbiosis: The Mudejar-Crusader Experience in Thirteenth-century Mediterranean Spain," in *International History Review,* **2** (1980), *Jaume I i els Valencians del segle XIII* (1981), "The Paper Revolution in Europe: Crusader Valentia's Paper Industry," in *Pacif-*

ic Historical Review, **50** (1981), *Muslims, Christians, and Jews in the Crusader Kingdom of Valencia* (1984), *Diplomatarium of the Crusader Kingdom of Valencia: The Registered Charters of Its Conqueror Jaume I 1257–1276,* 5 vols. (1985–), and, as editor, *The Worlds of Alfonso the Learned and James the Conqueror* (1985).

Antoni Ferrando i Francés *et al.*, eds., *Llibre del repartiment de València,* 4 vols. (1978); Ramón Ferrer Navarro, *La exportación valenciana en el siglo XIV* (1977); Thomas F. Glick, *Irrigation and Society in Medieval Valencia* (1970); Earl J. Hamilton, *Money, Prices, and Wages in Valencia, Aragon, and Navarre, 1351–1500* (1936); Felipe Mateu y Llopis, *La ceca de Valencia y las acuñaciones valencianas de los siglos XIII al XVIII* (1929) and *El pais valencià* (1933); Leopoldo Piles Ros, *Estudio documental sobre el bayle general de Valencia* (1970); Joan Reglá Campistol, *Approximació a la història del país Valencià* (1968); Francisco A. Roca Traver, *El justicia de Valencia, 1238–1321* (1970); J. C. Russell, "The Medieval Monedatge of Aragon and Valencia," in *Proceedings of the American Philosophical Society,* **106** (1962); Manuel Sanchis Guarner, *La ciutat de València: Síntesi d'història i de geografia urbana,* 2nd ed. (1976); José Sanchis y Sivera, *La catedral de Valencia* (1909) and *La diócesis valentina: Estudios históricos,* 2 vols. (1920–1921); Antonio Ubieto Arteta, *Orígenes del reino de Valencia: Cuestiones cronológicas sobre su reconquista,* 3rd ed., rev. (1977); Eliseo Vidal Beltrán, *Valencia en la época de Juan I* (1974); Jill R. Webster, "Francesc Eiximenis on Royal Officials: A View of Fourteenth-century Aragon," in *Mediaeval Studies,* **31** (1969).

.

Robert I. Burns, S.J.

[See also **Aragon, Crown of (1137–1479); Arnald of Villanova; Castellan; Catalan Language; Catalan Literature; Cid, the, History and Legend; Consulate of the Sea; Cortes; Eiximenis, Francesc; Expulsion of Jews; Fuero; Insanity, Treatment of; Jordi de S. Jordi; Law, Spanish; March, Ausiàs; Peter IV the Ceremonious; Spain, Christian-Muslim Relations; Spain, Muslim Kingdoms of; Vincent Ferrer, St.**]

VALHALLA (Old Norse: *Valhǫll*). In Scandinavian mythology, Valhalla is the hall of Odin. *Grímnismál* 8–10 locate it at Glaðsheimr (home of joy) and report that its rafters are spear shafts; gold bright, it is thatched with shields and its benches strewn with armor. A carving of a wolf hangs to the west of the door with an eagle over it. Valhalla has 540 doors, through each of which 800 of Odin's

warriors will pass to fight the wolf at Ragnarǫk (*Grímnismál* 23). The conception of Valhalla in the literary sources is closely associated with these warriors. They are the *einherjar,* dead heroes chosen by Odin to accompany him to the last battle. In Valhalla they do battle daily and then are reconciled (*Vafþrúðnismál* 41). An otherwise unknown figure, Andhrímnir, cooks Sæhrímnir (according to Snorri a boar) for their food (*Grímnismál* 18). Snorri cites these passages and adds such details as that Sæhrímnir, boiled each day, is whole by evening (*Snorra edda, Gylfaginning,* chap. 24).

The tenth-century poems *Hákonarmál* and *Eiríksmál* describe the arrival in Valhalla of Hákon the Good and Eiríkr Bloodaxe, great warrior kings, with their retinues.

Most scholars interpret Old Norse *Valhǫll* as "hall of the slain" and concur that it referred originally to a grave mound or rock where the dead were thought to dwell. Use of the term for certain rocks in southern Sweden has strengthened this assumption and may suggest that the second component, *hǫll* (hall), is a corruption from a word like *hella* (rock). Formally, however, *Valhǫll* can also mean "foreign hall," and Magnus Olsen suggested possible influence from European buildings, perhaps especially the Colosseum, where many doors led to scenes of combat. In either case, the conceptions of the Eddas appear late, more the property of literature than religious belief, and association with cult is difficult to discern.

BIBLIOGRAPHY

E. F. Halvorsen, "Valhall," in *Kulturhistorisk leksikon for nordisk middelalder,* **19** (1975), 464–465; Gustav Neckel, *Walhall: Studien über germanischen Jenseitsglauben* (1913); Magnus Olsen, "Valhall med de mange dører," in *Acta philologica scandinavica,* **6** (1931); E. O. G. Turville-Petre, *Myth and Religion of the North: The Religion of Ancient Scandinavia* (1964), 53–55.

John Lindow

[See also **Eiríksmál and Hákonarmál; Grímnismál; Gylfaginning; Odin; Ragnarok; Vafþrúðnismál.**]

VALKYRIE, a female figure of Scandinavian mythology and heroic legend. Old Norse *valkyrja* means literally "chooser of the slain," and thus the

VALKYRIE

Valkyries are understood as figures attendant at battle, choosing who will live and who will die. Although some scholars have seen the Valkyries as goddesses of death, in the extant sources they are purely literary figures.

Concluding his catalogue of the goddesses in *Gylfaginning*, Snorri Sturluson says that there are women who serve in Valhalla, Odin's hall. They bring drink to the *einherjar*, the dead warriors who inhabit Valhalla. Snorri cites *Grímnismál* 36, which names thirteen of these maidens, and adds: "These are called Valkyries. Odin sends them to every battle. They choose the arrival of death on men and control victory" (*Snorra Edda, Gylfaginning,* chap. 22). The close association with Odin, natural because he is a god of the dead, is further suggested by the Odin name *Valkjósandi* (one choosing the slain), found in the verse of a tenth-century Icelandic skald. *Voluspá* 30 names six Valkyries and says they are the women of Herjan (Odin). The names mentioned in these and other passages have generally to do with battle. A tenth-century poet used two of them, *Gondul* (shaft bearer) and *Skogul* (shaft), in *Hákonarmál* to choose Hákon the Good to fall in battle and thus to swell and improve the forces of the *einherjar*. Another poet, in the vision poem *Darraðarljóð*, used Valkyrie names for women who weave the fates of men in the Battle of Clontarf (1014). A third poem, *Haraldskvæði*, attributed to Þorbjorn hornklofi, presents a description of the warlike and courtly attributes of Harald Fairhair as a dialogue between a Valkyrie and a raven, a traditional beast of battle.

Valkyries appear too in heroic poetry, particularly the Helgi poems. Sigrún is the beloved of Helgi Hundingsbani and Sváva of Helgi Hjorvarðsson. The prose coda to *Helgakviða Hundingsbana* II states that Helgi and Sigrún were reincarnated as Helgi Haddingsbani and the Valkyrie Kára.

BIBLIOGRAPHY
Anne Holtsmark, "Vefr Darraðar," in *Maal og minne* (1939); Folke Ström, *Diser, nornor, valkyrjor* (1954).

JOHN LINDOW

[See also **Darraðarljóð; Eddic Poetry; Eiríksmál and Hákonarmál; Grímnismál; Gylfaginning; Haraldskvæði; Helgi Poems; Odin; Scandinavian Mythology; Skaldic Poetry; Snorra Edda; Snorri Sturluson; Valhalla; Voluspá.**]

VALLA-LJÓTS SAGA

VALLA-LJÓTS SAGA. The significance of *Valla-Ljóts saga* lies in its ethos. The saga unmistakably advocates restraint of violence as the sine qua non for an ordered social existence. Only after forbearance fails to effect peace, must force be exerted to inhibit social disruption. In endorsing forbearance as a social ideal and force merely as a tool of enforcement, the saga forwards a solution to the strife that rent thirteenth-century Iceland. In effect, this message is a rejoinder to a prophetic warning in *Íslendinga saga*, the major chronicle of the era: "Wound will requite wound/Where men fell one another./Each savage assault will breed another" (1.136).

In many sagas purportedly dealing with Iceland's historic matter, honor activates far-reaching, bloody events. The matrix of conflict is often the legal system. In order to maintain or attain honor, saga figures resort to specious litigation, impose unfair settlements, and engage in legal self-help, particularly in the form of blood revenge. Concomitantly, success frequently confers honor. In *Valla-Ljóts saga* honor is no longer conceived in the traditional mode. Blood revenge is shown to be wanton and futile. Deft legal manipulations and the exercise of brute force prove unreliable weapons in the pursuit of honor. The righteousness of the cause, fairness in legal and social dealing, become the cornerstone of worldly success. The model chieftain prefers peace to violent settlements of disputes, and acts of esteem to contests of honor.

The saga has a bipartite structure. The first half features Halli, the spiritual foil to Valla-Ljótr, with Valla-Ljótr appearing only toward the end of the section. The opening scene sets the moral tone of the saga. A dying father counsels his three sons to be mindful of their honor and not to be self-seeking. The father's foresight and advice in Halli's case are in vain. Halli cannot be deflected from his self-ordained path. Imbued with a lofty, self-centered concept of honor, he kills his mother's suitor, a worthy and wealthy freedman, ostensibly because of a legal insult. In reality, he would not accept, in contrast to his brothers, his mother's prospective marriage to a man socially inferior to them. Significantly, Halli exploits the exoneration that the law on verbal insults affords him. He similarly manipulates the law to attain stature, first in the service of Guðmundr the Powerful, and subsequently in his confrontations with Valla-Ljótr.

In his first encounter with Valla-Ljótr, Halli callously prosecutes him for having unwittingly violated the law against judicial transactions on religious holidays. From then on, Ljótr's equipoised sense of honor and forbearance dominate the saga. In a duel, interpreted religiously by Valla-Ljótr as trial by combat, he slays Halli. Ironically, obloquy was at issue, the pretext Halli used to kill his mother's suitor. After Halli's brother murders Valla-Ljótr's nephew in an unprovoked ambush, Valla-Ljótr remonstrates against a retaliative act of blood revenge on Halli's peace-loving son and younger brother. Nevertheless, Valla-Ljótr rallies to his kinsmen in order to effect an equitable legal settlement of the killing. He disregards an attempt on his life by Guðmundr the Powerful. By opportunely returning Guðmundr's spear and by offering him a costly sword as a symbol of friendship, Valla-Ljótr secures Guðmundr as a secular and spiritual ally. In concert they break the cycle of blood revenge and reestablish the social order.

The saga illustrates the attainability of true honor. During the course of the narrative, society, as exemplified within the narrow confines of single *thing* districts (judicial districts), gradually accepts the transformed concept of honor. Chieftains are the exponents and enforcers of the ideal. Individual men of the *thing* give incipient support by disapproving the senseless violence erupting in the wake of traditional disputes over honor.

By a curious coincidence the chronological setting of the saga and the dating of the original manuscript illuminate, from different angles, the author's didactic concern. Like many sagas of its kind, *Valla-Ljóts saga* aspires to a kind of historic verisimilitude. This required that the audience accept the contention that a transformed concept of honor would ultimately prevail. Events accordingly take place at the spiritual turning point in Icelandic history, at the closing of the heathen age and the beginning of the Christian era. Saga writers had posited that by this crucial time, distinguished protagonists occasionally had an intuitive understanding of the Christian meaning of life, which transmuted traditional values and beliefs.

The original version of *Valla-Ljóts saga* is dated either between 1220 and 1240 or between 1230 and 1280. Both datings place its composition within a period of pernicious civil disorder. However, no medieval manuscript is extant. Numerous paper copies from the seventeenth to the nineteenth centuries survive. Of these, only two seventeenth-century versions (AM 496, 4to, 86r–99v, and AM 161, fol., 36r–50v) have independent value.

BIBLIOGRAPHY

Editions are *Valla-Ljóts saga*, Jónas Kristjánsson, ed. (1952); *Valla-Ljóts saga, Islenzk fornrit, IX*, in *Eyfirðinga sǫgur* (1956). Translation: W. Bryant Bachmann, Jr., *Four Old Icelandic Sagas* (1985), 43–67.

Studies include Theodore M. Andersson, "The Displacement of the Heroic Ideal in the Family Sagas," in *Speculum*, 45 (1970), including bibliographical annotations; Marlene Ciklamini, "The Concept of Honor in *Valla-Ljóts saga*," in *Journal of English and Germanic Philology*, 65 (1966); Lars Lönnroth, "The Noble Heathen: A Theme in the Sagas," in *Scandinavian Studies*, 41 (1969); Maarten C. van den Toorn, *Ethics and Moral in Icelandic Saga Literature* (1955), 1–153.

MARLENE CIKLAMINI

[See also **Family Sagas, Icelandic; Iceland.**]

VALOIS DYNASTY, a cadet branch of the Capetian family of French kings. It produced thirteen kings of France between 1328 and 1589—as well as four dukes of Burgundy between 1363 and 1477 who achieved international stature as rulers of the Netherlands. The progenitor of the family was the second son of Philip III, Charles, count of Valois during 1285–1325. When the three sons of Philip IV died without male heirs to succeed them, the French magnates in 1328 turned to Philip, the son of Charles of Valois and first cousin of the last king, Charles IV. In doing so, they ruled that a claim to the throne could not be transmitted through a woman. John II, Charles V, and Charles VI, each the eldest son of his father, succeeded Philip VI.

Charles VI (1380–1422) suffered from mental disorders and in 1420 he was compelled to name as heir his victorious foe, Henry V of England, who had conquered northwestern France and married Charles VI's daughter, Catherine. This action disinherited Charles VII, predeceased by two older brothers, whose legitimacy was belatedly questioned because of Charles VI's condition and the queen's reputation for promiscuity. Although his position was desperate, Charles VII retained enough support so that the English succession could only be enforced militarily. Encouraged by Joan of Arc, Charles VII allowed himself to be crowned at Rheims in 1429. Thus, the Valois monarchy survived, although a long struggle against the English lay ahead.

In 1461 Charles VII's older son, Louis XI, succeeded him; Charles VIII, Louis' only son, followed in turn in 1483. The former's sudden death in 1498 brought to the throne a younger branch of the Valois, descended from Louis of Orléans, the brother of Charles VI. The dynasty became extinct in 1589 with the assassination of Henry III. Despite grave setbacks, the Valois kings did much to build the modern French state.

BIBLIOGRAPHY

Raymond Cazelles, *La société politique et la crise de la royauté sous Philippe de Valois* (1958), *Société politique, noblesse, et couronne sous Jean le Bon et Charles V* (1982), and *Catalogue de comptes royaux des règnes de Philippe VI et de Jean II (1328–1364),* I (Recueil des historiens de la France, VI) (1984); Philippe Contamine, *La France au XIVᵉ et XVᵉ siècles* (1981); Roland Delachenal, *Histoire de Charles V,* 5 vols. (1909–1931); Gaston Dodu, *Les Valois: Histoire d'une maison royale* (1934); Richard C. Famiglietti, *Royal Intrigue* (1986); Kenneth Alan Fowler, *The Age of Plantagenet and Valois* (1967, repr. 1980); Paul M. Kendall, *Louis XI* (1971); Françoise Lehoux, *Jean de France, duc de Berri: Sa vie, son action politique,* 4 vols. (1966–1968); Édouard Perroy, *The Hundred Years War,* W. B. Wells, trans. (1951); Malcolm G. A. Vale, *Charles VII* (1974).

JOHN BELL HENNEMAN

[See also **Charles V of France; Charles VII of France; France: 1314–1498; Hundred Years War; Joan of Arc, St.; Louis XI of France; Philip VI of Valois.**]

VALVENS ÞÁTTR. See Parcevals Saga.

VAN, LAKE (Armenian: Bznunikᶜ or Rštunikᶜ; Greek: Thospitis, Arsenē, or Arsissa). The largest of the three great lakes of the Armenian plateau, Lake Van lies at an altitude of 5,400 feet (1,646 meters), is 80 miles (129 kilometers) long and 40 miles (64 kilometers) wide, and has an area of 1,453 square miles (3,763 square kilometers). Its waters are alkaline rather than saline and are chiefly composed of sodium carbonate, sulfate, and borax, the last used as a detergent. The chief fish is the tarekh, a kind of herring formerly dried for export. The level of Lake Van varies up to 8 feet (2.44 meters) every five years and even more over longer periods, so that of its former seven islands only four are still visible: Lim, Arter, Ałtᶜamar, and Ktucᶜ. All of these were the sites of monasteries. The most im-

portant remains are those of the tenth-century church of the Holy Cross on Ałtᶜamar, built when the island was the capital of the Arcrunid kingdom of Vaspurakan.

BIBLIOGRAPHY

Vital Cuinet, *La Turquie d'Asie,* 4 vols. (1890–1895), II; Sowren T. Eremyan, *Hayastanĕ ĕst "Ašxarhacᶜoycᶜ"-i* (1963), 45, *s.v.* "Bznuneacᶜ cov."; C. F. Lehmann-Haupt, *Armenien einst und jetzt,* II (1926); H. F. B. Lynch, *Armenia,* II (1901): *Nagel's Encyclopedia-Guide: Turkey* (1968); Karl Ritter, *Die Erdkunde im Verhältnis zur Natur und zur Geschichte des Menschen,* IX (1840), 972–1,009.

ROBERT H. HEWSEN

[See also **Ałtᶜamar; Arcrunis; Armenia, Geography; Armenia: History of; Sewan, Lake; Urmia, Lake; Vaspurakan.**]

VANAND. A district of Armenia of about 1,823 square miles (4,722 square kilometers) located in the northern half of the Axurean Valley between the Axurean River (Kars-çay) and the upper Kura. Originally a part of Basean (Greek: Phasianē) and sometimes known as Upper Basean, Vanand formed a separate principality whose ruling house, which terminated in the seventh century, may have been a branch of the house of Orduni extinct since the fourth century. Located between Vanand and Basean, however, lay Aršarunikᶜ and Abełeankᶜ on the left bank of the Axurean, and Hawenunikᶜ and Gabełeankᶜ on the right. Since the princely houses of the last three states were younger branches of the house of Kamsarakan, which owned Aršarunikᶜ, it is possible that the house of Vanand was a Kamsarakan branch as well and, hence, of royal Arsacid descent.

As a result of the Byzantine-Persian partition of Armenia in 591, Vanand became a part of the new Byzantine province of Lower Armenia (Armenia Inferior), which corresponds to the (greater) Ayrarat of Armenian sources. The center of Vanand was the town and fortress of Kars, and here were also found the fortresses of Caṙakᶜar and Arnik, the towns of Zarehawan and Zarišat, and the lake called Cᶜeli (Turkish: Çıldır). The northern trade route from Iran to Anatolia and the Black Sea passed through Vanand and contributed much to its prosperity in the Middle Ages.

Overrun by the Arabs in the seventh century,

Vanand passed to the house of Bagratuni in the eighth century and became the independent kingdom of Kars in 962 when King Asot III of Bagratid Armenia gave it to his brother Mušeł I. Under Mušeł (962–984) the new kingdom expanded until it included Aršarunik^c, Basean, and a part of Ašoc^ck^c, which brought it the additional fortress of Kapoyt Berd (blue castle) and the town of Bagaran, both in Aršarunik^c. Mušeł was succeeded by his son Abas I (984–1029) and by his grandson Gagik-Abas II (1029–1064), the latter abdicating in favor of the Byzantine emperor Constantine X. Vanand, however, was immediately seized by the Seljuk Turks (1065) and then passed to the Georgians in the district of Kari. Overrun by the Mongols in the thirteenth century, Vanand ceased to exist as a separate entity and after a period of Turkoman rule passed to the Ottoman Turks. Under the Bagratids, Vanand enjoyed considerable prosperity and its capital, Kars, became an important mercantile and cultural center.

BIBLIOGRAPHY

Nicholas Adontz, *Armenia in the Period of Justinian,* Nina G. Garsoïan, trans. (1970); Sowren T. Eremyan, *Hayastanĕ ĕst "Ašxarhac^coyc^c"-i* (1963), 82; T^cadewos X. Hakobyan, *Hayastani patmakan ašxarhagrut^ciwn,* 2nd ed. (1968), 136–137, 276–277; Heinrich Hübschmann, *Die altarmenischen Ortsnamen* (1904, repr. 1969), 363–364; Cyril Toumanoff, *Studies in Christian Caucasian History* (1963).

ROBERT H. HEWSEN

[See also **Armenia: History of; Armenia, Geography; Arsacids/Aršakuni, Armenian; Ayrarat; Bagratids (Bagratuni), Armenian; Gagik of Kars; Kamsarakan; Kars; Kura River; Trade, Armenian.**]

VANDALS. The Vandals were a Germanic barbarian people that originated in Scandinavia or the Baltic region. They began to move south in the first century A.D., one group of them settling in the region of Silesia (the Silings) and another farther south and east, just west of the Carpathians (the Hasdings). For three centuries the Vandals remained in these regions, establishing close contacts with the Romans and with other Germanic peoples, especially with the Visigoths, who lived east of the Hasdings.

Pressure from the Huns in the late fourth century caused a general Germanic movement toward the west; the two groups of Vandals recombined and were joined by smaller groups of Alani and Sueves. They crossed the Rhine frontier in 406, moved through Gaul, causing much destruction, and in 409 crossed the Pyrenees into Spain. In Spain they broke up again, the Hasdings and Sueves moving into the northwest part of the peninsula (Galicia), the Silings into the south (Baetica), and the Alani settling in the middle region. In 416 the Visigoths, as federates of the empire, were sent into Spain to counter the Vandals and their allies; in the conflict that followed, the Visigoths (before returning to Aquitaine) nearly wiped out the Silings and badly defeated the Alani. The remaining Alani joined the Hasding Vandals and together they moved into the southern part of the peninsula. By 425, under king Guntharic, they captured Cartagena and Seville from the Romans and, using captured Roman vessels, temporarily occupied the Balearic Islands. At this point, Vandal attention shifted to North Africa, which was much disturbed by military rebellion, Donatist schism, and Berber uprisings; the population was restless under heavy fiscal exactions.

In 428 Guntharic died and was succeeded by his brother Genseric (Gaiseric), who proved to be one of the most able Germanic leaders of the fifth century. Under his leadership, the Vandals crossed into Africa in May 429, leaving Spain and the Balearics behind. A census taken just before the departure indicated that some 80,000 people were involved—a small group to occupy the rich Roman provinces of North Africa.

The Vandals passed through the Mauretanias and into Numidia without opposition. Further east they were able to occupy the countryside without difficulty, but some of the towns held out, notably Cirta, Carthage, and Hippo (St. Augustine died in Hippo in 430 during the Vandals' unsuccessful fourteen-month siege of that city). A Western army under Count Boniface and an Eastern army under *magister militum* Aspar were defeated in 431. In 435 a treaty with Rome gave the Vandals a position as imperial federates in Africa similar to the Visigothic position in Aquitaine. This treaty gave Genseric time to regroup his forces and to equip a fleet with which he attacked Palermo and the fortress Lilybaeum. Without naval protection, the Western Empire agreed to a new treaty in 442 whereby the Vandals received the richest parts of North Africa (Africa Proconsularis with Carthage, Byzacena, and part of Numidia with Hippo) in something like full sovereignty.

Thereafter until 455 relations with Rome continued undisturbed, but the murder of General Aetius in that year followed by the assassination of Emperor Valentinian III shortly thereafter left a political vacuum that invited Vandal intervention. In spite of entreaties from Pope Leo I, the Vandals sacked Rome, pillaging it for two weeks, although conceding to Leo's pleas not to kill or to burn. From Rome the Vandals carried off great quantities of booty and a number of captives, including the widow and two daughters of Valentinian (one of the daughters would be married to Huneric, son of Genseric). The unopposed Vandal fleet then took Corsica, Sardinia, the Balearics, and the remainder of Sicily, and raided the coast of the Peloponnesus, virtually paralyzing Mediterranean commerce. A united imperial attempt to check the Vandals was defeated and in 476 a treaty recognized Vandal dominion over the western islands as well as the African provinces. From this territory Sicily (except Lilybaeum) was shortly thereafter ceded to Odoacer, the Germanic "king" who had deposed the last of the Western emperors in 476.

Under Genseric the Vandal kingdom had reached its height. Following his death in 477, Vandal power slowly weakened, disturbed by internal and external pressures (partly political, partly religious) and threatened by disruption from the ever-rebellious Berbers. The later Vandal kings were Huneric, 477–484 (a son of Genseric), Gunthamund, 484–496 and Thrasamund, 496–523 (nephews of Huneric), Hilderic, 523–530 (son of Huneric and Eudoxia), and (following the deposition of Hilderic) Gelimer, 530–534 (great-grandson of Genseric). The Vandals recognized a royal family, although the means of determining which member should be king are not known. The Vandal kingship was a strong one, the king exercising greater authority over the Vandal nobles than did any of the other Germanic rulers.

Our knowledge of the organization of the Vandal state and life in the Vandal kingdom is very limited. If the Vandals issued a code of law, it has not survived, although the few legal instruments that have been found (see the *Tablettes Albertini*—forty-five wooden tablets written in black ink that record thirty-two acts of property transfer or sale between 493 and 496) indicate that many Roman forms were retained, at least in private law. Other information comes primarily from Roman writers,

who were very hostile to the Vandals. The most important of these were the Byzantine writer Procopius and the African bishop Victor of Vita, writing in exile. Much of the antagonism between the Vandals and their Roman subjects was caused by religious differences—the Vandals were Arians while the Romans were Catholics—and from the Vandal attitude toward the land of Africa. The Vandals claimed complete sovereignty—the fiction of federates had been dropped in 442—and felt no obligation to share the land with their Roman provincials. As a result, the Vandal land regime was harsher than that of the other Germanic kingdoms. Most of the Vandals were settled in Proconsularis (one of the most fertile of the African provinces): there was apparently extensive expropriation of the Roman landholders there. Outside of Proconsularis, the land was considered property of the state and was used for distribution among the king's followers or allowed to remain under Roman administration for the benefit of the king. The wealthier Roman landholders thus felt Vandal exactions heavily, but although many of them lost their most valuable estates, they retained their freedom. For the lower classes and coloni, Vandal rule offered little change from the previous regime except lower fiscal exactions.

The Vandal land policy was aimed at providing a firm economic base for Vandal society, but it may also have been aimed at depriving the Roman provincials of the means to support resistance to Vandal rule. The same may be said for the Vandal religious policy. Arianism received official support and Catholicism was restricted to private observation if not subjected to actual persecution. The Catholics lost their churches and many of the bishops were sent into exile; thus the African bishops were removed as a source of leadership for resistance or of collaboration with the Eastern Empire.

The Eastern emperor Justinian justified his attack on the Vandal kingdom as a move against the Arian heresy and as punishment for the Vandal deposition in 530 of King Hilderic (who had been on good terms with Justinian). For whatever the reason (internal dissension caused by Berber uprisings, possible loss of military readiness as a result of the easy life of North Africa, or poor leadership), the Vandal army was easily defeated by Justinian's general, Belisarios, in 533. The king was taken captive to Constantinople and many Vandal warriors were impressed into the Byzantine army for service on the Persian frontier. The Byzantines overthrew the Vandal administration, restored the Catholic church and bishops, and confiscated much of the Vandal property; within a short time, all Vandal traces disappeared. It would seem that the Byzantine-Roman provinces of North Africa tried to wipe out all memory of Vandal rule. But this picture is almost surely misleading, based on the strongly biased writing of Procopius. Certainly the lesser people had no reason to rejoice, for the Vandal regime had burdened them less heavily than the earlier Roman regime or the Byzantine one that was then coming into being.

BIBLIOGRAPHY

Sources. Christian Courtois *et al.*, eds., *Tablettes Albertini: Actes privés de l'époque vandale* (1952); Procopius, *The Vandalic War*, in Henry B. Dewing, trans., *Procopius*, II (1916), and *Wandalenkriege*, in Otto Veh, ed. and trans., *Prokopwerke*, IV (1971).

Studies. Christian Courtois, *Victor de Vita et son oeuvre* (1954) and *Les vandales et l'Afrique* (1955); Émile F. Gautier, *Genseric roi des vandales* (1935); Arnold Hugh Martin Jones, *The Later Roman Empire, 184–602*, 2 vols. (1964); Charles-André Julien, *Histoire de l'Afrique du Nord—Tunisie, Algérie, Maroc—des origines a la conquête arabe*, 2nd ed. rev. and updated by Charles Courtois (1951); Ludwig Schmidt, *Geschichte der Wandalen*, 2nd ed. (1942), trans. into French by H. E. del Medico as *Histoire des vandales* (1953); Malcolm Todd, *Everyday Life of the Barbarians: Goths, Franks, and Vandals* (1972).

KATHERINE FISCHER DREW

[See also **Alani; Barbarians, Invasions of; Roman Empire, Late.**]

VANIR. In Scandinavian mythology, the Vanir (Old Norse; sing., *vanr*) are a group within the family of gods. The only gods named as Vanir are Njǫrðr and his son and daughter, Freyr and Freyja. As each is associated with fertility, scholars usually understand the Vanir as fertility gods.

The only occasion when the Vanir act as a group in the mythology is during the great war with the Æsir, the other and major group of gods. *Vǫluspá* (strophes 21–24) accounts this the first war in the world and mentions an otherwise obscure figure, Gullveig or Heiðr, thrice killed by the Æsir and yet still alive, the possessor of powerful magic. When battle was joined the Vanir gave a good account of themselves, but the conclusion of the war is unclear in *Vǫluspá*.

Snorri treats the story more coherently. After neither side emerged victorious, they exchanged hostages: Njǫrðr and Freyr went to the Æsir, Hœnir and Mímir to the Vanir (*Ynglinga saga*, chap. 4). As a token of peace, both sides spat into a kettle. From the spittle the gods made a man, Kvasir. Dwarfs murdered him and fermented the mead of poetry from his blood (*Snorra edda, Skáldskaparmál*, chaps. 4–6). Later Odin obtained the mead for both gods and men.

Many scholars have regarded this myth as a reflection of the subduing of an indigenous agrarian people in Scandinavia, worshipers of fertility gods like the Vanir, by more warlike invaders, perhaps Indo-Europeans, worshipers of gods like the Æsir. On the other hand, Dumézil has drawn attention to Indo-European parallels and suggested that the myth is an inheritance from Indo-European times, an explanation of how and why farmers and warriors must live together to create a whole society. In either case, the myth is well integrated. The mead of poetry, derived from the truce between the two groups, is a powerful symbol of mythic wisdom.

Tacitus (*Germania*, chap. 40) describes the worship of a fertility goddess, Nerthus, whose name is linguistically equivalent to that of Njǫrðr.

BIBLIOGRAPHY

Ólafur Briem, *Vanir og æsir* (1963); Georges Dumézil, *Gods of the Ancient Northmen* (1973), 3–25; Anne Holtsmark, "Vanir," in *Kulturhistorisk leksikon for nordisk middelalder*, XIX (1975), 493–494.

JOHN LINDOW

[See also **Æsir; Hœnir; Mímir; Vǫluspá.**]

VANNI, ANDREA (*ca.* 1332–1414), Sienese painter. Influenced by Barna, Simone Martini, and Ambrogio and Pietro Lorenzetti, he collaborated with Bartolo di Fredi in 1353 and with Antonio Veneziano in the Siena Duomo in 1370 and was documented in Naples in 1375 and 1383. His principal surviving works include the portable altarpiece

Crucifixion. Small portable altarpiece attributed to Andrea Vanni (or possibly Paolo di Giovanni Fei). ISABELLA STEWART GARDNER MUSEUM, BOSTON

Victory of the Sienese over Nicola di Montefeltro in 1363. Monochrome fresco by Lippo Vanni in the Palazzo Pubblico, Siena, 1373. ALINARI/ART RESOURCE

with *Crucifixion* (Isabella Stewart Gardner Museum, Boston), the polyptych with *Madonna and Child Enthroned with Saints* (S. Stefano, Siena, 1400), and the triptych with *Crucifixion* (1396) in the Siena Pinacoteca. The long-lived Vanni was a painter whose style evolved from a naturalistic to an increasingly hieratic one, and it seems to have found favor with conservative patrons throughout Tuscany and Naples.

BIBLIOGRAPHY

Bernhard Berenson, *Italian Pictures of the Renaissance: Central Italian and North Italian Schools*, 3 vols. (1968); Millard Meiss, *Painting in Florence and Siena After the Black Death* (1951).

ADELHEID M. GEALT

[See also **Antonio Veneziano; Barna da Siena; Bartolo di Fredi; Lorenzetti, Ambrogio; Lorenzetti, Pietro; Siena; Simone Martini; Trecento Art.**]

VANNI, LIPPO (*fl.* 1341–1373), Sienese miniaturist and painter. His style was influenced by Simone Martini, Lippo Memmi, and Ambrogio and Pietro Lorenzetti. His signed and dated works include a reliquary triptych of a *Madonna and Child Enthroned* (1358; Rome, SS. Domenico e Sisto) and the frescoes depicting the *Victory of the Sienese over Nicola di Montefeltro in 1363* (1373). Numerous portable triptychs, altarpieces, and miniatures have been ascribed to him.

BIBLIOGRAPHY

Bernhard Berenson, *Italian Pictures of the Renaissance: Central Italian and North Italian Schools*, 3 vols. (1968).

ADELHEID M. GEALT

[See also **Lippo Memmi; Lorenzetti, Ambrogio; Lorenzetti, Pietro; Siena; Simone Martini.**]

VÁPNFIRÐINGA SAGA (The story of the people of Vápnafjörðr) relates a feud between two families in the Vápnafjörðr district of northeastern Iceland.

The chieftains Helgi Þorgilsson of Hof and his brother-in-law Geitir Lýtingsson of Krossavík have a Norwegian merchant murdered in order to acquire his cargo and valuables, a golden armlet and a chest believed to be filled with money. The merchant's Icelandic partner, Þorleifr the Christian, frustrates their design, however, and delivers the merchandise to the murdered man's heirs in Norway. Helgi now persuades a certain Ketill to summon Þorleifr for nonpayment of the heathen temple tax, but during a storm Ketill is forced to take shelter with Þorleifr, who returns good for evil by providing generous hospitality. The close friendship between Helgi and Geitir gradually turns to bitter enmity, partly because each suspects the other of having purloined the Norwegian's valuables and partly because Helgi becomes increasingly more ruthless in his encroachments upon Geitir's liege men. Among his most heartless misdeeds is his abandonment of his dying wife, Geitir's sister. Finally Geitir and his men ambush Helgi—there is a lacuna in the text at this point—and he is killed.

Incited by his stepmother, Helgi's son Bjarni avenges his father's death by killing his uncle Geitir, but regrets this act immediately and holds Geitir's head on his knees until he dies. Geitir's son Þorkell repeatedly attempts to wreak vengeance on Bjarni, but without success. In a battle between the two kinsmen and their followers, both leaders are seriously wounded. Bjarni has his friend, the physician Þorvarðr, heal Þorkell's wounds. When Þorkell finds himself in straitened circumstances, Bjarni invites him and his household to move to Krossavík. At the urging of his wife, Þorkell accepts the invitation, and the two kinsmen become reconciled and remain close friends as long as they live.

Although the author was not a good stylist, he was an excellent craftsman. To the finest detail he constructed his story according to the principle of contrastive parallelism. Whereas Helgi is ruthless and aggressive, Geitir is wise and unassertive. In the second generation—an interesting variant of the generation-gap theme—Þorkell is stubborn and belligerent, while Bjarni is patient and conciliatory. Symbolically, the woman as inciter to vengeance in the first half of the story is balanced by the woman as co-initiator of reconciliation in the second. Since family loyalty was one of the highest virtues in the *Íslendingasögur* (family sagas), the author sought to explain the conflict among kinsmen as the result of a curse placed on Helgi for his first killing. This curse, however, is neutralized by Bjarni's conciliatory bearing, which, in turn, has a counterpart in the exemplary behavior of Þorleifr the Christian.

Older oral traditions about the people of Vápnafjörðr are preserved in the poem *Íslendinga-drápa,* by Haukr Valdísarson. The author of the saga has radically ennobled the character of Bjarni, who is known in older sources as Víga-Bjarni (Killer-Bjarni) and described as "quarrelsome." The story ends with a list of Þorkel's descendants, among whom were Bishop Þorlákr the Holy and his nephew, Bishop Páll Jónsson.

BIBLIOGRAPHY

The text is in Jón Jóhannesson, ed., *Austfirðinga sögur* (1950); the translation is in Gwyn Jones, trans., *Four Icelandic Sagas* (1935). See also Theodore M. Andersson, *The Icelandic Family Saga* (1967); Rolf Heller, "Studien zum Aufbau und Stil der Vapnfirðinga Saga," in *Arkiv för nordisk filologi,* 78 (1963); Paul Schach, *Icelandic Sagas* (1984), 132–134, 164.

PAUL SCHACH

[See also **Family Sagas, Icelandic; Haukr Valdísarson.**]

VARANGIAN GUARD. The Varangians, or "companions," guarded the person of the Byzantine emperor in the palace and on campaign both night and day. They also guarded the emperor's secretarial office and his reception chamber. They accompanied him to religious services and in public processions and festivities, and probably had special guard rooms in the palace.

The Varangian Guard as a distinct unit of the Grand Hetairia (mercenary bodyguards) began in 987–988 as a contingent of some 6,000 Rus sent to aid Emperor Basil II to repress a revolt of Bardas Phokas, even though some Rus and Norse served as early as the 830's and certainly throughout the tenth century. In addition to Scandinavians, Anglo-Saxons started serving in the eleventh century. The unit was most famous in the eleventh and twelfth centuries (the most famous Varangian was Harald Sigurdson, later King Harald III Hardråde of Norway. In 1204 the Guard ignominiously surrendered to the crusaders; it never regained its vigor even though modest numbers of Varangians are reported in the thirteenth and early fourteenth centuries, perhaps as a vestigial and symbolic reminiscence and tradition.

The Varangians carried famous one-edged axes and, if serving on horse, also spears and swords. They wore coats of mail, greaves, steel helmets, and round shields. They had an interpreter and worshiped in a special church. Their commander was called an *akoluthos.* They probably numbered about 500 when accompanying the emperor on campaign, but there are no reliable figures. Although famous for their loyalty to the emperor, they occasionally were charged with accumulation of excessive and improper wealth. They received monthly pay as high as forty gold nomismata, war booty, and occasional presents (such as for the accession of an emperor), but they may have bought their entrance to the guard.

BIBLIOGRAPHY

Sigfús Blöndal, *The Varangians of Byzantium,* trans., rev., and rewritten by Benedikt S. Benedikz (1978).

WALTER EMIL KAEGI, JR.

[See also **Bardas Phokas; Basil II "Killer of the Bulgars."**]

VARDAN AREWELC⁣ᶜI (1200/1210–1271/1272). Biographical information is lacking on the early years of the Armenian historian Vardan Arewelc⁣ᶜi (the Easterner), also called "the Great." One of his early teachers was Yovhannēs Vanakan (d. 1251), whom Vardan refers to in his *Universal History* as "our glorious father," and whose now-lost historical work Vardan, like Kirakos of Ganjak, employed. Around 1239/1240, Vardan visited Jerusalem on a pilgrimage and then went to Cilicia (*ca.* 1240/1241), where he was received very favorably by King Hetᶜum I (1226–1269/1270) and the reigning *katᶜołikos,* Constantine. In his own *History of Armenia,* Kirakos, Vardan's friend, fellow historian, and classmate, states that Constantine entrusted Vardan with an encyclical, which the latter brought back to eastern Armenia for the signatures of the somewhat reluctant bishops, monks, and princes. This journey would have taken him from Erzurum (Karin) to Ani, Kars, Bǰni, Amberd, and other eastern Armenian monasteries, as well as to Caucasian Albania. Vardan spent his remaining years in eastern Armenia.

In writing his *Universal History,* Vardan made use of Kirakos' work. Another source of his information derived from personal acquaintance with the principals of the day. In addition to his intimacy with prominent Armenians, Vardan was acquainted with the Mongol Hulagu and his Christian wife, Doquz Khatun. Vardan attended the Mongol New Year celebration in Iran in 1265/1266 at Hulagu's invitation, and described it in chapter 96 of his work. Hulagu apparently was greatly impressed by Vardan, sought his advice on politics, and invited him to return the next year. After Hulagu's death, Doquz Khatun secretly contacted Vardan for advice. In addition to its relevance for Armenian and Mongol history, Vardan's work is valuable for the early history of the Seljuks, since it preserves a lengthy extract from the now-lost history of Mχit^{c}ar of Ani on Seljuk origins.

BIBLIOGRAPHY

Sources. Mkrtič [Joseph] Emin, ed. and trans., *Mecin Vardanay Barjrberdc^{c}woy patmut^{c}iwn tiezerakan* (1861) (this edition was incorrectly attributed to another Vardan, from Barjrberd in Cilicia); Ališan, ed., *Hawak^{c}umn patmut^{c}ean* (1862); Édouard Dulaurier, trans., "Les Mongols, d'après les historiens arméniens," in *Journal asiatique,* 5th ser., **16** (1860), and "Extrait de L'Histoire Universelle de Vartan le Grand," in *Recueil des historiens des croisades: Documents arméniens,* I (1869).

Studies. Robert Bedrosian, "The Turco-Mongol Invasions and the Lords of Armenia in the 13–14th Centuries" (diss., Columbia, 1979); Dickran K. Kouymjian, "Mχit^{c}ar (Mekhithar) of Ani on the Rise of the Seljuqs," in *Revue des études arméniennes,* n.s. 6 (1969); H. Oskean, "Vardan Arewelc^{c}i," in *Handēs Amsoryea* (1921).

ROBERT BEDROSIAN

[See also **Armenian Literature; Het^{c}um I; Historiography, Armenian; Hulagu; Karin; Kirakos of Ganjak; Mongol Empire; Seljuks.**]

VARDAN MAMIKONEAN, ST. (*d.* 451), *tanutēr* (lord) of the Mamikonean house and *sparapet* (grand marshal) of Armenia in the first half of the fifth century. Despite his earlier temporizing and outward religious compromise, Vardan led the revolt of the Armenian naχarars against the attempt of the Sasanian king of kings, Yazdgard II, to force Zoroastrianism on Armenia in 450. Together with his supporters, Vardan fell at the Battle of Avarayr, 26 May/2 June 451, but Armenia remained Christian. The Armenian church raised Vardan and his companions, the *Vardanank^c*, to the rank of saints and martyrs. Enshrined in Ełišē's epic *History of the Vardan and the Armenian War,* which compares them to the Maccabees, they became the symbols, par excellence, of Armenian religious and national resistance, and they continue to be commemorated to the present day.

BIBLIOGRAPHY

Ełishē, *History of Vardan and the Armenian War,* Robert W. Thomson, trans. (1982); René Grousset, *Histoire de l'Arménie dès origines à 1071* (1947); Cyril Toumanoff, *Manuel de généalogie et de chronologie pour l'histoire de la Caucasie chrétienne* (1976).

NINA G. GARSOÏAN

[See also **Avarayr; Ełiše; Mamikonean; Naχarar; Sasanian History; Sparapet; Tanutēr.**]

VARDAPET (**vartabed**; Armenian, "teacher" or "doctor"). There is still debate about the etymology of *vardapet.* According to one theory, it derives from the Middle Persian *varda* (work) and *pati* (Armenian: *pet,* "chief"). It was used by the translators of the Armenian version of the Scriptures to render the Greek *didaskalos* and *epistates* and the Hebrew *rabbi.* Until the tenth century the word was used in a general sense, but thereafter it was restricted to designate priests who taught in monasteries and were doctors of the faith. By the thirteenth and fourteenth centuries the term was used for those who had attained the highest academic rank in monastic schools. Vardapets in the Armenian church have the right to hold staffs when they preach. In medieval Armenian inscriptions the word and its derivative *vardpet* are occasionally used in the sense of "architect."

BIBLIOGRAPHY

E. Benveniste, "Titres iraniens en arménien," in *Revue des études arméniennes,* 9 (1929), 10; Robert W. Thomson, "*Vardapet* in the Early Armenian Church," in *Le muséon,* 75 (1962).

KRIKOR H. MAKSOUDIAN

[See also **Armenian Church, Structure.**]

VARDZIA. See Wardzia.

VARIATIO. *Variatio* refers to the opening notes of antiphons. Each musical mode has a limited number of *variationes*. Sung at the beginning of the antiphon and psalm combination, the *variatio* also occurs when the antiphon is repeated at the end of the psalm. In this position, it immediately follows the psalm termination (differentia). In order to ensure a smooth musical transition from psalm to antiphon, the psalm termination is chosen according to the *variatio,* or how the antiphon begins. Rules and groupings for differentia and *variatio* are given in the Tonary. Although *variatio* and intonation are not equated in medieval theory, they are probably identical in practice, consisting of a few notes setting one or two syllables of the text, and sung by a soloist to set the pitch.

BIBLIOGRAPHY
Willi Apel, *Gregorian Chant* (1958).

ANDREW HUGHES

[See also **Antiphon; Differentia; Tonary.**]

VARNA, city in Bulgaria on the Black Sea coast where an army consisting of Hungarian and other Christian troops led by Hungarian King Wladislas I and János Hunyadi was defeated on 10 November 1444 by the Turkish forces of Murad II (Wladislas was killed). This battle marked the end of the last Christian anti-Ottoman crusade.

B. KREKIĆ

[See also **Bulgaria; Crusades of the Later Middle Ages; Hunyadi, János.**]

VASPURAKAN (Georgian: Aspurakani; Arabic: Asfaradjān or al-Asfuradjān; Greek: [B]Asprakania/Basprakan), the Armenian name for the Sasanid Iranian province of Armn, organized after the Byzantine-Persian partition of Armenia in 591. Persarmenia at this time consisted of the city of Dwin, the Armenian principalities of Siwnik^c and Mokk^c, and some thirty-five districts between the two, most of which belonged to one Armenian principality or another but otherwise had never previously been organized as a unit. It was these thirty-five districts that were gathered to form Vaspurakan.

Overrun by the Arabs by 653, Vaspurakan came to be dominated by the house of Arcruni, which had been gradually acquiring one principality of the region after another ever since the fourth century. The Arcrunids are believed to have been the scions of the old Orontid royal house of Sophene, transplanted by the kings of Armenia to the southernmost borderlands of their realm, probably in the first century B.C. After the conversion of Armenia to Christianity in the early fourth century, they claimed descent from the sons of King Sennacherib of Assyria, who, the Bible says, fled to Armenia (2 Kings 19:37; Isa. 37:38). Originally holding the districts of Greater and Lesser Ałbak in the valley of the upper Zab, with their seat at the castle of Hadamakert (now Başkala), the Arcrunids appear to have been the viceroys (*bdeašk^c* or *vitaxae*) of Adiabene, the Median March of the Armenian kingdom, before 371. They later acquired the extensive holdings of the house of Mardpetakan after the latter became extinct by the fifth century, as well as the principality of Anjevac^cik^c about 867. Between 772 and 890 the Arcrunids gradually spread their rule to the whole of Vaspurakan, as well as to the former Bagratid principalities of Kogovit, Tamoritis (Tmorik^c), and later Moxenē (Mokk^c), thereby reducing the surviving princely houses of the province to vassalage.

Prince Xač^cik-Gagik II was recognized in 908 as (anti-) king of Armenia by the Arabs and as prince of princes (*archōn tōn archontōn*) in 921/922 by the Byzantines. Thereafter, in spite of repeated Arab invasions, wars with other Armenian kingdoms, and various internal struggles, Vaspurakan prospered. New fortresses were built, old ones were restored, and an extensive building program was inaugurated, especially at the town of Ostan and on the island of Ałt^camar in Lake Van, where the magnificent church of the Holy Cross (915–921) survives. Under Gagik II (908–*ca.* 943) Ałt^camar became the capital of the kingdom, with a city containing schools, magazines, warehouses, treasuries, armories, and a palace with orchards and terraced gardens. Gagik also built a palace overlooking the lake on nearby Mt. Artos.

Spreading their rule from the basin of Lake Van to the upper course of the river Zab, the Arcrunids became masters of the southern Armenian trade routes linking northern Iran with Mesopotamia, and they rivaled the Bagratunids for primacy as rulers of the most important Armenian kingdom of the period. Eventually weakened by its wars and internal strife, Vaspurakan was subject to Turkish raids as early as 1016/1018. As a result, King Sennacherib (Senek^{c}erim) made the extraordinary decision to cede his entire kingdom to Basil II in return for lands located in Cappadocia, within the Byzantine Empire. According to contemporary chroniclers, Vaspurakan consisted at this time of 10 cities, 72 fortresses, and 3,400 villages.

In his migration to his new lands in 1021/1022, the king was said to have been accompanied by 14,000 men, women, and children. There is evidence, however, that the Armenian population that remained in Vaspurakan offered some resistance—though it was soon crushed—to the arrival of the Byzantine authorities, especially from the fortress of Amiwk^c.

Byzantine Vaspurakan was administered as the catepanate of Basprakania, with its center at Van, until it was overrun by the Turks in 1071. Thereupon Vaspurakan ceased to exist as a separate entity, the term being used by the later Armenians for the general vicinity of Van. The Arcrunid line that settled in Cappadocia is last heard of at Tarsus in Cilicia in the eleventh century, and a branch survived at Mahkanaberd (Mankaberd) in southern Georgia, holding high office until it disappeared early in the fourteenth century. Several Armenian families (Berozian, Zedayan, Dadian, Dedeyan) subsequently claimed descent from the Cappadocian line.

The chief towns of Vaspurakan were Van, Ostan, Arčēš, Berkri, Naχčawan, Maku, Moks, Arckē, Artamet, and Xizan. Of its nearly forty castles and fortresses, the chief were Hadamakert, Ašotakert, Kotor, Ampriotik, Kangavar, Ĭłmar, Šatax, Smbataberd, Šamiram, Hayk, Zṛel, and, briefly, Manazkert (Greek: Manzikert) and Xlat^c. Its major monasteries were Varag, Narek, Ałt^{c}amar, Holy Cross, Aṛna, and St. Thaddeus at Maku. In 1113 the bishop of Ałt^{c}amar, primate of Vaspurakan, assumed the position of an independent kat^{c}ołikos (supreme patriarch) of the Armenian church, a title he retained even after the schism was healed in 1409. The area of the original Sasanid Vaspurakan was 15,775 square miles (about 40,870 square kilometers); of the Arcrunid kingdom (whose boundaries did not exactly coincide with the original province), about 13,370 square miles (about 34,636 square kilometers), expanding at its height to about 17,000 square miles (about 44,030 square kilometers).

BIBLIOGRAPHY

Nikolai Adonts, Armenia in the Period of Justinian, Nina G. Garsoïan, ed. and trans. (1970), 179–182, 246–251; H. Bartikian, "La conquête de l'Arménie par l'empire byzantin," in Revue des études arméniennes, n.s. 8 (1971); Sowren T. Eremyan, Hayastaně ěst "Ašxarhac^c oyc^c"-i (Armenia according to the Geography) (1963), 82, 117; T. X. Hakobyan, Hayastani patmakan ašxarhagrut^{c}iwn (Historical geography of Armenia), 2nd ed. (1968), 173–191, 274–275; Heinrich Hübschmann, Die altarmenischen Ortsnamen (1904, repr. 1969), 261–263, 339–347; J.-M. Thierry, "Monastères arméniens de Vaspourakan," in Revue des études arméniennes, n.s. 2–12 (1965–1977); Cyril Toumanoff, Studies in Christian Caucasian History (1963) and Manuel de généalogie et de chronologie pour l'histoire de la Caucasie chrétienne (1976), 87–93; V. M. Vardanyan, Vaspurakani Arcrunayc^c t^{c}agavorut^{c}yune (The Arcruni kingdom of Vaspurakan) (1969); K. N. Yuzbashian, "L'administration byzantine en Arménie aux Xe–XIe siècles," in Revue des études arméniennes, n.s. 11 (1975–1976).

ROBERT H. HEWSEN

[See also Ałt^{c}amar; Archōn tōn Archontōn; Arcrunis; Armenia, Geography; Armenia: History of; Armenian Art; Armenian Church, Doctrine; Bagratids, Armenian; Gagik II; Naχčawan.]

VASSALLETTUS (Vasallectus, Vassalletto) is the surname of a family of marble workers who produced Cosmati work and sculpture in Rome and Latium from the mid twelfth century through the mid thirteenth century. Inscriptions usually contain only the family name; hence, the genealogy of the family and the composition of the workshop are not entirely secure. The name Petrus Vassallettus appears in Cori (along with his brother, Johannes), in the cathedral at Segni, and on the famed paschal candelabrum in S. Paolo Fuori le Mura, Rome. The family name appears, inter alia, on the paschal candelabrum in the cathedral at Anagni and the cloister of S. Giovanni Laterano, Rome. To the Vassallettus family are also attributed the cloister of S. Paolo Fuori le Mura, Rome, and the portico of S. Lorenzo Fuori le Mura, Rome.

BIBLIOGRAPHY

Peter C. Claussen, Magistri doctissimi romani: Die römischen Marmorkünstler des Mittelalters (Corpus cosmatorum, I) (1987), 101–144, with extensive bibliography; Dorothy F. Glass, *Studies on Cosmatesque Pavements* (1980); Edward Hutton, *The Cosmati* (1950).

DOROTHY F. GLASS

[See also **Cosmati Work; Lateran.**]

VATNSDŒLA SAGA (The story of the people of Vatnsdalr), which was probably written around 1270 at the monastery of Þingeyrar, is the chronicle of the chieftaincy (*goðorð*) of the Vatnsdalr district of northern Iceland. In the fanciful introduction, which takes place in Norway, Þorsteinn Ketilsson mortally wounds a highwayman named Jökull. Despite his wound, Jökull overpowers Þorsteinn, yet spares his life. Þorsteinn is pardoned by Jökull's parents and marries their daughter Þórdís. Their son Ingimundr wins fame and fortune as a Viking, supports King Haraldr Fairhair in his struggle for supremacy in Norway, and emigrates to Iceland, where he becomes chieftain (*goði*) of the district in which he was destined to settle. When old and nearly blind, Ingimundr is mortally wounded by his foster-brother's nephew Hrolleifr, whose life he seeks to save.

After Ingimundr's slaying has been avenged by his four sons, the eldest, Þorsteinn, acquires the chieftaincy. Þorsteinn and his brother devote themselves to purging the district of an assortment of witches, warlocks, and other evildoers. Following Þorstein's death, his son Ingólfr holds the chieftaincy until he is slain in a foolhardy attack on a band of robbers. The chieftaincy remains unoccupied for a time since Ingólfr's sons are too young to manage it. When a certain Þorkell silfri attempts to acquire the *goðorð* by means of sorcery, he is slain by Þorkell krafla, in return for which Þorgrímr á Karnsá acknowledges Þorkell as his natural son. Þorgrímr holds the chieftaincy until he is succeeded by his son Þorkell, who has gained wealth and renown abroad and in Iceland. When the National Assembly adopts Christianity (999), Þorkell submits to baptism and remains firm in the faith to his dying day.

The structure of the first part of *Vatnsdœla saga* is firm, but after the death of Ingimundr the work disintegrates into a series of more or less independent anecdotes that are held together by two themes: family good fortune and the ideal chieftain.

The style is characterized by the frequent use of alliteration, antithesis, and pairs of synonyms. More than two dozen different designations are used for the many scoundrels in the story, and the concept of fame and fortune is expressed by a wide variety of terms. The author of *Vatnsdœla* outdoes even the creator of *Laxdœla saga* in his subjective use of psychological motivation. There is evidence to suggest that part of the story is a reworking of a lost older saga that was excerpted by Sturla Þórðarson (d. 1284) in his redaction of *Landnámabók*. Instead of using the generation gap theme, the author has Ingimundr develop from a Viking warrior to a peaceful farmer-chieftain. Even more than *Eyrbyggja saga*, *Vatnsdœla saga* extols the virtues of moderation and conciliation. Although most of the action takes place in heathen times, the chieftains exemplify the virtues of Christianity. The characterization of Haraldr Fairhair as a stern but just ruler has been interpreted as an indication of the author's hope that submission to Norwegian rule (1262–1264) would bring peace and justice to Iceland after the brutal Sturlung Age.

BIBLIOGRAPHY

Theodore M. Andersson, *The Icelandic Family Saga: An Analytic Reading* (1967); Gwyn Jones, trans., *The Vatnsdalers' Saga* (1944); Paul Schach, *Icelandic Sagas* (1984), 145–147; Einar Ól. Sveinsson, ed., *Vatnsdœla saga*, in *Íslenzk fornrit*, VIII, *Vatnsdœla saga* (1939, repr. 1958); Walther Heinrich Vogt, ed., *Vatnsdœla saga* (1921).

PAUL SCHACH

[See also **Eyrbyggja Saga; Family Sagas, Icelandic; Landnámabók; Laxdœla Saga.**]

VAULT, a masonry ceiling or roof; a self-supporting structure of stones or bricks disposed so as to cover an interior space, usually carried by walls, piers, or columns. The term can also be used to describe an enclosed space covered by such a masonry ceiling, especially a lower or underground room, or undercroft; it is in this sense that "vault" is used to describe a crypt, burial chamber, or vaulted drain or sewer. A unit of vaulting is called a bay. There are many kinds of vaults; the most important and most common are given below.

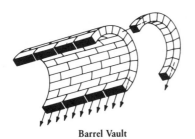

Barrel Vault

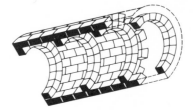

Banded Barrel Vault

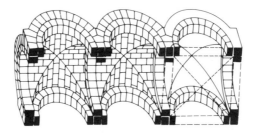

Groin Vault

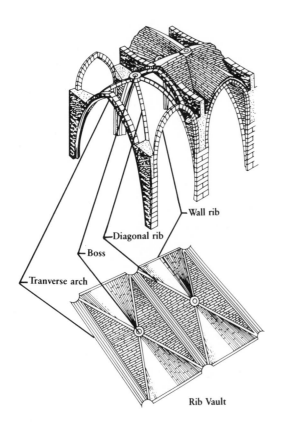

Wall rib

Diagonal rib

Boss

Tranverse arch

Rib Vault

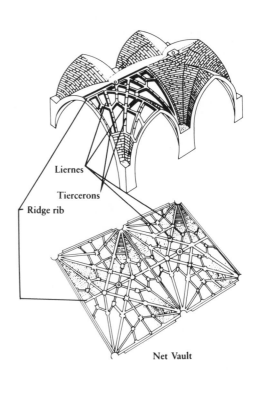

Liernes

Tiercerons

Ridge rib

Net Vault

TYPES OF VAULTS
Adapted from Fitchen, *The Construction of Gothic Cathedrals*

Annular vault, a vault that follows a curved plan, as in the barrel vaults of early Christian ambulatories.

Barrel vault. The basic form of any vault is the arch, and the simplest form of vault is the barrel vault, which may be conceived as an arch extended in depth or as a series of contiguous arches. The weight of a barrel vault is continuous along its length, requiring heavy walls to counter the downward and outward thrusts of the semicylindrical or slightly pointed vault. It is also called a tunnel or wagon vault.

Banded barrel vault, a semicylindrical or barrel vault reinforced at intervals by transverse arches (built before the vault itself) that project below the surface of the vault. Banded barrel vaults are fairly common in Romanesque architecture, where they may be given a slightly pointed profile. (See the illustrations of the nave of La Madeleine, Vézelay, and of the abbey church of Fontenay at "Romanesque Architecture.")

Cloister vault, a type of cupola vaulting consisting of four, eight, or twelve curved surfaces, solid along their bases and rising to a common crown, often with a pointed profile. It may be conceived as the intersection of two, four, or six barrel vaults of equal height and diameter. Brunelleschi's cupola for the cathedral of Florence is a double-shell cloister vault. (See illustration at "Brunelleschi.") In England such a construction is called a domical vault.

Corona vault, in Byzantine churches of the domed-octagon type, an octagonal ring of spandrels or pseudo-pendentives above the four main arches and the angle squinches of the central space and below a circular dome, serving as a transitional device. This area has the appearance of an inverted crown, and so is called a corona vault.

Cross vault, a vault formed by the intersection on cross axes of two semicylindrical vaults. Quadripartite groin and rib vaults are cross vaults.

Diamond vault. See *Prismatic vault.*

Dome, a hemispherical vault.

Domical vault. See *Cloister vault.* This term is also used to describe a groin or rib vault whose crown is higher than its boundary arches, causing it to dome upward; a domed vault.

Fan vault, a type of vaulting peculiar to the English Perpendicular style, in which all the ribs have the same curve, resembling the framework of a fan. The structure of a fan vault is a shell of inverted conoids, joined at the center by flat vault-ing and carried by transverse arches. The ribs may be connected by panels of blind Perpendicular tracery. In late examples, like the chapel of Henry VII at Westminster Abbey, pendant cones of masonry are suspended from hidden transverse arches (a pendant vault or fan vault with pendants). (See illustrations at "Gothic, Perpendicular" and at "Westminster Abbey" in this volume.)

Folded vault. See *Prismatic vault.*

Groin vault, a cross vault produced by two barrel vaults of identical shape intersecting at right angles. The edges or lines of intersection are called groins. The thrust of a groin vault is not continuous along its sides, as with a barrel vault, but is channeled outward to the four corners of the vault bay and down the corner piers. The profile along the groin of a simple groin vault is a semi-ellipse; in a domed groin vault this profile is semicircular, causing the two intersecting barrel vaults to bow upward, and yielding a domed or domical vault that is higher in the center than at the sides.

Lierne vault, a rib vault that employs liernes or secondary ribs, which link diagonal ribs (tiercerons) and ridge ribs to create geometric patterns, as in net vaults and some star vaults. (See illustration at "Lierne.")

Net or *mesh vault,* an elaborate rib vault employing liernes and tiercerons to create an overall reticulated pattern of lozenges, stars, and other shapes, which gives the effect of a net or mesh suspended beneath the vault. The ribs of a net vault are often purely decorative.

Oblique or *skew vault,* a vault spanning a space between two parallel walls that are not directly opposite each other. The ends of such a vault are not at right angles to its axis, but at oblique angles to it; thus the vault is skewed in relation to its axis.

Prismatic vault, a late Gothic vault type developed in Eastern Europe, built without ribs and composed of folded panels of brickwork that produce a prismatic surface effect. It is also called a diamond vault (from the faceted shapes) or a folded vault (from its resemblance to a sheet of intricately folded paper).

Quadrant vault, a half-barrel vault, that is, a vault whose arc is one quarter of a circle. Like quadrant arches, it is used in the galleries of Romanesque and Gothic churches to buttress the nave walls. (See illustration of St. Étienne, Caen, at "Romanesque Architecture.")

Quadripartite vault, a cross vault divided into

four compartments, cells, or fields by two diagonal ribs, with the vault bay defined by transverse arches and wall ribs; the simplest form of groin or rib vaulting. (See illustrations of the St. Denis ambulatory and the nave of Chartres Cathedral at "Gothic Architecture.")

Rib or *ribbed vault,* a cross vault erected over diagonal ribs that reinforce the groins of the vault; the ribs were erected first to help support the thin shells of masonry laid between them. The simplest form is the quadripartite vault, with two diagonal ribs, two wall ribs, and two transverse arches; in a sexpartite vault a third transverse arch or rib is added, producing a vault with six cells or fields. In late Gothic architecture, ribs tend to lose their structural function and become decorative, with additional ribs added (liernes, tiercerons). In English Gothic vaulting a ridge rib runs along the longitudinal axis of the vaults, often with transverse ridge ribs crossing it on the minor axis of each vault bay. In some late examples, the ribs break loose from the masonry shell of the vault and move freely through space as flying ribs.

Sail vault, a pendentive dome, used in place of groin or rib vaulting. See *Dome.*

Sexpartite vault, a square bay of rib vaulting in which a third transverse arch or rib divides the vault into six compartments, cells, or fields rather than the usual four (quadripartite). It is used in early Gothic architecture. Because each vault bay embraces two bays of the nave elevation, with an alternating rhythm of principal and secondary piers, a sexpartite vault is also a type of double-bay vault. (See illustration of Laon Cathedral nave in "Gothic Architecture.")

Star vault, a vault in which the ribs describe a star pattern. Star vaults are fairly common in Islamic architecture, where the ribs are usually structural. In the West, star vaults often cover an octagonal space such as that of a chapterhouse, and the ribs are largely decorative. It is also called a stellar vault.

Stilted vault, a cross vault in which the springing along one or both of the cross axes is raised, or stilted, by the insertion of horizontal courses above the impost. Used in Gothic ribbed construction to adjust the vault to an irregular or elongated bay.

Tierceron vault, a rib vault that employs tiercerons or intermediate ribs, which rise from the springing to the crown or apex of the vault. In a net vault, tiercerons are joined by secondary ribs or liernes to produce complex geometric patterns.

BIBLIOGRAPHY

James H. Acland, *Medieval Structure: The Gothic Vault* (1972); John Fitchen, *The Construction of Gothic Cathedrals: A Study of Medieval Vault Erection* (1961) and *Building Construction Before Mechanization* (1986).

GREGORY WHITTINGTON

[See also **Arch; Archivolt; Bay System; Buttress; Construction: Building Materials; Construction: Engineering; Dome; Gothic Architecture; Gothic, Decorated; Gothic, Flamboyant; Gothic, Perpendicular; Lierne; Masons and Builders; Pendentive; Romanesque Architecture; Tierceron; Voussoir.**]

VEGETIUS (**Renatus Flavius Vegetius,** *fl.* late fourth–mid fifth century) wrote the four books of his military manual *Epitoma rei militaris* (or *Rei militaris instituta*) between 383/384 and 450. He dedicated the work to his emperor, probably Theodosius I, and in it lamented the decline of Roman military efficiency. Among the authorities he claimed to have used in his somewhat disordered compilation were Cato the Elder, Celsus, Frontinus, and Paternus. The *Epitoma* was less influential in its own time than in the Middle Ages, when, surviving in multiple manuscripts, it was translated several times for contemporary purposes (for instance, by Jean de Meun in prose and by Jean Priorat in verse). Each book of the *Epitoma* has a preface, an epilogue, and rubrics (the latter not supplied by the author). Book I deals with the recruit; book II with military discipline and organization; book III with strategy; and book IV with naval warfare and siegecraft. Vegetius may also have been responsible for the compilation on veterinary science attributed to a P. Vegetius of the same period.

BIBLIOGRAPHY

An edition is Flavi Vegeti Renati, *Epitoma rei militaris,* Charles Lang, ed., 2nd ed. (1885, repr. 1967).

Studies include Andreas Andersson, *Studia Vegetiana* (1938); Dankfrid Schenk, "Flavius Vegetius Renatus: Die Quellen der *Epitoma rei militaris,*" in *Klio: Beiträge zur alten Geschichte, Beiheft,* 22 (1930).

JEANETTE M. A. BEER

[See also **Chivalry; Fachschrifttum; Jean de Meun; Warfare.**]

VEHICLES, EUROPEAN. During the course of the Middle Ages, vehicles were notably improved over what they had been in antiquity, and at the end of the medieval period there were more carts, wagons, and carriages in use than had been the case in Roman times, despite a decrease in the number of miles of surfaced roads. Before 1500, technological advances had ensured superior traction, more efficient construction, especially as regards the wheels, and a higher degree of comfort for passengers.

THE CLASSIFICATION OF VEHICLES

Vehicles may be classified in various ways: by the number of animals required to pull them, by the number of wheels, or by the purposes to which they were put. In classical times one reads of the *biga* pulled by two horses or mules, and of the *quadriga* with its four-horse team. In the Middle Ages in France it was no longer the number of horses but the number of wheels that distinguished among vehicles. In fourteenth-century France a *quadriga* was a vehicle with four wheels. In American English a cart always has two wheels and only two, and a wagon invariably four. In British English, however, a cart may have two or four wheels. Over the centuries, carts and wagons have been used for hauling freight and for bringing in the harvest; chariots and cars for carrying heroes, generals, and racing drivers; and passenger vehicles for pleasure, for ceremonial purposes, and for social status and prestige.

THE LEGACY FROM ANTIQUITY

Probably the earliest evidence for wheeled vehicles comes from Mesopotamia toward the end of the fourth millennium B.C. During most of antiquity vehicles were equipped with a pole and two yokes and were drawn by either two or four draft animals abreast, or sometimes by three or more. Two were hitched under the yokes, and the outside animals pulled on their neighbor's yoke. The harness included two straps, the one encircling the animal's belly and the other either its shoulders or its breast. Lefebvre des Noëttes named this arrangement the throat and girth harness and declared that it tended to strangle horses and mules, so that they could not pull heavy loads. Since the harness was appropriate to oxen, they were employed to draw bulky goods, like marble for construction. However, J. Spruytte, in his more recent experiments and investigation of sculptures of the ancient period, claimed in 1977 that Lefebvre des Noëttes was in error. He had confused two ancient harnesses: one in which the yoke rested on the neck and shoulders, so that traction was effected by the shoulders, and one in which the horse pulled with his breast. Spruytte claims that there could never have been a throat and girth harness and that the men of antiquity were not inefficient in the manner in which they harnessed horses. The earliest Mesopotamian chariots were drawn by onagers—wild asses of western India and Baluchistan. The wheels in that region were disk wheels, that is, wheels made of three solid pieces of wood fastened with tranverse struts and strengthened with a swelling around the hub. It has been suggested that the reason for this construction was a scarcity of large trees in the Middle East, whereas in northern Germany with its immense forests in prehistoric times there were disk wheels made from a single section of a tree trunk. This latter type of disk wheel, however, was much more likely to break than a tripartite disk wheel. Actual wheels have survived from ancient times; pictures and toy vehicles supply additional details. The rims of the earliest tires were studded with bronze nails; specimens fitted with bronze tires (*ca.* 2000 B.C.) have been unearthed. Circular axle holes and the use of linchpins to secure the wheels indicate that in most cases wheels turned on the axletree.

By the third millennium B.C. wheeled vehicles had become part of ritual and funerary practices, as for example at Ur and in southern Russia. The practice later spread to Europe, as discovered in Hallstatt and La Tène graves, and continued as late as the ninth century A.D., as discovered in the Oseberg burial in Denmark. Linguistic evidence suggests that the main regions for the diffusion of wheeled vehicles in Europe were the Germanic and Celtic areas plus Greece. They appeared later in central and southern Italy (with the exception of the southeast).

The first noteworthy improvements in vehicles occurred around 2000 B.C., when the horse was domesticated and used for traction and when spoked wheels first appeared. These innovations made possible the fast, light, two-wheeled chariot drawn by a pair of horses. About 1550 B.C. the war chariot had reached Crete and Mycenae, and by 1300 B.C. it was in Sweden. In the eighth century B.C., Homer describes the Achaean heroes as riding to battle in chariots but not fighting from them. In classical times the infantry was the most effective formation in battle. When the two-wheeled chariot became obsolescent for military purposes in the Mediterranean region, it nevertheless continued to be used for races, both in Greece at the Olympic games and in Rome in the Colosseum. Its unrivaled prestige and glamour meant that it continued to be the vehicle of the gods and of the Roman emperors. In outlying parts of Europe the chariot continued in use for war. In prehistoric Britain chariots were the preferred military arm, and Caesar was confronted with them there in the first century B.C.

Evidence for Minoan and Mycenaean vehicles is both literary and pictorial. Wheels had four fellies and four spokes, were fastened with a linchpin, and, at Knossos, were stored separately from the rest of the vehicle. However, the barbarian practice of burying the hearse with the hero, plus the preservative qualities of northern bogs, has meant that most archaeological evidence for early vehicles has come from northern Europe rather than from Mediterranean lands. Celtic wheels were skillful examples of the wheelwright's art. Wheels of hornbeam, ash, elm, or oak revolved on the axle and were held on by linchpins. There were ten to fourteen spokes, lathe-turned, mortised or doweled into the hub and felly, and fitted with iron or bronze collars. Hubs, too, were turned and bound with bronze, sometimes both inside and outside. Those from the Dejbjerg wagon (first century B.C.) had a further refinement: channels inside the hub, perhaps for wooden rods to act as roller bearings. Celtic wheels had fellies that were made of a single piece of heat-bent wood and, by the second century B.C., iron tires shrunk into place while hot rather than fastened with nails. According to Diocletian's Edict on Maximum Prices (A.D. 301), wagons with fellies in one piece sold for nearly twice the price of wagons with composite fellies.

If historians agree on the nature of ancient and medieval wheels, they have hotly debated the question of the wagon body and chassis and especially the existence of the pivoted axle. For example, some scholars have criticized the reconstruction of the Dejberg and Vix funeral wagons with a pivoted axle. One difficulty is that ancient paintings and bas-reliefs show four-wheeled vehicles from the side, an angle from which the kingpin is hard to see. In the early Middle Ages, artistic representations commonly ignore the chassis and, sometimes, the pole, and depict vehicles that could not possibly have been usable. Only in the fourteenth century was there a real interest in technological realism in illustrations. The remains of ancient hearses buried

with the deceased have not been as helpful as could be wished, because almost all wooden parts have decayed. Some archaeologists have postulated a wooden kingpin. In at least three cases, however, the iron kingpin of the pivoted front axle has been found in place. One was at Hochmichele Grave 6 in southern Germany, one at Les Jogasses in the Marne—both from the late Hallstatt period (roughly from 700 to 500 B.C.), and the third at Somodor in Hungary, dating from the second or third century A.D. It is therefore certain that antiquity knew the turning train. It is impossible, however, to be certain how widely it was used. Obviously the difficulties of using a four-wheel vehicle with rigidly fixed axles would be formidable. If the vehicle was too large or too heavily loaded to be lifted from time to time and set on the correct course, the wheels would tend to be forced off the road and turns could take place only by describing a very wide circle. Wagon technology of the northern barbarians was very well known and much admired among the Romans, who were the first to make very frequent, routine, and extensive journeys for administrative and other purposes. The preferred method of travel was in four-wheeled carriages. It does not seem possible that so many journeys would have been made had the vehicles been plagued by incessant breakdowns, especially when the Romans had available to them a convenient alternative, the two-wheeled carriage. Throughout history, however, superior convenience has not always forced people to adopt the most efficient technology. (In Poland in recent times, for example, farmers were still using wagons with rigidly fixed axles to haul the harvest into the barn. This state of affairs is understandable. Getting in the harvest happened only once a year; homemade wagons were probably less expensive than a superior product; and, if money were in short supply and labor very cheap, the size of the farm probably would not have justified the purchase of an efficient wagon.) Nevertheless, one can safely conclude that, at least on long journeys, the Romans used wagons with the pivoted front axle.

In the first century B.C., vehicles began to proliferate among the Romans. At least seventeen different names are given, some half of them Celtic. Two-wheelers included the *carpentum, carrus, cisium, covinus,* and *essedum,* and four-wheelers included the *carruca, petorritum,* and *raeda,* all of which were used for luxury travel. Whether the *raeda* was considered a carriage or a freight vehicle seems to have been determined by the fittings. There was also the *carruca dormitoria* fitted up for sleeping. Heavy-duty hauling was the chief purpose of the *petorritum, ploxenum,* and *serracum.* Luxury vehicles were comfortable and fast. Julius Caesar, according to Suetonius (*Lives of the Caesars*), made the longest journeys in a hired *raeda* with extraordinary rapidity, and Plutarch states that the trip from Rome to the Rhône took him eight days. Carriages were popular not only because they were fashionable, but also because they provided an opportunity for conspicuous consumption. Emperors gave such privileges to the senatorial class as the decorating of their *carrucae* with silver plaques, and in the fourth century Ammianus Marcellinus made note of the competition among senators as to who should have the highest carriage.

FIFTH TO TWELFTH CENTURIES: THE DECLINE IN THE USE OF PASSENGER VEHICLES

In antiquity, transport had been organized around the pole and double yoke, so that vehicles were drawn by two, three, four, or more animals. Almost without exception, representations show the mules or horses harnessed abreast. No doubt, in depictions of the god Jupiter, it was simply a matter of prestige for him to be shown in a two-wheeled chariot drawn by six horses abreast. In the real world, such extravagance was not practical and may not even have been allowed. In A.D. 438, the Theodosian Code declared that three mules were adequate for a two-wheeled vehicle, while eight mules should be yoked to a *raeda* in the summer and ten in the winter. The question then arises as to how ten animals could be harnessed abreast to pull a carriage. Roman roads were not ordinarily wide enough for so many animals to walk side by side. The solution may be found in a relief at Langres, executed perhaps in the second century A.D., that depicts a four-wheeled vehicle drawn by two pairs of horses, one behind the other. It is unclear, however, how the front pair is harnessed to the wagon. This method of harnessing seems to be unique in the illustrations.

Other provisions of the Theodosian Code have been cited as proving the inefficiency of ancient harnesses. The *raeda* was not to carry more than two or three men and 1,000 pounds (almost 457 kilograms), while a two-wheeled conveyance was to carry 200 pounds (90.7 kilograms) only. These weights were exceeded by those allowed on ox-drawn post wagons, for which the limit was 1,500 pounds (about 680 kilograms). The latter is not much above those weights allowed on horse-drawn vehicles, which may argue that ancient oxen were smaller and less powerful than their descendants. It has been pointed out, however, that these weights are not very different from those in effect in eighteenth-century France.

Early in the Christian era there begins to be evidence of innovations in vehicles, notably in the use of a competitor to the pole wagon: the shaft cart, a vehicle that opened the way for the use of a single draft animal. Frescoes from Pompeii, painted prior to A.D. 79, show a two-wheeled chariot with shafts drawn by a goat. These paintings have been dismissed as fanciful, but there is no doubt about the shafts shown on a chariot drawn by one animal at Igel, near Trier, in a bas-relief from the third century. Vehicles with shafts are shown on a number of funerary monuments from the regions of Arlon in Belgium, Metz in France, and Igel around this time. Some of the two wheelers are pulled by a single animal.

In the fifth and sixth centuries, as their world fell apart, the Gallo-Romans attempted to continue an earlier way of life, while the Merovingians tried their best to adopt it. Their princesses on their bridal journeys rode in a *pilentum,* a *carruca,* or a *currus.* The poet Fortunatus (530–609) celebrated the Gallic *raeda,* flying on swift wheels behind a double-yoked team. He wrote an excessively complimentary tribute to a bishop for his kindness in inviting him to dismount and ride on the soft cushions of his carriage, where Fortunatus was comfortable and protected from the weather. Nevertheless, there is evidence that passenger vehicles were declining in numbers and variety. They are mentioned less and less frequently. A saint's life written in the first half of the tenth century about a seventh-century holy woman, Odilia, states that she rode from the convent of Baume-les-Dames (Doubs) to her father, the duke of Alsace, at Hohenburg *in curru,* as the custom then was. Beginning in the sixth century, writers do not seem to be making the distinctions between vehicles that the Romans had made. Fortunatus not only mentions that Galeswintha was riding in a *pilentum* (a luxury vehicle) but at one point he has her in a *serracum* (a heavy-duty freight cart of wagon). Ancient Roman authors had mentioned at least seventeen different vehicles; Isidore of Seville (*ca.* 570–636) in his *Etymologies* lists eight, and Hrabanus Maurus (*d.* 856) in his *De universo* only five. Hrabanus Maurus was a contemporary of Einhard, who found that the last of the Merovingian kings rendered the Frankish people ridiculous by driving into town in a wagon drawn by oxen led by a cowherd. It has been suggested that it was the rusticity of riding behind oxen that was the cause of Einhard's contempt. It was probably more than that, however, because during the remainder of the Middle Ages no man with any pretensions to gentle blood would be seen in a wheeled vehicle, unless he were too ill to sit a horse. For example, Chrétien de Troyes emphasizes the devotion of Lancelot to Guinevere by showing he was even willing to undergo the humiliation of riding in a cart, if only he could rescue her.

As the historian searches for reasons for the decline of riding in passenger vehicles, he or she cannot fix on the deterioration of the Roman roads as a major cause. Although maintenance on these roads had largely ceased, there continued to be much carting in the Carolingian Empire over considerable distances. The *Capitulary aquisgrense* (801–813) provided that the equipment of kings, bishops, counts, and abbots was to be carried in carts. Carts or wagons were necessary to military expeditions and to agricultural production. In the ninth century, to get crops to points where they could be sold, tenants of the great Rhineland abbey of Prüm, west of Coblenz, carried them to Coblenz, Bonn, Cologne, and Worms as well as to Metz, Verdun, and Frankfurt am Main. On the lands of St. Germain-des-Prés, according to the polyptych of the abbot Irmion, the dependents carted various crops, predominantly wine, to Quentovic, Paris, Orléans, Angers, and elsewhere. The vehicles were pulled by two oxen, but whether they were two-wheelers or four-wheelers is unknown. They are referred to as *angaria*. However, it was in fifteen wagons (four-wheelers), each pulled by four oxen, that the Avar treasures were carted back to Aachen by Charlemagne. In the tenth century, some abbeys in what is today Belgium owned grape-producing properties farther south, entailing the necessity of transporting the wine to the convent by vehicles for religious services. And in Anglo-Saxon England, cartage was one of the services owed to the king.

Nor can the disfavor into which passenger vehicles fell be attributed to deterioration in the carriages themselves. On the contrary, numerous improvements in harnessing and traction, the appearance of nailed-on horseshoes, and other refinements should have made such vehicles more attractive to riders. Perhaps it was the superior inducements of the improvements in horseback riding that drew travelers away from carriages. The introduction of saddles with stirrups, which reached the West at least by the sixth century, was such an improvement. Prior to this introduction it had been much harder to mount a horse. To ride a horse without stirrups was dangerous, so that being on horseback conveyed panache and taking part in a mounted hunt meant a contempt for danger; but these factors did not necessarily make horseback riding popular with a broad spectrum of the population. Other improvements involved physical changes in the horses themselves. The history of the horse in the Middle Ages shows more and more attention to breeding, which produced an increase in size, in types, and in numbers.

It has sometimes been mistakenly supposed that medieval wheels were clumsier than earlier ones, a supposition based on the wheels of the Oseberg wagon of about 850 and of a few other vehicles, chiefly from Swedish bogs. The four wheels of the Oseberg funerary vehicle have high fellies, almost half the diameter of the wheel, and with correspondingly short spokes. Such wheels are by no means as graceful as the ancient high Celtic wheels, many of them a little over 35 inches (90 centimeters) and more in height and made from a single piece of heat-bent wood. Technologically, the nature of the material limits the diameter of the rim, so that if one wishes to have a heavier wheel with a deeper felly, it is necessary to make it of a series of pieces of wood. In the Middle Ages, where a picture clearly depicts the rims of the wheels they are usually of a series of fellies. The disadvantage of the narrow tread is it will cut into the roadbed, although it is unlikely to stick in mud. On the other hand, a broader tread holds up better on a rocky or uneven roadbed, although it is likely to stick in mud. Narrow wheels with long spokes are more likely to break from the pressure of sideways thrust, but those with short spokes and very deep fellies stand up better. These observations on sideways thrust apply only to wheels in one plane before the introduction of the dished wheel, which was in use at least by the fifteenth century.

The body of the Oseberg wagon is clinker-built, a technique borrowed from boat-building. It has been suggested that the Oseberg wagon would not have been practicable for a journey much longer than that of a hearse. It has been maintained and denied that the wagon could have had a turning

Miniature from the Trier Apocalypse showing the first modern horse collar. German, *ca.* 800. FOTO MARBURG / ART RESOURCE

train. (The Oseberg wagon is among the last in the tradition, going back at least to the early third millennium B.C., of burying the funerary vehicle with the corpse. With the conversion of the Scandinavians to Christianity, the custom lapsed.)

The early Middle Ages was a period in which inventions that had first appeared in late antiquity, like the shaft cart, were widely adopted. Nailed-on horseshoes were in use certainly by the tenth century. The Romans had had a horseshoe that was tied onto the animal's hoof. Nailed-on horseshoes provided better traction for the horse and protected the horse's hoofs against injury, a most important consideration, since lame horses were (and are) usually considered unfit for use.

Technological invention also improved the horse's harness. The horse is faster than the ox and has greater endurance, so it can work more hours per day. As far as the actual harnessing of the horse is concerned, the subject remains controversial. With the medieval harness, like the modern, the horse can pull a much heavier weight than seems to have been common in ancient times. The breast-strap harness seems to have been much used. In a tapestry found with the Oseberg ship there is a picture of a horse with a breast strap and withers yoke, the traces attached at the juncture of the breast strap with the yoke. Superior harnesses are

documented in Scandinavia, where plowing with horses was common in the ninth century. Metal harness mountings have been found in ninth-century Swedish graves. The improvement in the harness may not, however, originally have been Swedish. The breast-strap harness was in use in China by the second century; and the word *hames*, referring to the rigid sidepieces of the horse collar, is from a Turkic dialect of Central Asia. Philological evidence shows that the breast strap may have been borrowed by the Slavs before the sixth century and the horse collar by the Germans in the eighth or ninth century. A picture in the Trier Apocalypse (*ca.* 800) has been hailed as the first to depict the modern horse collar. Some scholars prefer the tenth century for the introduction of the modern horse collar into Western Europe, and even after that, some illustrations continued to depict the ancient horse collar. Nevertheless, the modern version had been widely adopted by the twelfth century. With it a single horse harnessed between shafts could pull a cart holding several people, and could also back up and exert a braking effect when going downhill.

Other distinctive medieval inventions were the whippletree and tandem harnessing. The whippletree was a wooden bar whose ends were hooked to the horse's traces and whose center was connected to the front of the vehicle. It provided greater

Elijah Taken into Heaven. Cast bronze relief on door of Novgorod Cathedral, 1154, showing early whippletree. FOTO MARBURG/ART RESOURCE

maneuverability and, as an alternative name, splinter bar, indicates, was the part of the harness expected to break under pressure to spare other parts of the vehicle. The whippletree appears in the Bayeux tapestry and on the bronze doors of Novgorod Cathedral (made at Magdeburg in 1152–1154). In antiquity, the use of a single horse to pull a chariot was a late innovation. There is only one piece of evidence that the Romans had employed pairs of draft animals, one behind the other, leaving it doubtful that this method was much used in antiquity. In the Middle Ages, however, horses were harnessed in single file, the horse nearest the cart harnessed between shafts and the animals in front attached by ropes or traces. The team was controlled by a postilion riding the horse nearest the vehicle, and in the case of a team of several horses harnessed in tandem, by an additional postilion on one of the front horses.

In illustrations of vehicles from the Carolingian period through the twelfth century, passengers in the vehicles seem to be either villeins or, if important personages, biblical or allegorical characters, like Elijah going up to heaven in the fiery chariot or the virtues and vices of Prudentius' *Psychomachia*. In keeping with the inspirational nature of the material, the artist in many cases did not find it worthwhile to indulge in realism to the extent of depicting reins or a pole for the cart. Frequently the

wheels are placed so as to render the vehicle nonfunctional. Vehicles are drawn by two horses abreast, and most have two-wheeled, square bodies. Except for the fact that they lack a railing and instead have two boards for sides, they bear a marked resemblance to an English farm cart depicted in a manuscript of Aelfric's vernacular paraphrase of the Hexateuch produced at St. Augustine's in Canterbury in the second quarter of the eleventh century (fol. 67v).

Occasional illuminations in manuscripts of the period show a curved rear on the cart; but the chief exceptions to the rule of the boxlike shape occur in two manuscripts of the eleventh century. An illustration in Prudentius' *Psychomachia* (Brussels, Bibliothèque Royale, MS 9968–9972, fol. 93r) shows a four-wheeled, bathtublike body without a pole. Another notable departure from the norm is furnished by pictures in a manuscript of Aelfric's paraphrase mentioned above: for example, a wagon with an upright (or uprights) supporting by means of hooks the corners of a cloth, thus making a kind of hammock, in which Joseph is improbably sitting bolt upright, apparently riding in superior comfort to meet his father. In the same manuscript, in illustrations of pharaoh's chariots sent to bring Joseph's father and brothers to Egypt, the body of the chariot is shaped like a crescent moon, but the pictures show no evidence either of supports or of the springiness of a hammock: four men are sitting upright in the vehicle. Each chariot is drawn by one pair or two pairs of mules, in the latter case one pair hitched in front of the other. It is obvious that the Anglo-Saxon artist never completed illuminating the manuscript: some wheels have spokes outlined but not colored. But this fact does not account for the lack of realism; such a lack was, at least partly, a question of the temper of the times.

The suspension of pharaoh's chariots in this Anglo-Saxon manuscript seems to be unique in Western Europe at the time, although already in the tenth century suspended chariots had been reported in Hungary by a traveler, Ibrahim ibn Yaᶜqūb. He wrote that the kings there rode in big, high wagons with four wheels and with a post rising at right angles from each corner axle end, and that from these posts a litter or sedan chair, covered with brocade, hung from strong chains. Those sitting in it were not subjected to the jolting of the wagon.

Altogether, the body of Joseph's chariot in the illumination from the Aelfric manuscript bears so strong a likeness to the Hungarian vehicle that the former may indeed be the drawing of an Anglo-Saxon artist who has heard of the suspended wagons but has not seen one. Early in the reign of Cnut (1017–1035) the sons of Edmund Ironside took refuge from the new king in Hungary. Perhaps reports of life there reached England and influenced our artist. Nevertheless, there are obvious differences between the Hungarian vehicle and that in the Anglo-Saxon manuscript. For instance, one may speculate whether the artist meant to show two or four posts with hooks (in any case they are not chains). In addition, the Hungarian vehicle had a roof, whereas Joseph's did not. Almost all representations of chariots from the Carolingian period through the twelfth century show them uncovered, but a tilt (canopy) appears on a vehicle depicted on a capital from the crypt of St. Denis.

THIRTEENTH TO FIFTEENTH CENTURIES

In some thirteenth-century illuminations, there begins to be much more interest in the details of harnesses. A manuscript of Herrad of Hohenberg's *Hortus deliciarum* (*ca.* 1200) shows pharaoh in a six-sided, two-wheeled cart pulled by two horses abreast with a postilion on the near horse. The animals have bits, bridles, collars, and ropes from the collars to the vehicle. In the same manuscript the sun's chariot is drawn by two pairs of horses, one behind the other, with a modern horse collar and whippletrees. The wheels have five fellies and ten spokes.

Fourteenth-century illustrations not only document the medieval inventions and adoptions in the field of transportation made long before: the stirrup, horseshoes, the modern horse collar, the whippletree, and the shaft cart; they also show technological advances that some writers have denied to the Middle Ages, like the suspended carriage, the turning train, and the pivoted front axle. The existence of the turning train has been doubted before modern times, but it has now been proved that it was known in ancient times, and in the fourteenth century a number of illuminations indicate it. For example, a fourteenth-century manuscript of *Les Métamorphoses d'Ovide allégorisées* (Paris, Bibliothèque Nationale, MS 373, fol. 251v) shows what is almost certainly a turning train. The wagon is making an abrupt turn. Two animals are harnessed to the vehicle, with the whippletree consisting of a single-tree, double-tree arrangement, which was still current in the twentieth century. The pin fastening the double tree to the pole or

tongue of the wagon is plainly visible. The pole is forked where it is rigidly attached to a trapezoidal piece of wood with the wider side fastened to the front axle. Since the pole is at an angle to the front of the wagon, one can assume the presence of a kingpin connecting the wagon bed and front axle. The front wheels are not smaller than the rear ones, so they could not have passed under the wagon body, but they are at the ends of extended axles, a feature which meant that wider turns could be made without the wheels being stopped by the sides of the vehicle. Two features that are recognized evidence of the turning train are the sway bar and front wheels that are smaller than the rear ones. Both are noticeable features in a fourteenth-century manuscript (London, British Museum, Sloan 3983, fol. 12) that shows two four-wheeled baggage wagons. Nevertheless, in the fourteenth century there are numerous illustrations that do not bother to give details of the chassis, however clearly they show the rest of the vehicle. For example, on the Luttrell Psalter carriage (*ca.* 1340), the carvings on the vehicle are depicted with meticulous care, but there is no undercarriage. In the fifteenth century many pictures show the sway bar and front wheels smaller than the rear ones, amply documenting the use of the pivoted front axle.

Suspension was a refinement added to the baggage or farm wagon to make a luxury vehicle, and before and after its invention there was a remarkable resemblance between the two.

Transportation was by packhorse, chariot, or cart. The *carecta* or *charrette* each had two wheels; the *currus, curriculum, char,* and *chariot* were four-wheeled vehicles. Purchases of "two wheels for the *charrette* and four for the *chariot*" were among the expenses of the abbey of St. Jean-le-Grand of Autun in 1399–1400. The parts of a cart were the frame or body, the wheels, and the pole or shafts. The railing that formed the sides could be removed in favor of boards, and in England at harvest time, hurdles were added to extend the carrying capacity. A *chariot* was described as consisting of a body with a perch, wheels, axles, and shafts. Iron was used for nails, linchpins, axle spindles, hurters, chains for braking, and bands around the futchels and the hubs of the wheels, and frequently around the wheels themselves. The hurters were iron plates on the axletree to keep it from wearing. In 1385 a chariot belonging to the duchess of Burgundy contained 417 *livres* of iron—370 to 441 pounds (167.8 to 200 kilograms), according to which *livre* was used. The iron tire was made up of several pieces fastened with great protruding nails, which must have been why some towns, such as London and Millau, forbade iron-shod carts to enter. They were also barred from crossing London Bridge or the bridge at Toulouse.

Pictures show wheels made up of a number of fellies and, in the fourteenth and fifteenth centuries, of six or, more usually, eight spokes, sometimes with one spoke to a felly. These wheels had fewer spokes than Celtic wheels, but the fellies were narrow like the ancient ones, much more so than had been the case with the wheels of the Oseberg wagon or those found in Scandinavian bogs. Dished wheels protect the wheel against the horizontal thrust to which it is subjected when going over uneven ground. However, although known to Villard de Honnecourt in the thirteenth century, dished wheels do not seem to have been popular before the fifteenth century.

By far the most complicated part of the vehicle was the wheels, the only part made by specialists. In England, if there was no wheelwright in the village, wheels were bought at fairs, but the rest of the cart could be made locally. At Paris in the thirteenth century wheelwrights, according to Étienne Boileau's *Livre des métiers,* had their own guild, which was listed with the carpenters' guild. Wheelwrights produced only the wooden wheel; iron was applied by blacksmiths, locksmiths, or spurriers. Both a wheelwright and a blacksmith accompanied a convoy of carts carrying money from Paris to Toulouse in 1285 for the use of Philip III in his invasion of Aragon. The journey lasted from 23 February to 31 March 1285, and almost every day there was

something for the blacksmith to do. Perhaps his work consisted mostly of shoeing horses, but he also renewed the iron on the carts. One of the important repairs to cart wheels consisted in replacing the iron nails protruding from the tread. The expense accounts show that the blacksmith bought planks, iron tires and nails for them, and iron for the axles, including axle clouts. Under the expenses for the wheelwright are listed repairs to the carts, fellies, and axles; new wheels and iron for the wheels; and frequent purchases of grease for lubrication. Altogether one has the impression that only incessant care kept the convoy rolling.

Carts were not the only vehicles used in France at this time. In 1231 the four-wheeled wagon was part of the equipment of a royal military expedition, one chariot to every fifty men. Before the fourteenth century the front and back wheels of a wagon were the same size, and it could not make the abrupt turns possible for the cart. Also, the capacity of the cart was much less than that of the wagon. If one may judge by tolls of the twelfth to fifteenth century at Paris, Harfleur, and Crépy, the *chariot* or *char* (wagon) of the period carried twice the load of the cart and occasionally more. In the early thirteenth century a *chariot* was taxed at Givors at two and a half times, and at Sens at four times, a cart. More horses were ordinarily required to pull a wagon than a cart. *Chariots* were pulled by two, three, four, or frequently five and even six horses, whereas carts made do with one, two, or three. Of these, the one-horse vehicle seems to have been less common than the others. Carts seem always to have been equipped with shafts, as was frequently true of the *chariot*. Finally, the wagon

Carriage depicted in the Luttrell Psalter, *ca.* 1340. British Library, Add. MS 42130, fols. 181v–182.

could carry bulkier articles and was more stable than the cart, which tipped when the horse or horses were removed.

In comparing medieval carts and wagons with their modern counterparts, it is important to remember that the twentieth-century vehicles have diverged considerably from their predecessors. The modern *charrette* and *chariot lorraine* have approximately the same capacity, but the *charette*'s weight is poised on only two points, not four. Consequently, it requires a firmer surface than the *chariot*, which is better able to traverse marshy terrain and unimproved roads. Also, the *chariot lorraine* has the front wheels smaller than the rear, rendering it more maneuverable than its medieval predecessor.

In England in the Middle Ages, the wagon was rarely employed, and the cart was mainly relied upon for transportation. All types of goods were carried in carts, and they were essentially farm carts. When abbeys commuted services of their villeins, they preferred to retain the obligation of cartage. The king had the right of purveyance of carts. Only with the introduction of the Dutch wagon in the sixteenth century did four-wheeled vehicles become popular.

It was otherwise in France. In the eleventh century, documents mention wagons and carts in toll exemptions, and the *Chanson de Roland* refers to fifty Spanish *chars* carrying gifts to Charlemagne. In the twelfth century a charter of Philip I fixed charges on a wagon to be paid to the canons of Notre Dame at twice that of a cart and four times that of a donkey. However, in the same century the only vehicles mentioned by six Angevin toll lists are carts. In the thirteenth century chariots were used to carry goods from the river Oise to the fairs of Champagne, and of Sens and Givors. They are mentioned again and again in Boileau's *Livre des métiers*, although by no means so frequently as carts. The toll at Bapaume listed charges on *chariots*, and Beaumanoir's *Coutumes de Beauvaisis* explains that if chariots, carts, packhorses, or men carrying loads encounter each other on a narrow road, the one least heavily loaded or with the least perishable stuff should turn out. On the other hand, in the thirteenth century in the south of France, even carts, but especially chariots, seem to have been rare, to judge from toll lists. In the fourteenth century there was an increase in the use of vehicles in this area, for although between Marseilles and Avignon pack animals, especially mules, continued

as the chief means of transportation, chariots and carts were also used.

Pack animals were sometimes more economical than wheeled vehicles, and for this reason in 1284/1285 the ordinance of the household of Philip IV called for a decrease in the number of carts and wagons belonging to the household and the substitution of sumpter animals. Packhorses or mules can negotiate difficult trails, whereas wheeled vehicles require roads; and carriage roads were by no means to be found in all parts of medieval France. At Toulouse in the fourteenth and fifteenth centuries, goods went by wagon from Toulouse to southern Languedoc, to Béarn and Bayonne, but went across the Pyrenees or the Massif Central to northern France by pack mule. In Dauphiné in the fourteenth and fifteenth centuries, there were wagon roads only on either side of the Rhône and up the Isère as far as Grenoble; from Marseilles carriage roads went to Aix and to the Rhône. Northern France seems to have been much more fully provided with wagon roads, and efforts were made to keep them open. There were still other reasons for preferring pack animals to carts. Evidently they were considered to cause less wear on the merchandise: In the late thirteenth century professional carriers of woolen cloth from the fairs of Champagne to southern France signed contracts promising to use pack animals, not carts.

There seems to have been an increase in the use of wagons in the fourteenth and fifteenth centuries. For example, the departments of the royal household deprived of their carts by Philip IV in 1284/1285 are found in subsequent ordinances again to be furnished with vehicles. Furthermore, whereas in 1284/1285 only the king's *chambre* had a chariot, and vehicles attached to other departments were carts, in 1317 and 1328 two other divisions each had a wagon, and in 1380–1381 royal household accounts mention repairs to five chariots, each maintained for a different purpose. In the fourteenth and fifteenth centuries noble households—such as those of the dukes of Burgundy and Orléans—employed chariots, and in 1393 Anne of Bohemia, queen of Richard II of England, paid an annual stipend to the "purveyor of our chariots," which conveyed her wardrobe. There are instances of professional carriers using wagons to transport goods between Normandy and Paris, and between Paris and Navarre.

In the thirteenth century, illuminations continue to show the same riders in vehicles as previously—

Old Testament figures or personifications—and the prejudice against men of quality using vehicles was still strong. Matthew Paris reported that no royal bailiff or other official was to ride in a cart. The thirteenth-century toll at Bapaume lists as exempt from charges carts carrying the ill or pilgrims. (Perhaps the pilgrims were so enfeebled that they were unable to walk and required transportation. Or they could be demonstrating their humility by traveling that way instead of on horseback.) Only illness reduced Eudes Rigaud, archbishop of Rouen, to riding in a cart. Ordinarily his extensive travels to make his ecclesiastical visitations were accomplished on horseback. In Western Europe, vehicles were the proper conveyance for weaklings, rustics, and criminals. Farther to the East, however, the mores were different, as has already been noted in the case of Hungary. In parts of what is now East Germany there was nothing unknightly in riding in vehicles. In 1279, when the Magdeburg and Brandenburg warriors advanced to attack Brunswick, they were riding in wagons, something the chronicler from the West found laughable.

In spite of the Western prejudice against gentlemen and warriors riding in vehicles, no opprobrium was attached to noble ladies doing so. In 1217–1219 the widowed countess of Champagne, Blanche of Navarre, ordered repairs to her *currus,* and in 1266, when Charles I of Anjou made a ceremonial entry into Naples, the ladies of the party rode in a covered, wheeled vehicle. By the end of the century a beautifully decorated chariot was the luxurious appointment of a great lady. In a sumptuary ordinance of 1294, Philip IV expressly provided that no bourgeois woman was to have a *char.* It has been suggested that the reason was to alleviate traffic congestion in Paris, but a reading of the document makes it clear that the purpose was to limit the number and types of costumes and luxuries permitted to various ranks of society and to keep the lower orders in their place. The prestige of a great lady in the fourteenth century required that she own two of these gorgeous conveyances, one for herself and one for her ladies, in addition to a litter for her personal use. Illustrations show these vehicles in use in Flanders, Germany, France, and England. In England the Luttrell Psalter carriage was a type of whirlicote, as it was then called. Ladies of the royal family used whirlicotes in the time of Richard II. We know that his mother rode in one and that his second queen, Isabella of France, owned a state chariot.

By the late medieval period, changes in Western attitudes toward luxurious vehicles for gentlemen made it possible for both men and women of the upper classes to use and own four-wheeled conveyances. In late medieval art, it was almost always in a four-wheeled vehicle, the *char* or chariot, that distinguished people are portrayed as riding. In the fifteenth century the sun's chariot and even triumphal Roman chariots were depicted with four wheels. Also, in contrast to ancient types, medieval ceremonial vehicles almost all have tilts (canopies). Before the introduction of the suspended chariot or *char branlant,* the chassis of a lady's personal *char* was the same as that of the wagon in which her luggage was transported.

The body of the chariot proclaimed its aristocratic connections and afforded opportunity for that display so much in vogue in court circles around the turn of the fifteenth century. The body of the chariot in many cases was so high that a ladder was necessary for passengers to climb in from the rear, the only entrance. There was no driver in the vehicle, which was controlled by a postilion mounted on the near horse. The vehicle might have either a pole or shafts. There were low wooden sides, which were gilded and painted. A series of arches covered the chariot from side to side and, with longitudinal rods, held up the covering. (There was a certain family resemblance between such a chariot and the American Conestoga wagon, but the latter is a country cousin compared with the magnificent medieval chariot.)

The *char* of a great lady was painted by a well-known artist of the day with the initials and coats of arms of the owner; the bosses were decorated with gilt and enamel; the ends of the rods were carved; the nails were gilded; and the covering was of the finest cloth—white, azure, scarlet, or (a favorite color) green. Other chariots had a leather tilt—King René of Sicily ordered a leather covering dyed scarlet for his in 1477. The leather kept out the rain, and luxury was ensured by a lining of bright woolen cloth. Nor was the arched tilt the only shape. In the *Très riches heures* of Jean, duke of Berry, the sun god's chariot has a square tilt with perhaps a hint of the tents used during the Hundred Years War. Inside such a chariot were two coffers furnished with locks and benches with an ample supply of cushions. Cushions were stuffed with feathers and covered with tapestry or the most expensive wool fabrics. The duchess of Burgundy had some showing white sheep under pine trees against a green background. Some chariots had as many as seven cushions. In 1403 Madame de Savoy's had five vermilion cushions in cloth of gold, two for her to sit on, one to be placed behind her back, and one for either side of her. Illustrations imply that passengers rode one behind the other, and accounts tell us there were gilded, carved knobs, apparently for riders to hold on to, so as to minimize the jolting of the vehicle.

A lady's litter had the same appearance and decorations as her chariot, but instead of wheels it was supported on two long poles. A litter was carried by two horses, one in front and one behind it. It was essential for the comfort of the occupant that the gaits of the two horses be matched. Carelessness on the part of those riding the horses or of footmen leading them resulted in the lady being shaken up. It is probable that the litter provided a more comfortable ride than did the first suspended carriages; but in England, after Anne of Bohemia introduced the sidesaddle, litters and whirlicotes were used on ceremonial occasions only. When Margaret, daughter of Henry VII, made her bridal journey to Scotland for her marriage to James IV in 1503, she and most of her ladies rode on hackneys, while four of her attendants journeyed in her chariot. In her cortège was a "very rich litter borne by two fair coursers very richly dressed," but she used it only occasionally, except when entering the good towns.

The suspended chariot seems to have been known in Germany at least as early as 1330/1350, when one was very distinctly depicted by the illustrator of Rudolf von Ems's *Weltchronik*. Six wives of Jacob's sons are shown going to Egypt in a carriage whose body is of basketwork hanging from straps, presumably of leather, running longitudinally from supports in front and back. Suspended chariots or *chariots branlants* (rocking or trembling chariots) were in use in France at least from 1374. In that year the records of Jean, duke of Berry, note expenditures for the carters of the *chariot branlant*. This may have been the small German chariot purchased the same year. By 1384–1385 the duchess of Burgundy and her daughter-in-law each owned one of these *chars*, and in 1396 the duchess of Orléans had a *chariot branlant*. In 1405 Queen Isabeau entered Paris in great pomp, accompanied by litters, *chariots branlants*, and hackneys. There are frequent mentions of *chariots branlants* in the course of the fifteenth century.

Instead of being suspended by leather straps, French *chariots branlants* used chains, as shown in

expense accounts. The extravagant and fashionable wife in Eustache Deschamps's *Miroir de mariage* demands a *curre à cheannes,* for a chariot suspended by chains was the last word in style and elegance. She says: "When the weather is fresh as butter, I must have a chariot with chains, well-ordered, painted inside and out, covered with cloth of camlet. . . . Why shouldn't I have one, drawn by four horses?" Enameled chains were part of the luxurious appointments of the chariot of the daughter of the king of Hungary, according to *The Squire of Low Degree,* a fourteenth-century English poem.

The exact method of suspension may be clearly seen in a Burgundian illustration in the Breslau manuscript of Froissart's *Chronicle* painted about 1470. From the front and back axletree beds, just inside the wheels, rose two slightly curved, strong posts, tilted forward and backward, respectively. From the tops of these posts, chains passed transversely under the chariot body to support it. There is a strong resemblance to the tenth-century description of the suspended Hungarian chariot in which the Magyar kings rode. There were still carriages hanging from chains in the sixteenth century. However, compared with coaches of that period, with their sturdy, carved standards, the Breslau Froissart chariot looks improvised and almost fragile.

Fourteenth- and fifteenth-century chariots seem to have required frequent repairs. The *char* of Mahaut, countess of Artois, in 1317 was given four new wheels with iron tires, and new coverings for the cushions and chariot. In addition it was painted and provided with bosses and nails. Two years later there were repairs to axles and wheels. In 1322 the old chariot was retired in favor of a new one, which lasted only four years, being replaced in 1326. In 1478 a locksmith was paid for redoing the ironwork on a chariot belonging to King René, because as done before it was worthless.

There were no professional carriage makers. As indicated earlier, the only specialist certain to be employed in the construction of a chariot was the wheelwright. Ironwork was done by a blacksmith, a locksmith, or a spur maker; the body was constructed by a joiner or wheelwright, painted or decorated by an artist, and covered with cloth or leather by a draper, saddler, or harness maker. It is probable that wheelwrights and blacksmiths also made bodies of chariots.

Construction and maintenance of vehicles involved considerable travel. The duchess of Burgundy sent her chariot to Paris for repairs and ordered cushions for it from Arras. Parts of King René's chariots were made or assembled at Miľau, Beaucaire, Avignon, and Marseilles.

In the late fourteenth and in the fifteenth century, German, and later Hungarian, carriages enjoyed a considerable reputation in France. Evidently the suspended carriage was introduced into France from Germany. Jean, duke of Berry, owned a small German *chariot branlant* in 1374, and a century later, in 1477, King René ordered one made by two Germans, and in 1478 one made by a Hungarian. Still dissatisfied, King René in 1478 and 1479 obtained plans for chariots from a physician of Carpentras and from a Hungarian gentleman. Bertrandon de la Broquière, who visited Hungary about 1425, praised Hungarian chariots. One presented to the queen of France in 1457 by King Ladislaus of Hungary was described as a very sumptuous and rich *chariot branlant*. In 1479 King Louis XI of France purchased a complete chariot in the Hungarian style for the captain of his Swiss guards.

One of the most admired features of the Hungarian chariot was evidently its lightness. At this time French chariots, heavy with iron, ordinarily required at least two, and frequently four, five, or even six, horses to draw them. King René was especially anxious to learn how to construct a chariot that could be drawn by one horse. Bertrandon de le Broquière praised the lightness of the Hungarian chariot, which could hold eight men but nevertheless was drawn by a single horse. Its weight was so little that Bertrandon suspected a single man could pull it. It had very light wheels, the rear ones much higher than the front, and the ride was so comfortable a passenger could fall asleep. The exceptional riding comfort of Hungarian coaches may have been due to their longitudinal suspension by leather straps. This type had already been used in a German chariot illustrated in the Zurich manuscript of Rudolf von Ems, and eventually completely superseded the French and Flemish suspension in which chains passed transversely under the body.

The features of the Hungarian chariot in the sixteenth century spread over Europe. At first the familiar arched tilt continued, as did the square one. In the course of the sixteenth century, however, it became the rule to have a door in the side and the coachman seated in front. This arrangement was a return to antiquity, when the horses had been controlled by a driver riding in the vehicle rather than by postilions mounted on the horses or a footman leading them. The superior ride of the Hungarian coach meant that it gradually became respectable for men to ride in them. In 1378, during Emperor Charles IV's visit to France, it was only when the emperor became too ill to ride horseback that King Charles V of France sent him a *char* drawn by four beautiful white mules and two coursers with a very elegant litter belonging to the queen. In 1474 Emperor Frederick III, with no apologies, rode into Frankfurt in a covered and suspended carriage. After this, despite objections from various quarters, more and more men, as well as women, rode in the vehicles to which, in the sixteenth century, the name "coach" was applied. Because of the fame of the Hungarian chariots, the name of the Hungarian town of Kocsi came to be applied to all passenger vehicles of whatever description.

CONCLUSION

The achievements of medieval people in improving vehicles were considerable. In ancient times the barbarians of northern Europe were already very competent in wagon construction, and medieval people continued their predecessors' interest in transportation. During the course of the first millennium, technological discoveries and innovations meant the more efficient use of animals pulling vehicles. Nailed-on horseshoes meant fewer hoof injuries and a firmer grip on the road; the modern horse collar was so placed and fashioned as to allow the horse to exert maximum strength without hindrance. The introduction of the whippletree contributed to the development of a superior harness. Tandem harnessing came in, allowing the combination of the forces of several animals. The shaft cart became popular, and by the end of the period the one-horse wagon was increasing in numbers. After improvements in harnessing and in breeding, horses and mules became preferred to oxen for pulling vehicles. As compared to Roman times, horses were larger and more powerful, and their numbers in the fifteenth century seem to have been about the same as in the nineteenth.

There is no doubt that medieval people knew the turning train at least by the fourteenth century and may have been using it long before. They always had the choice of using two-wheelers. Therefore, if they used four-wheelers on long journeys, it argues for the use of the pivoted front axle. Fourteenth-century illuminations have in some cases elaborate pictures of undercarriages with futchels and sway-bars. Dished wheels, a superior construction, were in use at least by the fifteenth century. A lighter vehicle came into use, and suspension was introduced. It is one of the triumphs of the wagon-builders' art that in the course of the sixteenth century, carriages became so comfortable that they outdistanced their competitors, the litter and the riding horse, and became the preferred method of travel. This development had behind it a long history, traceable through the medievals' preference for vehicular transportation and their insistence (not shared by the Romans) that bridges be provided at all important river crossings, all the way back to the ancient Celts, whose expertise in wagon building had been so admired by the Romans.

BIBLIOGRAPHY

William Bridges Adams, *English Pleasure Carriages: Their Origin, History, and Capabilities* (1837); Gösta Berg, *Sledges and Vehicles* (1935); Marjorie Nice Boyer, "Medieval Suspended Carriages," in *Speculum,* **34** (1959), and "Medieval Pivoted Axles," in *Technology and Culture,* **1** (1960); Richard C. Bronson, "Chariot Racing in Etruria," in *Studi in onore di Luisa Banti* (1965); Ann Burford, "Transport in Classical Antiquity," in *Economic History Review,* 2nd ser., **13** (1960); M. Cagiano de Azevedo, *I trasporti e il traffico* (1938); Robert Capot-Rey, *Géographie de la circulation sur les continents,* 5th ed. (1946); Lionel Casson, *Travel in the Ancient World* (1974); Charles Victor Daremberg and Edmond Saglio, eds., *Dictionnaire des antiquités grecques et romaines* (1887–1919); Jean-Pierre Devroez, "Un monastère dans l'économie des échanges," in *Annales: Economies, sociétés, civilisations,* **39** (1984); Richard Lefebrve des Nöettes, *La force motrice à travers les âges* (1924); Albert C. Leighton, *Transport and Communication in Early Medieval Europe, A.D. 500–1100* (1972); Robert Lopez, "Evolution of Land Transport in the Middle Ages," in *Past and Present,* **9** (1956); J. H. Markland, "Some Remarks on the Early Use of Carriages in England, and on the Modes of Travelling Adopted by Our Ancestors," in *Archaeologia,* **20** (1824); Stuart Piggott, *The Earliest Wheeled Transport from the Atlantic Coast to the Caspian Sea* (1983); Henri Polge, "L'amélioration de l'attelage, a-t-elle réellement fait reculer le servage?" in *Journal des savants* (1967); J. Spruytte, *Études expérimentales sur l'attelage* (1977); P. Vigneron, *Le cheval dans l'antiquité grecque et romaine* (1968); James F. Willard, "The Use of Carts in the Fourteenth Century," in *History,* **17** (1932).

MARJORIE NICE BOYER

[See also **Animals, Draft; Codex Theodosianus; Oseberg Find; Roads and Bridges, Western European; Rudolf von Ems; Technology, Western; Trade, European; Travel and Transport, Western European.**]

VEHICLES, ISLAMIC. The most striking fact about vehicles in the medieval Islamic world is their absence. Although the disappearance of wheeled transport was not in any way a result of the rise of Islam and the Arab conquest of the Middle East in the seventh century, it occurred within a short enough time span prior to those events that Islamic society was the first to be deeply affected by it.

Wheeled vehicles existed in various forms in the ancient Middle East—chariots, ox carts, passenger vehicles—and the dry, treeless terrain of much of the region made road building, or even cross-country travel, comparatively easy. At the same time, the sparsely vegetated desert areas afforded free pasturage to herds of camels that did not compete with agriculture in the way that oxen and horses did. Since technological and other considerations militated against trying to harness camels to carts (though this was done effectively in Tripolitania and the Indus Valley), the way was prepared for competition in the transport economy between ox carts and pack camels. The integration of the Arabs into the Middle Eastern economy that resulted from the rise of a profitable, Arab-dominated caravan trade in the second and first centuries B.C. activated this latent economic competition.

By A.D. 301, according to Emperor Diocletian's Edict on Maximum Prices, camel transport was 20 percent cheaper than transport by wheeled vehicle. A gradual disappearance of wheeled transport was the result, although the precise stages of that disappearance over several centuries, including deterioration of roads and decline of vehicular crafts, are difficult to distinguish.

That vehicles had disappeared by the beginning of the Islamic period is testified to in several ways. ʿAjala and gardūn, the words for cart or wagon in Arabic and Persian, respectively, seldom occur in medieval texts, and more extensive vocabulary relating to vehicles and associated crafts is virtually nonexistent. Depictions of vehicles in Islamic art are rare, and when they do occur, they are often fanciful, technologically impossible creations used in scenes from pre-Islamic legends. Moreover, those references to vehicles that do occur in texts are often accompanied by indications that the vehicle in question was regarded as an oddity.

The primary areas presenting exceptions to this situation within the domain of Islam are Spain, parts of Tunisia and Tripolitania, Anatolia, the Indus Valley, and the Turko-Mongolian steppe of Central Asia. The technological relations extending across Christian-Muslim borders in southern Europe and North Africa are still too poorly known to ascertain whether Tunisia and Spain may have been linked in a pattern of vehicle use extending through Sicily and Italy, but there does seem to have been a shared technological vocabulary. The degree of vehicle use is likewise unknown. In Anatolia, rudely constructed Byzantine carts and wagons continued in use after the Muslim conquest of the eleventh century. They are designated by the Turkish words *kağnı* and *araba*. Vehicle use in the Indus Valley region and eastward across northern India was ancient and continuous, but the use of one-humped camels as draft animals, with attendant adaptation of harnessing technology, became common only after 1000.

The most important area of persistent vehicle use was the Turko-Mongolian steppe. The word *araba* derives from this area and entered several of the languages of Muslim peoples, including Arabic, in the fourteenth century. Both harnessing technology and spoked wheel design were of a high order on the steppe from ancient times, and the round felt homes (yurts) of the nomads were sometimes mounted on wagons and transported by that means during migrations.

The Mongol invasions of the thirteenth century brought the *araba* sporadically into use in the eastern regions of the Islamic world, where vehicles had long since disappeared, and the Mamluk regime in Egypt and Syria and the Ottoman regime in Anatolia did the same thing for the western regions. Yet the *araba*, or the various vehicles called by that general term, never became common and apparently was not economically competitive with pack animal transport. It remained an occasional, military, or luxury vehicle until the nineteenth century, when, under European influence, wheeled vehicles came back into frequent use.

The consequences for medieval Islamic society of the general absence of vehicles were far-reaching. Road maintenance and paving were unimportant in comparison with bridge building and the construction of caravansaries. Vehicular considerations were of no consequence in the laying out of city streets, the result being narrow, winding lanes of irregular width and surface, and comparatively few

large open areas. Maximum load size tended to be limited to the carrying capacity of the camel, which had effects on the transport of heavy building materials that probably helped bring about a brick-oriented architecture. Vehicle-related crafts, which generated significant technological innovation in Europe, were nonexistent, although waterwheels, potter's wheels, and other wheel-using devices were constructed.

As a whole, Islamic culture developed a non-vehicular cast. Languages lacked extensive vehicular vocabulary; animal caravans rather than carts and wagons appeared in poetic imagery; and vehicular symbolism was absent from religious thought.

BIBLIOGRAPHY
Richard W. Bulliet, *The Camel and the Wheel* (1975); Maxime Rodinson, "Sur l'*araba*," in *Journal asiatique*, **245** (1957), "ᶜAdjala," in *The Encyclopedia of Islam*, new ed., I (1960), and, with G. L. M. Clauson, "Araba," *ibid.*

RICHARD W. BULLIET

[See also **Animals, Draft; Roads in the Islamic World; Tools, Agricultural: Islamic; Trade, Islamic; Travel and Transport, Islamic.**]

VELLUM, fine, strong, white parchment made, in theory, from calfskin (or lambskin or kidskin). In practice, high-quality parchment from older animals is also often designated as vellum. Uterine vellum refers to the highest-quality parchment, sometimes made from the skin of unborn animals.

BIBLIOGRAPHY
Ronald Reed, *Ancient Skins, Parchments, and Leathers* (1972), 132–144.

LESLIE BRUBAKER

[See also **Parchment.**]

VENANTIUS FORTUNATUS (*ca.* 540–*ca.* 601), churchman and writer, sometimes regarded as the last classical poet. Born in Venetia in northern Italy, Venantius Honoratus Clementianus Fortunatus received a classical education in grammar, rhetoric, law, and poetry. About 565 he journeyed to Gaul in fulfillment of a vow to visit the tomb of St. Martin of Tours, and in the course of his travels he established his reputation as a poet. After a two-year stay at the court of King Sigisbert, he ultimately settled at Poitiers, where, after his ordination as a priest, he became chaplain of the convent of St. Radegunda. In 599 he was made bishop of the city.

A prolific writer, Venantius' surviving works include prose lives of Sts. Hilary of Poitiers, Germanus of Paris, Albinus of Angers, Paternus of Avranches, Radegunda, Marcellus of Paris, and Severinus of Bordeaux. In verse he wrote a *Life of St. Martin* in four books, eleven books of poems (including many epitaphs and descriptive pieces), and several hymns, some of which, such as the *Vexilla regis prodeunt* and *Pange, lingua,* became church standards.

BIBLIOGRAPHY

Sources. Venanti Fortunati Carmina, F. Leo and Bruno Kusch, eds., in *Monumenta Germaniae historica: Auctores antiquissimi,* IV.1–2 (1881–1885); Bruno Kusch, ed., *Monumenta germaniae historica: Scriptores rerum Merovingicarum,* II (1888), 1–54, and, with W. Levison, *Vita Germani episcopi Parisiaci,* VII.1 (1920), 219–224, 372–418; *Patrologia latina,* LXXXVIII (1862), 59–596.

Studies. Clavis patrum latinorum, 2nd ed. (1961), nos. 1033–1052; Frederic J. E. Raby, *A History of Secular Latin Poetry in the Middle Ages* (1934), 127–142, and *A History of Christian-Latin Poetry* (2nd ed. 1953, repr. 1966), 86–95; D. Tardi, *Fortunat: Étude sur le dernier représentant de la poésie latine dans la Gaule merovingienne* (1927).

RALPH W. MATHISEN

[See also **Hymns, Latin; Latin Literature.**]

VENDĪDĀD. See Vidēvdād.

VENETS (Russian, "crown") is the technical word for a completed horizontal layer one log thick in the *klet* or *srub,* the basic log cube element in a Russian wooden building. The logs comprising a single *venets* were notched to join each other at the corners.

The same word is used for the metallic ceremonial crowns held over the heads of the bride and groom in the Russian Orthodox wedding service (the Greek Orthodox prefer crowns of flowers), for royal and imperial crowns, and for the crowns of

precious metal occasionally attached to sacred figures in icons.

GEORGE P. MAJESKA

[See also **Russian Architecture; Russian Art.**]

VENI CREATOR SPIRITUS, a celebrated medieval Latin chant, an invocation of the Holy Spirit constructed on the model of the Ambrosian hymn. The number of stanzas varies from one source to another, but is most often six or seven. Of these the first states the theme of the hymn; the next two enumerate the titles and activities of the Holy Spirit; and the following three restate the invocation in detail.

Stanza six reads as follows:

> *Per te sciamus, da, patrem*
> *noscamus atque filium,*
> *te utriusque spiritum*
> *credamus omni tempore.*

Grant that we may know through you the Father and the Son; and grant that we may believe for all time in you, the Spirit of them both.

The words "utriusque spiritum" have suggested to some scholars (notably Lausberg) the expression of a point of view relative to the *Filioque* controversy dealt with in the Synod of Aachen in 809, a controversy that had political as well as theological aspects. This suggests an attribution to Hrabanus Maurus, though there are no reliable indications of this in the manuscript tradition. Adopted into the liturgical collection known as the New Hymnal (a term used by Gneuss and others), "Veni creator spiritus" was assigned to Pentecost, where it was sung either in vespers or terce (the sources vary). It was sung at the beginning of church councils and in services of ordination; in later liturgical books it has other uses in addition to these.

In an extremely broad and comprehensive study of the melodies of medieval hymns, Stäblein found only one melody for this text (with a single, unimportant exception), a melody that is transmitted with remarkable uniformity in the many sources. Though it appears in a hymnal of Milan as the setting for a text by Ambrose himself, "Hic est dies verus dei," it has a quality unlike that of the typical Ambrosian melody. There is a purposefulness in the movement—away from the tonic in the first line, further away in the second, reaching a climax at the beginning of the third, and returning to the tonic at the end—that contrasts with the static and decorative qualities of Ambrosian melodies. Thus there are questions about the authorship and place of origin of the melody, just as there are for the text.

There are several translations into German; one is by Martin Luther—"Komm, Gott Schöpfer, heiliger Geist"; others date back to at least the twelfth century, and perhaps earlier. Medieval translations of it into English have been surveyed by Gneuss; there are three translations into Anglo-Norman that can be dated at intervals of about fifty years from the middle of the thirteenth century to the middle of the fourteenth. Polyphonic arrangements of this chant were made by a number of composers of the Renaissance; among more recent treatments may be cited the use of the text (though not the melody) in the opening of the Eighth Symphony of Gustav Mahler, composed in 1906.

BIBLIOGRAPHY

Guido M. Dreves, ed., *Analecta hymnica medii aevi*, L (1907), 193–194; Helmut Gneuss, *Hymnar und Hymnen im englischen Mittelalter* (1968); John Julian, ed. *A Dictionary of Hymnology*, II (1907, repr. 1985), 1,206–1,211; Heinrich Lausberg, *Der Hymnus "Veni Creator Spiritus"* (1979); Bruno Stäblein, *Monumenta monodica medii aevi*, I (1956); S. Harrison Thomson, "Three Anglo-Norman Translations of the *Veni Creator Spiritus*," in *Medium aevum*, 8 (1939).

Ruth Steiner

[See also **Ambrosian Chant; Divine Office; Gregorian Chant; Hymns, Latin; Mass, Liturgy of the; Sequence.**]

VENICE. The people of medieval Venice saw themselves as denizens of a unique city. Geographically, politically, and economically they felt atypical, but in a positive sense that was most meaningful for their great success during the Middle Ages. Andrea Dandolo, a fourteenth-century chronicler and doge, believed this singularity had developed right from the city's foundation. According to his account, the Apostle Mark, who was proselytizing in Roman Venetia, a region of northeastern Italy, found himself forced to take cover from a sudden storm on a deserted group of little islands and mudbanks that would eventually become the Rialto—the economic focus and first physical center of Venice. While seeking refuge there from the storm that had broken around him—and implicitly from the storm that

was about to engulf the Roman world—an angel appeared to comfort him. The angel's first words were "Pax tibi Marce" ("Peace be with you, Mark"). These words, which by Dandolo's time would adorn the banner of the city, held a double meaning. First, they were simply a reassurance to the Apostle that he was in a safe place where no harm would come to him. But there was a deeper meaning in his promise of peace insofar as the angel made perfectly clear that "here your body will rest [after your eventual death] and here a devoted and loyal people will build a marvelous city where finally your body will have its deserved peace, dwelling in highest veneration while your merits pass on to them many benefits."

Dandolo's vision of the apostolic foundation of Venice implied both literally and physically that the city existed in a unique time and space. Unlike virtually every other city in the West except Rome, Venetian time was directly tied to the beginning of Christian time: the Apostle Mark founded Venice as he spread Christianity through the West, just as the Apostle Peter refounded Rome by preaching Christ's message there. The space of Venice was also meaningful: the city was a sacred place of refuge from a troubled world. This mythic vision of Venice's foundation had many additional layers of meaning. To the modern eye it also highlights the city's uniqueness. For Venice was primarily an urban center of merchant capitalism ruled by traders in a world largely rural and feudal, dominated by churchmen and warriors.

Yet this mythic vision of Venice's beginnings, even with its levels of deeper truth, presents serious problems for an accurate account of the city's foundation. When one begins to ask such questions as who founded the city, when was it founded and why, one continually runs up against very strong elements of myth. Venice's chroniclers saw in the beginnings of their city matters of too great a significance to be limited by mere mundane events. This tendency to tie local history into the great moments of Christian and Roman time was not unique to Venice, but Venetian history provides an extreme example. There the myths of the city's origin and early triumphs continued to grow through the Renaissance into the early modern period and to a degree continue in much of the modern history of the city.

Even if one must doubt Mark's role in Venice's founding, the myth is suggestive. The isolated nature of Venice's setting did make it an ideal place of refuge in the times of turmoil that accompanied the collapse of Roman imperial domination of the Mediterranean. The northeastern Adriatic coast of Italy was washed by a strong current that formed the silt deposited by the rivers of the region into long, thin islands (*lidi*). Behind these islands were trapped large bodies of shallow water and marsh called lagoons. During Roman times these regions were inhabited primarily by fishermen with perhaps an occasional vacation villa for those seeking privacy. The shifting channels in the lagoons made access difficult; but more importantly, settlement was inhibited by a variety of problems with the water. In saltwater areas a shortage of fresh water impeded the foundation of major settlements; yet in freshwater regions (generally near the mouths of the rivers that opened into the lagoons), the freshwater pools provided excellent breeding grounds for the mosquitoes that in turn provided the basis for malarial "bad air." Physically isolated and unhealthy, the northeastern lagoons remained relatively undeveloped during the height of the Roman Empire.

THE PERIOD OF INVASIONS

The Germanic invasions of the empire that began at the end of the fourth century made the lagoons' disadvantages seem less daunting. In the turmoil of those invasions the very isolation of the lagoons made them a most attractive place of refuge for Romans from major mainland cities such as Padua and Aquileia. Even the Roman capital in the West moved eventually to a lagoon location at Ravenna, an island city to the south of the Venetian lagoons. For the development of Venice two events stand out in the invasions: the capture and sacking of Aquileia by Attila and the Huns (452), which caused many (including the archbishop of the region) to flee to the lagoons, and the invasion of Italy by the Lombards (568) after the abortive attempt of the Eastern Empire's armies to reunite East and West under Justinian's rule. According to the *Cronaca altinate*, after more than a century and a half of the Roman population rising and falling in the lagoons, the destruction caused by the Gothic wars followed by the Lombard invasions finally convinced many Romans to remain permanently in the lagoons, rejecting all hope of a successful wedding of Germanic and Roman civilization.

There is much that is logical in this vision of a Roman flight to safety in the lagoons. But one must be wary of the mythic perceptions that caused this aspect to be stressed over equally compelling reasons for the region's development. As a refuge for fleeing Romans, Venice became a pure continuation of Roman civilization against the barbarians. Many medieval cities made similar claims, but Venice's foundation by fleeing Roman nobles was an especially powerful version of the genre. Perhaps even more important in the lagoons' growth was the Byzantine attempt to use the area as a base for continuing contact with the West. Especially after the Lombards had succeeded in taking much of the interior of Italy, Byzantine policy was predicated upon holding coastal cities. In this they were aided to a degree by the relative lack of interest that the early Lombards had in Roman cities and trade. Venice's growth in these terms was crucial to Byzantine interests in northern Italy and became even more important with the fall of Ravenna in 751.

In any event the Lombard invasion was a key moment. Following quickly there appeared in the Venetian lagoons twelve townships: Grado, Bibione, Caorle, Jesolo, Heraclea, Torcello, Murano, Rialto, Malamocco, Poveglia, Chioggia, and Sottomarina. According to the *Cronaca altinate* it was also at this point that there was a spate of church building, signifying the commitment of immigrants to stay on in the lagoons and providing the spiritual base for permanent major settlements. It is important to keep in mind that the Rialto settlement, the heart of the future city, was by no means the most important. Heraclea, Grado, Malamocco, and Torcello were each at particular moments in the early period much more significant population centers.

The early development of the region has two primary themes: the rise to power of the Rialto settlement as the center of Venice and the growing independence of the city. Again the mythic tradition stressed that the region was an independent entity from the beginning. According to this view, after the Lombard invasions both the Western and the Eastern parts of the Roman Empire ceased to have any authority in the West. At that very moment Venice was born as the successor to Rome, owing no allegiance to any political authority. Actually Venice's early maritime development and ideal eastward orientation, combined with Byzantine interests in Italy, presaged, from the beginning, close ties with Byzantium. Even before the Lombard invasions the Byzantine general Belisarios had used the lagoons during the Gothic wars as a military outpost in attempting to regain control of Italy

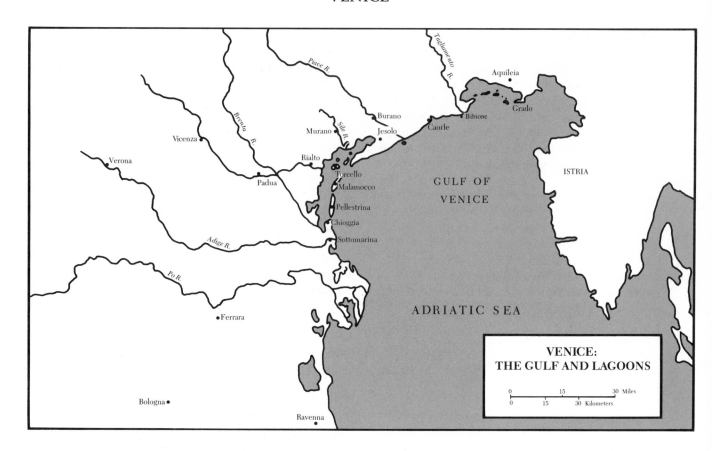

VENICE:
THE GULF AND LAGOONS

from the Ostrogoths. As a result, at the time of those invasions the region was already at least nominally part of the Eastern Empire.

Various claims have been advanced to argue that Venice quickly escaped this status. Narses, Belisarios' successor, was reported to have recognized the lagoons' independence against Paduan claims. It was also said that the lagoons asserted their independence to the Byzantine envoy Longinus, who was attempting to gain their support against the Lombards. Aid was promised, but they rejected his request to recognize Byzantine control, claiming that "God who is our help and protector has saved us that we might dwell upon these waters. This second Venice which we have raised in the lagoons is our mighty habitation; no power of emperor or prince can touch us."

To a great extent the relationship was a symbiotic one where Venice had much to gain economically and little to lose politically from its nominal subservience to a distant emperor. By the end of the seventh century the lagoon area was formally recognized as a military province of the Eastern Empire ruled by a *dux* under the command of the *exarch* of Ravenna. Primarily a military official

overseeing the lagoons from Heraclea, this duke had to compete for power with the tribunes of each township and the local clergy. How effective or even significant his rule was remains problematic. Yet as the antecedent of the later chief executive of the city, the doge (a Venetian corruption of the Latin title *dux*), it has become a commonplace to envision a gradual growth of the office's power from these military beginnings. It might be more meaningful, however, to see the office being radically reoriented in response to specific problems during the eighth century, so radically reoriented that an evolutionary view has little to offer.

The first major break developed with the inauguration of an iconoclastic policy by the Eastern emperor Leo III in 726. In response, the tribunes of the lagoons and the local clergy elected independently their own doge, Ursus (Orso). This assertion of independence, however, was tacitly overcome when the emperor offered Ursus the Byzantine court title of *hypatos* and the offer was accepted. With Ursus' death in 737, the emperor again appointed his own military leader in the lagoons. But once more in 742 the tribunes and clergy elected a new doge, Deusdedit, and moved the seat of gov-

384

ernment to Malamocco. The doge was becoming a locally elected official; without much of a formal break the office had begun to change significantly.

THE CAROLINGIAN PERIOD

The rise of the Carolingians and their attempts to gain hegemony in northern Italy brought some clarity to the question of Venetian status and in the process made the doge the major political figure in the lagoons, precipitating perhaps the least mythical founding of Venice. The story of the papacy's search for military support against the Lombards and the consequent elevation of the Carolingians first to royal, then to imperial, status is familiar. For the lagoons the development of Carolingian power in Italy created a division between pro-Carolingian and pro-Byzantine factions. The conflict came to a head when the pro-Byzantine doge Giovanni Galbaio murdered the pro-Carolingian patriarch of Grado, Giovanni. The patriarch, the most powerful ecclesiastic in the area, was succeeded by his nephew Fortunatus, who was if anything more pro-Carolingian. Fortunatus' name, however, was not particularly apt; his plan to counter violence with violence by assassinating the doge was discovered, forcing him to flee to the Carolingian court, where he counseled an invasion of the lagoons.

The test came when Charlemagne's son Pepin was dispatched to the lagoons to bring the region under the control of the renewed Western Empire. Attacking from the south in 810, he captured first Chioggia and then the capital, Malamocco. But the inhabitants of the lagoons and the doge fled before the invader, this time to the Rialto, a settlement on the group of islands and mudflats in the center of the lagoons clustered around a high bank (*rivo alto*). Pepin was unable or unwilling to follow and with the coming of summer withdrew. Without winning a battle the city had won its claim to independence, in the West at least. Paradoxically, it was this Carolingian failure that marked the beginning of the Rialto as the center of Venice, just as (in the view of Henri Pirenne) it was the Carolingian success that spelled the end of the Roman Mediterranean as a focus of Western civilization.

Venice was still formally subject to the Eastern Empire, for the move to the Rialto had secured victory for the pro-Byzantine party. A treaty of 810 between the Western emperor and the Eastern emperor Nikephoros I clearly placed Venice within the Eastern orbit, while granting Venetian the right to trade in Carolingian territory in the West. Soon after the move to the Rialto, however, another important event contributed to Venetian claims to independence. Though less concrete than a military campaign and less clearly readable than a treaty, the reported arrival of the remains of St. Mark taken from Alexandria created yet another base for the city's importance. A ducal chapel was built for these relics, thus fulfilling the prophecy reported by Dandolo that the saint would find in Venice his final resting place and glory. This chapel, which would eventually become the splendid cathedral of S. Marco, replaced an earlier ducal chapel dedicated to a Greek warrior, St. Theodore. For a mere Byzantine military official St. Theodore was a fitting ally; for a locally elected doge ruling an increasingly aggressive merchant people the Apostle St. Mark implied an independent spiritual support spanning both East and West.

Significantly, this ducal chapel was not the primary ecclesiastical establishment in the region. That honor was disputed between the bishops of Grado and Aquileia. Each bishop claimed to be the true successor to the archbishop of Aquileia, Paolo (Paulinus), who had fled to Grado in 568 after the Lombard invasions. In 683 the Synod of Pavia attempted a compromise that made the "new" Aquileia responsible for the mainland regions of the northeast and Grado responsible for the lagoons and Istria. Squabbles continued, but as a result Grado became the ecclesiastical center of the lagoons, underscoring once more Venetian independence from mainland authority. The distinction between Grado as the seat of the archbishop and S. Marco as the private chapel of the doge and the eventual state church helped the city to escape the conflicts that developed between powerful bishops and secular authorities over who would rule, conflicts typical of most other medieval Italian towns. In Venice the Apostle had founded his own church and state, independent of all other authority and ruled by a quasi-theocratic doge, at least according to the myth that grew up around these events.

EMERGING INDEPENDENCE

Originally the lagoon townships had been merely the western outlet of a Byzantine trade network that continued to exploit the northern Mediterranean. Their primary role had been as a transshipping center moving goods up the rich Lombard plain to cities like Cremona, Pavia, and Milan. But even there they faced strong competition, especially from nearby Comacchio, a city formally part of the Lombard and later of the Carolingian domains. That city's special privileges put Venice locally at a disadvantage, a problem solved by the Venetian conquest and sacking of its competitor in 886. Thus Venice assured itself of a dominant position on the river systems of northern Italy and in turn secured a local base for more adventuresome commercial ventures. With its Eastern connection the city had much to offer at the fairs of the mainland towns. Incense, silks, spices, even the supposedly restricted imperial purple cloth, were among the luxury goods reportedly offered. Closer to home along the smaller rivers—the Adige, Brenta, Piave, and Tagliamento—and in Istria, the Venetians sought to control the markets in basic staples such as salt, fish, and wheat.

As the Eastern Empire became weaker in the West, Venice began a policy of aggressively guaranteeing its trade. The key element of this program was the domination of the Adriatic Sea, especially its pirate-infested eastern coastline. Three stages marked this primarily military progression. First Istria in the north of the Adriatic was incorporated as a quasi-feudal dependency of Venice. The way was prepared for this by a tradition of close commercial ties with the region; by the progressive penetration of the area by Venetian churches under the leadership of Grado; by the establishment of estates in the area and marriage ties with some of the leading Venetian noble families; and by the acceptance of a few of the more powerful families from the region into the Venetian nobility. The end product of this gradual process was the formal performance of homage to Venice by the people of Capodistria (Koper) in 932. This peaceful ceremony was reinforced by a short military campaign against the local count, Wintero, that secured Venetian dominance in the area.

The mid Adriatic, especially Dalmatia and its coastal waters dotted by islands that were ideal pirate lairs, presented a more difficult obstacle. As early as 948 Doge Pietro III Candiano launched two military expeditions against the area. Although the first accomplished little, the second wiped out an important pirate lair at the mouth of the Narenta River. This victory led a number of other pirate groups to promise peace, but periodic military expeditions were required to enforce those promises. By means of a series of military campaigns at the end of the century, Doge Pietro II Orseolo systematically destroyed the pirate strongholds in the area,

took the major cities of Zara and Trau, and established military garrisons to police the zone. These successes were to some degree facilitated by the growth of the Venetian slave trade in the tenth century. This trade, involving largely mainland Slavs captured in the Dalmatian interior, converted many pirates into Venetian partners who rounded up the victims. In the year 1000 Doge Pietro added to his other titles that of duke of Dalmatia, signifying Venetian control of the mid Adriatic. The growth of Venetian naval power and prestige is perhaps best reflected in the fact that Pietro managed to marry a son to the niece of a Byzantine emperor and another son to a sister-in-law of the Western emperor. Control of the mid Adriatic, however, did not go unchallenged, especially by the rising power of the Christian kings of Hungary.

To a great extent Venice never did control the lower Adriatic between modern Apulia and Albania. Ultimately the city had to settle for a military balance of power in the region that allowed her ships access to the eastern Mediterranean. Regular naval policing, capped occasionally by major naval victories like that of 1002, when the Muslim advance from Sicily up the east coast of Italy was checked before Bari, kept the seas open. The Normans replaced the Muslims as an expansive force in the area with their conquest of the south in 1071. Again, however, Venetian naval power was used to keep the southern Adriatic open until the Norman expansion became somewhat dissipated in the East as a result of the success of the crusades.

TRADE AND COMMERCIAL GROWTH

It should be noted that this clearing of the Adriatic occurred at a time when northern Europe was just beginning to recover from the invasions of the Vikings, Muslims, and Hungarians. As northern prosperity developed, the East lay open and receptive, thanks in large part to the commercial expansion of cities like Venice. Confirming Venice's aggressive growth in the Mediterranean, the Eastern emperor granted the city the Bolla d'Oro in 992 as a reward for military aid against the Muslims. This grant gave Venetian traders a reduction in customs duties in the empire and an advantage over other merchants, even the emperor's own subjects. In 1082, as a reward again for military aid, this time against the Normans, these concessions were extended to allow Venetians to trade in the empire exempt from all duties; to live under their own laws there; and to have their own commercial districts in the cities of the empire. Such privileges, though they caused much resentment, assured Venice a predominant role in the trade of the empire and Mediterranean trade in general.

The products involved were lumber, metal, skins, and slaves from the West in return primarily for luxury goods from the East, for example silk, fine cloth, spices, dyes, and precious stones. Much of this trade was triangular, with Venice's primary products being sold to Muslims in return for gold and silver that were used to buy the luxury goods of Constantinople for consumption in the West. Locally, Venetians also made solid profits by controlling trade in staples such as fish, wheat, and salt. Given its naval strength and trade advantages, it is not surprising that Venice quickly became one of the richest cities of Europe.

Venetian commercial growth, however, created political pressures at home to break the quasi-monarchical power of the doge in the late eleventh and twelfth centuries. It has been argued that the attack on the dogeship originated in a split in the city's elite between a group of old wealthy families intent on using the dogeship to protect their position and wealth and a group of more aggressive families interested in developing further the city's Mediterranean and local trade. Both groups had found the basis of their wealth in commerce. But the older group, influenced by the feudal world that surrounded them, had invested heavily in land and become involved in church affairs to secure their power and status. The newer group believed trade was central and saw growing involvement in feudal society as not only unnecessary but dangerous. The result was a concerted effort to limit the powers of the doge; to break the virtually hereditary rule of families like the Participazi, Candiani, and Orseoli; and to develop institutions more responsive to the communal interests of the more aggressive merchant group without allowing political participation to spread too far.

REFORM OF POLITICAL STRUCTURES
Early on there was an attempt to use judicial officials as a counterbalance to the doge. But growing recourse to violence and assassination led to the implementation of more formal limits. Most important perhaps was the establishment of a regular group of ducal councillors, an institution that seems to have developed out of the practice of periodically appointing ducal advisory groups. These councillors gained the power not only to advise the doge, as their name implies, but also crucially to limit his authority. Progressively the doge was not allowed to act without their consent. With the election of Enrico Dandolo as doge in 1192 this process was reinforced by the requirement that he swear a coronation oath prepared for him—the *promissione ducale*—that formally limited his power. Each doge thereafter swore a revised oath. It should be noted, however, that although the doge was theoretically limited by these controls, changes in the election procedure initiated with the election of Sebastiano Ziani in 1172 rendered those controls moot to a certain degree. Essentially, the election of the doge was taken out of the hands of the people; previously the election had been carried out before a general assembly of the people (the *Concio*). After Ziani a formal nominating procedure developed. Dominated by the merchant families of Venice, it pretty much assured that the doge would be one of their own number. Thus doge, councillors, and *promissione ducale* all tended to aim at common goals, with the result that there was a continued commitment to commercial growth in the Mediterranean arena.

That commitment produced great wealth for the city and changed its physical aspect significantly. As early as 900 growth was so rapid in the settlements near the *Rialto* that doges were granting permits to build up mudflats in the area near Dorso Duro for additional housing. Almost all the area of the present city was built by 1150. By 1224 a zoning board, the *Magistrato del Piovego*, had been set up to adjudicate conflicts over the proper utilization of increasingly scarce urban space. The houses were still primarily of wood (the ornate marble facades of the palaces of the present city are mostly a product of the period from 1350 to 1700). Bridges were also still of wood and without steps, to permit passage to horses. Only in the fourteenth century were horses prohibited from certain areas and required to wear bells to warn pedestrians of their approach.

The population growth that made expansion and regulation so necessary cannot be documented in any secure way. Still it has been estimated that by 1200 the city numbered some 70,000 inhabitants, making it one of the largest cities in the West and, incidentally, more heavily populated than it is today on a year-round basis. Wealth and a highly organized urban environment were the keys to this demographic growth. Wealth provided an attraction that drew immigrants to the city not only to man the fleets or engage in trade, but also to develop the service industries that supplied the daily needs of the community. In addition it allowed the government to obtain a relatively constant food supply, and, for the financially secure, it encouraged reproduction and survival.

COMMERCIAL PREDOMINANCE

The growth of Venice was in part stimulated by and reflected in a highly organized approach to commerce typified by a combination of governmental control and private financing. The merchant-dominated government was anxious to ensure that the city would become a center for shipbuilding, both military and commercial. The famous *Arsenale* (state shipyard, originating not long after 1100), along with many private shipbuilders, constructed ships to governmentally imposed standards. The fleets (*mude*) that sailed to the primary Venetian ports of call in the East were state organized, led, and protected. In the early period they sailed only the Adriatic together, then broke up into smaller units to pursue their individual goals. Later, increasingly, the whole voyage fell under governmental control.

The capitalization of commerce, however, remained largely private and was restricted to Venetian citizens. Money was raised in a number of ways: the sea loan, a straight loan at a high rate of interest; the *cambio,* or bill of exchange, carrying a hidden rate of interest; and most popularly the *colleganza* (known in most of the rest of Italy as the *commenda*). Theoretically, the *colleganza* involved splitting the costs between a passive investing partner, who contributed significantly more capital, and an active partner, who invested primarily his time and effort in addition to taking the physical risks of the trading voyage. Partners split profits on a varying scale depending upon the amount of capital and risk involved. The advantage of this system was that it allowed a certain security to the more established investor, who could divide his capital between several contracts, thus not risking it all on one venture; it also allowed him to stay more permanently in one place to oversee his investments and avoid the personal dangers of the merchant-venturer. For the active partner it provided an opportunity for the bold to make considerable profits with little capital.

The career of Romano Mairano is instructive. From humble beginnings as an active partner in *colleganza* contracts, he built up a large enough fortune over a period of ten years to be the principal owner of a ship trading between Venice, Alexandria, and Constantinople in the late twelfth century and to control considerable wealth. The bubble burst, however, when he lost the entire cargo of his ship because of disturbances in the Eastern Empire. It took him at least twelve years to repay his debts; yet by the end of the century he had recouped his losses and was a major shipowner again. Not all, however, were as successful as Mairano; the major benefits of the system went to the passive investors who could divide their risks by investing in many *colleganze*.

Great wealth and power in the Mediterranean did not come without problems for Venice. These centered in two areas: competition with the aggressive commercial interests of other merchant cities, especially Genoa, and a growing animosity to Venice by people who felt exploited by the city's monopolistic trade practices and special privileges, especially in the Eastern Empire. The trade privileges granted by the Eastern emperor in 1082 went too far in making Venetians a privileged commercial caste, allowing them to undercut Greek competition, dominate the markets of the empire, and escape paying customs duties. To a degree the empire in this way lost considerable revenues by undermining its own customs-paying merchants. The result was a general animosity toward Venetians, directed especially at their highly visible trading quarters in major cities. Reports of from 30,000 to 80,000 Venetians living in Constantinople in the second half of the twelfth century may be an exaggeration, but they reveal that such communities were perceived to be very large.

The attack on Venetian privilege came from both above and below in the late twelfth century. Several popular uprisings as well as periodic petty violence harassed Venetian traders and communities in the empire. At the same time the emperor and his bureaucracy stepped up attempts to limit Venetian privileges. Venice, in turn, heightened tensions by periodically slipping from trade to piracy and pillaging to demonstrate that its privileges were a small price to pay for the city's peaceful support. Finally in 1171 the emperor Manuel I Komnenos felt strong enough to take decisive action. He ordered the arrest of all Venetians in the empire and the seizure of their property. In response, Doge Vitale II Michiel led a major naval expedition against the East. But even though the Venetians had a clear military superiority, Komnenos controlled the situation because of the hostages he held. As a consequence the expedition was a failure, and it resulted in the fall of the doge.

THE CRUSADES

A new doge, advised by a new elective council (which would eventually evolve into the Major Council), followed a policy of diplomacy and piracy that slowly and grudgingly secured the release of hostages and a renewal of trade. But it was the crusades that finally allowed Venice to solve its Eastern problems. In the beginning, because of its close alliance with Byzantium and its suspicions of Norman interests in the East, Venice stayed aloof from the First Crusade, preached by Urban II in 1095. Yet once the crusaders had taken Jerusalem and become a factor to be reckoned with in the East, the city sent out a fleet to aid against a Muslim counteroffensive. In return for this crucial, if tardy, help the Venetians were granted the right to have a church and a market area in every city taken. They were also freed from customs duties in the crusader Kingdom of Jerusalem. But problems in the Adriatic engendered by the expansionist policies of the Hungarians and Normans left little freedom to do more than take advantage of those trade privileges, while Pisa and Genoa moved out aggressively into the East. Later, in a campaign of 1123–1124, the Venetians defeated a major Egyptian fleet off Ascalon and helped in the conquest of Tyre that assured the West a naval predominance in the area for a generation. This was Venice's primary formal contribution to the early crusades.

The Fourth Crusade saw the entrance of Venice into the crusading movement in a major way, primarily as a naval power contracting to deliver approximately 200 ships to carry 4,500 knights and their horses, 9,000 squires, and 20,000 foot soldiers to the Holy Land for a price of 85,000 marks. It was an ambitious undertaking, but by the summer of 1202, thanks to a general communal effort, the Venetians had the fleet ready. Unfortunately, as the French chronicler of the crusade, Villehardouin, admitted, the number of crusaders who arrived in the city fell far short of the number promised and they were able to pay only slightly more than half their fare. With the crusade about to founder for lack of funds and Venice likely to sustain a considerable loss as well, the ancient doge Enrico Dandolo (d. 1205), reportedly over eighty and nearly blind, suggested a solution. In return for

the crusaders' help in subduing Zara (that mid-Adriatic city had recently revolted against Venetian rule with the aid of the king of Hungary) the debt would be deferred until it could be repaid with booty captured on the crusade. After considerable discussion, the majority of the crusaders agreed to the plan and Zara, a Christian city, fell to them in mid November 1202.

While wintering at Zara, a second and even more significant diversion was planned. A claimant to the Byzantine throne approached the crusaders with an offer of 200,000 marks of silver and 10,000 Greek soldiers to aid their cause in return for their help in securing his claims to the emperorship. The debate was acrimonious and a number of crusaders defected, but the main body accepted the offer of this "young Alexios." Thus the crusaders in the spring sailed not for Jerusalem but for Constantinople, a turn of events that could not have displeased the Venetians. The crusaders, in the end, resorted to a military attack on the Christian capital of the East not once but twice. First, in July 1203, the once impregnable city was forced to accept Alexios after the crusaders captured a major section of the city's wall and put the adjoining neighborhoods to the torch. Then again, in April 1204, the city was taken and sacked when it became clear that Alexios, unable to rule the empire, was going to renege on his promises.

Baldwin, count of Flanders, was elected emperor, but Venice did very well in the division of the spoils, receiving officially three-eighths of the empire, the right to choose the Latin patriarch of the East, and the reconfirmation of all previous trading rights and privileges. In addition the Venetians received a large share of the plunder, including not only gold, silver, precious stones, and monuments such as the four bronze horses that adorn the facade of S. Marco, but also highly valued relics from the churches of the empire. Significantly, Venice did not attempt to exercise fully her territorial rights. Rather the city concentrated on securing naval bases to solidify commercial dominance. Commercial exploitation, not dominion, remained the goal. Crete and Negroponte were major exceptions to this policy, but even these larger islands were strategic points on Venetian commercial routes. Some individual Venetian nobles, however, were not so reluctant about territorial acquisition. Most notably, Marco Sanuto carved out an island empire for himself in the Aegean, the duchy of Naxos, which he held as a fief of the empire.

POLITICAL READJUSTMENTS: 1205–1381

The immense wealth gained as a result of the Fourth Crusade solidified Venice's position as one of the leading powers in Europe. The triumph over her Byzantine opponents was so complete that it has been claimed that the redirection of the crusade was a Venetian plot from the beginning. There is little evidence to support such a position, and it seems more likely that the conquest of Constantinople gradually evolved as a viable goal as contractual problems moved crusading leaders away from their original goals, with Venetian support and ultimately to Venice's advantage. But the leadership of the crusade as a whole profited from the conquest, and the likelihood of such a redirection of crusading fervor had long been feared by Byzantine rulers.

Once again success brought problems as well. At home new wealth promoted the rise of new families ready to compete for political power and social status. Along with ancient families like the Morosini, Michiel, or Falier, who could trace their lineage of wealth and leadership back to the first civic memories of Venice, and relatively newer families like the Ziani, Malipiero, and Dandolo, who reached prominence in the twelfth century, now an even newer group rose to prominence on the wings of Venetian imperial expansion. The process was not a smooth one. New families like the Tiepolo faced considerable resistance from older families and turned for support to the growing numbers of artisans and small merchants. Thus, for all Venice's success abroad, at home there grew up considerable political and social tension.

Such tensions were not unique to Venice. Throughout the Italian north in the thirteenth century new wealth rose to power under the banner of *il popolo* (the people). *Il popolo,* however, did not mean all the people; rather it was predicated upon an alliance of artisans, merchants, bankers, and professional people against old wealth. Guilds, in a sense communes within the commune, were the primary vehicle for the *popolo*'s conquest of power using superior organization and violence where necessary to capture government. Although the old wealth of Venice was less land-oriented than in most other cities, the dogeship of Giacomo Tiepolo (1229–1249) reveals that a form of the new wealth–old wealth conflict expressed in terms of *popolo* power had its day even in Venice. His hotly contested election was seen as a victory for the *popolo*. True to the form of such regimes, as doge he busied himself with legal reforms codifying civil and criminal law and issued a maritime code especially protective of the lesser men involved in trade. But even with such measures and continued Tiepolo support, the *popolo* never attempted to restrict or drive out the old wealthy elite and thus take power in Venice.

Central in the failure of the *popolo* was the weakness of the guild structure as an independent power base for the newly wealthy and the artisans. The government controlled the guilds by means of the *Giustizieri Vecchi,* a council that oversaw and limited guild action by monitoring guild elections, adjudicating guild problems, and periodically passing rules for guild operation. Moreover, government favored a fragmentation of the guilds—which eventually numbered more than one hundred—that splintered their limited power to such an extent as to render them less and less meaningful. Carefully monitored and divided guilds lacked the ability to organize the *popolo* in Venice. Finally, the merchants formed no guild as they fought for power in the halls of government itself, where eventually new wealth and old made their accommodations; the lesser men of the city who helped to force that accommodation found in their guilds at best a form of social support and economic discipline.

But those accommodations took time, and tensions remained high. In fact, dissension at home was, if anything, accentuated as Genoa emerged as the major competitor for commercial domination in the East. A long series of wars with Genoa severely tested the city. Already in the twelfth century a rivalry had developed, punctuated by periodic raids and privateering. The Fourth Crusade gave Venice an advantage, but Genoa's response was to ally with the forces seeking to reestablish a Greek empire. Finally, a formal war broke out between the two powers in 1258, with the first victory going to Venice. The triumph was short-lived, however, as three years later Michael VIII Palaiologos regained Constantinople, reestablishing a Greek empire in the East. The Genoese alliance had borne fruit, and Venice found itself in a precarious position vis-à-vis an emperor who saw himself as the legitimate successor to an imperial line that Venice had played a major role in overthrowing. Nonetheless, in 1266 Venice once again defeated Genoa, in a major battle near Sicily that allowed the city to regain some standing in the Eastern Empire: the emperor could not ignore Venice's demonstration of naval power. Late in the century the conflict blazed up again with a series of major defeats for Venice, capped by the Battle of Curzola in 1298. This Pyrrhic victory for the Genoese caused both sides to withdraw and attempt to recoup their losses.

THE END OF VENETIAN DOMINANCE

This half century of war, really only the beginning of a conflict that would stretch on until 1381, signaled the end of Venetian dominance in the East. A growing competition for the remaining goods and a general slowing of economic growth (probably traceable to the peaking of the medieval demographic boom), in conjunction with a constriction in markets, contributed to a perception that the seemingly unlimited growth potential of the early thirteenth century existed no longer. In this context political power became even more important than it had been previously. Increased competition for shrinking profits had to be regulated, and a large public debt had to be administered. New wealth and old finally had to work out a political accommodation that would preserve as much of the city's commercial strength as possible.

The result was a gradual definition of political status that spanned approximately a generation from 1292 to 1323. Conflict flared openly with the death of Doge Giovanni Dandolo in 1292, when, in a reassertion of ancient custom, the people of Venice attempted to acclaim Giacomo Tiepolo doge (his father and grandfather had both been doges). The Tiepolo name still carried a promise of *popolo* power, but the government overrode this challenge by following formal electoral procedures to elect Pietro Gradenigo doge. Either to preserve order or to avoid almost certain defeat, Tiepolo retired from the city, leaving Gradenigo and the old wealth still in power.

Yet tensions remained, and continuing losses in the war with Genoa plus the burden of its cost forced a political compromise that united new commercial wealth and old in an alliance to rule Venice. The *Serrata* (closing) of the Major Council in 1298 initiated the process of creating a hereditary ruling class. The first legislation, though lost, apparently merely began the process by limiting who could sit on the council. Limitations became progressively tighter until legislation passed in 1323 clearly stated that membership was hereditary. As the Major Council elected virtually all other officeholders from its own members, this meant that political participation was limited to

approximately 180 families who comprised most of the new merchant elite as well as the old.

A compromise had been reached, but it did not go unchallenged. As early as 1300 Marin Boccono and a group of followers were executed for an obscure conspiracy to gain admittance to the Major Council. A more serious threat grew out of factional strife within the ruling class over the unsuccessful military policies of Doge Gradenigo in 1310. A war with Ferrara that had promised easy success at little expense had escalated into a major confrontation with the papacy. The Querini family, leading the faction opposed to the war, sought the help of Baiamonte Tiepolo, heir to the Tiepolo tradition of *popolo* popularity, in the hope of securing broader support for their plot to overthrow Gradenigo. The Querini-Tiepolo conspiracy failed, however, and the triumph of Gradenigo and his supporters assured the success of the *Serrata*.

POLITICAL RESTRUCTURING

In the aftermath of the conspiracy the Council of Ten was created, a secret executive committee with rights of summary justice in cases involving treason, sedition, and conspiracy. It reorganized the policing of the city with an eye toward maximizing patrols and seeing to it that reserve units were ready to defend the government at the sound of the communal bell. At this time a centralized bureaucracy also began to coalesce, based upon the Major Council as the source of political power and the doge as its personification. But with a hereditary membership of about 1,100, the Major Council was too unwieldy to act effectively; thus it progressively delegated its power to two already existing councils: the *Quarantia*, or Forty, concerned mainly with criminal and internal matters and the *Rogati*, or Senate, concerned primarily with diplomatic and commercial concerns. The doge, in turn, came to act more within the context of an executive committee, the *Signoria*, including himself, the three leaders of the *Quarantia*, and the ducal councillors. In that same wave of reorganization the *Avogadori di Comun*, or state attorneys, were put in charge of organizing the legislation of the government and ensuring its implementation. What emerged was an unusually centralized government with an ordered conception of how authority flowed through a system checked periodically by institutions such as the Council of Ten, the *Avogadori*, and the *Signoria*. Behind this structure lay a legally unified class of merchants, who made the government work as much through their shared vision and interests as by the logic of their institutions.

This process of political restructuring of society was closely associated with a new definition of social status. Following the Querini-Tiepolo conspiracy, there was a legal pronouncement that noble status belonged to those who had the right to sit on the Major Council. In other words, political and social status became synonymous and hereditary. The importance of this association cannot be overstated. While other cities were struggling with nebulous definitions of status, both intellectually in discussions of *virtù* and physically in bloody battles in the streets, Venice settled down to defend a legally defined and established merchant nobility. It did so with amazing success. Faced with strong competition and constricting economic possibilities, and saddled with war debts, Venice nonetheless sustained a measured economic expansion led by the Senate. Venetian fleets retooled and adjusted to the striking changes in nautical technology of the early fourteenth century. Those fleets penetrated the Atlantic and continued the conflict with Genoa. In addition Venice began to attempt to control more closely local markets and trade routes in northern Italy. Control and discipline, made necessary by a changing economic environment and made possible by a closed ruling group with relatively common interests, became the keys to economic success.

Tensions remained, but they were progressively denied by a vision of Venice that stressed a tradition of cooperation within the nobility and between the nobility and those below for the common good of society. Perhaps the best example of this was the cooperation of Doge Andrea Dandolo (1343–1354) and his non-noble chancellor Benintendi dei Ravignani. Together they developed a civic mythology that saw Venice as a divinely appointed place of peace and tranquillity—the Apostle Mark's refuge—where under a benign doge's leadership nobles and people cooperated to create a third power independent of the spiritual claims of the papacy and the political claims of emperors. It was a classic vision that contrasted starkly with the problems of Dandolo's rule. For during his reign the city was racked by the first wave of the plague in 1347–1348, losing at least half its population. Rapid immigration from the mainland introduced many new people unaccustomed to the restricted political and social status of artisans and guilds there. And

once again Venice became involved in an open phase of its war with Genoa.

Fortunately for Dandolo, he died before these realities came to a head. And fortunately for the "history" he and his chancellor helped to formulate, the realities of his rule were quickly forgotten while the myths endured and grew. Immediately, however, disunity seemed to have won out. A conspiracy to overthrow the state was discovered in 1355, led by the new head of that state, the doge Marin Falier. Apparently, Falier, disappointed by the war policy forced upon him by his government, decided to become a *signore* (tyrant) on the model of many mainland rulers. The Council of Ten, with its typical efficiency and silence, arrested the doge when it became aware of the plot; called in a special group of the most important men of the city to aid in his trial; and had him beheaded in private, noting in its secret registers on a page still unfilled that they would report the particulars of the case later, when tensions subsided.

THE WAR WITH GENOA
Perhaps the greatest challenge Dandolo's myth faced occurred during the last phase of the city's war with Genoa that began in the 1370's. After a series of naval victories the Genoese admiral Pietro Doria was able to sail up the Adriatic and capture Chioggia, the major city at the southern edge of the lagoons, in 1379. Venice lay open before him, but lacking knowledge of the channels that would allow his ships to sail across the lagoons, Doria decided to starve the city into submission with the help of his mainland allies, who were anxious to destroy Venice's local power. To break the blockade, the government tried to man a fleet from the populace of Venice, but with little success. Only when the very popular Vettore Pisani was freed from the jail where he had been imprisoned for his alleged cowardice in battle was it possible to recruit crews. Pisani, with audacity, and the support of men more loyal to him than to the nobility, blockaded the Genoese by sinking ships in the channels that led from Chioggia to the open sea. With small boats and hand-to-hand fighting he prevented the enemy from clearing a path to the sea and slowly starved them into submission. What had seemed a hopeless situation became Venice's greatest victory. If Pisani had thoughts of transforming his popularity with the people into something more, they were thwarted by his untimely death in mop-up operations against Genoese ships still at large in the

Adriatic before a formal peace had been signed. Ultimately, once again the nobility had won.

For them the victory was especially sweet. Thirty of the most loyal commoners were elevated to noble status as a reward for their support. Again the vision of noble leadership and popular loyalty was preserved. Genoa, in contrast, dissolved in factional strife and eventually fell under foreign control. As a result, Eastern trade, though clouded by the ominous rise of Turkish power, seemed to promise much. Closer to home the growth of *signori* on the mainland meant Venice would have to take a more aggressive stance in Italian affairs to protect her commercial interests and the growing number of noble estates on the mainland. Thus, in the early fifteenth century, Venice took advantage of the internecine warfare of the neighboring *signori* of Padua, Verona, and Milan to conquer a territorial state of her own in northeastern Italy. That expansion broadened Venetian economic interests and potential and made the city a major power in the Renaissance diplomacy of Italy.

CONCLUSION

With its triumph over Genoa and its move onto the mainland Venice had to a degree completed its medieval development, consolidating the rule of a merchant nobility over a commercial empire that connected East and West and a territorial state that dominated some of the richest lands in Italy. The city had become a suitable resting place for the Apostle Mark: with a strange logic, myth had to a degree become reality. Raffiano Caresini, a commoner and civil servant enobled after the war of Chioggia, appropriately summed up Venice's triumph in the face of tensions and adversity with a metaphor that continued Dandolo's vision:

> For just as the ship of St. Peter was tossed about but did not sink, so too the ship of St. Mark, his disciple (who by divine grace oversees the city of Venice), when it appeared to be endangered by the waves was brought safely to port, not only for the private good, but for the general welfare of all.

BIBLIOGRAPHY

Giorgio Cracco, *Società e stato nel medioevo veneziano (secolo XII–XIV)* (1967); Otto Demus, *The Church of San Marco in Venice: History, Architecture, Sculpture* (1960); Frederic Chapin Lane, *Venice and History: The Collected Papers of Frederic C. Lane* (1966) and *Venice: A Maritime Republic* (1973); Gino Luzzatto, *Storia economica de Venezia dall XI al XVI secolo* (1961); William H. McNeill, *Venice: The Hinge of Europe, 1081–1797* (1974); Pompeo Gherardo Molmenti, *Venice: Its Individual Growth from the Earliest Beginnings to the Fall of the Republic,* Horatio F. Brown, trans., 6 vols. (1906–1908), the later Italian edition (1927) contains more information; Edward Muir, "Images of Power: Art and Pageantry in Renaissance Venice," in *American Historical Review,* 84 (1979); Donald E. Queller, *The Fourth Crusade: The Conquest of Constantinople, 1201–1204* (1977); Samuele Romanin, *Storia documentata di Venezia,* 10 vols. (1853–1861); Guido Ruggiero, "Modernization and the Mythic State in Early Renaissance Venice: The Serrata Revisited," in *Viator* 10 (1979), and *Violence in Early Renaissance Venice* (1980); Freddy Thiriet, *Histoire de Venise* (1952) and *La romanie vénitienne au moyen âge* (1959).

GUIDO RUGGIERO

[See also **Byzantine Empire: History; Carolingians and Carolingian Empire; Constantinople; Crusades and Crusader States; Dalmatia; Genoa; Italy; Lomards, Kingdom of; Navies, Western; Navigation, Eastern European; Ostrogoths; Ravenna; Roman Empire, Late; San Marco, Venice; Ships and Shipbuilding, Mediterranean; Trade, European; Urbanism: Western European.**]

VERECUNDUS OF JUNCA (*d.* 552), theologian and biblical commentator, became bishop of Junca in North Africa in 534. He opposed some of the theological rulings of the emperor Justinian and fled to Chalcedon, where he died in 552. Verecundus wrote the *Liber in cantica,* which are largely allegorical commentaries on nine Old Testament canticles, a poem of 242 hexameters on penitence (*De satisfactione poenitentiae*), and 406 hexameters on resurrection (*De resurrectione mortuorum*).

BIBLIOGRAPHY

Max Manitius, *Geschichte der lateinischen Literatur des Mittelalters,* I (1911), 153–156; Frederic J. E. Raby, *A History of Christian-Latin Poetry,* 2nd ed. (1953), 99–100; Verecundus, *Commentarii super cantica ecclesiastica; Carmen de satisfactione paenitentiae,* R. Demeulenaere, ed. (1976).

W. T. H. JACKSON

[See also **Byzantine Church; Justinian, Emperor.**]

VERGIL IN THE MIDDLE AGES. Publius Vergilius Maro (70–19 B.C.) was esteemed during the Latin Middle Ages as the most important of all poets. A *Life of Vergil,* attributed to Donatus but probably by Suetonius, commonly preceded his *Eclogues, Georgics,* and *Aeneid.* It said that Vergil was the author of a number of minor poems, now

considered spurious, such as the *Priapea, Culex,* and *Moretum.* It also said that Vergil left the *Aeneid* unfinished, but that the emperor Augustus preserved the manuscript. As the national epic of Rome, the *Aeneid* was soon used in the schools, and in the first century Quintilian recommended Vergil's works for study. Poets like Ovid, Lucan, Statius, Silius Italicus, and Claudian wrote in Vergil's shadow.

Throughout the Middle Ages, to study grammar was to study Vergil. It is safe to assume that anyone who could read in the Middle Ages, even the author of *Beowulf,* probably knew Vergil in some form, With the Bible and Ovid, Vergil provided educated men with a common denominator for over 1,500 years. He is discussed by church fathers such as Lactantius, St. Jerome, and St. Augustine, who wept over the episode of Dido. Vergil was a model for the early Christian poets Juvencus (*Evangeliorum libri, ca.* 330), Prudentius (348–405), Sedulius (*Carmen paschale,* mid fifth century), Arator, and Dracontius. Steeped in the *Aeneid* were works like Corippus' *Johannis,* an epic poem in eight cantos on Justinian's general (546–548), Gregory's *History of the Franks* (*ca.* 590), and Aldhelm's *De virginitate.*

Opinions varied among Christians as to whether pagan works were fit to read, but the more educated authors, particularly encyclopedists like Bede, Cassiodorus, and Isidore, recommended and studied Vergil. In the ninth century, sometimes called the *aetas Vergiliana,* Lupus of Ferrières revised and annotated Tiberius Claudius Donatus' commentary on the first six books of the *Aeneid.* Alcuin borrowed Vergil's dialogue form, and his eclogue on the cuckoo prefigured the use Petrarch and many writers in the Renaissance made of the pastoral form.

In the fourteenth century, Dante noted that Providence made Aeneas and David contemporaries, and he turned Vergil's praise of Rome into hope for the contemporary church and empire. Unlike countless medieval poets and Renaissance humanists, Dante did not imitate Vergil's Latin hexameters; nonetheless, in the *Divine Comedy* Dante tells the figure of Vergil, who has been sent to guide him through Hell and Purgatory: "You are my master and my author. You alone are he from whom I took the fair style that has done me honor" (*Inferno,* I, 85–87).

The values Christian readers found in Vergil's work assured Vergil's popularity in the Middle Ages. Already by the fourth century, ecclesiastical writers had found a prophecy of the coming of Christ in Vergil's fourth eclogue, which utilized a traditional vision of the Golden Age to announce the peace and harmony that were to be ushered in by the birth of a boy:

> The great line of the centuries begins anew. Now the Virgin returns, the reign of Saturn returns; now a new generation descends from heaven on high. . . . He shall have the gift of divine life, shall see heroes mingled with gods, and shall himself be seen of them, and shall sway a world to which his father's virtues have brought peace. (H. Rushton Fairclough, trans.)

This eclogue was written in 41–40 B.C., and the boy may have been the son of Antony and Octavia. Nonetheless, Vergil as a prophet of Christ is a common theme in medieval art and literature. In the twenty-second canto of Dante's *Purgatorio,* Statius claims that the fourth eclogue converted him to Christianity.

Dante has dominated studies of Vergil in the Middle Ages, but recent researches have looked at Vergil through other eyes. Comparetti and Spargo reviewed Vergil's reputation as a magician among the common people of Europe, particularly around Naples, where Vergil was buried. Recent work has concentrated on the way in which numerous commentators understood Vergil's works.

394

Servius is the best-known commentator. He incorporated the work of earlier scholars who for several hundred years had analyzed Vergil's grammar, lexicography, philosophy, religious and political history, and use of antiquities. His work has survived in two forms, one from the fourth or very early fifth century, and the other, printed in 1600 by Pierre Daniel and known as Servius Auctus or Servius Danielis, which relies on ninth- and tenth-century manuscripts, possibly representing a seventh-century text in which someone had included material from Aelius Donatus, the teacher of St. Jerome.

Servius' work is generally assigned to the late fourth century, the time of the pagan revival, just before the final triumph of Christianity. This period produced the *Saturnalia* of Macrobius, a work in which the figure of Servius takes part in a symposium on the *Aeneid*. Members of the senatorial aristocracy, like Macrobius, Servius, Donatus, and Symmachus, discussed antiquarian problems, superintended the last remnants of pagan religious worship, and commented on Vergil. They passed on uncorrupted texts and gave direction to medieval Vergilian exegesis.

Whereas modern scholars propose that Vergil followed a tradition of allegorical readings of Homer and in fact wrote the *Aeneid* as an allegory, in the Middle Ages many commentators believed that beneath the veil of allegory the adventures of Aeneas showed the perils of the Christian life. Popular in the eighth and ninth centuries was the sixth-century *De continentia vergiliana* of Fabius Planciades Fulgentius, which claims that the books of the *Aeneid* represent the stages of human life—birth in book one, childhood in the marvelous adventures of books two and three, the time of love in book four, and on through manhood in book six. Less absurd than Fulgentius were later allegorizers such as Bernard Silvester and Christopher Landino. The size of commentaries increased until, in the 1490's, a series of Venetian publishers produced some of the most heavily annotated books ever printed, surrounding the text of Vergil by the commentaries of Servius, Donatus, Landino, Mancinelli, and Calderini.

BIBLIOGRAPHY

Herbert Bloch, "The Pagan Revival in the West at the End of the Fourth Century," in Arnaldo Momigliano, ed., *The Conflict Between Paganism and Christianity in the Fourth Century* (1963); Robert R. Bolgar, *The Classical Heritage and Its Beneficiaries* (1954); Domenico Comparetti, *Vergil in the Middle Ages*, Edward F. M. Benecke, trans. (1929); Raymond J. Cormier, *One Heart, One Mind: The Rebirth of Virgil's Hero in Medieval French Romance* (1973); G. P. Goold, "Servius and the Helen Episode," in *Harvard Studies in Classical Philology*, **74** (1970); Gilbert Highet, *The Classical Tradition* (1949); Robert Kaster, *Guardians of Language: The Grammarian and Society in Late Antiquity* (1988); Max L. W. Laistner, *Thought and Letters in Western Europe, 500 to 900 A.D.* (1957); Alexander G. McKay, "Recent Work on Vergil: A Bibliographical Survey (1964–1973)," in *Classical World*, **68** (1974); Michael Murrin, *The Allegorical Epic* (1980), 27–50; Elizabeth Nitchie, *Vergil and the English Poets* (1919), 1–71; Ettore Paratore, "Ancora sulla vita Donatiana di Virgilio," in *Philologus*, **121** (1977); Brooks Otis, *Virgil: A Study in Civilized Poetry* (1963); David Thompson, *Dante's Epic Journeys* (1974); J. H. Whitfield, "Virgil and Dante," in D. R. Dudley, ed., *Virgil* (1969).

CHARLES STANLEY ROSS

[See also **Allegory; Classical Literary Studies; Epic, Latin; Latin Literature; Ovid in the Middle Ages; Prudentius.**]

VERMANDOIS is located in upper Picardy near the Belgian province of Hainaut. Today it is a part of the French *département* of the Aisne. Its terrain is very flat, punctuated here and there by low sandy hills. From premedieval to modern times this flatness has facilitated the passage of armies and trade. It sits athwart the routes that connect the Parisian basin with Flanders. Vermandois derives its name from the *Veromandui,* a group of people noted by Caesar in his *Gallic War* and which he located as living near the heads of the Oise, Sambre, and Scheldt rivers. The two principal towns of Vermandois, as in the Middle Ages, are Péronne and St. Quentin, between which is situated the small village of Vermand.

During the Carolingian period (eighth and ninth centuries) Vermandois was organized into an administrative circumscription called a *pagus* and was known as *Veromanduensis pagus.* It was administered by an official subordinate to a count; the count in turn wielded power over a larger area known as a county. With the breakup of the Carolingian Empire in the second half of the ninth century, Vermandois became a feudal county whose first count was probably Herbert I, a descendant of Charlemagne. Killed in 902 by an assassin in the pay of the count of Flanders, he was succeeded by his son Herbert II (902–943), who increased the territorial extent of the county and who kept the Carolingian ruler Charles the Simple a captive for six years. In 1077 Herbert IV, the last male heir of the first Vermandois house, acquired the countship of Valois by marriage. Succeeding him was his daughter Adela, who married Hugh, the brother of Philip I of France (r. 1060–1108). One of the leaders of the First Crusade, Hugh died at Tarsus in Cilicia in 1102. Following the rule of several of his descendants, his granddaughter Isabelle succeeded to the countship in 1167 and also acquired control over the territory around Valois and Amiens. Her marriage with Philip of Alsace, count of Flanders, cemented ties with that strong feudal state. By an agreement of 1186 Philip Augustus of France recognized Philip of Alsace as count of Vermandois. The Flemish counts held Vermandois into the early thirteenth century, when it was ceded to Philip Augustus. Henceforth Vermandois was ruled by the French kings.

After becoming a part of the kingdom of France, Vermandois was organized into a *bailliage,* an administrative district under the authority of a royal official known as a *bailli* who wielded local military, financial, and judicial powers. During the thirteenth century the strategically located towns of Vermandois became important trade centers, and some of them, such as St. Quentin, excelled in the fabrication of cheap wool cloth.

In 1435 the area around Péronne was ceded by Charles VII of France to Duke Philip the Good of Burgundy by the Treaty of Arras, but it was repurchased by Louis XI of France in 1463. Having fallen into the hands of Duke Charles the Bold of Burgundy in 1468, Louis XI was held prisoner in the château of Péronne and forced to sign the disastrous Treaty of Péronne, which handed over the territory and revenues of northeastern France. Paradoxically, it was in this château that Charles the Simple had been held prisoner by Herbert II.

BIBLIOGRAPHY

Jan Dhondt, *Études sur la naissance des principautés territoriales en France, IXe–Xe siècle* (1948); E. Lemaire, "Essai sur l'histoire de Saint-Quentin," in *Mémoires de la société historique de Saint-Quentin,* **2** (1887); Léon Vanderkindere, *La formation territoriale des principautés belges au moyen âge,* 2 vols. (2nd ed. 1902, repr. 1981); Henri Waquet, *Le bailliage de Vermandois aux XIIIe et XIVe siècles: Étude d'histoire administrative* (1919).

BRYCE LYON

[See also **Bailli; Carolingians and the Carolingian Empire; Charles VII of France; County; Flanders and the Low Countries; Louis XI of France; Pagus; Pierre de Fontaines.**]

VERMICLE ENAMEL. See **Enamel, Vermiculé.**

VERNICLE (Middle English; from Latin *veronicae, veroniculae,* from *vera icona,* "true image"), a copy of the sudarium, the cloth upon which the likeness of Christ was imprinted miraculously when, according to the apocryphal Gospel of Nicodemus, a woman wiped his face during the procession to Calvary. This anonymous woman was later named St. Veronica. The relic was preserved in St. Peter's, Rome, where it became the focus of a popular cult during the thirteenth and fourteenth centuries. The image was worn also as a badge by pilgrims to Rome.

MICHAEL T. DAVIS

[See also **Pilgrimage, Western European; Relics.**]

VERS (from Latin *versus*), in Provençal troubadour poetry, the term used for a lyric poem of five to ten stanzas followed by one or two truncated dedicatory stanzas (*tornadas*). The term seems in this function to be equivalent to the later term *canso. Vers* was also used simply to indicate one line of a lyric poem in French or Provençal.

MARCIA J. EPSTEIN

[See also **Canso; Provençal Literature; Tornada.**]

VERTUE, ROBERT AND WILLIAM (d. 1506 and 1527, respectively), among the last and greatest English medieval architects. They were sons of Adam, a mason at Westminster in 1475. Robert, the elder, served as king's master mason from about 1475 until his death in 1506. He was succeeded by William from 1510 until the latter's death in 1527. Together they designed Bath Abbey, and William completed Robert's work on St. George's Chapel, Windsor. (See illustration at "Lierne.") Robert designed Henry VII's chapel in Westminster Abbey—

one of the most sumptuous late medieval buildings—and William completed it, with its lacelike pendant vaults, in 1519. (See illustrations at "Gothic, Perpendicular" and "Westminster Abbey.") Robert was also responsible for the design of Corpus Christi College, Cambridge.

BIBLIOGRAPHY

Eric Gee, "Oxford Masons, 1370–1530," in *Archaeological Journal*, **109** (1952), esp. 89–90; John Harvey, *Gothic England: A Survey of National Culture, 1300–1550* (1947), 29, 129–131, 183–186, and *English Mediaeval Architects: A Biographical Dictionary Down to 1550* (1954), 270–274; William R. Lethaby, *Westminster Abbey and the King's Craftsmen* (1906), 223–226.

STEPHEN GARDNER

[See also **Architect, Status of; Gothic Architecture; Masons and Builders; Westminster Abbey.**]

VESTMENTS, LITURGICAL. It is instinctive to wear special clothing for special occasions, and there is a tendency to wear conservative clothing for religious functions, which are in their nature usually conservative. Long before Christian times both Jewish and non-Jewish religious leaders wore distinctive vestments for liturgical occasions, and there is a tradition reaching back into patristic antiquity that vestments for Christian liturgical services were adaptations of these earlier precedents. It is now generally agreed, however, that in the practice of the early Christian church there was no distinction made between ecclesiastical and civil dress. Rather, Christian liturgical vestments derived from Roman dress, whose forms were later maintained out of a conservative attitude regarding liturgical functions. It was only later in patristic times and the early Middle Ages that commentators began to find precedents for Christian liturgical vestments in ancient Jewish and non-Jewish cultic usage. It was also in the early Middle Ages that councils and popes began to make distinctions between the dress of clergy at the altar or away from it. And slightly later in the ninth and tenth centuries vesting prayers containing allegorical and mystical meanings for the vestments were introduced as a cleric vested for liturgical functions. Moreover, from late patristic antiquity throughout the Middle Ages particular meanings were attached to the colors used for liturgical vestments.

It is important to remember that many pieces of clothing worn by religious men and women that are sometimes considered liturgical are not; for example, monastic habits, cassocks, and the like are not strictly speaking liturgical, although they are sometimes worn during liturgical ceremonies. In this article medieval liturgical vestments will be considered under four broad headings: liturgical undergarments; liturgical outer garments; insignia; and hand, foot, and head liturgical clothing.

LITURGICAL UNDERGARMENTS

Amice. This vestment, variously called *amictus, humerale, superhumerale, anabolagium,* and *anagolaium,* is thought to be derived from the classical neck cloth or scarf, examples of which may be seen on Trajan's column in Rome. Because it was an optional dress in classical times, it was not obligatory as a liturgical vestment in Western Christendom for many centuries. In fact, the ancient *Ordo Romanus I* notes that the pope wears an *anagolaium,* but it is clear from the later eighth-century *Ordo Romanus IV* that it was not obligatory to wear the amice. The amice is a square or rectangular piece of material that covers the neck, shoulders (hence *humerale*), and breast and is tied by two strings around the waist. By the tenth century it was common to attach colored pieces of embroidered material (sometimes covered in gems, pearls, and gold and silver thread) to the amice. This perhaps arose from the method of donning the amice by placing it over the head as a helmet (the vesting prayer mentions the helmet of salvation) until the other vestments were pulled over it. When thrown back over the other vestments the heavier piece of material gave weight to the amice and held it back against the neck of the wearer.

Fanon. Related to the amice is the fanon (a word also used to describe the maniple), but unlike the amice the fanon is worn over, not under, the alb. The fanon is mentioned in *Ordo Romanus I* as an *anabolagium* and was used by several orders of clerics at more solemn Masses. By the end of the twelfth century it was reserved to the pope, and by the end of the Middle Ages the pope was wearing both the amice and fanon. The fanon, a piece of material with a head hole in the center, was made of white silk with red and gold stripes and like the modern papal fanon perhaps had a gold embroidered cross on it.

Alb. The alb, variously called a *tunica manicata, tunica linea, camisia, tunica talaris,* or *tunica po-*

deris, had its origins in the undergarment of classical times, although according to medieval commentators it was a continuation of the dress of Old Testament priests. Although the alb was worn by newly baptized Christians (and called the chrismal), it was the standard liturgical undergarment of clerics and could be used not only at Mass but also at synods and in the administration of communion to the sick. Since the thirteenth century the alb has usually been restricted to the orders of subdeacon, deacon, presbyter, and bishop, leaving the lower orders to wear the surplice or cotta. Of two major types, one reaching to the knees (sometimes without sleeves) and the other to the feet, the alb was early made of white linen or wool and, in the Middle Ages, occasionally of silk, either white or colored. Albs might be decorated in various ways, early with russet vertical stripes or *clavi* down the back and front and around the skirt, wrists, and *caputium* or head hole; and later with apparels on the sleeves, breast, and back and front of the lower part of the skirt.

Related to the alb and later the surplice is the rochet. Characterized by tight sleeves, it was a loose-fitting garment of white linen or cotton generally reaching to the feet or shins. Until the thirteenth century, when it was called *roccus,* the rochet was usually designated as an *alba* or *camisia.* In Rome this *camisia* seems to have been a garment for upper clerics, but elsewhere all clerics might wear it.

Cincture. The girdle that was tied around the waist to keep the alb from impeding the movement of the wearer was called a *cingulum* or *zona* and was a part of everyday clothing in classical times. Perhaps a cincture was used liturgically by priests in the Gallican rite, and in *Ordo Romanus I* a cincture is mentioned. In any event, as is shown in the special vesting prayers, the cincture was recognized at least by the early tenth century as liturgical attire, especially for the bishop and presbyter. The earliest examples of liturgical cinctures are not the simple cords used today, but either narrow or very thick bands of highly ornamented silk or brocade, sometimes with gold and silver thread-work and with tassels attached.

Related to both the cincture and maniple is the subcinctorium, also called a *balteus, semicinctium,* or *praecintorium.* This was a cincture worn on the cincture, perhaps originally intended to secure the stole to the cincture. First used in France by bishops and a few priests before the year 1000, it gradually

spread to Italy, and its use was reserved there to the bishop of Rome.

Surplice. From its name, *superpelliceum,* it appears that the surplice was designed as a more ample form of the alb to go over a fur gown (*pelisse*) for the night Office in the colder climes of northern Europe. Used at least from the tenth century especially for the choir Office, the surplice came to replace the alb by the twelfth century as the choir habit and was accepted as a liturgical garment in Rome by the thirteenth century. Originally it seems to have been like an ample alb with wider sleeves. These could be split or even missing and by the fifteenth century might be almost like those of a Benedictine habit. Although the surplice might reach only to the knee and ankle, it generally extended to the feet. Because of its ample folds the surplice was rarely decorated, although there are some rare examples with geometrical ornaments on front and back.

LITURGICAL OUTER GARMENTS

Tunicle. The tunicle was called by a large variety of names: *tunica, tunicella, subtile, roc, rocca, roquo, linea dalmatica, dalmatica minor, dalmatica subdiaconlis, tunica subdiaconalis, tunica stricta, subdiaconale,* and even *alba.* There are a number of theories as to its origin but generally they can be divided into secular and liturgical. According to the former the tunicle derives from the Roman second tunic with short sleeves or no sleeves whatsoever that reached only to the knees. According to the latter theory, it is said that as a liturgical vestment the tunicle goes back to Pope Gregory I, who distinguished between the tunicle for subdeacons and the dalmatic for deacons. But against this and for an earlier date it is pointed out that Gregory forbade subdeacons to wear tunicles, which one of his predecessors had allowed. After this time, it is thought by liturgiologists, Roman subdeacons wore the *planeta* or chasuble until the eighth century, after which they wore the tunicle. Outside Rome the change was made earlier, and the First Council of Braga (561) implies that a subdeacon wore a tunicle. But even in the ninth century the tunicle was not necessarily common for subdeacons, as can be seen on the covers of the Drogo Sacramentary (Paris, Bibliothèque Nationale, MS lat. 9428), where subdeacons are dressed in albs.

Although the tunicle became the garment par excellence of the subdeacon, other ecclesiastical functionaries might wear it: acolytes, crucifers, and thurifers in the greater churches; deacons under their dalmatics; and cardinal presbyters without dalmatics. By the time of *Ordo Romanus I* in the seventh and eighth centuries, the pope would wear one, and by the twelfth century bishops and sometimes important abbots would wear both the tunicle and dalmatic.

During the Middle Ages there were at least three major types of tunics. The first, found in an illustration in a manuscript in Rome, Biblioteca Vallicelliana, MS B-25, is a long, tight-fitting garment reaching to the feet, with narrow, long sleeves (*tunica talaris*). The second, found in the ninth-century Raganaldus Sacramentary (Autun, Bibliothèque Municipale, MS lat. 19 [19 bis]), is a full garment reaching below the knees and with wide sleeves. A third type, leaving the shoulder free, was called an *exomium*. Gradually slits were made in the sides of the tunicle, and in the later Middle Ages these reached up to the sleeve. The material of the tunicle was linen or silk, and by the ninth century they also were noted as being colored. By the tenth century they could be decorated in gold. In any event, they were generally made to match the color of the chasuble and dalmatic for a feast or season.

As the symbol of the subdiaconate, the tunicle was commonly given to holders of this office at their ordination. By the twelfth century this was the case in some areas, and by the fourteenth and fifteenth centuries it was the common practice in most places.

Dalmatic. The origins of the dalmatic, almost always called only *dalmatica,* were said to have been in Dalmatia, from a special wool there. Clearly Roman emperors wore dalmatics as early as the second century, and Christians very early wore them ornamented with *clavi,* as can be seen in catacomb frescoes.

Popes in Rome and bishops and archbishops in Milan and Ravenna early on wore this vestment, as did deacons in Rome, but only gradually did it become the distinguishing mark of these latter officers, who with other persons of honor (for example, abbots) might be given the dalmatic by the pope. Throughout Europe the dalmatic had become by the ninth century the usual liturgical dress of deacons. By the tenth century, Roman cardinal presbyters were granted the privilege of wearing the dalmatic, as were certain chosen presbyters outside Rome.

Because the dalmatic was seen (as the vesting

Above: Bishop with scarlet and gold chasuble (center) between presbyter with full gold chasuble and deacon with wide-sleeved dalmatic decorated with red and black *clavi. Below:* Subdeacon with gold tunicle. Miniature from the Raganaldus Sacramentary of *ca.* 845. AUTUN, BIBLIOTHÈQUE MUNICIPALE, 19 bis, fol. lv

prayer notes) as a garment of praise and joy, it was omitted in penitential seasons, a practice virtually universal by the twelfth century. On such occasions the deacons simply wore an alb or the folded chasuble.

By at least the eighth century the dalmatic was given to the deacon in Rome as a symbol of his office. Outside Rome this practice was not universal until the later Middle Ages, and the commentator Sicard mentions it with some hesitation.

In its earliest form the dalmatic was a long, wide tunic reaching to the feet, with very wide sleeves. In Rome it remained that way until the High Middle Ages, when it became shorter, with narrowed sleeves, as had been the case in northern Europe from at least the ninth century. Originally the garment was made of linen or wool, and as silk became more common this material was used as well and even became dominant. Before the tenth century dalmatics were usually white; thereafter they were colored, and by the thirteenth century they were often made of a color to match the priest's chasuble. Dalmatics were early ornamented with *clavi* or two bands on front and back with a narrow band on the sleeves. In the ninth century tufts of red fringe were sometimes added to the *clavi* and bands on the sleeves. In Italy it was common to ornament the dalmatic with an apparel above the front and back hem of the garment.

Chasuble. The chasuble, called a *planeta, penula, amphibalus,* or *casula* (because with its head hole it resembled a little house), was probably identical with the outer garments of the lower classes in classical times. Originally all clerics wore this vestment, but gradually it was restricted to the *sacerdotes* (priests). In *Ordo Romanus I* all ranks of clergy wore the penula, but only the pope kept his on at entering the church for liturgical functions. By the ninth century it seems that its use by deacons was being restricted, inasmuch as the liturgical commentator Amalarius mentions that the deacon retained his *penula* only until after the Alleluia in the Mass, at which time he put off the vestment, rolled it on his left shoulder, and passed its two ends together with the stole across and under his right arm, fastening it there. This eventually led to the so-called *planeta plicata* or folded chasuble.

Originally the chasuble was a round or square piece of material with a head hole. By the early Middle Ages it had become conical, made with a semicircular piece of material, folded with a straight edge in the middle, and sewn together leaving a head hole. Sometimes two semicircular pieces of material were sewn together, with a seam down the front and back. This was then covered with a decorative orphrey, although on occasion the front seam might be left open almost to the top. This conical-shaped chasuble was common in the twelfth century, when a change was made to a type in which slits were made from the hem upward to the arms or the sides were cut away so as to free the arms of the priest as he elevated the host and chalice in the Mass. After the thirteenth century the chasuble became excessively ornamented with embroideries and decorative orphreys sometimes made in the form of a cross, crucifix, or the like.

A variant form of the chasuble is depicted in the eleventh-century frescoes of S. Clemente in Rome and in the Bayeux Tapestry: a chasuble that is long in back but shorter in front, reaching to a point below the breast.

Cope. Called a *pluviale* (because it protected the wearer against the rain) or *cappa,* the cope goes back to classical antiquity and probably derived from an open-fronted *penula.* It was only by the late ninth century that they were distinctively liturgical, although even after that there were certainly nonliturgical copes. When they became common liturgical vestments they were used at great festal masses by all the clergy, and at Cluny by all monks. Secular canons picked up this use, and cantors might have especially elaborate copes to go with their own important function in the choir. Outside the church they would be used in processions, benedictions, burials, and the like. The *cappa nigra* was the cope for the Divine Office, and it was out of this that the *cappa magna* or *cappa choralis* worn by cardinals and privileged prelates grew. Also, the *mantum,* the red vestment with which the pope was invested (the *inmantatio*), developed out of the cope.

The cope was made like the chasuble, but the folded front was not sewn together. Over the years the most important change was in the hood, which evolved from a triangular practical hood to an ornamental appendage looking like a shield held by buttons to the lower edge of the orphrey on the back of the cope. Copes were often splendidly decorated, and some of the best embroidery work in the Middle Ages was devoted to these vestments. Particularly famous was the embroidery work called *opus anglicanum.* (A chasuble with *opus anglicanum* embroidery is shown in volume 9.) The cope was fastened together with a brooch called a morse or *pectorale,* which might be enameled or decorated with gems or pearls.

INSIGNIA

Maniple. There are many theories as to the origin of the vestment called a *mappula, sudarium, mantile, fanon, manuale, sestace,* or *manipulus:* that it was a towel, sweat cloth, nose cloth, simple mark of office, or cloth used by Roman emperors to begin the games. In any event, it seems first to have been used by clerics in Rome and then in Ravenna. By the ninth century it was almost universally used. Although mainly worn by the higher orders of subdeacon, deacon, presbyter, and bishop, it was occasionally worn by acolytes (as in Rome) and even lay brothers at Mass (as was the case in Cluny until the late eleventh century).

Very early the symbolic gifts given to a subdea-

The Mass of St. Clement. 11th-century fresco in the church of S. Clemente, Rome, showing the pope in a chasuble. HIRMER FOTOARCHIV

con on his ordination were the pitcher, basin, and towel. But by the tenth century and the Egbert Pontifical the maniple is given to the subdeacon as the insignia of office. That this was not common everywhere is shown in a letter of Lanfranc of Bec to John of Avranches, which states that there is no call for it in the old canon law collections such as the *Statuta ecclesiae antiqua* and the Pseudo-Isidorian *Epistula ad Leudefredum*. But as the subdiaconate became a sacred order in the eleventh century, the gift of the maniple or *fanon* became common throughout Europe.

Until the twelfth century the maniple might be worn on the wrist, left or right, or carried in the hand or fingers, as is shown in the Carolingian Vivian Bible. But in the twelfth century it became common to wear it on the left arm, attached by small bands so as not to slip off. Generally the maniple was worn only at Mass, but it could be used during anointing. The subdeacon, deacon, and presbyter put on their maniples before Mass, and the bishop after the *Confiteor*.

Originally the maniple was a folded piece of cloth and hence functional, but by the tenth century they were becoming decorative objects in themselves, made with simple strips of valuable fabric, adorned with gold and silver thread, pearls, and gems, and finished with tassels or bells.

Stole. According to some scholars, the *orarium* or *stola* was originally the outer garment of Roman matrons, as suggested by the word *stola* itself. This is probably incorrect, however, because the early term used for this insignia was *orarium*. Moreover, the full chasuble could also be called a *stola*. It is probable that the liturgical stole derived from a Roman consular insignia. The Theodosian Code ordered that a scarf or pall was to be worn over the alb and *penula* of senators and consuls; this garment showed a close resemblance to the pallium or *omophorion* worn by bishops and perhaps was the same thing. Hence, perhaps when the term *orarium* was applied to bishops it meant pallium, and when applied to presbyters and deacons it meant stole. In any event, it was usual to

Landulf of Benevento, dressed in blue chasuble over a green and gold stole, wearing a gold pallium with red crosses, and shod with episcopal shoes and stockings, places a gold stole around the neck of a presbyterial ordinand dressed in a white alb tied with a cincture around the waist. Other presbyterial candidates wear gold stoles; the archdeacon to the left wears a gold stole over the left shoulder of a wide-sleeved dalmatic adorned with bands. Miniature from the Landulf Pontifical, after 969. ROME, BIBLIOTECA CASANATESE, 724 B.I 13

relate the word *orarium* to *orare* (to pray, which the medieval deacon bid the people to do in liturgical ceremonies). In northern Europe by the eighth century the term used was *stola,* but in Rome the term *orarium* was preferred.

As to its use, the stole was commonly worn by bishops, presbyters, and deacons; early, however, subdeacons and acolytes might wear it but with special restrictions as a mark of honor. By the sixth century Spanish and Gallican councils were legislating about the use of the stole as the mark of the deacon and presbyter. The Third Council of Braga (675), for example, notes that the priest is to cross over his breast. From the ninth century the stole could be worn out of doors as a mark of honor, and in Spain, Gaul, and Italy it might be worn over the dalmatic of the deacon.

Just as the maniple was the insignia of the subdeacon, so the stole was the mark of the deacon, who wore it over his left shoulder, and the presbyter, who wore it around his neck. It was a narrow band usually made of valuable fabric and decorated with orphreys or apparels and finished with fringe, tassels, and occasionally with bells. Like the maniple, the color of the stole usually contrasted with the chief vestments worn.

Pallium. Over the centuries there have been many theories as to the origin of the pallium: that it derived from the Old Testament ephod, that it was like Peter's mantle, that it derived from the investiture of Emperor Constantine, that it was a liturgical mantle of the pope folded into a band, that it was a folded ordinary mantle, or that it was a papal liturgical garment of broad, oblong, folded cloth. In any event, it probably originated as a type of liturgical badge of the pope and was the counterpart of the *omophorion* used by bishops in the East.

In the *Liber pontificalis* it is said that Pope Mark (336) gave the pallium to the bishop of Ostia because it was his duty to consecrate the pope. It was certainly in use by the popes by the sixth century, when Pope Symmachus is said to have given one to Caesarius of Arles. By the eighth century the giving of the pallium had come to be controlled by the pope, but earlier there is evidence that in Spain and Gaul all bishops might use the pallium. Although the pope might give the pallium to ordinary bishops, it was usually reserved to metropolitans. By the ninth century in order to receive the pallium metropolitans were directed to send a petition with a solemn profession of faith, without which they could not exercise their jurisdiction. From early times the pallium was used only in church and at masses on great feasts.

From at least the sixth century the pallium was a long white band of wool ornamented with crosses and finished off with tassels. It was draped around the neck, breast, and shoulders in such a manner as to form a V in front with the ends hanging from the shoulders, one in front and the other in back. By the ninth century the ends were allowed to fall down the middle of the wearer, front and back, and were fastened with pins. Eventually the pallium was sewn into a Y-shape with front and back tails. The present circular form originated in the tenth and eleventh centuries. Small crosses were sewn into the pallium, but there was no regulation as to the number or color. The wool used for the pallium came from lambs (*agni*) blessed on the feast of St. Agnes at the basilica outside the Roman walls where her relics are buried.

Rationale. This insignia, not to be confused with the large pectoral clasp worn on the chasuble, dates back to the tenth century. It was in use mainly in German territories, Poland, and Aquileia. It was probably an equivalent or imitation of the pallium and was worn by bishops. If a bishop had both the pallium and *rationale* (as did Poppo of Aquileia in 1027), he wore the former on festal occasions.

In the Middle Ages the *rationale* took several forms. As with humeral collar, there were two bands that crossed the shoulders and joined at the breast, like a Y- or T-shaped pallium. The edges of the *rationale* were at times trimmed with small bells.

HAND, HEAD, AND FOOT CLOTHING

Pontifical gloves. Called *chirothecae, manicae,* or *wanti,* these gloves probably were first used in France as a proper adornment for the bishop's hands and not for any practical purpose. By the tenth century the custom had gone to Rome, and by the eleventh century even abbots might use them by special permission. They were worn at solemn pontifical masses after communion, at solemn offices, and in processions.

Pontifical gloves were usually knitted or made of woven white material. In the later Middle Ages the lower end was enlarged into a cuff or gauntlet or into a cuff with a long point and tassel. The backs of the gloves were often highly ornamented, sometimes with pearls, gems, and decorated roundels.

Shoes and stockings. Shoes were early called *campagi* and stocking *udones,* but by the eighth century the term *sandalia* was used for shoes, and by the eleventh stockings could be called *caligae.* Both derive from the sandals and stockings worn by persons of high rank as a mark of honor. In Rome subdeacons and acolytes might wear a type of sandal called *subtalares,* but these were simple, with no straps. But by the tenth century the wearing of these sandals and stockings had become a pontifical prerogative, although occasionally it was granted to abbots.

Visigothic bishops wearing reddish-orange and yellow headdresses in conical miter-tiara form. Miniature from the 10th-century Visigothic Codex Vigilianus. El Escorial RBSL d.I.2, fol. 344r. FOTO MAS

The stockings were usually made of white linen, perhaps decorated with gold or silver threadwork. The sandals originally covered only the toes and heels and were fastened to the foot with straps. By the tenth century the straps were replaced by three to five tongues caught up at the ankle by a string. By the thirteenth century the sandal had become a regular shoe with slits on the sides to facilitate use; occasionally the leather was covered with silk. Only from the fourteenth century on do crosses appear on the shoes.

Miter-tiara. Although it was said by Pope Innocent III that the tiara was a symbol of *regnum* and not a liturgical vestment and although it is commonly said that episcopal miters do not antedate the eleventh century, it is clear from documentary and pictorial sources that the tiara was indeed used in liturgical ceremonies and that episcopal headdresses of a tiara-miter type go back to at least late patristic times.

The tiara-miter had, in fact, a long history even before the Christian era, and in early Christian times there seems to have been no distinction between a tiara and miter, which were of two types: a rather low, round cap and a tall, stiffer conical headdress. Multiple examples of these being worn by episcopal figures are depicted in the canon law manuscripts El Escorial d.I.1 and d.I.2, which, although made in the tenth century, are very likely based on Visigothic exemplars of the seventh century. In these codices popes and bishops are shown as having tall, conical headdresses attached to a cowl (as a monastic bishop might be expected to wear) and round, almost halo-like headdresses. By the early eighth century, so the *Liber pontificalis* reports, Pope Constantine (708–715) wore in procession in Constantinople a *camelaucum,* which was probably a derivative of the round episcopal cap of antiquity. From the early eleventh century there are illustrations in the Bari benedictional Exultet roll of a bishop with a tiara-like miter in the ceremony of baptism; and in the slightly later central Italian manuscript of the canonical *Collection in Five Books* (Vat. lat. 1339), there are numerous illustrations of bishops with a miter shaped like the papal tiara. It is at this time that literary sources speak of the *mitra romana* being given to cardinals, bishops, canons, abbots, and lay lords.

In the late-eleventh-century Exultet roll Vatican, Barb. lat. 592, there appears to be a further development of the *mitra romana* into the *mitra bicornis* or "horned" miter, in which the sides of the miter are raised into points. From this it was a short step to the *mitra biplana,* which became very widely spread. Attached to the lower band of the miter were two bands called *fasciae, fimbriae, vittae, penduli, fanones, linguae,* or *ligulae,* and later *infulae;* it was common from the twelfth century on to depict miters with these appendages.

As for the development of the papal tiara, there was perhaps as early as the period of the Gregorian reform a tiara in which the diadem and crown were combined. Then in the later *Vita Gregorii IX* a *diadema duplex* is mentioned. And finally, at the time of Pope Boniface VIII, about 1300, there is the combination of the diadem with two crowns or the so-called *triregnum,* or triple-crowned tiara. Gerhart Ladner has shown that there never was a fully nonliturgical symbolism attached to the tiara and that it continued to have sacerdotal symbolism. Moreover, the tiara was worn elsewhere than in Rome; the bronze doors of the cathedral of Benevento, destroyed in World War II, depicted the archbishop of Benevento in a tiara with a mitered suffragan, and the acts of the provincial Council of Benevento of 1374 note that a headdress called a *camaurum* and shaped like that worn by the pope was used at Benevento.

Skullcap. Called a *calotte, subbiretum, submitrale, solideo,* or *pileolus,* the skullcap had its origins in the High Middle Ages, when it was worn with a *cappa.* It was eventually worn under the miter-tiara, as can be seen in various funereal monuments of popes and bishops. It seems first to have been worn in Rome and its use spread northward. It was not simply the skullcap known today, as it covered more of the head.

Biretta. The biretta, also called a *pileus,* probably originated in the twelfth century and was used as a choir hat, especially by cantors. At first it was a type of skullcap, perhaps with a small, soft tuft in the center, and eventually it evolved into a small round cap. Since the cap was easily indented by the fingers when putting it on the head, by the end of the fifteenth century it was stiffened on the top into three or four ridges. It was worn while sitting, judging, giving absolution, and when out-of-doors.

BIBLIOGRAPHY

The somewhat dated but classical study of vestments is Joseph Braun, *Die liturgische Gewandung im Occident und Orient nach Ursprung und Entwicklung: Verwendung und Symbolik* (1907). See also Gerhart B. Ladner, "Der Ursprung und die mittelalterliche Entwicklung der päpstlichen Tiara," in Herbert A. Cahn and Erika Simon, eds., *Tainia: Roland Hampe zum 70. Geburtstag . . . ,* I (1980); Robert Lesage, *Vestments and Church Furniture* (1960); Cyril E. Pocknee, *Liturgical Vesture: Its Origins and Development* (1960); Roger E. Reynolds, "The Portrait of the Ecclesiastical Officers in the *Raganaldus Sacramentary* and Its Liturgico-Canonical Significance," in *Speculum,* 46 (1971), "Image and Text: The Liturgy of Clerical Ordination in Early Medieval Art," in *Gesta,* 22 (1983), "Image and Text: A Carolingian Illustration of Modifications in the Early Roman Eucharistic *Ordines,*" in *Viator,* 14 (1983), and "Rites and Signs of Conciliar Decisions in the Early Middle Ages," in *Settimane di studio del Centro italiano di studi sull'alto medioevo,* 33 (1987).

ROGER E. REYNOLDS

[See also **Colors, Liturgical; Costume; Dalmatic; Law, Canon; Mass, Liturgy of; Omophorion; Pallium; Processions, Liturgical.**]

VÉZELAY, CHURCH OF LA MADELEINE, a Burgundian Benedictine abbey church famous for its hilltop site, its groin-vaulted Romanesque nave (after 1121–*ca.* 1130/1132), its rib-vaulted Gothic choir (*ca.* 1185–*ca.* 1205/1210), and its rich sculptural program on the west portals and the historiated capitals. Eugène-Emmanuel Viollet-le-Duc extensively restored the church between 1840 and 1859, but saved it from certain ruin.

The Mission of the Apostles. Tympanum sculpture on the center portal of the narthex in La Madeleine, Vézelay, *ca.* 1120–1130. SCALA / ART RESOURCE

St. Bernard and Pope Eugenius III preached the Second Crusade at Vézelay on Easter Sunday (31 March) 1146, a theme symbolized in the tympanum of the central portal of the west facade.

BIBLIOGRAPHY
Robert Branner, *Burgundian Gothic Architecture* (1960), 30–32, 192–194; Adolf Katzenellenbogen, "The Central Tympanum of Vézelay: Its Encyclopedic Meaning and Its Relation to the First Crusade," in *Art Bulletin,* 26 (1944), 141–151; Francis Salet, *La Madeleine de Vézelay* (1948).

CARL F. BARNES, JR.

[See also **Benedictines; Crusades and Crusader States to 1192; Romanesque Architecture; Romanesque Art.**]

VIA MODERNA (Latin, the modern way) is a term used in philosophical and theological discussions in European universities of the late Middle Ages. The *moderni*, those identified as followers of the *via moderna*, were distinguished from the *antiqui*, followers of the *via antiqua* (the old way). Modern scholars use the German term *Wegestreit* (conflict between the ways) to refer to the rivalry that developed between the *moderni* and the *antiqui* within the university faculties and that was a prominent feature of late medieval intellectual life. This rivalry has roots in the fourteenth century, although the evidence suggests it was not until the fifteenth century that the terms *moderni* and *antiqui* became party labels. When it did become a party label the term *moderni* was often used interchangeably with the terms *nominales* (nominalists) and *terministae* (terminists). Thus, in general terms, the *via moderna* represented late medieval nominalism in a context in which it was distinguished clearly from other philosophical and theological positions of the fifteenth century.

The *moderni* varied considerably with time and place. The characteristics discussed below do not apply to all in the century to whom the name *moderni* was applied. Furthermore, much research remains to be done before scholars will have an adequate picture of the *via moderna*.

The *moderni* held to the epistemological hallmark of nominalism: a denial of the reality of universal mental concepts that enable us to recognize individuals as belonging to the same species on the basis of similarities to such concepts. Furthermore, the *moderni* affirmed the principle of economy or parsimony, known as Ockham's razor: do not multiply entities beyond necessity.

These familiar characteristics of nominalism are not the only marks of the *via moderna*. It appears that the earliest distinguishing characteristic was a distinctive approach to logic. The *moderni* may have acquired their name by continuing a fourteenth-century approach to logic that emphasized the meaning and reference of terms (hence the name "terminists"). These masters turned to the logical treatises not only of William of Ockham but also of Jean Buridan, Marsilius of Inghen, and other logicians of the fourteenth century. Their approach to logic was distinguished from that of other members of the arts faculties, who urged a return to the approach taken in the thirteenth century based on the logic of Aristotle and Averroës (Ibn Rushd) and their thirteenth-century commentators. Be-

cause these latter scholars favored a return to an earlier approach, they came to be called *antiqui*. Those who opposed them thus acquired the label *moderni*.

The *moderni* were not found among masters of the arts faculties alone. Faculties of theology were involved as well, and certain theological themes were associated with the *moderni*. Theologians among the *moderni* emphasized a theme found earlier, especially in Duns Scotus: the freedom of God as sovereign Agent. God is not bound by anything outside the divine nature; indeed, radical freedom is a basic characteristic of the divine nature. The *moderni* elaborated on this freedom by making extensive use of the distinction between the absolute and the ordained power of God. God's absolute power was invoked to emphasize that God is free to act in whatever way God chooses. Whatever God does, he does freely, contingently. The realm of God's ordained power comprises those things God actually chooses to do. If the absolute power of God is invoked to emphasize divine freedom, the ordained power is invoked to emphasize the contingency of what happens in the orders of nature and history.

Many scholars have found the seeds of radical skepticism in the *moderni*'s emphasis on God's absolute power. While it is true that the *moderni* placed limits on the power of logic in matters of theology, it seems clear that their intention was not so much to undermine the power of reason as to emphasize the sovereignty of God and to limit speculation in theology. They did not challenge the reliability of either empirical knowledge of the created order or revealed knowledge of God.

One way in which the *moderni* combined the theme of the reliability of knowledge of the created order with that of the sovereignty of God was to use the idea of a covenant or pact between God and humanity. Although the divine freedom is boundless, God has made a covenant with the human race and can be relied upon to act in accordance with the terms of that covenant.

There is a positivism embedded in this approach. If God acts according to a covenant contingently established, then we must seek to find what the terms of the covenant are. To know God's acts of grace we are dependent on the sources of revelation, which tell what God has in fact done. To know how God acts in nature, we arrive at our conclusions not a priori but a posteriori, on the basis of empirical observation. This latter point has led some scholars to claim that there is a link between the *via moderna* and the rise of modern empirical science.

Since the middle of the nineteenth century, generations of scholars have assumed that the rivalry between the *moderni* and the *antiqui* began before 1350 in controversies over the thought of William of Ockham. Carl Prantl and many thereafter believed that from the second quarter of the fourteenth century the words *moderni* and *antiqui* referred to rival intellectual parties, the nominalists and realists respectively.

Scholarship since the 1970's by Neal Gilbert has challenged that view. He has argued persuasively that throughout most of the fourteenth century a *modernus* was not a representative of a particular intellectual party but simply a contemporary. Similarly, *antiquus* had a temporal and not a philosophical meaning. Prantl and others read fifteenth-century meanings back into their fourteenth-century sources and posited a full-blown *Wegestreit* generations before one actually existed.

Gilbert explains the equation of *antiqui* with realists and *moderni* with nominalists as a consequence of the controversy over the teaching of John Wyclif. Wyclif heaped scorn upon modern logicians at Oxford and used the term *modernus* in a wholly pejorative way. His contempt was directed not at logical but at theological error. Wyclif's disciple Jerome of Prague was even more scornful of modern logicians, who were for the most part nominalists. After the condemnation of Wyclif at the Council of Constance (1415), the followers of Thomas Aquinas and Albertus Magnus, realists like Wyclif, wishing to avoid any association with the condemned Wyclif, adopted the name *antiqui* as a safer label than *reales*. In the same period the nominalists began to accept the term *moderni*. Because Wyclif and Jerome of Prague had attacked their approach on theological grounds, the nominalists were constrained to defend the usefulness of their approach in theology as well as the arts. Gilbert finds the earliest official use of the phrase *via modernorum* at Cologne in 1425.

Was there no sign before the fifteenth century of the coming rivalry between the *moderni* and *antiqui*? Gilbert suggests that an informal pattern of rivalry was developing before the official reference of 1425. William Courtenay goes further and argues that what was to be the division between the *moderni* and the *antiqui* has roots not only in controversies over Wyclif after Constance but also

in events at the University of Paris in the middle of the fourteenth century.

Courtenay explains that in the late 1330's Paris saw a rapid influx of new English philosophical and theological works that precipitated a conflict between terminist and modist logicians. Terminists believed that linguistic structures are human creations. Modist logicians, on the other hand, assumed that structures of language are part of the nature of things, not human conventions. The newer English works represented terminist logic and challenged the modist logic that had previously dominated at Paris. In many respects William of Ockham was only one of a number of terminist logicians. His brand of terminist logic, however, led him to a reinterpretation of Aristotle's categories, particularly in the areas of physics. Conservative masters at Paris contrasted Ockham's "new" interpretation of Aristotle with what they perceived as the proper interpretation associated with the older commentators Albertus Magnus, Thomas Aquinas, and Giles of Rome (Egidius Colonna). This controversy gave some content to a growing distinction between *antiqui* and *moderni*. Courtenay finds that by 1380 there were the elements of two parties at Paris. On one side were, for example, Pierre d'Ailly and Marsilius of Inghen, who were terminists in logic and nominalists in epistemology. On the other side were those who preferred modist logic, rejected nominalism, and appealed to the thirteenth-century commentators on Aristotle rather than to Ockham and his followers. The rivalry at Paris was a forerunner of the later *Wegestreit,* Courtenay concludes, even though the terminology and the issues of the fifteenth century were often different from those of the earlier setting.

By the early fifteenth century these two sides were being labeled *antiqui* and *moderni,* first perhaps at Cologne and Louvain and then at other universities. Rivalry between the two became intense. An act of 1425 at Cologne prohibited the approach of the realists. Two years later at Louvain it was the nominalists' turn to be prohibited. Early in the century the majority of German electors favored the nominalist approach, perhaps because of the association of realism with the condemned Wyclif and Hus.

While one can accurately say that throughout the fifteenth century the *via moderna* was represented at most European universities, its history was distinctive at each institution. At Cologne the earliest statutes of the university (1398) call for lectures on the logical treatises of Peter of Spain or Buridan. In 1415, however, the masters specified that Aristotle was to be interpreted along the lines of the realists Thomas and Albert. Ten years later the electors ruled, against the resistance of the faculty, that masters should follow the *moderni*. For most of the century the *antiqui,* especially Thomas and Albert, dominated at Cologne. Even so, it was at Cologne in mid century that Gabriel Biel encountered Ockham's works and became committed to his thought.

The *antiqui* also dominated at Louvain, where the faculty in 1427 forbade the teaching of "Buridan, Marsilius, Ockham, or their followers." In 1447 Ockham's exposition of Aristotle was again banned at Louvain (together with Wyclif's exposition).

At Paris, as we have noted, already by 1380 there was something of a polarization of approaches, although the two parties were not yet called *moderni* and *antiqui.* As the *Wegestreit* at Paris developed, Jean Buridan, Pierre d'Ailly, Marsilius of Inghen, and to some extent Jean Gerson came to be recognized as leaders of the Parisian *moderni.* Wessel Gansfort testifies that in the mid fifteenth century representatives of both (or perhaps three) *viae* were active in the Paris faculty: he went to Paris a follower of Thomas and Albert, became a Scotist, then a nominalist. In 1474 a royal edict temporarily drove the nominalists out of Paris, but they were reinstated in 1481.

Evidence from Heidelberg suggests that the *moderni* there were especially associated with the name of Marsilius of Inghen. There is evidence that by 1469, although both *viae* were represented in the university, hostility between the two was minimal. In the persons of Wessel Gansfort and Jakob Wimpfeling, furthermore, there are links at Heidelberg between the *moderni* and an emerging humanism.

The University of Basel (founded 1460) began under the domination of the *moderni* but soon developed an approximate parity between the two and a reduction of tensions. At Tübingen (founded 1478) it was the *antiqui* who first dominated. The *via moderna* came to Tübingen in 1484 in the person of Gabriel Biel. It was subsequently represented by Biel's disciple Wendelin Steinbach and then by Peter Braun of Kirchheim. These three masters constituted a continuous line of *moderni* at Tübingen from 1484 until 1534, when the university was reorganized as a result of the Protestant Reformation. Tübingen, like Heidelberg and Basel, saw the reduction of tension in the *Wegestreit*. The

nominalist Biel had much in common with Conrad Summenhart, a leader of the Tübingen realists. One reason for the convergence was the fact that both Summenhart and Biel owed much to Scotus. Summenhart was a Scotist rather than a Thomist, and Biel turned often to Scotus when his mentor Ockham was not helpful. Another reason for the reduction was that Biel himself sought to be a mediating figure, using nominalist methods to show that apparent discrepancies were not substantive but semantic.

The *via moderna* dominated at Erfurt and from there was introduced to Wittenberg. The first *modernus* to teach at Wittenberg was Iodocus Trutvetter, formerly a master at Erfurt.

Not only did the *via moderna* experience different fates at the various universities; it also appeared under different labels. While it is true that the *moderni* were often identified as followers of William of Ockham, other names were often substituted for Ockham's. At Heidelberg the *moderni* were called the *via Marsiliana,* for Marsilius of Inghen. At Wittenberg they were apparently called the *via Gregorii,* after Gregory of Rimini. At Cologne, the two most prominent names associated with the *via moderna* were those of Marsilius and Jean Buridan. At Paris, Buridan and Nicole Oresme were as prominent as any among the *moderni*'s authorities, but the nominalists were often called—especially by their opponents—Ockhamists. The fact that Ockham was a foreigner may have been one of the reasons his name was chosen.

The *via moderna* constituted one of the most significant intellectual movements of the fifteenth century and continued as a viable approach well into the sixteenth. Despite claims by Hermelink and others that the *via antiqua* provided the crucial link between scholasticism and humanism, there is evidence that often it was the *via moderna*, especially through its emphasis on careful use of language, that found common ground with the humanists.

BIBLIOGRAPHY
William J. Courtenay, "Nominalism and Late Medieval Thought: A Bibliographical Essay," in *Theological Studies,* 33 (1972), "Nominalism and Late Medieval Religion," in Charles Trinkaus and Heiko A. Oberman, eds., *The Pursuit of Holiness in Late Medieval and Renaissance Religion* (1974), "Late Medieval Nominalism Revisited: 1972–1982," in *Journal of the History of Ideas,"* **44** (1983), and "*Antiqui* and *Moderni* in Late Medieval Thought," in *Journal of the History of Ideas,*

48 (1987); *idem* and Katherine Tachau, "Ockham, Ockhamists, and the English-German Nation at Paris, 1339–41," in *History of Universities,* II (1982); Astrik L. Gabriel, "'Via Antiqua' and 'Via Moderna' and the Migration of Paris Students and Masters to the German Universities in the Fifteenth Century," in Albert Zimmermann, ed., *Antiqui und Moderni* (1974); Neal W. Gilbert, "Ockham, Wyclif, and the 'Via Moderna,'" in Albert Zimmermann, ed., *Antiqui und Moderni* (1974), and "Comment," in *Journal of the History of Ideas,* **48** (1987); Heinrich Hermelink, *Die theologische Fakultät in Tübingen vor der Reformation, 1477–1534* (1906).

Leonard A. Kennedy, "Late-Fourteenth-century Philosophical Scepticism at Oxford," in *Vivarium,* **23** (1985); Alister E. McGrath, "*Homo Assumptus?* A Study in the Christology of the *Via Moderna,* with Particular Reference to William of Ockham," in *Ephemerides Theologicae Lovaniensis,* **60** (1984); Heiko A. Oberman, *The Harvest of Medieval Theology: Gabriel Biel and Late Medieval Nominalism* (1963, repr. 1983), *Masters of the Reformation,* Dennis Martin, trans. (1981), "*Initia Lutheri—Initia Reformationis,*" in *The Dawn of the Reformation,* Heiko A. Oberman, ed. (1986), and "*Via Antiqua* and *Via Moderna*: Late Medieval Prolegomena to Early Reformation Thought," in *Journal of the History of Ideas,* **48** (1987); Olaf Pluta, "Albert von Köln und Peter von Ailly," in *Freiburger Zeitschrift für Philosophie und Theologie,* **32** (1985); Carl Prantl, *Geschichte der Logik im Abendlande,* III (1867, repr. 1955); Gerhard Ritter, *Studien zur Spätscholastik,* II, *Via antiqua und via moderna auf den deutschen Universitäten des XV. Jahrhunderts* (1922).

WALTER L. MOORE

[See also **Ailly, Pierre d'; Albertus Magnus; Aquinas, St. Thomas; Aristotle in the Middle Ages; Biel, Gabriel; Buridan, Jean; Councils, Western; Duns Scotus, John; Egidius Colonna; Gerson, John; Gregory of Rimini; Hus, John (Jan); Nominalism; Ockham, William of; Oresme, Nicole; Oxford University; Paris, University of; Peter of Spain; Philosophy and Theology, Western European; Realism; Rushd, Ibn (Averroës); Scholasticism, Scholastic Method; Terminism; Thomism and Its Opponents; Wyclif, John.**]

VICAR. The office of vicar was created by Diocletian as the deputy of the praetorian prefect, the full title being *vices agens praefectorum praetorio.* The vicar was the head of the subdivision known as the diocese and deputized for the praetorian prefect in a number of his functions. He was the judge of the court that heard appeals from the provincial governors, but it is probable that these courts were little used and that appeals went directly to the courts of the praetorian prefects. The vicar could not raise troops in an emergency without first applying to the praetorian prefects. It appears that the vicars were often bypassed in the chain of command by both the provincial governors and the prefects, and the power of the vicar gradually declined throughout the fifth and sixth centuries until the office was abolished by Justinian I.

BIBLIOGRAPHY
Arnold H. M. Jones, *The Later Roman Empire, 284–602: A Social, Economic, and Administrative Survey,* I (1964).

LINDA C. ROSE

[See also **Diocese, Secular; Praetorian Prefect; Roman Empire, Late.**]

VICTOR III, POPE. See **Desiderius of Monte Cassino.**

VICTORINES. See **Hugh of St. Victor.**

VICTORINUS (Gaius Marius Victorinus, *fl.* mid fourth century), an African rhetorician who taught in Rome. Victorinus numbered such men as St. Jerome among his students, and he was granted a statue in Trajan's Forum. An account of his conversion from paganism to Christianity may be found in Augustine's *Confessions* (8.2). In 362 he was prohibited from teaching because of his new religion. His surviving works include not only writings on grammar and rhetoric, such as *On Definitions,* the *Art of Grammar,* and the *Explanations of the Rhetoric of Cicero,* but also religious tracts, such as *Against Arius, On the Generation of the Divine Word, On the Reception of Homoousios,* and the *Commentaries on the Letters of Paul.* Victorinus was but one of several pagan writers of this period who turned their talents to the service of the church.

BIBLIOGRAPHY
Clavis patrum latinorum, 2nd ed. (1961), nos. 94–98; Karl Felix von Halm, *Rhetores latini minores* (1863),

153–304; A. H. M. Jones, J. Morris, and M. R. Martindale, *Prosopography of the Later Roman Empire,* I (1971), 964; Heinrich Keil, *Grammatici latini,* VI (1874), 3–31; *Patrologia latina,* VIII (1844), 1,019–1,294, and LXIV (1847), 891ff.; M. Schanz, C. Hosius, and G. Krüger, *Geschichte der römischen Literatur,* IV, pt. 1 (1920), 157–158; Albert H. Travis, "Marius Victorinus: A Biographical Note," in *Harvard Theological Review,* 36 (1943).

RALPH W. MATHISEN

[See also **Aristotle in the Middle Ages; Dialectic; Rhetoric: Western European.**]

VIDAS, short Provençal prose biographies of the troubadours, written in the thirteenth and early fourteenth centuries by Uc de Saint-Circ, Miquel de la Tor, and some anonymous authors. There are *vidas* for 101 of the 450 known troubadours.

In the earliest manuscripts containing *vidas,* the biography, which was probably recited as a prelude to a lyric, precedes the poet's work, often introducing it by a phrase such as "Et aici son escritas de las soas cansos" (And written here are some of his lyrics). Later the biographies were collected and copied separately from the poetry.

The authors clearly followed a pattern, although not all *vidas* contain all the types of information found; those of the earliest troubadours are among the shortest. Usually the author began by stating the poet's birthplace or home, occupation and social position; then he listed personal qualities, such as poverty or wealth, generosity, chivalry, courtliness, appearance, education, and eloquence, followed by mention of the poet's professional ability and reputation and his love affairs. Finally, the end of the troubadour's career or his death was evoked.

Fact and fiction are both present. The precise mention of places, events, and people, especially patrons, helps situate a troubadour in a region, period, and society. Details about love affairs, not as amplified or as imaginative as the *razos* (prose texts focusing on the poet's role as a lover), tend to be derived from interpretation of the lyrics; the "coeur mangé" legend is fancifully attributed to Guillem de Cabestaing. Nevertheless, frequently for the biographer, the quality of the words and melody of a troubadour's lyrics depends on his personality and love experience, just as his success in love and society are related to the pleasure his poetry provides. Critical evaluation of the poetry is summary,

but an individual feature or fault of style is sometimes noted and praise may be bestowed for outstanding achievement.

Written in a clear, simple style containing Italianisms, the *vidas* have their own eloquence.

BIBLIOGRAPHY

The texts are in Jean Boutière and A.-H. Schutz, eds., *Biographies des troubadours: Textes provençaux des XIIIe et XIVe siècles* (1964), trans. by Margarita Egan as *The Vidas of the Troubadours* (1984).

See also Egan, "Commentary, *Vita Poetae,* and *Vida*: Latin and Old Provençal 'Lives of Poets,'" in *Romance Philology,* 37 (1983); Elizabeth W. Poe, *From Poetry to Prose in Old Provençal: The Emergence of the Vidas, the Razos, and the Razos de Trobar* (1984); Elizabeth R. Wilson, "Old Provençal *Vidas* as Literary Commentary," in *Romance Philology,* 33 (1980).

GLYNNIS M. CROPP

[See also **Provençal Literature: After 1200; Troubadour, Trouvère.**]

VIDERUNT OMNES, the gradual for the Mass of Christmas Day, whose text is drawn from Psalm 97, verses 3 and 2 respectively:

> *Viderunt omnes fines terrae salutare Dei nostri: jubilate Deo omnis terra. Notum fecit Dominus salutare suum: ante conspectum gentium revelavit justitiam suam.*

> All the ends of the earth have seen the salvation of our God. The Lord hath made known his salvation: his righteousness hath he openly shewed in the sight of the heathen. (King James Version, Psalm 98)

The chant is the basis for two organal settings included in the *Magnus liber organi,* one in four parts, the other in two. The latter is one of only two complete *quadrupla.* The other is the gradual "Sederunt" for St. Stephen's Day. (A four-part setting of the clausula "Mors" from the "Alleluia: Christus resurgens" is also preserved in the *Magnus liber* sources.) Both are ascribed by Anonymous IV to Magister Perotinus. The two-part *organum purum* setting is preserved in the three principal Notre Dame manuscripts in two variant forms, one of which is considerably shorter than the other. The *quadruplum* version stands at the beginning of the four principal *Magnus liber* sources and is the most extended example of four-part counterpoint prior to the works of Machaut. The gradual "Viderunt" offers two opportunities for substitute clausulae, and thus motets. The melisma on "Omnes" in the response exists in eleven different two-part settings and one four-part setting. The "Dominus" melisma from the verse was set once in four parts and fourteen times in two parts, including a unique "nusmido" setting in which the pitches are presented in retrograde motion. "Omnes" in turn spawned twenty-eight motets, ranging from those that simply add a text to one of the pre-existent clausulae to late *ars antiqua* motets, including one by Adam de la Halle. There are altogether seven two-part motets on "Omnes," two in four parts, and nineteen in three. "Omnes" thus belongs to a select group of the three or four most popular motet tenors of the thirteenth century. "Dominus," however, was used only seven times, six in two parts, one in three. The reasons for the rather disproportionate popularity of "Omnes" over "Dominus" are not difficult to discover. The former is a simple, incisive melody of ten notes. It lends itself ideally to the multiple repetition, with or without varied rhythm, most characteristic of the *ars antiqua* motet. "Dominus," by contrast, is longer, subtler, and more diffuse—characteristics that make it not only less memorable but more difficult to use as the basis for a motet.

A study of "Viderunt omnes" and its relatives would cover a very broad spectrum of *ars antiqua* music and introduce virtually every problem that the student of this music is likely to encounter. It would likewise be a convincing demonstration of both the unity and the variety of the *ars antiqua* tradition.

BIBLIOGRAPHY

Friedrich Gennrich, *Bibliographie der ältesten französischen und lateinischen Motetten* (1957); Heinrich Husmann, *Die Drei- und Vierstimmigen Notre-Dame-Organa* (1940, repr. 1967), 10–19, edition of the four-part setting; Friedrich Ludwig, *Repertorium organorum recentioris et motetorum vetustissimi stili* (1910, 2nd ed. 1964); Fritz Reckow, *Der Musiktraktat des Anonymus IV* (1967); Ethel Thurston, ed., *The Works of Perotin* (1970), 3–30, edition of four-part setting with two motets; William Waite, *The Rhythm of Twelfth-century Polyphony* (1954), 67–73, edition of the two-part setting.

ROBERT FALCK

[See also **Adam de la Halle; Anonymous IV; Ars Antiqua; Clausula; Gradual; Magnus Liber Organi; Melisma; Motet; Notre Dame School; Perotinus.**]

VIDĒVDĀD (also **Vidēvdāt** or **Vendīdad** [Middle Persian, "law against the demons," from the Avestan: *vī-daēvō-dāta*]). One of the latest books of the Avesta, the Zoroastrian scriptures, the *Vidēvdād* dates from the Arsacid or early Sasanian period. The Avestan text is accompanied by an extensive commentary in Middle Persian. Indeed, in places the Avestan seems to have been influenced by Middle Persian syntax.

The central concern of the *Vidēvdād* is the performance of *yaozhdāthra* ("making whole"). Encompassed in this concept are rites of purification, acts of atonement, medical treatment, and the meting out of punishment for various sins or forms of contamination. The elaborate rituals prescribed in the *Vidēvdād* are the logical extension of the fundamental Zoroastrian belief in the oneness of "truth" (*asha*) and its manifestations in order, health, cleanliness, and good thoughts, words, and deeds; and in the reality of the "lie" (*druj*) as it finds expression in disorder, illness, contamination, and evil thoughts, words, and deeds. Priests, who administer the rites of the *Vidēvdād,* are those who counteract or cancel out (Avestan: *par*) the effects of evil in the world. Although it was composed as a book of instruction for priests, the *Vidēvdād* became a part of the liturgy recited over the dead, perhaps because it outlines the rituals to be followed for the proper disposal of corpses.

The Avestan text of the *Vidēvdād* is corrupt and replete with grammatical irregularities that can be attributed neither to dialect nor to the vagaries of oral transmission. Although there are in the *Vidēvdād* fragments of what would seem to be early Avestan compositions, such as the hymn to the earth in chapter 3, much of the text is derivative or clumsily patched together from other parts of the Avesta. Taken as a whole, however, the *Vidēvdād* is a composition with a degree of unity and logical development.

The first three chapters of the book are devoted to the earth, a creation of Ahura Mazdā, the Wise Lord, and its contamination by Angra Mainyu. The most grievous sin against the earth is the burial of a corpse. The *Vidēvdād* then prescribes at length the procedure for the exposure of corpses on *dakhmas*, originally rocky hilltops where vultures and dogs consume the rotting flesh, whose putrescence is caused by Druj ī Nasu, a demon who attacks at the time of death. Subsequently *dakhma* came to mean a structure for the exposure of corpses, as in the Indian Parsis' "towers of silence." There are also chapters on animals, both Ahuric and demonic; the treatment of women during menstruation; and disposal of hair and nails, which are considered to be dead matter.

Chapter 19 recounts the creation by Ahura Mazda of the first priest (*yaozhdātar*), Zarathustra, whose birth occasions an unsuccessful assault by the demons. Zarathustra repels the attack by uttering true words, the Yathā Ahū Vairyō prayer. There follows a list of priestly incantations that are particularly effective for healing.

BIBLIOGRAPHY

Mary Boyce, *A History of Zoroastrianism*, I (1973), and *Zoroastrians: Their Religious Beliefs and Practices* (1979); Maneckji N. Dhalla, *Zoroastrian Theology* (repr. 1972); Martin Haug, *Essays on the Sacred Language, Writings, and Religion of the Parsis*, E. W. West, ed., 2nd ed. (1878).

DALE L. BISHOP

[See also **Avesta; Pahlavi Literature; Zoroastrianism.**]

VIE D'EDOUARD LE CONFESSEUR, an Anglo-Norman poem, written between 1163 and 1170, recounting the life of Edward the Confessor. This version, by a nun of Barking Abbey (Essex)—possibly Clemence, author of the *Vie de sainte Catherine*—is based on Ethelred of Rievaulx's *Vita sancti Edwardi et confessoris* (1163). Another verse life, the *Estoire de seint Aedward le rei*, was written around 1250 by Matthew Paris, using Ethelred and other sources, including his own *Chronica majora*.

BIBLIOGRAPHY

La estoire de seint Aedward le rei, in H. R. Luard, ed., *Lives of Edward the Confessor* (1858); Osten Södergard, *La vie d'Edouard le confesseur: Poème anglo-normand du XIIᵉ siècle* (1948); Kathryn Wallace, *La estoire de seint Aedward le rei* (1983).

BRIAN MERRILEES

[See also **Anglo-Norman Literature; Edward the Confessor, St.; Ethelred of Rievaulx; Hagiography, Middle English; Matthew Paris.**]

VIE DE ST. ALEXIS. There were numerous versions of the life of St. Alexis. The first is one of the earliest great monuments of French literature. Based on a Latin prose model of the late tenth century, it was apparently composed in Normandy by an anonymous cleric in the mid eleventh century (though an early-twelfth-century date has been argued). This *aimiable cançun* (pleasing song) composed presumably to be sung or recited in church on Alexis' feast day, consists of 625 lines: 125 five-line stanzas, with decasyllabic assonanced lines. This early version relates in beautiful, concise language the life of the saint: his birth to a noble Roman Christian family; his marriage to his bride, whom he abandons on his wedding night; his parents' and bride's despair, and their fruitless search for him. The account continues with his seventeen-year stay among the beggars in Edessa; his return to Rome, where he spends the last seventeen years of his life living under the stairs in his parents' house, mocked by servants; his holy death; the voice heard in the city, telling the people to find the holy man; the finding of Alexis' body bearing a letter he wrote just before he died disclosing his identity; his family's despair on learning this news; the miracles performed by his body; the burial of this *gemme celeste* (celestial gem); and, finally, the reunion of Alexis and his bride in heaven.

Alexis is of course the central figure, the saint to whom the audience and the narrator alike must pray for aid. But the narrator devotes considerable attention to Alexis' wife and family, to their long and deeply poetic laments. This contrast between the hardness—the superhuman virtue—of Alexis, who loves only God, and the humanity of his family adds pathos and narrative tension to the story.

An interpolated version dates from the mid twelfth century. The narrator, probably a *jongleur*, keeps the original poem, but amplifies it from 625 to 1,355 lines; the original 125 five-line stanzas become 140 laisses of varying length. The narrator adds details in the taste of the period: Alexis visits Jerusalem, and the bride is developed as a character (indeed, the story is billed as that of Alexis *and* his wife). The basic spirit of the original version has been generally retained, but this work is clearly destined for a more secular public.

In the thirteenth century, a narrator familiar with the interpolated version retold the story in fashionable rhymed laisses, thus updating the still-popular story. This latest version was then redone in the fourteenth century in uninspired mono-rhymed quatrains of twelve-syllable lines, apparently for private reading. These three reworkings of the Norman original were all apparently Norman or Picard.

There were also several other versions of the life of Alexis, independent of the eleventh-century life but also based on the Latin original.

The *Life of St. Alexis* is also included in Vincent of Beauvais's *Speculum historiale*, which served as one of the sources of the *Legenda aurea*, which in turn influenced the fourteenth-century *Miracle de Nostre Dame de Saint Alexis.* This dramatic version, which consists of 2,659 lines and portrays thirty-six characters, greatly amplified the Alexis story.

Three late-fifteenth-century mystery plays devoted to Alexis have not survived.

BIBLIOGRAPHY
Paul Meyer, "Légendes hagiographiques en français," in *Histoire littéraire de la France,* 33 (1906); Gaston Paris and Leopold Pannier, eds., *La Vie de Saint Alexis: Poème du XIe siècle et renouvellements des XIIe, XIIIe, et XIVe siècles, publiés avec préfaces, variantes, notes, et glossaire* (1872); Gaston Paris and Ulysse Robert, eds., *Miracles de Nostre Dame, par personnages,* VII (1883), 279–369; Louis Petit de Julleville, *Histoire du théâtre en France: Les mystères,* II (1880); Christopher Storey, ed., *La Vie de Saint Alexis* (1968).

EVELYN BIRGE VITZ

[See also **Drama, French; French Literature: To 1200; Golden Legend; Hagiography, French; Hagiography, Western European; Laisse.**]

VIE DE ST. AUBAN, a verse life in 1,846 alexandrine lines of the first British martyr, St. Alban (*d. ca.* 209), composed in Anglo-Norman by Matthew Paris (*d.* 1259), a monk and chronicler of St. Alban's Abbey (Hertfordshire). The text and illustrations of the sole manuscript (Dublin, Trinity College MS E.i.40) are from the author's own hand.

BIBLIOGRAPHY
Arthur Robert Harden, ed., *La Vie de Seint Auban,* (1968); Mary Dominica Legge, *Anglo-Norman in the Cloisters* (1950), 19–31, and *Anglo-Norman Literature and Its Background* (1963), 269–270; W. R. Lowe and Ernest F. Jacob, *Illustrations to the Life of St. Alban* (1924); Richard Vaughan, *Matthew Paris* (1958), 168ff.

BRIAN MERRILEES

[See also **Anglo-Norman Literature; Hagiography, Middle English; Mathew Paris.**]

VIE DE ST. GILLES, a late-twelfth-century Anglo-Norman verse life of St. Giles by Guillaume de Berneville (perhaps Barnwell). According to this story, St. Giles, born in Greece, abandoned a life of wealth to become a hermit near Arles in Provence. Wounded accidentally while protecting a hind that fed him, Giles earned a reputation for holiness that led to a meeting with Charlemagne in Orléans. There he obliged the emperor to confess his sin of incest with his sister, Gisla, a union that produced the epic hero Roland. Giles journeyed to Rome before returning to Arles to die.

BIBLIOGRAPHY
Mary Dominica Legge, *Anglo-Norman Literature and Its Background* (1963), 254–257; Gaston Paris and Alphonse Bos, *La vie de Saint Gilles par Guillaume de Berneville,* (1881).

BRIAN MERRILEES

[See also **Anglo-Norman Literature.**]

VIE DE ST. LAURENT, a twelfth-century Anglo-Norman verse account, written by an anonymous nun, of the martyrdom of St. Lawrence. The saint, a deacon of Rome, was put to death in 258, shortly after the beheading of Pope Sixtus II. According to this and most versions of the story, St. Lawrence was roasted to death on a gridiron, though it is more likely that he was also beheaded.

BIBLIOGRAPHY
D. W. Russell, ed., *La Vie de Saint Laurent: An Anglo-Norman Poem of the Twelfth Century* (1976).

BRIAN MERRILEES

[See also **Hagiography, Middle English.**]

VIE DE ST. THOMAS BECKET, the title given to the Old French versions of the life and violent death of Thomas Becket, archbishop of Canterbury, who was murdered in his cathedral in 1170. An early version, written before 1172, was done by Guernes de Pont-Sainte-Maxence and based on a Latin account by an eyewitness of Thomas' death, Edward Grimm. Fragments of this text survive in London (Society of Antiquaries MS 716). Dissatisfied with this text, Guernes visited Canterbury in 1172 to gather further information about the events surrounding the murder, and over the next three or four years produced a *Vie de Saint Thomas* that has come down to us in its entirety. In this work Guernes is concerned not only with providing a factual and reliable account but also with interpreting the significance, political and moral, of the archbishop's martyrdom. A monk of St. Albans, Beneit, wrote a third *Vie de Saint Thomas Becket* between 1183 and 1189. This poem, based on a lost Latin life by Robert of Cricklade, prior of St. Frideswide's (Oxford) from 1140 to 1177, is cast in six-line stanzas with a tail rhyme, a form borrowed from English tradition. There also exist fragments of another *Vie de Saint Thomas* written in the thirteenth century and based on a historical compilation known as the *Quadrilogus* (1198 or 1199).

BIBLIOGRAPHY

Börje Schlyter, ed., *La Vie de Thomas Becket par Beneit: Poème anglo-normand du XIIe siecle* (1941); Ian Short, "An Early Version of Guernes' *Vie de Saint Thomas Becket*," in *Medium aevum*, **46** (1977); Emmanuel Walberg, *La Vie de Saint Thomas le martyr, par Guernes de Pont-Sainte-Maxence: Poème historique du XIIe siècle (1172–1174)* (1922) and, as ed., *La Vie de Saint Thomas Becket* (1936).

BRIAN MERRILEES

[See also **Guernes de Pont-Sainte-Maxence; Hagiography, French.**]

VIE DE STE. CATHERINE D'ALEXANDRIE, an Anglo-Norman verse life by Clemence, a nun of Barking Abbey near London. The legendary St. Catherine was reputed to have been tortured on a spiked wheel that fell apart beneath her (*ca.* 307), and the incident gave rise to the term "catherine wheel." The French text, which dates from the last third of the twelfth century, is based on a so-called *vulgata* version. The author adds her own digressions and moral comments and imparts a courtly tone to the poem with passages reminiscent of the *Tristan* of Thomas.

BIBLIOGRAPHY

Mary Dominica Legge, *Anglo-Norman Literature and Its Background* (1963), 70–72; William MacBain, ed., *The Life of St. Catherine by Clemence of Barking* (1964).

WILLIAM MACBAIN

[See also **Anglo-Norman Literature.**]

VIE DE STE. MARGUERITE, a medieval French legend surviving in at least nine poems and ten prose versions. The former include works by the Norman poet Wace and the Anglo-Norman Nicole Bozon (*fl.* late thirteenth–early fourteenth centuries). All are independently derived from Latin prose texts, the later ones from Jacopo da Voragine's (*d.* 1298) *Legenda aurea* (*Golden Legend*). A fifteenth-century *mystère* has also survived. St. Margaret of Antioch (third century) was the patron saint of childbirth.

BIBLIOGRAPHY

David Clandfield, "Édition critique des versions anglo-normandes de *La Vie de Sainte Marguérite*" (diss., Paris, 1976); Elizabeth A. Francis, *Wace: La Vie de Sainte Marguérite* (1932); Aristide Joly, *La Vie de Sainte Marguérite* (1879); M. Amelia Klenke, ed., *Three Saints' Lives by Nicole Bozon* (1947); I. Orywall, "Die alt- und mittelfranzösischen Prosafassungen der Margaretenlegenden" (diss., Cologne, 1968); G. Tammi, *Due versioni della legenda di S. Margherita* (1958).

BRIAN MERRILEES

[See also **Anglo-Norman Literature; Golden Legend; Nicole Bozon; Wace.**]

VIE DE STE. MODWENNE, an anonymous Anglo-Norman poem of 8,692 lines written about 1230 that recounts the life of Modwenna, a nun of Burton Abbey (Burton-on-Trent). The character appears to be a conflation of two saints, one Irish, St. Moninne, said to have been veiled by St. Patrick, the other an obscure English woman, St. Edith of Polesworth. The original Anglo-Norman text may have preceded the extant version and like it have been based on a Latin life of Modwenna by Geoffrey, abbot of Burton, during the first half of the twelfth century.

BIBLIOGRAPHY

A. T. Baker and Alexander Bell, eds., *St. Modwenna* (1947); Mary Dominica Legge, *Anglo-Norman Literature and Its Background* (1963), 261–263.

BRIAN MERRILEES

[See also **Anglo-Norman Literature; Hagiography, Middle English.**]

VIE DES ANCIENS PÈRES, LA, a collection of seventy-four pious tales written in verse in the mid thirteenth century. The *Vie* is composed of two sets of quite similar stories by different authors (one Champenois, one Picard), which were combined in manuscripts by the later thirteenth century. Sources include the *Vitae patrum*, Gregory the Great's *Dialogues*, and Caesarius of Heisterbach's *Dialogue on Miracles*. Among the tales are numerous miracles, and the stories of Thaïs and of Barlaam and Josaphat. Thirty-one extant manuscripts and two incunabula (1486 and 1495) attest to the late medieval popularity of the *Vie*.

BIBLIOGRAPHY

Paul Meyer, "Versions en vers et en prose des Vies des Pères," in *Histoire littéraire de la France*, 33 (1906); Constance Rosenthal, *The "Vitae Patrum" in Old and Middle English Literature* (1936), 22–52; Édouard Schwan, "La Vie des anciens Pères," in *Romania*, 13 (1884).

EVELYN BIRGE VITZ

[See also **Barlaam and Josaphat; Caesarius of Heisterbach; Gregory I the Great, Pope; Hagiography, French.**]

VIE ST. EDMUND LE REI, LA, a long (4,033 lines) but incomplete Anglo-Norman verse account of the life, martyrdom, and miracles of St. Edmund, king of East Anglia, killed in 869 by invading Danes. It was written around 1170 by Denis Piramus, who names himself in his prologue and has been identified, though not conclusively, with the monk Dionysius mentioned in Jocelin of Brakelond's *Chronicle* of the abbey of Bury St. Edmunds. Piramus knew Abbo of Fleury's *Passio sancti Eadmundi* (composed 985–987) but called on many other sources. The poem, the most extensive of the accounts of the martyrdom of St. Edmund written in French, has been edited four times. A second manuscript, discovered in the John Rylands University Library, Manchester, although incomplete, presents significant new material.

BIBLIOGRAPHY

Hilding Kjellman, *La vie Seint Edmund le rei: Poème anglo-normand du XIIᵉ siècle par Denis Piramus* (1935); William Rothwell, "The Life and Miracles of St. Edmund: A Recently Discovered Manuscript," in *Bulletin of the John Rylands University Library*, 60 (1977–1978).

JUDITH GRANT

[See also **Anglo-Norman Literature; Hagiography, Middle English; Jocelin of Brakelond; Passiun Seint Edmund, La.**]

VIENNE, COUNCIL OF. See **Councils, Western (1311–1449).**

VÍGA-GLÚMS SAGA (The story of Killer-Glúmr; *ca.* 1230–1240) is the biography of Glúmr Eyjólfsson (*b. ca.* 928) of Þverá in northern Ireland, the site of the Benedictine monastery Munkaþverá (founded in 1155). The saga is preserved complete in an abbreviated redaction in *Mǫðruvallabók* and in fragments of a fuller older version. Except for two interpolations the structure is cohesive, with each episode leading logically to the next. Nevertheless the story is sometimes difficult to follow because of the extreme narrative compaction resulting from stylistic condensation, the obscurity of mythological and contemporary allusions for modern readers, and the devious machinations of the protagonist in his struggle to maintain his prestige and property. Although the story is based on historical events, the chronology is not precise.

Glúmr's father wins the daughter of a Norwegian lord in marriage after ridding him of a berserk, and Glúmr is rewarded by his maternal grandfather for a similar exploit with three heirlooms—a cloak, a spear, and a sword—that preserve his good fortune as long as he retains them. Upon returning to Iceland, Glúmr, incited by his mother, punishes a neighbor named Þorkell for his encroachment on their farm by slaying Þorkell's son Sigmund and forcing him to surrender his own land to them at half price. This is the first of a series of clashes between Glúmr and the people of Espihóll, in which he remains undefeated until he swears an ambivalent oath to escape charges of manslaughter. In a skaldic verse he betrays the truth and, having lost his talismans, is convicted and banished from his estate. Even as a blind old man Glúmr seeks vengeance by scheming to stab two of the leading men of the district. With the advent of Christianity (999) Glúmr is converted, and he dies around 1003.

The only fully drawn character is that of Glúmr, and the plot of the story develops logically from his increasingly imperious, ruthless, and deceitful dealings with his adversaries. But the story also preserves vestiges of a struggle between religious cults. Glúmr, who seems to have come under the influence of the Viking deity Odin, the god of his maternal ancestors, three times offends Freyr, the patron deity of his paternal kinsmen. His banishment from Þverá can be understood as an answer to Þorkell's plea to Freyr that Glúmr be forced from his lands, as he was. With the loss of his talismans Glúmr is at the mercy of his enemies, of Freyr, and of fate. But the saga also reflects contemporary events. Not only does Glúmr resemble Sighvatr Sturluson in behavior and temperament; in the episode called *Ingólfs þáttr*, which is based on a parable from the *Disciplina clericalis*, there are thinly veiled allusions to the suspected guilt of Sighvatr in a murder committed in 1222.

The main sources of this anonymous work are skaldic stanzas, local traditions, and older sagas, including a lost *Esphœlinga saga*.

BIBLIOGRAPHY

Theodore M. Andersson, *The Icelandic Family Saga: An Analytic Reading* (1967); Lee M. Hollander, trans., *Víga-Glúms Saga and the Story of Ögmund Dytt* (1972); Jónas Kristjánsson, ed., *Víga-Glúms saga*, in *Íslenzk fornrit*, IX: *Eyfirðinga sǫgur* (1956); Paul Schach, *Icelandic Sagas* (1984), 138–140; G. Turville-Petre, ed., *Víga-Glúms Saga*, 2nd ed. (1960).

PAUL SCHACH

[See also **Berserks; Disciplina Clericalis; Family Sagas, Icelandic; Freyr; Odin.**]

VIGILIUS, POPE (r. 537–555), was a protégé of the Byzantine empress Theodora I. In the midst of the controversy over the Monophysite heresy that was threatening to tear apart the Eastern Roman Empire in the middle of the sixth century, Vigilius proved highly indecisive. Brought from Rome to Constantinople in 547 to aid in an attempt at arriving at a religious compromise, Vigilius alienated all sides, while accomplishing nothing. He boycotted the Fifth Ecumenical Council held in Constantinople in 533 and died en route back to Rome.

BIBLIOGRAPHY

J. B. Bury, *History of the Later Roman Empire*, 2 vols. (1923, repr. 1958); Harry J. Magoulias, *Byzantine Christianity: Emperor, Church, and the West* (1970).

ROBERT E. LERNER

[See also **Councils (Ecumenical); Monophysitism; Theodora I, Empress.**]

VÍGLUNDAR SAGA (The story of Víglundr), which was composed around 1400, is preserved in two vellums, from the fifteenth and sixteenth centuries respectively, and in numerous paper transcripts from the seventeenth century. *Rímur* cycles were derived from it, the latest one by Sigurður Breiðfjörð (d. 1846). The model and chief source for this late romantic work is *Friðþjófs saga,* but the author also drew upon various other *fornaldarsögur, riddarasögur,* and *Íslendingasögur,* as well as *Landnámabók* for names, themes, and motifs, and the style reflects these sources. The story takes place in Iceland and Norway during the tenth century. For the most part the characters are either unblemished heroes and heroines or villains with no redeeming virtues. *Víglundr,* which means "battletree," is an old kenning for warrior and appears here for the first time as a personal name. The name of the heroine, Ketilríðr, appears nowhere else in the sagas of Icelanders. The twenty-two skaldic verses, most of which are attributed to Víglundr, were probably composed by the author.

Víglundar saga is the only love story among the *Íslendingasögur* that has a happy ending. Like *Tristrams saga,* this work begins with a prelude that foreshadows the main story. Þorgrímr, the illegitimate son of a Norwegian farmer, and Ólof geisli (Sunbeam), the daughter of Earl Þórir, plan to get married, but the earl promises her to a man of greater prominence. Þorgrímr abducts the bride from the wedding feast and elopes with her to Iceland. Their sons are Trausti and Víglundr. Þorgrímr's friend Hólmkell and his wife Þorbjörg have two sons and a daughter named Ketilríðr. For no apparent reason Þorbjörg hates her daughter and incites her sons, who are unregenerate scoundrels, to mischief. Víglundr and Ketilríðr fall in love, but Hólmkell is hounded by his wife and sons to promise her to a Norwegian merchant named Hákon. Hákon and Ketilríðr's brothers with a band of men ambush Víglundr and Trausti, but the chief attackers are killed in the fight. After recovering from their wounds, Víglundr and Trausti go abroad. When they return to Iceland, they take lodging with an old farmer named Ketill, to whom Ketilríðr has been married during their absence. Eventually they learn that the fake marriage has been arranged by Þorgrímr and Hólmkell to protect Ketilríðr and that Ketill is Víglundr's uncle. The story ends with general reconciliation and the marriage of the two lovers.

A pale imitation of the stirring thirteenth-century *Íslendingasögur, Víglundar saga* is typical of the escape literature that flourished in Iceland after the fall of the commonwealth in 1262–1264.

BIBLIOGRAPHY
Sources. "The Story of Viglund the Fair," in *Three Northern Love Stories and Other Tales,* Eiríkr Magnússon and William Morris, trans. (1875); *Víglundar saga,* in *Íslendinga sögur,* III, Guðni Jónsson, ed. (1946); *Víglundar saga,* in *Íslenzk fornrit,* XIV, Jóhannes Halldórsson, ed. (1959).

Study. Paul Schach, *Icelandic Sagas* (1984), 157–158;

PAUL SCHACH

[See also **Family Sagas, Icelandic; Fornaldarsögur; Iceland; Kenning; Riddarasögur; Rímur; Tristrams Saga ok Ísöndar.**]

VIKING ART. The Viking Age art of Scandinavia from the late eighth to the early twelfth century is characterized throughout by the use of stylized animal motifs, ultimately derived from those that had been developed during the fourth and fifth centuries, based on late Roman provincial art. A limited range of plant motifs borrowed from Western European art were popular additions to the artistic repertoire from the mid tenth century, only to be largely abandoned in the mid eleventh century. It is notable that there existed throughout Scandinavia in the Viking Age a series of basically uniform modes of artistic expression, following well-defined conventions. Several of its style phases are also well represented in the areas of Scandinavian settlement from Iceland to Russia, but particularly in the British Isles.

Most surviving art of the Viking Age takes the form of applied art—the decoration of functional objects of everyday life, most notably personal metalwork, such as brooches. Representational art was probably always uncommon, although some sculpture, a tapestry from the Oseberg ship burial, and references in the literary sources indicate that narrative art did exist, most notably, it seems, for religious purposes. Three-dimensional images are particularly rare, although small-scale carvings of figures are known for use as gaming pieces, but larger figures existed, such as the idols referred to by Adam of Bremen as standing in the pagan temple at Uppsala. Such idols would have been carved in

Watercolor reconstruction of a tapestry from the Oseberg ship burial, Norway, 9th century. UNIVERSITETETS OLDSAKSAMLING, OSLO

wood, which undoubtedly was the natural medium for Viking Age artists in Scandinavia, although little such wood carving survives, leaving us with incomplete sources for assessing their achievements.

There are, however, two groups of Viking Age wood carvings in Norway that illustrate the quality and richness of Viking art, which is otherwise now only to be seen in fine metalwork. The earliest of these, the elaborately carved objects found in the ninth-century Oseberg ship burial (now in the Viking Ship Museum at Bygdøy, Oslo), reveal the essential continuity of Scandinavian art from the eighth to the ninth century, with the beginning of Viking art being marked by the appearance of a new motif—the "gripping beast," so called because of its characteristic tendency to grip whatever is available. The gripping-beast motif developed during the second half of the eighth century, as is demonstrated by the excavation in the 1970's of a metalworker's workshop in Denmark, but it remained popular in one form or another well into the tenth century.

The last style in Viking art, the Urnes style, has been named for the eleventh-century decoration on a small wooden church (rebuilt) in the Norwegian village of that same name; at the church the visitor may still appreciate the high standards of design and craftsmanship to which Viking art aspired. Even at Urnes, in a specifically Christian context, the motifs employed are limited to stylized animals, with a few foliate details.

Between the Oseberg and Urnes styles there are generally recognized to be four further phases of Viking art: the Borre, Jellinge, Mammen, and Ringerike styles. (Each of these phases is the subject of a separate illustrated article in this Dictionary.) The Borre and Jellinge styles were in contemporaneous use from the latter's development in the late ninth century through much of the tenth; the two styles are occasionally found on the same object. The Borre style makes further use of the gripping beast, alongside other motifs (notably an interlace pattern known as the "ring chain"), although it is adapted for use singly so that it grips its enclosing frame or its own body rather than those of its neighbors, as in the wild melees to be found in the Oseberg style. The Jellinge style's ribbon-shaped animal in profile is descended from those of the Oseberg style, and from it there developed the more massive animal (the "great beast") of the Mammen and then the Ringerike styles. It was the Mammen and Ringerike styles that made

use of plant motifs, tendril patterns adopted and adapted from Anglo-Saxon and Ottonian art, alongside their variations on the native animal motifs, the meaning of which (if any) remains obscure.

The Borre and Jellinge styles were brought by the Vikings to the British Isles and to Russia, where regional variations were developed. The Ringerike and Urnes styles became established to a lesser extent in England in the eleventh century, but they had a notable influence in Ireland, where the Irish version of the Urnes style flourished well into the twelfth century, as may be seen on such masterpieces of metalwork as the Cross of Cong (*ca.* 1123).

The popularity of wood carving may go some way to explaining why stone carving was a neglected art in Scandinavia until the late tenth and eleventh centuries. Its eventual widespread introduction was in imitation of Western European traditions of stone monuments; Scandinavian settlers in northern England and the Isle of Man had earlier followed and modified native practices in this respect. The Danish king Harald Bluetooth may have started a fashion for stone sculpture in southern Scandinavia: he erected a great stone monument at Jelling, most probably in the 960's, but certainly between 960 and 985, bearing a runic inscription, a representation of the Crucifixion, and a "great beast" (in the Mammen style). In the early Viking Age it was only on the Baltic island of Gotland that there had existed an important school of sculpture, one that produced distinctive memorial stones lightly incised with elaborate scenes that were originally painted (as would have been most Viking Age stone and wooden sculpture). These "picture stones" display representations of Viking warriors, women, riders, and ships under sail, of particular interest to the archaeologist and student of Norse mythology, but they stand apart from the mainstream of Viking art.

The gradual conversion of Scandinavia to Christianity popularized the use of stone sculpture to commemorate the Christian dead and their good deeds, recorded in runic inscriptions borne on serpents' bodies in the late Viking styles. It was, however, the church that brought Viking art to the end of its vigorous and independent life by encouraging the spread of European Romanesque art, to which it succumbed during the twelfth century, although some of its elements were to survive in medieval Scandinavian folk art.

The Jellinge stone, Denmark, showing the Crucifixion, 960–985. SECOND SECTION, NATIONALMUSEET, COPENHAGEN

Picture stone from Alskog, Gotland, Sweden, 9th century. The scene at top may depict Valhalla. STATENS HISTORISKA MUSEUM, STOCKHOLM

BIBLIOGRAPHY

Richard N. Bailey, *Viking Age Sculpture in Northern England* (1980); Signe Horn Fuglesang, *Some Aspects of the Ringerike Style* (1980), "Stylistic Groups in Late Viking and Early Romanesque Art," in *Acta ad archaeologiam et artium historiam pertinentia*, series altera **1** (1981), and "Early Viking Art," *ibid.*, series altera **2** (1982); James A. Graham-Campbell, "From Scandinavia to the Irish Sea: Viking Art Reviewed," in Michael Ryan, ed., *Ireland and Insular Art, A.D. 500–1500* (1987); David M. Wilson and Ole Klindt-Jensen, *Viking Art*, 2nd ed. (1980).

JAMES A. GRAHAM-CAMPBELL

[See also **Adam of Bremen; Anglo-Saxon Art; Borre Style; Celtic Art; Denmark; Jellinge Style; Mammen Style; Metalworkers; Norway; Oseberg Find; Ringerike Style; Romanesque Art; Urnes Style; Vikings.**]

VIKING NAVIGATION. During the Viking period (*ca.* 800–*ca.* 1050), Scandinavian navigational practices may have been the most skillful in Europe. True, the Viking sailor may have been no better than others while traveling coastal waters, for knowing the location of sandbars, skerries, and other hazards and the tendencies of tides, coastal winds, and currents was part of any sailor's stock-in-trade since at least the time of Odysseus. What distinguished the Viking as a navigator were his methods of crossing wide and open seas during the traditional sailing season from April to October.

As is often the case with the history of early navigation, direct contemporary evidence for Viking navigation is lacking: the northern navigator passed along only orally what he learned for himself and what he knew of the cumulative experience of past generations. We are forced to glean what we can about his practices from mostly casual references in sagas and other accounts of his time that were written considerably afterward, usually by men who themselves were inexperienced at sea. Inadequate as it is, this evidence reveals at least the Viking's most important navigational methods.

So far as can be known with certainty, he used no instruments beyond the simple lead and line for soundings, useful enough in shallow waters but not in deep seas, where he relied upon his senses and rudimentary celestial observations. A passage

419

in *Landnámabók* (Book of [Icelandic] settlements, *Hauksbók* version) says that one should sail west from Hernar in Norway, just north of Bergen (60° 24′ N), to reach Hvarf, at the southern tip of Greenland (59° 41′ N). On his way a mariner will pass "north of the Shetlands, which can be seen on a clear day, and south of the Faeroes, so that the sea will appear to be halfway up the slopes, and then to that point south of Iceland where there are birds and whales." The island promontories, as well as sightings of glaciers on Iceland and Greenland mentioned by other authors, were of obvious importance for getting one's bearings, and haunts of whales, together with familiar schools of fish, could indicate that an island destination was near even if it was enveloped by fog. Seabirds not far from land—and first sighted as much as 150 miles south of Iceland by modern trawlers—would provide similar aid.

We must suppose too that such visual clues to location as typical cloud formations, varying color of the sea, drift ice and icebergs, and occasional pieces of driftwood and floating seaweed were not ignored. Nonvisual aids also must have been valuable: the sounds of cracking icebergs, blowing whales, and squawking birds; the relatively fresh taste of water emptying into the sea from an island's river; the feel of the comparatively cold East Greenland polar current; and the fresh, earthy smell of land, recognizable from quite far out at sea. Knowledge of location gained in these ways was particularly important when lost in fog or when on an exploratory voyage. And all sensory clues were used whenever possible to confirm a position that was learned as a result of astronomical observations made during periods of fair weather.

The passage in *Landnámabók* does not say how one was able to sail west from a particular point in Norway to one in Greenland, but obviously celestial navigation was involved. In northern waters during the long summer days of the sailing season, the star that helped most was the sun, not Polaris. Certainly the Viking sailor was well aware that the farther north he sailed the lower the sun reached at its zenith, midway through its heavenly transit; and conversely the farther south, the higher it reached—in other words, he knew what we would call relative latitude. Thus if he could keep the sun at the same distance above the horizon at midday, day after day, he would be traveling in a due easterly or westerly line, thereby practicing what is sometimes known as "latitude sailing." This apparently simple feat

was not easy to accomplish. The sun's distance above the horizon could be consistently measured with anything conveniently available—the length of an upraised arm, for example—but for this measurement to be even reasonably accurate, the ship itself had to be on an even keel, not usual in the North Atlantic. Furthermore, the best opportunity for measuring the sun's distance above the horizon is presented only at midday; at another time—halfway between rising and the zenith, for example—it is much more difficult to judge without reference to a fixed geographical point and without a timekeeping device (such as even a small water-clock), something which the Viking sailor evidently did not use. During the twenty-four-hour period between middays, his ship surely would leave a due easterly or westerly course before the error could be corrected with another observation of the sun's meridian.

Though it had these limitations in practice, as well as others, latitude sailing still was much appreciated. Whenever new land in the west was discovered—progressively, the Faeroes, Iceland, and Greenland—the height there of the sun at midday would be ascertained several times during the sailing season; when traveling from Norway, which faces all of these places, a sailor first would sail up or down the Atlantic coast to the point where the sun's altitude was the same, then make his departure across the sea. Latitude sailing was also indirectly useful for north-south sailings. For instance, if an Icelander knew the height of the midday sun in northern Ireland at various times during the sailing season, he could sail south of his island until he reached the latitude of Ireland, then sail east until he struck land. Though he knew about relative latitude, the Viking navigator had no way of determining even relative longitude at sea; rather he gauged his voyage's progress by the number of days it took, a practice reflected in other sailing directions preserved in *Landnámabók*: for instance, a voyage from the most westerly point of Norway to the east coast of Iceland, a distance of about 530 nautical miles, required a sailing of seven days, a period which should be understood only as the average under favorable circumstances.

Currents and winds were of course most welcome to the Viking seafarer, provided he wanted to travel in their direction; otherwise they could be most distressing. Flowing from west to east, the North Atlantic current is the main one in the open waters he sailed. Prevailing winds come from the

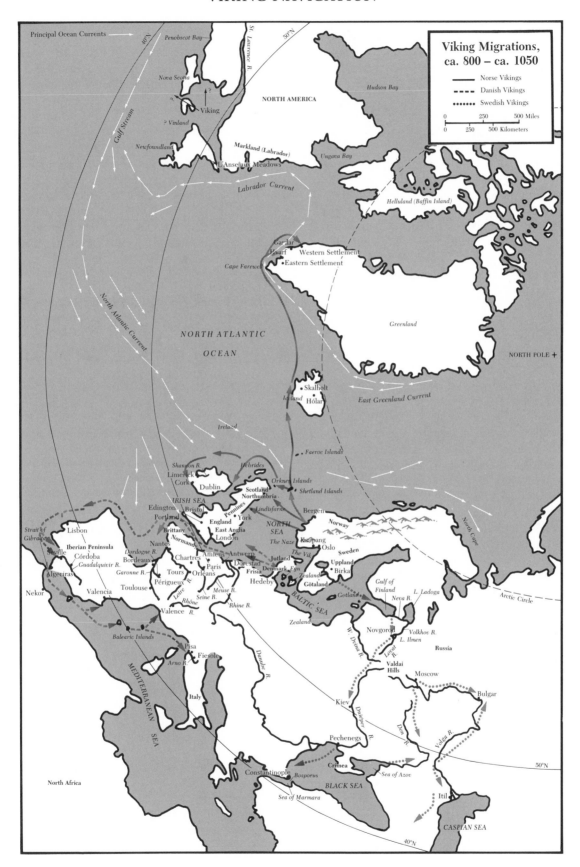

same direction. Sailing from Norway westward against both of them usually required a considerable amount of tacking, an additional reason for the only approximate nature of Viking latitude sailing. Until the comparative latitude of a western destination had been well ascertained by repeated and constantly more refined observations throughout the sailing season, and until a considerable body of sea lore had been accumulated for the route to help make up for the unavoidably inaccurate estimations of latitudinal position along the way, the need for tacking against wind and current could make a voyage to the west quite hazardous. On early direct voyages to Greenland from Norway, for example, if one tacked too far to the north, or was prevented from making adequate compensation for it by a new adverse wind, the ship might not just reach the drift ice off the eastern coast of Greenland but be stranded on the isolated and desolate coast itself; if one tacked or was driven too far to the south, the ship might reach North America. It was because of "prolonged difficulties at sea" on his way from Norway to Greenland that Leif Eriksson discovered America, according to *Eiríks saga rauða* (Erik the Red's saga).

Difficulties in sailing from Norway to Greenland persisted even thirty to forty-five years after the island was first settled by Norsemen, if we can believe the words that Snorri Sturluson, author of *Óláfs saga helga* (St. Olaf's saga), put into the mouth of an experienced sailor when speaking to Olaf, ruler of Norway from 1015 to 1030: "'Now, it may happen, King, as is not unlikely and can easily occur, that we cannot make Greenland but are driven to Iceland or to other lands.'" Because of ignorance of the route or some unusual ill-luck, fourteen of the thirty-five ships that left western Iceland to first settle Greenland in 984 or 985 were either lost at sea or driven back home. Nevertheless, the passage to Greenland was generally easier from Iceland than from Norway. After crossing the Denmark Strait from western Iceland to some distance off the east coast of Greenland, taking care to avoid the drift ice, an Icelandic sailor would be aided by the Greenland current, which flows down the eastern side of the large island and around its southern tip to the west coast, where the Norse settlements were located. He was also assisted by the prevailing northerly winds of the island's east coast and, once he got around the southern tip, by the prevailing southerlies of the west coast. The main difficulty was in rounding the tip, for there he would encoun-

ter the same westerlies that caused difficulties for a Norwegian as soon as he left his home shores. An agreement of about 1022 between St. Olaf and the Icelanders refers to this problem when it takes into account that Icelanders who were on their way to Greenland, or on an exploratory voyage, might unintentionally be driven to Norway by that troublesome wind.

Beset with dangers of sudden shifts of wind or lack of it altogether, blanketing fog, and other perils of the North Atlantic, the Viking who crossed this ocean was always an adventurer. That the mishaps he had, as recounted in sagas and other sources, are the exception rather than the rule owes much to his navigational skill.

BIBLIOGRAPHY

Paul Adam, "Problèmes de navigation dans l'Atlantique Nord," in *Vikings et leur civilisation: Problèmes actuels*, Régis Boyer, ed. (1976); *Bibliography of Old Norse-Icelandic Studies* (1963–), s.v. "Navigation"; Hjalmar Falk, "Altnordisches Seewesen," in *Wörter und Sachen*, 4 (1912); Bruce E. Gelsinger, "The Norse 'Day's Sailing,'" in *Mariner's Mirror*, 56 (1970); G. J. Marcus, "The Navigation of the Norsemen," in *Mariner's Mirror*, 39 (1953), "The Greenland Trade-Route," and "The Norse Traffic with Iceland," in *Economic History Review*, 2nd ser., 7 (1954–1955), and 2nd ser., 9 (1957); Roald Morcken, "Norse Nautical Units and Distance Measurements," in *Mariner's Mirror*, 54 (1968); Thorkild Ramskou, *Solstenen: Primitiv Navigation i Norden før Kompasset* (1969), reviewed by Bruce E. Gelsinger in *Scandinavian Studies*, 42 (1970); Uwe Schnall, *Navigation der Wikinger: Nautische Probleme der Wikingerzeit im Spiegel der schriftlichen Quellen* (1975); Carl V. Sølver, "Leiðarsteinn: The Compass of the Vikings," in *Old Lore Miscellany*, 10 (1946); Gustav Storm, ed., *Islandske annaler indtil 1578* (1888, repr. 1977); Heinrich Winter, "Die Nautik der Wikinger und ihre Bedeutung für die Entwicklung der europäischen Seefahrt," in *Hansische Geschichtsblätter*, 62 (1937).

Bruce E. Gelsinger

[See also **Exploration; Iceland; Landnámabók; Navigation; Norway; Óláfs Saga Helga; Ships and Shipbuilding; Vinland Sagas.**]

VIKINGS

INTRODUCTION

The term "Vikings" is used today to refer to Scandinavians of the period from about 800 to about 1050 (that is, the Viking Age). In that period the term meant "adventurers" and "pirates." It probably derives etymologically from the Old Norse *vik,* meaning "inlet": thus, the "inlet folk." During the decades immediately before or after the year 800 the Vikings came out of their northern homelands and traveled west to the British Isles, Iceland, Greenland, and, finally, to the shores of the North American continent; south to the lands of the Franks and further south to the Iberian Peninsula, and even through the Strait of Gibraltar to Italy and North Africa; and east through the river systems of Russia to found a capital at Kiev and to challenge mighty Byzantium itself.

The two northern European peninsulas—the Jutland and the Norwegian-Swedish—and their attendant islands were the lands from which these warrior-seamen sailed. Of these, Norway was the largest, a thousand miles long from Cape North to the Naze, yet its generally mountainous terrain—its mountain range, the Keel, resembled a ship turned upside down—meant that most of the population lived scattered along the coast and on the fjords (deep-water inlets reaching in some instances over a hundred miles inland). People living in scattered settlements by the sea and along the fjords made contact only with immediate neighbors and only by ship. No unified Norway existed in 800 and, many would say, for hundreds of years afterward. Sweden, on the other part of this peninsula, was much less mountainous. Thickly wooded and dotted with bogs, Sweden had at this time three principal areas of settlement: Uppland, Götaland, and the island of Gotland in the Baltic Sea. Again, as in Norway, no national government existed, and no "Swedish sense" united the peoples living in this land. Denmark, because of its size, had a more homogeneous population and a greater likelihood of producing strong local rulers exercising control beyond their own localities. One of these rulers, Godefred, successfully confronted the mighty Charlemagne in the years after 800. Jutland itself, the islands of Fyn (Funen) and Zealand (Sjælland), and the southern part of present-day Sweden formed medieval Denmark.

Three major trading centers—one in each of these lands—allowed contact with a wider world: Kaupang on the Vik (Oslofjord) in Norway, Hedeby (near modern Schleswig) in the neck of the Jutland peninsula, and Birka in central Sweden. An Arab merchant from Spain, al-Tartushi, visited Hedeby about 950 and described it as "a large town at the other end of the world sea . . . not rich in goods and wealth . . . a place where the dreadful singing of the people is worse even than the barking of dogs." Excavations at these sites show that they were relatively small and were involved in international trade.

Separateness characterized the living situations of the peoples in these northern lands, yet unifying forces were at work. Among them was a common language (*dönsk tunga*), which meant that Vikings from Kiev would have been able to understand Vikings from Newfoundland. Similar artistic styles were in use (not independent of Germanic and Celtic influences), which generally took the form of semi-naturalistic ornamentation applied on wood, stone, and metal. These peoples also shared the same pantheon with its anthropomorphic deities: the aristocratic Odin, the thundering Thor, and the phallic Freyr (Frey). Their dead heroes were taken up by the beautiful Valkyries to the glorious hall of Odin, Valhalla. Moreover, in a society stratified by social distinctions between king, noblemen, freemen, freedmen, and slaves, decisions were made by men of power (local property holders); they made these decisions locally in a *thing* (a local assembly) and more broadly in an *althing* (a general assembly). Actual laws no doubt reflected local concerns. The island of Gotland, for example, levied a scale of fines for touching a woman: 4 ounces of silver for touching her wrist or ankle, 2⅔ ounces for touching her elbow or her leg between knee and calf, 1 ounce for touching her breast, and no fine at all for the "touch dishonorable" above her knee (because consent was presumed). Outlawry was a penalty common to the north; common, too, were many of the judicial procedures.

The explosion of the Vikings out of their northern homelands around the year 800, an explosion that sent waves of warriors west to northern England, Scotland, and Ireland, south to Frisia and Francia, and east to Russia, remains far from satisfactorily explained by historians. Once underway, dynamic forces kept this outward movement, this centrifugal force, in motion for over two centuries. But what started it in the first place? Since the late nineteenth century historians have stressed the population factor, and modern analysis continues this emphasis. Widespread polygamy in a society in which manhood was measured in the number of children sired provides a context in which a population might grow rapidly. King Harald Fairhair of Norway, for example, sired at least nine sons who survived to adulthood; each of these, in turn, might have done likewise, and so their sons and their son's sons, until a point of crisis would be reached. We are reminded, rightly, that childbearing women and not siring men are crucial to population growth. Even monogamous societies, however, can experience striking growths in population. From soil analysis in Denmark the conclusion is drawn that in the ninth century an increasing amount of land was used for tillage and that the crops grown were high in protein content (for instance, cereals like rye) and were obviously intended for an expanding human population. Marginal lands in some places were brought under cultivation. A point was reached, the argument runs, when the resources of the land were unable to satisfy the needs of the population and (a thousand years before Malthus) emigration became the safety valve to resolve the population crisis. Other factors no doubt existed; principal among these was the mercantile network between Scandinavia and the outside world. Birka in Sweden had trading lines running as far east as the upper Volga, and Denmark traded with Dorestad in Frisia. The construction of the Danevirke by King Godefred in the early ninth century is often alleged as further evidence of commercial activity, for this earth mound stretching across the Jutland neck provided a road (and shortcut) from the Baltic Sea to the North Sea. Actually, the wall whose construction Godefred ordered in 808 was the second of three walls to be built in this area: the first was constructed about 730 and the third about 960. Hostile neighbors to the south, in addition to increased trade, might explain the building and rebuilding of the wall across southern Denmark.

Not a cause but surely a sine qua non was the sail or, more exactly, the sailing boat. Without it the Viking Age would be inconceivable. The vessels of northern Europe were legendary. As early as A.D. 90 the Roman historian Tacitus said that the northern ships were different: a prow at each end and no sails. By the end of the eighth century the full sail and the developed keel had come to the north, and it was by sail that the raiding ships traveled. The Viking ship as such did not exist: there were a variety of ships differing in length and purpose. The underwater excavations in the Roskildefjord at Skuldelev in Denmark in the 1960's show five Viking Age vessels: two warships, two cargo boats, and a small coastal boat. The so-called Viking longship was undoubtedly used for long voyages, particularly across the North Atlantic. A number of

these have been excavated in the area of the Oslofjord. Best known is the Gokstad ship, dating perhaps from the second quarter of the ninth century. She measures 76 feet 6 inches (23.33 m) long by 17 feet 6 inches (5.25 m) wide amidship. Made almost entirely of oak, the Gokstad ship weighed eighteen tons but drew only three feet of water. To the long keel, cut from an oak tree over 80 feet (about 24 m) high, were added bow and stern posts and then sixteen overlapping strakes per side. Sixteen oars were used on each side, and the sail rose perhaps to a height of 40 feet (about 13 m). A replica of the Gokstad ship sailed from Bergen to Newfoundland in the spring of 1893 and on a test day averaged 9.3 knots, a speed the equal of cargo steamers of the same time. Longer ships may have been used by the Vikings: the *Long Serpent,* built by Olaf Tryggvason about 998, if we can believe literary sources, was over 110 feet (about 37 m) long. Viking shipbuilding was without rival in all of Europe with the possible exception of Frisia. The Vikings did not possess refined navigational skills, merely the common sense that came from experience. Latitudinal sailing in the open seas, the "smell" of land by noticing coastal fish and birds, the recognizing of landmarks, and an oral tradition that kept this experience alive contributed to make the Vikings skillful sailors. With such skills and sails the Viking Age was possible.

The first record of a Viking attack appears in the *Anglo-Saxon Chronicle* and can be dated to the years 789 to 793. This raid was against Portland in Dorset on the English south coast: "There came for the first time three ships of Northmen," who slew the reeve. The suspicion exists that these raiders were perhaps Danish and that the emphasis given to this incident in the chronicle betrays the southern origin of the chronicler. In a very real sense the Viking raids began in the north of England with the attack on the monastic island of Lindisfarne in 793. At Lindisfarne on 8 June 793, preceded by heavenly portents, the Vikings attacked, and, in the words of the chronicler, "their ravages miserably destroyed God's church on Lindisfarne with plunder and slaughter." Alcuin, the English adviser to Charlemagne, wrote from the Frankish court upon hearing the dire reports: "It has been nearly three hundred and fifty years that we and our fathers have lived in this most beautiful land and never before has such a terror appeared in Britain and never was such a landing from the sea thought possible." Landings indeed were possible as further raids proved. During the next decade raids by Norwegian Vikings were felt in other parts of northeastern England, the Scottish coast, the islands of Orkney and Shetland, and on both sides of the Irish Sea. Soon, the Danish Vikings were attacking in the Low Countries, and the Swedish Vikings were sailing into what was to become Russia.

FROM SCOTLAND AND THE ISLES TO IRELAND

Further raids took the Vikings from Norway beyond Northumbria to the coast of Scotland. Attempts to see the Orkney Islands as the center of all these raids, including Northumbria, have not proven successful. Archaeological excavations at Jarlshof (Shetland) and Birsay (Orkney) have revealed graves dating from about 800. The Annals of Ulster for the year 794 record "a devastation by the heathen of all the islands of Britain." These two islands, Orkney and Shetland, were to remain politically in the Scandinavian orbit until the fifteenth century and culturally even longer. Six miles (10 km) separate the Scottish mainland from Orkney, from which Fair Isle can be seen and from which, in turn, Shetland is visible. Caithness, the nearest point in Scotland to the northern isles, was itself greatly influenced by Viking settlers: scores of Norse place-names still exist there (such as Thurso, "Thor's mound"). The Hebrides and, to their south, the Isle of Man and Anglesey were also raided and became satellites of Viking Orkney.

The Norsemen, following a geographical logic, reached Ireland, giving it and three of its four provinces (Ulster, Leinster, Munster) their names. In 795 they came to the island of Lambey, north of Dublin. Raiders came again in 798, 802, 806, 812, and frequently thereafter, and these are only the raids known through surviving records. How many went unrecorded and how many were recorded in records now lost will never be known, but the pattern is clear: frequent raids from the late 790's, striking not only along the east coast near Dublin and in Ulster, but also on the west coast in Sligo, Mayo, and Kerry. By the 830's the Vikings had penetrated up the Shannon to the monastery at Clonmacnois and to other places in the midlands.

This period (ca. 795–ca. 830) of hit-and-run raids in all parts of the country was followed by a period of settlement, dating from the 830's, when the Vikings established ports that later developed into towns: Duiblinn (Dublin), Hlymrekr (Limerick), Veigsfjörth (Wexford), Vethrafjörth (Water-

ford), Vikingalo (Wicklow), and Cork. Excavations in Dublin at High Street, Christ Church Place, and Winetavern Street have produced over thirty thousand objects, mainly from the later Viking Age; the Dublin they reveal was a mercantile town, an entrepôt, yet a town with its own specialized craftsmen, especially bronzesmiths, combmakers, and leatherworkers. This first settling ended about 870; by then some alliances had been formed between Irish and Viking chieftains and some conversion and intermarriage had occurred. But the process was not a peaceful one: in 845 alone, for example, the Vikings attacked Terryglass, Clonenagh, Dunamese, Clonmacnois, Clonfert, Lorrha, Kildare, and Armagh. The brief appearance of the Norse leader Turgeis ended in 845, when the Uí Néill overking captured him and drowned him in Lough Owel; legends grew out of these meager facts. Briefly, also, some Danish Vikings appeared (851 to 853), but they were merely a distraction. The attacks and settlements were carried out by Norsemen coming either directly from Norway or, more likely, from intermediate lands such as Orkney and the Hebrides. The "forty-year rest" described by the annalist as beginning in 873 is only an approximate description, for in 902 the Dublin Vikings were defeated by Irishmen from Meath. From 914 the Vikings came again in what can be called a second settlement. Dublin was reconquered, links were made with the Vikings at York, and there came into being a political alliance between these two Viking towns. The second settlement ended about 940. During that settlement period, as indeed later, the Vikings in Ireland did not form a single political unit—there were several distinct groups of Vikings—nor did the Vikings always establish alliances with one another. Frequently some Vikings would ally themselves with particular Irish factions only to find that they were fighting against brother Vikings allied with other Irish factions.

The drama connected with the Battle of Clontarf in 1014 and the story of the success of Brian Boru are mostly make-believe. This battle was not, as tradition would have us believe, a battle between native Irish and foreign Vikings, a battle that brought the definitive defeat of the Norsemen, in a word, the battle that ended the Viking Age in Ireland. Brian Boru, the southern overking, did in fact win a battle at Clontarf in 1014, but he led a confederation of Irish factions and even some Vikings against his fellow Irishman, the king of Leinster, who was supported by the Dublin Vikings.

The slower process of absorption had begun perhaps two centuries earlier and was to continue for another hundred years, accelerated by the gradual conversion of the Vikings to Christianity and by their intermarriage with the native Irish.

Recent attempts to deemphasize the destructive force of the Vikings in Ireland underline the fact that, although the Vikings visited violence upon the centers of high Celtic civilization—the monasteries—the Irish themselves also attacked these sacred places, leaving much ruin in their wake. Quantification of extant sources, because of their incompleteness, provides little help in assessing the Vikings' effect on Ireland. Destructive they indeed were, particularly in the first three-quarters of the ninth century. The memory of these and subsequent years led a twelfth-century writer, the anonymous author of *The War Against the Foreigners,* to wail: "If one neck had a hundred heads of hardened steel and if each head had a hundred sharp tongues of tempered metal and if each tongue shouted incessantly in a hundred thousand voices, they could never list the sufferings which the Irish—men and women, laity and clergy, young and old—endured from these warlike, savage people." The age of illuminated manuscripts and ornamental metalwork and stonework ended, and its ending coincided with the period of Viking attacks and settlement. Causal connections are not easily established.

THE NORTH ATLANTIC

The islands of the North Atlantic lie at such intervals as to encourage adventurous seafarers with excellent ships to explore them. From Shetland to the Faeroes is 190 miles (305 km), from there to Iceland only 240 miles (390 km), and from there to the nearest point in Greenland another 190 miles. The Norse Vikings explored and settled in these three lands; only the Greenland settlement failed to survive the Middle Ages.

When they landed at the Faeroes around the year 800 these Vikings found Irish monks, who had gone there as "pilgrims for Christ." Dicuil, an Irish geographer writing in 825, described islands to the north of Britain that could be reached by a two-day journey under favorable winds: "On these islands hermits sailing from our country Scotia [Ireland] have lived for nearly a hundred years. But . . . now because of the Northmen pirates they are emptied of anchorites. . . ." These Vikings probably came from the south (that is, the northern and western isles off Scotland). They soon took to sheep raising. Their population increased when in the 880's or 890's political émigrés arrived from Norway, but political dissidence is only part of the picture of the settling of the Faeroes, for good grazing land was attraction enough for the land-hungry Norse. Christianity came to these people about the year 1000.

The crowning jewel of Viking overseas settlements must be Iceland. Uninhabited save, again, for Irish monks on their *peregrinatio pro Christo,* Iceland became the only large Viking settlement in a place without a native population: no need to conquer, no danger of absorption. The literary achievements alone, belonging to the post-Viking age, far surpassed the accomplishments not only of other places of settlement but also of Scandinavia itself. This oval-shaped island with a protruding peninsula in the northwest had for the Viking settler green meadows rimmed along the sea and rivers and, in contrast, lava plains, the result of the activity of more than 200 volcanoes.

The accounts found in versions of the *Landnámabók* (The book of settlements) variously ascribe the discovery to Naddod, Gardar, and Floki: the first called the place Snowland, the second Gardarsholm, and the third Iceland. This preoccupation with the identity of the discoverer (that is, Viking discoverer) should not obscure the essential fact that Viking adventurers sighted and explored Iceland in the 860's. A period of intensive settlement followed. In the sixty years from 870 to 930 an enormous migration occurred, numbering perhaps between 15,000 and 25,000 souls. Who were these settlers? The *Landnámabók* describes 400 of the principal settlers. These were the great men, the landowners, and they came mainly from Norway but also from Ireland and the Outer Hebrides. Some took with them Celtic wives and Celtic slaves, who were Christians. Attempts to see a significant Celtic strain among the settlers and thus to explain the later literary achievements should not distract us from recognizing that this was a Norse settlement and that the great men who came from Ireland and the Hebrides were Norsemen. The impetus for this migration was probably not singular; there were some political émigrés fleeing Harald Finehair, but, more importantly, there were the land-hungry, who could have land for the taking.

The ruling chieftains set up their althing probably in 930; it met in the open at a place they called *thingvellir* (the assembly plain). Remarkably, no single chieftain was to emerge as ruler, and Iceland remained non-monarchical. The constitutional provisions helped to provide Iceland with the stability that brought to that island relative prosperity and, in time, a golden age. The key to the conversion of the Icelanders to Christianity was the accession in 995 to the Norwegian kingship of Olaf Tryggvason, a recent convert. He, in turn, converted two visiting Icelandic chieftains and in 1000 sent them home with an evangelizing priest. The converted chieftains met their brothers at the althing, and in a decision of profound consequences the lawspeaker judged that division among the people would be harmful and that all Icelanders, whatever they did privately, must be Christians publicly. Bishoprics were established at Skalholt in 1056 and at Hólar in 1106, and Icelandic bishops were to attend general councils. When the Reformation came to Iceland under Danish auspices in the sixteenth century, the bishop of Hólar, married and the father of two sons, died defending the old Catholic order and Icelandic liberties.

For almost 500 years Vikings lived in Greenland in two settlements near its southern tip, Cape Farewell. Icelanders knew of a massive land to the west, and, when the choice lands of Iceland were taken, land hunger and adventure took men to this land. Eric (Eirik) the Red, the moving force in this movement west, was not a creature of the fashioners of legend: the site of his farm is known and, also, the location of his wife's church and the family cemetery. He had come to Iceland from Norway probably about 870 but fought with his new neighbors over marginal lands. When he was outlawed for a period of three years, probably about 983, he explored the land to the west. The selection of the name Greenland by Eric may have been part of his scheme to promote settlement. Upon his return to Iceland he organized a colonizing party, which, if we can believe the saga, left Iceland in twenty-five ships, only fourteen of which arrived in Greenland. Subsequently other colonists joined them. From the beginning there were two settlements, both in the southwest: the Eastern Settlement in the very southwest and the Western Settlement four hundred miles "west" (actually northwest). At their height the Eastern Settlement, always the larger, had 190 farms and the Western Settlement half as many. Eric settled at Brattahlid (Brattahlíð) in the Eastern Settlement, and the thing was held near his farm. Christianity came to Greenland directly from Iceland about the year 1000, and a diocese was erected at Gardar in 1126. In addition, two monastic

communities and sixteen parish churches provided care for the 4,000 or so Christians at this outpost of the Western world.

Among the rich results of archaeological activities in Greenland has been the discovery of Eric's farm at Brattahlid. The original building, to which extensions were added, was a great hall, which measured 45 by 15 feet (15 × 5 m). A short distance away were cow barns with room for twenty-eight cows. In 1961 workmen accidentally discovered some human bones nearby, and archaeologists have unearthed at that place not only a cemetery for 150 bodies but also a church (only 11 by 6 feet in size [3.5 × 3 m]), the church, it was concluded, of Eric's wife, Thjodhild. The site of the cathedral and the bishop's house at Gardar have also been identified. The cathedral was cruciform in shape and measured 90 by 54 feet (28 × 17 m). Of particular interest is the cemetery found at Herjolfsnes in the Eastern Settlement, where archaeologists discovered thirty dresses with low décolletage and full skirts, seventeen hoods, and five hats.

The European settlement in Greenland ended in the fifteenth century with virtually no explanation. Climatic rather than political or economic factors were probably responsible. The people living in these two settlements were self-sufficient to a very large extent but stood in the path of a minor ice age that affected Greenland from the thirteenth century with increasing severity. The temperature of the seawater dropped at least 3° C (5.4° F), and perhaps as much as 7° C (12.6° F), enough to send, first, ice floes into their sea lanes and, later, icebergs. The thirteenth-century author of the *King's Mirror* reported that "when one has sailed over the deepest part of the ocean, he will encounter huge masses of ice in the sea . . . and also ice of a much different shape (like mountains rising high out of the sea), which people in Greenland call icebergs." The Eskimos living for centuries in the northern part of Greenland were driven south and the Europeans abandoned their Western Settlement in response to this pressure. In 1377 the bishop of Gardar died; in 1410 the last Icelandic ship known to have sailed to Greenland returned home; and in 1492 Pope Alexander VI wrote Greenland's epitaph:

The diocese of Gardar lies at the bounds of the earth in the land called Greenland. The people there have no bread, wine, or oil; they live on dried fish and milk. Very few sailings to Greenland have been possible because of the ice in the seas and these only in the month of August, when the ice has melted. No ship has sailed there for eighty years and no bishop or priest has resided there during that time. For this reason many inhabitants have abandoned the faith of their baptism. (J.C. Heywood, *Documenta selecta e tabulario secreto vatic . . .* [1893], 12)

The sixteenth century was to see the European rediscovery of this land.

THE NEW WORLD

The controversy over who discovered America reveals a Eurocentric preoccupation. America was probably discovered by Asians 30,000 years ago. Who were the first Europeans to discover America? The short answer is the Vikings. The evidence of the Viking discovery is incontrovertible; the evidence for a discovery by pre-Viking European or Mediterranean sailors has not come to light. The suggestion that a Celtic community lived at Mystery Hill in New Hampshire is not supported by hard evidence. The allegedly second-century-A.D. stone with a Hebraic inscription found at Bat Creek, Tennessee, lacks credibility. The story of legendary Atlantis, known to the ancients as a once mighty land somewhere west of Spain that was devoured by the sea, is but a tale. Moreover, the story of the real-life sixth-century St. Brendan, who in curragh boats with fellow monks is said to have traversed the waters west of Ireland and landed on several lands, belongs to the *immrama* tradition of spinning yarns about sea voyages.

The Vikings landed on the shores of North America about the year 1000. This fact is supported by literary and archaeological evidence. The earliest mention of this achievement was made by Adam of Bremen in 1075, when he wrote in *The History of the Archbishops of Hamburg* that he was told by King Swein of Denmark (1047–1074) that "still another island has been discovered in that ocean and it is called Vinland, because there grow wild vines which produce wine." For the year 1121 the *Icelandic Annals* record that "Bishop Eric of Greenland set out in search of Vinland." Also, the Icelandic historian Ari Thorgilsson, writing about five years later, displayed a knowledge of Vinland.

The best-known accounts of the Vikings in the New World come from two sagas: *Greenlanders' Saga (Grœnlendinga saga)* and *Eric's Saga (Eiríks saga rauða)*. These sagas were committed to writing in the early and later thirteenth century, respectively, and exist today only in later copies. Their stories are very similar, but the *Greenlanders' Saga* is pre-

ferred by scholars. It tells how the Icelander Bjarni Herjolfsson, sailing for Greenland in 985 (or 986), went off course in a violent storm and, when the winds and seas calmed, sailed west and sighted land. Rather than land, Bjarni sailed north and sighted two other lands, which again he failed to explore. The first of these three lands was a verdant place with woods and low hills; the second a flat, thickly forested land; and the third a barren, glaciered land. He finally reached Greenland. Years later Leif, the son of Eric the Red, bought Bjarni's ships and retraced Bjarni's route. He found and landed at all three places. The barren land of glaciers and rocks he called Helluland (Slab-land). The flat land with thick forests and long strands of sandy beaches he called Markland (Forest-land). Two days later he sighted another land: a bay with an island standing sentrylike at its opening to the sea. It was a land in which grapes and grain grew wild and salmon were large and plentiful. Night and day were more equal than in their northern homeland. He called it Vinland. Three subsequent Viking expeditions were made to this site; their purpose was to colonize. They involved other children of Eric the Red: his son Thorvald, his daughter Gudrid with her husband, Karlsefni, and his wicked daughter, Freydis. The most successful of these settlements was the Gudrid-Karlsefni settlement, but, like the others, it was abandoned because of hostile contact with native people, whom they called Skraelings (probably Uglies); it lasted but three years. These saga accounts in their general outlines demand acceptance: Vikings from Greenland, with prominent participants from the family of Eric the Red, attempted unsuccessfully sometime around the year 1000 to colonize at some point along the North American littoral.

What was the location of Vinland? Distinctions need be made. The Vikings gave names to large areas (the Faeroes; Iceland) and used the name Vinland in this sense rather than in a particularized sense. Virtually unanimous opinion places Helluland at Baffin Island and Markland at Labrador. Vinland lies to the south and, perhaps, the west. Claims of Viking sites in Nova Scotia, Massachusetts, Rhode Island, Ontario, Minnesota, and even Oklahoma can be dismissed as spurious. The tower in Newport, Rhode Island, which inspired Longfellow to write "The Skeleton in Armor," is a seventeenth-century windmill. The twelfth-century Norse objects that came to light in 1936 at Beardmore, Ontario, had been planted by their finder.

The runic stone discovered at Kensington, Minnesota, in 1898, which told of Vikings journeying there from Vinland, had probably been cut shortly before its discovery. Of a more serious nature are two locations in Canada. The first, at Ungava Bay in northern Quebec, has revealed several longhouses and some stone implements, which are variously judged to be Viking or Eskimo. The second site—at L'Anse aux Meadows in Newfoundland—was thoroughly examined in annual digs from 1961 to 1968 under the supervision of Dr. Anne Stine Ingstad. She uncovered the remains of an early-eleventh-century community, small in size and unquestionably Norse in character. This Viking site is situated on a marine terrace overlooking Epaves Bay and Great Sacred Isle, which stands at its opening to the sea. Three clusters of houses were found, each with a longhouse and one or more outbuildings. The walls of the buildings were constructed of layers of turf and resemble other known buildings in Greenland and Iceland. The site of a smithy nearby contained hundreds of fragments. Among the objects found at L'Anse aux Meadows that bear close resemblance to other Viking objects and no resemblance to Eskimo objects are a soapstone spindle whorl, a lamp-stone, a bone needle with a drilled eye, and a bronze pin with a ring through its eye. Dozens of pins of this latter type have been found at other Viking settlements of the same period. The radiocarbon testing conducted on sixteen samples has produced a mean date of 920 ± 30, which is clearly meaningless since mean dating cannot be used to negate the fact that charcoal samples date from as early as 670 ± 140 and 740 ± 140. The charcoal samples aside—they derive from driftwood that might have been used hundreds of years after a tree had died—three samples remain (two turf and one bone), and C^{14} tests produce for them the dates 1020 ± 100, 1020 ± 60, and 1040 ± 110. The Viking site at L'Anse aux Meadows was inhabited for a short time only, at most twenty or thirty years: no signs of rebuilding appear and middens are relatively small. It is one thing to say that this is the place of a short-lived eleventh-century Viking community, but it is quite another to say that it is the site where Leif landed and where his relatives came to live. No signs of hostile encounters with native people have been found, and soil analysis concludes that no grapes grew there at that time. There did grow there, however, red and black currants, still called wineberries in parts of Norway.

How far south of northern Newfoundland did the Vikings explore? How far south did Vinland extend? These are questions answerable only by some future discovery of Viking Age objects. The examination in 1978 of a silver coin found at Goddard's farm near the eastern mouth of Penobscot Bay in the state of Maine led to the conclusion that it is an authentic Norse coin from the 1070's that had been in situ since pre-Columbian times. Its singularity as a Viking artifact in a field containing 50,000 objects precludes Goddard's farm from being the site of a Viking settlement. The presence of the Norse coin there, when taken together with Labradoran chert and a Dorset-Eskimo tool, strongly suggests a trade network along the North American littoral connecting, no doubt in many stages, the Maine coast and the lands in the north where in the early years of the new millennium Europeans explored and tried to settle.

Ranking with the Piltdown Man as one of the great forgeries of the twentieth century must be the Vinland Map. Published by Yale University Press on the eve of Columbus Day, 1965, this map of the world clearly showing Vinland, labeled as such, was hailed as the only pre-Columbian map containing North America. The failure of its handlers to disclose the library from which the map was bought and the secrecy in which it was studied invited close scrutiny by scholars. Doubts were raised about the legend bearing the account of the discovery of Vinland and about the strikingly accurate delineation of Greenland. In 1972 sophisticated microanalysis was used—at the university's insistence—to examine the map. The conclusion that the ink on the map contained a chemical compound unavailable before 1920 forced even its staunch supporters to acknowledge that the map is a forgery. (Further examination of the ink, conducted at the University of California at Davis in the mid 1980's, has, however, forced a reopening of the question.)

DANES IN FRANCIA AND BEYOND

As Charlemagne lay dying in 814, we are told, he feared what harm the Vikings might cause his descendants and the Frankish people. His deathbed foreboding was amply realized in the events of the next century. Minor raiding began even before his death (in 799 in Aquitaine and in 810 in Frisia), but the major Viking attacks against the lands of the Franks (Francia) began in 834, at a time when King Louis the Pious (814–840) was countering the ambitions of his sons. His successor in the western

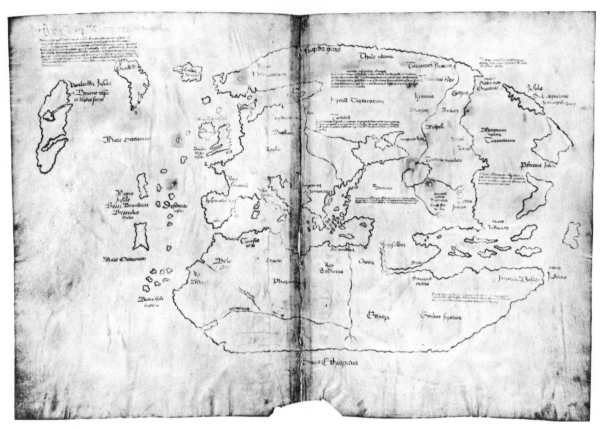

The contested Vinland Map. Reproduced from R. A. Skelton *et al.*, eds., *The Vinland Map and the Tartar Relation* © 1965 YALE UNIVERSITY PRESS

Frankish lands, Charles the Bald (*d.* 877), likewise was involved with problems internal to his kingdom. With the Frankish rulers distracted, the attacks of the Vikings, from their point of view, could scarcely have come at a more advantageous moment.

Generally speaking, the Viking attacks on Francia came in four phases. First, the raids from 834 to about 850 were seasonal raids: the Vikings came between spring and autumn and attacked at random along the coast and up the rivers. Frisia was struck in 834, and two years later the town of Antwerp on the river Scheldt was fired. Also in 834, Viking ships landed at the island of Noirmoutier near the mouth of the Loire; it was to become in time their base for raiding in the Loire. Up the Loire at Nantes in 843 Vikings murdered the bishop at his altar, and, later chronicles say, a fearsome massacre of the Christians followed. Meanwhile, others had sailed into the Seine. On 14 May 841 they burned Rouen; on 24 May they burned the monastery at Jumièges; on 25 May the monks at Fontenelle paid

six pounds to spare their monastery; on 28 May the monks of St. Denis near Paris paid twenty-six pounds to ransom captives; and on 31 May the raiders returned to the sea after a profitable three-week campaign. And so it went: the Vikings were appearing in other rivers (Gironde, Garonne, Dordogne, Meuse) and attacking other places (Chartres, Amiens, Bordeaux, Toulouse, Tours, Angers, Orléans, Poitiers, Blois, and Paris).

During the second phase (*ca.* 850–*ca.* 875) the Vikings wintered in Francia, first at island bases near the mouths of the greater rivers and, later, at other places inland. More like campaigns than raids, the Viking activities in Francia were sustained for longer periods. For example, for six years (856–862) a band of Vikings remained, raiding on the Seine. Ermentarius of Noirmoutier commented that the ships of the Vikings were growing in number and that the attackers "captured Bordeaux, Périgueux, Limoges, Angoulême, and Toulouse, destroying Angers, Tours, and Orléans, and in ships beyond number sailed up the Seine, attacking, pillaging, burning Rouen, seizing Paris, Beauvais, and Meaux, occupying Chartres, pillaging Évreux and Bayeux, and attacking all the other towns."

Frankish defenses were unequal to this assault. Meeting with his advisers at Pîtres in 862, Charles the Bald ordered the construction of fortified bridges. Work began in 862 on such a bridge at Pîtres, the first fordable place on the Seine, but was not completed till 873; in fact, in 869 laborers from other parts of the kingdom had to be conscripted to work on its construction. The program was not a success, and resistance became localized. Neither flight nor ransom is truly defensive. Where possible, monks left their monasteries and fled inland to the expected safety of Burgundy, the Auvergne, and Flanders, taking with them their revered relics. The body of St. Martin was taken from Tours to Comery in 853, taken back to Tours in 854, probably moved again in 862 and 869, and moved in 877 to Chablis, Auxerre, and, finally, back to Tours. The ransom paid to attackers by a community as a price of being spared an attack, later called danegeld, proved merely a temporary and regional remedy. The Vikings simply took their silver and went elsewhere to attack other parts of Francia. Charles the Bald, for example, in 866 paid a Viking army 4,000 pounds of silver and a quantity of wine to lift the siege of Melun, and the foreigners left the Seine. Relative peace ensued in the region of the Seine, but not elsewhere, and the Vikings were to return. Later, in 886, they besieged Paris and, when the danegeld was paid, left Paris to attack Burgundy.

Viking ships sailed beyond Francia to Spain and through the Strait of Gibraltar into the Mediterranean Sea. As early as 844 they raided along the western coast of Iberia. For thirteen days they raided near Lisbon and later sailed up the Guadalquivir, held Seville briefly, and raided the countryside before being forced to withdraw. A daring adventure lasting nearly four years (859–862) brought other Vikings into these regions. After raiding with indifferent success along the Iberian west coast, a fleet, reportedly of sixty vessels, sailed into the Mediterranean. They burned the mosque at Algeciras and then they crossed over to North Africa, where they captured Nekor in what is now Morocco, held captives for ransom, and after a total of eight days sailed away. They raided along the east coast of Spain and in the Balearic Islands before wintering on the island of Camargue near the Rhône mouth. In the spring the raiders went up the Rhône as far as Valence. Later they attacked Italy, penetrating up the Arno to devastate Pisa and sack Fiesole. A twelfth-century French account relates the story of their attacking Luna, thinking it Rome, but the story is probably not true. After further raids in the lands of the Moors these Viking adventurers were back in Frankish lands and waters.

The most prolonged period of devastation in Francia began in 879 and lasted thirteen years. This third phase saw the so-called Great Army of the Vikings moving virtually unchecked in the regions between the Seine and the Rhine while other Vikings were active in the Loire region. Events in Francia were never far removed from events in England, and it was the news of King Alfred the Great's victory over the Danes at Edington in 878 that convinced a newly arrived Viking army to sail at winter's end for the Continent. At first this army used Ghent as the center for raiding, but soon ranged more widely. In 884 the annals of St. Vaast mourned that "along all the roads there lie bodies of the clergy and laity, of nobles and others, of women, children, and infants: there is not a road not strewn with the bodies of slain Christians." The following year the army headed south to the Seine Valley and from November 885 to November 886 besieged Paris. In 892 the great Viking army and the army of the Loire (by then in Picardy) sailed from a land suffering from famine and disease, consequences of an exceptionally bad harvest. Many went to England.

The settlement—and final—phase began about the year 900. The Vikings who came to the lands of the Franks at this time were intent on settlement. An attempt was made to establish a settlement in the region of the Loire around Nantes, and Viking rule there was recognized in the 920's by the Franks, but in 937 Alan Crooked-Beard, the Breton leader, drove them out. The settlement in Normandy, their only successful settlement in Francia, has its origins clouded in mist: no document exists to establish that an agreement was made in 911 between King Charles the Simple and the Viking leader Rollo. In that year Rollo's army was defeated at Chartres and by 913 he was described as a Christian ruler having authority in Rouen. Some agreement was reached at that general time by which the Vikings settled the lower Seine and, in return, undertook the defense of the region. The original area—its precise size is unknown—was added to in 924 and again in 933 to form the extent of the medieval duchy of Normandy. Within two generations the new colony had largely taken shape. Settlers came mainly from Denmark, but others migrated from northeastern England and from Ireland. Assimilation took place rapidly, and in the third generation Rollo's grandson Richard I (942–996) was sent from Rouen, the Viking capital, to Bayeux to learn Viking ways. His mother was a Frankish princess, and Richard himself was to become espoused to a Frankish princess. Normandy was a French province by the middle of the tenth century. The Northmen entered into a feudal society, took Christian names, and abandoned their language. Few traces of the Viking past survive in France, only some nautical words (such as *bâbord* [larboard], *hâvre* [harbor]) and place-names ending in *-bec, -bu, -dique,* and *-tot.*

THE DANES IN ENGLAND

For nearly 200 years the Vikings dominated English history. Scarcely a page of the *Anglo-Saxon Chronicle* for the period fails to mention the "heathen." The attacks on Lindisfarne and northern England in the 780's and 790's were by Norwegians and belong to the migrations that took them to Scotland and then island-hopping across the North Atlantic. But it was the Danish Vikings who attacked England in 835 and remained a presence till the time of Cnut (*d.* 1035). They came to England in two waves (835–954 and 980–1035), a period of relative peace intervening. A settlement of sizable proportions accompanied these waves.

The same forces in Denmark that propelled the Vikings into northern Francia in 834 undoubtedly sent them to England in the following year. For the first thirty years they attacked regularly but only seasonally, striking mainly coastal places in southern England, according to the *Chronicle* (which may provide only part of the picture). The pattern changed in 865: "A great army came to England and set up winter quarters in East Anglia" (*Anglo-Saxon Chronicle*). Its purpose was to take land and establish settlements. With horses taken in East Anglia this Viking army moved north to take York, which, weakened by internal discord, fell easily on All Saints Day, 866. The following year they traveled south, moving at ease through the kingdom of Mercia, and returned to York in 869. Later that year the Danes were in East Anglia, where they defeated the East Anglians, giving the local king, Edmund, martyrdom and sainthood.

Wessex lay before them. The rich lands of the West Saxons, watered by the Thames and lesser rivers, were to be defended by Alfred, the local king. His brother Ethelred led the Wessex defense in 870/871. Soon after his brother's death Alfred sued for peace, and the Vikings turned on London and other parts of Mercia. In 875 the Viking army split. Halfdan, one of the Viking leaders, went north and in the following year "shared out Northumbria between himself and his men, and his army was soon ploughing land and living off it" (*Anglo-Saxon Chronicle*). The other part of the army turned on Wessex. No effective defense was made and the Vikings moved easily in Wessex before making peace. They then divided Mercia in two, sharing out for themselves the lands of East (Danish) Mercia. The remaining Vikings returned to Wessex in January 878, intent upon taking land. Alfred retreated into the marshes of Somerset to prepare for a spring offensive. When spring came, Alfred's men defeated the Danes, led by Guthrum, at Edington. Defeated but not nearly decimated, the Danes returned to their base at Chippenham, where, after a two-week siege by Alfred, Guthrum sued for peace. The battles at Edington and Chippenham did not witness total victory for the West Saxons nor unconditional surrender by the Vikings. Guthrum was baptized and confirmed in the Christian religion and agreed to leave Wessex. The Vikings were still active in Mercia, East Anglia, and Northumbria. In 886 Alfred seized London and established the Mercian ealdorman (king?) Ethelred in authority. Guthrum and Alfred agreed to a boundary between their lands: west along the Thames from its mouth, up the Lea, then the Ouse to Watling Street, its western boundary. How far north Guthrum's kingdom extended is unclear, perhaps to the Welland and upper Avon. Other Viking kingdoms existed further north. To call these Danish-held lands north of the Alfred-Guthrum line the "Danelaw" implies a political unity and a single law north of that line, which, in fact, was not the case at that time.

Alfred had still to contend with fresh Viking invasions. The great army driven from Francia in 892 by famine and pestilence sailed for England. Alfred's defensive system consisted of fortified places principally along the coast and the rivers Avon (Bristol) and Thames, that is, on the perimeter of Wessex: it was a defense of Wessex, not England. The Danes during the four years of this campaign used Watling Street freely and enjoyed successes in Mercia and East Anglia. A stalemate was obvious in 896, and some of the Viking soldiers settled in Northumbria and East Anglia, while others returned to the Continent in search of adventure.

The picture of Viking ships sailing up the riverways of England in these campaigns is far from the truth. The Viking attacks upon the inland portions of England were not by ships but by horse over Roman roads and, to some extent, over the prehistoric and Anglo-Saxon trackways. Roman engineers had constructed thousands of miles of road, still in sufficient repair in the ninth century to allow men on horse to pass. Horses were used in the campaigns in the 860's in Northumbria and Mercia. Roman roads led the Vikings into Wessex and, after the Battle of Edington, into the rich fields of East Anglia. A system of roads centered on Cirencester. Later, in 893, the Danes took Buttington on the river Severn, and, while being besieged there by the English, "they despaired for lack of food and ate most of their horses" (*Anglo-Saxon Chronicle*).

The extension of the power of the West Saxon kings to the Midlands was accomplished by King Alfred's son and daughter. Edward the Elder (899–924) and his sister the Mercian queen Ethelfled (Æthelflæd, 911–918), "the lady of the Mercians," successfully engaged the Vikings in battles between 911 and 917—fortresses built in Mercia featured in this success—with the result that in 918 Edward the Elder controlled all of England south of the Welland and, soon, extended his authority to the Humber. Northumbria remained under Viking control.

The Viking kingdom of York lasted about three-quarters of a century (876–954), falling then to the descendants of Alfred, who were destined to unify England. This Viking kingdom replaced the English kingdom of Northumbria on the northern political scene. Its western boundary was not permanently fixed at the Pennines; in a situation that was never static, the kings of York at times exercised power west of the Pennines and even, for a short time, as far as Dublin. An early Viking king, Guthfrith, received Christian obsequies at York Minster about 895, and coins bearing Christian symbols were being minted at York by about the year 900, symbols of the rapid conversion of the Viking settlers. A hoard of coins, numbering over 7,000, was found at Cuerdale on the river Ribble in Lancashire in 1840. The hoard contained no coins minted after 903, when they were buried. Cuerdale is situated on what was the Dublin-to-York route,

and this hoard is an early testimony to what was to become the Dublin-York axis. When three Danish kings of York died in battle at Tettenhall in 910, a power vacuum was created in the north, and into this moved Ragnald, a Norseman from Dublin. He set himself up as king in York by 919, and Norse kings were to rule York till 954 save for a twelve-year period (927–939) of English rule under Athelstan, grandson of King Alfred. After Athelstan's death the restoration of Viking power was never complete and was always vulnerable. Eric (Eirik) Bloodaxe (an undeserved soubriquet) died at Stainmore in 954 and with him the political control of Northumbria by the Vikings.

Excavations at York in the years after 1972 have exposed aspects of life in the city of York during the Viking period. At the Coppergate site the remains of three buildings were discovered, as were evidences of woodworking and jewelry making. Other sites revealed signs of other manufacture, particularly metalwork and leatherwork. Trade is also shown by the discovery of goods manufactured abroad: silk probably from the East, wine jars from the Rhineland, and whetstones from Norway. Like Dublin, York was part of a northern trading network. St. Oswald's biographer, writing about the year 1000, described York as "a city greatly enriched by the wealth of merchants, who came from everywhere but especially from the Danish people."

A major migration of Danes came to England behind the shield of their conquering armies and settled large portions of England north of the Alfred-Guthrum line. Their coming is unrecorded by contemporary sources but is compellingly evidenced by place-name and linguistic arguments. The density of places bearing Scandinavian names argues for a density of settlement. In parts of Lincolnshire, for example, nearly 75 percent of the place-names are Scandinavian. Hybrid place-names, such as those with English -*tun* preceded by a Scandinavian name (Grimston, Barkston) probably indicate lands previously held by English and seized by Danes. Place-names ending in -*by* (Danby, Selby), of which there are nearly 800, probably refer to lands not previously in use. Place-names ending in -*thorp* (Scunthorpe, Weaverthorpe) seem to indicate poorer lands that were settled later. The English language has been influenced more by the Danes than by any other external agent. Hundreds of words came into the language—often ordinary words (*happy, ill, law, call*) that simply replaced the existing English equivalents. Profound changes in the structure of the language occurred; a clear pronominal form developed for the third-person plural. A period of bilingualism was followed by "Anglo-Scandinavian," that is, a conflation of Old English and the *dönsk tunga*.

The size of the Danish migration can never be known with certainty, but it must have numbered in the thousands and clearly outnumbered the Danish settlers in Normandy. The assumption that the Danish settling of England was virtually complete by the fall of Eric Bloodaxe in 954 needs revision in view of evidence of continued Danish migration even into the eleventh century.

The second wave (980–1035) of Viking attacks reflects the development in Denmark of the early stages of a state. These campaigns were led by national leaders—members of the royal family and their generals—and were, in fact, national campaigns. The English king Ethelred, known to posterity as "the Unready," was unequal to the challenge. He paid danegeld in 991, 994, 1002, 1007, and 1009, an aggregate sum of over 100,000 pounds of silver. On St. Brice's Day (13 November), 1002, he ordered the slaughter of all the Danes, probably the new Danes, in England. To no avail, for Svein in 1014 and Cnut in 1016 seized the English crown. Cnut, king of England from 1016 to 1035, became king of Denmark in 1019 and king of Norway in 1028, the leader of a mighty Scandinavian "empire," but he made no attempt to create a unitary rule. As befitted his prominence in European affairs, Cnut attended the imperial coronation in Rome in 1027 and in the 1030's arranged his daughter's marriage to the eldest son of the emperor. The attempt of Harald Hardråde, king of Norway, to gain England failed in 1066 at Stamford Bridge, days before the descendants of Rollo attacked England from Normandy.

THE SWEDES IN RUSSIA

The river systems of eastern Europe were to the Swedes what the Roman roads of England were to their Danish cousins. The Valdai Hills, situated about 200 miles (355 km) northwest of modern Moscow, contain the sources of four great Russian rivers: Western Dvina, Lovat, Dnieper, and Volga. They and their tributaries, connected by portages, provided the Vikings with access to the deepest parts of eastern Europe and beyond. When they came to rule at Novgorod, they entered the area through the Gulf of Finland and the river Neva into Lake Ladoga, and from there along the river Vol-

khov to Novgorod. *The Russian Primary Chronicle* tells the story under the years 860/867:

> The tributaries of the Varangians drove them back beyond the sea and, refusing them further tribute, set out to govern themselves. There was no law among them, and they began to war one against another. They said to themselves, "Let us seek a prince who may rule over us and judge us according to law." They, accordingly, went overseas to the Varangian Rus. These particular Varangians were known as Rus just as others are called Swedes, others Norse, others Angles, and others Goths, for they were thus named. The Chuds, the Slavs, the Krivichians, and the Ves said to the people of the Rus, "Our land is great and rich, but there is no order in it. Come to rule and reign over us." They thus selected three brothers, with their kinfolk, who took with them all the Rus and migrated. The oldest, Rurik, located himself in Novgorod; the second, Sineus, at Beloozero; and the third, Truvor, in Izborsk. On account of these Varangians the district of Novgorod became known as the land of the Rus.

Soon thereafter, the chronicle continues, two Varangians and their men set sail from Novgorod in Lake Ilmen, then went down the Lovat to the Dvina and thence to the Dnieper, portaging where necessary. They seized a hilltop town, Kiev, which was to become their principal city.

No doubt should exist about the identity of these Varangian Rus: they were Swedes. The chronicle is not the only witness. Under the year 839 the *Annals of St. Bertin,* the contemporary Frankish court chronicle, relates that in that year an embassy from Constantinople came to Louis the Pious at Ingelheim near Mainz. With the embassy were two men who called themselves "Rhos." The emperor inquired who they were, and he was told that they were Swedes. Liutprand of Cremona corroborates this testimony. In addition, artifacts of Scandinavian origin were unearthed at Staraya Ladoga on the Volkhov seven miles (11.2 km) south of Lake Ladoga at ninth-century levels: a runic-inscribed wooden stick, a bronze brooch, four gaming pieces, a bronze needle case, and leather shoes tapering to a triangle in the Swedish fashion. The date of the coming of the Rus into these places cannot be given precisely despite the dating in the chronicle, notorious for its unreliability in matters of chronology. Probably sometime during the first or second decade of the ninth century those Viking Swedes called Rus came to the area near Novgorod and not much later to Kiev. The earliest reference, in the Frankish chronicle under 839, concerns ambassadors from the *chaganus* (king) of the Rus to Constantinople. Their leader lived most likely either at Novgorod or, many suggest, at Kiev.

In 860 the Vikings, already well established at Novgorod and Kiev, were attacking Constantinople itself. With a force perhaps 8,000 warrior-seamen strong they appeared unexpectedly on the Bosporus, struck the Golden Horn, and attacked the Islands of the Princes in the Sea of Marmara, where the exiled patriarch Ignatius witnessed the sacred vessels stolen and twenty-two of his servants cut in pieces by Viking axes. The patriarch Photios preached during the raid and asked his hearers, "Why has this dreadful bolt fallen on us out of the farthest north?" He lamented, "Woe is me that I see a fierce and savage tribe fearlessly poured round the city, ravaging the suburbs, destroying everything, ruining everything—fields, houses, herds, beasts of burden, women, old men, youths—thrusting their swords through everything, taking pity on nothing, sparing nothing." The aim of the Rus was to seize booty and, perhaps, to see the world's greatest city (Michelgard or Miklagarðr, as they called it, "the great city"). After they sailed back into the Black Sea, Photios once again mounted his pulpit:

> An obscure nation, a nation of no account, a nation ranked among slaves, an unknown nation now gaining fame because of its expedition against us . . . a nation dwelling somewhere far from our country, barbarous, nomadic, armed with arrogance, unwatched, unchallenged, leaderless, has suddenly appeared in the twinkling of an eye like a wave of the sea, poured over our frontiers, and, as a wild boar, has devoured the inhabitants of our land like grass or straw or a crop.

But peaceful days and peaceful pursuits followed. Trade agreements were reached in 907 and 911, by which Rus merchants were encouraged by promise of food supplies and even baths and by freedom from taxes on their goods to trade with the Greeks. Thirty years of peaceful commercial relations between the Kievan Rus and Byzantium apparently followed these agreements. The Rus king Igor broke the peace when, in 941, he sailed with a fleet of a thousand vessels against Constantinople. The Italian envoy to Constantinople, Liutprand of Cremona, did not reach there till 949, but his stepfather, an eyewitness of the Viking attack, told him of it. The attackers, he related, were *Nordmanni* (the term used in the West for the Scandinavians), who took advantage of the absence of the Greek fleet. The emperor put into service fifteen retired ships, outfitted them with fire-throwers fore and aft, and sent them into the midst of the Viking ships. Burning oil was shot through tubes upon the Rus. "Seeing the flames," Liutprand reported, "they hurled themselves into the sea, preferring water to fire; some sank, weighed down by their breastplates and helmets, and others caught fire." Three years later a formidable Viking fleet reappeared, but the emperor Romanos I Lekapenos bought peace with tribute and gifts. Shortly thereafter, about 950, a manual on diplomacy (*De administrando imperio*) was prepared secretly by Emperor Constantine Porphyrogenitos for his son. The Pechenegs, it said, lived between the Rus and Byzantium, and it was central to the foreign policy of the Greeks to be at peace with the Pechenegs, who would hold the Rus in check. In 957 the same emperor received at court the Swedish-born princess of the Rus of Kiev, Olga, Igor's widow. She returned to Kiev a Christian and sent for a German missionary, Adalbert of Trier, whose mission was not successful. Her son Svyatoslav tried to establish a Rus settlement on the Danube. He was defeated by Emperor John I Tzimiskes, and the two leaders met to conclude peace at the Danube: the emperor with a magnificent retinue, the Rus king pulling an oar with fellow oarsmen, distinguished only by the cleanness of his clothes and a gold earring.

Christianity came to the Rus in the years immediately after 989, when their ruler Vladimir, a notorious womanizer—"erat enim fornicator immensus et crudelis" (Thietmar)—was converted. A mass baptizing took place in the Dnieper at Kiev. The new religion was to be Greek in form but Slavonic in language. Thereafter, the already existing commercial ties with Byzantium became even closer. By the year 1000 a band of Rus (the Varangian Guard) formed the palace guard for the emperor in Constantinople. Harald Hardråde, who fell at Stamford Bridge in Yorkshire in 1066, had served as a prominent member of the Varangian Guard.

Contacts were also made by the Rus with the world of Islam, mostly business dealings but also occasionally hostile encounters. They met at commercial centers like Bulgar at the Volga bend. The Vikings dealt in furs and, less importantly, slaves. Ibn Fadlan, the Arab ambassador from Baghdad to the Bulgars in 922, met these traders there. He had never seen such perfect physical specimens, he wrote. Each Rus man was armed with an axe, a sword, and a knife, and his arms were totally tattooed. Ibn Fadlan witnessed a Russian funeral, in which the body of a chieftain was placed on a ship with a slave girl and then cremated. A Rus standing nearby said to him, "You Arabs are fools because you take the people whom you love and respect and put them in the ground to be eaten by worms, whereas we burn our loved ones and in an instant they enter paradise."

Into the Caspian Sea the Rus relentlessly came. Whether they reached Baghdad in the ninth century is not clear and probably not of great moment, for the questionable account of such an adventure must refer to a very small group. Of undoubted importance is their later activity in the region of the Caspian. A fleet of perhaps 500 Viking vessels entered this area in 913 from the Crimea by way of the river Don and a portage to the Volga. They raided at will along the shores of this hitherto peaceful sea, seizing slaves and valuable objects. The Khazars, who guarded the lower Volga, hearing of these devastations, inflicted a stinging defeat on the Rus upon their return. A later band of Rus tried in 943 to establish themselves at Berda in Azerbaijan but failed. And twenty-two years later the great Svyatoslav destroyed the Khazar capital of Itil, "leaving," in the words of a visitor, "not a grape or a raisin, not even a leaf on a tree."

The Rus became Slavs: not in a moment, but when the slavicization was completed, it was total. Between 839 and 1043 the Rus (never more than a minority) became Slavs, and the Slavic people with whom they lived took their name. The eleventh-century Rus can be called Russians, a truly Slavic people. In this steady absorption the reign of Vladimir (ca. 978–1015) may be crucial. When he was converted to Christianity, he insisted that the language of the liturgy of the Rus be the language of the Slavs. Many graves of the early tenth century in the Kiev region still show definite Scandinavian characteristics, whereas by the second half of that century very few such graves are found and soon none at all. The process was so complete that the Russian language, save for a few place-names, bears no traces of Scandinavian influence.

CONCLUSION

The Viking Age ended in the mid eleventh century. New forces—a strong German emperor, a reformed church, new economic patterns—changed the complexion of Europe. The Viking force was spent. The Northmen had had their day, and an argument can be made that they provided the historical focus for the years from 800 to 1050. The dynamic factor in European history during these years was not the kingdom of the Franks, growing weaker each year with internal discord and a fracturing of authority. Impelled by forces that are still not clearly understood, warrior-seamen sailed out of the fjords of the northern peninsulas, soon reaching Vinland in the west, the Volga in the east, and Valencia in the south; England, Ireland, Scotland, France, and the Low Countries felt their impact; in uninhabited Iceland and Greenland they created communities; the river systems of eastern Europe led them to a land to which they gave their name. That such a forceful people, once settled in England, Scotland, Ireland, Normandy, and Russia, was absorbed and, in time, lost its Scandinavian character still puzzles. Their only surviving settlement, in Iceland, reached its zenith in the post-Viking period of poems and sagas, a testimony of fulfilled promise.

It would be wrong to see the Vikings as either farmers or barbarous warriors. Indeed, they were both. Their early raids were motivated by a thirst for silver, their later raids by a thirst for land. Neither silver nor land are taken from their owners without violence. After the thieving and the killing and the land-taking, they farmed and gradually became Englishmen, Irishmen, Scotsmen, Frenchmen, and Slavs. Meanwhile, at their old home, behind a veil not yet lifted, states were being formed, and the migration was over.

BIBLIOGRAPHY

Among the general books on the subject the reader should consult Holger Arbman, *The Vikings* (1961); Johannes Brøndsted, *The Vikings* (1965); Gwyn Jones, *A History of the Vikings* (1968, rev. ed. 1984); Thomas D. Kendrick, *A History of the Vikings* (1930); F. Donald Logan, *The Vikings in History* (1983), with bibliography at the end of each chapter; Lucien Musset, *Les invasions: Le second assaut contre l'Europe chrétienne (VIIe–XIe siècles)*, 2nd ed. (1971); and David M. Wilson, *The Vikings and Their Origin*, new ed. (1980). Dealing with Viking society is Peter G. Foote and David M. Wilson, *The Viking Achievement* (1970). James Graham-Campbell and Dafydd Kidd, *The Vikings* (1980), was published in conjunction with a Viking exhibit. Two studies on Denmark should be consulted: Klaus Randsborg, *The Viking Age in Denmark* (1980); and E. Roesdahl, *Viking Age Denmark* (1982).

For art see David M. Wilson and Ole Klindt-Jensen, *Viking Art*, 2nd ed. (1980); for religion see Edward O. G.

Turville-Petre, *Myth and Religion of the North* (1964); for ships see Anton W. Brøgger and Haakon Shetelig, *Viking Ships*, Katherine John, trans. (1951). Useful essays on various topics are found in Peter H. Sawyer, *The Age of the Vikings*, 2nd ed. (1971).

The Scottish aspect is discussed in A. W. Brøgger, *Ancient Emigrants: A History of the Norse Settlements of Scotland* (1929); and A. A. M. Duncan, *Scotland: The Making of the Kingdom* (1975). For Ireland see Françoise Henry, *Irish Art During the Viking Invasion, 800–1020* (1967); Kathleen Hughes, *Early Christian Ireland: Introduction to the Sources* (1972); and Donnchadh Ó Corráin, *Ireland Before the Normans* (1972). For the Vikings in the North Atlantic the reader may consult, in general, Gwyn Jones, *The Norse Atlantic Sagas* (1964); and Magnus Magnusson, *Viking Expansion Westward* (1973). Essential for Iceland are Knut Gjerset, *History of Iceland* (1924); Jón Jóhannesson, *A History of the Old Icelandic Commonwealth* (1974); and Dag Strömbäck, *The Conversion of Iceland* (1975). Greenland is discussed with magisterial authority in Finn Gad, *The History of Greenland*, I, *Earliest Times to 1700*, Ernst Dupont, trans. (1970). For Vinland see Jones, *Norse Atlantic Sagas* (above); the still-useful Geoffrey M. Gathorne-Hardy, *The Norse Discoverers of America* (1921); the translation by Magnus Magnusson and Hermann Pálsson of *The Vinland Sagas: The Norse Discovery of America* (1965); and Eric Wahlgren, *The Vikings and America* (1986). On specific issues see Anne Stine Ingstad, *The Discovery of a Norse Settlement in America: The Excavations at L'Anse aux Meadows, Newfoundland, 1961–1968*, 2 vols. (1977); Raleigh A. Skelton, Thomas E. Marston, and George D. Painter, *The Vinland Map and the Tartar Relation* (1965); and T. A. Cahill *et al.*, "The Vinland Map Revisited," in *Analytical Chemistry*, 59 (1987). A valuable interpretive essay on the Frankish lands is J. M. Wallace-Hadrill's *The Vikings in Francia* (1975). Much of interest can also be found in Marc Bloch, *Feudal Society*, L. A. Manyon, trans. (1961), esp. book 1, chap. 2; and in Einar Joranson, *The Danegeld in France* (1923). The essential books on England are Peter H. Blair, *An Introduction to Anglo-Saxon England*, 2nd ed. (1977); Henry R. Loyn, *The Vikings in Britain* (1977); Peter H. Sawyer, *From Roman Britain to Norman England* (1978) and *Kings and Vikings* (1982); and Sir Frank M. Stenton, *Anglo-Saxon England*, 3rd ed. (1971).

The reader may use as an introduction to the vast (and indeed, contentious) literature on the Vikings in Russia such general works as Hilda R. Ellis Davidson, *The Viking Road to Byzantium* (1976) and "Varangian Problems," in *Scando-Slavica*, suppl. 1 (1970). Of specific interest are Robert J. Kerner, *The Urge to the Sea: The Course of Russian History* (1942); and A. P. Vlasto, *The Entry of the Slavs into Christendom* (1970).

F. DONALD LOGAN

[See also **Alfred the Great; Byzantine Empire: History; Cnut the Great; Danelaw; Denmark; England, Anglo-Saxon; Exploration by Western Europeans; Gotland; Iceland; Ireland; Kievan Rus; Landnámabók; Luitprand of Cremona; Navies, Western; Navigation: Western European; Normans and Normandy; Norway; Novgorod; Photios; Runes; Scandinavia (Before 800); Scandinavian Mythology; Scotland; Ships and Shipbuilding, Northern European; Sweden; Varangian Guard; Vinland Sagas; Vladimir, St.**]

VILLAGES: COMMUNITY. Each village settlement created during the Middle Ages physically framed the lives of its inhabitants. They formed therein a little local society, a village community. Daily face-to-face encounters among neighbors in these small rural communities were the principal social environment for most Europeans from the early Middle Ages to the nineteenth century.

The solidarity of common interests encouraged development of village institutions. Many communities came to exercise more or less de facto autonomy in local affairs, to regulate the collective life of their members, and even to obtain formal recognition as collectivities. By the end of the Middle Ages village communities were becoming in much of Europe the primary territorial unit of government as well as of social interaction in the countryside.

For a long time, historians failed to recognize that there *was* a history of villages in medieval Europe—that there was in fact change over time. The common impression was of rural stability "from time immemorial," and this impression was aided by the documents from which history is written. Village affairs penetrated but rarely into the consciousness of the literate elite and the records they kept. Only when villages started to disappear in the nineteenth century did historians begin to explore the individual social and institutional histories of medieval villages, to delineate regional patterns, and, as here, to suggest provisionally some general features of medieval village life and development.

SOCIAL STRUCTURE

Medieval villages were more usually hierarchical than egalitarian places. Nearly everyone lived and worked in a household whose members combined household resources and their productive labor to provide for their collective needs. The core of most households was a single nuclear (or conjugal) family—a married couple and their unmarried children—around whom often clustered unmarried relatives and servants. Individual roles in the household derived largely from age and sex, with the senior active male normally preeminent within and spokesman without for the entire household. From many regions for much of the Middle Ages our usual historical documents tell only about the heads of household, the recorded tenants, who often bore legal responsibility for all who lived under their authority. A village community thus grouped households, not individuals. Also in the village, but not of it, would be the parish priest. In addition, the village might contain the residence of a seignior, who would live in his house only part-time if, as was often the case, he had other lands and residences.

Village households varied significantly in their economic standing. Where documents survive to measure households' command over productive resources, notably farmland, precise or even rough equality is an exception limited to settlers recently endowed with equal shares in a newly established village. More normal were situations like that in the thirteenth-century English West Midlands, where but one tenant household in four possessed thirty acres (twelve hectares), one in three about half that much, and nearly one in two was an almost landless cottar. In areas less overpopulated than the grain-growing plains of the West Midlands, the largest group of village households often had farms of middling size (by whatever local standard) and lesser numbers larger and smaller holdings.

Population density varied in the Middle Ages not only by region but also over time. Just as the fertile plains were the most heavily exploited areas, so the thirteenth and early fourteenth centuries saw, in most areas, the peak of population for the entire Middle Ages. Peasants living after the Black Death of the fourteenth century generally encountered less competition for land; and in the lightly populated early Middle Ages there was no shortage of land, but rather a shortage of peasants. In such circumstances, peasants were far less likely to hold lands too small to support their households.

The economic disparities of the village were paralleled by social ones, with members of some families holding village office repeatedly through generations, more obtaining only occasional authority, and others none at all. Commonly, but not invariably, holders of the larger peasant farms exerted a dominant and lasting influence in village affairs, while the poorly endowed tended to be powerless and even ephemeral members of the community.

EARLY COMMUNITY DEVELOPMENT

No single influence shaped the medieval European village community. It grew from physical proximity, neighborly cooperation, economic needs, the decentralization of judicial authority, and the pressures of lordly interests. Communities identified with villages emerged during the ninth through twelfth centuries and spread and developed through the later Middle Ages because they proved useful to people living in them and ruling them.

The conjugal family households that inhabited the isolated farms, hamlets, and other motile sites of the late Iron Age and earliest Middle Ages did not identify their settlement units as communities. Their sense of community extended from family to kindred to a larger ethnic or tribal entity. But with the progressive weakening of kinship ties these families formed new groupings based less upon blood links than upon residence in the same territory and the consequent mutual economic and social interests. Where genuine village settlements emerged precociously, these nucleations could themselves become foci for social cooperation. More commonly, however, our documents reveal (at different times in different parts of Europe) a prior stage of territorial communities, associations of people who lived in a common neighborhood, though not necessarily in a single or even a spatially stable site. Vernacular names for these communities varied, but written texts as distant as early Germanic law codes from the west and ducal charters from twelfth-century Poland indicate by their use of the same Latin term, *vicinia*, or neighborhood, the essential quality of the territorial community. Territorial communities enforced local law and order, met the demands of public or other authority, and regulated access to the non-arable resources of the neighborhood used by all resident households. Land under the plow, however, belonged to and was controlled by individual households, not the collectivity. Of mechanisms for common action in the *viciniae* we know little, though they clearly assumed cooperation among relative equals. Beside such territorial communities coexisted more hierarchical structures, the great households with their *familiae* of slaves and their *villae* (manors) of dependent peasants, both under the direct authority of a master and hence not communal in quality at all.

As early in some places as the ninth century new pressures caused the incremental replacement of territorial communities with more tightly integrated village communities. The essential prerequisites were the concentration of settlement and consequent intensification of interaction among farming households. These variously reflected and reinforced the effects of expanded seigniorial control over rural people, of safety in numbers, and of increasing emphasis on arable agriculture to meet the demand of growing populations. The enduring double function of the village as a lordly and a neighborly institution permanently revealed its mixed origin.

Common interests of inhabitants made of the village a primary node in the web of their collective relationships and reciprocal obligations. They increasingly shared subjection to the authority of a landowner and seignior. Most lords imposed some obligations on the collectivity of their subjects living in one place; both lord and peasants saw the usefulness of at least informal structures jointly to allocate, collect, disburse, or even oppose these. Labor services in particular required some degree of organization, most usefully provided by the peasants themselves—or at least by a knowledgeable member of their community.

Village churches, mostly established at local initiative about this same time, also drew allegiances to the village. In much of England, France, Italy, and Germany parish boundaries coincided with those of villages; elsewhere they could encompass several settlements. Normally the parishioners came to claim some joint responsibility for the church building.

Almost everywhere villagers also possessed the right of the collective use of economically critical nonarable resources: waste pasture, woodlands, water, and meadows. Common agreement assured access to each household. And wherever people lived in the new or increased propinquity of a village, everyday interactions heightened their sense of familiarity, group consciousness, and concern for what the Germans called *Nachbarschaft* and the French *voisinage,* their mutual "neighbor-hood." A degree of de facto mutual self-governance was inevitable.

The clearest forms of new village communities appeared by 1200 on the open fields of the northern European plain, where the symbiosis of grain and stock-raising on intermingled and unfenced strips of all farming households compelled a shift from neighborly cooperation to collective control over farming practice. In what from the institutional perspective is best called a "common-field" village, adjacent strip parcels of different landholders were managed in common. The labor input and grain output of each strip were exclusive to its holder, but a parcel not under crop lay open to the common use of animals grazing on the stubble or the weeds of the fallow.

This common use compelled agreement among all holders of strips in a furlong on such issues as crop rotations and dates of planting and harvest. Individual management had to defer to the collective benefit of augmented pasture resources and improved manuring of the land. Joint management of furlongs was perhaps known in some northern French and Flemish villages by the time of Charlemagne.

Collective control over farming practice by furlong units could, however, interfere with each household's need always to have equal parts of its land at each phase of the rotational cycle. The logical next step was to coordinate management of the village's furlong units on a village-wide basis, and even to redistribute the land. This was evidently occurring by the twelfth century, when closely regulated village-wide cropping systems were being installed in villages of, for example, the Rhine Palatinate, southern Sweden, and parts of the English Midlands.

Because the agricultural practices of local peasants differed little one from another and formed an annual routine, collective decisions soon became a matter of locally recognized custom, later written down as village bylaws, *Weistümer,* or *coutumes.* Even where several lords had divided a village, intermingled peasant lands and interests compelled villagers to recognize their own community.

COMMUNITY INSTITUTIONS AND THEIR OPERATION

From the twelfth century village institutions can be seen evolving to meet the needs of peasants, who were exploited by nonpeasants but also internally divided in their interests.

The notion of the village itself as a legal entity probably arose first from practical recognition that its territory comprised a special jurisdiction, a "peace." *Paix* even came to denote "village territory" or "township" in parts of France. But that the human community of villagers had corporate identity emerged more slowly, in part because secular legists saw these people, if at all, as dependents and objects of lordly rights. Organizations of ostensibly religious purpose thus commonly first achieved recognized standing: in pious confraternities or parish councils (which came to be elected by French villagers in the thirteenth century at the latest), villagers identified and developed community solidarity. Secular equivalents appeared when groups of neighbors negotiated with their lord to replace dues in labor or produce with cash; or, as is seen after the fact in some twelfth-century English villages, when they moved jointly to take over demesne land for a fixed annual sum.

Secular sworn associations of villagers, frequently called communes, drew upon such rural traditions and also emulated better-documented urban precedents. The recognized village communes that spread eastward in Germany after 1150 were likely modeled on municipal charters from the eleventh-century Low Countries. In northern France the Law of Beaumont-en-Argonne, granted in 1182 and much copied, established genuine self-governing rural communes. Less formal (or perhaps simply less well-recorded) Italian analogues were soon absorbed by the expanding Italian city-states as tools of local administration. By the thirteenth century such arrangements were familiar enough that legists debated (inconclusively) whether a village might be a *universitas,* or a "mystical body," or some other recognized form of corporation.

Most medieval village communities had no corporate charter, just tacit acceptance as associations somehow capable of dealing with their lords, concluding agreements, or acting collectively in other ways. These oral activities of illiterate villagers became historically visible when they affected members of the literate elite. Whole villages in twelfth- and thirteenth-century France negotiated charters of liberties from their lords. Others there and in England brought to royal courts their suits opposing seigniorial demands or threats against their own use of commons. Still other communities are recognizable only in the "conspiracies" against which elite authors railed.

Both officially sanctioned associations and more covert village communities had comparable internal features and functions.

Active participation in communal decision-making was almost always restricted to certain people. The decision-making group normally included all heads of village households, but often enough it was restricted to an even smaller group of the better-endowed. In most German-speaking areas these were the "full peasants" (*Vollbauer*), with a certain, usually sizable, holding; around Zurich, in Lower Saxony, and in much of England they possessed specific farms, presumably the oldest in the village. Control over village decisions let the better-off villagers defend their relative position by managing common resources in their own interests, by restricting the entry of newcomers, or by allowing only those smallholders who had labored in the harvest to glean fallen grains from the emptied fields. This power was exercised at a public village assembly, which met at regular intervals or at the call of a headman, a village council, or a lord, and might be combined with sessions of the local court.

Where communities had only informal identity, temporary syndics or proctors might act for them on specific matters as they arose, but in most communities the terms of local officials gave continuity from one assembly to another. They provided both lord and peasants a person who was responsible for their interaction. In England and other regions of strong lordly authority this official was often the reeve, a local man assigned by the lord each year the task of tending his interests and overseeing peasant performance of obligations. In eastern Germany the hereditary holder of a certain large farm held for life the office of *Schulze*; he chaired the village court and collected dues owed the lord or other claimants. Elsewhere, villagers might select their own head or rotate the office among them. Whatever the source of a headman's appointment, he played a key role as chief among the peasants, enforcer of external authority, and spokesman for the community. Associated with the headman in most villages was a small village council of prominent members of the community, who might be called elders, selectmen, assessors, or jurors. These elders often made up the court panel for the village, declaring the law (custom) and reaching a verdict under the leadership of the lord's judge.

Village communities served real needs of both the dominant and the less powerful villagers. Like the territorial communities before them, villages took much responsibility for local law and order, so dispute settlement was normally an important function. In much of central Europe, village courts handled most minor offenses, but elsewhere the court of first instance belonged to a seignior or territorial sovereign, even though local people there presented charges and participated in the judgment. Offenders against village sensibilities could also feel communal resentment more informally in the public mockery of a shivaree or even ostracism or expulsion. But preventive action to maintain social peace was even more generally pervasive. Communities fined the violent, the drunken, and the sharptongued; they appointed constables, ale-tasters, and keepers of stray beasts; some even enacted fire-prevention ordinances and invested in fire-fighting equipment. Emergency relief for the deserving local poor was "neighborly" and "Christian charity." It also meant that the poor were less likely to steal from their betters or to leave the village in search of a better life (thereby depleting the village's supply of agricultural laborers).

Besides managing common fields or common-land resources, village communities provided other economic facilities and services. Villages collectively built or leased from their lord mills, bake ovens, wine presses, and even forges. Where their pastoral needs required it, they pooled their beasts and hired a communal herder. Highly autonomous and self-conscious southwest German villages even had by the late fifteenth century their own local rules for weights, measures, prices, and wages.

The corporate village community provided a good vehicle for peasants to deal with the world surrounding the village. Defense of common rights took villages to court against lords and against nearby villages accused of encroaching on the lands or waters of the township. In parts of southern Germany groups of adjacent villages formed so-called *Mark* associations to manage jointly their corporate rights to the upland pastures that lay between them. Village vestrymen represented parishioners' interests against local rectors and more distant patrons or bishops. In Italian city-states village communes were responsible for tax collection, and their councils functioned as the local arm of the state government. First the bureaucratic church and then the growing state of the later Middle Ages presaged, in fact, the eventual modern subjection of European village communities to larger sociopolitical identities.

BIBLIOGRAPHY

Most rural social and institutional history is local or regional in scope and written in the language of the area studied. The following representative selection, mostly in English, covers topics relevant to medieval village communities and will lead to important earlier scholarship.

Warren O. Ault, *Open-Field Farming in Medieval England: A Study of Village By-laws* (1972); Karl S. Bader, *Studien zur Rechtsgeschichte des mittelalterlichen Dorfes*, 3 vols. (1957–1973); Marc Bloch, *French Rural History: An Essay on Its Basic Characteristics*, Janet Sondheimer, trans. (1966), 167–189; Jerome Blum, "The European Village as Community: Origins and Functions," in *Agricultural History*, 45 (1971), and "The Internal Structure and Polity of the European Village Community from the Fifteenth to the Nineteenth Century," in *Journal of Modern History*, 43 (1971)—the two Blum articles are together the best compendium of earlier scholarship on medieval and modern village communities throughout Europe; Edward Britton, *The Community of the Vill: A Study in the History of the Family and Village Life in Fourteenth-century England* (1977); Jean Chapelot and Robert Fossier, *The Village and House in the Middle Ages*, Henry Cleere, trans. (1985); Helen Clarke, *The Archaeology of Medieval England* (1984), esp. chap. 1; Barbara A. Hanawalt, *The Ties That Bound: Peasant Family Life in Medieval England* (1986), 90–107; R. H. Hilton, *A Medieval Society: The West Midlands at the End of the Thirteenth Century* (1966, repr. 1983), 65–166, and *The English Peasantry in the Later Middle Ages: The Ford Lectures for 1973 and Related Studies* (1975), 20–53; Richard C. Hoffmann, "Medieval Origins of the Common Fields," in William N. Parker and Eric L. Jones, eds., *European Peasants and Their Markets: Essays in Agrarian Economic History* (1975), 23–72.

George C. Homans, *English Villagers of the Thirteenth Century* (1941), a classic and pioneering work in village social history; William Chester Jordan, *From Servitude to Freedom: Manumission in the Sénonais in the Thirteenth Century* (1986), 61–96; Emmanuel Le Roy Ladurie, *Montaillou: Cathars and Catholics in a French Village, 1294–1324*, Barbara Bray, trans. (1978), filled with passing glimpses of social life in a pastoral community; J. Ambrose Raftis, *Tenure and Mobility: Studies in the Social History of the Mediaeval English Village* (1964) and, as ed., *Pathways to Medieval Peasants* (1981); Werner Rösener, *Bauern im Mittelalter* (1985), 155–176; Walter Schlesinger, *Die deutsche Ostsiedlung des Mittelalters als Problem der europäischen Geschichte* (1975).

RICHARD C. HOFFMANN

[See also **Agriculture and Nutrition; Class Structure; Commune; Corvée; Court Leet; Estate Management; Family; Feudalism; Fief; Field Systems; Hide; Magic and Folklore; Parish; Reclamation of Land; Reeve; Serfs and Serfdom; Syndic; Tenure of Land; Tithes; Tools, Agricultural; Urbanism.**]

VILLAGES: SETTLEMENT. From at least the tenth century onward, most medieval peasants lived in villages. These, and not the "manor" or equivalent forms of lordships (entities of domination and revenue extraction and not, strictly speaking, places where people lived), were the fundamental units of the medieval countryside.

Villages were the residences not just of peasants but of nobles and clergy as well. The English manor house and the Mediterranean castle were both integrated into the village fabric, indeed often determined both its location and its layout. Thirteenth-century Languedocian lords lived in houses next door to their peasant tenants, and everywhere village priests lived next door to their parishioners. Neighborliness led to sociability, even to intimacy, despite the pervasive sense of hierarchy. But, as villages developed political independence and self-consciousness, social differences also became fruitful sources of conflict.

The village organization of rural space dominated the grain-growing regions of northern Europe, the Mediterranean plain, and the pioneer lands of Spain and central and eastern Europe. Elsewhere—in the pastoral and mining areas of Devon and Cornwall and the west of France, in isolated regions of the southern Massif Central, in parts of the Pyrenees, the Alps, and the highlands of central Europe—individual farms remained scattered about the countryside, and village territories might be shared by several hamlets. Even where highly nucleated (and often fortified) village centers had become the rule in the thirteenth century, as in Provence and northern Italy, the taste for individual farms developed in the fourteenth, especially among the merchants, lawyers, and newly made nobility of prospering market, industrial, and administrative towns. Later, in the fifteenth and sixteenth centuries, numerous villages that had disappeared in the plague and wars of the fourteenth century were revived as individual farms, their fields incorporated into the parish and political structures of neighboring villages.

Historians commonly distinguish villages from market towns and cities. The word "village," however, applies to settlements of many different sizes, physical plans, and forms of economic activity, of differing social complexity and types of political organization. The boundary distinguishing villages from market towns is wide and vague, and in some exceptional cases a city by one definition may have been an agricultural village by another. In Italy,

Provence, and Languedoc, where some ecclesiastical dioceses were quite small, a few episcopal sees (commonly called *civitates*—"cities"—by medieval writers) were inhabited only by clergy and peasants, and thus looked—and smelled—like villages (for instance, Cavaillon and St. Papoul). In Provence, where a household census of settlements survives from the early fourteenth century, the places we would call villages ranged from hamlets with less than 10 households (less than 50 people) to well over 200 (over 1,000 people). These differences in population between one village and another suggest differences among them in economic and social complexity and a hierarchical ordering of the kind described by geographical "central-place theory"; but this problem has been little investigated by historians of medieval Europe.

A village consisted of both the built-up area (or areas) of houses, outbuildings, and gardens, and the surrounding fields from which its inhabitants drew their livelihood. In this it resembled the modern French rural *commune* or the New England town, and the most precise translation of the Latin word *villa,* at least from the eleventh century on (and perhaps before), is thus "township." The history of the village is the history of both fields and settlement.

ORIGINS

Unlike the village countryside of the Middle Ages, the Roman countryside was organized around individual farmsteads (*villae*) and trading posts (*vici*) along the roads. Except on the fringes of the empire (Wales, northern England, Frisia and other coastal regions of the Low Countries), there is as yet no archaeological evidence for pre-Roman rural settlements surviving into the Middle Ages in the lands conquered by Rome. Arguments have long been made that continuity of place-names from the Roman world to the medieval proves continuity of settlement from the fourth century to the eleventh, but such arguments are no longer widely accepted. The occasional location of medieval rural churches—often with associated cemeteries—on the sites of Roman villas suggests one possible form of continuity from antiquity to the Middle Ages, but such coincidences can be variously interpreted, and, in the absence of clear stratigraphical evidence, arguments drawn from them must remain hypothetical.

When in the Middle Ages did rural populations first begin to congregate in villages? Historians and archaeologists have proposed dates from the sixth century onward. Everywhere during the death throes of the old empire, rural dwellers reoccupied pre-Roman hill forts (as early as the third century at South Cadbury, England). Saxon and Frankish migrants brought with them into Britain and Gaul both their building techniques and their practice of hamlet settlement. Other Germanic peoples swept up in this migratory movement brought similar practices to western Germany. But these settlements, revealed by archaeology, were impermanent; we do not know how many may have given rise to later villages. Berber invaders brought to Spain a complex arrangement of castle-refuges and associated hamlets. These, likewise, were replaced by other forms of village settlement during the Reconquest.

Part of the problem in understanding the nature of discontinuities during the early Middle Ages comes from the complex and changing relationships between settlements and their associated townships.

Topographical studies in England show that village settlement sites were remarkably mobile. Saxon (and occasionally successive Saxon) sites were abandoned in favor of others in the eleventh century, and these were sometimes again abandoned in the twelfth and yet again in the reconstructions of the fifteenth and sixteenth centuries. Thus, although all but a few percent of the 13,418 place-names in Domesday Book have been identified, in the absence of archaeological work there is no way to tell how many surviving village centers that bear Domesday names are located on the same sites as those canvassed by King William's men. Similar mobility has been discovered on the Mediterranean coast of France and in the pioneer lands of central and eastern Europe. The transfer of parish rights from one church to another, abandoned churches in the countryside, abandoned hillside sites near lowland villages and vice versa, phenomena one finds widely on the Continent, show that this mobility was not peculiar to the British Isles.

It took many centuries for the rural settlement patterns of the central Middle Ages to come into being, and those patterns were rudely altered by the demographic and economic crises of the fourteenth and fifteenth centuries. Thus, the period when the individual farmsteads of the Roman countryside were abandoned (between the third and the seventh centuries, depending on the region) was not neces-

sarily the same period when the village centers of the period after 1000 were first settled, nor were those village centers necessarily the same as those that now exist. In some cases, of course, there may have been continuity from the early Middle Ages to the present; in one small region of western France, for example, Merovingian cemeteries have been found next to twenty village churches. But these cases, in all likelihood, were the exceptions rather than the rule.

By the year 1000, however, if not well before, inhabited sites appear to have moved within already well-defined village territories, territories that have remained relatively stable down to the twentieth century. Townships, therefore, have a different history from that of the settled sites within them. The oldest of them most probably had their boundaries defined and fields laid out well before the built areas within them achieved some measure of stability.

Continuity between late Roman estate boundaries and the boundaries of village territories has been suggested for England, but the evidence is highly indirect and circumstantial. A break in continuity can be demonstrated in those Mediterranean areas where the Romans imposed their checkerboard centuriation on the countryside. There, though village boundaries often follow major Roman roads as well as natural features of the landscape, they do not conform to the rectilinear, quadrilateral constraints of Roman field tracks. (Those parts of Italy where centuriation survives to the present day—parts of the Po Valley, the lower Arno—may prove to be exceptions.) And some Carolingian monastic estates that may have descended from late- or sub-Roman estates (for example, those of St. Victor of Marseilles) encompassed territories that by the year 1000 were divided among several villages. Yet documents from tenth-century Mediterranean lands reveal village territories with fixed boundaries, field roads (which can sometimes be identified with roads still in use), and organized fields. The most likely period for their creation seems to be the ninth century.

Within these village territories, the pattern of settlement evolved slowly, at rates that varied from region to region. In the Lazio, near Rome, seigniorial entrepreneurs were calling permanent walled settlements into being as early as the tenth century. In Languedoc the same reshaping began in the eleventh century and continued unabated in the twelfth. In Béarn, in the western Pyrenees, it did not occur until the thirteenth. On the Iberian Peninsula fortified villages progressed south with the Reconquest.

Data from a 1975 survey of 108 village excavations (principally in the Rhineland and north-central Europe) provide some idea of the settlement process over time. Between the first century B.C. and the third century A.D., settlement occurred on twenty-eight of the sites. Between the fourth and the sixth centuries A.D., settlement took place on twelve of the sites. Between the seventh and the ninth centuries, roughly the period of the great Carolingian expansion, thirty-nine sites were settled. In the troubled tenth century only six sites were newly settled; in the eleventh, seven were settled. Then, in the twelfth century, a period of rapid expansion, fifteen were settled. In the thirteenth century, only five were settled, and in the fourteenth, three.

A number of the sites were abandoned and resettled at a later date, which points up again the danger of assuming continuous occupation of a known village site. In addition, only fifteen of the settlements occupied between the sixth and the ninth century were still occupied in the twelfth, which reinforces the idea that the villages of the High Middle Ages cannot always—or even usually—trace their pedigrees back to Carolingian or earlier times.

Because excavation can only be done on abandoned sites, and many villages that are still inhabited were probably founded between the eighth and thirteenth centuries, the survey seriously undercounts the new foundations of the central Middle Ages. It nevertheless shows two significant peaks: in the Carolingian period (with the large majority disappearing by the end of that period), and in the twelfth century. These two peaks coincide with periods of rapid growth in the medieval economy, and therefore they are where we would expect them to be.

The data on abandonments are less easily explained, because the peaks occur in the ninth century (eleven cases) and the thirteenth (fourteen cases). These were both periods of economic expansion, and considerable new settlement was actually taking place while these sites were being abandoned.

Village abandonment, however, was not always the result of disaster. Some desertions, especially in the tenth, eleventh, fourteenth, and fifteenth centuries, were indeed provoked by destructive war, as in England when William the Conqueror brutally "harrowed the North," or in Normandy and southern France when equally brutal armies of the Hundred Years War scorched the countryside. Villages disappeared, however, not just because of plague and war but also because their inhabitants left for better opportunities elsewhere.

Much migration in the twelfth and thirteenth centuries was promoted by new seigniorial foundations, as lords and their hired agents (called *locatores, populatores,* or other similarly explicit terms) led Flemish peasant pioneers and drainage engineers to Germany, Germans to Bohemia, Silesia, Hungary, and Poland, Czechs to Hungary, Poles to the Ukraine, English to Ireland, French to Spain. Promoters were active not just in frontier areas but in the heartland of western Europe as well, offering forests to be cleared, swamps to be drained, moors and mountains for sheep and shepherds, and above all the privileges of low, fixed rents, a place along a trading road, markets, freedom from arbitrary justice and arbitrary demands. Kings, bishops, monasteries, petty lords, and urban governments individually and jointly turned into real-estate developers. Many migrants, however, may have gone no farther than from a hamlet to a village center in the same township, or from a settlement around a church to a settlement around a newly built castle. Many villages doubtless moved when villagers of their own initiative reorganized their fields and their settlements along with them, or simply built on the edge of the inhabited area and abandoned the older center, thus allowing the village to "drift" along a road, down a hill, or around a common.

This wave of twelfth- and thirteenth-century pioneering left on the map a permanent memento in the form of place-names that can definitely be traced to this period, of which the many Newtons, Villeneuves, Villanovas, Chateauneufs, Castetnaus, and Neuburgs are only the most obvious. It also left identifiable town and village forms, such as the grid plan of the *bastides* in southwestern France and the German and eastern European types described below.

FIELD STRUCTURES

By the thirteenth century, three kinds of field systems dominated the landscape. The English Midlands and the rich plain that stretched from northwestern France as far as Poland were lands of grain and grazing. This was the Europe of "open fields," where the arable was composed of long, narrow strips (10 to 20 meters wide, and anywhere from 100 to more than 1,000 meters long), grouped together in blocks that the English called "furlongs." When the village territory was most intensively organized (perhaps only after the thirteenth century), these furlongs in turn were grouped together for cropping purposes into large "fields." Both the individual peasant holdings and the lord's demesne lands consisted of strips scattered among different furlongs and fields. No hedges or other permanent barriers closed off the strips or the furlongs, which in the intervals between croppings were left open to grazing animals. The furlongs were physically divided from each other by field tracks, "headlands" (where turning plows threw up mounds of earth), or by natural features such as streams. In heavy soil, the strips themselves left physical remains in the form of alternating ridges and furrows that can still be seen in some English pastures. One example was found under a motte built before 1100, thus dating this feature to pre-Conquest England.

Documentary evidence shows open fields already in existence in the tenth century. There was no continuity, however, between Roman or "Celtic" fields and those of the Middle Ages. An eighth- or ninth-century date for the beginnings of open-field agriculture thus seems likely.

Several explanations have been offered for the creation and use of long strips: heavy plows drawn by teams of oxen worked most efficiently when turns were few (since turning took time), and thus the ideal length of a strip was the distance a team could pull before needing to rest ("furlong" means "furrow length"); clearing new furlongs was collective work, and long strips, with access at either end, were the most logical divisions of the new land; when dividing a block of land among heirs, or selling a portion of it, strips were likewise the most logical form of division. All of these reasons may have played a role. But the predominant reason may have been the symbiosis of grain and stock raising that this agricultural system assumed. Animal manure restored the fertility of the fields; and large fields (furlongs or groups of furlongs) over which the animals could freely graze were the most practical way to allow this.

In northern areas unsuited for the large-scale grain production of the open fields, another form of land use predominated: extensive pasture, orchards, and gardens were mixed with small fields wherever grain might easily grow. In the so-called "infield-outfield" system, a grain field near the settlement was cropped intensively (the "infield"), while elsewhere in the village (the "outfield") a portion of the rough pasture might be ploughed and cropped for a few years and then allowed to return to grass. When the fields and pastures in such areas were surrounded by permanent hedges these agrarian practices gave rise to the so-called *bocage* (hedgerow) landscape of northwestern France.

Sometimes these different types of agricultural landscapes came into being in close proximity to each other, as they did in the vicinity of Chartres (France): immediately to the west of the city was a region of dispersed farms, tiny hamlets, and *bocage*; immediately to the south and east was a plateau of nucleated settlements and open fields.

Mediterranean agriculture continued the Roman practice of mixed production. Gardens of beans, pulses, and root crops were planted just outside the village settlement, where they could be fertilized with household waste. Intensively cropped grain fields (*ferraginalia*) were created nearby. Beyond them lay vineyards, extensive grain fields, and olive and chestnut groves that supplied the rest of the Mediterranean diet, and also fields of flax and cannabis for industrial use. Hay fields along streams and rivers, pasture in the hills, and waste (*garriga*) were used to feed animals and to supply herbs for the table and plants and cochineal for dye. Here, as in the north, both seigniorial and peasant holdings were scattered, sometimes not just in the fields of their own village but in those of neighboring villages as well. The fields themselves were compact and approximately rectangular, bounded by field tracks and occasionally by stone walls, but, like the furlongs of the north, grouped together in sections that bore individual names. Hillsides were terraced, and, as in antiquity, irrigation, drainage, and flood control—with their attendant constraints—continued to preoccupy both lords and tenants. Vineyards, grain fields, and gardens tended to be grouped together, but this was never a general rule.

The reason for the shape of these fields may be that these lighter soils demanded only an ard for plowing, which was easier to maneuver than the heavy wheeled plow. It may also be the result of shifting use, as old vineyards were put to grain, and grain fields planted with vines or olives. But the principal reason may again have been the place of animals in the strucure of agriculture, here relegated to the margins of productive land because their appetites were so dangerous to vines, orchards, and gardens. Without the constraining need to convert arable to pasture and back again, fields could be more compact, self-contained, and ready for changing productive use.

None of these field systems were invented all at once. Around the Mediterranean, as in northern Europe, woods, swamp, open pasture, moor, garigue—and the pastoral and gathering activities they served—occupied a far larger portion of the countryside in the ninth and tenth centuries than they did in the thirteenth. With much land available, arable at that time may have consisted everywhere of large blocks of land held in severalty. Such an arrangement would have been consistent with a habitation pattern of hamlets and farmsteads (as it continued to be in those areas where nucleated village centers did not later develop), allowing easy access from houses and stables to fields nearby. Increasing population in the late Carolingian world must finally have required that more land be put to grain. The organization of Mediterranean fields, like those of the open fields, suggests cooperative assarting (land clearing) under seigniorial or communal direction, followed by division into separate holdings. With the spread of arable to the farther reaches of the village territories and further scattering of holdings, only a concentration of habitat near the center would have equalized everyone's access to their fields. Thus the enlargement of the arable and the nucleation of villages would have gone together. For the moment, however, this scenario is only a working hypothesis.

SETTLEMENT FORMS

In the late tenth century, lords began to build castles across the countryside. In the Mediterranean lands, these castles attracted settlements around them or nearby, settlements that in the course of the eleventh and twelfth centuries acquired their own fortifications. So common did these fortified villages become that by the year 1200 in many Mediterranean regions *castrum* was the usual Latin word for village. Fortification imposed a nearly circular or rectangular form on these settlements, with concentric rings forming as their population expanded.

Circular villages (*Rundlingen*) were also built in the Saale and middle Elbe regions of Germany, where German-speaking newcomers came into (sometimes hostile) contact with settled Slavic populations. Other settlement forms also reveal the origins and history of villages. Planned villages were often built on a regular grid around a central green or square or church or village meeting place (green villages, *Angerdörfer*). Woodland pioneer villages were often but one street wide (*Strassendörfer, Waldhufendörfer*), with fields stretching out towards the forest on either side. Marshland villages (*Marschhufendörfer*) along the North Sea coast and in the lower reaches of central European rivers were built where there was dry land, with the drained fields and canals stretching out into the water. If the settlement was also a parish center it had its church and cemetery, which served the community as meeting hall, market place, and occasionally as refuge or warehouse as well.

In the years of plague and war of the mid and late fourteenth century, most villages lost part of their population, and many villages disappeared entirely. (In Provence, 157 of the 577 settlements listed by the tax surveyors in 1471 had no inhabitants.) Reconstruction at the end of the fifteenth century often meant settling a new site. In the north, especially, it commonly meant more lasting construction. Village houses of earlier centuries rarely lasted more than one generation; some of those built around 1500 still survive. But, where the arable had not been totally abandoned, the new villagers continued to use the fields their earlier medieval predecessors had laid out. Thus the fields, rather than the settlements themselves, are often the best surviving physical testimony to the medieval village.

BIBLIOGRAPHY

Village history has tended to be local, regional, or national, rather than European-wide. The following are a few recent titles whose extensive notes or bibliographies will direct the reader to older literature.

England. Christopher Taylor, *Village and Farmstead: A History of Rural Settlement in England* (1983); Trevor Rowley, ed., *The Origins of Open-Field Agriculture* (1981). Studies of individual English counties have appeared since 1955 in the series *The Making of the English Landscape,* edited by W. G. Hoskins and Roy Millward. M. W. Beresford and J. K. S. St. Joseph, *Medieval England: An Aerial Survey,* 2nd ed. (1979), presents photographs of villages and field systems with commentary.

France. Jean Chapelot and Robert Fossier, *The Village and House in the Middle Ages,* Henry Cleere, trans. (1985). G. Démians d'Archimbaud, *Les fouilles de Rougiers* (1980), is a model excavation report.

Germany. Herbert Jankuhn, Rudolf Schützeichel, and

and Fred Schwind, eds., *Das Dorf der Eisenzeit und des frühen Mittelalters* (1977); Werner Rösener, *Bauern im Mittelalter* (1985).

Italy. G. Cherubini, "La campagne italiane dall'XI al XV secolo," in G. Galasso, ed., *Storia d'Italia,* IV (1981); Aldo Settia, *Castelli e villaggi nell'Italia padana* (1984). R. Comba, "*Stirpere nemus et colere terram*: Espansione dei coltivi e restrutturazioni insediativi fra X e XIII secolo," in R. Comba, *Metamorfosi di un paesaggio rurale* (1983), 25–102, and Pierre Toubert, *Les structures du Latium médiéval* (1973), 199–549, are examples of Italian regional studies.

The essays in Walter Schlesinger, ed., *Die deutsche Ostsiedlung des Mittelalters als Problem der Europäischen Geschichte* (1975), also include studies of new settlement in Spain, southwest France, the Netherlands, and Russia.

The major medieval archaeology journals publish annual reports on current excavations: *Medieval Archaeology* (1957–), *Archéologie médiévale* (1971–), *Zeitschrift für Archäologie des Mittelalters* (1973–), and *Archeologia medievale* (1974–). The *Annual Reports* (1952–) of the Medieval Village Research Group, National Monuments Record (Great Britain), are devoted entirely to village archaeology.

FREDRIC L. CHEYETTE

[See also **Agriculture and Nutrition; Barbarians, Invasions of; Bastide; Black Death; Castles and Fortifications; Castrum; Climatology; Domesday Book; Famine in Western Europe; Field Systems; Reclamation of Land; Roman Empire, Late; Surveying; Tools, Agricultural: European.**]

VILLANCICOS. In its original and broadest sense, the villancico is the Castilian popular song of the fifteenth and sixteenth centuries. Derived from *villano* (peasant, folk), the term begins to appear in the songbooks of the fifteenth century when these songs were collected for the first time. The name is also applied later to some courtly, nonpopular songs with certain stanza features derived from the popular villancico. After 1600 the term refers to religious songs, especially Christmas carols.

Various distinctive features of the villancico point to an ancient oral tradition related to other forms of the medieval romance lyric: the Mozarabic *kharja,* the Galician-Portuguese *cantiga de amigo,* and the French *refrain.* Like all of these, the villancico is typically the love complaint of a young maiden, addressed either to her mother or to her lover-friend (*amigo*). The villancico is invariably brief, consisting of two, three, or four lines, usually of unequal meter, of variable length, which when they rhyme are in assonance. These short compositions can be sung alone or followed by one or more stanzas, of varying length, referred to as *glosas* (the most characteristic being the parallelistic and the *zéjel* types; parallelism is also typical of the Galician-Portuguese *cantigas de amigo,* while the *zéjel* is a stanza of popular Arabic origin).

An example of a villancico with a parallelistic *glosa* can be found in *Cancionero musical de Palacio:*

> *Amigo, el que yo más quería,*
> *venid al alba del día.*
>
> *Amigo, el que yo más amaba,*
> *venid a la luz del alba.*
>
> *Venid a la luz del día;*
> *non tragáis compañía.*
>
> *Venid a la luz del alba;*
> *non traigáis gran compaña.*

Beloved, the one I love the best, / come at the dawn of day. / Beloved, the one I love most, / come at the light of dawn. / Come at the light of day; / do not bring company. / Come at the light of dawn; / do not bring many companions.

The same source also provides an example of a villancico with a *zéjel* type of *glosa:*

> *Tres morillas me enamoran*
> *en Jaén:*
> *Axa y Fátima y Marién.*
> *Tres morillas tan garridas*
> *iban a coger olivas;*
> *y hallábanlas cogidas*
> *en Jaén:*
> *Axa y Fátima y Marién.*

Three little Moorish girls make me fall in love / in Jaén: / Aisha and Fátima and Marién. / Three lively little Moorish girls / were going to pick olives; / but found them already picked / in Jaén: / Aisha and Fátima and Marién.

BIBLIOGRAPHY

José María Alín, *El cancionero español de tipo tradicional* (1968); Dámaso Alonso and José Manuel Blecua, *Antología de la poesía española: Lírica de tipo tradicional* (1964); Eugenio Asensio, *Poética y realidad en el cancionero peninsular de la Edad Media* (1957); *Cancionero musical de Palacio (siglos XV–XVI),* an edition and study, in *La música en la corte de los Reyes Católicos,* vols. IV-1, IV-2 (1965); John G. Cummins, ed., *The Spanish Traditional Lyric* (1977); Margit Frenk, "Glosas de tipo popular en la antigua lírica," in *Nueva revista de filología hispánica,* **12** (1958), as editor, *Lírica hispánica de tipo popular: Edad Media y Renacimiento* (1966), *Estudios sobre lírica antigua* (1978), and *Corpus de la antigua lírica popular hispánica (siglos XV a XVII)* (1987); Pierre Le Gentil, *La poésie lyrique espagnole et portugaise à la fin du moyen âge,* 2 vols. (1949–1953); Ramón Menéndez Pidal, "La primitiva poesía lírica española," in his *Estudios literarios* (1920), "Cantos románticos andalusíes," in his *España: Eslabón entre la Christiandad y el Islam* (1968), and "Sobre primitiva lírica española," in *De primitiva lírica española y antigua épica,* 2nd ed. (1968); Josep Romeu Figueras, "La poesía popular en las cancioneros musicales españoles de las siglos XV y XVI," in *Anuario musical,* **4** (1949); Antonio Sánchez Romeralo, *El villancico: Estudios sobre la lírica popular en los siglos XV y XVI* (1969).

ANTONIO SÁNCHEZ ROMERALO

[See also **Cantigas de Amor, Amigo, and Escarnio; Kharja; Mozarabic Literature; Spanish Literature: Dawn and Spring Songs; Spanish Literature: Lyric Poetry.**]

VILLARD DE HONNECOURT, Picard artist, active about 1220 to 1240, known exclusively through thirty-three leaves of pen-and-ink drawings preserved in Paris (Bibliothèque Nationale, MS fr. 19093). Since 1849 Villard (Wilars) has been called an architect, but no building anywhere can be attributed to him with certainty. His drawings indicate he visited Cambrai, Chartres, Laon, Lausanne, Meaux, and Vaucelles, and that he traveled to Hungary. He was interested in antique sculpture, and his finest drawings are of drapery, the rendering technique of which suggests he was trained as a metalworker. The claim that his bound drawings constituted a shop manual or textbook for masons is unacceptable.

BIBLIOGRAPHY

The most thorough facsimile edition of the Villard de Honnecourt is by Hans R. Hahnloser, *Villard de Honnecourt: Kritische Gesamtausgabe des Bauhüttenbuchs ms. fr. 19093 der Pariser Nationalbibliothek,* 2nd rev. ed. (1972); the most recent facsimile edition is by François Bucher, "Villard de Honnecourt," in *Architector,* **1** (1979), 15–193. Complete bibliography and introductory essay is found in Carl F. Barnes, Jr., *Villard de Honnecourt: Critical Bibliography, 1666–1981* (1982).

CARL F. BARNES, JR.

[See also **Mullion; Technology, Western** (both with illustrations).]

VILLEHARDOUIN, GEOFFROI DE (*ca.* 1150–*ca.* 1213), leader and chronicler of the Fourth Crusade, was born in the Château de Villehardouin near Troyes. An important figure in Champagne before he took the cross (apparently at Écry in late November 1199), Villehardouin had high diplomatic and military responsibility as a crusader and was marshal of Romania. In 1203 he participated in negotiations involving the Byzantine emperor Isaac II Angelos and the latter's son Alexios. In 1204 Villehardouin, who had earlier (June 1201) proposed his friend Boniface, marquis of Montferrat (*ca.* 1155–1207), as commander in chief of the crusaders (and who should not be confused with a nephew of the same name who followed Boniface on the Fourth Crusade), was emissary and guarantor in a dispute between the marquis and the Latin emperor Baldwin I (*r.* 1204–1205). Villehardouin led Baldwin's troops at Adrianople in the spring of 1205 and joined the emperor Henry's expedition against the Bulgars in 1208. Beyond this, we know only that Villehardouin witnessed the Acts of Ravennika on 2 May 1210 and acted as guarantor in December 1212. In 1218 his son established memorials for him.

Villehardouin's narrative, *La conquête de Constantinople,* written in unadorned French, begins with the preaching of Fulk of Neuilly in 1198 and ends with the death of Boniface on 4 September 1207. It is not a diary, for it shows awareness of events to come; nor was it written without preparation, for its accuracy is confirmed in detail by surviving documents. Written from above, as it were, by a leader prominent in counsel and action, it surveys the whole of the crusade. Strategy and politics dominate Villehardouin's account, whereas vivid details were emphasized by the *troupier* Robert de Clari in his chronicle of the same title. As a leader describing his own actions, Villehardouin has been charged with dissembling, especially regarding the diversion of the crusade to Constantinople. Whether his account of an unpremeditated diversion is accurate or conceals a plot by the chief crusaders is now a matter for conjecture rather than proof.

BIBLIOGRAPHY

Source and translation. Geoffroi de Villehardouin, *La conquête de Constantinople,* Edmond Faral, ed., 2 vols. (1938–1939); *Memoirs of the Crusades, by Villehardouin and De Joinville,* Sir Frank Marzials, trans. (1908).

Studies. Jeanette M. A. Beer, *Villehardouin: Epic Historian* (1968) and "Villehardouin and the Oral Narrative," in *Studies in Philology,* 67 (1970); Claude Buridant, "Motifs et formules dans *La conquête de Constantinople* de Villehardouin," in *Revue des sciences humaines,* 151 (1973); Edmond Faral, "Geoffroy de Villehardouin: La question de sa sincérité," in *Revue historique,* 177 (1936); Jean Larmat, "Sur quelques aspects de la religion chrétienne dans les chroniques de Villehardouin et de Clari," in *Le moyen âge,* 80 (1974); Jean Longnon, *Les compagnons de Villehardouin* (1978); Colin Morris, "Geoffroy de Villehardouin and the Conquest of Constantinople," in *History,* 53 (1968); Albert Pauphilet, "Robert de Clari et Villehardouin," in *Mélanges de linguistique et de littérature offerts à M. Alfred Jeanroy par ses élèves et ses amis* (1928).

SUSAN M. BABBITT

[See also **Baldwin I of the Latin Empire; Boniface of Montferrat; Châtelain de Coucy; Chronicles, French; Crusades and Crusader States: Fourth; Robert de Clari.**]

VILLENA, ENRIQUE DE (also called Enrique de Aragón) (*ca.* 1384–1434) is one of the more curious figures of early Spanish humanism. The studious son of Pedro of Aragon (*d.* 1385) and Juana, the illegitimate daughter of Henry II of Castile, he was brought up by his grandfather Alfonso of Aragon, the first marquis of Villena. The year of his birth is generally given as 1384, but documents in the Archivo del Reino de Valencia suggest an earlier date. The same archive should yield valuable information about his early education, of which little is known. Politics prevented Enrique from inheriting the marquisate of Villena, and attempts to obtain compensation were a major motivating force in his life. After a short public career, chiefly in Aragon, he retired to relative obscurity in the province of Cuenca, dedicating himself to literary pursuits. His reputation as a sorcerer was further enhanced after his death in 1434, when part of his library was burned by order of John II of Castile. A highly latinized diction generally characterizes Villena's surviving works. They are: *Los doze trabajos de*

Hércules (1417); *Tratado de la lepra* (*ca.* 1420); *Arte cisoria* (1423); *Tratado de la consolación* (1424); *Exposición del salmo "Quoniam videbo"* (1424); *Tratado del aojamiento* (1425); translation and glosses of the *Aeneid* (1427–1428); translation of the *Divina Commedia* (1427–1428); the fragmentary *Arte de trovar* (1433?). The consolatory *Epístola a Suero de Quiñones* probably belongs to the period from 1422 to 1428. The *Tratado de astrología* is of doubtful attribution, and there are other apocrypha. Lost works include a translation of the *Rhetorica ad Herennium* (*ca.* 1427); some *epístolas e arengas,* a treatise on *El coro de las nueve Musas* (*ca.* 1422), and possibly an *Historia de Vulcano* or *Tratado de los esperimentos de los fuegos* (*ca.* 1417). Contemporary references seem to point to the existence of poetry by Villena, but none has been identified.

BIBLIOGRAPHY

The standard study of Villena is that of Emilio Cotarelo y Mori, *Don Enrique de Villena: Su vida y obras* (1896). Other studies include Russell V. Brown, ed., *Arte cisoria* (1984); Derek C. Carr, ed., *El tratado de la consolación: A Critical Edition* (1971); Pedro M. Cátedra, *Exégesis-ciencia literatura: La "Exposición del salmo 'Quoniam videbo'" de Enrique de Villena* (1985); Margherita Morreale, ed., *Los doze trabajos de Hércules* (1958); José A. Pascual, *La traducción de la "Divina Comedia" atribuida a D. Enrique de Aragón: Estudio y edición del "Infierno"* (1974); Ramón Santiago Lacuesta, ed. and trans., *La primera versión castellana de "La Eneida" de Virgilio* (1979); Antonio Torres-Alcalá, *Don Enrique de Villena: Un mago al dintel del Renacimiento* (1983).

DEREK C. CARR

[See also **Spanish Literature: Translations.**]

VILLON, FRANÇOIS (*ca.* 1431—after 1463), French poet. "De moy, povre, je vueil parler" (Of my poor self I wish to speak), says he, thus prefacing a personal anecdote; but the line may serve as an introduction to his whole literary output. No major poet was more autobiographical than Villon; yet in many ways he speaks for humankind. His life was crammed with incident; his acquaintanceship reflects a cross-section of society at his time; his mental world embraces religious fervor, scholastic philosophy, classical literature, popular wisdom, and the survival tactics of the outcast and the outlaw. The dramatic and unforeseen ups and downs of his personal experience echo in his verses.

Born in poverty, he was adopted by a Parisian canon, given minor orders, treated to a university education, disappointed of a profession, obliged to live by expedients, deprived (apparently) of benefit of clergy, charged with theft and the murder of a priest (1455), imprisoned, released in a celebratory amnesty, received at the court of Charles of Orléans, reduced to tramping the highways, sentenced to death for a trivial offense, released on appeal, and exiled from Paris; his story ends there. In his odd moments (perhaps sometimes in hiding or in prison), he rehearsed these and other experiences and attempted to make sense of them; the result was some of the greatest French verse ever penned.

Its profoundly personal character may in some measure be due to circumstance. Although Villon sometimes tried his hand at occasional verse, attempting thereby to please real or hoped-for patrons ("Ballade pour Robert d'Estouteville," "Louange à Marie d'Orléans"), most of his production seemingly is addressed to his rather disreputable companions: unemployed academics, semiprofessional thieves, tavern-keepers, jailers, mummers, prostitutes. He also conducts debates with his own divided ego. A generous slice of the teeming lower stratum of mid-fifteenth-century French life, with its sights, sounds, and smells, comes to us in nearly 3,000 verses, as filtered through a highly subjective sensibility.

Villon's works comprise two unified compositions and a number of independent pieces. In his *Lais* (1456), pretexting a disappointment in love, he announces his intention of leaving Paris and his uncertainty of returning; he therefore undertakes to distribute his worldly goods to a series of named beneficiaries. Of these goods, many are fictitious (arms and armor, tents, rich foods, dogs, money); others, although real, are not his to bestow (taverns, castles, stolen ducks); still others are insulting (bales of straw for a brothel floor, his hair clippings) or threatening (discomfort, disease, blows of all kinds). All this youthful exuberance, this mingling of high-flown sentiment, obscene jokes, personal allusions, and scholastic vocabulary, is squeezed into forty stanzas of octosyllables rhyming *ababbcbc*—a framework made amazingly elastic by the strains of syntax and passion.

The *Lais,* in itself interesting, served as a trial piece for a greater work: the *Testament.* In it the poet gives his age as thirty and the year as 1461,

although sections may have been composed earlier or later. Again he takes up the format of the legacy, this time postulating not departure but imminent death; again he bethinks himself of his kin and acquaintances; once more he utilizes legal language, here extended to the whole framework of last will and testament (down to such minutiae as which executors, which bells, which burial place, which epitaph); as before, he turns to the eight-syllable octave.

He has, though, matured as an artist and as a person. Life has educated him more effectively than the university curriculum:

> Travail mes lubres sentemens
> Esguisez comme une pelote,
> M'ouvrit plus que tous les Commens
> D'Averroÿs sur Aristote.

His slippery wits, "sharp as a ball," have been more opened up by hardship than by the study of formal philosophy. Much has happened in the intervening years. He has been treated with, so he thinks, unnecessary rigor by assorted authorities, and chiefly by the bishop of Orléans, Thibaut d'Aussigny; at this man, the cause of his ruined health, the poet spits his powerless rage, and thus begins his major work. The *Testament* proper (once Villon attends to it), like the *Lais,* includes many satirical bequests, some of them to the same legatees; like the earlier poem, it draws on legal formulas and refers to specific persons, places, events, and institutions.

A striking aspect of the *Testament,* missing in the *Lais,* is the insertion at intervals of pieces in fixed form, primarily ballades, giving an intensified expression to the train of thought in the preceding octaves. The fixed forms, and the octaves as well, called for a degree of discipline that was seemingly absent from the poet's private life; yet technical mastery is only the beginning of his art. There is a startling contrast between the solidity of rhyme and meter, strophe and refrain, and the ease and naturalness of what is communicated.

The *Testament* is organized not by a formal or logical or even chronological principle, but by an association of ideas carried on recurrent images. Villon is haunted by the flight of time; by the transitoriness of beauty, fame, and happiness; and by the approach of death. The ancient topos *ubi sunt?* here acquires a highly personal note: Where have my good years gone? Where are the companions of my youth? Where are the rulers and the lovely ladies of the past? Such thoughts are memorably expressed in the "Ballade des dames du temps jadis" with its murmuring refrain "Mais où sont les neiges d'antan?" (But where are last year's snows?). At other times, remembering that he is a testator, he occupies himself with his benefactors: his adoptive father, "plus doulx que mere" (more tender than a mother), his careworn mother, whose legacy is a ballade with which to address the Virgin. Far more often, though, he remembers his raffish acquaintances and his tormentors. The many individuals and institutions that have (so he thinks) victimized him are in turn victimized, and immortalized, in satirical bequests.

This is a work full of contrasts: sometimes mocking, sometimes obscene, occasionally tender, often bitter and cruel, and frequently difficult to interpret. For Villon was a master of many styles, including the teasingly ambiguous, and could shift from one to another in a single stanza. Language fascinated him; he caught the accents of Paris and Poitou, the technical terms of schoolroom and law court, the jargon of the underworld, the grave rhythms of the liturgy and the Bible, the set formulas of proverbs.

This variety spills over from the two main works to the independent poems: six (eleven?) ballades in jargon, and fifteen or sixteen other pieces. Among these are some of his most justly famous, for example the "Débat de Villon et de son coeur," and the "Ballade des pendus," a condemned man's vision of his own executed corpse and his appeal to his brother humans for their prayers. Here matter and substance are in perfect equipoise; it is one of the sublime moments in poetry.

BIBLIOGRAPHY

Pierre H. Champion, *Histoire poétique du quinzième siecle*, II (1923), 57–131, and *François Villon: Sa vie et son temps*, 2nd ed., 2 vols. (1933); Jean Dufournet, *Recherches sur le "Testament" de François Villon*, 2nd ed., 2 vols. (1971–1973), and *Nouvelles Recherches sur Villon* (1980); John H. Fox, *The Poetry of Villon* (1962); Galway Kinnell, *The Poems of François Villon* (1977); André Lanly, trans., *François Villon: Ballades en jargon* (1971); Auguste Longnon and Lucien Foulet, eds., *François Villon: Oeuvres*, 4th ed. (1932); Odette Petit-Morphy, *François Villon et la scolastique*, 2 vols. (1977); Winthrop H. Rice, *The European Ancestry of Villon's Satirical Testaments* (1941); Jean Rychner and Albert Henry, eds., *Le Testament Villon*, 2 vols. (1974), and *Le Lais Villon et les poèmes variés* (1977); Italo Siciliano, *François Villon et les thèmes poétiques du moyen âge* (1934) and *Mésaventures posthumes de maître Françoys Villon* (1973); Evelyn Birge Vitz, *The Crossroad of Intentions: A Study of Symbolic Expression in the Poetry of François Villon*, 2 vols. (1954); Armand Ziwès and Anne de Bercy, *Le jargon de maître François Villon*, 2 vols. (1954).

BARBARA NELSON SARGENT-BAUR

[See also **French Literature: After 1200.**]

VILMUNDAR SAGA VIÐUTAN is an Icelandic romance preserved in three fifteenth-century vellum manuscripts and some forty-one paper manuscripts. Probably composed around 1400, the saga has been edited in one unpublished and three published editions.

This saga has borrowed from several sources, including *Hálfdanar saga Eysteinssonar* and the *Perceval* material of Chrétien. It concerns the two daughters of King Vísivaldr, Gullbrá and Sóley, whose future is predicted by a visiting wise woman. Gullbrá's half-brother, Hjarandi hviða (Whirlwind), sequesters her in a fortress and sets on stakes the heads of all her suitors who are not his equal in knightly achievement. Sóley promises herself to the hideous slave Kolr kryppa (Hunch) in return for his assassination of a suitor, but after his success she tricks him by changing appearances and clothes with a kitchen servant. Meanwhile, Vilmundr, grandson of Bögubósi, grows up in a remote valley, believing no human beings exist except his parents. After finding a gold-adorned shoe, he learns by overhearing a conversation coming from a large rock that the owner will marry none other than the man who returns the shoe to her. Dressed in a bearskin coat and otter-skin hood, he sets out to find his father's prized goat and comes to Vísivaldr's kingdom, where he is thought to be a fool. After defeating Hjarandi's surrogate in a wrestling match, as well as Hjarandi and a ferocious polar bear in aquatic battles, he becomes Hjarandi's sworn brother. They then annihilate the army of an unwanted suitor for Gullbrá's hand and set out to attack Kolr, who has become an outlaw with "Sóley" and who worships a destructive sow. Subsequently banished because the king believes Vilmundr has killed his daughter in the battle, the hero returns to the large rock, mentions the golden shoe to the inhabitants, and returns the real Sóley to her father.

Two *rímur* versions composed prior to 1600

exist, one in sixteen stanzaic divisions edited by Ólafur Halldórsson and one in twenty-four stanzaic divisions. Three *rímur* versions from the nineteenth century are also extant but unedited.

BIBLIOGRAPHY

Ólafur Halldórsson, ed., *Vilmundar rímur viðutan* (1975); Guðmundur Hjartarson, ed., *Sagan af Vilmundi viðutan* (1878); Finnur Jónsson, *Den oldnorske og oldislandske litteraturs historie*, 2nd ed., III (1924), 118; Agnete Loth, ed., *Late Medieval Icelandic Romances*, IV (1964); Nils W. Olsson, ed., *Vilmundar Saga Vidutan* (diss., Univ. of Chicago, 1949); Margaret Schlauch, *Romance in Iceland* (1934); Franz Rolf Schröder, ed., *Hálfdanar saga Eysteinssonar* (1917); Finnur Sigmundsson, *Rímnatal*, I (1966); Jón Thorkelsson, *Om digtningen på Island i det 15. og 16. århundrede* (1888), 273–275, 358; Björn K. Thórólfsson, *Rímur fyrir 1600* (1934), 498–501; Bjarni Vilhjálmsson, ed., *Riddarasögur*, VI (1954).

PETER A. JORGENSEN

[See also **Chrétien de Troyes; Hálfdanar Saga Eysteinssonar; Rímur.**]

VIMARA, a Spanish monk of the Leonese region responsible for the production of the Bible of 920 (León Cathedral, Cod. 6), though in what capacity is not clear, since a Iohannes signed it as scribe and painter. It is the first surviving major work of the Mozarabic school, with its hallmarks (flattened figures, brilliant color) fully evident.

BIBLIOGRAPHY

Manuel Gómez-Moreno, *Provincia de León* (1925), 151ff; John Williams, *Early Spanish Manuscript Illumination*, (1977).

JOHN WILLIAMS

[See also **Manuscript Illumination, European; Mozarabic Art.**]

VINCENT FERRER, ST. (1350–1419), Dominican preacher and healer, born in Valencia. He entered the Order of Preachers on 2 February 1367, took vows the following year, and was ordained in 1379. For four years he served as confessor for Queen Yolanda, wife of Juan I of Aragon. In 1378 at Valencia Vincent had met Cardinal Peter de Luna of Aragon, papal legate of the antipope Clement

St. Luke. Full-page miniature by Vimara from the Bible of León, 920. León Cathedral, cod. 6, fol. 211. HIRMER FOTOARCHIV

VII, who had come to solicit the support of King Pedro IV of Aragon for the Avignon papacy. When the cardinal was elected pope (Benedict XIII) at Avignon in 1391, Vincent was called to be his confessor and chaplain. Offered a cardinalate in addition, Vincent refused.

On 3 October 1398 in the midst of a serious illness, Vincent had a vision of Christ standing between Sts. Dominic and Francis telling him "to go forth and preach." Reluctantly, Benedict a year later granted Vincent permission to leave Avignon as "legatus a latere Christi," that is, as one deputed to preach anywhere he wished, exempt from local ecclesiastical jurisdiction; thus began Vincent's extraordinary life as an itinerant mendicant preacher. For the next twenty years until his death Vincent preached throughout Europe, at first traveling by foot and then, for health reasons, on an ass.

Thousands followed him on his mission, and on several occasions as many as 20,000 heard him preach. A small company of flagellants formed around him and assisted him on his journeys.

Vincent preached repentance, conversion, and the imminence of the Last Judgment during this time of the Black Death and the Great Schism. Although fluent only in his native tongue, he was understood wherever he preached. This phenomenon was attributed to the gift of tongues.

Vincent was also called upon to mediate local and international disputes. At Vercelli in 1406 he secured a peace between the Guelphs and Ghibellines. In 1412 he was chosen, along with his brother Boniface (master general of the Carthusians), as one of nine judges to decide the succession to the crown of Aragon. He eventually declared with the majority in favor of Ferdinand of Castile.

As early as 1408 Vincent had urged Benedict XIII to resign his papacy as a means to facilitate the end of the Great Schism. By 1416, frustrated by Benedict's obstinacy, Vincent urged King Ferdinand to withdraw Spanish obedience to Benedict, which left Benedict virtually isolated and allowed the Council of Constance to decide on one pope (Martin V). John Gerson, the famed Parisian theologian, wrote to Vincent, "But for you, this union could never have been accomplished."

In Spain Vincent converted thousands of Muslims and Jews. Among the latter were Solomon ha-Levi (d. 1435), known as Paul of Burgos or Pablo de Santa María, and Josue Harloqui (Gerónimo de Santa Fé), the talmudist. He assisted in drawing up the "Valladolid laws," which placed restrictions on Jews and Muslims and created the *juderías* and *morerías* to keep the unconverted separate from the conversos. In 1391 there were severe riots against the Jews throughout Spain. Although some have accused Vincent of fomenting such agitation, he in fact condemned the anti-Jewish violence in Valencia. In February 1414 he participated in the great disputation at Tortosa between Christians and Jews. Many Jews, including several rabbis, converted, some from conviction, others, no doubt, from fear or convenience.

In 1418 he preached before the English king Henry V at Caen in Normandy. He returned to Vannes in Brittany, where he died on 5 April 1419.

BIBLIOGRAPHY

Vincent's works were edited by Henri D. Fages in *Oeuvres de Saint Vincent Ferrier* (1909). Studies include Yitzhak F. Baer, *A History of the Jews in Christian Spain*, Louis Schoffman and H. Halkin, trans., 2 vols. (1961–1966); Fages, *Histoire de Saint Vincent Ferrier*, 4 vols. in 2 (1901–1905), and *Notes et documents de l'histoire de Saint Vincent Ferrier* (1905); Matthieu M. Gorce, *Les bases de l'étude historique de Saint Vincent Ferrier* (1923); Jesús E. Martínez Ferrando, ed., *San Vincente Ferrer y la casa real de Aragón* (1955); John A. Trentman, "The *Questo de unitate universalis* of Vincent Ferrer," in *Mediaeval Studies*, 44 (1982).

GEOFFREY B. GNEUHS

[See also **Aragon, Crown of; Castile; Councils, Western; Dominicans; Flagellants; Gerson, John; Jews in Christian Spain; Preaching and Sermon Literature; Schism, Great.**]

VINCENT OF BEAUVAIS (*ca.* 1190–*ca.* 1264). In the mid thirteenth century Vincent, a Dominican monk, compiled a colossal compendium or summa known as the *Speculum maius*; this large encyclopedia mirrors the culture and thought of Scholastic society as it records a very comprehensive overview of all of the classical and ecclesiastical knowledge and information available to late medieval man. In addition to this major compilation, Vincent also wrote pedagogical, theological, and devotional works.

As an individual, Vincent has been completely overshadowed by his voluminous and varied writings and treatises. What he wrote is known, but who he was and what he did are wrapped in uncertainty. All that is available to modern scholars is a scanty outline of his personal life and activities—and even some of these are plausible approximations rather than known facts.

Vincent apparently was born at Beauvais during the last years of the twelfth century. While various scholars give dates from 1184 to 1200, the most frequently cited year is about 1190. The date of his death is traditionally listed as 1264, probably at his native Beauvais. This date is more certain than that of his birth, as the year 1264 comes from a statement by the historian Luis of Valladolid (d. 1436) and from a puzzling epitaph noted in and logically interpreted by Jacques Quétif and Jacques Échard.

Vincent's life and career are as problematic as the years of his birth and death. He was apparently a student at the University of Paris and one of the first to join (*ca.* 1220) the newly established Dominican house of St. Jacques in Paris. Plausible conjecture then has Vincent transferred to the new priory established in his hometown of Beauvais (*ca.* 1230), since the Dominicans of St. Jacques followed the policy of sending members home when they established a new house in the region of their origin. There is no evidence to prove that the Vincent who was subprior at Beauvais in the 1240's was the great encyclopedist, however. This theory is based primarily upon the indisputable fact that Vincent became very closely associated with the monks of the nearby Cistercian abbey of Royaumont. Through his friendship with Abbot Ralph, Vincent entered into an ongoing friendship with King Louis IX of France, who had founded Royaumont about 1228 and whose favorite residence was in the Royaumont-Beauvais area. Through Ralph, Louis IX became acquainted with Vincent's work, and thus Vincent came to enjoy the favor and financial assistance of the French king.

Prior to his friendship with the king, Vincent had already begun to think in terms of organizing all sacred and profane literature into a systematic compilation that would make the hitherto inaccessible wisdom of earlier authors more readily available to others. Louis IX, hearing of Vincent's growing compilation of quotations and excerpts, wanted a copy for himself and offered the financial assistance needed to finish the project. Accordingly, Vincent sent the first half of the second part, the *Speculum historiale,* to the king and explained that its prologue summarized the entire first part, the *Speculum naturale.* The date of composition of the *Speculum* is difficult to determine precisely, since Vincent revised it several times; the first draft is usually dated 1244 and the last about 1260, with one or more revisions by Vincent as he compiled and expanded his text.

The *Speculum maius,* Vincent's masterpiece, is a composite of quotations and excerpts from earlier pagan and Christian authors; Vincent made no claim to originality and took pride in being the master organizer who collected, classified, and arranged his summary of human knowledge into a single unified entity. Originally the *Speculum* contained only two parts, the *Naturale* and the *Historiale;* reorganization and additional material that he did not deem suitable for inclusion in these two volumes resulted in a third part, the *Doctrinale.* Despite the fact that all printed editions consist of four parts, Vincent wrote only the above three; sometime between 1310 and 1325 an anonymous author added a *Morale* that was drawn chiefly from the *Summa theologiae* of Thomas Aquinas.

The three authentic components of the *Speculum maius* reveal that Vincent's encyclopedia was theologically oriented—knowledge helps carry man from sin and ignorance to God. The *Naturale* (thirty-two books) deals with nature as created by God, the *Historiale* (thirty-one books) is a universal history of mankind from creation until 1254, and the *Doctrinale* (seventeen books) summarizes the theoretical and practical learned arts and sciences. While Vincent's careful organization and his masterful orchestration of divergent sources reveal a very logical and rational mind, he is somewhat gullible at times, periodically intermingling superstition, fable, and miracles with verifiable scientific and rational knowledge. This master compiler is as good as his sources (over 400), which are cited with amazing regularity and accuracy. Thus Vincent's *Speculum maius* not only is the best medieval encyclopedia, it is also the largest: the three parts together consist of over 3 million words in 9,885 chapters in eighty books. It would require over fifty modern octavo volumes to print the entire *Speculum maius,* according to current estimates.

The influence and popularity of the *Speculum maius* can be ascertained from the numerous extant manuscripts, excerpts, epitomes, and summaries, and from the fact that the whole or parts of it were translated into French, Catalan, Spanish, Dutch, and German. It was well known to the humanist scholars of the Italian Renaissance and was printed four times in the fifteenth century, once in the sixteenth, and once in the seventeenth. Unfortunately, no new edition of the *Speculum maius* has been published since the early seventeenth century. This 1624 Douai edition is the most readily available and most frequently cited version, especially after a facsimile reprint at Graz in 1964, even though the 1473–1476 Strasbourg edition of Johann Mentelin is generally considered to contain the most reliable text. Since these early editions do not have trustworthy texts because of editorial corrections, revisions, interpretations, and rearrangements, a modern critical edition of the *Speculum maius* is highly desirable and is one of the major goals of scholars currently working on Vincent. Needless to say, the lack of a reliable text makes it very difficult to study and evaluate the sources, content, and organization of Vincent's great encyclopedia.

Due to his favor with Louis IX as well as to his accomplishments, Vincent was appointed lector at the abbey of Royaumont; but despite his close ties with the royal family, he was never the tutor of the king's children. So intimate was Vincent with Louis IX that on the death of the dauphin Louis, in 1260, he sent the king a moving letter of sympathy entitled *Epistola consolatoria super morte filii.* At the request of Queen Marguerite and the cleric Simon, tutor of Prince Philip, Vincent wrote a pedagogical treatise dealing with the education of royal children, *De eruditione filiorum nobilium* (1246/1247–1249). This was to be part of a planned larger work, *Opus universale,* designed to deal with royal governance and political science. The only other part of this intended treatise that Vincent produced was entitled *De morali principis institutione* (1260–1263), and it dealt with the moral duties and virtues of rulers. These two educational works were influential then and still merit serious study but, unfortunately, are frequently obscured by the monumental *Speculum.* Vincent's pedagogical works have been attracting the study they deserved during the last decades of the twentieth century, but also have been producing a certain degree of controversy—especially over whether Vincent's educational ideas should be viewed as precursors of Renaissance humanistic ideas or as the traditional views of a typical medieval ascetic.

While Vincent's historical fame rests primarily on his vast encyclopedia, he is usually credited with writing several additional theological and devotional works—on Christ, Mary, John the Baptist, the Trinity, and Christian life, among others. Not all of these minor works attributed to Vincent are necessarily authentic, and they do not merit the attention and research that his major works have attracted. Thus, while not representing the sum total of his literary productivity, his major contributions, the *Speculum maius* and his educational treatises, give Vincent of Beauvais a legitimate and respected role in the development of medieval European history and culture.

BIBLIOGRAPHY

Sources. Editions are *De eruditione filiorum nobilium,* Arpad Steiner, ed. (1938); "The *De morali principis institutione* of Vincent of Beauvais: Introduction and Critical Text," Robert J. Schneider, ed. (diss., Notre Dame, 1965).

Studies. W. J. Aerts, E. R. Smits, and J. B. Voorbij, eds., *Vince of Beauvais and Alexander the Great: Studies in the Speculum Maius and Its Translation into Medieval Vernaculars* (1986); Anna-Dorothee von den Brincken, "Geschichtsbetrachtung bei Vincenz von Beauvais: Die Apologia actoris zum *Speculum maius,*" in *Deutsches Archiv für Erforschung des Mittelalters,* 34 (1978); Pierre F. C. Daunou, "Vincent de Beauvais, auteur du *Speculum maius* terminé en 1256," in *Histoire littéraire de la France,* XVIII (1835); Thomas R. Eckenrode, "Vincent of Beauvais: A Study in the Construction of a Didactic View of History," in *The Historian,* 46 (1984); Astrik L. Gabriel, *The Educational Ideas of Vincent of Beauvais* (1956, 2nd ed. 1962); Gregory G. Guzman, "The Encyclopedist Vincent of Beauvais and His Mongol Extracts from John of Plano Carpini and Simon of Saint-Quentin," in *Speculum,* 19 (1974), and "A Growing Tabulation of Vincent of Beauvais' *Speculum historiale* Manuscripts," in *Scriptorium,* 29 (1975); Michel Lemoine, "L'oeuvre encyclopédique de Vincent de Beauvais," in Maurice de Gandillac *et al., La pensée encyclopédique au moyen âge* (1966); Serge Lusignan, *Préface au Speculum maius de Vincent de Beauvais* (1979); Joseph M. McCarthy, *Humanistic Emphases in the Educational Thought of Vincent of Beauvais* (1976) and "Research on Vincent of Beauvais: Trends and Possibilities," in *Vincent of Beauvais Newsletter,* 2 (1977).

C. Oursel, "Un exemplaire du *Speculum maius* de Vincent de Beauvais provenant de la bibliothèque de Saint-Louis," in *Bibliothèque de l'École de chartes,* 85 (1924); Monique Paulmier [-Foucart], "Les *flores* d'auteurs antiques et médiévaux dans le *Speculum historiale,*" "Étude sur l'état des connaissances au milieu de XIIIe siècle: Nouvelles recherches sur la genèse du *speculum maius* de Vincent de Beauvais," and "Le portrait de César dans le *Speculum historiale,*" in *Spicae: Cahiers de l'Atelier Vincent de Beauvais,* 1 (1978), and "Écrire d'histoire au XIIIe siècle: Vincent de Beauvais et Helinand de Froidmont," in *Annales de l'Est,* 5th ser., 33 (1981); Jacques Quétif and Jacques Échard, *Scriptores Ordinis Praedicatorum,* I (1719), 212–240; Jean Schneider, "Vincent de Beauvais: Orientation bibliographique," in *Spicae,* 1 (1978), and, with Helen Naïs, "L'Atelier Vincent de Beauvais," in *Revue d'histoire des textes,* 4 (1974); Rosemary Barton Tobin, *Vincent of Beauvais' De Eruditione Filiorum Nobilium: The Education of Women* (1984); B. L. Ullman, "A Project for a New Edition of Vincent of Beauvais," in *Speculum,* 8 (1933); James A. Weisheipl, "Is a Critical Edition of the *Speculum maius* Possible?" in *Vincent of Beauvais Newsletter,* 3 (1978). See also M. C. Duchenne, Gregory G. Guzman, and J. B. Voorbij, "Une liste des manuscrits du *Speculum historiale* de Vincent de Beauvais," in *Scriptorium,* 41 (1987).

GREGORY G. GUZMAN

[See also **Alchemy; Bestiary; Bible; Dominicans; Encyclopedias, Western European; Fables; Louis IX of France.**]

VINCENTIUS HISPANUS (*fl. ca.* 1210–1248), Bolognese canonist. Born on the Iberian Peninsula in the late twelfth century, he studied law at

Bologna and afterward taught canon law there from about 1210 to 1217. He was appointed dean of the cathedral chapter at Lisbon in 1212 (perhaps in absentia), administrator for the diocese of Lisbon in 1217, and chancellor of Sancho II in 1224. In 1228 he was bishop-elect of Idanha-Guarda (confirmed in 1235); he died in 1248. Javier Ochoa Sanz has maintained that he was bishop not of Idanha but of Saragossa and that he died in 1244. Stephan Kuttner has pointed out, however, that a Bishop Vincentius, "rector iuris canonici et glossator," was appointed to a commission at the Council of Lyons in 1245. If this man was our canonist, Ochoa's contention that Bishop Vincentius of Saragossa was the Bolognese canonist cannot be accepted.

Vincentius was a remarkably prolific author of works on canon law. He is the only canonist to have glossed the *Compilationes antiquae* (1191–1210) and the *Decretals* of Pope Gregory IX, compiled by Raymond of Peñafort in 1234. During his stay in Bologna he composed an apparatus to the *Compilationes prima et tertia* (First and third compilations) and a commentary on the constitutions of the Fourth Lateran Council. After Vincentius became bishop—he began his apparatus with a reference to himself: "Vincentius episcoporum Hispanie minimus"—he completed a comprehensive commentary on the *Decretals* of Gregory IX. He also wrote a number of minor works: glosses to Gratian's *Decretum* and to the *Compilatio secunda* (Second compilation), a *casus* for the *Compilatio tertia*, and glosses to the *Arbor consanguinitatis et affinitatis* (Tree of consanguinity and affinity). Several other minor works have been attributed to him.

Vincentius had a lively, fertile mind. In one manuscript he is called Vincentius Hilaris, and whether this was a common nickname or not, it suits his character. He had great influence on other canonists, particularly Johannes Teutonicus and Tancred, who borrowed much from his apparatus to the First and Third Compilations, and he often punctuated his glosses with acerbic or witty comments. He called Johannes a *bavecha* (it might mean "dull-witted") and Tancred "acephalic." He mentioned Spanish conditions frequently in his glosses. Unlike most other canonists, Vincentius wore his nationality on his sleeve. In several famous comments to decretals of Innocent III, he declared his love of Spain and rejected any claim that the medieval German emperor had jurisdiction over the old Roman province.

BIBLIOGRAPHY

Sources. Only one of Vincentius' major works has been edited: *Apparatus in Concilium quartum Lateranense*, in Antonio García y García, ed., *Constitutiones Concilii quarti Lateranensis una cum Commentariis glossatorum* (1981). García has also edited Vincentius' glosses to *Arbor consanguinitatis et affinitatis*, in *Zeitschrift der Savigny-Stiftung für Rechtsgeschichte*, Kan. Abt. 68 (1982). The manuscripts of Vincentius' works are listed in the works of Ochoa and Kuttner below.

Studies. The dispute about whether Vincentius was bishop of Idanha or of Saragossa has been stimulated by the work of Javier Ochoa Sanz, *Vincentius Hispanus* (1960) and "El glosador Vincentius Hispanus y títulos comunes 'de foro competenti' canónico," in *Miscellanea in onore dei Professori Anastasio Gutiérrez e Pietro Tocanel* (1982). Also see Stephan Kuttner, "Vincentius Hispanus," in *Traditio*, 17 (1961), and "Wo war Vincentius Hispanus Bischof?" *ibid.*, 22 (1966); and A. D. de Sousa Costa, *Mestre Silvestre e Mestre Vincente* (1963). On Vincentius' nationalism, see Gaines Post, "'Blessed Lady Spain': Vincentius Hispanus and Spanish National Imperialism in the Thirteenth Century," in *Speculum*, 29 (1954), repr. with changes as "Vincentius Hispanus and Spanish Nationalism" in Post's *Studies in Medieval Legal Thought* (1964).

KENNETH PENNINGTON

[See also **Councils, Western; Decretals; Johannes Teutonicus; Law, Canon: Post-Gratian; Raymond of Peñafort; Tancred.**]

VINLAND SAGAS. The story of what is commonly known as the "Norse" (more precisely, the Icelandic) discovery of North America around 1000 is told in two differing versions, which are united under the term "Vinland sagas." "Vinland" was the name given by the discoverers to the most remote of the areas explored and the only one they reportedly attempted to settle.

Grœnlendinga saga (The Greenlanders' saga; GS) is uniquely preserved as interpolations in a saga of King Olaf Tryggvason of Norway (r. 995–1000). The interpolation stems from one of the compilers of the huge and handsome manuscript of around 1388 known as the *Flateyjarbók* (GkS 1005 fol.). The date of original composition of GS is not known; Jóhannesson surmises that it dates to about 1200 and is based on oral tradition.

Eiríks saga rauða (Eric the Red's saga; ES) is preserved in two compilations of sagas: *Hauksbók* (AM 544 4°), from the early 1300's, and *Skál-*

456

holtsbók (AM 577 4°), from around 1400. These go back to a common original, which is more faithfully preserved in the later manuscript (Jansson, Reeves). The account in *ES* is more coherent and sophisticated than that in *GS,* which lent it credibility for most commentators following Storm and Finnur Jónsson. But Jóhannesson reversed the field, claiming that *ES* is based on *GS* and reveals a churchly bias insofar as it makes Leif Ericson a missionary, for which there is no independent evidence. He dated *ES* to 1264 or later.

These two major sources of the Vinland story differ markedly in terms of narrative, and the problem of their respective validity has been endlessly and inconclusively debated. Both of them are late mixtures of genuine traditions and romantic accretions. In both, however, the Norse Greenland settlements are presupposed as *points d'appui* of the voyages, while Norway and Iceland form their background. Both bring Greenlandic explorers to more southerly lands, where the coastline runs from southwest to northeast; relate initially peaceful but eventually disastrous encounters with natives, the Skrælings; include as leaders in the exploration of Vinland Leif Ericson, son of Eric the Red, with his family, and Þorfinn Karlsefni, with his wife Guðríð; find three successive lands, Helluland (flat rock land), Markland (forest land), and Vinland (vine or wine land). In the last of these they find wild grapes and wheat. There can be no doubt that the sagas are talking about the same events, and that the Norsemen reached some point on the North American east coast.

But the discrepancies are disturbing. In the *GS,* Vinland is sighted by Bjarni Herjólfsson, blown off course while sailing from Iceland to Greenland in search of his father. In the *ES,* Bjarni is absent, but Leif Ericson is similarly diverted off course while sailing from Norway to Greenland, having been sent by King Olaf as a missionary to bring Christianity to Greenland. He sights and explores Vinland. In the *GS,* Leif's contribution is reduced to exploring a land already discovered by Bjarni. Three later expeditions are headed by Leif's brothers Þorvald and Þorstein and his half-sister, Freydís. In the *GS* the narrator gives special attention to Eric's family, which, with Þorfinn as a brother-in-law, heads five out of six expeditions (counting Þorstein's disastrous one). In the *ES* there are only three expeditions, headed by Leif, Þorstein, and Þorfinn; most of the *ES* is devoted to Þorfinn and Guðríð and their explorations and attempts to settle

in the new country. Their son Snorri is born there and is three years old when they give up and return to Iceland, where they become progenitors of an illustrious family, three of whose members become bishops in the Icelandic church.

The discrepancies of the two versions are such as to have led the Norwegian explorer Nansen to dismiss the whole story of Vinland as fabulous, a version of classical tales about the Fortunate Isles in the western ocean. Others, like the American naval expert William Hovgaard, have found both versions "essentially of equal value" and held that the truth lies somewhere between. As mentioned, Jóhannesson claimed that *ES* is a clerical reworking of the *GS,* but close study of the texts does not substantiate this view. There is no parallel in saga writing for such violent disparities in distinct sagas about the same events: not only are the episodes differently told and ordered, but there is scarcely a single verbal echo such as one might expect from a mere rewriting. The intervening link seems more likely to be oral narration, with all its potential for distortion over a period of two centuries.

There is controversy also about the meaning of "Vinland" itself. A theory advanced by Söderberg and accepted by some scholars, including the Ingstads, holds that the first element is Old Norse *vin* (with short "i"), a word meaning "meadow," not *vín* (with long "i"), meaning "vine" or "wine." The problem could only arise because medieval Icelandic manuscripts rarely mark length. However, an unbroken tradition of pronunciation in Iceland testifies to the long vowel. That grapes were associated with the Vinland story from the first is attested not only by the sagas, but also by the German clerical historian Adam of Bremen, in his *Gesta ecclesiae Hammaburgensis* (*ca.* 1075), the first known reference in literature to Vinland. Adam heard the story at the Danish court from Icelanders who had "been there." *Vin* is not attested as a living word in Old Norse and was probably obsolete by 1000. In place-names it is common as a suffix in Norway, though not in Iceland or the Faeroes; as a first element it is extremely rare. While wine was not produced in Scandinavia, it was imported from southern Europe and was well known as an aristocratic luxury.

Attempts to locate the places so vividly described in the sagas have ranged from Labrador in the north to Virginia in the south, with Newfoundland and the Cape Cod region as favorite contenders. In excavations in 1961 the Norwegian explorer Helge

Ingstad made a sensational breakthrough by discovering what proved to be an authentic Norse site near the northern tip of Newfoundland at L'Anse aux Meadows. Many others have been claimed, but not authenticated. The Ingstads claim to have found Leif's Vinland, but neither climate nor topography agrees well with the sagas' accounts. But it is a natural enough point of initial landfall and brief settlement, located at the shortest distance across from the Greenland settlements. The sagas reflect what is clearly a much more southerly exploration to more clement landscapes, so that Vinland is a region of indefinite extent. So far, searches along the coast have not been fruitful, although much credence was once given to researches by Horsford claiming successful excavations at Gerry's Landing on the Charles River in Cambridge, Massachusetts (Holm). A so-called Vinland map launched by Yale University Press in 1965 has been discredited as a forgery, but its origin is still unknown.

We suggest that the two versions represent differently slanted oral traditions. *GS* is associated with northern Iceland, where Þorfinn and Guðríð settled and where their episcopal offspring had their see (at Hólar). *ES* is associated with the region of Snæfellsnes in western Iceland, from which Guðríð and her family emigrated. Any hope of locating Vinland with the help of these sagas is bound to fail; the finds in Newfoundland are the beginnings of a solution, but surely not the end.

BIBLIOGRAPHY

Einar Haugen, ed. and trans., *Voyages to Vinland* (1942); Gustav Holm, "Small Additions to the Vinland Problem," in *Meddelelser om Grønland*, 59 (1925); Eben Norton Horsford, *The Landfall of Leif Erikson*, A.D. 1000 (1892); William Hovgaard, *The Voyages of the Norsemen to America* (1914); Anne Stine Ingstad, *The Norse Discovery of America*, I, *Excavations of a Norse Settlement at L'Anse aux Meadows, Newfoundland, 1961–1968*, Elizabeth S. Seeberg, trans. (1985); Helge Ingstad, *Westward to Vinland*, Erik J. Friis, trans. (1969) and *The Norse Discovery of America*, II, *The Historical Background and the Evidence of the Norse Settlement Discovered in Newfoundland*, Elizabeth S. Seeberg, trans. (1985); Henrik M. Jansen, *A Critical Account of the Written and Archaeological Sources' Evidence Concerning the Norse Settlements in Greenland*, in *Meddelelser om Grønland*, 182 (1972).

Sven B. F. Jansson, *Sagorna om Vinland I: Handskrifterna till Erik den Rödes saga* (1945); Jón Jóhannesson, "The Date of the Composition of the Saga of the Greenlanders," Tryggvi J. Oleson, trans., in *Saga-Book of the Viking Society for Northern Research*, 16 (1962–1965); Gwyn Jones, *The Norse Atlantic Saga*, 2nd ed. (1986); Magnus Magnusson and Hermann Pálsson, *The Vinland Sagas* (1965); Fridtjof Nansen, *In Northern Mists* (1911); Arthur M. Reeves, ed. and trans., *The Finding of Wineland the Good* (1890); R. A. Skelton, Thomas E. Marston, and George D. Painter, *The Vinland Map and the Tartar Relation* (1965); Gustav Storm, *Studies on the Vinland Voyages* (1889); Matthías Þórðarson, *The Vinland Voyages* (1930).

EINAR HAUGEN

[See also **Adam of Bremen; Exploration by Western Europeans; Iceland; Norway; Skrælings; Viking Navigation; Vikings.**]

VIRELAI (from the Latin *vertēre*, Old French *virer*, to turn), a French poetic and song form, one of the *formes fixes* of the fourteenth and fifteenth centuries. The virelai begins with a refrain, usually of four to ten lines, set to the first section of the music, followed by two verses set to the second section of the music, then one verse to the first section, and the refrain: thus, the musical scheme is $A b b a A$. The text may include two to six stanzas: in performance, the refrain presumably should be stated only once between stanzas ($A b b a A b b a A$). The virelai is structurally identical to the Italian ballata.

The virelai appears to have developed from the loosely structured refrain forms of the thirteenth century. One of its first manifestations is in Adam de la Halle's polyphonic *Fines amouretes ai*. Jehannot de l'Escurel wrote five monophonic examples around 1300, by which time the form was firmly established. Monophonic virelais remained the rule in the fourteenth century: of thirty-three written by Guillaume de Machaut, only eight are polyphonic, and all but one of these are for one voice with instrumental tenor.

Virelai texts were primarily love songs until the latter half of the fourteenth century, when a "programmatic" variety, with polyphonic music, took on the dimensions of a fad. Texts of this type described battle, market, or pastoral scenes, each with appropriate cries, calls, and onomatopoeic noises reflected in the music. The pastoral type, the most popular, abounded in birdcalls and may have been showcase pieces for virtuoso singers. The onomatopoeic devices are also reminiscent of the Italian caccia and its French relative, the canonic chace.

Of the three *formes fixes,* the virelai was most closely associated with the devices of wordplay—short metrical phrases, internal rhyme, patter declamation, coined words—although these devices were sometimes distorted by the musical settings. The form declined in popularity during the fifteenth century.

BIBLIOGRAPHY

Willi Apel, ed., *French Secular Compositions of the Fourteenth Century,* 3 vols. (1970–1972); Marcel Françon, "On the Nature of the Virelai," in *Symposium* (Syracuse, N.Y.), **9** (1955); Gilbert Reaney, "Fourteenth Century Harmony and the Ballades, Rondeaux, and Virelais of Guillaume de Machaut," in *Musica disciplina,* **7** (1953), "The Ballades, Rondeaux, and Virelais of Guillaume de Machaut: Melody, Rhythm, and Form," in *Acta musicologica,* **27** (1955), and "The Development of the Rondeau, Virelai, and Ballade Forms from Adam de la Halle to Guillaume de Machaut," in Heinrich Hüschen, ed., *Festschrift Karl Gustav Fellerer* (1962).

MARCIA J. EPSTEIN

[See also **Ars Nova; Ballade; Ballata; Caccia; French Literature: Lyric; Machaut, Guillaume de; Rondeau; Trecento Music.**]

VIRGIL THE GRAMMARIAN (Virgilius Maro Grammaticus) (*fl.* mid seventh century), wrongly labeled Virgil of Toulouse, was almost certainly an Irishman, possibly active on the Continent. His curious treatises, *Epitomae* and *Epistolae,* deal with grammar, meter, cryptograms, etymologies, secret languages, and lore surrounding hitherto unidentified schools and scholars. His writings were widely utilized to the end of the Carolingian period.

BIBLIOGRAPHY

Sources. Johann Huemer, *Virgilii Maronis grammatici opera* (1886); G. Polara and L. Caruso, *Virgilio Marone grammatico Epitomi ed Epistole* (1979).

Studies. Michael Herren, "Some New Light on the Life of Virgilius Maro Grammaticus," in *Proceedings of the Royal Irish Academy,* **79,** C, 2 (1979), 27–71; Louis Holtz, "Irish Grammarians and the Continent in the Seventh Century," in H. B. Clarke and Mary Brennan, eds., *Columbanus and Merovingian Monasticism* (1981), 135–152; Vivien Law, *The Insular Latin Grammarians* (1982), esp. 42–52.

MICHAEL HERREN

[See also **Hiberno-Latin; Hisperic Latin.**]

VIRGATE, an area or superficial measure for land in England that was generally synonymous with the yardland and in Sussex with the wista. Like other land measures, its total acreage depended on local soil conditions, regional topography, and the impact of custom and tradition: but virgates of 15, 16, 20, 24, 28, 30, 32, 40, and 60 acres (6.07 to 24.30 hectares) were the most common. It was generally equal to 0.25 hide and was occasionally the sum of 2 or 3 bovates or 4 farthingdales. The medieval Latin form *virgata* was derived etymologically from the Latin *virga,* a twig or rod; hence, originally, the virgate was calibrated according to some local measuring rule or stick.

RONALD EDWARD ZUPKO

[See also **Weights and Measures, Western European.**]

VIRGIL. See **Vergil in the Middle Ages.**

VIRGIN MARY IN THEOLOGY AND POPULAR DEVOTION. Devotion to Mary as well as theology about her can be traced to the New Testament, where, in addition to the Nativity narratives of Matthew and Luke, Mary is mentioned as being present at the foot of the cross (John 19:25–27) and in the upper room at Pentecost (Acts 1:14). Paul describes Jesus as "born of a woman" (Gal. 4:4), and Igantius of Antioch (*d. ca.* 110) appealed to Mary in support of the authentic humanity of Christ.

The formula "born of the Virgin Mary" in the early creeds asserted the doctrine of the Virgin Birth, and gradually Christians intuited that Mary remained always a virgin, despite gospel references to "brothers and sisters." This belief in the perpetual virginity of Mary was reflected in apocryphal writings (such as the Gospel of James) from the second century and was treated theologically by Origen (*d.* 254) and other writers, achieving common acceptance by about 400. It was Athanasius (*d.* 373) who both reflected and promoted the bond between piety and belief in his use of the title *Theotokos* (Godbearer, or Mother of God) and

459

praised Mary as patroness of freely chosen virginity for the sake of the kingdom.

The New Testament references to Mary already had ecclesial significance. For Irenaeus (*d.* 202) Mary sang her Magnificat in the name of the church. Like Mary, the church is virgin mother: as the Virgin conceived Christ, so the church at the baptismal font brings forth children in purity of faith (Leo, *d.* 461).

The Council of Ephesus sanctioned the term *Theotokos* to defend the truth that the Son of Mary is the very Son of God become man. How early did Christians call on the Virgin Mary in prayer? Perhaps by the late third century. A late-fourth-century prayer has survived, *Sub tuum praesidium confugimus* (We fly to thy patronage), which addresses Mary as *Theotokos* and asks her assistance, much like the medieval *Memorare* (Remember, O most gracious Virgin Mary . . .). In the communion of saints the martyrs were first to be invoked in Christian prayer, then Mary and others, so that "by their prayers and intercessions God may receive our supplications."

Christian reflection on Mary's holiness focused first on freedom from personal, actual sin, and gradually extended to immunity from original sin. Remote indications of her "immaculate conception" are found from the second century—fancifully in apocryphal stories, and theologically, perhaps by implication, in Mary's association as the "new Eve" with the victory over sin of her son, the "new Adam." The question arose explicitly only in the fourth century; St. Augustine (*d.* 430) could not reconcile freedom from original sin with being the child of two human parents. Augustine's view prevailed into the Western Middle Ages, even when original sin was recognized as a spiritual deprivation, not the inescapable result of normal procreation (St. Anselm, *d.* 1109).

In the eighth century Eastern homilists such as Andrew of Crete, Germanus of Constantinople, and John of Damascus extolled Mary's total holiness, though without raising Western questions about original sin. By the late seventh century there was a Syrian liturgical feast of the conception of Mary, which spread through Byzantium, reaching England about 1050 and France and Spain in the twelfth century, though St. Bernard (*d.* 1153) chided the canons of Lyons for keeping the feast. Great Scholastics, such as Albert, Bonaventure, and Thomas Aquinas, could not fit Mary's freedom from original sin into the universality of redemp-

tion. Duns Scotus (*d.* 1309) overcame this impasse in terms of anticipatory, preservative redemption "in view of the merits of Jesus Christ."

Piety played a major role in the growing belief in the Immaculate Conception, as exemplified in a book by Eadmer (*d.* 1124), the Saxon secretary of St. Anselm, on the conception of Mary. This treatise made an appeal on behalf of popular devotion and an earlier English feast that the Normans had suppressed. It also offered the theological argument that Divine Wisdom formed for his dwelling place the all-holy Mother of God, which is a prime example of monastic theology that, in Jean Leclercq's phrase, demonstrated a "love of learning and the desire for God." Nevertheless, despite many instances of medieval piety and theologizing, the doctrine of the Immaculate Conception was not formally accepted by the Roman Catholic church until 1854. The churches of the Christian East, Orthodox and others, extol Mary's holiness extensively, but do not accept this doctrine.

Belief in the Assumption, that the Mother of Jesus was taken body and soul to heavenly glory, also developed gradually, beginning with the notion of her "dormition" or "koimesis" (falling asleep), which was observed in the liturgy on 15 August as early as the sixth century, in a way similar to the "birthday into heaven" of martyrs on the anniversaries of their deaths. Only in 1950 did Pope Pius XII define the Assumption as a dogma of Catholic faith.

Apart from the creeds, the oldest liturgical reference to Mary is the remembrance prayer of the Eucharist. Early in the fourth century a Syrian anaphora had a Marian commemoration; by the mid fourth century the liturgy of St. Basil, still in use today, reads, "remembering in the first place the Blessed Virgin Mary, Mother of God, and all the saints," a pattern followed by the West. Marian feast days were introduced first in the East, then the West.

The second Council of Nicaea (787), in answer to iconoclasm, reiterated the church's veneration of the *Theotokos* in doctrine and devotion. Homilists and theologians such as John of Damascus (*d. ca.* 750) praised the blessed Virgin as all-holy (*panagia*). In the Middle Ages Mary's role as spiritual mother and as sharing in her Son's saving work as mediatrix came to the fore, particularly through the influence of St. Bernard. In a prayer Anselm wrote: "He who was able to make all things out of nothing refused to remake it by force but first became the

Son of Mary. So God is the Father of all created things, and Mary is the mother of all recreated things."

Alcuin of York (*d.* 804) promoted Saturday as Our Lady's day. Devotion to Mary in the High Middle Ages reflected the communion between the pilgrim church and the glorious church. Many sermons and prayers come from this period, such as the "Hail, Holy Queen" (*Salve regina*). Great cathedrals bore Marian dedications, and theological masters such as Bonaventure, Albertus Magnus, and Thomas Aquinas wrote prayers and hymns to Mary for popular use.

The invention of printing encouraged the spread of such popular devotions as the rosary and scapular. The "mantle Virgin" captures the late pre-Reformation outlook—the merciful Mother of Jesus sheltering her many children under the cloak of her celestial protection. At the Reformation Luther, Calvin and other leaders reacted to abuses in devotion to Mary and the saints and forbade all calling on their assistance in prayer. After the Catholic reform at Trent (1545–1563) Mary's place remained strong in Catholic belief and practice. In recent centuries a prominent feature of popular devotion has been pilgrimages to Marian shrines. In the East traditional icons have continued to be foci of prayer, both liturgical and popular.

BIBLIOGRAPHY

Henri Barré, *Prières anciennes de l'Occident à la Mère du Sauveur* (1963); R. E. Brown, K. P. Donfried, *et al.*, *Mary in the New Testament* (1978); Michael Carroll, *The Cult of the Virgin Mary: Psychological Origins* (1987); Hilda Graef, *Mary: A History of Doctrine and Devotion* (1986); Frederick M. Jelly, *Madonna: Mary in the Catholic Tradition* (1986); Henri de Lubac, *Splendor of the Church* (1986); A. Stacpoole, ed., *Mary's Place in Christian Dialogue* (1983); Benedicta Ward, *The Prayers and Meditations of St. Anselm* (1984).

EAMON R. CARROLL

[See also **Annunciation; Assumption of the Virgin; Ave Maria; Blessed Virgin Mary, Little Office of; Book of Hours; Councils (Ecumenical, 325–787); Eleousa; Koimesis; Lactatio; Marian Feasts; Nativity; Nestorianism; Pietà; Platytera; Presentation in the Temple; Theotokos; Visitation; Vladimir Virgin.**]

VIRGINAL is the title given to a Middle High German narrative poem from the cycle of stories about Dietrich von Bern. The poem survives in a number of late redactions, all of which must be considered corruptions of late-thirteenth-century originals. These original versions were only modest poetic achievements, and the surviving versions border on unintelligibility. There is no recent edition of the poem. Zupitza's edition has been reprinted, and it forms the basis for the following summary.

Dietrich rides out from Bern (Verona) with his mentor and vassal Hildebrand. Upon reaching a wild region, they hear a strange voice and Hildebrand rides off to investigate, leaving Dietrich alone. Hildebrand finds a maiden, who bewails the fact that she is to be part of the annual tribute her queen is forced to pay to the heathen Orkise, who has held sway over the region for many years. Orkise appears and is killed by Hildebrand. The latter returns to Dietrich and finds him in a battle with Orkise's followers. After Dietrich and Hildebrand kill the heathens, they set out for the mountain where the queen Virginal lives. Along the way, however, they are embroiled in a sequence of battles with "young dragons," freeing a knight from the maw of one of them. The young knight turns out to be a grandnephew of Hildebrand, and they set out to his father's castle (inexplicably forgetting all about the journey to Virginal's castle). The heroes are received with great ceremony and celebration. The messenger from Virginal arrives and invites all present to the queen's court.

On the way, Dietrich is separated from the others and finds his way to the castle Muter, where he is imprisoned by its lord, Nitger, with the help of the giant Wicram. Nitger's daughter saves Dietrich from starvation and helps him get word to his friends of his whereabouts. They assemble an army to march to Muter. Eleven individual battles are fought with the giants, and Dietrich is freed. Nitger is forced to accept his lands as a fief from Dietrich. All return to Virginal for a great festival. Word arrives that Bern is under siege. Dietrich returns home and restores order. In some versions the episode at the castle Muter is missing, and in others Dietrich marries Virginal. Most of the narration consists of messenger journeys.

The story seems to have no basis in German heroic legend beyond the use of traditional names. The plot seems to be the result of a long process of addition and subtraction of motifs. At least three plot types can be seen, all of them having to do with the freeing of someone from oppression, imprisonment, or imminent death. Zupitza and others in the nineteenth century attributed the poem to Albrecht von Kemnaten, the poet who names himself in *Goldemar,* but the consensus now rejects this attribution. The poem is composed in the thirteen-line stanza known as the *Bernerton.*

BIBLIOGRAPHY

An edition is Julius Zupitza, ed., *Virginal,* in *Deutsches Heldenbuch,* V (1870, repr. 1968), based on the longest manuscript.

Studies are Joachim Heinzle, *Mittelhochdeutsche Dietrichepik* (1978): content of different versions (34–37), complete list of manuscripts (329–333), and bibliography (335–346); Carl von Kraus, "Virginal und Dietrichs Ausfahrt," in *Zeitschrift für deutsches Altertum und deutsche Literatur,* 50 (1908), an attempted reconstruction of the original poem; Hugo Kuhn, "Virginal," in his *Dichtung und Welt im Mittelalter,* 2nd ed. (1969), the best textual and literary criticism of the poem.

EDWARD R. HAYMES

[See also **Alpharts Tod; Buch von Bern, Das; Eckenlied; Middle High German Literature.**]

VIRTUES AND VICES. The Virtues and the Vices are represented by human figures acting as personifications of abstract ideas. The Virtues are a degree of the second order of angels. These figures are usually female and are typically represented in armor carrying pertinent attributes. This type of anthropomorphization is common in classical antiquity and is prevalent in medieval times as well. In the Christian church, the Virtues and Vices serve a didactic function in the dissemination of the church's ideas on moral righteousness. The canon of Christian Virtues is comprised of three theological virtues—faith, hope, and charity—and four cardinal virtues—prudence, justice, temperance, and fortitude. The opposing vices are popularly depicted as idolatry, despair, avarice, pride, cowardice, anger, and sloth or any of the Seven Deadly Sins.

The concept of the Virtues is found as early as Plato's *Republic* (4:427ff.) as necessary traits of the ideal citizen. The church sanctioned these same traits for Christians, considering them as acquired by the Eucharist. The conflict of the Virtues with Vices is a prevalent theme in both art and literature: Prudentius, a fourth-century Spanish poet, pitted the Virtues against the Vices in battle in his allegorical work the *Psychomachia.* The depiction of

Envy. Fresco by Giotto from the Arena (Scrovegni) Chapel, Padua, *ca.* 1310. ALINARI / ART RESOURCE.

the Virtues and Vices is popular in medieval frescoes, sculpture, and illuminated manuscripts. For example, the sculptural programs at Chartres Cathedral and the fresco cycles in the Scrovegni Chapel, Padua, by Giotto depict the Virtues and Vices. In Gothic art, until roughly the thirteenth century, personifications of the Virtues are often depicted as treading on their corresponding Vices. In the Renaissance they are usually found in separate figures. Charity and Justice are the most common Virtues reproduced. In Renaissance painting the Seven Virtues are often accompanied by the Seven Liberal Arts, the Labors of the Months, or the Wise and Foolish Virgins.

BIBLIOGRAPHY

Gilbert Cope, *Symbolism in the Bible and the Church* (1959); Adolf Katzenellenbogen, *The Allegories of the*

Virtues and Vices in Medieval Art (1939) and *The Sculptural Programs of Chartres Cathedral* (1959).

JENNIFER E. JONES

[See also **Allegory; Angel/Angelology; Prudentius; Seven Deadly Sins.**]

VĪS U RĀMĪN (Vis and Rāmīn), a Persian romance in verse by Fakhr al-Dīn Asᶜad Gurgānī (*fl.* mid eleventh century). Completed around 1050, the poem consists of 8,905 rhyming distichs in the *hazaj* meter. Almost nothing is known of the poet's life.

The story relates that Queen Shahrō of Māh promises her daughter Vīs to King Mōbad of Merv (Mary). Vīs is brought up with Rāmīn, Mōbad's younger brother. When Vīs grows up, Shahrō breaks her pledge to Mōbad and marries Vīs to her own son, Virō, Vīs's brother. Mōbad learns that the marriage is unconsummated and induces Shahrō to surrender Vīs to him. While on a journey, Rāmīn sees Vīs and falls in love with her. Vīs persuades her old nurse, a sorceress, to prepare a talisman to render Mōbad temporarily impotent, but the talisman is lost and Mōbad remains impotent for life. The lovers elope and later return to Merv, where Vīs rejoins Mōbad. On one occasion Vīs has the nurse take her place in Mōbad's bed so that she can meet Rāmīn. Rāmīn leaves Merv and in another city marries Gul. He tires of her and returns to Merv, where he and Vīs quarrel and are later reconciled. Rāmīn raises an army and prepares to overthrow Mōbad. The king marches against Rāmīn but is gored to death by a boar in Amul. Rāmīn reaches Amul, where he is proclaimed king, and then returns with Vīs to Merv, where he rules in prosperity for eighty-three years.

The romance of Vīs and Rāmīn shows a number of striking similarities of plot and character to that of Tristan and Isolde, although no actual connection has been demonstrated. Vladimir Minorsky has argued that *Vīs u Rāmīn* has a Parthian background and reflects historical events during the reign of that dynasty (*ca.* 237/247 B.C.–A.D. 224/226), but this thesis has been disputed by ᶜAbdal-Ḥusayn Zarrīnkūb and other Iranian scholars. *Vīs u Rāmīn* was translated into Georgian, probably during the reign of Queen Tamar (1184–1213).

BIBLIOGRAPHY
Sources. The best Persian edition is by M. A. Todua, A. A. Gwakharia, and S. Aini (1970). There are translations into English (George Morrison, 1972), French (Henri Massé, 1959), and Georgian (M. A. Todua and A. A. Gwakharia, 1962), the last translated into English by Sir John Oliver Wardrop (1914, repr. 1966).
Studies. Works in Western languages include Julie Scott Meisami, *Medieval Persian Court Poetry* (1987); Vladimir Minorsky, "Vīs u Rāmīn: A Parthian Romance," in his *Iranica* (1964), 151–199; R. Zenker, "Die Tristansaga und das persische Epos von Wīs und Rāmīn," in *Romanische Forschungen,* **29** (1911). Studies in Persian include: Sādiq Hidāyat, "Chand Noqta dar bāra-ye Vis o Rāmīn," in his *Neveshtahā-ye Parākanda* (1955); Mojtabā Minova, "Vis o Rāmīn," in *Sukhan,* **6** (1954); ᶜAbd al- Ḥusayn Zarrīnkub, "Vis o Rāmin," in his *Yād-dashthā va andīshah-hā* (1972).

WILLIAM LIPPINCOTT HANAWAY, JR.

[See also **Georgian Literature; Iranian Literature.**]

VISCHER, PETER (THE ELDER) (*fl.* 1489–1520's), metal sculptor. Son of a bronze founder, Vischer became the leading bronze sculptor in Nuremberg. He was head of a large workshop that included his two sons (after *ca.* 1510) and produced bronze tombs as well as small-scale works for export. His masterwork is the tomb of St. Sebaldus at Nuremberg (commissioned 1507, completed 1514–1519; illustration overleaf), filled with references to humanist subjects and Italianate figures and ornaments.

BIBLIOGRAPHY
Michael Baxandall, *The Limewood Sculptors of Renaissance Germany* (1980), 289–290; Simon Meller, *Peter Vischer der Ältere und seine Werkstatt* (1925); Kurt Pilz, *Das Sebaldusgrabmal . . .* (1970); Heinz Stafski, "Die Vischer-Werkstatt und ihre Probleme," in *Zeitschrift für Kunstgeschichte,* **21** (1958), and *Der jüngere Peter Vischer* (1962); Dieter Wuttke, "Die Handschriften-Zeugnisse über das Wirken der Vischer," in *Zeitschrift für Kunstgeschichte,* **22** (1958).

LARRY SILVER

[See also **Gothic, International Style; Metalworkers.**]

VISCONTI. The Visconti family held the lordship of Milan from 1277 to 1447. They were one of the

Tomb of St. Sebaldus in the Sebalduskirche, Nuremberg. Bronze sculpture by Peter Vischer the Elder, 1507–1519. FOTO MARBURG/ART RESOURCE

families, called "captains," to whom Landulf, archbishop of Milan (978–999) gave lands of the church as fiefs in return for their support. In the twelfth century the Visconti had a fief at Marliano and lands on the shore of Lake Maggiore. Their rise to power began in 1262, when Pope Urban IV named Ottone Visconti, archdeacon of the cathedral of Milan, archbishop of the city. At the time Ottone was accompanying Cardinal Ubaldini on his legations in Italy and in France. The Della Torre, a powerful noble family of Milan, opposed the appointment of Ottone and barred his entrance to the city. In the Battle of Desio (20–21 January 1277) Ottone defeated the Della Torre and so was able to enter Milan. He was an able politician and succeeded in gaining the support of all classes in the city.

In 1287 Ottone had his grandnephew Matteo (1287–1322) proclaimed captain of the people. For the old flag of the city (a red cross on a white field) he substituted the Visconti banner (a blue serpent with a red man in its mouth). In 1294 Adolf of Nassau (emperor-elect) made Matteo imperial vicar of Milan and its region. In June 1302 an uprising organized by the Della Torre forced Matteo to leave Milan. In 1310, however, Emperor Henry VII came to Italy and reinstated Matteo in Milan. Matteo extended Visconti domination over Pavia, Piacenza, Tortona, Bergamo, Como, and Alessandria and defied excommunication by the Avignon pope John XXII.

Matteo's son Galeazzo (1322–1328) thwarted a papal offensive led by Cardinal Bertrand of Poggetto. Azzo (1328–1339), son of Galeazzo, bought the title of imperial vicar for 25,000 florins, crushed the rebellion of his cousin Lodrisio in the Battle of Parabiago (1339), and introduced the silk industry. Azzo was succeeded by his brothers Luchino and Giovanni (1349–1354); the latter became archbishop of Milan in 1342. He established the lordship of the Visconti over Bologna (1350) and Genoa (1353). His nephews succeeded him: Galeazzo II (1354–1378), who settled in Pavia, and Bernabò (1354–1385), who lived in Milan.

Gian Galeazzo (1378–1402), son of Galeazzo II, put Bernabò in prison in 1385 and became the sole lord of the Visconti lands, which he extended to include Verona, Padua, Pisa, and Siena. In 1389 Gian Galeazzo married his daughter, Valentina, to Louis, duke of Orléans, brother of King Charles VI of France. (This was the origin of Louis XII's claim to Milan in the sixteenth century.) In 1395 he bought the title of duke from Emperor Wenceslas for 100,000 florins. Gian Galeazzo, however, thought of his vast political construction as a family property and not as a state, and wanted to divide his lands among his three sons. Years of anarchy followed; finally Filippo Maria (1412–1447) rebuilt the duchy. By marrying Beatrice, widow of the condottiere Facino Cane, he increased the size of the Visconti lordship. His foolish attacks on Florence and on Venice, however, forced him to entrust the fate of the duchy to the condottiere Franchesco Sforza (who had married Bianca Maria, Filippo Maria's illegitimate daughter). Filippo Maria died in 1447 without a legitimate heir, thereby ending the Visconti lordship.

BIBLIOGRAPHY
Useful for background information are the following: Fondazione Treccani degli Alfieri per la storia di Milano,

Storia di Milano, V, *La Signoria Viscontea (1310–1392)* (1955); Giorgio Giulini, *Memorie spetanti alla storia, al governo ed alla descrizione della città e campagna di Milano, ne' secoli bassi*, 2nd ed., 7 vols. (1854–1857); Gino Luzzatto, *An Economic History of Italy from the Fall of the Roman Empire to the Sixteenth Century*, Philip Jones, trans. (1961); Lauro Martines, *Power and Imagination: City-States in Renaissance Italy* (1979).

ANGELO PAREDI

[See also **Guelphs and Ghibellines; Italy in the Fourteenth and Fifteenth Centuries; Milan; Sforza.**]

VISIGOTHIC ART can been seen as a symptom of a civilization in which a certain artistic unity was achieved despite tremendous cultural diversity. It is primarily the work of the indigenous Hispano-Roman population of the Iberian Peninsula, challenged and invigorated by the rule of a Visigothic oligarchy. This was a juxtaposition that existed in other European arts contemporary to the Visigoths, but both cultural dichotomy and cohesion were emphasized in the Iberian Peninsula by its isolation from the rest of Western Europe and by its geographical remoteness from the center of the Eastern Roman Empire.

ARCHITECTURE

Built of fine, fitted ashlar by indigenous craftsmen, Visigothic buildings reflect roots in the finest type of Roman masonry. We can identify no two monuments constructed by the same atelier but rather see in each a different and original manner of interpreting the ashlar technique. The decoration, both geometric and figural, however, exhibits an interest in complex, textured, patterned ornament that must to some degree reflect Visigothic decorative traditions.

The surviving churches of Visigothic Spain are extraordinary for a formal preoccupation with the partitioning of spaces, hierarchy, and division. In massing, articulation of walls, and sculpting of space, these churches share a common approach, a common means of answering certain formal questions, that distinguishes them from their contemporaries in Europe and the Mediterranean, and that disassociates them from stylistic and typological ancestors. These are concerns reasserted through the consistent use of chancel barriers, or at times actual walls, that exclude the laity from the most important part of the cult. Complete partitioning

can be seen in the small church of S. Gião near Nazaré, in Portugal. Here a wall punctured by a thin door and two windows obscured the laity's view of the rite performed in the choir. At the churches of S. Pedro de la Nave in Zamora (late seventh century), S. Comba de Bande in Orense (*ca.* 672), S. Maria at Quintanilla de las Viñas in Burgos (late seventh century), and S. Fructuoso de Montelius in Portugal (mid seventh century), an aesthetic of partitioned space predominates, one in which the crossing is marked, significantly, by a series of horseshoe arches. Though the horseshoe arch had existed before on a very limited scale in Roman Iberian architecture, it enjoyed widespread use once it was adopted by the Visigoths. Such arches occur when more than the semicircle is defined. The horseshoe arch that inscribes three-fourths of a circle became a constant in the repertory of the Visigothic mason. Its springer juts out into the door or window opening, forming a more decorative transition that deemphasizes the architectural weight-bearing principles so clearly articulated in a conventional, semicircular arch. It existed in both interiors and exteriors; the western entrance and arcade of King Recceswinth's tiny basilica of S. Juan de Baños in Palencia (661) are composed of horseshoe arches that serve to both embellish and partition the church's interior.

The horseshoe arch and its effect augment the partitioned and hierarchical space that is the most original and characteristic of Visigothic architecture. The evolution of this style occurred at a time when concerns over secrecy and division were being expressed in the councils of the Hispano-Roman church. Parallel to this are studies of Manuel C. Díaz y Díaz, who notes in the liturgy an esoteric development that turns away from the instruction of the laity, one that in its literary elaboration was intended uniquely for the clergy's ears. These changes are to some extent explained by Josef A. Jungmann, who sees in Spanish liturgical developments of the same time prayer types and modes of referring to Christ that reflect to a high degree the "defensive stance" taken by the indigenous Spanish Catholic church against the religious, social, and economic threat of its Arian Visigothic rulers.

Perhaps the secrecy and mystery of Visigothic architecture, the successive closing off of spaces in Visigothic churches, might be the unconscious expression of this same defensive battle. It is an architectural and spatial consideration that began, with these liturgical changes, at the time when the

S. Juan de Baños, Palencia, 661. HIRMER FOTOARCHIV

Spain stemmed initially from an interest in the Eastern Roman Empire, where it was extremely popular in the fifth and sixth centuries. The exterior of the funerary chapel of S. Fructuoso de Montelius, in particular, seems to reflect Eastern influence, as a comparison with the mausoleums of Galla Placidia in Ravenna readily demonstrates. Its ashlar masonry and geometric wall decorations are all that identify its geographical location. S. Fructuoso might reflect lost buildings in the Visigothic capital of Toledo, where royal patrons might have exercised their influence in typology. Within, screens of columns recall Justinian's buildings in particular. This is not surprising when one remembers the dual nature of the close contact that existed between the Visigothic rulers and the Byzantines. Though often at war with the Eastern Empire, the Visigoths never lost their sense of awe at their enemy's sophistication and wealth, nor their own desire to exist "amid royal insignia and abundant wealth, secure in the felicity of the Empire," as Isidore of Seville proclaims in his *De laude Hispaniae*.

SCULPTURE

The work of Visigothic sculptors reveals many of the same themes that were evident in architecture, as we may see in two of the earliest sculptural fragments to survive Visigothic Spain: two sculpted pillars now preserved in the church of S. Salvador in Toledo (early seventh century). One, a fluted pilaster, betrays from the front direct development from a classical tradition of architectural decoration, and the other, which is carved with four scenes from the life of Christ, includes iconography that carefully continues Early Christian tradition. Nevertheless, we can see differences between these and Late Antique work that set the Visigothic pillars apart. The sides of the pilasters are not fluted like the fronts but covered instead with a busy and spontaneous relief that might ultimately find its roots in Byzantine textile design. The depictions from the Life of Christ on the second pillar are carved in a flat, etched style that evokes the metalwork that constituted the Visigoths' primary artistic tradition before settling in Spain. If we skip to the late seventh century, the divers traditions feeding into Visigothic sculpture are less distinguishable with the appearance of a more integrated style. At S. Pedro de la Nave, a continuous vine-scroll relief is applied to the church's fine ashlar walls, and the capitals and bases of the crossing columns are

oppression of the new Arian rulers must have been felt. It can be viewed as the desire on the part of churchmen to reassert in permanent and monumental architectural language divisions that complemented the conceptual separations noted by Jungmann. Such a system of partitioning space also had the effect of enhancing the clergy's position, of rendering them more remote and formidable. The veiling of parts of the sacraments increased the authority of the clergy as arbiters between a gradually excluded laity and their lord—a role of mediatorship denied Christ in the need to associate him with the Father and to shield him from the separateness and humanity of Arian belief.

There were also external influences on the buildings of the Visigoths that are just as evocative of their culture as the ones discussed above. The plans of S. Pedro de la Nave, S. Comba de Bande, S. Fructuoso de Montelius, and S. Pedro de la Mata (Toledo), for instance, are all variations of the cross plan. Though it is a digested part of a Visigothic tradition in most of these cases, there is reason to believe that the popularity of this plan in Visigothic

466

adorned with Old Testament scenes, saints, apostles, and Evangelist symbols. Helmut Schlunk, in 1970, showed the decoration to be a cohesive system evoking the teachings of the Gospels, directed primarily at the occupants of the nave of the church. He suggested that the iconography and style derive from a lost Visigothic manuscript, the missing rescension for a series of tenth-century miniatures that survive today. The reliefs at S. Pedro are indeed executed on one plane and reflect a great interest in linear surface decoration, but these are characteristics that seem intrinsic to Visigothic sculpture in general. The rich figurative remains of the Visigothic sculptural tradition bear witness that the aniconic (anti-image) tenets of the fourth-century Council of Elvira—precepts aimed at genuine pagan idolatry—were no longer of concern to artists and patrons by the seventh century.

PAINTING

The question of what the Visigothic tradition of manuscript illumination might have been remains unresolved. Only one drawing survives—a "Rose of the Winds," executed in a provincial workshop and quite dependent on classical models. Perhaps the Asturian Bible in the monastery of La Cava dei Tirreni, near Naples, reflects the continuation of a Visigothic tradition of illumination, as John Williams suggests. There has also been speculation that the Ashburnham Pentateuch (Paris, Bibliothèque Nationale, MS nouv. acq. lat. 2334) might have been executed in seventh-century Spain, an idea based on certain exotic details in setting and on affinities with later Mozarabic manuscripts.

METALWORK

Visigothic kings, like their contemporaries in Constantinople, dedicated luxurious crowns to important churches. These would hang above the altars, both proclaiming the piety of the king and reinforcing as well the metaphorical connection between him and Christ. Scholars have found, not surprisingly, that Visigothic royal workshops aspired to imitate Byzantine metalwork in fashioning these crowns. Perhaps the most spectacular is one dedicated by King Recceswinth (653–672; Madrid, Museo Arqueológico Nacional) to the church of Toledo, a wide gold band encrusted with gems and pearls, found with the treasure of Guarrazar in Toledo. Suspended below its center is a jeweled cross, and hanging from its perimeter is the king's dedication: RECCESVINTHUS REX OFFERET.

Daniel in the lions' den. Capital at southwest corner of the crossing of S. Pedro de la Nave, Zamora, *ca.* 691. HIRMER FOTOARCHIV

Both the style and function of these crowns serve as indications of their cohesion, the "royal insignia" and "felicity of empire" sought by the Visigoths. (See illustration at "Votive Crown.")

The Visigothic arts that most reflect Gothic traditions are also objects fashioned in a metalwork tradition. In the belt buckles and eagle fibulae of the sixth and seventh centuries a nearly uninterrupted artistic tradition can be noted that was shared by most of the migratory peoples of Europe. In the eagle fibulae of the Walters Gallery in Baltimore the schematization of feathers and other natural forms creates an abstract pattern that covers the works' entire surfaces. This is perhaps the aesthetic principle that most binds the sculpture of the Visigoths to that of the other migration cultures of Europe.

CONCLUSIONS

The seeds of this same formal system of abstract patterning can be noted in one of the most hauntingly beautiful monuments of Visigothic Spain. At the seventh-century church of S. María at Quintanilla de las Viñas, vine scrolls like those at S. Pedro de la Nave wrap around the east or apsidal end of the church like the border of a delicate fabric.

Though such motifs, ultimately derived from Byzantine textile patterns, had long been in the repertory of Visigothic sculptors, they did not lose the sense of delicate, linear articulation associated with that original media, even against a ground of austere, flat ashlar. The decoration indeed binds the entire exterior of S. Maria into one formal unit. Within the church are found side by side reliefs of Christ and Mary and personifications of Sol and Luna, all cut in a dynamic troughed style. Perhaps the vitality lent to this classical iconography by its formal presentation can be our barometer of the extent to which the life and originality of Visigothic art grew from the cultural diversity in which it was produced.

BIBLIOGRAPHY
Manuel C. Díaz y Díaz, "Literary Aspects of the Visigothic Liturgy," in *Visigothic Spain: New Approaches,* Edward James, ed. (1980), 61–76; Jacques Fontaine, *L'art préroman hispanique,* I (1973), offers an excellent historical context and a balanced art historical treatment; Josef A. Jungmann, "Die Abwehr des germanischen Arianismus und der Umbruch der religiösen Kultur im frühen Mittelalter," in *Zeitschrift für Katholische Theologie,* 8 (1954); Carl Nordenfalk, "Late Roman Illumination," in André Grabar and Carl Nordenfalk, eds., *Early Medieval Painting from the Fourth to the Eleventh Century* (1957); Pedro de Palol [Pedro Palol de Salellas], "Escencia del arte hispanico de epoca visigoda romanismo y germanismo," in *Settimane di studio del Centro Italiano di Studi sull'alto medioevo,* III (1956), 65–126, contains an excellent discussion of major questions and definitions; Helmut Schlunk, "Arte visigodo," in *Ars hispaniae: Historia universal del arte hispanico,* II (1947), 225–323, has the most solid, cautious treatment of the formal problems of Visigothic art and architecture, and *Die Denkmäler der frühchristlichen und westgotischen Zeit* (1978); John Williams, *Early Spanish Manuscript Illumination* (1977), 12, 40–43.

J ERRILYNN D. D ODDS

[See also **Early Christian and Byzantine Architecture; Metalsmiths, Gold and Silver; Migration and Hiberno-Saxon Art; Pre-Romanesque Architecture; Pre-Romanesque Art.**]

VISIGOTHS. The Visigoths were part of a larger grouping of Germanic peoples known as Goths. The Goths seem to have had their origin in the southern part of Scandinavia and the northern part of Jutland. For reasons that have never been adequately explained, this people started moving east and south in the early centuries of the Christian era. By the middle of the third century, the Goths in loosely organized bands occupied a large area stretching along the northern shore of the Black Sea westward to the boundary of the Roman province of Dacia.

The Goths took advantage of the crises that faced the Roman Empire in the third century to cross the Roman frontier and to ravage eastern parts of the empire, including Thrace, the Balkan Peninsula, and parts of Asia Minor; the empire suffered greatly from these invasions. Eventually, however, the Gothic menace was repulsed, but at a cost so high that the province of Dacia north of the Danube River was abandoned by Rome (about 271). That portion of the Gothic people coming to be known as the West Goths or Tervingi (later to be known as the Visigoths) moved into Dacia and thus became immediate neighbors of the Romans. The other Goths, the East Goths or Greutungi (later to be known as the Ostrogoths), continued to dwell in an extensive area along the northern shore of the Black Sea.

Internally, both groups of Goths were becoming more cohesive, a process that advanced more rapidly among the Ostrogoths than among the Visigoths. By the time the Huns conquered the Ostrogoths in the late fourth century, the Ostrogoths had already accepted the leadership of a chieftain whose position was essentially that of a king. Historians can discern among the Visigoths by this time more firmly organized groups under dukes or judges, and occasionally one of these chieftains seems to have enjoyed some preeminence over the others. The concept of kingship, however, had not yet developed and would not until after the Visigoths had entered the Roman Empire.

FROM DACIA TO GAUL

The Visigoths lived in Dacia as neighbors of the Roman Empire for approximately one hundred years. During this time, relations between the two peoples were essentially peaceful, with the exception of friction during the reign of Constantine, which resulted in a Visigothic defeat and recognition of the Visigoths as federates (*foederati*) of the empire, rendering military service in time of need in return for yearly subsidies. During the time they lived in Dacia, the Visigoths undoubtedly felt Roman influence, especially in matters of trade, the exportation of slaves and cattle and the importation of grain, clothing, wine, and coins.

They also had contacts with Christianity from several sources—from those Christian Roman provincials of Dacia who remained behind after Rome abandoned the province and from Christians captured by the West Goths during their raids in Asia Minor in the third century and carried north when the Visigoths retreated. Ulfilas, a descendant of third-century Christians from Asia Minor, was born about the year 310. He grew up as a Goth among the Goths although he remained a Christian. About 340 he was consecrated by Eusebius of Nicomedia, the Arian bishop of Constantinople, to be bishop for the Christians in Gothia. Thus the fateful association between the Goths and Arianism was created, although not all Visigoths, nor even a majority of them, converted to Christianity during the episcopacy of Ulfilas. In fact, a strong reaction against Ulfilas' proselytizing developed, and about 348 Visigothic leaders instituted a persecution of Christians. Ulfilas and his followers were forced into exile. From this time until his death about 380, Ulfilas lived and worked in Nicopolis (in the Roman province of Lower Moesia) as the religious (and political) head of the Christian Goths who had gone into exile with him. During this period much of Ulfilas' important religious and cultural work was done and Arian Christianity began to spread among the Goths and was carried to other Germanic neighbors of the Visigoths. From Greek Ulfilas developed a Gothic alphabet, which he used to translate part of the Bible into the language of the Goths.

Relations between the Visigoths and the empire began to deteriorate in the late 360's. The Romans began to interfere north of the Danube River, and at the same time there developed internal tensions among the Goths that strained cooperation among the various Visigothic groups and eventually led to conflict among them. Contributing to the tension were differences on the subject of paganism versus Christianity (which had continued to spread slowly after the departure of Ulfilas) and on the subject of how to face the menace of the Huns, who pushed ever nearer. The two opposing Visigothic leaders who emerged from this confusion were Fritigern and Athanaric.

By 375 the Huns had defeated the Ostrogoths and pressed on toward the Visigoths. The leader Athanaric led out a Visigothic army to meet this advance, but finding himself outmaneuvered, he abandoned resistance and led part of the Visigoths into the mountainous region west of the Carpa-

thians. The greater part of the Visigoths, however, weary of hardship and privation, sought permission in 376 to enter the Roman Empire under the leadership of Fritigern.

Permission to enter was given and for a time the entry proceeded peacefully. Attempts on the part of Roman officials to take advantage of the Visigoths' dire need for food, however, led to resistance and eventually to war. The decisive encounter between the two forces occurred at Adrianople in 378, where the Visigoths defeated the Roman army and the Roman emperor Valens was slain. This battle is sometimes mistakenly regarded as symbolizing the shift from predominantly infantry warfare to predominantly cavalry warfare; the main units of the Visigothic army fought on foot, and only the reconnoitering and foraging parties were mounted. The timely return of these Visigothic cavalry units at Adrianople to take the Roman army in the rear accounts for the undue emphasis given to the cavalry action of this battle.

The Battle of Adrianople was followed by a confused period during which Roman defense grew more effective under the new emperor, Theodosius I, and during which the Visigoths sought by diplomatic and military pressure to secure land for permanent settlement in the Eastern Empire. Neither side was in a strong position: the Visigoths were still not a single people (Fritigern's group had been joined by other Visigoths and even some Ostrogoths, and the role of leader was in dispute); and the Roman Empire was in a period of transition. So long as Theodosius lived, the personal ambitions of the military leaders of the Roman army (many of whom were Germanic, even Gothic) were held in check, but following the death of Theodosius in 395, political leadership declined rapidly under the nominal rule of the sons of Theodosius, Arcadius in the East and Honorius in the West. In effect, it was now the Germanic commanders of the army who largely determined policy, and the policies of these barbarian commanders alternately protected the empire against the barbarian invaders and utilized some groups of barbarians against other barbarians. The Visigoths suffered from this vacillation in policy, but they also profited by it. Settled for a time in Moesia, the Visigoths regarded this area as less desirable than other land; in the process of forcefully moving south and west in the Balkan Peninsula, they temporarily settled in Epiros. By now the role of the Visigothic leader had become stronger, although it was still elective and basically military. The leader or chieftain by this time was a man named Alaric (*ca.* 370–410), and either during the Visigoths' stay in Epiros or during their later travels in Italy he began to be referred to as "king."

By the year 401, conditions in the West encouraged the Visigoths under Alaric to leave Epiros and move into Italy. This first move into Italy was halted by the Vandal Stilicho, *magister militum* in the Western Empire, and the Visigoths were forced to return to Epiros. But the following years were utterly disastrous for the Western Empire. Beginning in 406 the Rhine frontier was penetrated by a series of Germanic peoples, including the Vandals, Sueves, and Burgundians. In Italy, the position of Stilicho was undermined by his enemies, and in 408 his execution was ordered by Emperor Honorius. In the confusion that resulted, the Visigoths again demanded land or subsidies; following the refusal of Honorius to grant these, they re-entered the Italian peninsula and almost without opposition moved to Rome, where after fruitless negotiations they laid siege to the city. Rome fell after suffering terribly from famine, and the Visigoths subjected the city to a three-day sack (August 410). At this time Rome was stripped of much of its movable wealth, although this sack was not especially destructive. Laden with booty, the Visigoths moved south intending to make their way to the fertile fields of North Africa. After losing part of their shipping to bad weather and their leader Alaric to death, the Visigoths reconsidered their plans. Electing Alaric's brother-in-law, Athaulf, as their king, the Visigoths returned north through Italy and passed into Gaul, carrying with them Galla Placidia, sister of the emperor, who had been taken during the sack of Rome.

The Visigoths entered Gaul in 412, but it was not until 418 that they concluded a treaty with Rome regularizing their position. During the earlier part of this interval Athaulf attempted to secure food supplies and political concessions from the Romans and to encourage the advance of Romanization among his people, and at some time in this period he married Galla Placidia. But Athaulf was killed in 415, and after a brief period Wallia was elected king. By 418, both Visigoths and Romans were tired of the continuous struggle and a treaty of alliance was signed whereby the Visigoths were assigned the province of Aquitanica Secunda and Galla Placidia was returned to Italy. When Wallia died, the Visigoths elected Theodoric I (*r.* 418–

451). Although the date that the Visigoths as a nation accepted Arianism is disputed, they were certainly Arians by the time they arrived in Aquitaine. Their Arianism became a point of serious friction with the Gallo-Roman provincials, although the Visigothic kings generally pursued a policy of toleration toward the Gallo-Roman Catholics.

When the Visigoths first took over their new territory, they held a rather ambiguous position: they had been given land in return for military service to Rome. So far as the Visigoths themselves were concerned, they were subject to the authority of their king, but their king was subject to the authority of Rome. The position of the Roman provincials in the Visigothic area was uncertain, but the military superiority of the more warlike Visigoths in effect extended the authority of the Visigothic king over them also, even though the Roman civil administration remained in place and maintained the Roman provincial and city organization.

The new king, Theodoric I, steadily increased his authority as well as the territory controlled by his people. The means of accomplishing this was the continued military need of Rome: on a number of occasions the Visigoths responded to requests for protection against the Vandals and Sueves in Spain, and in 451 the Visigoths joined an army assembled by the Roman commander Aëtius to face the Huns, who had penetrated deep into Gaul. Much of the credit for the Roman victory at the Battle of the Catalaunian Fields (Châlons) belonged to the Visigoths and to their king, Theodoric I, who fell during the course of the battle. The reputation of the Visigoths as loyal but ambitious *foederati* was high.

After Theororic's death, his son Thorismud succeeded as king until 453, when he was assassinated at the instance of a brother who became Theodoric II. Theodoric II was in turn removed by another brother, Euric (466–484). When Euric died he was succeeded by his son Alaric II, who ruled the Visigoths until his death in battle with the Franks in 507 (Vouillé), bringing to an end the most serious attempt in Visigothic history to establish an hereditary dynasty. But even these kings ultimately owed their positions to the choice made by the Visigothic people (or rather by the army). After the death of Alaric II in 507 the continued operation of election virtually ruled out the establishment of heredity as the ruling principle in deciding the kingship, and in the process guaranteed recurrent internal struggles for the throne. This proved to be a serious constitutional weakness for the Visigothic kingdom.

In the interval between the original treaty with Rome in 418 and defeat by the Franks in 507, the Visigoths built up an extensive territory that became largely independent of Rome even before the deposition of Romulus Augustulus in 476 and the end of formal control from Rome. This territory stretched from the Loire River in the north to the Rhône in the east and across the Pyrenees through most of the Iberian Peninsula, with the exception of a territory in the northwest occupied by the Sueves and a territory in the western Pyrenees occupied by the Basques.

THE VISIGOTHS IN SPAIN

After defeat by the Franks in 507, the Visigoths were forced to withdraw south from most of their territory in Gaul, with its capital at Toulouse, and thereafter to base their kingdom in Spain. The actual settlement of Visigothic peoples was concentrated in the north-central part of the Iberian Peninsula, although the capital of the kingdom would be established in the extreme south of this area in the city of Toledo.

Rule of Amalaric. Follwing the death of Alaric II in 507, the throne passed after an interval to Alaric's son Amalaric (511–531). During this period the Visigoths enjoyed the protection of the Ostrogoths, whose king, Theodoric, was Amalaric's maternal grandfather. It was Ostrogothic intervention that had allowed the Visigoths to retain Gallic Septimania (along the Mediterranean coast) in spite of Frankish attempts to occupy it. Following Theodoric the Ostrogoth's death in 526, Ostrogothic influence waned but did not entirely disappear until 548 (Theudis, king of the Visigoths during this period, was an Ostrogoth who had married a Hispano-Roman provincial). Ostrogothic influence was partially replaced by Byzantine influence from 552 to about 624, during which time the southeastern part of the peninsula was under Byzantine control. With incorporation of the Suevic kingdom in the northwest in 585 and expulsion of the Byzantines from the southeast between 623 and 625, foreign influence in the peninsula was largely extinguished until the arrival of the Moors in 711.

Sixth century. The most important of the Visigothic kings in the later sixth century include Leovigild (568–586), who incorporated the kingdom of the Sueves into the Visigothic kingdom; he revised an earlier Visigothic law code issued by Euric (between 476 and 483)—a revision that included a provision that lifted the earlier prohibition on intermarriage between Goth and Roman—and developed a concept of a united state held together in a single religious faith. Since Leovigild was Arian, this single faith was at first conceived of in terms of Arianism, and accordingly some pressure was exerted to convert Catholics to that faith. Even before his death, however, Leovigild seems to have realized that the attempt would fail: too many of the Visigoths had already become Catholic; too few Catholics were lured to Arianism. Leovigild's own son Hermenegild had openly been a Catholic (a factor in his rebellion, which began in 579–580 and ended with his death in 585), and another son of Leovigild, Recared, was favorably inclined toward Catholicism. In any event, by the time Leovigild died in 586 and was succeeded by Recared, the way was evidently open to Recared's renunciation of Arianism. Recared accepted Catholicism in 587, and in 589 the Third Council of Toledo declared Catholicism to be the religion of the state. Thereafter, all traces of Arianism rapidly disappeared in the Visigothic realm, and the religious unity thereby produced removed one factor of internal discord in the kingdom.

Seventh century. Under Chindaswinth (642–653) a revision of Leovigild's law code was begun, and a new edition of the law was issued about 654 during the reign of Chindaswinth's son, Receswinth (653–672). This version of the Visigothic law (the *Leges Visigothorum* or the *Forum Judicum*) replaced all earlier versions and likewise repealed the *Breviary of Alaric*, which had been issued in 506 as a code of Roman law for the Roman population of the Visigothic kingdom. Since the religious distinction between Roman and Goth had already been removed and the ban on intermarriage lifted, the legal homogeneity of the kingdom established by the new territorial law code facilitated a more rapid fusion between the Roman and Germanic parts of the population.

Conquest by the Moors. The kings after Receswinth faced increasing unrest in the kingdom, as a result of which few of the later Visigothic kings enjoyed peaceful reigns but rather faced sporadic rebellions from ambitious nobles. Assassination, deposition, and civil war plagued the kingdom in its last years and contributed largely to the weak resistance put up against the Moors in 711. These rebellions were not rebellions of Romans against

Goths, but were struggles among the powerful to gain more power. This was the Gothic disease that eventually destroyed the state.

INSTITUTIONS AND SOCIAL STRUCTURE OF VISIGOTHIC SPAIN

Information about the history and institutions of the Visigothic kingdom comes from a number of sources. The most important literary source is Isidore of Seville's *History of the Goths* (619–624), although this work is in general very disappointing. Legal and ecclesiastical materials provide better information. The Visigothic kings beginning with Theodoric II concerned themselves with issuing laws for their people. But the *Edictum Theodorici* (458) dealt primarily with the resolution of cases that had arisen between Goths and Romans and was a very incomplete statement of the law. More important was a codification of Visigothic law code issued by Euric between 476 and 483 (a code that has not survived) and a codification of Roman law issued by Alaric II (the *Breviary*) in 506. Although the *Breviary* does not seem to have been revised after its original issue, it remained the basis of law for the Roman part of the population of the Visigothic kingdom until its repeal in 654. The Visigothic legislation, on the other hand, went through a series of revisions, each revision reflecting greater Roman influence. When the revised *Leges Visigothorum* was issued in 654 by Receswinth it became a territorial code for the entire kingdom. But although Visigoths and Romans lived under different personal laws until 654, the two systems had been converging for some time. In any event, the abrogation of the *Breviary* seems to have caused no protest from the Hispano-Romans.

In addition to the Visigothic laws, the canons issued by the councils of Toledo tell us much about the Visigoths and their institutions. The councils of Toledo were technically church councils, but since they met irregularly at the call of the king and were attended by various royal officials as well as by members of the diocesan and provincial church hierarchy, the canons that they issued assumed the role of supplements to the law codes as well as guides to church doctrine and discipline. The council that met in 589 (the council that renounced Arianism) was the Third Council; the conciliar legislation came to an end with the Seventeenth Council in 694.

There is a considerable contrast between the theory of Visigothic government revealed in these sources and its practice. Heavily influenced by Roman concepts, the Visigothic kingship was in theory a powerful institution, the king combining the old Germanic notion of the king as military leader responsible for the defense of his people with the Roman concept of the ruler as responsible for the health of the civil order as well; thus he was the ultimate source of law and justice in the kingdom. To this was added a religious sanction: the Visigothic king ruled with divine approval. The king controlled appointment of all civil and military offices in the state and he also controlled ecclesiastical appointments. Although the officers of the church and those members of the civil administration who enjoyed special influence or favor with the king met in frequent councils at Toledo and these councils issued canons affecting both state and church, this institution did not constitute a check or limitation on the king's authority. The canons drawn up by the councils were always submitted for approval to the king before going into effect, and they were ultimately enforced by the king's justice. At law, to act against the king was treason (*maiestas*), a concept lacking in other Germanic legislation.

So in theory the Visigothic king held all the means of converting his position into an effective autocratic one, but in practice this did not happen. The failure of the notables to accept the hereditary principle coupled with their refusal to place royal or national interests before personal ambition led to frequent rebellion and a refusal to render requested military service. The Visigothic state was a badly divided one by the early eighth century; in 711 a party of invading Moors found itself invited to intervene on behalf of one of the contending parties. Thereafter, it required only a short while for the Moors to overcome the disorganized Visigothic resistance.

Despite the unhappy picture presented by the dissension between the Visigothic king and his nobles, other aspects of Visigothic history offer more positive achievements. The religious and legal assimilation of the Roman and Gothic parts of the population was more than just an idealistic goal. Visigothic Spain became a vigorous Catholic state, its Catholicism somewhat hostile to Rome and aggressively hostile to Jews. A truly unified state such as the Visigothic kings sought to create had no place for religious dissent; therefore, the anti-Semitic legislation of the Visigoths after 589 was designed to bring about either genuine conversion or exile for the Jews of the kingdom. This legislation did not succeed in accomplishing its goal, but the severity of the laws against the Jews of the Visigothic kingdom would guarantee that the Jews of Spain would put up no resistance to the Moorish conquest.

The Visigothic king's government was organized in a hierarchy that owed much to its Roman model. At the king's court were to be found officials who presided over such central bureaus as treasury, chancery, chamber, and stable. At the provincial governorship level were officials with the title of duke; and at the local level (the Roman *civitas*) there were the city counts. Paralleling this civilian hierarchy there was a military hierarchy. Normally the same individual did not serve in a civil and military office at the same time, but it was not unknown for the same individual to combine both civil and military power. Both Romans and Goths served in all these offices, but there was some tendency for the Hispano-Romans to dominate the provincial offices and the ecclesiastical hierarchy and for the Goths to dominate at court, in the military commands, and among the city counts. Little is known about Visigothic taxation, but it seems that some of the Roman taxes were continued and that both Goths and Romans were subject to them.

The social structure of the Visigothic kingdom evolved from Roman and Gothic precedents: it consisted of the free and the unfree. The Roman half-free (the *coloni*) had disappeared by the time the *Breviary* was abrogated, the more fortunate members of the Roman colonate probably making their way into the class of the free and the more unfortunate depressed into the ranks of the unfree. At the level of the unfree or slave there was no distinction at Visigothic law between slaves performing various services (for instance, between those employed in the household or in the field), but there was some distinction based on ownership. Royal slaves enjoyed greater privileges than the slaves of ordinary freemen or of the church.

The class of the free was divided into a more powerful group on top and a more humble one below. The legal status of both groups was the same, but the more powerful (sometimes called nobles) were subject to higher fines than the more humble and were subjected to torture less frequently. Membership in neither category was strictly hereditary, and as a result a member of either could be reduced to the status of a slave (through capture in battle, voluntary sale, penal slavery, or failure to pay a fine or a debt). Freed slaves suffered some limitations on their legal capacity, but their children were completely free. There was thus no rigid class structure in the Visigothic state, and considerable social mobility was possible within the law.

City life continued in Visigothic Spain. The civil administration of the kingdom continued to be concentrated in the cities. A considerable amount of internal commerce survived from the earlier period as well as some external trade directed mainly toward the Mediterranean Sea. In the cities some of the institutions of classical education also survived (some of the most learned scholars of the West in the sixth and seventh centuries came from Spain, for instance Leander and his brother Isidore, successive bishops of Seville).

Although city life continued on a somewhat reduced scale in the Visigothic kingdom, the majority of the population was rural. The rural economic regime was based on the Roman villa system, the large agricultural estate worked by free tenants or unfree slaves. Doubtless there were free smallholders also, but they are difficult to trace. The land had been distributed among the Visigothic invaders according to a system of "hospitality" that was put into effect in Gaul following the original agreement with Rome in 418; it may well have been applied also in Spain after the Visigoths moved out of Gaul (except for Septimania) and into Spain. This system of hospitality involved a sharing of land as well as agricultural workers between a Roman host and a Visigothic guest, but the Visigothic laws referring to this system take much for granted and there is no precise knowledge of how this system worked in practice. It does not seem to have occasioned strong protest from the Roman landholders: the fact that the land had been underpopulated and the Visigoths were not numerous allowed the Visigoths to settle on the land with a minimum of resistance. It should be noted, however, that the main Visigothic settlement in Spain (as indicated by archaeological evidence from cemeteries) was concentrated in the north-central part of the peninsula; elsewhere the Roman population and its descendants predominated.

Visigothic familial institutions combined Roman and Germanic influences. The Visigothic family was a small one, consisting of husband, wife, minor sons, unmarried daughters, and other legal dependents. The father's power over his children was less than that of the Roman *pater familias,* and his legal control over his wife less than that among other Germanic peoples. Visigothic law, like the laws of other Germans, kept separate the property of husband and wife, but among the other Germans women were not legally competent, and administration of the wife's property normally was exercised by her husband during his lifetime, and by an adult kinsman after his death. The Visigothic woman, however, enjoyed a limited legal competence of her own. She administered her own property, even after marriage, though she normally could not administer the property of anyone else unless she acted as guardian for her minor children; a husband could administer his wife's property only with her written consent. Sons became independent of their father's control at the age of twenty (after which they could arrange their own marriages, although they could not force the distribution of their father's estate). Unmarried daughters always remained subject to the control of their fathers or other male relatives so far as their marriage was concerned, except that women over twenty could arrange their own marriages if they were willing to forfeit their places in their family's inheritance. Reminiscent of the early imperial Roman marriage, the Visigothic marriage could be dissolved by mutual consent.

The composition of the Visigothic kin group was essentially the same as among the other Germans: it consisted of an individual's relatives to the seventh degree, and the kin group differed for each set of people with the same father and mother. The role played by this kin group was basically the same as for the other Germans in matters of private law—for instance, in arranging marriages, claiming inheritance, assuming guardianship, and so on. In the public area, however, the role of the kin group was considerably reduced. There is little or no evidence of the continuation of the blood feud in the Visigothic kingdom, and Germanic modes of proof (depending principally on compurgation and ordeal) had been replaced by the Roman methods of judicial investigation, witnesses, and torture. The role of the kin group in public law was now limited to the kind of indirect support needed to give an individual strength to charge his enemies before the courts.

The composition of the Visigothic court was like that of the Burgundians and Lombards and unlike that of the Franks and Anglo-Saxons. It was a court presided over by a royal justice who rendered his decision in accordance with his own knowledge of or interpretation of the law. He was not assisted by any group of men elected from or representing the community. Justices investigated the charges brought before them, heard the proof, and rendered their verdict. Hearing the proof consisted, in both civil and criminal types of actions, in bringing witnesses into court, placing them on oath, and hearing the evidence (given under torture, in some cases). The judge made his decision, announced it, and supervised its being carried out—which might entail punishment as well as a fine in the case of criminal offenses.

Although the Visigothic kingdom came to an end in the early eighth century, the influence of Visigothic institutions did not die. As the Moors advanced in the peninsula, parts of the Visigothic population retreated and eventually created a separate Christian state in the northwest part of the peninsula (known as the kingdom of Asturias). Here many aspects of Visigothic life lived on. But such was the case not only in the kingdom of the Asturias: even in those parts of the peninsula directly under Muslim rule, the small number of Moors combined with their tolerant attitude toward their subjects produced groups of "Spaniards" who were largely autonomous—in any event, they were allowed to practice their own Christian religion and to govern their private lives by Visigothic law.

BIBLIOGRAPHY

Sources. Latin texts containing Visigothic material are "Concilia hispaniae," in *Patrologia latina*, CLXXXIV (1862), 301–626; Karl Zeumer, ed., "Leges Visigothorum," in *Monumenta Germaniae historica*, Legum sectio I, I (1902).

For modern editions and translations, see Guido Donini and Gordon B. Ford, Jr., trans., *Isidore of Seville's History of the Kings of the Goths, Vandals, and Suevi* (1966); Charles C. Mierow, trans., *The Gothic History of Jordanes* (1915); Samuel P. Scott, *The Visigothic Code* (1910).

Studies. Dietrich Claude, *Geschichte der Westgoten* (1970); Felix Dahn, *Die Könige der Germanen*, VI, 2nd ed. (1885); Pierre P. Courcelle, *Histoire littéraire des grandes invasions germaniques*, 3rd ed. (1964); Thomas Hodgkin, *Italy and Her Invaders*, I, 2nd ed. (1892); Edward James, ed., *Visigothic Spain: New Approaches* (1980); P. D. King, *Law and Society in the Visigothic Kingdom* (1972); Marie R. Madden, *Political Theory and Law in Medieval Spain* (1930); Álvaro d'Ors, *Estudios visigóticos*, I (1956); Eduardo Pérez Pujol, *Historia de las instituciones sociales de la España goda*, 4 vols.

(1896); Edward A. Thompson, *The Visigoths in the Time of Ulfila* (1966) and *The Goths in Spain* (1969); Manuel Torres *et al., Espana visigoda,* in R. Menéndez Pidal, ed., *Historia de España,* II (1940); Joseph Vogt, *The Decline of Rome* (1967); Herwig Wolfram, *Geschichte der Goten* (1979); Aloysius K. Ziegler, *Church and State in Visigothic Spain* (1930).

KATHERINE FISCHER DREW

[See also **Alaric; Arianism; Asturias-León; Barbarians, Invasions of; Huns; Isidore of Seville, St.; Jews in Europe; Law, German: Early Codes; Law, Spanish; Mozarabic Art; Mozarabic Literature; Mozarabic Rite; Ostrogoths; Pre-Romanesque Art; Roman Empire, Late; Toledo.**]

VISION. See **Optics.**

VISION OF MAC CONGLINNE. See **Aislinge Meic Con-Glinne.**

VISIONS. During the Middle Ages and the Renaissance, there was tremendous interest in the phenomena and literature of visions and dreams of all kinds. The literary artifacts of this interest occur in two main forms. The first and generally less important is the visionary interlude in a longer work, the dream that helps to further the narrative in an epic or romance, or to comment on it. Such visions—Arthur's dream of the dragon in Malory's *Le Morte D'Arthur* is a good example—are generally enigmatic and prophetic; they are often also, as here, admonitory, beckoning a character toward some experience even as they also warn of its possible consequences. The dragon dream is one of several visions in the *Morte* that seem, in the midst of immediate victory, to speak of ultimate fall.

The second form has traditionally been called the "dream vision"; in it, typically, the narrator recounts in the first person a vision or a series of visions that constitute the frame and the focus of the piece as a whole. Such works are extremely common in French literature from the thirteenth century on; the flowering of the form occurred a little later in Germany, Spain, Italy, and England, but in all the European literatures the dream vision represents a signally important body of material, a tradition extending to the sixteenth century and beyond. As A. C. Spearing comments in *Medieval Dream Poetry,* the dream vision "had as long a run as a major literary form as has been granted to the novel so far."

The literary ancestry of the form is extremely complex. Its classical sources include Odysseus' journey to Hades in book XI of the *Odyssey,* Aeneas' visit to the underworld in book VI of the *Aeneid,* and, most important, the *Somnium Scipionis* of Cicero; this work, with Macrobius' commentary on it, offered not merely a pattern of dream experience but also what was perhaps the seminal system of dream classification for the Middle Ages. The New Testament and the Apocrypha offered biblical models: the *Apocalypse* of St. John, for example, and the *Vision of St. Paul,* which dates from the third or fourth century. The latter work was translated from Greek into Latin by the sixth century; the history of its many versions is typical of the tradition as a whole.

During the early Middle Ages, influences from Persia, from Islam, and from Celtic mythology brought to Judeo-Christian mysticism an extraordinary corpus of images and motifs to enrich a Latin literature in which visions of heaven and hell—Hincmar's *Visio Bernoldi,* for example, and the vision of Dryhthelm in book V, chapter 12, of Bede's *Ecclesiastical History*—played a significant part.

There were also in the earlier Middle Ages Latin visions expressing great philosophical and doctrinal truths and systems, in the tradition of Boethius—the twelfth-century *De planctu Naturae* of Alan of Lille is an example. But by the end of the twelfth century, the development of a vernacular literature in France spurred translations of existing visions from the Latin and seems to have fostered a French dream tradition which produced the *Roman de la Rose* and the love visions of, among many others, Froissart and Machaut. This French tradition stimulated and influenced the production of vernacular dream visions in England and (though the line of transmission is less certain here) in Spain. In the later thirteenth and especially in the fourteenth century, as Chaucer, Langland, and the *Pearl* poet in England, and Boccaccio and Dante in Italy, experimented with the form, the vision became perhaps the most important metaphor and structure for exploring the philosophical, religious, and literary issues of the age.

This is hardly surprising. Carolly Erickson has postulated that an understanding of the medieval concept of "vision" is seminal to an understanding of an age in which the visionary imagination had a central role. In her view, metaphors of the vision were commonly the vehicle for many types of formal writings, and the many-leveled reality of allegory and of apocalyptic literature was familiar ground to men and women of the twelfth through fourteenth centuries.

Certainly medieval Christianity urged its believers to look beyond this world to another, and the intellectual structures of the school of Chartres fused Christian and Neoplatonic doctrine into a poetic of illumined sight and ultimate verities. Thus educated and ignorant alike tended to perceive a many-leveled reality, for the imaging of which the vision, with its interplay of world and otherworld, was an apt and convenient vehicle.

Certainly the use of the visionary mode was intensely popular from the thirteenth century on, as a great variety of works in many languages attest. However, so great is the disparity among these works—ranging from the frankly erotic to the mystical—that critics have long been reluctant to consider love and religious visions alongside one another, as products of a single tradition defining a particular kind of poem. Whatever the surface similarity in frame, the arguments run, there can surely be little significant connection between a work such as Chaucer's prologue to the *Legend of Good Women* and the high and holy seriousness of the *Pearl*.

It has been suggested that though the dream poem may not be a separate literary category, it does tend to present a certain type of subject: an ideal and often symbolic landscape in which a dreamer meets an authoritative figure who imparts a religious or secular doctrine. It clearly has a beginning and an end (marked by the falling asleep and awakening of the narrator); there is a narrator, whose experience is the subject of the poem; and it is imaginative fiction. Thus, it is a work of art.

Hence, the dream vision can be seen as in some ways a very self-conscious form, anticipating (or perhaps inventing) some modern concerns. It is important to remember, however, that the vision being articulated by these works is essentially a medieval one, in which the erotic and religious traditions are significantly connected. A dream vision, linking two or more worlds or levels of reality, juxtaposing landscapes of the mind and heart with views of this world and the next, records the process of an education—the dreamer's—so

that readers or hearers may profit from it, may themselves be educated in the mysterious forces that govern our world but may be encountered directly only in a state of heightened vision. Whether a dreamer visits the Courts of Love or approaches the Holy City, he generally learns something—whether willingly or not.

The dream vision is a definable, though by no means homogeneous, literary form—a tradition within which several subcurrents of tradition operate, interchanging motifs, images, and more. Likewise, the very climate of fascination with dream and vision was a heterogeneous one. Doubts and questions were common, as the many conflicting systems of dream classification and interpretation attest. If God could speak to man in a dream, so might the devil; and of course there are mental and physical causes that must be taken into account. Macrobius himself admits indigestion as a primary cause of nightmare. Many theorists sought to introduce order into the chaos of material and nomenclatures, as Carolly Erickson has shown in her consideration of Augustine, Bacon, and Nicholas of Cusa, among others.

However, while the term "vision" may in some works and authors signify a higher and holier state than dream—a state in which the waking soul communicates as directly as possible with God—there is nothing resembling a universal practice for the period. All that can be said with certainty is that some writers—Dante, for example—seem to have made a distinction in terminology, and it is perhaps significant that the *Divine Comedy* is one of many important medieval and Renaissance works—Gower's *Confessio Amantis* is another example—that are clearly "visionary" but are not cast explicitly as dreams or visions. Such an implicit form allowed the clear portrayal of varying states and degrees of vision.

However, dreams and visions with explicit frames continued to be tremendously influential in European and British literature. The *Pèlerinage de la vie humaine* and *Pèlerinage de l'âme* of Guillaume de Deguileville stem from the mid fourteenth century but exist in many later verse and prose redactions in both English and French, testifying to the enduring popularity of vast visionary allegories. In England, several skilled Middle Scots writers—Robert Henryson, William Dunbar, and Gavin Douglas—continued to write visions of love and poetry that extended the Chaucerian tradition into the sixteenth century, when it was taken up by

Stephen Hawes and John Skelton. Editions of Langland's *Piers Plowman* were popular in the mid sixteenth century, and the collected works of Chaucer into the seventeenth. In Italy, Boccaccio's use of the dream for satire in his *Amorosa visione* and *Il corbaccio* helped to fix Renaissance practice in the form, as did (though in another direction) Petrarch's highly emblematic *Trionfi*. In Spain the satirical visions of hell created by Francisco de Quevedo in the seventeenth century continued a rich vernacular dream tradition that had included Gonzalo de Berceo in the thirteenth century and the Marqués de Santillana and Juan de Mena in the fifteenth.

In fact, it could be argued that the dream vision proved as protean a form in the early Renaissance as it had in the Middle Ages. Both dream visions and visionary interludes in longer works are of tremendous significance. However, the later Renaissance saw the decline of the form. The Reformation, with its distrust of traditional allegorical theory and practice, and the new science and philosophy, with their emphasis on the phenomena of the world, on material causes and effects, shattered the medieval vision of the world. For a time the tradition of the occult sciences kept alive the concept of a universe composed of mysterious forces, of interlocking realities, but by the seventeenth century such views were becoming increasingly unpopular. And although dreams and visions continued to be written, few—with the exception of Bunyan's *Pilgrim's Progress*—are of any literary merit. Increasingly, the form became debased into a tool for literary hacks, for warring religious and political pamphleteers. The visionary power evoked by poets for more than four centuries had finally been lost.

BIBLIOGRAPHY

Sources. Alan of Lille, *The Plaint of Nature*, James J. Sheridan, trans. (1980); Giovanni Boccaccio, *The Corbaccio*, Anthony K. Cassell, trans. and ed. (1975); Boethius, *The Consolation of Philosophy*, S. J. Tester, trans., rev. ed. (1973); Geoffrey Chaucer, *The Book of the Duchess, The House of Fame, The Parliament of Fowls*, and the prologue to the *Legend of Good Women*, in *The Poetical Works of Chaucer*, Fred N. Robinson, ed., 2nd ed. (1961); Dante Alighieri, *The Divine Comedy*, Charles S. Singleton, trans., 3 vols. in 6 (1970–1975); Gavin Douglas, *The Palice of Honour*, in *The Shorter Poems of Gavin Douglas*, Priscilla J. Bawcutt, ed. (1967); William Dunbar, "The Goldyn Targe" and "The Thrissil and the Rois," in *The Poems of William Dunbar*, James

Kinsley, ed. (1979); Guillaume de Deguileville, *The Pilgrimage of the Life of Man*, John Lydgate, trans., F. J. Furnivall and Katharine B. Locock, eds., 3 vols. (1899–1904).

Guillaume de Lorris and Jean de Meun, *The Romance of the Rose*, Charles Dahlberg, trans. (1971); Stephen Hawes, *The Conforte of Louers*, in *The Minor Poems of Stephen Hawes*, Florence W. Gluck and Alice B. Morgan, eds. (1974); James I of Scotland, *The Kingis Quair*, John Norton-Smith, ed. (1971); William Langland, *Piers the Plowman*, J. F. Goodridge, trans. (1959); John Lydgate, *The Temple of Glass*, John Norton-Smith, ed. (1966); Macrobius, *Commentary on the Dream of Scipio*, William H. Stahl, trans. (1952); *The Parlement of the Thre Ages*, M. Y. Offord, ed., (1959); *Pearl*, Eric V. Gordon, ed. (1953, repr. 1980); Francesco Petrarch, *Lord Morley's Tryumphes of Fraunces Petrarcke*, D. D. Carnicelli, ed. (1981); John Skelton, "The Bowge of Court," in *The Poems of John Skelton*, Robert S. Kinsman, ed. (1969); [*A Good Short Debate Between*] *Winner and Waster*, Sir Israel Gollancz, ed. (1921, repr. 1974).

Studies. Judith H. Anderson, *The Growth of a Personal Voice* (1976), 12–76; Ernest J. Becker, *A Contribution to the Comparative Study of Medieval Visions of Heaven and Hell* (1899, repr. 1976); Walter Blank, *Die deutsche Minneallegorie* (1970), 139–142; Carolly Erickson, *The Medieval Vision* (1976); John V. Fleming, *The Roman de la Rose* (1969); Denton Fox, "The Scottish Chaucerians," in *Chaucer and Chaucerians*, Derek S. Brewer, ed. (1966); Sigmund Freud, *The Interpretation of Dreams*, James Strachey, trans. and ed. (1955, repr. 1965); Pamela Gradon, *Form and Style in Early English Literature* (1971), 93–151; Constance B. Hieatt, *The Realism of Dream Visions* (1977); George Kane, *The Autobiographical Fallacy in Chaucer and Langland Studies* (1965); Elizabeth D. Kirk, *The Dream Thought of Piers Plowman* (1977); Ernest Langlois, *Origines et sources du Roman de la Rose* (1890, repr. 1973).

Alice E. Lasater, *Spain to England: A Comparative Study of Arabic, European, and English Literature of the Middle Ages* (1974), 56–95; Alice Cornelia Loftin, "Such Shaping Fantasies: Traditions of Visionary Narrative from the Fourteenth Through the Seventeenth Century" (diss., Univ. of Michigan, 1977); Isabel G. MacCaffrey, *Spenser's Allegory: The Anatomy of Imagination* (1976), 5–75; Norman I. Mackenzie, *Dreams and Dreaming* (1965); Michael Murrin, *The Allegorical Epic* (1980), 37–42, 55–56, 110–111, 124–127; William A. Neilson, *The Origins and Sources of the Court of Love* (1899, repr. 1967); Francis X. Newman, "St. Augustine's Three Visions and the Structure of the *Commedia*," in *Modern Language Notes*, 82 (1967); Anthony D. Nuttall, *Two Concepts of Allegory* (1967); Arnold B. van Os, *Religious Visions* (1932); Douglas D. R. Owen, *The Vision of Hell* (1970); Howard R. Patch, *The Other*

World (1950), chap. 4; Derek Pearsall, "The English Chaucerians," in *Chaucer and Chaucerians,* Derek S. Brewer, ed. (1966).

Paul Piehler, *The Visionary Landscape* (1971); Chandler R. Post, *Mediaeval Spanish Allegory* (1915, repr. 1974); Wilhelm Schmitz, *Traum und Vision in der erzählenden Dichtung des deutschen Mittelalters* (1934); Meredith Anne Skura, "Revisions and Rereading in Dreams and Allegories," in *The Literary Freud,* Joseph H. Smith, ed. (1980); Wilbur O. Sypherd, *Studies in Chaucer's Hous of Fame* (1907, repr. 1965); Keith V. Thomas, *Religion and the Decline of Magic* (1971), 25–253; Rosemond Tuve, *Allegorical Imagery* (1966), 145–218, 233–264; Winthrop Wetherbee, *Platonism and Poetry in the Twelfth Century* (1972); James I. Wimsatt, *Chaucer and the French Love Poets* (1968); James Winny, *Chaucer's Dream-Poems* (1973); Frances A. Yates, *The Occult Philosophy in the Elizabethan Age* (1979), 9–22, 61–71.

ALICE CORNELIA LOFTIN

[See also **Alan of Lille; Allegory; Berceo, Gonzalo de; Boccaccio, Giovanni; Chaucer, Geoffrey; Dante; Douglas, Gavin; Dunbar, William; Gower, John; Henryson, Robert; Langland, William; Mena, Juan de; Pearl, The; Petrarch; Roman de la Rose; Santillana, Marqués de.**]

VISITATIO SEPULCHRI, visit to the sepulcher (of the three Marys and the angel), is a term used in the history of the medieval drama. It refers to the development of the trope *Quem quaeritis,* sung before the introit of the Easter Mass, into an independent office and ultimately into an Easter play (a view not universally accepted). The earliest reference is in the *Regularis concordia* of Ethelwold of Winchester (*ca.* 965–975).

BIBLIOGRAPHY
C. Clifford Flanigan, "The Liturgical Context of the *Quem quaeritis* Trope," in *Comparative Drama,* 9 (1974); Timothy J. McGee, "The Liturgical Placements of the *Quem quaeritis* Dialogue," in *Journal of the American Musicological Society,* 29 (1976), and "The Role of the *Quem quaeritis* Dialogue in the History of Western Drama," in *Renaissance Drama,* n.s. 7 (1976); Sr. Marie Dolores Moore, R.S.M., "The *Visitatio sepulchri* of the Medieval Church" (diss., Univ. of Rochester, 1971).

W. T. H. JACKSON

[See also **Drama, Liturgical.**]

VISITATION, the meeting of Mary and Elizabeth after the Annunciation, described in Luke 1:39–56. Elizabeth, greeting Mary as the "mother of my Lord" (*mētēr tou kuriou; mater Dei*), was the first to recognize the Incarnation. Representations of the scene first appeared in the fifth century (for example, a relief carving on a Ravenna sarcophagus) and, until the fifteenth century, almost invariably were accompanied by an image of the Annunciation. Two prevalent types surfaced early. One, always more popular in the Byzantine East, showed the two women embracing (as in the *Homilies* of Gregory of Nazianzus, 879–883; Paris, Bibliothèque Nationale, gr. 510, fol. 3r); the other, particularly common after the thirteenth century in the Latin West, pictured them in conversation (as on the west portal of Rheims Cathedral, of about 1225). More extensive narrative sequences survive from the Middle Byzantine manuscripts of the *Homilies* of James the Monk, called Kokkinobaphos, while late medieval variants in the West included glimpses of the infant Christ and Elizabeth's son John the Baptist hailing each other from inside their mothers' wombs, and Elizabeth kneeling in homage before Mary.

BIBLIOGRAPHY
Émile Mâle, *Religious Art in France,* Harry Bober, ed., Marthiel Mathews, trans. (1978); Gertrud Schiller, *Iconography of Christian Art,* Janet Seligmann, trans. (1971), I, 55–56.

LESLIE BRUBAKER

[See also **Annunciation; Ave Maria; Byzantine Art, 843–1453; Early Christian Art; Gothic Art: Sculpture; James the Monk; Romanesque Art (with illustration); Virgin Mary.**]

VITA OF KOTOR, a Franciscan priest from Kotor (Montenegro, Yugoslavia), master builder of the mausoleum church of the Serbian king Stefan Dečanski (*d.* 1331) at Dečani Monastery (built 1327–1535). The church is the largest medieval church in Serbia, and one of the most successful products of the fusion of Byzantine, Romanesque, and Gothic styles.

SLOBODAN ĆURČIĆ

[See also **Byzantine Art; Early Christian Architecture; Serbian Art and Architecture.**]

VITAE PATRUM (Lives of the fathers), a collection of lives and legends of the early saints put together in the sixth century. The ten books include writings by Jerome, Rufinus, Sulpicius Severus, Cassianus, and others. Much of the material concerns the early hermits in the Egyptian desert and is important for the history of the beginnings of monasticism.

BIBLIOGRAPHY

The text of *Vitae patrum,* edited by Heribert Rosweyde, is in *Patrologia latina,* LXXIII and LXXIV.

W. T. H. JACKSON

[See also **Cassian, John; Church Fathers; Jerome, St.; Monasticism, Origins.**]

VITAL OF BLOIS, Latin poet of the mid twelfth century associated with the literary schools of Blois, Orléans, and Tours. Only the manuscript tradition connects him specifically with the city of Blois; he may have taught there. All that is known for certain of Vital's identity is what he writes of himself in the prologue to one of his poems:

> *Curtavi Plautum; Plautum haec iactura beavit;*
> *Ut placeat Plautus, scripta Vitalis emunt.*
> *Amphitryon nuper, nunc Aulularia tandem*
> *Senserunt senio pressa Vitalis opem.*
> (*Aulularia,* vv. 25–28)

I abridged Plautus and this has enriched him. Vital wrote that Plautus might find favor. Recently the *Amphitryo* and now, at last, the *Aulularia,* both old-fashioned, have been modernized by Vital.

Vital's versions of the *Amphitryo* and the *Aulularia* are two of the earliest of a small group of extant Latin *coemediae,* comedies or versified plays, a genre popular in the literary schools about 1150–1175.

The first of these, known both as the *Amphitryo* and, more commonly, as the *Geta* is, as Vital writes, modeled on Plautus. The basic plot is the same, but the deceived husband (Amphitryo) is transformed from a soldier into a scholar; he and the servant Geta, who plays a more prominent part in Vital's version, are vehicles for satirizing the vain pretensions of scholars and for expressing the contempt the more traditional masters of the literary schools felt for the dialectical reasoning then the rage in Paris. Geta especially makes a complete fool of

himself trying to use logic to make sense of the situation.

Vital's version of the *Aulularia* is a less successful comedy; it is, in fact, based not on Plautus but on a fourth-century text, the *Querolus sive Aulularia,* commonly attributed to Plautus at the time. Despite the popularity of *Geta* and its success in the schools, Vital remains a more obscure figure than other poets (such as William of Blois and Matthew of Vendôme) who experimented with writing *coemediae,* perhaps as his students.

BIBLIOGRAPHY

Vital's comedies have been edited with an introduction and commentary by Gustave Cohen in *La "comédie" latine en France au XIIᵉ siècle,* I (1931), 1–106. See also Joseph de Ghellinck, *L'essor de la littérature latine au XIIᵉ siècle,* 2nd ed. (1955), 476–484; Frederic J. E. Raby, *A History of Secular Latin Poetry in the Middle Ages,* 2nd ed., II (1957), 54–69.

S. C. FERRUOLO

[See also **Drama, Western European; Latin Literature.**]

VITAL OF SAVIGNY, ST. (also known as Vitalis, *ca.* 1050–1122), preacher, monk, and founder of the Norman abbey of Savigny. He was born of well-to-do parents in Tierceville, about nine kilometers (five miles) from Bayeux, in Normandy. His charm, strong intelligence, and early theological training won him the patronage of Bishop Odo of Bayeux, who supported his further study, probably at Liège. At the completion of Vital's formal education, Odo ordained him as a priest and recommended him to the service of his brother, Count Robert of Mortain. From about 1082 to 1094, Vital served as chaplain in Count Robert's household and as a canon in the collegiate church that Robert founded at Mortain.

About 1094, supposedly desiring a more solitary life, Vital withdrew from Mortain and settled in a hermitage in the nearby forest of Dompierre. He continued, however, to advise Count Robert. Vital made extensive preaching expeditions throughout Anglo-Norman territory, preaching at the London Council of 1102, at which he supported the goals of the papal reformers, and at the Council of Rheims in 1119. Vital's zealous and inspirational preaching, described by the chroniclers as eloquent, learned, and heavily scriptural, earned him a reputation as one of the great preachers of his day, the recognition of Pope Calixtus II and of King Henry I of England, and the role of adjudicator in a number of baronial disputes. His preaching also attracted a large number of followers.

In 1104/1105, Vital decided to establish a monastery, and because of widespread disorders he moved his followers into the forest of Savigny on lands of the lords of Fougères, who were vassals of the counts of Mortain. The foundation of Savigny dates from 1112/1115, when conventual buildings were completed and occupied. Vital died on 16 September, which is kept as his feast day.

BIBLIOGRAPHY
Claude Auvry, *Histoire de la congrégation de Savigny,* Auguste Laveille, ed., 3 vols. (1896–1899); John Marshall Carter, "'Fire and Brimstone' in Anglo-Norman Society: The Preaching Career of St. Vital of Mortain and Its Impact on the Abbey of Savigny," in *American Benedictine Review,* **34** (1983); Bennett D. Hill, *English Cistercian Monasteries and Their Patrons in the Twelfth Century* (1968) and "The Counts of Mortain and the Origins of the Norman Congregation of Savigny," in William Chester Jordan *et al.,* eds., *Order and Innovation in the Middle Ages: Essays in Honor of Joseph R. Strayer* (1976); Eugène P. Sauvage, ed., "Vitae BB. Vitalis et Gaufridi, primi et secundi abbatum Saviniacensium," in *Analecta Bollandiana,* I (1882); Johannes von Walter, *Die ersten Wanderprediger Frankreichs: Studien zur Geschichte des Mönchtums* (1906).

BENNETT D. HILL

[See also **Cistercian Order; Preaching and Sermon Literature, Western European; Savigny.**]

VITALE DA BOLOGNA (Vitale d'Aimo de' Cavalli; *fl.* 1330–1359/1361). Although no longer considered the founder of the Bolognese school, Vitale continues to occupy a major place in the history of trecento painting in north Italy. Open to both Italian and transalpine influences in the cosmopolitan milieu of Bologna, he forged a strong artistic identity characterized by a lyrical, often emotional use of line, a rich density of tone, and refined surface decoration. His narratives, infused with psychologically expressive details, have an earthy realism. Reference points for the reconstruction of Vitale's oeuvre include the signed and dated *Madonna dei Denti* (1345; Bologna, Galleria Davia Bargellini), his frescoes in the St. Nicolas Chapel of the cathedral of Udine (1348/1349) and in the apse

Madonna dei Denti. Vitale da Bologna, 1345. ALINARI / ART RESOURCE

of the abbey church of Pomposa (1351), and the *Coronation of the Virgin* polyptych from S. Salvatore, Bologna (1353; Bologna, Pinacoteca).

BIBLIOGRAPHY
Rosalba D'Amico and Massimo Medica, *Vitale da Bologna* (1986); Cesare Gnudi, *Vitale da Bologna and*

Bolognese Painting in the Fourteenth Century, Olga Ragusa, trans. (1964); Roberto Longhi, "Mostra della pittura bolognese del trecento" (1950), repr. in his *Lavori in Valpadana* (1973); 155–187.

CAROL TALBERT PETERS

[See also **Simone da Bologna; Trecento Art.**]

VITRY, JACQUES DE. See **Jacques de Vitry.**

VITRY, PHILIPPE DE (1291–1361), poet, musician, official at the French royal court under Charles IV (*r.* 1322–1328), Philip VI of Valois (*r.* 1328–1350), and John II (*r.* 1350–1364), and bishop of Meaux from 1351. His services to Charles IV and to Philip VI were rewarded by the conferral of several benefices between 1323 and 1332 (Cambrai, Clermont, Soissons, Verdun, St. Quentin, Vertus, Aire en Artois).

Vitry's career in royal service (his father may have been a notary in the royal chancellery) eventually brought him close to the king. He was a notary under Charles IV and at the beginning of the reign of Philip VI. By 1340, he was one of the *maîtres clercs des requêtes du Palais,* dealing with petitions to Parlement. By 1346, Vitry had become a *maître des requêtes de l'Hôtel,* indicating that he had moved from Parlement to the king's household, where he dealt with the petitions addressed directly to the king and to the duke of Normandy. This position required that Vitry accompany his masters, and indeed he followed the duke in 1346 on campaigns in Gascony (to the siege of Aiguillon).

In 1350, before his coronation, John II sent Vitry on a mission to Pope Clement VI in Avignon, possibly to prepare the way for John II's visit to Avignon after the coronation. On 3 January 1351, undoubtedly at the request of the king, who was still in Avignon, Vitry was elected bishop of Meaux (such promotions were frequent for *maîtres des requêtes de l'Hôtel*). He served in this capacity until his death, but remained a counselor to John II and to Charles, duke of Normandy (the future Charles V). Petrarch congratulated Vitry on his appointment in a letter of 23 October 1351, expressing surprise at Vitry's taking on the burdens and responsibilities of a bishop, especially after his previous undemanding position at the royal court

(in Vitry's time, the *maîtres des requêtes de l'Hôtel* served only three months out of the year).

Many references to Vitry as poet and musician are found in contemporary literary works, in musico-theoretical treatises, and even in texts of musical works. Petrarch's friendship with Vitry is witnessed by two letters in Petrarch's *Rerum familiarium libri,* where Vitry is termed "truly always the keenest and most ardent seeker of truth" and "now the only poet of France" (this latter may be meant ironically).

Pierre Bersuire, a Benedictine whom Vitry knew in Avignon and Paris, called him "a man of especially excellent genius, a distinguished zealot of moral philosophy and of ancient history and erudite in all mathematical sciences." Vitry was in contact with the Jewish mathematician and astronomer Levi ben Gershom (Gersonides) in Avignon. Levi's treatise *De numeris harmonicis,* dealing with a mathematical proof of a certain hypothesis relating to rhythmic notation, was written in 1343 in answer to Vitry's specific request. Vitry was also a friend of the mathematician, astronomer, and music theorist Jehan de Murs. A passage in a treatise of Jehan refers to a philosophical tract of Vitry that has not survived.

Other references attest to Vitry's skill as a musician. In two motets of the fourteenth century that name several composers, Vitry's name is placed near the beginning of the list, directly after Jehan de Murs. An anonymous music theorist (Pseudo-Simon Tunstede) writing *ca.* 1350 called Vitry "the flower of the whole world of musicians." Gace de la Buigne, chaplain to Philip VI, John II, and Charles V, stated in his *Roman des deduis* (1359–1377), "Philippe de Vitry was the name—he composed motets better than anyone." An anonymous author of a rhetorical treatise of the early fifteenth century (*ca.* 1411–1432) is quite specific in enumerating Vitry's contributions to poetry and music. Vitry is cited between Jean de Meun, the author of the second part of the *Roman de la Rose,* and Guillaume de Machaut: "After [Jean] came Philippe de Vitry, who found the [new] style of motets, and ballades, and lais, and simple rondeaux, and in music discovered the four prolations, red notes, and novel proportions [among note values]." The last three elements concern musical notation (perhaps the last refers to the proportional diminution of rhythmic values in motet tenors, a characteristic of many isorhythmic motets). As for the musical-poetical forms mentioned, only a few

481

extant motets can be tentatively ascribed to Vitry. No practical evidence survives supporting the assertion that Vitry may be credited with innovations in the composition of *formes fixes,* though some music historians believe that Vitry must have invented the polyphonic chanson of the type cultivated from about 1340 by Guillaume de Machaut.

The central problem concerning Vitry as a musician is that his fame, documented by many contemporary references, is not matched by a large body of works that can definitely be attributed to him. Today Vitry is primarily associated with the *ars nova,* a new development in music formulated and documented in the first quarter of the fourteenth century. Vitry's part in the development, in the capacity of poet, musician, and theoretician, is seen in a few motets attributed to him by modern scholars and in a tradition of theory associated by modern scholars with a supposed treatise by Vitry, the *Ars nova* (early 1320's). There are serious textual problems with the treatise, since no extant source transmits a complete or unambiguous text; it is likely that what remains are the notes by several of Vitry's students. His own main contributions seem to be the description of certain notational advances (minims and red notation) and the full admission of duple ("imperfect") time alongside triple ("perfect") time. In essence, Vitry points the way toward the codification of our modern time signatures $\frac{9}{8}$, $\frac{3}{4}$, $\frac{6}{8}$, and $\frac{2}{4}$, something that was more systematically carried out by about 1330. By means of red notation, a certain flexibility was introduced in shifts between triple and duple relationships within a piece. This rational, hierarchical organization of rhythm contrasts with the freer treatment of rhythm in motets during the previous generation, epitomized by the works of Petrus de Cruce.

The first practical source containing examples of the Vitry-style motet is an especially sumptuous copy of the *Roman de Fauvel* from ca. 1316. Some of the musical interpolations in this copy may be by the young Vitry. Among the motets often attributed to him by modern scholars are two datable 1314 on the basis of historical references in the texts, "Firmissime fidem / Adesto sancta / Alleluya," with the tenor in diminution for the second half, and "Garrit Gallus / In nova fert / N(euma)," with coloration (red notes) in the tenor and a sophisticated numerical phrase structure. Among the later motets that may be by Vitry is a four-voice work, possibly from the 1330's, with the acrostic ROBERTUS in the motetus voice ("O canenda / Rex quem / Rex

regum"), referring to King Robert d'Anjou, and "Petre Clemens / Lugentium," a three-voice motet possibly for the coronation of Pope Clement VI in 1342.

Of Vitry's poetry, there survive two *dits,* a ballade, and a few lines in a Latin *jeu-parti* (*partitura amoris*), written with Jean de Savoie and Jean Campion. The *Chapel des trois fleurs de lis* (1,148 lines) concerns Philip VI's planned crusade of the mid 1330's. The *Dit de Franc Gontier* (32 lines), which praises the virtues of country life, was imitated in the early fifteenth century by Pierre d'Ailly, bishop of Cambrai, who wrote of the miserable life of a tyrant. In the late fifteenth century, Vitry's poem was parodied by François Villon in *Les contrediz Franc Gontier* (*Testament,* verses 1,473–1,506). Both the ballade *De terre en grec Gaulle appellée* (27 lines), replete with mythological images, and the "judgment" section from the Latin *jeu-parti, Ulixea fulgens facundia,* are closely associated with certain members of Vitry's intellectual circle. Indeed, most of Vitry's poetry and music consists of occasional works, associated with particular personages and historical events.

BIBLIOGRAPHY

Sources. Le chapel des trois fleurs de lis, the *Dit de Franc Gontier,* and the companion piece by Pierre d'Ailly are edited by Arthur Piaget in "Le chapel des fleurs de lis par Philippe de Vitry," in *Romania,* **27** (1898). An English translation of all but the second stanza of *Franc Gontier* is found in Johan Huizinga, *The Waning of the Middle Ages* (1924, repr. 1937), 117–118. Vitry's only extant ballade is edited with English translation and extensive commentary in James I. Wimsatt, *Chaucer and the Poems of 'CH'* (1982), 51–60. The Latin *jeu-parti* and a four-part motet (for which no music survives) are published in Edmond Pognon, "Du noveau sur Philippe de Vitri et ses amis," in *Humanisme et renaissance,* **6** (1939).

Leo Schrade edited fourteen motets of Vitry in *Polyphonic Music of the Fourteenth Century,* I (1956), including many of uncertain attribution. Readily available editions of single motets include Richard H. Hoppin, *Anthology of Medieval Music* (1978), 120–126; and W. Thomas Marrocco and Nicholas Sandon, eds., *Medieval Music* (1977), 120–126. Material relating to the body of musico-theoretical teachings of Vitry is collected in Gilbert Reaney, André Gilles, and Jean Maillard, eds., *Philippi de Vitriaco: Ars nova* (1964); an English translation of one source is in Leon Plantinga, "Philippe de Vitry's 'Ars Nova': A Translation," in *Journal of Music Theory,* **5** (1961).

Studies. The most important study of Vitry's life is

Alfred Coville, "Philippe de Vitri: Notes biographiques," in *Romania*, 59 (1933). Studies of the music include Ernest H. Sanders, "Vitry, Philippe de," in *New Grove Dictionary of Music and Musicians,* XX (1980), and "The Medieval Motet," in *Gattungen der Musik in Einzeldarstellungen: Gedenkschrift Leo Schrade,* I (1973), 554–573. A revisionist view of Vitry's activity as a composer is given by Daniel Leech-Wilkinson, "Related Motets from Fourteenth-century France," in *Proceedings of the Royal Musical Association,* 109 (1982–1983); while Sarah Fuller, "A Phantom Treatise of the Fourteenth Century? The *Ars nova,*" in *Journal of Musicology,* 4 (1985–1986), reassesses the question of Vitry as music theorist.

LAWRENCE M. EARP

[See also **Ars Nova; Fauvel, Roman de; Motet; Musical Treatises.**]

VIZIER (Arabic: *wazīr*), the title borne from the late eighth century onward by the chief administrator of the Abbasid caliphate and, through imitation, by the chief administrators of most successor states throughout the Islamic world. The post arose from the need to coordinate the activities of an increasingly complicated bureaucracy, but the term appears in the Koran.

BIBLIOGRAPHY
Dominique Sourdel, *Le vizirat ᶜabbāside, de 749 à 936* (1959–1960).

RICHARD W. BULLIET

[See also **Abbasids; Caliphate; Islamic Administration.**]

VLACHS. The term "Vlach" refers to several groups of people descended from Latin speakers living in the Balkan Peninsula. Although much concerning them is disputed by historians, there is agreement on a few facts. It is known that they spoke a Romance language, preferred to reside in mountainous territory, and pursued a largely pastoral and often nomadic way of life. The Vlachs were the ancestors of the Romanian-speaking population in Walachia, Moldavia, and Transylvania, as well as of other small Romance-language communities scattered in parts of the Balkans. "Vlach" is from the Slavic word *Vlah* (Bulgarian and Serbian), which in turn is derived from the Germanic **Walh* (referring to Celtic and Latin peoples); other

variants are Greek: *Bláchoi*; Latin: *Blachi* or *Vlachi*; German: *Wlach*; and Hungarian: *Oláh*. These terms were used by neighboring peoples to designate those who called themselves *rumîni* (from the Latin *romani*, Romans).

The earliest recorded use of the term "Vlach" occurs in an eighth-century reference found in the monastery of Kastamunitu. The next reference does not occur until the latter part of the tenth century, the time given by the Byzantine historian John Skylitzes for the Vlachs' murder of a brother of the Bulgarian tsar Samuil in the region between Lake Prespa and Kastoria in northern Greece. In the eleventh century, references in Byzantine sources become more frequent.

Kekaumenos, describing the Vlach revolt in Thessaly (1066) in his *Strategikon,* took note of their practice of transhumance and their reputation for bad faith. In the *Alexiad,* Anna Komnena mentions the existence of Vlachs in Macedonia and Thrace. She reports that on one occasion Emperor Alexios I sent agents into the Balkan provinces "to enroll new men for a term of duty from the Bulgars and the nomads (commonly called Vlachs)," thereby stressing the association of Vlachs with Bulgars and identifying nomadism with the Vlach culture. Around the turn of the century, the Vlachs scandalized Byzantine religious sensibilities when approximately 300 Vlach families, fleeing from imperial tax collectors, moved to Mount Athos to sell provisions, especially cheese, to the monks. The Vlach women, disguised in men's clothing, had free entry into the monks' private quarters. Emperor Alexios ordered the Vlachs to be expelled, touching off a violent reaction among the monks.

In the twelfth and thirteenth centuries Vlachs are mentioned regularly in Serbian monastic deeds recording gifts to religious communities. Most important, they are associated with the Bulgarians in the revolt against the Byzantine emperor Isaac II in 1186, which led to the creation of the Second Bulgarian Empire. The leaders of the revolt, the brothers Asen, Peter, and Kalojan, were most probably Vlachs. North of the Danube, Vlachs are attested by the middle of the twelfth century, at the latest, in the works of Niketas Choniates and John Kinnamos. The Hungarian king Béla IV, in a charter of 1247, mentions Vlach political leaders—specifically, voivodes and chiefs—between the Carpathians and the Danube in the region that later became Walachia. By the fourteenth century the Vlachs are documented as residents throughout the Balkan Peninsula and speaking a number of related dialects: Northern Romanian or Dacoromanian, Istro-Romanian, Aromanian, and Megleno-Romanian.

There are numerous scholarly questions about the origins, language, culture, migration, and settlement of the Vlachs. The literary evidence is more than normally fragmentary. The evidence of archaeology, place-name studies, and linguistics, while helpful, is often equivocal. The problems of Vlach history have been compounded by national rivalries among Eastern European historians since the end of the nineteenth century. Many Romanian historians argue that the Vlachs were the descendants of Roman settlers from the province of Dacia, created north of the Danube by Emperor Trajan. The short-lived history of this Roman province and the lack of evidence for the continuous occupation of the area seriously weaken this hypothesis. Other historians have argued that the preservation of the Slavonic liturgy among the later Walachians at a time (twelfth century) when the Bulgarians had abandoned this rite for the Greek liturgy confirms the early presence of the Vlachs north of the Danube. Linguistic analysis, however, shows a pattern of close association with South Slavic peoples (Bulgarians and Serbs) and almost no contact with West Slavic peoples (Czechs, Slovaks, and Poles), which suggests that the earliest homeland of the northern Romanian Vlachs lay south of the Danube. How and when they established themselves in the Carpathian region has not been satisfactorily explained. Contemporary Bulgarian and Yugoslav historians, moreover, have asserted that references to Vlachs in twelfth- and thirteenth-century Byzantine documents do not mean Vlachs but rather Bulgarians. This interpretation, not surprisingly, has found little support outside Bulgarian historical circles. These disputes should not obscure the remarkable historical achievement of the Vlachs in preserving their Romance language and culture amid a sea of Slavic, Magyar, and Eurasian steppe peoples.

BIBLIOGRAPHY

André Du Nay, *The Early History of the Rumanian Language* (1977), the best modern scholarly synthesis; John V. A. Fine, Jr., *The Early Medieval Balkans* (1983) and *The Late Medieval Balkans* (1987); Manfred Huber, *Grundzüge der Geschichte Rumäniens* (1973); Robert W. Seton-Watson, *A History of the Roumanians* (1934, repr. 1963); T. J. Winnifrith, *The Vlachs* (1987), the most

recent survey from ancient times to the present; Robert L. Wolff, "The 'Second Bulgarian Empire': Its Origin and History to 1204," in *Speculum*, **24** (1949), with an excellent summary of the earlier literature.

JAMES ROSS SWEENEY

[See also **Bosnia; Bulgaria; Romanian Language and Literature; Romanian Principalities; Walachia/Moldavia.**]

VLAD ȚEPEȘ (the Impaler), also known as Vlad III Dracula or Dracula, reigned as voivode (prince) of Walachia in 1448, 1456–1462, and 1476. Born about 1431, he was a member of the Drăculești branch of the princely house of Basarab, the son of the voivode Vlad II Dracul. His life was intimately linked with the fifteenth-century crisis in the Balkans symbolized by the Ottoman Turkish conquest of Constantinople in 1453 and its consequences. In the fifteenth century the semi-autonomous principality of Walachia, while espousing Orthodox Christianity, was nominally a dependency of the Catholic kings of Hungary, and at the same time was obligated to pay an annual tribute to the Ottoman sultan. Vlad Țepeș found it expedient to use the Hungarian-Ottoman struggle to enhance the independence of Walachia. In 1447 the Hungarians, under János Hunyadi, overthrew Vlad II Dracul and after a short interval installed Vladislav II, a pro-Hungarian voivode. In the following year Vlad, at the head of a largely Turkish army, seized the princely seat of Tîrgoviște, where he proclaimed himself voivode. This first reign lasted only a few months, for late in 1448 the pro-Hungarian faction drove him out. For the next eight years Vlad Țepeș wandered in exile, first to the Turkish capital of Edirne (Adrianople), then to Moldavia, and later to Transylvania. While in Transylvania he cultivated better relations with the Hungarians, paving the way for his second reign.

In 1456, with Hungarian encouragement, Vlad rallied his Walachian supporters to drive out Vladislav II, his earlier rival. On 6 September 1456, he swore an oath of vassalage to the Hungarian king. During the next six years he pursued a largely anti-Turkish policy that also was not pro-Hungarian. Tensions between Vlad Țepeș and the Hungarian king Matthias Corvinus were numerous and exacerbated by his brutal treatment of Transylvanian Saxon merchants from the towns of Brassó (German: Kronstadt; Romanian: Brașov) and

Nagyszeben (German: Hermannstadt; Romanian: Sibiu). In a series of raids into Transylvania he burned and looted a number of villages, impaling on wooden stakes those men, women, and children who had survived the initial attacks. Later young Saxon apprentices resident in Walachia were gathered in a single place and burned alive. Numerous other incidents of atrocity, especially impalement, are reported throughout his reign. As his relations with the Walachian boyars deteriorated, he strove to check their independence, and they, too, suffered impalement.

Militarily, the high point of this reign occurred in 1461–1462, when Vlad in reprisal for a Turkish attack led a daring invasion of Ottoman territory south of the Danube killing, by his own account, thousands of Turks. The Walachian advance, however, was repulsed by Sultan Mehmed II, who then invaded Walachia (in 1462). A faction of pro-Turkish Walachian boyars took advantage of Vlad's discomfiture, overthrowing him and installing with the Sultan's approval his younger brother, Radu. Vlad took refuge in Hungary, where for the next twelve years he was kept under house arrest. During this period he converted to Roman Catholicism. In 1476, as part of a Hungarian-sponsored Christian offensive against the Turks, he was for the third time installed as voivode, but only for a matter of weeks. Outnumbered and surrounded, his forces were defeated by a combined Walachian-Turkish army, and he was killed—whether by treachery or in the thick of battle is uncertain.

Assessments of Vlad's personality and achievements vary. Whereas Robert Seton-Watson views him as "a man of diseased and abnormal tendencies, the victim of acute moral insanity," modern Romanian scholars—for example, Ștefan Andreescu—believe him to be "an outstanding figure of the fifteenth century, an embodiment of the Romanians' aspirations for freedom and independence." There is also disagreement about the nickname Dracula, a diminutive of Dracul, meaning either "devil" or "dragon." A plausible case has been made for understanding the name as a reference to the fact that he was the son of a knight of the Order of the Dragon (Vlad Dracul). The sobriquet Țepeș, meaning "impaler" in Romanian, dates from shortly after his death. By the end of the sixteenth century his reputation for cruelty, especially within the German-speaking community, far outweighed his deeds as a fighter against the Turks. This lasting image of Vlad Țepeș as a bloodthirsty monster helps to explain how in the nineteenth century he came to be identified with the legendary vampire immortalized in Bram Stoker's novel published in 1897.

BIBLIOGRAPHY

Radu Florescu and Raymond T. McNally, *Dracula: A Biography of Vlad the Impaler, 1431–1476* (1973), is the best biography in any language. McNally and Florescu also produced the somewhat more popular *In Search of Dracula* (1972). A brief, traditional assessment of Vlad's accomplishments is given in Robert W. Seton-Watson, *A History of the Roumanians* (1934, repr. 1963). Ștefan Andreescu, *Vlad Țepeș (Dracula): Între legendă și adevăr istoric* (1976), with English summary, 275–284, and Nicolae Stoicescu, *Vlad Țepeș* (1976), with English summary 231–238, present the prevailing Romanian view of Vlad as a national hero. The earlier part of his life is treated more technically in Radu Constantinescu, "Quelques observations sur l'époque de Vlad Țepeș," in *Revue roumaine d'histoire*, **17** (1978). Further documentation on the evolution of the Dracula legend and the novel of Bram Stoker is provided in Leonard Wolf, ed., *The Annotated Dracula* (1975).

JAMES ROSS SWEENEY

[See also **Hungary; Romanian Principalites; Walachia/ Moldavia.**]

VLADIMIR, ST. (*fl.* 970's–1015), son of Grand Prince Svyatoslav of Kiev, captured that principality from his brother in 978. After a campaign to spread a uniform pagan cult throughout the land of Rus, Vladimir accepted Christian baptism at the hands of Byzantine clergy, doubtless with political considerations in mind. The traditional date is 988. Having put away his several wives and "800 concubines," he married Anna, sister of the Byzantine emperors Basil and Constantine. Vladimir then ordered the baptism of all his subjects and brought Byzantine architects, painters, clergy, and singers to the Kievan land to build and staff churches and to instruct the people in Christianity and Slavic letters. He died in 1015 and was eventually enrolled in the lists of saints as the "baptizer of Russia."

BIBLIOGRAPHY

The main source for the reign of St. Vladimir is *Povest vremennykh let*; for an English translation see Samuel H. Cross and Olgerd P. Sherbowitz-Wertzer, eds. and trans., *The Russian Primary Chronicle: Laurentian Text*. This account of Vladimir and Russia's conversion is, however, enveloped in a mass of legendary material. There is an excellent treatment of Vladimir and Russia's conversion in George Vernadsky, *Kievan Russia* (1948). See also Yevgeny Golubinsky, *Istoria russkoi tserkvi*, I, 2 pts. (1901–1904); Andrzej Poppe, "The Political Background to the Baptism of Rus," in *Dumbarton Oaks Papers*, 30 (1976); *Vladimirsky Sbornik* (1938).

GEORGE P. MAJESKA

[See also **Byzantine Church; Byzantine Empire: History (330–1025); Kievan Rus; Russian Orthodox Church.**]

VLADIMIR MONOMAKH (1053–1125) was the son of Vsevolod I, grand prince of Kiev, and probably of Maria, a daughter of the Byzantine emperor Constantine IX Monomachos. He succeeded his cousin Svyatopolk II as grand prince of Kiev at the latter's death in 1113, in accordance with the "rotation principle" agreed upon at the Lyubech congress of princes (1097). He took power in Kiev in the midst of a riot against moneylenders and merchants, particularly Jews, which induced him to limit interest rates and debt slavery. After spending much of his life fighting steppe nomads, he died in 1125. Later his imperial Greek name was attached to ceremonial regalia of the Muscovite tsars, particularly to the crown or "cap of Monomakh."

BIBLIOGRAPHY

There is extensive material on Vladimir Monomakh in *Povest vremennykh let*, D. S. Likhachev, ed., 2 vols. (1950), ed. and trans. by Samuel H. Cross and Olgerd P. Sherbowitz-Wetzer as *The Russian Primary Chronicle: Laurentian Text* (1953). Both versions include the text of his "testament."

Studies include Boris D. Grekov, *Kiev Rus*, Y. Sdobnikov, trans., Dennis Ogden, ed. (1959); Aleksandr Orlov, *Vladimir Monomakh* (1946, repr. 1969), repr. ed. by C. H. Van Schooneveld, both editions in Russian; Boris A. Rybakov, *Early Centuries of Russian History*, John Weir, trans. (1965); George Vernadsky, *Kievan Russia* (1948).

GEORGE P. MAJESKA

[See also **Kievan Rus.**]

VLADIMIR VIRGIN, also known as the *Mother of God of Vladimir,* is a famous Byzantine icon long connected with the rulers of Russia. Brought from Kiev to the city of Vladimir when the latter became the capital of Russia in the mid twelfth century, this icon of the Mother of God became the national palladium, often being carried into battle by Russian forces. In 1395 it was brought to Moscow, and in 1480 it was enshrined in the new Dormition Cathedral, where it remained until 1918, when it was cleaned and restored. It is now displayed in the Tretyakov State Gallery in Moscow. An exquisite example of the finest early-twelfth-century Constantinopolitan style, although badly damaged and much repainted, it shows a half-length Mary in a gold-trimmed maroon robe holding the Christ child on her right arm; the child hugs his mother, touching his cheek to hers. The iconographic type is called "tenderness" (Greek: *eleousa*; Russian: *umilenie*).

BIBLIOGRAPHY

The basic study of this painting is Aleksandr I. Anisimov, *Our Lady of Vladimir*, N. G. Yaschwill and T. N. Rodzianko, trans. (1928); see also Konrad Onasch, "Die Ikone der Gottesmutter von Vladimir," in *Ostkirchliche Studien*, 5 (1956), and *Icons* (1969). An up-to-date bibliography can be found in *Iskusstvo Vizanty v sobraniakh S.S.S.R.*, II (1977), 24.

GEORGE P. MAJESKA

[See also **Bogoliubskii, Andrei; Byzantine Church; Eleousa (with illustration); Icon, Theology of; Iconography; Icons, Manufacture of; Icons, Russian; Rublev, Andrei; Russian Art; Russian Orthodox Church.**]

VLADIMIR-SUZDAL, the northeast Russian principality that flourished in the twelfth and thirteenth centuries, originally "the Rostov land" (so named from its first capital and chief ecclesiastical center). The capital was moved to Suzdal under the first locally based prince, Yuri Dolgorukii (1113/1125–1157), and to Vladimir under his son Andrei Bogoliubskii (1157–1174). The pinnacle of its power was achieved under Andrei, his half brother Vsevolod "Big Nest" (1176–1212), and the latter's son Yuri (1212–1217, 1218–1238). Its power fell somewhat following the Mongol conquest (1238), but Yuri's brother Yaroslav (1238–1246) and his sons Alexander Nevsky (1252–1263) and Yaroslav (1263–1271) were commanding figures. The children of the latter two developed fully the autonomy of the principalities of Moscow and Tver, which superseded Vladimir in the fourteenth century.

By the 1220's the territory of Vladimir-Suzdal, or Suzdalia, extended somewhat east of Nizhnii Novgorod, south of Vladimir, west of Moscow and Tver, and well north of Beloozero and Ustiug in the northwest and northeast, respectively. It extended about 600 kilometers (375 miles) along either axis and was the richest and most powerful Russian principality. Suzdalian influence reached directly into neighboring Great Novgorod (key to preeminence in Russia), Ryazan, and Murom, and indirectly touched the neighboring East Finnish tribes, the Volga Bulgar state, and most other Russian principalities. The grand prince of Vladimir aided Novgorod against its Scandinavian and German rivals in the Baltic, but otherwise commanded more help than he gave.

Some historians have considered Vladimir-Suzdal to have been peculiarly monarchical or autocratic during the pre-Mongol period. In fact, local magnates, townsmen, and militias, and sometimes outside forces, played a role in the politics of princely succession before the Mongol period.

Suzdalian culture was characterized by its distinct form of ecclesiastical architecture (raised domes, Kama white stone, and exterior sculpture), laconic local chronicles, a local patriotic cult of the Virgin, and some cynical political literature.

After 1238, the Mongols, while not interfering with the principles of princely succession, did appoint or approve the grand princes of Vladimir, sanctioned local dynasties, supervised local politics, controlled foreign policy, took censuses, and taxed harshly, but left the grand princes sufficiently strong to continue to protect and influence Novgorod, and thus guard the northwestern flank of the Mongol Empire.

Moscow supplanted Vladimir as the center of power in Suzdalia in the 1330's and consciously appropriated the Vladimirian legacy in the latter 1400's, when the Moscow princes extended their power beyond the confines of Suzdalia. "Grand prince of Vladimir" remained part of the title of the Russian sovereigns down to 1917.

BIBLIOGRAPHY

John L. I. Fennell, *The Crisis of Medieval Russia: 1200–1304* (1983); Yuri A. Limonov, *Letopisanie Vladimiro-Suzdalskoi Rusi* (1967); A. N. Nasonov, *"Russkaya zemlia" i obrazovanie territorii drevnerusskogo gosudarstva* (1951); Aleksandr E. Presniakov, *The Formation of the Great Russian State*, A. E. Moorhouse,

trans. (1970); Nikolai N. Voronin, *Zodchestvo Severovostochnoi Rusi XII–XV vekov*, 2 vols. (1961–1962).

DAVID GOLDFRANK

[See also **Bogoliubskii, Andrei; Kievan Rus; Mongol Empire; Muscovy, Rise of; Nevsky, Alexander; Novgorod; Russian Architecture.**]

VOCABULARIUS SANCTI GALLI. The abbey of St. Gall possesses a manuscript containing on 126 of its pages a Latin-German glossary of parts of the body, human qualities, houses and land, and other categories known as *Vocabularius Sancti Galli* because, according to an entry in the manuscript, it was written by the saint himself. This is no longer believed; recent scholarship suggests that the whole manuscript, perhaps written at Murbach about 790, was the work of the Anglo-Saxon mission to Germany and its source was the *Hermeneumata*, a widely used Greek-Latin glossary of the third century. The pages are less than 4 inches (10 cm) square; the parchment is dirty and worn.

BIBLIOGRAPHY

An edition is *Die althochdeutschen Glossen*, Elias Steinmeyer and Eduard Sievers, eds., III (1895, repr. 1968), 1–8. Extracts can be found in Wilhelm Braune, *Althochdeutsches Lesebuch*, 16th ed., rev. by Ernst A. Ebbinghaus (1979), 1.2. See also John Knight Bostock, *A Handbook on Old High German Literature*, 2nd ed., rev. by Kenneth C. King and David R. McLintock (1976), 100. For a detailed study see Georg Baesecke, *Der Vocabularius Sancti Galli in der angelsächsischen Mission* (1933).

DAVID R. MCLINTOCK

[See also **Old High German Literature; St. Gall, Monastery and Plan of.**]

VOGT. See **Advocate.**

VOLGA BULGARS, a highly urbanized people of Oghur Turkic origin occupying the Middle Volga region who today constitute one of the ancestral components of the Kazan Tatars and perhaps the Chuvash. A tribal confederation called *Bulghar* (mixed ones) arose out of the mass of Oghur tribes and joined with Hunnic elements that reappeared in the Pontic steppes following the collapse of Attila's state (*ca.* 460). Linguistically differentiated from speakers of Common Turkic and possessing a culture that placed somewhat greater emphasis on sedentary pursuits, elements of the Oghurs found themselves under successive Avar and Turk overlordship in the mid sixth century. By the early seventh century, the Onoghur-Bulghar union had formed an important but short-lived state (Magna Bulgaria) under their khan Qubrat/Kuvrat (of Western Turk origin). Wars with the Khazar Khaghanate, a successor state of the Turks, led to the breakup of Magna Bulgaria in the late seventh century and caused the migration of some Bulghar hordes to the Balkans. The latter gave rise to Danubian-Balkan Bulgaria.

Scholarly opinion is divided as to the chronology of the other Bulghar migrations. One view places the migrating Bulghars in the hitherto Finno-Ugric Volga-Kama area at this time and suggests that they coalesced with other Oghur groupings believed to have arrived there in Hunnic times. A contrary view places the appearance of the Oghur-Bulghar tribes in the Middle Volga region in the late eighth or early ninth century.

The nucleus of the Volga Bulgars' state was undoubtedly formed by the late ninth century. They were visited in 921/922 by emissaries of Caliph al-Muqtadir billāh who had gone there to convert the Bulgars to Islam. According to the account left by the secretary of this mission, Aḥmad ibn Faḍlān, the Bulgars' tribal composition indicated ties with the Oghur-Bulghar tribes of the Caspo-Pontic steppes. The Bulgar ruler, Almush ibn Shilkī, who bore the title *yıltavar* (Common Turkic: *elteber*), a rank given to subject tribal leaders in the Turko-Khazar hierarchy, was seeking at this time to end Khazar hegemony in his lands.

In the tenth century, Volga Bulgaria was rich in agriculture and cattle, and traded extensively in furs and other products of the forest-steppe zone with the Islamic Caspian and Central Asian lands. The wealth derived from this trade, furthered by continuing expansion into the fur-rich northern lands, promoted the growth of towns.

Expansion led to confrontations with Kievan Rus (beginning in 985) as well as peaceful commercial contacts. By the late twelfth century, the Bulgaro-Rus competition for control over the forest peoples led to increasing hostilities that culminated in major wars in the early thirteenth century. This rivalry was cut short by the appearance of the Mongols in 1223. Volga Bulgaria fell to them in 1236/1237. It was incorporated into the Golden Horde, ultimately becoming the Chinggisid khanate of Kazan. During this period, the Bulghar Turkic tongue was gradually replaced by Kipchak Turkic (the language of the Cumans, the dominant ethnic element of the Golden Horde). The fusion of Bulgars, Kipchaks, and Mongols produced the modern Volga Tatars.

BIBLIOGRAPHY

V. V. Bartol'd (W. Barthold), "Bulghār," in *Encyclopaedia of Islam,* I (1913), also in his *Sochinenia,* V (1968); Abdullah Battal Taymas, *Kazan Türkleri* (1966); J. Benzing, "Das Hunnische, Donaubolgarische und Wolgabolgarische," in Jean Deny *et al., Philologiae Turcicae fundamenta,* I (1959); Károly Czeglédy, "From East to West: The Golden Age of Nomadic Migrations in Eurasia," Peter B. Golden, trans., in *Archivum Eurasiae Medii Aevi,* 3 (1983); C. Gérard, *Les bulgares de la Volga et les slaves du Danube* (1939); *Ibn Faḍlān's Reisebericht,* Ahmed Z. V. Togan, ed. and trans. (1939); Josef Markwart (Marquart), "Ein arabischer Bericht über die arktischen (uralischen) Länder aus dem 10 Jahrhundert," in *Ungarische Jahrbücher,* IV (1924); Julius (Gyula) Moravcsik, "Zur Geschichte der Onoguren," in *Ungarische Jahrbücher,* X (1930); Omeljan Pritsak, "Kāšġarī's Angaben über die Sprache der Bolgaren," in *Zeitschrift der deutschen morgenländischen Gesellschaft,* **109** (1959); A. Róna-Tas, "A Runic Inscription in the Kujbyšev Region," in *Acta orientalia hungarica,* **30** (1976), "Some Volga Bulgarian Words in the Volga Kipchak Languages," in Gyula Kaldy-Nagy, ed., *Hungaro-Turcica: Studies in Honour of Julius Németh* (1976), and "A Volga Bolgarian Inscription from 1307," in *Acta orientalia hungarica,* **30** (1976).

PETER B. GOLDEN

[See also **Barbarians, Invasions of; Bulgaria; Golden Horde; Mongol Empire; Russia, Nomadic Invasions of; Scandinavia in Arabic Sources.**]

VǪLSUNGA SAGA (The saga of the Volsungs), classified as a *fornaldarsaga* (legendary saga), is largely a prose recasting of the heroic sections in the *Poetic Edda.* It survives in one medieval manuscript from around 1400 and in paper transcripts. Chapter 23 is borrowed from *Þiðreks saga* (ca. 1220–1250). Unless this chapter is a later interpolation, the composition of *Vǫlsunga saga* can therefore be dated no earlier than the mid thirteenth century. On the other hand, nothing in the style suggests a date later than the end of the thirteenth century.

The content may be divided into six sections: (1) the genealogy of the Volsung family (Odin, Sigi, Rerir, Volsung, Sigmund, and Signy); (2) the story of Volsung's death at the hands of Signy's husband, Siggeirr, and the vengeance carried out by Sigmund and Sinfjǫtli (the son of an incestuous union between Sigmund and his sister Signy); (3) the adventures of Sigmund's son Helgi; (4) the story of Sigurd, Brynhild, and Gudrun; (5) the story of Atli's treacherous slaying of Gudrun's brothers and her revenge; (6) the story of Svanhildr (Gudrun's daughter by Sigurd), her murder by Jǫrmunrekkr, and the vengeance of her half brothers Hamðir and Sǫrli.

The genealogy from Odin to Sigmund is not found in the *Poetic Edda* and has been attributed by some critics (Finnur Jónsson, Per Wieselgren) to a lost "Sigurðar saga." The story of Sigmund and Signy is also missing in the *Poetic Edda* and is probably derived from a lost poetic source or sources (half of a stanza is cited). The action appears to be modeled on the story of Gudrun and Atli. The Helgi material is taken from the Eddic Helgi poems. The story of Sigurd and Brynhild derives from the Eddic *Reginsmál-Fáfnismál* and *Sigrdrífumál* (with probable supplements from the Sigurðar saga), the three Sigurd poems, and *Guðrúnarkviða II*. The section on Atli and Gudrun interweaves the Eddic poems *Atlakviða* and *Atlamál,* and the final section on Svanhildr and Jǫrmunrekkr is based on the Eddic *Hamðismál.*

The chief value of *Vǫlsunga saga* lies in its preservation of some narrative not found elsewhere—for example, the story of Sigmund and Signy. Most important, the saga was composed when the Eddic collection was still complete and thus can be used to reconstruct the central poems *Sigurðarkviða in forna,* half of which is lost in the Eddic manuscript, and *Sigurðarkviða in meiri,* all of which is lost in the lacuna. As a consequence, only *Vǫlsunga saga* gives a full version of the most famous of the Norse heroic legends, the story of Brynhild and Sigurd. In particular, our understanding of Brynhild's dominant personality depends very largely on the narrative of *Vǫlsunga saga.*

The author of the saga saw his mission in the harmonization of his poetic sources and not in a particular conception of the legends. The task was not easy, because he was sometimes confronted with variant versions of the same tale (especially in sections 4 and 5). Certain contradictions result from the fusion, but on the whole the author succeeded in shaping a consistent narrative that can be read for pleasure without reference to the sources.

BIBLIOGRAPHY

Sources. Vǫlsunga saga ok Ragnars saga loðbrókar, Magnus Olsen, ed. (1906–1908); *The Saga of the Volsungs,* R. G. Finch, ed. and trans. (1965).

Studies. R. G. Finch, "The Treatment of Poetic Sources by the Compiler of *Vǫlsunga saga,*" in *Saga-book of the Viking Society for Northern Research,* **16** (1962–1965), and *"Atlakviða, Atlamál, and Vǫlsunga saga:* A Study in Combination and Integration," in Ursula Dronke *et al.,* eds., *Speculum Norrœnum: Norse Studies in Memory of Gabriel Turville-Petre* (1981); Andreas Heusler, "Die Lieder der Lücke im Codex Regius der Edda," in *Germanistische Abhandlungen Hermann Paul dargebracht* (1902), repr. in his *Kleine Schriften,* II, Stefan Sonderegger, ed. (1969), and "Altnordische Dichtung und Prosa von Jung Sigurd," in *Sitzungsberichte der Preussischen Akademie der Wissenschaften,* Phil.-hist. Kl. (1919), repr. in his *Kleine Schriften,* I, Helga Reuschel, ed. (1943, repr. 1969); Per Wieselgren, *Quellenstudien zur Vǫlsunga-saga* (1935).

THEODORE M. ANDERSSON

[See also **Atlakviða; Atlamál; Eddic Poetry; Fornaldarsögur; Guðrúnarkviða II; Hamðismál; Helgi Poems; Reginsmál and Fáfnismál; Sigurðarkviða in Forna; Sigurðarkviða in Meiri; Sigurðarkviða in Skamma.**]

VOLTO SANTO (Holy countenance), a celebrated votive image of the Crucifixion in Lucca Cathedral, showing Christ in a long, belted tunic. The original statue of the late eleventh century was replaced in the early thirteenth century by a wood copy that survives today (see illustration overleaf). First mentioned about 1100, the *Volto Santo,* according to legend, was carved by Nicodemus, who used the impression Christ's body made on his shroud as a model, and enclosed relics of the Passion in the statue's head. Numerous crucifixes of the twelfth and thirteenth centuries were modeled on the Luccan *Volto Santo.*

LESLIE BRUBAKER

VOLUMEN (Latin, "roll"), technical term designating the ancient form of book, the roll, in which sheets of papyrus or parchment were joined end to

The *Volto santo*. Carved wood crucifix from Lucca Cathedral, early 13th century. ALINARI / ART RESOURCE

end and rolled for storage. In late antiquity, the codex supplanted the *volumen* for most kinds of books. However, rolls, often called *rotuli*, continued in use throughout the Middle Ages for certain legal or archival documents and for special musical, liturgical, or related texts, such as obituary rolls.

BIBLIOGRAPHY

Richard H. Rouse, "Roll and Codex: The Transmission of the Works of Reinmar von Zweter," in *Paläographie 1981: Colloquium des Comité International de Paléographie, München, 15.–18. September 1981* (1982).

MICHAEL MCCORMICK

[See also **Codex; Kollema; Kollesis; Manuscript Books, Production of; Paper, Introduction of; Papyrus; Parchment; Pipe Rolls; Writing Materials, Western European.**]

VǪLUNDARKVIÐA (Lay of Vǫlundr), an Eddic poem of undetermined date, preserved in toto only in the Codex Regius of the *Poetic Edda*. The poem is composed in irregular *fornyrðislag* (old-lore meter) and contains an extensive introductory prose passage as well as two additional small prose inserts. Because of several unique words, obscure passages, and unusual syntactical characteristics, scholars concur that *Vǫlundarkviða* is one of the oldest poems in the collection.

The poems relates the story of Vǫlundr the smith (elsewhere known as Wieland or Wayland), who lives in Wolfdale (Úlfdalir) with his two brothers. One day they discover three swan-maidens bathing in a lake and they capture and marry them. Eight years later the swan-maidens fly away, and Vǫlundr's brothers set off in search of their wives. Vǫlundr remains alone at home waiting for his wife to return and forging rings for her. At the bidding of King Níðuðr the smith is taken captive; the king steals one particular ring and his sword, hamstrings Vǫlundr, and banishes him to a deserted island to forge treasures. Filled with hatred toward the king, Vǫlundr plots revenge. First he secretly slays the king's sons, returning their skulls, eyes, and teeth in the form of goblets and jewelry. Then he rapes the king's daughter; laughing, he informs the king that she will bear his child, and flies away, leaving Níðuðr behind, forever broken and dishonored.

The popularity of the story of Vǫlundr the smith in ancient Germanic times is attested by the numerous references to the tale in the literature and art of England, Scandinavia, and Germany, as well as the widespread identification of his name in folklore with the figure of the master smith, who produces works of unsurpassed excellence. The earliest pictorial records of the tale are found carved in the front of Franks Casket (*ca.* 700) and on the pre-Christian Gotland picture stone, Ardre VIII. From approximately the same time we have literary testimony in the Anglo-Saxon poem *Deor*, dated to the eighth, ninth, or tenth century, and in *Vǫlundarkviða*. A third version of the tale is contained in the Old Icelandic *Þiðreks saga* from the thirteenth century, based ultimately on German sources. The version in *Þiðreks saga* differs in some respects from the account in *Vǫlundarkviða*.

The focal point of these ancient records of the tale is Vǫlundr's revenge against King Níðuðr, and all concur that this action consisted of slaying the king's sons and ravishing his daughter. For information on the early life of Vǫlundr and the reasons for his capture and maiming and his escape we have only the divergent accounts in *Vǫlundarkviða* and *Þiðreks saga*. Much attention has been devoted to the two related problems of defining the nature of the central character and explaining his escape. Most scholars consider *Vǫlundarkviða* to be a heroic poem and explain the smith's escape by means of either artificial wings (with reference to the account in *Þiðreks saga*) or a magic ring (with reference to the fairy-tale swan-maiden episode at the beginning of the poem). Both explanations contain flaws and leave unsolved puzzles in the text of the poem. A less popular but more satisfactory interpretation identifies Vǫlundr as an elf or dwarf who, like the gods, has the ability to transform himself into a bird and fly away. The structure of the poem can then be seen as analogous to that of *Grímnismál,* in which the supernatural being triumphs over his human opponent and vanishes. Accordingly, the poem belongs together with *Alvíssmál* among the mythological poems of the collection.

BIBLIOGRAPHY
Alfred Becker, *Franks Casket* (1973); Henry A. Bellows, trans., *The Poetic Edda* (1957); Kaaren Grimstad, "The Revenge of Vǫlundr," in *Edda: A Collection of Essays,* Robert J. Glendinning and Haraldur Bessason, eds. (1983); Alexander H. Krappe, "Zur Wielandsage," in *Archiv für das Studium der neueren Sprachen und Literaturen,* **158** (1930), **159** (1931), **160** (1931), **161** (1932); Edith Marold, "Die Gestalt des Schmiedes in der Volksage," in *Probleme der Sagenforschung,* Lutz Röhrich, ed. (1973); Gustav Neckel and Hans Kuhn, eds., *Edda; Die Lieder des Codex Regius* (1962); Paul B. Taylor, "The Structure of *Vǫlundarkviða,*" in *Neophilologus,* **47** (1963); Jan de Vries, *Altnordische Literaturgeschichte,* I (1964), 81–87.

Kaaren Grimstad

[See also **Alvíssmál; Eddic Meters; Eddic Poetry; Grímnismál; Þiðreks saga.**]

VǪLUSPÁ. The Codex Regius manuscript of the *Poetic Edda* begins with a mythological poem of sixty-two stanzas in the *fornyrðislag* meter that deals with the creation of the world and its eventual destruction. Another version containing fifty-nine stanzas is found in the manuscript *Hauksbók* (*ca.* 1300). In his *Prose Edda,* Snorri Sturluson calls this poem *Vǫluspá* (The sibyl's prophecy) and quotes thirty stanzas from it, paraphrasing sixteen others. It is quite likely that each surviving version of the text represents a separate recension. Sophus Bugge's reconstruction of the poem contains sixty-six stanzas; and while not all editors agree with Bugge's arrangement, his numbering has become standard.

Vǫluspá is a rather late poem, composed in Iceland between 950 and 1000, at a time when Christianity and northern paganism were moving toward their final confrontation. While its meter is regular, the influence of skaldic verse can be detected in the number of kennings in the poem, simple though they may be. Nine stanzas have the refrain "Do you still understand—or what," and stanza 44 is repeated in whole or in part three times. These stylistic features contribute to a general sense of urgency and apprehension in the poem, but this does not mean that the poem is written in response to the millenarian pressures sweeping Europe in the latter part of the tenth century. Virtually every line in the poem is controversial in one way or another, and there is an enormous body of scholarship from every ideological viewpoint on all aspects of the text.

The poem is a monologue delivered by the sibyl (*völva*) to the inquiring god Odin, sometimes in the first person and sometimes in the third. The first nine stanzas deal with the creation of the world and how the gods in council begin time (and history) by naming it and then enjoy a brief golden age. There is almost universal agreement that stanzas 9–16, the Catalog of the Dwarfs, is an "interpolation"; but it is common to all three recensions. Catalogs similar to it are found in other Eddic poems, such as *Grímnismál,* and they seem to be a feature of mythological and epic poetry as far back as the *Iliad.* The best that can be said is that the purpose and aesthetic function of these stanzas are now obscure.

Among other matters, stanzas 17–29 deal with the creation of humankind and the war between the two races of gods, the Vanir and the Æsir. Stanzas 30–37 are full of foreboding. Baldr is slain and Loki is punished, a prelude to stanzas 38–58, which recount the terrors of final days, the *ragnarǫk* ("fate of the gods," but corrupted as early as the time of Snorri to *ragnarøkkur,* "twilight of the gods"): the monsters Fenrir (Fenris Wolf) and Midgardsormr (Midgard Serpent), Loki's children, get loose; it is an ax age, a sword age, a storm age, a wolf age, before the world topples; the gods go out to their final battle; the sun darkens, the earth sinks into the sea, the stars vanish, and the great conflagration rages to the very heaven.

The conclusion of the poem, stanzas 59–66, has

been described as being colored by Christianity, but it points back to a much older worldview found in the *Rig-Veda* and expounded in the *Bhagavata Purana*. The universe is destroyed, to be created again. There will be a second creation, the gods will once again assemble on another Iðavöllr, and Baldr will come again. The world will seem a paradise in Gimlé, but the final stanza, which reintroduces the dragon Niðhöggr, carrying corpses, serves as a reminder that this universe, like the one just described, is created only to be destroyed. The last line of the poem ("Now she must sink") is usually interpreted as the cessation of the sibyl's vision. However, the "she" [*hon*] may not refer to the sibyl at all but, rather, to the feminine noun *iorð*, the world that rose anew in stanza 59 and that must, in its own turn, suffer its own *ragnarok*.

Snorri also refers to a *Vǫluspá hin skamma* (Short *Vǫluspá*), part of which is preserved as stanzas 29–44 of the mythological poem *Hyndluljóð*, found in the manuscript *Flateyjarbók*. The reference to a pantheon of twelve gods (stanza 29) and other stylistic and linguistic features place the composition of the fragment in twelfth-century Iceland. It consists mainly of genealogical information, such as the nine mothers of Heimdallr and the offspring of Loki, and accounts of the origins of sibyls (*völur*), wizards (*vitkar*), spell-casters (*seiðberendr*), giants (*jötnar*), and female monsters (*flögð*). Whereas in *Vǫluspá* the world comes to an end in a conflagration, in this fragment the gods perish in snows and fierce gales (stanza 42).

BIBLIOGRAPHY

Editions. Norrœn fornkvæði . . . almindelig kaldet *Sæmundar Edda hins fróða*, Sophus Bugge, ed. (1867, repr. 1965), *Vǫluspá*, 1–42; *Vǫluspá*, Sigurður Nordal, ed. (1923, 2nd ed. 1952); *Vǫluspá*, commentary by Sigurður Nordal, B. S. Benedikz and John McKinnell, trans. (1978); *Vǫluspá*, Sigurður Nordal, ed., Ommo Wilts, trans. (1980); *Hávamál og Vǫluspá*, Gísli Sigurðsson, ed. (1986), same text and annotations, with some additional charts and diagrams, in *Sígild kvæði*, I: *Eddukvæði*, Gísli Sigurðsson, ed. (1986), 9–25, 78–79.

Studies. Haraldur Bessason, "Um byggingu Vǫluspár," in *Morgunblaðið*, April 1, 1984, 72–74, and "Innra samhengi Vǫluspár," in *Morgunblaðið*, July 5, 1987, B 6–7; Joseph Harris, "Eddic Poetry," in Carol J. Clover and John Lindow, eds., *Old Norse-Icelandic Literature: A Critical Guide* (1985), 68–156 (bibliography of *Vǫluspá* criticism, 154–156); Sigurður Nordal, "Three Essays on *Vǫluspá*," in *Saga-Book*, 18 (1970–

1971), 79–135; Elenore C. Pritchard, "The 'Vǫluspá': A Commentary" (diss., Univ. of Pennsylvania, 1972).

SHAUN F. D. HUGHES

[See also Æsir; Eddic Meters; Eddic Poetry; Fenris Wolf; Grímnismál; Hyndluljóð; Odin; Ragnarok; Scandinavian Mythology; Skaldic Verse; Snorra Edda; Snorri Sturluson; Vanir.]

VOTIVE CROWN. The votive crown served to emphasize the greatness or sanctity of a person or place. Ultimately derived from the ancient practice of giving a crown of laurels and the symbolic surrender of sovereignty by the vanquished in Roman imperial ceremonies of triumph, votive crowns continued to be used and depicted throughout the Middle Ages. Often embellished with hanging crosses and jewels, they served as reliquaries ("iron crown" of Monza), were suspended from ciboria above altars and thrones (Pola casket; crown of Recceswinth), or were depicted above the heads of

The crown of Recceswinth. Visigothic, 7th century. HIRMER FOTOARCHIV

saints (nave mosaics of S. Apollinare Nuovo, Ravenna; Cuthbert Gospels).

BIBLIOGRAPHY

Oleg Grabar, "The Umayyad Dome of the Rock in Jerusalem," in *Ars orientalis,* **3** (1959), esp. 47–50; Peter Lasko, *Ars sacra: 800–1200* (1972); Henri Leclerq, "Guarrazar (Couronnes de)," in *Dictionnaire d'archéologie chrétienne et de liturgie,* VI, pt. 2 (1925), and "Monza," in XI, pt. 2 (1934); Percy Ernst Schramm, *Herrschaftszeichen und Staatssymbolik,* I and II (1954–1955).

MICHAEL T. DAVIS

VOUSSOIR, a stone or brick used to form an arch or a vault, usually in the shape of a truncated wedge with two converging sides. The voussoirs are disposed radially along the curve of the arch, with their narrower ends downward, so that the wedges lock together to sustain the arch or vault.

GREGORY WHITTINGTON

[See also **Arch; Vault.**]

VOYAGE DE SAINT BRENDAN, LE, an Anglo-Norman verse adaptation of the *Navigatio Sancti Brendani,* written in the first quarter of the twelfth century by a poet who qualifies himself as *li apostoiles danz Benedeiz,* possibly an ecclesiastical envoy or missionary. The *Voyage* follows the pattern of its Latin source, with numerous abridgments of integral episodes and incidental detail. In Old French literature it fits neither the model of the typical saint's life nor that of an adventure romance, but, being the first major French text to use octosyllabic rhyming couplets and exploiting a quest theme, it can be seen as pointing the way to romances later in the twelfth century.

BIBLIOGRAPHY

Editions include Edwin G. R. Waters, ed., *The Anglo-Norman Voyage of St. Brendan by Benedeit* (1928, repr. 1974), reprinted with German introduction and facing translation in Ernstpeter Ruhe, trans., *Le voyage de Saint Brendan/Benedeit* (1977); and Ian Short and Brian Merrilees, eds., *The Anglo-Norman Voyage of St. Brendan/Benedeit* (1979).

A modern French translation is by Jean Marchand, "Le voyage de Saint Brendan à la recherche du paradis, par Benoît," in *L'autre monde au moyen âge: Voyages et visions* (1940).

BRIAN MERRILEES

[See also **Anglo-Norman Literature; Irish Literature: Voyage Tales.**]

VRELANT, WILLEM (*fl.* before 1454–1481), illuminator, born in Utrecht, was a citizen of Bruges in 1456 and leader of its guild of illuminators, on whose behalf he commissioned an altarpiece from Hans Memling in 1477/1478. Volume II of Wauquelin's *Chroniques de Hainaut* was (despite recent skepticism about the spelling of the illuminator's name by the French-speaking ducal accountant who recorded it in 1468) almost certainly illustrated by Vrelant and his assistants, for several manuscripts connected with Bruges present the same general style of doll-like figures in deep blue and wine-red garments. These manuscripts are by various hands, but among those closest in style to the *Chroniques* are the 1455 breviary of Philip the Good and a treatise on the Ave Maria (both in Brussels), some gatherings in a late copy of Wauquelin's *Alexander Romance* (Paris, Petit Palais), and a *Golden Legend,* now divided between Mâcon and New York.

BIBLIOGRAPHY

Bibliothèque Royale de Belgique, *La miniature flamande: Le mécénat de Philippe le Bon,* L. M. J. Delaissé, ed. (1959), an exhibition catalog; Jean M. Caswell, "A Double Signing System in the Morgan-Mâcon *Golden Legend,*" in *Quaerendo,* **10** (1980); James D. Farquhar, "The Vrelant Enigma: Is the Style the Man?" *ibid.,* **4** (1974), and *Creation and Imitation* (1976); Victor Leroquais, *Le bréviaire de Philippe le Bon* (1929); W. H. J. Weale, "Documents inédits sur les enlumineurs de Bruges," in *Le beffroi,* **4** (1872–1873), 117, 253–328, 299, 301, 336, and "Memlinc's Passion Picture in the Turin Gallery," in *Burlington Magazine for Connoisseurs,* **12** (1907–1908); Friedrich Winkler, *Die flämische Buchmalerei des XV. und XVI. Jahrhunderts* (1925).

ANNE HAGOPIAN VAN BUREN

[See also **Manuscript Illumination, European.**]

VULGAR LATIN. Despite the ambiguity of the appellation, Vulgar Latin is now a generally accepted term applied to the historical development of the Latin language as it is thought to have been spoken in everyday situations. It is to be contrasted with the literary language, Classical Latin, a form of speech that remained more or less fixed from the middle of the first century B.C. to about the end of the fifth century A.D. It may also be seen as a succession of stages in the development of the Romance languages. Nonetheless, it is not identical with "Proto-Romance" (a reconstructed prototypal language that is the direct parent of the Romance languages) but overlaps it, since there are a number of Vulgar features that do not survive in Romance but remain of interest to the student of Latin. Vulgar Latin also overlaps, but is not identical with, "Late Latin" (*ca.* A.D. 200–*ca.* A.D. 600), which embraces a somewhat more restricted period and concerns itself with learned as well as popular developments of the language.

The so-called Vulgar Latin period extends from the middle of the first century of the Christian era (from which the earliest evidence dates) to the latter part of the eighth century. Because of the homogeneity of many of the data, no hard and fast historical divisions have been established within this span, but there is an increasing tendency to refer to "early" and "late" Vulgar Latin. For the early period, there has been much debate regarding who the speakers of Vulgar Latin were, and numerous attempts have been made to assign its traits to one social level or another. The evidence for the early period is too scanty for broad generalities. By the fourth century, however, the language of daily life employed by virtually everyone must have differed radically from the written language promoted tenaciously in the schools. "Foreign" and "substrate" influences on Latin also have been much discussed, but some recent studies now discount these influences (such as Oscan) in favor of traits native to Latin.

The question of dialects within Vulgar Latin is still much debated. Attempts to show local divisions in the language of the early period have largely foundered on the paucity of materials. The apparent homogeneity of the written evidence has led some scholars to conclude that formation of dialects did not get under way until the very end of the Vulgar Latin period. But studies using charters written in France and Italy in the seventh and eighth centuries have established local variations for significant phonological features in the seventh century, and it seems probable that the beginnings of the formation of dialects must be pushed back to the sixth century at the very latest.

For the early Roman Empire the best evidence is provided by inscriptions on stone, wall paintings, ostraca, and papyruses; in the latter two classes new materials are still coming to light. The evidence of the Pompeian wall inscriptions has been confirmed in considerable detail by analysis of the letters (preserved on papyrus) of the soldier Claudius Terentianus (*fl. ca.* 115). Also of value is Petronius' *Satyricon* (written in Nero's reign), particularly the portion known as the *Cena Trimalchionis* (Trimalchio's feast). Unfortunately, that section is transmitted in a single manuscript written in the early fifteenth century; thus the dependability of the phonological and morphological evidence is considerably reduced.

From about the fourth century on, the data given by inscriptions and papyruses are supplemented, to an increasing extent, by the literary language, at least in certain classes of texts. Of special importance are technical treatises, such as the *De re coquinaria* (culinary treatise) of "Apicius," the veterinary treatise known as the *Mulomedicinae Chironis,* and the dietary work under the name of Anthimus, *De observatione ciborum.* While historical writing preserved its learned character up to about 500, this changed in the latter part of the sixth century with Gregory of Tours's *Historiae Francorum,* a work of great importance for tracing changes in Latin morphology (thanks to its preservation in a seventh-century manuscript). In the sixth century there originated the collections of legal formulas and charters that are of exceptional value because the surviving manuscripts are often originals or are copies not far removed from the time of composition. Another class of evidence is the popular Christian literature, among which special importance must be attached to the pre-Hieronymic versions of the Bible known generically as the *Vetus Latina* and the *Itinerarium Egeriae* (fourth century). To all this evidence must be added the statements of the later grammarians. Of special interest is the *Appendix Probi.* It is certain that the work was not compiled by Probus (first century); it has been dated to as early as about 200 or as late as the sixth or seventh century. The work is a list of 227 corrections to incorrect spellings or censored forms; many of the "incorrect" entries reveal phonetic developments that were productive in Romance: *vetulus non veclus; calcostegis non calcosteis; frigida non fricda; mensa non mesa; camera non cammarra,* and so on.

Some of the chief features of Vulgar Latin are the

following: (1) In phonology, the classical Latin vowel system was simplified, especially by the falling together of *ē* and *ĭ, ō* and *ŭ, ae* and *ě*; the yodification of *e* and *i* in hiatus; the extension of syncope. (2) The consonants *b* and *u* [*w*] fell together into an intervocalic spirant; intervocalic voiced consonants became spirants; the combination *tl* became *kl* (after syncope); in the combination *kt, k* became a spirant (then disappeared); most final consonants were lost. (3) Prothetic *e* or *i* before *s* + consonant was widespread.

Classical vowel quantities were gradually lost, though the accentuation system was largely preserved. Phonetic changes prompted widespread changes in morphology, especially in the classical Latin case system, which was greatly simplified. This in turn necessitated changes in the standard Latin word order and the introduction of prepositional phrases to compensate for decreased inflection. The role of the pronoun was greatly extended, and a definite and an indefinite article were introduced.

Vocabulary changes are characterized (in part) by the replacement of classical Latin words by metaphorical terms or words with formerly restricted meanings. Thus *testa* (jar) vies with *caput*; *caballus* (workhorse) ousts *equus*; *spatha* (practice sword) replaces *ensis* and *gladius*. Word formation also underwent considerable change, a chief feature being the extension of the diminutive.

BIBLIOGRAPHY

J. N. Adams, *The Vulgar Latin of the Letters of Claudius Terentius* (1977); Wilhelm A. Baehrens, *Sprachlicher Kommentar zur vulgärlateinischen Appendix Probi* (1922); Johann Baptist Hofmann, *Lateinische Umgangssprache*, 3rd ed. (1951); Bengt Löfstedt, *Studien über die Sprache der langobardischen Gesetze* (1961), with excellent bibliography; Einar Löfstedt, *Late Latin* (1959); Frieda N. Politzer and Robert L. Politzer, *Romance Trends in 7th and 8th Century Latin Documents* (1953); Arnulf Stefenelli, *Die Volkssprache im Werk des Petron im Hinblick auf die romanischen Sprachen* (1962); Veikko Väänänen, *Le latin vulgaire des inscriptions pompéiennes*, 3rd ed. (1966), and *Introduction au latin vulgaire*, new ed., rev. (1967); Roger Wright, *Late Latin and Early Romance* (1982).

MICHAEL HERREN

[See also **Bible; Indo-European Languages; Italian Language; Itinerarium Egeriae; Latin Language.**]

VULGATE. When the Latin word *vulgata* (common, widespread) was first used, it designated the Greek Bible of the early church in the lands surrounding the Mediterranean, but it soon referred also to the Latin translations from the Greek that were beginning to appear. Then *vulgata* was restricted to St. Jerome's version (end of the fourth century). Roger Bacon (*d. ca.* 1291) contributed to the general adoption of the word, and the Council of Trent, using the phrase *vetus vulgata latina*, gave the Vulgate official status in the Latin church (1546).

The nucleus of Jerome's rendering was the Old Latin, often extempore, versions intended to make the liturgical pericopes accessible to hearers unfamiliar with Greek (second century). According to Jerome's preface to the New Testament, he found "as many forms of text as manuscripts." Books or passages of the Old Latin versions, riddled with Grecisms and colloquialisms, and not free from misconstructions, were in use as late as the twelfth and thirteenth centuries.

Shortly before 400, at the request of Pope Damasus I, Jerome revised the texts in circulation. To secure conformity with the sources, a correspondence he called "veritas graeca, veritas hebraica," Jerome consulted the originals—his Greek reference was Origen's *Hexapla*—but he avowedly limited his corrections to essentials in order to disturb as little as possible the faithful accustomed to their scriptural phrasing. Indeed, he left untouched the deuterocanonicals, and the other books were either translated afresh (Samuel, Kings) or only revised (New Testament).

The success of the Vulgate was immediate. In Gaul, Spain, and Italy, it was quoted and copied. Some extant parts date back to the fifth century, among them Paris, Bibliothèque Nationale, nouvelles acquisitions, latin 1628, a palimpsest containing the Gospels. An indication of Jerome's influence was the growing proportion, among codices that are still in existence, of Vulgate texts (left figure) versus Old Latin ones (right): fifth century, 7/26; sixth century, 24/15; seventh century, 37/11; eighth century, 142/15. So it seems that by the ninth century, the supremacy of the Vulgate was definitely established.

Quite predictably, in the process of copying, corruptions, inherited and multiplied by later scribes, were introduced into Jerome's text. Correcting it was the endeavor of Cassiodorus (*d. ca.* 583), Bede (*d.* 735), Alcuin (*d.* 804), and Lanfranc of Bec (*d.* 1089), who collated various Latin manuscripts, sometimes with the Greek. From the twelfth century on, the Vulgate, in more or less successfully emended texts, was used for preaching and teaching. Even printed Bibles introduced and propagated mistakes, which prompted Erasmus to elaborate an alternative translation from the Greek of the whole New Testament (1506–1509, printed 1516). In spite of the textual weaknesses in the Vulgate, the Council of Trent declared it "authentic" (exempt from dogmatic or moral error), recommending at the same time that the text should be printed in as correct a form as possible. This was provisionally done in the Clementine *Biblia sacra* (1604), which, after almost 400 years, gave way to the *Nova vulgata* (1979), the latest edition and the nearest to "Jerome's Vulgate."

BIBLIOGRAPHY
Editions are John Wordsworth and Henry J. White, eds., *Novum Testamentum Domini nostri Iesu Christi latine . . .*, 3 vols. (1889–1954); Bonifatius Fischer, ed., *Vetus latina*, 6 vols. (1949); *Nova vulgata Bibliorum sacrorum editio* (1979).

Studies include Samuel Berger, *Histoire de la Vulgate* (1893, repr. 1958); *Cambridge History of the Bible*, II, Geoffrey W. H. Lampe, ed. (1969); Hans H. Glunz, *History of the Vulgate in England from Alcuin to Roger Bacon* (1933); Bruce M. Metzger, *The Early Versions of the New Testament* (1977); Henri Quentin, *Mémoire sur l'établissement du texte de la Vulgate* (1922); Hermann Rönsch, *Itala und Vulgata*, 2nd ed. (1875); Beryl Smalley, *The Study of the Bible in the Middle Ages* (2nd ed. 1952, 3rd ed., rev. 1983); Arthur Vööbus, *Early Versions of the New Testament; Manuscript Studies* (1954).

HENRI GIBAUD

[See also **Bible; Jerome, St.; Translation and Translators.**]

WACE (after 1100–*ca.* 1175), Norman verse chronicler and author of saints' lives. Born on the Isle of Jersey, he was the grandson of Duke Robert the Magnificent's chamberlain. He grew up in Caen, pursued his studies in Paris, and returned after many years to Caen, where he evidenced a great literary activity by composing a number of works in vernacular: poems for the occasion, pious works, and translations of several saints' lives. Of this production the following are preserved (probably composed in this chronological order): *La vie de Sainte Marguerite*, a translation of a Greek legend; *La conception Nostre Dame*, three episodes in the life of the Virgin Mary; and *La vie de Saint Nicolas,* a collection of tales about the saint. Other works of this genre may be extant but are not recognized as his because they lack his signature.

Wace's fame is based on his translation of Geoffrey of Monmouth's *Historia regum Britanniae*, entitled *Roman de Brut* (finished in 1155 and dedicated to Eleanor of Aquitaine), in which he also introduces elements of the Arthurian legend not mentioned by Geoffrey, for example the creation of the Round Table. This work inspired much of the Arthurian literature in French, notably that of Chrétien de Troyes, and was later freely adapted into English by Layamon. The success of the *Brut* prompted Henry II to ask Wace for a work justifying the right of the Norman rulers to the English throne. Wace labored on the *Roman de Rou* (Rollo) intermittently from 1160 to 1174 without ever completing it (part of it is in alexandrine verse, a meter he later abandoned for his familiar octosyllables), despite the fact that Henry II tried to encourage him with a prebend in Bayeux. Around 1175 the Plantagenet king finally entrusted Benoît de Sainte-Maure, author of the *Roman de Troie*, with the same task. Wace's language and style are somewhat archaic, yet precise, elegant in simplicity, and rich in vocabulary.

BIBLIOGRAPHY
Editions and translations. Ivor D. Arnold, ed., *Le roman de Brut,* 2 vols. (1938–1940), and *idem* and M. M. Pelan, eds., *La partie arthurienne du roman de Brut* (1962); William R. Ashford, ed., *The Conception Nostre Dame* (1933); Elizabeth A. Francis, ed., *La vie de Sainte Marguerite* (1932); A. J. Holden, ed., *Le roman de Rou,* 3 vols. (1970–1973); David A. Light, *The Arthurian Portion of the Roman de Brut of Wace* (diss., New York Univ., 1970); Eugene Mason, trans., *Arthurian Chronicles Represented by Wace and Layamon* (1912); Edgar Taylor, trans., *Master Wace: His Chronicle of the Norman Conquest from the "Roman de Rou"* (1837).

Studies. Benjamin F. Carpenter, *The Life and Writings of Maistre Wace* (diss., Univ. of North Carolina, 1930); Charles Foulon, "Wace," in Roger S. Loomis, ed., *Arthurian Literature in the Middle Ages* (1959, repr. 1969); Urban T. Holmes, "Norman Literature and Wace," in William Matthews, ed., *Medieval Secular Literature* (1965), esp. 55–67; Margaret E. Houck, *Sources of the Roman de Brut of Wace* (1941); John S. P. Tatlock, "Wace," in his *The Legendary History of Britain* (1950).

HANS-ERICH KELLER

[See also **Arthurian Literature; Benoît de Sainte-Maure; Brut, The; Geoffrey of Monmouth; Hagiography; Middle English Literature.**]

WAITS (Waytes, Wayghtes). Mentioned in English documents from about the thirteenth century, waits were professional musicians who, after serving an apprenticeship, were given official status and wages from a city or town. Waits were employed by civic authorities, but often they received payment from the royal purse and from private individuals. In this they were similar to those minstrels who were employed by a court or a patron, and unlike jongleurs, who wandered from town to town playing instruments and entertaining in other ways. Their counterparts in southern France were *gaychatores,* and in Germany *stadtpfeiferen*; the Saxon equivalent was "gleemen."

"Wait" is derived from the Anglo-Saxon word *wacian* (to watch or guard); other terms are *gaite* (Normandy) and *wacht* (Germany). Many of these terms were taken up by the performers as their names; for example, Gait, Wait(e), or Wakeman.

Waits had many duties; principal among them, as the term suggests, was that of guarding or watching over the town. They patrolled the streets, walls, and towers, playing instruments at certain times to show that someone was guarding the city and that "all's well." Various accounts indicate that the waits were obliged to play every night and morning through the entire year: "Every trumpeter . . . had . . . sworn to play each hour of the day and night—until death." During the day, when the city was less vulnerable to attack and only a few watchmen were needed, waits assisted at medieval plays, weddings, and other social functions such as royal visits. They also "piped watch" for the changing of the guard and had to awaken certain people at given hours by softly playing music at their door. "A wayte [shall] nightly from Mychelmas to Shreve Thorsdaye pipe the watche within this courte fowere tymes; in the somere nightes iij tymes, and maketh Bon Gayte at every chambere doare, and offyce, as well for feare of pyckers and pillers."

To fulfill their function, it was necessary to have an efficient method of alerting the townsfolk to danger. Visible signs were obviously useless at night, and not very effective by day. As a consequence, loud instruments characterized the music performed by the waits. Guards were roused by horns, and bell ringers alerted the rest of the city to prepare for an attack. Commonly used instruments were the shawm ("wayte pipe"), a double-reed woodwind instrument; the sackbut, an early form of trombone; various trumpets; and the horn. The

watchman's horn was nicknamed "thunder horn" because of its loud, strong noise.

In smaller towns there were usually from four to six waits. Larger cities had more: London had as many as nine. Although anyone could become a wait so long as he was an accomplished musician, the position tended to be hereditary: as soon as a man gave up his job, usually because of death, his son took over. A wait could also keep two boys as musical apprentices, at his own expense, as long as his fellow waits approved. In London it was resolved that no strangers would be allowed to play within the city and that waits would not be allowed to leave the city except to play on special occasions, when licensed to do so by the mayor.

Waits had certain privileges. They wore special dress or a uniform, usually of bright colors, easily distinguished from that of other groups. Badges were embroidered or pinned onto the clothing or hung from a chain; presented by the municipality for certain jobs well done, they were called "escutcheons" or "cognizances."

BIBLIOGRAPHY

Hugh Baillie, "A London Gild of Musicians, 1460–1530," in *Proceedings of the Royal Musical Association*, 83 (1956–1957); Edmund Bowles, "Tower Musicians in the Middle Ages," in *Brass Quarterly*, 5 (1962); Francis W. Galpin, *Old English Instruments of Music*, 4th ed. (1965); Lyndesay G. Langwill, "The Waits: A Short Historical Study," in *Hinrichsen's Musical Year Book*, 7 (1952).

PENELOPE HUGHES

[See also **Joglar/Jongleur; Minstrels; Music in Medieval Society; Musical Instruments.**]

WAKEFIELD PLAYS. See **Towneley Plays.**

WAKHTANG GURGASLANI. See **Waχtang I Gurgaslani.**

WALACHIA/MOLDAVIA. The name Walachia (Wallachia, Valachia, Vlachia) as a medieval geographical term was applied to any settlement of Vlachs, a pastoral and migratory Romance-language people, in the Balkan Peninsula and adjacent regions. Linguistically the name is related to other terms used originally by Teutonic peoples to describe Latin peoples: Walloons, Welsh, (German) *wälische*. Medieval sources, therefore, locate the land of the Vlachs in different places, because groups of these people were settled in widely scattered locations. Twelfth-century Byzantine and Western writers—for example, Anna Komnena and Rabbi Benjamin of Tudela—refer to "Great Wallachia," by which they mean that portion of the Rhodope Mountains inhabited by Vlachs in the provinces of Macedonia and Thessaly roughly coextensive with the region later called Rumelia. Other Byzantine writers identified Vlach settlements in Epiros as "Little Walachia" and those in portions of northern Albania as "Upper Walachia." In the thirteenth century, Western sources—Robert of Clari and Geoffrey of Villehardouin, for example—use the term "Walachia" to refer to all or part of the lands of the Second Bulgarian Empire, an ethnically composite state formed by Bulgarians, Vlachs, and Cumans. In the later Middle Ages, however, Walachia was understood to refer to the lands of the Romanian-speaking population south of the Transylvanian Alps and north of the Danube. A further terminological refinement placed "Great Wallachia" to the east of the river Olt, a region which in the Romanian language was called Muntenia, "land of the mountains," or Ţara Românească, "land of the Romanians." West of the Olt, the region was known as "Little Walachia" or Oltenia, which in political terms was coextensive with the banat of Severin (Hungarian: Szörény). When the latter region was absorbed into the principality of Walachia, it, too, became a part of Ţara Românească.

No such complexities existed for the region of Moldavia, which takes its name from the Moldova River, a tributary to the Siret (Siretul, Seretz). The political and economic center of the principality lay in the north, in the region which postmedieval writers designate as the Bukovina (the beech woods). Between the rivers Siret and Dniester, extending south to the Black Sea, lay the Moldavian region of Bessarabia.

The Romanian principalities of Walachia and Moldavia in the fourteenth and fifteenth centuries, while politically distinct, shared a common ancestry, language, and religion. Each was ruled by a prince known as a *voivode* (or *vaivode*, from the Slavic for governor). In the later Middle Ages both principalities exhibited the characteristics of frontier states located along major lines of cleavage: linguistic (Romance versus Slavic and Hungarian), religious (Orthodoxy versus Catholicism, and Christianity versus Islam), and cultural (Byzantine versus Latin European). For that reason both principalities were often drawn into protracted warfare during which the voivodes submitted to the lordship of Hungarian, Polish, or Turkish rulers in order to preserve a measure of autonomy until the day when they might be strong enough to reassert political independence.

ORIGINS

Although Walachia and Moldavia, like most Eastern European principalities, contained an ethnically diverse population, the overwhelming majority were Romanian-speaking Vlachs. How and when this Vlach population came to inhabit the Carpathian Mountains and its foothills has been the subject of one of the best-known, possibly notorious, historical debates. The controversy, begun in the nineteenth century but with antecedents as far back as the sixteenth and seventeenth centuries, has produced two seemingly irreconcilable theories: the hypothesis of Daco-Roman continuity and the migration theory. While the issues at stake are ostensibly purely historical, the competing territorial claims of rival ethnic groups in east-central Europe have lent the debate a considerable measure of partisanship and heated polemic. The debate has been waged in terms of archaeology, place-name studies, linguistics, and social and political history. In general, Romanian scholars and some German and English authorities have been proponents of the continuity theory, while Hungarian, German, Bulgarian, and Yugoslav scholars have tended to support the migration theory. At its heart the continuity theory holds that the Romanian-speaking populations of Walachia and Moldavia are the direct descendants of the Romans and romanized Dacians who remained north of the Danube after Aurelian abandoned the Roman province of Dacia in 271, and persisted continuously in the Carpathians from that time until the thirteenth and fourteenth centuries, when documentation for them in Transylvania, Walachia, and Moldavia becomes abundant. The weakness of this theory, as its critics point out, is that there is no evidence for the presence of Vlachs north of the Danube for a period of nearly seven centuries (from the fourth to the eleventh century), while there is abundant evi-

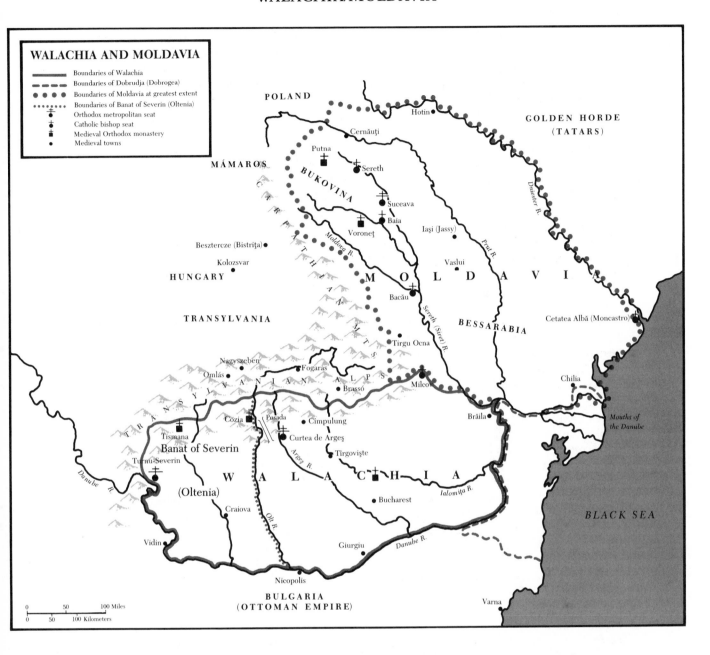

WALACHIA AND MOLDAVIA

Boundaries of Walachia
Boundaries of Dobrudja (Dobrogea)
Boundaries of Moldavia at greatest extent
Boundaries of Banat of Severin (Oltenia)
Orthodox metropolitan seat
Catholic bishop seat
Medieval Orthodox monastery
Medieval towns

dence for Vlachs south of the Danube from the ninth century.

The central argument of the migration theory is that of ethnic discontinuity north of the Carpathians. According to this theory, under successive waves of Gepids, Avars, Slavs, Magyars, Pechenegs, and Cumans the Romano-Dacians were overwhelmed, decimated, and assimilated. In the thirteenth century, especially after the withdrawal of the Mongols in 1242 opened up lands that had recently been depopulated, Romanian-speaking people migrated from areas south of the Danube into the Carpathians. The strengths of this theory lie in the proven discontinuity of Latin place-names north of the Danube in the medieval period, the fact that the north Romanian dialect has affinities with Albanian and South Slavic (rather than West Slavic) dialects, which accords better with a southern origin for people living in the Carpathians, and the fact that the northern Vlachs were not converted by Latin missionaries but by Orthodox missionaries associated with the Bulgarian spiritual center at Ochrid, which used Old Church Slavonic as its liturgical language. The weaknesses of this theory are shown by the fact that Vlachs are now known to have been north of the Danube in the eleventh and twelfth centuries, well before the Mongol invasion of Central Europe, and by the equally valid observation that for the migration of the Vlachs there is the same lack of evidence as for the continuity theory. An observer without strong attachments to either side might note that even if the proponents of the continuity theory are minimally correct that a Romanian-speaking population resided continuously in the Carpathians, the lack of clear evidence for its existence suggests that it would have been so feeble as to have been incapable by itself of preserving Romanian language and customs and of creating the medieval principalities of Walachia and Moldavia. In the Middle Ages, rivers united peoples more frequently than they divided them, and the crossing and recrossing of the Danube should be assumed as a matter of course. The expansion of the First Bulgarian Empire in the tenth century and the dislocations that followed its total and precipitous collapse in the early eleventh century would have provided the stimulus for the migration over several generations of the already migratory Vlachs from the Balkan Mountains north to the Carpathians, where they possibly joined the small continuous settlements or merely started life afresh. There can be no certainty here.

The regions that would become Walachia and Moldavia were in the tenth and eleventh centuries subject to the Pechenegs, who in the twelfth century were displaced by the Cumans. Robert of Clari, identifying Walachia with the Second Bulgarian Empire, places "Cumania" beyond Walachia to the north of the Danube. The Cumans were defeated by the Mongols in the thirteenth century, some of the Cumans fleeing to Hungary, others taking service with the Mongol khanate of the Golden Horde or the Tatars. Many scholars believe the Cuman contribution to the ethnic, social, and cultural life of Walachia and Moldavia has been undervalued, but a lack of evidence from this formative period prevents a carefully documented reassessment.

WALACHIA TO THE DEATH
OF MIRCEA THE OLD (1418)

Around 1230 the Hungarian king Andrew II organized a military district south of the Carpathians around the Danubian fortress of Severin (Szörény). The apparent purpose was to create a buffer area between Hungary and the Second Bulgarian Empire to the south and the Cumans along the lower Danube to the east. The dignity of ban of Severin was initially bestowed on Hungarian lords who held high office at the royal court. In 1247, in the aftermath of the Mongol invasion, Andrew's son, King Béla IV, attempted to reorganize this frontier province by granting lordship to the Order of the Knights Hospitaler. The text of the royal charter provides the first mention of the existence of four Vlach political leaders (identified by the Slavonic title *knez*, "chieftain"): Ioan, Farcaş, Litovoi, and Sănislau. According to the charter, "all of Cumania from the Transylvanian Alps to the river Olt" was to be subject to the Hospitalers, including the lands of Ioan and Farcaş, but not the lands of the voivodes Litovoi and Sănislau, which "they shall hold on the same conditions as before." The reorganization apparently failed, for the list of Hungarian bans of Severin resumes in 1263 and the office was continuously filled by royal appointment throughout the rest of the century.

To the east of the banat of Severin, by the late thirteenth century, a new center of power emerged around Cîmpulung and Curtea de Argeş. These mountain fortresses became the possessions of the Vlach voivode Basarab (ca. 1310–1352), the son of Thotomer (Tihomir). As the fourteenth-century *Hungarian Illuminated Chronicle* (chap. 209) narrates at length, Basarab had been a faithful vassal of the Hungarian king Charles Robert. But the king, wishing to seize Basarab's lands to give them to his friends, rejected the voivode's protestations of loyalty and in 1330 led a large army via the banat of Severin to attack Argeş. As a result of a serious shortage of provisions, however, the king concluded a truce and began to withdraw toward Transylvania. While the Hungarian army was in very mountainous terrain near Posada, Basarab sprang a surprise attack. Charles Robert and his army "came to a defile where the road was shut in on either side and ahead the way was blocked by stone barriers." The chronicler reports that the army, "like fishes trapped in a weir or caught in a net," was decimated by a deadly assault of spear, clubs, and boulders for four days. The Battle of Posada (9–12 November 1330) traditionally marks the political independence of Walachia.

Basarab succeeded in consolidating his authority, extending his domain as far south as the Danube. Upon his death his son, Nicolae Alexandru, succeeded as voivode (1352–1364), thereby launching the Basarab dynasty. The family ruled Walachia throughout the Middle Ages, dying out only in the seventeenth century. Nicolae Alexandru persuaded the patriarch of Constantinople to create the metropolitan see of Ungro-Walachia at Curtea de Argeş in 1359, thereby establishing the first Walachian ecclesiastical province. In 1368, during the reign of Nicholae Alexandru's son, Vladislav I (1364–ca. 1377), the Hungarian king Louis I of Anjou led an army against Walachia in the hope of compelling obedience. This military campaign failed, and in late 1369 Louis and Vladislav concluded an important treaty. In return for acknowledgment of Hungarian suzerainty over Walachia, Vladislav received the banat of Severin and the Transylvanian castles of Omlás (Amlaş) and Fogaras (Făgăraş) as hereditary fiefs of the Hungarian crown. The grant of the Transylvanian fiefs, located in an area with a large Romanian-speaking population, was intended to bind the Walachian voivode more securely within the Hungarian political orbit. In effect, however, the resources and political stature of the voivode were enhanced without any significant diminution of his political independence.

The long reign of Mircea the Old (Mircea cel Bătrîn, 1386–1418) is often seen as a golden age in Walachian history. Mircea, whose principal seat was now at Tîrgovişte, not only retained the banat of Severin and the Transylvanian fiefs, but he also acquired control of the mouths of the Danube and extended his rule to the Dobrudja (Dobrogea), a region on the Black Sea. Mining, trade, and commerce significantly increased. The voivode was a generous patron of the church, especially of the monastery at Cozia. Mircea was above all an able politician and military leader who maintained friendly relations with Hungary, Moldavia, and Poland. During his reign the principal threat to Walachia came from the south as a result of the Ottoman conquest of the Balkan Peninsula. Following the defeat of the Serbs at Kossovo in 1389, Walachia became the front line of Christian resistance to the Muslim advance. Mircea defeated a large Turkish invading army under the sultan's command at Rovine on 17 May 1395. Thereafter the Turks withdrew south of the Danube. Mircea joined the anti-Ottoman coalition forged by the Hungarian king Sigismund of Luxembourg, which met with disaster at the Battle of Nicopolis on 25 September 1396. Although the Ottomans were unable to exploit their advantage and press beyond the Danube because of their own defeat at Ankara (1402) at the hands of Tamerlane, they ultimately compelled Mircea in 1415 to pay an annual tribute

of 3,000 gold ducats in return for peace. At the same time, however, Mircea was active in fostering political discord within the Ottoman Empire by supporting rival candidates for the sultan's throne. At the time of Mircea's death in 1418, Walachia was a respected, independent principality enjoying European-wide political prestige.

MOLDAVIA TO THE DEATH OF ALEXANDER THE GOOD (1432)

The emergence of a Romanian principality east of the Carpathians was a by-product of the joint effort to subjugate Ruthenia by Louis I of Hungary and Casimir III of Poland. To secure the southern flank of Ruthenia for Hungary, King Louis, in 1345, sent an army under Stephen Lackfi, voivode of Transylvania, across the mountains into the region between the Moldova and the Siret rivers. Here a district dependent upon the Hungarian crown, with a certain Vlach lord, Dragoş, as voivode, was established as a buffer against the declining power of the Tatars of the Golden Horde. The dates and sequence of these developments have been much debated by specialists. Nineteenth-century scholars and modern works based on them place these events in 1342, but recent scholarship has provided a revised chronology of Moldavian origins. The voivode Dragoş (ca. 1347–1354) established his seat at the town of Siret. Although Dragoş was succeeded by Sas (1354–1363), who was presumably his son, Bogdan I (1363–1367) entered the region at the head of a large group of Vlach migrants from Máramaros (Maramureş) county in northern Hungary and seized the voivodal dignity, throwing off Hungarian suzerainty.

Under Bogdan's successors the principality expanded to the east and south as a result of successful campaigns against the Tatars. During the reign of the voivode Petru I Muşat (1375–1391) the town of Suceava served as the prince's main residence. To resist the continuing efforts of the Hungarians to reassert dominion over Moldavia, Petru submitted to the suzerainty of Poland in 1387 in return for Polish help. In the next year Petru concluded a treaty with Jagiełło, grand duke of Lithuania and king of Poland, whereby Pocutia, the southernmost province of Ruthenia, adjacent to Moldavia, was pawned to the voivode in return for a substantial loan with the proviso that if the loan were not repaid the Moldavian could retain the province. As the Polish king repaid only three-quarters of the amount, the lordship of Pocutia became a long-standing issue of Polish-Moldavian contention. Petru's successor, Roman I (1391–1394), extended the principality's frontiers to the Black Sea, styling himself "the great and only Master, Lord, by the grace of God, Voivode . . . who rules over Moldavia from the mountains to the sea."

The early period of Moldavia's history concludes with the reign of Alexander the Good (Alexandru cel Bun, 1400–1432). Under his leadership Moldavia played a more prominent role in the international affairs of Eastern Europe. Alexander acknowledged the suzerainty of Poland when he swore homage to Jagiełło of Poland and Lithuania at Kamenitz in 1404. Thereafter, Moldavian troops fought on the Polish side at the Battle of Tannenberg (Grunwald) in 1410, when the Teutonic Knights suffered a resounding defeat. The renewal of the Polish-Moldavian alliance was directed principally against the Hungarian king, Sigismund of Luxembourg. Growing Polish influence and the voivode's practice of marrying Catholic princesses led to the establishment of Catholic bishoprics and monasteries. During Alexander's reign, however, the first Orthodox incumbent in the metropolitan see of Moldo-Vlachia at Suceava obtained recognition of his title from the patriarch of Constantinople. Alexander's policy of religious toleration is also reflected in the fact that Hussite refugees sought and received sanctuary in Moldavia. The reign was marked by increased trade and the growing importance of the southern towns of Cetatea Albă and Chilia (taken from the Walachians in 1427), where Genoese factors dominated commercial activity.

WALACHIA IN THE FIFTEENTH CENTURY

In the fifteenth century bitter dynastic struggles and frequent interventions, or even invasions, by Hungarian kings and Ottoman sultans created an era of instability and political decline. Two factions emerged in the Basarab dynasty following the death of Mircea the Old, which persisted for several generations: the Dănești, descendants of Mircea's brother Dan, and the Drăculești, Mircea's legitimate and illegitimate sons and their offspring, named for one of his illegitimate sons, Vlad II Dracul. Between 1418 and 1456 the leadership of the principality changed at least eighteen times, with one voivode, Radu II the Bald, occupying the throne four separate times. While the Walachian boyars had a role in elevating or overthrowing individual voivodes, the principal powers contending for ascendancy were the Turks, who frequently supported Drăculești candidates, and the Hungarians, who often backed the rival Dănești.

Shortly before 1450 the dominant figure in Walachian politics was the great Hungarian general János Hunyadi, who was himself of Vlach ancestry. Hunyadi was the leader of the Christian campaign against the Turks. In 1444, Hunyadi's army, which contained a large Walachian contingent sent by the voivode Vlad II Dracul, was overwhelmed at the Battle of Varna on the Black Sea. Although named regent of Hungary in 1446, it was as ban of Severin and voivode of Transylvania that Hunyadi was advantageously positioned to intervene in Walachian affairs. In 1447, Hunyadi invaded Walachia, defeated Vlad II Dracul, who shortly thereafter was assassinated, and proclaimed himself "prince of Walachia." He may have governed the principality directly for a brief time, but fell back upon the traditional expedient of installing a political client, Valdislav II, as voivode. When, in 1456, news reached Walachia of Hunyadi's death only weeks after his great victory over the Turks at Belgrade, Vladislav II was defeated and killed by Vlad III Țepeș.

Vlad III Țepeș ("the Impaler," also known as Dracula) ruled Walachia at three different times: 1448, 1456–1462, and 1476. Of all the Walachian voivodes of the fifteenth century he was the most effective defender of the principality's political independence. While initially swearing vassalage to the Hungarian king and paying annual tribute to the sultan, Vlad III invaded Transylvania in 1458 and refused to pay the Ottoman tribute in 1459. Despite his victory over Mehmed II and his reputation as a staunch fighter in the anti-Ottoman struggle, Vlad was captured by the Hungarian king, Matthias Corvinus, Hunyadi's son, in 1462. After years of Hungarian captivity he was once again installed as voivode by the Hungarians in 1476. Within weeks, however, he was killed in the midst of a struggle with partisans of his pro-Turkish rival Basarab Laiotă ("the Old").

After Vlad III the voivodes of Walachia found it increasingly difficult to participate in the anti-Ottoman cause, the leadership of which passed to Moldavia. For Walachia the issue became the struggle to resist becoming a pashalic and to preserve political autonomy within a framework dominated by the Turks. With the death of Stephen the Great of Moldavia in 1504 and the decisive Ottoman victory over the Hungarians at Mohács in 1526,

Walachia was deprived of the possibility of receiving help from neighboring rulers. Thereafter, with the notable exception of the meteoric career of Michael the Brave (1593–1601), Walachia was governed by Christian rulers appointed by the sultan and remained until the nineteenth century a docile dependency of the government in İstanbul.

MOLDAVIA UNDER STEPHEN THE GREAT

During the quarter century following the death of Alexander the Good, Moldavia was seriously weakened by a bitter dynastic feud among Alexander's sons and grandsons. The intensity of the family strife may be gauged by the blinding of the voivode Iliaş by his brother Stephen II and by the de facto partitioning of the principality into northern and southern halves. The internal political turmoil was turned to advantage by Poland, which supported groups of boyars backing certain claimants and opposing others. Some historians assert that the emergence of the boyars as an independent factor in Moldavian political life dates from this period. The principality was rescued from further internal disintegration by the energy and forceful persistence of Stephen III, a grandson of Alexander the Good, commonly known as Stephen the Great (Ştefan cel Mare).

In the second half of the fifteenth century Stephen the Great (1457–1504) was a ruler of European-wide stature. His court at Suceava became one of the great princely centers in Eastern Europe. Although capable of acts of brutality (he was said to dine while watching prisoners being put to death), he was a munificent benefactor of the church and an indefatigable defender of Moldavian autonomy. During his reign Moldavia faced the triangulated threat of invasion from Hungary, Poland, and the alliance of the Turks with the Crimean Tatars. In response he improved the defenses of Suceava and other market towns, constructed a chain of fortresses southward from Hotin along the Dniester in the east, and rebuilt fortifications in the mountains and along the lower Danube. In the generation after János Hunyadi and the Albanian George Castriota (Skanderbeg, d. 1468), Stephen the Great rose to preeminence as the Eastern European champion of the anti-Ottoman cause. For his tireless efforts and his battlefield victories over the Turks, Pope Sixtus IV hailed him in 1475 as the "Athlete of Christ."

Stephen seized the throne from his uncle, Peter III (Petru Aron), who had murdered his father, Bogdan II (d. 1451), and spent the early years of the reign guarding against Peter's return from exile (first in Poland and then in Hungary). Late in 1467, the overconfident Hungarian king Matthias Corvinus invaded Moldavia with the object of compelling the recognition of Hungarian suzerainty but was decisively defeated at the Battle of Baia (14–15 December 1467). After this Hungary ceased to be a threat to Moldavia. In 1471, Stephen openly defied the sultan by refusing to pay the customary annual tribute and thereafter sent troops into Walachia to oust the pro-Turkish Radu the Handsome, replacing him in 1473 with Basarab Laiotă. In response, a Turkish army—joined by the ungrateful Walachian voivode Basarab—invaded Moldavia. Stephen won a major victory at Vaslui in 1475, as the commander of the combined Moldavian, Hungarian, and Polish forces. Buoyed by his victory, Stephen addressed a letter to all the Christian princes of Europe in a vain effort to win their support for a new anti-Ottoman "crusade." In the following year Sultan Mehmed II personally commanded an invasion force that besieged Stephen at Suceava. But the advance of Hungarian troops sent by Matthias Corvinus, to whom Stephen had sworn homage in 1475, threatened the Turkish lines of communication and caused the sultan to withdraw south of the Danube.

After the death of Vlad III Ţepeş and the restoration of Basarab Laiotă, Stephen again invaded Walachia (in 1477) and installed Basarab the Younger (Basarab cel Tînăr, 1477–1482), who subsequently also defected to the Turks. Meanwhile, in 1479, Stephen agreed to resume paying tribute to the sultan, as the price for an end to Turkish incursions into southern Moldavia. But in 1481 he invaded Walachia and replaced Basarab the Younger with Vlad IV the Monk (Vlad Călugărul, 1481, 1482–1495), an illegitimate half-brother of Vlad III. Only a few years later, in 1484, this new Walachian voivode also actively assisted the Turks in attacking Moldavia, further destroyed Stephen's efforts to keep Walachia in the anti-Ottoman camp.

Although for several years Stephen worked to defend Moldavia's position along the lower Danube and on the Black Sea, Chilia, wrested earlier by Moldavia from the Hungarians, and Cetatea Albă (Turkish: Akkermān) were taken by Sultan Bāyazīd II after long sieges in the summer of 1484. Stephen's only hope for aid in expelling the Turks lay with Casimir IV of Poland, to whom he swore homage on 15 September 1485. When King Casimir, however, concluded a peace with the sultan confirming Turkish possession of the two lost Moldavian towns, Stephen turned instead to Hungary. In 1490, he invaded Polish-controlled Ruthenia in an effort to secure the much-disputed province of Pocutia. Following the death of Matthias Corvinus, however, Wladislas Jagiełło (Ulászló), brother of the Polish king John Albert, ascended the Hungarian throne, making it more difficult for Stephen to play one king off against the other. Instead, the Polish king launched a major invasion of Moldavia in 1497, for the purpose of overthrowing Stephen and providing a throne for another Jagiellonian prince, his youngest brother Sigismund. But by autumn, after a series of Moldavian victories, the last at Cernăuți (Czernowitz) on 30 October 1497, the Poles withdrew in defeat and in April 1498 concluded a peace treaty in which in addition to ending hostilities both sides agreed to mutual freedom of trade for their merchants and to reciprocal obligations in the event of Turkish or other attack.

Under Stephen the Great's sons Bogdan III the Blind (Bogdan cel Chior, 1504–1517) and Peter IV (Petru Rares, 1527–1538, 1541–1546), and his grandson Stefăniţa (1517–1527), the capacity of Moldavia to resist the Ottomans was gradually eroded by disputes with Walachia, boyar uprisings, the Turkish conquest of Hungary, and an unsuccessful war with Poland over Pocutia. In 1538, Suleiman I the Magnificent established an Ottoman protectorate over Moldavia that, although punctuated by periodic efforts to regain independence, would prevail until the nineteenth century.

RELIGION AND CULTURE

The practice and traditions of Orthodox Christianity shaped the religious and cultural development of both principalities. No reliable evidence exists for a discussion of the first stage of the conversion of the Vlachs to Christianity, a topic linked to the controversy over origins. When incontrovertible evidence exists, for example the listing in a Byzantine document *ca.* 839–856 of a bishop for the Vlachs who was dependent upon the archbishopric of Ochrid, it is clear that certain Romanian-speaking peoples were already Christians. What is not certain is where the jurisdiction of this bishop was located. More important, however, the liturgy was celebrated in Old Church Slavonic, a fact that points to the Bulgarian church as the agent of conversion. Before the establishment of an au-

tonomous church in Walachia, the Bulgarian bishops of Vidin and Silistria exercised episcopal functions north of the Danube. There is evidence for the existence of local Vlach bishops along the eastern slopes of the Carpathians in northeastern Walachia and southwestern Moldavia early in the thirteenth century. In a letter written in 1234 to the future Hungarian king Béla IV, Pope Gregory IX expressed distress that these schismatic Greek-rite "pseudobishops" administered the sacraments not only to the Vlachs, but also to Hungarians, Germans, and other orthodox peoples living to the east of the Carpathians.

The creation of an autonomous ecclesiastical hierarchy coincided with the erection of permanent political institutions in each principality. In keeping with Byzantine traditions, the existence of an autonomous ecclesiastical jurisdiction coextensive with the political jurisdiction was a mark of princely independence. The patriarch of Constantinople, who alone could confer this status, recognized the establishment of the metropolitan see of Ungro-Vlachia at Curtea de Argeş in Walachia in 1359, and a second metropolitan see was created at Turnu-Severin in 1370. Recognition of the metropolitan of Moldo-Vlachia at Suceava was delayed until 1401 because the Moldavian metropolitan had initially received orders from the Ruthenian metropolitan of Halicz.

Most of the great Orthodox monasteries were founded in the period from the latter half of the fourteenth century until the beginning of the sixteenth century. Cozia, Tismana, and Snagov were among the more important in Walachia. Tismana, in particular, achieved a reputation for spiritual enlightenment under the leadership of the hesychast Nicodim. The hesychast movement later spread to Moldavia as well, where the principal monasteries were Neamţu, Voroneţ, and Putna, the last founded by Stephen the Great after his great victory at Vaslui in 1475. Ties between Mt. Athos and Walachia were established around 1371, when one of the monasteries on the Holy Mountain, Koutloumousiou, was placed under the patronage of the voivode, and its abbot, Chariton, was installed in 1372 as metropolitan of Ungro-Vlachia. In the fifteenth century, after the fall of Constantinople, Stephen the Great's benefactions to Mt. Athos helped preserve the traditions of the spiritual center of Orthodox monasticism.

The Western, Latin church coexisted uneasily and sporadically with the Orthodox. The papacy,

Hungary, and Poland were the principal sponsors of Latin missionaries, usually Franciscans and Dominicans. Around 1220 Hungarian Dominican friars set out to convert the Cumans living east of the Carpathians. The seat of the bishop of the Cumans was at Milcov (Hungarian: Milkó; Latin: Milcovia) near the frontier between Walachia and Moldavia. The bishopric was destroyed by the Mongols in 1241–1242, but when the diocese was reestablished in the fourteenth century, the seat was moved to Bacău. In Walachia in the fourteenth century a Latin bishop resided at Severin, and for a time another, an Italian Dominican, was established at Argeş as a suffragan of the Hungarian archbishop of Kalocsa. In Moldavia a Catholic bishopric was founded at Siret in 1370. Under Alexander the Good, as a concession to his Hungarian wife, a Latin-rite monastery was founded at Baia, where in 1413, probably as a result of Polish influence, a Latin bishopric was also established. On the Black Sea, Cetatea Albă (Italian: Moncastro) had an Italian bishop who ministered to the large Genoese trading population. The spread of Latin-rite Christianity, therefore, was linked directly to the growth of foreign influence and appears not to have had lasting effect upon the Romanian-speaking majority. Moldavian Orthodox prelates are reported to have attended the Council of Constance (1415–1418) and to have participated in discussions about the union of the churches at the Council of Florence in 1439.

The cultural life of Walachia and Moldavia as expressed in literature, art, and architecture reflected a largely mediatized Byzantine tradition acquired through Bulgaria and Serbia and only occasionally directly through Constantinople. Although Romanian was the spoken language of both principalities, the literary language was Slavonic, the liturgical language of the church, written in Cyrillic characters. Almost all manuscripts written earlier than the mid fifteenth century contain Slavonic translations of Greek theological and hagiographical works or copies of texts derived from Bulgarian or Serbian originals. The most original literary product was the late-fifteenth-century *Chronicle of the Days When the Land of Moldavia Was Founded by the Will of God* (known today only through later translations), written in Slavonic by command and under the supervision of Stephen the Great. His death in 1504 is the last entry in the *Chronicle*, which was subsequently translated into Polish, Russian, and German. The first printed book, a Slavonic prayer book, was published in Walachia in 1508.

The Byzantine artistic tradition as adapted in the Balkans spread to Walachia and Moldavia. The fourteenth-century monastic church at Cozia, for example, has architectural features similar to those found in churches in northern Serbia. The court church of the voivodes at Curtea de Argeş, built between 1366 and 1377, contains a cycle of frescoes apparently inspired by the interior decoration of the church of St. Savior in Chora (Kariye Çamii) in Constantinople. In Moldavia the Balkan practice of painting the exterior walls of churches with religious scenes was enlarged to cover entire walls with elaborate cycles of paintings. The earliest surviving example of this characteristic Moldavian artistic achievement is the church of St. George at Suceava, which dates from 1522.

SOCIETY AND ECONOMY

The privileged members of society in Walachia and Moldavia included the princely families, the nobility or boyars, the higher clergy, and members of the urban patriciate. The lower classes included free peasants, artisans, serfs, miners, and salt workers. The position of the voivode (styled *domn* [lord] in Romanian, and in postmedieval times also known as *hospodar*) was that of a hereditary prince exercising supreme political authority within the principality. Chosen in theory by the mixed practice of hereditary right and election by the "country" (in fact, only members of the princely family could participate in the election and be elected), the voivode received the homage of the boyars, commanded the army, conducted relations with neighboring powers, meted out justice together with his council, and appointed the church hierarchy. The hereditary voivodes of the houses of Basarab in Walachia and Muşat in Moldavia each presided over a court, the principal offices of which were modeled on Bulgarian and Serbian adaptations of Byzantine functionaries. There was also some Hungarian influence. The chief officer was the *vornic* (from the Slavic *dvor* [court]), who exercised supreme command of the army in the absence of the voivode and who carried out judicial functions similar to those of the neighboring Hungarian count palatine. In addition, there was the *logofat* (similar to the Byzantine "logothete"), who directed the chancery, and the *vistier* (similar to the Byzantine "protovestiarios"), who functioned as treasurer. The more ceremonial positions were those of *spatar* (sword-bearer), *paharnic* (cup-bearer, similar to the Hungarian *pohárnokmester*), *stolnic* (chamberlain), and *cluciare* (keeper of the keys).

The boyars, the principal landowners, were the descendants of Vlach chieftains whose ranks were increased by the absorption of the leading families of the Slavs, Pechenegs, and Cumans residing within each principality. As the politically and economically dominant class in society, the boyars were personally exempt from the payment of direct taxes but were subject to levies on agricultural produce. Boyars and peasants alike were obligated to pay to the voivode the *cîbla* or *galeata* in Walachia, the *ilisul* in Moldavia, which was a payment in kind of one-tenth of the harvest. A similar impost on wine was collected, known as the *vinarici* in Walachia and the *deseatina* in Moldavia. Politically the boyars emerged as a major influence on public affairs in the civil wars in both principalities during the first half of the fifteenth century. The boyars together with the higher clergy took part in the representative assemblies variously called *seim* (from the Polish *soïm*, "assembly"), *congregatio*, *parlamentum*, or *stari generale* (estates general), the first of which was convened in Moldavia in 1441. Similar occasions are recorded for 1448 and 1457.

The lower classes included a free peasantry, which had the right to unlimited disposition of property, but which over time shrank in numbers as members of this class were compelled to accept servile status. Chosen from the ranks of the freemen was the headman (*knez*) and the local judge (*vataman*) of each village. The largest class of peasants consisted of dependent serfs who worked tenements belonging to the boyars. The serfs had hereditary rights to their farms and full property rights over their animals and agricultural implements. Below the social order were slaves, for the most part Gypsies and Tatars. Since the first half of the fourteenth century, Gypsies, originally from India, are attested as enslaved artisans attached to the courts of the princes, noble households, and monasteries. The Tatars were originally prisoners of war who were deprived of all rights and treated as the movable property of the boyars.

Even before the political organization of the two principalities was established, the region was traversed by trade routes linking Central and Eastern Europe with the Black Sea. These routes became the commercial highways of Walachia and Moldavia in the fourteenth and fifteenth centuries. In Walachia one route followed the course of the Danube. Another began in Brassó (German: Kronstadt; Romanian: Braşov) in Transylvania, crossed the Carpathians and passed by Cîmpulung, and then proceeded to Tîrgovişte, where it divided, going either southward to the Giurgiu on the Danube or eastward to Brăila near the frontier with Moldavia. A third route began at Nagyszeben (German: Hermannstadt; Romanian: Sibiu) in Transylvania and crossed the Carpathians via the Turnu-Rosu (Red Tower) pass, proceeding to Curtea de Argeş and down the Olt Valley to the Danube. The trade routes through Moldavia connected Poland in the north with the Black Sea via Cernăuţi (Czernowitz), Siret, Suceava, and the course of the river Siret to Chilia in the Danube Delta. The famed Tatar route also passed through Cernăuţi but followed a more easterly course to Iaşi (Jassy) and then due east to Caffa in the Crimea, crossing the Dniester considerably north of Cetatea Albă. Lesser routes connected the Siret Valley via Tirgu Ocna with Brassó in the south and with Beszterce (Bistriţa) and Kolozsvár (Klausenburg, Cluj) to the north.

Trade along these routes included the shipment of agricultural products from Walachia and Moldavia to Poland, Hungary, and destinations on the Black Sea, including Caffa and Constantinople, as well as imports of manufactured goods from these regions. In the fourteenth century, for example, Constantinople received valuable shipments of Walachian and Moldavian wheat as well as wine, wax, and honey shipped from the Danube Delta and Cetatea Albă by the Genoese to their trading quarter at Pera. Western cloth and other manufactured items passed into the principalities from Brassó, where Walachian and Moldavian commodities, including cattle, fish, wax, and honey, were transshipped to more western destinations. In addition, there was a transit trade where goods from more distant areas merely passed through the principalities. Although the voivodes of Walachia and Moldavia coined money, the supply was augmented by the widespread use of Byzantine, Hungarian, and Polish coinage.

The towns that arose along the trade routes possessed limited privileges conferred on them by the princes. The chief officers of the town who exercised administrative, judicial, and fiscal responsibilities were called *judeţi* in Walachia and *soltuzi* or *vornici* in Moldavia. The urban population was overwhelmingly made up of Germans, Poles, Armenians, Jews, Greeks, Ragusans, and Italians. The last, especially the Genoese, dominated the Black Sea trade until the Turks captured Chilia and Cetatea Albă (1484).

BIBLIOGRAPHY

The most complete modern, nonpartisan guide to the literature is the annotated bibliography compiled by Manfred Stoy and Max-Demeter Peyfuss, "Rumänien," in Mathias Bernath, ed., *Historische Bücherkunde Südosteuropa,* I, *Mittelalter,* (1980), pt. 2, 1,454–1,618. A critical edition of the documentary sources in the original languages (Latin, Slavonic, Romanian) may be found in the multivolume Eudoxiu de Hurmuzaki *et al.,* eds., *Documente privitóre la istoria Românilor* (1887–1942). More modern source collections for each principality unfortunately translate the documents into modern Romanian: Mihail Roller *et al., Documente privind istoria Romániei,* Series A: *Moldova,* I, *1384–1475* (1954); and Series B: *Țara Românească,* I, *1247–1500* (1953).

Short general accounts may be found in Miron Constantinescu, Constantin Daicoviciu, and Ștefan Pascu, *Histoire de la Roumanie,* Micaela Slavescu, I. Niculita, and I. Baciu, trans (1970); Manfred Huber, *Grundzüge der Geschichte Rumäniens* (1973); Nicolae Iorga, *A History of Roumania: Land, People, Civilisation,* Joseph McCabe, trans. (1925); Robert W. Seton-Watson, *A History of the Roumanians* (1934). The best detailed study of the medieval development of both principalities remains Iorga, *Histoire des Roumains,* III: *Les fondateurs d'état,* and IV, *Les chevaliers* (1937).

Major contributors to the controversy over origins, listed chronologically, have been the advocates of the continuity theory: Alexandru D. Xenopol, *Une énigme historique: Les Roumains au moyen âge* (1885); Constantin Daicoviciu, *Le problème de la continuité en Dacie* (1940); and Constantin C. Giurescu, *Formarea poporului român* (1973). The arguments in favor of the continuity theory and the defects of the migration theory are summarized in Daicoviciu, Emil Petrovici, and Gheorghe Ștefan, *La formation du peuple roumain et de sa langue* (1963). Proponents of the migration theory are Robert Rösler, *Romänische Studien: Untersuchungen zur älteren Geschichte Romäniens* (1871); Pál Hunfalvy, *Die Rumänen und ihre Ansprüche* (1883); and Petŭr Mutafčiev, *Bulgares et Roumains dans l'historie des pays danubiens* (1932). An excellent summary of the strengths of the migration theory and the weaknesses of the continuity theory is provided in André Du Nay, *The Early History of the Rumanian Language* (1977).

Useful specialized studies include N. Constantinescu, "La résidence d'Argeș des voivodes roumaines des XIIIe et de XIVe siècles," in *Revue des études sud-est européenes,* 8 (1970); Radu Florescu and Raymond T. McNally, *Dracula: A Biography of Vlad the Impaler, 1431–1476* (1973); Ștefan D. Gorovei, "Îndreptări cronologice la istoria Moldovei din veacul al XIV-lea," in *Annuarul Institutului de istorie și arheologie: Iași,* 10 (1973), for the revised dating of the first Moldavian voivodes; Maria Holban, "Contacts balkaniques et reálités roumaines au confins danubiens du royaume de Hongrie: À propos de la publication de nouvelles sources concernant Basarab," in *Revue des études sud-est européenes,* 3 (1965); Dimitri Obolenski, *The Byzantine Commonwealth: Eastern Europe, 500–1453* (1971); George Ostrogorsky, *History of the Byzantine State,* Joan Hussey, trans. (1969), for Byzantine connections and the correct date of the battle of Rovine; T. J. Winnifrith, *The Vlachs* (1987); Robert Lee Wolff, "The 'Second Bulgarian Empire': Its Origin and History to 1204," in *Speculum,* 24 (1949).

JAMES ROSS SWEENEY

[See also **Bulgaria; Hungary; Hunyadi, János; Ottomans; Romanian Language and Literature; Romanian Principalities; Vlachs; Vlad Țepeș.**]

WALAFRID STRABO (*ca.* 808–849), abbot, teacher, and poet. During his lifetime, short even by medieval standards, Walafrid Strabo built a reputation as a teacher, author, and abbot of the monastery of Reichenau. After studying with Hrabanus Maurus at Fulda, Walafrid Strabo joined the court of Emperor Louis the Pious. His career as an abbot was affected by the wars between Louis' sons, which, at one point, drove Walafrid from his abbey. His writings cover a wide range. Many, such as his condensations of the biblical commentaries of Hrabanus Maurus and his revision of Einhard's *Vita Karoli Magni,* were editorial and pedagogical. He also wrote a liturgical handbook, several saints' lives, and a book on gardening. Walafrid was one of the most accomplished poets in an age known for skilled versification. His poems, including *Visio Wettini,* are imaginative and employ a wide range of meters. The *Glossa ordinaria* sometimes attributed to Walafrid Strabo is a work of the twelfth century.

BIBLIOGRAPHY

Franz Brunhölzl, *Geschichte der lateinischen Literatur des Mittelalters,* I (1975), 345–358, 557–559; Peter Goodman, *Poets and Emperors: Frankish Politics and Carolingian Poetry* (1987); Eleanor Shipley Duckett, *Carolingian Portraits: A Study in the Ninth Century* (1962), 121–160; Wesley M. Stevens, "Walafrid Strabo: A Student at Fulda," in *Canadian Historical Association, Historical Papers* (1971).

JOHN J. CONTRENI

[See also Carolingian Latin Poetry; Einhard; Exegesis, Latin; Fulda; Hagiography, Western European; Hrabanus Maurus; Latin Literature.]

WALDEF, L'ESTOIRE DE, a long (22,304 lines) though incomplete adventure romance in Anglo-Norman verse written late in the twelfth century or early in the thirteenth. The story relates the genealogy, life, and many adventures of Waldef, son of a King Bede and the sister of the king of Normandy, and the adventures of Waldef's own sons, Gudlac and Guiac. The anonymous author claims to have used an English source, which has never been identified. A fifteenth-century Latin epitome of the story, based on a lost Middle English version, also exists.

BIBLIOGRAPHY

John Bramis, *Historia Regis Waldei*, Rudolf Imelmann, ed. (1912); Mary Dominica Legge, *Anglo-Norman Literature and Its Background* (1963).

Brian Merrilees

[See also Anglo-Norman Literature.]

WALDENSIANS were Western European Christian heretics who existed from the late twelfth century to the end of the Middle Ages and beyond (an Italian Waldensian church exists even today). At first Waldensians followed their leader, named Waldes, in desiring only to lead lives of voluntary poverty and preaching, but when church officials refused to allow them to preach they soon became outright heretics.

Waldensian beliefs were rigorously evangelical. They taught that only those who lived in strict accordance with the literal teachings of the Gospels could be saved and that the Gospels called above all for adherence to the apostolic model of poverty. In the Waldensians' view, the Roman church had been damned since the time of Constantine because of its attachment to wealth. Convinced of the perdition of the church, the Waldensians created their own counterchurch, which had its own priesthood and ministered its own sacraments. The attractiveness of Waldensian beliefs gained the heresy numerous converts and the efficiency of Waldensian organization helped it to endure. Certainly Waldensianism was the most geographically widespread and the longest-lived of all medieval popular heresies; most likely it was also the largest in terms of aggregate numbers of believers.

ORIGINS

The founder of the movement, one Waldes, was a merchant (and perhaps also a moneylender) of Lyons who underwent a radical conversion experience around 1173. According to the most detailed surviving contemporary source, the rich and usury-stained Waldes happened upon a crowd one Sunday that was listening to a minstrel sing about the life of St. Alexis, an early Christian saint who gained blessedness by giving up his wealth for begging. Supposedly Waldes was so moved by this narrative and its possible relevance to his own career that he brought the minstrel home with him to hear more about the story. Still unsatisfied, the following day he went to consult an expert theologian about his soul's welfare. In response to Waldes' demand to know the surest way of reaching God, the theologian offered Christ's words to the rich man: "If you wish to be perfect, go and sell what you have, and give it to the poor . . . and follow me" (Matt. 19:21). Hearing this, Waldes immediately did as the words commanded.

Some of the details of this story may be fictional, but there seems little doubt that in the midst of a prosperous career Waldes was moved so intensely by learning of the New Testament criticisms of wealth that he decided to become a beggar. If it seems strange that a man could have reached maturity without having learned of Christ's teachings in the Gospels, it must be remembered that in Waldes' day the Bible was available only in Latin, a language that laypeople could not understand, and that sermons summarizing biblical teachings for laypeople were as yet unheard of. Thus a second source seems worthy of belief when it reports that after Waldes' initial awakening he sought to inform himself more fully about the Gospel messages by hiring two priests to translate and copy for him many books of the Bible and extracts from patristic theological writings. In the words of this account, after studying the revered texts so intensively that he learned many of them by heart, Waldes "resolved to devote himself to evangelical perfection, just as the apostles had pursued it." In practice this meant giving away all his wealth to the poor—except for a small portion he reserved to support his wife and two daughters—and embarking on a career of begging and preaching the Gospels to all who would listen. In response to the many who said he was crazy, he insisted that he was only seeking his own salvation and striving to teach others that they too should place all their hopes in God and "trust not in riches."

Waldes quickly gained many followers in and around Lyons who adopted his way of life and his calling to preach the Gospels. Terming themselves simply "the poor," they were all laypeople who resolved "never to possess silver or gold, or to take thought for the morrow." The early Waldensians had no fixed dwellings and begged for a living. According to one eyewitness, they went about "two by two, barefooted, dressed in wool, possessing nothing, but holding all in common after the example of the apostles: naked following the naked Christ." They studied and circulated their own Bible translations and preached "against their own sins and those of others." One of the major targets of their preaching was the Albigensian, or Cathar, heretics, who were then at the height of their strength in southern France.

Although the Waldensians thought of themselves as models of orthodoxy, they were immediately viewed with distrust by church officials because their profession of poverty tended to put members of the clergy in a bad light. Even though the early Waldensians seem not to have criticized clerical wealth openly, their very existence constituted an implicit criticism of rich prelates because the glaring contrast between a voluntarily barefooted Waldensian and a splendidly accoutred bishop must have led many observers to conclude that the former was more Christlike and hence more holy than the latter. Certainly some prelates found the Waldensians far too conspicuous. Shortly after Waldes' conversion the archbishop of Lyons ordered him to desist from begging publicly and to take food only with his wife at home, but the zealous convert to the "apostolic life" disregarded this injunction in favor of going out with his followers into the streets and highways.

Another and more legally valid objection to the Waldensians was that they not only begged but also preached. Had the Waldensians not insisted on preaching, they might never have been formally condemned, because lives of poverty and begging were not in contravention of contemporary church law. But lay preaching without special license was illegal on the grounds that all laypeople were assumed to be theologically ignorant. Fully aware

of this problem and realizing that he would never gain enduring consent to preach from the hostile archbishop of Lyons, Waldes journeyed with some followers to Rome in 1179 to bring his case before the Third Lateran Council, presided over by Pope Alexander III.

The meeting between the Waldensians and the highest authorities of the church at the Third Lateran was fateful for both parties. Although a major goal of the council was to fight the Albigensians, and although the Waldensians wished nothing more than to be commissioned as evangelical shock troops for this purpose, the officials of the church could not see their way to employing the lay volunteers. Most likely they were resentful of the Waldensians' ostentatious poverty; without question they refused to allow the possibility that the Waldensians were qualified to preach. Even though the men of Lyons brought their biblical and theological translations for inspection, they were subjected to hostile theological questioning. Asked successively whether they believed in God the Father, the Son, the Holy Spirit, and the Mother of Christ, they answered affirmatively each time and thus were caught in a well-laid trap: if they had said that they did not believe in the Mother of Christ they would have been accused of heresy, but because they said that they did they were derided for their "ignorance" in putting the Virgin Mary on the same level with the Trinity. Apparently Pope Alexander III was not as hostile to the Waldensians as other clerics at the council, perhaps because he recognized that they could be put to positive uses. According to one account, the pope "embraced" Waldes and approved of his dedication to poverty. Nonetheless Alexander drew the line at preaching and reaffirmed canon law by ruling that the Waldensians could preach only if they were authorized to do so by their local priests.

The outcome of this decision was that the church lost the services of a vital lay force and the Waldensians were rapidly driven into resistance and heresy. For Waldes and his followers the issue of preaching allowed no compromise, because the Lord had commanded the apostles to "preach the Gospels to every creature" (Mark 16:15). Back in Lyons, the Waldensians were not given the authorization to preach that they desired and soon chose disobedience over compromising their consciences. Allegedly, when Waldes was told to stop preaching by the archbishop of Lyons, he assumed the role of the Apostle Peter by saying, "We ought to obey God rather than men" (Acts 5:29). Whether or not he actually said that, around 1182 the Waldensians were excommunicated and expelled from Lyons because of their continued insistence on preaching the Gospels. Forced to move elsewhere, they found welcome and gained recruits in many cities and towns of southern France and northern Italy. In short order Waldes' movement was condemned by Pope Lucius III in 1184, but this condemnation by no means put an end to its spread. Quite to the contrary, by the time Waldes died (between 1205 and 1218) the movement he founded had become entrenched in many areas of Western Europe.

DOCTRINES

By the time of Waldes' death Waldensianism had also become thoroughly heretical. It is true that Pope Lucius had already condemned the Waldesians for heresy in 1184, but close attention to the wording of his decree reveals that he neglected to accuse them of upholding doctrinal error, charging them instead solely with defying authority in preaching without authorization. Thus the Waldensians of 1184 were, properly speaking, schismatics rather than doctrinal heretics. But in the following years they began to formulate their own truly heretical teachings, a development that came about because they had been forced into a position whereby they had either to accept church discipline and thereby lose their identity, or else justify their resistance on the grounds of a thorough re-evaluation of church doctrine and usage. Once the Waldensians turned toward criticism they very quickly worked out a full-fledged set of heretical doctrines that remained the basis of their faith until the end of the Middle Ages.

Discounting regional variations in emphases and occasional atypical borrowings from other heresies, the main tenets of Waldensianism from around 1200 to 1500 can be grouped under three headings: (1) an attack on the authority of priests and the church similar to the ancient heresy of Donatism; (2) a denial of the doctrine of purgatory and its attendant beliefs and practices; and (3) a radically evangelical morality.

The early-fourteenth-century inquisitor Bernard Gui was no doubt correct in saying that "the principal heresy of the Waldensians was and still remains the contempt for ecclesiastical power." Like the Donatists of the fourth century, the Waldensians argued that priestly ordination in itself conferred no rights to preach or administer the sacraments: only "merit" conferred those rights. From this it followed that all unmeritorious priests had no sacramental powers and should be ignored and, if necessary, disobeyed. Since Waldensians quickly concluded that the entire hierarchical church had been poisoned by wealth and sin, they soon came to believe that all priests were lacking in merit and that the church as an institution should be held in contempt. Meritorious laypeople (including women), on the other hand, could preach, hear confessions, and celebrate the Eucharist. In practice, such people, usually known among the Waldensians as "the perfect," became the new priests of a Waldensian counterchurch.

As Waldensian Donatism resulted in creating an alternate church, the Waldensian denial of purgatory helped strengthen the heretics' confidence in their new church and provide a basis for further criticism of the old one. The Waldensians refused to accept the doctrine of purgatory because they found no explicit statement of it in the Bible. For them there were only two roads after death—straight to heaven or straight to hell. Not surprisingly they also concluded that members of their own community would go to heaven, while their enemies were damned without any chance of purgation in the afterlife, and this belief gave the Waldensians psychological support for enduring persecution.

Denying purgatory furthermore meant denying some associated orthodox beliefs, which in turn meant calling into question some basic foundations of the Roman church. Specifically, since all souls went straight to heaven or hell there was no point in praying for the dead and no rationale for the granting of indulgences (that is, the remission of temporal punishment in purgatory in return for certain good works). Given that most monasteries and capitular churches gained most of their wealth from praying for the dead and that the theory of indulgences was a major prop behind crusades, pilgrimages, and much of the theoretical and financial pretensions of the papacy, it can be seen how threatening the Waldensians' criticisms were to the entire life of the church. Less strictly tied to the denial of purgatory was the Waldensian denial of the cult of saints: without purgatory saints could not serve as intercessors for dead souls, but many Waldensians went further and denied the cult of saints altogether (sometimes making exceptions for the Virgin and the Apostles).

The last class of Waldensian errors was a literalness in interpreting biblical moral teachings. Waldensians refused to take oaths, in obedience to Christ's pronouncement that men should "swear not at all" (Matt. 5:34). They also believed that even the most trivial lie was a mortal sin, that all legal procedures were sinful because Christ said, "Judge not, that ye be not judged" (Matt. 7:1), and that all warfare and capital punishment were strictly forbidden on the grounds of the commandment "Thou shalt not kill" (Exod. 20:13) and Christ's statement that "all they that take the sword shall perish by the sword" (Matt. 26:52). Since most Waldensians followed in the path of Waldes himself in learning the Bible as thoroughly as they could—reading it in vernacular versions if they were literate or listening to it being read aloud if they were not—they could usually offer the appropriate biblical chapter and verse to support their moral teachings when challenged.

In addition to their specific heresies, the Waldensians developed a set of legends that strengthened their sense of mission. According to them, the church that Christ founded on Peter had remained pure until the advent of Constantine and Pope Sylvester I because it was unsullied by wealth and temporal power. But when Constantine "donated" rule over Italy and the West to the papacy, an angel was heard to cry from heaven: "This day poison has been spread in the church." Neither the story of the "donation of Constantine" (in fact unhistorical) nor that of the angelic voice was invented by the Waldensians, but the heretics drew their own unorthodox conclusions from them. Once poison was spread by the flow of wealth, the Roman church ceased being the church of Christ, and became instead the "whore of the Apocalypse" or "synagogue of Satan." According to this account, an associate of Pope Sylvester fortunately refused to accept earthly riches and, after being excommunicated for his defiance, went underground with his followers to keep the fire of the true church burning. From then on there was a continuous line of truly Christian priests and believers, but they remained hidden until the twelfth century, when Waldes brought the underground movement once more into the open. These legends gave Waldes the name of Peter because he had "restored" the church that was founded on the first Peter, and because he supposedly insisted, like the first Peter, that "we ought to obey God rather than men." All of Waldes' followers were thus heirs of two great Peters and the only true heirs of Christ.

ECCLESIASTICAL ORGANIZATION

Waldensian organization was shaped by a compromise between Waldensian beliefs and practical realities. Although theoretically all people who wished to be saved should follow Christ's model of absolute poverty, and although all "meritorious" people theoretically could be priests, in practice not everyone could live off alms if there were none to dispense them, and not everyone could be a shepherd if there were no flocks. As a result, from the time of the movement's early spread until the end of the Middle Ages, Waldensian organization paralleled Catholic ecclesiastical organization in resting on a distinction between the "perfect" who served as priests and the ordinary faithful.

The "perfect," who were also sometimes known as "masters" or "preachers," lived off the charity of the Waldensian faithful. Like Catholic priests, they were ordained by "bishops," practiced celibacy, preached, heard confessions, and celebrated the Eucharist. Their greatest difference from Catholic priests was that they were customarily itinerant because they were in short supply. Often disguised as merchants, they traveled widely to visit numerous congregations. Waldensian bishops, the highest among the perfect, presided over the organization of larger regions. Occasionally bishops and the perfect from different regions held meetings with each other, but there never was a Waldensian "pope" because after Waldes' death no one had sufficient international prestige to keep the movement united. Without a doubt full international centralization would also have been impossible for a persecuted movement that was faced by the enormous difficulties of long-distance communication.

The Waldensian faithful were usually called "believers," "friends," or "the known" (that is, known by God). Like ordinary Catholics, they pursued their own lay occupations. Very often they were not recognizable as Waldensians by outsiders. The religious lives of the Waldensian believers varied greatly according to whether one of their priests was in their vicinity or not. When a Waldensian priest was present—customarily only two or three times a year—the believers would confess and take what they regarded to be proper communion. As occasion demanded, the Waldensian priest might also preside over clandestine baptisms and weddings, and there would usually be clandestine meetings of all the faithful to hear sermons and discuss the Bible. Throughout the rest of the year the Waldensian believers would customarily attend Catholic churches in order to escape detection. This meant that they were sometimes obliged to duplicate the rites they had practiced in secret.

The evangelical appeals and effective organization of Waldensianism allowed it to spread rapidly throughout Western Europe. From southern France and northern Italy the movement spread to Aragon and Lorraine by the 1190's, and it became well ensconced in many parts of Germany, Austria, and Bohemia in the course of the thirteenth century. In 1315 a captured heretic estimated that there were more than 80,000 Waldensian heretics in Austria and an "infinite number" in Bohemia and Moravia; although he was certainly exaggerating, it is certain that entire villages had gone over to the heresy in Bohemia as well as Brandenburg and Pomerania by around that time.

THE RESPONSE OF THE CHURCH

The reaction of the church to the spread of Waldensianism was fitful. At first when Waldensians were detected in a given town they were excommunicated and expelled, but that only accelerated their proliferation. Occasional episcopally directed inquisitions in the early thirteenth century did force some Waldensians to abjure or be burned, but such inquisitions were too isolated in their occurrence to have much cumulative effect. Thus it was only when Pope Gregory IX started commissioning papal inquisitors to fight heresy on a large scale in the 1230's that the heretical tide began to be stemmed. Throughout the thirteenth century the efforts of the papal inquisitions were directed primarily against Cathars in southern France and northern Italy because Cathars were perceived to be the greatest threat to the church. But southern European inquisitors also caught Waldensians in their nets, with the result that by around 1300 Waldensianism had been wiped out or made negligible in most Mediterranean urban areas. Yet the inquisitors seldom ventured into isolated mountains and valleys, which meant that Waldensianism survived in the more inaccessible regions of Provence, Dauphiné, Savoy, and Piedmont until the end of the Middle Ages.

North of the Alps, where there were hardly any Cathars, concerted inquisitorial activity began only in the fourteenth century and even then it operated on a patchwork basis. Recent manuscript discoveries have revealed that inquisitions against Waldensians in Bohemia during the second third of the

fourteenth century were ruthless: between 1335 and 1355 at least 4,000 alleged Waldensians were brought before Bohemian inquisitorial tribunals and at least 200 burned at the stake. Yet elsewhere in the north Waldensians were allowed to go their inconspicuous ways for long periods. Sometimes a determined inquisitor would comb through heretically infested territories and succeed in gaining large numbers of abjurations, but usually his work would not be repeated for decades and many of the heretics who had abjured would revert to their Waldensianism. The sources do not allow certainty about the numbers of Waldensians in Central Europe at any given time, but there is no doubt that some Waldensian communities survived in scattered German-speaking areas at least until the Reformation.

INFLUENCE AND DECLINE

Generalizations concerning the social status of Waldensians are made difficult by the fact that the heresy existed in so many different regions over such long durations. Most of the early Waldensians came from burgeoning cities and towns, and apparently most of them were prosperous inasmuch as the sources speak of their having imitated Waldes in giving away their wealth. But Waldensianism was by no means always a "bourgeois" heresy of prosperous townsfolk. Not only did Waldensianism virtually disappear in urban areas of the south after the thirteenth century, surviving primarily in mountain villages, but recent scholarship has shown that in Central Europe Waldensianism flourished at least as widely in the countryside as in the towns. Inquisitors did find Waldensians in such cities as Strassburg, Nuremberg, and Prague, but at least as often they found them in small farming communities on the German-Slavic frontier. There Waldensianism was characteristically a heresy of simple peasants and artisans. Sometimes relatively prosperous leaders of village communities would be Waldensians too, but even they were in no sense "bourgeois" since they gained their livelihood from agriculture rather than trade or industry.

If it is difficult to generalize about the Waldensian social base, it is possible to say with assurance that the heresy always had a pronounced appeal for women. The exact numbers or proportions of female "perfect" will never be known, but there is no question that the Waldensian theory of female priesthood was consistently put into practice. To the horror of his contemporaries, Waldes encouraged even converted prostitutes to be preachers, and there remained Waldensian women who preached and heard confessions in Pomerania and Strassburg as late as 1393 and 1400. In addition to the existence of female Waldensian priests, there were so many female Waldensian believers that Waldensian women often outnumbered Waldensian men. Such women often played crucial roles in the religious lives of their communities. Repeatedly, inquisitorial sources reveal how Waldensian women recruited men, acted as underground emissaries, and ensured the continuity of the faith within families over the course of generations.

Aside from its effects on the lives of believers, the Waldensian movement had little influence on major developments of medieval history. There was no "Waldensian Crusade" as there was an Albigensian Crusade to change the political fortunes and cultural patterns of large geographical areas; institutions associated with the papal inquisition originated in response more to Catharism than to Waldensianism; and Catholic doctrine probably would have been defined carefully by church councils and scholastic theologians even had Waldensians not attacked it. Nor can it be said that aspects of Waldensian thought rubbed off on non-Waldensians. Numerous orthodox medieval critics of the church attacked ecclesiastical wealth and temporal power, but such critics were evangelically inspired cousins of the Waldensians rather than descendants of them. Indeed it is uncertain whether any other heretics, such as Lollards or Hussites, were influenced by Waldensianism.

But the longest-lived and probably largest of all medieval heresies should be evaluated in its own terms. The fortunes of medieval Waldensianism reveal how piety can be driven into heresy, demonstrate that a proscribed movement could survive for centuries, prove how heretics and orthodox Catholics could live peacefully for long periods side by side, and provide evidence of the varieties of medieval Christian piety.

BIBLIOGRAPHY

Carl T. Berkhout and Jeffrey B. Russell, *Medieval Heresies: A Bibliography, 1960–1979* (1981), 53–61; Jean Gonnet and Amedeo Molnár, *Les Vaudois au moyen âge* (1974); Gottfried Koch, *Frauenfrage und Ketzertum im Mittelalter* (1962); Malcolm Lambert, *Medieval Heresy: Popular Movements from Bogomil to Hus* (1977); Robert E. Lerner, "Les communautés hérétiques (1150–1500)," in Pierre Riché and Guy Lobrichon, eds., *Le moyen âge et la Bible* (1984), and "A Case of Religious Counter-culture: The German Waldensians," in *The American Scholar*, 55 (1986); Alexander Patschovsky and Kurt-Victor Selge, eds., *Quellen zur Geschichte der Waldenser* (1973) and *Quellen zur böhmischen Inquisition im 14. Jahrundert* (1979); Christine Thouzellier, *Catharisme et Valdéisme en Languedoc*, 2nd ed. (1969); Walter P. Wakefield and Austin P. Evans, trans., *Heresies of the High Middle Ages: Selected Sources Translated and Annotated* (1969).

ROBERT E. LERNER

[See also **Albigensians; Bible, French; Bohemian Brethren; Cathars; Councils, Western; Dominicans; Donation of Constantine; Donatism; Heresies, Western European; Heresy; Indulgences; Inquisition.**]

WALDRAMMUS (late ninth–early tenth century), a monk of St. Gall known for only one poem, a lament on the death of Waldo, the brother of Bishop Salomo. This elegy (906) is a cento taken from the *Consolation of Philosophy* of Boethius and from Venantius Fortunatus' consolation poem to Fredegund and Chilperic.

BIBLIOGRAPHY

Ernst L. Dummler, *St. Gallische Denkmale aus der karolingischen Zeit* (1859), 229–247; Max Manitius, *Geschichte der lateinischen Literatur des Mittlelalters*, I (1911), 594; *Patrologia latina*, CXXXII (1853), 574.

NATHALIE HANLET

[See also **Boethius; Carolingian Latin Poetry; Salomo of Constance; Venantius Fortunatus.**]

WALES: HISTORY. Medieval Wales emerged from the twilight world of the end of Roman Britain. After the withdrawal of the Romans in the early fifth century and during the subsequent Germanic invasions and settlements, Britain was transformed. Britons were either slowly assimilated by the newcomers or gradually isolated, mainly in the western parts of the island. Their Celtic language, British, became "Welsh," the language of "foreigners" (the name given to Britons by those who displaced them). It was only slowly, as a result of new pressures from the Scots of Ireland added to the continuing expansion of Anglo-Saxon settlements, that Welsh-speaking people became confined to the area we know as Wales. Irish raiders from the west soon began to settle, on Anglesey and in the northwest, but to greater effect in Dyfed and the southwest. Here stones bearing ogham inscriptions and the Irish place-names still witness their lasting presence. They were part of the cultural mix that was to produce Wales. But more important to North Wales was the continuing contact with Britons in the north of the island. The earliest surviving Welsh poetry may have been composed in what today is lowland Scotland; it certainly preserves memories of northern British heroes whom it mourns or praises. There is also a strong tradition, preserved in the ninth-century *Historia Brittonum* (History of the Britons, attributed to Nennius), of a migration of a northern British tribe from the lowlands of Scotland, led by Cunedda, from whom the royal dynasty of Gwynedd was to claim descent.

EMERGENCE OF KINGDOMS

By the early sixth century several distinct kingdoms had emerged in Wales. Of these the most important were Gwynedd in the northwest, Powys in the east midlands, Dyfed in the southwest, and Gwent (later Glywysing) in the southeast. Their origins are lost in time. It is unlikely that they grew out of Roman settlements, though some continuity may be assumed. Later genealogists certainly traced royal lines back through Roman Britain to important ancestors: that of Dyfed was supposedly descended from Constantine the Great, while the royal dynasty of Gwynedd claimed to have begun with no less a person than Anna, the cousin of Mary, the mother of Jesus! But there is strong evidence suggesting an Irish connection for the Dyfed dynasty, while Gwynedd preserved a tradition of descent from Cunedda of north Britain. This confusion makes certainty impossible. All we can say is that a mosaic of petty kingdoms covered Wales and that out of them emerged some strong rulers who were to force their authority on others, thus creating larger kingdoms from which a kingdom of Wales would later develop. Fixed boundaries were slow to appear and it was long before natural geographical features were used to mark the limits of kingdoms.

The most dominant of these kingdoms, and the one which was to have the greatest influence on the future of Wales, was undoubtedly Gwynedd. Based on Anglesey (the Welsh Môn), which the Welsh called "the mother of Wales," it controlled a secure island fortress, protected by the Menai Strait and by the massif of Snowdonia. The island was the granary of Wales and provided a safe refuge if Gwynedd kings were under military pressure. But in the seventh century it was invaded by Edwin, king of Northumbria, and its ruler, Cadwallon, was forced to seek refuge in Ireland. From there he later formed a desperate alliance with Penda, the pagan king of Mercia, and together they defeated and killed Edwin. This success enabled Cadwallon to dream of expanding Gwynedd eastward at the expense of the English. But the dream was short-lived. He was killed far from home, somewhere near the old Roman wall, by Oswald, the new king of Northumbria. Nevertheless, the poets kept his memory alive, and with it the impossible dream of expansion.

But by now Wales was isolated and something like a border was being fashioned out of territory subject to a long series of attacks by the English. This territory had acquired something of the character of a march when the Romans turned it into a military frontier. Powys in particular was vulnerable, especially from Mercia. But the English, too, suffered from raids from Wales, and in the late eighth century the Mercian king Offa began the construction of the great earthwork which bears his name. Offa's Dyke stretches for more than 120 miles (190 km) from the estuary of the Dee southward almost to the river Severn, and it symbolizes the border that was to mark off Wales from England in the future. It was never an iron curtain separating the two cultures: English place-names are to be found on the western (Welsh) side of the dyke, just as Welsh names survive on the other side. But in general it became a real national divide between Wales and England.

For a long time, too, there was another heritage that sharply distinguished the Welsh from the English. The Welsh were Christians, guardians of a religion that they inherited from Rome, refusing to share it with the despised Saxon pagans who had invaded their island. Monasticism from Gaul was well established in Wales by the early sixth century. This initiated the "age of the saints," when holy men wandered through the country founding churches and monasteries that bear their names. Most lives of these saints, however, were written as late as the eleventh and twelfth centuries and therefore cannot be trusted in detail. But there is no reason to doubt the tradition of Iltud setting up his

514

monastery in South Wales, which reputedly trained Samson (the founder of the monastery on Caldy, among others) as well as Gildas (author of the important *The Ruin and Conquest of Britain*). By far the most important for the future was David (Dewi), whose foundation in Dyfed became the seat of a bishopric. So did Bangor, Llandaff, and Llandeilo Fawr, all founded before the late sixth century.

The church in Wales was therefore not exclusively a monastic one. Though few in number, the bishops possessed authority in clearly defined areas (for example, churches could not be founded except by their license) and administered these areas from their own church. Even though St. David's was claiming metropolitan status in the twelfth century, there is no historical basis for the claim. The few references to "archbishops" imply that the title was honorific and conferred no canonical status. Welsh bishops were not organized into a hierarchy. Indeed some were attached to monasteries where they had no administrative function. Here the abbots possessed authority, which they also exercised over the federations of monasteries that existed. But however prominent they were, even the greater abbots were subject to episcopal direction at times. It was a monastic church, then, dominated by bishops, and thus very different from the church that grew among the English. This difference was symbolized in a famous meeting on the Severn estuary in 602, when the leaders of the Welsh church rejected St. Augustine, who had brought the English church into conformity with Rome.

If the Welsh and the English were different in ecclesiastical organization, they were similar in the way in which political authority came to lie with kings presiding over kindreds that controlled the lives of individual members of the kin. In Wales, lordship never developed along feudal lines; towns remained alien to the people; the economy, though it did eventually use money, remained simple and relatively poor; kings never developed the kind of sophisticated administration that enabled their English counterparts to realistically expand to the extent of a kingdom the size of England. Perhaps the biggest disadvantage that distinguished Welsh kings from those in England was the Welsh law that made kingdoms partible among the royal heirs. Primogeniture had no place in this law. Nevertheless, some Welsh kings did succeed, however temporarily, in uniting kingdoms and giving hope of uniting Wales.

TOWARD WELSH UNITY

If the history of pre-Conquest Wales is essentially the history of four separate kingdoms, there were occasions when a kingdom of Wales seemed a realistic possibility. The tenth-century poem *Armes Prydein* went even further and urged all Britons to unite and expel the English. Such promptings encouraged some kings in their ambitions, none more so than the ninth-century king of Gwynedd, Rhodri, the first Welsh king to be styled *Mawr* (the great). Through his mother, Nest, he acquired Powys in 855, and by 877, when he extended his lordship over Ceredigion, he had become overlord of a good part of Wales. He had shown great military skills, not least when he gained a famous victory over the Vikings in Anglesey in 856. But he did not live to unite Wales under his rule. He was killed by the English in 878. His fame, however, lived on and inspired others. His sons pushed on into the south, forcing rulers there to seek the protection of the English king Alfred. His grandson Hywel Dda ("the good," the only Welsh king ever granted this title) married the daughter of the king of Dyfed and through her he inherited that kingship, thus ruling much of Wales. The English called him "king of the Britons," though this was an exaggeration since the whole of the southeast lay outside his control.

Hywel was remarkable in a number of ways. He was the first Welsh king to issue his own coinage, though it was minted for him in Chester. It is to him, too, that tradition ascribes the compilation of the Welsh law tracts that bear his name. The story of his initiative in assembling skilled lawyers and educated clergy, to whom he gave elaborate instructions on the codification of the laws, might be spurious; but the association of his name with the work of compilation testifies to his enduring reputation as a great king. It was largely due to him, too, that St. David's became the ecclesiastical center of Wales and that the cult of the saint became a national one. His approximately forty-year reign seemed to augur well for the future of Wales. He died in 949 or 950, having earned the appellation "head and glory of the Britons."

But with his death his achievement fell apart. Chaos followed, marked by English attacks and renewed violence among the kingdoms. The *Brut y Tywysogion* (Chronicle of the princes) records the death by violence of no fewer than thirty-five rulers between then and the Norman Conquest. Viking raids continued, and even though they established few permanent settlements of the kind they made in England and Ireland, they still caused havoc and destruction. In 1049, for example, the annals record that "for fear of the Gentiles" the whole of South Wales had been deserted. Some Welsh kings also employed Vikings as allies, which added to the fragmentation of Wales. It seemed that Wales was fated not only to endure the attacks of English and Vikings, but to be kept in a state of turmoil by the rivalry of her own kings and the inability of any one dynasty to establish an overlordship that would be permanent.

Then a new hope appeared. In 1039 Gruffydd ap Llywelyn became ruler of Gwynedd and Powys and for the next sixteen years he fought to become ruler of the south. His success meant that for a brief period of eight years, until he died in 1063, Gruffydd was the nominal master of the whole of Wales. But he lacked the institutions of government to make his rule effective. It remained personal, depending on his own ruthless ability to force his overlordship on reluctant subordinate rulers. His raids across the border into England brought him material rewards as well as a prestige that helped him to consolidate his rule on a personal basis.

England was forced to take notice. Finally, Edward the Confessor traveled to the Severn and made peace with Gruffydd. No wonder the *Brut y Tywysogion* hailed the "fame and glory" that he won because of his "innumerable victories and taking of spoils and treasures of gold and silver and precious purple raiment," so that he had become "head and shield and defender of the Britons."

But the same chronicle records that Gruffydd was killed "through the treachery of his own men," emphasizing what was a fatal weakness in any attempt to unify Wales politically: the lack of any real tradition of unity and the dangers that threatened any ruler when he moved outside the bounds of his own kingdom. Gruffydd ap Llywelyn was killed because an English invasion in the dead of winter isolated him from his northern retreat and forced him to fall back into mid Wales. There he was at the mercy of Welsh enemies, who killed him. His head was sent, significantly enough, to Edward the Confessor, an indication of the formidable challenge he had presented to the English. But it also shows the comparative ease with which his Welsh hegemony could be destroyed in the end.

NORMAN CONQUEST

Once again Wales was fragmented, and three years later a new and more formidable enemy was to replace the English. The Normans who invaded England in 1066 under Duke William were quick to exploit the internal divisions that now bedeviled the Welsh. There had already been a shadowy Norman presence on the border, under the patronage of Edward the Confessor. But very soon after he became king of England, William the Conqueror installed Normans experienced in border situations. Hugh of Avranches was made earl of Chester; Roger of Montgomery, earl of Shrewsbury; and William fitz Osbern, earl of Hereford. Before long, advances were made across the border into Wales. From the new castle at Montgomery the Normans penetrated deep into mid Wales. From Chester others pushed along the coast to Bangor and then on to Anglesey. Yet another Norman advance reached Cardigan, where a new castle was built; and from there they moved southward through Dyfed, where another castle was built at Pembroke.

All of this was possible because of a deliberate policy of attracting settlers to the border areas. New boroughs were established, with extensive privileges given to the burgesses. Earl William fitz Osbern, for example, extended to French settlers in

Hereford the customs enjoyed in his Norman borough of Breteuil. These customs of Breteuil became the model for many a new borough and indeed were later imported into Ireland by the Welsh-Norman invaders of the following century. New manors were also created, often using pre-Norman patterns and a fusion of Welsh and new French practices. These manors and the new fortified boroughs were novelties. But the new settlers were greatly outnumbered by the indigenous Welsh, except in a few areas such as Pembroke, where there was particularly heavy foreign settlement. The large numbers of Welsh were left to continue their traditional agriculture in the highland areas, while the settlers in the new towns and manors of the more fertile lowlands followed the imported methods. The distinction between what later became the "Englishries" and "Welshries" was therefore established quite early in the history of Norman occupation.

With the new settlers came ecclesiastical change. For all their ruthlessness the Normans were often truly religious and endowed new religious foundations on a prodigal scale. Benedictine monasticism now appeared in Wales, often associated with the new boroughs and manors. Before long, new orders appeared, especially the Cistercians, who moved into Welsh areas bringing with them new practices of the reformed Roman church. More important than the arrival of new orders, however, was the gradual transformation of the Welsh bishoprics into dioceses of the new continental type. Staffed by new men trained in the new ways of the "schools," they were brought firmly within the province of Canterbury, bishops swearing an oath of obedience to the archbishop. This had obvious political advantages for the king of England, who exercised his regalian rights in the choice of bishops for the Welsh sees. When the Welsh reacted to the Norman presence, they naturally tried to assert the independence of the Welsh church and procure for St. David's a metropolitan status free of Canterbury, just as Dublin procured a similar status from the pope in 1152. But all efforts were to fail, and the Welsh church remained part of the province of Canterbury.

The arrival of the Normans, then, was to have momentous results for the political, ecclesiastical, and economic life of Wales. Along the border the settlers were carving out lordships that were inevitably expanding into Wales proper. They were creating the March of Wales, that ill-defined area which straddled the border between the two countries, as well as embracing wide lands deep within Wales itself. The wedge of marcher lordships replaced older political divisions and the new marcher lords inherited many of the privileges, and even something of the status, of the rulers they replaced. They exercised financial, military, and legal rights that they claimed with their lordships, so that while not altogether outside the control of the king of England, they were far less susceptible to royal authority than were the feudal barons of England. Successive kings may have tried to impose their will, but they never succeeded in restricting the freedom of action that the marcher lords claimed within their lordships.

Unlike their conquest of England, the Normans' attempted conquest of Wales was piecemeal, the work of individual enterprise, without any central direction until the time of Edward I. Even so, by the 1090's such was the success of the different advances into Wales that much of the country seemed to be firmly in their hands. The southeast, a good part of the southwest, and the whole of the border area—all of the country that came to comprise the march—remained Norman. But in the north there was a strong Welsh reaction that forced the Normans to withdraw. Gruffydd ap Cynan, after many vicissitudes, succeeded in regaining Gwynedd and for the next century and a half it remained unconquered. It even expanded, forcing Henry I to lead an expedition into Wales in 1114. But Gruffydd and his ally, Owain ap Cadwgan of Powys, came to terms with Henry, did homage, and gained the favor of the king. When the death of Henry I led to civil war in England, Gwynedd was able to profit.

OWAIN GWYNEDD AND RHYS AP GRUFFYDD

Gruffydd's eldest son, Owain, advanced almost as far as Chester. Known as Owain Fawr (the fair), he proved to be the most formidable ruler of Gwynedd since Gruffydd ap Llywelyn. When the powerful Henry II returned to England in 1157 he led an invasion of North Wales to curb Owain. But he met with disaster and was nearly killed. Still, Owain had been given a taste of the Angevin's power and agreed to come to terms. He gave homage to the king, surrendered hostages, and returned some recently usurped territory. In accepting the overlordship of Henry II, he believed that he had secured his own position in Gwynedd against future Norman aggression. For seven years he stuck to his bargain. But in 1164, with Henry embarrassed by the great quarrel with Becket and with England divided, he decided to seize his chance. Gwynedd was joined by Powys and other Welsh kingdoms in a widespread revolt. Henry II gathered troops from all his dominions, hired mercenaries from Flanders, assembled war supplies on a huge scale at Shrewsbury, and hired the Dublin fleet to harry the North Welsh coast. The conquest of Wales was to be his answer to Owain. But he failed disastrously and never tried again.

Owain had secured Gwynedd's independence and consolidated his own position as leader of Wales. Two years before he died, his ambassador was received in the court of Louis VII of France, to whom Owain offered help in his war against Henry II. By the time of his death in 1170 he had been excommunicated because of his unorthodox promotion of Arthur of Bardsley to the see of Bangor despite the opposition of both King Henry and Pope Alexander III. To the end he retained his independence.

In the south another great leader had appeared. Rhys ap Gruffydd, the powerful prince of Deheubarth, had wrested lands and castles from the Norman settlers throughout a long career. First with his two brothers, and then with Owain Gwynedd, he had been in the van of resistance to the Normans. But after Owain's death the lord Rhys stood without challenger as the greatest leader in Wales. He was helped by the quarrel between Henry II and Becket, but more especially by the Anglo-Norman involvement in Ireland. This not only removed from southwest Wales men like Richard de Clare, earl of Pembroke, and other enemies, but it diverted Henry II's interest away from Wales toward Ireland. Henry also appreciated the importance of a friendly Rhys in this now dangerous part of Wales and he made it his business to cement good relations with the Welshman. He formally recognized Rhys as lord of all the lands he had won and then appointed him justiciar of South Wales. This was an unprecedented gesture and it clearly signalled the unchallenged position of Rhys ap Gruffydd as superior of all the lesser rulers in that part of Wales. It also secured for Henry the loyalty of Rhys, who now attended some meetings of the king's council in England, including the important Council of Oxford in 1177. But when Henry II died in 1189 Rhys felt free to take advantage of the long absence of Richard I from England. He had to meet new challenges to his position from Welsh as well as Norman enemies. When he died in 1197

he had succeeded in holding what he had gained and in maintaining Deheubarth in a position of supremacy.

But his kingdom died with him. With Powys, the middle kingdom, unable to overcome the fatal weakness of succession disputes, only Gwynedd was left as a potential base for a revival of Welsh independence. When Henry II received the homage of Welsh rulers, he had naturally insisted that the traditional style of "king" should give way to the more normal feudal style of "lord," so that the rulers might appear as little more than ordinary feudatories. Owain Gwynedd, however, was the exception and retained the style "prince." As prince of Gwynedd he initiated a dignity that was to become the focus of political action by his successors, the two great Llywelyns.

Meanwhile, the successes of Owain and Rhys had helped restore confidence in traditional Welsh institutions. In the winter of 1176 Rhys held what has often been called the first eisteddfod at his castle of Cardigan, attended by competitors from not only Wales but Ireland, Scotland, and even England as well. It was in Gwynedd that the great literary revival was most in evidence, the poets reflecting the new confidence in the future, celebrating victories over the Normans, and praising the achievements of heroic leaders.

Despite Norman successes in conquest and settlement, spreading new languages, law, ecclesiastical and social institutions, a distinctive Welsh culture was now strong enough to survive even conquest itself. It became possible for a rich legacy of a Welsh language, literature, and law to be passed on to posterity. A sense of Welsh nationality had been born, in part the result of the pressure of a foreign culture, and it was never to die. Gerald of Wales, himself of mixed Norman-Welsh blood and not one to adopt a purely "national" stance, tells a story of an old Welshman addressing the mighty Henry II as he marched through Wales: "This nation . . . can never be totally subdued through the wrath of man, unless the wrath of God concur. Nor do I think that any other nation than this of Wales, or any other language, whatever hereafter may come to pass, shall, on the day of severe examination before the Supreme Judge, answer for this corner of the earth."

LLYWELYN THE GREAT
By the beginning of the thirteenth century, then, Welsh Wales had survived and foreign conquest had

been thwarted. Gwynedd in the north now produced a ruler who seemed to fill the aspirations of court poets for a hero to unite Wales. He was the grandson of Owain Gwynedd, Llywelyn ap Iorwerth, known to history as Llywelyn the Great, and he had a clearer vision than any Welshman before him of the kind of constitutional relationship that should exist between England and Wales. He strove to gain for Wales, as a principality, the same kind of independent status that Scotland possessed in relation to the English crown. As prince of Wales, he would do homage for all others to the king of England; Welsh lords in turn would do homage to him. In this way Wales would be united. He had a further, and in the Welsh context revolutionary, ambition. To prevent the kind of fragmentation that disputed successions and divided inheritance had brought to Welsh kingdoms in the past, he would secure the undisputed succession and universal recognition of his son David (Dafydd). Primogeniture in the English fashion would guarantee the continuation of a united Wales.

The greatness of Llywelyn's achievement is that when he died both of his aims had been realized. As a young man he had to fight against the claims of uncles and cousins before he finally succeeded in securing the whole of Gwynedd. In 1204 he did homage for this to King John and, as a sign of the king's favor, was given John's illegitimate daughter Joan in marriage (later she was legitimized by the pope as a favor). No less significant, in 1202 the ruler of Meirionydd became his vassal. After a successful campaign against Powys, to which he had a claim through his mother, he installed vassal chieftains in lands there. The expansion of his overlordship beyond Gwynedd was well under way. This alarmed King John, himself a marcher lord (Glamorgan) with some experience of Wales. John decided to encourage Llywelyn's enemies among the lesser Welsh lords. The situation became more alarming for the king when in 1210 he pursued the powerful marcher lord William de Braose into Ireland. Llywelyn made the mistake of supporting William. As a result he had to face the full force of an expedition led by King John, with the strong support of minor Welsh chieftains, in the summer of 1211. Llywelyn endured a humiliating defeat, being granted peace terms only through the intercession of his wife.

But King John had overreached himself. His grants of land to favorites such as Falkes de Breauté and the building of castles at places such as Aberystwyth alarmed some of his erstwhile Welsh allies, who rebelled against him. By the summer of 1212 they were reconciled with Llywelyn, who then led them on a campaign of destruction. The fact that the king had been excommunicated by the pope, who released all his subjects from their allegiance, greatly helped the rebels. King John could do little to cope with the situation in Wales, even after making his peace with the pope in 1213, and had to negotiate a truce through the papal legate. But by then John's troubles with his own barons in England had escalated and Llywelyn brought the Welsh into alliance with them. When the king sealed Magna Carta at Runnymede on 19 June 1215, the charter restored to the Welsh "all lands, or franchises, or other things" of which they had been dispossessed "without legal judgment of their peers." Where disputes arose, they were to be settled by English law in England, Welsh law in Wales, and march law in the march. All hostages, and in particular the son of Llywelyn, were to be returned immediately, together with "the charters which had been delivered to us as a security for peace."

This was a remarkable victory for Llywelyn. But when the pope later denounced the charter and the hostages had been freed, civil war broke out in England and the Welsh took arms against the king. Llywelyn led an army of Welsh chieftains such as had rarely been seen before in Wales and invaded South Wales. He divided his conquests among his allies and became their overlord. Then he drove out the ruler of south Powys and was so strong that when in 1218 he made his peace with the representatives of the young Henry III, he was able to win recognition of all his new possessions (including the castles of Cardigan and Carmarthen). For these he did homage to the king.

Back in Wales, trouble broke out in the south. Llywelyn invaded Dyfed in 1220, ravaged widely, and extorted a large fine for sparing Pembroke castle. The new earl of Pembroke, William Marshal, was naturally incensed, and in 1223 he returned from Ireland, bent on revenge. From England came a royal army in support of the earl. By the time Llywelyn made his submission in October he had lost much of what he had gained in recent conquests. It was a serious setback to his plans. The intrusion of the justiciar Hubert de Burgh into South Wales and the speed with which he steadily augmented his power there seriously alarmed Llywelyn. He went on a rampage of destruction and conquest again, provoking royal reaction. But de Burgh was now out of favor, and knowledge of this persuaded Llywelyn to negotiate with the king. He was proved right when de Burgh fell from power in 1232. Ironically, however, Llywelyn again became involved in a struggle with King Henry in 1233, when he supported the new earl of Pembroke, Richard Marshal, who had come under attack from the king. The new alliance was successful and many important castles fell into their hands. When a truce between Llywelyn and the king was negotiated at Middle in June 1234, a significant advantage was gained by the Welshman. All conquests made before Earl Richard rose in rebellion were to be retained, which gave him Builth and Cardigan. Now his authority stretched through most of Wales and was unchallenged until his death in 1240.

At the outset he had styled himself "prince of Gwynedd," a style he retained officially until 1230. This style placed him above the other Welsh "lords" and was a symbol of the special status claimed by the ruler of Gwynedd. But after 1230 he adopted the new style of "prince of Aberffraw and lord of Snowdon," a deliberate attempt to indicate that his lordship extended beyond the traditional seat of the Gwynedd dynasty on Anglesey. He had made the lesser lords his vassals, built up a centralized administration to buttress his rule, and created a staff of trained civil servants to execute his wishes. A great and a privy seal were used by his clerks. Law was brought up to date in revised legal texts. Even though the kindred survived as an important element in law enforcement, jurists were now stressing the importance of individual responsibility rather than the kindred. Economic change was also accelerating, most notably with the spread of urban institutions and associated trade. A modest money economy was developing. All of this had grown to the extent that the next ruler of Gwynedd was able to commute renders in kind into cash payments and even to collect a tax on movable property.

Llywelyn the Great knew full well that his achievements must be protected by guaranteeing the succession of his son David to an inheritance that was indivisible. He procured David's marriage to Isabella, daughter of William de Braose. Such marriages were an important element in Llywelyn's statecraft. His own marriage to Joan helped greatly his relations with the king. He had daughters married to other important marcher lords: Reginald de Braose, Ralph Mortimer, William de Lacy, John de Braose, and John the Scot, earl of Chester.

But David's marriage was the most important of all. In 1220 Llewelyn procured Henry III's formal recognition of David as sole heir and then in 1238, at the monastery of Strata Florida, he made the assembled rulers swear allegiance to his successor. The plan succeeded and David inherited an undivided patrimony after his father's death.

But he lived for only six more years and during that time had to surrender many of his father's gains. When he came to do homage to the king in 1240, Henry refused to allow him to represent the other Welsh lords; indeed three of them did homage individually to Henry at Windsor and became tenants-in-chief. In 1237 Chester had escheated to the crown; instead of a friendly earl at his back, David now found a royal official determined to use every opportunity to push the interests of the king. Old enemies of Gwynedd appeared, Welsh and marcher, who regained lands and castles they had formerly lost to Llywelyn. A royal expedition in 1241 forced David to make other restorations and diminished his power still further. But in 1244 the advantage fell to him. A potentially dangerous rival, his older brother Gruffydd, fell to his death in attempting to escape from the Tower of London. Nearly all Wales now rallied to David's side and went to war against the English. The king led an expedition along the north coast in August 1245 but achieved nothing and was forced to retire. David was safe, and with him much of his father's achievement. Significantly, too, he had adopted the style "prince of Wales," the first to do so, an earnest of his claim to overlordship over the other Welsh lords.

In February 1246, however, he died without an heir. Partition became a reality again. The two claimants, Owain and Llywelyn, nephews of David, agreed to share his lands, so that Gwynedd was at least spared the damage of a war of succession. They also continued the war against Henry III. But in April 1247 in the Treaty of Woodstock, which recognized their rights in Gwynedd, and for which they did homage to the king, they ceded not only their lands but, more significantly, the homage of other lords in North Wales. Homage of the Welsh lords was once again due to the king of England, and a key element in Llywelyn's pretensions to overlordship had been lost.

For some years an uneasy peace was maintained. In 1254 there was an ominous development. As part of a package (which included all crown lands in Wales) designed to provide an income worthy of a royal heir, Henry III granted the earldom of Chester to his son Edward. For a long time the earls had been well disposed toward Gwynedd, and a marriage alliance had secured that important part of the border. That position had been eroded after 1237 when the earldom had escheated to the crown, so that security could no longer be taken for granted. But after 1254 the situation greatly deteriorated. Edward was aggressive and was to use Chester as a base for attacking Gwynedd and ultimately for conquest. In retrospect his acquisition can be seen as one of the decisive turning points in relations between the ruler of Gwynedd and the English crown.

LLYWELYN AP GRUFFYDD

In 1255 the harmony between Llywelyn and Owain was at last broken. Llywelyn defeated and captured his brother, held him prisoner, and thus became sole ruler. But the rest of Wales was now once again highly fragmented and the idea of a principality seemed more of a chimera than ever. It was the remarkable achievement of Llywelyn ap Gruffydd that not only did he resume the title Prince of Wales in 1258, but he won recognition of the reality of that position from the king of England in the 1267 Treaty of Montgomery. This great achievement was largely the result of his shrewd exploitation of the political difficulties of Henry III in England itself. Already he had shown considerable military skills as well. In a series of campaigns in 1256, 1257, and 1258 he not only made many territorial gains, defeated and drove back royal expeditions sent against him, and showed his genius in the logistics of warfare (including the successful naval defense of his coastline against the threat of attack from Ireland), he also gained the support of all but one of the important Welsh lords, and at an assembly held in 1258 they all did homage to him as vassals.

At first he held aloof from the dissident English barons who were trying to impose reforms on the king, despite invitations to join them. The arrival of Simon de Montfort in 1263 threw England into civil war and Llywelyn took his side, becoming betrothed to his daughter Eleanor. Despite de Montfort's defeat at the decisive battle of Evesham in August 1265, Llywelyn was more than able to hold his own. Finally, on 25 September 1267, Henry III sealed the Treaty of Montgomery with him. This gave formal recognition to Llywelyn and his heir of the title Prince of Wales, secured to him the vassalage of the Welsh lords, and provided a considerable augmentation of his lands. For this he and his heirs would do homage to the English king.

The principality of Wales was a last a reality, guaranteed by formal treaty. But there were still serious flaws that were to undermine Llywelyn's achievement. His three brothers, Owain, David, and Rhodri, were still alive, and whatever the new order in Gwynedd might proclaim, Welsh law still recognized their claims to an inheritance that was divisible. Welsh lords, too, could be bound in allegiance to a prince of Wales only so long as his power was strong enough to compel them. The marcher lords had gotten a severe fright at the success of the Welsh prince, and new men like Gilbert Clare and Roger Mortimer, both supporters of the lord Edward, looked forward to the opportunity of bringing him down. Clare built his astonishing castle at Caerphilly as a sign of his antagonism to Llywelyn. And the ruler of England was similarly poised to take advantage of the first chance to deny the validity of the Welsh principality. The fact was that Llywelyn had the support of neither history nor Welsh law for his claims, and he lacked the necessary institutions of government to secure his rule despite this disadvantage.

Yet he remained unaware of the danger, conscious only of the rights he had gained. He told English royal officials that "the rights of his principality are entirely separate from the rights of the king's realm," a view hardly likely to be welcome to the ambitious and unbending Edward. Worse was his behavior to the new king when Edward returned to England in 1274. Llywelyn had defaulted in payment of the money promised under the Treaty of Montgomery, was involved in disputes that required the new king's intervention, failed to attend Edward's coronation (despite earlier acknowledging the invitation), and, worst of all, withheld the homage due to the king. Despite orders from the king, Llywelyn refused to travel to do homage. One excuse that he offered was that Edward was harboring his enemies, particularly his rebel brother David, who had joined a conspiracy against him in early 1274 and had later sought refuge in England. Between November 1274 and early 1276 Llywelyn refused to obey five separate summonses to attend the king. To make relations between the two even worse, the king took Eleanor de Montfort into custody late in 1275 while she was on her way to Llywelyn, whom she had married by proxy shortly before that. This marriage to the daughter of Edward's old enemy was a great mistake and gave the impression that Llywelyn was posing as de Montfort's political heir, a dangerous affront to the ruler of England.

In November 1276 Edward finally lost patience, proclaimed Llywelyn a rebel and disturber of the peace, and prepared for war. The campaign of 1277 was masterly. The English armies outflanked Llywelyn, preventing him from retreating to a safe refuge on Anglesey. Edward succeeded in driving along the north coast and occupying Anglesey, where his army harvested the rich crop. Llywelyn was forced to capitulate. Naturally the terms were harsh. Under the Treaty of Conway, Llywelyn kept his Prince of Wales title but was now confined to his original territory of Gwynedd and lost the homage of all but a handful of minor Welsh lords. His brother David was rewarded with land and other Welsh lords were restored. Marcher power, too, was buttressed and the king himself gained a vast extension of royal power through the annexation of lands. Finally, the long-postponed homage was rendered by Llywelyn when he traveled to London in December 1277.

EDWARD I'S SETTLEMENT

Now that he had brought the Welshman to submission, Edward was prepared to be generous. He released Eleanor, was present when she completed her marriage to Llywelyn, and freed the hostages whom the prince had surrendered on capitulating. Llywelyn for his part seemed satisfied to abide by the Conway agreement, despite all the real grievances he had with some of the lords who were restored in 1277. In one important case, which under the terms of the Treaty of Conway should have been dealt with by Welsh law, King Edward insisted that English law and procedures should apply, much to the discomfiture of Llywelyn. Edward seemed to be breaking the 1277 terms, which boded ill for the future. Then Llywelyn's brother David, frustrated by the way he was treated by officialdom, burst into rebellion in 1282. Others soon joined him, royal castles were attacked, and the rebellion quickly spread. Llywelyn had been taken by surprise and may even have been embarrassed by the speed of the action. He had to assume command and once more Welsh Wales was fighting for its independence.

The English reaction was severe. Marcher lords were left to cope with the south, while the king led an army through the north. Once again Edward

assaulted Anglesey, cutting off retreat and penning the enemy into Snowdonia. By an unfortunate chance Llywelyn was killed in a minor skirmish while trying to rouse the south. His death really marked the end of the rebellion. David continued to hold out in the north, but Edward was ruthless, keeping his army in the field all through the winter and pressuring the fugitive David until he was captured. Typically, David was handed over to the king by other Welshmen. Condemned as a traitor, he was hanged, drawn, and quartered in October 1283. Welsh independence was at an end. The heads of the two brothers, Llywelyn and David, were placed side by side over the Tower of London, a terrible symbol of the end of a century of hope.

There is little doubt that after 1277 Edward I had decided to extend the law of England in Wales, and with it the English administrative system. In effect he intended to conquer Wales, even though he may never have consciously formulated such a policy until pushed into it by the rebellion of David in 1282. Now he began a thorough reorganization of the conquered territory. The principality of Llywelyn, now annexed to the crown, was divided into three shires. The rest of Wales, outside the marcher lordships, was also shired. These complicated arrangements were set out in the Statute of Wales (or Rhuddlan) in 1284, which also established that while civil law might remain essentially Welsh, English criminal law was to be applied in all other cases. Edward also proceeded with the program of castle-building that he had already commenced in 1277: building at Aberystwyth, Flint, Rhuddlan, and Builth had begun in the spring of that year. But now he began the building of Conway, Caernarvon, Criccieth, Harlech, and, later, after the rising of 1295, Beaumaris. Ringing Snowdonia, these huge fortresses, incorporating the very latest ideas in military architecture, were to prevent the spread of Welsh rebellion in the future. They cost the king a fortune, demanding huge labor forces as well as enormous quantities of materials. During building operations at Beaumaris alone in 1295 an average of 2,600 men were employed. The castles rank as one of the greatest defensive systems ever built in Europe.

But they were more than just castles. They also contained new boroughs, garrison towns colonized by English settlers attracted by the monopoly of trade and other privileges that burgess status conferred. They were to support English rule in a foreign environment, planted with Englishmen, as the burgesses of Newborough (Anglesey) reminded the Black Prince in 1347: "Our town was established for the habitation of Englishmen." Existing boroughs were also encouraged by the king, as was trade. Wales was expected to pay her way and the flow of money had to be increased. Rents were collected in cash, as were the profits of justice. This naturally caused some social disturbance, at a time when division between English and Welsh was already acute. Not all Welshmen acquiesced in the new settlement imposed by Edward I. There was serious rebellion in 1294–1295, led by Madog ap Llywelyn, which caught the king by surprise and in which the new castles showed their value. Edward himself had to take refuge in Conway, which successfully resisted attack until rescue arrived. Harlech was completely cut off; but victualed by sea from Ireland, it was able to hold out. Caernarvon, which was only half-built, was taken and subsequently took forty years to complete. The revolt itself was eventually ruthlessly crushed, but resentment at English officialdom continued to smolder.

The formal inauguration of the future Edward II as Prince of Wales in 1303 may have helped to heal the wounds, especially as he had been born on Welsh soil in April 1284, in a temporary building used during the construction of Caernarvon Castle. There were many Welshmen willing to serve in English armies. Already, thousands had joined the king during his wars in Wales. They served in great numbers in Flanders, Scotland, and in France during the Hundred Years War. Their famous longbow was a fearsome weapon and more than 3,000 Welshmen were to demonstrate its efficiency by annihilating the French at Crécy. Other Welshmen became administrators in the new system of shires and still more were active in the government of lordships. Some even reached the top as sheriffs or stewards. These civil servants, administrators, lawyers, and leaders of military retinues were in time to found landed families that became a new gentry. They were Welsh-speaking, patrons of poets, and preservers of Welsh native culture, but at the same time supporters of the new order in Wales. Many retained an affection for the descendants of Edward I, warmly supporting his son Edward II and later his great-grandson Richard II after they were deposed.

OWAIN GLYN DŴR

Yet there were others who continued to resent the English and sporadic conflict in the fourteenth century sharpened differences. The effects of prolonged plague and sharp population decline produced social change that caused further tension. In the marcher lordships tenants had faced difficulties before, not least during times of rebellion, when they had to choose between loyalty to their immediate lords and revolt. After the 1282 and 1294 wars the earl of Lincoln sealed elaborate agreements with his tenants of Denbigh, remitting his anger and granting his peace in return for pledges of future loyalty. This shows how fragile was the contract that bound lords and their communities together. The kind of stress that in England produced the Peasants' Revolt in 1381 was in Wales preparing the ground for a similar revolt that had convenient targets in the English. Disaffected peasants were lacking a leader. In 1400 such a leader appeared.

Owain Glyn Dŵr (Glendower) descended from princes and so represented the kind of claim to leadership that the times demanded. He had a respectable career: study of law at the London Inns of Court, service in Scotland in 1385, a successful manager of his estates bordering the march. But a dispute over boundaries led him to resort to arms in September 1400. English settlements were attacked and quickly the revolt spread to the whole of Wales. It is significant that at the September meeting where Owain took up arms, he was proclaimed prince of Wales. The widespread support he received from old families and new Welsh gentry indicates how much resentment existed. Of the families who were with him from the start, however, none was more important than the Tudors, a name long since associated with Welsh leaders such as Llywelyn the Great and his son David. And it was their capture of Conway castle that symbolized the remarkable early success of the rebellion.

Owain now had high ambitions. He sent messengers to Ireland and to the king of Scotland with plans for a grand alliance against the hated Saxon. Nothing came of this, but it mattered little. Students from Oxford and Welsh laborers from different parts of England rushed home to join their new prince. As had happened before, the successful Welsh rebel allied with the baronial opposition in England against an unpopular Lancastrian dynasty. He also found an active ally in Charles VI of France. He summoned two parliamentary assemblies and was formally crowned prince of Wales. So strong was he in 1405 that he entered into a famous tripartite indenture with the earl of Northumberland and Edmund Mortimer, purporting to defend the realm of England against all men ("saving the oath of alliance sworn by Glyn Dŵr to the king of France") and fixing boundaries that gave the whole of Wales to the prince. He planned not one but two universities for Wales, and with the support of a national synod of the Welsh clergy in 1406 he proclaimed the independence of St. David's from Canterbury as a metropolitan see.

But once Henry IV overcame the plots that threatened his throne, the Welsh rebellion could at last be tackled. Guns were used to take key castles, support began to fall away, and by 1410 Owain was a fugitive. He was last heard of in 1415 and despite two public offers of pardon by the new king, Henry V, he never reappeared. His name lived on and his alliance with the Percy and Mortimer families anticipated the anti-Lancastrian opposition that was to embroil many Welsh in the so-called Wars of the Roses. And the name of Tudor, so prominent in this revolt, was to come from Wales to resolve the conflict finally with the accession of Henry VII.

TOWARD UNION

There can be no doubt of the immense impact of the Glyn Dŵr rebellion. It showed how vital were the boroughs in the defense of Wales for the English and sharpened at least for a time the difference between Welsh and English. It had a profound effect on the structure of Welsh society, paradoxically accelerating the change from Welsh to English tenures. It exposed the failure of the marcher lordships and focused English attention on the reputation of the march for lawlessness. The English parliament protested at the anomaly of the liberties claimed by the marcher lords and especially at the failure of the rule of law there, a fact that was highlighted in the 1536 act uniting Wales to England. That act was the end of a long political drama that had begun generations before. The growth of an anti-Lancastrian faction in England, which came to be centered on Richard, duke of York, was bound to have repercussions in Wales. Many of the leading figures were marcher lords. Richard of York, as heir to the Mortimers, was himself a marcher, as was his right-hand man, the earl of Warwick, who was lord of Glamorgan. On the Lancastrian side, probably the most important man in Wales was Jasper Tudor, earl of Pembroke at the outset of the war. His mother, Catherine, had been the widow of Henry V, so that he and his elder brother Edmund were half brothers of Henry VI. Edmund had married Margaret Beaufort, who was descended from Edward III. It was their son Henry who eventually became the first Tudor king of England. His uncle Jasper was a key figure in bringing this about.

In 1468 Jasper Tudor was involved in the plot to restore Henry VI to the throne, which roused part of Wales and provided a vital link with France and Brittany. During the restoration he and his nephew Henry were rewarded in Wales. But after Edward IV regained the throne, Jasper brought his nephew to safety in Brittany. In 1483, when Richard III was losing popularity, he made an abortive attempt at recovery in England. Finally, in 1485, another attempt was made, this time through Wales. Landing at Milford Haven, as the new Arthur of the poets, joined by Welshmen from North as well as South Wales as he moved east, Henry finally defeated and killed the Yorkist king at Bosworth. Crowned Henry VII, he rewarded his uncle Jasper, making him justiciar of South Wales as well as duke of Bedford and lord of Glamorgan. Other Welshmen were richly rewarded, Welsh bishops were promoted to four sees, Welsh sheriffs were appointed, and Welshmen filled offices at every level in the localities. Henry gave new life to the Council in the Marches of Wales, initiated by Edward IV, which was later based at Ludlow Castle, making it something like the capital of Wales. He even sent his young son to preside over the council, but he died within a few months.

Henry had named his son Arthur, a conscious attempt to pose as the descendant of the ruler of the ancient Britons. He also put professional genealogists to work on his descent. But it was another son, Henry, who came to the throne in England, and he showed none of the same awareness of the Welsh blood that flowed (however thinly) in his veins. He faced the problems of Wales as he faced similar ones in Ireland and the northern borderlands of England. The new gentry, which had slowly been acquiring land and position throughout the fifteenth century, provided the backbone of the new Wales. Most of the families that had dominated the old marcher lordships had disappeared and with a few exceptions these were now in the hands of the crown. Henry VIII himself showed little interest in Wales in the early years of his reign. But when Thomas Cromwell took over from Thomas Wolsey as the king's chief minister and began to shape the new England that was to be embodied in the king, it was inevitable that Wales, notorious as the most lawless part of Britain, should draw his attention.

Already Wales was undergoing drastic change. The church after 1529 was slowly subjected to the supremacy of the crown; religious houses were suppressed and their properties distributed among safe gentry; reforming bishops were appointed, such as William Barlow, who abandoned St. David's, age-old symbol of the Welsh national church, and moved to Carmarthen. Such changes were to be greatly accelerated in the future; but they do indicate a break with the medieval past that was to usher in modern Wales.

Nothing symbolizes this change more than the 1536 Act of Union. This stated that Wales was "a very member and joint" of the imperial crown of the realm of England, so that Henry VIII was its "very head, king, lord, and ruler." Yet its "divers rights, usages, laws, and customs" were "far discrepant from the laws and customs of this realm" and its people spoke a language different to "the mother tongue," so that "some rude and ignorant people have made distinction and diversity between the king's subjects of this realm and his subjects" of Wales. Therefore, with the consent of parliament, the king ordained that Wales shall "stand and continue from henceforth incorporated, united, and annexed to and with his realm of England." Union with England ended all hope of independence. Yet the names of national heroes survived, a sense of nationality had been created through the great upheavals of the Middle Ages, and a distinct culture had been preserved that was to distinguish Wales from England.

BIBLIOGRAPHY

R. R. Davies, *Lordship and Society in the March of Wales, 1282–1400* (1978) and *Conquest, Coexistence, and Change: Wales 1063–1415* (1987); Wendy Davies, *Wales in the Early Middle Ages* (1982); R. Ian Jack, *Medieval Wales* (1972); John E. Lloyd, *Owen Glendower* (1931) and *A History of Wales from the Earliest Times to the Edwardian Conquest*, 2 vols., 3rd ed. (1939); John E. Morris, *The Welsh Wars of Edward I* (1901); Lynn H. Nelson, *The Normans in South Wales, 1070–1171* (1966); William Rees, *The Union of England and Wales* (1948) and *An Historical Atlas of Wales from Early to Modern Times*, new ed. (1972); David Walker, *The Norman Conquerors* (1977); Albert H. Williams, *An Introduction to the History of Wales* (1941); Gwyn A. Williams, *When Was Wales?* (1985).

JAMES LYDON

[See also **Angevins; Bangor (Wales); Barons' War; Becket, Thomas, St.; Benedictines; Celtic Church; Cistercian Order; Conway, Peace of; Cunedda Wledig; Dyfed; Edward the Confessor, St.; Edward I of England; Edward the Black Prince; Eisteddfod; England; Gerald of Wales; Gildas, St.; Gruffudd ap Cynan; Henry II of England; Henry IV of England; Henry V of England; Historia Brittonum; Hundred Years War; Ireland; John, King of England; Justiciar; Law, Welsh; Llywelyn ap Gruffydd; Magna Carta; Marshal; Nennius; Normans and Normandy; Owain Gwynedd; Peasants' Rebellion; Rhodri Mawr; Richard I the Lionhearted; Richard III; St. David's; Scotland, History; Simon de Montfort the Younger; Vikings; Wars of the Roses; Welsh Literature.**]

WALES: MARCHER LORDS. The marcher lords were Anglo-Norman rulers of quasi-regal lordships in Wales. The marcher lordships first appeared during the Norman conquest of Wales; they continued as autonomous entities until Henry VIII's statute of 1536 abolished their peculiar status. The lordships of South Wales were augmented in the reign of Edward I and thereafter by analogous lordships in the north of the forbidding land. Geographically a frontier area, these units are best defined as the regions of Wales subject neither to the immediate jurisdiction of the English king nor to that of Welsh princes. The marcher honours varied dramatically both in extent and in the authority exercised therein by their lords. The lordships numbered about forty at their height of development in the fifteenth century. They included such major lordships as Iscennen, Kidwelly, Cemaes, Pembroke, Bromfield and Yale, Chirk, Builth, Brecon, Glamorgan, Ewyas Lacy, Radnor, Abergavenny, Usk, Caerleon, and Newport. The principality of Wales, ruled by native Welsh princes until its incorporation into the lands governed directly by the English crown in and after the reign of Edward I, stood outside the marcher lordships and their constitutional and political evolution.

NORMAN PERIOD

With all their diversities, the marcher lordships in the Norman period (1066–1154) exhibited two principal characteristics: an atmosphere of pioneering and of relative independence from the king coupled with innovative state-building. Their lords responded to the practical need to keep peace within their lands and to the corollary need to provide for their defense against native incursions and insurrections. This was a time in the history of the marches when the skies were ablaze with burning villages and castles, when warfare was endemic and Anglo-Norman rule had to be enforced by arms, men, and castles. David Walker has pointed out that, faced with integration or coexistence, the marchers of the Norman period chose coexistence; later in the Middle Ages, integration (at least among nobles of English and Welsh lineage) became common through marriage. The diversity among the marcher fees is explained principally by the topography of Wales, a land divided by rugged mountains and rushing streams, as well as by the equally rugged individuality of the Norman conquerors. R. R. Davies has alluded to the vital importance of the practices summed up by the term "feudalism" in the march of Wales from the reign of William the Conqueror throughout the Middle Ages; there castles, castle-guard, knight service, the incidents of services and aids, and tenurial arrangements maintained a practical operative importance much later than these characteristics are to be found in England, where feudal realities yielded early on to chivalrous ceremonial and to vestigial formalities.

It might have appeared that the marches of Wales were effectively subdued by the end of the reign of William I, but apparent subjugation was illusory—sporadic resistance by the native Welsh occasionally erupted into major conflicts throughout the Middle Ages, and few marcher lords slept easily in their strongholds since the potential to actuate hatred of the colonizers might at any time be converted into raw and terrible violence. As early as 1067 border jurisdictions were established in England to control the Welsh frontier—Hereford, soon followed by Chester (1070) and Shrewsbury (1074). Launched from Hereford and Shrewsbury, raids into South Wales provided the basis of the original marcher lords' conquests and of their jurisdictions. Norman expansion into Wales continued in the reign of William II Rufus, with marcher lordships founded in Brecon, Glamorgan, Pembroke, Gwynllŵg (later Newport), and Cardigan. During Henry I's reign, Gower joined the march. Anglo-Norman colonization, then, was well under way by the end of the Norman period, and the foundation for the future expansion of marcher lordships sturdily established. Yet this expansion did not resume on a major scale until the reign of Edward I.

EDWARD I AND WALES

The trigger action for this enlargement of the march was Edward's summer offensive of 1277 against the great Llywelyn ap Gruffydd, prince of Wales, whose power in the principality had been growing mightily since 1259; his position had been recognized by Henry III in the 1267 Treaty of Montgomery. Yet Llywelyn planned to marry the daughter of the late rebel against Henry, Simon de Montfort, earl of Leicester, and had failed to pay the expected homage at the coronation of Edward I; the king moved against him as a contumacious vassal in 1277. The royal forces were aided by marcher lords, and their joint success was reflected in the Treaty of Conway. The Welsh went to war again in 1282; this conflict lasted intermittently until 1295, despite the death of Llywelyn in 1282. Edward's Statute of Wales of 1284 modestly stated that "Divine Providence . . . has . . . wholly and entirely converted the land of Wales, previously subject to us by feudal right, with its inhabitants into a dominion of our ownership, and has annexed and united it to the crown of the said kingdom as a constituent part thereof."

Essentially, the statute extended English forms of government and legal actions into the former principality, which was now shired. But the marcher lords continued to rule where they had been accustomed so to do. As well, Edward erected new marcher jurisdictions: in Ceri and Cydewain, Chirk, Bromfield and Yale, Denbigh, Ruthin, Powys, and elsewhere. By the end of Edward's reign the march of Wales was for the most part complete.

LATER DEVELOPMENTS

Across the fourteenth century certain trends and developments ensued. One was the concentration of more and more land in the hands of fewer and fewer lords, who were among the great noble families from England; they included the houses of Beauchamp, Montague, Stafford, Despenser, Braose, Marshal, Mortimer, Bohun, Clare, Valence, Grey, Warenne, Talbot, fitz Allen, and Bigod. These were names associated with great landed aristocratic power in England, and it was in England that their leverage in English politics lay, not in the march. This development also led to absentee lordship in the march of Wales. It is interesting that as Welsh affairs quieted down in the fourteenth and fifteenth centuries (relatively speaking, of course), the place of the marcher barons as disturbers of border peace was taken by such northern

English border families as the Percys. As well, increasingly toward the turn of the fifteenth century, distinctions between free and bond tenure and status blurred, as did the demarcation between English and Welsh ethnicity, especially among the upper classes. Tenurial and legal distinctions also faded, the English customs prevailing over the native. Davies alludes suggestively to the "cultural assimilation" of English and Welsh literary traditions, beginning in the twelfth century with Geoffrey of Monmouth, Gerald of Wales, and Walter Map.

Few new marcher lordships were created in the fifteenth century; the chief constitutional development in Wales related to the royal principality rather than to the march. Edward IV, in the 1470's, made the first faltering steps toward exercising direct royal authority in the principality by means of the council of the prince of Wales at Ludlow, thus anticipating the Tudor Council of Wales. Henry VII improved royal administration in the crown lands of Wales, and Reeves points out that the methods he used in dealing with the march were "traditional ones, among them the conclusion of agreements or indentures with Marcher lords in an effort to ensure order and justice." The history of the march as a semi-independent congeries of lordships ended in the reign of Henry VIII, whose parliament of 1536 promulgated "an acte for Lawes and Justice to be ministred in Wales in like fourme as it is in this Realme." Reeves notes that "it was more an act for judicial and administrative integration, for there was no Wales, in the sense of an independent political entity, to be united with England."

JURA REGALIA

The marcher lords, within their Welsh lordships, enjoyed most of the powers and jurisdiction exercised in England by the king: *jura regalia,* in the phrase of the period. These practices were wideranging and set the lordships of the Welsh march apart from all English honours other than the palatinates of Chester, Durham, and Lancaster, which also claimed *jura regalia* (regalities). As the marches were so varied geographically and topographically, so were they in their constitutional peculiarities; but there were elements which they shared. Like the English palatine lords, the marcher lords held their lands of the king in chief and were thus bound by feudal ties and obligations to the

monarch as suzerain. One must not make too much of the distinctive features which follow—as Edward I's dictum ran, there could be but one king in England (and in Wales). The rights of justice in the march were royal rights: the lords had the right to judge in life and limb, to administer routine justice within their jurisdiction; legal officers and administration were answerable only to their lords, and only they could afforest and enforce forest law in their lordships. Unlike English barons, they had the right to make war on their own initiative, to raise armies without royal license, and likewise to raise castles. They could charter boroughs, establish markets and fairs, levy tolls, and set standards for the uniformity of weights and measures. They had the rights to treasure trove, wreck of the sea, and royal fish.

Obviously, the courts were not only the means by which marcher lords enforced their law and punished its transgressors; they were also the means whereby the lords governed their men, both English and Welsh. Two important marcher institutions deserve mention. The first is the Law of the March, what Reeves calls the "aggregate of laws of the Marcher lordships," customary law which persisted owing to the fact that the king's writ—even the writ of error (which did run in the palatinates)—did not run in the march; as in palatinates, the lord's writ replaced that of the king. The Law of the March was constantly changing, since it was unwritten law. Yet, in the fourteenth and fifteenth centuries, English common law slowly replaced Welsh custom—judge-made like Welsh custom, English law was more rational (for example, employing the trial jury), and more familiar to the increasing number of English settlers and royal administrators.

The other Welsh judicial institution alluded to above was the Great Sessions, extant in the fourteenth century and thereafter. In theory triennial, its sittings overrode all subordinate jurisdictions, and it was the ultimate court of appeal within the lordship. Perhaps here again is a mirroring of the judicial superiority of royal courts in England over lesser judicial bodies; like the courts bearing royal authority in England to the shire level, the Great Sessions were itinerant, judging in the lord's name. The quality of marcher justice obviously varied from lordship to lordship, but in general firm peace was preserved, despite the absence of a constabulary, lack of uniformity of justice either among the lordships or within each, and the persistence of recognizances.

The marcher lords were lords of all lands in their regions but those held by the church. The origin of these lordly rights is a matter of controversy—it is unclear whether they arose from the marches' position as frontier areas, whose defense necessitated the immediate exercise of regalian rights, or whether the marcher lords succeeded to the powers of their Welsh predecessors; perhaps the explanation lies in both elements. Clarity was lacking in the Middle Ages concerning these matters, and the same fuzziness is found in modern historical scholarship. Perhaps the essence of marcher rule was military, symbolized and effectuated by the castles which dotted the countryside, castles from which judicial and administrative, as well as military, power radiated. Legal and constitutional theories are important—perhaps vital—but the reality of power was encompassed in the brooding stone strongholds which dominated their districts.

Much of the power obviously embodies the right to exercise authority over land and over men; franchisal and seignorial rights also had their financial aspects, which augmented the attraction of the marcher lordships for their masters. There is little in the economic benefits accruing to these lords which does not find its analogy in feudal England. The marches were a source of fighting men and of such military technology as the longbow, so effectively employed by the armies of Edward I and of his successors. Any individual source of income for the marcher lords was rather paltry, whether profits of justice, feudal or seignorial income, or casual revenues, yet their aggregate was a sufficient annoyance to the natives that the profitability of lordship (as well as its foreign origin) was an important factor in the revolt begun under Owain Glyn Dŵr in 1400. Across the later Middle Ages, direct exploitation of the demesne (growing of food both for market and for consumption; raising of livestock) yielded to renting the land out to men who, having replaced a personal dependency with an economic relationship, illustrated the parallel tendency to convert the former personal services of the villein class and of knightly vassals into money payments to the lord; thus were undermined the social axes of the seignorial and feudal structures.

Yet some sources of agricultural income persisted: for example, the exploitation of forest and of hunting rights (to timber, estovers, and pannage, the purchased privilege of using waters for transport and for fishing, of pasturing flocks and herds upon meadows, and of access to waste). As well, the marcher lords monopolized (and charged for) access to water mills for grinding grain or for fulling cloth, market and fair tolls, the profits of urban courts (all towns of the march had been founded by marcher lords), reliefs, rents, death duties, entry fines, and other casual sources of profit. The destruction accompanying the revolt of Glyn Dŵr diminished much of the material base upon which these revenues were based, and harrowing, combined with the hostility between the Anglo-Norman lords and the native Welsh, reduced the economic resources of the marcher lords. As Reeves has pointed out, "Lordship in the March was still attractive, but it was not so profitable in the fifteenth and sixteenth centuries as it had been before."

RELATIONSHIP WITH THE ENGLISH KING

In theory, the king's authority in the march was confined to disputes concerning advowsons and to contested inheritances to lordships. But again Henry VIII brought into focus the legal and political realities. In his reign, the marchers were deprived of their right to judge pleas of the crown (primarily in cases involving punishment in life and limb, such as arson, robbery, theft, rape, murder, treason, and the like). While they continued to enjoy rights over their noble and base tenants, these were seignorial rather than royal rights. And the Act of 1543, enforcing the English common law in all of Wales, ended the legal autonomy of the march.

It may appear that the marcher lords of Wales were kings in their own dominions, not subject in any meaningful way to the king of England; legal niceties sometimes obscure political realities. Royal power was always present, as a threat and often in actuality; as noted, the marcher lords derived their chief importance on the English national scene as English lords, not as marcher lords, and their influence and position were formed in the arena of English politics and society. It is true that the thirteenth century encompassed more precise definition of marcher franchises, as well as of those of the great English palatinates; yet this mattered little in a period when the royal rights were more grandly defined and exercised. Of course, kings had dispossessed marcher lords previous to this without a theory—Norman kings had ruined marcher lords for rebellion, as King John did William de Braose. It all became very clear in the reign of Edward I, who not only exercised royal lordship over all British franchises but made beyond dispute the realities of power during his reign; Henry VIII, in emplanting his own direct authority in the marches, acted not without precedent.

Henry III's reign set two important legal precedents for the untrammeled exercise of royal power: In 1244 Henry's officials ordered that none was to employ regalities lacking either specific royal franchise or prescriptive tenure, and the 1266 Dictum of Kenilworth demanded return to the monarchy of all royal rights theretofore alienated. While these two statements do not apply specifically to the marches, they formed a precedent which, in hindsight, was ominous for the continued exercise of regalities by the great marcher lords. No ambiguities remain in the reign of Edward I. The 1275 Statute of Westminster I was straightforward: even where the king's writ does not run, "if it be in the Marches of Wales [or in any other franchise], the king who is sovereign lord over all will do right to any who complain to him if the lord of the liberty be remiss." The *Articuli super cartae* (1300) make it plain that "the complaints that shall be made of all those who contravene or offend [Magna Carta or the Charter of the Forest] as well within liberties as without" shall be amenable in royal courts.

And so the political reality which had been present from Norman times acquired legal form: petty kings the marcher lords may have been, but their authority must need bow before that of the one king from whom all regalities in Britain issued.

BIBLIOGRAPHY

R. R. Davies, *Lordship and Society in the March of Wales, 1282–1400* (1978) and "Kings, Lords, and Liberties in the March of Wales, 1066–1272," in *Transactions of the Royal Historical Society*, 5th ser. **29** (1979); Lynn H. Nelson, *The Normans in South Wales* (1966); A. J. Otway-Ruthven, "The Constitutional Position of the Great Lordships of South Wales," in *Transactions of the Royal Historical Society*, 5th ser., **8** (1958); Thomas B. Pugh, ed., *The Marcher Lordships of Wales, 1415–1536: Selected Documents* (1963); Albert C. Reeves, *Newport Lordship, 1317–1536* (1979) and *The Marcher Lords* (1983); David Walker, *The Norman Conquerors* (1977); Albert H. Williams, *An Introduction to the History of Wales*, II (1941).

JAMES W. ALEXANDER

[Conway, Peace of; Edward I of England; Feudalism; Henry III of England; Knights and Knight Service; Llywelyn ap Gruffydd; Nobility and Nobles; Westminster, Statutes of.]

WALĪD I IBN ᶜABD AL-MALIK, AL- (*d.* 715), the sixth caliph of the Umayyad line and a ruler remembered primarily as a great builder. His birth date is uncertain, and from the little that is known of his early life, it seems to have been rather undistinguished.

Upon ᶜAbd al-Malik's death in 705, al-Walīd acceded to the throne of an empire internally at peace. His reign was thus characterized by activities that would not have been feasible during his father's troubled caliphate. Campaigns of external conquest, renewed by the caliph's governors, met with great success. In the West, Umayyad forces crossed the Strait of Gibraltar in 711, and in three years conquered the Visigoths of Spain. More important were the campaigns in the East. Invading Arab armies made major inroads into Transoxiana, and another force advanced across Baluchistan, captured the port of Daybul (711) at the mouth of the Indus River, and moved up the Indus Valley as far as Multan.

These conquests provided enormous levels of revenue and booty to the Umayyad treasury and made possible a vigorous program of internal development. On the administrative level, the process of Arabization begun by ᶜAbd al-Malik was continued, though many of the non-Muslim Greek personnel remained. In war-torn Iraq, canals and irrigation systems were repaired and expanded. The pilgrimage routes in Arabia were patrolled with greater diligence, and new wells and way stations were established. Al-Walīd also laid down new roads, increased public services to the poor, and established endowments for lepers, the lame, and the blind.

The caliph's most renowned projects, however, were his building programs, the descriptions and surviving examples of which justify ranking al-Walīd as the greatest builder of the Umayyad dynasty. His first undertaking was to provide Damascus with a mosque worthy of the imperial capital. The temenos of the ancient temple of Jupiter, which by then had been converted into a church, was confiscated and completely remodeled on a grand scale. The resulting edifice was probably the most magnificent in the Islamic world at that time. Al-Walīd also rebuilt or enlarged the congregational mosques of other cities and established a number of rural estates in the countryside of Syria. The impressive ruins that remain of such establishments at ᶜAnjar, Jabal Says, Khirbat al-Minya, and Quṣayr ᶜAmra are all to be attributed to this caliph's reign.

As much of this building activity would suggest, al-Walīd was very much an Islamic ruler. He sought to advance Islam as the religion of his empire and actively promoted the teaching and study of the Koran. At his court, the early religious figure Rajāᵓ ibn Ḥaywa al-Kindī was an influential adviser.

Al-Walīd died at the age of about forty-five in 715. He is usually ranked among the greatest of the Umayyads, but this bears considerable qualification. His task as caliph was to consolidate a situation already restored to order by his father, who also left him a full treasury and a corps of able and experienced governors and generals. Many of his conquests and programs were in fact directed by his subordinates, and he was often highly solicitous in confirming their decisions and heeding their advice. He was very popular in Syria, the Umayyad heartland, but on other fronts the situation remained unsettled. Al-Walīd was never on very good terms with the Alids, and the east was kept quiet only through the harsh but able rule of al-Ḥajjāj ibn Yūsuf, who enjoyed practically sovereign authority there. Pious circles in the Hejaz were for a time placated by the appointment of al-Walīd's devout cousin ᶜUmar ibn ᶜAbd al-ᶜAzīz as governor; but when al-Ḥajjāj later objected, ᶜUmar's conciliatory rule was ended and more heavy-handed ways were restored. In sum, it would seem that al-Walīd recognized his own abilities and limitations and preferred to rule accordingly.

BIBLIOGRAPHY
Keppel A. C. Creswell, *Early Muslim Architecture,* I, 2nd ed. (1969), 142–196, 373–449, 472–481; Francesco Gabrieli, "Muḥammad ibn al-Qāsim ath-Thaqafī and the Arab Conquest of Sind," in *East and West,* 15 (1965); Hamilton A. R. Gibb, *The Arab Conquests in Central Asia* (1923), 29–58; Marshall G. S. Hodgson, *The Venture of Islam,* I (1974), 223–230; Évariste Lévi-Provençal, *Histoire de l'Espagne musulmane,* I (1950–1953), 1–34; M. A. Shaban, *Islamic History: A New Interpretation,* I (1971–1976), 117–119; W. Montgomery Watt, *A History of Islamic Spain* (1965), 5–16; Julius Wellhausen, *The Arab Kingdom and Its Fall,* Margaret Graham Weir, trans. (1927).

LAWRENCE I. CONRAD

[See also **Caliphate; Ḥajjaj ibn Yūsuf al-Thaqafī, al-; Islam, Conquests of; Islamic Art and Architecture; Mosque; Umayyads.**]

WALLINGFORD, RICHARD. See **Richard of Wallingford.**

WALO OF AUTUN (late ninth–early tenth century), bishop. He was bishop of Autun from 893 to 919. He appears in the minor writing of Remigius of Auxerre, questioning the latter on two points: the altercation of Michael the Archangel with the devil over the body of Moses and the response of God from the whirlwind to Job.

BIBLIOGRAPHY
Max Manitius, *Geschichte der lateinischen Literatur des Mittelalters,* I (1911), 517.

EDWARD FRUEH

[See also **Remigius of Auxerre.**]

WALSINGHAM, ALAN OF (*fl.* 1314–1364), monk and prior of Ely Cathedral. His greatest achievement was his supervision of the construction of parts of the cathedral, beginning with the Lady Chapel in 1321 and thereafter the octagon, lantern, and choir. Earlier hypotheses that Alan was himself an architect are unfounded.

BIBLIOGRAPHY
Frank R. Chapman, ed., *Sacrist Rolls of Ely,* I (1908), 8–72; John Harvey, *English Medieval Architects: A Biographical Dictionary Down to 1550* (1954), 276; Louis F. Salzman, *Building in England Down to 1540* (1967); Leslie Stephen, ed., *Dictionary of National Biography,* I (1885, repr. 1960), 215–216.

STEPHEN GARDNER

[See also **Chapel; Gothic Architecture; Masons and Builders.**]

WALTER MAP. See **Map (Mapes), Walter.**

WALTER OF BIBBESWORTH (*fl.* mid thirteenth century), author of *Tretiz pus aprise de langwage* (*Traité pour apprendre la langue*), a verse treatise on the teaching of French. It was written in England around 1240–1250 for an Essex noblewoman,

Dionysia of Munchensey, to aid in instructing her own children. The treatise is essentially a means of introducing vocabulary on various aspects of daily and particularly rural life, such as names of parts of the body, names of animals and plants, terms used in baking, spinning, brewing, and fishing, natural phenomena, and agricultural implements, as well as such lexicological problems as homonyms and synonyms. Many of the terms are glossed in English. Bibbesworth was also the author of a debate poem in which he discusses the Crusade of 1270 with Henry de Lacy, earl of Lincoln.

BIBLIOGRAPHY

Annie Owen, ed., *Le traitié de Bibbesworth sur la langue française* (1929).

BRIAN MERRILEES

[See also **Anglo-Norman Literature; French Language.**]

WALTER OF CHÂTILLON (Gaulteri de Castellione, Gautier de Châtillon, Walter of Lille) (*ca.* 1135—1202/1203), humanist poet and scholar, was born in Ronchin, near Lille. He studied the arts and theology in Paris and in Rheims, then taught at Laon and at Châtillon-sur-Marne. The chronology and details of his subsequent career are uncertain. He held a canonry at Rheims, probably first serving as secretary to Archbishop Henry I (1162–1175). His identification with a Master Walter de Insula, a cleric in the chancery of Henry II who undertook a royal mission to England in 1166, has been questioned; but his verse suggests a likely connection to the circle of English humanists (including John of Salisbury) who left the court during the Becket controversy. Perhaps then, like others who moved from the court to the schools, Walter went to Bologna, where he is known to have studied canon law, and also visited Rome, which he so often satirized. More certain is Walter's lengthy service in the chancery (as *notarius* and *orator*) of William, archbishop of Rheims (1176–1201), to whom he dedicated his epic poem the *Alexandreis*. After the archbishop's death, Walter retired to Amiens, where he died of leprosy.

The *Alexandreis*, Walter's most ambitious work, took more than five years to complete (*ca.* 1178–1182) and consists of 5,464 hexameter verses in ten books, each beginning with a successive letter from the name of his patron, Archbishop Wil-

liam (G-U-I-L-L-E-L-M-U-S). Based upon classical sources (including Quintus Curtius), it closely follows the major events of Alexander the Great's life in narrative form. One of the most successful medieval attempts to imitate a classical Latin epic, it became an established text in the schools and was itself widely imitated.

Walter was also a skilled lyricist who composed pastoral and erotic verse, but whose true mastery is displayed in popular moral and satirical pieces, which comprise the bulk of his lyrical verse. Many of these, such as *À la feste*, were composed for the Feast of Fools. Others were probably models composed for the schools, among them several conventional humanist laments over the decline of learning: for example, *Felix erat studium, Missus sum in vineam,* and *Tanto viro locuturi.* One, *in domino confido,* a lengthy combination of prose and verse, was delivered at the University of Bologna as a sermon criticizing the state of education and the study of law. In spite of its indignant attacks on the simony and corruption of the Roman Curia, Walter was no enemy of the papacy; he composed several poems, such as *Quis furor, o cives,* in support of Alexander III against the imperialist antipopes. The sharp and daring invective of his satire won him great influence among his contemporaries; the learning and quality of his verse rank him among the greatest Latin poets of the Middle Ages.

Walter also wrote a prose apologetic work, a *Tractatus contra Judaeos* in dialogue form (after Peter Abelard). The attribution to him of other prose works, most notably the *Moralium dogma philosophorum,* is still contested. The *Georgica,* a religious pastoral poem imitating Vergil and long attributed to Walter, has been shown to be the work of John of Garland.

BIBLIOGRAPHY

Sources. Walter's *Alexandreis* is in *Patrologia latina,* CCIX (1855), 459–572, and his *Tractatus contra Judaeos* is *ibid.,* 423–458. Walter's lyrical verse is in Karl Strecker, ed., *Die Lieder Walters von Châtillon in der Handschrift 351 von St. Omer* (1925) and *Die moralisch-satirische Gedichte Walters von Châtillon* (1939); A. Wilmart, "Poèmes de Gauthier de Châtillon dans un manuscrit de Charleville," in *Revue bénédictine,* **49** (1937).

Studies. J. Hellegouarc'h, "Un poète latin du XIIe siècle: Gautier de Lille, dit Gautier de Châtillon," in *Bullétin de l'Association Guillaume Budé,* 4th ser., **1** (1967); Max Manitius, *Geschichte der lateinischen Literatur des Mittelalters,* III (1931), 920–936; Frederic J. E.

Raby, *A History of Secular Latin Poetry in the Middle Ages,* II (1957), 72–80, 190–204.

S. C. FERRUOLO

[See also **Alexander Romances; Conductus; Epic, Latin; Latin Literature.**]

WALTER OF COLCHESTER (*ca.* 1180–1248), artist and monk, who was responsible for making the shrine of St. Thomas Becket at Canterbury for the translation of the saint in 1220. He was the founder of a distinct school of painting at his abbey of St. Albans, where from about 1214 until his death he produced figure paintings, sculpture, and carvings. He is generally confused with a Brother William of St. Albans, an artist who was active two decades earlier.

The Crucifixion. Drawing by E. W. Tristram of the decayed wall painting by Walter of Colchester on a nave pillar of St. Albans Cathedral, *ca.* 1220. FROM TANCRED BORENIUS AND E. W. TRISTRAM, *ENGLISH MEDIEVAL WALL PAINTING* © 1929 HARPER AND ROW

BIBLIOGRAPHY
William Page, "The St. Albans School of Painting, Mural, and Miniature: Part I, Mural Painting," in *Archaeologia,* **58** (1902); Margaret Rickert, *Painting in Britain: The Middle Ages* (1954, 2nd ed. 1965), 106–107, 120.

BARRIE SINGLETON

[See also **Canterbury Cathedral; William the Englishman; William of Sens.**]

WALTER OF EVESHAM. See Odington, Walter.

WALTER OF HENLEY (*ca.* 1240–*ca.* 1290/1300), the author of the most influential text on estate management in England in the High Middle Ages. His name is known from manuscripts copied about the time of his death or shortly thereafter, and there is no reason to doubt the attribution, for the biographical information was inserted by a contemporary, who appears to have known the author. He is identified as Sir Walter of Henley, knight, who in middle years entered the Dominican Order. There can be no certain identification with a known man, but among the candidates the most likely is Sir Walter of Henley, an estate administrator of the Clare family in the later thirteenth century. Inferences from the text indicate that the author was of the West Midlands, where the Clares had large estates, and the form of the treatise in a reliable early manuscript is evidence that it originated as a Dominican type of sermon-lecture. It was probably delivered at Oxford, where courses in management are known to have been available. The sermon can be reliably dated as written after the promulgation in parliament in 1276 of the *Extenta manerii* and before the compilation of *Fleta* (1290–1300), for it assumes the former, and the latter is partially based upon Walter's text.

The treatise is thus one of the numerous treatises and legislation concerning estate management of the late thirteenth century and rapidly became the most influential of the texts. This is of particular importance, for the thirteenth and fourteenth centuries are the epoch of medieval "high farming," the management of demesne agriculture directly by lords. Such management was in the hands of administrators who needed to know agricultural practice and stock management as well as accounting and the law. The age of Scholasticism produced an overlapping class of educated professionals, those lawyer-administrators in whose hands lay the English economy, judicial system, and formulation of much legislation. It is no coincidence that one of the earliest treatises on management was written by Bishop Robert Grosseteste or that the representation of the commons in parliament was a product of the epoch.

It was for an audience of such professionals that Walter wrote. A number of manuscripts are of a size that could be carried in the pocket of a busy steward, and the owners who are known were largely abbeys, lawyers, and estate stewards. The 1971 edition includes, along with Walter's, three closely related thirteenth-century texts addressed to the same audience: the *Rules,* a translation into French (*ca.* 1240) of the household and estate regulations in Latin compiled for his own household by Robert Grosseteste, and translated for the use of the countess of Lincoln; the *Seneschaucy,* a text on the duties of manorial officials and central oversight of their activities; and the anonymous *Husbandry,* a personal compilation, probably made for a Ramsey Abbey official.

Of these, the *Seneschaucy* is the most closely related to Walter; it too addresses and was copied by lawyers in charge of estates with large demesnes and numerous officials. Unlike the *Seneschaucy,* Walter's is not a treatise for central administrators of groups of seignorial estates, and unlike the *Rules* it is not meant for the lord himself who might wish his household to reflect his income. It takes for granted some knowledge of the *Seneschaucy* and is a commentary on that treatise's description of general practices. It is written for bailiffs or students of estate management on the best way to run a single manor enterprisingly. Thus it assumes a general knowledge of farming, describes improvements to current practice, and gives the results of experimental farming, some carried out by Walter. The reader is constantly enjoined to test for himself, before accepting the author's assertions, and ways of checking are suggested.

Walter calls attention to uses of the manorial extent that go beyond those of earlier treatises and beyond the uses envisaged in the statue of 1276. An extent was a description of the manor based upon the verdict of sworn jury; Walter suggests that the extent be used to address further questions—for example, about the amount of seed corn needed per acre and the number of livestock that could be maintained. From these, he demonstrates, the lord could check the management of the demesne. Further, he is quite original in showing how the extent could be used to assess the costs of plowing. His point of view is that of the practical farmer, concerned as he is with the necessity of knowing the qualities of the manor's different fields and the yields after costs of arable, dairy, and meat production. But the practical manager of a demesne of the thirteenth century worked with a large staff of free and customary servants. Thus Walter, preoccupied with yields after costs, is always conscious of fraud practiced by manorial servants and continually devises means of detecting and countering their dishonesty. By viewing the practical farmer as accountant, Walter's treatise is related to the didactic literature on accounting in England and, of course, to the actual manorial and centralized accounting systems that lay behind the precocious efficiency of demesne farming in England from the beginning of the thirteenth century until after the Black Death (1348–1350). The form of Walter's treatise reflects his concern with efficiency and improvement under conditions in which the manorial staff is fraudulent and many members uncooperative. It begins with a prologue in the form of maxims the wise man taught his son to inculcate the profitable virtues of prudence and honesty (caps. 1–15). The main body of the treatise is his advice on improvements in husbandry: lessons on increasing the yield of the demesne and on avoiding the fraud of servants (caps. 16–110). It concludes (caps. 111–113) with maxims on the moral requirements of manorial officials and warnings about their shortcomings.

His greatest contribution may have been in opening the eyes of lords to the expectations an improver might have, and to the conditions under which he must labor to achieve and increase profits. He never considers the question of whether renting out the land is more profitable than direct management, but addresses the steward retained for direct management. Yet his calculations for determining real costs and yield after costs made it possible for lords to calculate for themselves the more profitable course. When, with the "wage revolution" of the late fourteenth century, lords could begin to see their profits from direct management dwindling, the days of Walter's use to them were over. The extant manuscripts of the treatise clearly show the period of, and end of, the medieval agriculture about which Walter had written the key text.

There are numerous copies of the treatise from the late thirteenth and early fourteenth centuries throughout England. It continued to be copied until late in the fourteenth century. Two texts from the sixteenth century show a renewed interest, but the first shows the changed circumstances. The copy of 1523 by Fitzherbert shows that the agricultural advisor no longer need take account of the unreliable labor force provided by manorial servants. In the late sixteenth century John Smyth, steward of the Liberty and Hundred of Berkeley, was the last to take a practical interest in Walter. The treatise was later edited, but only for an audience of antiquarians, naturalists, and economic historians.

BIBLIOGRAPHY
P. D. A. Harvey, "Agricultural Treatises and Manorial Accounting in Medieval England," in *Agricultural History Review,* **20** (1972), and *Manorial Records* (1984); Edward Miller, "England in the Twelfth and Thirteenth Centuries: An Economic Contrast?" in *Economic History Review,* 2nd ser., **24** (1971); Dorothea Oschinsky, *Walter of Henley and Other Treatises on Estate Management and Accounting* (1971); Michael M. Postan, *The Medieval Economy and Society* (1972); L. F. Salzman, ed., *Ministers' Accounts of the Manor of Petworth, 1347–1353* (1955).

ELEANOR SEARLE

[See also **Accounting; Bailiff; Estate Management; Feudalism; Fleta; Grosseteste, Robert; Parliament, English; Tenure of Land, Western European.**]

WALTER OF LILLE. See Walter of Châtillon.

WALTER OF MAURETANIA (Walter of Mortagne) (*ca.* 1090–1174), theologian and bishop, who seems to have belonged to the lower aristocracy of Tournai. Walter studied at Rheims, becoming *scholasticus,* dean, and, in 1155, bishop of Laon, where he served until his death. He composed a treatise *De Trinitate* as well as *De sacramento conjugii,* which is often associated with the *Summa sententiarum* now ascribed to Odo of Lucca. Among the surviving letters is one addressed to Hugh of St. Victor. Walter may also be the author of an early treatise on the problem of universals.

BIBLIOGRAPHY
Sources. Patrologia latina, CLXXVI (1854), 153–174; CLXXXVI (1854), 1,052–1,054; and CCIX (1855), 575–590. For other works and bibliography, see Michael McCormick, *Index scriptorum operumque latino-belgicorum medii aevi: Nouveau répertoire des oeuvres médiolatines belges,* pt. 3, II (1979), 64–70.

MICHAEL MCCORMICK

[See also **Hugh of St. Victor; Philosophy and Theology: Western European; Universals.**]

WALTER, HUBERT (*ca.* 1150–1205), the principal governor of England from 1193 to 1205, when its kings were occupied in their continental dominions. Son of a Norfolk knight, he was brought up by his uncle, Ranulf de Glanville, chief justiciar of Henry II, and under him became adept at royal finance, learned in the common law, and an experienced diplomat. Although he had little scholastic training, Hubert, by his royal service, gained promotion in the church: in 1186 the deanery of York, in 1189 the bishopric of Salisbury, and in 1193 the archbishopric of Canterbury. From 1195 to 1198 he was papal legate as well. Impressed with his leadership on the Third Crusade, King Richard made Hubert chief justiciar of England in 1193. Although he was allowed to resign that post in 1198, he took the office of chancellor on John's accession in 1199 and held it until his death in 1205.

As head of both church and state in England, he provided the kind of united administration Henry II had wanted from Becket. The general eyre of 1194, which pacified England after Richard's crusade, was an administrative triumph, and Hubert was responsible for England's leadership in the keeping of permanent governmental records. Everyone was impressed with his energy, his industry, and his ability to choose aides of the highest quality. Generous, courteous, and magnanimous, keeping magnificent state, he perforce gave much attention to acquiring wealth. St. Hugh of Lincoln told him he was too worldly; other churchmen criticized his Latinity; still others complained of the taxes he collected from them for the king; but most found him a just judge and a protector against royal tyranny. Although his monks of Canterbury quarreled with him violently, Hubert died reconciled with them. Even Gerald of Wales retracted most of the unkind things he had written when Hubert frustrated Gerald's attempts to establish a separate Welsh church.

BIBLIOGRAPHY

Christopher R. Cheney, *Hubert Walter* (1967); Charles R. Young, *Hubert Walter, Lord of Canterbury and Lord of England* (1968).

FRED A. CAZEL, JR.

[See also **England: Norman-Angevin; Glanville, Ranulf de; Henry II of England; Justiciar.**]

WALTHARIUS, a Latin epic poem composed in the mid ninth century, recounts the exile and return of the legendary hero Walter of Aquitaine. The narrative, which consists of 1,456 hexameters, begins as Attila the Hun is leading his army against the kingdoms of the Aquitanians, Burgundians, and Franks. To avoid battle, the three kings send tribute and hostages. The hostages respectively are Walter, the maiden Hiltgunt (to whom Walter is betrothed), and the warrior Hagen, who is sent in place of the young prince Gunther. All three eventually rise to positions of prominence in Attila's court. Hagen, however, escapes and returns home when he learns that Gunther, who has acceded to the throne of the Franks, has abrogated his father's treaty with Attila. Then Walter makes plans to escape with Hiltgunt and return to Aquitaine. After arranging an elaborate banquet for the Huns, he and Hiltgunt flee while Attila and his men are sunk in drunken sleep. The exiles take with them two large boxes of treasure stolen from the Huns.

When Walter and Hiltgunt pass through Frankish territory, Gunther is driven by greed to wrest the treasure from them. He gathers a force of eleven warriors, including Hagen and Hagen's nephew Batavrid, to attack the two travelers. Hagen goes along but refuses to participate actively in what he considers to be a wrongful undertaking. Confronted by the force of Franks, Walter makes his stand in a mountain pass so narrow that only one man at a time can attack him. In a series of individual combats he kills the ten warriors sent against him by Gunther. Among those whom he slays is Hagen's nephew.

Only Gunther and Hagen remain. Hagen now agrees to join the fray in order to avenge the death of Batavrid and save the Franks from the disgrace of losing to a single foe. After luring Walter to open ground, he and Gunther attack. In the ensuing fight all three men suffer grievous wounds. Walter hacks off Gunther's right leg, but Hagen then cuts off Walter's right hand. Walter retaliates by grasping a dagger in his left hand and gouging out Hagen's right eye and six of his teeth. The injured men lay down their weapons, exchange joking insults, and depart for home. The poet concludes the tale with the information that Walter will reach Aquitaine, marry Hiltgunt, and rule happily for thirty years.

The three main components of Carolingian culture—Germanic, classical, Christian—are fused in the *Waltharius*. The poet, while imitating a classical literary genre, retells an episode from Germanic heroic legend so that it offers a Christian moral lesson. This poet was a monk, but we can say nothing more with certainty about him. He may have been the same Brother Gerald who composed a twenty-two-verse preface found in some manuscripts. Recent scholarship, by establishing that the *Waltharius* was composed between the years 840 and 875, has disproved an earlier attribution of authorship to Ekkehard I of St. Gall (*ca.* 910–973).

The *Waltharius* is the first literary treatment of characters and events from Germanic legend that appear in a wide range of medieval literature. The surviving fragments of the Old English epic *Waldere,* for example, contain statements by Walter and Hiltgunt that seem to occur just prior to the attack by the Franks in the mountain pass. Moreover, references both to the years spent by the hostages with Attila and to Hagen's initial refusal to fight against Walter appear in the *Nibelungenlied.*

The *Waltharius* poet has cast his version of the legend in the form of a classical Latin epic. The three classical poems that served as his models for language and diction are Vergil's *Aeneid,* Statius' *Thebaid,* and Ovid's *Metamorphoses.* The poet also makes extensive use of Prudentius' allegorical epic, the *Psychomachia.*

The Christian message of the *Waltharius* is contained in the poet's criticism of the concept of heroic excellence associated with both Germanic and classical epic. The *Waltharius* attacks the heroic ethos, with its emphasis on vengeance and the quest for worldly fame, as being rooted in the sin of avarice. The tone of the narrative is one of mocking humor. The mockery is used to condemn the actions of the main characters. Gunther, who desires to rob two fugitives passing through his territory, is utterly ignoble; he is described in language taken from Prudentius' description of the sin of Pride. Hagen too is portrayed as motivated by greed. He delivers a long speech criticizing his nephew's lust for glory as mere avarice; but when Hagen tells Walter that he wishes to exact vengeance on behalf of Batavrid, he expresses his own desire for glory. Even Walter, whose exploits the narrative seems to celebrate, is presented as sinning through greed. He fights boldly, but in so doing reveals the inadequacy of the heroic code; for he states openly that he fights to avoid the shame of losing treasure, which he originally stole from Attila.

The implied criticism of the main characters is made explicit in the final episode, which is based on Prudentius' account of the defeat of Avarice. The poet makes the following moralizing comment about the wounds suffered by Walter, Hagen, and Gunther:

Postquam finis adest, insignia quemque notabant:
Illic Guntharii regis pes, palma iacebat
Waltharii nec non tremulus Haganonis ocellus.
Sic sic armillas partiti sunt Avarenses!
(1,401–1,404)

After the end of the battle, marks branded each man. There lay King Gunther's foot, Walter's hand, and Hagen's still-twitching eye. Thus, thus did they share the treasure of the Huns!

This passage alludes to the biblical admonition (Mark 9:42–48) that it is better to lose one's eye or to cut off one's hand or foot, should those members cause one to sin, than to go uninjured to hell. The symbolic appropriateness of Hagen's injury is immediately recognizable, since he was motivated by a desire for vengeance; but all three injuries are to be understood as suitable retribution for sinful behavior. Walter rightly loses the hand with which he vows to protect his treasure.

The *Waltharius* is representative of much of the literary and artistic activity of the Carolingian renaissance. The pagan heritage is not rejected but transformed. Using the language and conventions of the classical epic tradition, the poet has refashioned a portion of Germanic legend into a vehicle for the expression of a Christian moral theme.

BIBLIOGRAPHY

Source. Monumenta Germaniae historica: Poetae latini aevi carolini, VI, pt. 1 (1951).

Studies. Peter Dronke, "Functions of Classical Borrowing in Medieval Latin Verse," in R. R. Bolgar, ed. (1971); Dennis M. Kratz, "Quid Waltharius Ruodliebque cum Christo?" in Harald Scholler, ed., *The Epic in Medieval Society* (1977), *Mocking Epic* (1980), and, as ed. and trans., *Waltharius and Ruodlieb* (1984); Karl Langosch, *Waltharius: Die Dichtung und die Forschung* (1973); Emil E. Ploss, ed., *Waltharius und Walthersage: Eine Dokumentation der Forschung* (1969); Karl Stackmann, "Antike Elemente im *Waltharius*," in *Euphorion*, 45 (1950); Wolfram von den Steinen, "Der *Waltharius* und sein Dichter," in *Zeitschrift für deutsches Altertum*, 84 (1952); Karl Strecker, ed., *Waltharius* (1947).

DENNIS M. KRATZ

[See also **Carolingian Latin Poetry; Ekkehard I of St. Gall; Epic, Latin; Latin Literature; Nibelungenlied; Prudentius; Ruodlieb.**]

WALTHER VON DER VOGELWEIDE (*ca.* 1170–*ca.* 1230), greatest medieval German singer and composer. Only one contemporary document mentions Walther, an entry in a bishop's account book recording a gift of five solidi to the singer Walther for a fur coat; otherwise his life is revealed only through remarks and references in his songs and through statements of contemporary and later writers. Walther states that he learned the art of minstrelsy in Austria, which then meant only lower Austria or the region around Vienna, and it is probable that he was native to that area even though nineteenth-century scholars put his birthplace in the south Tyrol. Most of Walther's political songs can be dated approximately, some of them very closely, by allusions to political events and personalities; but the dates of all other songs can be surmised only roughly by comparing their styles and melodies with those of the dated songs.

LOFTY LOVE AND NATURAL LOVE

It is generally assumed that Walther was a pupil of the Viennese court poet Reinmar der Alte (von Hagenau), a champion of *hôhiu minne* (exalted or lofty love), but there is no evidence of such tutelage, for the traits shared by their songs could be attributed to their common heritage. It is further supposed that, after composing songs of lofty love, Walther found them uncongenial and switched to songs of natural love.

The cult of *hôhiu minne*, sometimes called "courtly love," had been imported from the troubadours of Provence during Walther's childhood and had dominated the most fashionable courts. The singer in this tradition, the minnesinger, praised an unattainable lady, often the wife of the singer's patron, who was worshiped rather than desired, since her value would have diminished if she had stepped down from the pedestal on which the singer had placed her. Copying the terminology of *herrendienst* (feudalism), the minnesingers performed *frouwendienst,* or service to their lady. The courtly poet was the vassal (*dienstman*) of his lady (*frouwe*), whose grace (*hulde*) he aspired to win through his loyalty (*triuwe*). Should she deign to acknowledge his service (*dienst*), even through a mere greeting (*gruoz*), he would feel joy (*freude*) and high spirits (*hôher muot, hôchgemüete*), which would inspire him to noble deeds. The lover's reward was not the winning of his lady, but the elevating effect of his hopeless and selfless passion.

As a born teacher and preacher, Walther stressed the ennobling influence of pure womanhood, for "whoever has the love of a good woman will be ashamed of any misdeed" (*Swer quotes wîbes minne hât, der schamt sich aller missetât*). In contrast to Reinmar, Walther argued that the term *wîp* (woman) is more honorable than the term *frouwe* (lady), since true womanhood is superior to good birth and wealth. Walther and Reinmar composed opposing songs on the subject; and humorless scholars have traced a serious feud between them, unmindful that the two poets may have planned their disputation as an entertainment at court.

It is true that Walther composed some of Germany's best songs of lofty love and that he also sang songs of natural love between equals; but this does not prove that he progressed from the former to the latter, as critics would have us believe, for some of his songs of lofty love seem, on stylistic grounds, to have been composed after some of his songs of natural love. In other words, we cannot expect dependable autobiographical confessions in the songs of medieval singers, particularly of mendicant singers like Walther, whose profession required them to produce what their patrons requested rather than what they felt in their hearts.

In any case, after lofty love had ruled the courts for a decade or more, Walther's songs of natural love must have come as a refreshing change. Most famous among these is his *Under der linden,* in which a girl exults in the joy she feels after embracing her lover under a linden tree. This song appears so natural and naive that it is hard to recognize it as

an artful construction of topoi, or literary commonplaces, previously used in the sophisticated Latin poems of the goliard poets. In all the songs of natural love, the lovers are social equals and their love is reciprocal. Despite the current popularity of "dawn songs," or duets in which lovers lament having to part after a night of love, Walther left only one example of this genre, possibly because he found the requirements of the genre too restrictive.

Many of Walther's songs of natural love were dance songs, especially summer or May songs, which, like the songs of the vagabond poets, usually began with a "nature introduction" describing an ideal landscape with its linden tree, spring, brook, flowers, grass, and little birds. Fewer in number were his winter songs, in which he regrets the passing of summer and the advent of bleak winter. It is generally agreed that Walther's songs of natural love prepared the way for the boisterous rustic dances of Neidhart "von Reuental," which soon began to drive propriety from the courts, as Walther sadly complains.

WALTHER AND HIS PATRONS

After Duke Frederick I of Austria died in 1198, his brother and successor Leopold VI did not support Walther, who therefore had to take to the road to earn his bread. From the few scraps of information available, scholars have tried to reconstruct his itinerary. But this is obviously impossible, since forty years or more of wandering must have taken him to many courts and cities he failed to mention in his songs, and he must have visited some of them many times. In any case, one thing is certain: he never gave up hope of being called back to the court of Vienna, for which he cherished a strong sense of love-hate.

When Walther left Vienna in 1198, he found the Holy Roman Empire in turmoil. The emperor, Henry VI, son of the famous Frederick I Barbarossa, had died a year earlier and the princes were unwilling to recognize his infant son Frederick II as emperor. Because of their unwillingness, Henry's party, the Hohenstaufens, persuaded his brother Philip of Swabia to serve as emperor until the legitimate heir came of age. Philip, who would have preferred an ecclesiastical career, agreed only reluctantly. During this period of confusion Walther composed what remains perhaps his best-known song, a lament beginning "I sat upon a stone" (*Ich saz ûf eime steine*), which inspired our only picture of Walther, a stylized miniature not of Walther as an individual but of the contemplative poet in general in the traditional posture of deep thought. In this song Walther regrets that such turbulent times prevent a man from winning wealth and honor without losing God's grace, and it implies that only a strong emperor can bring the peace required to secure all three values. In a sequel to this song, beginning "I heard a river flowing," Walther laments that, whereas the birds and beasts elect rulers and obey them, only the German realm fails to do so, and he calls upon the German princes to crown Philip. This the princes did in September 1198 with the correct insignia but in the wrong city, Mainz. Meanwhile, the opposition party, the Welfs, had crowned Otto of Brunswick in the correct city, Aachen, but with the wrong insignia. The Hohenstaufen party under Philip prospered until Pope Innocent III, seeing an opportunity to weaken the Hohenstaufens' hegemony in Italy, recognized Otto and excommunicated Philip; for he did not wish the Hohenstaufens to encircle Rome by consolidating their rule in Sicily.

Outraged by the pope's meddling, Walther cast his lot with Philip and composed scathing denunciations of the papacy. One of these had the same melody and same meter as the two previously discussed songs, thereby making the three into a trilogy carefully interlocked by an intricate numerical scheme. This third strophe complains that, after being beaten at arms, the church party had resorted to excommunication to achieve their temporal goals; it also blamed the youth of the pope.

When Philip was crowned, Walther legitimized the coronation by the fact that the imperial crown exactly fitted the candidate's head. Of course, the crown could have been altered to fit the head, but this is irrelevant. The important thing was that Philip had been crowned with the proper insignia which had been in possession of his brother (Emperor Henry VI), even if he had been crowned in the wrong city. When Philip held a diet at Magdeburg on Christmas day some months later, Walther again stressed the insignia in a song that compared Philip on the earth below to the Trinity in heaven above, thus alluding to St. Augustine's City of Man and City of God. Nor did Walther consider it blasphemous to associate Philip's queen, the daughter of the Greek emperor, with the Virgin Mary, whose name she had assumed. This song had the same melody as the previous one, for it was Walther's custom to compose a fresh melody for a new patron and then to use it for all songs to, for, or even

against that patron. In this case he used his "First Philip's Tune."

Despite his initial support of Philip, Walther seems to have become disenchanted with his lack of generosity or largess, as is shown by an admonition in another song of the "First Philip's Tune," which holds up the Saracen king, Saladin, and the English king, Richard I the Lionhearted, as models of largess. It is to be remembered, however, that Walther may not have been complaining of Philip's lack of generosity to poor minstrels like himself but of his failure to reward his loyal vassals, whose spokesman Walther may have been. Another song, this one in the "Second Philip's Tune," again chastised Philip for his niggardliness, this time alluding to the fate of his father-in-law Isaac II Angelos, the emperor of Byzantium, who had lost his throne when he failed to share with the leaders of the Fourth Crusade. Since this song clearly censures Philip's lack of largess to his vassals, we may suspect that the previous song had done so too.

Walther's apparent break with Philip did him little harm, because Philip was murdered soon thereafter. This left as contender only Otto, whom the pope crowned in October 1209. Although the pope had supported Otto to weaken Philip, the new monarch followed his predecessor's Italian policy and soon came to blows with the pope, who excommunicated him within a year of crowning him. This justified Walther to champion the very ruler against whom he had just ranted, and he greeted Otto with a song of praise when he returned from Italy to hold a diet at Frankfurt in March 1212. Although written in the "First Ottonian Tune," this song was really written on behalf of Count Dietrich of Meissen, for whom it begged a pardon. Several more songs to Otto were not so much songs of praise as songs of advice, especially the advice to vindicate Germany's honor by restoring law and order.

During this period Walther composed a whole series of diatribes against the pope, two of the best being directed against the pope's efforts to collect money for a crusade against the Albigensians. The pope had placed a collection box in all German churches ostensibly for this purpose, but Walther questioned whether much of the money collected was actually used for the purpose intended. In one of these songs the pope cynically boasts how he has played two German kings against each other so that they will devastate the empire; at the same time he fills his chests with good German silver and the priests eat chicken and drink wine, while the German laymen fast and hunger. In another, Walther asks the collection box whether any of the money it collects will serve God, since priests' hands seldom share any money.

In other songs Walther accuses Innocent not only of simony but even of heresy and black magic, and he also chides his inconsistency in first demanding obedience to Otto but then excommunicating him, for two tongues fit unevenly in one mouth. Walther reminds Innocent that Christ clearly commanded men to give unto Caesar what is due unto Caesar. In one of his most devastating songs against the pope he deplores the "Donation of Constantine," a document attesting that Emperor Constantine had presented the Roman Empire to the pope and had received it from him as a fief, thus giving the papacy secular rule. Walther reminds his public that the angels in heaven had cried out "Alas!" three times when the tragic donation was made. He further complains that the clerics have used this donation to pervert secular law. It is ironic that, however much Walther detested the donation, he did not question its authenticity, as Lorenzo Valla did two centuries later with stylistic proof that it was a later forgery.

After excommunicating Otto, Innocent backed the youthful Hohenstaufen claimant, Frederick II, believing he could keep him under control. Frederick was elected in Frankfurt in December 1212, less than a year after Otto had held his diet there. Like most of Philip's supporters, Walther (or his patron) immediately went over to the young emperor's side. He justified his change of allegiance in a song accusing Otto of niggardliness. Frederick seems to have rewarded Walther with a small benefice, for which Walther expressed joyful thanks, but a later song implies that the income from the fief was inadequate.

When Walther denounced the clergy, he was denouncing only the papal party, not all churchmen; for many German prelates, being members of noble German families, were solidly behind the empire. This was true of Archbishop Engelbert of Cologne, who was appointed to serve as regent during Emperor Frederick's absence. During Engelbert's regency Walther praised him for maintaining law and order; and, when the regent's fervor caused him to be murdered by a discontented nephew, Walther called down the Lord's wrath upon his assassin. Whereas Walther wished hell to swallow

him alive, the courts wished swifter punishment and had him broken on the wheel.

Nineteenth-century critics spent much effort in trying to justify Walther's shift of loyalties from the Hohenstaufens to the Welfs and back to the Hohenstaufens. Most of them tried to show that his loyalty was to the empire rather than to any one incumbent, as one might expect of a German during the Wilhelmine period. When Philip offered the best chance of securing a strong centralized government, Walther sided with him against Otto. When Philip was assassinated and Otto was the only pretender, Walther upheld him; but he deserted him as soon as the young Frederick was crowned and Otto proved unable to control the empire. This argument has one major flaw: if Walther first opposed Otto because he enjoyed papal support, then he should have stood by him when he tried to oppose the pope and carry out the imperial policy previously fostered by the Hohenstaufens. Instead, Walther immediately went over to Frederick, who had been groomed and crowned by the pope as a means to assure papal domination over the empire.

All such arguments are beside the point. Walther's duty was neither to the emperor nor to the empire, but only to his immediate patron. Under feudal law, which had its roots in the comitatus, or retinue of the ancient German chiefs, a man's loyalty was to his immediate superior, to whom he was personally bound by oath. In battle a vassal was obliged to serve the lord who had nourished him in time of peace (the word "lord" is derived from "loaf-ward"), and medieval literature stressed the resulting obligation. The same relationship held between patron and poet, and no irony was intended in the minstrels' motto "Whose bread I eat, his song I sing" (*Swes brot ich ezz, des liet ich sing*). Walther's duty was to the patron who supported him, a fact that explains how he could ask Otto to pardon the traitor Dietrich of Meissen even though he usually demanded punishment of traitors who disturbed the peace. To be sure, a minstrel was free to seek out a patron whose policies he endorsed, but this was not demanded.

SINGER AND COMPOSER

Histories of German literature tended to attribute noble birth to any medieval poet whose humble birth could not be proved. They even accepted the fanciful ranks given to the early minnesingers by their later bourgeois successors. Most critics call Walther a knight, even though Walther himself made no such claim. Some seem to consider the "von" in his name a sign of nobility, not realizing that Vogelweide was probably a nickname given to Walther in derision, or perhaps assumed by himself, because he had no place of residence. A *vogelweide* was a reserve where birds such as herons were protected until being hunted by noble falconers. Never does Walther refer to bearing a sword, the hallmark of the knight.

One song confirms Walther's humble status, a scurrilous one telling how a nobleman named Atze shot Walther's palfrey (*pfert*) and refused to compensate him for it. Although injured in his honor, Walther did not challenge the offender, as a knight would have done; instead he complained to their mutual lord. Failing to gain satisfaction, Walther composed a malicious ditty explaining that Atze killed the palfrey because he thought it was related to the charger (*ross*) that bit off his finger. This was obviously not Atze's reason, but it made a humorous song at his expense. Had Walther been a knight, he would have ridden a charger rather than a palfrey, which suited women and clerics. Although aware that he was socially inferior at court, Walther had an immense professional pride and felt that, through his music, he had achieved as much dignity (*wirde*) as anyone else enjoyed.

Walther sang not only of love and politics. Along with his songs on these subjects he composed others instructing both children and adults, and many of his apparent love songs are really lessons in proper decorum. Several songs concern the rearing of children and warn that sparing the rod will spoil the child. It has been suggested that one or two of these alluded to Emperor Frederick's young son Henry VII, who was elected king of the Germans as a child and was married at the age of fourteen to the twenty-five-year-old Austrian princess Margaret. There is certainly no reason to suppose, as some scholars do, that Walther was tutor to the royal family, which position would hardly have been offered to a mendicant minstrel. If these allusions actually referred to Henry, then the song was more probably composed for Count Ludwig of the Palatinate, who had the misfortune to be little Henry's regent.

As a born teacher, Walther implored his audience to avoid hypocrisy, lying, and intemperance and to practice love, self-control, largess, and other virtues. Like his contemporaries, he was fond of addressing personifications such as Lady Love (*Frô Minne*), Lady Constancy (*Frô Stæte*), Lady Moderation (*Frô Mâze*), and Lady Impropriety (*Frô*

Unfuoge). Above all, he preached *mâze*, or balance and moderation in all things. Most of this didacticism appeared in *sprüche*, a genre of song previously cultivated only by lowly professional poets and first made acceptable at court by Walther himself. Such *sprüche* usually presented a pithy bit of wisdom derived from those parts of the Bible then attributed to Solomon or else from the church fathers or from folk wisdom. The political songs previously discussed were an outgrowth of this *spruch* tradition.

Because the word *spruch* is related to the word *sprechen* (to speak), critics assumed that they were recited rather than sung. But this was entirely wrong, for they were sung to the same melodies as the songs, the only difference being the subject matter. The same case is made in the case of the words *singen* and *sagen,* which critics interpret as "singing" and "saying." Here too there is no difference in the mode of performance, both being sung. *Singen* means "singing lyric matter" and *sagen* means "singing narrative matter."

Modern critics always refer to Walther as a poet (*Dichter*) who wrote poems (*Gedichte*), whereas he was actually a singer who composed and sang songs. In the Middle Ages composers spent much time in perfecting their melodies and considered them far more important than the lyrics, so much so that there was a word for "melody thief" (*dœne-diep*) but no word for "lyrics thief." The words of succeeding strophes, of course, were arranged to fit the melody made for the first. The miniatures in the Mannesse Manuscript, in which Walther's picture is found, show no composers in the act of writing; instead they are singing, and a scribe is busy writing down what they sing.

Walther, who compared himself to a nightingale, was praised by Gottfried von Strassburg and others for his voice; and it will be noted that Bishop Wolfger gave the five solidi to Walther as singer (*cantor*). It is regrettable that we have almost nothing of Walther's music. No musical notations survive from his period, and the few later transcriptions are so inadequate that modern musicologists reconstruct them differently. Germany had to wait two centuries, until the time of Oswald von Wolkenstein, to receive relatively reliable notations. Many of Walther's numerical relationships were misunderstood as long as his songs were treated as poems, because the number systems often relate to the beats of the music, whether or not these are covered by the words.

Despite Walther's attacks against the pope, it was the incumbent, not the office, that he attacked. He never questioned church authority or dogma, and his prayers and other religious songs consist of the usual religious clichés, albeit in uncommonly pleasing arrangements. He addressed no songs to any of the saints except the Virgin Mary, to whom he addressed many, including a long and intricate *leich*, or song based on the sequence and composed of strophes of varied length and meter. In this complex song of 164 verses one finds nearly all the standard epithets of the Virgin and many Old Testament prefigurations of Christ's conception and birth. Also very ambitious was his so-called "Palestinian Song," which is often considered a crusade song but is really a pilgrimage song, since it does not preach violence. In the first strophe the singer says that his life has been worthwhile now that he has seen the land that Jesus trod; but this does not prove that Walther himself ever visited the Holy Land, since it was only the poetic "I" who was speaking. The remaining six strophes are interrelated by very complicated numerical relationships and give a typical *Heilsgeschichte,* or story of salvation, describing Christ's birth, life, passion, harrowing of hell, and resurrection as well as the day of judgment. Walther composed several more songs about doomsday, that being a popular subject in those trying times, and also two crusade songs.

One of Walther's most significant works is his so-called *Elegy,* which he composed about 1227, or some two years before his death. It is a retrospective song beginning "Ouwe war sint verswunden alliu miniu jar?" (Whither have they vanished, all my many years?). The poet looks back on his life and wonders whether it was all a dream, since nothing remains as he remembered. On one level the singer finds that he cannot go home again, but on another he sees that the worldly life he lived was but a meaningless dream, an exile from God. Having voiced his own melancholy mood in the first strophe to set the tone for the song, he devotes the second to describing the unhappy state of the present world, and in the third he calls upon young men to join Frederick II's crusade. Thus it turns out to be less an elegiac confession than a well-contrived bit of recruiting propaganda. The meter Walther chose was appropriate, it being close to that of the tragic Austrian epic of the Nibelungs.

The remarkable thing about Walther is that his ideals and moral values pointed to the future and are still mostly valid today. Because he spoke so convincingly for God and for all humanity, we can understand why, a century later, the schoolmaster Hugo von Trimberg could say, "Her Walther von der Vogelweide, swer des vergæze, der tæte mir leide" (I would feel sorry for anyone who forgot Walther von der Vogelweide).

BIBLIOGRAPHY
Editions. Karl Lachmann and Carl von Kraus, eds., *Die Gedichte* (1959); Friedrich Maurer, ed., *Die Lieder,* 2 vols. (1956–1960); Hermann Paul and Hugo Kuhn, eds., *Gedichte* (1959); Helmut Protze, ed., *Gedichte* (1963), with excellent annotations.
Editions with modern German translations. Hans Böhm, ed., *Minne, Reich, Gott* (1949); Paul Stapf, ed., *Sprüche Lieder der Leich* (1963); Peter Wapnewski, ed., *Gedichte* (1962).
English translations. Edwin H. Zeydel and Bayard Q. Morgan, trans., *The Poems* (1952). Twelve of Walther's songs appear in free translation together with modern transcriptions of their melodies in Barbara G. Seagrave and J. Wesley Thomas, *The Songs of the Minnesingers* (1966), which reproduces the illuminations of the Manesse Manuscript and also contains a recording of sixteen minnesongs, three of them by Walther. See also George F. Jones, *Walther von der Vogelweide* (1968). For a summary of Walther scholarship and an exhaustive bibliography, see Kurt H. Halbach, *Walther von der Vogelweide* (1973).

GEORGE FENWICK JONES

[See also **Courtly Love; German Literature: Lyric; Germany; Goliards; Gottfried von Strassburg; Hugo von Trimberg; Middle High German Literature; Minnesingers; Neidhart "von Reuental"; Reinmar der Alte; Sequence; Troubadour, Trouvère.**]

WALTHER VON SPEIER (965–*ca.* 1030), poet and teacher at the cathedral school in Speier. He wrote prose and verse replacements for a life of St. Christopher by a nun, Hazecha, lost when sent to Speier. The poem's 1,272 hexameters contain a preface about Walther's education and literary interests. The style is highly ornamented and allusive. Walther was probably bishop of Speier from 1004 to about 1030.

BIBLIOGRAPHY
Waltheri Spirensis Vita et Passio Sancti Christophori martyris (1878). See also Wilhelm Harster, *Walther von Speier, ein Dichter des X. Jahrhunderts* (1877); Max

Manitius, *Geschichte der lateinischen Literatur des Mittelalters*, II (1923), 501–506.

W. T. H. JACKSON

WANDERING JEW LEGEND, the most widely extant of the various migratory legends concerning the Crucifixion. Like the legend of Cain (Gen. 4) or the Buddhist legend of Pindola, it is a extra-scriptural tale of punishment by eternal wandering for an affront, an insult, or actual physical violence offered to a deity. This legend represents the confluence of two other legends, both derived from the Gospel of John, that of John who waits for God (John 21:20–22), known as Cartaphilus (dearly beloved), and that of Malchus, the servant of the high priest, who struck Christ a blow (John 18:22).

The legend originated obviously in the first century, in or near Jerusalem. Two branches soon become discernible. One, the eastern, traveled from the region of Jersualem north through Asia Minor and the Balkans into Slavic territory, where it has survived almost entirely in oral folktales. The second, the western, came through Egypt and North Africa and took root in Italy. In the folktales from either branch, one can see that sometimes the Cartaphilus and sometimes the Malchean influence is present, although there is a definite tendency for the Malchean to predominate. Where the Cartaphilus stage dominates he becomes the symbol of immortality and long life and is frequently identified as Juan de los Tiempos or Jan van den Tyden.

Some 150 various examples of the folktale have been collected. In some of the earlier ones, especially in the eastern branch, the wanderings of the protagonist are limited—about a pillar, in a prison cell, on an isolated Aegean island. In others of the tales the wanderings become more extensive: the protagonist can appear anywhere—in all of Europe, in America, even at the North Pole. In some versions he ages indefinitely; in others, at the age of 100 he returns to his age at the time of the Crucifixion. These alterations are accompanied by seizures of a cataleptic or epileptic nature, and in one, the Icelandic *Bragda Magus saga* of about 1500, he sheds his old skin like a snake and, after dragging himself through a beam of wood, reappears carrying his old skin over his arm like a discarded cloak.

The legend also gets contaminated with others, such as with that of Fortunatus and the Inexhaustible Purse and that of the Treasure Finder.

The Jewishness of the wanderer is assumed from the first, although it is not always explicitly stated. After all, he was an inhabitant of Jerusalem at a time when Christ was known as the king of the Jews. It is very likely that the Fourth Lateran Council of 1215 fostered belief in the legend, for it was there decreed, inter alia, that any legend, however un-Christlike, should be encouraged if it expressed God's mercy to all. The continued existence of the killers of Christ in the legend would be such a case of God's mercy.

The oldest surviving written version of the legend is the mid-sixth-century *Leimonarion* by Johannes Moschos of Damascus, which emphasizes the Malchean form of the story. The next extant account is the Bolognese Latin chronicle *Ignoti Monachi Cisterciensis S. Mariae de Ferraria Chronica et Ryccardi de Sancto Germano Chronica Priora*, dating from 1223. It tells of a group of pilgrims who report that they had seen "a certain Jew in Armenia who had been present at the Passion of the Lord and, as He was going to His martyrdom, drove him along violently, with the words: 'Go, go, thou tempter and seducer, to receive what you have earned.' The Lord is said to have replied, 'I go, but you will wait until my return!'"

This report is repeated by the St. Albans chronicler Roger of Wendover in his *Flores historiarum* for 1228, which embellishes the details of the wanderer's rejuvenation, a motif that first appeared in a Latin chronicle of Bolognese origin in 1223. The tale is also recounted by Roger's successor at St. Albans, Matthew Paris, in his *Chronica majora* for the year 1238, and still again by the Flemish chronicler Philippe Mousket in his *Chronique rimée* (1243). By this time the wanderer was being "seen" by various people in various communities, and there are allusions to him in English mystery plays, Italian private correspondence, and Spanish proverbs as a symbol for old age or immortality.

There are examples of the folktale throughout Italy and in Sicily; it is there that the Malchean aspects begin to reveal themselves. The character was generally known in these areas under a new name, Botadeo (other versions being Botaddio, Buttadeus, Boudedieu, Puttidew), "God pusher." Pardoxically this name is easily altered to the rarer term, opposite in meaning, Votaddio, or "devoted to God," thus returning the protagonist to a passive, repentant state. Two noteworthy literary works contain references to these tales.

The first is Chaucer's Pardoner's Tale (lines 720–738), in which the impressive figure of the old man appears before the "three riotoures." He can find no one to exchange fates with him, though he "walked into Ynde"; he longs to die but cannot; he is wasting away but must continue to live "as long as it is Goddes wille." Various interpretations for the old man have been advanced: he represents Old Age, Death, Experience. One has even suggested that he is the fading Odin; I prefer Experience. But he may also be the Wandering Jew. The difficulty in recognizing him instantly as such is that (1) no specific reason is given for his predicament, and (2) his desire to die and his inability to find one who is willing to change places with him is not elsewhere heard of until the romantic age—in other words, Chaucer's version seems much more developed than other fourteenth-century versions of the legend. Yet it is altogether possible that Chaucer may have picked up the legend on one of his trips to Italy and fashioned it—like any great student of humanity—as he saw fit.

Another account comes from a manuscript in the Strozzi Palace in Florence, printed by Morpurgo. The account is ascribed to Antonio di Francesco di Andrea (*fl. ca.* 1400). Here the Wandering Jew, known as Giovanni Votaddio, rescues Antonio and his two nephews from a snowstorm near Florence in 1411, takes them to an inn, and tells them where the innkeeper keeps his money (the power to scent out treasure is a Central European commonplace in the folktales). He remarks that he can never stay longer than three days at the most in any one place, and although a suspicious character, he can never be hanged for any crime because the rope always breaks. He can perform healing miracles; this is vouched for by the learned Leonardo Bruni (Aretino). As elsewhere throughout the Middle Ages, he is invariably repentant when the Crucifixion is mentioned, shedding tears and groaning aloud.

The Iberian Peninsula, where he is known as Votaddio, or more commonly as Juan Espera en Dios, presents the protagonist as a milder, more submissive Cartaphilan type, contritely acknowledging his guilt for the blow he gave the Savior. The most interesting contribution it makes is that the folktales present the Jew as a shoemaker (*zapatero*). The explanation would seem to be that shoemakers are traditionally viewed as an independent, brusque

lot and that the Jew, from his constant wandering, is always in need of shoes.

From 1600 into the twentieth century, the legend continued to circulate in Europe—in Italy, Germany, France, England, and Scandinavia. It showed up in chapbooks, poetry, and novels, taking on new forms, adding detail, and sometimes even appearing in disguise. A vital literary motif, the legend found a place in the works of such writers as Goethe and Coleridge.

BIBLIOGRAPHY
George K. Anderson, *The Legend of the Wandering Jew* (1965), the most extensive survey of the subject, including postmedieval developments; Maurice Bataillon, "Pérégrinations espagnoles du juif errant," in *Bulletin hispanique*, 43 (1941); Moncure Conway, *The Wandering Jew* (1881); Josephus J. Gielen, *De wandelende Jood in Volkskunde en Letterkunde* (1931); Salamone Morpurgo, *L'ebreo errante in Italia* (1891), containing the story of Antonio di Francesco di Andrea; Leonhard Neubaur, *Die Sage vom ewigen Juden* (1884, rev. ed. 1893).

GEORGE K. ANDERSON

[See also **Anti-Semitism; Bruni, Leonardo; Chaucer, Geoffrey; Crucifixion; Matthew Paris; Mystery Plays; Philippe Mousket.**]

WAQF. A *waqf* (pl., *awqāf*; in North Africa, *ḥubs* in Maghrebi Arabic or *habous* in French) is a legal device by means of which a person devotes some piece of property to a charitable or pious purpose. The intentions of the founder (*wāqif*), as spelled out in a foundation deed (*waqfīya*), are observed and respected in the same manner as a legal document. The accepted definition of *waqf*, according to the Hanafite school, is "the detention of the corpus from the ownership of any person and the gift of its income or usufruct, either presently or in the future, to some charitable purpose." To create a *waqf*, an owner must make an oral declaration permanently reserving the income of the property for a specific purpose. Once this declaration has been made, the property may not be transferred or alienated by the founder, the administrator, or the beneficiaries, and it cannot be inherited by the founder's heirs.

The charitable purpose to which *waqf* property must be dedicated may be ultimate rather than immediate. The founder may reserve the income of the *waqf* property for his children and their descendants (*waqf ahlī* or *waqf dhurrī*), stipulating that, upon extinction of the family line, the income should be used for some charitable purpose, such as a mosque or religious school. Although the beneficiaries are normally the founder's descendants, this is not compulsory, and even strangers may be designated.

With the exception of certain differences in their manner of administration, family and public *awqāf* are essentially identical in their nature and in the legal rules applied to them. The *waqf* is supervised by an administrator (*mutawallī* or *nāẓir*). The founder may designate the first administrator in the *waqfīya* and set the conditions for the appointment of his successors. In the absence of such a provision, the judge will designate an administrator, usually favoring a descendant of the founder. The administrator maintains the property and distributes the income according to the provisions of the *waqfīya*.

The origins of the institution of *waqf* has been the subject of considerable discussion. The Koran makes no reference to *waqf*, and the development of the institution illustrates the composite nature of Islamic law and the flexibility of its institutions during its formative period. The *waqf* may have one of its roots in the sacred precincts (*himā'*) of pre-Islamic Arabia; another in the contributions to the holy war that Muḥammad had demanded of his followers; another in the need of the early Muslims to counteract some of the effects of the law of inheritance; a fourth in the pious foundations (*piae causae*) of the Eastern churches; and a fifth in the charities and benefactions of the early Muslims.

A family *waqf* can be used to avoid the limitations of the Islamic law of inheritance, such as the restriction of legacies to one-third of the estate. Such a *waqf* can also be used to avoid the fragmentation of property that is so frequently caused by the application of the Islamic law of inheritance. However, because of the rules of perpetuity and inalienability, *waqf* property is totally withdrawn from commercial circulation and therefore can hinder economic development and land reform.

Functionally, the public *waqf* (*waqf khayrī*) served as a kind of municipal authority by providing numerous essential urban services. Religious schools, alms kitchens, guesthouses, hospitals, bathhouses, caravansaries, and waterworks were founded and administered through *awqāf*. Revenues for such institutions were provided by rural and urban *awqāf* that included villages, hamlets, bazaars, tanneries, slaughterhouses, mills, and bakeries.

Waqf documents contain many different types of information. A typical *waqfīya*, for example, usually indicates the name of the founder and all living beneficiaries. This is followed by a careful description of the property or item designated as a *waqf*. It also delineates the boundaries of the property and mentions the adjoining property, including the name of its owner. In the case of buildings, the *waqfīya* sometimes lists the number of rooms and their uses; in the case of land it indicates the basic crops, the quality of the soil, and the annual yields. Supplementary documents specifying additions, deletions, and changes in the endowment property were often appended to the original *waqfīya*. Together, these documents make it possible to trace the history of many prominent families and institutions over periods of a century or more, and are therefore of immense value to social and economic historians, art historians, and archaeologists.

BIBLIOGRAPHY

For an extensive bibliography of books and articles published prior to 1953, see W. Heffening, "Waḳf," in H. A. R. Gibb and J. H. Kramers, eds., *The Shorter Encyclopedia of Islam* (1953).

See also Claude Cahen, "Réflexions sur le *waqf* ancien," in *Studia islamica,* **14** (1961); Henry Cattan, "The Law of *Waqf,*" in Majid Khadduri and Herbert J. Liebesny, eds., *Law in the Middle East,* I (1955); Daniel Crecelius, "The Organization of *Waqf* Documents in Cairo," in *International Journal of Middle East Studies,* **2** (1971); Fuad Köprülü, "L'institution du vakf et l'importance historique des documents du vakf," in *Vakiflar dergesi,* **1** (1938); Joseph Schacht, "Early Doctrines on *Waqf,*" in *Mélanges Fuad Köprülü* (1953).

DAVID S. POWERS

[See also **Inheritance, Islamic; Law, Islamic.**]

WĀQIDĪ, ABŪ ᶜABD ALLĀH MUḤAMMAD IBN ᶜUMAR AL- (748–823), an early Arab historian, born in Medina in 748. Though little is known of his youth, it is clear that from an early age he began to devote himself to the study of the Koran, prophetic tradition, law, and early Islamic history. Such studies were already fields of active inquiry in his native city, and in his time al-Wāqidī was their most eminent representative.

His early career was not successful from a financial standpoint, and he was often deep in debt. But in 786 Hārūn al-Rashīd and his vizier Yaḥyā ibn Khālid came on pilgrimage to Medina, and al-Wāqidī, as the leading authority on the holy places of the city, was recommended to them as a guide. The historian was henceforth highly favored by the Abbasids and often benefited from their generosity. Al-Maʾmūn appointed him to a judicial post in 819, and when the aged historian died in 823, the caliph acted as executor of his will.

Al-Wāqidī produced many works on the subjects he studied. These included monographs on the Koran, tradition, and jurisprudence, but in the main they dealt with historical topics: pre-Islamic history, the life of the prophet Muḥammad, the caliphate of Abū Bakr, the conquests of Syria and Iraq, the assassination of ʿUthmān, the battles of al-Jamal and Ṣiffīn, and the minting of Islamic coinage. Some of these were probably essays incorporated into his more substantial writings. His main works appear to have been his *Al-Taʾrīkh al-kabīr*, an annalistic account (to 796) of Islamic history, often quoted by al-Balādhurī (*d.* 892) and al-Ṭabarī (*d.* 923), and his *Kitāb al-ṭabaqāt*, a biographical dictionary, covering the years to 802. The latter work formed the nucleus for the book on the same subject by his student and secretary Ibn Saʿd. Of all his works, only the *Kitāb al-maghāzī*, a very important book on the military campaigns of Muḥammad, is extant.

Al-Wāqidī was a well-organized and systematic writer and an energetic scholar dedicated to the reconstruction of the early Islamic past. His library was reportedly enormous, and he is said to have visited old battlefields and queried anyone he met whose family had been involved in great historical events—a practice that makes his work a somewhat problematic historical source. He very often combines different accounts into a continuous narrative under a collective *isnād* (chain of authorities), which makes for smoother prose but also allows for the insinuation into the tradition of new material of dubious authenticity, particularly new minutiae, exegetical comments, and narrative coloring. That al-Wāqidī himself did not notice this is curious, since he was often more skeptical than other authors—for example, where fabricated poetry was concerned. Whether one attributes these amplifications to al-Wāqidī himself or sees them as reflective of the information gained from informants, the problem affects many important historical narra-

tives and thus makes the use of al-Wāqidī highly problematic.

Largely because he was so much more informative, his narratives were frequently cited by later historians. Accusations of sectarian and specifically Shiite partisanship are largely unfounded, though he does seem to have been rather circumspect in dealing with matters sensitive to his Abbasid patrons.

BIBLIOGRAPHY

Abd al-Aziz Duri, *The Rise of Historical Writing Among the Arabs*, Lawrence I. Conrad, ed. and trans. (1983); Josef Horovitz, "The Earliest Biographies of the Prophet and Their Authors," in *Islamic Culture*, 2 (1928); al-Wāqidī, *Kitāb al-maghāzī*, Marsden Jones, ed. (1966); Julius Wellhausen, *Muhammed in Medina: Das ist Vakidi's Kitab-al-Maghazi in verkürzter deutscher Wiedergabe* (1882), although this rendering is based on a defective manuscript text and can no longer be considered reliable.

LAWRENCE I. CONRAD

[See also **Caliphate; Historiography, Islamic.**]

WAQ-WAQ ISLANDS, an exotic place described in eleventh- and twelfth-century tales of Muslim sailors and geographers. Their exact location was unclear; some sources placed them near southern Africa, others far to the east of China. The islands were said to be ruled by a nude queen seated on a throne and served by 4,000 virgins, and were named for the native "Waq-waq" tree that bore fruit in the shape of human and animal heads. The tree is also described in the legends surrounding Alexander the Great (Iskandar), who encountered it at the ends of the earth and was counseled by its talking heads to go no further in his conquests. Depictions of the Waq-waq tree appear in illustrated copies of Firdawsī's *Shāhnāma* and in Zakariyā ibn Muḥammad al-Qazqwīnī's thirteenth-century cosmography, *The Wonders of Creation and Oddities of Existence.*

BIBLIOGRAPHY

Phyllis Ackerman, "The Talking Tree," in *Bulletin of the American Institute for Persian Art and Archaeology*, 4 (1935); Gabriel Ferrand, "Le Wāḳwāḳ: Est-il Japon?"

Iskandar (Alexander the Great) and the Talking Tree. Depiction of the Waq-waq Islands in the Demotte *Shāhnāmah,* 14th century. COURTESY OF THE FREER GALLERY OF ART, SMITHSONIAN INSTITUTION, WASHINGTON, D.C.

in *Journal asiatique,* **220** (1932), and "Waḳwāḳ," in *The Encyclopaedia of Islam,* 1st ed., IV (1934).

JULIE O. BADIEE

[See also **Geography and Cartography, Islamic; Zanj.**]

WARDZIA (Vardzia), a rock-cut monastic complex built between 1156 and 1205 in the southern Georgian province Mesχetᶜi. Thirteen stories high and 1,640 feet (500 m) wide, the complex lies 4,265 feet (1,300 m) above sea level. It consists of numerous churches and chapels, dwelling places for the clergy and secular inhabitants, hospices, a scriptorium, conference rooms connected by a web of intricated tunnels, storage rooms, and an elaborate irrigation system. Part of the furniture is cut from the living rock. Some of the churches contain wall paintings. The largest church, dedicated to the Virgin, contains well-preserved portraits of the donors and the Georgian rulers Giorgi III and his daughter Queen Tamar. A thirteenth-century typicon preserved in the Institute of Manuscripts in Tbilisi explains the peculiar characteristics of this monastery and its significance in medieval Georgia.

BIBLIOGRAPHY

G. Gapᶜrindašvili, *Vardzia* (1976), with English text, 1–14.

WACHTANG DJOBADZE

[See also **Giorgi III; Tamar.**]

WARFARE, BYZANTINE. Byzantium was not a militaristic empire, as the term is normally used. Its strategists regarded war not as an occasion for the winning of martial glory and renown, but as an unfortunate necessity, forced upon the Byzantines by their hostile neighbors. Throughout most of the empire's history, its conception of warfare was fundamentally defensive.

Divine aid, as the Byzantines understood it, was the most important element for military success, followed closely by the skill and enthusiasm of the commanders and soldiers. Sheer masses of troops and equipment were never considered the decisive element by Byzantine strategists and tacticians, who viewed war as a subject for intellectual study. These strategists and tacticians believed in the organization of men, materials, and transportation. They perceived and portrayed themselves as protagonists in a world filled with enemies who often possessed greater material resources than themselves; they did not regard that situation as hopeless. By rational reflection and organization, they believed, one could achieve the most effective use of existing human and material resources. It is from their *strategika* and *taktika,* that is, manuals of strategy and stratagems, and of tactics, and from historical narratives and some rhetorical works, that one can gain the best understanding of Byzantine warfare.

The Byzantine science of military tactics rested on the basic assumption that there was a repetitiveness in warfare and that therefore, by mastery of various alternative patterns, one could avoid being surprised and overcome by the unexpected—knowledge of military discipline and order in battle would help to overcome any surprises and unexpected enemy tactics. This was an attempt to make order and regularity out of what otherwise would be chaos.

The Byzantines always labored, in their analysis of war, under the burden of their Greco-Roman heritage. They used their knowledge of Greek and Roman history extensively to uncover precedents for particular military measures, and from time to time they attempted to understand and explain the reasons for Greek and Roman military successes. The format and language of Byzantine tactical and strategic manuals owed much to such Greek strategists as Aelian, Arrian, Onasander, and Aeneas Tacticus. Various Byzantine emperors encouraged the writing—or actually wrote manuals themselves—of tactics and strategy, and some of the great families influenced the tone and content of such manuals, which therefore must be read with appropriate caution and discounting of biases and self-interest and self-glorification.

Byzantium's prevailing commitment to a policy of avoiding decisive battle for most of its history probably contributed to its longevity. There was a readiness to exploit uncertainties while minimizing one's own casualties, preferring a combination of artifices, diplomacy, delay, dissimulation, sowing dissension, corruption, and, most of all, employing caution and an indirect approach to warfare, in an effort to reduce risk and gambling to a minimum in warfare. The Byzantines did not discover all of these approaches to warfare, but developed some proclivities in Greco-Roman military counsels.

The Byzantines appreciated order, discipline, the use of commonly understood verbal orders of command and drill, the use of advanced technologies, such as Greek fire, and experimentation with principles of mechanics and optics for the winning of military advantage.

The greatest weakness of Byzantine addiction to cleverness and deception in warfare was the development of excessive overconfidence and occasional intellectualism in military operations. It encouraged an admirable readiness to use one's head in studying war, yet it often created a dangerous or disastrous overconfidence in the ability of a strategist to overcome, through cleverness, quantitatively and perhaps qualitatively superior material and human resources and power.

The Byzantines appreciated the role of timing in warfare, the interdependence of strategic moves, and, above all, the unknown or unexpected element. Long distances and slow communications combined to affect the Byzantine armies and their foes. It was difficult to make intelligent decisions in Constantinople with outdated information filtered through many persons. Warfare was often slow-paced in that world of imperfect information.

Byzantine armies achieved a measure of success in protracted warfare, but those successes were precarious. In the long run, success in its wars of maneuvering and attrition depended upon two prerequisites. First, it was necessary for the emperor and his officials in Constantinople to have sufficient trust in their field commanders for the latter to be able to act flexibly and rapidly, with a wide latitude of authority to meet any contingency. Such absolute trust was impossible to achieve, and whatever trust there was broke down because of the rivalry of commanders who undercut and denounced each to the imperial court. Intrigues, rivalries, and envy thrived because of and in the midst of the indecisive and protracted warfare, and contributed to the failure of commanders to commit all of their talents to the struggle against external enemies. Emperors

Cavalry besieging a tower, depicted in an 11th-century miniature. PARIS, BIBLIOTHÈQUE NATIONALE, MS GREC. 74, fol. 92v

never succeeded in finding a way to conduct external military operations on a large scale without potentially strengthening an ambitious general so much that he might become a threat to internal security. There was an inherent contradiction between the needs of the army and its generals for adequate manpower and resources, and freedom of action for the sake of maximum military efficiency, on the one hand, and the fears of emperors and their officials that such generals might create a domestic threat, on the other hand.

The second prerequisite for success was the maintenance of an efficient flow of supplies and money, which proved to be impossible. Indeed, the frequently protracted warfare resulted from and intensified the armies' logistical and organizational problems. It was difficult to procure and transport adequate provisions and money to the armies without causing excessive hardship to domestic agriculture, commerce, and the civilian population.

Armies were small for operational purposes, probably exceeding 20,000 men very rarely, for a specific campaign; usually they were much smaller. Warfare often involved ambushes, ruses, and rapid maneuvers of cavalry, and only rarely involved masses of men fighting in fixed positions. It was adapted to the relatively large amount of territory over which it could spread, terrain that was suitable for horses. The Byzantines did not commit all of their manpower to defending their lengthy frontiers, but preserved mobile field armies that sought to engage larger groups of foreign invaders who penetrated deeply. The civilian population sought the safety of fortified hills, fortresses, islands, or even caves for the duration of a raid or invasion. Byzantine troops often endeavored to close mountain passes that the invading party would need to use for return to its own territory, as well as to cut off and destroy smaller units of the invaders. The normal practice was to avoid a bloody pitched battle unless one possessed overwhelming superiority and other circumstances were very favorable.

Emperors and commanders sought to produce the maximum results from their soldiers by rewarding the most successful individuals and units for their deeds on the battlefield. They also sought to instill religious zeal, to stress that the soldiers were fighting as Christians—often—against non-Christians rather than solely as defenders of the empire. Religious services often preceded battle.

Slow and protracted warfare was not always the norm. There were moments of decisive and rapid strikes, such as some expeditions of Leo I, Justinian I, Nikephoros Phokas, John Tzimiskes, Basil II, and Heraklios.

Although there were some improvements in techniques of combat, there was no disposition to believe that there would be further progress in

548

warfare—yet the historian Procopius was convinced in the sixth century that techniques in his day had progressed over those of antiquity. As their *taktika* and *strategika* attest, the Byzantines did adjust their methods of fighting to changing circumstances and the special techniques of their opponents, both in weapons and in ways of fighting. Yet there was no readiness to expect innovation in warfare—let alone to regard it as something desirable and positive, to be cultivated assiduously. The answers to success in warfare were thought to be found in the empire's past, including its Roman antecedents. In general, those who wrote about war believed that any faults in their military system lay in neglect of exercise, tactical maxims, and knowledge of ancient principles, and in the falling into disuse of older and correct military practices. From this followed, it was thought, lack of experience and knowledge, and the cowardice of soldiers and their commanders. The appropriate remedy was thought to be the revival of the older practices (*eutaxia* [discipline], *gymnasia* [exercise], and *taxis* [order]) that had worked so well.

It would be incorrect to attribute any grand strategy to the Byzantine practice of warfare. The slowness of communications and logistical problems, and the absence of anything approaching a general staff, prevented the implementation of grand strategy in the modern sense. This does not mean, of course, that emperors such as Justinian or Constantine VII did not have some conception of the interrelated features of diplomacy and warfare on various frontiers. Yet the *strategika* and *taktika* assumed that the general might have to direct his men in local situations in which he might be cut off from easy communication with his government; therefore he had to possess wide authority and initiative in waging war in the face of uncertainties and unknowns.

There was no refusal to borrow techniques, arms, and even soldiers from other peoples if they functioned well in warfare. Performance was the critical measure. It was recognized that there were many different ways of fighting.

Mounted archers were important, especially starting in the sixth century, although their difficult techniques were falling into neglect by the tenth century, and that neglect contributed to the Byzantine inability to present an adequate resistance to the Seljuk Turks in the eleventh century. Foot soldiers were far less important than cavalry to the effectiveness of Byzantine armies in combat.

Mounted archers required an ample supply of arrows, which were procured from specific districts, at least in the tenth century, and the supply train (*touldon*) might carry additional arrows among its many items, which included food, metals, leather, cloaks, containers, carpentry tools, chain-mail sleeves, shields, javelins, wine, siege machines, timber, cloth, and jars.

The empire's ability to wage war depended, of course, in part upon its financial resources and its financial, bureaucratic, and military institutions. Warfare cost money, and it resulted, because of invasions and raids, in extensive physical damage to towns and countryside.

No one emperor was responsible for creating a distinctive Byzantine way of waging war; it evolved slowly from Greco-Roman and late Roman antecedents, adjusting to changing circumstances and limited resources, both human and material. Yet there was a failure, noticeable especially from the eleventh century on, to adapt and respond adequately to changes in warfare; even the older *strategika* and *taktika* appear to have received less study and updating. The result was an increasing dependence on outsiders for maintenance of effectiveness in warfare. This process reached its culmination in the empire's final centuries, when it decisively failed to adapt to the new technology and ways of fighting required for firearms, and was forced to hire foreigners who had mastered them. Though the reasons for this failure to continue to adjust to newer methods of warfare after the tenth century are unclear, the consequences for the empire are unmistakable.

Byzantine strategists and generals expressed confidence in the utility of studying history and writings on war, but they always remained cautious about the unexpected turns that violent conflict could take, especially in large-scale decisive combat. They accepted the use of military force, but they often realized their inability to predict, to control, or to direct the course of a war once full-scale hostilities had commenced.

There usually was a prudent preference to avoid the maximum possible level of violence within existing levels of weaponry. (Basil II's final wars against the Bulgarians and Alexios I Komnenos' and Justinian I's respective annihilations of the Pechenegs and Vandals are exceptions.) It was repeatedly within the capabilities of Byzantium to exterminate a defeated population, but the actual cases in which such policies were elected are very rare. The comparatively modern doctrine of the maximum concentration of force did not dominate military wisdom. Byzantine commanders and emperors were usually mindful of the difficulty of replacing losses among the soldiers, who were relatively expensive and difficult to recruit and train in that era of relatively small armies.

It was sometimes difficult to terminate hostilities once they had commenced. In its protracted wars without absolute military victory, it was sometimes hard for the empire to decide when was the optimal time to agree to a settlement. It was the unexpected victories or campaigns that contributed the most to altering the course of negotiations in progress. In such wars the latest engagements exerted a multiplier effect on diplomatic bargaining. It was sometimes difficult for Byzantine leaders and negotiators to view matters in a long perspective in the midst of the pressures, uneven conditions, and limited information that was available. Thus the unexpected, the hitherto undiscounted or disbelieved, had a tremendous effect on the course of negotiations and on the peace terms.

Fighting was often conducted with an eye more to negotiations than to pure military objectives. Changes at the battlefront usually meant a quick change in the stance and mood of Byzantine diplomacy, yet it was impossible for Byzantine diplomats to maintain lengthy control of a military situation during negotiations. At least as important for the course of negotiations in Byzantium's wars were factors beyond the trend of the negotiations and even beyond the fortunes of battle: deaths, illnesses or other incapacitation of respected leaders, or internal dissension or conspiracy sometimes decisively affected the outcome of a war's diplomacy.

Byzantine diplomats and generals made many blunders and errors, but they were accustomed, in all the centuries of the empire's history, to simultaneous fighting and negotiating. The existence of mutual mistrust and mutual resort to stratagems, tricks, and deception surely impeded the Byzantine Empire's negotiations with its adversaries in war, but the lack of absolute trust did not prevent termination of hostilities or the implementation of reasonable terms for peace, including exchange of prisoners.

Repeated problems in Byzantium's wartime diplomacy were (1) the timing and sequence of approved military evacuations; (2) the omnipresent monetary factor, which proved to be an efficient expediter and compensator in complex contexts—

there were two varieties of monetary levers, outright bribery of negotiators or enemy commanders, and payments to Byzantium's opponent for some of its alleged losses or expenses; (3) matters of status and prestige—unreasonable insistence on certain points repeatedly led to costly and dubious resumptions of hostilities or protraction of existing wars, as well as jealousy and ruinous acts by proud generals; and (4) territorial issues.

It is difficult to study Byzantine warfare without an appreciation of longer-range continuities. In addition to historical narratives and *strategika* and *taktika*, archaeological evidence can be of value— yet few Byzantine battlefields are securely identified. Military references in astrological works and in manuscript illuminations of combat and weapons require caution. Investigation of Byzantine warfare is still in its infancy.

BIBLIOGRAPHY

Sources. George T. Dennis, ed. and trans., *Three Byzantine Military Treatises* (1985); Kekaumenos, *Strategikon*, in German as *Vademecum des byzantinischen Aristokraten*, Hans-Georg Beck, ed. and trans. (1956), and in Russian as *Sovety i rasskazy Kekavmena*, Gennadi Grigorevich Litvarin, ed. and trans. (1972); Leo VI, *Tactica*, in *Patrologia graeca*, CVII (1863), and in an edition edited by R. Vari (1917–1921); Maurikios, *Strategikon*, George T. Dennis, ed., and E. Gamillscheg, trans. (German edition) (1981), and *Maurice's Strategikon: Handbook of Byzantine Military Strategy* (1984); Procopius of Caesarea, *Procopius*, original text with English translation, H. B. Dewing, ed. and trans., 7 vols. (1953–1954); Nikephoros Phokas, *Le traité sur la guérilla (De velitatione) de l'empereur Nicéphore Phocas*, Gilbert Dagron and Haralambie Mihaescu, eds. and trans. (1986).

Studies. Alphonse Dain, "Les stratégistes byzantins," in *Travaux et mémoires*, 2 (1967); John Heldon and Hugh Kennedy, "The Arab-Byzantine Frontier in the Eighth and Ninth Centuries," in *Zbornik Radova, Vizantoloshki Institut* (Belgrade), **19** (1980); Walter Emil Kaegi, Jr., *Byzantine Military Unrest, 471–843: An Interpretation* (1981) and *Some Thoughts on Byzantine Military Strategy* (1983); Paul E. Lemerle, *Prolégomènes à une édition critique et commentée des "Conseils et récits" de Kékauménos* (1960); Agostino Pertusi, "Ordinamenti militari, guerre in Occidente e teorie di guerre dei Bizantini (secc. VI–X)," in *Settimane di studio del centro italiano di studio sull'alto medioevo, 15: Ordinamenti militari in Occidente nell'alto medioevo* (1968).

WALTER EMIL KAEGI, JR.

[See also **Byzantine Empire: History; Cavalry, Byzantine; Kekaumenos; Manazkert; Maurice, Emperor; Procopius.**]

WARFARE, ISLAMIC. Warfare in medieval Islam was conducted by a people in arms, by a warrior aristocracy, or by professional mercenaries, assisted by compulsory levies and by volunteer irregulars. Troops tended to shift from one category into another, so that warrior peoples like the Arabs, the Berbers, and the Turks became noblemen or professional soldiers, and professionals like the Turks became aristocrats; a common denominator was the bond of personal loyalty between equals, and between superiors and inferiors. The types nevertheless represented an Islamic society with a high percentage of tribal, and nomadic tribal, peoples in which the duty to fight for the faith was a constant inspiration; in which the successful warrior was rewarded with power, wealth, and prestige; but in which rulers preferred to rely for long periods upon paid troops of foreign, often servile, origin. Techniques varied in consequence, according to the community and the class from which the troops were drawn. While a tribal force, for example, might be homogeneous, most armies were formed from a variety of contingents whose different skills provided the separate arms of a composite whole. The aim was to use them in combination.

The problem was as much social and political as military. Tensions between units were with difficulty overcome by tactics that endeavored to exploit the virtues and minimize the vices of each. At the same time, antagonisms might be welcomed by the prince as a way of eliminating any threat to himself from a part or the whole of his army. The tendency for the horse to be the expensive luxury of a warrior aristocracy might be offset by its common use among nomads, for example the Turkomans of Central Asia, while the volatility of nomadic horsemen could be countered by the discipline of foreign infantry. Over the centuries, with many variations of time and place, the tactical balance tended to shift, so that a broad progression can be discerned toward a peak of professional horsemanship represented by the Mamluks of Egypt from the thirteenth century on. In the fifteenth century, however, the infantry reappeared in a central role, following the constitution of the Ottoman corps of janissaries at the end of the fourteenth century, and the introduction of firearms.

The importance of the infantry went back to the earliest days of the Arab conquests. Traditions regarding the battles of the seventh century are not necessarily reliable, but they point to popular armies of men on foot armed with spears and bows,

Cavalry charge of Alexander the Great against the Zangis. Miniature from the *Khamsah* of Niẓāmī. Persian, 1449–1450. THE METROPOLITAN MUSEUM OF ART, NEW YORK, GIFT OF ALEXANDER SMITH COCHRAN, 1913 (13.228.3)

commanded by wealthy, noble horsemen. At least in the Fertile Crescent and North Africa, mobility was provided by the camel, used for riding and for baggage; ranged around a camp, the animals could be used to form a laager for defense. Ditches were used to fortify an encampment or a position on the battlefield. Typically, the early conquerors constructed *amṣār* (singular: *miṣr*, garrison cities) to dominate each new territory: Basra and Al-Kufa in Iraq, Al-Fusṭāṭ in Egypt, and Al-Qayrawān (Kairouan) in Ifrīqiya. Originally tented or hutted, these were laid out around a central area comprising the residence of the commander and a place for meeting, prayer, and drill. By entry into these *amṣār*, Arab and non-Arab recruits were inducted into the community of the faithful with its military discipline. The central area might serve as an inner fortress in case of attack, but the *miṣr* itself was intended as a base for further conquest. It was the mustering point for expeditions that eventually led to the creation of yet another garrison city in another land, where new recruits might be formed into new armies.

Recruits from the eastern half of the empire probably included horsemen formed in the long Persian tradition of cavalry warfare. Horsemen grew in number with the wealth of the empire and the development of an Arab aristocracy. Infantry, however, continued to form the bulk of the army, though by the eighth century regulars were distinguished from irregulars, and the more highly paid from the more lowly paid. Ibn ʿAbd al-Ḥakam's account of the defeat of Kulthūm ibn ʿIyāḍ by rebellious Muslim Berbers in northern Morocco in 741 illustrates the operation of these forces of the late Umayyad period. Kulthūm's army consisted of men from the Middle East, reinforced with contingents from Ifrīqiya and preceded by a force of Syrian Arab cavalry. His enemies were Berber tribesmen who had previously provided the Muslim armies with recruits or had fought alongside them as allies. They had some horsemen, but the majority were on foot, wearing only trousers. Kulthūm, relying on his cavalry, sent it to attack the entire enemy horde. The charge was broken when the Berbers shouted, drew back, and stoned the Arabs with slings. In flight, the horses broke the line of battle formed by Kulthūm's infantry, leaving these troops helpless before the Berber rush. Kulthūm, on horseback in the center, refused to flee, and probably dismounted for the last stand. Only the remnants of the cavalry escaped, unsuccessfully pursued by the Berber horsemen.

This type of army continued to develop in Egypt, North Africa, and Spain. The slave trade with Europe and black Africa provided regiments of ʿabīd, footguards who protected the commander and his fairly small but fairly heavily armored mounted escort. Armed with swords, spears, and round shields, they gave stability at the center of a battle line basically of three ranks, in which archers and javelin throwers assisted in the defense until the enemy was broken. The bulk of the fairly light cavalry, which had harassed the enemy from the wings or remained in reserve, then completed the rout. A traditional fivefold division into center, van, and wings, with the baggage, including mangonels, in the rear, gave both a marching order and the

basis of a battle formation. Such an army, though effective when deployed, was vulnerable to surprise. At its most elaborate, in Fatimid Egypt in the eleventh century, it contained units of all nations, each with its own skill, in rivalry with the rest. At its simplest, with the Almoravids about 1068, it was a more homogeneous force from a single ethnic group. In the Maghrib, the type survived until the fifteenth century, changing in social composition rather than in technique.

In Iraq and Iran, from at least the ninth century, fairly heavily armored cavalry became more numerous and more important with the recruitment of Turkish slave troops by the Abbasids. Infantry, such as the Daylamites employed by the Buyids in the tenth century, nevertheless continued to be essential to a balanced force; moreover, tactics remained basically defensive. The Byzantine *Taktika* of Emperor Leo VI attributes to the Abbasid army a solid oblong formation on the march and in battle, where it was designed to resist attack until the opportunity came to advance.

On both the Spanish and the Central Asiatic frontiers of Islam, however, warfare against the infidel consisted of raids by lightly armed horsemen. The Seljuk Turks, who arose on the Central Asiatic frontier in the eleventh century, conquered Iran with a horde of such warriors drawn from the nomadic Turkomans who followed them into the Middle East. Although the Seljuks became armored knights in the manner of their predecessors, they were obliged to retain the aggressive mobility of the Turkoman tribesmen in order to offset the superior weight of the Frankish cavalry of the crusaders in the Levant. Emphasis therefore fell upon mounted archers, who used techniques employed since the eighth century, but now, in Turkoman fashion, were given a principal role in attack and defense. Most tasks in the army of Saladin were thus performed by cavalrymen who charged and retired, concentrated or scattered, until they formed for a final assault. A fivefold formation was still used—at Asrūf, for example, in 1911—but infantrymen were relegated to secondary roles as skirmishers or supporters, and as pioneers in siege warfare. They were mainly levies or volunteers. Irregular cavalry was provided by bedouin tribesmen.

This type of army reached its peak under the Mamluks of Egypt in the thirteenth century. At that time, in Spain, the forces of Granada attempted to match the increasingly heavy armament of their Christian neighbors by adopting it, but by the fourteenth century the experiment had been abandoned for a return to the extreme lightness and mobility of frontier warfare, whether on horse or on foot. In Iran the Mongol invasions of the period reaffirmed the supremacy of the mounted archers. In Anatolia, on the other hand, they disappeared in the wake of the Mongol defeat of the Seljuks of Rum. The Ottoman army, composed initially of horsemen raiding the Byzantine frontier, was reorganized in the fourteenth century on the basis of infantry regiments of archers and spearmen, notably the janissaries recruited from the subject Christian population of the new empire. As this recruitment became institutionalized, the janissary corps expanded to form the center of the line of battle, relegating the cavalry to the wings.

In the fifteenth century field artillery was drawn up in a row in front of this infantry formation, and by 1500 the transition to warfare of the early modern period was complete when the janissaries were armed with muskets. The Mamluks, in reply, experimented with field guns too little and too late, and refused to touch hand-held firearms. Their aristocratic dislike of such weapons—which were cumbersome and dirty and could not be used from horseback—was shared by the Ottoman cavalry, whose attitude to them accentuated the sharp tactical as well as social divisions within the Ottoman forces.

From at least the siege of Constantinople in 1422, the Ottomans employed heavy siege guns, inaugurating a process that by the sixteenth century had changed the art of fortification that the Arabs had inherited from the Byzantines. Ukhayḍir in Iraq—square, with semicircular bastion towers, and a gateway in the middle of each side, is the largest of a number of eighth-century fortresses—of which a perfect example is the *ribāṭ* of Sousse in Tunisia. In this two-story building around a central court, the flat roof forms a *chemin de ronde* with battlements for the archers of the garrison. In the ninth century, similar battlements on the minaret of the Great Mosque of Qayrawān converted the building, with its massive retaining wall, into a fortress; at Sousse, the Great Mosque was designed as a castle defending the harbor, and a tower like the minaret of Qayrawān stood in the angle of the town walls at their highest point on the hill. In the tenth century at Mahdia, the Great Mosque protected a corner of the enceinte surrounding the peninsula; access to the city was by a massive gateway in the form of a long, straight tunnel equipped with doors and portcullises. Boom towers guarded the entrance to the harbor.

The defenses of Mahdia, though substantial, were relatively simple. From the eleventh century on, castles, citadels, and city walls became more numerous and elaborate. Beginning, for example, with the rebuilding of the walls and gates of Cairo by Badr al-Jamālī between 1087 and 1091, the process culminated in the twelfth and thirteenth centuries in the citadels of Cairo and Aleppo, castles such as Shayzar in Syria, and walls like those of Seville. Ramparts were heightened against the trebuchet, which replaced the mangonel as the main war engine; outer walls protected inner walls with the aid of ditches and glacis; barbicans defended gateways. Entrances turned through one or more right angles inside the towers, approached by zigzag routes along the foot of each line of walls. The finest examples of such works were effectively impregnable to mining and assault by ladders and movable towers. Such strongholds, whether cities or fortresses, severely limited the efficacy of combat in the field, where victory was of little account without their capture. Thus the kingdom of Acre survived for a century after the fall of Jerusalem, and the Reconquest in Spain dragged out over 400 years.

Few great naval battles took place. Beginning with the Byzantine fleet in Egypt, whose Coptic commander transferred it to the Arabs, strong fleets operated in the Mediterranean. Between the seventh and tenth centuries these fleets conquered Cyprus, Crete, Sicily, and the Balearic Islands and raided the Christian mainland with galleys manned by rowers and fighting men. From the eleventh century, these raids turned to piracy by enterprising privateers. The navies of the dynasties of Egypt, North Africa, and Spain were normally used in support of land campaigns, especially those involving the blockade or relief of a coastal city. In the fifteenth century, from the siege of Constantinople in 1453 on, these two branches of naval warfare were successfully reunited in the Ottoman marine.

BIBLIOGRAPHY

David Ayalon, "Studies on the Structure of the Mamluk Army," in *Bulletin of the School of Oriental and African Studies,* **15** and **16** (1953 and 1954), *Gunpowder and Firearms in the Mamluk Kingdom* (1956), *Studies on the Mamluks of Egypt* (1977), and *The Mamluk Military Society* (repr. 1979); Maurice Canard, "Les expéditions des arabes contre Constantinople dans l'histoire et dans la légende," in *Journal asiatique*, **208** (1926); Vassilios Christides, "Two Parallel Naval Guides of the Tenth Century," in *Graeco-Arabica*, **1** (1982), and "Naval Warfare in the Eastern Mediterranean," *ibid.*, **3** (1984); Aly Mohamed Fahmy, *Muslim Naval Organization in the Eastern Mediterranean*, 2nd ed. (1966), and *Muslim Sea-Power in the Eastern Mediterranean* (1966); Hamilton A. R. Gibb and Harold Bowen, *Islamic Society and the West*, I, pt. 1 (1950), 45–71, 314–328; R. Stephen Humphries, "The Emergence of the Mamluk Army," in *Studia islamica*, **45** and **46** (1977); T. Kollias, "The *Taktika* of Leo VI and the Arabs," in *Graeco-Arabica*, **3** (1984); Wladyslaw B. Kubiak, "The Byzantine Attack on Damietta in 853 and the Egyptian Navy in the 9th Century," in *Byzantion*, **40** (1970); Yaacov Lev, "The Fāṭmid Navy, Byzantium, and the Mediterranean Sea," in *Byzantion*, **54** (1984); David Nicolle and Angus McBride, *The Armies of Islam, 7th–11th Centuries* (1982); Vernon J. Parry and M. E. Yapp, eds., *War, Technology, and Society in the Middle East* (1975).

MICHAEL BRETT

[See also **Aghlabid Art; Cairo; Castles and Fortifications; Cavalry, Islamic; Fatimids; Islam, Conquests of; Janissary; Mamlūk; Mamluk Dynasty; Mongol Empire; Navies, Islamic; Ottomans.**]

WARFARE, WESTERN EUROPEAN. Of all the major aspects of life in medieval Europe, warfare has been curiously neglected. Wars were chronic throughout the period, and it might be difficult to find a year in which hostilities were not being conducted somewhere in Western Europe. Yet only since the 1950's have scholars begun to turn their attention to serious study of the military institutions and practices of this thousand-year period.

The reasons for the neglect are twofold. First of all, Sir Charles Oman, for two generations the foremost authority on the subject, concluded that military operations during the Middle Ages were lacking in plan and were haphazard and aimless; that medieval commanders were little better than dolts, with no understanding of strategy or tactics; and that a study of medieval military history could lead to no true understanding of the art of war. This article, and those dealing with individual campaigns and battles, should demonstrate the fallacy of Oman's argument.

The second, and more important, consideration lies in the nature of the sources from which the military history of Western Europe in the Middle Ages must be reconstructed. At the time when the sophisticated Byzantine military treatises attributed to Maurice (582–602), Leo VI the Wise (866–912), and Nikephoros II Phokas (963–969) were written, the literate layman in Western Europe was a rarity. Annals and chronicles were written by members of the only literate element in society—the clergy. These were primarily monks who had no knowledge of, and little interest in, strategy and tactics. The purpose of historical writing was to glorify God, who awarded victory to the righteous, and defeat to sinners and heretics. This is not fruitful material from which to reconstruct just what happened on a particular occasion. Until the High Middle Ages, the lay writer of history is not to be encountered. Ranulf de Glanville's account of the siege and capture of Lisbon (1147), and the accounts of the Fourth Crusade written by Geoffroi de Villehardouin and Robert de Clari early in the thirteenth century, are early examples of military history written by laymen. Occasionally, too, a cleric wrote with keen awareness of military realities. One such was Walter the Chancellor of Antioch; another example is the *Expugnatio Hibernica* of Gerald of Wales, a first-rate account of the Anglo-Norman conquest of eastern Ireland in 1169–1175; his *Descriptio Kambriae* laid out the strategy that Edward I was to successfully follow in subjecting Wales to English rule a century later.

But in general, medieval military history must be gleaned from sources that were not written with this objective in mind. Most accounts are in Latin; the first vernacular narrative in English, written by an actual participant in the events it describes, is the anonymous *Historie of the Arrivall of Edward IV in England*, an invaluable account of the Barnet-Tewkesbury campaign of 1471. Such useful accounts as the *Chronique* of de Monstrelet (covering the years 1400–1444) and Comines' racy *Memoires* (written 1489–1498) also come late in the period.

Another problem is that of numbers. It is now recognized that the sizes of medieval armies as given by the monkish chroniclers can be dismissed as meaningless exaggerations. The population of Western Europe was much smaller than it had been in Roman times, and a much larger percentage of it was engaged in the production of necessary foodstuffs. It would have been impossible to find the surplus manpower to provide the 100,000 knights and 600,000 infantry who are alleged to have participated in the First Crusade (1096–1099).

By the second half of the twelfth century, however, official documents, such as the Pipe Rolls of the English Exchequer, make possible some informed estimates of the military establishment maintained by the Angevin monarchs of England. It becomes possible to determine with reasonable accuracy the sums spent by Henry II (1154–1189) on fortifications, such as the great castle at Dover, and for the pay of mercenary troops for garrison and field service during the baronial revolt of 1173–1174. Documentation for French military expenditures does not date from before the early thirteenth century, but by its second decade it can be determined that Philip II Augustus (1165–1223) was able to maintain a nucleus of some 2,700 mercenaries, horse and foot. There is also considerable information on the military institutions and expenditures of the Italian city-republics, such as Florence, Lucca, and Milan, as well as of the emerging Iberian kingdoms. By the second half of the fifteenth century, the sober reports of the Milanese ambassador to the court of Burgundy provide realistic statistics on the military establishment of Duke Charles the Rash (or Bold, 1467–1477).

For purposes of convenience, rather than strict accuracy, the military history of Western Europe in the Middle Ages will be divided into three rather unequal periods. The first, which can be labeled "Tribal Warfare," occupies just over two centuries—from 500 to *ca.* 730. The second, and longest, period—*ca.* 730 to *ca.* 1200—can properly be designated as "Feudal Warfare," although there were notable exceptions. Finally, the last three centuries of the Middle Ages could variously be called "Postfeudal" or "Transitional."

TRIBAL WARFARE

By 500, eight Germanic peoples had established themselves in the western provinces of the Roman Empire—Visigoths, Vandals, Franks, Burgundians, and Ostrogoths on the Continent, and the Angles, Saxons, and Jutes in Britain. Late in the sixth century the Lombards began the conquest of much of the interior of Italy. Unfortunately, little is known of the military organization of these Teutonic tribes before they entered Roman territory. The brief references in Caesar's *Commentaries,* and in the *Germania* of Tacitus, are suspect and cannot be considered reliable.

It would appear that during their sojourn on the Ukrainian steppes, the Visigoths had learned to fight mounted, as their victory over the Roman legions at Adrianople (378) clearly indicates. Thereafter the history of the Visigoths is ill recorded, and little is known of their military activities, although the upper classes apparently continued to fight on horseback. But only a single campaign, that of Wamba in 673, is recorded in any detail. Some light is thrown on Visigothic military organization by surviving royal codes and edicts, which reveal a rudimentary command structure. The king, of course, was the supreme commander. Below him were the dukes, who commanded the provincial armies, and *comes exercitum,* who were in charge of divisions of the provincial armies. There was also a nascent feudalism, for references are made to land grants in return for military service; whether this was mounted service is not clear. As for the obligation to serve in arms, it seems likely that such service was imposed on the Romanized population after the religious unification.

The field army, called out only when needed, apparently had no permanent organization. There were officers down to the squad level (*decanus*), but no evidence suggests that they were appointed unless a state of war existed. Military and civil authority were kept separate at the upper level, although at the king's convenience the two were sometimes combined. At the other end of the scale, slaves, especially those owned by the fisc, also had a military obligation, not as mere camp-followers, but as regular fighting troops with full military equipment. Provision was also made for the supply of garrison troops, as well as those on field service. On the face of it, Visigothic law provided for a rather elaborate military system; how well it worked under combat conditions, given the chronic instability of the Visigothic monarchy, and the lack of adequate narrative sources, it is impossible to determine. The whole system was swept away by the successful Islamic invasion in the early eighth century, and the "Spanish feudalism" that began to evolve three centuries later was of an entirely different character.

Some reconstruction of Lombard military organization in Italy after 568 can be hazarded. Although there was a Lombard king with his capital at Pavia, until nearly the end of Lombard rule his authority was but nominal. The Lombard conquest was piecemeal, and until the second half of the eighth century, when the exarchate of Ravenna was occupied, Byzantine naval power kept the Lombards from securing any significant outlet to the sea.

All free men had an obligation to military service; the free population was divided into three classes based on economic status. The first two classes were required to appear at the muster mounted, with suitable arms and armor, while the third class served as infantry. All classes were required to provide their own armor and weapons. It should be noted that by this time the merchant was sufficiently prosperous to be included for military service along with the landholders. The sources fail to indicate whether the mounted element fought on horseback, but there is some evidence to suggest that on occasions mounted engagements took place.

In the late sixth century, the great magnates, especially the dukes, revived the practice of recruiting bands of personal followers, sworn to loyalty, not unlike the comitatus of the primitive Germans. This threatened royal control over the armed forces, and it almost certainly reduced the importance of the military service due from freemen of the lesser sort. This fragmentation of military power doubtlessly contributed to the success of the Frankish invations of 755, 756, and 774. The Frankish occupation of Italy resulted in no great change in Lombard military institutions, although Frankish officials gradually replaced Lombards as offices became vacant for one reason or another. In the successful campaigns against the Avars in the Danube Valley during the late eighth and early ninth centuries, the commanders were usually Franks, but the armies were composed mostly of Lombards. It could reasonably be surmised that, by this time, the Lombards had adopted the Frankish practice of fighting on horseback.

The one Germanic people which did not find it necessary to alter its traditional tactical formation were the Anglo-Saxons. Until the demise of the Old English state on the bitterly contested field at Hastings, the Saxons fought as infantry. Some elements may have ridden to battle, but attempts to prove that they fought mounted have so far been fruitless.

While little is known of the military organization of the various Anglo-Saxon kingdoms before the reign of Alfred the Great (871–899), it is possible to reconstruct English military institutions after that time with some confidence. The king had at his disposal the entire levy of the kingdom. All able-bodied freemen were obliged to serve, when summoned, in the general levy, or *fyrd*. This would probably have been called out infrequently. For local campaigns, regional armies—surely survivals of the levies of the former kingdoms of the Hep-

tarchy—or the levies of one or more shires were summoned. The command structure was complex, and depending on whether the king or a specially designated lieutenant commanded the army in person, its field of operations might be restricted. Later (the date is uncertain) when campaigns not requiring "total mobilization" were involved, a "special" *fyrd* was developed. The kingdom was divided into units of five hides (the hide was a unit of land measurement of varying size), and towns were assessed for military service at arbitrarily fixed numbers of hides. Each five-hide unit was required to provide a solider on summons, and the unit furnished him with twenty shillings for sixty days' service.

In addition to the general levy, the regional and local units, and the "special" *fyrd,* the Old English kings had further sources of military manpower. The thegns (thanes) were either country gentry or the clients of great magnates. They were obligated to provide military service because they were of thegnly rank, and not because they held land on military tenure. A final element was the huscarl (housecarl). The huscarls were mercenary professionals, probably introduced into England during the reign of King Cnut (1016–1035). By the end of the Saxon period, they were employed not only by the king but by the great magnates as well, and they were the most reliable element in the Old English armed forces. On balance, it is likely that Anglo-Saxon England had a military organization superior to any west of Constantinople.

The Franks, who were to exercise so great an influence on later medieval institutions, emerged from their forested homeland, where cavalry was of little use, as infantry. Almost nothing is known of their military institutions or tactical formations. As with all the primitive German peoples, every free man was obligated to military service. Presumably they were organized into dense phalanges, which charged in a wild rush, and if a series of these failed to defeat the enemy, they melted away into the surrounding forest. The Franks wore no body armor; they were armed with shield, spear, and sword, but their special weapon was the *francisca,* a precisely balanced throwing axe, which was launched at the enemy just before contact was made.

After such defeats as Casilinum (Capua) in 554, in which a Frankish army was surrounded by the Byzantines and annihilated by their horse archers, the Franks gradually adopted body armor, and by the beginning of the eighth century the king, the great magnates, and their households rode to battle, although they usually fought on foot. It thus appeared that the infantry tradition, preserved by the Romans through eight centuries, might be restored by the Franks. But the eighth century saw changes that were to revolutionize Western warfare and to dominate military operations until well into the fourteenth century.

FEUDAL WARFARE

The Frankish state. Military feudalism in the Frankish state, especially in the lands north of the Loire, evolved as a response to three pressures. First, the centuries-long economic depression that followed the collapse of Roman government in its western provinces (and the establishment of the Germanic kingdoms in the fifth and sixth centuries) was only accentuated by the Muslim conquest of much of the Mediterranean littoral in the seventh and eighth centuries. Western European commerce dwindled, and the Germanic monarchs did not have monetary resources with which to maintain a professional civil service and a permanent military establishment.

The other two problems were political and military, and in the last half of the eighth century they became inextricably interconnected. Europe was faced with the first of a series of new enemies in the early part of the eighth century, when the Muslim conquest of Visigothic Spain brought with it a new menace. And after reducing all but the mountainous northwest of the peninsula, the Arabs pushed across the Pyrenees, occupied the Narbonnaise in southern Gaul, and raided Aquitaine almost at will. In 732 a large-scale raiding force pushed north almost as far as the Loire. Somewhere between Tours and Poitiers it was met and repulsed by the Frankish levy commanded by the mayor of the palace, Charles, who earned his nickname Martel (the Hammer) on that day. The Battle of Poitiers is no longer given the importance it once was. The Frankish victory did not prevent Muslim conquest of Western Europe; in fact, their foothold in southern Gaul was not eliminated until 759. But it must have been obvious to Charles that he was unable to exploit his victory because the slow-moving Frankish levy could not pursue the mounted Arabs. If the Franks were to cope successfully with the Muslims, at least some of the troops would have to be mounted and capable of fighting on horseback. Other factors, chiefly political, were involved in the

The campaign of Joab. Miniature from the Psalterium Aureum, a 9th-century Carolingian MS, depicting cavalry with stirrups, lances, and mail coats. ST. GALLEN, STIFTSBIBLIOTHEK

gradual shift to mounted service, but the necessity of a capability to cope with fast-moving enemies was the chief military consideration.

The introduction of the stirrup into Western Europe in the early eighth century was also an important factor. The stirrup gave the mounted warrior decided advantages over infantry armed with only a spear, sword, or axe, and protected only by a shield. With a firm seat in the saddle, protected by shield, iron cap, and mail shirt, the horseman could use his lance for striking, instead of throwing or thrusting it. Although shock tactics were some three centuries in developing, they eventually became standard in Western Europe. By rising in his stirrups, the trooper could deal highly effective blows with his sword. The infantry of antiquity never had to deal with such firmly seated cavalry as did the infantry of the Middle Ages. Indeed, until the appearance of the Swiss halberdiers and pikemen in the fourteenth century, no Western infantry could cope with the knight on equal terms at close quarters.

But the equipment of a mounted warrior was expensive. The ordinary free Frank, trying to scratch out a living from the soil, could not afford a horse and the arms and armor necessary for mounted service. Moreover, it required constant training and practice to be able to control a horse while managing a shield and wielding a lance or sword. In other words, if Charles Martel were to field an army of mounted warriors, they would have to be provided with the means of subsistence, without the necessity of having to work for a living. In a state such as the Carolingian monarchy, which provided neither pay nor equipment to its troops, there was but one practicable answer.

To provide a living for the warriors whom he recruited, Charles made revocable land grants, complete with agricultural tenants, first known as benefices, later as fiefs. The recipient of a benefice had to swear absolute fidelity to Charles. This was a contractual relationship; if the grantee died, proved disloyal, or for some reason was prevented from honoring his military obligation, the benefice was forfeited. Only an individual rich in lands could afford to do this on a large scale. Charles used the crown lands, but these proved to be inadequate. He then compelled bishops and abbots to grant benefices from their vast holdings. The land technically remained church land, but now the church was caught up in the military aspect of a developing feudal system. The fighting bishop or abbot was not an unusual sight on medieval battlefields.

Lay and ecclesiastical magnates soon followed the example of Charles Martel, parceling out much of their land into fiefs to support what amounted to private armies. In addition, lesser men, with land and tenants of their own, either voluntarily or through coercion, became the vassals of their more powerful neighbors. By the end of the ninth century, office, land tenure, and military service were tending to become hereditary. The Frankish army no longer consisted of the levy of free men, commanded by the king's officials, the counts, but of the vassals of the counts, over whom the king no longer had any effective control. The capitularies of Charlemagne (during 768–814) had attempted to increase the strength of the mounted army by requiring that free men of the lesser sort send one of their number, usually one of four, mounted to the host. This, however, served only to increase the status of the man on horseback. He gradually became lord over his fellows who tilled his fields while he was away at the wars.

The collapse of the Carolingian Empire in the middle decades of the ninth century only tended to accelerate the evolution of military feudalism. The imposing empire of Charlemagne had ceased to exist as a cohesive unit. Political and military power began to break down into ever-smaller units. The pressing need of society on every level was security, and in the absence of any effective central authority the weaker man everywhere sought the protection of the stronger. In the process, the ordinary freeman, no longer able to perform the military functions of his class, sank to the level of the dependent serf.

The Viking raids, beginning in the last decades of the eighth century, led to increasing reliance on mounted service. The Scandinavian raiders, relying at first on the mobility afforded by unchallenged sea power, were able to strike at times and places of their own choosing all the way around the Atlantic periphery of Europe and even into the Mediterranean as far as the mouth of the Rhône. Their shallow-draft vessels could penetrate far up such rivers as the Rhine, Somme, Seine, Loire, Garonne, Duero, Guadalquivir, and Rhône. As long as imperial defenses held up at all, the Norse raids were little more than a tolerable nuisance. But with the outbreak of the civil wars late in the reign of Louis I the Pious (814–840), the Vikings were not slow to take advantage of the situation. Soon they were landing, stockading their ships, rounding up all available horses, and embarking on long cross-country raids. The slow-moving Frankish infantry was helpless in this situation; only mounted troops could cope with the "horsed Vikings."

Through the late ninth, tenth, and early eleventh centuries, feudalism had the vitality of a growing organism, and it was impossible to check the further fragmentation of civil and military authority. This goes far to explain the almost continuous warfare of the early feudal period. The possessor of what amounted to a private army found it hard to resist the temptation to use it against his neighbors, his feudal superiors, and even against the king himself, if there seemed to be a chance of profit.

It should be noted that during this chaotic transitional period, there can have been very little difference among the warriors who received their pay in cash, as they did in Spain and southern Gaul, those who were maintained in their lord's household, and those who received benefices in return for their military services. All were professionals who fought for a living. It seems fairly certain that all were required to serve for as long as they were needed.

But the household knight eventually disappeared; and gradually a distinction began to develop between the beneficed knight, and the professionals who were paid in cash. This became the case in the twelfth century as kings and magnates began to employ mercenaries on an increasingly large scale. Due to a reviving economy, their monetary revenue had become more adequate to meet their military needs. In the meantime, the knight as landholder had begun to develop localized interests that were incompatible with those of the knight as soldier. Thus he sought to limit his military obligations as much as possible. By the twelfth century a fairly standard term of forty days' service at his own expense had been established in most of Western Europe; by about 1100 he could even escape this obligation (in England) by the payment of a fine in lieu of personal service. Thus the feudal knight, now a member of the aristocracy, became a part-time soldier at best, and therefore an indifferent one.

The mercenary soldier had always been available to those who could afford his services, and in certain areas—parts of Italy, southern France, and the Christian states of Spain, where Moorish booty and tribute provided a fairly steady cash inflow— soldiers seem always to have been paid in cash. Benefices or fiefs were given as rewards for past services, not for stipulated future military duty. Mercenaries from as far away as Apulia can be found in the invasion army with which Duke William of Normandy began his conquest of England in 1066. Hired troops are recorded in crusading armies as early as the siege of Antioch in 1097–1098. Henry II of England (1154–1189) used large numbers of mercenaries to suppress a serious baronial revolt in 1173–1174, and by the beginning of the thirteenth century the most reliable element in the French army of Philip II Augustus was a solid nucleus of horse and foot mercenaries. Stipendiary troops from Brabant and Poitou were hired by King John of England (1199– 1216) to suppress the revolt that began in 1214. Indeed it would be difficult to cite a campaign or engagement where the units can be identified in which paid troops were not involved.

The use of professional soldiery increased significantly during the fourteenth and fifteenth centuries. Specialists in various categories were in particular demand. Thus Genoese crossbowmen were to be found in most French field armies during the Hundred Years War. English longbowmen were

A Viking attack on Thetford, depicted in a 12th-century English *Miracles of St. Edmund*. NEW YORK, PIERPONT MORGAN LIBRARY, MS 736, fol. 10

employed by Duke Charles the Bold of Burgundy, and Swiss pikemen were hired by King Louis XI of France (1461–1483) as well as by sundry Italian tyrants.

By the mid eleventh century, military feudalism was most completely established in France north of the Loire—the old Carolingian Neustria. Here, almost all the land, ecclesiastical as well as secular, was obligated to provide military service. Warfare was endemic in even the best-run feudal states, such as Flanders, Normandy, and Anjou. It was epidemic in such loosely organized principalities as Brittany, and in the royal demesne until the accession of Louis VI (1108).

Elsewhere, military feudalism was greatly modified by existing social, economic, and military institutions. In places where feudal military service was a conscious import—in southern Italy and

Sicily, England, and in the crusader states of Syria and Palestine—it was largely the result of Norman enterprise. In Germany, southern France, northern Italy, and the Iberian Peninsula, the military aspects of feudalism were but superficial, and the military procurement systems of these areas will be noted later.

The Normans. Norman adventurers began to filter across the Alps down into southern Italy about 1016. Because of the incredibly confused political situation, they were able to profit from the turmoil. Sicily was held by the Muslims; the southern third of the peninsula was divided among the Byzantine theme of Langobardia, an assortment of Lombard duchies, and several maritime cities owing nominal allegiance to the Byzantine Empire, but virtually independent. Into this maelstrom of conflicting claims and jurisdictions, the Normans came with nothing but their skill at swordplay, a willingness to fight for the person who would pay them most, and a keen eye for the main chance. By the middle of the eleventh century, Norman mercenaries were serving in the armies of Lombard dukes, Byzantine *catapans,* and the maritime republics. By 1030 the Normans had begun to establish themselves as landed magnates. Bari, the last Byzantine foothold in Italy, fell in 1071 to the aggressive Normans, and by 1076 all of southern Italy with the exception of Benevento, Capua, and Naples was in Norman hands. In the meantime, the conquest of Sicily was well under way. It was facilitated by the inability of the three Muslim emirs who controlled the island to cooperate effectively to oppose the Norman offensive. The Normans conducted operations with ridiculously small forces. It does not appear that they ever disposed of more than 600 mounted troops, and for the campaign of 1062 no more than 130 heavy horses seem to have been available. With the union of Apulia and Sicily in 1128, Norman Sicily became perhaps the most powerful military state in Western Europe. Within the next half century, it was able to beat off attacks by popes and Byzantine and Holy Roman emperors, to mount amphibious assaults as far east as the Aegean Sea, and, for a brief period, to maintain a hold on a considerable stretch of the North African coast.

Unfortunately, little can be ascertained of the military forces at the disposal of the rulers of the Kingdom of Sicily. There were the regular feudal levies due from the Norman tenants, and the militia from the towns, but after the final reduction of Sicily in 1091, Norman rulers seem to have relied to a large extent on mercenaries recruited from among their Muslim subjects. Both infantry and cavalry were maintained on a permanent or semipermanent basis; Muslim engineers directed siege operations, and Muslim naval personnel were instrumental in securing Sicilian naval supremacy in the central Mediterranean for much of the twelfth century.

Fifty years after the first Norman adventurers began to seek their fortunes in lower Italy, the more publicized Norman conquest of England began. The English king Harold II was faced with a double invasion threat—from the Norwegians and from the Normans. The Norse threat materialized first, when an army commanded by King Harald Hardråde landed in the Humber estuary and occupied York. Harold marched north, met the Norwegians at Stamford Bridge on 25 September 1066, won a decisive victory, and left King Harald dead on the field of battle. But his march to the north left the south coast undefended, and on 28 September, Duke William landed unopposed on the Sussex coast. Harold's forced march from York and the subsequent Battle of Hastings on 14 October resulted, despite desperate English resistance, in the king's death, and a Norman victory. It should be noted, however, that so far as can be determined, no other medieval army fought two pitched battles within the space of three weeks.

The victory at Hastings did not ensure a Norman conquest by any means, and until 1071 England must be regarded as a military frontier, with what amounted to a small army of occupation—no more than 6,000 or 7,000 men—extending its authority piecemeal until the entire kingdom was under Norman control. By this date continental feudalism had been introduced into England, as fiefs were parceled out from the confiscated estates of the English magnates. It has been estimated that when the occupation was complete, the Conqueror had due him the service of about 6,000 knights. But the Normans were a practical lot who never discarded an institution that worked. For this reason the old English *fyrd* was retained, and as soon as native unrest had been quieted it was employed against baronial rebels, and even for campaigns in Normandy until well into the twelfth century.

The Norman and early Angevin kings of England also employed mercenaries on an increasingly large scale as their monetary resources became greater. William I and William II utilized paid professionals on occasions when feudal manpower appeared to be inadequate, such as the Danish "invasion scare" of 1085. Henry I employed them as castle garrisons, and during the civil wars of Stephen's reign stipendiary troops played a significant role, particularly on the royalist side. And the great baronial revolt of 1173–1174 was suppressed both in England and on the Continent largely by Henry II's mercenary units. Thus, by the end of the twelfth century, English monarchs were no longer entirely dependent upon feudal resources either to maintain internal order or to repel foreign invasion.

Crusader states. Crusader Syria and Palestine were, indeed, far removed from Western Europe, but the knights and infantry who maintained a bridgehead in the Levant for nearly two centuries were Westerners, and their adaptation to new enemies with unfamiliar tactics must be considered if a complete understanding of Western European warfare is to be achieved. The Latin princes were never more than outpost commanders of a military frontier that, after the fall of the county of Edessa in 1144, confined Christian control to the narrow coastal strip between the Mediterranean Sea and the Syrian desert. That with ever-decreasing resources they were able to hang on until 1291 is ample testimony to the military acumen of European commanders.

European settlement in the Near East was never on a sufficient scale to expand the bridgehead into what might have become a permanent European lodgment. For that reason, the Frankish rulers in the Latin East had to husband their scanty resources carefully. Operations had to be approached with extreme caution; battles were never to be hazarded if the objective of a campaign could be obtained by other means. Muslim armies could always be counted on to break up with the advent of the cold, wet weather of autumn. The primary purpose of a campaign was to maintain an army in being, and thus assure the safety of the castles and towns that had been stripped of their garrisons to provide a field army. A defeat in the open field could be utterly disastrous, as the campaign of 1187 was to prove.

The manpower resources of the Latin states were limited. It has been estimated that, in an extreme crisis, the king of Jerusalem could put about 1,000 knights into the field from feudal sources at the time of the kingdom's greatest extent. The knightly levy of the Principality of Antioch may have amounted to about 700 heavy horses, while the count of Tripoli owed the service of 100 knights to the king of Jerusalem. Account must also be taken of the contingents of the great military orders, the Knights of St. John and the Knights of the Temple. It would appear that the former could put some 500 troopers into the field, and the latter perhaps 300. The king of Jerusalem could, then, muster perhaps as many as 1,750 to 1,800 knights at the maximum. To these were added the Turcopoles, lightly armed cavalry who were useful for reconnaissance, but who were also put into the line of battle with the knights to augment their always undermanned squadrons.

The infantry levies are more difficult to estimate. The towns and monastic establishments were obligated to provide infantry, but a late source states that something over 5,000 sergeants could be mustered; this may not be far from the actual number. The Antiochene levy mustered 3,000 men for the campaign of 1119, but no figures are available for the counties of Edessa and Tripoli.

The mercenary appeared early in the annals of the Frankish East, but here the main problem was one of money. As loss of territory and the impoverishment of fiefs reduced the normal sources of manpower, increasing reliance was placed on paid soldiery. Finally the entire free male population could be called out in times of dire emergency. Even so, the largest army ever mustered in the Latin East, that which faced Saladin in 1183, numbered no more than 15,000 men. With such inadequate resources, the wonder is not that the Europeans were finally ejected from the Near Eastern mainland, but that they were able to maintain their foothold for so long in the face of insuperable odds.

Germany. In the rest of Western Europe—Germany, northern Italy, and the Iberian Peninsula—military feudalism never evolved, either as a native institution or as a consciously imposed system. In Germany only the duchies of Lorraine and Franconia, the heartland of the old Carolingian monarchy, were more than superficially feudalized. The remainder of the kingdom never adopted more than the external trappings of feudal structure. When Frederick I Barbarossa (1152–1190) attempted to bring the German nobility into something like a feudal relationship to the crown, the military aspects of feudalism were already of decreasing importance in the England of Henry II and the France of Philip II Augustus.

But two factors in the military structure of Germany before 1200 require notice. The first is the unusual reliance placed by the crown on the German bishops and abbots. The great lay magnates, notably the dukes, were notoriously untrustworthy. Indeed, no reign passed without at least one rebellion, even under such strong monarchs as Otto I the Great (936–973) and Henry IV (1056–1106). But the bishops and the abbots of the greater monasteries were, in effect, royal appointees, and the king could thus be assured of loyal support against noble rebellion and for his attempts to impose imperial rule on Italy. The surviving evidence suggests that German armies were composed largely of ecclesiastical contingents.

Moreover, as time went by, the kings and both lay and ecclesiastical magnates increasingly relied on a new source of military manpower: ministerials—unfree knights. The ministerial was, originally, a servile tenant who was entrusted with minor administrative and military duties on the crown lands. The evolution of this class, which began in the reign of Conrad II, had by the time of Henry III been widely accepted by both lay and ecclesiastical lords. Except possibly in the county of Champagne, whose count was a vassal of the German king for some of his lands, there is no parallel elsewhere in Western Europe. The advantages of the ministerials are obvious: not only were they entirely dependent on their patron for their status, and thus likely to prove more loyal, but their holdings were not at first hereditary, a factor of especial importance to the church, which could not canonically alienate its lands. These unfree warriors served as infantry and cavalry; they garrisoned castles, and the abler members of the class were eventually absorbed into the minor ranks of the nobility.

Thus, at the end of the twelfth century, there was no established pattern of military service in Germany. Royal and imperial armies were manned largely by ministerials, a large proportion of whom were furnished by ecclesiastics. On occasion the feudal levies of the Rhineland magnates would be summoned. The crown could usually rely on the support of the infantry of the Rhenish towns, and as late as Bouvines (1214) the majority of the Saxon contingent was still fighting on foot.

Central and northern Italy. The collapse of the Carolingian Empire in the middle ninth century resulted in indescribable anarchy in central and northern Italy. The descendants of Carolingian counts and Lombard nobles—many of whom claimed to be descended from Charlemagne—waged almost continuous war for the empty title of king of Italy, and lesser lords sought to increase their power and immunities by playing off one contender against another. It was against this background of civil strife that the towns, particularly those of Lombardy, began to play a role in the petty warfare of the period. At first they were content merely to hold their own against the nobles of the countryside, who regarded the merchants of the towns as legitimate objects for plunder. However, as urban life, perhaps never completely extinguished in Tuscany and Lombardy, began to revive, the towns began to surround themselves with walls, which enabled them not only to resist baronial assaults, but to launch offensive operations against the nobles of the *contado* (surrounding countryside). By the twelfth century, the townsmen had prevailed; the nobles, except in the remoter regions, had been subdued and had also been compelled to become residents of the towns for the greater part of the year. This provided the civic communes with a nucleus of heavy cavalry. As the urban centers prospered, civic ordinances required that citizens possessed of a certain amount of property must provide themselves with equipment suitable for cavalry service. Although they were not nobles, they were registered as "knights for the commune." The lesser sort of citizens and residents of the *contado* provided the infantry and auxiliary services.

On the basis of available evidence, towns were divided into "quarters," or wards. Depending on the importance of an impending campaign, the levies of varying numbers of quarters were called out for field service. Troops were paid while on active duty, and the officers received a small retainer during peacetime. It was this efficient military organization that enabled the cities of the Lombard League to destroy once and for all the imperial ambitions of Emperor Frederick I Barbarossa at Legnano in 1176. Had the Lombard towns been able to forgo their bitter rivalries, they might well have established a formidable military power in the Po Valley.

Spain. Medieval Spain has been aptly described as "a society organized for war." The Arab destruction of the Visigothic kingdom early in the eighth century had pushed the remaining independent Christians to the mountainous region of the Asturias, where the Arab mounted formations could not operate to advantage. Indeed, the levies of the kingdom of the Asturias were largely infantry until the Christians were able to establish themselves on the plain of the Duero. Here, the requirements of a new military environment led to the extensive fortification of the newly acquired territory, the development of cavalry capability, and the colonization of the desolated frontier area. This latter requirement resulted in the foundation of many new towns, with favorable terms offered to those who would settle on the frontier. The same conditions did not exist in northeastern Spain, where the Carolingian Spanish march had been established in the eighth century, when the Catalans began to encroach on the fertile and populous Ebro Valley. But in either case, the constantly shifting frontier required military responses that differed considerably from those of the highly feudalized principalities of Western Europe.

Although some of the aspects of feudalism penetrated south of the Pyrenees, it was never more than superficial (outside of the Spanish March). Benefices, granted as rewards for past military services, tended to become allodial property within a generation or two, thus effectively removing them from royal control. This led to the creation of an extraordinarily turbulent military aristocracy, ever ready to participate in the numerous civil wars or the almost constant strife among the Christian kingdoms. Nor were they loath to take service with the rulers of Moorish Spain if the price was right.

Fortunately the rulers of Christian Iberia had other sources of manpower than that provided by the unreliable nobility. The ecclesiastical magnates were required to appear with their tenants in campaigns against the Moors, and the establishment of the great military orders—Calatrava (1158), Santiago (1175), and Alcántara (1218)—gave the kings of Castile, in particular, a nucleus of reliable heavy cavalry on the Western model. Eventually, however, they became so powerful, as they did in the crusader states, that they became a threat to the monarchy itself.

So although the feudal structure of medieval Spain appeared to resemble that of Capetian France or Norman England, the appearances were deceiving. At the top were the great magnates (*ricos hombres*), corresponding to the dukes and counts of France, who were entitled to raise and maintain private armies, and who were entitled to an invitation rather than a summons to participate in a campaign. Below them were the *hidalgos,* roughly equivalent to the English baronage, and the knights (*caballeros*).

But knights on the Western model, with their heavy panoply, were ill-adapted to the frontier warfare of the *Reconquista*. Here mobility was required for the fast-moving raid and counter-raid, which seem to have been almost continuous between more formal campaigns. This led to the development of "non-noble" knights (*caballeros villanos*), who were most likely concentrated principally in the colonial towns established along the frontier. Since they had to be prepared to fight a type of warfare in which mobility was essential, they adopted the arms, weapons, and even the horsemanship of their Moorish enemies. From them evolved the celebrated Spanish light cavalry (*genitours*), who were excellent as scouts and skirmishers, but who were unable to stand up to the charge of the feudal heavy trooper. These non-noble knights have some resemblance to the mounted sergeants of Norman and Plantagenet England, and to the *milites pro commune* of the Italian city-republics.

Strategy and tactics. Although military manpower "procurement systems" operated in many different ways during the so-called feudal period, there were striking similarities in armor and weapons, in the proliferation of castles, and in the tactical disposition of armies throughout Western Europe during this era. Of strategical concepts or combinations, there was not much before the beginning of the thirteenth century. There were, of course, exceptions: Otto I the Great's decision to come down to the east bank of the Lech in the campaign of 955 showed real strategic insight, as did that of King Henry I of France in the Norman campaign of 1054. William the Conqueror's march around to the west and north of London, in October through December 1066, must also be regarded as a strategic move, since it cut off the metropolis from any possible aid from the north.

Tactical combinations on the other hand, tended to be simple. It could hardly be otherwise when a commander could not know until the muster was complete just what he would have to work with to achieve his objective; often the brigading had to be done on the battle site itself. Medieval armies were usually divided into three divisions, or "battles," and the divisions were customarily all put into the line of battle, with the commander leading the middle division. Provisions for a reserve were occasionally made; flanking detachments were not unknown. And it should be noted that Norman knights, in particular, were never reluctant to send their horses to the rear and fight on foot. On occasion the divisions were posted one behind another, usually with disastrous results. A repulse of the first "battle" threw it back in confusion on the rear divisions, which were thus unable to make an effective charge. Numerous examples of this irrational order of battle can be cited, and the French continued to use it into the fifteenth century, with notable lack of success. In the crusader states, commanders developed a marching tactical formation, which enabled them to move through a surrounding army without breaking formation.

The difficulty of keeping armies in the field for any great length of time does much to explain the comparative infrequency of pitched battles before the beginning of the thirteenth century. The limits on length of service imposed by feudal custom, and the inability of rulers to finance standing armies, reduced warfare largely to a matter of skirmishes and sieges.

Fortifications. Characteristic features of medieval fortifications were the castle, the fortified residence of greater and lesser magnates, both lay and ecclesiastical, and the fortified community—towns, or ecclesiastical establishments. Some communities retained their Roman walls, but, except in Italy until the twelfth century, most private and communal fortifications were simple structures of earth and timber. The typical castle, known as a "motte-and-bailey" castle, consisted of a high, ditched mound of earth—the motte—palisaded around the top, and within this enclosure stood the "keep" or "hall" of the proprietor. Adjacent was a larger enclosure, also ditched and palisaded, wherein stood the huts of the lord's more menial attendants, and quite frequently, the parish church.

A simple motte-and-bailey castle could often be carried by assault, and it was vulnerable to fire, but a determined garrison could usually hold out until relieved by hastily collected forces from neighboring garrisons. But in the late twelfth century, the increasing construction of masonry fortifications on the private and municipal level enabled the defense to obtain an advantage over the offense, which it was to retain until the late fifteenth century, when artillery had become a really effective weapon. Otherwise, starvation was the surest means of reducing a stronghold, and the besieging commander had to possess the means to keep an army in the field for a protracted period. The increasing use of masonry construction in fortifications led to the development of more sophisticated siege techniques. Mining and sapping were em-

ployed; the use of projectile-hurling engines became common. Movable towers that could be moved against the walls of a besieged town enjoyed occasional success. But the improvement in fortification, doubtless the result of crusaders' observation in the Byzantine Empire and Syria, more than offset the offensive advances.

Armor and weapons. Although recruitment systems differed widely in "feudal" Europe, as well as strategy and tactics, armor and weapons remained remarkably uniform throughout the period. Originally the warrior, when body-armor was uniformly adopted, whether mounted or on foot, was protected by a mail shirt, which reached to mid thigh, a conical iron cap, often provided with a nasal bar to protect the face from sword cuts, and a large oblong shield. By the end of the twelfth century, the mail shirt had been extended to cover both the arms and legs, and the steel cap was beginning to be replaced by the "pot-helm." For both infantry and cavalry the long cutting sword remained standard, although in England the two-handed Danish axe was in use until the middle of the twelfth century. The lance, as used by the trooper, is depicted as late as the mid eleventh century as being tossed, or thrust, or couched under the knight's arm. The latter usage eventually prevailed, for it put the impetus of horse and rider behind the shock, usually sufficient to break the infantry levies of the period.

POSTFEUDAL WARFARE

The thirteenth century saw the beginning of a change in the nature of warfare that was still in progress at the end of the Middle Ages. The reviving economy of Western Europe enabled monarchs—and recalcitrant vassals—to employ stipendiary troops on an ever-increasing scale. Even in France, where the feudal levy was employed until well into the fifteenth century, the noble contingents were paid for their services. But the major development, so far as military personnel is concerned, was the reappearance of infantry as a vital factor on Western battlefields.

There are two types of tactics to win battles: missile tactics and shock tactics. The former depends upon missiles to keep the enemy from closing or to so reduce his numbers that his impact on the line of battle will be minimal and can easily be beaten off. The latter are effective only if the attacking force has the impetus to carry away the enemy by its impact. Both systems were developed during the thirteenth and fourteenth centuries by the English and the Swiss.

During the campaigns fought by Edward I of England (1272–1307) in his subjugation of the Welsh, English infantry began to adopt the longbow, a weapon of south Welsh origin. By the end of the thirteenth century, a tactical system had evolved that, although it could be used offensively, was more effective in a defensive situation. This development took place during Edward's Welsh and Scottish campaigns, unnoticed by continental observers. Thus, during the early phases of the Hundred Years War (1337–1453), French commanders were at an utter loss as to how to respond to a tactical deployment that made the yeoman peasant the master of the mounted or dismounted knight. The English armies that fought the Hundred Years War were composed of professionals, recruited under the indenture system. The crown would "indenture" a captain of proven reputation to recruit a given number of men-at-arms, or spearmen, and archers. The indenture was a form of contract, the soldiers were paid by the crown, when and if the money was available, and it seems likely that the prospect of plunder and the possibility of profitable ransoms from prisoners of rank lured more men into the profession of arms than did the uncertain prospects of pay.

Only when the French refrained from engaging in pitched battles did the tide of war change. The English, through long cross-country raids, inflicted incalculable damage on the French countryside. But during the brief resumption of the war between 1369 and 1380, by adopting guerrilla tactics, the French managed to reconquer all that had been lost since 1346, except for the Calais bridgehead.

But when the war was resumed in 1415, after a long truce, the French were guilty of the same tactical blunders they had committed in the opening phases of the conflict. Agincourt (1415) and Verneuil (1424) were but repetitions of Poitiers (1356). But the revival of French morale wrought by Joan of Arc during the campaign of 1429–1430 led to a series of French victories such as Patay (1429), in which the English were not allowed time to take up their now-traditional defensive position. The innovation of Charles VII of France (1422–1461), who in 1445 created the first standing army in Western Europe since the days of imperial Rome, also had much to do with eventual French victory. And at Formigny (1450) and Castillon (1453), artillery played an important if not decisive role in reducing

English possessions in France to Calais and its environs. Thereafter, the use of the longbow was largely restricted to the English civil struggle known as the Wars of the Roses (1455–1485).

Contemporary with the development of English missile tactics was the evolution of Swiss shock tactics. The primitive Swiss weapon was the halberd, essentially an axe on a seven- or eight-foot shaft. While it could inflict ghastly wounds, it was unsuited for repelling mounted troops with their long lances. So early in the fourteenth century the pike, a fifteen-foot weapon, was adopted as the national arm. Universal military service was the rule, and a Swiss army could be mobilized with what was, for the fourteenth century, an incredible speed. The units from each valley, district, and canton marched under their own officers and flags to the mustering place. Each unit knew its place in the formation, and the army marched as it was to fight.

A Swiss army normally marched in three massed columns, banners and pennons flying above the upright forest of pikes, and it must have been an imposing if not frightening sight as it bore down on the enemy with three rows of pikes projecting from the front rank. The halberdiers were massed in the center of the phalanx, ready to issue from the flanks should the column be brought to a halt. For infighting the halberd was extremely effective, and for the first time since antiquity infantry was able to deal with cavalry at close quarters on equal terms. Should the column be outflanked, the Swiss formed the "hedgehog," with the pikes of the outer ranks and files projecting outward to repel an assault from any direction.

Although the Swiss had established themselves as redoubtable soldiers, who neither asked nor gave quarter, their reputation as almost invincible was established in the Burgundian Wars (1476–1477). Duke Charles the Bold of Burgundy had raised a standing army consisting, in addition to the heavy cavalry of his own domains, of auxiliary troops from those areas noted for a particular military specialty—English archers, Flemish pikemen, Savoyard light cavalry, and German arquebusiers. But in so doing, the duke lost sight of the principle that cohesion is the essence of any effective military organization. Troops who did not understand the tactics or even the language of the corps to the right or left could not have been expected to make a determined stand against so homogeneous an army as the Swiss put into the field. In addition to its cohesiveness, the Swiss had developed a tactical system that was both simple and flexible. The Confederate army, as noted above, marched in the three divisions common to most medieval armies. Deployment was based on the terrain and the position of the enemy. The Swiss never waited to be attacked; the forward division could move directly to the front, with the other divisions to the right or left in echelon as the situation required. Occasionally, as at Laupen (1339), the center opened the attack with the wings refused. But in any event, it was extremely difficult to outflank the Swiss battle order. This was proven in a series of engagements in 1476 and 1477 that ended with the death of Duke Charles at the Battle of Nancy in 1477. With the single exception of Arbedo (1422), European commanders were not able to develop tactics that could meet the onset of the Swiss phalanx until the beginning of the sixteenth century.

The political changes in fourteenth- and fifteenth-century Italy greatly altered the characteristics of its military institutions and practices. The communes of the twelfth and thirteenth centuries had defeated the imperial pretensions of Frederick I and Frederick II with their own communal levies. But, increasingly, the Italian states fell under the control of tyrants who had good reason to distrust their subjects. Therefore, the almost incessant wars of the fourteenth and fifteenth centuries were fought not by citizen armies, but by mercenary companies recruited by individual *condottieri*, who sold their services to the various Italian rulers.

The *condottieri* bands were largely composed of heavily armored cavalry, with a small percentage— rarely as large as twenty-five percent—of crossbowmen. The long and honorable Italian career of Sir John Hawkwood and his company of English men-at-arms and longbowmen failed to stimulate Italian emulators. Much of the Italian terrain was unsuitable for cavalry combat, which greatly reduced the field of operations. Various factors combined to turn Italian warfare into something like a gigantic chess game played over the level terrain of central and northern Italy. (See the painting of the Battle of San Romano at "Uccello" in this volume.) By the end of the fourteenth century, armor had become so heavy that knights tilting at one another rarely suffered serious injury. Moreover, the individual man-at-arms constituted the captain's stock-in-trade; and unless the tactical situation was such that the odds seemed overwhelmingly in a commander's favor or, conversely, he had allowed himself to be maneuvered into such a position that the only escape was by offering battle, general engagements were rare. In the latter situation, however, a captain might declare himself "checkmated" and surrender his entire army. Moreover, a dead soldier could pay no ransom; a captive could, and the taking of prisoners was, perhaps, more important to the individual mercenary than killing an opponent.

Thus it was that when Charles VIII of France came down into Italy in 1494, contemporary Italian chronicles wrote in shocked disbelief that these barbarians from beyond the Alps actually killed and wounded the enemy! This stemmed from the French belief that, even if tactically outmaneuvered, it was still possible to win battles by killing and damaging as many of the enemy as possible. By the end of the fifteenth century the formal, "chessboard" warfare of the *condottieri* had come to an inglorious end, and Italians were to see their states become mere pawns in the international power struggle for the next fifty years.

But the real military revolution of the later Middle Ages began with the introduction into warfare of an explosive mixture of saltpeter, sulphur, and charcoal. Who invented gunpowder is most uncertain, and who conceived the idea of confining the explosion in such a way that it would propel a missile is unknown. However, there is reference to the use of cannon at the siege of Metz in 1324, and in a Florentine document of 1326. The first pictorial representation of any kind of firearm appears in the English Milemete MS, which can be dated accurately to 1327.

From this time on, references to various types of firearms multiply, in both official documents, narrative chronicles, and manuscript illuminations. These show the increasing use of gunpowder weapons of various types. Two variations appear that were eventually to lead to modern hand-and-shoulder weapons, and to the later field and siege artillery.

Early experiments were conducted with what might be called anti-personnel weapons—pieces of small-bore and sometimes arrow-shaped shafts, firing iron or leaden pellets. These were often arranged in lines so that they could be discharged almost simultaneously. From these developed the early "hand-guns," at first mounted at the end of a stave braced against the ground. And from these primitive weapons evolved the arquebus of the German and Czech mercenaries who appeared on many a foreign field before the fifteenth century had run its course.

The larger guns, which, before the end of the fourteenth century, had risen to 500 or 600 pounds (230 or 270 kg) in weight, increased in size and bore throughout the fifteenth century. By the middle of the century pieces capable of casting projectiles of up to 600 pounds were being cast, which precluded the use of metal; iron and lead were too limited in quantity and too expensive to be used for such purposes. For this reason, stone cannonballs were the usual projectiles in the last half of the century.

But although they were awkward and difficult to move from one position to another, even after the addition of wheels to the gun carriages, the siege batteries had become effective well before 1500. The heavy guns of Charles VII of France reduced more than sixty English-held fortresses within little more than a year during the final phases of the Hundred Years War. And by the war's end artillery had achieved its first victory in the open field at Formigny and in defending field fortifications at Castillon. During the 1460's the siege train of Edward IV of England quickly blasted the northern rebels out of their strongholds. By the end of the fifteenth century, the medieval castle had become an anachronism. By this time also, casting techniques had improved and the long bronze guns of Renaissance workmanship bore little resemblance to the clumsy pieces of but a few decades earlier. Attempts were made to devise breach-loading artillery, but with little success; the muzzle-loader was not superseded until the second half of the nineteenth century.

CONCLUSIONS

Ten centuries in any area of the human experience will see significant changes, whether it be in religious, social, political, economic, or military institutions. Nor should any of these changes be viewed as if they existed as separate entities. All were interrelated in one way or another. The crusades, which established a Western European bridgehead in the Levant that was maintained for nearly two centuries, were undertaken as a result of popular religious zeal. But it should not be forgotten that papal political ambitions cannot be ruled out as a factor in the church's sponsorship of the crusades, and many crusaders were motivated more by the hope of material gain than by the promise of eternal salvation. The economic revival that en-

abled Western European monarchs to employ mercenaries on a large scale was largely instrumental in the destruction of military feudalism.

Only recently have scholars begun an attempt to relate military institutions and operations to their effect on society as a whole. Not much can be known about earlier centuries; chroniclers make reference to the devastation of a particular district due to the passage of an army through it. An occasional charter exists in which a baron makes restitution to an ecclesiastical establishment for damages inflicted during his military operations; Domesday Book notes the number of tenements destroyed to make room for the castle after the Norman Conquest of England. And that is about all. That warfare bore heavily on the civilian population there can be no doubt, but the degree to which the people were exposed to hardship can only be surmised.

By the thirteenth century, official documentation and political narrative begin to become more adequate, although never completely so. This ever-increasing amount of contemporary material continues throughout the remainder of the Middle Ages, except for England during the Wars of the Roses. It was always possible for scholars to turn to this readily available material, but earlier military historians were primarily concerned with military institutions—those which princes utilized to raise field forces—and the conduct of campaigns and battles.

Due to recent scholarship, it is now becoming possible to get a fairly accurate picture of how war finance affected the public and some notion of how governments attempted to sway public opinion toward a war policy and the reaction of various segments of the population to what would now be called propaganda. In general it can be said that society supported a war, however grudgingly it paid the extraordinary outlay of money, as long as it was going well. But popular unrest, often resulting in civil disturbances, followed hard upon the heels of continued reverses. Despite the incomplete record, it may well be suspected that medieval people reacted to the fluctuating fortunes of war much as do their twentieth-century counterparts.

BIBLIOGRAPHY

Sources. Many of the narrative sources are available in good translations, not only the English and continental chronicles, but also such epics as the Norse *Heimskringla,* the French *Chanson de Roland,* and the Spanish *Cantar de mío Cid,* which do much to make understandable the ethos of the medieval military caste.

General studies. A useful starting point is Charles W. C. Oman, *The Art of War in the Middle Ages, A.D. 378–1515* (1885), rev. and ed. by John H. Beeler (1953). Oman expanded his original essay in *A History of the Art of War in the Middle Ages,* 2 vols. (1924), which is still the only scholarly treatment in English of medieval warfare. See also Beeler, *Warfare in Feudal Europe, 730–1200* (1971); Hans Delbrück, *Geschichte der Kriegskunst im Rahmen der politischen Geschichte,* 6 vols. (1920–1932), II, *The Germans,* and III, *The Middle Ages,* Walter Renfroe, Jr., trans. (1980, 1982); Ferdinand Lot, *L'art militaire et les armés au moyen âge en Europe et dans la proche Orient,* 2 vols. (1946). Frederick H. Russell, *The Just War in the Middle Ages* (1975), admirably sums up the moral and scriptural sanctions for warfare among medieval states.

England. Michael Powicke, *Military Obligation in Medieval England* (1962), surveys the sources of military manpower of English kings throughout the Middle Ages. Anglo-Saxon England is covered in C. W. Hollister, *Anglo-Saxon Military Institutions on the Eve of the Norman Conquest* (1962). Post-Conquest England is discussed by Beeler, *Warfare in England, 1066–1189* (1966); Hollister, *The Military Organization of Norman England* (1965); and William E. Kappelle, *The Norman Conquest of the North: The Region and Its Transformation, 1000–1135* (1979). The thirteenth century is dealt with in John E. Morris, *The Welsh Wars of King Edward I* (1901), still the only account of the English conquest of Wales; and Michael Prestwich, *War, Politics, and Finance Under Edward I* (1972). John Schlight, *Monarchs and Mercenaries* (1968), concentrates on the use of paid troops by English monarchs.

Continental Europe. Bernard S. Bachrach, *Merovingian Military Organization* (1972), attempts to show, not quite convincingly, that Roman civic military formations survived in some Gallic towns until the mid eighth century. Édouard Audouin, *Essai sur l'armée royale au temps de Philippe Auguste* (1913), examines the composition of the French army in the late twelfth century. D. P. Waley, "The Army of the Florentine Republic from the Twelfth to the Fourteenth Century," in Nicolai Rubenstein, ed., *Florentine Studies* (1968), treats the military organization of Florence before the advent of the *condottieri.* The only serious study of medieval Spanish military history is Elena Lourie, "A Society Organized for War: Medieval Spain," in *Past and Present,* 35 (1966). Three studies deal with the medieval German *Drang nach Osten:* Eric Christiansen, *The Northern Crusades: The Baltic and Catholic Frontier, 1100–1525* (1980); and William Urban, *The Baltic Crusade* (1975) and *The Prussian Crusade* (1980). Major Charles Brusten, *L'armée bourguignonne de 1465 à 1468* (1954?), deals with the Burgundian army of Charles the Bold. The

"chessboard" warfare of the *condottieri* bands in Italy is treated in Joseph Jay Deiss, *Captains of Fortune: Profiles of Six Italian Condottieri* (1966), and, in a more scholarly way, in Michael E. Mallett, *Mercenaries and Their Masters: Warfare in Renaissance Italy* (1974).

The crusades and the military orders. R. C. Smail, *Crusading Warfare (1097–1193)* (1956), is probably the best monograph on any phase of medieval warfare. The military orders are discussed in Jonathan Riley-Smith, *The Knights of St. John in Jerusalem and Cyprus, ca. 1050–1310* (1967); Desmond Seward, *The Monks of the War: The Military Religious Orders* (1972); and Edith Simon, *The Piebald Standard: A Biography of the Knights Templars* (1959).

The Hundred Years War. This war is the most widely studied military confrontation of the Middle Ages. The best purely military accounts are Col. Alfred H. Burne, *The Crécy War* (1955) and *The Agincourt War* (1956). Herbert J. Hewitt, *The Black Prince's Expedition of 1355–1357* (1957), is an excellent detailed account of one phase of the war. Richard A. Newhall, *The English Conquest of Normandy, 1416–1424: A Study in Fifteenth-century Warfare* (1924) and *Muster and Review: A Problem of English Military Administration, 1420–1440* (1940), describe the English endeavor to maintain Henry VI's "Kingdom of France." Édouard Perroy, *The Hundred Years War,* W. B. Wells, trans. (1951), examines the impact of the war on the French civil population. Philippe Contamine, *Guerre, état, et société à la fin du moyen âge: Études sur les armées des rois de France, 1337–1494* (1972), is the most important study to date of the war from the French point of view. The essays in Kenneth Fowler, ed., *The Hundred Years War* (1971), and H. J. Hewitt, *The Organization of War Under Edward III, 1338–1362* (1966), examine the relationship between society and its spokesmen, and a government committed to a war of aggrandizement on the Continent. John Barnie, *War in Medieval English Society: Social Values in the Hundred Years War, 1337–1399* (1974), is a perceptive study of the ways in which the English government sought to gain public support for its French war.

Fortifications. Some basic assumptions of Sidney Toy, *Castles: A Short History of Fortifications from 1600 B.C. to A.D. 1600* (1939), have been modified by archaeological discoveries of the last four decades. William Anderson, *Castles of Europe from Charlemagne to the Renaissance* (1970), must be consulted for the numerous illustrations—many never before reproduced—assembled by the collaborator, Wim Swaan. Wolfgang Müller-Wiener, *Castles of the Crusaders,* J. Maxwell Brownjohn, trans. (1966), is an admirable survey. Philip Warner, *Sieges of the Middle Ages* (1968), is a good introduction to the topic.

Arms and armor. Two excellent studies are Claude Blair, *European Armour Circa 1066 to Circa 1700*

568

(1959); and Paul Martin, *Armour and Weapons*, René North, trans. (1968). A useful introduction on firearms is W. Y. Carman, *A History of Firearms from Earliest Times to 1914* (1955). The most definitive study to date is James R. Partington, *A History of Greek Fire and Gunpowder* (1960). See also Bryan H. St. John O'Neil, *Castles and Cannon: A Study of Early Artillery Fortification in England* (1960).

JOHN BEELER

[See also **Arms and Armor; Barbarians, Invasions of; Cannon; Castles and Fortifications; Cavalry, European; Chivalry, Orders of; Crusades; Feudalism; Fief; Hastings, Battle of; Hide; Hundred Years War; Knights and Knight Service; Lance; Lombards, Kingdom of; Ministerials; Normans and Normandy; Poitiers, Battle of; Swords and Daggers; Thegn; Vikings; Visigoths.**]

WARNERIUS OF BASEL (*d.* 1050), a cleric, perhaps abbot of Basel. Nothing is known about his life. He left two major works: *Synodicus,* a poem on the Old and New Testaments based on the Eclogues of Theodulus, and the *Paraclitus,* an elegiac dialogue between a sinner and Divine Grace. There are two hagiographies also attributed to Warnerius, the life of St. Adalbert and the life of St. Aegidius (Giles).

BIBLIOGRAPHY

Barthélemy Hauréau, *Notices et extraits de quelques manuscrits latins de la Bibliothèque nationale,* VI (1892); Max Manitius, *Geschichte der lateinischen Literatur des Mittelalters* (1911).

NATHALIE HANLET

WARS OF THE ROSES, a series of civil battles fought in England between 1455 and 1487 that arose from characteristic difficulties in the late medieval system of government.

The regular income of fifteenth-century English kings from crown lands, prerogatives, and customs was too small to finance a standing army, a national police force, or a large bureaucracy. Parliament was reluctant to supplement this income by taxation, often exhorting the king to "live of his own," something that only Edward IV succeeded in doing—and that only for a few years with the aid of a French pension. To rule the country, and especially to secure justice and order in the provinces, the king

had to depend upon the nobility, some sixty peers and a larger number of lesser, untitled landowners who exerted their authority in the areas of their respective holdings. None of these lords held such complete sway over a definable region that they could set themselves up in lasting opposition to royal power: their lands were scattered and were held in different degrees of feudal tenure that made them vulnerable to the intricacies of law and inheritance. The maintenance of general stability, the control of the frequent disputes among magnates, and a fair distribution of the prizes within the crown's prerogative all required an active, fairly intelligent, respected monarch. Politics, for fifteenth-century England, was the operation of this interdependency between kings and nobles. To be effective, government had to be cooperative.

HENRY VI

The Wars of the Roses started because this system broke down in a characteristic way. The accidents of birth to which a hereditary monarchy is subject produced in the Lancastrian Henry VI (*r.* 1422–1461, 1470–1471) a king of considerable piety, questionable intelligence, sporadic industry in worldly affairs, and no political or military talent. Lacking a reliable guardian of national stability and justice, men had to protect their interests by their own efforts. Lesser men did this by seeking the protection of greater, thus generating the growth of armed private retinues that could quickly extend any quarrel entered into by either retainer or lord. The greater lords sought to dominate the king, bending the machinery of government to their own service and provoking the anxiety of rivals who were excluded from crown favors. There ensued a breakdown of order, bitter efforts to dislodge factions in power, shifting alliances as men sought greater leverage, and private wars between factions. The final results were civil war and changes of dynasty, but these were reached slowly. The lords were reluctant to push their disputes into armed conflict involving the king himself, and even more reluctant to solve the problem by deposing him.

An explosion of discontent among the commons in 1450 demonstrated the unpopularity and ineffectiveness of Henry VI's regime. Anger over domestic injustices and the recent expulsion of the English from northern France led to several riotous incidents in which mobs murdered the king's favorite, the duke of Suffolk, and three other crown ministers. A Kentish rebellion led by Jack Cade occupied London for some days. These events effected no reform, however. Suffolk's place at the king's side was promptly taken by Edmund Beaufort, duke of Somerset, and soon challenged by Richard, duke of York. The quarrel between these two marked the next five years.

As descendant of Edward III through Lionel of Clarence and the Mortimer line, York felt he should be recognized as heir presumptive to the childless king. His feeling may have been the more anxious since Somerset, the senior male of the Beaufort descent from John of Gaunt, could be suspected of cherishing a similar claim. As a royal duke and the wealthiest magnate in the kingdom, York was entitled to a dominant place on the king's council. As lieutenant of Ireland and former commander in Normandy (replaced by Somerset), he was owed large sums for his services. York was aggrieved at Henry VI's generosity to his favorites and Somerset's ready access to crown revenues; he, moreover, detested the man he held responsible for the loss of France. Twice he tried to remove Somerset and reform the government, through parliamentary maneuver in 1450–1451 and in a military confrontation at Dartford in 1452. A better opportunity arose during the insanity of Henry VI (August 1453–December 1454). Although the queen, Margaret of Anjou, tried to assume the regency, York managed to have himself declared protector and head of the council.

York's first failures arose from lack of support from other lords; his success in achieving the protectorate came from an alliance with the Neville earls of Salisbury and Warwick. Through Henry VI's reign, Neville power in the north of England had gradually increased at the expense of the Percys of Northumberland. By 1453 this rivalry had produced a bloody clash between the Neville and Percy retinues, the most outrageous of a number of feuds that the weak government of Henry VI permitted in outlying districts of the realm. When Somerset quarreled with Warwick over lands forming part of the countess of Warwick's inheritance, the two rivalries became superimposed. The private northern war of Percy and Neville coalesced with and reinforced the struggle between Somerset and York over Henry VI's government.

Henry VI's recovery from insanity terminated the protectorate, threw York and the Nevilles out of office, and restored Somerset to power. Somerset called a great council to meet at Leicester in May 1455, to provide for the king's safety. York and the Nevilles, alarmed, gathered troops and intercepted the court at St. Albans. The subsequent fighting (22 May), the first open battle of the Wars of the Roses, was a half-hour melee producing a Yorkist victory when Somerset and Henry Percy, the earl of Northumberland, fell among the sixty slain.

St. Albans, settling nothing, ushered in another five years of rivalry. A second brief Yorkist protectorate followed the battle. Henry, putty to the strongest personality near him, was willing to retain York as chief councilor, and tried in various touching ways to reconcile his bickering peerage. Queen Margaret took the opposite line: anxious for the inheritance of her newly born son, Prince Edward, she rejected York and welded together a fanatical Lancastrian party that included the heirs of those killed at St. Albans. She moved the court from London to the Lancastrian Midlands, and in 1459 called a great council to meet in Coventry to pass indictments against York and his friends. The latter again amassed troops. After an indecisive battle between royalist troops and Salisbury at Blore Heath (23 September 1459), Henry VI's army confronted York and the Nevilles at Ludford Bridge on 12–13 October. Here some of Warwick's men, learning that they were to oppose the king, deserted, and the Yorkist leaders were obliged to flee: York to Ireland; his son Edward of March, along with the Neville earls, to Calais. A month later Parliament declared the Yorkist leaders to be rebels, their lives and lands forfeit.

This threat forced the Yorkists into decisive response. It also provoked greater support among the nobility for the Yorkists, hitherto a narrow faction. When Edward of March and the Nevilles returned to England in the summer of 1460, they were welcomed in Kent and allowed to control London, and won the Battle of Northampton (10 July). After the latter they captured Henry VI and took over the government in his name. York himself, however, drastically changed the stakes of the struggle when, returning from Ireland in October, he claimed the crown as his by right, condemning Henry VI and his Lancastrian predecessors as usurpers. This move, the first overt introduction of the dynastic issue, was also the first claim to the crown in English history on a purely hereditary basis, and the first assertion that such a claim was indefeasible: "Though right rest for a time and be put to silence, yet it rotteth not nor shall it perish." Despite the absence of the most ardent Lancastrians (regrouping in the north with Margaret), York could not carry his claim. When the judges declared the issue beyond their learning, the lords were forced to arrange a compromise. Recognizing both York's pedigree and their own oaths of loyalty to an anointed king, they devised the Act of Accord that declared Henry VI king for his natural life and made York his heir. Moving north to oppose the Lancastrians, York was defeated and killed in the Battle of Wakefield (30 December).

EDWARD IV

The crown that York's followers declined to give him in October was freely bestowed upon his son Edward of March five months later. March's judgment and timing were shrewder than his father's. Circumstances also forced the Yorkists' hand. Although March won the Battle of Mortimer's Cross (3 February 1461) in Wales, Warwick lost a second battle at St. Albans (17 February) against a marauding force brought south by Margaret. In losing, Warwick also lost the person of Henry VI and thereby all legitimacy for the Yorkist government. Taking advantage of London's refusal to admit Margaret for fear of sack by her army, the Yorkists seized control of the capital, revived the legitimist claim to the crown, and installed March as King Edward IV on 4 March. The new king's asserted authority was secured by his victory over Margaret's forces at Towton on 29 March, in the largest, longest, and bloodiest battle of the Wars of the Roses.

This first phase of the Wars of the Roses is a history of blundering but forceful aristocrats attempting to cope with the effect of a blundering but weak king until a shrewd opportunist rewrote the script on a claim of legitimism enforced by military success and eventual parliamentary confirmation of his title. Discontents lingered that could lead to renewal of the conflict. Edward IV and Warwick needed three years to crush lingering pockets of Lancastrian opposition; and although Henry VI was captured and put in the Tower, Margaret and her son remained at large. Open warfare need not have recurred, and when it did in 1469–1471, it differed in character and cause from the first phase of the wars.

Far fewer lords participated in the second phase than had in the battles that ended at Towton. Edward IV tried, with slow but growing success, to restore the authority and financial solvency of the crown, to reconcile old opponents by reversing attainders, and to quell the disorders and feuds Henry VI had permitted. Renewal of the war stemmed less from justifiable complaint about bad government and more from the disappointed ambition and vanity of two Yorkists: Warwick and Edward's brother, George, duke of Clarence. The will-o'-the-wisp Clarence felt he was kept short of money, prevented from marrying as he wished, and denied influence in the government. Warwick was incommoded by Edward IV's marriage to Elizabeth Woodville, which introduced her large family as a major new faction in court politics and the aristocratic marriage market, and more crucially snubbed when Edward's foreign policy in favor of Burgundy thwarted Warwick's interests in France.

Warwick and Clarence combined in a series of plots that led to two minor battles (Edgecote, July 1469; Losecote Field, March 1470) and a brief attempt to rule England with Edward as puppet. Then, driven out of England and denied access to Calais, they took refuge in France. With the help of Louis XI, Warwick established an alliance with the exiled Queen Margaret, betrothing his daughter to her son Edward of Lancaster. In September 1470 he returned to England in force. When Warwick's brother John Neville, earl of Montague, unexpectedly changed sides from Edward IV to Warwick, Edward fled to the Burgundian county of Holland, Warwick restored Henry VI to the throne and ruled in his name.

In March 1471, Edward IV returned with Burgundian aid. Swift movement, sound strategy, and good luck brought him victory over Warwick at Barnet (14 April) and over Margaret at Tewkesbury (4 May). Since Clarence had been persuaded to return to his brother's allegiance, since Warwick and Montague had died at Barnet and Edward of Lancaster and the remaining male Beauforts had died at Tewkesbury, and since Henry VI was murdered in the Tower after Edward IV's triumphant return to London, the house of Lancaster and its allies were crushed. Edward reigned successfully until his natural death in 1483. He was strong enough to carry out the execution of Clarence (again plotting) and energetic enough to reorganize crown finances and enforce justice in the localities. Had he survived until the majority of his sons, the Wars of the Roses would have had no third phase.

RICHARD III

Edward IV's death in April 1483 left his brother Richard of Gloucester as protector, confronting the

Woodvilles, who had control of the young princes Edward V and Richard of York. Gloucester and the Woodvilles, deeply fearful of each other, maneuvered uneasily until 26 June. Then Gloucester had himself proclaimed Richard III, using a legitimist claim that entailed bastardizing the princes and recognition by the estates of the realm. Woodville hostility to Richard, a sudden change of sides by his chief ally, the duke of Buckingham, and rumors of Richard's murder of the princes led to an abortive rebellion in October. This rebellion sought to place on the throne an obscure descendant of the Beauforts, the exiled Welshman Henry Tudor. Two years later Henry Tudor tried again, and the treachery of two lords cost Richard III his crown and life at Bosworth (22 August 1485).

HENRY VII

The new king, Henry VII, faced a similar rebellion on behalf of a Yorkist heir, John de la Pole, earl of Lincoln; it was settled when Lincoln was killed at the Battle of Stoke (16 June 1487). Although Yorkist heirs and pretenders vexed Henry VII for another decade, Stoke was the last open battle of the wars, and the last occasion in English history when a king faced a rival claimant for his crown in the field.

ASSESSMENT

The Wars of the Roses is a slight misnomer, although no better label has been advanced. "Wars" is an inflated term for some sixteen battles, many mere skirmishes, fought in occasional campaigning that occupied some sixty weeks over thirty-two years. There was no extensive sack or siege. Trade, agriculture, and the arts were unaffected. Loss of life was largely confined to royalty, the greater lords, and their immediate retainers. Even they did not suffer the slaughter once supposed: extinction of noble families continued at a rate normal for the Middle Ages. The "roses" are partly anachronistic. Although the Lancastrian kings included among their badges a red rose, and the house of York had inherited a white one from the Mortimers, these were little used by the combatants themselves. It was Henry VII's invention of the double rose, white superimposed on red, to symbolize the union of houses in his marriage to Elizabeth of York, that spurred later writers to use the roses as emblems of the conflict. Those emblems imply a massiveness and consistency of faction that is belied by the sporadic character of the conflict, the fre-

quent switching of sides, and simple nonparticipation by many peers. The roses also overstress the dynastic issue, which was injected into the conflict by the Yorkist legitimist claim a decade after it started.

Dynastic feeling was the result, not the cause, of the wars, used to justify the accessions of Edward IV, Richard III, and Henry VII, and forming the impetus for interpretation of the wars during the Tudor period. Tudor chroniclers backdated the issues to the usurpation of Henry IV, which disturbed the regular succession of Plantagenet kings, and converted the story of the wars into propaganda for national unity in support of the Tudor dynasty. Imaginative writers turned the propaganda to eloquence and high drama, most notably in Shakespeare's history plays, whose influence long supported a view of the wars as a catastrophic convulsion arising from rival dynastic ambitions. The fifteenth-century jurist Sir John Fortescue was more accurate when he attributed the troubles of Henry VI to the "lack of political rule and governance."

The wars do reveal stress lines in late medieval society. A powerful noble could temporarily pervert the course of local justice and defy or dominate the crown with relative ease. A dispute between magnates could eventually swamp the crown. Once a king's title was challenged, no public law existed that could readily settle the doubt. None of these problems seriously arises with a strong king: the threat of overmighty subjects and rivals exists only in the presence of an undermighty ruler. Even with an ineffective or unpopular king, it was far easier for a small body of determined opponents to make an immediate impact than for them to achieve the wide support necessary for permanent effect. Except when a crucial personage was killed, many military victories and shifts in power were mere seesawing.

Cumulatively, however, the wars did produce two significant developments: (1) the aristocracy's ability to disturb national life by force was curbed, partly through their own reluctance to take further risks and partly through the ruthless policies of the first two Tudor kings; (2) the authority of Parliament was strengthened. Whatever their claims and victories at the moment of accession, Edward IV, Richard III, and Henry VII each found it necessary to have their possession of the crown ratified. God might make a king, through inheritance or military success, but the king also required sanction from the kingdom, and this could be given by the estates of the realm in formal act of Parliament.

BIBLIOGRAPHY

William H. Dunham, Jr., and Charles T. Wood, "The Right to Rule in England: Depositions and the Kingdom's Authority, 1327–1485," in *American Historical Review*, **81** (1976); Anthony Goodman, *The Wars of the Roses: Military Activity and English Society, 1452–97* (1981); R. A. Griffiths, "Duke Richard of York's Intentions in 1450 and the Origins of the Wars of the Roses," in *Journal of Medieval History*, **1** (1975), and *The Reign of Henry VI* (1981); DeLloyd J. Guth, *Late-Medieval England, 1377–1485* (1976), annotated bibliography of printed sources and scholarship through 1974; Michael A. Hicks, *False, Fleeting, Perjur'd Clarence: George, Duke of Clarence, 1449–78* (1980); Jack R. Lander, *Crown and Nobility, 1450–1509* (1976) and *Government and Community: England, 1450–1509* (1980); Charles D. Ross, *The Wars of the Roses: A Concise History* (1976), *Patronage, Pedigree, and Power in Later Medieval England* (1979), and *Richard III* (1981); Peter Saccio, *Shakespeare's English Kings: History, Chronicle, and Drama* (1977); Bertram P. Wolffe, *Henry VI* (1981).

PETER SACCIO

[See also **Cade, Jack/Cade's Rebellion; England: 1216–1485; Fortescue, Sir John; Henry VI of England; Richard III.**]

WARTBURGKRIEG (Contest at the Wartburg). A collection of strophes from the mid thirteenth century forms the nucleus of the *Wartburgkrieg*. Klingsor, a figure apparently based on Clinschor in Wolfram's *Parzival*, challenges Wolfram von Eschenbach, who solves each of a series of riddles. Charges of black magic and consorting with the devil abound.

Around this central complex several elaborations developed. One of these, the "Praise of Princes," was probably conceived as the first half of a structure concluded by riddles, with the contest of singers serving as the common band. Heinrich von Ofterdingen claims the duke of Austria is more praiseworthy and more generous than any three other princes and challenges any singer to dispute his claim, the loser to forfeit his life like a thief (be hanged). Walther von der Vogelweide and the "Tugendhafter Schreiber" (virtuous scribe) enter the lists, Wolfram and Reinmar von Zweter are called

as judges, Biterolf joins in, Walther wins, but Ofterdingen asks that Klingsor be called to defend him. Klingsor's religious allegories are explicated by Wolfram, who proves the superiority of lay piety to scholastic erudition. In two manuscripts Walther returns between riddles to praise a solution.

Hedda Ragotzky derives the nucleus from the literary image of Wolfram as a pious, self-taught layman; this image was used by later *Spruchdichter* (didactic poets) to reinforce their self-image. Klingsor acquires the traits assigned Wolfram by Gottfried von Strassburg. Burghart Wachinger traces the development of subsequent accretions to the nucleus and puts them in relation to the developing self-awareness of the *Spruchdichter*.

Numerous other disputations and tales accompany the central complex, and Ragotzky sees its openness and lack of coherence (exemplified by the wide divergencies from manuscript to manuscript) as a genre characteristic. "Zabulon's Book" and, more remarkably, *Lohengrin* start as polemic dialogues, but rapidly turn into narratives. The polemic dialogue that introduces Kalogrenant's tale in Hartmann von Aue's *Iwein* gave rise to a literary debate poem; it may have also influenced the use of *Wartburgkrieg* material in *Lohengrin*, just as Walther's political songs may have inspired the comparison of Austria and Thuringia in the "Praise of Princes."

In the Jena Song Codex (1330's or 1340's) one finds two groups of strophes appended to their melodies, that is, the same sort of arrangement that underlies the rest of the codex. The two melodies (and the strophic forms) are in the tradition of didactic song and remain relatively constant over several centuries. References to a singers' contest are clearest in the Colmar Song Codex from the 1470's, especially in the new material. The Meistersinger clearly viewed the complex as an analogue and model for their own practice. In addition, the strife between the singers was presented as a part of Thuringian history in a hagiology of Elizabeth of Hungary (written 1289 to 1297, probably based on earlier accounts) and recurs subsequently in various Thuringian chronicles. Richard Wagner's *Tannhäuser* is based in part and indirectly on the *Wartburgkrieg*.

BIBLIOGRAPHY

Horst Brunner, *Die alten Meister: Studien zu Überlieferung und Rezeption der mittelhochdeutschen Sang-*

573

spruchdichter im Spätmittelalter und in der frühen Neuzeit (1975); Thomas Cramer, *Lohengrin: Edition und Untersuchungen* (1971); Erdmute Pickerodt-Uthleb, *Die Jenaer Liederhandschrift: Metrische und musikalische Untersuchungen* (1975), 195–210, 240–262, 507–508; Hedda Ragotzky, *Studien zur Wolfram-Rezeption: Die Entstehung und Verwandlung der Wolfram-Rolle in der deutschen Literatur des 13. Jahrhunderts* (1971), 45–91; Burghart Wachinger, *Sängerkrieg: Untersuchungen zur Spruchdichtung des 13. Jahrhunderts* (1973), 1–89, 299–319; Herbert Wolf, "Zum Wartburgkrieg Überlieferungsverhältnisse, Inhalts- und Gestaltungswandel der Dichtersage," in *Helmut Beumann*, ed., *Festschrift für Walter Schlesinger,* I (1973), 13–30.

HUBERT HEINEN

[See also **German Literature: Lyric; Gottfried von Strassburg; Hartmann von Aue; Lohengrin; Reinmar von Zweter; Tannhäuser; Walther von der Vogelweide; Wolfram von Eschenbach.**]

WĀSIṬ, a medieval city in south-central Iraq. The date of its foundation is disputed: work on the city probably began in 702; al-Ḥajjāj, its founder, had certainly taken up residence there by 703; and extant coins from the city's mint begin to appear in the following year.

Al-Ḥajjāj resolved to build a new city in Iraq after he had crushed the very serious rebellion of Ibn al-Ashᶜath in 701. This uprising, as well as earlier developments in the Second Civil War, had demonstrated that the Umayyads could not rely upon regional tribal contingents to maintain order in Iraq. Henceforth, Syrian troops would have to rule the province almost as if it were occupied enemy territory. To this end a garrison town was needed to keep the troops isolated from the local population, yet strategically positioned to respond to any trouble. The site al-Ḥajjāj chose was on the west bank of the Tigris River, approximately equidistant from Basra to the southeast, Al-Kufa to the west, and Al-Ahwāz in Khūzistān to the east— hence the name (or so we are told) Wāsiṭ (middle).

From 703 until the end of the Umayyad caliphate, Wāsiṭ was the capital and principal urban center of Iraq. Construction of the city cost over 40 million dirhams and took several years to complete. It was provided with a palace called Al-Qubba al-Khaḍrāʾ (the green dome) and a great congrega-tional mosque, and its mint soon became the primary producer of Umayyad silver coinage. Efforts to improve agriculture in the surrounding area were largely successful: Wāsiṭ became renowned for its vast groves of fruit trees and date palms and for the fertility of its soil. Agricultural production, combined with textile manufacturing, boatbuilding, and overland and maritime commerce, made Wāsiṭ a major economic as well as military center.

The city was at first populated only by Syrian military contingents and a small minority of Turkish tribesmen. But as Wāsiṭ became more important socially and economically, it became impossible to maintain this isolation. After the death of al-Ḥajjāj in 714, the exclusive principle was gradually abandoned. The city's population in time became very mixed, and Wāsiṭ eventually merged with Kaskar, its sister city across the Tigris.

Wāsiṭ expanded and prospered despite frequent destructive setbacks. It was ravaged by the plague several times under the Umayyads, withstood an eleven-month siege before surrendering to an Abbasid army in 750, and changed hands on several occasions during the internal conflicts of the early Abbasid caliphate. It was attacked several times during the Zanj rebellion (869–883), and in the centuries that followed, Wāsiṭ, like all of lower Mesopotamia, suffered repeated damage to its agricultural infrastructure as the declining power of the central authority made it difficult to maintain irrigation works or to control the depredations of bedouin raiders.

The city's economic importance nevertheless continued, and medieval geographers who visited it were almost all favorably impressed by its prosperity and the vigor of its intellectual life. Yāqūt Al-Rūmi attests that in his time, the early thirteenth century, Wāsiṭ was still a sizable town; and even after the Mongol invasion travelers praised it for its fine buildings and immense palm groves. In the late fourteenth century, Timur (Tamerlane) considered Wāsiṭ important enough to keep a strong garrison there.

The final decline of the city may be traced to the fifteenth century, when the course of the Tigris began to shift at Kūt al-ᶜAmāra, forty kilometers (twenty-four miles) to the northwest. This diverted the flow of the river to a bed further east and ultimately proved disastrous to Wāsiṭ. By the seventeenth century the town was a small one standing amidst arid wasteland, and by the early nineteenth the site was a desolate ruin.

BIBLIOGRAPHY
Keppel A. C. Creswell, *Early Muslim Architecture*, 2nd ed., I (1969), 132–138, and a full bibliography; Fuad Safar, *Wāsiṭ: The Sixth Season's Excavations* (1945).

LAWRENCE I. CONRAD

[See also Ḥajjāj ibn Yūsuf al-Thaqafī, al-; Iraq; Umayyads.]

WĀSIṬĪ, YAḤYĀ IBN MAḤMŪD AL- (*fl.* 1237), the spirited illustrator of the so-called Schefer Ḥarīrī (Paris, Bibliothèque Nationale, MS arabe 5847), one of the finest surviving manuscripts of al-Ḥarīrī's eleventh-century Arabic literary classic, the *Maqāmāt* (Assemblies).

Of the artist himself, nothing is known beyond the few facts that emerge from the manuscript colophon: the name al-Wāsiṭī indicates that he was associated with the town of Wāsiṭ in southern Iraq;

Bell Harry tower of Canterbury Cathedral, late 15th century.
PHOTO: WIM SWAAN

Scholars at the public library of Ḥulwān. Miniature by al-Wāsiṭī from the *Maqāmāt* of al-Ḥarīrī, mid 13th century. PARIS, BIBLIO-THÈQUE NATIONALE, MS ARABE 5837, fol. 5v

he was both the scribe and the illustrator of the manuscript, and he completed his work on Saturday, 3 May 1237. Pious formulas at the end of the colophon suggest that he was a Shiite Muslim.

His paintings, which include ninety-nine miniatures and a double frontispiece, are distinguished by the sheer variety of their subjects and compositions, ranging from bustling city scenes and desert vignettes to a visionary island landscape. In their visual expressiveness and narrative subtlety they attest to the flourishing urban culture of the thirteenth-century Arab world.

BIBLIOGRAPHY
Oleg Grabar, *The Illustrations of the Maqamat* (1984).

MIRIAM ROSEN

[See also Islam Art and Architecture; Manuscript Illumination, Islamic (with illustration).]

WASTELL, JOHN (*fl.* 1485–1515), a renowned master architect of late medieval England. Wastell was responsible for a great number of important building projects. Apart from many fine Perpendicular-style parish churches, such as Lavenham, his masterpieces are the central tower of Canterbury Cathedral (known as Bell Harry) and a substantial portion of Henry VII's King's College Chapel, Cambridge.

BIBLIOGRAPHY

John H. Harvey, *English Mediaeval Architects: A Biographical Dictionary Down to 1550* (1954, rev. ed. 1984), 316–325; Robert Willis and John W. Clark, *Architectural History of the University of Cambridge*, I (1886), 608–614; Francis Woodman, *The Architectural History of Canterbury Cathedral* (1981).

STEPHEN GARDNER

[See also **Architect, Status of; Gothic, Perpendicular.**]

WATER MILL. See **Mills.**

WATERMARKS. Manufacturing paper in the late medieval West involved dipping a frame or mold fitted with a screen into a tub filled with the raw material of paper. The screen left its imprint on the finished sheets. From the late thirteenth century, papermakers added characteristic designs or watermarks to the screens and, therefore, the finished paper. Since the molds wore out rapidly, the watermarks changed. Typically, watermarks might look like a crown, an anchor, or some similar emblem; sometimes the emblem included lettering. By comparing watermarks of a paper manuscript or printed book with specialized repertories, scholars can often identify the date and place of the paper's manufacture. Paper in the West without watermarks is usually of Spanish or Arab origin.

BIBLIOGRAPHY

Jean Irigoin, "La datation par les filigranes du papier," in *Codicologica*, V: *Les matériaux du livre manuscrit* (1980).

MICHAEL MCCORMICK

[See also **Paper, Introduction of; Writing Materials, Western European.**]

WATERWORKS. During the Middle Ages water was an extremely important resource, as it is today. It was needed not only to maintain daily health and yearly agricultural production, but also to support industrial processes and such necessary activities as the extinction of fire. It was a means of transportation, and, as a by-product, its use could provide a defensive network in case of a military offensive upon a particular area. But as beneficial as water was to medieval societies, it could prove quite destructive as a result of inundation. The individuals who were responsible for such devices as dams, bridges, and conduits were frequently motivated as much by problems of protection as by those of production. Consequently, entire fluvial systems, particularly in southern Europe, were changed to defend against the ravages of flooding.

EARLY MIDDLE AGES

During the early Middle Ages there are examples that indicate a significant awareness of the need to regulate waters both in the East and in the West. Acting in the Roman tradition, the emperor Justinian (r. 527–565) built a number of underground cisterns to supply the city of Constantinople with water. In Italy the church engaged in projects of reclamation. St. Frediano, the bishop of Lucca (561–589), took steps to drain the Lucchese plain by changing the location of the river Serchio from the east to the west of the city so that it emptied into the sea rather than the Arno. St. Zeno, the bishop of Verona, was renowned for his efforts to protect his city from floods. It is said that in 590 he saved Pistoia from similar difficulties and thereby was named its patron saint.

In addition, the secular powers were at work connecting rivers within their domains to create a more effective transport system. In 793, Charlemagne began the construction of a canal linking the Rhine and the Danube to improve the transfer of military supplies. Although this *fossa carolina* failed because of the incessant rains that washed away its foundations, it points to a conscious concern for the development of a more sophisticated hydraulic system to complement a growing network of river ports and coastal harbors in the northern reaches of the Carolingian Empire. Such concern may have been responsible for the initial efforts to reclaim the peat bogs along the coast of the North Sea during the eighth and ninth centuries.

MUSLIM CONTRIBUTIONS

From the middle of the ninth century until as late as 1300, the Islamic world contributed greatly to the development of medieval waterworks. The noria or hydraulic wheel, driven either by animal power or by the propulsive force of the water alone, spread into Spain and Sicily to activate irrigation systems that produced such new commodities for the West as sugar, rice, and oranges. Accompanying this mechanism was the process of digging wells deeper than previously known. Carefully located Muslim dams, whose subsidiary canals were furnished with sluices to remove silt, provide evidence of the traditional methods of construction employed by the Romans and Sasanians—the installation of heavy, durable masonry held together by mortar and sometimes metallic connectors. Muslim hydraulic engineers thus transmitted older procedures which could be used to produce such innovations as the first known arch dam, built by the Mongols at Kebar during the reign of Maḥmūd Ghāzān Khan (1295–1304), or the arched reservoir dam built by the Christians of Spain at Almansa in the late fourteenth century. These advances in the storage of water overcame the difficulties of the Roman gravity dam, which depended upon its sheer weight to direct water pressure vertically downward toward its base. The thinner arch dam, composed of a series of arches firmly secured at their ends, carried such pressure laterally toward the sides of the structure; the arched dam, essentially a hybrid form, remained heavy, but its curvature still added safety and stability.

ELEVENTH TO FOURTEENTH CENTURIES

After experiencing a population boom during the eleventh century, Western Europe in general responded to the need to perfect its hydraulic systems. Between 1100 and 1300 the waterways of the territory of Pistoia assumed their modern configuration. Because autumn rains in particular created raging torrents that carried mud and debris from the Apennines into the valley below, watercourses such as the Bure, the Brana, and the Stella were diverted away from their natural outlets south of the city into conduits further downstream, so that the plain could be converted from a quagmire into a fruitful prairie. Toward the end of the thirteenth century, Prato, Pistoia's eastern neighbor, had developed on the right bank of the Bisenzio a network of artificial canals to supply water

more efficiently to its mills. With the city of Prato at its center, this complex of some twenty square miles (*ca.* 48–49 sq km) also acted as a means of defense against sudden attack. In northern Europe, demographic growth in the Netherlands provided the stimulus for the reclamation and settlement of peat bogs on a scale far more extensive than what had occurred during the eighth and ninth centuries. By the early fourteenth century all of the Rijnland, or the area making up the delta formed at the mouths of the Rhine and Maas rivers, had been reclaimed by dikes and sluices to create polders that supported at least 3,250 households, or an estimated population of 13,000 inhabitants. As early as 1018, Count Diederik III (995–1039) used the large network of ditches at Vlaardingen, south of the Rijnland, to repel the imperial forces of Henry II—a concrete example of the tactical effectiveness of waterworks.

Urban water supply. Within the medieval cities of Western Europe, water was often supplied through pipes. In 1153 the cathedral and priory of Canterbury were supplied with water by means of lead pipes originating beyond the north wall of the city. They fed not only settling tanks, but also a fishpond that had a secondary function of flushing latrines. During the reign of Philip II Augustus (1179–1223), lead pipes began to convey water into the city of Paris from a reservoir at Pré-St.-Gervais. Medieval Nuremberg had water mains made of hollow tree trunks and special machines for boring them.

In cities where water was particularly scarce, the construction of aqueducts and fountains was of the utmost importance. Prior to the fourteenth century the Tuscan city of Siena, lacking natural watercourses, was fed by six major subterranean systems so that its inhabitants could properly manufacture its woolen cloth, prepare its leather, extinguish its fires, and be provided with potable water. The conduits, originating in numerous distant springs (*vene*) surrounding the city, had dimensions as large as six by three feet; frequently they were lined with brick to guarantee the best hygienic conditions. During the fourteenth century the complex was improved, while the government provided subsidies in money and materials for anyone wishing to build wells and cisterns either in the city or in its boroughs.

In 1469, Siena undertook the construction of a reservoir dam designed to create an artificial lake, which would be used to provide the city with fish. The Sienese, unfortunately, had no experience in building such large dams, and the design was therefore inappropriate. The dam, located in the remote Bruna Valley northwest of Grosseto, cracked in 1492, and the whole project failed.

Bridges. The increase in trade during the central Middle Ages greatly stimulated the construction of bridges. The surviving names for French bridges are five times more plentiful between 987 and 1100 than in the century before. After 1100, moreover, stone rather than wooden bridges became the norm as some of the widest and most difficult rivers were spanned. During the course of the twelfth century alone, the Loire, for example, saw new constructions at Saumur, Orléans, and Beaugency.

These as well as other European bridges were built on artificial islands called starlings. This method of construction was not without problems. The piers of a medieval bridge were normally close together, which increased the rate of flow of water through the restricted passages remaining. This rapidly flowing water could, and often did, scour away the material at the base of the artificial islands on which the piers rested.

By the fourteenth century, if not earlier, this problem was solved by the use of the cofferdam, which allowed the piers to be founded on bedrock or on stakes driven into the earth well below the bed of the river. The cofferdam is a watertight enclosure from which the water may be removed, thus exposing the riverbed to air. Most medieval cofferdams were formed by constructing two rows of interlaced piles and filling the intervening space with clay mortar to make the structure impermeable. It would appear that the water within was removed manually by buckets rather than by the pumps drawn and described by the Sienese engineer Mariano Taccola during the early fifteenth century. These devices were apparently too inefficient or, at least, too costly.

Cofferdams thus permitted the building of bridges that were safer and more durable. Nevertheless, pier thickness remained a problem for bridges even into the early modern period. Although the piers could have been built with a thinner frame to support vertical loads, the fear of rushing water, particularly during periods of inundation, kept them large. When the famed Ponte Vecchio at Florence was reconstructed between 1335 and 1345, the cumbersome semicircular vaults used by the Romans were replaced by three segmental arches that permitted greater spans. It was not until the latter half of the eighteenth century, however,

that the width of its piers was systematically reduced by Jean-Rodolphe Perronet (1708–1794).

Canals for transport. The Chinese were the first to develop river haulage in any sustained manner by their work on the Grand Canal from the beginning of the seventh through the thirteenth century. By comparison, water transport in the West was backward until increased commerce provided an impetus for change. By the end of the thirteenth century, diversionary dams throughout Western Europe were equipped with stanches or flash locks, which gave boats a means of passing through unimpeded.

In the meantime, the canals along the North Sea were enlarged and furnished with sluice gates that, when raised by windlasses, permitted the entrance of vessels. Soon two sluice gates were used to enclose a basin and thereby form a lock that would enable a vessel to overcome differences of water level. Locks such as these appear in Flanders and Holland from the twelfth century onward; their construction at Spaarndam, Vreeswijk, Delfshaven, Damme, and Schiedam during the late fourteenth century prove that by that time they had become quite common. Between 1391 and 1398 the Stecknitz Canal was built, connecting Lübeck with Lauenburg on the Elbe to form a passageway between the North Sea and the Baltic. For the first time this system utilized locks that overcame differences in the levels of land as well as water.

In Italy there were also significant improvements in water transport. After plans were prepared in 1387 for the construction of the new cathedral at Milan, the Naviglio Grande, originally an irrigation canal extending from the Ticino River to a basin outside the city, was used to move the building stone. In order to facilitate delivery, the canal was eventually connected to an old moat that passed near the cathedral. The water level of the moat was several feet above that of the canal, however, and it was not until 1438 that a lock was installed to surmount the difficulty. This prompted the enlargement of the moat, which came to be known as the Naviglio Interno. In 1492, Leonardo da Vinci began work on the construction of six new locks for this expanded waterway and soon produced the swinging miter gates that thereafter became a standard feature for European locks in general.

Conclusion. The design of medieval waterworks was often dictated by local conditions, with little, if any, outside influence to stimulate or regulate change. The achievements of the Chinese in canal construction during a period of some 700 years remained unknown in the West. The land reclamation of the Netherlands was an indigenous development that had no importance for the Italians, who contended with an entirely different geographical terrain. Even the hydraulic systems within the Italian region of Tuscany differed one from the other despite their proximity. Outside of common techniques developed for the essentials of bridge building or stanch construction, hydraulic achievements were basically isolated and without pattern.

There were, however, exceptions that cannot be ignored. The church or any strong secular power could act as a vehicle for transferring methods and ideas. Although the Muslims possessed an unstable political structure, their culture nonetheless served as an agency for conveying the principles of Roman and Sasanian dam construction to the Christians of Spain and the Mongols of Central Asia. Toward the end of the twelfth century, the undershot waterwheel, utilized for mills located on the banks of navigable rivers, appeared in southern France, particularly at Toulouse. By the middle of the thirteenth century, the city of Florence had adopted this mechanism for its major rivers while incorporating the overshot "French" mill as an apparatus to grind grain on smaller streams. During the second half of the fourteenth century, this latter development led to the novelty of combining the gearing system of the new mills with the older horizontal waterwheel. The notebooks of Mariano Taccola served as a means for the transmission of a hydraulic device from the East to the West. Copies made of his work caused the chain or "Tartar" pump to become common throughout Europe by the sixteenth century. Thus, despite the local individuality of medieval waterworks, there existed the necessary circumstances for the spread of new techniques.

BIBLIOGRAPHY

Nicholas Adams, "Architecture for Fish: The Sienese Dam on the Bruna River—Structures and Designs, 1468–ca. 1530," in *Technology and Culture*, 25 (1984); Duccio Balestracci and Gabriella Piccinni, *Siena nel Trecento: Assetto urbano e strutture edilizie* (1977), 145–149, 165–175; Marjorie Nice Boyer, *Medieval French Bridges: A History* (1976), chaps. 3, 10; R. J. Forbes, "Hydraulic Engineering and Sanitation," in Charles Singer et al., eds., *A History of Technology*, II (1957) 663–694; J. A. García-Diego, "The Chapter on Weirs in the Codex of Juanelo Turriano: A Question of Authorship," in *Technology and Culture*, 17 (1976); Thomas F. Glick, *Islamic and Christian Spain in the Early Middle Ages* (1979), 68–78, 96–99, 217–247; S. B. Hamilton, "Bridges," in Singer *et. al.*, III (1957), 417–437; Ahmad Y. al-Hassan and Donald R. Hill, *Islamic Technology: An Illustrated History* (1986), 31–54, 80–91, 235–244; William H. McNeill, "The Eccentricity of Wheels; or, Eurasian Transportation in Historical Perspective," in *American Historical Review*, 92 (1987); John Muendel, "The 'French' Mill in Medieval Tuscany," in *Journal of Medieval History*, 10 (1984); Elena Paderi, "Variazioni fisiografiche del bacino di Bientina e della pianura lucchese durante i periodi storici," in *Memorie della Società geografica italiana*, 17 (1932); Renato Piattoli, *Lo statuto dell'arte dei padroni dei mulini sulla destra del fiume Bisenzio (1296)* (1936); Frank D. Prager and Gustina Scaglia, *Mariano Taccola and His Book "De ingeneis"* (1972), pt. II, chaps. 2–4; Natale Rauty, "Sistemazioni fluviali e bonifica della pianura pistoiese durante l'età comunale," in *Bullettino storico pistoiese*, 69 (1967); Pierre Riché, *Daily Life in the World of Charlemagne*, Jo Ann McNamara, trans. (1978), 22, 34; Germain Sicard, *Les moulins de Toulouse au moyen âge: Aux origines des sociétés anonymes* (1953), 29–52; A. W. Skempton, "Canals and River Navigations Before 1750," in Singer *et. al.*, III (1957), 438–470; Norman Smith, *A History of Dams* (1971), 63–71, 87–93, 102–111; William H. TeBrake, *Medieval Frontier: Culture and Ecology in Rijnland* (1985), chaps. 3, 6.

JOHN MUENDEL

[See also **Agriculture and Nutrition; Castles and Fortifications; Flanders and the Low Countries; Florence; Irrigation; Italy, Rise of Towns in; Lübeck; Milan; Mills; Nuremberg; Reclamation of the Land; Roads and Bridges, Western European; Sicily, Kingdom of; Siena; Spain, Christian-Muslim Relations; Surveying; Toulouse; Travel and Transport, Western European; Venice.**]

WAUQUELIN, JEAN (d. 1452), bookseller and author, was born in Picardy and established by 1430 in Mons, where he composed histories and romances for high members of the Hainaut administration. He was commissioned to produce three works for Philip the Good in 1446 and was named valet de chambre in 1447. By April 1448 Wauquelin had been paid for the transcription of copies for the duke of his prose version of the *Alexander Romance*, the first volume of his three-volume translation of an Hainaut chronicle, and his new prose version of the *Romance of Girart de Roussillon*. He probably advised the illuminators of the *Chroniques de Hainaut* (now in Brussels, with a frontispiece attributed to van der Weyden), who had been working since autumn 1447. The other two manuscripts (in Paris and Vienna) were likewise illustrated by teams of established illuminators in Bruges or Brussels. In the four years remaining before his death, Wauquelin provided the duke with translations of a Brabant chronicle and of Giles of Rome's (Egidius Colonna) *De regimene principum,* a prose version of the *Histoire de Hélaine,* and three volumes of a copy of Froissart's chronicle.

BIBLIOGRAPHY

Félix Brassart, "Jehan Wauquelin, traducteur de Jacques de Guise, 1446–1452," in *Souvenirs de la Flandre Wallonne,* 19 (1879); L. M. J. Delaissé, "Les chroniques de Hainaut et l'atelier de Jehan Wauquelin à Mons dans l'histoire de la miniature flamande," in *Bulletin des Musées royaux des beaux arts,* 4 (1955); Ernest Matthieu, "Un artist picard à l'étranger: Jehan Wauquelin, traducteur, historien, et littérateur," in *Mémoires de la Société des antiquaires de Picardie,* 3rd ser., 10 (1889); Antoine de Schryver, "Pour une meilleure orientation à propos de Maitre de Girart de Rousillon," in *Rogier van der Weyden en zijn tijd* (1974); Anne H. van Buren, "New Evidence for Jean Wauquelin's Activity in the *Chroniques de Hainaut* and for the Date of the Miniature," in *Scriptorium,* 26 (1972) and 27 (1973), and "Jean Wauquelin de Mons et la production du livre aux Pays-Bas," in *Publication du Centre européen d'études burgondo-médianes,* 23 (1983).

ANNE HAGOPIAN VAN BUREN

[See also **Alexander Romances; Egidius Colonna; Froissart, Jehan; Manuscript Illumination, European; Picard Literature; Weyden, Rogier van der.**]

WAX TABLETS. The ancient and medieval equivalent of the modern note pad consisted of thin, rectangular boards which could be held in the hand and whose surface was hollowed and filled with colored wax. A stylus was used for writing and erasure. Because of their flexibility, medieval wax tablets were particularly valued for drafting, school exercises, and current record-keeping.

BIBLIOGRAPHY

Reinhard Büll *et al.,* "Wachs als Beschreib- und Siegelstoff: Wachsschreibtafeln und ihre Verwendung," in *Vom Wachs: Hoechster Beiträge zur Kenntnis der Wachse,* 1 (1968), 785–894.

MICHAEL MCCORMICK

[See also **Writing Materials, Western European.**]

WAXTANG I GURGASLANI (or Wakhtang, *ca.* 447—522/523), king of eastern Georgia (K^cart^cli-Iberia). Waχtang was at first a loyal vassal to the Iranian great king Yazdgard II and fought their common Roman enemy in western Georgia. But in 482 he broke with Iran, joined with the *marzpan* (viceroy) of Armenia, Vahan Mamikonian, and in alliance with Byzantium resisted Iranian control. Waχtang's request that the bishop of Mtskheta be elevated to katholikos was granted by Constantinople. The last decades of his reign marked the zenith of the religious unity of K^cart^cli-Iberia, Armenia, and the Byzantine Empire once the Caucasian churches adopted Zeno's *Henotikon* (482) at the Council of Dwin (506). Waχtang's last years were spent at war with Iran. He was driven from his capital, Tbilisi, a town he is reputed to have founded, and forced to flee westward to Lazika, where he died.

BIBLIOGRAPHY

William E. D. Allen, *A History of the Georgian People* (1932, repr. 1971); David M. Lang, *The Georgians* (1966); Cyril Toumanoff, "Christian Caucasia Between Byzantium and Iran: New Light from Old Sources," in *Traditio,* 10 (1954).

RONALD G. SUNY

[See also **Georgia: Political History; Georgian Church and Saints; Henotikon; Tbilisi; Zeno the Isaurian.**]

WEIGHTS AND MEASURES, BYZANTINE. In Byzantium, as in Islam and the West, weights and measures were of fundamental importance for the orderly exchange of goods (as well as coins). The place of these ubiquitous objects in the daily round of commercial transactions is illustrated in the *Book of the Eparch,* a tenth-century compilation of trade ordinances. When a consumer at Constantinople purchased salted fish, pork, vegetables, wax, or nails, the price which he paid for each of these commodities was determined by weight on a steelyard scale. Incense, myrrh, and cinnamon, on the other hand, were sold by weight on a balance scale. In the *Book of the Eparch,* then, two types of weighing implements are mentioned: the steelyard scale, for gross weighing, and the balance scale, for fine weighing. The balance scale was the traditional weighing implement of the east Mediterranean; the steelyard was introduced into this region by the Romans.

A steelyard is an unequal arm balance—a rod consisting of longer and shorter portions. Pans or hooks attached by chains to the shorter section hold the load to be weighed; a counterpoise is suspended from the longer portion, which is provided with engraved scale marks. The counterpoise is moved along the rod until the rod is horizontal; the load's weight is indicated by the scale mark where the counterpoise comes to rest. A popular type of counterpoise among the Romans was the lead-filled statuette or bust weight; they were produced in a variety of forms (including gods, goddesses, and animals). In the early Byzantine period, imperial busts and busts of Athena (Minerva) enjoyed special favor. The latest date assigned to most bust weights is the sixth century; an Athena bust weight survives, however, from a seventh-century shipwreck off the Turkish coast. Its weight, approximately sixteen pounds avoirdupois, reflects the use of steelyards and their counterpoises for gross weighing.

Such employment is further exemplified by the weighing capacity of a steelyard exhibited at the Chichester District Museum in 1978. It weighs a load up to sixty-four Roman pounds or approximately fifty pounds avoirdupois (the Roman pound is usually reckoned at 327.45 grams or 0.7221 pound avoirdupois, but this estimate may be too high; Schilbach's recent study, for example, employs the figure 326.16 grams). Examples of steelyard counterpoises dating from the mid Byzantine period (and later) have been excavated at Corinth; they exhibit a variety of forms, including bell-shaped, globular, and polygonal. Most Byzantine weights from Corinth, however, were intended for use with balance scales; a common type within this group is the disk-shaped weight (found in contexts from the ninth to the twelfth century). Many are inscribed with value symbols. Two groups of marks may be discerned: those indicating value in ounces (weights for commerce) and others relating to value in gold coins (weights for coinage), a dual system that is a continuation of Roman practice.

Prior to the reign of Constantine the Great, weights were issued in accordance with the Roman ponderal system of twelve ounces (unciae) to the pound. In the wake of Constantine's reform of the gold coinage, coin weights were issued based on a nomisma (gold coin) struck at 4.55 grams. By the end of the fourth century, coin weights (exagia)

were in common use along with uncial weights. Both categories often were issued in the form of square (or rectangular) flat weights (round and spherical-shaped weights are also known). Value designations (as well as engraved designs) were regularly filled with silver. Glass exagia were introduced in the sixth century and presumably were manufactured until at least the middle of the seventh century. Glass weights complemented bronze exagia; for, whereas bronze coin weights were used to weigh a quantity of coins, glass weights were employed for weighing a single gold coin or fractional denominations thereof (the semis, a gold coin of one-half weight, and the tremissis, a gold coin of one-third weight).

In the Roman weight system, the libra (pound) occupied a central position; this position was occupied in the Byzantine weight system by the logarike litra (reckoning pound). The logarike litra is a continuation of the libra and is identical with it, as is the oungia (ounce), the twelfth part of the logarike litra, with the Roman uncia (ounce). Subdivisions within the Byzantine weight system are as follows: 1 logarike litra = 12 oungiai = 72 exagia = 1,728 keratia = 6,912 sitokokka. Like the Roman libra, the Byzantine litra may refer to a pound of gold. In conformity with Constantine's coinage reforms, a gold pound (chrysaphike litra) was subdivided as follows: 1 litra = 72 nomismata.

Wheat was purchased in Byzantium by the modios, that is, by the bushel. As a rule the term modios in Byzantine sources signifies the sea bushel or thalassios modios (in weight, 40 logarike litrai); as a measure of capacity the sea bushel was equal to roughly 17 liters. Two smaller measures of capacity are termed modios: the monastery bushel (monasterikos modios = 4/5 thalassios modios, or approximately 13.6 liters) and the tax bushel (annonikos modios = 2/3 thalassios modios, or approximately 12.8 liters). In the later Byzantine period, the term modios also designated a "trade" bushel—a large measure of capacity employed in the grain trade and equal, it seems, to approximately 307.5 liters.

Wine was exchanged in Byzantium by the metron (measure). The largest measure was the sea measure (thalassion metron = 10.2 liters); smaller measures of capacity were the monastery measure (4/5 thalassion metron = 8.2 liters) and the tax measure (2/3 thalassion metron = 6.8 liters). Oil was also purchased by the measure: the sea measure (8.5 liters) and the tax measure (2/3 thalassion metron = 5.6 liters). Another measure of capacity for oil was the *soualia litra*, which equaled 0.24 liter. Both wine and oil were traded by the quarter measure (*tetartion*). The *tetartion* was 1/4 *thalassion metron*; as a measure of capacity for wine, the *tetartion* equaled 2.5 liters, and as measure of capacity for oil, the *tetartion* equaled 2.1 liters. All the units that have been discussed were official weights and measures; other systems, however, were also employed at the local level.

BIBLIOGRAPHY

G. Bass, "Underwater Excavations at Yassi Ada: A Byzantine Shipwreck," in *Archäologischer Anzeiger* (1962), 561–563; Gladys R. Davidson, *Corinth: The Minor Objects* (1952), 203–217; Erich Schilbach, *Byzantinische Metrologie* (1970).

JOHN W. NESBITT

[See also **Constantine I, The Great; Eparch, Book of the; Mints and Money, Byzantine; Nomisma; Weights and Measures, Western European.**]

WEIGHTS AND MEASURES, WESTERN EUROPEAN. The many weights and measures systems employed throughout Western Europe during the Middle Ages were developed by Germanic and Celtic peoples who fell heir to the western provinces of the Roman Empire following the breakdown of Roman power during the fourth and fifth centuries. Characterized generally by confusion and complexity, and dominated largely by custom and tradition, medieval weights and measures evolved on local or regional bases and were geared to needs, especially during the early Middle Ages, that were significantly different from those found in the earlier Roman world.

During most of the republican and imperial eras, Rome enforced a standardized systems of weights and measures in Italy and the provinces to ensure the proper functioning of its sophisticated political, legal, military, commercial, and urban institutions, and in so doing added yet another dimension to the universality and unity of Roman life. The linear, superficial, itinerary, and capacity measures of Rome, together with its weights, formed a cohesive system that, like the Latin language and Roman law, bound together this far-flung, multicultural empire. Merchants, craftsmen, agricultural laborers, military personnel, and others shared the bene-

fits of a unified system of weights and measures that had relatively few units, that was based on state-regulated physical standards, and that was subject to enforcement by a centralized bureaucracy.

This unity, simplicity, precision, and standardization—not to be witnessed again in Western Europe until the creation and dissemination of the metric system in the modern world—came to an end during the turmoil of the early Middle Ages. Native metrologies, long lying dormant in the hinterlands, together with those introduced by scores of conquering tribes, slowly supplanted the weights and measures of Rome. After the year 1000 rapid metrological growth set in; it gathered speed during the later Middle Ages because of many factors, the most important being economic development, commercial competition, demographic growth, increased urbanism, tax manipulations, transportation refinements, technological progress, territorial expansion, and the continuous impact of custom and tradition. In England, for example, there were about fifty major measurement units in the late tenth century; by the end of the Middle Ages there were several hundred major units with approximately 25,000 local variations. The situation in other European states demonstrated an even greater growth pattern, especially in France, the Italian republics, and the Holy Roman Empire. This article will analyze the dominant characteristics of these weights and measures by concentrating chiefly on those employed in the British Isles and France.

THE ROLE OF GOVERNMENT

The major problem with medieval weights and measures was the enormous disparity between the units employed by central governments and those employed regionally and locally. Beginning as early as the twelfth century, the English, French, and other European governments tried to rectify this situation by issuing decrees and promulgating legislative acts, by manufacturing and distributing physical standards to prominent cities and markets, and by instructing and supporting a corps of officials who were supposed to inspect local weights and measures, to verify their authenticity by comparing them to government prototype standards, and to enforce metrological laws. The goal was to bring regional or local systems into alignment with those of the central governments, but for the most part these programs failed, for the following reasons.

First, metrological decrees and conciliar and legislative acts were, on the whole, poorly framed throughout the Middle Ages. The wording in most of them was extremely ambiguous. Standards were mentioned, but usually they were not defined or even identified; this was especially true of linear standards. Capacity measures were described not as volumes, but rather by their weight when filled by certain dry products or river water. The multiples and submultiples of weights were listed, but rarely were the systems upon which they were based described in grains or linked to some government standard.

In addition, injunctions and prohibitions were repeated constantly, producing a prodigious number of enactments. This made a proper knowledge of weights and measures very difficult to obtain. Some laws provided exceptions, especially for the aristocracy and certain commercial interests. These exceptions set precedents for still more exceptions. Some laws favored certain regions or provinces to the detriment of others. Frequent repeals, necessitated by hasty lawmaking, made citizens hesitate to comply with new laws. Certain laws even acknowledged past failures but did not prescribe new approaches or stiffer penalties for noncompliance.

Second, no government ever produced enough physical prototype standards to allow for effective standardization within its jurisdiction. There were no benchmark prototypes at all for many units authorized by central governments, and there were virtually none available for the many local and regional exceptions.

The physical standards sent out to cities and markets normally varied from the masters. However, even the masters could vary. Often several different locations were authorized to construct and maintain masters. In England and Scotland, for example, as many as five or six metropolitan centers supplied standards.

Medieval standardization, then, normally consisted of making inexact copies of variant masters. The situation would be compounded on the local level, where artificers would make copies of the official copies. It was these second-order copies that were put into daily use as weights and measures.

Use and natural causes led to deterioration of physical standards at all levels. Wooden standards decayed; those constructed from lead, iron, or bronze oxidized. State standards suffered from constant handling by officials. Local standards, posted on municipal or market walls, became impaired by weather conditions and general neglect.

Finally, standardization efforts were stifled by the large number of officials entrusted with inspection, verification, and enforcement. Townsmen acting individually or as members of ad hoc commissions, manorial lords and courts, church dignitaries, university administrators, urban magistrates, guildsmen, port officials, justices, sheriffs, coroners, government ministers, market personnel, and many others performed one or more metrological duties.

Such officials often found their duties poorly defined, and they rarely received appropriate training. Jurisdictions frequently overlapped, and there were many opportunities for fraud and corruption. In most cases an official's remuneration depended on the number and amount of fines levied; this, of course, was a strong incentive to abuse.

In short, the actions of government contributed to metrological proliferation, not standardization. Ineffective legislation, an inadequate system for the production and copying of physical prototype standards, and a confused and frequently corrupt corps of enforcement officials all worked against the standardizing impulse of central governments. It was not until the seventeenth and eighteenth centuries that significant strides would be made in eradicating the outstanding metrological problems, and it was not until the advent of the metric system that they would be eradicated altogether.

PRINCIPAL TYPES AND CAUSES OF VARIATIONS

Central governments contributed substantially to weights and measures proliferation by promulgating several national standards for individual units that had widespread usage throughout their respective domains.

In France, for example, the arpent was the principal measure of area for land, but there were three official standards. The *arpent de Paris* contained 100 square perches, each perche of 18 pieds in length. It was a square whose four sides were 180 linear pieds each, totaling 32,400 square pieds (34.189 ares). The *arpent des eaux et forêts* contained 100 square perches, each perche of 22 pieds in length; its four sides were 220 linear pieds each, totaling 48,400 square pieds (51.072 ares). The *arpent de commun*—authorized for use outside the old royal domain—was 100 square perches, each perche of 20 pieds. This square had sides of 200 linear pieds each, totaling 40,000 square pieds (42.208 ares). The corde, a measure of volume for firewood, also had three national standards: the *corde des eaux et forêts* was a pile 8 pieds long, 4 pieds high, each billet being 3 pieds, 6 pouces, in length, or 112 cubic pieds (3.839 cubic meters) in all; the *corde de port* was a pile 8 pieds long, 5 pieds high, each billet being 3 pieds, 6 pouces, in length, or 140 cubic pieds (4.799 cubic meters) in all; and the *corde de grand bois* was a pile 8 pieds long, 4 pieds high, each billet being 4 pieds in length, or 128 cubic pieds (4.387 cubic meters) in all. In the late eighth century the perche was fixed under Charlemagne at 6 aunes or 24 Roman pieds (approximately 7.09 meters), and this remained the national standard until the end of the Middle Ages, when it was replaced by three other perches: the *perche de Paris* of 3 toises or 18 pieds (5.847 meters); the *perche de l'arpent commun* of 20 pieds (6.497 meters); and the *perche des eaux et forêts* of 3⅔ toises or 22 pieds (7.146 meters). Multiple national standards also existed in France for the mille, toise, and pied.

Regionally, the problem of multiple standards was, of course, even more acute, and two examples can suffice as illustrations. The canne was the principal measure of length in southern France for textiles, but the canne of Marseilles was 8 pans or 64 menus or 72 pouces or 892.22 Parisian lignes (2.013 meters), the canne of Montpellier was 8 pans or 881 Parisian lignes (1.987 meters), and the canne of Toulouse was 8 pans or 64 pouces or 796.2 Parisian lignes (1.796 meters). In Paris the *quintal poids de marc* or hundredweight was 100 livres (48.951 kilograms), but regionally the *quintal toulousain* was 104 livres (42.422 kilograms), the *quintal lyonnais* was 100 livres (41.876 kilograms), and the *quintal poids de table* at Marseilles and the *quintal d'eau-de-vie* at Montpellier were each 100 livres (40.79 kilograms).

Occasionally a common, local vessel would become so popular that it would become a unit of measure. A measure of capacity for coal at La Rochelle called the baille was eventually considered the equivalent of ⅟₈₀ muid. Originally it was any metal or wooden bucket used for carrying water. Most local measures, however, never reached this status. In England, the trendle was any round or oval tub used for wax; the prickle, a wicker or willow basket for fruit; the costrel, any leather, wooden, or earthenware vessel for wine that was carried at a man's side; and the coddus, any small bag for grain. The coste, fargot, and flin of France and the balla of the Italian republics were similar.

Product variations. Product variations were the single most important source for metrological proliferation. The English bale for buckram was 60 pieces, but 40 or 45 half pieces for fustian, and 10 reams for paper. A bunch of onions or garlic was 25 heads, while that for glass equaled ⅟₆₀ wey or ⅟₄₀ waw. A dicker of hides was 10; of horseshoes and gloves, 10 pairs; and of necklaces, 10 bundles, each bundle containing 10 necklaces. For grain a fatt contained 9 bushels (*ca.* 3.17 hectoliters); but for bristles, 5 hundredweight (254.010 kilograms); coal, ¼ chalder (*ca.* 3.17 hectoliters); isinglass, 3¼ to 4 hundredweight (147.417 to 181.436 kilograms); unbound books, 4 bales equal to ½ maund; wire, 20 to 25 hundredweight (1016.040 to 1270.050 kilograms); and yarn, 220 or 221 bundles. A kip of lambskins was 30; of goatskins, 50. A pack of cloth was 10 pieces, but for flax, 240 pounds (108.862 kilograms); teasels, generally 9,000 heads for kings and 20,000 heads for middlings; and yarn, 4 hundredweight or 480 pounds (217.724 kilograms). For barley, corn, and malt, a wey consisted of 40 bushels (*ca.* 14.09 hectoliters); but for cheese it was 180 pounds (81.646 kilograms); flax, 182 pounds (82.553 kilograms); glass, 60 bunches or cases; salt, generally 42 bushels (*ca.* 14.80 hectoliters); and lead, generally 182 pounds (82.553 kilograms), but occasionally 175 pounds (79.378 kilograms). A seron of almonds was 2 hundredweight (97.976 kilograms); of aniseed, 3 to 4 hundredweight (152.406 to 203.208 kilograms); and of castile soap, 2½ to 3¾ hundredweight (127.005 to 190.507 kilograms). The hogshead of ale was 48 ale gallons (*ca.* 2.22 hectoliters); while that for beer was 54 beer gallons (*ca.* 2.49 hectoliters); and for honey, oil, and wine, 63 wine gallons (*ca.* 2.38 hectoliters). In France a ballon of colored glass was 12½ bundles, each bundle consisting of 3 plates; white glass, 25 bundles, each bundle of 6 plates; and paper, 24 reams, each ream (this was originally an English measure) normally of 500 sheets. Hundreds of other units containing thousands of product variations existed in France and England and in other areas of Western Europe.

Urban and suburban measures. With the rapid growth of towns during the eleventh and twelfth centuries, weights and measures in certain locales tended to be separated into different standards, depending on whether they were employed within the original, early medieval, walled structures or outside these walls in the expanding suburbs. The

584

outstanding example of this was the danrée employed at Châlons-sur-Marne. As a measure of area for land, the *extra muros* or danrée employed outside the walls was 5,335⁵⁄₉ square Parisian pieds (5.630 ares), whereas the *intra muros* standard of the town proper was 5,555⁵⁄₉ square Parisian pieds (5.862 ares). To further complicate the situation, the danrée was always reckoned equal to ⅑ arpent or journal whether inside or outside the town.

Land and sea measures. Similarly, some measuring units had different standards depending on their usage on land or on sea. The French lieue, for instance, was originally the distance that a man could traverse in one hour of ordinary walking; it was used in Gaul before the Roman occupation. By the fifth century it was reckoned as 1,500 Roman paces of 5 feet each or, in metric terms, 2.216 kilometers (1.47 meters × 1,500). By the end of the eighth century it had increased to 3 Roman miles or 4.411 kilometers. During the later Middle Ages lieues of many different lengths were employed, most of them being between 2,000 and 3,000 toises, and the greater lengths were usually employed for sea distances. The *lieue marine* was eventually standardized at 3 *milles de marine* or 5,555.62 meters, while the *lieue de Paris* for common road measurement contained 12,000 pieds or 3898.08 meters.

National variations in the British Isles. In the British Isles a major problem adding to metrological proliferation was that the same measuring units had different standards in England, Scotland, Ireland, and Wales. A Scots acre, for example, consisted of 4 roods (*ca.* 0.51 hectares) or 6,150.4 square yards or slightly more than ⁵⁄₄ of an English statute acre of 4,840 square yards (0.405 hectares). The Scots standard pint for liquids and dry products contained 103.404 cubic inches (*ca.* 1.70 liters) or 2 choppins or 4 mutchkins, but the English pint for dry products contained 33.6 cubic inches (0.551 liters), and the pint for liquids contained 4 gills or 28.875 cubic inches (0.473 liters) for wine and 32.75 cubic inches (0.578 liters) for ale and beer. The Scots cloth ell was 37 inches (*ca.* 0.95 meters), equal to approximately 37⅕ English inches. A Scots furlong consisted of 40 falls (226.771 meters) or 240 ells, equal to 744 English feet. In Scotland the gallon was employed chiefly for wine and contained 827.232 cubic inches (*ca.* 13.60 liters). This was equal to 3.5811 English wine gallons. The Scots mile was 320 falls (1,814.170 meters) or 1,920 ells, equal to 1,984 English yards or 5,952

English feet. The tun of wine was standardized in Scotland at 60 gallons (*ca.* 8.16 hectoliters); the English wine tun contained generally 252 gallons (*ca.* 9.54 hectoliters). Most of the capacity measures for liquids and dry products in Ireland were smaller than their English prototypes. In Wales the variances were not so significant.

The livre. Measuring units also changed in size over time. In France the livre was the principal unit of weight. During the late eighth century the *livre esterlin* was fixed at 5,760 grains (367.1 grams) and consisted of 20 sous or 12 onces or 240 deniers or 480 oboles. In the middle of the fourteenth century the government of King John II the Good authorized the employment of a new, heavier livre called the *livre poids de marc*, which contained 9,216 grains (489.506 grams) and was subdivided in two different ways. Whenever such changes occurred, of course, most or all of a unit's submultiples were altered appreciably.

Multiple uses. Some units had the distinction of being used for more than one measurement division. The French aissin was a measure of capacity for grain, a measure of volume for wood and plaster, and a measure of area for land. A corde was a measure of length for agricultural and forest lands, a measure of area for small garden plots, and a measure of volume for firewood. Such unit diversity was commonplace throughout Western Europe.

Subunits. Even when there was only one standard and it did not fluctuate over time, it could have various methods of submultiple compilation. The best illustration of this was the fother, used in England as a weight of 2,100 pounds (952.539 kilograms) for lead. It was subdivided in four different ways: 30 fotmals of 70 pounds each (31.751 kilograms), or 168 stone of 12.5 pounds each (5.670 kilograms), or 175 stone of 12 pounds each (5.443 kilograms), or 12 weys, each wey of 175 pounds (79.378 kilograms).

Multiple names. Further confusion in medieval weights and measures systems was caused by the widespread tendency to designate a certain unit with more than one name. In France there were such multiple names as gros = treseau; absa = aune = canne; barrique = bussard; obole = maille; and denier = scrupule. In the British Isles there were the pint = jug = stoup; butt = pipe; hundredweight = quintal; virgate = wista; rod = perch = pole = goad = verge; yard = perch; plowland = hide = sulung; oxland = oxgang = oxgate. In the Italian states one finds the grosso =

dramma = quarro; degalatro = decimo = decina; danapeso = denaro; and cantaro = quintale = cantaio = carara = centinaio.

The herring cran. Sometimes a standard measure was defined in one way but measured in another. The English herring cran, for instance, was defined as the equivalent of 34 wine gallons (*ca.* 1.29 hectoliters), but it was based upon a completely different capacity measure. A standard but bottomless 30-gallon herring barrel was heaped full and the barrel then lifted, leaving the herrings in a pile on the ground or floor.

Units of account. The English last and French laste are examples of units of account—measures or weights that did not have prototype standards because of their enormous sizes or dimensions. They were simply computational units used for record-keeping.

The English last had the following standards: ashes and barrel fish, 12 barrels (*ca.* 17.76 hectoliters); beer, 12 barrels (*ca.* 19.92 hectoliters); bowstaves, 600; butter, 12 barrels (*ca.* 17.76 hectoliters); feathers, 1,700 pounds (771.103 kilograms); flax, 600 bonds; grain, 10 seams or 80 bushels (*ca.* 28.19 hectoliters); gunpowder, 24 barrels or 2,400 pounds (1,088.616 kilograms); herrings, 12,000; hides, 20 dickers or 200 in number; oatmeal, 12 barrels (*ca.* 17.76 hectoliters); pitch, 12 barrels (*ca.* 17.76 hectoliters); potash, 12 barrels or 2,688 pounds (1,219.248 kilograms); raisins, 24 barrels or 24 hundredweight (1,219.248 kilograms); salmon, 6 pipes or 504 gallons (*ca.* 19.08 hectoliters); salt, 10 weys or 420 bushels (*ca.* 148.00 hectoliters); soap, 12 barrels (*ca.* 17.76 hectoliters); tar, 12 barrels (*ca.* 14.28 hectoliters); and wool, 12 sacks or 4,368 pounds (1,981.290 kilograms).

In France the laste was used for dry products in the import and export trade of Lille, where it was 38 rasières for wheat and 40 rasières for oats; Marseilles, where it was 3 quintaux or 300 livres *poids de table* (12.238 dekagrams); and Montpellier, where it was 2 milliers or 20 quintaux or 2,000 livres (*ca.* 2,000 kilograms).

Coinage or income basis. It was customary in the Middle Ages to base agricultural area or superficial measures of land either on coinage standards or on units of income derived through production. The French soudée represented either the amount of land required to produce an annual income of one sou (monetary), or the amount that could be acquired or rented for one sou, or the amount that

was assessed on the tax rolls at one sou. The English librate was an amount of land worth one pound (monetary) a year. Its total acreage depended on local soil conditions and on the value of the pound, and it seems to have varied from several bovates or oxgangs (often four) to as much as ½ knight's fee.

The knight's fee probably originated as an amount of land needed to support a knight and his family. In this sense, the knight's fee was regarded as a unit of income for a fighting man just as the hide was probably a unit of income for a peasant. But, as early as the thirteenth century, the knight's fee was expressed as a land division containing a definite number of bovates, virgates, or hides, and, even though there was little uniformity, the following equivalencies were the most common: a knight's fee of 4 hides, each hide containing 120 acres, or 480 acres (*ca.* 194.40 hectares) in all; of 4 hides of 16 virgates, each virgate containing 4 farthingdales of 10 acres each, or 640 acres (*ca.* 259.20 hectares) in all; of 5, 5½, 6, 6½, 8, 10, and 12 hides, no standard acreage established for the hide; of 12 hides totaling 600 acres (*ca.* 243.00 hectares); and of 14, 16, 27, and 48 hides, no standard acreage established for the hide.

Production or tax assessment. Measures were also based on food production and tax assessments. The toltrey was an English measure of capacity for salt (*ca.* 1400) containing 2 bushels (*ca.* 7.05 dekaliters). It was derived etymologically from *tolt*, toll, + *rey*, king, and was so named because it was the fixed toll in kind on salt paid by the men of Malden to the bishop of London. In France the fourée was merely the amount of arable land on which a crop of wheat could be harvested. At Caithness in Scotland a boll of bear's sowing was equal to approximately an acre (*ca.* 0.51 hectares) and was used as a measure for the payment of rent.

Work functions and time allotments. Medieval land and product measures were also based on work functions and time allotments. In Lincolnshire the bescia was employed for turf-cutting on the fens. It represented the amount of land that could presumably be dug annually by one man with a spade between 1 May and 1 August. In Herefordshire a math equaled approximately 1 acre (*ca.* 0.40 hectares) or the amount of land that a man could mow in a day. Elsewhere in England a wash, containing approximately 1 gallon (*ca.* 4.40 liters), probably originated as the amount of oysters washed at one time, while a werkhop of grain of about 2½ bushels (*ca.* 8.81 dekaliters) represented one day's work in threshing. In many provinces of France agricultural laborers used the ouvrée for vineyards and hempfields; originally it was the extent of land that a worker (*ouvrier*) could work— for instance, plant, sow, or spade—in the course of one day. In the department of Eure-et-Loir a measure for prairie and meadowland varying in size from 100 to 200 square meters and called the andain was originally the space that a mower could cut on each side of him as he moved in a straight line from one end of a plot of land to the other. In the Charolais, Mâconnais, and Brionnais the bichetée was the amount of land that one was able to seed with a bichet of wheat; in other regions one boisseau of seed made the boisselée. A fauchée denoted the space that a mower (*faucheur*) cutting hay or other fodder could cover in one day. A soiture (derived ultimately from the Latin *sextura*, sixth) was the extent of land that a reaper was able to work in a day, or one-sixth of a workweek. The hommée (derived from *homme,* man) was either the amount of meadowland that a man could cut with a scythe in one day, or the amount of arable land that a man could plow in one day, or the amount of vineyard land that a man could cultivate with a spade in one day. Finally, the jour (from Middle French *jour,* time, hour, day) was simply the amount of land that a man could work within one working day.

Animal production. The production capability or strength potential of one or more animals constituted still another method by which medieval man established standards. A capacity measure for milk in Suffolk and Sussex known as the meal equaled the quantity taken from a cow at one milking. Along the Rhône River the ânée represented the stock of goods carried on the back of one ass; the actual amount depended on the size of the animal, the distance covered, and the condition of the roads. The benaton was originally any basket used to transport goods on the back of animals, generally asses, while the benne, used principally for the transport of coal, lime, and metal ores within mine shafts and on roadways, was usually a large, metal, rectangular receptacle fitted with wheels and pulled by a team of asses or mules.

Subdivision. It was customary in the Middle Ages to create additional weights and measures to fill ever-expanding agricultural and industrial needs by dividing existing units into halves, thirds, and fourths, and, where such subdivisions were not

practical or possible, into an irregular assortment of diminutives.

The most important of these units were the *demi-* (= half) series in France, where, in each of the following examples, the name indicated a weight or measure equal to 50 percent of some standard unit: demi-arpent, demi-aune, demi-baril, demi-barrique, demi-boisseau, demi-brasse, demi-caque, demi-carat, demi-gros, demi-lieue, demi-litron, demi-livre, demi-minot, demi-muid, demi-once, demi-pièce, demi-pipe, demi-posson, demi-quartaut, demi-quart(e), demi-quarteranche, demi-quarteron, demi-queue, demi-quintal, demi-roquille, demi-scrupule, demi-setier, demi-somme, and demi-voie. Measures such as the demion and demoiselle also fitted into this category.

French weights and measures equal to one-fourth of some existing standard were normally prefixed with *quart-,* and the most important among them were quartal (= ¼ baril); quartaut (= ¼ muid or queue); quarte (= ¼ pot, velte, or setier); quartée (= ¼ of any land unit); quartel (= ¼ of some larger land unit); quartelade; quartelée (= ¼ arpent or mine); quartelet (= ¼ quarte or any small quarte); quarteranche (= ¼ bichetée); quarterée; quarternel; quarteron (= ¼ livre *poids de marc,* cent, or centaine); quartier (= ¼ setier); quartière (= ¼ émine); and quartonnier (= ¼ boisseau). In England, fourths were usually prefixed with *far-thing-, fer-, for-, fur-,* or *quart-,* as in farthingdale, ferling, forpit, furendal, and quartern.

In both England and France submultiples of one-third were identified by the prefix *tierce-* or *ter-.* Common among the French series were tiercel (= ⅓ arpent); tiercelée (= ⅓ setier); tierceron; tiercière; tierçon (= ⅓ muid); and tierçuel. England had the tierce (= ⅓ pipe) and the tertian (= ⅓ tun of 252 gallons, synonymous with the puncheon, and double the tierce of 42 gallons).

Diminutives in France were customarily formed with the suffixes *-lot* (barillot), *-sel* (barisel), *-let* (bariselet), *-el* (pintel), *-elle* (coupelle), *-ette* (pinte-lette), and *-on* (peson). In the British Isles *-et* was the standard diminutive suffix, as in balet. In Italy, *-etta* (balletta), *-ciello* (ballonciello), *-ino* (granot-tino), and *-otto* (granotto) were used.

OTHER BASES FOR MEASURES

There were many other bases for weights and measures. Perhaps the most commonly used was the human body.

The human body. In the British Isles, the digit—

later standardized at ¾ inch (1.905 centimeters)—was originally a finger's breadth, equal to ¼ palm, 1/12 span, 1/16 foot, 1/24 cubit, 1/40 step, and 1/80 pace. The palm or hand's breadth was equal to ⅓ span or 1/6 cubit. The palm was equal to 3 inches (7.62 centimeters). A span was equal to the distance from the tip of the smallest finger to the tip of the thumb on the outstretched hand. The span was equal to 9 inches (2.286 decimeters). The cubit was the distance from the elbow to the extremity of the middle finger, which was generally taken as 18 inches (4.572 decimeters), or 6 palms or 2 spans. A step was ½ pace or approximately 2½ feet (*ca.* 0.76 meters), while a pace equaled 2 steps or approximately 5 feet (*ca.* 1.52 meters).

The shaftment was 6 inches (*ca.* 15.24 centimeters), or the distance from the tip of the extended thumb across the breadth of the palm. The nail, used principally for cloth, was the length of the last two joints of the middle finger, taken equal to ½ finger, ¼ span, and ⅛ cubit, and standardized at 2¼ inches (5.715 centimeters). The hand was reckoned at 4 inches (10.16 centimeters). The finger for cloth was equal to 2 nails or ½ span and generally reckoned at 4½ inches (1.143 decimeters). The fathom was the length of the arms outstretched. It generally contained 6 feet (1.829 meters).

The perch used in the British Isles is an example of how linear measurement varied according to the physical needs of men engaged in specific trades or crafts. Although the standard consisted of 16½ feet or 5½ yards (5.029 meters), variations of 9, 9⅓, 10, 11, 11½, 12, 15, 16, 18, 18¼, 18¾, 19½, 20, 21, 22, 22½, 24, 25, and 26 feet (2.743 to 7.925 meters) were also used. Perches of 16½ feet and smaller were usually agricultural land measures, while those larger than 16½ feet were used by woodsmen in the forest regions and by town laborers engaged in draining, fencing, hedging, and walling operations.

Other linear measures were based on a specific number of steps or paces, on bodily feats or capacity, and on the range of the human voice. The mile, for instance, had a number of special variations prior to its standardization under Elizabeth I at 5,280 feet (1.609 kilometers). The medieval English mile could be 5,000 feet (*ca.* 1.52 kilometers), or 1,000 paces of 5 feet each; 5,000 feet, or 8 furlongs of 125 paces each, the pace containing 5 feet; 6,600 feet (*ca.* 2.01 kilometers), or 10 furlongs of 660 feet each; or the Old English mile of 1,500 paces, the pace varying in size from one region to another. In

Wales the leap, a length of 6 feet 9 inches (2.057 meters) after its standardization, was originally a normal jump for a working man. A Welsh ridge, or space between the furrows of a plowed field, equaled 3 leaps or 20¼ feet (6.176 meters). A Scots fall of 6 ells (5.669 meters) was the distance covered by gently throwing a rod, staff, pole, or stick on the ground. In France the houpée was the distance recorded between one man who remained stationary and shouted "houp" or "hop" and another man who walked down the road and stopped at that point where he could no longer hear the shouts. The French culbutée and sabotée were related to the houpée.

Area measures from capacity measures. Occasionally superficial standards were based upon corresponding capacity standards, and this was particularly evident in France. The civadier of land, varying in size from 1.094 to 2.472 ares along the Rhône, was based on the grain civadier, and the same situation could be found in such area measures as the civayer, coupée, and eminée.

Area measures from linear measures. Additional methods of creating superficial measures included the squaring of some measuring rod, squaring of a commonly plowed furrow length, or manipulation of certain variations in linear submultiples. An example of the first of these is the lance (Middle French *lance,* from Latin *lancea,* lance or spear) used in Burgundy, which was any land parcel whose length and breadth were measured with a long pole. Another example is the dextre, which was derived in similar fashion and was found in several French provinces. For the second type one finds the English selion or sillyon, which was the strip of land or pathway between two parallel furrows of an open field; it was also called a butt of land or a ridge. The outstanding example of the third type was the English acre. Since the size of the acre was defined in terms of the linear perch, regional variations arose whenever the length of the perch (16½ feet by statute) or the number of square perches in the acre (160 by statute) differed from the statutory standards. In Westmorland the acre was 6,760 square yards (0.565 hectares) or 160 perches of 6¼ square yards each; in Ireland, 7,840 square yards (0.655 hectares) or 160 square perches, each perch of 7 yards on a side; in Dorsetshire, generally 134 square perches (*ca.* 0.34 hectares); in Worcestershire, 90 to 141 square perches (*ca.* 0.23 to *ca.* 0.36 hectares); in Hampshire, 107 to 180 square perches (*ca.* 0.27 to *ca.* 0.45 hectares); and in Sussex, 107,

110, 120, 130, or 212 square perches (*ca.* 0.27 to *ca.* 0.54 hectares).

Clear water of Tay. Scotland was unique in establishing its medieval standards for many capacity measures on the weight content in river water poured into certain vessels. The boll, first standardized under David I (1124–1153) at 12 gallons or the capacity of a vessel 9 inches deep and 72 inches in circumference, was commonly regarded throughout the Middle Ages as any vessel capable of holding 164 pounds of the clear water of Tay. By 1600 it was fixed at 4 firlots or 8,789.34 cubic inches (1.441 hectoliters) and equal to 4.087 Winchester bushels for wheat, peas, beans, rye, and white salt; and 12,822.096 cubic inches (2.101 hectoliters) and equal to 5.963 Winchester bushels for oats, barley, and malt. Both bolls were equal to 16 pecks or 64 lippies.

The firlot of Edinburgh was the standard (after 1600) for wheat, peas, beans, rye, and white salt. It was 21¼ pints (3.612 dekaliters) of 103.404 cubic inches each or 2,197.335 cubic inches in all and equal to 1.0218 Winchester bushels. The Linlithgow firlot was the standard (after 1600) for barley, oats, and malt. It was 31 pints (5.270 dekaliters) or 3,205.524 cubic inches and equal to 1.4906 Winchester bushels. Prior to 1600 the firlot was defined as a vessel holding 41 pounds of the clear water of Tay.

The Scots gallon for liquids and dry products contained 827.232 cubic inches (*ca.* 13.60 liters) or 4 quarts, 8 pints, 16 choppins, 32 mutchkins, or 128 gills. Throughout the Middle Ages it was defined as a vessel capable of holding 20 pounds and 8 ounces of the clear water of Tay.

Finally, the pint (also called a jug or stoup), after 1600 of 103.404 cubic inches (*ca.* 1.70 liters), was defined in medieval Scottish legislation and in several acts thereafter either as 2 pounds and 9 ounces of the clear water of Tay, or as 2 pounds and 9 ounces troy weight of clear water, or as 3 pounds and 7 ounces troy weight of water from the river of Leith.

Heaped, striked, or shallow. Capacity measures for dry products in Scotland and elsewhere in Western Europe were either heaped (*comble, coumble, cumulatus*), striked (*ras, rasa, rasyd, sine cumulo, sine cumulata, stricke, stryke*), or shallow (*cantel, cantell, grains sur bords*). The heaped measure contained an amount of grain extending above its rim. The actual amount in excess of a level measure depended on the proportions of the vessel.

If two vessels contained an equal capacity, yet one was shallow, with a wide diameter, and the other was deep, with a narrow diameter, the former, if both were heaped, would contain the greater amount. Examples of heaped measures found in the British Isles were the full, heap, ring, and fatt. A vessel in which the contents did not extend above the rim was a striked measure. A measure was striked by passing a straight piece of wood called a streek, strike, or strickle over and along its rim in order to remove any excess grain. The striked measure was thus a level measure. The French rasière and English strike, sleek, raser, and hoop fit into this category. A shallow measure was one in which the contents did not reach the rim. Either the vessel was purposely filled this way or the merchant or seller compressed its contents below the rim. The English cantel was a shallow measure limited for use in selling oats, malt, and meal.

The caritas. During the fourteenth century a measure of capacity for wine known as the caritas was standardized at Evesham, Abingdon, and Worcester at ¾ gallon (*ca.* 2.84 liters), 1½ gallons (*ca.* 5.67 liters), and 2 gallons (*ca.* 7.56 liters), respectively. This caritas or "charity," however, probably originated as an allotment of wine given by an abbot to his monks over a certain period of time rather than as a definite capacity measure. Such special measures were common throughout feudal and manorial Europe, particularly so on ecclesiastical estates.

Wholesale measures. Some capacity measures were reserved solely for wholesale shipments. In France the pièce for wine and brandy was employed specifically for regional and interregional wholesale shipments over highways and waterways. Generally it did not have fixed dimensions, but represented any large cask, vat, tun, barrel, or other container loaded on wagons or aboard ships, and sometimes it merely referred to a given number of smaller receptacles. However, in the following mercantile centers, it normally had standard values: Bayonne, 80 veltes; Bordeaux, 50 veltes or approximately 105 English imperial gallons; Bourgogne, 110 pots of Lille; Cognac and La Rochelle, 75 to 90 veltes; Marseilles, 700 to 1,700 livres weight content; Montpellier, 1,400 livres weight content or 5 to 5½ barils; and Nantes, 29 veltes.

Measures for wood. Volume measures for wood were frequently based on the name or on the length of some cord, string, rope, twine, or other substance used to bind or tie together the billets or sticks. In

England the cord was originally determined as the amount encompassed by a length of cord or string, equal to a double cube of 4 feet or 128 cubic feet (3.624 cubic meters), but there were local variations, ranging from 126 to 162½ cubic feet (3.568 to 4.601 cubic meters). In southern France the anneau, of unspecified dimensions, was generally considered equal to ⅓ voie. It derived its name (Middle French *anel*, ring, from the Latin *an[n]ellus*, a derivative of the Latin *annus*, year, circular revolution of the sun) from the circular hoop made of metal or other material used to bind the bundle of logs or sticks together.

The chambrée. Other volume measures originated as the amount of any goods stored within certain sheds, rooms, or cubicles. A chambrée in France was such a measure employed for animal fodder. It was simply the supply of hay or other fodder contained within a storage room or bin. Etymologically, it stems from Middle French *chambree*, roomful, or "all that a room could hold."

QUANTITY MEASURES

Perhaps no division of measurement contained as many special variations as quantity measures. First, many of them were indefinite in number, tale, or count, and were based on an irregular assortment of human, animal, and other capabilities. The French fascicule, for example, denoted the amount of any material that a man could hold or carry with both arms. The term was borrowed by physicians and cooks to represent a handful of ordinary medicinal or cooking ingredients. A jointée was the amount of grain that a man could scoop up and hold with both hands clasped together, while a manipule, as employed by physicians and apothecaries, signified a handful of any substance. The pincée (a pinch or spoonful) was an indefinite quantity of dry material, such as powder, sand, or grain, that could be picked up with two or three fingers and thumb. It was used primarily by the medical and culinary professions. A poignée was used by the medical and pharmaceutical trades to refer to the amount of material that one could hold in a closed hand, and a pugille was any pinch of material used in prescriptions or chemical formulas that did not require precision.

A number of French measures were used to refer to quantities of products that could be conveniently shipped by packtrain or other means of transport. Among these measures were the ballot, quarteron, gerbe, telleron, and membrure. Such quantities usually fit within some canvas sack, bag, or bale. Measures of this type were found in profusion throughout Western Europe. English examples would be the balet, bolt, fad, fadge, fardel, fardlet, fesse, flitch, packet, and trussell, while in the Italian republics one finds the balla, balletta, ballonciello, ballone, fagotto, mazzo, pezzo, torsa, and torsello.

Even when quantity measures had standardized counts, the actual number varied from product to product. The table on pages 592–593 presents the most important variations. (Metric equivalents, wherever applicable, can be found in the author's books and articles listed in the bibliography.)

VARIOUS FRENCH WEIGHTS

Among medieval weight systems the two major causes of variations were the specific needs of certain trades and professions, and the significant differences created in their multiples. Although the actual numbers of such variations were as prolific as for quantity measures, one can demonstrate the enormous complexity involved merely by examining a random sample of some of the more important weights employed in France, and they are included in the table on pages 594–596.

BIBLIOGRAPHY

This bibliography is a selective listing of some of the important published sources in the field of Western European historical metrology. Readers desiring additional metrological books and articles, or the numerous manuscripts and published works in other fields that contain weights and measures information, should consult Paul Burguburu, *Essai de bibliographie métrologique universelle* (1932), and those works below whose annotations indicate extensive bibliographies.

Wilfrid Airy, "On the Origin of the British Measures of Capacity, Weight, and Length," in *Minutes of Proceedings of the Institution of Civil Engineers,* **175** (1909); Hans-Joachim von Alberti, *Mass und Gewicht* (1957); Jean-Baptiste-Auguste Barny de Romanet, *Traité historique des poids et mesures* (1863); A. E. Berriman, *Historical Metrology* (1953); William Roger Breed, *The Guide to Weights and Measures* (1956) and *The Weights and Measures Act: 1963* (1964); Henry W. Chisholm, *On the Science of Weighing and Measuring* (1877); Maurice Denis-Papin and Jacques Vallot, *Métrologie générale* (1946); J.-A. Decourdemanche, *Traité pratique des poids du moyen âge* (1915); Allan Granger, *Our Weights and Measures* (1917); Philip Grierson, *English Linear Measures: An Essay in Origins* (1972); M. A. Grivel, *Les anciennes mesures de France* (1914).

P. Guilhiermoz, "Note sur les poids du moyen âge," in *Bibliothèque de l'École des Chartes,* **67** (1906) (extensive bibliography), and "Remarques diverses sur les poids et mesures du moyen âge," *ibid.*, 80 (1919); William Hallock and Herbert T. Wade, *Outlines of the Evolution of Weights and Measures* (1906); Walter R. Ingalls, *Systems of Weights and Measures* (1945); P. Kelly, *Metrology* (1816); Bruno Kisch, *Scales and Weights* (1965); Witold Kula, *Measures and Men*, Richard Szreter, trans. (1986); Frederic C. Lane, "Tonnages, Medieval and Modern," in his *Venice and History* (1966), 345–370; Armand Machabey, "Techniques of Measurement," in Maurice Daumas, ed., *A History of Technology and Invention*, Eileen B. Hennessy, trans., II (1969), 306–343; Edward Nicholson, *Men and Measures* (1912); John A. O'Keefe, *The Law of Weights and Measures* (1966); A. N. Palmer, "Notes on the Ancient Welsh Measures of Land," in *Archaeologia Cambrensis*, 5th ser., 13 (1896); Alexis J. Paucton, *Métrologie* (1780); W. H. Prior, "Notes on the Weights and Measures of Medieval England," in *Bulletin du Cange*, 1 (1924) (extensive bibliography).

"Report from the Committee Appointed to Inquire into the Original Standards of Weights and Measures in This Kingdom," in *Parliamentary Papers, Great Britain: Reports from Committees of the House of Commons*, 2 (1737–1765), 411–451; A. W. Richeson, *English Land Measuring to 1800* (1966); Jean B. Romé de L'Isle, *Métrologie* (1789); "Second Report of the Commissioners . . . to Consider the Subject of Weights and Measures," in *Parliamentary Papers, Great Britain: Reports from Commissioners*, 7 (1820), 1–40.

Frederic Seebohm, *Customary Acres and Their Historical Importance* (1914); *Select Tracts and Table Books Relating to English Weights and Measures (1100–1742)*, Hubert Hall, ed. (1929); Frederick G. Skinner, *Weights and Measures* (1967); M.-J. Tits-Dieuaide, "La conversion des mesures anciennes en mesures métriques," in *Contributions à l'histoire économique et sociale*, 2 (1963); Charles M. Watson, *British Weights and Measures* (1910); Harald Witthöft, *Umrisse einer historischen Metrologie*, 2 vols. (1979), and *idem*, ed., *Die historische Metrologie in den Wissenschaften* (1986).

Ronald E. Zupko, *A Dictionary of English Weights and Measures* (1968), "Notes on Medieval English Weights and Measures in Francesco Balducci Pegolotti's 'La pratica della mercatura,'" in *Explorations in Economic History*, 7 (1969–1970), "Medieval English Weights and Measures," in *Studies in Medieval Culture*, 4 (1974), *British Weights and Measures: A History from Antiquity to the Seventeenth Century* (1977), "The Weights and Measures of Scotland Before the Union," in *The Scottish Historical Review*, 56 (1977), *French Weights and Measures Before the Revolution* (1978), *Italian Weights and Measures from the Middle Ages to the Nineteenth Century* (1981), *A Dictionary of Weights and Measures for the British Isles: The Middle Ages to the Twentieth Century* (1985), and *Revolution in Measurement: Western European Weights and Measures Since the Age of Science* (1988). Most of the above items have extensive bibliographies.

RONALD EDWARD ZUPKO

[See also Acre; Arpent; Barrel; Boisseau; Boll; Bushel; Chalder; Clove; David I of Scotland; Field Systems; Food Trades; Gallon; Hide; Hundred (Land Division); Hundred and Hundredweight; Journal; Last; League; Livre; Marc; Masons and Builders; Mile; Mints and Money, Western European; Muid; Ounce; Peck; Perch; Pound, Weight; Quarter; Sack; Setier; Stone; Surveying; Taxation (various articles); Textiles; Trade, Regulation of; Virgate.]

Quantity Measures in the British Isles

Name and Location	Products	Description	Name and Location	Products	Description
Bale (England)	almonds	3 hundredweight	Bundle (England) (cont.)	birch brooms	1 or 2 dozen
	bolting cloth	20 pieces		brown paper	40 quires
	buckram	60 pieces		glovers' knives	10 in number
	caraway seeds	3 hundredweight		harness plates	10 in number
	cochineal	1½ hundredweight	(Gloucestershire)	hogshead hoops	36 in number
	cotton yarn	3 to 4 hundredweight	(Devonshire)	oat straw	40 pounds
	flaxen yarn	240 pounds	(Yorkshire)	straw	¹⁄₁₂ thrave
	fustian	generally 40 or 45 half-pieces	(Devonshire)	wheat straw	28 pounds
	hay or straw	generally 224 pounds	(Hamborough)	yarn	20 skein
	hemp	20 hundredweight	Cage (England)	quails	generally 28 dozen
	paper	10 reams	Carrata (Sicily)	pipe staves	3,800 in number
	pipes	10 gross or 1,440 in number	Cent (France)	most goods	100 in number
	raw silk	1 to 4 hundredweight	(Nantes)	small Norwegian boards	124 in number
	thread	100 bolts	(River Sèvre)	salt	28 muids
	wool	180 pounds	Fangot (England)	raw silk	1 to 2¾ hundredweight
Ballon (France)	colored glass	12½ bundles of 3 plates each		grogram and mohair	1½ to 2½ hundredweight
	white glass	25 bundles of 6 plates each	Fargot (France)	piece goods and cloth	150 to 160 livres
	paper	24 reams, generally of 500 sheets each	Flock (England)	piece goods	40 in number or sets
Bind (England)	eels	10 sticks or 250 in number	Glean (England)	herrings	¹⁄₁₅ rees or 25 in number
Binne (England)	skins	33 in number	(Essex and Gloucestershire)	teasels	1 bunch
Bottle (England)	hay or straw	7 pounds	Grenier (France)	onions	100 in number
Bouchée (Seine-et-Marnais)	onions	¹⁄₁₀₀ grenier	Gross (British Isles)	piece goods	small of 12 dozen or 144 in number; large of 12 small gross or 1,728 in number
Brawler (Somersetshire)	straw	7 pounds			
Bunch (England)	glass	¹⁄₄₀ waw	Gwyde (England)	eels	10 sticks or 250 in number
	onions or garlic	25 heads	Hank (England)	yarn (cotton or spun silk)	7 skeins or 840 yards
(Cambridgeshire)	osiers	45 inches around at the band		yarn (worsted)	7 wraps or 12 cuts or 560 yards
	reeds	28 inches around at the band	Hasp (England)	linen yarn	6 heers or ¼ spindle or 3,600 yards
(Essex)	teasels	25 heads	Hattock (Northern England)	grain	10 or 12 sheaves
(Gloucestershire)		20 heads for "regulars" and 10 heads for "kings"	Heap (Scotland)	limestone	4½ cubic yards = about 5 tons
(Yorkshire)		10 heads	Heer (England)	linen yarn	2 leas or ⅙ hasp or 600 yards
Bundle (Devonshire)	barley straw	35 pounds			
(England)	bast ropes	10 in number			

Quantity Measures in the British Isles

Name and Location	Products	Description
Hundred (British Isles)	most goods	100 in number
	balks, barlings, boards, canvas, capravens, cattle, deals, eggs, faggots, herrings, lambskins, linen cloth, nails, oars, pins, poles, reeds, spars, staves, stockfish, stones, tile, and wainscots	120 in number
	cod, ling, saltfish, and haberdine	124 in number
	"hardfish"	160 in number
	onions and garlic	225 in number
(Roxburghshire and Selkirkshire)	lambs and sheep	106 in number
(Fifeshire)	herrings	132 in number
Kip (England)	goat skins	50 in number
	lamb skins	30 in number
Knot (Essex)	wool yarn	80 turns around a reel
Knitch (Northern England and Scotland)	unbroken straw	34 inches around
Lest (France)	herrings	12 caques or barils
Load (Essex)	osiers	80 bolts
Loggin (Yorkshire)	straw	14 pounds
Marque (Normandy)	timber	300 chevilles of 12 cubic pouces each
Maund (England)	unbound books	2 fatts or 8 bales or 40 reams
Mease (England)	herrings	500 to 630 in number
Migliaio (Italy)	piece goods	1,000 in number
Nest (England)	piece goods	3 in number or sets
Piling (Staffordshire)	wheat straw	3 sheaves
Pwn (North Wales)	straw	160 pounds
Quire (British Isles)	paper	24 or 25 sheets = 1/20 ream

Name and Location	Products	Description
Ream (British Isles)	paper	"regular" of 20 quires
		"printer's" of 21½ quires
		"stationer's" of 504 sheets
Rees (England)	herrings	15 gleans or 375 in number
Roll (England)	parchment	60 skins
Rook (Yorkshire)	beans	4 sheaves
Rope (England)	onions and garlic	15 heads
Roul (England)	eels	1,500 in number
Ruck (Derbyshire)	bark	5¼ stacked cubic yards
Sack (Scotland)	sheepskins	500 in number
Score (British Isles)	most goods	20 in number
(Liverpool)	barley, beans, and oats	21 bushels
(Newcastle)	coal	21 chalders
(Roxburghshire and Selkirkshire)	grain	21 bolls
(Derbyshire)	lime	20 to 22 heaped bushels
(Dumbartonshire)	sheep	21 in number
Shock (England)	piece goods	60 in number
(Derbyshire)	corn	12 sheaves
Skive (Southampton)	teasels	generally 500 in number
Staff (Essex)	teasels	1,250 in number
(Gloucestershire)		500 in number for "middlings" and 300 for "kings"
Stick (England)	eels	25 in number
Stoke (England)	dinnerware	60 pieces
Thousand (British Isles)	piece goods	generally 10 times larger than the corresponding hundred
Thrave (England)	straw	12 to 24 sheaves
Timber (England)	fur skins	40 in number
Truss (England)	hay or straw	56 pounds
Warp (Sussex and Kent)	herrings	4 in number
Waw (England)	glass	40 bunches
Web (Scotland)	window glass	60 bunches
Wrap (England)	worsted yarn	80 yards

Weight Measures in France

Name and Location	Products	Description	Name and Location	Products	Description
Breton (Britanny)	dry products	100 livres	Livre (*cont.*)		
Carat	precious metals and jewels	4 grains valued at 3.876 grains *poids de marc* (2.059 decigrams)	(Aix-en-Provence)	all products	*poids de table* (379.1 grams)
			(Albi)	all products	(407.9 grams)
Charge	all products	300 livres *poids de marc* (146.85 kilograms)	(Allevard)	all products	*poids de fourneau* (532.5 grams)
				all products	*poids de fonte* (552.6 grams)
(Marseilles)	grain	300 livres *poids de marc* (122.38 kilograms)	(Apt)	all products	(397.5 grams)
			(Arles)	all products	(391.2 grams)
(Nantes)	all products	300 livres (148.32 kilograms)	(Aude)	all products	(469 grams)
			(Aveyren)	all products	(408 grams)
(Nice)	all products	300 livres (93.48 kilograms)	(Avignon)	all products	(408.7 grams)
			(Beaucaire)	all products	(412.9 grams)
(Toulouse)	all products	3 quintaux (127.26 kilograms)	(Bourges)	all products	(468.3 grams)
			(Cambrai)	all products	(470 grams)
Denier	generally gold, silver, precious metals, and jewels	24 grains (1.275 grams) = ⅓ gros or 1/24 once	(Carpentras)	all products	(400 grams)
			(Castres)	all products	(412 grams)
			(Clermont)	all products	same as Aire
Drachme	medical and pharmaceutical products	60 grains (3.824 grams) or 3 scrupules or 6 oboles = ⅛ once	(Douai)	all products	(425 grams)
			(Dunkirk)	all products	same as Aire
			(Embrun)	all products	*poids de table* (435 grams)
Estelin	gold and silver	28.8 grains (1.53 grams) or 2 oboles or 4 félins = 1/20 once	(Gap)	all products	*poids de table* (392 grams)
Félin	gold and silver	7⅕ grains (0.38 grams) = ½ maille, ¼ estelin, 1/10 gros, or 1/80 once	(Grenoble)	all products	*poids de table* (417.3 grams)
				all products	*poids de ville* (442.7 grams)
				all products	*poids de Savoie* (551.8 grams)
Grain	all products	24 primes (53.115 milligrams) = 1/12 félin, 1/24 denier, 1/72 gros, 1/576 once, 1/4,608 marc, or 1/9,216 livre		all products	*poids de fonte* (552.6 grams)
			(Istres)	all products	(388.5 grams)
			(La Rochelle)	all products	(404.4 grams)
			(Lavaur)	all products	same as Albi
			(Lille)	all products	(431.3 grams)
Gros	all products	72 grains (3.824 grams) or 2½ estelins, 3 deniers or scrupules, 5 mailles, or 10 félins = ⅛ once, 1/64 marc, or 1/128 livre	(Limoges)	all products	(481.9 grams)
			(Marseilles)	all products	*poids de table:* same as Albi
			(Mauberge)	all products	(467.1 grams)
			(Moissac)	all products	(429.1 grams)
			(Montauban)	all products	*poids de table* (425.6 grams)
Livre	all products	(see "Livre" in volume 7 of this *Dictionary* for government standards)	(Montpellier)	all products	*grosse:* same as Albi
			(Morlaix)	all products	(491.3 grams)
			(Nancy)	all products	(455.7 grams)
			(Nantes)	all products	(494.4 grams)
(Abbeville)	all products	(422 grams)	(Nîmes)	all products	*grosse:* same as Albi
(Aire)	all products	(428.3 grams)	(Rambereillers)	all products	(460.1 grams)
			(Rouen)	all products	*poids de vicomté* (509.1 grams)

Weight Measures in France

Name and Location	Products	Description	Name and Location	Products	Description
Livre (*cont.*)			Once	all products, but principally gold and silver	*once d'esterlin* of 480 grains (30.59 grams) or 20 deniers or 40 oboles = 1/12 livre *de Charlemagne*
(Rouen)	all products	*pour les laines* (528.6 grams)			
(Salon)	all products	(376.6 grams)			
(St. Chamas)	all products	(379.2 grams)		all products	*once poids de marc* of 576 grains (30.594 grams) or 2 demi-onces, 8 gros or drachmes, 24 scrupules or deniers, or 13,824 primes = 1/2 demi-quarteron, 1/8 marc, or 1/16 livre
(St. Mitre)	all products	same as Salon			
(Tarascon)	all products	(388.1 grams)			
(Toulon)	all products	(406.5 grams)			
(Toulouse)	all products	*poids de table* (413.6 grams)			
	all products	*carnassière* or *grosse* (1,240.8 grams)			
(Tours)	all products	(475.7 grams)			
(Troyes)	all products	(520 grams)			
(Uzès)	all products	(412.1 grams)		gold and silver; pearls and diamonds	576 grains (30.594 grams)
(Vienne)	all products	*poids de balance* (404.1 grams)			
	all products	*poids de crochet* (456.8 grams)	Pellet	weight of account	1/24 prime (0.092 milligrams) or 1/576 grain
(Villefranche)	all products	(436.8 grams)			
(Voiron)	all products	*poids de table* (417.3 grams)	Perrée	all products	generally 8 livres *poids de marc* (3.916 kilograms)
Maille	gold and silver	*maille d'esterlin* of 14.4 grains (*ca.* 0.8 grams) or 2 félins = 1/2 esterlin, 1/40 once, 1/320 marc, or 1/640 livre *maille de denier* of 12 grains (*ca.* 0.7 grams) = 1/2 denier	Prime	medical and pharmaceutical products	1/24 grain (2.213 milligrams)
			Quarteron	all products	4 onces (122.38 grams) or 2 demi-quarterons = 1/4 livre *poids de marc*
Marc	principally gold and silver	4,608 grains (244.753 grams) or 8 onces, 64 gros, 160 esterlins, 192 deniers, 320 mailles, or 640 félins = 1/2 livre *poids de marc*		all products	traditionally: 1/4 cent or hundredweight
			(Toulouse)	all products	26 livres *poids de table* (10.75 kilograms)
Millier	all products	1,000 livres *poids de marc* (489.51 kilograms) or 10 quintaux = 1/2 tonneau *de mer*	Sarcinée (Toulouse)	goods shipped by land transport	3 quintaux (*ca.* 127 kilograms)
			Scrupule	precious metals, jewels, medical and pharmaceutical products	24 grains (1.275 grams) = 1/3 gros or drachme, 1/24 once, or 1/384 livre
Obole	gold and silver	*obole d'esterlin* of 14.4 grains (*ca.* 0.8 grams) or 2 félins = 1/2 esterlin, 1/40 once, 1/320 marc, or 1/640 livre *obole de denier* of 12 grains (*ca.* 0.7 grams) = 1/2 denier	Sizain	generally valuable or scarce commodities	144 grains (7.648 grams) or 2 gros or 6 deniers = 1/4 once

continued

WEINSCHWELG, DER, a panegyric of 416 lines on wine and drunkenness preserved in codex 2705 of the Austrian National Library. The poem may have originated in the Tirol and was probably composed not long before the manuscript was written (*ca.* 1260–1290). A fifteenth-century codex contains a corrupt and much-abbreviated text.

Der Weinschwelg is a work of startling wit and originality. Written in octosyllabic couplets, it is divided into twenty-three sections by the refrain *dô huob er ûf unde tranc* ("then he raised [his beaker] and drank"). This refrain concludes the final couplet of each section, but is syntactically linked to the following section through the accusative object *tranc* ("a larger drink than ever before") or a dependent clause (for instance, "as though he would never stop"). Thus the refrain, rather than breaking the text into units, propels it forward from one hyperbole to another. One finds clever manipulation of language throughout (alphabetical order of rhymes, punning, verbal repetitions, and variations).

The poem begins with a narrator's assertion that he knows the archetype and champion of drinkers, one whose swallows surpass those of elk and bison. In line 14 the guzzler himself begins a monologue that constitutes the rest of the poem, interrupted only by the narrator's comments (for instance, "and drank so much that all said . . . it was his prize-winning drink"). The most extravagant claims are made: wine brings strength, wisdom, health, wealth, and beauty; drinking is better than jousting or courtly dancing; had Paris loved wine instead of Helen, no harm would have befallen him. Gradually the lush comes to eulogize not wine but himself, the peerless drinker, master of his art. Finally, with veiled allusions to the Book of Psalms, he lauds himself as "Ungenôz" (the Incomparable).

Though certain details link *Der Weinschwelg* to Latin drinking songs of the Middle Ages, it is a work sui generis. Some stimulus may have come to the author from Stricker's vignettes about drunkards, and it is plausible that *Die böse Frau*, a comedy of marital strife employing many techniques of *Der Weinschwelg*, was composed by the same person.

BIBLIOGRAPHY

Source. Hanns Fischer and Johannes Janota, eds., *Der Stricker. Verserzählungen II. Mit einem Anhang: Der Weinschwelg*, 3rd ed. (1984).

Studies. Helmut de Boor, *Die deutsche Literatur im späten Mittelalter: Zerfall und Neubeginn*, pt. 1: 1250–1350 (1962), 282–287; Stephen L. Wailes, "Wit in *Der Weinschwelg*," in *German Life and Letters*, 27 (1973–1974).

STEPHEN L. WAILES

[See also **Stricker, Der.**]

WELFS. See **Guelphs and Ghibellines.**

WELSH LITERATURE. The earliest literature in Welsh dates from the sixth century, by which time the language had developed a new analytic form out of the older, synthetic Brittonic (or Brythonic) language. Although the manuscript sources for this literature are much later, there is considerable evidence to support its authenticity. This panegyric and elegiac verse was written almost certainly by official poets for local rulers in the Brittonic-speaking areas of Wales and southern Scotland, in the context of the struggles with the Saxon invaders in the latter part of the sixth century. Kept alive by a conservative bardic tradition, this poetry is terse and epigrammatic in style and exhibits a remarkable technical facility as well as a considerable adeptness at striking imagery.

VERSE: THE EARY PERIOD (TO 1000)

The earliest direct reference to this poetry occurs in one of the *aliqua excerpta* of Nennius' *Historia Brittonum* (cap. 62), concerning the reign of Ida of Bernicia (547–559): "At that time Talhaearn Tad Awen [Father of Inspiration or Father of the Muse] was famed in poetry, and Aneirin and Taliesin and Bluchbard and Cian, who is known as Gwenith Gwawt [Wheat of Song], were all at the same time famed in British poetry." Works by two of these poets survive in the Book of Taliesin (*ca.* 1275) and the Book of Aneirin (*ca.* 1250). A considerable amount of legendary material later became attached to the name of Taliesin as soothsayer and shape-shifter as well as poet, but among the rather heterogeneous compilation of the Book of Taliesin twelve poems are in a much clearer narrative style, dealing with events in the sixth century and with historical figures of that period. Taliesin wrote principally for three patrons: Cynan Garwyn, a Powys chieftain whose son Selyf was killed in the Battle of Chester (*ca.* 615); Urien of Rheged (in southwestern Scotland) and his son Owain; and the north British chieftain Gwallawg of Elfed (in modern Yorkshire). Urien and Gwallawg, allies in the fight against the Saxon invaders, are both mentioned in Nennius' *excerpta* (cap. 63). These poems of praise and elegy lie firmly in the heroic mode, providing descriptive evidence of the subject's generosity and bravery.

In contrast to these short poems, the Book of

Aneirin contains two versions of rather different date of *The Gododdin*, a series of elegies on the warriors of a disastrous expedition sent by Mynyddawg Mwynfawr from Caer Eiddyn (in the vicinity of modern Edinburgh) to recapture the area of Catraeth in Yorkshire (once the site of the Roman fort of Caturactonium; modern Catterick, Yorkshire), lost earlier in the century to the English of Deira. The text as it has come down to us is in a very corrupt state, with numerous interpolations, but there is no reason that it could not have been written (as the epigraph claims) by Aneirin in the late sixth century. Like Taliesin's poetry it is cast in the heroic mold and makes considerable use of many of the technical devices (stanza linking, alliteration, consonance, internal rhyme) that later became the foundation of Welsh bardic poetry. The extraneous material in the *Gododdin* manuscript includes a poem referring to the death of Domnall Breac at the Battle of Strathcarron in 642 and a delightful cradle song. The poetry of Taliesin and Aneirin shows clear evidence of the professional bardic system that was to be the basis of Welsh poetry for centuries to come; though not fully developed, it also shows the beginnings of the elaborate system of alliteration, consonance, and internal rhyme that was later codified into the system of *cynghanedd*, which has provided the basis of Welsh metrics to the present day. That a class of such professional bards must have existed is attested by Gildas, who in his invective against Maelgwn Gwynedd (*De excidio et conquestu Britanniae*, 34/6) refers scornfully to Maelgwn's preference for hearing his own praises sung by the "voice of the rascally crew yelling forth" rather than the praises of God.

Very little survives of the literature of the following three centuries. A few poets are mentioned in documentary sources, such as Arofan, bard to Selyf ap Cynan, and Cadwallon's bard Afan Ferddig. A few individual poems survive, including an elegy for Cadwallon (d. 633) that may be by Afan Ferddig, and one for Cynddylan ap Cyndrwyn. One of the finest poems of this period is an anonymous praise poem directed not to a patron but to the fortress of Tenby (the late-ninth-century *Edmyg Dinbych* preserved in the Book of Taliesin). From the early tenth century *Armes Prydein* (The prophecy of Britain, also in the Book of Taliesin) envisages a mass uprising of Celts and Dublin Norse to drive out the Anglo-Saxon oppressors. To this period also belong some of the poems dealing with the legendary story of Taliesin preserved in the Book of Taliesin as well as the two groups of *englynion* written in the first half of the ninth century in the margins of a Cambridge University Library manuscript of Juvencus' paraphrase of the Gospels. Nine of these *englynion* (a stanza form of three, occasionally four, lines) form a traditional poem in praise of God, while the other three appear to be part of a lost narrative or saga, or perhaps a monologue. They are in a very archaic form of Welsh.

The most important poetry surviving from the tenth century is the series of *englynion* associated with Llywarch Hen (the Old), a sixth-century chieftain owing allegiance to Urien Rheged. Once thought to be the work of Llywarch, these poems are now generally accepted as a literary work in which he is the principal character. The poems deal primarily with Llywarch's aging and the deaths of his twenty-four sons. Their tone is elegiac, but not heroic in the manner of the poetry of Taliesin and Aneirin. In these highly dramatic monologues and dialogues, Llywarch is cast as a bitter old man who has outlived both his family and his lord, and who blames himself for their loss. A related set of poems deals with the story of Heledd, sister of Cynddylan ap Cyndrwyn, who laments the death of her brother and the fall of her family. Both Heledd's and Llywarch's stories are told with a high degree of art, concentrating on the opposition of ill fate (*diriaid*) and good fortune (*dedwydd*) and their relationship to pride (*traha*).

Other individual poems related to narrative material suggest that this form of literature was common: a dialogue between Arthur and the gatekeeper Glewlwyd Gafaelfawr and one between Arthur and Gwenhwyfar (Guinevere); a poem on Gereint, son of Erbin; a poem probably connected with the Tristan story; and a series of poems dealing with Myrddin Wyllt, cognate with the Irish Suibhne Geilt and Lailoken in Scotland, all of them heroes driven mad in battle who live as wild men in the woods, gifted with prophetic sight. Myrddin later became transformed into the Merlin of the Arthurian legends.

Most of these poems are preserved in the Black Book of Carmarthen (late twelfth or early thirteenth century), which also contains the *Englynion y Beddau* (Stanzas of the graves), a series of briefly allusive poems on the graves of heroes that provide a wealth of information on saga material now lost or obscure. The Book of Taliesin also preserves a few poems on religious subjects, as well as two poems of classical background (on Hercules and Alexander) and one on the Irish hero Cú Roí mac Dáiri. The poets of the period before the end of the eleventh century are usually called the *Cynfeirdd*, the early poets. Their work is rounded out with an assortment of nature and gnomic poetry.

VERSE: THE *GOGYNFEIRDD*

The political consolidation of Wales during the eleventh and twelfth centuries saw also the growth of an organized professional bardic class in service to the political leaders. The literature of the twelfth through the early fourteenth centuries is dominated by the work of these court poets, often called the *Gogynfeirdd* (rather early poets). Their work is primarily preserved in the Red Book of Hergest and the Hendregadredd Manuscript, a compilation from the late fourteenth and fifteenth centuries.

Poems by about sixty of the *Gogynfeirdd* survive, consisting largely of elegy (*marwnad*) and panegyric (*moliant*) as well as religious poetry; they are written primarily in the *awdl* form of lengthy single-rhymed stanzas. Their work is intensely traditional, even artificial, utilizing vocabulary and constructions that must have been archaic in their own day. The poetry is often allusive, difficult, and obscure in meaning, and yet their technical brilliance is often astonishing. These court poets are generally at their best in the composition of *marwnadau,* in which a sense of true emotion is often present, in contrast with the extensive lists of largess in the panegyric poems. Among the best-known poets of this period are Meilyr Brydydd (*fl. ca.* 1100–*ca.* 1137), his son Gwalchmai ap Meilyr (*fl. ca.* 1130–1180), Owain Cyfeiliog (*ca.* 1130–1197), Cynddelw Brydydd Mawr (*fl. ca.* 1155–1200), Prydydd y Moch (Llywarch ap Llywelyn, *ca.* 1173–1220), Dafydd Benfras (*ca.* 1220–1260), Bleddyn Fardd (*fl. ca.* 1257–1285), and Gruffudd ap yr Ynad Coch (*fl. ca.* 1280).

The training and the professional organization of the *Gogynfeirdd* were bardic. The Laws of Hywel Dda (earliest manuscript version *ca.* 1200) describes their division into grades. Chief among them was the *pencerdd* (chief of song), whose duty it was to eulogize his patron and to sing of God and the saints. These subjects were proscribed for the *bardd teulu* (household bard), who was to sing the praises of the retinue, was allowed to sing of nature and of love, and was expected to entertain the lady, when required, with "three songs in a low voice so as not to disturb the court." In addition to these official poets, there were a wide variety of *cerddorion* (minstrels), whose relationship to the bardic system may well have been tenuous, and whose work probably included a wide range of artistic expression. The profession of bard seems frequently to have been hereditary, and many of the *Gogynfeirdd* passed their positions on to their sons.

VERSE: THE *CYWYDDWYR*

In the period following the loss of Welsh independence in 1282, the court poets, such as Casnodyn (*ca.* 1290–1340), began to develop a rather simpler style, but this development is overshadowed by the work of a new "school" of poets who rose primarily under aristocratic patronage in the fourteenth century. Writing primarily in the new and complex *cywydd* meter, these poets are generally known as the *cywyddwyr,* or the poets of the *uchelwyr,* the native aristocracy. Principal among them are Dafydd ap Gwilym (*ca.* 1320–*ca.* 1380) and his contemporaries and successors Madog Benfras (*ca.* 1320–1360), Gruffudd ap Adda (*ca.* 1340–1370), Iolo Goch (*ca.* 1320–1398), Gruffudd Gryg (*ca.* 1360–1410), and Siôn Cent (*ca.* 1400–1430).

Although these poets were capable of writing praise poetry in the archaic style of their predecessors, their language is far closer to the spoken vernacular, and is usually called Early Modern Welsh. Their subject matter often departs entirely from the traditions of the previous period, concentrating on nature and love, and admitting such foreign influences as the lyric poetry of the trouvères and the songs of the *clerici vagantes.* Formally, their poetry is distinguished by a preference for the new *cywydd* meter, in which seven-syllable lines rhyme in couplets alternating masculine and feminine rhymes. They utilized to the full the elaborate system of *cynghanedd,* but they used it with a new elegance deriving from their return to a simpler language. The *cywyddwyr* also developed a technique of *sangiad,* or parenthetical comment, that allows multiple strands of thought to be presented simultaneously and frequently makes their poetry difficult to translate. It is this difficulty of translation that has kept Dafydd ap Gwilym from his recognition as one of the greatest medieval poets.

Dafydd's poetry is one of the great achievements of the Middle Ages; his surviving works (just over 150 poems in Thomas Parry's edition) show not only an absolute technical mastery of complex forms but also an ability to deal with intense personal emotion and, like his contemporary Geoffrey Chaucer, a keen sense of humor—often directed at himself. Dafydd's greatest poetry involves the contemplation of nature. His continual feeling of wonderment at God's plenitude and his sense of oneness with the natural world distinguish him from all other medieval poets. Though Dafydd is frequently cited as a love poet, many of his love poems are in fact thinly disguised nature poems in which the beloved, too, is set in the larger context of God's plenty. This blending of love and nature is especially strong in his *llatai* poems, in which a messenger (frequently a bird, animal, or natural element like the wind) is asked to convey a message to the beloved.

The later *cywyddwyr,* from the middle of the fifteenth century, became increasingly formalistic. At an eisteddfod held at Carmarthen around 1451, the poet Dafydd ab Edmwnd reorganized and codified the twenty-four canonical meters of Welsh poetry, and his successors Tudur Aled (*d.* 1525/1527; Dafydd's nephew) and Gutun Owain (*ca.* 1460–1500) became more and more obsessed with descriptive detail. Three poets from the second half of the fifteenth century carry on the tradition of the *cywydd* in the style of Dafydd ap Gwilym: Dafydd Nanmor (*ca.* 1450–*ca.* 1480), Guto'r Glyn (*fl.* 1440–1493), and Lewys Glyn Cothi (*ca.* 1420–1489).

Works written for the instruction of bards, usually called *gramadegau,* or bardic grammars, date from about the late fourteenth century; the earliest is attributed to Einion Offeiriad.

PROSE

The earliest Welsh prose texts consist primarily of notes and glosses on Latin texts. The earliest passages of continuous prose are the so-called *Surexit* memorandum, an account of a law case argued in Welsh and written down toward the end of the eighth century in the St. Chad Gospels, now preserved at Lichfield Cathedral, and a tenth-century fragment of an astronomical computus designed to assist in calculating the date of Easter. The laws traditionally codified by Hywel Dda (*d.* 950) survive in a wealth of manuscripts in both Latin and Welsh. It is generally accepted that they fall into three groups representing three different editions, but also reflecting geographical differences: the Books of Blegywryd, Cyfnerth, and Iorwerth. The earliest version in Welsh is in the Black Book of Chirk (*ca.* 1200).

The most important literary prose works of the Middle Ages are the comparatively few survivals of the vast repertoire of the *cyfarwyddiaid,* or storytellers. Principal among these is the collection known as the *Mabinogion* (almost certainly a scribal error for *Mabinogi*), preserved complete in the Red Book of Hergest and the White Book of Rhydderch, with a few fragments surviving in MS Peniarth 6. This miscellaneous group of tales comprises four connected stories (known as the "Four Branches"). These consist of three Arthurian romances (*Owain* or *The Lady of the Fountain, Gereint uab Erbin,* and *Peredur*) related in ways that are now unclear to Chrétien de Troyes's *Yvain, Erec,* and *Perceval,* and a fourth romance, *Culhwch and Olwen,* which, though connected with the Arthurian story, shows almost no French influence and is much closer to folktale. Its author often seems to be experimenting with, or perhaps parodying, style and structure. He takes what is in essence a simple tale, the Giant's Daughter story, and elaborates it in a very ambitious manner. If the result is structurally flawed, it is nonetheless one of the most energetic and thoroughly delightful of early Welsh tales. In addition to these stories, the collection includes a legendary story related to Geoffrey of Monmouth's tale of the fighting dragons (*Lludd and Llefelys*), and two dream tales, one (*The Dream of Rhonabwy*) a delightful parody of the conventions of romance and oral narrative and the other (*The Dream of Maxen Wledig*) a romantic tale dealing with Emperor Maximus and the beautiful British girl he sees in a dream.

The best of the collection is the group of tales known as the Four Branches of the Mabinogi, which may originally have been a series of tales dealing with a single hero, but which now show only partial interconnections. Their mythic origins have long been recognized, and their elegance of characterization, descriptive detail, and humor have served to negate any difficulties caused by inconsistencies in the narrative. The unknown compiler writes prose of a very high artistic level, far more balanced and fluid than most medieval romances with their elaborate descriptive passages. He has a fine knack for dialogue; this and his facility in setting a mood create an atmosphere of great richness. We know nothing of this highly literary artist; one of the greatest problems concerning the Four Branches is the extent to which he drew on oral traditions, how much of his work derives from previous literary sources, and how much is the product of his own imagination. Individual influences have long been recognized; for example, the Norman influence in the first and third branches (*Pwyll Pendeuic Dyuet* and *Manawydan uab Llŷr*) is contrasted with the strong Irish influence in the second and fourth branches (*Branwen uerch Lyr* and *Math uab Mathonwy*). The presence of well-known folklore motifs has also been demonstrated, but none of this has produced clear answers about the origins of the tales. Nor is the date of the compilation a settled question. Recent critics have argued for dates from the mid eleventh to the late twelfth century, with the largest measure of agreement settling on the period from about 1050 to 1120.

Several tales and romances deriving from Latin and French originals also survive, but their quality rarely approaches that of the *Mabinogion*. These include *Ystorya Bown de Hamtwn* (ca. 1250–1275), *Ystorya de Carolo Magno* (1265–1293), *Y Seint Greal* (late fourteenth century), and versions of the *Ami et Amile* story, *Tales of Odo of Cheriton, Tales of the Seven Sages of Rome,* and the *Epistola Presbyteri Joannis.*

Clear evidence for a great wealth of native story material survives in the Triads of the Island of Britain. These stories or characters in groups of three similar episodes or themes—perhaps mnemonic in origin—sometimes enhance tales known to us from the *Mabinogion* and other sources, but more frequently give precious information on stories now wholly or partly lost. Preserved in a variety of manuscripts, the Triads are frequently referred to in the *cyfarwyddyd,* often merely alluded to as if they were the stock in trade not only of the storyteller but also of the audience.

Most medieval Welsh historical writing is based on Latin originals, and includes three versions of the *Ystorya Dared,* translated from Dares Phrygius' *De excidio Troiae,* as well as at least sixty manuscripts of Welsh versions of Geoffrey of Monmouth's *Historia Regum Britannia.* This is normally called *Brut y Brenhinedd* or *Ystorya Brenhinedd y Brytanyeit,* and the earliest Welsh version dates from about 1200. Originally compiled as a continuation of Geoffrey's work, the *Brut y Tywysogion* (Chronicle of the princes) extends to 1282 in one version and to 1332 in another. Other chronicles include the *Brut y Saesson* (ca. 1375–1400) and *Brenhinedd y Saesson* (early fifteenth century). *Hystoria Gruffudd ap Cynan* (late twelfth century) is a translation of a lost Latin biography of this early-twelfth-century prince.

A considerable body of religious prose is dominated by the compilation known as the Book of the Anchorite (*Llyvyr Agkyr Llandewivrevi*, 1346), which includes a translation of the *Elucidarium,* and the very moving mystical text *Kyssegyrlan Uuched* (On holy living). Other texts include translations of saints' lives, the *Promptuarium Bibliae* (as *Y Bibyl Ynghymraec*), the *Officium parvum Beatae Mariae Virginis* (as *Gwasanaeth Meir*), the *Visio Sancti Pauli* (*Brendwyt Pawl Ebostol*), the apocryphal gospels of Nicodemus and Pseudo-Matthew, and the Fifteen Signs Before Doomsday.

Miscellaneous translations include versions of the *Imago mundi* of Honorius Augustodunensis (*Delw y Byd*), the *Disticha Catonis* (*Cynghorau Catwn*), the *Disputatio Hadriani imperatoris et Epicteti* (*Adrian ac Ipotis*), and several collections of proverbs.

Welsh prose of the later Middle Ages is, as has been indicated, highly derivative, and there are no true successors to the native brilliance of the *Mabinogion*. It was not until the sixteenth century that a comparable prose style was re-established in Wales, and at that time its purpose was principally religious and humanistic.

BIBLIOGRAPHY

Sources. Black Book of Carmarthen (MS Peniarth 1; late twelfth–early thirteenth centuries), ed. by Alfred O. H. Jarman as *Llyfr Du Caerfyrddin* (1982); Black Book of Chirk (MS Peniarth 29; *ca.* 1200), ed. and trans. by Arthur W. Wade-Evans as *Welsh Medieval Law* (1909); Book of Aneirin (MS Cardiff, Free Library 1; *ca.* 1250), ed. by John Gwenogvryn Evans as *Llyfyr Aneirin* (1908), by Sir Ifor Williams as *Canu Aneirin* (1938, repr. 1961), and by Kenneth H. Jackson as *The Gododdin* (1969, repr. 1978); Book of Taliesin (MS Peniarth 2; *ca.* 1275), ed. by John Gwenogvryn Evans as *Facsimile and Text of the Book of Taliesin* (1910) and by Sir Ifor Williams and John E. Caerwyn Williams as *The Poems of Taliesin* (1968, repr. 1975); White Book of Rhydderch (MS Peniarth 4; *ca.* 1300), ed. by John Gwenogvryn Evans as *Llyfr Gwyn Rhydderch*, 2nd ed. (1973) and by Sir Ifor Williams as *Pedeir Keinc y Mabinogi* (1930, 2nd ed. 1951), trans. Patrick Ford as *The Mabinogion and Other Medieval Welsh Tales* (1977); Red Book of Hergest (Oxford, Bodleian Library, Jesus College MS CXI; *ca.* 1375–1425), ed. by John Gwenogvryn Evans as *The Poetry of the Red Book of Hergest* (1911) and by Sir Ifor Williams as *Canu Llywarch Hen* (1935, 2nd ed. 1953), and ed. and trans. by Patrick Ford as *The Poetry of Llywarch Hen* (1974);

Hendregadredd MS (Aberystwyth, National Library of Wales, MS 6680C; fourteenth–fifteenth centuries), ed. by Rhiannon Morris-Jones, John Morris-Jones, and Thomas H. Parry-Williams as *Llawysgrif Hendregadredd* (1933, repr. 1971), and by Joseph P. Clancy as *The Earliest Welsh Poetry* (1970).

Studies. Sir H. Idris Bell, *The Development of Welsh Poetry* (1936 repr. 1970); Rachel Bromwich, "The Character of the Early Welsh Tradition," in Nora Chadwick, ed., *Studies in Early British History* (1954), *Trioedd ynys Prydein: The Welsh Triads* (1961, 2nd ed. 1979), *Dafydd ap Gwilym* (1974), *Medieval Celtic Literature* (1974), and, as editor with R. Brinley Jones, *Astudiaethau ar yr Hengerdd* (1978); D. Simon Evans, *A Grammar of Middle Welsh* (1964), which includes a list of works and sources, pp. xxi–xliv, and *Medieval Religious Literature* (1986); Margaret E. Griffiths, *Early Vaticination in Welsh* (1937); Alfred O. H. Jarman, *The Cynfeirdd* (1981); idem and Gwilym Rees Hughes, eds., *A Guide to Welsh Literature*, 2 vols. (1976–1979); John Lloyd-Jones, "The Court Poets of the Welsh Princes," in *Proceedings of the British Academy*, 34 (1948); Proinsias MacCana, *The Mabinogi* (1977); Thomas Parry, *A History of Welsh Literature*, H. Idris Bell, trans. (1955, repr. 1970); Thomas Parry and Merfyn Morgan, *Llyfryddiaeth Llenyddiaeth Gymraeg* (1976); Gwyn Williams, *An Introduction to Welsh Literature* (1978); Sir Ifor Williams, *Lectures on Early Welsh Poetry* (1944) and *The Beginnings of Welsh Poetry*, Rachel Bromwich, ed. (1972); John E. Caerwyn Williams, *The Poets of the Welsh Princes* (1978).

DAVID N. KLAUSNER

[See also **Ami et Amile; Aneirin; Arthurian Literature, Welsh; Bard; Bardic Grammars; Casnodyn; Celtic Languages; Chrétien de Troyes; Computus; Cynddelw Brydydd Mawr; Dafydd ap Gwilym; Eisteddfod; Elucidarium and Spanish Lucidario; Geoffrey of Monmouth; Gildas, St.; Grail, Legend of; Gruffudd ab yr Ynad Coch; Gwalchmai ap Meilyr; Historia Brittonum; Honorius Augustodunensis; Iolo Goch; Law, Welsh; Mabinogi; Meilyr Brydydd; Mythology, Celtic; Taliesin; Wales: History.**]

WELSH LITERATURE: POETRY. The history of Welsh poetry in the Middle Ages is traditionally divided into three periods: that of the *Cynfeirdd* (early poets), about 575–1100; that of the *Gogynfeirdd* (rather early poets), about 1100–1350; and that of the *beirdd yr uchelwyr* (poets of the nobility), about 1350–1650.

The earliest surviving poetry in Welsh is a body of aristocratic and heroic verse generally dated to the last half (and probably the last quarter) of the sixth century. It celebrates the exploits of British warriors in some of their last encounters with the Anglo-Saxons before the extinction of British power in the north of England and the emergence of Wales as the cultural and political center of Celtic Britain. Two names are associated with this poetry: the poets Taliesin and Aneirin, who are mentioned by the historian Nennius (*ca.* 800) as among the most renowned British poets of the mid sixth century.

Most scholars accept as the genuine work of Taliesin twelve of the approximately sixty poems contained in the Book of Taliesin, a manuscript that dates from about 1275. All twelve are praise poems that celebrate a warrior prince for the martial prowess that makes him an able defender of his people and for the munificence with which he provides for the peacetime prosperity of his followers—especially his poet. Nine of Taliesin's extant poems are addressed to members of one family: to Urien of Rheged, a British kingdom in what is now northwestern England, and his son Owain. Nennius' *Historia Brittonum* and early genealogical tracts attest to the historicity of Urien and Owain; according to Nennius, Urien was preeminent among a number of kings who fought against the Anglo-Saxon kings of Northumbria during the last quarter of the sixth century. Urien and Owain also developed a legendary dimension, in which they played prominent roles in the Arthurian story as told by Geoffrey of Monmouth, Chrétien de Troyes, and others.

Besides Urien and Owain, Taliesin composed poetry for Cynan Garwyn, probably a ruler of the kingdom of Powys in Wales, and for Gwallawg, another British king mentioned by Nennius as a leader of the northern resistance to the Anglo-Saxons. It has been conjectured that Taliesin began his career as court poet to Cynan Garwyn of Powys, moving into the service of Urien once his reputation was established. He may have offended Urien by composing praise poems for other rulers whose courts he visited, such as Gwallawg, and such offense may have been the occasion for a conciliatory poem (*dadolwch*) addressed to Urien, a poem that ends with a quatrain that concludes seven of Taliesin's twelve extant poems: "And when I'm grown old, with death hard upon me,/I'll not be happy save to praise Urien" (Anthony Conran, trans.).

The poetry of Aneirin is somewhat different. His extant work, called *Y Gododdin*, is a series of 103 stanzas of varying length, an elegy for a host of 300 noble warriors defeated in battle by the Anglo-Saxons. Here, as in the work of Taliesin, we have praise poetry rather than narrative verse, but, as there emerges from Taliesin's work a fragmentary image of some of Urien's exploits, so we are able to piece together a story from the allusions to history in *Y Gododdin*.

The British kingdom of Gododdin in southeastern Scotland, with its capital at what is modern Edinburgh, was apparently ruled about 600 by Mynyddog Mwynfawr. This prince gathered about him a retinue of 300 of the very best British fighting men, and during a year of feasting they planned and prepared a military expedition against the Angles of Deira. At the end of the year they set forth, engaging the enemy at a place called Catraeth, which is probably the present-day Catterick in Yorkshire. The outcome was disastrous for the Britons: as the poem puts it, "Of three hundred champions who charged on Catraeth,/Alas, only one man escaped."

Some of the stanzas commemorate individual heroes of the calamity, such as Owain ap Marro, whose courage is exalted and whose death is lamented in these lines: "Quicker his blood to earth/Than to his wedding,/Quicker the crows were fed/Than we could bury him" (Anthony Conran, trans.). Other stanzas concern the entire band of 300:

Men went to Catraeth, keen was their war-band.
Pale mead their portion, it was poison.
Three hundred under orders to fight.
And after celebration, silence.
Though they went to churches for shriving,
True is the tale, death confronted them.
(Joseph P. Clancy, trans., 1970)

Aneirin's work, like Taliesin's, is preserved in a single manuscript, the Book of Aneirin, written about 1250. There are, however, two texts of *Y Gododdin* in the manuscript, texts that correspond only partially. The so-called *B* text, comprising forty-two stanzas, is linguistically more archaic and appears to have been copied from a ninth- or tenth-century exemplar. The *A* text has eighty-eight stanzas, of which some nineteen have analogues in *B*. The wide variations in the two texts, together with the existence of variant versions of certain stanzas within the text, suggest a lengthy period of oral transmission—perhaps two or three centuries—before *Y Gododdin* was committed to writing.

Indeed, it is only by assuming such oral tradition, as well as fairly free modernization on the part of the scribes, that it is possible to argue that Aneirin's work and Taliesin's date from the sixth century; the linguistic forms in the Book of Aneirin and the Book of Taliesin are much later. Most Celtic scholars believe that the texts we have are essentially those of the two sixth-century poets, although not in their exact words.

The earliest Welsh poetry that has survived in its original form comprises twelve *englynion* (three-line stanzas) in Old Welsh, nine of them in praise of God and three describing the loneliness and sorrow of a warrior after some great loss. They are known as the Juvencus *englynion,* after the manuscript of Juvencus' Latin versification of the Gospels (Cambridge University Library MS Ff.4.42) in which they are preserved.

The next substantial body of poetry dates from the ninth century, and it is quite different from the work of the earlier *Cynfeirdd.* For one thing, the poems of Taliesin and Aneirin are built on lines of roughly uniform syllabic length, and most carry a single end rhyme throughout. This is a form known in Welsh tradition as the *awdl.* The great poetry of the ninth century, on the other hand, consists of *englynion.* The *englyn* is a stanza in the strict sense, consisting of a fixed number of lines (three or four, depending on the type), each of a fixed length and with a fixed place in the rhyme scheme. Both *awdl* and *englyn* are further ornamented with alliteration, internal rhyme, and *cymeriad,* a linking of lines or stanzas by repetition of words or sounds. Despite the similarities of the two forms, a number of scholars have speculated that the *englyn* was the more informal of the two, employed by poets other than the official court bards, or by the bards in an unofficial capacity.

Another difference is that in ninth-century poetry the elegiac note is very strong, virtually overwhelming the heroic. The *englynion* are often referred to collectively as "the poetry of Llywarch Hen" because much of the poetry is put in the mouth of a putative cousin of Urien of Rheged by that name, who may have been a minor sixth-century British prince in his own right. One series of verses laments a fallen and decapitated Urien and the decay of his home. Another, set not in the north but in Powys, in east-central Wales, depicts Llywarch as an aged warrior who has outlived twenty-four sons. The deeds of these sons are praised in heroic terms: Pyll was "a fort on the border," "like fire through a chimney." The emphasis, however, is on Llywarch's wretchedness and loss: "Before I was decrepit, I was splendid;/My spear was foremost, was first in attack./Now I am hunched over, I am weary, I am wretched" (Patrick K. Ford, trans.).

Other ninth-century *englynion* with no explicit connection to the figure of Llywarch Hen are similar in tone, such as the series in which a certain Heledd laments the death of her brother, Cynddylan ap Cyndrwyn of Powys, a historical king who died about 660: "The hall of Cynddylan is dark tonight,/Without fire, without bed./I weep awhile, then I am silent." A number of distinguished scholars have regarded the *englynion* as the remnants of sagas in which prose and verse were interspersed, the prose variable in form and therefore never committed to writing. Whether or not this is true, there is a strong narrative impulse in the *englynion,* as strong as, if not stronger than, what is to be found in *Y Gododdin.*

The poetry of the later *Cynfeirdd,* dating from about 850–1100, is varied. Some of it deals with the legend of Taliesin, which developed between the sixth and the ninth century. According to this legend, Taliesin was a poet-seer who had acquired perfect wisdom by drinking three drops of liquid from the Cauldron of Inspiration and Knowledge, which had been prepared by the sorceress Ceridwen for her son. His flight from her wrath involved a series of metamorphoses on both their parts, culminating when Taliesin, in the form of a grain of wheat, was swallowed by Ceridwen in the form of a hen, only to be reborn of her nine months later, in human form. The potion, the transformations, and the experience of rebirth gave the legendary Taliesin the extraordinary knowledge out of which he speaks in such lines as "I have been dead, I have been alive,/I am Taliesin."

Another legend that has left its trace in the poetry of the later *Cynfeirdd* is that of Myrddin. Geoffrey of Monmouth conflated this Myrddin with Ambrosius of Nennius' *Historia* to create the figure of Merlin for Arthurian tradition. The Myrddin of Welsh legend served a late-sixth-century northern British prince by the name of Gwenddolau and went mad when his lord was killed in battle. The verse ascribed to him at least 300 years later bemoans his miserable life in the woods, "wandering with madness and madmen," and offers political "prophecies" that were probably already history by the time they were composed. Some of it, as well as some verse not connected with Myrddin, combines observation of nature with gnomic wisdom, usually in the pithy *englyn* form: "Mountain snow; red feet of hens;/Where it chatters, water's but shallow;/Big words add to any disgrace" (Anthony Conran, trans.).

A very few poems, all of them extremely obscure, allude to the Arthurian legend. *Preiddiau Annwfn* (The spoils of Annwfn) is a report of a voyage to the otherworld (in which Arthur participates) to seize a magic cauldron. There is also a dialogue in verse between Arthur and a gatekeeper, Glewlwyd, that includes a list of Arthur's men.

The rest of the poetry associated with the *Cynfeirdd* is of various kinds. There are fragments of monologue and dialogue that may, like the Llywarch Hen and Myrddin poems, have been associated with lost sagas. There is religious verse—biblical and apocryphal narrative, sacred panegyric, a debate between body and soul. There is political prophecy, most notably the *Armes Prydein,* a tenth-century composition calling for an alliance of Scots, northern Britons, Cornishmen, Bretons, and Norse to drive the Anglo-Saxons out of Britain; in fact, such an alliance was forged, although without Welsh participation, and was defeated by Athelstan at Brunanburh in 937. In addition, there are a few pieces of panegyric addressed to princes, poems that link the praise poetry of Taliesin and Aneirin to the enormous corpus of eulogy produced by the *Gogynfeirdd* in the twelfth and thirteenth centuries. Much of this miscellaneous verse still needs to be fully edited; when that task has been accomplished, scholars will be able to study the poetry of the later *Cynfeirdd* more critically, and perhaps form a more complete and coherent picture of the literary life of Wales in this period.

The second period in medieval Welsh poetry, the era of the *Gogynfeirdd,* is often divided into two parts. The age of the earlier *Gogynfeirdd,* or *beirdd y tywysogion* (poets of the princes), comprises the years 1137–1282. After the fall in 1282 of Llywelyn ap Gruffudd, last of the native Welsh princes, the court poets addressed their verse not to princes but to lesser noblemen, bishops, and abbots. Nevertheless, the later *Gogynfeirdd* continued to compose verse in the manner of their predecessors well into the fourteenth century.

The *Gogynfeirdd* were court poets, first and foremost, and courtly conventions defined both the subject and the style of their verse. The subject was most often the prince of one of the medieval Welsh kingdoms or, among the later *Gogynfeirdd,* the lord of a great manor or the abbot of a large monastery. Almost all of the surviving poetry of the twelfth and thirteenth centuries is eulogy and elegy of such men and of their families, panegyric with a very self-conscious link to the tradition established by Aneirin and Taliesin.

According to the conventions of this celebratory verse, a prince is praised—in terms literal, figurative, and allusive—for his nobility of blood, his munificence, and his valor. So, for example, Gwalchmai ap Meilyr (*fl. ca.* 1130–1180) exalts Owain Gwynedd as a descendant of heroes both historical and legendary—Gruffudd, Iago, Rhodri, and Aeneas—while Cynddelw Brydydd Mawr (the great poet; *fl. ca.* 1155–1200) describes Madog ap Maredudd of Powys as the "golden lion of warlike stock." The generosity of princes to their war bands and to their poets is recognized in phrases like the one in which Bleddyn Fardd (*fl. ca.* 1257–1285) describes Llywelyn ap Gruffudd as "most fertile for bounty, in the high, lovely fashion of Mordaf and Nudd," or in epithets like Cynddelw's for Madog ap Maredudd, "mansion of meadhorns" (Anthony Conran, trans.). It is martial imagery, however, that lends this poetry its dominant tone. The poems abound in descriptions of battle and in panegyric epithets like "the chosen hawk of mighty hawks" (Y Prydydd Bychan [the small poet], *fl. ca.* 1222–1270; said of Rhys Gryg), "the oaken door of Aberffraw" (Gruffudd ab yr Ynad Coch, *fl. ca.* 1282; said of Llywelyn ap Gruffudd), and "the roar of the sea surge beating against the shore" (Cynddelw; said of Madog ap Maredudd). Both eulogy of the living and elegy for the dead are cast in this heroic mode, the only real difference being that prayers for the repose of the prince's soul are added to the terms of praise in the latter.

The conventional nature of bardic eulogy is evident not only in the poetry itself but also in a fourteenth-century treatise on "the way in which each thing should be praised" that is included in a grammar (conventionally referred to as "the bardic grammar") containing various kinds of information of use to professional poets. That conventions also governed the performance of courtly poetry and the social position of the poet is clear from laws current in the twelfth century, though perhaps they were much older. The laws, for example, identify the *bardd teulu* (poet of the household) as one of the twenty-four officers associated with a court and define his duties thus:

> When it is desired that a song be sung, the chaired bard begins, first of God, with the second of the king to whom the court belongs, and if he has nothing to sing of him, let him sing of another king. After the chaired bard, it is proper for the bard of the household to sing three songs of another genre. If it happens that the queen wants a song, let the bard of the household go and sing to her unstintingly, and that quietly, so that the hall is not disturbed by him.

The laws then go on to describe some of the courtly privileges and material rewards that are the bard's right.

It appears, then, that in the twelfth and thirteenth centuries poetry was a highly esteemed and highly regulated craft; there is even evidence that its practitioners sometimes engaged in public contests (*ymrysonau*) in order to establish their relative status in the profession. One became a bard through apprenticeship to a poet of high standing, and in some cases, at least, the profession may have been hereditary. We know of one line that began with Meilyr (*fl. ca.* 1100–1137), court poet to Gruffudd ap Cynan of Gwynedd; continued with his son Gwalchmai ap Meilyr, bard to Gruffudd's son Owain Gwynedd and to his sons Dafydd and Rhodri, as well as to Madog ap Maredudd of neighboring Powys; and produced at least two poets in the third generation: Einion ap Gwalchmai (*fl. ca.* 1203–1223), who continued to eulogize the royal line of Gwynedd; Meilyr ap Gwalchmai (*fl. ca.* 1170–1220), of whose work only religious poetry remains; and possibly Elidir Sais (*fl. ca.* 1195–1246), another northern bard.

Besides the predominant *molawd* (eulogy) and *marwnad* (elegy), bards in their official capacity composed *rhieingerddi* (maiden songs), rather formal poems of praise addressed to women in the voice of a would-be suitor; *dadolychau,* which are conciliatory poems addressed to offended patrons; and religious poems of praise, contrition, and petition that apparently served as a kind of extraliturgical public prayer and that were mandated, as we have seen, by the laws. They may have composed satire (*dychan*) as well, but none has survived. There is also a small body of bardic poetry in a less formal mode, some of it composed by the court poets themselves, some of it by the two "poet princes," Hywel ab Owain Gwynedd (*fl. ca.* 1140–1170) and Owain Cyfeiliog of Powys (*ca.* 1130–

1197). This verse includes love poetry, personal elegies, meditative religious poetry, and two celebrations of life and love (*gorhoffeddau,* boasts)—one by the professional bard Gwalchmai ap Meilyr and one by Prince Hywel ab Owain Gwynedd.

Whether formal or informal, public or private, however, all *Gogynfeirdd* poetry employs *awdl* and *englyn* meters. By the twelfth century these meters, especially the *awdl* forms, had become far more rigidly codified than they had been in the era of the *Cynfeirdd.* Indeed, in the fourteenth century, the bardic grammar would establish twenty-four meters, including twelve *awdl* measures and eight kinds of *englyn,* as acceptable for use by professional poets.

While not all of these meters can be found among the work of the *Gogynfeirdd,* none of these poets employs a meter that does not turn up later on the official list. An *awdl* measure can be as simple as the *cyhydedd naw ban,* a nine-syllable line with end rhyme, or as complex as the *gwawdodyn,* a four-line form in which a couplet of *cyhydedd naw ban* is followed by a nineteen-syllable unit such as the *cyhydedd hir,* which is divided into three sections of five syllables and one of four syllables, the final section carrying the main rhyme while the first three rhyme with one another. It is not uncommon for several *awdl* measures to be incorporated in one poem, so that odes of several hundred lines avoid monotony while preserving unity by means of rhyme and *cymeriad.* The *englyn* is less common than the *awdl* measures. When it does occur in *Gogynfeirdd* verse, it is the four-line *englyn unodl union,* consisting of lines of ten, six, seven, and seven syllables, rather than one of the three-line forms common among the *Cynfeirdd.*

The poetry is extensively ornamented with final and internal rhyme and with alliteration. Throughout a passage of as many as 100 lines, an *awdl* can sustain a single end rhyme, and the juncture of passages with different end rhymes is always reinforced with *cymeriad.* These stylistic features combine with a strong predilection for obscure and archaic diction, as well as syntactic compression and rearrangement, to produce verse that is often aurally magnificent but sometimes semantically cryptic.

Poetry survives by some thirty *beirdd y tywysogion* and another twenty-five or so later *Gogynfeirdd,* most of them associated with North Wales. The primary manuscript sources for their poetry are the Hendregadredd manuscript (*ca.* 1300), the

Red Book of Hergest (*ca.* 1375), and National Library of Wales MS 4973 (seventeenth century). There are in addition a few *Gogynfeirdd* poems in the Black Book of Carmarthen (*ca.* 1225–1250). Because there are so many poets, and because until now so little of their work has been edited, most students of Welsh literature have a very imperfect sense of individual poets. Nevertheless, while much of the verse is no more than conventional, there is a great deal of very fine poetry from this period, particularly by the *beirdd y tywysogion*. The most prolific of them, and probably the most gifted, were Cynddelw and Llywarch ap Llywelyn Prydydd y Moch (poet of the pigs, *fl. ca.* 1173–1220). The single best-known *Gogynfeirdd* poem, however, is the elegy of Gruffudd ab yr Ynad Coch for Llywelyn ap Gruffudd, the last independent native Welsh prince, who was killed by the forces of Edward I in December 1282. It is an *awdl* of 104 lines with a single end rhyme (*prifodl*) throughout. The poem celebrates Llywelyn's glory and mourns his loss:

> A soldier's head, a head for praise henceforth;
> A leader's head, a dragon's head was on him,
> Head of fair, dogged Llywelyn; it shocks the world
>   that an iron stake should pierce it.
> My lord's head, a harsh-falling pain is mine,
> My soul's head, which has no memorial;
> A head which owned honor in nine hundred lands,
>   with the homage of nine hundred feasts;
> A king's head, iron flew from his hand;
> A king's head, a proud hawk breaching a gap;
> A regal head of a thrusting wolf,
> A king's head this; may Heaven be its refuge!
>   (Gwyn Williams, trans.)

It is distinguished from other bardic elegies by the authenticity of its sorrow, not only for the personal loss of Llywelyn but also for the implications of his downfall for the future of Wales.

The third period, that of the *beirdd yr uchelwyr*, extends beyond the end of the Middle Ages. The first half of this era, so called because in the absence of native princes professional poets devoted their energies to the praise of the lesser nobility and of well-placed clerics, is by far the more important; indeed, the years 1350–1500 were the golden age of Welsh poetry. In marked contrast with the *Gogynfeirdd* period, that of the *beirdd yr uchelwyr* is clearly dominated by one man, Dafydd ap Gwilym (*ca.* 1320–1370), a great innovator in both form and content.

Dafydd composed the first substantial body of love poetry in Welsh, work that clearly participates in the continental tradition of *fin'amors*. Scholars disagree about the relative importance in Dafydd's poetry of Latin, French, Provençal, Catalan, and other specific influences. They all acknowledge, however, that as a skilled poet with access to the homes of the gentry and as scion of a family whose members had held various offices of the crown, he was well acquainted with the Anglo-Norman culture of his day, and was able to make use in his own verse of the subject matter, imagery, and flexibility of tone that he encountered in continental literature.

Dafydd's love poetry is marked by the preoccupation with a lady's charms, frustrated longing, and exalted fulfillment that we associate with courtly love poetry throughout Europe in the late Middle Ages. Two ladies figure most prominently: blond and married Morfudd, the subject of thirty poems, and dark, virginal Dyddgu, the subject of nine. He describes the latter thus:

> Her hair's blacker, proud forest,
> Than blackbird or brooch of jet.
> Smooth skin's unblemished whiteness
> Darkens her hair, flawless praise.
>   (Joseph P. Clancy, trans.)

The love messenger (*llatai*) figures frequently in Dafydd's poetry: he apostrophizes an animal or object, begging it to bear word of his love to some inaccessible mistress, and makes the situation an occasion for various figurative descriptions of the messenger. His invocation of the wind, for instance, is riddlelike in its imagery:

> No need for a swift horse under you,
> Nor bridge nor boat at river-mouth,
> You will not drown: you have been indeed
>   forewarned,
> You have no corners, so you will not get
>   entangled.
> Though you might winnow leaves, seizing the
>   nests,
> None will indict you. . . .
>   (Rachel Bromwich, trans., 1982)

These love message poems and others are full of a pleasure in nature that is very rare in Welsh poetry before Dafydd. He often chooses outdoor settings for his trysts, his meditations, and his laments, a habit that affords him ample opportunity for description of nature in terms of culture, as in the poem that describes the dawn songs of the thrush and the nightingale as a woodland Mass.

Humor is as characteristic of Dafydd's poetry as

is his sensuous pleasure in women and nature, and it constitutes another new element in the Welsh poetic tradition. Dafydd's is a ribald, bitter, ironic humor that betrays the influence of the fabliau. He often refers, for example, to the stock figure of the jealous husband, whom he calls Yr Eiddig (the jealous one) or Y Bwa Bach (the little hunchback). Merely because the husband stands between the poet and his mistress, Dafydd expresses the wish that when he journeys to France to fight, Eiddig will be drowned during the crossing or felled by a bowman. He urges the latter:

> Look for, shooter of straight shafts,
> His lank and scrawny whiskers.
> Shabby beard, a fennel bush,
> Time's come, good were his taking.
> (Joseph P. Clancy, trans., 1965)

Dafydd also excels in comic accounts of the interruption or frustration of his amorous adventures by others, as when a shepherd stumbles into the grove where he lies with his love:

> Who had, public enemy,
> A harsh-horned sag-cheeked rattle.
> He played, cramped yellow belly,
> This bag, curse its scabby leg.
> So before satisfaction
> The sweet girl panicked: poor me!
> (Joseph P. Clancy, trans., 1965)

Dafydd's meter is the *cywydd deuair hirion,* a rhyming couplet of seven-syllable lines in which one line has a masculine ending and the other a feminine ending. Along with three other *cywydd* measures, it is among the twenty-four meters laid down as permissible for professional Welsh poets by the bardic grammars. *Cywydd* measures were not employed by the *Gogynfeirdd,* however, and the evidence points to Dafydd as the first poet important enough to have had his work preserved who made extensive use of it. This turned out to be a very important innovation, for the *cywydd* soon became so much the norm in Welsh poetry that the poets of the nobility, with the exception of the late *Gogynfeirdd,* who clung to the old forms of panegyric until about 1350, are sometimes known as the *cywyddwyr* (*cywydd* men).

With the ascendancy of the *cywydd* came the full development of another important feature of Welsh poetry, *cynghanedd.* This term, whose literal meaning may be best described as "harmony," refers to an elaborate system of alliteration and internal rhyme. These features had characterized Welsh

verse from the time of Taliesin and Aneirin on, but their use according to certain fixed patterns became obligatory among the *cywyddwyr* and was codified by the bardic manuals of the fifteenth and sixteenth centuries.

The principles of *cynghanedd* may be illustrated by a description of just one of the four main kinds, which are *cynghanedd sain* (sonorous *cynghanedd*), *cynghanedd lusg* (trailing *cynghanedd*), *cynghanedd groes* (cross *cynghanedd*), and *cynghanedd draws* (traversing *cynghanedd*). The first of these involves both internal rhyme and alliteration. The line is divided into three parts, with the last syllable of the first rhyming with the last syllable of the second, while the second and third parts alliterate with one another according to the rules of either *cynghanedd groes* or *cynghanedd draws.* This means that all the consonants of one section, with the exception of the last, must be repeated in the same order in the other. In *cynghanedd draws* there is a short non-alliterative section between the two echoing sequences; in *cynghanedd groes* there is not. Below is a couplet from Dafydd's poem to the seagull that employs *cynghanedd sain* in the first line and *cynghanedd groes* in the second. In the first line italics mark the rhyming syllables, boldface the alliterating consonants.

> E**dr**y*ch*/a we*lych*/**w**ylan,
> **Eigr** o liw ar/y **g**aer lân.

> Look that you may see, seagull,
> One of Eigr's hue on the castle wall.

Although many of the *cywyddwyr* adopted not only the meter but also the subjects popularized by Dafydd, the tradition of professional panegyric remained strong during the fourteenth and fifteenth centuries, though changed by the drastically altered circumstances of Wales after 1282. It was extremely rare that a patron could maintain a full-time family bard, as had the princes, so that poets typically traveled around the countryside, visiting various houses of the affluent gentry, a practice known as *clera.* The content of their encomia changed as well: although martial valor in the old heroic style was still a part of the idealized portrait of the patron of letters, it was less prominent than it had been in the poetry of the *Gogynfeirdd.* There was also a new emphasis on physical beauty and gracious living.

On occasion this preoccupation with the amenities of a settled and civilized life expressed itself in poems of praise focused on a place rather than a person, such as Iolo Goch's (*ca.* 1320–1398) *cywydd* to the court of Owain Glyndwr (Owen Glendower) at Sycharth, near the Shropshire border. This poem lingers lovingly over every architectural and domestic detail of the place; it celebrates, for example, the

> Tile roof on each building,
> And chimney which nurtures no smoke,
> Nine halls of proportioned shape,
> And nine wardrobes in each one.

An even more common convention in the professional poetry of the period was the *cywydd* requesting a specific gift from a patron. In such pieces it was the object of the poet's desire, rather than the patron himself, that served as the subject to be elaborated in metaphor and simile showing the poet's imagination and versecraft to advantage.

Despite, or perhaps because of, the many changes in their circumstances and practices during this period, the bards became increasingly organized and self-regulating. The poets held an occasional eisteddfod (assembly) in order to discuss and establish the rules of meter and *cynghanedd,* and to award appropriate licenses to bards of varying degrees of expertise. The first of these meetings whose historicity is certain was held at Carmarthen about 1451, and there is some evidence that the tradition may have been established as early as 1176, when the lord Rhys hosted a gathering of poets and musicians at Cardigan Castle.

The process of codification of subject, meter, and ornament continued, with written treatises on poetic art gradually replacing, at least in part, the oral training of disciple by master that had been the backbone of the Welsh poetic tradition for centuries. The exercise of the craft, too, involved writing during this period, whereas earlier it is likely that the Welsh bards composed as did their Irish counterparts, lying on their backs in the dark. From the fourteenth and fifteenth centuries we have a collection of *areithiau* (orations), prose compositions in which novice poets practiced the creation of compound words and metaphors that were characteristic of the poetry of the nobility.

Further evidence for the interest of the period in "correct" practice and the maintenance of standards are the surviving *ymrysonau* (poetic debates), which often deal with matters of propriety in subject and meter. The most famous of these is Dafydd ap Gwilym's debate with Gruffudd Gryg, comprising eight *cywyddau* of about fifty lines each—four by each poet. In their good-humored exchange they discuss the relative merits of love and the excellence of a patron as subjects, of the *cywydd* and the *awdl* as forms.

Despite the dominance of a single poetic form—the *cywydd* with *cynghanedd*—the late Middle Ages was a period of exuberant variety in Welsh poetry. Verse has survived by some 150 poets. There is love and nature poetry, not only Dafydd's but also that of his numerous disciples, including Dafydd ap Edmwnd (*fl.* 1450–1497), who played an important role in the codification of meter and *cynghanedd* at the Carmarthen eisteddfod, replacing two obsolete *englyn* forms with measures of his own devising in the traditional scheme of twenty-four meters. There is traditional bardic fare—eulogy, elegy, petition—by such accomplished poets as Iolo Goch, Guto'r Glyn (*ca.* 1435–*ca.* 1493), Gutun Owain (*fl.* 1450–1498), and Tudur Aled (*ca.* 1465–*ca.* 1525). There is political vaticination by, for example, Lewys Glyn Cothi (*ca.* 1420–1489); this very old tradition of prophecy veiled in obscure animal imagery reached its zenith during the Wars of the Roses, as Welshmen saw their hopes embodied in Henry Tudor. There is, in the *ymrysonau,* poetry about poetry. And there is social and religious commentary and satire, most notably in the jeremiads of Siôn Cent (*ca.* 1400–1430), who reminds his audience:

> Futile the frantic plotting
> Of weak clay, dead in a day.
> From bare earth he came, dark cold,
> Coldly he goes in ashes.
> (Joseph P. Clancy, trans., 1965)

All of the poetry, however, is characterized, as is Welsh poetry throughout the Middle Ages, by great craftsmanship and self-conscious artistry.

BIBLIOGRAPHY

Rachel Bromwich, *Medieval Celtic Literature: A Select Bibliography* (1974), includes excellent sections on diplomatic editions and facsimiles, manuscript catalogs, texts and translations, and literary history and criticism. Each of these has a subdivision for Welsh poetry, or at least for Welsh.

Significant contributions to scholarship in the field of medieval Welsh poetry since 1974 include a new edition of the poems in the Black Book of Carmarthen, Alfred O. H. Jarman, ed., *Llyfr Du Caerfyrddin* (1982). There is an important article on the Hendregadredd Manuscript, in Welsh, by Daniel Huws in *National Library of Wales Journal,* **22** (1981).

Among recently published texts and translations of medieval Welsh poetry is Gwyn Jones, ed., *The Oxford Book of Welsh Verse in English* (1977). Richard M. Loomis, ed., *Dafydd ap Gwilym: The Poems* (1982), translates all of Dafydd's verse. There are several editions in Welsh of other *cywyddwyr*, including E. D. Jones, ed., *Lewys Glyn Cothi* (1984); and Eurys Rolant, ed., *Gwaith Owain ap Llywelyn ab y Moel* (1984).

Among recent critical and literary historical studies, the most useful to the beginning student of Welsh poetry are Rachel Bromwich, *Dafydd ap Gwilym* (1974) and *Aspects of the Poetry of Dafydd ap Gwilym: Collected Papers* (1986); Alfred O. H. Jarman, *The Cynfeirdd* (1981) and *idem* and Gwilym Rees Hughes, eds., *A Guide to Welsh Literature*, 2 vols. (1976–1979); Meic Stephens, ed., *The Oxford Companion to the Literature of Wales* (1986); J. E. Caerwyn Williams, *The Poets of the Welsh Princes* (1978).

The best sources for current bibliography are *Celtic Studies Bibliography*, published triennially by the Celtic Studies Association of North America; and the "List of Books, Articles, etc." that appears, accompanied by "Theses and Dissertations on Celtic Studies," in each double volume of *Studia celtica* (biennial).

Quotations in this article can be found in the following works: Rachel Bromwich, ed., *Dafydd ap Gwilym: A Selection of Poems* (1982), rev. as *Selected Poems of Dafydd ap Gwilym* (1985); Joseph P. Clancy, ed., *Medieval Welsh Lyrics* (1965) and *The Earliest Welsh Poetry* (1970); Anthony Conran, ed., *The Penguin Book of Welsh Verse* (1967); Patrick K. Ford, ed., *The Poetry of Llywarch Hen* (1974); Thomas Parry, ed., *Gwaith Dafydd ap Gwilym* (1952); Gwyn Williams, ed., *The Burning Tree* (1956).

CATHERINE A. MCKENNA

[See also **Aneirin; Bard; Bardic Grammars; Casnodyn; Cynddelw Brydydd Mawr; Dafydd ap Gwilym; Einon ap Gwalchmai; Eisteddfod; Elidir Sais; Elucidarium and Spanish Lucidario; Gruffudd ab yr Ynad Coch; Gwalchmai ap Meilyr; Hywel ab Owain Gwynedd; Iolo Goch; Meilyr Brydydd; Taliesin; Wales: History; Welsh Literature.**]

WELSH LITERATURE: PROSE. Medieval Welsh literature distinguishes both in form and in function between prose and verse. Poetry, as practiced by the bards and patronized by princes and aristocracy, was largely reserved for the eulogy and elegy of patrons, though a substantial body of verse, similar in style and metrics, consists of religious poetry. There are examples of other types of poetry, such as prophecy, nature, gnomic, and religious lyrics. Though some poems seem to require a context in some form of prosimetron narrative, there is no narrative poetry and there is little didactic verse. Narration and instruction are the roles of Middle Welsh prose, which is used as the medium for stories and for learned functional texts. Many in the latter category are translations, and it is a temptation to classify Welsh prose as "native" or "translated." This, however, is an oversimplification; the true division is "learned," "functional," and "entertainment," as both groups contain texts from both native and foreign sources.

The earliest examples of continuous passages of Welsh prose belong to the Old Welsh period. These are records of title to land (ninth century), a fragment of a computus used to ascertain the date of Easter (tenth century), and a description of the privileges of the church and diocese of St. Teilo at Llandaff, Glamorgan, which is in two parts, one from about 950–1090 and the other from about 1110–1129. The "Privilege of Teilo" (Braint Teilo) in the Book of Llandaf (first half of the twelfth century) is an original composition in Welsh (which also exists in a Latin version), and it seems to confirm the evidence of the Old Welsh passages and related glosses that Welsh had been used for writing legal and utilitarian memoranda and translations from an early period. The earliest extant prose texts of any length derive their consistent orthography, their standard form of language almost wholly free from dialect variations, and their stylistic conventions from a continuous tradition of writing.

The Welsh learned classes (lawyers, mediciners, and bards) were responsible for the conservation and development of a broadly based native culture comprising traditional history, myth and legend, genealogies, and toponymics and geography. Though such knowledge was essentially orally transmitted, probably in narrative forms, and had a basic social function, the native learned classes appear to have formed a fruitful relationship with others trained in a book-based Latin ecclesiastic culture. The result was that native culture achieved written prose form and foreign texts were translated into an accepted literary language at an early period. Native law texts, showing Roman and canonical influences, are the first fully developed examples of Welsh prose; but native tales, when their written forms first appear, are also marked by a mature, self-confident literary style and by consciously created structures.

The extant native tales are collectively known as

the *Mabinogion*. This is a modern title (deriving from a scribal error in the White Book of Rhydderch text) that unfortunately suggests a greater degree of homogeneity for these stories than is the case. Ten of these eleven tales are found in the fourteenth-century White Book of Rhydderch and, together with one other, are in the late-fourteenth–early-fifteenth-century Red Book of Hergest. In neither do they form a single group; individual stories belong to different periods, and their literary contexts vary.

The oldest is probably *How Culhwch won Olwen* (or *Culhwch and Olwen*), the extant redaction of which has been dated to the end of the eleventh century. This is a literary and extended version of a folktale describing how the hero, Culhwch, fated to marry Olwen, the giant's daughter, overcomes the difficulties placed in his way, and with the help of King Arthur succeeds in fulfilling the seemingly impossible tasks set him. After a short introduction that sets the scene, a rhetorical passage describes the arrival of Culhwch at Arthur's court, where he claims assistance in his quest in a roll call of Arthur's men, a catalog that effectively closes the first section of the story. The quest follows, Olwen is found and claimed, and after scenes of barbarous but comic parleys the giant's list of tasks closes this section of the tale. The rest of the story is an account of fulfilling some, but by no means all, of these tasks and comprises a number of independent folktales, some told in greater detail than others, set within the context of the winning of Olwen.

Culhwch and Olwen follows one or two recognizable folktale types, but its length, structure, elaboration of incidents, and inclusion of other narrative material suggest that it is a literary composition by an author who not only was knowledgeable in the content of native tradition but also was able effectively to give written form to a variety of oral styles and to sustain a buoyant narrative throughout.

The four stories—Pwyll, Prince of Dyfed; Branwen, Daughter of Llŷr; Manawydan, Son of Llŷr; Math, Son of Mathonwy—invariably follow one another in this sequence and together form the "Four Branches of the *Mabinogi*," dated between the mid eleventh and early twelfth centuries. *Mabinogi* apparently means an account of the youthful exploits characteristic of heroic prodigies that foreshadow their later greatness. The "four branches" form a loose unity, but in its present form the sequence of stories is not a single coherent tale.

Analyses and analogues suggest that the basic material is myth and that the protagonists are in origin Celtic deities, but successive redactors have conflated and adapted the material, shaped it to their own ends, and given it literary form. Comparative studies can reveal the nature and significance of the basic narrative, but this is far removed from the use made of the developed material by the final author. He writes succinctly and suggestively, with a restrained objectivity more reminiscent of the study than of the mead hall, and his aim seems to be not simply entertainment or even guidance for society but the expression of a personal view of life. The logical ordering of episodes is not the strong point of the narrative, but the author uses each branch to portray themes of human relationships that together present a view of life which is realistically somber but always just and ultimately hopeful. Though superficially the most removed from the real world, the "Four Branches of the *Mabinogi*," on account of their restrained style and compassionate attitude, are the most moving and classical of all the Middle Welsh stories.

Another finely wrought piece is the brief *Dream of Maxen Wledig* (the Roman general Magnus Maximus, proclaimed emperor by his troops in Britain in 383). In the native historical tradition he gave the Britons a basis for their claim to be a remnant of the Roman Empire and inheritors of *romanitas*, while his return to the Continent at the head of his British army became one of the explanations of the colonization of Brittany. In the *Dream* these themes are expressed imaginatively in terms of the love of the emperor for a woman seen in a dream and later discovered to be a British princess; this love story is combined with antiquarian items to make a jewel of a story.

Another brief story is *Lludd and Llefelys (Lleuelys)*, first found as an insert in a thirteenth-century Welsh version of Geoffrey of Monmouth's *Historia regum Brittanie* but extant also as an independent story in an expanded version in the Red Book of Hergest and the fragment in the White Book of Rhydderch. The narrative, based on a repetition of incidents, shows little imagination or skill. What must have been a traditional tale, reflecting either a mythological tradition of successive settlements of Britain or a reflex of Dumézilian tripartite functions, has been retold in a flat, factual style that, unlike the other tales, shows few signs of the art of the oral storyteller.

At the other extreme of narrative conventions is

the *Dream of Rhonabwy*, perhaps the latest of the so-called *Mabinogion*. The narrative is full of noisy, colorful scenes but almost devoid of any progression. It is a tour de force of rhetorical description and embellishment, and a good example of the use of triadic repetition; but if one is looking for a "story," it is a disappointment. The *Dream* is best regarded as a comic satire that irreverently looks at the heroic presentation of the Arthurian past and the unheroic reality of the present, and expresses these attitudes in a narrative form that parodies contemporary literary fashions.

The accepted Arthurian scene is found in the three stories now commonly referred to as romances: *Peredur Son of Efrog*, *The Lady of the Fountain*, and *Geraint and Enid*. These stories have an obvious similarity to three romances by Chrétien de Troyes: *Perceval*, *Yvain*, *Erec et Enide*. Such resemblance, varying in degree in each of the tales, has to do with plot, sequence of episodes, and the names of the characters. It has raised the question of the relationship between the Welsh and Old French texts. Many of the themes seem to be of Celtic origin, as are the names of the protagonists, so that Chrétien's sources have been claimed to be *contes* recited by Breton and Welsh storytellers and represented by these Welsh stories, which therefore have a common origin with the French poems. The Welsh versions are not, however, uninfluenced by contemporary French usage, and in ethos they appear different from the other eight tales we have described. Another view would emphasize such influence and attribute it directly to Chrétien's poems, seeing these Welsh prose tales as retellings, probably from memory, of the French works. Their adaptation to the strong tradition of Welsh narrative prose and its conventions would have led to a refashioning of the source material.

All eleven stories have a boldly marked narrative line, and minimal characterization and descriptive elaboration, but they are written in a vivid style that moves the narrative along and presents colorful or mysterious scenes with both an economy of words and rhetorical flashes. There is no analysis of motive or any introspection, nor is there any authorial comment or intervention.

Middle Welsh narrative is objective, "epic," and linear, drawing its strengths from the conventions of the oral storyteller but tempering his excesses with a disciplined awareness of the different needs of written literary composition. For the most part the Welsh tales bear only their surface meanings

although, as has been suggested, this is not true of the "Four Branches of the *Mabinogi*." The three "romances" seem to have a deeper significance and to have been designed to explicate implicitly chivalric themes of education, self-awareness, and marital relationships. It is this development, more than details of external resemblance, that truly justifies their claim to be "Welsh romances."

The composition of the "native" texts extended over the whole of the Middle Welsh period, from the late eleventh century to the fourteenth century (when the Welsh adaptation of the *Tales of the Seven Sages of Rome* was compiled, following the same tradition of what we may call the literary form of oral narrative tradition). Throughout this period Welsh prose was enriched by translations of foreign material. The stylistic confidence, the strength of vocabulary and syntax, and the faithfulness to the original of the majority of these translations suggest that native skills and conventions were being fruitfully used by writers who were well versed in Latin and Anglo-Norman/French culture.

In spite of the strong traditional "Celtic" element in medieval Welsh literature, Wales and its culture had from earliest times looked eastward and had been aware of the European inheritance. The re-invigoration of intellectual life in the twelfth century was experienced by Welsh writers and learned classes, and from the end of the century on, the Welsh aristocracy shared French literary interests and fashions. The appeal of Arthurian romance (or at least those examples felt to be inherently Welsh) led to the re-creation of the genre according to Welsh prose conventions at the same time as the chansons de geste, their foreign origins more apparent, were being translated rather than adapted.

A collection of Charlemagne texts was translated and set in a linked sequence by different writers in the period extending from the mid thirteenth to the mid fourteenth century and known in its modern edition as *Ystorya de Carolo Magno*. The first of the series was a version of the Latin *Pseudo-Turpin* chronicle. At a later date the Roncevaux section of the *Chanson de Roland* was inserted in place of the brief chronicle account (or, as has been suggested, this section was abstracted from an earlier translation of the full *Chanson*). At subsequent stages the *Pérelinage de Charlemagne* and the romance of Otuel were added to form a cycle of texts that must have become popular, judging by the number of manuscript copies. An

611

Anglo-Norman *Bevis de Hamtoune* was translated by someone who commanded a wide vocabulary.

To the fourteenth century also belongs an interesting attempt to adapt French prose romance for a South Wales patron. The narrative convention of a strong story line with little authorial comment was too strong to allow any allegory, and though techniques of interlace and simultaneous episodes caused some difficulties, the translator(s) did not iron them out completely. This Welsh *Ystoryaeu Seint Greal* is a composite text, the first part a version of the *Queste del Saint Graal* and the second of *Perlesvaus*; together with a few other fragments it reveals how new French romance was becoming acceptable in Wales. The Welsh *Friendship of Amlyn and Amig* is derived from a Latin original and was translated at the beginning of the fourteenth century by an author able to slip into the formulas and familiar expressions of the native writers, further proof that the prose tradition was thriving even at the end of the Middle Welsh period.

Most of what may be termed functional prose is, not unexpectedly, translated and is representative of Western European medieval learning in history, religion, geography, and didactic or exhortatory texts. Other categories, however, such as law, medicine, and grammar, derive from native learning in these fields combined with their Latin forms. Fourteenth- and fifteenth-century bardic grammars, formalized as a response to the crisis in the bardic order after the demise of the last Welsh royal line in 1282, present a stylized ideal of Welsh metrics and a systematized hierarchy of social grades to be praised for their proper virtues; their linguistic analysis, however, is taken largely unadapted from Latin grammars. Medical texts are based on common medieval practices and are not peculiarly Welsh in their material. The organization of the material, however, may reflect traditional methods of teaching, and the common European nature of the medicine is somewhat concealed by the texts' being ascribed to a family of mediciners who acquired this body of learning supernaturally. The most important category of native learning is the law texts. The codification of native law is traditionally ascribed to King Hywel the Good (d. 950), and Welsh medieval law was termed by its practitioners the "Law of Hywel Dda." This law (what we would call "the law of the land") is found in its different aspects, recensions, and copies in many different manuscripts. "Law" is the unified system; the books contain its expression. They have a

general similarity but differ in the details of the tractates contained in them and the law set out. Later law books appear to be more closely related to the needs of practicing lawyers, and still others are collections of pleadings, procedures, and verdicts. Welsh legal texts are obviously of prime importance for the legal and social historian, but they are also of interest in the study of the development of Welsh prose styles. The law books describe the structures of society in a number of separate discussions. The material is collected, systematized, argued, and in some sections is presented as textbook material in condensed forms for easy recall.

Some law books are in Latin, but as there can be no doubt that the language of instruction and the courts was Welsh; the Welsh books echo the traditional styles and forms of the law as practiced. They open with an account in traditional narrative style of the supposed conference at which the law was promulgated, but this drifts into a list of the officers of the court and their privileges that is less analytical in style. The discussion of specific topics follows. The strength of the law books lies in their ability to define unambiguously and to explain clearly, logically, and reasonably.

Though they lack the more obvious embellishments of the tales, the law books have their own techniques—rhetorical questions, direct speech, catalogs, triads, alliteration, pairs of synonyms or terms. Paragraphs often have a balance of sentences or progress to a logical conclusion that is aesthetically pleasing. It is fine utilitarian prose forged and constantly refined in the oral discussions of law schools and courts, and it may well have been one of the agents that taught the writers of saga prose the virtues of economy and precision.

Another large body of learned prose is historical texts, all translated from Latin. Unique among them is the only Welsh secular biography, the *History of Gruffudd ap Cynan*, the twelfth-century king of Gwynedd and founder of the successful dynasty that came to an end in 1282. The Latin original of this text, apparently composed toward the twelfth century, is lost, and the thirteenth-century translation had a limited circulation. The antecedents of the work are not clear, but it probably belongs to a contemporary genre of regal biographies.

More popular are the six or seven Welsh versions of Geoffrey of Monmouth's *Historia regum Britanniae* extant in some 60 manuscripts. Three separate

612

translations were made in the thirteenth century, and others were being prepared and amalgam versions composed up to the fifteenth century. Together they are a clear indication of the importance of the *Historia* in Welsh historical consciousness throughout the Middle Ages. The *Historia* became the center point of Welsh historiography. Several manuscripts precede the Welsh version with a translation of Dares Phrygius' account of the Trojan War, and even more contain versions of the "Chronicle of the Princes," the Latin original of which is lost and which continues the history of the thirteenth century. These translations owe little to the style of the native storyteller and, unlike the law texts, have no oral antecedents. The authors seem to be uninfluenced by oral conventions or formulas. The different schools of writers and the changed expectations of their audience combined to produce a Latinate style more periodic than native narrative. Syntactically it moves away from the colloquial, and its vocabulary is full of loan translations and calques, but nevertheless it has its own sonorous dignity. Similar features are found in the translations of religious texts, though the greater variety in the types of texts translated leads to more varied styles.

Other translations from Latin are *Delw y Byd* (*Imago mundi* of Honorius Augustodunensis), *Ffordd y Brawd Odrig* (*Itinerarium fratris Odorici*), and from French, presumably for a Welsh gentleman, an abbreviated version of Walter of Henley's *La dite de hosbondrie* (*Llyfr Hwsmonaeth*). This text, more than any other, suggests the context for the patronage we should seek for the compiling and copying of many of these texts. The White Book of Rhydderch and the Red Book of Hergest, the two major manuscripts referred to above (as were the main collections of religious material), were compiled for gentry who were local officials having a political role but who also were custodians of native culture. Some had significant libraries, and the few attributions that exist reveal members of this class in the thirteenth and fourteenth centuries commissioning translations and employing scribes. These translations are an important element in Middle Welsh prose. Reflecting as they do the range of medieval book learning (the clearest omission is philosophical discussions), they extended the possibilities of Welsh writing beyond the amalgam of native learning and writing as seen in the law texts. Nevertheless, the true basis of the Welsh prose style resided in the oral tradition, and it is the written form of the tradition that is its glory.

BIBLIOGRAPHY

Daniel Simon Evans, *A Grammar of Middle Welsh* (1964), xxix–xliii, gives a list of Welsh prose texts with details of published editions. The *Mabinogi* has been translated by Gwyn Jones and Thomas Jones as *The Mabinogion* (1949, new ed. 1974) and by Patrick K. Ford as *The Mabinogi and Other Welsh Tales* (1977). Many of the topics mentioned in this article are discussed in Geraint Bowen, ed., *Y Traddodiad Rhyddiaith yn yr Oesau Canol* (1974); Alfred O. H. Jarman and Gwilym R. Hughes, eds., *A Guide to Welsh Literature*, 2 vols. (1976–1979); Thomas Parry, *A History of Welsh Literature*, H. Idris Bell, trans. (1955, repr. 1970); Meic Stephens, ed., *The Oxford Companion to the Literatures of Wales* (1986). More specific are Dafydd Jenkins, *Cyfraith Hywel* (1970); Thomas Jones, "Historical Writing in Medieval Welsh," in *Scottish Studies*, 12 (1968); Proinsias MacCana, *The Mabinogi* (1977); A. T. E. Matonis, "The Welsh Bardic Grammars and the Western Grammatical Tradition," in *Modern Philology*, 79 (1981–1982); Morfydd E. Owen, "Meddygon Myddfai: A Preliminary Survey of Some Medieval Medical Writing in Welsh," in *Studia celtica* 10/11 (1975/1976).

BRYNLEY F. ROBERTS

[See also Ami et Amile; Arthurian Literature, Welsh; Bardic Grammars; Chrétien de Troyes; Computus; Geoffrey of Monmouth; Grail, Legend of; Honorius Augustodunensis; Law, Welsh; Mabinogi; Mythology, Celtic; Wales: History; Walter of Henley.]

WELSH LITERATURE: RELIGIOUS. Most extant Middle Welsh verse is eulogy and elegy written usually, but not exclusively, for lay patrons by professional court poets. From the twelfth century on (and perhaps earlier), many of these poets used their skills to produce religious verse similar in its high style and conventions of praise to their secular poems. Praise to God the King, however, frequently becomes a poem of repentance in the face of the reality of the Last Judgment and pains of Hell, so that reconciliation is a more obvious theme than eulogy. The suffering of the Christ-man is vividly described in an appeal to the sinner to seek forgiveness, and even in poems claimed to be deathbed confessions, the threat of judgment and descriptions of punishment are as much a part of the poem as the catalog of sins. Descriptions of the Day of Judgment, sometimes associated with the *Fifteen Signs Before Doomsday,* reflections on the Mass, and the Debate of the Body and Soul are other common themes.

This somber and majestic religious court poetry is followed in the fourteenth century by more personal lyrics that have as their themes *ubi sunt, de contemptu mundi,* the worm in the grave, and devotion to the Blessed Virgin Mary. These personal poems are foreshadowed in the earlier period by the work of such intense poets as Gruffudd ab yr Ynad Coch and the friar (perhaps a Franciscan) Madog ap Gwallter, who wrote a delightful song on the Nativity.

Side by side with the religious poems written following the court poetry conventions there existed verse, much of it probably by clerics, that was more varied in theme and more obviously didactic, and that seems to represent a body of "unofficial" poetry that is popular in aim. The earliest example is a series of *englynion* (stanzas) to God the Creator in the ninth-century Juvencus manuscript. Six poems in the thirteenth-century Black Book of Carmarthen may be the work of a single poet. Some are hymns of praise to God and the Trinity, Creator and Savior, while others, sometimes composed in the style of contemporary nature poetry, reveal an intense awareness of God's immanence and a resulting consciousness of the impermanence of the world and of the need for reconciliation. Still other poems reflect on the awful certainty of judgment: one seems to be a prayer before a journey; and another, in the form of a series of questions, draws on the instruction offered by manuals to describe the mortal sins, the acts of mercy, and right living. This poem had some circulation as a popular mnemonic guide to the Christian life. A few stanzas from it are attached to another poem in which Arthur converses with an eagle, his transformed nephew. Dialogue poems are a well-known narrative genre in Middle Welsh, but the form is used didactically here to emphasize virtues of the faith. Stanzas from a dialogue on the need to attend Mass were also incorporated into the eagle poem, and in yet another narrative dialogue a spirit reveals to his former colleague how to gain salvation. Such poems as these suggest that popular poetic forms were being employed to instruct laity, just as some of the translators of Latin manuals occasionally inserted *englynion* into their texts to underline the teaching.

Instruction, popular devotion, and judgment all find fuller treatment in the prose translations of the late thirteenth, fourteenth, and fifteenth centuries. At their simplest many of these texts merely set out the basic tenets of the faith in schematic form. They are lists of the seven deadly sins and the seven cardinal virtues, the seven acts of mercy, the seven gifts of the Holy Spirit, the seven sorrows of the Virgin, five joys of Mary, and the pains of Hell. Other catalogs justify church ordinances, such as why Friday is a fast day, and the virtues of attending Mass. The most comprehensive of these schematizations is *How a Man Should Believe in God (Py fodd y dyly dyn gredu),* which takes the reader through a logical sequence of the bases of belief and their implications: an exposition of the Creed leads to a description of the believer's love for God and the desire to obey Him in the Ten Commandments; a simple analysis of sins, virtues, and works of mercy concludes this brief tract of practical theology. Other handbooks that are extended catalogs of Christian teaching (some set out in question-and-answer form) are a version of *L'enfant sage,* the related but less substantial *Disputatio Adriani . . . et Epitici,* and *Agoriad Cyfarwyddyd* (Key to guidance), which attempts an exposition to the Nativity, the Passion, and the Mass.

More ambitious than these simple series of statements, in that they offer an intellectual and historical commentary, are versions of the Apostles' Creed, *How the Trinity Is One God,* and, more especially, a commentary on the Lord's Prayer, based on the work of Hugh of St. Victor, and two versions of the Nicene Creed, one of which has an original commentary by the Welsh translator. In such works, as in versions of portions of Scripture with exegesis, translators were obliged to forge a new vocabulary and to create a lucid style capable of expressing abstract concepts and affective theology.

The handbooks of instruction and exposition achieve their highest level in four texts: a popular compendium of theology and science, Honorius Augustodunensis' *Elucidarium*; a confessional manual for priests, *Penityas,* the title of which recalls the poem *Peniteas* cito but which is probably based on one or another of the popular *summae de peonitentia* of the thirteenth century; *Drych yr Ufudd-dawd (Speculum humilitatis),* based on the *De contemptu mundi* of Innocent III; and an incomplete treatise on mystical love, *Cysegrlan Fuchedd* (Holy living), which reflects aspects of Victorine mysticism. The strength of these translations

614

lies in their style, the first two being marked by an unforced prose appropriate for practical works (*Penityas* especially is reminiscent of the style of the law books). *Drych* has a flowing style that draws on preachers' rhetoric to make its appeal, while *Cysegrlan Fuchedd* combines native rhetorical embellishments with Latin imagery to present the ecstasies of love.

The impetus for these translations is to be sought in the reforms in clerical education and attention to pastoral instruction resulting from the Fourth Lateran Council of 1215. Successive bishops' instructions enjoined parish clergy to instruct their flock in the basic tenets of the faith and to hear confession regularly. Archbishop of Canterbury John Peckam's Constitutions of 1281 describe the instruction to be given to laymen and the articles of faith to be expounded in the vernacular, and Archbishop Thoresby's Canons of 1357 further elaborate upon these. *How a Man Should Believe* and other instructional handbooks would fulfill the demands of such canons at a simple level; and though other, more developed commentaries and tracts were designed for clerics (*Penityas* is a clear example), evidence suggests that many of these were in fact commissioned and used by devout laypeople. One version of the Athanasian Creed and a translation of *Transitus beatae Mariae* were prepared for a brother and sister in the late thirteenth century, and laymen of the fourteenth century had compiled for them major collections of religious texts in the White Book of Rhydderch, the *Book of the Anchorite,* and the Red Book of Talgarth. Peniarth MS 190, containing *Penityas, Elucidarium,* and *Cysegrlan Fuchedd,* probably was the property of a cleric.

Improving reading was provided for laymen and clerics by apocryphal legends, collections of miracles, and saints' lives. The most popular of the first group were the *Gospel of Nicodemus, Transitus beatae Mariae, Yita Adam et Evae,* and *Finding of the True Cross.* The two earliest saints' lives, both of native origin, are those of David (Dewi) and Beuno, and there are a number of thirteenth-century lives of female saints. Another popular narrative genre that is more obviously didactic consists of the various visions of Hell—such as *Visio sancti Pauli, St. Patrick's Purgatory,* and *Guido's Ghost*—that are intended to shock readers into repentance. Descriptions of the Day of Judgment and of the Fifteen Signs tend simply to be catalogs of disasters. These eschatological tracts have an effective vigor lacking in the translations of the legends, which generally are written in the Latinate style found in the secular historical texts.

There are no texts that guide the layman's devotions or expound the services of the church for him, but together with versions of the Ave Maria and Pater Noster (in prose and verse) there are a number of private prayers, some for use on occasions during the day, some to the Virgin, and others at the elevation of the Host or Post-Communion during the Mass. In the fourteenth century a translation of the Little Office of the Virgin (*Gwasanaeth Meir*) was produced, presumably for private use, but there is no information regarding the commissioning of this sole example of a Welsh version of an office. The use by this translator of prose and of verse in both bardic and free meters reminds us that religious literature was produced for the whole community by writers both lay and clerical, and that one cannot differentiate sharply between the various types of writing.

BIBLIOGRAPHY

The best introduction is John E. Caerwyn Williams, "Medieval Welsh Religious Prose," in *Proceedings of the Second International Congress of Celtic Studies, 1963* (1966). See also his "Rhyddiaith grefyddol Cymraeg Canol," in Geraint Bowen, ed., *Y Traddodiad Rhyddiaith* (1974); and D. Simon Evans, *Medieval Religious Literature* (1986). Glanmor Williams, *The Welsh Church from Conquest to Reformation* (1962), 85–104, gives the wider context. See also Idris L. Foster, "The Book of the Anchorite," in *Proceedings of the British Academy,* **36** (1950). For the poetry see John E. Caerwyn Williams, *Canu Crefyddol y Gogynfeirdd* (1976).

BRYNLEY F. ROBERTS

[See also Councils, Western (1215–1274); Gruffudd ap yr Ynad Coch; Honorius Augustodunensis; Peckham, John; Penance and Penitentials; St. Patrick's Purgatory; Seven Deadly Sins; Virtues and Vices.]

WENDS. The term "Wends" is used with several different and sometimes confused meanings. As employed in the Middle Ages (and in later times with reference to that era), "Wends" signified all the various Slavic tribes on the borders of Germany (that is, east of the rivers Elbe and Saale) or the Slavic splinter groups within it. As the Czechs and Poles consolidated, they began to be called by their own specific names, so that "Wends" was left to designate the various other Slavic tribes between the

Elbe-Saale and the Oder (approximately the territory of present-day East Germany). After the Middle Ages, nearly all of these other tribes had been conquered by Germany and assimilated into the Germans, and "Wends" meant the few remaining Slavic groups in Germany and Austria. Thus the small group in the former province of Hannover (remnants of the Drevani tribe, which had infiltrated west of the Elbe into Germany and which retained a Slavic language until about 1700) was called Wends and even today the area is called Wendland. Similarly a group of Slovenes in Austria came to be called "Windish."

In modern times, with the demise of the Hannover Wends, the term "Wends" has normally meant the still unassimilated Slavic minority of Lusatia (Lausitz) in the area of Bautzen and Cottbus. Since 1945 these people usually have been called "Sorbs," because of feelings that "Wends" was too vague and was sometimes pejorative, even though "Sorbs" is also inexact and often confused with the South Slavic "Serbs." These Lusatian Wends, or Sorbs, are the remnants of two small Slavic tribes, the Lužiči (around present-day Cottbus) and the Milčani (around present-day Bautzen), which were subgroups of the medieval Sorbs (the major tribe of which, the Sorbs proper, was located to the west of Lusatia). There remain in 1988 perhaps 50,000 people who still can speak Wendish (Sorbian) along with German, and who retain some other aspects of Slavic culture.

In reference to the later Middle Ages, "Wendish" took on the very different meaning of "North German"; this is what is meant by the "Wendish cities" of the Hanseatic League, for example. Finally, the similarity of the terms "Wend" and "Vandal" caused a confusion with that Germanic tribe.

MEDIEVAL ORIGINS

Returning to the major medieval meaning of "Wends" as "Slavs along the eastern German borders," it should be recalled that in the pre-medieval period of the migrations, before the formation of Germany, Germanic tribes had settled from the Rhine to the Vistula, as described in Tacitus' *Germania*, written about A.D. 100 (the Veneti mentioned there as the eastern neighbors of the Germans, around the Vistula, are not considered to have been Slavs, but may have given their name to the Slavic Wends who supplanted them). The Ger-

manic peoples later withdrew from the area east of the Elbe and Saale. In the sixth century, the Asiatic Avars advanced northward from the Balkans, pushing those Slavic tribes which had been in the region of present-day Hungary into the largely vacated lands east of the Elbe-Saale, while other Slavs came west across the Oder; they absorbed the remaining Germans in the area.

The Slavic peoples east of the Elbe-Saale, in the area that is now East Germany, Czechoslovakia, and Poland, are grouped together as the West Slavs. They consisted of many different small tribes that were only loosely attached to each other to form larger associations. Some of the major tribes were, in the north, the Obodrites (Abodrites) and the Ljutici or Veletians (Vilci); in the center, east of German Thuringia, the Sorbs (with several subgroups, including the above-mentioned Lužiči and Milcăni); in the south, the Czechs (Bohemians), Moravians, and Slovaks; and in the east, the Poles. There were many other tribes. Smaller groups, such as the Drevani mentioned above, infiltrated into the German areas west of the Elbe-Saale; other such groups were the "Main-Wends" and the "Regnitz (Rednitz)-Wends," who settled along those rivers in southern Germany, subjecting themselves to German rule.

In the seventh and ninth centuries, the Franks were molding Merovingian and Carolingian Germany and beginning the expansion of Germany to the east that was destined, in the following centuries, to bring the Wendish areas into Germany, both by military might and by peaceful colonization. Conversely, the Slavs sometimes invaded Germany, so that the German military moves were at times defensive in nature (note, for example, the erection of a defense line along the Saale against the Sorbs, the *Limes Sorabicus,* under Charlemagne). And, of course, the Slavic tribes also often battled each other.

In many respects, the culture of these Slavs was similar to that of the Germans. After about 600, new methods of farming were being developed (for example, using the horse and the iron plowshare) that greatly increased productivity and laid the economic basis for the development of feudalism. However, the Slavs clung to their old religion centuries after the Germans had exchanged theirs for Christianity. Also, their tribes tended to remain independent, rather than uniting to form states, and they were similarly reluctant to make the transition to feudalism. These two trends left them weaker than the feudal states of the Germans, Czechs, Poles, and Danes, all of which pressured them.

POLITICAL HISTORY

Only a few of the turbulent political events can be noted here. To defend against the Avars and the Franks in the seventh century, many tribes did unite for several decades under Samo to form the "first Slavic state" (in the area of present-day Czechoslovakia), defeating the Avars in the south in 623 and the Franks at Wogastisburg in 631. However, the Franks continued their campaigns against the Wends, and their overlordship was established under Charlemagne, with whom the Obodrites even joined in his wars against the Saxons. At the end of the eighth century, Charlemagne's armies destroyed the kingdom of the Avars, ending that major threat from the south and enabling the settlement of present Austria by Germans and Slavs. In the ninth century, Mojmír (Moimir), Rastislav, and Svatopluk united the Moravian and neighboring tribes in present Czechoslovakia and Hungary, forming "Great Moravia," which was, however, crushed by the Magyars in 906.

German annexation of the Wendish territories began under Henry I in 928, with conquest and forced Christianization going hand in hand. Within the following decades, German rule was established as far as the Oder. However, in 983 the Slavs revolted, destroying the institutions of Christianity and regaining much of their independence. German influence in the following century was consequently slight, and the Slavic nobles consolidated their personal power, introducing feudalism and Christianity and oppressing their peasants. The Slavic and German nobles often joined forces against the peasants, so that the struggle frequently was more of a class war than that of German against Slav. The Obodritic prince Gottschalk, an ally of the Saxons and Danes, succeeded in forcibly uniting the Obodritic tribes and others, but they rebelled in 1066, killing Gottschalk, reestablishing their independence, and repulsing Christianity. There was a similar rebellion in 1093 against Gottschalk's son, Henry, who, however, put down the rebellion and went on to conquer all the Slavic tribes in the north. The fact that such rebellions were directed against Christianity unfortunately caused the Germans to view the Slavs as heathen barbarians who had to be conquered and Christianized or annihilated. The result was the "Wendish Crusade" of 1147 under Henry the Lion, which had only limited success but

caused great destruction among the Slavs. Thereafter, there was little Slavic opposition to German rule, to Christianity, or to the influx of German settlers. During the course of the following centuries, in the formerly Wendish regions between the Elbe-Saale and the Oder, the Germans became the majority and began the process of assimilating the remaining Slavic inhabitants.

BIBLIOGRAPHY

Francis Dvornik, *The Slavs: Their Early History and Civilization* (1956) and *The Making of Central and Eastern Europe*, 2nd ed. (1974); Marija Gimbutas, *The Slavs* (1971); František Graus, *Die Nationenbildung der Westslawen im Mittelalter* (1980); Joachim Herrmann, ed., *Die Slawen in Deutschland* (1985), an excellent, up-to-date handbook covering every aspect of the subject, and *Die Nordwestslawen und ihr Anteil an der Geschichte des deutschen Volkes* (1973).

JOSEPH WILSON

[See also **Avars; Bohemia-Moravia; Germany: 843–1137; Poland; Slavs, Origins of; Slavic Languages and Literatures.**]

WERGILD, in Germanic law, was the sum of money that a manslayer owed the kin of the victim to compensate them for the death. The amount to be paid was established by royal code and varied, as would be expected, from one system of law to the next.

An important feature of the system of wergild was the schedule of tariffs that differentiated between the value of the lives of individuals of various social classes. In Lombard law, for example, the wergild of a landowner was set at twice the price of the life of a landless man. In Anglo-Saxon law the wergild of a thane, a man who held five hides of land, was set at six times the wergild of a common *ceorl* (churl). At 1,200 shillings the price for killing a thane would be ruinous even for a very rich lord.

This careful calculation of the value of lives was not meant to reflect the economic losses suffered by the kin; rather, the intention seems to have been to express a belief that the value of some lives really was greater than others. Thus, Anglo-Saxon law recognized the value of a man's oath as compurgator in terms of the size of his wer, so that a thane's oath was worth six times that of a churl. Similarly, in situations where a person had committed a deed for which his life was forfeit, it typically could be redeemed by paying the sum of his wergild.

The system of compensation by wergild existed as an alternative to the bloodfeud, by which the enraged kin sought vengeance upon the kin of the slayer. Sometimes the slayer might refuse to pay any compensation and prefer to bear the feud. Sometimes, too, the kin of the victim might refuse to accept compensation and take their own vengeance, though this choice was frowned upon by those in authority. Occasionally it seems to have been possible for the kin of the slayer to escape the feud by handing him over to the kin of the victim in lieu of wergild or by swearing to offer him nothing in the way of assistance.

The system of wergild and the other compensations of Germanic law perished with the establishment of effective government in the twelfth and thirteenth centuries. In England, for example, Henry II treated manslaying as a crime against the whole community by requiring a jury to swear out complaints against those suspected of homicide. The state then took over the prosecution of the malefactor, with the side effect that the kin lost all right to seek damages of any kind. The disappearance of wergild elsewhere in Europe took longer but generally seems to have been accomplished by 1300.

CHARLES M. RADDING

[See also **Compurgation; Felony; Law, English Common: to 1272; Law, German: Early Codes; Lombards, Kingdom of; Oath.**]

WERNHER DER GARTENÆRE (*fl.* second half of the thirteenth century), minstrel and writer. The colophon to the better manuscript of the verse novella (*Meier*) *Helmbrecht* (MS *A*) names Wernher der Gartenære as its author. Research and speculation since the mid nineteenth century have yielded no direct information about the man. It is difficult to believe that a poem as skillfully constructed as *Helmbrecht* can have been its writer's sole opus, but no other work is attributed or attributable to him. We are limited in our suppositions concerning the poet to our interpretation of the scant internal evidence.

A specific reference to Neidhart "von Reuental" as being dead (verse 219), the possible influence on—more likely topical similarities with—*Seifried*

Helbling, and a mention in Ottokar's *Österreichische Reimchronik* (verse 26,217) place the *Helmbrecht* during the period from about 1240 to 1320. Although the two *Helmbrecht* manuscripts, *B* (1457) and the more conservative *A* (1504–1516), are transposed to contemporary language, they do preserve traces of the dialect of the original poem in the rhyme. From such traces, characteristic of Middle Bavarian spoken in the later thirteenth century, it is possible to narrow the date of composition to a period from about 1250 to 1300. Place-names (verses 192, 897) in *A* localize the action east of the Inn and south of the Danube in an area now part of Austria but politically part of Bavaria until 1779; in *B* different names point to a site in Austria 100 kilometers (about 60 miles) farther east. Either or neither set of names might be original; the poet probably changed them to suit his audience, and lost versions may have designated still other places. There are other clues in the work as to its provenance, however. *Gîselitze* (v. 473), thought to have been an Austrian dish, the Austrian *clamirre,* which the father urges his son to eat (vv. 445ff.), and the Bohemian greeting *dobraytra* (v. 728), perhaps more apt to have been known in Austria than in Bavaria, all strongly suggest Austria as the place of origin. Furthermore, as Kurt Ruh points out in the introduction to his edition (§4), it is on Austrian literature that we see the influence of the *Helmbrecht.* Besides his reference to Neidhart, Wernher mentions *Herzog Ernst* (v. 957), shows the possible stylistic influence of Wolfram von Eschenbach and Gottfried von Strassburg, and evinces a somewhat vague acquaintance with the legends of King Arthur (vv. 1,478ff.) and the tales of Dietrich von Bern (vv. 76ff.), Charlemagne (vv. 62ff.), and Troy (vv. 45ff.); he was obviously not unread. Suggestions concerning the derivation of the appelation "der Gartenære" include the possibility that the poet was a gardener in a monastery or member of the noble Gartner family in Krems, or even that he came from the region of Lake Garda in Italy. There is no internal evidence for these suggestions, however. More inviting is Franz Pfeiffer's derivation of the name from *garten* (wander about, beg); but the agential noun *gartenære* (vagrant) appears to be a more probable source.

Wernher's remark that he would find little favor with women compared to the young dandy Helmbrecht (vv. 208ff.) does not necessarily prove he was not a cleric, nor does his ascribing the embroidery of Helmbrecht's hood to a nun who, like many others, had left her cell for erotic pleasures (vv. 107ff.). He was not identical with Bruoder (Bruder) Wernher, whose solemn style lacks der Gartenære's drama and irony. By his own witness he was not a nobleman (vv. 864, 884). Finally, he speaks of himself as a poet (v. 1,933) and as one who has traveled about much and has not always received the best treatment (vv. 848ff., 840ff.). In summation, then, Wernher was most probably a professional minstrel of Upper Austria who wrote in the second half of the thirteenth century.

BIBLIOGRAPHY

Editions are *Helmbrecht,* Friedrich Panzer, ed. (1902), 9th ed., rev. by Kurt Ruh (1974), the standard scholarly edition; and *Helmbrecht,* Helmut Brackert, Winfried Frey, and Dieter Seitz, eds. (1972), which includes the original text, a modern German translation, good bibliography, and a discussion of older theories. Translation by Linda B. Parshall, *Helmbrecht* (1987), includes German text edited by Ulrich Seelbach. See also Charles E. Cough, ed., *Meier Helmbrecht: A Poem by Wernher der Gartenære* (1942, 2nd ed. 1947, repr. 1969).

FRANK G. BANTA

[See also **Ambraser Heldenbuch; Austria; Middle High German Literature; Neidhart "von Reuental."**]

WERNHER VON ELMENDORF *(fl.* second half of the twelfth century), a priest and chaplain from Elmendorf (in the province of Oldenburg?) who adapted and translated very freely parts of the moral treatise *Moralium dogma philosophorum* (*MDP*) into German verse. The work was composed using short lines in rhymed couplets (of which 1,209 lines have been preserved; most of the conclusion, probably about fifty to one hundred lines, is missing). Wernher wrote his highly didactic poem sometime in the 1170's, having been commissioned by Dietrich von Elmendorf, provost (head) of the principal church in Heiligenstadt, in Thuringia. The language of the poem is mainly Thuringian (*mitteldeutsch*), but it contains as well many Low German elements, especially in the rhymes.

Although Wernher's main material source is clearly the *MDP,* he appears to have transformed this material into a didactic poem no longer philosophical and theoretical, but empirical and practical; he doesn't altogether give up the conceptual framework of the cardinal virtues as expounded in the *MDP* but organizes his thoughts and examples according to the mirror of princes (*Fürstenspiegel*) model, in which the specific virtues and values pertaining to a lord and ruler are highlighted.

Thus, after a general prologue (lines 1–72), the poet deals with the virtue of prudence but discusses particularly the issue of the good versus the bad counselor (*gute und schlechte ratgeber,* lines 73–236). Under the rubric justice, he treats justice itself (*reht*), but more explicitly the judicial system and the just judge (lines 237–290). Then the apparently very important virtue of generosity (*milte*) is discussed at great length and in detail (lines 291–554), followed by a section on religiousness (trust in God and prayer) and on love of one's relatives and friends (lines 555–730). In the realm of fortitude the poet is especially concerned with the right attitude in warfare (lines 731–804), adding strong praise of the virtue of constancy (*stæte*) and of patience (lines 805–855). The discussion of the last cardinal virtue, temperance (*mâze*), is very elaborate and detailed; *mâze* in almost all areas of feudal life is explained and emphasized (lines 856–1,200). The poet buttresses his arguments by quoting from or referring to such classical authorities as Seneca, Horace, Juvenal, Sallust, Lucan, Boethius, Cicero (Tullius), and occasionally also Solomon; he also makes some strong points by adducing *exempla* from the lives of rulers (Darius, Alexander, Antigonus).

The source of Wernher's poem is a version of the very popular *MDP* as edited by John Holmberg and attributed by him and others to William of Conches (*d. ca.* 1154). Yet Wernher very probably used an interpolated version of Holmberg's Latin text: there are too many differences between the received Latin text and Wernher's adaptation. A Latin version closer to Wernher's translation has yet to be found.

Although Wernher writes poetry, his diction is very simple, unadorned, and almost dry; he frequently uses the method of direct appeal to his listener or reader (second-person singular), thus setting a clearly didactic, even admonitory, tone. But this is only to be expected in a work belonging to the genre of literature for everyday use (*Gebrauchsliteratur*).

Wernher's poem has been preserved in two manuscripts: one dating from the end of the twelfth century with a very good text (Berlin, Staatsbibliothek Preussischer Kulturbesitz, MS germ. oct. 226, a fragment only, two double folios, about 134 lines); and one from the fourteenth century with a somewhat modernized text (Klosterneuburg, Stifts-bibliothek, cod. 1056, fols. 65–74, 1,203 lines, only the end is missing).

BIBLIOGRAPHY
Sources. Wernher von Elmendorf, Joachim Bumke, ed. (1974) (Altdeutsche Textbibliothek, no. 77). A source for the *MDP* is *Das Moralium dogma philosophorum des Guillaume de Conches: Lateinisch, altfranzösisch und mittelniederfränkisch,* John Holmberg, ed. (1929).

Studies. Hartmut Beckers, "*Gelücke* und *Heil* bei Wernher von Elmendorf," in *Beiträge zur Geschichte der deutschen Sprache und Literatur* (Halle), **99** (1978); Joachim Bumke, "Die Auflösung des Tugendsystems bei Wernher von Elmendorf," in *Zeitschrift für deutsches Altertum,* **88** (1957), and his introduction to the edition cited above; Hans Eggers, "Wernher von Elmendorf," in *Die deutsche Literatur des Mittelalters: Verfasserlexikon . . . ,* Wolfgang Stammler and Karl Langosch, eds., IV (1953), 914–920; Günter Eifler, ed., *Ritterliches Tugendsystem* (1970); R. A. Gauthier, "Les deux recensions du *Moralium dogma philosophorum,*" in *Revue du moyen âge latin,* **9** (1953), and "Un prologue inédit au *Moralium dogma philosophorum,*" *ibid.,* **11** (1955); Martin Last, "Die Herkunft des Wernher von Elmendorf," in *Zeitschrift für deutsche Philologie,* **89** (1970); Albert Leitzmann, "Zu Wernher von Elmendorf," in *Zeitschrift für deutsches Altertum,* **82** (1948/1951); John R. Williams, "The Authorship of the *Moralium dogma philosophorum,*" in *Speculum,* **6** (1931), and "The Quest for the Author of the *Moralium dogma philosophorum,* 1931–1956," *ibid.,* **32** (1957).

PETRUS W. TAX

[See also **Latin Literature; Middle High German Literature; Mirror of Princes; William of Conches.**]

WERVE, CLAUS DE (*fl. ca.* 1390–1439). Hailing from Hatheim in Holland and registered in the guild of *steenbickeleren* (stonemasons) of Brussels, the sculptor Claus de Werve in 1396 joined his uncle, Claus Sluter, in Dijon, where Sluter was engaged on the monumental tomb of Philip the Bold.

At Sluter's death in 1406, when de Werve was placed in charge of the project, only a few of the forty-one alabaster figures of weeping, hooded monks (*pleurants*) had been completed. Although Sluter must be credited with the masterly conception of the funeral cortege and the powerful treatment of the figures in their heavy cowls almost as anonymous symbols of grief, the great majority of

Pleurant from the tomb of Philip the Bold. Alabaster figure probably carved by Claus de Werve, before 1410. Musée des Beaux Arts, Burgundy. PHOTO: WIM SWAAN

the figures are undoubtedly by de Werve. It is a striking testimony to his skill that an overall stylistic unity pervades the whole, making it impossible to distinguish the individual contributions of uncle and nephew.

The tomb was finally completed in 1410 and de Werve was commissioned to execute a similar monument for John the Fearless. However, due to unsettled political conditions, the work was repeatedly delayed until 1435 and the aged de Werve died virtually penniless in 1439.

BIBLIOGRAPHY

Josef Duverger, *De Brusselsche steenbickeleren der XIVᵉ en XVᵉ eeuw* (1933); Theodor Müller, *Sculpture in the Netherlands, Germany, France, and Spain, 1400–1500* (1966); *Les pleurants dans l'art du moyen âge en Europe, Musée des Beaux-arts, Dijon, 1971* (1972); Pierre Quarré, "Les pleurants des tombeaux des ducs de Bourgogne à Dijon, in *Bulletin de la Société nationale des antiquaires de France* (1949); Domien Roggen, "Klaas van de Werve," in *Gentsche bijdragen tot de Kunstgeschiedenis* (1941).

WIM SWAAN

[See also **Dijon, Chartreuse de Champmol; Sluter, Claus.**]

WESSOBRUNNER GEBET (Wessobrunn prayer), an Old High German text in a Wessobrunn manuscript, now in Munich, dating from about 800. The first section, usually thought to consist of nine lines of somewhat irregular alliterative verse, describes the primeval void and the presence of God and his glorious spirits (angels). The second section, which follows without a break, is a prayer to God the Creator; this appears to be in prose, though it employs alliterative phrases. The text is headed *De poeta.* The first five lines of the "verse" contain echoes of Germanic mythological poetry (notably the Old Icelandic *Vǫluspá*), the last four the heroic phrase *manno miltisto,* used in *Beowulf* (line 3,181: *manna mildust*) to describe the hero, but here applied to God. The dialect is Bavarian, though there are some possibly alien elements in the phonology and vocabulary, and some insular scribal features. The mixture of pagan, heroic, and biblical elements may indicate a missionary purpose.

BIBLIOGRAPHY

Text is in Theodor Wilhelm Braune, *Althochdeutsches Lesebuch* (1875 and later editions), no. 29. See also John Knight Bostock, *A Handbook on Old High German Literature,* 2nd rev. ed. (1976), 126–135; Cyril Edwards, "Tôhuwâbôhû: The *Wessobrunner Gebet* and Its Analogues," in *Medium Ævum,* 54 (1984); J. Sidney Groseclose and Brian O. Murdoch, *Die althochdeutschen poetischen Denkmäler* (1976), 43–48.

DAVID R. MCLINTOCK

[See also **Missions and Missionaries, Christian; Old High German Literature; Saxony.**]

621

WESTMINSTER ABBEY. For almost a thousand years, Westminster Abbey has been the principal church of the English monarchy. Not only the traditional site for coronations and burials of kings and queens, it also served until the Reformation as the shrine of the English national saint, King Edward the Confessor, and still houses the tomb today. In fact it was Edward—the last of the Anglo-Saxon kings—who first made Westminster a royal abbey, although a monastic community had probably existed there even earlier. Edward began building a large new church about 1050, perhaps the first in England of the Romanesque style. Built near Edward's palace at Westminster and intended as his burial church, the abbey was soon the site of William the Conqueror's coronation in 1066.

The present church was begun in 1245 by Henry III in order to foster the cult of the English saint and, thereby, to ennoble the English nation. He strove to emulate the royal churches of France then under construction for Louis IX, and he probably sent his architect, Henry of Reynes, to study the latest French styles at buildings such as Rheims and Amiens cathedrals, the royal abbeys of Royaumont

Chapel of Henry VII in Westminster Abbey, completed by William Vertue, 1519. PHOTO: WIM SWAAN

and St. Denis, and the king's Parisian chapel, the Ste. Chapelle. Thus, although the architecture is still English in spirit, Westminster Abbey has been called "the most French of all English Gothic churches," especially in its sense of soaring height and its use of flying buttresses.

The church that almost emptied Henry III's coffers was still unfinished at his death in 1272. The nave was not completed until the fifteenth century, and the facade, partially designed by Christopher Wren, was finished only in 1734 by Nicholas Hawksmoor. Among the other additions to the building are the spectacular chapel of Henry VII at the east (designed by Robert Vertue and completed by William Vertue in 1519) and the myriad tombs and monuments of national figures.

BIBLIOGRAPHY

Francis Bond, *Westminster Abbey* (1909); Robert Branner, "Westminster Abbey and the French Court Style," in *Journal of the Society of Architectural Historians,* **23** (1964); Peter Brieger, *English Art, 1216–1307* (1957), 106–134; Edward Carpenter, ed., *A House of Kings: The Official History of Westminster Abbey* (1966); John Flete, *The History of Westminster Abbey,* J. Armitage Robinson, ed. (1909); William R. Lethaby, *Westminster Abbey and the King's Craftsmen* (1906) and *Westminster Abbey Reexamined* (1925); Jocelyn Perkins, *Westminster Abbey: Its Worship and Ornaments,* 3 vols. (1938–1952); George G. Scott, *Gleanings from Westminster Abbey* (1863); Herbert Francis Westlake, *Westminster Abbey,* 2 vols. (1923).

STEPHEN GARDNER

[See also **Edward the Confessor, St.; Gothic Architecture; Gothic, Perpendicular (with illustration); Henry III of England; Henry of Reynes; Thirsk, John (with illustration); Vertue, Robert and William.**]

WESTMINSTER, STATUTES OF. Three statutes framed at Westminster—I (1275), II (1285), and III (1290)—are part of the flood of new legislation that Edward I sponsored in England. The Edwardian statutes, issued at parliaments, were more carefully recorded and publicized than earlier legislation. Each statute treats many diverse topics, with Westminster I containing fifty-one chapters introducing numerous changes in procedure. These changes aimed at protecting subjects from royal officials; some provisions echo Magna Carta's guarantees.

Westminster II touches almost every aspect of law in its fifty clauses. Chapter 24 authorized the

chancellor, as custodian of legal writs, to make available new ones "in like case," new remedies for litigants who found no writ suitable for their needs. Chapter 30 made royal justice more readily available in the counties. It authorized the nisi prius, allowing assize justices to take juries' verdicts in the counties and report them to Westminster, saving the jurors a long and costly journey.

The most important provisions of Westminster II and III sought to cope with the increasing complexity of feudal land law, recognizing legitimate rights of both lord and tenant. The general tendency, however, was to strengthen the lord's position. The lords wished to preserve strict rules of primogeniture, encouraging the possibility that tenures might revert to them. This conflicted with their tenants' desire to have complete control of the land, including the right to alienate freely, in order to provide for younger sons and daughters. Chapter 1 of Westminster II, *De donis conditionalibus* (Concerning conditional gifts), legalized the fee tail, a gift of land descending only in a strict line of male descent. Westminster III, or *Quia emptores,* provided an alternative to subinfeudation. Under the statute, a tenant could alienate, but the new tenant, instead of becoming his subtenant, held directly of the lord, owing him the accustomed services.

BIBLIOGRAPHY

John M. W. Bean, *The Decline of English Feudalism, 1215–1540* (1967); Stroud F. C. Milsom, *Historical Foundations of the Common Law* (1969), 88–102, 140–168; Theodore F. T. Plucknett, *Legislation of Edward I* (1949) and *A Concise History of the Common Law,* 5th ed. (1956), 27–31, 318–321; F. Maurice Powicke, *Oxford History of England,* IV, *The Thirteenth Century* (1962); Harry Rothwell, ed., *English Historical Documents,* III, *1189–1327* (1975), 397–410, 428–457, 466.

RALPH V. TURNER

[See also **Edward I of England; England, 1216–1485; Feudalism; Fief; Jury; Justices Itinerant; Law, English Common; Parliament; Provisions of Oxford.**]

WESTWORK, the developed west facade of a church, usually consisting of at least one tower containing a chapel over the entrance vestibule. The earliest known example appeared at the monastery of St. Riquier near Abbeville, France, dedicated by the lay abbot Angilbert in 799. Once introduced, westworks became a standard component of Caro-

West facade of *Münster*, Bad Gandersheim, 11th–12th centuries.
FOTO MARBURG / ART RESOURCE

lingian, Romanesque, and Gothic architecture, especially in France and Germany.

BIBLIOGRAPHY
Kenneth John Conant, *Carolingian and Romanesque Architecture: 800–1200* (1959, rev. ed. 1974, 1978).

LESLIE BRUBAKER

[See also **Angilbert, St.; Basilica; Gothic Architecture; Pre-Romanesque Architecture; Romanesque Architecture.**]

WEYDEN, ROGIER VAN DER (*ca.* 1399–1464), an outstanding Flemish painter of the fifteenth century, was born at Tournai. He took his apprenticeship there with Robert Campin (Master of Flémalle) in 1427 and became a master in the painter's guild in 1432. By 1435 Rogier had settled in Brussels, where he became "city painter" until his death.

Rogier organized a huge atelier that produced altarpieces and devotional panels that had overwhelming influence on later painters in the Netherlands and in the Rhineland. In 1439 he executed four panels of the *Justice of Trajan* and the *Justice of Herkinbald* for the Town Hall in Brussels, now lost but partially preserved in drawings and copies in tapestries in Berne. In 1450 Van der Weyden traveled to Rome for the Holy Year. His earliest works (for example, the *Annunciation,* Paris, Louvre) show the strong influence of his master, Robert Campin. Other influences may be seen in his works. Rogier based the composition of a panel surviving from an altarpiece for the painters' guild, *Saint Luke Drawing the Madonna* (*ca.* 1435–1438; Boston, Museum of Fine Arts), on Jan van Eyck's *Madonna of Chancellor Rolin* (Paris, Louvre).

Sometime before 1443 Rogier painted one of his masterpieces, the *Deposition from the Cross* (Madrid, Prado) for the chapel of the Crossbowmen's Guild in Notre-Dame-hors-Ville at Louvain.

Rogier's art is distinguished by highly inventive compositional motifs and by a heightened emotional content enhanced by tears, the first in Flemish painting. One invention was the pseudo-*Schnitzaltar* (carved altarpiece), in which he painted frames about the compositions resembling sculptured Gothic portals. His *Granada-Miraflores Altarpiece of the Virgin* (Berlin, Staatliche Museen) is the most successful of these, with the narratives reduced to the most essential figures, placed beneath the painted arches like actors performing on a theater stage. Sometime around 1450 Van der Weyden executed a huge polyptych, the *Last Judgment,* for the high altar of the hospital in Beaune founded by Nicholas Rolin, where it is today. About 1455 he was commissioned to paint a *Nativity Altarpiece* (Berlin, Staatliche Museen) for the church of Middelburg, a city founded near Bruges by Pierre Bladelin in 1444.

During or shortly after his trip to Italy in 1450, Rogier painted two works, the *Madonna and Child with Four Saints* (Frankfurt, Staedelsches Kunstinstitut) and the *Entombment* (Florence, Uffizi), that were based on Italian compositions but executed in a style wholly Flemish. Exuberance and festive color are displayed in the famous *Columba Adoration of the Magi Altarpiece* (Munich, Alte Pinakothek), executed about 1460; but in general his late style exhibits an increasingly iconic character through abstraction and reduction of secondary

Deposition from the Cross. Panel painting by Rogier van der Weyden, before 1443. Madrid, Prado.
ANDERSON/ART RESOURCE

details. These features are particularly apparent in two late Crucifixions (Philadelphia, John G. Johnson Collection, Museum of Art, and Madrid, Escorial), where only Mary and John the Evangelist appear below the cross that is placed against an abstract background. Van der Weyden excelled in bust portraiture, endowing his sitters with a special dignity and intelligence. He executed a number of devotional diptychs with the Madonna and Child paired with the portrait of a male donor. Rogier van der Weyden and Jan van Eyck represent the poles between which Flemish painting vacillates during the course of the fifteenth century.

BIBLIOGRAPHY
Martin Davies, *Rogier van der Weyden* (1972); Max J. Friedlander, *Early Netherlandish Painting,* Nicole Veronee-Verhaegen, trans., II (1967); Craig Harbison, "Realism and Symbolism in Early Flemish Painting," in *Art Bulletin,* 66 (1984); Erwin Panofsky, *Early Netherlandish Painting,* 2 vols. (1953), I, 247–302.

JAMES SNYDER

[See also **Campin, Robert; Eyck, Van; Flemish Painting.**]

WHEAT. See **Grain Crops, Western European.**

WHEEL OF FORTUNE. The allegorized goddess Fortuna and her constantly turning wheel represent one of the key images of medieval culture. The image of the wheel, symbolizing the mutability and transience of success in the sublunary world, derives from the second book of Boethius' *Consolation of Philosophy* and was taken up by such authors as Alan of Lille, Jean de Meun, Dante, Chaucer, and many others.

In art, the wheel of fortune is often depicted with kings placed radially around the rim. The top figure sits securely on his throne, crowned and holding a scepter. Around the wheel, moving clockwise, figures fall and lose crowns down to the bottom figure, then become more stable on the left side as they rise again toward the top. The wheel thus gives visual form to the realities of political life.

BIBLIOGRAPHY

For full bibliography, see the article **Fortune** in volume 5. For illustrations, see **Machaut, Guillaume de** and the last page of the present volume.

CARL F. BARNES, JR.

WHEEL WINDOW. A large circular window in the terminal wall of a church in which the tracery radiates outward from a "hub" in the center of the window to its rim, resembling the spokes in a wheel. Early examples are quite plain (St. Étienne at Beauvais, north transept terminal). Fully developed

Wheel window in the south transept of Notre Dame de Paris, 1258–1261. PHOTO: WIM SWAAN

examples (Paris Cathedral, both transept terminals) are more complex, their radial design giving rise to the stylistic term "rayonnant" for mid-thirteenth-century French Court Style architecture.

BIBLIOGRAPHY

Illustrations are found in Victor Leblond, *L'église de Saint-Étienne de Beauvais* (Petites monographies des grands édifices de la France) (1929), 37, for Saint-Étienne de Beauvais; Whitney S. Stoddard, *Monastery and Cathedral in France* (1966), figs. 183 and 194, for Paris.

CARL F. BARNES, JR.

[See also **Gothic Architecture; Gothic, Rayonnant; Rose Window; Tracery.**]

WHITBY, SYNOD OF. Church council held in September or October 663 (possibly 664) at the double monastery of Streaneshalch (Old English for Whitby, meaning Bay of the Beacon or Lighthouse) on the Northumbrian coast and attended by King Oswy (654–670) of Northumbria and his son Egfrith; Colman, bishop of Lindisfarne; Wilfrid, abbot of Ripon; Hilda, abbess of Whitby; and other royal and ecclesiastical dignitaries. King Oswy, who probably summoned the synod, took an active part in its debates.

In the mid seventh century, the question of the proper method for calculating the date of Easter, the principal feast of the Christian year and the one on which the entire liturgical calendar was based, sharply divided the Christian community in Britain. Christians of northern England, following the traditions of the Celtic missionaries from Ireland, such as Sts. Columba and Aidan, who had converted them, calculated the date differently from those of southern England, who had accepted Christianity from Roman missionaries led by Augustine of Canterbury. Thus Queen Eanfleda, who followed the Roman rule, was fasting and keeping Palm Sunday, while her husband, King Oswy, was celebrating Easter. Defenders of Celtic custom, the future saints Colman and Chad, argued from tradition and claimed theirs was the method of St. John the Apostle. Supporters of the Roman practice, led by Wilfrid, argued from the authority of the Apostolic See and the decrees of the Council of Nicaea. Wilfrid's eloquence apparently proved decisive, and King Oswy settled the controversy, stating that he must follow St. Peter, who had been

given the keys of the kingdom of heaven. Northumbria eventually accepted the Roman custom, and in 669 Archbishop Theodore of Canterbury imposed it on all England. The synod of Whitby marked the decline of Celtic ascendancy in northern England and the establishment of the Roman Easter and Roman church organization there. It prepared the way for a unified English church open to the continental influences of Latin Christianity from Western Europe.

The correct form of the clerical tonsure represented a major secondary issue; according to Bede, "there was much controversy about that also." A religious custom among many Eastern peoples, tonsure or the cutting of the hair became common for Western monks in the fourth or fifth centuries and then was adopted generally in the church as the symbol of entrance to the clerical state. The Celtic practice was to shave the hair in front of a line going from ear to ear, whereas the Roman custom was to shave the crown of the head, leaving a fringe of hair around the head symbolizing Jesus' crown of thorns. Although the sources do not specify the synod's decision on tonsure, presumably the Roman practice was gradually adopted and enforced through the influence of bishops formed according to the Roman custom.

BIBLIOGRAPHY

The sources are Bede, *Ecclesiastical History of the English Nation*, 3.25–26; and Eddius Stephanus, *Life of Wilfrid*, B. Colgrave, trans. (1927), chap. 10.

See also Peter Hunter Blair, *Northumbria in the Days of Bede* (1976); Margaret Deansley, *Augustine of Canterbury* (1964); and Paul Grosjeans, "La date de Pâques et le concile de Nicée," in Academie royale de Belgique, *Bulletin de la classe des sciences*, 5th ser., 48 (1962).

BENNETT D. HILL

[See also **Celtic Church; Colman, Bishop of Lindisfarne; Theodore of Canterbury.**]

WIBALD OF STAVELOT (1098–1158), Benedictine monk, political and diplomatic figure in the German Empire. Born at the end of the eleventh century to a family of lesser officials of the abbey of Stavelot, Wibald studied at Liège before climbing the monastic ranks to become abbot of Stavelot in 1130. For two months in 1137 he served as abbot of Monte Cassino, until he was driven from the abbey by King Roger II of Sicily; in 1146 he also became abbot of Corvey. Wibald played an administrative and political role of no little significance in the government of the German king Conrad III. Frederick I Barbarossa entrusted him with delicate diplomatic missions to the Byzantine emperor Manuel I Komnenos. It was en route home from his second trip to Constantinople that Wibald died, in July 1158. The original register of his correspondence has survived from the years 1147 to 1157 and is a historical source of prime importance.

BIBLIOGRAPHY

Wibald's letters can be found in P. Jaffé, ed., *Monumenta corbeiensia* (Bibliotheca rerum germanicarum, 1 1864), 76–602. See in addition Michael McCormick, *Index scriptorum operumque latino-belgicorum medii aevi: Nouveau répertoire des oeuvres médiolatines belges*, pt. 3, II (1979) 307–308; and Franz-Josef Jakobi, *Wibald von Stablo und Corvey (1098–1158): Benediktinischer Abt in der frühen Stauferzeit* (1979).

MICHAEL MCCORMICK

[See also **Frederick I Barbarossa; Germany: 1138–1254; Hohenstaufen Dynasty; Manuel I Komnenos; Monte Cassino.**]

WIBERT OF CANTERBURY (*fl.* mid twelfth century). As prior of Canterbury Cathedral Priory (1152/1153–1167), Wibert constructed a vast new series of cloisters, monastic buildings, and accommodations for pilgrims. Known from surviving elements and from a remarkably detailed twelfth-century drawing, the complex was renowned for its elaborate decoration and its extensive system of lead water pipes.

BIBLIOGRAPHY

David Knowles, ed., *The Heads of Religious Houses: England and Wales, 940–1216* (1972), 34; William Urry, *Canterbury Under the Angevin Kings* (1967), 391–394; Mackenzie E. C. Walcott, "On the Conventual Arrangement of Canterbury," in *Transactions of the Royal Institute of British Architects*, 21 (1863), 58–76; Robert Willis, "The Architectural History of the Conventual Buildings of the Monastery of Christ Church in Canterbury," in *Archaeologia cantiana*, 7 (1868), 1–206; Francis Woodman, *The Architectural History of Canterbury Cathedral* (1981).

STEPHEN GARDNER

[See also **Canterbury; Monastery; Pilgrimage, Western European.**]

WIBERT OF TOUL (**Wibertus**) (*fl.* eleventh century), archdeacon of Toul (in northeastern France on the Moselle River) and author of a life of Pope Leo IX (*r.* 1049–1054), who had been bishop of Toul and Wibert's companion. Book I tells of Leo's early life and clerical career; book II covers the period from his election as pope to his death.

BIBLIOGRAPHY

Max Manitius, *Geschichte der lateinischen Literatur des Mittelalters*, II (1923), 345; *Patrologia latina*, CXLIII (1853), 465–504.

EDWARD FRUEH

[See also **Leo IX, Pope.**]

WICHRAM OF ST. GALL (*fl.* second half of the ninth century), a monk of St. Gall, is possibly identical with the Wichram whose name appears in documents between 860 and 895. He was the author of a *Computus* in question-and-answer form, based on the work of Bede, to teach students about the astronomical year and how to calculate the feasts of the church.

BIBLIOGRAPHY

The full text of the *Computus* has never been printed. See Max Manitius, *Geschichte der lateinischen Literatur des Mittelalters*, II (1923), 727–729.

W. T. H. JACKSON

[See also **Bede; Calendars and Reckoning of Time; Computus; Easter.**]

WICLIF. See **Wyclif, John.**

WIDUKIND OF CORVEY (*ca.* 925–after 973), a monk of Corvey on the Weser and a leading tenth-century historian whose *History of the Saxons* is a major source for the reigns of Henry I and Otto I of Germany. Widukind completed his *History* in 968 and subsequently revised it to include events up to 973, the death date of Otto I. It is made up of three books. The first begins with the origins and early history of the Saxons and then concentrates on the deeds of Henry I. The second and third books treat the reign of Otto I. Widukind followed some written sources in writing the earliest chapters of his *History,* but starting with the career of Henry I he relied on what he heard and saw himself. Because many leading German political figures spent time at Widukind's monastery of Corvey, he was in an excellent position to gain reliable news of current political events. It is certain too that on at least one occasion Widukind saw Otto I. Widukind was best informed about events that transpired in and around Saxony; the farther Otto I traveled away from Germany the less Widukind has to say about his affairs.

Although Widukind was a monk, he came from an aristocratic Saxon family and wrote to extol the greatness of the Saxon tribe and the glory of its leaders, Henry and Otto. In Widukind's view both men were endowed with supernatural charisma, and their accomplishments were almost epic in character. Widukind had no interest in spiritual affairs; he says nothing about German missionary activity in the East and has very little to say about the papacy. (For him the "highest priests" were the archbishops of Mainz or Cologne.) But Widukind had a consuming interest in dynastic and military affairs. His descriptions of battles, modeled on the style of the historian Sallust, are extremely lively and vigorous. His account of the Battle of the Lechfeld (955), in particular, is one of the most engaging pieces of medieval Latin narrative prose. Widukind is also noted as an exponent of the "non-Roman imperial idea." In his account Henry I and Otto I were acclaimed as emperors by their troops after winning crucial battles over the Hungarians. Their imperial title was thus Germanic rather than Roman and owed nothing to papal award or confirmation. In reality neither Henry nor Otto took the title of emperor as a result of military acclamation, but Widukind's tendentious rendering of events gives evidence of how some aristocratic Germans resisted the Roman and papal conceptions of empire that were soon to prevail. (An alternative but less convincing interpretation is that Widukind was simply unaware of the Roman and papal theories.) In this and other ways Widukind's work provides valuable insights into tenth-century German secular attitudes.

BIBLIOGRAPHY

Albert Bauer and Reinhold Rau, *Quellen zur Geschichte der sächsischen Kaiserzeit* (1971), 3–183, German trans. with facing page in Latin; James A. Brundage, "Widukind of Corvey and the 'Non-Roman' Imperial Idea," in *Mediaeval Studies,* **22** (1960); Boyd H. Hill, Jr., *The Rise of the First Reich: Germany in the Tenth Century* (1969), 9–18; Wilhelm Wattenbach and Robert Holtzmann, *Deutschlands Geschichtsquellen im Mittelalter,* Franz-Josef Schmale, ed., rev. ed. (1967), 25–34.

ROBERT E. LERNER

[See also **Germany: 843–1137; Germany: Idea of Empire; Historiography, Western European; Otto I the Great, Emperor; Saxon Dynasty.**]

WIGBODUS (*fl.* late eighth century), a monk in the court of Charlemagne. Asked by Charlemagne to write a commentary on the Octateuch, the first eight books of the Old Testament, he compiled the teachings of the early church fathers concerning this part of the Bible.

BIBLIOGRAPHY

Max Manitius, *Geschichte der lateinischen Literatur des Mittelalters,* I (1911), 195, 248; *Patrologia latina,* XCVI (1851), 1,102–1,168.

NATHALIE HANLET

[See also **Octateuch.**]

WIGMORE ABBEY, CHRONICLE OF, a fourteenth-century prose account in Anglo-Norman French of the years leading up to the establishment of an abbey at the Augustinian monastery of Wigmore, Herefordshire, in 1172; its dedication by the founder, Hugh Mortimer II, in 1179; and the reconciliation of Hugh's son Roger to the maintenance of his father's benefactions to the abbey. The *Chronicle* is found in University of Chicago Library, MS 224. The Wigmore house also has two Latin records, the *Historia* and the *Annales Wigmorienses.*

BIBLIOGRAPHY

J. C. Dickinson and P. T. Ricketts, eds., "The Anglo-Norman Chronicle of Wigmore Abbey," in *Transactions of the Woolhope Naturalists' Field Club,* **39** (1969).

BRIAN MERRILEES

[See also **Anglo-Norman Literature.**]

WILD, HANS. See **Hemmel, Peter.**

WILDE ALEXANDER, DER (*fl.* second half of the thirteenth century), German poet. Almost nothing is known of the life of Der wilde Alexander. That he was a wandering poet-composer of non-noble origins from the German south is a matter of scholarly consensus; whether he was active mainly in the mid or late thirteenth century is in dispute. Manuscript *J* (Jena) gives him the title *Meister Alexander,* whereas Manuscripts *C* (Heidelberg) and *W* (cod. vind. 2701) list his name as *Der wilde Alexander.* The appelation "wild" may apply either to his unsettled existence as a singer or to the strange, that is, allegorical, mode he favored in his work (compare "Der wilden rede nim ich den kern," II.19.1). Just over thirty of Alexander's lyrics have come down to us, although scholars suspect textual corruption and the presence of redactors. Noteworthy is the careful preservation of the melodies. They attest both the facility of his composition and the correspondences between his text and musical form. Judging from extant works, Alexander did not strive for musical innovation.

Notwithstanding the most searching analysis, no clear silhouette of Alexander's work has emerged. Influenced by prophecy, the sermon, and epic material, Alexander found the wellhead for his imagery and themes in the canon of medieval German didactic or gnomic poetry (*Spruchdichtung*): the nature and conditions of true love (*minne*); the worth and decline of art; experiences of the traveling poet; Dame World; the moral state of mankind; the Deadly Sins; the Last Things; and the Antichrist. Animal imagery plays a significant role. Although the range of topics he considered is traditional, Alexander achieved individuality by virtue of his often dark and virtuoso style, the arrangement of his material, the fusion of lyric forms, and several inventive, striking poems—among them, a Christmas song drawn on multiple motifs (I); a *Leich* on love (VII); enigmatic verses on Zion, *Das Zion-Lied* (IV); and the much-debated song of childhood the *Kindheitslied* (V). The last begins with reminiscences of a bucolic strawberry hunt (compare Vergil's third Eclogue), moves to warnings of danger, and concludes with references to Scripture. A key term, *pherierlin,* identified both as "pony" and a form of *patrinus,* is cryptic. The song is characteristic of Alexander's work, inasmuch as the poet relies on religious allegory, which his listening audience must fully decode.

A central concern in Alexander's poetry is eschatology. Through song Alexander sought to move the Christian community to repentance and preparation for the Final Judgment. The degree to which his biblical allusions are topical and "political" is contested (for example, the scholarly attempt to equate *Sîon, trûre* [IV] with the fall of Acre in 1291). Twentieth-century research, however, places Alexander in the anti-Ghibelline camp on the basis of II.4 (by identifying King William of Holland, *d.* 1256, with the eagle). Now recognized as an important milestone in the development of German modes of lyric expression, Alexander's poetry must also be considered within the larger framework of medieval political and religious rhetoric.

BIBLIOGRAPHY

Source. Carl von Kraus and Hugo Kuhn, eds., *Deutsche Liederdichter des 13. Jahrhunderts,* 2nd ed. (1978), I, 1–19, II, 1–17.

Studies. Jürgen Biehl, *Der wilde Alexander: Untersuchungen zur literarischen Technik eines Autors im 13. Jahrhundert* (1970); Helmut Birkhan, "Altgermanische Miszellen 'aus funfzehen Zettelkästen gezogen,'" in *Festgabe für Otto Höfler zum 75. Geburtstag,* Birkhan, ed. (1976), 54–58; David Blamires, "*Pherierlin* in Der wilde Alexanders 'Kindheitslied,'" in *Medium aevum,* **45** (1976); Thomas Cramer, "Das Zion-Lied des wilden Alexander," in *Euphorion,* **65** (1971); Helmut de Boor, "Das Antichristgedicht des wilden Alexander," in *Beiträge zur Geschichte der deutschen Sprache und Literatur* (T), **82** (1960); Ingeborg Glier, "Meister Alexander (Der wilde Alexander)," in *Die deutsche Literatur des Mittelalters: Verfasserlexikon,* 2nd ed. (1978), I, 213–218; Rudolf Haller, *Der wilde Alexander: Beiträge zur Dichtungsgeschichte des XIII. Jahrhunderts* (1935); Günther Hase, *Der Minneleich Meister Alexanders und seine Stellung in der mittelalterlichen Musik* (1921); Peter Kern, "Das 'Kindheitslied' des wilden Alexander: Zur verhüllenden Redeweise in mittelhochdeutscher Lyrik," in *Festgabe für Hugo Moser: Zeitschrift für deutsche Philologie,* **98** (1979); William C. McDonald, "A Pauline Reading of Der wilde Alexander's *Kindheitslied,*" in *Monatshefte,* **76** (1984); Marvin S. Schindler, "Structure and Allegory in Der wilde Alexander's 'Hie vor dô wir kinder wâren,'" in *German Quarterly,* **46** (1973); Norbert Wagner, "Die Lebenszeit des wilden Alexander," in *Zeitschrift für deutsches Altertum,* **104** (1975).

WILLIAM C. McDONALD

[See also **Antichrist; German Literature: Lyric; Middle High German Literature; Music in Medieval Society; Rhetoric, Western European.**]

WILHELMUS. See **William.**

WILIGELMO DA MODENA (Willegelmus) (*fl.* late eleventh–early twelfth centuries), a northern Italian early Romanesque sculptor best known for the four Genesis reliefs at S. Geminiano, the cathedral of Modena (*ca.* 1099–*ca.* 1106/1110). Wiligelmo—believed to be one of the originators of Romanesque sculpture—worked in a style often compared to and contrasted with that of coeval monuments in Spain and southern France. Wiligelmo's work influenced many other northern Italian monuments, including the cathedral at Cremona (S. Maria) and the abbey of S. Silvestro at Nonantola.

BIBLIOGRAPHY

George H. Crichton, *Romanesque Sculpture in Italy* (1954), 3–21; *Lanfranco e Wiligelmo: Il Duomo di Modena* (1984).

DOROTHY F. GLASS

[See also **Romanesque Art.**]

WILLIAM IX OF AQUITAINE (Guillaume de Poitiers, 1071–1126) is known today primarily for his poetry. He is the first of the troubadours whose works have come down to us, the first poet in whom we find evidence of the "courtly love" tradition that soon dominated Western literature. William is not only the first known troubadour poet; he is also one of the best and is unrivaled in his appeal to modern audiences.

However, William was also an important and powerful member of the aristocracy of his day. As the seventh count of Poitiers and the ninth duke of Aquitaine, he was the heir of a distinguished noble family whose holdings exceeded those of the king of France. This family was accustomed not only to wealth and power, but also to the pleasures and luxuries of court life. Members of William's family displayed an interest in culture and education and sponsored ambitious building projects within their domains. William's granddaughter, Eleanor of Aquitaine, married first the king of France and then the king of England.

Because William was an important aristocrat, the chroniclers of the time recorded his activities and their impressions of his personal characteristics, so that we have much more biographical information about him than we have for most other troubadour poets. This is fortunate, for William differs from later poets in that he was not primarily a poet in his own eyes or in the eyes of his contemporaries. He was an aristocrat who made poetry. To appreciate his poems properly, we need to see them in the context of the life of which they were a part.

The chronicles show, first of all, that William's political and military achievements were mediocre at best. The first of the two crusades he undertook

Genesis scenes. One of the four reliefs by Wiligelmo from the facade of Modena Cathedral, early 12th century. ALINARI/ART RESOURCE

(1101) was a major disaster. While crossing Anatolia most of the army he had raised was massacred in an ambush. (It is true that his second crusade, in Spain in 1120, was a smashing success.) At home, William's devious efforts to increase his holdings resulted in persistent local warfare and conflict with the church, rather than in any significant territorial gains. In 1097 he temporarily annexed Toulouse after its lord had left for the First Crusade and while the land was under the protection of the church. Finally, his flagrant adultery and open devotion to promiscuity led him into further conflict with the church, and he was excommunicated in 1114. The excommunication was not lifted until 1117.

The accounts of William's relationship with the church, the many anecdotes illustrating his worldliness, and the chroniclers' evaluations of his personality show that William drew attention to himself less by his official acts in battle or politics than by his ostentatious violation of church-sponsored standards of conduct. The chroniclers acknowledge William's charm and charisma, noting that he took delight in entertaining others with jokes, comic acting, and the performance of his own songs. William's skill as an entertainer doubtless helped to spread the anecdotes that the chroniclers use to illustrate his pursuit of sexual pleasure and his hostility toward the church. The historian William of Malmesbury reports that William sang of how he planned to set up an Abbey of Whores in which various known prostitutes would hold the positions of authority. In the same passage, this historian describes William's violent behavior toward Peter, bishop of Poitiers, when Peter excommunicated him because of his famous affair with Maubergeonne, viscountess of Châtellerault. While Bishop Peter was speaking, William seized him by the hair and, waving his drawn sword, threatened to kill him. Peter, seeking martyrdom, invited William to do so. William, in turn, changed his mind and declined to help the bishop on his way to heaven. Later, he threw Peter into prison, and when the bishop died there William joked that he'd helped him to heaven after all.

Whether or not William made a particular escapade a topic for jokes or songs, he seems to have behaved in ways likely to catch attention and to give rise to anecdotes, to have dramatized repeatedly and colorfully his commitment to a life of worldly pleasure and his scorn for all who disapproved.

William's eleven surviving poems, like his behavior as described in the chronicles, celebrate worldliness, aggressively affirming the preference for it over obedience to the teachings of the church. William's six burlesque poems are especially close to the William of the chronicles. Not only do they reflect deliberate defiance of the church's teachings in favor of the delights of amorous adventures, but they are the kind of poem William is likely to have used in performances to entertain his aristocratic friends. All of the burlesque poems place the essentially private experience of sex within the context of social values, taking for granted the agreement of the immediate audience and challenging more or less obviously the dissenting church-sponsored view. They invite laughter by crude obscenity, by clever and inventive expression of themes, by unexpected and inappropriate borrowings from the church, by deliberate contrasts with accepted standards of thought and behavior, and by conspicuous virtuosity in form.

One poem, "Farai un vers, pos me sonelh," tells a fabliau-like story in which the poet passes himself off on two ladies as unable to speak intelligibly by saying only the nonsense words "Babariol, babarial / Babarian" even when they test him by having a large cat scratch him. The ladies, once convinced that he will be unable to speak of his adventures, have sexual intercourse with him 188 times in eight days.

Two poems condemn husbands for trying to prevent their wives from taking on lovers at will. One of these, "Companho, tant ai agutz d'avols conres," is so obscene that Alfred Jeanroy offers no translation of it in his 1913 edition of William's poems, though his policy of not translating obscene passages permits all the other poems to be translated at least in part. Even some modern editors and critics in this permissive age avoid the poem or speak of it with some embarrassment. Into this poem William deliberately inserts a full stanza of prayer in which he rhetorically questions why the "Lord God, you who are the leader and king of the world," did not destroy the first man who ever tried to guard his wife's sexual organ. This blasphemous prayer exploits the contrast between the "doctrine" of free love in the poem and the doctrine taught by the church.

The William of the burlesque poems is the William in whom the chroniclers, judging from the clerical perspective, saw only unbridled sensuality, a foolish disregard of the judgment to come, and

WILLIAM IX OF AQUITAINE

absence of purpose, a man who made a joke of everything and whose wit masked superficiality. The remaining poems are serious, indicating that William found spiritual and intellectual pleasure as well as physical pleasure in his life, that he was no gross sensualist but a man of sensitivity and intelligence, capable of a wide range of moods. But the poet of the serious poems is still the iconoclast of the burlesque poems, deliberately drawing attention to the contrast between the values implicit in his poems and those of the church, and also, very probably, to his impatience with the tendency of fellow poets to spiritualize secular love, to deny it sexuality. William's characteristic ways of incorporating iconoclastic elements are the same as in the burlesque poems: the unexpected intrusion of something jarringly inappropriate and, simply, the expression of unabashed delight in pleasures that his society considered sinful.

All but one of the serious poems are about love. They praise noble love between two people who are worthy of it as the source of "joy," the highest earthly good. This love both demands and mysteriously confers spiritual strength and refinement, making the lovers more noble than they were before. William's portrayal of love is consistent with what we find in later "courtly love" lyrics. The techniques also are familiar from later poets; these include the spring opening, the incorporation of religious terminology to characterize the lover's devotion to his beloved, the language used to portray the lover's symptoms, and the sophistication of the highly polished artistry of the poetry. The only conspicuous difference between William and the later troubadours is William's blunt inclusion of sex, felt by some critics to indicate that the tradition still lacked the refinement it was to achieve; but more probably, as I stated above, this inclusion represents William's protest against what he regarded as the overrefinement that was already part of the tradition.

Characteristic of the serious love poems is "Ab la dolchor del temps novel." This poem begins with a spring opening. The poet cannot share in the joy of the season because no word has come from his beloved. "Our love," he says, in lines universally praised and often quoted, "goes in this way":

> As a branch of hawthorne
> which trembles on the tree
> during the night in the rain and frost

until on the morrow when the sun shines through the green leaves and the branch.

He recalls next a morning of past happiness when the lady granted him her love. Up to this point, the poem is a skilled expression of the high-minded sentiments that characterize the genre. The poem is unusually beautiful, but not otherwise distinctive. William, however, now moves abruptly from memory of the past to hope for the future, a hope not at all in keeping with idealized love: "Still may God grant me," he prays, "to live long enough / that I may put my hand under her dress!" In these disconcertingly earthy lines, William insists that the "joy" of love is to be achieved only through sexual contact. Any illusions that we are—or ought to be—above such thoughts, that beautifully expressed sentiments will suffice, are quickly shattered. William follows this sharp reminder of our inelegant physical desires by an appeal to common sense that also calls into question the legitimacy of the traditional poem that he has just crudely interrupted: "We have the food and the knife," the essentials of love, and do not need fine talk. The appeal to God in which the poet expresses his hope for the future and a later reference to the beloved as a "good neighbor" serve as reminders that the religion of love is not that of the church.

"Pos de chantar m'es pres talenz" is the only surviving poem not concerned with sex or sexual love. In this, William's farewell to chivalry, the rival claims of the spiritual and worldly domains, implicit in his other poems and in his biography, are openly discussed. Although William characteristically inverts the traditional Christian depiction of life on earth as a period of exile, portraying instead his departure from world pleasures as an exile, he nevertheless acknowledges that he must accept God's will, give up the life he has enjoyed, and leave his homeland. Although this poem reads as if William were anticipating his death, we do not know when it was written. It shows, however, that William's delight in worldly enjoyments and his anger at individual churchmen did not blind him to recognition of God's will as the ultimate authority to which he owed obedience.

BIBLIOGRAPHY
Bibliography. Robert A. Taylor, *La littérature occitane du moyen âge: Bibliographie selective et critique* (1977), 75–81. Additional bibliographic sources are listed on pages 3–6.
Editions. Gerald A. Bond, ed. and trans., *The Poetry*

of William VII, Count of Poitiers, IX Duke of Aquitaine (1982); Alfred Jeanroy, ed., *Les chansons de Guillaume IX, duc d'Aquitaine (1071–1127)* (1913, 2nd ed. rev. 1927, repr. 1972); John D. Niles, ed. and trans., "Guilhem IX: Texts and Translations," in Peter Whigham, ed., *The Music of the Troubadours,* (1979), 121–189, a popular introduction for the general reader with very free translations, not a scholarly edition; Nicolò Pasero, ed., *Gugliemo IX: Poesie* (1973).

Studies. Reto R. Bezzola, *Les origines et la formation de la littérature courtoise en occident (500–1200),* part 2, *La société féodale et la transformation de la littérature de cour,* II (1960), 243–326; Gerald A. Bond, "Philological Comments on a New Edition of the First Troubadour," in *Romance Philology,* 30 (1976–1977), a review of Pasero's 1973 edition that also discusses Jeanroy's earlier edition and gives an overview of the current scholarship, and "The Structure of the *Gap* of the Count of Poitiers, William VII," in *Neuphilologische Mitteilungen,* 79 (1978); Douglas R. Butturff, "From Cynicism to Idealism: Psychology and the Genesis of Courtly Love in the Lyrics of Guillaume Neuf," in *Kentucky Romance Quarterly,* 24 (1977); Peter Dronke, "Guillaume IX and Courtoisie," in *Romanische Forschungen,* 73 (1961); Frede Jensen, *Provençal Philology and the Poetry of Guillaume of Poitiers* (1983); Jack Lindsay, "Guilhem of Poitou," in his *The Troubadours and Their World* (1976), 1–24; Stephen G. Nichols, Jr., "Canso → Conso: Structures of Parodic Humor in Three Songs of Guilhem IX," in *L'esprit créateur,* 16 (1976); Jean Charles Payen, *Le prince d'Aquitaine: Essai sur Guillaume IX, son oeuvre et son erotique* (1980), concerning which see F. R. P. Akehurst's review in *Speculum,* 56 (1981); L. T. Topsfield, "The Burlesque Poetry of Guilhem IX of Aquitaine," in *Neuphilologische Mitteilungen,* 69 (1968), and "Guilhem IX of Aquitaine and the Quest for Joy," in his *Troubadours and Love* (1975), 11–41; James J. Wilhelm, "Duke William IX of Aquitaine: The Whole Medieval Man," in his *Seven Troubadours: The Creators of Modern Verse* (1970), 21–59.

FRANCES RANDALL LIPP

[See also **Aquitaine; Cercamon; Class Structure, Western; Courtly Love; Eleanor of Aquitaine; Fabliau and Comic Tale; Family, Western European; Jaufré Rudel; Languedoc; Marcabru; Marie de Champagne; Prostitution; Provençal Literature; Quinze Joies de Mariage, Les; Robert d'Arbrissel; Troubadour, Trouvère; William of Malmesbury.**]

WILLIAM I OF ENGLAND, known to history as "the Conqueror" or "the Bastard," was count or duke of the Normans from 1035 and king of the English from 1066 until his death in 1087. He was born very probably at Falaise in 1027 or 1028, the illegitimate son of Robert I ("the Magnificent" or "the Liberal"), duke of the Normans, and Herleve, daughter of Fulbert, traditionally a tanner in the town.

When he was no more than seven years old, his father decided to make a pilgrimage to the Holy Land. Before leaving, Robert secured the acceptance of his young son as his heir. He did not return. William's succession was assured by his great-uncle Robert, archbishop of Rouen, but when the archbishop died in 1037 Normandy fell into great disorder as members of the ducal family strove for positions of power. The crisis came in 1046/1047, when William may already have been trying to assert a personal authority, and it took the form of a determined attempt to replace him by his cousin Guy of Burgundy, supported ominously by several lords in the west of the duchy. He was saved on this occasion by the timely assistance of King Henry I of France (in some sense his feudal superior), to whose support he may well have owed his survival to that point; though in the critical battle of Val-ès-Dunes (1047) William himself showed great valor.

In retrospect the next two decades of his life seem almost like a deliberate preparation for his greatest achievement, the conquest of England. In 1054, when he defeated the last aristocratic rebellion led by two of his uncles, William, count of Arques, and Mauger, archbishop of Rouen, he was able to establish an authority over and a personal relationship with his aristocracy that was without contemporary parallel. At the same time, working within the tradition of his immediate predecessors, he also assumed an authority over the church in Normandy that was almost equally exceptional. The scanty evidence suggests that his justice and his financial administration were at least up to eleventh-century standards. Certainly they enabled him to mobilize the resources of his duchy to the full.

Beyond the duchy, his position was threatened by a sudden change in the attitude of the king of France from benevolent protectiveness to open hostility and by the attempts of the count of Anjou to establish himself in Maine. William defeated two Franco-Angevin invasions (Mortemer, 1054; Varaville, 1057), annexed a part of Maine (Le Passais, 1051), and achieved an insecure hold on the whole of Maine in 1063. William maintained the traditional Norman dominance of eastern Brittany to protect his western frontier. In the east he strengthened his position by marrying Matilda, daughter of Baldwin V, count of Flanders (the marriage took place sometime between 1050 and 1052), and by establishing feudal lordships over the counts of Ponthieu and (most probably) Boulogne.

When King Henry of France and Count Geoffrey Martel of Anjou both died in 1060, and when Lanfranc of Bec had negotiated his reconciliation with the papacy (which had condemned his marriage for reasons unknown), William could finally afford to think seriously of such promises of succession as King Edward of England may have given him; for by that time he led an exceptionally well-ordered principality and his neighbors were either friendly or powerless. Even in England events played into his hands. Earl Harold's visit to Normandy in 1064, whatever its object, enabled William to maintain that Harold had recognized his claim to England and to denounce the earl's "usurpation" two years later. Furthermore, a Norse invasion had weakened Harold's army before William's own expedition could land.

The climax of William's career was his coronation in Westminster Abbey on Christmas Day, 1066. Thereafter his life was spent defending the Normanno-English realm he had created. Military expeditions were required to maintain the traditional relationship between the kings of England and rulers in Wales and Scotland and to translate it into a form of feudal lordship. In France he had to defend his lands against the king of France, who intervened in Brittany (1076), established himself in the Vexin Français (1077), and exploited the discontent of William's oldest son, Robert Curthose. Maine had to be reconquered in 1073. A Danish invasion of England threatened in 1085, and though it did not materialize William made elaborate preparation to meet it. He was mortally wounded at Mantes while trying to recover the Vexin Français, died at Rouen (9 September 1087), and was buried in the abbey he had founded at Caen.

William has to be judged as a military leader and as a ruler. As a commander he was bold and completely ruthless. No one can say to what degree his great victory at Hastings was due to Harold's mistakes or bad luck or to William's own generalship or good fortune, but the mobilizing of his army, its transportation to England, and the discipline he imposed on it were very remarkable achievements. He suffered several defeats after 1066 (Dol, 1076; Gerberoy, 1079; Mantes, 1087),

yet he understood that his vast composite state had to be defended as a whole and carried out his campaigns accordingly. In the end he lost very little. His unifying work in Normandy, particularly the development of Caen and the integration of the far west, his unquestioned leadership of the Norman aristocracy, and the honor gained from his relationship with the Norman church, made the conquest of England possible. His decision to govern the two countries together (personally and by moving frequently from one to the other) and his adaptation of the institutions of each to his rule showed the instincts of a statesman in the conditions of his time. His great authority was shown in the degree of control he exercised over the Norman aristocratic colonization of England, in the assembly he held at Salisbury in 1086, and in his command of an administration that could produce the Domesday Book. William initiated and to some extent established the medieval relationship between England and France that had such an enormous influence on the development of both countries.

BIBLIOGRAPHY

David C. Douglas, *William the Conqueror* (1964), supersedes all earlier biographies and provides a comprehensive list of published documents and historical works, though Frank M. Stenton, *William the Conqueror* (1908), can still be read with profit. A French interpretation is Michel de Boüard, *Guillaume le Conquérant* (1984).

There are descriptive and critical accounts of the evidence and literature in Frank M. Stenton, *Anglo-Saxon England*, 3rd ed. (1971), 688–730, and in David C. Douglas and George W. Greenaway, eds., *English Historical Documents, 1042–1189* (1953).

For the activities of William's principal clerical adviser, see Margaret Gibson, *Lanfranc of Bec* (1978).

JOHN LE PATOUREL

[See also Bayeux Tapestry; Brittany, Duchy; Caen; Domesday Book; Edward the Confessor, St.; England: Norman-Angevin; Flanders and the Low Countries; France: 987–1223; Hastings, Battle of; Lafranc of Bec; Normans and Normandy; Ordericus Vitalis; Rouen; William of Malmesbury; William of Poitiers.]

WILLIAM CARVER. See **Carver, William** (Bromflet).

WILLIAM DE BRAILES. See **Brailes, William de.**

WILLIAM MARSHAL (*ca.* 1146–1219) rose from relative obscurity to become the outstanding statesman of England by the time of his death. His career is a medieval success story par excellence, and it provides a running commentary on the political fortunes of the early Plantagenet kings. Shortly after his death, his heir commissioned a verse biography of his father, and the *Histoire de Guillaume le Maréchal* is both a major example of and a source for the chivalric culture of the High Middle Ages.

William owed his surname to his grandfather Gilbert (*d.* 1130), marshal of the court under King Henry I, and his Plantagenet connection to his father, John (*d. ca.* 1165), a partisan of Matilda in the struggles against King Stephen in the 1140's. John was subsequently rewarded for his loyalty with some grants of land made by King Henry II in the 1150's.

John sent William, his fourth son, to Normandy, where he served as squire to William of Tancarville, the chamberlain of the duchy, acquiring there his first experience of tournaments and of battle. He came also to the attention of Henry II's wife, Eleanor of Aquitaine. It was presumably through her influence that he became, in the 1170's, the military tutor and leading knight of the household of Henry II's eldest son, the "young king" Henry (*d.* 1183). William quickly established his reputation not only as a chivalrous knight but also as a military leader and political adviser, whose skills and intelligence enabled him to survive and to surmount Plantagenet family feuding.

After a sojourn in the Near East on a crusading pilgrimage in 1185–1187, William returned to England and entered the household of King Henry II. The final two years of Henry's reign were crucial for William's subsequent career and power: they established a firm tradition of service to, and patronage from, successive Plantagenet monarchs. Henry granted William some small fiefs, but far more importantly promised him marriage to Isabel, heiress of Richard fitz Gilbert de Clare ("Strongbow"), which conveyed the lordships of Pembroke and Striguil in the Welsh marches, Leinster in Ireland, and Orbec and Bienfaite in Normandy. After Henry's death in 1189, the marriage arrangement was confirmed by King Richard I, and

William and Isabel were promptly married. William acquired not only his wife's vast inheritance but also (from Richard) one-half of the Giffard estates, including Longueville in Normandy. He had become, almost overnight, a major landed baron, one of the wealthiest, most influential, and most trusted figures in the realm.

Henceforth William was almost always at the very center of public affairs. He held a number of important administrative and military positions in England and the marches on behalf of King Richard, and, although by now more than fifty years old, served actively in the field as a soldier in wars against King Philip Augustus of France.

William had supported the claims of John as Richard's heir presumptive throughout the 1190's, and, when John became king in 1199, William's loyalty was further rewarded. He was named sheriff of Gloucestershire and constable of Gloucester and Bristol castles, and was at last granted the comital title, earl of Pembroke, that had not been conveyed with his marriage to Isabel de Clare a decade earlier. He fought for John in the climactic struggle for Normandy against Philip Augustus (1202–1204), and after its absorption in the French realm was allowed to give liege homage for Longueville and his other Norman lordships to King Philip.

Not even a William Marshal, however, could stay forever in the good graces of a King John. His sons were taken hostage, he was stripped of his posts in government, and he spent most of the next four or five years in a sort of self-imposed exile or retreat in his great Irish lordship of Leinster. Here he harbored for a time William de Braose, head of the family that was the target of John's most murderous vendetta; but William Marshal's own relations with John, while strained, never completely snapped.

The causes of the estrangement are not fully clear. John may have had second thoughts about suffering William's divided loyalties between himself (for William's lordships in the British Isles) and Philip Augustus (for William's Norman lands); and John may have seen a more specific conflict between his own interests as lord of Ireland and William's substantial autonomy as lord of Leinster within it.

Whatever the precise causes of the estrangement, William and John were reconciled in 1211–1212, and for reasons that are not hard to discern: John simply could no longer afford the luxury of depriving himself of William's talent, experience, support, and prestigious reputation. William was entrusted with the military command of southern Wales and the marches, and he served loyally in the supreme crisis of the reign, the civil strife that culminated in Magna Carta (1215) and the invasion of England by Prince Louis of France.

William was not, however, simply a careerist or royal creature. He had sufficient independent stature to earn the trust of both the royalist and the antiroyalist sides, and he may well have played a vital if concealed role in the drafting, or at least the acceptance, of Magna Carta.

On his deathbed in 1216, John entrusted the young Henry III to William, and William's position, and his public career in general, was capped in 1217 when he assumed the role of guardian of the king and kingdom (rector regis et regni) shortly after John's death. As guardian, William defeated the French forces at the Battle of Lincoln, was largely responsible for the issuance of the revised version of Magna Carta, and in general should be given major credit for the crucial and successful first steps in the restoration of political stability and royal authority within the kingdom.

William resigned his position in April 1219 and died the following month, aged about seventy-three. The Histoire ends with a long, romanticized series of deathbed scenes; but the simplest and finest epitaph was that given at his funeral by Archbishop Stephen Langton: William Marshal was "the best knight who ever lived."

BIBLIOGRAPHY
Source. Paul Meyer, ed., L'histoire de Guillaume le Maréchal, 3 vols. (1891–1901).
Studies. Georges Duby, William Marshal: The Flower of Chivalry, Richard Howard, trans. (1985); James C. Holt, Magna Carta (1965); Kate Norgate, The Minority of Henry the Third (1912); Sidney Painter, William Marshal: Knight-Errant, Baron, and Regent of England (1933) and The Reign of King John (1949); Sir Frederick Maurice Powicke, The Loss of Normandy, 1189–1204: Studies in the History of the Angevin Empire (1913, 2nd ed. 1961).

MICHAEL ALTSCHUL

[See also Eleanor of Aquitaine; England: Norman-Angevin; Henry II of England; Henry III of England; John, King of England; Knights and Knight Service; Langton, Stephen; Magna Carta; Marshal; Nobility and Nobles; Normans and Normandy; Philip II Augustus; Richard I the Lionhearted.]

WILLIAM OF APULIA (*fl. ca.* 1100). Little is known of William beyond his authorship of the *Gesta Roberti Wiscardi* (Deeds of Robert Guiscard), an epic poem in five books devoted to the early history of the Normans in southern Italy. William was probably not a Norman. He may have been a monk or cleric, since he wrote at the request of Pope Urban II. The *Gesta* was dedicated to Robert Guiscard's son, Duke Roger of Apulia, who died in 1111. Written in hexameters with numerous classical allusions, especially to Vergil, it is both an important historical source and a literary monument.

BIBLIOGRAPHY
Sources. Marguerite Mathieu, ed., Guillaume de Pouille: La geste de Robert Guiscard (1961), contains both the Latin text and a French translation. See also Antonio Pagano, Il poema Gesta Roberti Wiscardi di Guglielmo Pugliese (1909); Filippo Roscimi, ed., Guglielmo Appulo: Monaco giovinazzese del secolo mille e autore del poema latino sulle Geste di Roberto il Guiscardo (1967), containing historical and critical commentary and an Italian translation.
Studies. Ferdinand Chalandon, Histoire de la domination normande en Italie et en Sicile, I (1907, repr. 1960), xxxviii–xl.

JAMES M. POWELL

[See also **Amatus of Monte Cassino; Anna Komnena; Italy, Byzantine Areas of; Monte Cassino; Robert Guiscard; Roger I of Sicily; Sicily, Kingdom of; Urban II, Pope.**]

WILLIAM OF AUVERGNE, French theologian and bishop of Paris from 1228 until his death in 1249. As a youth, he studied in Paris, and in 1225 he became a professor of theology at the University of Paris. After becoming bishop he maintained close ties to the university. His best-known work is the *Magisterium divinale*, which includes seven major sections. He also wrote at least twenty other treatises.

Influenced most notably by Augustine, William tried "to rescue Aristotle from the Arabians." His monumental attempt to combine Neoplatonism with Aristotelian philosophy was not successful, but he is credited with paving the way for his successors Alexander of Hales, Albertus Magnus, and Thomas Aquinas.

William was also concerned with the art of rhetoric and composed a large number of sermons.

BIBLIOGRAPHY
Sources. *Guilelmi Alverni Opera omnia,* 2 vols. (1674, repr. 1963); William of Auvergne, *De Trinitate,* Bruno Switalski, ed., (1976).
Studies. Helmut Borok, *Der Tugendbegriff des Wilhelm von Auvergne (1180–1249)* (1979); Steven P. Marrone, *William of Auvergne and Robert Grosseteste* (1983); Albrecht Quentin, *Naturkenntnisse und Naturanschauungen bei Wilhelm von Auvergne* (1976); Jan Rohls, *Wilhelm von Auvergne und der mittelalterliche Aristotelismus* (1980).

HARRY HAZEL, III

[See also **Albertus Magnus; Alexander of Hales; Aquinas, St. Thomas; Aristotle in the Middle Ages; Augustine of Hippo, St.; Neoplatonism; Paris, University of.**]

WILLIAM OF BRIANE (*fl. ca.* 1215) was the author of an Anglo-Norman prose version of the *Pseudo-Turpin Chronicle.* The original Latin version of this chronicle, the *Historia Karoli Magni et Rotholandi,* was spuriously attributed to Turpin, the archbishop of Rheims who appears in the *Chanson de Roland.* William of Briane was a clerk to Warin fitz Gerold, chamberlain of the royal Exchequer under Richard the Lionhearted and John. William's chronicle was probably written in the second decade of the thirteenth century.

BIBLIOGRAPHY
Ian Short, ed., *The Anglo-Norman Pseudo-Turpin Chronicle of William de Briane* (1973).

BRIAN MERRILEES

[See also **Anglo-Norman Literature; Chronicles, French; Forgery; Pseudo-Turpin; Roland, Song of.**]

WILLIAM OF CANTERBURY. See William the Englishman.

WILLIAM OF CHAMPEAUX (*ca.* 1068–*ca.* 1122) was an early philosopher at Paris and a teacher of Peter Abelard. He became bishop of Châlons-sur-Marne in 1113.

Born at Champeaux in Brie, William began his studies at Paris with Manegold of Lautenbach, but probably the teachers who had the greatest influence on him were Roscelinus (at Compiègne) and Anselm of Laon (at Laon). As these examples show, Paris in the eleventh century was far from being the leading educational center in France (Chartres was probably superior and Laon at least equal). William was to be one of the men who gave the schools of Paris their preeminence.

Roscelinus probably interested William in the problem of universals—that is, does an abstract noun such as "man" denote something that has a real, independent existence (realism) or is it simply a convenient name (nominalism)? To take one of William's examples, does the word "man," as applied to Plato and Socrates, mean that where Plato is then Socrates (in his essential humanity) is also there? Or is "man" simply a convenient name? Either position, taken in its most extreme form, leads to heresy. How can there be a Trinity if the essential element in each Person is the same? And yet, if that essential element is not equally present, then do we have three Gods?

Roscelinus' views, which tended toward nominalism, were questioned, and William was never to work out a satisfactory answer to the problem. He was not helped by having Abelard as a pupil. Abelard took particular delight in contradicting his old teachers, and he found it easy to point out inconsistencies in William's thought. William seems to have begun as a realist and then modified his views little by little until he was fairly close to the nominalist position.

The fact that William was important enough to draw an attack from Abelard shows his significance in the Parisian intellectual world. He was one of the teachers in the cathedral school who attracted students, and he eventually became its head. As he grew older he became less interested in scholarly debates, and in 1108 he retired to the hermitage of St. Victor in Paris. His presence there attracted students, and St. Victor's soon became an abbey and one of the more important elements in the intellectual community in Paris.

William died around 1122. He was recognized by his contemporaries as one of the leaders of the French church—praised by Bernard of Clairvaux and by Otto of Freising, called the "chief support of scholarship" (*columna doctorum*) by the bishop of Soissons at a council in 1120, and the "shining example of scholarship" among French bishops by the author of the *Chronicle of Maurigny*. Even Abelard admitted that William was the leading teacher of dialectic of his time. But the greatest praise came from Hugues Metel of Toul, who said that with the deaths of Anselm of Laon and William it was as if the "flame of the word of God had been extinguished on earth."

BIBLIOGRAPHY

E. Michaud, *Guillaume de Champeaux et les écoles de Paris* (1867), is old and outdated in many respects, but still the fullest treatment. See also Jean Châtillon, "De Guillaume de Champeaux à Thomas Gallus," in *Revue du moyen âge latin*, 8 (1952); André Forest, F. van Steenberghen, and M. de Gandillac, *Le mouvement doctrinal du XIe au XIVe siècle* (1951), 71–73; Georges Lefèvre, *Les variations de Guillaume de Champeaux et la question des universaux* (1898); Odon Lottin, "Les 'sentences' de Guillaume de Champeaux," in his *Psychologie et morale aux XIIe et XIIIe siècles*, V (1959), 189–227; Hans Zeimentz, *Ehe nach der Lehre der Frühscholastik* (1973).

JOSEPH R. STRAYER

[See also **Abelard, Peter; Anselm of Laon; Bernard of Chartres; Dialectic; Manegold of Lautenbach; Nominalism; Paris, University of; Realism; Roscelinus; Schools, Cathedral; Universals.**]

WILLIAM OF CHAMPLITTE was the first prince of the crusader state of Achaea, in Greece (r. 1205–ca. 1209). A baron from the county of Burgundy, he took the cross in 1201 and participated in the campaigns of the Fourth Crusade, culminating in the conquest of Constantinople in 1204. Then he helped Boniface of Montferrat, the newly created king of Thessalonica, to secure his domains in Greece. While Boniface's army was besieging Nauplia, Geoffroi de Villehardouin, nephew of the chronicler, suggested to William that they move on to seize lands in the Peloponnese that were less well-defended. William agreed and, with Boniface's permission, the two set out with 100 knights and about 400 mounted sergeants. They conducted a successful campaign and organized the feudal principality of Achaea (known more commonly to the Franks as Morea), with William as its first prince. He died around 1209, while on a visit to Burgundy to claim his inheritance there. The state he founded in Greece lasted until 1432.

BIBLIOGRAPHY

Jean Longnon, "The Frankish States in Greece, 1204–1311," in Kenneth M. Setton, ed., *A History of the Crusades*, II (1969), 235–276, and *Les compagnons de Villehardouin: Recherches sur les croisés de la quatrième croisade* (1978), 209–212.

PETER TOPPING

[See also **Boniface of Montferrat; Burgundy, County of; Constantinople; Latin Empire of Constantinople; Latin States in Greece; Morea; Morea, Chronicle of; Nobility and Nobles; Villehardouin, Geoffroi de.**]

WILLIAM OF CONCHES (*ca.* 1080—1154/1160) was a philosopher and theologian associated with the school of Chartres. John of Salisbury was one of his pupils.

William was born at Conches in Normandy, studied grammar and logic under Bernard of Chartres, and became a master by 1125. Chartres seems to have been his main center of learning and teaching, although he taught for a short time in Paris. From about 1140, he was attacked by William of St. Thierry, who had earlier opposed the teaching of Peter Abelard. In the tractate *De erroribus Guillelmi a Conchis*, William of St. Thierry accused William of modalism in his Trinitarian doctrine and of materialism in his presentation of the relationship of the Trinity to creation. William of Conches subsequently withdrew from the schools to the Norman court, where he was appointed tutor to the sons of Geoffrey Plantagenet, including the future King Henry II of England. He died some time between 1154 and 1160.

In addition to two major works, the *Philosophia mundi* and the *Dragmaticon*, William produced glosses on Priscian's *Institutiones grammaticae* and Boethius' *De consolatione Philosophiae*, two versions of glosses on Plato's *Timaeus*, a gloss on Macrobius' *De somnio Scipionis*, and a gloss on Martianus Capella. A florilegium of biblical and classical texts on ethics, entitled *Moralium dogma philosophorum*, may also be his work.

Like many of the thinkers associated with Chartres, William wrote extensively on cosmological questions, seeking to explain the Genesis account of creation and to harmonize it with the cosmological myth in Plato's *Timaeus*. His *Philosophia mundi* considers the divine nature in relation to creatures, the structure of the universe, the elements, geography, and human nature. Composed in the 1120's, it was reworked in the later 1140's into the *Dragmaticon,* written in the form of a dialogue with Duke Geoffrey. Besides showing signs of concessions to William of St. Thierry, the *Dragmaticon* displays significant influences from Greek and Arabic medical writings, recently translated for the first time into Latin. William's writings were to have considerable impact, in turn, on later cosmological and encyclopedic literature, including Alan of Lille's *Anticlaudianus,* Vincent of Beauvais's *Speculum naturale,* and Thomas of Cantimpré's *De natura rerum.*

BIBLIOGRAPHY

Guillaume de Conches, *Glosae in Iuvenalem,* Bradford Wilson, ed. (1980), with a biographical essay and extensive bibliography. See also Guillaume de Conches, *Glosae super Platonem,* Édouard Jeauneau, ed. (1965); Gregor Maurach, ed., *Philosophia mundi: Ausgabe des 1. Buchs von Wilhelm von Conches' "Philosophia"* (1974).

WANDA CIŻEWSKI

[See also **Alan of Lille; Bernard of Chartres; John of Salisbury; Plato in the Middle Ages; Schools, Cathedral; Thomas of Cantimpré; Translation and Translators, Western European; Vincent of Beauvais; William of St. Thierry.**]

WILLIAM OF HIRSAU (*ca.* 1026—4 July 1091), Benedictine monk, astronomer, and music theorist. He was educated at St. Emmeram in Regensburg (Bavaria) and appointed abbot of Hirsau (Wurtemberg, near Stuttgart) in 1069, where he introduced the customs of Cluny, adopted thereafter by more than ninety German and Austrian monasteries. Strong in character, with a definite propensity toward mysticism, William stood firmly for Pope Gregory VII (1073–1085) and against Henry IV (1056–1106), at the time of the investiture conflict, to preserve the immunity of his abbey from political and episcopal interference. He introduced, around 1076–1078, the custom of external brothers (*fratres exteriores*) for the domestic service of the monastery, a custom which led to the later Benedictine tradition of lay brothers (*fratres conversi*).

BIBLIOGRAPHY

Sources. Haimo's biography of William is available in G. Pertz, ed., *Monumenta Germaniae historica: Scriptores,* XII (1856), 211–225, reprinted in *Patrologia latina,* CL (1880). For a modern edition of William's treatise on music, see Denis Harbison, ed., *Willehelmi Hirsaugensis Musica* (1975).

Studies. Robert Bultot, "'Quadrivium,' 'natura,' et 'ingenium naturale' chez Guillaume d'Hirsau," in *Rivista di filosofia neo-scolastica,* **70** (1978); Hermann Jakobs, *Die Hirsauer* (1961); Maurus Pfaff, "Abt Wilhelm von Hirsau," in *Erbe und Auftrag,* **48** (1972).

YVES CHARTIER

[See also **Benedictines; Cluny, Order of; Gregory VII, Pope; Henry IV of Germany; Hirsau; Investiture and Investiture Conflict.**]

WILLIAM OF JUMIÈGES (William Calculus), a Benedictine monk, is known for his *Gesta Normannorum ducum,* an abridgment and continuation of the Norman history by Dudo of St. Quentin. Written in 1070–1071, and covering events up to that time, William's work is an important source for Norman history during the century preceding the pacification of England. It was the most widely read of Norman histories until superseded by the work of Ordericus Vitalis (*b. ca.* 1075).

BIBLIOGRAPHY

Guillaume de Jumièges: Gesta Normannorum ducum, Jean Marx, ed., Société de l'histoire de Normandie (1914); Elisabeth M. C. van Houts, "The *Gesta Normannorum ducum:* A History Without an End," in *Proceedings of the Battle Conference on Anglo-Saxon Studies, III, 1980* (1981), 106–115.

EDWARD A. SEGAL

[See also **Chronicles, French; Dudo of St. Quentin; Normans and Normandy.**]

WILLIAM OF MALMESBURY (*ca.* 1090–1143), precentor and librarian of Malmesbury, where he was educated and professed as a Benedictine monk, is generally recognized as the first major English historian to follow Bede. Born of mixed Norman and Anglo-Saxon parentage, William composed several devotional works, including a collection of miracles of the Virgin, a life of St. Dunstan, and a translation from English of a life of St. Wulfstan. He is best known, however, for his historical works.

William's career as a historian falls into two phases. The first, from around 1118 to 1125, encompasses his two great works, the *Gesta regum*

Anglorum (Deeds of the kings of the English), a history of England from the Anglo-Saxon period to 1120, and the *Gesta pontificum Anglorum* (Deeds of the archbishops and bishops of the English), an account of saints, bishops, and monasteries from the conversion of England to 1125. Both are in a literary, rather than annalistic, form, and they display the conscientiousness and critical skill that have earned him the praise of historians ever since. The second phase, from 1135 to 1143, finds William revising his earlier works, usually in the direction of increased caution and an overall tempering of his criticism of several important figures, including William the Conqueror, William Rufus, and several contemporary bishops. During this period he also wrote some local history, including the *De antiquitate Glastoniensis ecclesiae* (On the antiquity of the church of Glastonbury), and composed the *Historia novella* (Recent history), a contemporary history in chronicle form which describes the chaotic events of Stephen's reign. William was a witness to several events which he describes in the *Historia novella,* and his bias towards the empress Matilda is quite evident.

William's work is notable for his elegant Latin style, his vivid character sketches, and his use of a wide variety of source material—literary, oral, and physical. He traveled widely in England, recognized the importance of architectural and monumental evidence for historical research, and consulted both Anglo-Saxon and Norman historical, hagiographical, and biographical works, as well as archival materials. His works were widely read, copied, and used by other historians throughout England. Garrulous about his methods, interests, and beliefs, William makes his character evident on nearly every page of his writings, and the survival of a large number of early manuscripts makes it possible to reconstruct his changing interests and ideas.

BIBLIOGRAPHY

Sources. John Scott, *The Early History of Glastonbury: An Edition, Translation, and Study of William of Malmesbury's De antiquitate Glastonie ecclesie* (1981); William of Malmesbury, *De gestis pontificum Anglorum libri quinque,* N. E. S. A. Hamilton, ed. (1870), *De gestis regum Anglorum libri quinque: Historiae novellae libri tres,* William Stubbs, ed., 2 vols. (1887–1889), *The "Vita Wulfstani" of William of Malmesbury,* Reginald R. Darlington, ed. (1928), *The Historia Novella,* K. R. Potter, ed. and trans. (1955); *Polyhistor: A Critical Edition,* Helen Testroet Ouellette, ed. (1982).

Studies. Hugh Farmer, "William of Malmesbury's Life and Works," in *The Journal of Ecclesiastical History,* **13** (1962), and "Two Biographies by William of Malmesbury," in T. A. Dorey, ed., *Latin Biography* (1967), 157–176; Antonia Gransden, "William of Malmesbury," in her *Historical Writing in England c. 550 to c. 1307* (1974), 166–185; Montague R. James, *Two Ancient English Scholars: St. Aldhelm and William of Malmesbury* (1931).

MARY LYNN RAMPOLLA

[See also **Anglo-Saxon Literature; Asser; Bede; Eadmer of Canterbury; England: Norman-Angevin; Geoffrey of Monmouth; Gildas, St.; Historiography, Western European; Ordericus Vitalis; William of Jumièges; William of Poitiers.**]

WILLIAM OF MOERBEKE (also known as Guillelmus de Moerbeka, *ca.* 1215/1235–*ca.* 1286), a Dominican, was one of the most productive and influential translators from Greek into Latin of Aristotelian and other philosophical and scientific texts. He was born in the town of Moerbeke near the border of Flanders and Brabant, may have entered the order in the convent of Louvain, and belonged to the priory of Ghent. He may have studied at Paris or in Cologne under Albertus Magnus. He is known to have been at the Dominican priory in Thebes, Greece, in early 1260, and at Nicaea on 24 April of that year. In November 1267, May 1268, and June 1271 he was at Viterbo, then a papal residence. He was papal confessor and chaplain from 1272 to April 1278, but may have held that office as early as the pontificate of Clement IV (1265–1268). During that time, he visited the courts of Savoy and France to raise help for the Ninth Crusade (March 1272) and took part, as personal advisor to Gregory X, in the Second Council of Lyons (May–July 1274), where he was a keen promoter of reunion between the Greek and Latin churches. In April 1278, he was appointed archbishop of Corinth, where he resided until his death. The Greek village of Mermpaka, about thirty miles from Corinth, is probably named after him.

Moerbeke is known to have been in contact with some of the leading scientists of his time. During his stay at Viterbo, he made the acquaintance of Witelo, the Polish student of optics, whose *Perspectiva* was influenced by Moerbeke's translation of Hero's *De speculis* (1269) and Eutocius' commentary on *De sphaera et cylindro* (1269). The dedicatory epistle of *Perspectiva,* addressed to Moerbeke, suggests a Neoplatonic bent to his philosophy. At Lyons he met the astronomer Henry Bate of Malines, who dedicated to him the *Magistralis compositio astrolabii* (1274). It is possible that the mathematician Campanus of Novara, who knew Moerbeke at the papal court, influenced him to translate Archimedes and Eutocius. Moerbeke's translation of Galen's *De alimentis* (1277) was dedicated to the physician Rocellus of Arezzo. While there is no direct evidence for Moerbeke's acquaintance with Thomas Aquinas, he may well have been in touch with him at or near Rome before 1269 or between 1271 and 1274. It is certain that Aquinas used some, if not all, of Moerbeke's translations of Aristotle soon after they had been made.

Moerbeke produced only one original work, the *Geomantia.* His numerous translations—which remained influential well into the fifteenth, sixteenth, and later centuries—were produced over the course of more than twenty years. His translations are exact, literal, word-for-word renderings of the Greek originals, intended to complete and improve Western knowledge of Aristotle's works and some of the writings of Proclus, Archimedes, Eutocius, Ptolemy, Hero, Galen, and Hippocrates. Of the writings of Aristotle, Moerbeke translated from Greek into Latin for the first time the *Politica,* the *Poetica* (1278), *Metaphysica* (book XI), *Historia animalium, Meteorologica* (books I–III), and *De caelo* (books III–IV). He entirely retranslated the *Categoriae* (1266), *De interpretatione* (1268), *Meteorologica* (book IV), *De caelo* (book I–II), and the *Rhetorica,* and revised several of the earlier translations of Aristotle. His translations of commentaries on Aristotle included those by Alexander of Aphrodisias, Themistius, Ammonius, Philoponus, and Simplicius.

Moerbeke's translation of Proclus' *Elementatio theologica* (1268) had the effect of revealing the original text behind the *Liber de causis,* and of contributing to the development of Neoplatonism in the later Middle Ages and Renaissance. The careful and literal style of his work continues to provide evidence of Greek originals now lost or poorly preserved, thereby enriching scholarly comprehension of the history and transmission of Greek texts.

BIBLIOGRAPHY

Translations. For a complete list of Moerbeke's translations, with editions cited where works have been edited, see Lorenzo Minio-Paluello, "Moerbeke, William of," in *Dictionary of Scientific Biography,* IX (1974). Moerbeke's translations of Aristotle appear in the series *Aristoteles latinus* (1953–); some of his translations of Aristotelian commentaries are included in the Corpus Latinum commentariorum in *Aristotelem graecorum* (1957–), and those of his translations commented upon by Thomas Aquinas are found in *Opera omnia* (1882–), the Leonine critical edition of Aquinas' works. Also important is Marshall Clagett, *Archimedes in the Middle Ages,* II, *The Translations from the Greek by William of Moerbeke* (1976), which includes a valuable short account of William's life as well as his translations of Archimedes.

Studies. The article by Minio-Paluello cited above includes an extensive bibliography of secondary literature up to 1974, which can be updated from relevant sections of the *Bulletin thomiste* and *Bulletin de théologie ancienne et médiévale.* Of earlier studies, the most extensive is Martin Grabmann, *I papi del duecento e l'Aristotelismo,* II, *Guglielmo di Moerbeke, O.P.: Il traduttore delle opere di Aristotele* (1964).

WANDA CIŻEWSKI

[See also **Archimedes in the Middle Ages; Aristotle in the Middle Ages; Aquinas, St. Thomas; Councils, Western (1215–1274); Dominicans; Neoplatonism; Philosophy and Theology, Western European; Plato in the Middle Ages; Translation and Translators, Western European.**]

WILLIAM OF OCKHAM. See Ockham, William of.

WILLIAM OF POITIERS (*ca.* 1020–*ca.* 1087/ 1101) is best known for his only surviving work, the *Gesta Guillelmi ducis Normannorum,* a life of William the Conqueror written within the Norman historical tradition. As a youth, the author received training in arms, attended schools in Poitiers between 1045 and 1050, and subsequently became a cleric and served as personal chaplain to the Conqueror. Firsthand knowledge makes William's work a particularly important source for the life of the Conqueror, despite its pro-Norman bias.

BIBLIOGRAPHY

Raymonde Foreville, ed., *Guillaume de Poitiers: Histoire de Guillaume le Conquérant* (1952), Latin text and French translation.

EDWARD A. SEGAL

[See also **Cambridge Songs; William I of England.**]

WILLIAM OF ST. THIERRY, Benedictine abbot and Cistercian monk, contemplative and theologian, was born at Liège, Belgium, around 1085 and died in 1147 or 1148 at the Cistercian monastery of Signy, France. Known for centuries as the friend and biographer of Bernard of Clairvaux, he has come to be recognized as one of the principal authors of twelfth-century monastic letters. William's career touched most of the significant men and ideas of his time and was especially interwoven with the work of Bernard. Recently scholars have revised the chronology of William's life proposed by his first modern biographers, replacing exact dates with more approximate ones; this reflects the lack of precise data from documented sources.

Born of noble parents, William received some formal schooling at Rheims (formerly it was thought that William studied at Laon, where he was supposed to have met Abelard). William entered the Benedictine monastery of St. Nicaise of Rheims about 1113 or 1115; he was elected abbot of the Benedictine monastery of St. Thierry near Rheims about 1119 or 1120. He held the post for almost fifteen years and was honored by his contemporaries as an excellent administrator and spiritual counselor.

At St. Thierry he studied the Fathers and produced the first of his many works on the love of God—the *De natura et dignitate amoris* (On the nature and dignity of love) and the *De contemplando deo* (On contemplating God)—as well as many of his *Meditations,* a series of personal reflections on monastic life. Early in this period of intense community service and private study, William met Bernard and soon expressed a desire to join the Cistercians. Bernard, however, discouraged this, urging William to continue his work as abbot. The two friends shared an enthusiasm for the Song of Songs, which later led them both to devote works to its explication. William dedicated his *De sacramento altaris* to Bernard, and Bernard dedicated to William both his *Apologia,* directed against the Cluniacs (part of the controversial literature that surrounded the formation of reforming orders like the Cistercians), and the *De gratia et libero arbitrio* (On grace and free will).

About 1134 or 1135, William retired to the new Cistercian foundation at Signy; ill health forced him to devote himself to writing in lieu of the rigors of manual labor required under the order's rule. He wrote there his *Expositio in cantica canticorum* (Exposition on the Song of Songs) but left the work unfinished to take up the theological questions of the day, both by refuting Abelard and William of Conches and by preparing works of his own on the Trinity, *Speculum fidei* (Mirror of faith) and *Aenigma fidei* (Enigma of faith). William also moved Bernard to take part in Abelard's trial at Sens, which ended with Abelard's condemnation in 1140.

Near the end of his life, William was inspired by a visit to the Carthusians at Mont Dieu to write *Epistola ad fratres de Monte Dei* (A letter to the brethren at Mont Dieu), or the "Golden Epistle," as it is called, a celebration of contemplative love that is an acknowledged classic of Western spirituality. This text, like many other works by William, expresses the core of his teaching about love between God and man. The soul of man is related to God most intimately as an image of the Trinity. The analogy between the three incarnations of God (Father as creator, Son as wisdom, Holy Spirit as love) and the faculties of the soul was taken from the Fathers and transformed in William's work into a key for contemplating the Trinity and for charting the soul's proper progress to loving union with the Godhead.

BIBLIOGRAPHY

Sources. Editions of William of St. Thierry's works include: *Meditations et prières par Guillaume de St.-Thierry,* Jean-Marie Déchanet, ed. (1945); *Deux traités de l'amour de Dieu: De la contemplation de Dieu et de la nature et de la dignité de l'amour,* Marie M. Davy, ed. (1953); *Deux traités sur le foi: Le miroir de la foi, l'enigme de la foi,* Marie M. Davy, ed. (1959); *Exposé sur le Cantique des cantiques,* Jean-Marie Déchanet and M. Dumontier, eds. (1962); *Lettre aux frères du Mont-Dieu: Lettre d'or de Guillaume de St.-Thierry,* Jean-Marie Déchanet, ed. (1975). For the English translations of many of William's works, including *On Contemplating God, Meditations, Exposition on the Song of Songs, The Enigma of Faith,* and *The Golden Epistle,* see the Cistercian Fathers series, *The Works of William of St. Thierry,* 4 vols. (1971–1974); also important is *The Mirror of Faith,* Thomas X. Davis, trans. (1978). Other works by William appear in *Patrologia latina,* CLXXX (1855).

Studies. O. Brooke, "The Trinitarian Aspect of the Ascent of the Soul to God in the Theology of William of Saint Thierry," in *Recherches de théologie ancienne et médiévale,* **26** (1959); Jean-Marie Dechanet, *Aux sources de la spiritualité de Guillaume de St.-Thierry* (1940), "Amor ipse intellectus est: La doctrine de l'amour intellection chez Guillaume de St.-Thierry," in *Revue du moyen âge latin,* **1** (1945), and *William of St. Thierry: The Man and His Works,* Richard Strachan, trans. (1972); E. Rozanne Elder, "The Way of Ascent: The

Meaning of Love in the Thought of William of St. Thierry," in *Studies in Medieval Culture*, I, J. R. Sommerfeldt, ed. (1964), 39–47, and (as editor) *A Guide to Cistercian Scholarship* (1974); Étienne Gilson, *The Mystical Theology of Saint Bernard*, A. H. C. Downes, trans. (1940), 198–214; L. Malvez, "La doctrine de l'image et de la connaissance mystique chez Guillaume de St.-Thierry," in *Recherches de science religieuse*, **22** (1932); A. Wilmart, "La serie et la date des ouvrages de Guillaume de Saint-Thierry," in *Revue Mabillon*, **14** (1924).

THERESA MORITZ

[See also **Abelard, Peter; Benedictines; Bernard of Clairvaux, St.; Carthusians; Cistercian Order; Exegesis, Latin; Philosophy and Theology, Western European.**]

WILLIAM OF SENS (*fl.* late twelfth century). Certainly a Frenchman, William was the first truly Gothic architect in England. Chosen to rebuild Canterbury Cathedral after the fire of 1174, he completed a substantial portion before a near-fatal fall from the scaffolding in 1178 forced his return to France. No other works by William have yet been identified; our only knowledge of him comes from the writings of Gervase of Canterbury.

BIBLIOGRAPHY

Gervase of Canterbury, "Tractatus de combustione et reparatione Cantuariensis ecclesiae," in William Stubbs, ed., *The Historical Works of Gervase of Canterbury*, I (1879), 3–29; John H. Harvey, *English Mediaeval Architects: A Biographical Dictionary Down to 1550* (1954, rev. ed. 1984), 274; Kenneth Severens, "William of Sens and the Double Columns at Sens and Canterbury," in *Journal of the Warburg and Courtauld Institutes*, **33** (1970); Robert Willis, *The Architectural History of Canterbury Cathedral* (1845); Francis Woodman, *The Architectural History of Canterbury Cathedral* (1981).

STEPHEN GARDNER

[See also **Architect, Status of; Canterbury Cathedral; Gothic Architecture; Masons and Builders.**]

WILLIAM OF TYRE (*ca.* 1130–29 September 1186), chancellor of the Latin Kingdom of Jerusalem from 1174, archbishop of Tyre from 6 June 1175, and historian of the earlier crusades. Born in the Kingdom of Jerusalem, into a Western (likely French or Italian bourgeois) family, he studied the liberal arts, theology, and law in France and Italy from about 1145 to 1165. After returning to Jerusalem, he served King Amalric I (1163–1174) as tutor to his son Baldwin (later Baldwin IV). William then undertook royal and papal missions to Constantinople (in 1168 or 1169 and 1179/1180, respectively), and in 1179 attended the Third Lateran Council, the enactments of which he compiled. He lost hope of his greatest ambition when Heraclius of Caesarea was made patriarch of Jerusalem on 16 October 1180.

William apparently was encouraged to write by King Amalric. The original history, a narrative of Amalric's reign, was diverted and expanded, perhaps by new requests from the king, and was suspended after his death. William compiled his comprehensive history of the Kingdom of Jerusalem principally from three of his own works: the *Gesta Amalrici*, a history of the kingdom from 1094, and a now-lost history of the Islamic princes of the Orient.

William's achievements in assembling and evaluating sources, and in writing in excellent and original Latin a critical and judicious (if chronologically faulty) narrative, make him an outstanding historian, superior by medieval, and not inferior by modern, standards of scholarship. He used all available materials, comparing written (including Arabic) accounts and interviewing Amalric and others, to produce what his English translators have called "the main trunk of the literature on the crusades," a narrative admired (and appropriated) by successors, including Jacques de Vitry, Roger Wendover, and Matthew Paris.

BIBLIOGRAPHY

For William's history, see the *Historia rerum in partibus transmarinis gestarum*, Recueil des Historiens des Croisades, Historiens Occidentaux, (1844); and the annotated English version by Emily Atwater Babcock and A. C. Krey, *A History of Deeds Done Beyond the Sea*, 2 vols. (1943).

For the older literature, see the bibliography in Babcock and Krey. More recent work includes P. W. Edbury and J. G. Rowe, "William of Tyre and the Patriarchal Election of 1180," in *English Historical Review*, **93** (1978); Rudolf Hiestand, "Zum Leben und zur Laufbahn Wilhelms von Tyrus," in *Deutsches Archiv für Erforschung des Mittelalters*, **34** (1978); R. B. C. Huygens, "Guillaume de Tyr étudiant: Un chapitre (XIX, 12) de son 'Histoire' retrouvé," in *Latomus*, **21** (1962), and "La tradition manuscrite de Guillaume de Tyr," in *Studi medievali*, 3rd ser., **5** (1964); Hans E. Mayer, "Zum Tode Wilhelms von Tyrus," in *Archiv für Diplomatik*, **5–6**

(1959–1960); Rainer Christoph Schwinges, *Kreuzzugs-ideologie und Toleranz: Studien zu Wilhelm von Tyrus* (1977); D. W. T. C. Vessey, "William of Tyre and the Art of Historiography," in *Mediaeval Studies,* **35** (1973), and "William of Tyre: Apology and Apocalypse," in Guy Cambier, ed., *Hommages à André Boutemy* (1976).

SUSAN M. BABBITT

[See also **Chronicles, French; Crusades and Crusader States: To 1192; Historiography, Western European.**]

WILLIAM OF VOLPIANO (**Guilermo Volpiano**) (*fl.* early eleventh century), abbot of St. Bénigne, Dijon, Lombard monastic reformer and builder for the Cluniac order in France, first in Burgundy, then in Normandy. William was highborn and well educated. As a reformer-builder, he was both architect (*mēkhanikos*) and clerk of works (*arkhitektōn*) of his most famous project, the rotunda of St. Bénigne, constructed between 1001 and 1018 in imitation of the Holy Sepulcher in Jerusalem.

BIBLIOGRAPHY

Kenneth John Conant, *Carolingian and Romanesque Architecture, 800–1200* (1959, rev. ed. 1973, 1978); Sergio Luis Sanabria, "Metrics and Geometry of Romanesque and Gothic St. Bénigne, Dijon," in *Art Bulletin,* **62** (1980).

CARL F. BARNES, JR.

[See also **Burgundy, Duchy of; Cluny, Order of; Masons and Builders; Romanesque Architecture.**]

WILLIAM OF WINCHESTER, a mason who was paid 6*d.* per day for the year 1365–1366 at Westminster Palace, when the main work was a new Clock Tower and Jewel Tower, designed by Henry Yevele (who was paid 1*s.* per day) and built by Thomas Hardgrey and Maurice Yonge of Maidstone. He was entitled *apparator operantium* (warden or foreman of the workmen); his relationship with Yevele and the others is unclear. He may have been the son of the homonymous carpenter mentioned at Westminster in the 1320's.

BIBLIOGRAPHY

Howard M. Colvin, ed., *The History of the King's Works,* I: *The Middle Ages* (1963), 509–10; John H. Harvey, *English Mediaeval Architects: A Biographical Dictionary Down to 1550* (1954, rev. ed. 1984); William

R. Lethaby, *Westminster Abbey and the King's Craftsmen: A Study of Mediaeval Building* (1906), 188, 212.

BARRIE SINGLETON

[See also **Architect, Status of; Construction: Building Materials; Masons and Builders; Westminster Abbey; Yevele, Henry.**]

WILLIAM OF WYKEHAM (1324–1404). Bishop of Winchester, lord chancellor, and founder of New College, Oxford, and of Winchester College School, Wykeham is an outstanding example of a talented man of humble background who rose in the medieval church.

Born at Wickham, Hampshire, of peasant origin, perhaps the son of a serf, William, probably through the influence of William Edington, treasurer of the Exchequer, entered the service of King Edward III about 1347. From the position of clerk and keeper of the king's dogs, he rose steadily, becoming in 1356 surveyor of the king's works at Windsor Castle, Edward's favorite residence. In that post William supervised the enlargement of Windsor as a royal palace and home of the new Order of the Garter. His building achievement at Windsor so thoroughly won the king's confidence and gained him such authority that the French chronicler Froissart reported that at the English court "all things were done by him and without him nothing was done," and the papacy in 1363 and 1364 sought William's intervention with the king. Though he was not ordained a priest until 1362, ecclesiastical benefices, including the rich archdeaconry of Lincoln, rained upon him. In 1364, William became keeper of the Privy Seal; in 1366, bishop of Winchester (one of the wealthiest sees in Western Europe; he was consecrated 10 October 1367); and in 1367, lord chancellor.

Scholars dispute William's influence on government policy, but they agree he was an able administrator, though a calculating politician. As the king's chief minister, he was held responsible for the mismanagement of royal finances and for royal extravagance, and was blamed for continued taxation in peacetime. The Parliament of 1371 demanded his removal from office, and on a rising tide of anticlericalism he was dismissed. William later returned to favor, serving again, under Richard II, as chancellor in 1389–1391, and played a part in political affairs until his death.

Though William was one of the most notorious

pluralists of his day, though he may have been a sharp businessman who increased his annual income of £873.6s.8d (an early figure) by lending money at interest, and though the reformer Wyclif could cuttingly refer to a bench of bishops that included a clerk "wise in building castles," nevertheless he used his wealth nobly, in the service of education and religion. In 1369 he began buying land for St. Mary College of Winchester in Oxford, known since its foundation (1379) as New College. Designed in the early Perpendicular style by the architect William Wynford (fl. 1360–1405), and planned for a warden and seventy scholars, New College was on a larger scale than any other college at either Oxford or Cambridge.

William had maintained a school in Winchester since 1373. In 1382 he founded, and in 1387 ordered construction begun on, Winchester College, which, with a strong architectural resemblance to New College, was completed and occupied in 1394. Planned for ninety-six poor students, Winchester was the largest school then completed; it also enjoyed exceptional privileges as an independent, self-governing body. William saw the school as a nursery for New College and restricted entrance to it to the founder's kin, those from places where St. Mary's held property, men from the diocese of Winchester, and men from shires where the college held property.

In 1394, again using the architectural services of William Wynford, William began remodeling the nave of his cathedral, at 556 feet the longest Gothic church in the world. The twelve bays of the Norman building were reconstructed, and the triforium was removed and replaced by the Perpendicular arches of the present nave, giving a total effect of great height, length, and dignity.

William died 27 September 1404 and is buried in one of the chantries in the nave of his cathedral.

BIBLIOGRAPHY
For general background, see May McKisack, *The Fourteenth Century, 1307–1399* (1959); William A. Pantin, *The English Church in the Fourteenth Century* (1955). More recent evaluations of Williams and corrections to the above studies are in Roger Custance, ed., *Winchester College: Sixth-Centenary Essays* (1982), especially Peter Partner, "William of Wykeham and the Historians," and Guy F. Lytle, "Partonage and the Election of Winchester Scholars in the Late Middle Ages and the Renaissance"; William Hayter, *William of Wykeham: Patron of the Arts* (1970); Guy F. Lytle, *An English Bishop's Household in the Later Middle Ages* (1982);
Norman Sykes, *Winchester Cathedral* (1976). Though it is unreliable, the serious student will have to consult Thomas F. Kirby, ed., *The Register of William of Wykeham*, 2 vols. (1896–1899).

BENNETT D. HILL

[See also **Edward III of England; England: 1216–1485; Oxford University.**]

WILLIAM THE CONQUEROR. See **William I of England.**

WILLIAM THE ENGLISHMAN (*fl.* late twelfth century) is known only for completing the choir of Canterbury Cathedral between 1179 and 1184, the reconstruction of which had been started by William of Sens in 1174. William the Englishman introduced changes that more firmly related Canterbury to northern French architecture, such as reducing the height of the main arcade and employing a Gothic triforium. He also raised the floor level, elevating the tomb of Thomas Becket, to better display the shrine.

BIBLIOGRAPHY
Jean Bony, "French Influences on the Origins of English Gothic Architecture," in *Journal of the Warburg and Courtauld Institutes,* 12 (1949); Francis Woodman, *The Architectural History of Canterbury Cathedral* (1981), 87–130.

BARRIE SINGLETON

[See also **Canterbury Cathedral; Gothic Architecture; William of Sens.**]

WILLIAM TOREL. See **Torel, William.**

WILLIRAM VON EBERSBERG (*ca.* 1010–1085), abbot and exegete, born into a noble family in Franconia, Germany. He entered the famous Benedictine monastery of Fulda, where be became a monk. Around 1040 he moved to Bamberg as a teacher in St. Michael's Monastery. From 1048 until his death in 1085 he was abbot of the small monastery of Ebersberg in Upper Bavaria. He maintained connections with the imperial court, especially with Emperor Henry III. In Ebersberg, Williram was an energetic administrator and organizer. He was active as an architect and very much, albeit somewhat conservatively, interested in the liberal arts, especially in the trivium and in theology and exegesis.

Williram's main work is his *Expositio in Cantica canticorum* (Exposition on the Song of Songs, *ca.* 1065). In the original manuscripts it shows a remarkable form. The Vulgate text stands in the center column of each page in large letters; in the right column this text appears translated and commented upon in vernacular prose (East Franconian dialect), in which the exegete keeps certain key Latin words (*Mischprosa*). In the left column, the Vulgate text appears rendered into Latin leonine hexameters; then an exegetical explanation follows, also in leonine hexameters. The right and left columns are in a small script. The whole text is divided into more than 149 sections (the Vulgate text consists of 114 verses in eight chapters). With the prologue (in Latin prose), the total comes to 150 sections, a number which might have a symbolic meaning. Williram interprets the Bridegroom of this quite erotic text as Christ, the Bride solely and quite conservatively as the church (*ecclesia*); both speak in monologues and dialogues. A third voice is that of the synagogue.

Williram took most of his exegetical material from standard commentaries on the Song of Songs (Haimo of Auxerre, Angelomus of Luxeuil, and perhaps Bede and Gregory the Great). He shows a real mastery in his use of the vernacular prose, conveying the deeper religious meaning with a great sense of clarity, style, and rhythm by placing in his *Mischprosa* the Latin theological terms at carefully selected spots. The net result is the emergence of theological prose of high quality. Although the similar *Mischprosa* of Notker Teutonicus (*d.* 1022) probably served as a model, Williram's achievement still merits high praise. His verse is rhetorically embellished and quite elegant, but it is often complex and not easy to understand because of its more learned and profound contents.

Volker Schupp has tried to elucidate the genre as well as the form of Williram's *Expositio,* connecting the former with the Christian religious eclogue, the latter with the *opus geminatum,* the double (in prose and verse) biblical or hagiographical paraphrase or exegesis practiced by early Christian and medieval writers. But certain Psalter manuscripts (large Vulgate text in the center column, a commentary in small letters in the right and left columns) could very well have served as a model, too. Williram's work on the Song of Songs was enormously popular during the Middle Ages and later; over twenty manuscripts have been preserved. We know about several more that once existed.

Williram is also credited with sixteen mostly quite short poems in Latin. According to Schupp's convincing demonstration three of them (nos. 13–15) are not his. For Abbot William of Hirsau, he wrote sometime after 1065 an improved version of the *Vita S. Aurelii* in Latin prose (Aurelius was the patron saint of Hirsau Monastery in the Black Forest).

BIBLIOGRAPHY

Sources. Erminnie H. Bartelmez, ed., *The "Expositio in Cantica canticorum" of Williram, Abbot of Ebersberg, 1048–1085: A Critical Edition* (1967); Marlies Dittrich, ed., "Sechzehn lateinische Gedichte Willirams von Ebersberg," in *Zeitschrift für deutsches Altertum,* 76 (1939); Willy Sanders, ed., *(Expositio) Willerammi Eberspergensis abbatis in Canticis canticorum: Die Leidener Handschrift* (1971); *Vita S. Aurelii* in *Acta sanctorum,* IV (1925).

Studies. Marlies Dittrich, "Willirams von Ebersberg Bearbeitung der *Cantica canticorum,*" and "Die literarische Form von Willirams Expositio in *Cantica canticorum,*" in *Zeitschrift für deutsches Altertum,* 82 (1948–1950) and 84 (1952–1953); David A. Krooks, *The Semantic Derivation of the Modal Verb in the Old High German Williram* (1975); Willy Sanders, *Der Leidener Williram: Untersuchungen zu Handschrift, Text und Sprachform* (1974); Volker Schupp, *Studien zu Williram von Ebersberg* (1978).

PETRUS W. TAX

[See also **Angelomus of Luxeuil; Exegesis; Fulda; Haimo of Auxerre; Notker Teutonicus; William of Hirsau.**]

WINCHCOMBE, RICHARD (*fl.* 1398–1440), English architect who worked almost exclusively in and around Oxford. He may have built parish churches in the area and smaller buildings for New College and Balliol, but he is best known for designing the Divinity School (begun 1430), completed only later by William Orchard.

BIBLIOGRAPHY

Eric Gee, "Oxford Masons, 1370–1530," in *Archaeological Journal,* 109 (1952), 54–131 (esp. 69–70); John H. Harvey, *Gothic England: A Survey of National Cul-*

ture, 1300–1550 (1947), 80, and *English Mediaeval Architects: A Biographical Dictionary Down to 1550* (1954, rev. ed. 1984), 336–337; Geoffrey Webb, "The Universities of Oxford and Cambridge: The Divinity School, Part I," in *Country Life*, 65 (1929).

STEPHEN GARDNER

[See also **Orchard, William; Oxford University**.]

WINCHESTER TROPER, the name given to two manuscripts copied at the Old Minster in Winchester: Cambridge, Corpus Christi College, MS 473 [CC 473]; and Oxford, Bodleian Library, MS Bodley 775 [Bo 775].

CC 473 has 198 parchment folios, 146 × 92 millimeters. The main corpus was copied by two scribes (one text, one music) between 996 and 1006 (Planchart) or in the first quarter of the eleventh century (Holschneider). The contents are as follows: 10r–52v, proper tropes; 55r–70r, Kyries and Glorias with and without tropes; 70r–73v, tonary; 73v–78r, Sanctus and Agnus with and without tropes; 81r–88v, sequences; 89r–134r, proses; 135r–155r, organa (to Kyrie tropes, Kyries, Gloria tropes, tracts, sequences); 163r–189r, organa (to alleluias, *doxa*, responsories, antiphons). The copying of the manuscript was suspended at a relatively late stage, and miscellaneous additions were entered throughout the eleventh century as follows: 1r–9v (added fascicle, after 1050), miscellanea and alleluias; 53v–54r, introit tropes, organa to antiphons, *Ite missa est;* 78v–80v, introit tropes, Kyrie trope, Sanctus trope; 134v, Kyrie; 156v–161v, proses and organa to introit tropes; 189v–190v, organa (to responsory, alleluias, Kyrie); 191r–198v (added fascicle, before 1025), miscellanea.

Bo 775 has 191 parchment folios, 273 × 167 millimeters. The main corpus was copied by three scribes (two text, one music) about 1050. Its contents are as follows: 8r–61v, gradual-troper; 61v–75v, ordinary chants with and without tropes; 76r–87v, alleluias; 88r–97r, tracts; 97r–121v, offertories with verses and *prosulae;* 122v–129r, sequences; 136r–181v, proses. The manuscript shows additions of the late eleventh and early twelfth centuries: 1r–7v (added fascicle, after 1100), proses, alleluias, Kyrie and Gloria tropes; 87v, alleluias; 121v, Agnus trope; 130r–136r, proses; 182r, antiphon, Kyries; 182r–190v (added fascicle, before 1100), proses. In the early twelfth century many proses were erased and rewritten on crudely drawn staves.

These two manuscripts and a closely related fragmentary troper (British Library, Cotton Caligula A.xiv, fols. 1–36, copied at Canterbury *ca.* 1050) are the most extended chant sources and the only tropers to survive from Anglo-Saxon England.

The scripts in these tropers, except that in the first fascicle of Bo 775, are typical of Winchester hands of the tenth and eleventh centuries. The music is notated in staffless, unheightened Anglo-Saxon neumes that are closely related to north French neumatic notations. There is some alphabetic notation in CC 473, and the first fascicle of Bo 775 is notated in the slightly squared neumes typical of the early-twelfth-century English and north French notations.

Unlike most French and German tropers, the Winchester Tropers are carefully organized liturgical books with numerous rubrics. Bo 775 is an anachronistic source that reflects the state of the Winchester repertory about 978–985. The litany in the troper mentions King Ethelred (crowned 978) and gives 24 November as the date of the *Dedicatio ecclesiae* (the Old Minster was first rededicated 20 October 980). But the former date appears in the alleluias and offertories, and there is a prose in honor of St. Ethelwold (*d.* 984). CC 473 shows a careful revision of this repertory undertaken after 996, when St. Ethelwold was proclaimed a confessor.

Given the close relations between Winchester and Blandinium, Corbie, and Fleury, it is not surprising to find numerous Rhenish and French concordances in the Winchester repertory, though liturgical considerations led the Winchester cantors to write a number of new tropes and proses. Thus the Winchester Tropers are important sources of Anglo-Latin liturgical poetry. Most Insular tropes do not survive in later sources, and thus their melodies are not recoverable. Some of the proses do survive in transcribable sources, but they often use "international" melodies.

The problem posed by the notation also affects the most notable repertory of CC 473, the 174 organa copied in the manuscript. They are notated with care but show only approximate heightening of local neume groups. The organa are set down as individual parts. The principal voice for each (which is always a preexisting chant) was to be sung from another book, a gradual or an antiphoner. No graduals or antiphoners from the Old Minster survive, but enough music from the gradual appears in the tropers that the principal voices for sixty-eight organa appear in CC 473 and Bo 775 has principal voices for ninety-one. This allows the reconstruction of these voices with the aid of later sources in staff notation. When the principal voice can be reconstructed, a plausible transcription of the organum becomes possible, since Winchester polyphony seems to follow the relatively rigid contrapuntal rules found in the *Musica enchiriadis* and Guido of Arezzo's *Micrologus* for organum at the fourth with unison openings and cadences. Convincing reconstructions of Winchester organa have been published by Ewald Jammers and Andreas Holschneider.

Both tropers transmit a short Easter play that is similar but not identical to the *Visitatio sepulchri* described in the *Regularis concordia*. The play is provided with an ambiguous rubric, *Angelica de Christi resurrectione,* and its liturgical position and function are not made clear in either manuscript. In CC 473 the text of the play is so abbreviated that it could not have been performed from that manuscript. Its function might have been similar to that of the several pieces rubricated *Versus ante officium* found in both tropers. These are works that function as general introductions to the entire Mass. But the absence of a similar rubric for the play, and its position in Bo 775 before the Easter Vigil litany, cast doubts on this view as well.

Together with the Canterbury Troper, the two Winchester Tropers are among the most important witnesses of the artistic and liturgical revival produced in England by the reforms of St. Dunstan and St. Ethelwold. They transmit a considerable number of native works and provide us with detailed information on liturgical practice. The organa of CC 473, which according to Holschneider may be the work of Wulfstan of Winchester (*fl.* 990–1006), a disciple of St. Ethelwold, are the earliest major monument of European composed polyphony.

BIBLIOGRAPHY

Heinrich Besseler and Peter Gülke, *Schriftbild der mehrstimmigen Musik* (1973); Clemens Blume, "Wolstan von Winchester und Vital von Saint-Évroult," in *Sitzungsberichte der kaiserlichen Akademie de Wissenschaften zu Wien,* phil.-hist. Kl., **146** (1902–1903); Walter Howard Frere, ed., *The Winchester Troper: From Manuscripts of the Xth and XIth Centuries* (1894, repr. 1973); Jacques Handschin, "The Two Winchester Tropers," in *Journal of Theological Studies,* 37 (1936); O. B. Hardison Jr., *Christian Rite and Christian Drama in the Middle Ages* (1965); Andreas Holschneider, *Die Organa von Winchester* (1968); Heinrich Husmann, *Tropen- und Sequenzen Handschriften* (1964); Gunilla Iversen, *Corpus troporum,* IV, *Tropes de l'Agnus Dei* (1980); Ewald Jammers, *Anfänge der abendländischen Musik* (1955), 11–21, 74–75; Ritva Jonsson, *Corpus troporum,* I, *Tropes du propre de la messe,* 1, *Cycle de Noël* (1975).

Timothy J. McGee, "The Liturgical Placements of the *Quem quaeritis* Dialogue," in *Journal of the American Musicological Society,* **29** (1976); Armand Machabey, "Remarques sur le Winchester Troper," in *Festschrift Heinrich Besseler* (1961); *The Monastic Agreement of the Monks and Nuns of the English Nation,* Thomas Symons, trans. (1953), the Regularis *concordiae;* Alejandro Enrique Planchart, *The Repertory of Tropes at Winchester,* 2 vols. (1977); Gilbert Reaney, *Manuscripts of Polyphonic Music, 11th–Early 14th Century* (1966); Klaus Rönnau, *Die Tropen zum Gloria in excelsis Deo* (1967); Marius Schneider, *Geschichte der Mehrstimmigkeit, historische und phänomenologische Studien,* 2 vols. (1934–1935; 2nd ed., 3 vols. in 1, 1969); William L. Smoldon, *The Music of the Medieval Church Drama,* Cynthia Bourgeault, ed. (1980); Bruno Stäblein, *Schriftbild der einstimmigen Musik* (1975), "Sequenz (Gesang)," in *Die Musik in Geschichte und Gegenwart,* XII (1965), and "Tropus," *ibid.,* XIII (1966); Karl Young, *The Drama of the Medieval Church,* 2 vols. (1933, repr. 1967)

ALEJANDRO ENRIQUE PLANCHART

[See also **Agnus Dei; Antiphon; Drama, Liturgical; Ethelwold; Gloria; Guido of Arezzo; Introit; Ite Chant; Kyrie; Organum; Sanctus; Sequence (Prosa); Tonary; Troper; Tropes to the Ordinary of the Mass; Tropes to the Proper of the Mass.**]

WINDMILL. See Mills.

WINE AND WINEMAKING. Wine played a much more important role in daily life during the Middle Ages than it does today. Other stimulants, such as coffee and tea, had not yet been introduced into Western Europe. Distilled spirits were known toward the end of the Middle Ages but were valued only for their medicinal qualities. The water supply was often unsafe, and, at a time when even kings died of dysentery, fear of intestinal disorders could not be exaggerated. In much of Western Europe, wine was the basic beverage of rich and poor alike, and, even in those areas which did not produce wine, it was a ritual necessity.

WINE AND WINEMAKING

HISTORICAL BACKGROUND

The cultivation of the vine had been introduced throughout the entire Mediterranean basin during the Greco-Roman era, but subsequent political and religious developments shattered the agricultural as well as the political unity of that world. In those parts of the former Roman Empire which fell to the armies of Islam, the Koranic prohibition of wines was rigorously enforced. The vineyards were uprooted. In those lands which were formerly part of the Persian Empire, a much more tolerant attitude toward intoxicating beverages was adopted. Wine was still recommended for medicinal purposes in the Islamic world, but there is little information available on how widespread was this use and what were the sources of supplies.

The process of distilling alcohol was probably discovered in the context of medicinal experimentation in the Islamic world. The word "alcohol" appears to be Arabic in origin. In any event, alcohol was probably introduced to Western Europe along with classical and Arabic medical treatises from the Islamic world, but its properties were not understood for centuries. Accounts of the death of Charles II "the Bad," king of Navarre, in 1387 illustrate European unfamiliarity with the substance. Charles' physicians prescribed that he be wrapped in bandages soaked in alcohol. Unfortunately, a servant bearing a lit torch approached too close to his lord, and Charles' flaming death seemed an appropriate moral commentary on his reputation in life.

The Byzantine world was also the heir to the viticultural heritage of Rome as well as the more ancient traditions of the Greek world. The Greek practice of adding retsina to wine may go back to ancient times, but it is clearly attested in the tenth century, when Bishop Liutprand of Cremona complained that the Greek wine was "undrinkable because of the mixture in it of pitch, resin, and plaster." The crusaders from Western Europe did not find Greek wines to their taste but commented favorably on the quality of the wines produced by the Jewish communities in the Byzantine East.

With the decline of the Western European economy in the early Middle Ages, the commerce in wines that had flourished under the Roman Empire came to a virtual halt. Since wine was a necessity throughout Christian Europe for ritual purposes, areas unfavorable to production of wine had recourse to a variety of ways to obtain supplies when commercial sources were not available. Vineyards were cultivated in many areas inhospitable to the vine. The wines they produced were *verjus* rather than true wine, but they satisfied the needs of the faithful.

In the sixth century, St. Columba brought wine with him from the Loire Valley on his first journey to Ireland, but church institutions needed continual and reliable sources of supplies. Some communities received gifts of wine from correspondents in more favored regions. Wealthier institutions acquired properties in wine-producing areas to supply their needs.

COMMERCE IN WINES

By the time of Charlemagne, Frisian traders were active in transporting the wines of the valleys of the Rhine and the Moselle to England. Other supplies reached England from the Île de France and the valley of the Loire through Rouen. With the marriage of Eleanor of Aquitaine to the future Henry II of England in 1152, England's imports of wines from Bordeaux increased dramatically. The Bordeaux wines at this date were very thin and pale and were often fortified with the heavy wines of Cahors. The sources do not quantify the importance of the twelfth-century wines of Cahors, but these wines seem a likely source for the accumulation of capital in Cahors to such an extent that the term *cahorsin* became synonymous with "money-lender."

No statistics are available regarding the volume of exports from Bordeaux to England until the beginning of the fourteenth century, when Bordelais exports to England probably reached their peak. From 1308 to 1309 they amounted to 102,724 tuns. (A "tun," literally a large cask, here signifies a measure of approximately 250 gallons.) War, harvest failures, and the Black Death severely curtailed Bordelais exports in the middle of the fourteenth century. The volume of trade between Bordeaux and England eventually stabilized at a level of about a fifth of its 1308–1309 level.

The phrase "the wines of Burgundy" was used in the Middle Ages to refer to the white wines produced in the valleys of the Loire, the Cure, and the Yonne. These valleys were part of a vast and celebrated wine-producing area of which only a vestige around Chablis remains in production today. In the thirteenth century, the Franciscan monk Salimbene visited the area and exclaimed at the vast expanse he saw, whose "mountains, coasts, plains, and fields were covered with vines." The wines of this region were sent up the rivers to Paris and from there transshipped north to the lowlands or west to England.

The wines produced in the region of the Côte d'Or, the home of the great Burgundies of today, were referred to as the "wines of Beaune." The wines of Beaune were not as important commercially as the wines of Bordeaux or Burgundy. Much of the territory that produced the great wines of Beaune was held by the dukes of Burgundy or by the great ecclesiastical institutions, such as Cluny and Cîteaux, and the bulk of their production did not enter into the stream of commerce.

Commerce in the wines of Beaune was also discouraged by the fact that they did not enjoy easy access by water to the wine-starved markets of the north but were required to take the more difficult overland routes to Flanders or Paris. Supplies were also sent south by the rivers to Provence, where local wines were plentiful but lacked finesse. The wines of Beaune were so celebrated at the papal court at Avignon that Petrarch declared that the pope's fondness for them was prolonging the Babylonian captivity.

By the late Middle Ages, the markets of the major commercial centers of Western Europe offered a great variety of wines for sale. The volume of trade in the wines of Burgundy and Beaune probably never approached the volume of exports from Bordeaux, but they were nevertheless standard items in the northern markets. The markets of Bruges, for example, offered wines of the Mediterranean, Spain, Gascony, Poitou, the Île-de-France, Beaune, St. Pourçain, and the valley of the Rhine.

The ancient world used wineskins and pottery vessels to contain wines. Pottery vessels could be kept airtight and stored for some time, but the wines kept in them did not age. Nevertheless, the Romans prized some wines for their longevity, such as the Falernian wines that were served at Trimalchio's feast in the *Satyricon* of Petronius. During the Middle Ages vintners and retailers contained wines primarily in wooden vessels, which were porous, admitting air as well as bacteria. The wines were highly susceptible to spoilage and could not be stored for any significant time. They were normally consumed young, during the year they were produced. Wines that aged well could not be successfully marketed before the availability of bottles and corks in the eighteenth century.

In the Middle Ages, new wines were put into barrels for sale after only a short, initial period of fermentation ranging from a few hours to several days, and then they went on the market immediately. In Beaune, in the heart of the Burgundy region, the major wine sales took place at the St. Luke's Fair, which began on 18 October. The wines were probably still swollen at that date from the turbulence of the fermentation. One account described the shipment of a queue (barrel) of new wine, "still warm." Measures were sometimes adjusted to compensate for the expansion in volume during this period. The customs of Châtillon stipulated that a barrel of wine should contain 18 *setiers* until the feast day of St. Martin in winter (11 November). The barrel normally contained 16 *setiers*.

By the time the new harvest was in, the wines of the previous year were known as "old wine" and were sold at a discount. In areas that produced inferior wines, the costs of storage vessels might be greater than the value of the old wines. The old wines would be poured out at the time of the harvest to accommodate the new.

The fact that wines were normally consumed young, prior to the completion of the fermentation process, made them a much more important element in the diet than wines of today. The young wines still contained yeasts and unfermented sugars with more nutritional value than their modern counterparts. Far from being a luxury item to accompany the meal, wines were a basic part of the diet, and the per capita rate of consumption of wines in wine-producing areas was many times that of today.

Wines that have not fully completed the fermentation process, however, are much more vulnerable to spoilage. Since wooden barrels "breathe," their contents are subject to evaporation, acetification, and the introduction of bacteria. During the medieval period the barrels had to be inspected frequently and replenished to reduce the contact with the air. Inferior wines could not withstand the rigors of shipment. Merchants were therefore concerned with purchasing only the best quality of young wines, which would be better able to support the hardships and expenses of the journey.

The services of someone with professional expertise in wines were sorely needed. By the fourteenth century, foreign merchants could use the services of wine brokers in making their purchases. A papal register of 1355 records the payment of two florins to the brokers in St. Pourçain, an important wine center in the Bourbonnais, who guided the papal procurer "to the wines and cellars and led him to the village, and were always present during business."

The statutes of the corporations of brokers provide the most complete picture of the their functions. The 1607 statutes of the brokers of Beaune undoubtedly preserve provisions from a much earlier time when they state: "Let the brokers faithfully conduct the merchants through the caves and cellars of the town. Let them taste, drink wines with them, and let them not allow the purchase of any wines unless they are good and true." Once an agreement was reached between the buyer and the seller, the broker put his official mark on the barrel.

The brokers were directed to show preference to local residents who had wines to sell from their own property rather than those who purchased wines, perhaps a bias toward local property owners, but just possibly an adumbration of the preference for "estate-bottled wines" over those of *negotiants* found to this day. Otherwise, the brokers were to "conduct the merchants to good cellars of local residents, without favoritism to anyone, whether relative, friend, or distinguished citizen." They were not to accompany their clients to purchase wines outside the town, its faubourgs, or its banlieue, without the express permission of the mayor or the aldermen.

Retail sales of wine were conducted differently and were subject to different controls from wholesale sales. Retail sales took place in taverns, where wines were also available for consumption on the premises. The medieval tavern was a simple establishment. In Dijon, the capital of the duchy of Burgundy, all one had to do to open a tavern was to hang a green branch outside the door of the house to signify that wines could be bought "by the pot and by the pint." Wines offered for sale in the taverns were generally of inferior quality, often the wines from the third or fourth pressing, or "piquette," a beverage made by pouring water over the residue from the press.

Retail sales were strictly regulated and supervised, but there were other reasons for taverners to deal fairly with their customers. Regulations designed to keep the peace in taverns were very common. Gambling in taverns was frequently denounced, and women were sometimes prohibited from frequenting cabarets and taverns. The Fourth Lateran Council (1215) forbade clerics from visiting taverns except in a case of necessity, as when traveling. Local authorities sometimes tried to deal with such problems by limiting the hours of business or prohibiting all-night drinking. Nevertheless, the records of justice abound with reports of tavern brawls and resulting deaths. A taverner would be inclined to think twice before cheating such a raucous crew—although fear of their wrath did not stop the alewife in the Chester cycle who was condemned to "endless pains and sorrow cruel" for cheating her customers.

Taverns offered only wine, whereas in cabarets some food was also served, and in hostelries customers could be fed and lodged. Cabarets and hostelries were governed by members of professions involved in guilds, but taverners were broadly representative of the community. All classes of society, lay and religious, from the mightiest lord to the humblest worker, were involved in retail sales in taverns. The number of taverns was probably very large by the fourteenth century. Guillebert of Metz may have exaggerated when he described Paris around 1400 as having more than 4,000 taverns, but Milan in 1288 had 150 hostelries servicing foreigners alone. In Dijon in the late sixteenth century, there were more than seventy hostelries. There were undoubtedly many times that number of taverns.

PRODUCTION OF WINES

The organization of the production of wine varied considerably according to the geographic conditions in the area of production and the economic circumstances of the producer. The most common unit of production in most areas was probably the small, individual holding in which some grapes were cultivated, perhaps in a garden or a trellis adjacent to the house, as one of a number of crops for consumption by the producer. It is impossible to determine how widespread this form of organization was since it has left no records susceptible to systematic analysis, but it was undoubtedly the norm in all but the most favored wine-producing areas.

Contractual arrangements for production, whether oral or written, are much better known. One arrangement, *metayage*, was a form of sharecropping in which the cultivator agreed to give the owner a share of the crops, usually between a third and two-thirds, in exchange for the possession of the land. This practice went at least as far back as the twelfth century in Burgundy but became more and more important in the course of the thirteenth and fourteenth centuries. It was an important means of attracting workers when there was a shortage of labor, such as during the period after the Black Death, when many productive vineyards were being abandoned. In 1351, for example, most of the vineyards in Volnay belonging to the duke of Burgundy, which had formerly been cultivated by day laborers under the supervision of the ducal officials, were given over to *metayage*.

Metayage was often linked to a seignorial regime that imposed additional obligations on the occupant of the land. For example, the cultivator sometimes had to postpone harvesting his grapes until those of the lord's estates had been harvested. When he finally did harvest his grapes, he sometimes had to postpone processing them to permit the officials of the lord to make the division of the shares of the harvest. Then, he was required to use the lord's winepress, paying the keeper of the press a certain amount in coin or in wine for the service. Finally, he could not offer his wines for sale at certain times when the lord had a monopoly on sales. Such restrictions would be a major source of discontent from the twelfth century on. In popular manifestations of that time, such as the communal revolt of Vézelay in 1152, the local wine producers appear to have played an active role.

The practice of *metayage* has left a strong imprint on the customary law in much of Western Europe. Less well known but perhaps even more important for the production of wines for commerce is the use of professional contractors to cultivate vineyards. The notarial records of Dijon, the capital of the fourteenth-century duchy of Burgundy, contain numerous contracts with winegrowers (*vignerons*). They were hired for a season to cultivate a vineyard in exchange for a payment, sometimes in the form of money, sometimes in fruit or wine. Administrative records for great estates also report the use of contractors who would be responsible for assembling the labor force, particularly for such tasks as pruning the vines. This practice also seems to be more common at times when there was a shortage of skilled labor.

The most comprehensive information about the cultivation of the vineyards in the Middle Ages comes from the administrative records of the estates of great lords. These provide a mine of details concerning the production of wines on the great estates. The officials provided information for each day as to the location of the work, the task undertaken, the number of workers employed that day, and the amount of money paid to each worker for that day's labor. A typical entry might read, "Item,

for 39 men to prune in the vineyard of St. Romain at 7 *deniers* for a day's labor, 22 *sous* 9 *deniers*."

Most of the time, the laborers were day workers. *Corvée* labor was used in more remote areas, such as St. Romain in the hills behind Beaune, especially for such tasks as harvesting, which did not require skilled labor. During times of labor shortage, contractors were used more and more, especially for semiskilled tasks, while at times when there was a genuine crisis in the labor supply the records show more and more recourse to sharecropping, which offered more of an inducement to the laborer.

Normally, the day laborers on the large estates could be reasonably certain of employment from one day to the next. Laborers on smaller holdings were in a more tenuous position. Those seeking employment would gather at six o'clock in the morning at a specified place in the town with their tools and food for the day, so that, once hired, they were prepared to go directly to the vineyards. Municipal ordinances sometimes prohibited hiring day laborers outside of the designated places and often stipulated the maximum wages for a day's work. A lower rate was sometimes prescribed for day laborers who did not reside in the town. Food was usually not provided by the employer except at harvest time, but there may have been a distribution of wines—of the cheapest grades, to be sure—to the workers. The workday customarily ended around three o'clock in the afternoon, which would have allowed the day laborers time to cultivate their own holdings, if any.

There does not appear to have been any significant difference in methods of production whether or not a vineyard was in lay or religious hands. There was some difference between lay and religious institutions in the distribution of their wines, particularly those of the highest qualities. Much of the better-quality wines produced by ecclesiastical institutions were sent to the cellars of affiliates in locations that were less well suited to wine production, while lay lords were more likely to introduce their wines into the stream of commerce. Even here, the difference would be merely one of degree, since the importance of gift-giving among members of the upper classes and the prestige that already attached to the highest-quality wines would minimize even this contrast. The inferior grades of wine on both lay and ecclesiastical estates would be consumed on the estate or sold in the local taverns.

The agricultural cycle revealed in the accounts of the great estates would be equally relevant to more modest holdings. The fiscal year for the accounts of the dukes of Burgundy began on the feast day of St. Martin in winter (11 November). By that date, the wines of the previous fiscal year had been harvested, processed, and distributed. A new wine year was ready to begin.

The first task of the new wine year was to gather in the vine props that had been used in the previous year and sharpen them to prepare for their use in the new season. This had to be accomplished as soon as possible, because if the props were left lying around, they were likely to be gathered in by the poor and used for firewood. Then it was time for the "winter works," the tasks necessary to maintain the fertility of the vineyards, such as the remounting of the soil—which tended to slide down the slopes on which the vineyards were planted—and the application of fertilizer.

The most common fertilizer used in medieval vineyards was the waste material from the previous year's wine pressing. The use of animal waste is recorded in early-fourteenth-century Burgundy, but the practice was apparently abandoned in the chaotic aftermath of the Black Death. It was reintroduced at the end of the century, but its use was highly controversial. Critics claimed that the use of animal fertilizer in the vineyard gave a peculiar taste to the wine. In 1394 the duke of Burgundy forbade its use.

Around February the vineyards were pruned to direct and regulate the growth of the vines. Pruning was one of the more skilled tasks and was more highly paid than other labors in the vineyards. Women were employed at the same time to gather up the cuttings and were paid at a rate approximately one-third the rate paid to the men hired as pruners. Shortly after the Black Death, the officials of the duke of Burgundy permitted the poor to gather up the cuttings, but unauthorized gathering was severely punished. In 1385, a thief caught stealing the shoots was beaten and pilloried with a bundle of cuttings hung from his neck.

In March the "first work" was performed to loosen the earth around the vines and permit the fertilizer to penetrate the soil. Around April the props were carried into the vineyards, a task normally performed by women, and in May the vines were attached to them. In May, June, and July, second, third, and sometimes fourth works were performed. Suckers were cut off to permit the fruit to mature. By August, the vines were heavy with the fruit, and the accounts report expenses for guard-

ians to protect them from human and animal marauders while the grapes ripened.

September was the time of the harvest. The exact date varied from one year to the next, depending on the climate and the variety of grape. The exact date was proclaimed by the local authorities, whether seignorial, ecclesiastical, or municipal, and anyone whose vineyards were not enclosed was forbidden to harvest prior to the date set for the harvest. This practice was defended by agrarian writers in the Middle Ages as a means to ensure high-quality production. In the absence of an authoritative determination, a grower might be tempted to harvest the grapes prematurely to ensure against unfavorable weather or to get a jump on the market.

Men and women worked side by side in the vineyards at harvest time, the women receiving about half the pay of the men. The harvesters carried wicker baskets that varied from one locality to the next in size and shape. The baskets were emptied into small carts that were, in turn, emptied into two- or three-horse wagons, which brought the harvested fruit to the press. The harvesters were provided with food (bread and sometimes meat, cheese, and onions) and wine.

The wine harvest was a common subject in art, particularly in calendars or books of hours, where the month of September was represented by a scene of the harvest. These representations sometimes show the pressing of the grapes, depicting the fruit being trampled underfoot in large wooden vats. This was probably the most common method of pressing the grapes, but on the larger estates mechanical presses were constructed that, in some cases, have survived to this day. The huge presses constructed in 1238 by Alix de Vergy, widow of Duke Eudes III of Burgundy in Chenoves, continued to be used into the nineteenth century. At the Clos de Vougeot, a Cistercian estate, four gigantic presses were used to prepare the wine for the cellars that held 1,600 *pièces,* each of which held 228 gallons. Carpenters were on hand at the press to repair equipment and assemble the barrels.

There were probably a larger number of varietal types of grapes under cultivation in the Middle Ages than today. The sixteenth-century agrarian Olivier de Serres recommended the cultivation of at least six different varieties to give some protection against natural catastrophes that might attack one variety more seriously than others. He suggested that each variety of grape be planted in a rectangle, which would facilitate harvesting that particular type as well as afford greater ease of access to the plants for cultivation.

In Burgundy, however, the pinot noir played a predominant role at a very early date, a fact that undoubtedly accounts for the fame of the "wines of Beaune" among contemporaries. Around the end of the fourteenth century, the gamay grape was introduced and, despite the efforts of the duke of Burgundy to legislate against this grape, its area of cultivation expanded. Although it did not produce the high-quality wine of the pinot, it was much more fecund and could double the productivity of a given vineyard.

The more expansive growth of the gamay vines required the construction of more elaborate supports for the vines that may have contributed to the increased regularity of rows of plants in the vineyards. It seems to have been the custom in Italy from a very early date to plant the vineyards in rows, but this may not have been the custom in northern Europe. The representations of the vineyards from the early fourteenth century show a disorderly growth of vine shoots. By the end of the fourteenth century, the vineyards were shown as neatly planted in rows.

The late medieval innovations in vine production set the stage for the early modern period by introducing ways of increasing the production of wines to supply mass markets, paving the way for the ultimate triumph of the commercialization of the vineyards over seignorial and ecclesiastical domination.

BIBLIOGRAPHY

Arnaldus de Villanova, *The Earliest Printed Book on Wine*, Henry E. Sigerist, trans. (1943); Jacques Beauroy, *Vin et société à Bergerac du moyen âge aux temps modernes* (1976); Rosalind Kent Berlow, "The 'Disloyal' Grape: The Agrarian Crisis of Late Fourteenth-century Burgundy," in *Agricultural History*, 56 (1982); Émile Chatelain, "Notes sur quelques tavernes fréquentées par l'Université de Paris aux XIVᵉ et XVᵉ siècles," in *Bulletin de la Société de l'histoire de Parie et de l'Île-de-France*, 25 (1898); Jan Craeybeckx, *Un grand commerce d'importation: Les vins de France aux anciens Pays-Bas (XIIIᵉ– XVIᵉ siècles)* (1958); J. Délissey and L. Perriaux, "Les courtiers gourmets de la ville de Beaune," in *Annales de Bourgogne*, 34 (1962); Roger Dion, *Histoire de la vigne et du vin en France dès origines au XIXᵉ siècle* (1977); Renée Doehaerd, "Ce qu'on vendait et comment on le vendait dans le bassin parisien au temps de Charlemagne et des normands," in *Annales: Economies, sociétés, civilisations*, 2 (1947), and "Un paradoxe géographique: Laon, capitale du vin au XIIᵉ siècle," *ibid.*, 5 (1950); Henri Dubois, "Peste noire et viticulture en Bourgogne et en Chablis," in *Economies et sociétés au moyen âge: Mélanges offerts à Édouard Perroy* (1973), 428–436; Georges Durand, *Vin, vigne, et vignerons en Lyonnais et Beaujolais* (1979); Alan David Francis, *The Wine Trade* (1972); Margery K. James, "The Fluctuations of the Anglo-Gascon Wine Trade During the Fourteenth Century," in *Economic History Review*, 2nd ser., 4 (1951– 1952), and "The Medieval Wine Dealer," in *Explorations in Entrepreneurial History*, 10 (1957); Pietro de Crescenzi, *Liber commodorum ruralium* (1303); Yves Renouard, *Études d'histoire médiévale*, 2 vols. (1968); Desmond Seward, *Monks and Wine* (1979); Gérard Sivéry, *Les comtes de Hainaut et le commerce du vin au XIVᵉ siècle et au début du XVᵉ siècle* (1969); Claude Tournier, "Le vin à Dijon de 1430 à 1560: Ravitaillement et commerce," in *Annales de Bourgogne*, 22 (1950), and "Notes sur la culture de la vigne et les vignerons à Dijon entre 1430 et 1560," *ibid.*, 24 (1952).

Rosalind Kent Berlow

[See also **Agriculture and Nutrition; Aquitaine; Bordeaux; Burgundy, Duchy of; Fairs; Fairs of Champagne; Food Trade; Inns and Taverns; Markets, European; Trade, European; Trade, Regulation of.**]

WINSBECKE is the author of a courtly didactic poem of fifty-six stanzas written between 1210 and 1220 in Middle High German. The name has been identified with the von Winsbach family, who lived on the river Rezat southwest of Nuremberg. A closer personal identification of the poet is not possible, but the poem reveals clearly that its author was a knight and father who, incapacitated by old age, gives his only (remaining?) son advice for courtly conduct (*rehte tuon*). In each stanza the son is addressed directly.

Der Winsbecke is transmitted in eleven manuscripts and fragments that also contain unauthentic additions. All are listed and evaluated in the re-edition of the work by Ingo Reiffenstein. In perhaps the best manuscript (J) the work has the title "Ditze bůch heizzet der werltlich råt" (This "book" is called Advice for life in this world). The other manuscripts have various titles. The Grosse Heidelberger Liederhandschrift has (fol. 213r) an illustration depicting the author and his coat of arms and gives the name "Winsbeke"; in the margin as directive for the illustrator is "von Winsbach." In the Kolmarer Liederhandschrift, CGM 4997, the melody of the stanza is also preserved. All lines have four stresses, are upbeat, and are rhythmically joined to form a strophe with the rhyme scheme *a b a b b x b c x c*. In general each stanza is a thematic unit, although several may be devoted to one topic, and on occasion a stanza may be thematically split to introduce a new theme.

Stanzas 1–5 praise the wisdom that is derived from the love of God and the realization of the transitory nature of worldly life; 6–7 urge the reader to show consideration for the clergy regardless of their deeds; 8 extols the blessings of a harmonious marriage; 9–10 state that one should keep secrets, remain sober, loyal, and compassionate, and have admiration for women (*wîp*); 11–16 concern the beatific relationship of man and woman; 17–21 praise honor and the ennobling nature of knighthood. In stanzas 22–28 virtue and various modes of practical conduct are the subjects; 29–33 discusses possessions and the problem of greed, and how moderation (*mâze*) is the arbiter of good sense; 34–38 treat the willingness to accept good counsel and practical advice emphasizing the value of good habits (often given in proverbial form); 39–46 warn against specific vices, such as capriciousness, spite, haughtiness, pride, laziness, gambling, gluttony, and folly. Stanzas 47–51 concern how the virtuous direction of household or estate ennobles, so that it invites the blessing of God and wins the esteem of the world (*gote und der werlte wære er wert* [50.6], *gotes lôn, der werlde habedanc* [51.8]); 52 discusses ennobling quality of veracity; 53–55 warn against excommunication, banishment, or the incurrence of legal sanctions; 56 is a final summary: above all, one should keep three things firmly in mind—the love of God, truthfulness, and courtly conduct without fail (*wirt gotes minne nimmer vrî,/wis wârhaft, zühtic sunder wanc*, 56.6–7).

The poem had several inauthentic additions. In a continuation of twenty-four stanzas (57–80) the son responds to the father and is the principal speaker, but his discourse is interrupted by stanzas spoken by the father or by prayers addressed to God, so that a dialogue quality prevails. An ascetic mentality suggests a clerical author. The world is viewed as treacherous, and the son proposes withdrawal into a hospital that the father is to establish. There is also a thirteenth-century addition under the name *Die Winsbekin*. In it a mother admonishes her still naïve and innocent daughter in matters of love and advises her not to reject love outright, because it might cause harm and hurt. In this dialogue the speeches generally alternate. A four-

teenth-century *Winsbecke Parody* has survived, but only in fragmentary form.

BIBLIOGRAPHY

The best and most recent edition, with a good introduction, is *Winsbeckische Gedichte nebst Tirol und Fridebrant*, Albert Leitzmann, ed., 3rd ed. (1962), a completely new edition by Ingo Reiffenstein.

Studies include Bruno Boesch, *Lehrhafte Literatur* (1977), 43–48; Ewald Jammers, *Das königliche Liederbuch des deutschen Minnesangs* (1965); Alfred Mundhenk, "Der *Winsbecke* oder die Erziehung des Ritters," in Günther Jungbluth, ed., *Interpretationen mittelhochdeutscher Lyrik* (1969).

F. W. VON KRIES

[See also **Courtesy Books**.]

WIPO OF BURGUNDY (*d. ca.* 1050), historian and poet, is an important source for the period of Emperors Conrad II (*r.* 1024–1039) and Henry III (*r.* 1039–1056), which is not entirely well represented in many of the sources. Wipo's life is little known. In the 1040's, he was several times with the imperial court, moving from one place to another. A teacher of the future Henry III, he must have been a member of the imperial chapel. Even if he came from Burgundy (and this is indicated by the interest in Burgundian affairs shown in his writings), Wipo must have originated in the upper (German) parts that were attached to the German Empire after 1032. His writings bear witness to his wide knowledge and intellectual horizons, as well as to his poetic talent and his insight into contemporary international politics.

A number of Wipo's works are lost. From his allusions in the life of Conrad II, we know of his lost epic poem, *Gallinarius*, on the incorporation of Burgundy into the empire; his versified *Breviarium*, praising Henry III's victories over the Slavs; and a lost panegyrical "hymn" to the same Henry. Wipo's *Gesta Chuonradi imperatoris* (The deeds of Emperor Conrad) was composed after 1040, probably in 1045/1046, and he had the intention of covering as well the history of Henry III, whose early deeds are also recorded in the work. In its first part, Wipo drew on his own reminiscences and memories about Conrad's election, coronation, and early deeds, while in the second part he used a now lost chronicle of Reichenau, which served as a source for other contemporary historical works. Wipo, however, improved his source, corrected it, and, in general, took a more independent approach to the subject. He selected the motto "Legem servare est regnare" (To reign is to serve the law) as a leading theme for his presentation. Holtzmann terms his historical work one of the best royal biographies of the German Middle Ages.

Wipo's "Sutri song" (*Rhitmus ad Henricum*) is a political documentat encouraging Henry's intervention in Roman affairs ("Romana superstitio indiget iudicio"). His authorship is supported by the *Pöhlder Annals*. His *Proverbia centum* (Hundred proverbs), his oldest work, dedicated to Henry III (1028?), is a versified collection intended to serve as an inspiration for the future ruler. They express a definite "program," just as do the 326 hexameters of his *Tetralogus* presented to Henry III on Christmas Day, 1041, together with his *Versus ad mensam regis* (ten distichs for the royal table). Wipo's *Tetralogus,* as its title indicates, is a conversation with four participants: the poet and three Muses. Johannes Spörl considers it a turning point in the eleventh-century development of imperial ideology (*Kaisergedanke*). The panegyrical sections take second place behind the programmatic passages, which express basic axioms of a political program. The basis for the ruler's activities is represented by Christian virtues; "law and right" (*lex et ius*) are supporting elements of "peace" (*pax*), a goal of peacemaking emperors. With this, the foundation for the deeds of a reform-minded emperor is laid in this ideological work, satisfying both the requirements of the age and Wipo's own views.

Wipo's importance as an ideologist, a princely educator, and a historian does not obliterate his poetic significance. His *Cantilena* (stanzaic song) on the death of Conrad II is a spirited lament; its text is found also in the *Cambridge Songs*. In the same source, two other royal poems may have been written by Wipo. His Easter sequence "Victimae paschali laudes" (Praise to the Paschal victim), a dramatic Resurrection song, features Mary Magdalen in the role of announcer of the great event. Its dramatic mood and forceful language and imagery are coupled with an apologetic tendency contained in the part later suppressed in the liturgy as offensive to the Jews. It had a well-established place in Easter liturgies and inspired a large number of sequences, which used its melody, its external structure, and even a similar incipit. Wipo's sequence retained its place in the Easter Mass until the Second Vatican Council.

BIBLIOGRAPHY

Franz Bittner, *Studien zum Herrscherlob in der mittellateinischen Dichtung* (1962), 136, 157–160; Helmut A. de Boor, *Die Textgeschichte der lateinischen Osterfeiern* (1967); Harry Bresslau, ed., *Die Werke Wipos* (1915); Walther Bulst, "Zu Wipo's *Versus pro obitu Chuonradi imperatoris,*" in *Festschrift Percy Ernst Schramm,* Peter Classen and Peter Scheibert, eds., I (1964); Percy E. Schramm, *Kaiser, Rom und Renovatio,* 2 vols. in 1 (1929); Johannes Spörl, "Pie rex caesarque future!" in *Unterscheidung und Bewahrung: Festschrift für Hermann Kunisch,* Klaus Lazarowicz and Wolfgang Kron, eds. (1961); Gertrud Marie Stahl, *Die mittelalterliche Weltanschauung in Wipos Gesta Chuonradi II. imperatoris* (1925); Joseph Szövérffy, *Die Annalen der lateinischen Hymendichtung,* I (1964), 372–374, "Kultgeschichte und Politik," in *Archiv für Kulturgeschichte,* 55 (1973), and "Hymnologische Streifzüge, 2: Zur Frage der Kontrafaktur in Hymnodie: Victimae Paschali," in *Literatur and Sprache im europäischen Mittelalter: Festschrift für Karl Langosch* (1973).

JOSEPH SZÖVÉRFFY

[See also **Cambridge Songs; Chronicles; Germany: 843–1137; Henry III of Germany; Historiography, Western European; Hymns, Latin; Poetry, Liturgical.**]

WIRECKER, NIGEL. See **Nigel of Longchamp.**

WIRNT VON GRAFENBERG. The scanty information about Wirnt von Grafenberg indicates that he was a member of a minor noble family whose ancestral home was the present-day Gräfenberg, a walled town north of Erlangen. If he was the Wiritto de Grefenberc who appears among the witnesses to a document of 1170, he was middle-aged or older when he composed his only extant work, *Wigalois: Der Ritter mit dem Rade,* an Arthurian verse novel that was probably written between 1204 and 1210. A reference to Wirnt by Heinrich von dem Türlin about 1220 seems to imply that he was deceased at that time. Around the middle of the thirteenth century he became the hero of Konrad von Würzburg's verse tale *Der Welt Lohn,* which describes him as a wealthy young baron, well known as a poet and famous for knightly deeds, who went on a crusade. This account, however, is of dubious value as biography.

Using a symmetrical, five-part structure, *Wigalois* relates the adventures of a youthful favorite of fortune and describes his education for kingship. It tells how Gawain enters a remote land, marries a princess there, leaves to visit King Arthur's court, and is never able to find his way back. Twenty years later his son comes to this court to learn knightly skills, leaves to free a country from a heathen usurper, and fights a succession of combats to win the right to represent it. Having passed the tests, the hero is named the lawful sovereign of the land by the spirit of its former ruler, and strengthens his legitimacy by killing a dragon that has preyed upon its people. A second series of combats follows, which culminates in the death of the usurper and the crowning of the hero. In a final adventure the young king shows that he can be a force for justice at home and abroad by conquering the land of a duke who committed wanton regicide.

The chief source of *Wigalois* is a story that appeared in England, France, Germany, and Italy during the Middle Ages in considerably differing versions, the earliest of which is Renaut de Beaujeu's *Le bel inconnu*. Other Arthurian works from which Wirnt borrowed to some extent are Hartmann von Aue's *Erek* and *Îwein*, Ulrich von Zatzikhoven's *Lanzelet*, and the first part of Wolfram von Eschenbach's *Parzival*. In addition one can see the influence of the *Gospel of Nicodemus* and the *Revelation*, for the adventures of Wirnt's hero obviously parallel the account of Christ's death, descent into hell, defeat of Satan, redemption of the souls of the dead, and resurrection, as well as the millennium, the final battle against Satan, and the establishment of New Jerusalem.

Wigalois is carefully organized and, in spite of didactic discursions, well told. It was very popular during the later Middle Ages and was passed on to the modern period in prose translation as a fifteenth-century chapbook, *Wigoleis vom Rade* (1493). A large number of manuscripts (thirty-nine) of the medieval version have been discovered, but seven are now missing.

BIBLIOGRAPHY

An extensive bibliography of the literature on Wirnt von Grafenberg and the Wigalois story up to 1974 appears in *Wigalois: The Knight of Fortune's Wheel*, J. Wesley Thomas, trans. (1977), 88–99.

Studies dealing with Wirnt's novel include Christoph Cormeau, *"Wigalois" und "Diu Crône": Zwei Kapitel zur Gattungsgeschichte des nachklassischen Aventiureromans* (1977); Ingeborg Henderson, "Selbstentfremdung im *Wigalois* Wirnts von Grafenberg," in *Colloquia germanica*, **13** (1980); Gert Kaiser, "Der *Wigalois* des Wirnt von Grâvenberc: Zur Bedeutung des Territorialisierungsprozesses für die 'höfisch-ritterliche' Literatur des 13. Jahrhunderts," in *Euphorion*, **69** (1975).

Works concerned with later versions of *Wigalois* include Wulf-Otto Dreessen, "Zur Rezeption deutscher epischer Literatur im Altjiddischen: Das Beispiel *Wigalois-Artushof*," in Wolfgang Harms and L. Peter Johnson, eds., *Deutsche Literatur des späten Mittelalters: Hamburger Colloquium 1973* (1975); John L. Flood, "Der Prosaroman 'Wigoleis vom Rade' und die Entstehung des 'Ulenspiegel,'" in *Zeitschrift für deutsches Altertum und deutsche Literatur*, **105** (1976); Siegmund A. Wolf, ed., *"Ritter Widuwilt": Die westjiddische Fassung des "Wigalois" des Wirnt von Gravenberc, nach dem jiddischen Druck von 1699* (1974).

J. WESLEY THOMAS

[See also **Arthurian Literature; German Literature: Romance; Konrad von Würzburg**.]

WIRT, DER. Manuscript 1655 of the University Library, Erlangen, preserves a 580-line tale known as *Der Wirt*. This title derives from the last line of the text (*hie endet sich des wirtes maer*). The manuscript was written about 1350, and the tale likely dates from the first half of that century. Dialectal features imply an origin in the northwestern part of the Bavarian linguistic region.

A *Märe*, *Der Wirt* has a simple and unoriginal plot: three men, who have tricked an innkeeper's wife into sleeping with them all in a single night, oblige her to copulate with them again in the inn, before the eyes of her husband, but fool him so that he is unaware of their actions. Were this story the substance of the text, it would hardly attract attention. In fact, the story is the least interesting element of the composition.

Der Wirt contains long descriptive passages in courtly style, eulogies of two heroes, and extensive digressions by the narrator. The time is glorious May, full of flowers and birdsong. Two heroes are stereotypes of chivalric romance, one being a knight of King Arthur's court sent into Germany to serve ladies. The diction of these passages is modeled on the masters of ornate style (such as Wolfram von Eschenbach and Konrad von Würzburg), and the strong presence of the narrator, manifest in exclamations, praise and censure of events, rhetorical questions, and appeals to the audience, recalls Wolfram especially. The dissonance between highly rhetorical manner and crude plot poses the main interpretive problem of *Der Wirt.*

Because the narrator seems to place all moral responsibility for events on the third seducer, a servant versed in black magic, and on the witless husband, some (for instance, Schirmer) deny that the tale is persiflage. Examining closely the comments of the narrator and his figures, however, one may infer that *Der Wirt* is a complex parody of romantic conventions.

In plot, though not in style, *Der Wirt* closely resembles the later tale by Hans Rosenplüt, *Der Wettstreit der drei Liebhaber.*

BIBLIOGRAPHY
An edition is *Neues Gesamtabenteuer,* I, Heinrich Niewöhner, ed., 2nd ed., rev. by Werner Simon *et al.* (1967), 125–133.

Studies include Heinrich Niewöhner, "Des Wirtes Maere," in *Zeitschrift für deutsches Altertum und deutsche Literatur,* 60 (1923); Karl-Heinz Schirmer, *Stil- und Motivuntersuchungen zur mittelhochdeutschen Versnovelle* (1969); Stephen L. Wailes, "An Analysis of 'Des wirtes maere,'" in *Monatshefte,* 60 (1968).

STEPHEN L. WAILES

[See also **Mären.**]

WITAN. See **Witenagemot.**

WITCHCRAFT, EUROPEAN

THE CONCEPT OF WITCHCRAFT

European witchcraft was a unique phenomenon, differing both from European high magic and from the low magic or simple sorcery found around the world. The tradition of high magic was sophisticated, coherent, and characterized by a desire to understand the cosmos. Examples of such high magic are astrology and alchemy. These subjects, however superstitious they may appear today, cannot profitably be understood as superstitions in the Middle Ages or Renaissance, since their assumptions were based upon carefully thought-out philosophical systems and empirical observations. The difference between science and high magic is difficult to define in these periods, as Lynn Thorndike demonstrated in his *History of Magic and Experimental Science.*

European witchcraft, on the other hand, grew out of the tradition of low magic, which relied upon spells or charms to effect simple, practical results such as curing a friend's headache or drying up the milk of an enemy's cow. In its origins, witchcraft was indistinguishable from low magic or simple sorcery, and the word itself derives from the Old English *wicca* (pronounced "witcha"), "sorcerer." The Latin *maleficus,* the French *sorcier,* and the German *Hexe* all originally designated a simple sorcerer. In the course of the Middle Ages, these terms gradually changed their meaning from "simple sorcerer" to "witch." The essential difference between the sorcerer and the witch is that the latter, in addition to practicing sorcery, also venerates the Devil. European witchcraft, in other words, was in large part an anti-Christian religion and is not understandable except in terms of the Christian intellectual and moral context against which it was reacting. Thus in essence and in detail it differed substantially from the sorcery found in non-Christian societies.

European witchcraft developed out of simple sorcery through a series of stages. In the early Middle Ages, elements of pagan religion and folklore modified the underlying component of sorcery. The transformation was gradually completed through the addition of elements of heretical thought (from the eleventh century), Scholasticism (from the twelfth century), and the Inquisition (from the thirteenth century). By the fifteenth century the idea of diabolical witchcraft had been firmly established, and by the end of that century the great witch craze had begun.

One of the perennial questions about European witchcraft is whether it existed merely as a concept, a body of beliefs, or whether it existed objectively. Put bluntly, the question is whether diabolical witches ever existed. Scholars are still not agreed on this point. But whether witchcraft ever existed outside of the minds of its opponents, the concept of witchcraft was one of the dominant aspects of European thought from the late Middle Ages through the Renaissance and Reformation and down to the eighteenth century. At a conservative estimate, 100,000 to 200,000 people were executed for witchcraft in Europe during that period, and millions more were tortured, harried, or otherwise terrified. Witchcraft is therefore one of the most important phenomena, as well as one of the darkest, in European history.

Interpretations of the meaning of European

witchcraft have varied in the extreme. Serious writing about witchcraft from the nineteenth century was limited to polemical attacks upon, or defenses of belief in, witchcraft. The first serious modern study of witchcraft was Wilhelm Gottlieb Soldan's *Geschichte der Hexenprozesse* (1843); a thorough study of medieval witchcraft was done by another German, the archivist Josef Hansen, in 1900–1901. Meanwhile a school of interpretation that can be labeled "liberal secularist" was developing in England and America.

The first critical historical study of witchcraft by a writer in English was Henry Charles Lea's *History of the Inquisition of the Middle Ages* (1887). Lea also planned a multivolume work on the history of witchcraft but did not live to do it. Lea studied witchcraft in the context of its repression, particularly by the papal Inquisition. For Lea, witchcraft was an imaginary crime whose significance lay in its part in the history of intolerance and cruelty, particularly that of the church. The church in Lea's writings appears as a stumbling block in the road to a new age of science, tolerance, and light. Much the same view was taken by George Lincoln Burr (who with the assistance of Andrew Dickson White amassed at Cornell University the finest witchcraft collection in the world); by George Gordon Coulton; and, most recently, by Rossell Hope Robbins, author of *The Encyclopaedia of Witchcraft and Demonology* (1959) and of the introduction to the catalog of the Cornell University collection.

A second school of thought, which dominated the field from the 1920's through the 1950's, was the folklorist or Murrayite school, so called after its leading exponent, Margaret Alice Murray. The essential argument of this school was that witchcraft did indeed exist, but instead of being the evil Satanism described by the church it was really the survival of an ancient pagan religion centered on the worship of a horned god that Murray called Dianus. Having little historical basis, and often carried to absurd extremes, the Murrayite theory is now rejected by all scholars, although some continue to argue for the importance of the folklore element in the witch concept.

A third school, currently quite influential, is that of the historians who emphasize the social history of witchcraft, attempting to establish social patterns of accusation and belief. Excellent work has been done in this field by Keith Thomas and Alan Macfarlane for England, by E. William Monter and H. C. Erik Midelfort for the Continent, and by Paul Boyer and Stephen Nissenbaum for America. A fourth school comprises those who treat the history of witchcraft as part of the history of ideas or concepts. This approach has been used by Richard Kieckhefer, Norman Cohn, H. R. Trevor-Roper, Edward Peters, and Jeffrey Burton Russell, although these writers often disagree with one another. Other interpretations, too weak to merit serious consideration, include remnants of the fundamentalist-ecclesiastical view that witchcraft was in actual fact a Satanist conspiracy against Christianity, and the neo-pagan, "modern witchcraft" view (similar to Murray's) that witchcraft was the survival of an ancient religion of "the Goddess."

EVOLUTION OF WITCHCRAFT

The roots of European witchcraft are in European simple sorcery, some of it Mediterranean in origin, some of it Celtic and Teutonic. Teutonic sorcerers used herbs, sieves, and figures of wax, dough, or lime in their work. Practitioners used charms to hurt or to heal. The Germans, for example, called upon the Valkyrie Hilda to cure injury by pronouncing over the wound the phrase "Sprach Jungfrau Hille, Blut stand stille" (The maiden Hilda has spoken, the flow of blood is stanched). To destroy an enemy the Anglo-Saxons reduced him to nothing by associating him with the tiniest things in nature: "May you become as small as a linseed grain,/and much smaller than the hipbone of an itch mite,/and may you become so small that you become nothing" (Storms, p. 54). Some magic was simple and mechanical: "Against warts. Take the water of a dog and the blood of a mouse, mix together, smear the warts with this; they will soon disappear" (*ibid.*, p. 65). Sometimes the curse mingled religious elements with the mechanical: "If a man is troubled by tumors near the heart, let a girl go to a spring that runs due east, and let her draw a cupful of water moving with the current, and let her sing on it the Creed and an Our Father (*ibid.*, p. 247).

Christian penitentials, guides for priests in the early Middle Ages for use in hearing confessions and assigning penances, condemned simple magic. "If any woman," prescribed the penitential of Theodore about 600, "puts her daughter upon a roof or into an oven for the cure of a fever, she shall do penance for seven years" (McNeill and Gamer, p. 198). Many charges of evil magic that were later common during the witch craze derived from phenomena ascribed to ancient sorcery: making storms, causing disease or death in animals or humans, and inducing impotence.

Pagan religion and folklore were the next elements in the formation of European witchcraft. The Wild Hunt, for example, was a prototype of the witches' sabbat (sabbath). The Wild Hunt was a procession of spirits or ghosts who roamed through the countryside, particularly forests and deserted moors, reveling and destroying. Any mortal whom they chanced to meet would be slain. The members of the Wild Hunt were akin to the "wild men and women," part human and part animal, who were believed to roam the medieval forests. The leader of the ghastly rout was often perceived as female; in Germany she was called Hilda or Berta, and by the end of the ninth century this shadowy figure had been merged with the Roman goddess Diana. The spirits that followed Berta/Diana gradually became human witches, and the *Canon episcopi* (*ca.* 900), the first important legal document relating to European witchcraft, condemned those who believed that "they ride out at night on beasts with Diana and a horde of women," that they traversed long distances, and that they were "called out on Diana's service." A century after the *Canon episcopi*, Burchard of Worms called the leader of the Hunt "the witch Hilda."

Many pagan festivals of light and fertility were preserved in modified form, especially the "need-fire" festival of 31 October, transformed by the Christians into Hallows' E'en (Halloween), the Eve of All Saints' Day or All Hallows' Day, and later by the Protestants into Guy Fawkes' Day, 5 November. Other such festivals, designed to regenerate the light of the waning sun, to celebrate its renewal, or to assure plenitude of game, occurred on 1 January (when dancers dressed as stags), 1 February, 30 April (the fertility festival of May Day, transformed by Christians into the Eve of St. Walpurga's Day, Walpurgisnacht, and by the Marxists into a workers' festival), and 23 or 30 June (Midsummer Eve). The familiars of the later witches originated in the dwarves, fairies, trolls, kobolds, and other small nature spirits of northern folklore, who were equated by the church with minor demons.

Sorcery, pagan religion, and folklore were the first three elements in the formation of European witchcraft; Christian heresy was the fourth, and most important. The most common charges brought against witches during the witch craze all derived from, or were transformed by, medieval heresy: the ride by night; the pact with the Devil; the formal repudiation of Christianity; the secret, nocturnal meeting; the desecration of the Eucharist or the crucifix; the orgy; sacrificial infanticide; and cannibalism. The idea of a pact was crucial. A simple sorcerer at one time had been believed to practice magic without the help of spirits, but St. Augustine had already declared that much magic required the invocation of demons, and this view became the accepted one. Magic worked by compelling spirits to effect it; good spirits could not be compelled; the spirits were thus demons; they were under the command of the Devil; therefore the sorcerer was, whatever his conscious intention might be, a servant of the Devil. A witch, or *maleficus* (the most common term in Latin), was now no longer merely a magician but also a heretic and a Satanist. Once the witches were seen as servants of Satan, the Christian community felt that it had a positive and compelling duty to destroy them. By transforming sorcerers into heretics, the church made it possible to proceed against them legally.

The church's definition of witchcraft as heresy was not without reason. Many medieval heresies themselves added to the concept of witchcraft. In 1022, the first major trial and execution of heretics in the Middle Ages occurred at Orléans, at the order of Robert II (the Pious) of France. The heretics were accused of a variety of beliefs and practices, some of which resembled those that would later be alleged against the witches at the height of the witch craze: they were said to hold sex orgies at night in a secret place, either underground or in an abandoned building. The assembled heretics, it was charged, would hold torches and chant the names of demons until one of the evil spirits appeared. Then they would extinguish the lights and have an orgy where "each seized the person nearest to him," regardless of sex or family relationship. Any children conceived at such orgies were burned eight days after birth (a parody of Christian baptismal practice), and their ashes were baked in a bread used in parody of the Christian Eucharist. They were transported by the Devil from place to place; they adored the Devil in the shape of a beast, an angel of light, or black man; and they did formal homage to him, renouncing their Christian faith and desecrating the Cross. Whether any reality existed behind these charges, they became standard in the later history of witchcraft. Of these charges sexual orgy, human sacrifice, and cannibalism are significant in that they have a long literary history dating back through Christian accusations against Gnostics, Roman accusations against Christians, and Syrian accusations against Jews.

These charges became *topoi,* or clichés, of European witchcraft, but they were not made indiscriminately against all heretics. They were leveled only against those whose ideas were influenced by dualism, the tradition of a cosmic conflict between the powers of light, spirit, and goodness on the one hand and the powers of darkness, matter, and evil on the other. The Orléans heretics were apparently merely exaggerating dualist tendencies already inherent in orthodox Christianity; but then, beginning in the 1140's, Bogomil missionaries imported their own radical dualism from the Balkans, the result being a new heresy in Western Europe, Catharism. The Cathars taught that the material world was the creation of an evil spirit, whom they often equated with the God of the Old Testament. This power of evil, one of whose names was the Devil, created the human body in order to imprison and humiliate the spirit; Christ came to teach us how to evade the flesh and free our souls. The Catholic church was founded by Satan, but by following Cathar teachings a person might find salvation. The Cathars emphasized the enormous power of the Devil as lord of this world, matter, and the body, and as prince of all sensual pleasures and worldly satisfactions. Catharism opposed such works of the Devil even more vehemently than Catholicism. But the insistence on the Devil's power permitted an essential misinterpretation. The true, spiritual God is hidden from us; the Devil has huge powers over all the world; and he controls and can dispense wealth, sex, fame, and other earthly rewards; with such beliefs some people apparently preferred to worship Satan. Evidence that this occurred is found, for example, in fourteenth-century Italy. The potential ambivalence of dualism, already seen in the Gnosticism of the second and third centuries A.D., can unite the ascetic with the licentious and can identify disgust for matter with indulgence of matter. Thus Catharist doctrines and practices were open to such antinomian interpretation. Other heretical groups whose doctrines were susceptible to antinomian interpretation, such as the Brethren of the Free Spirit, also reinforced the idea that there existed groups of heretics who practiced rituals in defiance of church and society. Libertinism was probably not in fact widespread among these heretics, but it is clear that the Cath-

olics thought it was, so that the *topoi* later characterizing witchcraft were firmly fixed in popular opinion.

Theological discussion was the next major element in the formation of witch beliefs. Diabology, the theology of the Devil, had been thoroughly discussed by the church fathers and fairly settled by the time of St. Augustine in the fifth century. From the mid twelfth century onward, partly in response to Catharist dualism, both popular and theological interest in the Devil increased. The old idea of the Fathers that the cosmos was divided into two warring camps was revived with new strength and was used as justification for harsh treatment of heretics, who were perceived as recruits in the army of Satan. Scholastic theology, which dominated medieval thought from the twelfth century onward, emphasized the idea that heretics and sorcerers were members of Satan's army. The idea that witches had at least an implicit pact with the Devil became a central assumption of the Scholastic view. Scholastics named the witches' meeting the "synagogue" (from the twelfth century) or "sabbat" (from the fifteenth century), an indication of their assumption that witches, heretics, and Jews were equally servants of Satan. They firmly established the tradition that witches were more likely to be women than men, since witches had sexual intercourse with the Devil, and the Devil (although he could assume any shape or either sex) almost always chose to appear as a male.

Ideas introduced by inquisitorial and other courts are the sixth major element in witchcraft. In deciding to use the laws against heresy rather than against sorcery in the prosecution of witches, the continental courts finalized the separation of witchcraft and sorcery, although in England that distinction was never firm. In England, witchcraft remained a civil crime, so that convicted witches were hanged; whereas on the Continent witchcraft was a religious crime of heresy, the penalty for which was burning.

After the first execution of heretics at Orléans in 1022, the practice gradually became more common. In 1198, Pope Innocent III ordered that all who persisted in heresy after having been convicted and excommunicated should be re-arrested and burned at the stake. Between 1227 and 1235, Pope Gregory IX established the papal Inquisition; and its power was repeatedly confirmed by subsequent popes, notably Innocent IV, whose bull *Ad extirpanda* of 1252 authorized the imprisonment, torture, and execution of heretics. As witchcraft was assimilated to heresy, burning was extended to witches. Pope Alexander IV, while denying the Inquisition's request for jurisdiction over all cases of sorcery, did place under its authority all cases of sorcery "clearly involving heresy." This was a spur to the Inquisition to introduce charges of diabolism into sorcery accusations, thus diverting them to its own courts. In 1326 Pope John XXII issued the bull *Super illius specula,* which specifically authorized the Inquisition to proceed against all sorcerers on the grounds that they had made a pact with hell. In 1398 the University of Paris declared the working of *maleficia* a heresy when it was accomplished by means of a pact with Satan.

Conviction rates began to soar. The Inquisition prepared lists of standard witch accusations, put lists of standard, prepared questions to accused witches, and tortured and threatened them until they confessed. The list of obligatory questions prepared for the judges at Colmar—and used throughout the witch craze—is typical: "How long have you been a witch? Why did you become a witch? . . . What was the name of your master among the evil demons? What was the oath you were forced to render him?" and so on (Robbins, pp. 106–107). The question was not whether one had practiced witchcraft, but why and how. The confessions elicited were then used as corroboration that the charges were valid and could be used again in the next trial. In this way thousands were accused, convicted, and executed.

THE WITCH CRAZE

The witch craze, properly speaking, extended roughly from 1450 to 1700, with its peak between 1560 and 1660. It is thus a phenomenon of the Renaissance, Reformation, and early modern periods. Though the concept was formed in the Middle Ages and the theological and juridical bases for prosecution had been laid, it was the peculiar social, intellectual, and religious tensions of early modern Europe that made witchcraft one of the worst horrors of history. Legal sanctions grew harsher as the idea spread that all sorcery involved an implicit pact with the Devil. Theologians and jurists agreed that witchcraft was the greatest possible heresy, since it argued that God's worst enemy, the Devil, should be worshiped. Diabolical witchcraft developed earliest, and remained strongest, in the cities of France, Germany, Switzerland, and

northern Italy—precisely those areas where heresy had been strongest.

A trial at La Tour du Pin in southern France in 1438 is typical of the early years of the witch craze. An old man named Pierre Vallin was arrested by the Inquisition on the charge of witchcraft. The trial record says that he confessed "voluntarily," which simply means that he was tortured, removed from the place of torture, and then given the choice of confessing "voluntarily" or being returned for more torture. Under such pressures, Vallin confessed that he had summoned up the Devil, to whom—under the name of Beelzebub—he knelt and paid tribute. He thereafter served the Devil for sixty-three years, denying God, trampling and spitting on the Cross, and offering up his own baby daughter as human sacrifice. He went regularly to the "synagogue," copulated there with Beelzebub, who had taken the form of a girl, and ate the flesh of murdered children. Vallin was convicted, and all his possessions were confiscated. He was then sent back for more torture to force him to name his fellow witches. He resisted, but after being tortured at intervals for a week, he yielded and named a number of others. They too must have been tried and tortured, thus extending the circle of convictions. Because literally anyone could be a witch, the prospect existed of indefinitely extending the circle, and in fact the accusations, convictions, and new accusations continued for centuries.

The sixteenth century was to be much worse than the fifteenth. One reason was the invention of printing, which occurred just at the same time that a particularly notorious inquisitor, Heinrich Institoris, was at work. Born in 1430, Heinrich entered the Dominican order and, since he was an astute politician, obtained much influence in Rome. He received an appointment as inquisitor for southern Germany in 1474 and after 1476 concentrated his efforts on uprooting witchcraft. Completely unscrupulous, he was eventually condemned by his own order (1490), but in the meanwhile he had persuaded Pope Innocent VIII to issue the bull *Summis desiderantes affectibus* (1484), confirming full papal support for the efforts of the Inquisition to destroy witchcraft. In 1486, Institoris published the *Malleus maleficarum,* the "hammer against witches," with the pope's approval and the bull of 1484 as a preface. The *Malleus* soon became one of the most widely read of all early printed books, going into fourteen editions by 1520. Defining the four essential points of witchcraft as renunciation of the

Catholic faith, total devotion to the service of the Devil, sacrificing unbaptized children to the Devil, and having sexual intercourse with the Devil, the *Malleus* fixed the assembled *topoi* of witchcraft firmly in the European mind for centuries.

Medieval witchcraft had moved and changed over the centuries; from 1486 until the end of the witch craze in the eighteenth century few important changes in the picture of witchcraft occurred, and this stereotype was defended by scholars for centuries. Among the most virulent aspects of the *Malleus* was its explanation of the reason that more women than men were convicted of witchcraft: it was because women were more fickle, weaker, stupider, and more lustful. Thus theological theory and inquisitorial procedures united to spread the terror of witchcraft throughout Europe.

Throughout the Middle Ages and most of the period of the witch craze, English witchcraft remained substantially different from that of the Continent. On the Continent, heresy, law, theology, and the Inquisition transformed sorcery into witchcraft; but in England there was no Inquisition, little heresy, and a different legal system. The *Malleus maleficarum* was not published in England until the twentieth century. With some notable exceptions, such as the bizarre case of Dame Alice Kyteler in Ireland in 1324, there were few trials for witchcraft before the sixteenth century. As late as the 1560's, English witches differed markedly from their continental colleagues: they were not supposed to fly through the air, meet for orgies and feasting, have intercourse with the Devil, or sign a pact with him. Like sorcerers worldwide, however, they supposedly caused disease and fits, harmed livestock, and hurt babies and children.

English witches were most noted for their keeping of familiars. The practice was known on the Continent, particularly in Germany, but never to the extent as in England. Familiars were in historical origin the "little people" of folklore—kobolds and fairies—transformed by Christian theology into minor demons. With names such as Vinegar Tom and Grizel Greediguts, they retained an air more of mischief than of pure evil. These demons were supposed to take the form of animals, who kept the witch company, ran errands for her, and took their sustenance by sucking her blood through a "witch's teat." The search for the "witch's mark" was one of the most common ways of detecting witches in England. The witch was stripped and shaved, and any excrescence such as a wart or pimple was deemed evidence that the accused was a witch and kept a familiar. It was not until the reign of James I that continental ideas were introduced into Britain on a large scale.

The concept of witchcraft arose from a peculiar amalgamation of magic, paganism, and Christianity. That witchcraft had enormous power over the European mind for centuries requires further explanation in terms of the functions of witchcraft in society. First, it had the psychological function of shifting blame. If one is impotent, it is less embarrassing to blame a witch than oneself; if crops fail, it is more prudent to blame a witch than to blame God. Furthermore, witchcraft shifts blame for misfortune onto an individual who can be identified and punished; by destroying that person, the supposed victim feels that the evil spell is broken and good fortune will return. Witchcraft also had the broader psychological function of defining the boundaries of the Christian community and enhancing its sense of unity against a sinister foe.

SOCIAL HISTORY OF WITCHCRAFT

Social historians of witchcraft have investigated a number of correlations between accusations of witchcraft and social conditions. Since the caricature of the witch is an ugly hag, physical appearance appeared to be a likely positive correlation, but investigation has not brought this out. Instead, the most important traits in drawing witch charges were begging, grumbling, cursing, and quarreling. The witch is thought of as being old, and in fact some positive correlation does exist between age and witchcraft; children, for example, although frequently "bewitched," were themselves seldom accused. Many young men and women were accused and convicted, but the incidence of accusation did increase with age, possibly because age was supposed to enhance magical knowledge and wisdom, possibly because older people tended to be more isolated.

A strong positive correlation exists between periods of disaster and witchcraft. Famine, plague, and warfare all increased the incidence of accusations. In general, however, the correlation was not direct: the witches were not necessarily blamed for this or that disaster. Rather, the tensions generated by the disaster and the accompanying generally high levels of anxiety made people more fearful of witches in general and therefore more ready to lodge accusations on any basis.

Correlations between witchcraft and social class

are inconclusive. The "liberal" school of historians, cynically observing the legal procedure of confiscating a convicted witch's property, suggest that the witch craze was an excuse to secure the property of the wealthy, but the facts do not substantiate this view. In southwest Germany, there was a fairly proportional distribution of income groups among those convicted. In England, witches were marginally poorer than their victims, the witches tending to come from the laboring classes and the victims from the yeoman class. A broad but generally correct generalization is that through most of the witch craze all income levels were represented among the accused, with a bias toward the poorer end of the scale. Toward the end of the craze, when accusations in some areas went completely out of control and began touching everyone in the community, the rich and powerful were accused more frequently than before, and this was one of the reasons for the rapid decline of the craze in the late seventeenth century.

The firmest correlation coming out of the careful study of witchcraft in southwestern Germany is that the two groups most subject to accusation were people of either unusually bad or unusually good reputation. Thieves, sex offenders, brawlers, and quarrelers on the one hand, and magistrates, merchants, and teachers on the other, were most likely to be accused, the principle being that those who were in any way egregious were more vulnerable simply because they were more visible.

Demographic change has been cited as another cause of the witch craze. In periods of rapid social change, for example during increased migration from countryside to city, social tensions are heightened and the incidence of witch accusations increased; but no evidence exists that newcomers to the town were any more likely to be accused than older families. In the countryside, accusations most commonly arose among neighbors: typically the alleged witch was supposed to have practiced magic against one of her neighbors who had been rude or uncharitable to her.

The strongest correlation is that between witchcraft and women. Although about one-third of accused and convicted witches were male, the great majority were women, and the stereotyped witch is female to the point that the word itself has in general usage come to denote the female. (Historically, however, the term applies to both sexes; the modern idea that a male witch is a "warlock" is a baseless innovation.) The ultimate reasons for this

discrimination possibly lie in depth psychology and in the ancient history of religions. In the Judeo-Christian tradition and those upon which it draws, the principle or chief of the forces of evil is usually male, and female evil spirits are subsidiary. The Judeo-Christian tradition generally considered women inferior, weaker, and more easily led astray, and the power of such ideas is manifest in such writings as the *Malleus maleficarum*. Social and demographic considerations reinforced these stereotypes. Men much more often had power than women, and the possession of power is always a great help in avoiding prosecution of any kind. Women tended to live longer, even with childbirth death statistics included, and they survived plagues and famines better. This meant that many women lived alone, without the legal and social protection of father or husband. The increased incidence of lonely women in time of plague helps explain the rise of accusations at such times. Midwives, who were always women, were prone to being accused of causing the deaths and deformities that inevitably arose in connection with childbirth.

The kinds of social and political tensions provoking severe outbreaks of the witch craze have been well documented for some incidents of the craze.

H. R. Trevor-Roper observed of the witch craze in general that once a "great fear" takes hold of a society, "that society looks naturally to the stereotype of the enemy in its midst; and once the witch had become the stereotype, witchcraft would be the universal accusation" (p. 190).

BIBLIOGRAPHY
Paul Boyer and Stephen Nissenbaum, *Salem Possessed* (1974); Katharine M. Briggs, *Pale Hecate's Team* (1962); Peter R. L. Brown, *Religion and Society in the Age of Saint Augustine* (1972), 119–146; Norman Cohn, *Europe's Inner Demons* (1975); Martha J. Crowe, ed., *Witchcraft: Catalogue of the Witchcraft Collection in Cornell University Library* (1977), with introduction by Rossell Hope Robbins; Joseph Hansen, ed., *Zauberwahn, Inquisition, und Hexenprozess in Mittelalter . . .* (1900) and *Quellen und Untersuchungen zur Geschichte des Hexenwahns und der Hexenverfolgung im Mittelalter* (1901); Richard Kieckhefer, *European Witch Trials* (1976); Henry Charles Lea, *Materials Toward a History of Witchcraft* (1957); Alan Macfarlane, *Witchcraft in Tudor and Stuart England* (1970); John T. McNeill and Helena M. Gamer, *Medieval Handbooks of Penance* (1938); E. William, Monter, ed., *Witchcraft in France and Switzerland* (1976); Edward Peters, *The Magician,*

the Witch, and the Law (1978); Rossell Hope Robbins, *The Encyclopaedia of Witchcraft and Demonology* (1959); Elliot Rose, *A Razor for a Goat* (1962); Jeffrey Burton Russell, *Witchcraft in the Middle Ages* (1972); Jeffrey Burton Russell and Mark W. Wyndham. "Witchcraft and the Demonization of Heresy," in *Mediaevalia*, 2 (1976); Godfrid Storms, *Anglo-Saxon Magic* (1948), esp. 54, 65, 247; Lynn Thorndike, *A History of Magic and Experimental Science*, 8 vols. (1923–1958); H. R. Trevor-Roper, *The European Witch-Craze of the Sixteenth and Seventeenth Centuries and Other Essays* (1956); Wolfgang Ziegeler, *Möglichkeiten der Kritik am Hexen- und Zauberwesen im ausgehenden Mittelalter* (1973).

JEFFREY BURTON RUSSELL

[See also **Alchemy; Astrology; Heresies; Inquisition; Magic and Folklore, Western European; Magic, Bookish (Western European)**.]

WITTELSBACH FAMILY. The counts of Scheyern, who were the advocates of the bishopric of Freising, adopted in 1116 the name of their new castle, Wittelsbach, which they had built northeast of Augsburg (they had converted their ancestral castle of Scheyern into a monastery). After the fall of Henry the Lion in 1180, Frederick I Barbarossa enfeoffed the count palatine of Bavaria, Otto of Wittelsbach (*ca.* 1111–1183), with the duchy of Bavaria (16 Sept. 1180). The Wittelsbachs acquired the Rhenish Palatinate in 1214. Otto II's (*ca.* 1206–1253) sons divided Bavaria in 1255, the first of many partitions that left Bavaria fragmented until 1505. The Bavarian branch of the dynasty died out in 1777 and was succeeded by the Palatine line, the descendants of Rudolph I (1274–1319), who was the brother of Emperor Louis IV, the Bavarian (1283–1347). As kings of Bavaria, the Wittelsbachs ruled that country until 1918.

BIBLIOGRAPHY

Hubert Glaser, ed., *Wittelsbach und Bayern, I–II: Die Zeit der frühen Herzöge: Von Otto I. zu Ludwig dem Bayern* (1980); Max Spindler, ed., *Handbuch der bayerischen Geschichte*, I (1967, 2nd ed. 1980), and II (corr. ed. 1977).

JOHN B. FREED

[See also **Bavaria; Frederick I Barbarossa; Germany: 1138–1254; Germany: 1254–1493; Germany: Principalities; Henry the Lion; Palatinates**.]

WITENAGEMOT, a meeting of important figures from within the realm who were called upon to advise the king during the Anglo-Saxon period in England. "Witan," from the Anglo-Saxon word meaning "wise men," is frequently used to describe both the men who attended such gatherings and the witenagemot (meeting of wise men) itself. Most historians who have studied charter witness lists agree that the witan were a relatively fluid group of lay and ecclesiastic nobles who advised the king and formed a council of sorts. However, here the agreement ends and the historiographical dispute begins.

In the nineteenth century, most historians considered the witenagemot to be either a direct descendant of the Germanic comitatus or a direct precursor of the English Parliament. To them, the witan were champions of the common people, men who defended the rights of the people against royal encroachment and who exercised considerable influence on the king in a proto-democratic institution.

Historians in the early twentieth century did much to dispel this anachronistic interpretation of the witenagemot and focused their attention on three aspects of the problem: Who were the members of the witenagemot? What was its function? How institutionalized was it? These three questions continued to dominate the discussion of the witenagemot in the mid and late twentieth century as well. Most twentieth-century scholars agree that the higher church officials (the archbishops, bishops, and abbots) and the more powerful lay nobles (the ealdormen and royal household officials) were usually, indeed if not always, present at meetings of the king's council. The dispute arises over lesser nobles, particularly the thegns, and when, where, why, and how often they attended. The general consensus links a thegn's participation in a gemot to the location of the meeting; because the king and his court were constantly on the move, the lesser nobles generally served only when the court was in their own territories.

Because the size, composition, purpose, and location of the witenagemot changed according to specific circumstances, it is difficult for historians to define its function fully. However, modern scholarship holds that the witenagemot met when summoned by the king and basically advised the ruler, not as representatives of the common people or even of the aristocrats, but simply as individuals who knew the law. Their job was to work with the king to preserve society through the proper execution of traditional law and justice. Even though the king ultimately held all governmental authority, a wise ruler was careful to consult his witan and attempted to gain their consent to his plans because they could combine their military and legal powers to rebel against him, and they could rule the land without a king in times of crisis.

Given the variability of the witenagemot, it is difficult to believe that it was an institution in the modern sense of the word. In other words, the Anglo-Saxon witenagemot was not a corporate body that met at specific intervals to discuss a set agenda; rather it was a meeting of king and counselors that occurred when the need arose. The witenagemot was any discussion between the ruler and the important men of the realm on a particular problem at hand.

BIBLIOGRAPHY

Simon Keynes, *The Diplomas of Æthelred "The Unready" (978–1016): A Study in Their Use as Historical Evidence* (1980); Laurence M. Larson, *The King's Household in England Before the Norman Conquest* (1904); Felix Liebermann, *The National Assembly in the Anglo-Saxon Period* (1913, repr. 1961); H. R. Loyn, *The Governance of Anglo-Saxon England, 500–1087* (1984); Bryce D. Lyon, *A Constitutional and Legal History of Medieval England,* (1960, 2nd ed. 1980); Tryggvi J. Oleson, *The Witenagemot in the Reign of Edward the Confessor* (1955).

JANET M. POPE

[See also **England: Anglo-Saxon.**]

WITTENWILER, HEINRICH (*fl. ca.* 1400), author of *Der Ring,* a comic-didactic mock epic written around 1400 in northeastern Switzerland. The author, who identifies himself in verse 52 as "Haynreich wittenweylär," has not been definitely identified; but his extensive legal knowledge suggest that, of all recorded Heinrich Wittenwilers, he was most probably the *advocatus curiae Constantiensis,* or advocate at the episcopal court at Constance, mentioned in a document of 1395. Place-names in the poem, particularly that of the Necker, a little stream near Lichtensteig in Toggenburg, suggest that the poet and his public were familiar with, and probably resided in, that area.

The source of Wittenwiler's work was a short Swabian poem known as "Metzi's Wedding," which has survived in two later manuscripts. Into his peasant satire, consisting of 672 verses, Wittenwiler interpolated comical episodes and learned digressions until it reached a length of 9,699 verses He retained the simple verse scheme of his source, sometimes even incorporating entire rhyming couplets into his work.

The *Ring* begins with a peasant tournament in Lappenhausen (Foolsville), in which Bertschi Triefnas (Dripnose) woos his ladylove, Metzi (Metzli) Rüerenzumpf, whose name, as the author himself admits, is too obscene to utter. The humor of this long episode is unfortunately lost on any reader unfamiliar with the high-flown chivalrous language it parodies. When two peasants die in the tournament, the others wish to confess their sins before resuming the dangerous fray, and this introduces a mock confession in which they are duped by Neidhart Fuchs, a peasant-baiting nobleman of popular legend. After the tournament Neidhart proposes an "after-tourney," in which he pummels the peasants with an iron bar concealed in his straw club. The humor of the poem is largely malicious, being directed against the stereotype of the stupid and brutish peasant who no longer knows his place.

The tournament is followed by a series of farces in which the lovelorn Bertschi is frustrated in his attempts to see his sweetheart. His suit is successful only after her family holds a long debate, a debate that should decide whether they should give Metzi to Bertschi, but actually deals with the abstract question of whether a man should take a wife. This family council, a major part of the entire work, enables Wittenwiler to flaunt his knowledge of many scholarly subjects by having them discussed, most inappropriately, by the peasants themselves. Among the authors he quotes are Cicero, Ovid, Vergil, Juvenal, Horace, Terence, Seneca, Statius, Sallust, Theophrastus, Jerome, Boethius, Isidore, Gregory, and Pseudo-Bernard.

Returning to his basic source, Wittenwiler next describes the wedding feast, at which the peasants' gluttonous swilling and spilling illustrate how one should not behave at the table, for much of the *Ring*'s didacticism depends on negative examples. The feast is followed by a raucous dance that becomes ever wilder until it degenerates into a brawl, during which the men of Lappenhausen eject those of the neighboring town of Nissingen but detain and abuse their women.

Unable to win allies among the burghers of the great cities of the world, who wisely refrain from becoming involved, and among the knights of the

Round Table, who must remain at home to defend their castles against the cities, the villagers recruit heroes from German epics and mercenaries from Canton Schwytz, as well as witches, dwarfs, and giants from folktales. Through the tactics of these combatants and the instructions and harangues of their leaders, Wittenwiler teaches the art and law of war as formulated by Vegetius and Giovanni da Legnano. In this apocalyptic battle Lappenhausen is destroyed, together with Metzi and all other inhabitants except Bertschi, who withstands a siege by fortifying a haystack. When the enemy withdraws, he returns to Lappenhausen, sees the destruction, recognizes the vanity of the world, and saves his soul by retiring as a hermit.

Despite Wittenwiler's absurd plot and grotesque scenes, critics now generally agree that he wished to instruct as well as to entertain and that he included his "peasant shouting" only to sweeten the instruction, which he has marked with red in contradistinction to the green marking of the narrative parts. If this be the case the *Ring* should be considered a serious manual on how to live in this world while preparing for the next. In his monumental commentary to the *Ring,* Edmund Wiessner showed how accurately Wittenwiler rendered his classical, biblical, patristic, and scholarly sources, while retaining the fluidity of the spoken language.

Even if sometimes jolted by contrasts of serious and humorous matter, those who read the *Ring* carefully will see that Wittenwiler was a consummate artisan who could manipulate his language to serve any purpose and that he excelled in lively dialogues, quick repartees, and spirited descriptions of dancing and fighting. His humor includes unexpected twists, incongruous juxtapositions, and sudden suspension of illusion, as when a peasant woman ends her long argument lest further talk might make the book too heavy, or when, after several thousands of verses, the arbiter at the debate renders his decision in prose because "wise matter wants no rhyme."

In addition to verbal virtuosity, Wittenwiler showed great organizational skill in fitting his disparate matter into his received plot. Unless one counts the verses one hardly sees that most passages are arranged according to strict numerical relationships and that most dialogues are symmetrically constructed. Also, Wittenwiler keeps his many characters in mind and gives them persistent character traits. Whereas most of his rhymes are pure, he does allow himself occasional use of assonance,

but only when acoustically pleasing: tenues rhyme only with tenues, mediae with mediae, and nasals and liquids with nasals and liquids. Unlike the courtly minnesingers he was less concerned with unaccented syllables than the editor, Wiessner, would have us believe.

The *Ring* met no response, and only one manuscript has survived. When rediscovered in the nineteenth century, it was at first avoided because of its vulgarity and was cited only as a source of folklore; but now its basis in folklore is being questioned, since much of it can be proved to be based on literary tradition. On the other hand, the *Ring* is now considered a good illustration of the educational and literary interests of the urban "intelligentsia" of the late Middle Ages.

BIBLIOGRAPHY

George F. Jones, trans., *Wittenwiler's "Ring" and the Anonymous Scots Poem "Colkelbie Sow"* (1956); Bernwart Plate, *Heinrich Wittenwiler* (1977); Winfried Schlaffke, *Heinrich Wittenwilers Ring: Komposition und Gehalt* (1969); Edmund Wiessner, ed., *Heinrich Wittenwilers Ring* (1931) and *Kommentar zu Heinrich Wittenwilers Ring* (1936, repr. 1964).

GEORGE FENWICK JONES

[See also **Bauernhochzeit, Die; Mären; Middle High German Literature; Minnesingers.**]

WITTINGAU, MASTER OF (**Třeboň Master**) (*fl.* late fourteenth century), Bohemian painter, named after the Augustinian cloister (Wittingau in German, Třeboň in Czech) that housed his *Passion Altarpiece* (three panels, *ca.* 1385–1390; Prague, National Gallery). Tall, slender figure types, detailed landscape motifs, and architectural frameworks link this altarpiece to Franco-Flemish paintings of the 1390's (for example, the work of Melchior Broederlam, *fl.* 1381–1395) and may result from the Wittingau Master's possible training in northwestern Europe.

BIBLIOGRAPHY

Antonín Matějček and Jaroslav Pešina, *Czech Gothic Painting, 1350–1450* (1950), 55–58; Jaroslav Pešina, "Der Wittingau Meister," in *Die Parler und der schöne Stil, 1350–1400* (1978), II, 765–769; Gerhard Schmidt, "Bohemian Painting Up to 1450," in Erich Bachmann,

Resurrection. Panel painting by the Master of Wittingau, from his *Passion Altarpiece,* ca. 1386–1390. NATIONAL GALLERY, PRAGUE

ed., *Gothic Art in Bohemia* (1977), 55–56; Alfred Stange, *Deutsche Malerei der Gotik,* II (1936), 53–61.

LARRY SILVER

[See also **Broederlam, Melchior.**]

WITZ, KONRAD (*fl.* 1434–1446), Swiss painter, active in Basel. Witz's earliest large ensemble was the Basel *Heilspiegel Altarpiece,* based on the typological text of the *Speculum humanae salvationis* (Mirror of human salvation); the altarpiece is now only partly extant and is scattered in museums in Basel, Berlin, and Dijon. A signed work ("Conradus sapientis") now in Geneva is the *St. Peter Altarpiece,* dated 1444. One panel of this altarpiece, the "Miraculous Draft of Fishes," features a landscape view of the Lake Geneva shoreline. Witz's figures are solid, sculpturesque, yet charming.

BIBLIOGRAPHY

Daniel Burckhardt, "Studien zur Geschichte der alt-oberrheinischen Malerei," in *Jahrbuch der königlichen preussischen Kunstsammlungen,* **27** (1906), esp. 189–197; Mela Escherich, *Konrad Witz* (1916); Joseph Gantner, *Konrad Witz* (1943); Paul Ganz, *Malerei der Frührenaissance in der Schweiz* (1924), 51, and *Meister Konrad Witz von Rottweil* (1947); Alfred Stange, *Deutsche Malerie der Gotik,* IV (1951)127–147; Walter Ueberwasser, *Konrad Witz,* 2nd ed. (1942).

LARRY SILVER

[See also **Gothic Art: Painting; Speculum Humanae Salvationis.**]

WIZLAW III VON RÜGEN (*ca.* 1265–1325), German minnesinger and the prince of Rügen, was born into a family who had ruled the small Baltic country throughout its 200-year existence as a separate state. His reign (1302–1325) was marked by almost constant strife, caused largely by a shift in the balance of power as Brandenburg began to challenge the hegemony of Denmark in the southwestern Baltic area and the coastal cities became increasingly independent of their respective princes. Wizlaw displayed neither political nor military talent during these troubled times, but did distinguish himself as a poet and composer.

His twenty-six (possibly twenty-seven) extant songs present a variety of subjects—moral and religious teachings, biblical matter, a classical legend, a eulogy of a friend, a panegyric of harvest time, nature, and courtly love—in language which, for the most part, is stylized and conventional. The best compositions are the twelve minnesongs, most of which were intended to accompany summer and winter dances. These dance songs have extended nature introductions and are characterized by light-hearted humor; an affirmation of sensual pleasure in color, sound, smell, taste, and movement; and a frank sexuality that, however, is never coarse. The verse displays a high degree of structural virtuosity, an exceptional ability to compose smoothly in very complex metrical and rhyme patterns. The melodies reveal diverse styles, some simple and almost austere, others with a wealth of melodic ornamentation. All use *Barform* and all but three repeat a part or the whole of the *Stollen* in the *Abgesang* (*AA BA*). The scales used in the

The Miraculous Draft of Fishes, from the *St. Peter Altarpiece* by Konrad Witz, 1444. COLLECTION MUSÉE D'ART ET D'HISTOIRE, GENEVA

melodies include both plagal and authentic modes, and the range of several songs is quite wide, encompassing an octave and a half. For all his technical skill, Wizlaw was not outstanding as a poet. His music, however, belongs to the best of the minnesong tradition.

BIBLIOGRAPHY

Ewald Jammers, "Anmerkungen zur Musik Wizlaws von Rügen," in *Quellenstudien zur Musik: Wolfgang Schmieder zum 70. Geburtstag,* Kurt Dorfmüller, ed. (1972); Wesley Thomas and Barbara Garvey Seagrave, *The Songs of the Minnesinger, Prince Wizlaw of Rügen* (1967); Sabine Werg, "Die Sprüche und Lieder Wizlavs von Rügen: Untersuchung und kritische Ausgabe der Gedichte" (diss., Univ. of Hamburg, 1969).

J. WESLEY THOMAS

[See also **Minnesingers.**]

WOLFDIETRICH. The story of Wolfdietrich, Dietrich von Bern's ancestor and Ortnit's successor to the throne of Italy in the medieval German tradition of popular fiction, was known over the southern parts of the German-speaking area from the thirteenth to the sixteenth centuries, as is attested by its survival in complete or fragmentary form in fifteen manuscripts and one printed version. Though all versions are written in the four-line *Hildebrandston* strophe, no two are identical. Some differences are the result of different performers, scribes, or editors working at different dates in different places, feeling free to add or subtract material to suit their audience. Others are so great that they must be considered the result of independent development.

These major differences in plot and style distinguish four separate Wolfdietrich epics: *Wolfdietrich A,* or Wolfdietrich of Constantinople; *Wolfdietrich B,* or Wolfdietrich of Salonika; *Wolfdietrich C,* or Wolfdietrich of Athens, a series of short fragments; and *Wolfdietrich D,* or "the great" Wolfdietrich, an expanded version based on *B,* including what survives of *C,* and more.

Though all versions begin with a prologue explaining how Wolfdietrich got his name, the only common features of *A, B,* and *C* are contact with a wolf in infancy and the presence of Berhtung, a loyal vassal (*D* follows *B*). In *A,* Duke Saben persuades Hugdietrich, Wolfdietrich's father, to have Berhtung kill Wolfdietrich. When the child is left unharmed by wolves, Berhtung rescues him. In *B*, Hugdietrich, educated by Berhtung, disguises himself as a girl to court the daughter of the king of Salonika. Wolfdietrich, their child, is kidnapped, but not harmed, by a wolf. In *C*, Wolfdietrich, son of the king of Athens, is kidnapped by wolves. Berhtung is in Russia. Following the prologue, *A*, *B*, and *D* tell the same basic story. Wolfdietrich's two brothers do not wish to acknowledge him. Berhtung and his sixteen sons support Wolfdietrich, but are defeated. Wolfdietrich leaves the country, encounters a mermaid, and eventually reaches Lombardy, where he kills dragons and marries Ortnit's widow. He then returns home to free Berhtung's sons. Wolfdietrich's encounter with a knife-throwing heathen and his daughter occurs in *B* and *D* prior to, in *A* following, his defeat of the dragons. In *C*, Wolfdietrich, aided by Berhtung and his eleven sons, defeats the heathen king Olfant. Wolfdietrich leaves home and fights a dragon. Some of the many differences in *A*, *B*, *C*, and *D* lie in their relation to the *Ortnit* plot, their treatment of common material, and, in the case of *D*, expansion with material from *C*, legends, and other sources.

The deep structure of *Wolfdietrich* resembles that of Old French chansons de geste, which may reflect some common connection with Merovingian history. More important, it is a characteristic product of the late Middle Ages. All versions show much the same mixture of popular literary elements as do the *Spielmannsepen* (minstrel narrative poems) and the fairy-tale Dietrich epics.

BIBLIOGRAPHY

Sources. Arthur Amelung and Oskar Jänicke, eds., *Deutsches Heldenbuch*, III–IV, *Ortnit und die Wolfdietriche* (1871–1873, repr. 1968); Edward Haymes, ed., *Ortnit und Wolfdietrich: Abbildungen zur handschriftlichen Überlieferung spätmittelalterlicher Heldenepik* (1984); *Ortnit and Wolfdietrich*, J. W. Thomas, trans. (1986).

Studies. Werner Hoffman, *Mittelhochdeutsche Heldendichtung* (Grundlagen der Germanistik, XIV) (1974), 133–158; Hugo Kuhn, "Wolfdietrich," in *Verfasserlexikon des deutschen Mittelalters*, Wolfgang Stammler, ed., IV (1953).

RUTH H. FIRESTONE

[See also **Chansons de Geste; Middle High German Literature; Ortnit.**]

WOLFENBÜTTEL, HELMSTEDT MS 628 (St. Andrews MS), in the Herzog August Bibliothek (numbered 677 in the Heinemann catalogue of the library), has long been regarded as an important source of the music of the Parisian Notre Dame School of the late twelfth and early thirteenth centuries. But only in the 1930's did scholars realize that *W1* (as the manuscript is known) is of British rather than Parisian origin. Its precise date and provenance within the British Isles, as well as the age of its contents, are matters still in debate.

W1 is a composite source in that three of its eleven fascicles were copied by different though probably contemporaneous hands. The main body of the manuscript, fascicles 1–5 and 8–10, emphasizes the Parisian genres of organum, clausula, and conductus. Fascicles 6 and 7 supplement this with additional clausulae and organa, while fascicle 11 adds an Insular collection of works for the Mass of the Virgin, or Lady Mass. On blank leaves in fascicles 3, 9, and 10 the main hand has added a number of non-Parisian Sanctus and Agnus tropes.

An ex libris in a fourteenth-century hand (fol. 64) tells us that the book belonged to the Augustinian cathedral priory of St. Andrews in Scotland, where it remained until 1553, when it was acquired by the Protestant theologian Flacius Illyricus. At the sale of his library in 1597, the manuscript passed to the ducal library at Wolfenbüttel. The question is whether St. Andrews merely possessed the manuscript by the later fourteenth century or whether it was in fact produced for use there. Roesner's extensive study of the liturgical and paleographical evidence concluded that *W1* was almost certainly written for St. Andrews.

Dating proposed for the manuscript has ranged from the mid thirteenth century to the early fourteenth century. Most scholars acknowledge that the state of the Parisian repertory included is in general an early one, but opinion is divided as to whether *W1* is also the earliest extant source of this repertory. Roesner tended to agree with the paleographer J. H. Baxter, the editor of the facsimile edition and an expert in medieval Scottish sources, that the manuscript was copied in the first half of the fourteenth century, probably after the start of a liturgical renaissance at St. Andrews that began about 1314. More recently, the important studies by Brown, Patterson, and Hiley argue for a mid-thirteenth-century date.

Of the manuscript's original 215 folios, only 197 now remain; they measure 8.5 × 5.9 inches

(215 × 50 mm) and have been trimmed to the point that the old foliation in the top center recto has frequently disappeared. The modern foliation in the top right recto proceeds consecutively without noting lost folios; as a result, modern citations of *W1* use either the old foliation alone or the old and new together. Twenty-six of the original twenty-seven gatherings survive, and they are nearly all quaternions. There are twelve staves per page, ruled in red ink, in all but fascicle 10, which has only ten staves per page to accommodate text under each musical line.

The first three fascicles, containing four-voice, three-voice, and two-voice organa respectively, are each composed of a single quaternion, though in fascicle 1 the two outer double leaves of the gathering are missing. This leaves the first and third works, Perotinus' four-voice *Viderunt omnes* and the clausula *Mors*, incomplete; only the second piece, Perotinus' *Sederunt*, is present in full.

Fascicle 2 (fols. 9–16) begins with four three-voice organa, followed by what appear to be four three-voice conductus. But the first of these, *Serena virginum*, is actually a four-voice conductus-motet whose liturgical tenor has been omitted, thereby converting the piece into a conductus. This procedure, which happens five other times in *W1*, has been taken to reflect a certain Insular resistance to the motet as a genre.

Fascicle 3 (fols. 17–24) contains a selection of eleven two-voice organal settings of responsories for the Office; two more at the end of this group are unica works for the feast of St. Andrew. They are probably of Insular origin, as are two later additions by the main hand, a Marian gradual (almost all unicum), and a Sanctus trope.

The fourth fascicle (fols. 25–48) originally comprised three quaternions, but the middle one is now missing fols. 36–37, its central double leaf. The contents include two-voice organa for the Mass: thirteen graduals and nineteen alleluias plus probably one more of each on the missing folios. Fascicles 3 and 4 thus contain an Insular choice of works from the so-called *Magnus liber organi* of the Parisian Leoninus.

Both the fifth and sixth fascicles contain collections of two-voice clausulae which could be used to replace the corresponding section in an organum. Fascicle 5 is a ternion (fols. 49–54, with 51–52 missing) which now contains thirty-four clausulae, including two for organa not included in W1's collection. Fascicle 6, a quaternion by another hand

(fols. 55–62), contains sixty-eight clausulae, including seven for organa not found in *W1*, plus a unique conductus. These two groups of clausulae are, overall, stylistically the most recent among the several Notre Dame sources.

Fascicle 7, which seems an afterthought, adds five more three-voice organa for Mass and Office, including a Benedicamus Domino. Copied by another hand, the quaternion covers folios 63–69, with two leaves numbered 68. It is in this fascicle that the ex libris appears.

Fascicles 8 and 9 are both catchalls, the former emphasizing three-voice works and the latter two-voice pieces. The three gatherings of fascicle 8 (fols. 70–94, including one of nine leaves and two quaternions) contain eighteen conductus (one for two voices), three organa, one clausula, another four-voice conductus-motet with tenor removed, three Sanctus tropes, and two Agnus tropes. Folios 83–84 are missing. In similar fashion, fascicle 9 emphasizes two-voice conductus (a total of seventy-eight) but also includes four Benedicamus Dominos, four motets with tenors removed, and three Agnus tropes. The first four conductus begin with three-voice sections. This fascicle takes up more than a third of the manuscript (fols. 95–176), and its ten gatherings are all quaternions except for the third, a quinternion.

Fascicle 10, made up of two quaternions (fols. 177–192), was meant to be a collection of monophonic conductus, but the first gathering is lost and the second includes only three such works (the first without its beginning) before concluding with six Sanctus and six Agnus tropes, all monophonic.

The last fascicle, in another hand, comprises two quaternions and a ternion (fols. 193–214) and includes forty-seven two-voice works for the Lady Mass, which in the thirteenth century gradually spread from Saturday to daily observance because of its popularity. Significant in this polyphonic collection is the wide variety of liturgical types that set it apart from the Parisian repertory: Kyrie and Gloria tropes, Alleluias and a Tract, Sequences, pieces for the Offertory (including rhymed and troped Offertories), and Sanctus and Agnus tropes. This music today appears to be later than the Paris repertory (hence later than the early thirteenth century) but not necessarily more "advanced" in stylistic terms.

Despite the lack of firm answers to many questions about this manuscript, *W1* still offers an important and valuable perspective on both the central Parisian and the peripheral and Insular repertories of polyphony in the twelfth and thirteenth centuries.

BIBLIOGRAPHY

J. H. Baxter, ed., *An Old St. Andrews Music Book (Cod. Helmst. 628)* (1931, repr. 1973); Julian Brown, Sonia Patterson, and David Hiley, "Further Observations on W1," in *Journal of the Plainsong and Mediaeval Music Society,* **4** (1981); Bryan Gillingham, *The Polyphonic Sequences in Codex Wolfenbüttel 677* (1982); Friedrich Ludwig, *Repertorium organorum recentioris et motetorum vetustissimi stili,* I, pt. 1 (1910, repr. 1964), 7–42; Gilbert Reaney, ed., *Manuscripts of Polyphonic Music, 11th–Early 14th Century* (1966), 97–171; Edward H. Roesner, "The Manuscript Wolfenbüttel, Herzog-August-Bibliothek, 628 Helmstadiensis: A Study of Its Origins and of Its Eleventh Fascicle," 2 vols. (diss., New York Univ., 1974), and "The Origins of *W1,*" in *Journal of the American Musicological Society,* **29** (1976); Norman E. Smith, "Organum and Discant: Bibliography VI, France: Notre Dame," and "VIII, England," in *The New Grove Dictionary of Music and Musicians,* XIII (1980), 813–817.

REBECCA A. BALTZER

[See also **Agnus Dei (Music); Benedicamus Domino; Clausula; Conductus; Gloria; Gradual; Kyrie; Leoninus; Magnus Liber Organi; Mass, Liturgy of; Motet; Music, Western European; Notre Dame School; Offertory; Organum; Perotinus; Responsory; Sanctus; Tropes to the Ordinary of the Mass; Viderunt Omnes.**]

WOLFGER VON ERLA (*ca.* 1136–1218), bishop of Passau (1191–1204) and patriarch of Aquileia (1204–1218), a famous ecclesiastic known for his extraordinary diplomatic skill. His noble family had its seat in Erla, east of Enns in Lower Austria. His name is often erroneously given as Wolfker von Ellenbrechtskirchen. In early documents he appears as a layperson, has a son, Ottokar, and seems to have entered lower orders as a widower. He became provost of Zell am See and of Pfaffmünster, near Straubing, as well as a canon at the cathedral of Passau. On March 11, 1190, the Passau chapter elected him to succeed Bishop Diebold. During Wolfger's tenure as bishop, his episcopal domain extended over the entire Danube region from the Hungarian border to Passau and became the largest ecclesiastical principality in Germany.

Wolfger was a staunch supporter of the Hohenstaufens and maintained good relations with the Babenberg dukes of Austria. He attended the Imperial Diet of Bari (April 1195) and was chosen by the emperor to negotiate peace with Pope Celestine III. At the Diet of Worms (December 1195) he took the cross and, with the Babenberg duke Frederick I, left for the Holy Land. There, Wolfger was among the princes who, at Acre, elevated the Fraternity of the Hospital of St. Mary of the Germans into the Teutonic Order of Knights; later he succeeded in having its charter approved by the pope. In the civil war that followed the dual election of Otto of Brunswick and Philip of Swabia, Wolfger showed unwavering loyalty to the Hohenstaufen cause and as a result was certainly banned.

Despite Wolfger's continuing support of Philip, Innocent III allowed him to accept the election of the chapter of Aquileia in 1204. Prompted by a request of the pope, Wolfger traveled to Germany in 1206, met Philip and persuaded him to write a conciliatory letter to the pope. This letter clearly laid the ground for the later peace agreement. Wolfger received the regalia of the church of Aquileia in Nuremberg (11 June 1206) and became the driving force in bringing about an agreement between the pope and the Hohenstaufen, and between the Hohenstaufen and Otto of Brunswick. In July 1207, Philip was formally released from the ban of the church and Wolfger appeared in a large number of documents as witness. For his loyal service Philip rewarded Wolfger by granting him the imperial castle of Monselice near Padua. The patriarch became Philip's principal legate and negotiated a final agreement with the pope for the imperial candidacy of Philip. After receiving the news of Philip's murder on his journey from Rome, Wolfger returned to Aquileia while the pope rallied and received support for a renewed candidature of Otto. A marriage between the Welf Otto and Beatrix, the daughter of Philip, was arranged to pacify the hostile camps. Wolfger attended the Diet of Augsburg (January 1209), and, having secured the protection and favor of Otto for his church, he was also granted the duchy of Istria. As Otto's imperial legate he was sent to Italy to reclaim and restore imperial rights and properties, and also to prepare the way for the pending coronation. With great diplomatic skill and forcefulness he reclaimed what had been lost since the time of Henry VI, not knowing that Otto had secretly made certain territorial concessions to the pope. Wolfger would not have any part in Otto's designs upon Sicily and withdrew from the service of the ill-advised emperor.

When Otto was excommunicated in 1211 and Frederick II elected, Wolfger remained aloof, certainly realizing that the election of Frederick would eventually lead to a renewal of struggle between empire and papacy through the eventual union of the kingdom of Sicily and the empire. He advised Otto to consummate his betrothal to Beatrix in order to safeguard the loyalty of his Hohenstaufen liegemen in Germany. But when the youthful empress died less than three weeks after her marriage to Otto, most of his followers left camp and Frederick won nearly universal acclaim. In February 1214 Wolfger appeared at the Diet of Augsburg, and Frederick II confirmed all privileges granted by his predecessors and deeded to Wolfger and his church Monselice, which Otto inexplicably had reclaimed.

In 1215 Wolfger participated in the Fourth Lateran Council at the insistence of Innocent III. Wolfger's last major accomplishment was to negotiate peace between Treviso and Venice, and between Venice and Padua. He had been asked by Pope Honorius III to endeavor to bring an end to the violence. Upon his death, he was honored as a man of sound judgment and moderation, and as a friend of the arts. Already at Passau his court was somehow connected with the poet of the *Nibelungenlied,* with Albrecht von Johansdorf and Walther von der Vogelweide, while at Aquileia he was the lord of Thomasin von Zerclaere, and his court attracted, among others, Boncompagno of Signa.

BIBLIOGRAPHY

Viktor von Handel-Mazzetti, "Ellenbrechtskirchen," in *Verhandlungen des historischen Vereins für Niederbayern,* **48** (1912); Hedwig Heger, *Das Lebenszeugnis Walthers von der Vogelweide* (1970); Paul Kalkoff, *Wolfger von Passau, 1191–1204* (1882); Pio Paschini, "Il patriarcato di Wolfger di Ellenbrechtskirchen (1204–1218)," in *Memorie Storiche Forogiuliesi,* **10–11** (1914–1915); Eduard A. Winkelmann, *Philipp von Schwaben und Otto IV. von Braunschweig,* 2 vols. (1873–1878, repr. 1963).

F. W. VON KRIES

[See also **Babenberg Family; Frederick II of the Holy Roman Empire, King of Sicily; Germany: 1138–1254; Hohenstaufen Dynasty.**]

WOLFRAM VON ESCHENBACH (*ca.* 1170– after 1217), to judge by the number of extant manuscripts of his works and by the influence he exerted upon the literature of his time, was one of the most popular German poets of the Middle Ages. For his time he was extremely prolific, having composed over 40,000 verses. He is best known today for his massive Grail romance, *Parzival,* but the unfinished epic *Willehalm* seems to have been equally popular in his time. In addition to these major works he is also the author of a few fragments of an addendum to *Parzival,* called *Titurel,* and a handful of lyrics.

PERSONALITY

Almost all that we know about Wolfram we must deduce from the internal evidence of his works, and very few hard facts can be garnered. He names himself four times in his writings as Wolfram von Eschenbach, but Eschenbach is a fairly common toponym, and he does not tell us its location. Scholars have debated the merits of several towns of this name and are in general agreement today that Wolfram meant the Middle Franconian Ober-Eschenbach, a few miles southeast of Ansbach (near Nuremberg) in present-day Bavaria, a town that in 1917 changed its name officially to Wolframs-Eschenbach. Wolfram mentions many small towns in the area that probably would not be known to anyone save a native, and also speaks of the count of Wertheim, who held land nearby. There is archival evidence of the presence of a family of Eschenbachs from 1268 to about 1350, some of whose members held names like Wolverinus and Wolframus. And finally, the humanist Jakob Püterich von Reichertshausen claimed to have seen his grave there in 1462, and, according to the traveler Hans Wilhelm Kress, it was still to be seen in 1608.

The only difficulty with this locality is the fact that Wolfram calls himself a Bavarian, whereas this Eschenbach did not become a part of Bavaria until the middle of the nineteenth century. This has been explained away by the theory that Wolfram's family had moved to that area from some part of Bavaria, and its members still considered themselves Bavarians.

A few other passages in Wolfram's works appear to point to connections between him and other known personages of his era. In a passage in *Parzival* (230.12–13) he implies he is staying at a castle called Wildenberc, which may have been the model for Wolfram's Grail Castle. This may well have been a castle so named, south of Amorbach in the Odenwald, that was owned by Rupert von Durne. It is conceivable that Rupert may have been one of Wolfram's patrons during the writing of *Parzival*. There is further evidence that Wolfram may have spent some time at the Thuringian court in the famous castle called the Wartburg, and enjoyed the patronage of the best-known literary patron of the time, Landgrave Hermann of Thuringia. While in a *Parzival* passage (297.16–29) Wolfram criticizes Hermann, apparently for not being selective enough with his patronage, in *Willehalm* (417.22–26) he praises his generosity and states that he furnished him with the source of this work (3.8–9). This relationship lived on in tradition, as Wolfram is among the participants in the strange poetry contests that are described in the *Wartburgkrieg* (The song contest of Wartburg) as taking place at Hermann's court.

It is generally assumed that Wolfram was a knight, as his proud assertion "schildes ambet ist mîn art" (the office of the shield is my birthright, *Parz.* 115.11) seems to indicate. Also, his contemporaries and near-contemporaries refer to him by the title *hêr* (her) or "sir," which they would hardly do if he were not of the knightly classes; and in the stylized portrait of him in the famous Manessian manuscript (from the first half of the fourteenth century) he is decked out as a knight and given a coat of arms. On the other hand, there is little likelihood that he was a member of the higher nobility. He was probably a *ministerialis,* and therefore dependent upon patronage for a living.

While Wolfram interjects his personality into his works more than other poets of his time, in a number of asides, interpolations, and digressions, most of these remarks do not tell us much about him. Many of them are jocular in nature, and may have had little to do with reality. He tells us, for instance, when describing the plight of the starving inhabitants of besieged Pelrapeire, that the people in his house, where even the mice have difficulty finding enough to eat, fare almost as badly (*Parz.* 184.27–185.8). He laments that Lady Love has not been kind to him (*Parz.* 292.5–12), and that there is no one in his life as glamorous as the Lady Jeschute (*Parz.* 130.14–16). At one point in *Parzival* he mentions a wife, but the context is such that she could have been a hypothetical one (216.26–

217.6). However, in *Willehalm* he twice mentions a young daughter with an air of affection (11.23; 33.24). There are other, more convoluted passages that hint at a complex relationship between Wolfram and one woman or another, but there seems little hope of determining at this distance just what or who was involved.

Wolfram's writings contain many references to or reflexes of works of medieval German literature, including Hartman von Aue's *Erec* and *Iwein,* Heinrich von Veldeke's *Eneide,* Eilhart von Oberge's *Tristrant,* the *Nibelungenlied,* and the poetry of Walther von der Vogelweide and Neidhart von Reuental. Other influences are not so clear, but scholars have also scented evidence of Ulrich von Zazikhoven's *Lanzelet,* Gottfried von Strassburg's *Tristan,* the clerical literature of the twelfth century, such as the *Kaiserchronik, Annolied, Alexanderlied,* and such pre-courtly minstrel epics as *König Rother* and *Herzog Ernst.* Besides his French sources, there is evidence that Wolfram was also familiar with Chrétien de Troyes's *Roman de la charette,* and perhaps other Old French romances.

One of the major controversies in Wolfram scholarship revolves around whether or not he was illiterate. In *Parzival* (115.27) Wolfram states "I don't know a single letter," while in *Willehalm* (2.19–20) he notes, "I have remained ignorant of what stands in books." Older scholarship for the most part took this to mean literally that Wolfram could not read or write. While this view has its adherents today, the majority of scholars seem to believe that Wolfram meant not that he was illiterate but that he was no scholar. Some think he was ironically mocking the pedantry of Gottfried von Strassburg or Hartman von Aue by exaggerating his own ignorance.

Wolfram included numerous bits of erudite lore and scraps of French in his works, which has caused some critics to consider him more of a scholar than he admitted to, but the fact is, he could easily have picked this information up by word of mouth. Many of his remarks have been overinterpreted, particularly those pertaining to religion. Some have seen in them evidence of great theological learning; some mystic influences; others evidence of the Cathar heresy. In actuality, the religious views he expressed were quite orthodox, and the knowledge he displays does not go beyond that which any layman could easily have acquired in Sunday sermons.

STYLE

Ever since Karl Lachmann's edition of 1833, scholars have spoken of Wolfram's "obscure style," by which they have meant a kind of ornateness of vocabulary, a profusion of figurative language and a complexity of syntax that are comparable to the "Asian style" of antiquity, the *ornatus difficilis* of medieval Latin rhetoric, and the *trobar clus* of the Provençal troubadors, whether or not there is any direct connection with them. Indeed, Wolfram does employ many of the traditional characteristics of this mode of writing, including circumlocutions of all kinds, antiphrasis, ellipsis, hyperbole, and personification. In fact, by the use of abnormal word order, unusual grammatical constructions, and semantic overloading he sometimes stretches the resources of the language almost to the breaking point. He also employs a number of outrageous conceits that anticipate the euphuistic style of later centuries. For example, Wolfram says of Herzeloyde that "she was so radiant that if all the candles were extinguished there would be light enough from her" (*Parz.* 84.13–15). And of Parzival himself he says: "Many a woman has looked upon her face in a glass dimmer than his red mouth. The color of the skin on his cheeks and chin is such that it is like a tongs that could hold constancy to scrape away the fickleness of women who waver and have second thoughts about their love affairs. His radiance is a bond that holds women constant and causes their fickleness to disappear. Just to look at him makes them faithful: he passes through their eyes into their hearts" (*Parz.* 311.3–312.1).

Wolfram's style does not merit the reputation it has for being highly figurative or metaphorical. While there are some highly metaphorical passages in Wolfram's works, they are mostly concentrated in a few sections scattered throughout *Parzival* and *Willehalm,* which in most cases constitute digressions that stand apart from the narrative proper. These passages are filled with personal references and probably were meant to be ambiguous and mystifying even in his own time. Unfortunately, the Prologue to *Parzival* is one of these passages, and scholars tend to speak of the style of the entire work as if this passage were representative. Actually, for the length of most of the narrative, Wolfram's style, while it contains an occasional high-flown conceit, simple stereotype personification, or stylized topos, is not extremely metaphorical. The occasional more or less original metaphor or simile is realistic and emphatic, and derived from such spheres of everyday life as the joust, the chase, and dicing.

Wolfram's style contains many elements that give it an extremely original and individual cast. There is often a colloquial character to it that is not present to the same degree in the works of his contemporaries. There are many grammatical inaccuracies typical of colloquial usage, such as constructions apo koinou (conflation of two clauses with a common grammatical element), sudden switches from direct to indirect discourse, lack of congruence between subject and verb, shifting back and forth between past tense and historical present, strange examples of asyndeton, and anacolutha of all types. These traits are characteristic of the nonchivalric folk epic and minstrel epics, and Wolfram also has in common with them the use of a number of words and constructions that the chivalric writers mostly avoid. Like the authors of these popular works, Wolfram frequently addresses himself to his audience. But he does not limit himself to exhorting the audience to listen, or promising wonders to come, or protesting the truth of his account by citing the source, as do these authors, but interposes his personality in many other ways, sometimes to the extent of quite long interpolations of a personal or semipersonal nature. Nothing is more characteristic of Wolfram's style than these frequent authorial intrusions. They add a liveliness to the work and establish a rapport between the author and his audience. At the same time they sometimes produce a kind of "alienation effect," in that the continuity of the narrative is broken and the real world is interposed between the audience and the make-believe world of the story. Sometimes by protesting the truth of the story Wolfram raises doubts in the minds of his audience and establishes an atmosphere of irony in which author and audience together smile at the narrative. In fact, these digressions often evidence Wolfram's ambivalent feelings toward his material: while he cannot take many of the details of the plot seriously, he is deadly serious about the development of his hero and the message he wishes to convey.

In spite of all that has been said about Wolfram's "obscure" style, his narration is often quite lively, and not particularly difficult. There is a good deal of dialogue and action laced with zestful short descriptions and a good deal of humor. His accounts of duels and battles, which are often monotonous beyond description in other medieval romances, are kept to reasonable length, with the emphasis on the results rather than on the details of the fight. His narrative technique reaches a kind of peak in books III–IV of *Parzival,* which recount Parzival's youth and early adventures; in later chapters he tends to become more discursive, but at the same time exhibits a greater breadth of interest, a greater insight into institutions and emotions.

CHRONOLOGY

We must also rely on the internal evidence of Wolfram's works for our knowledge of their composition and their comparative chronology. Since a passage in *Willehalm* (4.20) mentions *Parzival* as a finished work, the precedence of *Parzival* is established. Within *Parzival* one passage (379.16–20) gives us some hope of establishing an absolute chronology. Here Wolfram mentions the vineyards of Erfurt as still showing the damage done by horses' hooves at the siege of Erfurt, which took place in 1203, when King Philip of Swabia took refuge there from the onslaught of Hermann and his allies. Wolfram may well have been at Hermann's court in 1204 (the year peace was established) or shortly thereafter, and it is conceivable that the first six books of *Parzival* were finished in this period. Many scholars suppose that there was a long interval between the composition of the first six books (some say books III–VI) and the rest of the work, during which period the unfinished work circulated. There is little further evidence within *Parzival* that can help us. A reference to the Margravine of Heitstein (Elizabeth of Vohburg) in book VIII (403.29–404.6) seems to demand a date after 1204, when she was widowed, as does another passage in book IX, which alludes to the plundering of Constantinople in that year (563.7–11). The closest we can come to pinning down the complete work is the span of 1200–1210.

A passage in *Willehalm* (393.30–394.5) mentions the coronation of Otto IV (1209) in a disrespectful way, which was probably not possible until after 1212, when Frederick II was elected as a rival emperor. There is also a mention of a *drîboc,* a war-engine first used in 1212, in *Willehalm* (111.9; 222.17). When the Prologue was written, Herman of Thuringia was still alive, but a later passage (417.22–26) sounds as if he were already dead. As he died in 1217, this would give us a span from about 1212 to 1217 or later for its composition.

The lyrics and the fragments of *Titurel* are not so easy to place with reference to his two major works. The lyrics, however, do have reminiscences in wording and tone of the first six books of *Parzival,* particularly books III–IV, and may well have been composed at roughly the same time. The *Titurel* fragments, on the other hand, contain two names (Ahkarin [Akerin] and Berbester) found in *Willehalm* that were derived from the French source of *Willehalm.* They also contain an instance of the word *admirât,* which Wolfram explains in the last book of *Willehalm.* It is thus generally supposed that the *Titurel* fragments were composed after *Willehalm,* or at least after Wolfram had become acquainted with its source. There is also the testimony, for what it is worth, of the author of *Der jüngere Titurel,* who claims that Wolfram died while composing *Titurel.*

PARZIVAL

Parzival, like most German Arthurian romances, is written in rhymed couplets. Wolfram also composed it in blocks of (mostly) thirty lines. The editor, Karl Lachmann, in his 1833 edition divided the work into sixteen books, which does not altogether agree with the manuscripts. A definitive study of the many manuscripts remains to be done—up until now no one has even attempted an edition that does more than correct a few of Lachmann's quirks, and his edition is still the standard one.

There is a preliminary story (books I–II), which deals with Parzival's parents. His father, Gahmuret, the younger son of the king of Anjou, takes service with a heathen king in the Middle East, where he accomplishes great exploits, among them the winning of the hand of the black queen Belakane, whom he marries, but soon deserts, leaving her pregnant. Back in the West, he wins a tournament that gives him the land of Herzeloyde. With bad conscience he marries her, this being possible because his first marriage was to a pagan. His brother having died, he becomes king of Anjou and of Herzeloyde's lands, Waleis and Norgals, as well. He goes off to the East to help his former liege, and is killed in battle. Herzeloyde is in the final stages of pregnancy when she hears the news, and soon after gives birth to Parzival.

The Parzival story proper begins with book III. Herzeloyde, a prototypical overprotective mother, brings her son up in the forest of Soltane in order to keep the existence of knighthood from him. When he is about fifteen, he encounters some knights in the forest; his blood will out, and he decides to go to King Arthur's court immediately to become a knight himself. His mother decks him out in fool's garb in the hope that the world will so ridicule him that he will return. When Parzival leaves, her faithful heart bursts, and she dies.

Outside of Arthur's court Parzival secures the trappings of knighthood from Ither, whom he kills in an unchivalric fashion. He is taught combat skills by Gurnemanz, and soon after relieves the siege of the castle of Pelrapeire and marries the beautiful queen, Condwiramurs. A year later he leaves to find his mother, and one evening, lost in a forest, he is directed by a fisherman to the Grail Castle. The fisherman turns out to be King Anfortas, who is suffering from a crippling ailment. Because he has been told not to ask questions, Parzival does not ask his host what is wrong with him, a question which would have cured him. He is later shamed for this dereliction by a Grail messenger in front of everyone at Arthur's court. Embittered, he renounces God, and goes off to find the Grail. His quest is in vain for five years, when chance brings him to his uncle, the hermit Trevrizent, who tells him the history of the Grail Castle, and its king, who is also Parzival's maternal uncle. The Grail Castle cannot be found unless it is predetermined that one should find it. Parzival repents his renunciation of God, and continues on his way.

A large portion of *Parzival* is devoted to Gawan, who has adventures parallel to Parzival's. He rescues a number of women held captive in a magic castle, Schastel Marveile, among them his mother, grandmother, and sisters. Without knowing each other's identity, he and Parzival engage in a duel, a requisite of the Arthurian romance as developed by Chrétien, but, with Parzival winning, they recognize each other before the culmination. He later battles with an unknown knight and is just about to vanquish him when his sword breaks. The other is too magnanimous to dispatch him, and he turns out to be Parzival's half-brother, Feirefiz, mottled black and white, the son of Belakane and Gahmuret. They go to Arthur's court, where Cundrie, the Grail messenger, appears, apologizes to Parzival, and leads him, his brother, his wife and twin sons to the Grail Castle. Parzival asks the redeeming question and becomes Grail king. Feirefiz marries Parzival's aunt, Repanse de Schoye, and goes to India, where he founds the famous dynasty of Prester John of the Indies. One of Parzival's sons remains in the Grail Castle to inherit the Grail Kingdom, and the other,

Loherangrin, becomes the famous, legendary Swan King.

Sources. Wolfram states that the source of his work was Kyot the Provençal, who wrote in Old French using Latin sources he had unearthed in Anjou on the basis of information pagan astronomers in Toledo had gathered from the stars. Older scholarship took this literally, and there are still some scholars today who believe it. However, it has been conclusively demonstrated that Wolfram very closely follows Chrétien de Troyes's unfinished Perceval romance from the beginning of book III up to the point where Chrétien's work leaves off. Wolfram finished the work by using in large measure structural elements that Chrétien used in his other romances. The origin of the first two books is obscure. It may have been a lost French poem, perhaps by the known French poet Guiot of Provins, which Wolfram merged with Chrétien's work.

Wolfram changes Chrétien's work to the extent that many more of his characters have names and identities, and most of them are of higher rank than their counterparts in Chrétien. Wolfram has also worked out very elaborate genealogies, so that almost all of his characters belong to one of two prestigious and interrelated families, the Grail family and the lineage of King Arthur, founded by Mazadan. Also, Wolfram presents three worlds in the work: the real world in the Gahmuret part; the world of the Arthurian romance in the Parzival parts; an in-between world in the Gawan sections, in which the real world comes into contact with the world of romance, and in which the predominant mood is satirical.

The problematics of *Parzival* center around two interrelated questions: the significance of the Grail and the Grail Kingdom, and the significance of the question that Parzival failed to ask at the Grail Castle. Often the Grail is considered to be a religious symbol, more or less representing salvation, and the Grail Kingdom is symbolic of heaven, or at least, an earthly paradise. Then Parzival's failure to ask the question that would provide him with the Grail and make him lord over the Grail Kingdom would be indicative of his sinful state. He is frequently described as lacking compassion or steadfast devotion, in not being able to determine when compassion should take precedence over propriety. Some see Parzival's renunciation of God as his principal transgression. But he does not renounce God until after he has been censured for failing to ask the question at the Grail Castle.

However, there is good reason to believe that Wolfram's principal concern in *Parzival* was political rather than religious. Wolfram's Grail is not a chalice, as we are accustomed to think it, nor yet a ciborium, as it is in Chrétien's work, but a magic stone called *lapsit exillis,* which receives its power annually from heaven and is capable of providing food and drink in a miraculous way, and of keeping all those who have gazed upon it alive for a week. The Grail Kingdom is a kind of training ground for rulers and consorts of rulers. Parzival is led to the Grail Castle and eventually becomes its lord because of his birthright. He appears not to have been accepted as king upon his first appearance there because of his immaturity. While he committed some grievous sins, he did so mostly out of ignorance and naïveté. His renunciation of God is more a form of madness than it is a sin. His excoriation seems to have been aimed at shocking him into seeing his faults, and improving himself.

Seen against the background of Wolfram's times, with the intense rivalry between Welf and Staufer for the possession of the imperial crown, the Grail Kingdom appears to be an analogue of the Holy Roman Empire, the Grail itself symbolic of the imperial crown with its famous gem, the Orphanus. The two great interrelated families of Mazadan and Titurel are reminiscent of the two great lines of the Guelphs and Ghibellines, likewise interrelated. *Parzival* thus bears the message that Wolfram considered the most important for the age in which he lived: only through a well-ordered system of succession to the imperial throne could lasting peace and prosperity be achieved. This meant that the throne must be handed down from father to son and belongs by divine right to only one dynasty. Only by mutual loyalty and assistance among its members can the dynasty survive. To avoid the chaos that is caused when an unfit person or a minor comes to the throne, there should be some kind of system to test the prospective monarch's fitness and maturity before he is allowed to reign, and to depose him if he reigns incompetently. The basis of this monarchy—as well as for all human actions—must be the courtly virtues of propriety, morality, and devotion. But beyond all human endeavor there is an area where only God can help, and this the Christian knight must recognize in a proper spirit of humility.

OTHER WORKS

The source of Wolfram's other great epic, *Willehalm,* is an Old French chanson de geste, *La bataille d'Aliscans,* from a cycle centering upon Guillaume d'Orange, a grandson of Charles Martel. Wolfram has changed the form of the poem from the *laisses* of the original to the rhyming couplets usual in the chivalric romance, and in tone and style likewise written in the manner of this genre. In the tradition of its first editor, Karl Lachmann, the work is divided into nine books, although the manuscript evidence for this division is scanty.

Willehalm has abducted and married a Saracen princess, Arabel, who became converted to Christianity and changed her name to Gyburg. Her father, Terramer, leads an army into southern France to rescue her, and this army annihilates Willehalm's forces at Alischanz. Willehalm alone escapes, and makes his way to Munlêûn (Laon), where he beseeches the French king, Loys, who is married to his sister, for assistance. Reluctantly the king agrees, and Willehalm leads the French army and arrives at his castle in Orange just in time to save it from the Saracen siege. There is a second tremendous battle at Alischanz, which the Christian army finally wins. In this battle Rennewart, who is a kind of clownish lout of whom everyone makes fun, a huge man who fights with a giant staff, often takes the center of the stage. He turns out to be Willehalm's brother-in-law, and distinguishes himself outstandingly in the battle. When the work ends abruptly, Rennewart is missing, and many other ends of the story remain loose.

It is generally assumed that Wolfram never finished his work, and if one compares the untidy ending with the way that all ends are neatly tied up in *Parzival,* it is hard to believe that he considered it finished, in spite of the contrary assertions of some scholars.

Many scholars have noted that the spirit of this work is much more pessimistic than that of *Parzival,* and lay this in general at the door of Wolfram's advancing age—although it seems unlikely that he was much past the forties when he wrote it. However, the difference in spirit is to a large extent inherent in the work itself, with its great amount of carnage, compared to the Arthurian romance, where the emphasis is on individual combat that seldom amounts to much more than a rough game. Perhaps if Wolfram had finished this work it would have ended on a more positive note.

In startling contrast to his contemporaries, in

Willehalm Wolfram preaches tolerance, at least to the extent that he decries the needless slaughter of the heathen, as they too are God's creatures. It is this modern-sounding message that leads many scholars to value *Willehalm* even higher than *Parzival*. However, it lacks the great panoply of life, the zestful writing, the humor, the swift, brilliant characterizations, the sense of awe and mystery, the great charm of *Parzival*.

Wolfram's third epic work is extant only in two fragments of some 680 lines, and it is generally thought unlikely that Wolfram completed much more of the work, if any. Although it is known as *Titurel* (Parzival's great-grandfather, the first person to be named in the work), it deals chiefly with the love that Parzival's cousin Sigune and Schionatulander bear toward each other in a period preceding their appearance in *Parzival*. The first and longer fragment deals with their youth and the early days of their love, while the second depicts the events that led immediately to Schionatulander's untimely death, which has already taken place when Parzival first encounters Sigune in *Parzival*. There is a certain melancholy, elegiac mood prevalent throughout the fragments, a lamentation for the devastation wrought by time and fortune, a kind of nostalgic evocation of the golden days of the past. This mood is considerably enhanced by the static quality of the unique stophic form that the poet chose for the work.

Eight lyric poems have come down to us under Wolfram's name. One of these (Wapnewski's no. VIII), it is generally agreed, is falsely ascribed to him. Of the other seven, two (VI and VII) are fairly conventional love songs (*minneliet*), while the other five are dawn songs (*Tagelieder*), the traditional lament of secret lovers who must part at break of day. Wolfram bears the dubious distinction of being the first poet in German, so far as we know, to include in his poems the figure of the watchman who warns the lovers of the approach of dawn, although he must have borrowed this feature, as well as the other details of the genre, from Provençal or French sources.

While the dramatic situation of the dawn song apparently appealed strongly to Wolfram, as did the frank sensuality, more realistic than could be expressed in the other traditional varieties of the chivalric lyric, there are enough disquieting and ironic elements in the poems to make it apparent that Wolfram had strong reservations about the content. He seems to have felt that it was dishonorable or at least undignified to engage in secret amours and have to sneak home in the early light of dawn, as well as being utterly stupid to put one's honor in the hands of a lowly watchman. His disapproval becomes so strong in one poem (V) that it has been termed an "anti–dawn song."

CONTINUATORS AND MODERN SCHOLARSHIP

Like Hartmann von Aue and Gottfried von Strassburg, Wolfram had many admirers among his contemporaries and successors. Many particularly admired his style, and sought to emulate him, such as Heinrich von dem Türlin in his mammoth Arthurian romance, *Diu Crône*, and Wirnt von Gravenberg in *Wigalois*. Scholarship has frequently contrasted Wolfram's style with that of Gottfried, who in a discursive passage in *Tristan*, without mentioning Wolfram by name, criticizes "finders of wild tales," who use unacceptable language to deceive people with untrue stories—perhaps an allusion to Wolfram's claiming that his source was a work by Kyot. Many scholars have seen hidden insults to the other's work in a number of other passages in both works, as well as *Willehalm*, but it is all very unlikely. Their contemporaries and immediate successors do not seem to have felt such a contrast in the style of the two poets that they felt compelled to champion one against the other; rather we often find the same poet praising both of them. In fact, Ulrich von Türheim wrote continuations both of Gottfried's *Tristan* and of Wolfram's *Willehalm* (called *Rennewart* after its main character). Among other continuations or adaptations of Wolfram's work were Ulrich von dem Türlin's prehistory of *Willehalm; Der jüngere Titurel* (probably by Albrecht von Scharfenberg), an expansion of Wolfram's *Titurel* and *Parzival; Lohengrin,* an anonymous continuation of *Parzival; Der neue Parzival,* by Claus Wisse and Philipp Colin, an addition to *Parzival* that is supposed to fit in between books XIV and XV; the *Buch der Abenteuer* of Ulrich Füetrer, a collection of many Arthurian epics redone in strophic form, including Wolfram's *Titurel* and *Parzival*. Wolfram is numbered among the chief contestants in the *Wartburgkrieg,* where he bests his own creation, the necromancer Clinschor. He was so well known throughout the late Middle Ages that he was numbered among the twelve masters who invented the *Meistergesang*.

Wolfram became known to the modern world through Johann Jakob Bodmer's translation of *Par-*

zival, published in 1753, followed by an edition of the original text edited by Christoph Heinrich Müller in 1784. However, it was not until the publication of Lachmann's edition of Wolfram's works in 1833 that modern Wolfram scholarship began. Since then his works have drawn the attention of many famous scholars, so that a tremendous amount of secondary literature has developed, especially in the decades since World War II. So many monographs and articles continue to be devoted to almost every aspect of his work that it is becoming increasingly difficult to keep abreast of the scholarship. The general trend seems to be a slow movement away from the almost mystical, over-intellectualized approach of such scholars as Bodo Mergell, Walter Johannes Schröder, and B. H. Willson to a more practical, rationalistic view of the poet as a layman and a German knight concerned with the political issues of his day.

BIBLIOGRAPHY

Editions. Wolfram von Eschenbach, Karl Lachmann, ed., 6th ed. rev. by Eduard Hartl (1926, repr. 1960), 7th ed. (without *Willehalm*) (1952); *Wolfram von Eschenbach*, Albert Leitzmann, ed., 5 vols. (1902–1906 and many later editions and revisions); *Parzifal und Titurel*, Karl Bartsch, ed., 4th ed. rev. by Marta Marti (1927–1932); *"Parzival": Abbildungen und Transkription zur gesamten handschriftlichen Überlieferung des Prologs*, Uta Ulzer, ed. (1974); *Willehalm, mit der Vorgeschichte des Ulrich von dem Türlin und der Fortsetzung des Ulrich von Türheim: Vollständige Faksimile-Ausgabe im Originalformat des Codex Vindobonensis 2670 der Österreichischen Nationalbibliothek*, Hedwig Heger, ed. (1974); *"Titurel": Abbildungen sämtlicher Handschriften mit einem Anhang zur Überlieferung des Textes im jüngeren Titurel*, Joachim Bumke, ed. (1973); *Die Lyrik Wolframs von Eschenbach: Edition, Kommentar, Interpretation*, Peter Wapnewski, ed. (1972).

Translations. Parzival: A Romance of the Middle Ages, Helen M. Mustard and Charles E. Passage, trans. (1961); *Parzival*, A. T. Hatto, trans. (1980); *Schionatulander and Sigune: An Episode from the Story of Parzival and the Graal as Related by Wolfram von Eschenbach*, Margaret F. Richey, trans. (1960); *The Middle High German Poem of Willehalm*, Charles E. Passage, trans. (1977); *Titurel*, trans. and studies by Charles E. Passage (1984).

Manuscripts. Gesa Bonath, *Untersuchungen zur Überlieferung des Parzival Wolframs von Eschenbach*, 2 vols. (1970–1971); Joachim Bumke, "Zur Überlieferung von Wolframs Titurel: Wolframs Dichtung und der jüngere Titurel," in *Zeitschrift für deutsches Altertum*, 100

(1971), and "Titurelüberlieferung and Titurelforschung: Vorüberlegungen zu einer neuen Ausgabe von Wolframs Titurelfragmenten," *ibid.*, **102** (1973); Rudolf Anton Hofmeister, "Manuscript Evidence in Wolfram's *Parzival*" (diss., Univ. of Illinois, 1971) and "A New Aspect of the *Parzival* Transmission Through a Critical Examination of Manuscripts G and G^m," in *Modern Language Notes*, **87** (1972); Jürgen Kühnel, "Wolframs von Eschenbach 'Parzival' in der Überlieferung der Handschriften D (Cod. Sangall. 857) und G (CGM. 19): Zur Textgestaltung des 'Dritten Buches,'" in *Festschrift für Kurt Herbert Halbach zum 70. Geburtstag* (1972); Werner Schröder, *Der Text von Wolframs "Willehalm" vom 327. bis zum 343. Dreissiger* (1977); Manfred von Stosch, *Schreibereinflüsse und Schreibertendenzen in der Überlieferung der Handschriftengruppe *WWO von Wolframs "Willehalm"* (1971).

Bibliographies. Joachim Bumke, *Die Wolfram von Eschenbach Forschung seit 1945: Bericht und Bibliographie* (1970); Ulrich Pretzel and Wolfgang Bachofer, *Bibliographie zu Wolfram von Eschenbach*, 2nd ed. (1968).

General studies. Joachim Bumke, *Wolfram von Eschenbach*, 5th ed. (1981); Dennis H. Green and Leslie P. Johnson, *Approaches to Wolfram von Eschenbach: Five Essays* (1978); Stephen C. Harroff, *Wolfram and His Audience* (1974); Friedrich Maurer, "Wolfram und die zeitgenössischen Dichter," in *Typologia litterarum: Festschrift für Max Wehrli* (1969); Friedrich Neumann, "Wolfram von Eschenbach auf dem Wildenberg," in *Zeitschrift für deutsches Altertum*, **100** (1971); James F. Poag, *Wolfram von Eschenbach* (1972); Margaret F. Richey, *Studies of Wolfram von Eschenbach* (1957); Werner Schröder, ed., *Wolfram-Studien*, 5 vols. (1970–1979).

Style. David Blamires, *Characterization and Individuality in Wolfram's "Parzival"* (1966); Kurt Gärtner, "Die Constructio apo koinou bei Wolfram von Eschenbach," in *Beiträge zur Geschichte der deutschen Sprache und Literatur*, **91** (1969); Henry Kratz, *Wolfram von Eschenbach's "Parzival"* (1973), 82–133; Patricia C. Kutzner, *The Use of Imagery in Wolfram's "Parzival": A Distributional Study* (1975); Rainer Madsen, *Die Gestaltung des Humors in den Werken Wolframs von Eschenbach* (1971); Eberhard Nellmann, *Wolframs Erzähltechnik* (1973); Christa Ortmann, *Die Selbstaussagen in "Parzival": Zur Frage nach der Personengestaltung bei Wolfram von Eschenbach* (1972); Hans Günter Welter, "Zur Technik der Wortwiederholungen in Wolframs Parzival," in *Zeitschrift für deutsche Philologie*, **93** (1974).

Reception. Erich Kleinschmidt, "Literarische Rezeption und Geschichte: Zur Wirkungsgeschichte von Wolframs *Willehalm* im Spätmittelalter," in *Deutsche Vierteljahrsschrift für Literaturwissenschaft und Geistesgeschichte*, **48** (1974); Hedda Ragotzky, *Studien zur Wolfram-Rezeption* (1971); Werner Schröder, "Wolfram-Rezeption und Wolfram-Verständnis im 14. Jahrhundert," in *Euphorion*, 70 (1976).

Parzival. Walter Blank, "Mittelalterliche Dichtung oder Theologie? Zur Schuld Parzivals," in *Zeitschrift für deutsches Altertum*, 100 (1971); Michael Curschmann, "Das Abenteuer des Erzählens: Über den Erzähler in Wolframs *Parzival*, in *Deutsche Vierteljahrsschrift für Literaturwissenschaft und Geistesgeschichte*, 45 (1971); Hans Dewald, *Minne und "sgrâles âventiur": Äusserungen der Subjektivität und ihre sprachliche Vergegenwärtigung in Wolframs "Parzival"* (1975); Walter Falk, "Wolframs Kyot und die Bedeutung der 'Quelle' im Mittelalter," in *Literaturwissenschaftliches Jahrbuch*, 9 (1968); Dennis H. Green, *The Art of Recognition in Wolfram's "Parzival"* (1982); Ursula Hennig, "Die Gurnemanzlehren und die unterlassene Frage Parzivals," in *Beiträge zur Geschichte der deutschen Sprache und Literatur*, 97 (1975); Dagmar Hirschberg, *Untersuchungen zur Erzählstruktur in Wolframs "Parzival"* (1976); Henry Kratz, *Wolfram von Eschenbach's "Parzival": An Attempt at a Total Evaluation* (1973); Carl Lofmark, "Zur Interpretation der Kyotstellen im *Parzival*," in Schröder, ed., *Wolfram-Studien*, V (1977); Friedrich Maurer, "Zur Bauform von Wolframs *Parzival*-Roman," in *Mélanges pour Jean Fourquet* (1969); Eberhard Nellmann, "Die Komposition des *Parzival*: Versuch einer neuen Gliederung," in *Wirkendes Wort*, 21 (1971); Christa Ortmann, "Ritterschaft: Zur Frage nach der Bedeutung der Gahmuret-Geschichte im *Parzival* Wolframs von Eschenbach," in *Deutsche Vierteljahrsschrift für Literaturwissenschaft und Geistesgeschichte*, 47 (1973); Josef Quint, "Der Gralstein in Wolframs *Parzival* und der Paradiesstein im Strassburger Alexander," in *Festschrift Helmut de Boor* (1966); Maurice Riehl, *La religion dans "Parzival" de Wolfram von Eschenbach* (1970); Hugh Sacker, *An Introduction to Wolfram's "Parzival"* (1963); Bernd Schirok, *Der Aufbau von Wolframs "Parzival"* (1972) and "Trevrizent und Parzival," in *Amsterdamer Beiträge zur älteren Germanistik*, 10 (1976); Franz R. Schröder, "Kyot und das Gralproblem," in *Beiträge zur Geschichte der deutschen Sprache und Literatur*, 97 (1975); Otto Springer, "Wolfram's *Parzival*," in Roger S. Loomis, ed., *Arthurian Literature in the Middle Ages* (1959); Petrus W. Tax, "Gahmuret zwischen Äneas und Parzival: Zur Struktur der Vorgeschichte von Wolframs *Parzival*," in *Zeitschrift für deutsche Philologie*, 92 (1973), and "Trevrizent: Die Verhüllungstechnik des Erzählers," in *Studien zur deutschen Literatur und Sprache des Mittelalters: Festschrift für Hugo Moser zum 65. Geburtstag* (1974); Hermann J. Weigand, *Wolfram's "Parzival": Five Essays with an Introduction*, Ursula Hoffmann, ed. (1969); Hans Günther Welter, *Die Wolframsche Stilfigur: Untersuchungen zu einem Strukturschema im "Parzival" Wolframs von Eschenbach* (1970); Herbert E. Wiegand, *Studien zur Minne und Ehe in Wolframs "Parzival" und*

Hartmanns Artusepik (1972); Peter Wieners, *Das Gottes- und Menschenbild Wolframs im "Parzival"* (1973); Marianne Wynn, *Wolfram's "Parzival": On the Genesis of Its Poetry* (1984); Gisela Zimmermann, "Untersuchungen zur Orgeluseepisode in Wolfram von Eschenbachs *Parzival*," in *Euphorion*, 66 (1972), and *Kommentar zum VII. Buch von Wolfram von Eschenbachs "Parzival"* (1974).

Willehalm. Marion E. Gibbs, *Narrative Art in Wolfram's "Willehalm"* (1976); Walter Haug, "Wolframs 'Willehalm'—Prolog im Lichte seiner Bearbeitung durch Rudolf von Ems," in *Kritische Bewahrung; Beiträge zur deutschen Philologie: Festschrift für Werner Schröder zum 60. Geburtstag* (1974); Helga Kilian, *Studien zu Wolframs "Willehalm"* (1969); Erich Kleinschmidt, "Die lateinische Fassung von Wolframs 'Willehalm'—Prolog und ihr Überlieferungswert," in *Zeitschrift für deutsches Altertum*, 103 (1974); Fritz Peter Knapp, *Rennewart: Studien zu Gehalt und Gestalt des "Willehalm" Wolframs von Eschenbach* (1970); Carl Lofmark, *Rennewart in Wolfram's "Willehalm": A Study of Wolfram von Eschenbach and His Sources* (1972); Uwe Pörksen and Bernd Schirok, *Der Bauplan von Wolframs "Willehalm"* (1976); Alois Schmidt, "Kampfschilderungen in Wolframs 'Willehalm,'" in Schröder, ed., *Wolfram-Studien*, III (1975); Werner Schröder, "Das epische Alterswerk Wolframs von Eschenbach," *ibid.*, I (1970); Friederike Wiesmann, *Le roman du "Willehalm" de Wolfram d'Eschenbach et l'épopée d'Aliscans* (1976).

Titurel. Joachim Heinzle, *Stellenkommentar zu Wolframs "Titurel"* (1972); Henry Kratz, "A View of Wolfram's Lyrics," in *Semasia*, 2 (1975); Ulrich Wyss, "Selbstkritik des Erzählens: Ein Versuch über Wolframs Titurelfragment," in *Zeitschrift für deutsches Altertum*, 103 (1974).

HENRY KRATZ

[See also **Arthurian Literature; German Literature: Romance; Middle High German Literature; Wartburgkrieg;** and individual authors and works.]

WOLGEMUT, MICHAEL (1434–1519), German painter and graphic artist. Assistant and successor in Nuremberg to Hans Pleydenwurff (d. 1472), Wolgemut is known for the dated *Hofer Altarpiece* (1465; Munich) and the *Zwickau Altarpiece* (1479; Zwickau, Marienkirche), which reveal the influence of Flemish painting, of which he had firsthand knowledge. He is equally famous as the teacher of Albrecht Dürer from 1486 to 1489 and for his woodcuts; Wolgemut supervised the vast project of 645 woodcuts for Hartmann Schedel's *Nuremberg Chronicle* (*Weltkronik*), published in 1493. Schedel's work is considered a landmark in the history of illustrated books.

BIBLIOGRAPHY

Richard Bellm, *Wolgemuts Skizzenbuch im Berliner Kupferstichkabinett* (1959); Gerhard Betz, "Der Nürnberger Maler Michael Wolgemut (1434–1519)" (diss., Freiburg, 1955); Franz Izra Stadler, *Michael Wolgemut und der Nürnberger Holzschnitt im letzten Drittel des XV. Jahrhunderts* (1913); Wilhelm Wenke, "Das Bildnis bei Michael Wolgemut," in *Anzeiger des Germanischen Nationalmuseums* (1932–1933), 61–68.

LARRY SILVER

[See also **Fachschrifttum; Nuremberg (with illustration); Pleydenwurff, Hans; Woodcut.**]

WOLVINUS (Wolvinius) (*fl.* mid ninth century), Carolingian goldsmith who created (and signed) the Paliotto, or Golden, Altar of S. Ambrogio, commissioned by Angilbert II, archbishop of Milan (824–859). Wolvinus combined embossed relief, enamel work, and inlaid gems with great technical mastery. On the back, he pictured himself handing the altar to Angilbert, who passes it on to St. Ambrose. The altar panels also contain scenes from the lives of Christ and St. Ambrose, Christ in Majesty surrounded by evangelist symbols, and the twelve apostles.

BIBLIOGRAPHY

Karl der Grosse: Exhibition Katalog (1965), no. 559; Peter Lasko, *Ars Sacra 800–1200* (1972), 50–55.

LESLIE BRUBAKER

[See also **Angilbert of Milan; Metalsmiths, Gold and Silver (with illustration); Milan; Paliotto of S. Ambrogio; Pre-Romanesque Art.**]

WOMEN, STATUS OF. See **Family.**

WOMEN'S RELIGIOUS ORDERS.

FOURTH–EIGHTH CENTURIES

In the fourth century, monasticism was transplanted from the East and began to develop rapidly in the decadent Western Empire. Houses for women predominated among those first established in Rome. St. Jerome (*d.* 420) stated that there existed in Rome a multitude of monasteries of virgin girls.

Monasticism spread in quick succession from Rome to other parts of the Western Empire. In Italy, the invasions of the Ostrogoths, Byzantines, and Lombards did not prevent the establishment of monasteries, both male and female. The monastic foundations of Pope Gregory the Great (590–604) came after St. Benedict (*ca.* 480–*ca.* 547) wrote his Rule requiring monks to devote certain hours daily to labor and reading, in addition to prayer. In 612 the monastery at Bobbio was established by the Irish monk St. Columbanus, who also issued a monastic rule. The Lombard period became rich in the foundation of both male and female Benedictine houses in the first half of the eighth century.

Meanwhile, at the end of the fifth century in Gaul, the Franks established a kingdom remarkable for its monastic foundations. Several men—Caesarius of Arles, Aurelian of Arles, Donatus of Besançon, and Waldabert of Luxeuil—wrote female rules, and female monasteries were established throughout the kingdom, mainly in cities. Best known are St. John of Arles, built at the beginning of the sixth century by Caesarius for his sister Caesaria, and Holy Cross of Poitiers, constructed in 530 by Radegunda with her husband Chlothar's money. By the end of the sixth century, when St. Columbanus arrived in Francia, the women flocked to his lectures. His followers in the monastery of Luxeuil, with the help of women, created the double monastery, an institution comprising two houses, one female and the other male, most often both supervised by an abbess.

In France, double establishments such as Faremoutiers, Jouarre, Remiremont, and Chelles were popular. There were some fourteen or eighteen in number, usually run by abbesses. They exerted a great influence in the seventh and eighth centuries. The abbesses heard members' confessions three times a day and punished offenders with the rod. In addition, they gave daily benediction to the nuns and monks. Their monastery functioned as a school for both girls and boys and had a library and probably also a scriptorium.

In Italy, by contrast, the powerful priesthood and pope did not generally permit double houses. An exception, St. Maria and St. Peter at Alife in Compania, was founded in 730 with Crispina as the abbess and Natalis as the abbot. But young women from England raised in the ascetic tradition were so impressed by the monasteries in France that, according to Bede, they traveled to take the veil at the double houses of Faremoutiers and Chelles or at Andelys, a female monastery. England itself was home to twelve double monasteries fashioned after the Frankish ones. Nuns and monks attended the divine service and probably also the choir service together; otherwise they were totally separated. Monks attached to the monastery provided the heavy labor, performed the priestly function, and gave the nuns some protection. Abbesses exercised influence commensurate with their function. For example, Hilda of Whitby founded several monastic institutions, was consultant to her royal relatives, and gave shelter to the Synod of Whitby in 663, which acknowledged Rome's superiority. Five bishops received their education under her and she promoted English poetry by encouraging the poetic talents of the shepherd Cædmon. The Viking invasions, which began in the mid ninth century, gradually wiped out this flowering monastic culture in England.

THE CAROLINGIANS

The early eighth century brought the Anglo-Saxon missionaries to the Continent. Their leader, St. Boniface, undertook a reform of the Frankish church that included placing all monasteries under the Benedictine Rule. The Rule provided that the head of the monastery be consecrated by the local bishop, which brought religious life in the Frankish kingdom under episcopal control. The Carolingian dynasty eagerly assisted in placing the monasteries within episcopal jurisdiction. But in return, the Carolingians expected help from bishops in creating a *Reichskirche,* or imperial church, in which the greatest abbeys were to be subordinated to the power of the monarch. In this manner, most of the monasteries ceased to enjoy their former independence and their resources were placed in the hands of royal administrators. Abbots, as royal advisers and friends of bishops, were able to ease previous restrictions placed upon their communities. Female monasteries, on the other hand, caught between haughty treatment by bishops and financial demands by the king, declined in importance.

Boniface applied the Rule of St. Benedict to both male and female communities. But in 755 the Council of Verneuil called for the incarceration of uncooperative nuns and their subjection to forced labor; there is no mention of similar treatment for reluctant monks. The council also declared that women who veiled themselves were to enter a monastery or were to live under subjection to a bishop *sub ordine canonica,* in a canonically regulated fashion. Beginning with the Council of Frankfurt in 794, abbesses were regularly offered the choice between Benedictine and canonical life, the distinction being that canonesses could hold possessions outside the monastery. Earlier, a canoness was considered part of the clerical order, able to instruct women in the faith and baptize them.

In 810, during the second phase of the Carolingian reforms, Benedict of Aniane undertook the consolidation of earlier improvements. The Council of Chalon-sur-Saône in 813 issued guidelines for the behavior of canonesses. Three years later, in 816, the Council of Aachen (Aix) expanded these regulations into a rule, *Institutio sanctimonialium.* The only difference between the Benedictine Rule and the *Institutio* was that, according to the latter, a canoness had the right to retain private property but not to manage it. This provision did not appear in the order of canons. Canons had the right to manage both ecclesiastical and private property. Canonesses moreover were strictly cloistered and were required to cover their faces in public and to wear a veil in church. They were to be guarded carefully from all contact with men. Even the abbesses could meet men only in the presence of other sisters. Conversation with relatives had to be monitored by three or four members of the community.

The reformers sought to avoid contact between the sexes in monasteries and forbade canonesses and nuns to teach boys. Abbesses of both types of institutions, canonical and Benedictine, lost their freedom of movement and also their former influence. Emperors and kings periodically summoned them, most probably to discuss their monastic resources. The abbesses, unlike the abbots, did not participate in synods that dealt with discipline. They were also deprived of any function thought to be sacerdotal. Because they could no longer give benediction to women, they were also forbidden to consecrate women. The concept that canonesses were members of the clerical order lingered on, but the functional distinction between canonesses and Benedictine nuns was abolished.

The transformation of the double monastery into a house of canons and a community of nuns or canonesses proceeded. It was easier to support a few canons than a house of monks. The canons were priests and ministered to the sacramental needs of the female members of the community. This arrangement nevertheless had certain disadvantages from the viewpoint of the nuns. The canons were not cloistered and enjoyed a greater freedom of movement than the female members. Although the canons were economically dependent on the abbess, they did not come under her jurisdiction. Their clerical status, moreover, gave them magisterial authority that abbesses had formerly exercised.

The strict Benedictine rules gradually became less prominent after the Treaty of Verdun in 843. Benedictine houses were no longer the exclusive recipients of royal privileges, and more Benedictine nunneries were transformed into institutes of canonesses. Also the attempt to cloister canonesses was abandoned. Local families, whose daughters administered the female monasteries, took charge of monastic revenues. Furthermore, in France, female houses tended to disappear.

Although the Carolingian reforms were enacted into law, their application to female monasteries in Italy was limited. The popes and the bishops made certain that the abbesses did not rule over men in religious orders; their power concerned only the women they were leading and the economic, social, and political influence they commanded as owners of great property. Their authority in social and political spheres was confined to hearing cases through an advocate, and their property had to be administered by a villicus, who was of somewhat higher status than the rest of the people attached to and working in the monastery. In addition, the Carolingian emperors imposed tremendous financial demands on the nuns. The properties of the largest female communities were farmed out among the Carolingian princesses and wives who, on occasion, held this property as lay abbesses. The monasteries were also frequently the target for expropriations by the local nobility. Moreover, in the middle of the ninth century, female institutions in the south became the prey of the Saracen plunderers, and in the late ninth and early tenth centuries, the victims of the Hungarian raiders from the north.

All these events did not prevent the foundation of new monasteries. For example in Milan, two new female monasteries were established in the ninth century, S. Radegonda and S. Maurizio, known to all as "Monastero Maggiore." In other towns the Carolingians and their nobles occasionally established monasteries for women, but their activity did not compare with Lombard or Merovingian foun-

dations. In the tenth century, the Italian kings favored some women's communities. But the real benefactors of monasteries were the German kings and the Italian aristocracy.

By the twelfth century there were approximately forty-five women's monasteries in Lombardy. Seventeen had been founded in the eleventh century, and nine each in the tenth century and the Lombard period. Only three had been founded in the Carolingian era, plus five each from the fifth and sixth centuries, and two from the fourth century. The great number of monasteries established in the eleventh century was probably a result of the investiture controversy and the resulting tendency of wives and concubines of Nicolaitic priests to withdraw to the monasteries. Some, however, were established in the early part of the century by nobles who were very observant in their religious devotion. In the twelfth century, a very devout epoch, twenty-five houses were founded. The thirteenth century follows with ten, the fourteenth century with three, and the fifteenth century with one. If we compare these figures with those of Puglia, in southern Italy, we find for the eleventh century five Benedictine monasteries, for the twelfth century sixteen, and for the thirteenth, twelve monasteries. The fourteenth century stands with nine and the fifteenth century with one religious house for women.

In central France, at least nineteen houses were dissolved before the year 1100. Only eighteen of the early female foundations survived. Three new communities were founded in the tenth century, and thirty-five new houses were created in the eleventh. These statistics indicate a disappearance of women's monasteries mainly in the ninth and tenth centuries and their replacement in the eleventh century by approximately the same number, thirty-five, which represents very nearly the number of female institutions existing throughout the previous five centuries.

THE ELEVENTH CENTURY

Cluny. In the eleventh century the reforms of Cluny, which followed the Benedictine Rule, came to be well known in France. Women began to clamor for their own communities, and the female monasteries that were founded in the eleventh century in France were exclusively Benedictine (whereas many that survived in the ninth and tenth centuries were canonical not only in France but also in Germany). Some religious houses had the freedom of selecting the abbess, but frequently, even if they had the liberty, the election was held in the presence of the founder or his or her family. The abbess was consecrated by the bishop, but, beginning in the mid eleventh century, the pope frequently claimed this privilege. In Italy, notwithstanding the Benedictine Rule in the earlier centuries, the king, the emperor, or a lesser founder held the right to nominate the person who could appoint an abbess. The rulers and the nobles often designated the abbots of the large male abbeys under whose jurisdiction a female monastery existed, but at other times they would propose their own male relative to govern the female house. In this manner quite a few Italian female houses were subjugated early. In France, by contrast, the female institutions established in the eleventh century set up dependencies. Only in the latter part of the eleventh century were new double houses, for example Marcigny and Molesme, headed by an abbot.

Germany. In Germany some sixty-one female houses existed in the tenth century, thirty-six of them in Saxony. In the ninth century only twenty-two were founded in this province. Female institutions were generally established by women alone or with their husbands or clerical relatives. Some fathers who lost their sons prematurely in war created them for their daughters. To be an abbess in these monasteries was coveted, with several Ottonian princesses holding this position. Some of the abbesses were appointed to the princely rank of *Reichsfürstinnen.* As such they could participate in imperial diets and approve the advocate selected for their monastery, although they could not choose him. Only with Emperor Henry II's reign in the early eleventh century did Saxon men perceive that the founding of monasteries irretrievably alienated land from them. They required, therefore, frequently by force, the marriage of noble widows and daughters. From 1070 on we do not find any new female establishments; and many existing ones were placed by bishops under the jurisdiction of reformed Benedictine male houses, which annexed their land.

NEW ORDERS OF THE TWELFTH CENTURY

The twelfth century was characterized by the creation of houses for women in the various orders.

Premonstratensians. When Norbert of Xanten founded Prémontré in 1120, he gave the monastery the Rule of St. Augustine and divided the men and women in canons and canonesses. Men and women at the Premonstratensian abbey were strictly separated; only the church was common to both. The sisters had to keep complete silence and very rigid enclosure. They were supervised by the prioress, who was responsible to the abbot, with whom she communicated through the *magister exteriorus,* always appointed by the abbot. It was he who regulated what vestments the sisters wore, what books they read, and what fasts they kept. The sisters were totally subjected to the brothers. Singing was forbidden to them; they said the offices in a low voice; and they worked in silence in making and keeping the brothers' robes in order.

This double house lasted only till 1137, and thereafter we must speak of the monastery of the Norbertines. In that year the order decided it could not keep double houses and the sisters were sent to faraway female communities, for example from Prémontré to Fontenelle. About a century later, in 1240, the order changed its attitude and established the sisters at Bonoeil. But according to the papacy the monks could not have more than twenty sisters in a monastery. The prioress was still their head, but she was often called *magistra,* to illustrate that she did not have jurisdiction. The abbot charged a prior with the government of the women's houses. The sisters were contemplatives, divided between the *sorores cantantes* and *conversae.* They could not have property and could not exit from the monastery without authorization from the abbot. Notwithstanding these rules, in 1270 a general chapter forbade the reception of sisters in the future. The female order thus died out, except in Belgium.

England. In England, Gilbert of Sempringham (*d.* 1189) organized canons and canonesses into one order. Depending on the number of canonesses, he placed not fewer than seven and not more than thirty canons in each house. The head of the monasteries, the *magister,* was named by the female house heads, the *praepositae.* The *magister* annually appointed two female members to visit the women's houses. The brothers worked outside and also did the buying and selling, but all their earnings were brought to the sisters; they could do nothing without the sisters' agreement. The male and female houses were strictly separated. The sisters could converse with the brothers through a small opening in the wall of their house, but they could not see

685

each other. There was only one church, but again the men and the women were separated by a heavy curtain.

In Italy in the thirteenth century hermits living in Tuscany, Umbria, and the Marche tended to adopt the Rule of St. Augustine; this led to the opening of numerous Augustinian female houses.

Cistercians. The first Cistercian female community was organized at Tart, in the neighborhood of Cîteaux, around 1123. After the death of the founder of this order, Stephen Harding, in 1134, the abbeys declared that there would not be any additional female monasteries within the order. But some female houses were exceptional. For example, the community of Obazine was accepted in 1147, and several female houses that were not integrated into the order were directed by neighboring Cistercian abbots. A chapter general meeting in 1213 incorporated a group of women's houses, but in 1228, 1239, and 1241 Cîteaux repeated its position of nonreception of female monasteries. The papacy kept imposing women's communities upon the order until Innocent IV renounced it in 1251. Nonetheless, people in high offices continued to request affiliation, which was often granted. Among the houses that were incorporated, most remained under diocesan jurisdiction. They were run by neighboring abbots, who assigned chaplains and furnished occasional economic assistance.

The Cistercian female houses were affiliated either under Clairvaux or Cîteaux or under the authority of a neighboring abbey. Tart had eighteen houses under her governance. The abbess of Tart visited the houses under her command annually, but ultimately she depended on the abbot of Cîteaux. One source indicates that in the thirteenth century Cîteaux had 136 and Clairveaux 75 female communities. Another cites 320 female communities for Germany, 160 for France, 90 for Spain, 100 for England, 70 for Italy, 57 for Belgium, 10 for Portugal, and 19 for Holland. There was also a house in Cyprus, one in Palestine, and one in Tripoli.

The abbot confirmed and could depose the abbess, but for other decisions he placed his will under the authority of the general chapter. He held the jurisdictional power, abbesses only the dominative. Girls younger than ten years of age could not enter the female community. The nuns were cloistered, wore white robes, could not eat any meat, and had affiliated lay brothers and sisters (*conversae* and *conversi*). Their life was spent in prayer, reading, and work. They sewed and embroidered liturgical vestments, gave instruction to girls, and transcribed manuscripts.

The Cistercian Las Huelgas was founded near Burgos in 1187 by King Alfonso VIII of Castile (1158–1214). It had an extensive organization. Six kings and queens and some thirty princes and princesses lie buried here. It was the royal monastery of 100 Cistercian nuns, and the abbess was usually a princess palatine. The third abbess of the Cistercian Las Huelgas, Doña Sancha García, arrogated to herself the powers of blessing the nuns, receiving their profession, confessing them, giving them the sacraments, preaching the Gospel, and pronouncing the act of absolution. She was condemned by Innocent III. That Sancha García claimed such powers is not surprising given that in the diocese of Astorga nine double houses were established in the tenth century. Farther to the northeast, five were founded in that century; and in the north in the eleventh century, four more were founded.

Fontevrault. The order of Fontevrault was founded by Robert d'Arbrissel between 1101 and 1115. First he settled his followers at Fontevrault in 1101, bidding the men to build an oratory and the women to consecrate themselves to prayer and contemplation. Then in 1106 Pierre II, bishop of Poitiers, placed the women's community under papal protection. Finally, in 1115, Robert gave Pétronille de Chemillé authority over Fontevrault and the neighboring male community. By this time Fontevrault had sixteen priories under her dependence; the number grew to thirty-three priories, one being in England. The women were under the Rule of St. Benedict and the men under the Rule of of St. Augustine. The abbess had full powers not only over Fontevrault but over all dependencies and over women as well as men. The novices were admitted at fourteen years; and the abbess chose the most gifted males to become priests when they reached eighteen. She had supreme say over the temporal that belonged to the order—woods, arable land, vineyards, fisheries, and mills. She was assisted by the brothers in supervising the management of properties. Although each priory had financial independence, it was responsible to the abbess, who could punish faulty administrators. Meat-eating was forbidden, even by the sick. The women had white apparel with black belts and the men wore black tunics.

686

Carthusians. The female order of the Carthusians, the Chartreusian nuns, originated at the monastery at Prébayon, in Provence. Around 1140, the nuns expressed the desire to adopt the Carthusian Rule, and Blessed John of Spain, then prior of Montrieux, modified the *Consuetudines* (Customs) to their use. Prébayon and the female communities founded up to 1260 had only a prioress governing them; the connection with the order was loose. Male visiting inspectors were sent out and a vow of obedience to the chapter general was taken by the prioress. The prioresses, though, were not represented at the chapter general; but they were assisted by the clerks assigned by the visitors. These intermediaries between the fathers and brothers acted as chaplains in the female monasteries and were charged with exterior affairs. In 1260 the clerks submitted to a prior, but this decision was not well received by the houses for women. Prébayon separated from the order, and in 1283 the order changed the name of the prior to vicar. Although in some affairs the prioress had superiority over him, the clerks and *conversi* (lay brothers) nevertheless owed obedience to him. Moreover, he was named with the prioress in the formula of profession. And he directed the conventual chapter, where his voice was the first and foremost in deliberations. He was the sole confessor, and with the prioress he gave the nuns the right to correspond with the outside world. In all other affairs the decision of the prioress prevailed, but she had to promise him obeisance. Consecration had ancient vestiges, and as a result nuns could read the Gospel at the mess and at nightly Office if they donned certain vestments or cerements. Seventeen communities were founded between 1140 and 1507. But in 1510 there remained only seven, in 1677 five, and thereafter only four.

Humiliati. The twelfth century brought to northern Italy the foundation of the order of Humiliati and Humiliatae. About 275 houses prevailed in thirteenth-century Lombardy, either double cloisters with a *praepositus* as the head or single female houses. They used mainly the Benedictine Rule. The general magister, Beltram II (1309–1317), however, ordered the sisters to take a lower position, and in 1327 Pope John XXII passed a constitution forbidding the admittance of women, giving the excuse that concubines and dishonest women were being taken into the order. In 1332 double monasteries were ordered divided; in 1344 and 1345 each *praepositus* was threatened with removal if he did not comply; by 1404 there was not a single double monastery left.

THE MENDICANT ORDERS

The two orders whose houses were called convents in Italian are the Dominicans and the Franciscans—the mendicant orders. The very first house that St. Dominic created, at Prouille in 1207, was a female institution, as was S. Damiano, established by Francis of Assisi for Clare in 1212.

Dominicans. In 1207 Dominic obtained episcopal permission to establish at Prouille in the church of Notre Dame a convent for twelve women devoted to a life of prayer. A nearby male monastery directed it. He founded thus a double monastery, reserving the spiritual direction for himself and giving temporal jurisdiction over the female convent to Guillelmine Fanjeux, prioress until her death in 1225. Dominic gave a rule, now lost, to the female community, probably in 1213. In 1215 papal protection was extended to Prouille, and in 1216 the Augustinian Rule was extended to the male convent. A papal bull in 1218 recognized Prouille as an independent community belonging to the Order of Preachers.

In 1218 the Madrid house for women was established, and the following year St. Sisto in Rome. In 1223 St. Agnes of Bologna was founded and requested St. Dominic's Rule from Prouille, but was turned down. Thus the Rule of St. Sisto, which resembled the Premonstratensian Rule, became the form of life at the second order of the Dominicans. In 1224 the chapter general held at Paris declared that the foundation of female houses was to be suspended, and this pronouncement was repeated in 1228 and 1235. Only Prouille and Madrid were able to obtain from the papacy the plan to have a prior and four brothers at their convent. The pope's policy varied on the question; Innocent IV from 1244 to 1252 gave licenses to nineteen female convents. However, in 1252 and 1253, once again the convents came under the supervision of the bishops. The situation lasted until 1267, when Clement IV withdrew the 1253 privilege of Innocent IV (which had been renewed by Alexander IV in 1259) and reconstituted the government of the sisters in the hands of the brothers. He made it somewhat easier for the priors to accommodate their program to the women's convents. They did not have to live in the monastery but could nominate chaplains who did.

In 1303 there were forty-two convents in Italy,

seventy-four in Germany, thirteen in France, eight in Spain, six in Bohemia, three in Poland, and three in Hungary. Bernard Gui spoke of two in Scandinavia; actually there were two in Sweden and one in Denmark. In England, the first Dominican female convent was founded in 1356. After the Council of Trent (1545–1563) these convents fell under the episcopal jurisdiction.

The Dominicans had also to accept Gregory IX's wish that they supervise the convents of St. Mary Magdalene, founded by the canon Rodolphe of the cathedral of St. Maurice at Hildesheim in 1225. In towns where there was not a Dominican convent, St. Mary Magdalene had to rely on the available Augustinian community.

Franciscans. The story of the Franciscan Second Order—known variously as Poor Ladies, Poor Recluses, Order of S. Damiano, the Clarisses, Order of St. Clare—was similar to that of the Dominican sisters; the friars were reluctant to care for them despite the sanctity of the nuns' lives. Clare, who lived at S. Damiano, determined to hold fast to the principles set down by St. Francis, causing such concern that Hugolino (Ugolino) was appointed cardinal protector by Honorius III in 1217. Hugolino extended a new rule to the female communities that came to be founded after S. Damiano. But Hugolino's Rule omitted two points that were essential to Clare: deepest penury and spiritual direction by the Friars Minor. When Hugolino changed his mind about spiritual direction and appointed a visitor and put the government of the Clarisses into the hands of the Minors, poverty was still not satisfied. Hugolino, promoted to Pope Gregory IX, offered property and income to all the Poor Ladies and was rejected by Clare. San Damiano obtained from Pope Gregory an order, not a bull, that the sisters might live there in absolute indigence. Hugolino's Rule, however, remained in effect until 1248 in most female houses.

Many of the communities accepting Hugolino's offer were not poor. Some convents, of course, adhered to the principle of poverty. The famous house at Prague was established by Agnes, daughter of the king of Bohemia. Another royal lady, Isabella, the sister of Louis IX of France, composed a rule for the convent she founded at Longchamps, Paris. Although it was accepted for other foundations in 1263 by Urban IV, its influence remained limited.

In the meantime, Innocent IV conceived of the plan of placing the supervision of the sisters in the hands of the brothers. All the responsibility for the sisters fell to the friars, but it came to be attacked from two sides—from the side of the brothers and also of the sisters. Finally, Urban IV together with the Franciscan minister general Bonaventure appeased the two sides. Urban approved a rule according to which the Friars Minor had to protect the Clarisses. Bonaventure let the sisters know that the brothers accepted this out of fraternal love and intervened only in convents willing to sign it. The brothers thus had only to provide spiritual direction; they were merely assistants to the cardinal protector. The 1298 bull of Boniface VIII gave the sisters all immunities enjoyed by the friars. Their chaplain was to hear confession and administer the sacraments, but he was not necessarily a Friar Minor.

By the year 1400 there were about 400 convents, of which some 250 were in Italy. The communities in France and Spain were next most numerous. In Germany there were only about twenty-five convents. England had only three houses by 1364–1365, and there is no trace of Clarisses in Scotland or Ireland. Poland, Dalmatia, and Hungary had a significant number of convents, and there were also houses in Cyprus, Crete, and Negroponte. The convents varied in size. Kraków and Naples had at least 250 nuns, but they were exceptionally large. Generally, the larger houses had between fifty and eighty members, and the smallest only three. It has been estimated that around 1400 there were about 15,000 sisters.

In the fourteenth century many houses fell short of the ideals Urban IV had set for them. Thus, the reforms of Colette Corbie (*b*. 1381 at Corbie, Picardy) became quite popular in the early fifteenth century. Indeed, by her death in 1447 she had restored seventeen monastic houses, and these came to be referred to as Colletine Poor Clares.

In Italy the preaching of Bernardino of Siena and John of Capistrano had such an effect that several female convents decided on correction and placed themselves under the oversight of the Observant Friars in the fifteenth century. A number of the Benedictine and Augustinian orders began to adopt the strict discipline of the Clarisses. In Spain, the Conceptualists founded in Galina by Beatrice were taken from the Cistercians after her death in 1495 and tied to the Rule of the Observants. In France, at about the same time, the Order of Annunciation was linked with the Observants, although it developed as an exclusively female order.

BIRGITTINES

In Sweden the double monastery, the Order of the Birgittines, was established by Birgitta (*d.* 1373). It was primarily a women's order, supplemented with monks, also under the supervision of the abbess. The first monastery that she founded was Vadstena in Sweden in 1369, and she also wrote a rule for it. The order was dedicated to honoring Mary, beloved by Christ. The abbess named the confessor, and under him were the monks. The monks and nuns lived separately but shared one church, with the monks worshiping downstairs and the nuns in the gallery. They did not sing the psalms together; the monks sang first and the nuns after. The Birgittine Order also had houses in England and Germany.

CONCLUSION

The women's orders of the Middle Ages have left us an enduring legacy—that women are capable of leading an ordered and disciplined life, not only under the leadership of monks but also by themselves or ruling over monks. The mystical writings of religious women in the Middle Ages reveal an extensive culture that was typically feminine. The manuscripts they copied, the vestments and the beautiful altar cloths they sewed and embroidered, and the lovely buildings with the works of art they commissioned are the evidence of their cultural activity. Such medieval accomplishments provide a rich background for the many female monasteries that exist today.

BIBLIOGRAPHY

Mary Bateson, "Origin and Early History of Double Monasteries," in *Transactions of the Royal Historical Society,* n.s. **13** (1899); Ursmer Berlière, *Les monastères doubles aux XIIe et XIIIe siècles* (1923); Jean de la Croix Bouton, *Les moniales cisterciennes* (1986); Otmar Decker, *Die Stellung des Predigerordens zu den Dominikanerinnen (1207–1267)* (1935); Micheline de Fontette, *Les religieuses à l'âge classique du droit canon: Recherches sur les structures juridiques des branches féminines des ordres* (1967); F. Discry, "La règle des pénitents de Ste. Marie Madeleine, d'après le manuscrit de St. Quir de Huy," in *Academie royale de Belgique, Bulletin de la Commission royale d'histoire,* **121** (1956); Lina Eckenstein, *Women Under Monasticism: Chapters of Saint-lore and Convent Life Between A.D. 500 and A.D. 1500* (1896); Ambros Erens, "Les soeurs dans l'ordre de Prémontré," in *Analecta Praemonstratensia,* **5** (1929); José María Escriva de Balaguer, *La abadesa de Las Huelgas* (1944); Penny Schine Gold, "Male/Female Cooperation: The Example of Fontevrault," in John A. Nichols and Lillian Thomas Shank, eds., *Medieval Religious Women,* I (1984); Albert Hauck, *Kirchengeschichte Deutschlands,* III, IV (1904–1920), 1,011–1,040; Stephanus Hilpisch, *Die Doppelklöster: Entstehung und Organisation* (1928), and *Aus deutschen Frauenklöstern* (1931); E. G. Krenig, "Mittelalterliche Frauenklöster nach der Konstitution von Citeaux," in *Analecta sacri ordinis cisterciensis,* 10 (1954); K. J. Leyser, *Rule and Conflict in an Early Medieval Society: Ottonian Saxony* (1979), 63–73; John Moorman, *A History of the Franciscan Order: From Its Origins to the Year 1517* (1968), 32–39, 205–215, 406–426, 548–559; John A. Nichols and Lillian Thomas Shank, eds., *Medieval Religious Women,* I (1984); Michel Parisse, *Les nonnes au moyen âge* (1983); Eileen E. Power, *Medieval English Nunneries* (1922); H. Ch. Scheeben, "Die Anfänge des zweiten Ordens des heiligen Dominikus," in *Archivum Fratrum Praedicatorum,* 2 (1932); Mary Skinner, "Benedictine Life for Women in Central France, 850–1100: A Feminist Revival," in John A. Nichols and Lillian Thomas Shank, eds., *Medieval Religious Women,* I (1984); Suzanne Fonay Wemple, *Women in Frankish Society: Marriage and the Cloister, 500 to 900* (1981), 149–188.

Suzanne Fonay Wemple

[See also **Anchorites; Angela of Foligno; Augustinism; Beguines and Beghards; Benedict of Nursia, St.; Benedictine Rule; Benedictines; Birgitta, St.; Bonaventure, St.; Brethren of the Common Life; Carthusians; Celibacy; Church, Latin: Organization; Cistercian Order; Clergy; Cluny, Order of; Devotio Moderna; Dominic, St.; Dominicans; Family, Western European; Francis of Assisi, St.; Franciscans; Hildegard of Bingen, St.; Mechthild von Magdeburg; Mendicant Orders; Monastery; Monasticism, Origins; Mysticism; Nicolaitism; Premonstratensians; Robert d'Arbrissel.**]

WOODCUT, the earliest method for the exact repetition of images, evolved in Europe around 1400, at least six centuries after it had become firmly entrenched in the Orient. There is no way to account for its rather tardy appearance in the West, other than to point out that only during the late fourteenth century were the requisite materials and crafts joined to the impulse to create multiple, standardized pictures.

The stamping of patterns from woodblocks onto textiles was a common practice during the late Middle Ages. This form of printing provided important models for exactly repeatable motifs, for the mass production of printed objects, for the division of labor in the production of images, and for the craft of preparing blocks of wood for printing. Further, the increasing supply of paper (introduced into Italy in the late thirteenth century) provided a cheap and flexible support for the new imagery. Yet, until recently the shift from abstract textile patterns to figurative motifs on paper was thought to have proceeded naturally from the increasing sophistication of the woodcutter's craft rather than from a change in attitudes and needs. The support for such a technologically based view is limited, however, to two major but isolated monuments of early printing, the so-called *Sion Printed Textile* and the *Bois Protat*.

As Hans Körner has shown, the woodcut was the ultimate development of the portable devotional object that proliferated at the end of the Middle Ages. It may now be seen as one of a number of methods of casting and stamping used in the manufacture of many fourteenth- and fifteenth-century artifacts. The early woodcut was rarely site-specific, either stylistically or iconographically, since the general subject matter tended to be regional if not pan-European. Most important, the woodcuts of 1400 to 1440 absorbed numerous stylistic and iconographic refinements that reflected the increasingly private, meditational, and mystical character of popular devotions. Only later in the century, when the cult of images had become a full-blown commercial venture, would woodcuts be associated with specific shrines or endowed with magical attributes.

The effectiveness of the first woodcuts may be attributed to their great beauty and perfection, qualities that generally were lost for the remainder of the century. Although there survive only one or two documents that mention these first efforts of about 1400 (see Hind), it is surmised that for a short time they served a fairly sophisticated clientele whose patronage would soon turn to the far more sophisticated pictorialism and detail of the engraving.

The basic problems that frustrate the researcher of the fifteenth-century woodcut are those of date, localization, and the craft-identities of the artists or artisans who designed, cut, and printed them. It is still not resolved whether the first woodcuts were designed by one hand and executed by a second. The early works that are composed of thick (one to three millimeters) swelling lines, branching curves and loops, and cascading drapery patterns typical of the International Style are incredibly unified both stylistically and technically. Art historians of

the eminence of Max J. Friedländer and Curt Glaser have argued for a single creator. Self-consciously decorative, both line and image adhere to the picture plane by avoiding sharp contrasts of color and scale, or sudden indications of depth. Single, emphatic borders often merge with the image in the same way two figures may share a common contour within the picture space. Although glass painting has often been cited as the obvious model for such compartmentalized drawing, no convincing correspondence between a surviving woodcut and a stained-glass panel has been adduced. It is also conceivable that the practice of painting in black on gold ground, generally popular in upper Germany during this period, might have provided a congenial model for the early woodcut style.

Given our uncertainties, it is impossible to decide whether an early woodcut was designed by a painter or by a more specialized craftsman, and similarly whether it was actually cut by either of them or by a trained block cutter (*Formschneider*). Certainly, design and execution were combined in the copyist workshops that flourished in Germany during the second half of the century, as Rosenthal (1925) has demonstrated; but a division of labor persisted throughout the fifteenth century, and is still seen in the collaborative printmaking from the sixteenth century down to our own day. This makes it imperative to distinguish between style and technique.

Many of the first woodcuts, such as *Christ Before Herod* (London, British Museum, Schreiber [S.] 265), *Christ on the Mount of Olives* (Paris, Bibliothèque Nationale, S. 185), or *St. Dorothy* (Munich, Graphische Sammlung, S. 1394), are sufficiently divergent in style and technique to be attributed to different workshops. One or two groups exist, however, that share a common style and/or technique. The well-known *Rest on the Flight into Egypt* (Vienna, Graphische Sammlung Albertina, S. 637), *Virgin and Child* (Vienna, Graphische Sammlung Albertina, S. 1098a), and *St. Francis and St. Louis of Toulouse* (Graz, Universitätsbibliothek, S. 1432p) suggest the existence of a long-standing workshop tradition whose changes in style, technique, and hand are all visible. Yet it has not been possible to locate this workshop convincingly in a specific town (Olmütz and Vienna are the most probable choices), nor have the specific dates of its woodcuts been agreed upon (1410–1440). Because prints, especially popular images like the woodcut, tend to satisfy eclectic tastes, they are often stylistically *retardataire*. Generally, therefore, the historian has favored technique in the admittedly risky determination of date and locale.

Nowhere is a firm correspondence between technical and stylistic criteria more evident than in the Buxheim *St. Christopher* (Manchester, John Rylands Library, S. 1349), yet nowhere is there more disagreement about the significance of the date of 1423 cut into the block itself. The dispute is crucial because this woodcut represents a marked departure from the other works of the generation between 1410 and 1430. Elements of description and narration, suggestions of a deeper space and angular motion, the presence of a thinner, more flexible line, the first signs of regularized shading, the more elaborate hand coloring, and a xylographic text all appear in the work—and for the very first time, if one accepts the date (as has virtually everyone but Schreiber and the present writer). Yet every one of these characteristics is normally associated with woodcuts of the second third of the fifteenth century (1430–1460), and corresponds to the second of Paul Kristeller's technical-stylistic divisions.

St. Christopher. German woodcut from Buxheim, 1423(?). MANCHESTER, JOHN RYLANDS LIBRARY, S. 1349

Regardless of how one views the *St. Christopher* controversy, it was during this second phase that the character and audience of the woodcut changed radically. It became a genuinely popular item, and the craving for such images was quickly satisfied by professional publishers (*Briefmaler*) who, for the most part, copied older woodcuts or contrived rather crude translations of images from other media. Since they were trained as cutters rather than as artists, the work of these *Briefmaler* was strikingly backward if not outright crude. But that very quality seems to have been the hallmark of the popular woodcut (as it would continue to be in the nineteenth-century *Images d'Épinal*). Despite their crudeness and directness, these woodcuts increasingly appropriated the trappings of painting. A growing naturalistic and expressive emphasis, a greater variety of line and complexity of hatching, all probably traced their sources to Netherlandish painting and printmaking of the period between 1430 and 1460.

Rest on the Flight into Egypt. German woodcut, before 1440. VIENNA, GRAPHISCHE SAMMLUNG ALBERTINA, S. 637

In addition, the mid-century woodcut was often enhanced with an extended range of color, given more elaborate framing lines and borders, and associated with expanding texts. A growing number of cuts were "signed" by their publishers—probably in emulation of the publishers of illustrated books. (A few of the most representative works of this phase are Schreiber numbers 98, 151ff., 267aff., 930, 1150b, 1218, 1271, 1398, 1435, 1684, and 1730m).

The third period, 1460 to 1490, was a time of enormous production throughout Europe. Because of its association with printed texts (the block book in the 1450's and the typeset book in the 1460's), the woodcut became a vehicle for an extraordinary range of imagery, even outdistancing engraving (which almost never ventured beyond the realms of religious, mythological, and ornamental subject matter). At the same time, the demand for single images burgeoned, as did the range of technical and artistic quality. From 1465 until 1485 the woodcut was rigorously formularized, especially in such centers as Ulm, Augsburg, and Basel. Thick, sometimes sinuous, sometimes angular contours played against registers of finer hatching. At best the works were remarkably clear, forceful, and even monumental, while others were marked by a wooden, sculptural quality. For the past 150 years (as of 1988) these works have been regarded as bearing the stamp of a so-called German national character. Among the most characteristic woodcuts of this period are Schreiber numbers 62a, 214, 471, 600, IX853m, 1215, 1283, 1527b, 1607, and *1676c.

Toward the end of the century in Lübeck, Mainz, Nuremberg, and Strassburg, new draftsmanly styles were adapted to the woodcuts that illustrated books. A looser, more flexible, but still disciplined hatching and cross-hatching achieved tone and modeled form, described surface textures and settings, and generally catered to a new taste for spatial and narrative complexity. Although often brightly painted, these woodcuts were increasingly able to survive without benefit of color. The woodcut had been carried to the point where it could illustrate any text or adequately reproduce any class of image save one, the work of art (painting and sculpture). But even this limitation was challenged in Nuremberg. In the workshop of Anton Koberger (1440–1513), where the young Albrecht Dürer (1471–1528) was an apprentice, the woodcut assimilated a loose, scratchy style of Franconian pen drawing. With Dürer's first mature work at the end of the 1490's, the woodcut had incorporated the language of engraving.

Although it is clear from Cennino Cennini's accounts that textile printing was widely practiced in Italy around 1400, the printing of images on paper (with the possible exception of playing cards) is singularly lacking in documentation. In this author's opinion, surviving examples cannot be dated before the second third of the century. While some scholars accept the miraculous woodcut of the *Madonna del Fuoco* (not in Schreiber; Forlì Cathedral) as a work of 1428, no modern scholar has been permitted to examine it. Stylistic and technical evidence suggest a later date (*ca.* 1450) consonant with the two very large Madonnas in London (British Museum S. 1158; Victoria and Albert Museum, S. 1058n). The only other convincing group of early Italian woodcuts that might be assigned to the midcentury are the Venetian woodcuts assembled by Erwin Rosenthal. These are characterized by their frontality and long, graceful, but uninflected vertical lines.

Another slightly later group is in the Biblioteca Classensa, Ravenna, but many of these either are German (Kristeller's "Master of the Last Supper," S. 169) or were executed by German craftsmen in Italy. Mention must also be made of the so-called *Block-book Passion* in Nuremberg (S. 34c ff.; a later version is in Berlin), a series of masterful woodcuts that combine elements of mid-century Florentine and north Italian painting. So small a percentage of the 7,000 or so woodcuts cited by Schreiber are of Italian origin that one would gather that private devotional images did not attain the popularity in Mediterranean lands that they had north of the Alps. Even the number of French woodcuts (aside from Germanic Alsace) that may be dated prior to 1480 is not more than two dozen, including a set of the *Nine Heroes* (*Neuf preux*), fragments of a Passion cycle, a set of the twelve Apostles, and a most intriguing *Virgin and Child Surrounded by the Four Elements* (S. 1945ff., 21c, 1759; the latter was not described by Schreiber).

The situation in the Netherlands was otherwise. Around the middle of the century, woodcut production of the highest rank was in evidence. Netherlandish technique generally was marked by its precision, fine scale, and pictorial subtleties. In Flanders the woodcut reached a peak of calligraphic subtlety, its thin, short strokes able to evoke the flexible drawing of a fine brush or metalpoint. In the northern Netherlands, a more angular, wooden, and less graceful technique prevailed, but it was more utilitarian and served as a long-lived style of book illustration. The most accomplished of the Flemish woodcuts (S. 1108 and S. 1039b) must be counted as far more artistically accomplished than the best mid-century German work, which, like German painting of the same period (1450–1480), was dependent on Netherlandish innovations.

The most important Netherlandish contribution to the woodcut was the block book, which was eagerly marketed and copied in Germany. The dense, neat, wooden hatching of the *Biblia pauperum* group of block books broke up the white of the page in a manner quite similar to that of type. Its mechanical regularity revolutionized German techniques just at the time (*ca.* 1460) when type-printed books were beginning to use woodcut illustrations.

Scholarship in the field of fifteenth-century woodcuts is indebted to the lifework of Wilhelm Schreiber (1855–1932), whose *Handbuch* is arranged by subject rather than by size. Schreiber's judgments about dating and localization have generally been the most reliable, although one must heed Dodgson's warning about overly ambitious specificity.

Despite all the research devoted to the early woodcut, comparisons with painting have not yielded particularly helpful results (but see Jahn and Benesch). Because there survive only five or six dozen woodcuts that are securely associated with the International Style, and virtually none of these are demonstrably derived from painted or sculptured models, our chronology has remained highly conjectural and is still being refined. It is clear, however, from a few instances of iconographic analyses, such as that of the *Coronation of the Virgin* (Munich, Graphische Sammlung, S. 729), that none of these survivors may be dated earlier than about 1400, if not a decade or so later. Until recently the manifest connections, both stylistic and thematic, with Bohemian, Austrian, and Bavarian painting of 1380 (the Trebon Master in particular) have led many scholars to assign the first surviving woodcuts to the period 1380 to 1400. But advances in paper analysis (Körner, and still unpublished studies by Piccard and Stromer) have tended to support Schreiber's original conclusions.

Virgin and Child. Flemish woodcut, after 1450. STAATLICHE MUSEEN PREUSSISCHER KULTURBESITZ, BERLIN (S. 1108)

BIBLIOGRAPHY

Otto Benesch, "Zur altösterreichischen Tafelmalerei," in *Jahrbuch der Kunsthistorischen Sammlungen in Wien,* n.s. **2** (1928); André Blum, *Les primitifs de la gravure sur bois* (1956); Cennino Cennini, *The Book of Art,* Daniel V. Thompson, Jr., ed. and trans. (1933, repr. 1954, 1960), chap. 173; Werner Cohn, *Untersuchungen zur Geschichte des deutschen Einblattholzschnitts im 2. Drittel des XV. Jahrhunderts* (1934); Campbell Dodgson, ed., *Woodcuts of the XV Century in the Department of Prints and Drawings, British Museum,* 2 vols. (1934–1935); Richard S. Field, *Fifteenth Century Woodcuts and Metalcuts from the National Gallery of Art* (1965), a catalog, and "A New Woodcut of Saint Joseph by Ludwig of Ulm," in *Cahiers de Joséphologie,* **17** (1969); Max J. Friedländer, *Der Holzschnitt* (1917, 4th ed. 1970).

Curt Glaser, *Gotische Holzschnitte* (1923); Franz M. Haberditzl, ed., *Die Einblattdrucke des XV. Jahrhunderts in der Kupferstichsammlung der Hofbibliothek zu Wien,* 2 vols. (1920); Paul Heitz, ed., *Einblattdrucke des fünfzehnten Jahrhunderts,* 100 vols. (1901–1942); Christian von Heusinger, *Studien zur oberrheinischen Buchmalerei und Graphik* (1953); Arthur M. Hind, *An Introduction to a History of Woodcut,* 2 vols. (1935, repr. 1963); Johannes Jahn, *Beiträge zur Kenntnis der ältesten Einblattdrucke* (1928); Hans Körner, *Der früheste deutsche Einblattholzschnitt* (1979); Paul Kristeller, *Kupferstich und Holzschnitt in vier Jahrhunderten,* 4th ed. (1922),

"Holzschnitte des Meisters des Abendmahls in Ravenna," in *Festschrift für Max J. Friedländer* (1927), and, as editor, *Holzschnitte im Kupferstichkabinett zu Berlin* (1915); Max Lehrs, *Holzschnitte der ersten Hälfte des XV. Jahrhunderts im Königlichen Kupferstichkabinett zu Berlin* (1908).

Paul A. Lemoisne, *Les xylographies du XIVe et du XVe siècle au Cabinet des estampes de la Bibliothèque Nationale*, 2 vols. (1927–1930); Friedrich Lippmann, *Der italienische Holzschnitt im XV. Jahrhundert* (1885), enl. and trans. by the author as *The Art of Wood-engraving in Italy in the Fifteenth Century* (1888, repr. 1969); Wilhelm Molsdorf, *Gruppierungsversuche im Bereiche des ältesten Holzschnitts* (1911) and *Beiträge zur Geschichte und Technik des ältesten Bilddrucks* (1921); Erwin Rosenthal, "Der Formschneider Casper," in *Beiträge zur Forschung, n.s.* 2 (1929), and "Two Unrecorded Italian Single Woodcuts and the Origin of Wood Engraving in Italy," in *Italia medioevale e umanistica*, 5 (1962); Giancarlo Schizzerotto, *Le incisioni quattrocentesche della Classense* (1971); Wilhelm L. Schreiber, *Handbuch der Holz- und Metallschnitte des XV. Jahrhunderts*, 8 vols. (1926–1930, repr. 1969–1976); Walter Stengel, *Holzschnitte im Kupferstichkabinett des germanischen National-Museums zu Nürnberg* (1913); Ernst Weil, *Der Ulmer Holzschnitt im 15. Jahrhundert* (1923); Martin Weinberger, *Die Formschnitte des Katharinenklosters zu Nürnberg* (1925) and "Kleine Beiträge zur Lokalisierung früher Holzschnitte," in *Mitteilungen der Gesellschaft für vervielfältigende Kunst*, 53 (1930).

RICHARD S. FIELD

[See also **Biblia Pauperum; Block Book; Bois Protat; Engraving.**]

WOOL. No single agricultural product was more important in the unfolding of the economic history of the Middle Ages than wool. Each step in the manufacture of cloth from wool gradually became the province of specialists, and by the late thirteenth century the various stages of manufacture had become quite mechanized and centralized. The Flemish towns owed their prosperity to this development.

English wools dominated the market from the twelfth through fifteenth centuries, although toward the end of this period French wool and especially Spanish merino wool became important exports in the wool trade. Sheepherding was the predominant agricultural industry in medieval England. Some episcopal lords, such as the bishop of Winchester, kept more than 15,000 sheep by the opening of the thirteenth century; by 1259 the size of the Winchester flocks had doubled. Most flocks, however, were smaller, numbering between 100 and 1,000 animals, and the smaller sheep farmers supplied most of the export demand for English wool.

Types of English wool varied with the climate and fodder available to the flocks. In the fourteenth century the best wools, those commanding the highest prices per sack, were those of the Ryeland sheep of the Welsh border and the short-haired sheep of the West Midlands. Following these in quality were the wools of the long-haired sheep of Leicestershire, Lincolnshire, and Shropshire. The wools of sheep raised in East Anglia and the southeast were classed as medium quality; the southwest produced only poor and coarse wools used primarily for home consumption.

Towns in the wool-producing areas thrived along with the fortunes and reputations of the wools they finished into cloth. Beverly, Lincoln, Stamford, and Northampton were the preeminent cloth-working towns in the thirteenth century, and produced cloth often purchased by the royal wardrobe. York, Louth, and Leicester produced cheaper cloths. The best-quality cloths were the scarlet of Lincoln, the burnet of Beverly, and the hauberget of Stamford. London's burel and the russet of Colchester and Oxford were of cheaper quality, and when purchased by the royal wardrobe were meant for distribution to the poor.

Making cloth from wool involved five operations. The raw wool was first carded and then combed by hand to remove burrs, knots, and other detritus. After carding the wool was spun into thread, usually on the distaff. The thread was then woven on a loom, which produced a loosely woven cloth. This cloth was then fulled, either by hand in a tub or in large stone vats by foot. Fulling shrank and tightened the weave, giving a greater fabric strength; it also served to compress individual fibers, imparting a smoother and softer surface. Fulling also cleaned the wool of any detritus left over from carding.

The finished cloth was then dyed. Three major dyes were used in thirteenth-century England: woad, madder, and grain. The woad plant grew naturally in England, but supplies were limited and much of the difference was imported from Picardy. Woad imparted a deep blue color. Madder also grew in England; it gave a tomato-red color, and when mixed with woad produced shades of blue ranging into purple. "Grain," imported from the Spanish and French Mediterranean littoral, was obtained from the bodies of a small insect (*Coccus ilicis*) dried in the sun. Grain was a rare and expensive dyestuff, and the scarlet color it set was a badge of high social position.

After dyeing, the cloth was cut into specific widths and lengths, these being set by law for the different qualities of cloths produced. Wrapped into bolts, the cloth was ready for sale.

BIBLIOGRAPHY

Eleanora M. Carus-Wilson, "The Woolen Industry," in M. M. Postan and E. E. Rich, eds., *The Cambridge Economic History of Europe*, II, *Trade and Industry in the Middle Ages* (1952), and "The English Cloth Industry in the Late Twelfth and Early Thirteenth Centuries" and "An Industrial Revolution of the Thirteenth Century," in her *Medieval Merchant Venturers: Collected Studies* (1954); R. A. Donkin, "Changes in the Early Middle Ages," in Henry C. Darby, ed., *A New Historical Geography of England* (1973); Walter Endrei, "Changements dans la productivité de l'industrie lainière au moyen âge," in *Annales: Économies, sociétés, civilisations*, **26** (1971); J. Geraint Jenkins, ed., *The Wool Textile Industry in Great Britain* (1972); T. H. Lloyd, *The English Wool Trade in the Middle Ages* (1977); Eileen E. Power, *The Wool Trade in English Medieval History* (1941, repr. 1965).

MICHAEL J. HODDER

[See also **Costume; Cotton; Dyes and Dyeing; Hemp; Linen; Scarlet; Silk; Textile Technology**.]

WORCESTER POLYPHONY. It is an indication of the lamentable state of preservation of medieval English polyphony that no codex is extant from about 1050 to about 1400. Unlike France, England, with its predominantly French aristocratic culture, developed no significant secular polyphonic repertoire. Polyphony was a clerical phenomenon (at first centered in monasteries, later in cathedrals and collegiate churches, and, beginning in the late fourteenth century, in court chapels) and was not preserved in libraries once a particular style was no longer fashionable. By contrast, enough French polyphony was collected in volumes presented to and kept in aristocratic libraries to provide us with reasonably comprehensive evidence. Nevertheless, how significant a role polyphonic music played in medieval England, at least from the thirteenth cen-

tury on, is indicated by the quantity of surviving scraps, flyleaves, pastedowns, stray leaves, and isolated jottings. Several of the fragmentary sources were once sizable codices, some of them numbering over 200 pages. While all of them are in more or less tattered and scattered condition, it has rightly been said that England has more sources of medieval polyphony than any other country.

The most significant source of English medieval polyphony after the Winchester Troper is the collection of leaves known as the Worcester Fragments. The so-called Worcester repertory comprises more than 100 anonymous polyphonic compositions, many of them fragmentary, roughly datable from between 1200 and 1350. It is contained in fifty-nine detached manuscript leaves, forty of which are preserved in Worcester, Cathedral Library, Add. 68. Sixteen leaves are in Oxford, Bodleian Library, Lat. lit. d. 20, and the remainder in London, British Library, Add. 25031. It seems that the leaves originated in several separate volumes, about which we have no information. Nothing definite is known about their provenance. The preservation in Worcester of so relatively large a number of leaves makes it reasonable for scholars to have assumed that most of the polyphony was written or at least used there; concordances, almost all of them somewhat younger, show that at least some of the music contained in the Worcester Fragments was also used elsewhere in England. In fact, the Worcester Fragments contain little more than a third of all completely preserved polyphonic works composed in thirteenth-century England and preserved in widely scattered sources.

While more than four-fifths of the entire Worcester repertoire is written for three voices, the ten earliest compositions are mostly two-voice settings of sequences, written in a largely note-against-note technique that is also known from other sources of the time, both Insular and Continental. A notable feature of many of the English pieces is the relative frequency of the contrapuntal interval of the third. The eighteen latest compositions, which may be dated from the first third of the fourteenth century, are not characteristic of the main corpus of the Worcester polyphony and will therefore be excluded from this discussion. Most of the main body of the Worcester music (about three-fifths) may be dated from about 1270; the remainder (thirteen pieces) can be dated from about 1280–1290. The categories of this central group are conductus and rondelli, motets on a cantus firmus, motets on a pes (with or without voice exchange), and troped chant settings (settings of a cantus firmus, itself often troped, in which the original text is elaborated, intermittently or throughout, by poetic tropes in the newly composed upper voices).

Voice exchange ("phrase exchange" might be a more appropriate term) is a medieval polyphonic technique that involves two voices of more or less equal range in the mutual alternation of phrases:

$$b\,a\,d\,c\,\ldots$$
$$a\,b\,c\,d\,\ldots$$

While it was widely practiced in the twelfth century, it is particularly characteristic of much English polyphony of the thirteenth century. *Rondellus,* a technique cultivated in thirteenth-century England, is triple voice exchange (also a piece completely composed in this manner):

$$c\,a\,b\,f\,d\,e\,\ldots$$
$$b\,c\,a\,e\,f\,d\,\ldots$$
$$a\,b\,c\,d\,e\,f\,\ldots$$

It is a procedure that, as horizontal projection of a simple harmonic scheme, depends on thirds, fifths, and octaves as constitutive intervals. An alternative technique developed by English composers of the time to apply voice exchange to the three-part texture preferred by them was to restrict it to the two upper voices and support it with a pes. The term, in this Insular context, generally denotes a strict or varied melodic ostinato, in contrast to the purely rhythmic ostinato into which continental composers fashioned their cantus firmi. Pedes were freely invented or, more rarely, borrowed from a song or dance tune. Both English conductus and English pes motets often contain sections made up of voice exchange over a pes. For example,

$$c\,b\,e\,d\,g\,f\,\ldots$$
$$b\,c\,d\,e\,f\,g\,\ldots$$
$$A\,A\,A'\,A'\,A''\,A''\,\ldots$$

There are also pes motets without voice exchange, where the repeated elements are quite long, though generally also subdivisible into variant segments.

The stylistic distinctions between conductus and motet were not so rigid in thirteenth-century England as knowledge of the French repertory might lead one to expect. The role played by the techniques of voice exchange and *rondellus* shows that the English predilection for extensive homogeneity in a composition accounts for much greater stylistic homogeneity in the repertory as a whole than is the

case in the French polyphony of the time. Homogeneity also characterizes the texts of the Worcester repertory. A large percentage of the poetry is Marian, and all the compositions set Latin texts. In England there was no parallel for the process by which the French *ars musica* early in the fourteenth century came to cultivate the polyphonic chanson, a primarily courtly species, and the Latin or French motet, a kind of university music with both ecclesiastical and courtly outlets. Not only were the composition and performance of polyphony in the hands of qualified members of the clergy, but nearly all their compositions are appropriate for divine service or special devotions, though some of the pieces may also have been produced in the hall on suitable occasions.

In the surviving English repertory of the second half of the thirteenth century most of the *rondelli,* most of the conductus with voice exchange or rondellus sections, and most of the pes motets are in F major or in a mixture of Lydian and F major. In almost every case the combined effect of the voices is the frequent reinforcement of the tonic by means of elaborations of a tonic ostinato, with the supertonic, because of its cadential function, holding a place of structural importance second only to that of the tonic. What gives much of the Worcester polyphony its characteristically English sound is the frequency of the major mode (F major, because the thirteenth-century tonal system generally caused major to be expressed as a variant of Lydian); the stress on the chords of tonic and supertonic, and the emphasis on thirds and triads; frequency of four-square phrase design; and an almost exclusive predilection for rhythms with trochaic ingredients, including the rhythmic pattern known on the Continent as the first mode. The phrase endings emphasize certain degrees of the scale and relate them to one another and to the tonic, nearly always outlining a composition with well-planned tonal unity.

The English preference for fashioning tonally unified compositions is also evident in many of the chant settings, of which the most brilliant and structurally elaborate specimens are the Alleluias, presumably to a large extent composed by W. de Wycombe (Whichbury). In many cases the cantus firmi were changed so as to yield tonally unified tenors; at times the alteration amounts to no more than one or two notes, while in other cases the changes are more extensive. Troping texts in the upper voices are usually arranged in the manner of the old troped organa; that is, they include the liturgical words of the cantus firmus, which are placed so as to permit their simultaneous declamation by all three voices. To apply motet terminology to such settings would be inappropriate, since the rigid disposition of preconceived rhythmic patterns for structural purposes is untypical of this repertory. Instead of reinforcing the concept of stratification, as embodied in the continental motet, the English uses of both polytextuality and polyphony produce a diversity that is carefully integrated to maintain the effect of organic homogeneity. It is not surprising, therefore, that cantus firmus motets constitute a very small part of the Worcester repertory. In contrast to the continental clausula motet, which is texted music, an English pes motet with its related texts gives the impression of a musical setting of poetry.

BIBLIOGRAPHY
Ernest H. Sanders, "England: From the Beginnings to c. 1540," in Frederick Sternfeld, gen. ed., *A History of Western Music,* I (1973), and "Worcester Polyphony," in *The New Grove Dictionary of Music and Musicians,* XX (1980).

ERNEST H. SANDERS

[See also **Conductus; Motet; Music, Western European; Rondellus; Winchester Troper.**]

WORMS, CONCORDAT OF, an agreement reached on 23 September 1122 between Emperor Henry V and the legates of Pope Calixtus II through the mediation of the German princes that ended the Investiture Conflict. In the imperial privilege, Henry renounced in perpetuity the right to invest bishops and abbots with the ring and crosier and accepted the canonical election and free consecration of all prelates in the empire. Calixtus conceded to Henry specifically that all elections were to occur in the emperor's presence, that is, at the imperial court. With the advice of the responsible metropolitan and his suffragans the emperor could determine the better candidate in a disputed election. Henry was to invest a German prelate with the regalia by means of a scepter prior to his consecration; in Burgundy and Italy investiture was to occur within six months of the candidate's election. The emperor thus retained considerable influence in the selection of German prelates but lost control over the Burgundian and Italian churches.

While Henry's death terminated Calixtus' concession, it was in fact perceived as a formal recognition by the papacy of existing German customs, which, unlike a privilege issued to a specific ruler, could not be revoked by a future pope. The concordat was deliberately ambiguous on a number of key points, such as the definition of the regalia and the emperor's right not to invest a prelate-elect. Both sides viewed it as an armistice rather than a definitive settlement of their differences and tried to revise it to their advantage at a more favorable moment. The practice of holding elections in the royal presence was soon abandoned, but Frederick Barbarossa reasserted his right to invest bishops. The acceptance after 1200 of the principle that confirmation rather than investiture authorized the bishop-elect to use the regalia made royal investiture less significant.

BIBLIOGRAPHY
Robert L. Benson, *The Bishop-Elect: A Study in Medieval Ecclesiastical Office* (1968); Bruno Gebhardt, *Handbuch der deutschen Geschichte,* 9th ed., Herbert Grundmann, ed., I (1970), 360–361; Adolf Hofmeister, "Das Wormser Konkordat: Zum Streit um seine Bedeutung," in Hofmeister, ed., *Forschungen und Versuche zur Geschichte des Mittelalters und der Neuzeit: Festschrift Dietrich Schäfer zum siebzigsten Geburtstag dargebracht* (1915), summarized in Geoffrey Barraclough, *Mediaeval Germany, 911–1250: Essays by German Historians,* I (1938), 98–101; Brian Tierney, ed., *The Crisis of Church and State, 1050–1300* (1964), 91–92.

JOHN B. FREED

[See also **Church, Latin; Concordat; Elections, Church; Frederick I Barbarossa; Germany; Holy Roman Empire; Investiture and Investiture Conflict.**]

WRITING MATERIALS, ISLAMIC. There are Koranic references to parchment and papyrus as being among writing materials known to the classical Mediterranean world, and both were employed by the early Muslim rulers. Muᶜawiya, the first Ummayad caliph (661–680), favored parchment, perhaps because erasures were more difficult. Papyrus was also in common use, however, and a large body of early Arabic texts, mostly from Egypt, has been preserved on papyrus. With the spread of Islam, the need for writing materials grew, for both religious and administrative purposes.

The Chinese art of papermaking was, according

to tradition, imparted to the Muslims in 751, after the conquest of Samarkand, on Islam's easternmost frontier; thereafter the manufacture and use of paper gradually spread westward. The term used for paper was *kāghad*, a Persian word derived from the Chinese *kog-dz*, and even until modern times the term *kāghadkhāna* was used in Arabic for "paper mill." Paper factories were known at Baghdad in 794, in Egypt in the 800's, at Damascus in 985, at Tripoli (Syria) in 1040, and at Ḥamā and Fēs and in Spain by the end of the twelfth century. During the tenth century parchment, papyrus, and paper were all used in the Islamic world, but by the middle of that century papyrus fell into disuse. The important paper manufactories of Europe date from the thirteenth century; thus five centuries lapsed between the introduction of this technology in the Islamic East and its adoption in Western Europe.

From the earliest days of papermaking, the Muslims produced several grades of paper. Ibn al-Nadīm, writing in tenth-century Baghdad, distinguishes a papyruslike paper (*firᶜawnī*), and *sulaymānī*, *jaᶜfarī*, *ṭalḥī*, *ṭāhirī*, and *nūḥī*, all named after famous rulers and officials of the Abbasid caliphate. Some of these terms became international trade names. Egyptians, for instance, in the Middle Ages produced a *ṭalḥī* paper, which was named for the ninth-century Abbasid governor of Khorāsān. All paper was expensive and thus was probably restricted to the ruling, administrative, and religious classes.

In time papers made in certain locales were preferred over others. Samarkand paper retained a high reputation throughout the Middle Ages; Damascus- and Ḥamā-made papers also were highly regarded. The Egyptians made paper at al-Fusṭāṭ, Fuwwa, and Fayyūm, but the Mamluk rulers of Egypt and Syria tended to use *waraq ḥāmawī* (Ḥamā-made paper) for important diplomatic and religious documents. According to the genizah documents, Syrian paper was regularly shipped to Egypt, the Red Sea ports, and India. Good-quality papers could be used as gifts to sultans or as currency.

As early as the ninth century, colored papers were in use, blue, yellow, red, olive green, and violet being popular hues. Yellow paper was favored in religious circles; it was thought to facilitate the memorization of texts. According to Ibn Bādīs, author of *The Book of the Staff of the Scribes and Implements of the Discerning*, paper was dyed after it was manufactured, rather than being colored before the pulp was put into molds.

In the Islamic world, paper was made from linen and cordage (processed flax), and the pulp was poured into molds, pressed, sized, and polished. Watermarking was unknown until the modern era, and the presence of a watermark on paper thus betrays a paper's European origin. The inks were made of lampblack, soot, tannin, vitriol, and gallnuts. Inks favored by scribes tended to be dark and heavy, and as a result paper was usually glazed before being written upon. European paper, when it came to be used in the East, was glazed after being shipped.

Pens (sing., *qalam*) were made of reeds, and Ibn Bādīs gives explicit directions for the cutting of the nibs to enhance the flow of ink. Reed pens were thought to work better than quills with thick inks and glazed paper. Scribes might own expensive writing sets (*dawā* or *dawiya*), known as early as the twelfth century, consisting of a container for reeds, an inkpot, and possibly an "inkpad" (*liq*). This implement was made of wool or flax, and, when placed in an inkwell, it facilitated the even spread of ink on writing tools.

The development of European papermaking centers in Italy in the thirteenth century and of advanced technologies enabling the production of large quantities of paper for export resulted in a flood of cheap European papers to the East in the fourteenth and fifteenth centuries. Al-Qalqashandī, the great fourteenth-century Egyptian encyclopedist, complained of their poor quality. But by the fifteenth century, Muslims were regularly using European-made paper—documents from the Ottoman chancellery dated 1402 are written on Genoese paper watermarked with a gloved hand—and in due course the local Muslim industry died out, to be restored only in modern times.

BIBLIOGRAPHY

Charles Moïse Briquet, "Le papier arabe au moyenâge et sa fabrication" and "Recherches sur les premiers papiers employés en Orient et en Occident du Xᵉ au XIVᵉ siècle," in his *Opuscula* (1955); Solomon D. Goitein, *A Mediterranean Society*, I (1967); Josef Karabaček, *Das arabische Papier* (1887); Martin Levey, "Mediaeval Arabic Bookmaking and Its Relation to Early Chemistry and Pharmacology," in *Transactions of the American Philosophical Society*, n.s. 52 (1962); Vsevolod Nikolaev, *Watermarks of the Ottoman Empire*, I: *Watermarks of the Medieval Ottoman Documents in Bulgarian Li-*

braries (1954); Johannes Pedersen, *The Arabic Book,* Robert Hillenbrand, ed., Geoffrey French, trans. (1984).

TERENCE WALZ

[See also **Ink; Manuscript Illumination, Islamic; Paper, Introduction of; Papyrus; Parchment; Watermarks.**]

WRITING MATERIALS, WESTERN EURO-PEAN. Codicological analysis of medieval manuscripts, joined with texts and pictures of scribes at work, clarifies how writing materials and technical procedures were synthesized into the modern book's immediate ancestor, the medieval codex. Since the same basic materials went into producing books and charters alike, a discussion of the former is not without value for the latter. This article offers a highly selective account of the materials on which Western medieval people wrote, what they wrote with, and how they combined materials, instruments, and techniques into the medieval codex.

Medieval writing occurs on a wide variety of materials, ranging from stone, glass, or textiles (graffiti, commemorative inscriptions, captions on tapestries) to lead or wax (tags for saints' relics, seals). Here specific function dictated the choice of material. For the more usual kind of text, the cost or unavailability of manufactured writing materials sometimes encouraged recourse to readily available natural ones. Thus the inhabitants of medieval Sweden or Russia wrote on birch bark when the document's nature did not require a more permanent and expensive material. In Visigothic Spain, Ireland, and France, various sorts of documents were scratched on pieces of slate. Wax tablets had been used extensively in classical times, and they continued to serve medieval scribes; specimens survive from the eleventh century. Such tablets were often bound together into small codices that could be held in the hand. Because they were easy to erase, wax tablets were particularly favored for writing rough drafts, current accounts, lists, and other texts that required revision.

At the outset of the Middle Ages, more permanent texts were copied on papyrus, which had to be imported, chiefly from Egypt, and on parchment. The dislocation of Mediterranean commercial networks in the upheavals of the seventh century helped drive papyrus from Western book production. Locally manufactured parchment now reigned supreme. This early medieval writing material is often thicker and stiffer than the luxury parchment produced in late antiquity, and specialists can detect some regional differences in its manufacture. For instance, parchment made in early medieval Ireland and Britain was generally polished with pumice so that the natural differences between every sheet's hair and flesh sides disappeared. In the late Middle Ages, techniques of parchment production were so perfected that the best material's thinness, whiteness, suppleness, ink retention, and durability have never been equaled.

Paper first crept into Western writing habits in eleventh-century Spain and Sicily, areas subject to Arabic influence. Early paper was imported from Mediterranean producers, but by the second half of the thirteenth century paper mills were manufacturing writing material in Fabriano, Italy, and in the next century paper challenged parchment as the dominant writing material of Western books. The nature of a writing material naturally influenced the instruments and operations by which it came to bear a text. This article focuses on parchment, since that material dominated medieval book production from the eighth to the fourteenth century.

Two types of pens seem to have prevailed among Western medieval book men and women: the classical *calamus,* made from a carved reed, and the quill pen (*penna*). The quill's nib was split down the middle. This improved ink flow and retention. The angle of the nib is thought to have influenced the appearance of the script the nib produced. A symmetrically cut nib was apt to produce a handwriting whose vertical strokes were thick and horizontal ones thin. If the nib's right half was cut shorter, the script would be fine and regular. When the left half was so treated, thick strokes alternated with hairlines. Whence the theory that ninth- and tenth-century scribes sharpened their nibs symmetrically, thereby producing the characteristics of Caroline minuscule; the Gothic nib is supposed to have had a shorter left half. Because nibs wore out quickly, scribes needed a sharp knife for frequent recutting. Pens and related instruments might be kept in a special pouch called a *calamarium.*

Early medieval scribes also made extensive use of the stylus (*graphium*), both when jotting notes on wax tablets and when working with parchment. The stylus was valued for ruling pages or sketching illustrations; it was much used for nearly invisible annotations—called drypoint—lurking in a surprising number of manuscripts. From the twelfth century, black lead increasingly replaced the stylus for these purposes, and during the thirteenth century, ink began to be more widely used for rulings.

Ink was kept in an inkstand or in hollowed horns that could be set in holes sunk into the writing table. When miniatures or texts show scribes working with two horns, one presumably contained black ink for the text, while the other would have held red ink for rubrics, titles, and critical apparatus.

Medieval copyists also utilized pumice stones and razors. With these they removed minor irregularities in their parchment before writing, or, once they had begun, erased their mistakes. The compass would seem a natural instrument for designing page layouts and illuminations on blank sheets of parchment; one is shown among scribal tools in a miniature in Codex Amiatinus (Florence, B. Laur. Amiatinus 1, fol. Vr). A straightedge and an awl were necessary for laying out the text, regardless of the instrument used to draw lines. Special wheel-like instruments may have been devised to apply line prickings. None, however, have come to light, and an awl combined with some kind of stiff parchment pattern may in fact explain the recurring irregularities observable in some line prickings. Wooden pattern boards with slots cut into them to guide the drawing of the lines were used for ruling in the late Middle Ages. They are mentioned in documents and a few specimens survive. Another instrument attested from the thirteenth century consisted of a parchment or paper wheel showing the numbers one through four, which slid up and down a string. It has been suggested that this was a place finder, by means of which a scribe could mark where he had left off copying an exemplar. Medieval illustrations depict copyists writing in books held on their laps or on lapboards. Desks with either slanted or flat tops also appear to have come into wide use.

The first step when transcribing a text in book form was to set out parchment for individual quires. Several sheets or bifolia, each the size of two folios, might be placed on top of each another to form a quire. Alternatively, one large sheet could be folded several times in such a fashion as to constitute a quire; various sequences of folds have been detected. Since the hair and flesh sides of a parchment sheet naturally look and feel different, finished quires were assembled so that one folio's hair side always faced another folio's hair side, and flesh side faced flesh. The result was an even appearance when the book was opened. This folio arrangement is named Gregory's Rule, after the nineteenth-century biblical scholar who discovered it. Isolated deviations from Gregory's Rule may indicate that the manuscript has been mutilated. However, Irish and British scriptoria and some writing centers influenced by them often ignored this rule in the centuries preceding the Norman Conquest. Typically, the quires of Western medieval manuscripts were arranged so that the outside folios displayed their hair side. Again, Insular practice sometimes went its separate way by assembling quires with the flesh sides to the outside, as in Byzantine manuscripts.

Next, the scribe had to line his parchment using, we may think, an awl, a compass, a straightedge, a stylus, black lead or ink, and sometimes, a pattern board. Tiny pinholes or prickings would be made in a few places near the parchment sheet's extremities. These master prickings were generally positioned according to geometrical formulas (whence the compass) and the special requirements of the text to be copied (such as long lines or two columns, ruling for text, glosses and other marginalia). Master prickings define and structure the writing space of each page. Line prickings were made in a vertical row or rows down the side of the sheet. Each of these tiny holes would correspond to one horizontal line on the final ruled page. Normally, the instrument that punched the master and line prickings into the top sheet of the prepared quire also perforated the sheets set under it. In this way, the same punctures would govern the overall design, measurements, and lines of the writing space on every folio of the quire. To create the page layout, the copyist aligned a straightedge with the various sets of master prickings and, applying pressure, drew a stylus along the ruler so as to leave a faint impression. Later, black lead or ink replaced the stylus. A similar procedure was followed for drawing the lines intended for the script. Use of a slotted pattern board to line the page would probably have simplified these procedures. Two characteristics of rulings executed in this manner are their absolute regularity and the absence of prickings. The finished design of the writing space is known as the ruling pattern. Codicologists describe ruling patterns by means of certain formulas developed by Léon Gilissen or by comparison with a repertory of ruling patterns, such as the one published by J. Leroy.

The process of ruling the folios of a quire might be accomplished in a number of ways, the details of which may reflect a specific scribal tradition. Thus

Early-12th-century miniature showing St. Michael surrounded by medallions illustrating aspects of the bookmaking process at the abbey of Michelsberg, near Bamberg. Note the sharpening of the goose-quill *penna* (*top left*); creasing of the parchment (*top right*); use of stylus and wax tablets (*2nd row left*); and stretching and cutting of parchment (*3rd row*). BAMBERG, STAATLICHE BIBLIOTHEK, MS MISC. PATR. 5, fol. 4

lines might be applied before folding the bifolia, as was most common in the Middle Ages, or after folding, as was customary in insular manuscripts down to the end of the ninth century. Again, ruling with a stylus might be applied to several sheets at a time or it might be applied to single sheets; it might be started from the inside or the outside sheet of the quire; it might be drawn on the hair or the flesh side of the folios. The side from which drypoint ruling was applied is usually clear from the impression, which will be concave. This process of applying the ruling is known as the ruling system and can easily be diagrammed:

In this example of a typical ruling system > represents direct application of a stylus to produce the ruling; > represents subsidiary impression of the direct application on other folios. H is the hair side, F the flesh side. This quire of eight leaves was probably ruled before the bifolia were folded. The hair side of the bifolium comprising folios 4 and 5 would have been face down on the worktable, while the hair side of the bifolium formed by folios 1 and 8 would have been on the top and facing the scribe. The ruling was then applied directly to the hair side of the top bifolium (folios 1 and 8); at the same time, the pressure of the stylus would have impressed the same ruling on the bottom bifolium (folios 4 and 5), as well as on the bifolia placed in between.

Once the quires had been assembled and lined, the scribe could begin copying. A few medieval manuscripts have survived with folios still unseparated. This proves that sometimes the text was copied onto a quire made from one large sheet, before that sheet was folded and cut, in much the same manner that modern books are printed. Very rarely, detailed written instructions guiding the scribe's work have been discovered in the manuscripts. Typically, the text itself would be copied in brown or black ink, and spaces would be left blank for chapter headings, initials, and whatever else needed to be written in red or other colors. The scribe frequently left tiny instructions for the rubricator in or around the blank space. Sometimes these annotations can still be detected, especially when, as often happened, the final rubrication was never accomplished, or when the margins were not trimmed excessively during binding.

To ensure that the binders assembled a book's component quires in the proper order, signatures or quire marks were written on the verso of the last folio of each quire. In the eleventh and twelfth centuries, catchwords increasingly replaced signatures. Here the first words of the next quire were written at the bottom of the preceding quire's last page. Pagination began to play a significant role in medieval books only in the thirteenth century.

BIBLIOGRAPHY

General works are Bernhard Bischoff, *Paläographie des römischen Altertums und des abendländischen Mittelalters* (1979), 19–64, translated by Hartmut Atzma and Jean Vezin as *Paléographie de l'antiquité romaine et du moyen âge occidental* (1985); Léon Gilissen, *Prolégomènes à la codicologie* (1977), a pioneering work of fundamental importance; James J. John, "Latin Paleography," in James M. Powell, ed., *Medieval Studies: An Introduction* (1976); Colin H. Roberts and T. C. Skeat, *The Birth of the Codex* (1983); Jacques Stiennon and Geneviève Hasenohr, *Paléographie du moyen âge* (1973), 37–163; Wilhelm Wattenbach, *Das Schriftwesen im Mittelalter*, 4th ed. (1958), 203–261. For a general description of how manuscripts were made in the early Middle Ages, see Jean Vezin, "La réalisation matérielle des manuscrits latins pendant le haut moyen âge," in *Codicologica*, II: *Éléments pour une codicologie comparée* (1978). On rulings: Léon Gilissen, "Les réglures des manuscrits," in *Scrittura e civiltà*, 5 (1981), with references to his other studies; J. Leroy, *Les types de réglure des manuscrits grecs* (1976) and "Quelques systèmes de réglure des manuscrits grecs," in Kurt Treu, ed., *Studia codicologica* (1977); E. K. Rand, "How Many Leaves at a Time?" in *Palaeographia latina*, 5 (1927).

On instruments: Jean Destrez, "L'outillage des copistes du XIIIᵉ et du XIVᵉ siècle," in Albert Lang *et al.*, eds., *Aus der Geisteswelt des Mittelalters: Festschrift Martin Grabmann*, I (1935); Michèle Dukan, "De la difficulté à reconnaitre des instruments du réglure: Planche à régler (*mastara*) et cadrepatron," in *Scriptorium*, **40** (1986); Leslie W. Jones, "Pricking Manuscripts: The Instruments and Their Significance," in *Speculum*, **21** (1946); Jean Leclercq, "Pour l'histoire du canif et de la lime," in *Scriptorium*, **26** (1972); Bruce M. Metzger, "When Did Scribes Begin to Use Writing Desks?" in F. Dölger and H. G. Beck, eds., *Akten des XI. Internationalen Byzantinistenkongresses München 1958* (1960). On scribal instructions: Léon Gilissen, "Un élément codicologique méconnu: L'indication des couleurs des lettrines jointes aux 'lettres d'attente,'" in *Paläographie*

1981: Colloquium du Comité international de paléographie, München, 15.–18. September 1981 (1982); A. Vernet, "Notes à l'usage des copistes," in *Bibliothèque de l'École des chartes*, **99** (1938). New publications in the field are reviewed systematically in the "Bulletin codicologique" published at the end of each issue of *Scriptorium*.

MICHAEL MCCORMICK

[See also **Codex; Codicology, Western European; Ink; Manuscript Books, Production of; Paper; Paleography; Papyrus; Parchment; Pecia; Prickings; Ruling; Scriptorium; Stylus; Volumen; Watermarks; Wax Tablets.**]

WULFSTAN OF WORCESTER, ST. (also spelled Wulstan, *ca.* 1008–1095), bishop of Worcester and ecclesiastical statesman. Born at Long Itchington in Warwickshire, Wulfstan was educated first at the abbeys of Evesham and Peterborough, then in the household of Brihtheath, bishop of Worcester, who ordained him priest. For a short time Wulfstan held the church of Hawkesbury in Gloucestershire. He then became a monk at Worcester Cathedral Priory, where in a uniquely English arrangement the monks performed the liturgical services in the cathedral church. In the monastery Wulfstan held a number of offices before becoming prior *ca.* 1050. As superior of the monastic community Wulfstan not only regained alienated property, reformed the finances, and raised the general level of monastic observance, he also gained a wide reputation as a preacher. At the time, the archbishop of York claimed Worcester as a suffragan see, but in 1062 the papal legates ordered the separation of the York and Worcester dioceses, affiliated Worcester to Canterbury, and, with the approval of King Edward, recommended the appointment of Wulfstan to Worcester. He was canonically elected on 29 August and consecrated bishop on 8 September 1062.

On the death of King Edward, Wulfstan supported Harold, but he accepted the Battle of Hastings as decisive and was one of the first bishops to submit to William the Conqueror, to whom thereafter Wulfstan gave his complete loyalty. Thus, he supported William in the baronial revolt of 1074 and defended Worcester Castle against the insurgents. For his loyalty, he was one of the very few Anglo-Saxon bishops retained in high office through William's reign and beyond.

As bishop Wulfstan combined the responsibilities of monastic superior and diocesan bishop. So far as was possible, he followed the monastic horarium and led a life marked by simplicity, frugality, solitude, and prayer. His chaplain, the monk Coleman, who wrote his *Life*, described him as "of middle height . . . neither lavish nor parsimonious in the choice of clothes and in his general standard of living." Wulfstan's administration witnessed the growth of the monastic community from twelve to fifty; the flourishing of scholarship, including the preparation of an important cartulary by the monk Hemming, the chronicle of Worcester, and other manuscripts; and the development of a flourishing school that served as the basis for the work of the twelfth-century chroniclers John and Florence of Worcester. Under Wulfstan, Worcester priory became an important center of Old English culture.

Wulfstan was assiduous in administering the sacrament of confirmation and was the first English ecclesiastic known to have made a systematic visitation of his diocese. As a suffragan bishop of Archbishop Lanfranc of Canterbury, Wulfstan supported the moral goals of the Gregorian reformers, giving his clergy the choice of their wives or their churches. Scholars credit Wulfstan with doing more than any other contemporary to combat chattel slavery. His sermons as bishop show not only a strong sense of pastoral responsibility but very great humanity: he taught that a Christian man should not be put to death for a small thing and God's handiwork so lightly destroyed.

Wulfstan died during the night of 19–20 January 1095 in his eighty-seventh year, a venerable memorial to an earlier age. Immediately cures were reported at his tomb, which King William Rufus covered with silver and gold. Careful records of the miracles attributed to him were kept, and in 1203 Pope Innocent III added his name to the list of saints. Wulfstan's feast day, 19 January, was popularly kept in medieval monastic houses.

BIBLIOGRAPHY

Sources. William of Malmesbury, *Vita Wulfstani,* Reginald R. Darlington, ed. (1928), trans. into English by J. H. F. Peile as *The Life of St. Wulfstan, Bishop of Worcester* (1934); D. H. Farmer, "Two Biographies by William of Malmesbury," in Thomas A. Dorey, ed., *Latin Biography* (1967).

Studies. Rosalind and Christopher Brooke, *Popular Religion in the Middle Ages* (1984); Antonio Gransden, "Cultural Transitions at Worcester in the Anglo-Norman

Period," The British Archaeological Association, Conference Transactions for 1975, in *Medieval Art and Architecture at Worcester Cathedral* (1978); David Knowles, *The Monastic Order in England*, rev. ed. (1950), 74–78, 159–163; *idem et al.*, eds., *The Heads of Religious Houses: England and Wales, 940–1216* (1972); Richard W. Southern, *Medieval Humanism* (1970).

BENNETT D. HILL

[See also **England: Anglo-Saxon; Worcester, School of.**]

WULFSTAN OF YORK (*d.* 1023) was bishop of London during 996–1002/1004; bishop of Worcester during 1002–1016; and archbishop of York during 1003–1023. Ecclesiastical statesman, homilist, and author of important treatises and law codes, Wulfstan was originally perhaps a monk of Ely or Winchester, but little certain knowledge of him survives before he became a bishop. He is representative of the late-tenth–early-eleventh-century Benedictine cultural revival associated with Sts. Dunstan, Ethelwold, and Oswald.

Wulfstan took a serious interest in the problems of government, and he may well have been a member of the royal witan (council). Between 979 and 1008, he drew up the law code that king Ethelred the Redeless (or Unready—so called because he was so ineffectual) issued to suppress lawlessness in the north. This code is considered noteworthy because it provided that twelve leading thegns in each wapentake (geographical division of the shire) should seize habitual wrongdoers and compel them to come to court; these twelve thegns have been considered by some scholars as precursors of the presentment jury established by King Henry II. Some scholars also attribute to Wulfstan the laws published by King Cnut. In his lengthy treatise, *Institutes of Polity, Civil and Ecclesiastical,* Wulfstan defined the public duties of the different classes of society, urged Cnut to govern as a Christian king, for "a Christian king is Christ's deputy in a Christian people," and promoted the assimilation of Danish and Anglo-Saxon cultures. As bishop, Wulfstan pressed the reforms begun by Dunstan and Ethelwold: parish priests should remain celibate, avoid drunkenness and fighting, and attend to their duties of preaching and administering the sacraments. Monks should live a cenobitic life according to the Rule of St. Benedict.

An able scholar and one of the best writers of

Old English, Wulfstan while at Worcester made its scriptorium a center of learning, especially in canonistic studies. His reputation, however, rests on his power as a forceful and eloquent preacher. His homilies, primarily expository instructions of the Christian faith, though some are eschatological, reflect familiarity with the ancient Latin authors, with Gregory the Great, Bede, Alcuin, and the Rule of St. Benedict. Wulfstan often wrote under the pen name of Lupus (Wolf), and in his famous homily *Sermon of the Wolf to the English* he paints a grim picture of English society in the early eleventh century, reveals the dependence of ecclesiastical officials on the king, describes the difficulties of enforcing Christian standards on the new Danish settlers, and laments how little his own efforts have brought success. Wulfstan's distinctive style has been discerned in the northern recension of the Anglo-Saxon Chronicle. He died on 28 May 1023 and was buried at Ely.

BIBLIOGRAPHY

Editions. *The Homilies of Wulfstan,* Dorothy Bethurum, ed. (1952); *Die "Institutes of Polity, Civil and Ecclesiastical,"* Karl Jost, ed. (1959), with an introduction in German; *Sermo Lupi ad Anglos,* Dorothy Whitelock, ed., 3rd ed. (1963).

Studies. Milton M. Gatch, *Preaching and Theology in Anglo-Saxon England: Aelfric and Wulfstan* (1977), with an extensive bibliography; David Knowles, *The Monastic Order in England*, rev. ed. (1950), 64; Dorothy Whitelock, "Archbishop Wulfstan, Homilist and Statesman," in *Transactions of the Royal Historical Society,* 4th ser., **24** (1942).

BENNETT D. HILL

[See also **Anglo-Saxon Literature; Ethelwold and the Benedictine Rule.**]

WUNDERER, DER. The *Wunderer* is usually classified as one of the fairy-tale medieval Dietrich epics, though all surviving versions, from the late fifteenth and early sixteenth centuries, are postmedieval. Further, one version is not an epic but a *Fastnachtspiel,* a short play performed during the pre-Lenten carnival season. Three versions of the text are in rhymed couplets. Of these, two are short fragments and the third is the *Fastnachtspiel.* The three other versions, two complete and one a fragment, are in the eight-line strophe known as the *Heunenweise* or *Hildebrandston,* a variant of the

Nibelungen strophe. The strophic versions are closely related to one another. The *Fastnachtspiel* is similar in content to the strophic versions, the differences being dictated by the dramatic form.

All three complete versions tell the following story: A beautiful princess interrupts a feast at King Etzel's court. She implores Etzel to protect her from the "Wunderer," a giant who wishes to devour her because she has refused to marry him. Etzel cannot act as her champion because his station is too high; in the strophic versions he is also a coward. Rüdinger cannot help because his station is too low. Only the youthful hero Dietrich von Bern can protect her from the monster. The "Wunderer" bursts into the hall. In the strophic versions his dogs try to attack the princess. He and Dietrich duel. After a long fight Dietrich beheads him. Amid general rejoicing the princess reveals that she is "Fraw Seld," whereupon, in the strophic versions, she vanishes.

All surviving versions of the *Wunderer* are intended for the casual entertainment of a mixed audience of the postmedieval period, as is shown by the focus upon bizarre and satirical elements. Nonetheless, its combination of historical, folkloristic, and courtly elements is similar to the late medieval literary tradition of Bavaria and Austria—a tradition that includes not only the earlier Dietrich epics but also the *Nibelungenlied*. Dietrich, whose name reflects that of Theodoric the Great, was viewed more positively by the Bavarians than by the Franks, who, historically bound to Rome, portrayed him as a dangerous Arian heretic. The story itself probably originated in Tyrolean folklore and became attached to Dietrich to refute Frankish tales that he was in league with the devil. In folklore the devil, like the "Wunderer," whose name means either "monster" or "wonder-worker," often takes the form of a wild man with a pack of dogs. Etzel and Rüdinger resemble Etzel and Rüdeger in the *Nibelungenlied*. As in the *Nibelungenlied*, the social criticism rising from the disharmony between status and character shows the influence of courtly literature. This influence is also seen in the name "Fraw Seld," a blend of "Fraw Selga," the wild maiden of Tyrolean folklore, and the allegorical "Frau Saelde" (lady luck) of Arthurian literature.

BIBLIOGRAPHY

Sources. Texts of complete versions of *Der Wunderer* include MS *H*, part of Kaspar von der Rhön's *Dresdner Heldenbuch* of 1472, in Friedrich Heinrich von der Hagen and Alois Primisser, eds., *Deutsche Gedichte des Mittelalters*, II, pt. 2, *Der Helden Buch in der Ursprache* (1825), 55–73; MS F, in Lutz Rörich, *Erzählungen des späten Mittelalters und ihr Weiterleben in Literatur und Volksdichtung bis zur Gegenwart*, II (1967), 34–38; MS B, a printed strophic version of 1503, *ibid.*, 7–25.

Studies. Helmut de Boor, *Geschichte der deutschen Literatur von den Anfängen bis zur Gegenwart*, III, *Die deutsche Literatur im späten Mittelalter: Zerfall und Neubeginn* (1962), 168–169; George T. Gillespie, "Probleme um die Dichtungen vom 'Wunderer' oder König Theoderichs Glück und Ende," in Wolfgang Harms and L. Peter Johnson, eds., *Deutsche Literatur des späten Mittelalters: Hamburger Colloquium 1973* (1975); Joachim Heinzle, *Mittelhochdeutsche Dietrichepik* (1978), 37–38, 334; Hans H. J. de Leeuwe, "Die dramatische Komposition des Fastnachtspiels vom 'Wunderer,'" in *Neophilologus*, 33 (1949); Lutz Rörich, *Erzählungen des späten Mittelalters*, II (1967), 393–407.

RUTH H. FIRESTONE

[See also **Middle High German Literature; Nibelungenlied.**]

WUZURG FRAMADĀR, Sasanian title meaning "great commander" in Middle Persian (written *RBA plmt'l*; as a Hephthalite title, *OAZOPKO PHPOMALAPO*; in Armenian transcription, *vzurk hramatar*). *Framadār* (commander, equivalent to Greek *epitropos*) seems to have been the title of the royal steward under the Achaemenians and Parthians. But under Bahrām V Gōr (420–438) the title, with the epithet *wuzurg* added, replaced the office of the *hazārabad*, and a wealthy landowner and nobleman of Arsacid descent, Mihrnerseh, was appointed to the post. The latter figures prominently in the Armenian *History of Vardan* by Ełišē, and has left an inscription at Fīrūzābād to commemorate an act of civic piety: his construction of a bridge. Xusrō I replaced the office of *wuzurg framadār* with four *spāhbad*s, perhaps because the concentration of power in the hands of the prime minister threatened the monarchy.

BIBLIOGRAPHY

Cambridge History of Iran, III (1983); Theodor Nöldeke, trans., *Geschichte der Perser und Araber zur Zeit der Sasaniden: Aus der arabischen Chronik des Tabari übersetzt und mit ausführlichen Erläuterungen und Ergänzungen versehen* (1879, repr. 1973), 109–111; Henrik S. Nyberg, *A Manual of Pahlavi*, I (1964), 125; Eruand Ter-Minasean, ed., *Ełishei: Vasn Vardanay ew Hayoc^C*

Paterazmin (1957); Robert W. Thomson, trans., *Elishē: History of Vardan and the Armenian War* (1982).

JAMES R. RUSSELL

[See also **Arsacids; Bahrām V Gōr; Ełišē; Hazārabad; Parthians; Sasanian Culture; Sasanian History; Spāhbad; Xusro I Anōšarwan.**]

WYCLIF, JOHN (*ca.* 1335/1338–1384). The date and place of John Wyclif's birth are uncertain; from the fact that he graduated as bachelor of arts at Merton College, Oxford, by 1356 it may be assumed that he was born not later than 1335/1338. Though it may be reasonable to conclude that he came from Yorkshire, attempts to make him a member of the family of Wycliffe at the village of that name near Richmond in the North Riding must be regarded as unproven. In May 1360, Wyclif is recorded as Master of Balliol, a post he vacated a year or so later. He was presented to the living of Fillingham, Lincolnshire, in 1361; he may have resided there for a while but, as with his later holdings, seems to have been absent for most of the time.

In 1363, Wyclif was granted a license to study theology at Oxford for a year; a similar license was granted in 1368 for two years. He rented a room at Queen's College in 1363–1364 and again in 1364–1365. In December 1365 he was appointed warden of Canterbury College by Archbishop Simon Islip. Early in 1367 he lost this position, following the decision of Islip's successor, Simon Langham, that the college should again be only for Benedictines; it was not, however, until the failure of his appeal to Rome in 1370 that Wyclif was ejected. In 1362 Wyclif had been granted a canonry at Westbury-on-Trym, Gloucestershire, with the prebendary of Aust; despite some troubles, it seems clear that he held this until his death. He was also presented to the rectory of Ludgershall, Buckinghamshire, in 1368, a post he did not vacate until death. In 1371 he was provided to a canonry of Lincoln, but the promised prebend never materialized. In 1374 the king presented him to the rectory of Lutterworth, Leicestershire, to which living he retired from Oxford in 1381. Despite these various livings, it is clear that for the majority of the years between 1356 and 1381 Wyclif lived mainly in Oxford. He gained eminence as a teacher of philosophy in the 1360's; by 1371 he had begun to lecture on theol-

ogy, and incepted as a doctor in the subject the following academic year.

Wyclif seems to have entered the political field in 1371. He was present at the parliament that year when two Austin friars argued that it was legitimate in times of emergency for the secular authorities to seize the property of the church, property given in the first place by laymen and now resumed for the preservation of the commonwealth. This argument was used to justify the levying of a heavy tax on the clergy, a tax that grudgingly was largely admitted later by convocation. Wyclif joined in the controversy, apparently at the instigation either of John of Gaunt or of the Black Prince, against the claims of the established church and of Rome, and began to develop the ideas about dominion that first brought him under censure. In 1374 he was sent to Bruges as a representative of the English king to assist in negotiations with the papal nuncios about financial affairs; the negotiations, for only six weeks of which Wyclif was present, were not particularly successful. In 1376 he was employed by John of Gaunt, partly in the latter's campaign against William Wykeham and the actions of the Good Parliament. An attempt by Bishop William Courtenay of London to cite Wyclif before the archbishop's court in Februrary 1377 was frustrated by the disorder of the London crowd, disorder apparently not connected directly with Wyclif.

In 1377 Pope Gregory XI issued a list of eighteen erroneous conclusions of Wyclif and called for his arrest and examination; the pope's actions seems to have been provoked by Benedictine opponents of Wyclif. Various attempts to produce a condemnation in England in 1378 failed, in part apparently because of the protection afforded by Joan, the widow of the Black Prince and mother of Richard II. In October 1378 Wyclif appeared before parliament in defense of a breach of sanctuary by soldiers at Westminster Abbey, an episode referred to in the *De ecclesia*. In 1380 a narrow majority of a commission in Oxford pronounced Wyclif's teaching on the Eucharist heretical. The following year Wyclif retired to Lutterworth, where he continued writing.

In May 1382 Archbishop William Courtenay summoned a council at Blackfriars, London; the council was marked by an earthquake in the capital, an event seen as significant by both Wyclif and his opponents, and one that gave rise to the common description of the meeting as the Earthquake Council. There, twenty-four of Wyclif's conclusions were condemned as heresies or errors, and demands were made that some of Wyclif's followers recant. Wyclif himself was, however, allowed to continue in his living at Lutterworth and no moves were made to excommunicate him. He continued writing despite worsening health following a stroke in November 1382; he suffered a second stroke on 28 December 1384 and died on 31 December. Despite frequent condemnations after his death, culminating in the execrations and listing of heresies at the Council of Constance in 1415, it was not until 1428 that his body was exhumed and burnt, and the ashes thrown into the river Swift.

Wyclif's prolific writing falls into two categories: texts on philosophical questions and texts on theological and ecclesiastical matters, with many connections from the first group to the second. The purely philosophical writings all seen to have been written before 1371. Of the 132 separate works that can reasonably be assigned to Wyclif, considerably fewer than half survive in mansucripts written and preserved in England; for the remainder we are dependent upon copies made on the Continent, mostly in the area of Hussite influence. Wyclif's philosophical ideas were familiar in Prague by 1380; his teaching was taken up, though with modifications, by John Hus, and his writings circulated within the Hussite movement through the first half of the fifteenth century. S. Harrison Thomson suggested an order for the early philosophical writings; it is likely that some works from this period have been lost, and possible that the surviving form of others may incorporate revisions made by Wyclif later in his life. A short *Sumula sumulorum magistri Johannis Wiclif* has been identified in a manuscript now in the Houghton Library, Harvard University; it is an elementary summary of certain logical propositions.

The attitude taken by Wyclif in these philosophical writings, perhaps after a youthful flirtation with terminism, was one of extreme realism. For Wyclif, anything exists only insofar as it partakes of the *esse intelligibile* that is in God. Equally, since it must be supposed that God knows everything possible, the possible (and hence the conceivable) must have reality; as such they cannot be annihilated. If being is, then, necessary and eternal, it must be indestructible. Thus, all creatures are linked in an indissoluble chain to God and, hence, to each other. If one being could be destroyed, this would entail the destruction of all—and of God, a conclusion both impossible and blasphemous. In all its impli-

cations and complexities it is clear that Wyclif's philosophy incorporates eclectic elements that need further analysis.

Wyclif's theological writings are more numerous and more diverse in form. From an early date (between *ca.* 1370/1371 and 1375/1376) comes his commentary on the entire Bible, *Postilla super totam bibliam,* pieced together by Beryl Smalley from a number of manuscripts whose ascriptions either are defaced or had been ignored; some of the parts—on the Pentateuch, the historical and apocryphal books of the Old Testament, and the book of Proverbs—have not yet been found. Early critics assembled a *Summa theologiae* in twelve books; though this grouping covers some, but not all, of the most important of Wyclif's theological writings, it is plain that the collection was not conceived by its author as a whole and that its components were written at various dates. It is a grouping better abandoned.

Wyclif wrote extensively on law, both divine and human, in *De dominio divino* (an early work), *De mandatis divinis* (1373/1374), *De statu innocenciae* (1373/1374) and *De civili dominio* (1376–1378). In these he developed the theory of dominion that featured in the earliest condemnations. Taking ideas from Marsilius of Padua, and more particularly from Richard Fitz-Ralph, Wyclif propounded the idea that only a man in a state of righteouness can properly exercise authority, whether over inanimate or animate nature. The practical deduction from this view was that authority did not automatically inhere in any office—the clergy, and even the pope, could not claim jurisdiction solely because of their occupancy of positions held by the early apostles; properly, they could do so only if they were truly righteous. Though this theory was capable of application to both secular and ecclesiastical authority, Wyclif purused its implications more fully with regard to the latter.

On its own the idea was largely theoretical, especially since Wyclif admitted that only God could correctly assess any man's righteousness. But at the time of the Great Schism few would have claimed that any of the contenders for the papal throne could have been regarded as "the most righteous man on earth" and, hence, the "true pope." Wyclif himself at times drew back from the logical conclusions of his own theory, acknowledging the chaos that would ensue, but he constantly used it as a weapon against aspects of the contemporary church that he disliked.

Of more immediately practical application was Wyclif's associated view on the nature of the church. Wyclif took Augustine's distinction between the heavenly and earthly cities to its logical conclusion: all men were divided into those predestined for the heavenly city and those foreknown to damnation; this distinction was eternally established by God, and affected the present life as well as the life to come. Only those predestined to salvation were properly members of the church: the church was the *congregatio omnium predestinatorum*. This idea is found in *De civili dominio* and was more fully developed in *De ecclesia* (1378/1379); it underlies all Wyclif's subsequent writings.

The actual church, with the pope as its head and the clergy as its ministers, bore only an accidental, temporary relationship to this true church: membership in the actual church could not, even—or perhaps especially—among the hierarchy, be regarded as any indication of membership of the true church. Obedience to the edicts or officials of the actual church was not obligatory unless these edicts conformed to the will of God and its officials were members of the true church. A member of the true church was, by virtue of that membership, nearer to God than any other person, even the pope. Here Wyclif came near to denying the need for ordination to the priesthood and to espousing the concept of the priesthood of all believers, a concept further developed by his followers.

Criticism of the abuses in the contemporary church arose here, as Gordon Leff has argued, not from an awareness of individual failings but from a radically different concept of the nature of the church. Wyclif admitted that only God could discern the predestined from the reprobate, but this human ignorance did not invalidate certain corollaries of the view. Only the predestined could properly receive absolution for sin; therefore the absolution of the actual church was merely confirmatory if in accord with God's judgment, and was blasphemous if it departed from that judgment. Excommunication, the church's final refusal to grant absolution, was subject to the same proviso.

Coupled with these originally theoretical positions was Wyclif's insistence upon the Bible as the sole and ultimate source of Christian doctrine. His *De veritate sacrae Scripturae* (1378) examined this question and took further the attitudes to the Bible found in his scriptural commentary. Though Wyclif by no means rejected the writings of the Fathers (his quotations from Augustine especially are legion),

the Bible was the final arbiter; patristic writers, canon law, and the Scholastics were valid only insofar as they conformed to Scripture. This did not entail a narrow literalism: Wyclif was well aware that Scripture contained different levels of truth, and that at places allegory was built at into its structure. But, along with the definition of the church, it meant that the Bible could serve as a touchstone for all aspects of the contemporary ecclesiastical world.

Insofar as the life of the clergy did not conform to the life of Christ and the early apostles, it stood condemned; every practice of the fourteenth-century church that had no counterpart in the Gospels or Epistles was redundant. The chief casualty of such a view was the temporal and political claim of the church: there could be no justification for the wealth of the clergy, for their claims to exemption from various forms of secular jurisdiction, for their existence as a separate estate of the realm. From an early stage of his teaching Wyclif had condemned the monastic life, not just because of the departure of contemporary monks from the ideals of their founders, but because of their misunderstanding of the biblical model inherent in those ideals. At first the friars escaped Wyclif's condemnation to some extent, but after 1380 they, too, were brought under a general anathema on all forms of "private religion," that is, any form of religious life that separated the individual from the ordinary life of the church, a separation for which Wyclif could find no justification in Scripture. Other aspects of contemporary piety fell under the same condemnation: the worship of images, pilgrimages, pardons and indulgences, prayers for the dead.

The subject, however, that produced the final condemnation of Wyclif by the authorities was the Eucharist. It appears that Wyclif's views on the major sacrament of the church had been unsettled for some time during the 1370's. His teaching seems first to have been formulated in 1379 and is found in the *De eucharistia* and in many later works. The condemnation of 1382 identifies the main points in Wyclif's argument: "that the substance of material bread and wine remains after the consecration in the sacrament of the altar," "that accidents do not remain without a subject after the consecration in the same sacrament," and "that Christ is not in the sacrament of the altar identically, truly, and really in his bodily person."

The first of these statements involves a denial of the contemporary doctrine of transubstantiation, the second disagrees with one explanation of this doctrine (that while the accidents of color, texture, taste, and dimension in the bread and wine remain identical after the words of consecration, the subject or reality of bread and wine is displaced by the body and blood of Christ), and the third departs from the view that this new subject is to be identified with Christ's corporeal body, born of Mary and now in heaven. In supporting his views, Wyclif relied mainly upon two arguments: first, the evidence of biblical proof texts, from which later writers developed their opinions and to which they and liturgical practice must be subordinated; second, the realist philosophy holding that the essence of matter was indestructible and that the alteration proposed by transubstantiation was therefore impossible. By the time Wyclif propounded these views, the doctrine of the Eucharist had been too closely defined to admit this radical reinterpretation without upheaval. The teaching alienated the friars and eventually led to the opposition of the university of Oxford, both hitherto defenders of Wyclif against the intrusion of episcopal scrutiny. In all condemnations of Wyclif from 1382 on, the Eucharistic teaching figures most largely.

After his withdrawal to Lutterworth in 1381, Wyclif continued to write prolifically. As well as a vast number of short polemical tracts on all aspects of the contemporary church, he put together three sets of sermons: on the dominical Gospels, on the dominical Epistles, and on the Gospels for the *commune sanctorum* and for feasts of major named saints. A few of his sermons from an earlier period, known as the *Sermones quadraginta,* remain; the three sets, while possibly drawing on earlier delivered versions, were composed in sequence. Most of the views already described appear frequently, along with an increasing concern with the need for preaching to the laity.

Also from the final years of his life is the *Trialogus,* a relatively brief, and consequently tendentious, account of his views on many topics. The importance that Wyclif attached to the Bible, and the respect in which he held Augustine and (pseudo-) Chrysostom, are revealed in the last work he wrote, the *Opus evangelicum,* completed, as one scribe explained, along with his life. This is a commentary on Matthew 5–7 and 23–25, and John 13–17, using extensive quotations from these two patristic sources.

Apart from the formal lists of condemned conclusions, criticisms of Wyclif's ideas began early. A number of texts survive showing Wyclif's arguments within the university; in some cases, as with Friar John Kynyngham (or Kenningham), both sides of the discussion are still extant. The same is true of the later argument between William Rymington and Wyclif. In other instances—for example, the disagreements with Ralph Strode and with William Binham—only Wyclif's side is preserved. The discussion with William Woodford seems to have begun as a friendly argument, but later Woodford became an implacable opponent and one of the first to analyze systematically and refute Wyclif's views.

Despite the condemnation of 1382 and the edicts that ensued, Wyclif's opinions continued for some time to attract interest and even support. Oxford university was persuaded to reject Wyclif's views soon after the Blackfriars Council; Philip Repingdon, one of Wyclif's closest Oxford disciples, recanted the same year, and friends such as the chancellor Robert Rygge gave open support no longer. But the number of both ecclesiastical and secular edicts, and the evidence, direct and indirect, of texts show that this reassertion of orthodoxy was not altogether easy.

The culmination of a series of proclamations and inquiries was the introduction in 1401 of the death penalty for heresy, in the act *De heretico comburendo.* A few years later the Constitutions of Archbishop Thomas Arundel (initiated in 1407 and promulgated in 1409) attempted to control the academic discussion further: discussion of controversial issues such as transubstantiation was curtailed, preachers and teachers had to be licensed rigorously, the views of Oxford students were to be investigated regularly, the ownership of books by Wyclif and of recent biblical translations was forbidden. The revolt of Sir John Oldcastle, an adherent of Wycliffite views, in 1413–1414 brought a further spate of refutations. Most notable among these was the enormously long, though uncompleted, *Doctrinale* of Thomas Netter, composed with papal and royal encouragement between 1421 and 1427.

Much scholarship has been devoted in recent years to assessing the sources of Wyclif's ideas and the influence of his thought on the later Reformation. Apart from the Bible, Wyclif acknowledged Augustine, Gregory, and Grosseteste as his especial masters. He cited a wide range of patristic and later writers; though some of these doubtless reached him indirectly, or in summary or florilegia, it is clear that his reading in *originalia* was wide. Certainly important, though rarely alluded to by Wyclif, was Richard FitzRalph, who helped to form Wyclif's views about dominion and, later, about the friars. Early opponents mentioned John of Jandun, Marsilius of Padua, Egidius Colonna, Berengar of Tours, William of St. Amour, and William of Ockham as Wyclif's teachers.

It is clear that Wyclif was well versed in canon law: despite his virulent criticism of its practitioners, he often used passages from canon law to support his own case. It is equally evident that Wyclif gathered up a number of views current at the time whose paternity is hardly ascertainable. His desire for the disendowment of the church can be found independently in the demands of the 1371 parliament. Involved in his eucharistic views was an element of materialistic skepticism discernible elsewhere in the late fourteenth century, and also a desire to shift the discussion from the arid technicalities of metaphysics to a more spiritual level—a desire visible in devotional writers of the time far removed from Wyclif's intellectual milieu.

Wyclif's appeal to many of his time resulted in large measure from this attunement with contemporary attitudes; in many cases he merely took current ideas to their logical conclusions. From the testimony of foes as well as of friends, it is evident that he was a compelling teacher, the only first-rate philosopher of his generation at Oxford, and a persuasive theologian. The modern reader of his polemical and often repetitive writings finds this magnetism hard to credit, but it is plain that Wyclif could attract the scholars of his time as no one else could.

Whether Wyclif himself instigated the translation of the Bible into English, a translation that became known as the *Wycliffite Bible,* is unclear. Though his stress on the availability of Scripture to the laity may have been the inspiration for the versions, it seems on balance improbable that Wyclif took part in the immense labors of the actual translation and its revisions. [See entry on Lollards.]

Wyclif's influence upon later reforming movements is difficult to measure. Certainly his writings affected Hus and his followers in a major way: large sections of Wyclif's works are quoted by Hus, the copying of Wyclif's works was rife in Hussite Bohemia, the Hussites were often known as *Wyclifistae,* and Wyclif himself was named in Bohemia as the "fifth Evangelist" (his Latin byname had been Doctor Evangelicus). Hus did not share all of Wyclif's heretical views, notably those about the

Eucharist; conversely, one of the most characteristic Hussite views, utraquism, cannot be found in Wyclif. Through Hus, some of Wyclif's ideas came to the notice of Luther and other sixteenth-century reformers.

In England the main channel of influence was the Lollard movement. By the end of the fifteenth century it was hard to come by copies of Wyclif's own writings in England (none of the vernacular writings that echo his views can safely be regarded as composed by the heresiarch); episcopal suppression had been fairly effective. The *Trialogus* was printed, probably at Basel, in 1525, but none of the works was printed by an English press before the Reformation. Transmission of Wyclif's ideas to the early reformers in England seems to have come through two channels: from Hus and the Hussite movement to the continental reformers and thence back to England, or through popularization in the vernacular works by the Lollards. In these latter, Wyclif's ideas had certainly suffered a coarsening and radicalization. But one strand of the master's thought came through clearly: the fundamental nature of the Bible, the need for all to know and understand the biblical message, and the necessity to measure the contemporary church against that source.

BIBLIOGRAPHY
Sources. The majority of Wyclif's Latin writings were edited by various scholars for the Wyclif Society between 1883 and 1922. To these the following should be added: *De officio pastoralis,* Gotthard V. Lechler, ed. (1863); *Trialogus,* Gotthard V. Lechler, ed. (1869); S. Harrison Thomson, "Three Unprinted Opuscula of John Wyclif," in *Speculum,* 3 (1928), and "A 'Lost' Chapter of Wyclif's *Summa de Ente,*" in *Speculum,* 4 (1929); *Summa de ente,* S. Harrison Thomson, ed. (1930); S. Harrison Thomson, "John Wyclif's 'Lost' *De fide sacramentorum,*" in *Journal of Theological Studies,* 33 (1932); I. H. Stein, "The Latin Text of Wyclif's *Complaint,*" in *Speculum,* 7 (1932), "The Vatican Manuscript Borghese 29 and the Tractate *De versuciis Anti-Christi,*" in *English Historical Review,* 47 (1932), "Another 'Lost' Chapter of Wyclif's *summa de ente,*" in *Speculum,* 8 (1933), and "An Unpublished Fragment of Wyclif's *Confessio,*" *ibid.; Tractatus de Trinitate,* Allen D. Breck, ed. (1962).

A list of Wyclif's works is given, together with much information concerning date and manuscripts, in Williel R. Thomson, *The Latin Writings of John Wyclyf: An Annotated Catalog* (1983); this supersedes earlier lists. *Studies.* Lives include Joseph H. Dahmus, *The Prosecution of John Wyclyf* (1952); Alfred B. Emden, *A Biographical Register of the University of Oxford to*

A.D. 1500, III (1959), with a full survey of earlier literature; Kenneth B. McFarlane, *John Wycliffe and the Beginnings of English Nonconformity* (1952), reissued as *The Origins of Religious Dissent* (1966); Herbert Workman, *John Wyclif,* 2 vols. (1926, repr. 1 vol. 1966).

Other studies include Gustav A. Benrath, *Wyclifs Bibelkommentar* (1966); William R. Cook, "John Wyclif and Hussite Theology 1415–1436," in *Church History,* **42** (1973); James Crompton, "John Wyclif: A Study in Mythology," in *Transactions of the Leicestershire Archaeological and Historical Society,* **42** (1966–1967); Joseph H. Dahmus, "John Wyclif and the English Government," in *Speculum,* **35** (1960); Lowrie J. Daly, *The Political Theory of John Wyclif* (1962); William Farr, *John Wyclif as Legal Reformer* (1974); Aubrey Gwynn, *The English Austin Friars in the Time of Wyclif* (1940); T. J. Hanrahan, "John Wyclif's Political Activity," in *Medieval Studies,* **20** (1958); M. Hurley, "*Scriptura sola:* Wyclif and His Critics," in *Traditio,* **16** (1960); Robert Kalivoda, "Johannes Wyclifs Metaphysik des extremen Realismus und ihre Bedeutung im Endstadium der mittelalterlichen Philosophie," in *Miscellanea mediaevalia,* **2** (1963); Howard Kaminsky, "Wyclifism as Ideology of Revolution," in *Church History,* **32** (1963), and *A History of the Hussite Revolution* (1967); Malcolm D. Lambert, *Medieval Heresy: Popular Movements from Bogomil to Hus* (1977), 217–271; Gordon Leff, "John Wyclif: The Path to Dissent," in *Proceedings of the British Academy,* **52** (1966), and *Heresey in the Later Middle Ages,* II (1967), 494–558; A. K. McHardy, "John Wycliffe's Mission to Bruges: A Financial Footnote," in *Journal of Theological Studies,* n.s. **24** (1973); W. Mallard, "John Wyclif and the Tradition of Biblical Authority," in *Church History,* **30** (1961), and "Dating the *Sermones quadraginta* of John Wyclif," in *Medievalia et humanistica,* **17** (1966).

A. Minnis, "'Authorial Intention' and 'Literal Sense' in the Exegetical Theories of Richard FitzRalph and John Wyclif: An Essay in the Medieval History of Biblical Hermeneutics," in *Proceedings of the Royal Irish Academy,* **75**, sec. C, no. 1 (1975); V. Murdoch, "John Wyclif and Richard Flemyng, Bishop of Lincoln: Gleanings from German Sources," in *Bulletin of the Institute of Historical Research,* **37** (1964); W. A. Pantin, "A Benedictine Opponent of John Wyclif," in *English Historical Review,* **43** (1928); John A. Robson, *Wyclif and the Oxford Schools* (1961); František Šmahel, "'Doctor Evangelicus super omnes evangelistas': Wyclif's Fortune in Hussite Bohemia," in *Bulletin of the Institute of Historical Research,* **43** (1970); Beryl Smalley, "John Wyclif's *Postilla super totam Bibliam,*" in *Bodleian Library Record,* **4** (1953), "The Bible and Eternity: John Wyclif's Dilemma," in *Journal of the Warburg and Courtauld Institutes,* **27** (1964), and "Wyclif's *Postilla* on the Old Testament and His *Principium,*" in Oxford Historical Society, *Oxford Studies Presented to Daniel Callus* (1964); Edith C. Tatnall, "John Wyclif and *Ecclesia*

Anglicana," in *Journal of Ecclesiastical History,* **20** (1969); S. Harrison Thomson, "The Order of Writing of Wyclif's Philosophical Works," in *Českou Minulostí, práce venované profesoru Karlovy University Václavu Novotnému* (1929), and "The Philosophical Basis of Wyclif's Theology," in *Journal of Religion,* **11** (1931); Michael J. Wilks, "The *Apostolicus* and the Bishop of Rome," in *Journal of Theological Studies,* n.s. **13** (1962) and **14** (1963), "Predestination, Property, and Power: Wyclif's Theory of Dominion and Grace," *ibid.,* (1965), "The Early Oxford Wyclif: Papalist or Nominalist?" in G. J. Cuming, ed., *The Church and Academic Learning* (1969), and "*Reformatio regni*: Wyclif and Hus as Leaders of Religious Protest Movements," in Derek Baker, ed., *Schism, Heresy, and Religious Protest* (1972).

Addenda: The above list was prepared in 1980. The sexcentenary of Wyclif's death in 1984 prompted a number of publications, of which the most important are:

Editions. Ivan J. Mueller, ed., *Tractatus de universalibus,* Anthony Kenny, trans. (1985); Paul V. Spade and Gordon A. Wilson, eds., *Summa insolubilium* (1986).

Studies. Anne Hudson and Michael Wilks, eds., *From Ockham to Wyclif* (Studies in Church History Subsidia, 5) (1987); Anthony Kenny, *Wyclif* (1985), and, as ed., *Wyclif in His Times* (1986).

ANNE HUDSON

[See also **Church, Latin: 1305–1500; Councils, Western (1311–1449); Ecclesiology; England (1216–1485); Heresies, Western European; Hus, John; Lollards; Marsilius of Padua; Oxford University.**]

YNFORD, WILLIAM (*fl.* 1360–1405), English master mason and architect, is one of the best-documented men of his profession in the medieval period. His career and major works generally involved one of two patrons, the king or William of Wykeham (1324–1404). He is first recorded at Windsor Castle in 1360 during Wykeham's clerkship of the works as warden of the masons and soon became the director or "disposer." After Wykeham became provost of Wells Cathedral, Wynford was the master mason from 1364/1365 till his death in 1405. He designed the west towers and built the south one. Among other jobs for Wykeham he built New College, Oxford, from 1379/1380 and Winchester College from 1387. From 1394 he completed the inchoate remodeling of Winchester Cathedral's nave. For the king he worked abroad in 1370, at Corfe Castle 1377/1378, at Southampton Castle 1378/1379, at Winchester Castle 1389–1403, and elsewhere. From 1371 till his death he received a royal pension, probably as a retaining fee.

BIBLIOGRAPHY

Howard M. Colvin, *The History of the King's Works*, I, II (1963); John H. Harvey, *English Medieval Architects: A Biographical Dictionary Down to 1550* (1954), 307–310.

               BARRIE SINGLETON

[See also **Architect, Status of; Masons and Builders; William of Wykeham.**]

WYNKYN DE WORDE (*d.* 1534/1535), from Wörth in the duchy of Lorraine, was William Caxton's assistant at Westminster by at least 1479. At Caxton's death early in 1492, de Worde took over his old shop near the chapter house, received denization papers in 1496, and printed there until late 1500, when he moved to the Sign of the Sun in Fleet Street, London. By 1509 de Worde also had a shop in St. Paul's churchyard at the Sign of Our Lady of Pity. De Worde, the most important English printer of his age, published over 700 books, mostly inexpensive quartos of devotional works, practical manuals, dictionaries, Latin grammars, sermons, almanacs, romances, and satirical poems and plays. Caxton himself had translated large folios, often of continental chivalric literature for an elite audience, but de Worde's tastes after 1500 were inclined to be more popular and insular, and he sought out contemporary English authors like Robert Copland, Stephen Hawes, Henry Watson, and Alexander Barclay.

De Worde's assets were valued at over 200 pounds in 1523–1524, three times that of his nearest competitor, Richard Pynson, the king's printer. Aside from Margaret Beaufort, Henry VII's mother (to whom de Worde was printer irregularly from 1494 to 1509), his patrons were generally churchmen, not nobles. He has been called a primitive mechanic, but he printed some fine folios, made authors such as Erasmus widely available, introduced Greek, italic, and music types into England, and consistently exercised over his texts a remarkable editorial control that modernized and simplified archaic English. His books were illustrated profusely with his own woodcuts (occasionally with the authors' cooperation). De Worde's will (dated 5 June 1534 and proved 19 January

1535) enabled others to maintain his shop well into mid century. Despite his many extant books and a variety of contemporary records (including his presentment for publishing a heretical work in 1525–1526, a partial ledger from around 1525, and a shop inventory in 1553), no well-documented biography or study of his press exists.

BIBLIOGRAPHY

H. S. Bennett, *English Books and Readers, 1475 to 1557*, 2nd ed. (1969), with handlist of publications by de Worde (239–276); N. F. Blake, *Caxton: England's First Publisher* (1976), 171–191, and "Wynkyn de Worde," in *Gutenberg-Jahrbuch*, Hans Widmann, ed. (1971 and 1972); Robert Grabhorn, *A Short Account of the Life and Work of Wynkyn de Worde* (San Francisco, 1949); Howard M. Nixon, "Caxton, His Contemporaries and Successors in the Book Trade from Westminster Documents," in *The Library*, **31** (1976): Henry R. Plomer, *Wynkyn de Worde and His Contemporaries from the Death of Caxton to 1535* (1925), the standard biography and printing history.

               IAN LANCASHIRE

[See also **Caxton, William; Printing, Origins of; Pynson, Richard; Woodcut.**]

WYSBECK, JOHN (*fl.* first half of the fourteenth century), a monk of Ely Cathedral responsible for construction of the Lady Chapel attached to the north arm of the transept of that cathedral. The chapel was begun in 1321 and completed in 1348, the year before John died of plague (16 June 1349). It is reported that, while excavating the chapel foundations, Wysbeck found an urn of coins, with which he paid the workmen.

BIBLIOGRAPHY

Louis F. Salzman, *Building in England Down to 1540* (1952), 393–394.

               CARL F. BARNES, JR.

[See also **Chapel; Masons and Builders.**]

XAČᶜKᶜAR (**khatchkᶜar**), an Armenian type of stele that appeared from the ninth century on, is a rectangular slab of stone (*kᶜar*) with a cross (*χačᶜ* or *khatch*) carved on one surface. The cross is often ornate and framed with geometric motifs, sometimes with a medallion carved below it. Some *χač^ck^cars* resemble lacework; others include saintly figures, such as the *Amenap^crkič^c* (savior) type. Freestanding or on a pedestal, often beside portals, *χač^ck^cars* were erected as donations to churches and to commemorate the deceased, the completion of religious or secular structures, military victories, and other events. *Xač^ck^cars* with inscriptions giving names and dates are valuable historical documents.

BIBLIOGRAPHY
Lewon Azaryan, *Armenian Khatchkars* (1973) and, with Armen Manoukian, *Khatchkar* (1970); Sirarpie Der Nersessian, *The Armenians* (1969) and *Armenian Art* (1978).

LUCY DER MANUELIAN

[See also **Armenian Art.**]

XAXULI (Khakhuli, Ḥaḥuli), a significant monastic center in the southern Georgian province Tao-Klarjet^ci (now under Turkish domination). Among its six churches and oratories the most significant and best preserved is the main church dedicated to the Virgin. It was built by the local ruler, David of Tao, in the second half of the tenth century. It is a cruciform domed structure with an elongated west arm which is divided by fluted piers forming a wide nave and two aisles. The only access to the church is from the southern side. A gallery was added here later, and toward the end of the tenth century the church was decorated with wall paintings which in part still remain.

BIBLIOGRAPHY
Rusudan Mepisashvili and Vakhtang Tsintsadze, *The Arts of Ancient Georgia* (1979); Euthymius Takaishvili, *Arkheologičeskaia ekspedicia 1917 goda v iuznye provincii Gruzii* (1952), 68–75.

WACHTANG DJOBADZE

[See also **David of Tao; Georgia: Political History; Georgian Art and Architecture; Tayk^c.**]

XLAT^c (Khlat^c; Arabic: Khilāṭ or Akhlāṭ; modern Ahlât), a town on the northwestern shore of Lake Van in the old Armenian principality of Bznunik^c, located on the southern trade route connecting Tabriz and Khoi with Bitlis and northern Mesopotamia. Xlat^c first became significant in the Arab period and by 918 was important enough to be attacked by the Byzantine general John Kurkuas and in 998 by the Iberians. After being held by the Qaysites, the most important Arab emirs of the Bagratid period (884–1045), Xlat^c became the seat of the Kurdish Marwanids from 983 to 1071, except for brief periods of Armenian rule, and was damaged in the Byzantine offensive of 993. In 1071 the city fell to the Seljuks, whose emirs ruled the city as an independent dynasty calling themselves the shahs of Armenia (Shāh-Arman).

Xlat^c was taken by the Ayyubids in 1207 and by the Khwārazmshāh Jalāl al-Dīn after a six-month siege in 1230. The city was sacked and destroyed by the Mongols in 1244 but was then given to a Georgian princess of the Mχargrjelid house and did not become definitively Mongol until 1259/1260. Thereafter it became the capital of the Armenian province of the Ilkhanids, the successors of the Mongols in Iran. The Jalayirids held Xlat^c in the fourteenth century, then the White Sheep (Aq Qoyunlu) and Black Sheep (Qara Qoyunlu) Turkomans. The Ottoman Turks captured the city in 1548 but it was leveled by Shah Tahmasp and did not become definitively Turkish until 1554/1555, when Sultan Süleyman I rebuilt the citadel. Thereafter, quasi-independent Kurdish chieftains held the declining town until it was suppressed by the Ottomans in 1847. Xlat^c is notable for its Islamic tombs and tombstones, most of which date from the Seljuk period. A walled city in a ravine in the Middle Ages, it was a great commercial center and an Arab base and stopover on the road from Mesopotamia to Dwin.

BIBLIOGRAPHY
T^cadewos X. Hakobyan, *Hayastani patmakan ašxarhagrut^cyun*, 2nd ed. (1968); H. A. Manandian, *The Trade and Cities of Armenia in Relation to Ancient World Trade*, Nina Garsoïan, trans. (1965); F. Taeschner, "Akhlāt," in *Encyclopaedia of Islam*, new ed., I (1960); Aram Ter Ghewondyan, *The Arab Emirates in Bagratid Armenia*, Nina Garsoïan, trans. (1976).

ROBERT H. HEWSEN

[See also **Aq Qoyunlu; Armenia: History of; Armenian Muslim Emirates; Ayyubids; Bagratids; Ilkhanids; Khwārizmshāhs; Mongol Empire; Qara Qoyunlu; Shāh-Arman; Trade, Armenian; Trade, Islamic.**]

XUSRŌ I ANŌŠARWĀN (Khusrau, Khosrau) (*d.* 579), Sasanian king (531–579). Xusrō earned his surname (meaning "of immortal soul") from the Zoroastrians for his suppression of the heresy of Mazdak in the last years of the reign of his father, Kawād I. Mazdak's communistic movement had shaken the foundations of the Sasanian state and the Zoroastrian church, and Xusrō moved swiftly to reestablish the authority of the crown by instituting tax reforms and encouraging through grants of land the growth of the lower ranks of the nobility, the *āzādān* (freemen). For easing the burden of the poor and building a strong base of support in Iranian society he gained a legendary reputation for justice in Persian literature. Even Muḥammad is described in Muslim sources as having been born "in the reign of the just king."

Xusrō, according to al-Balxī, kept golden thrones for the emperors of Byzantium, China, and the Khazars at the capital, Ctesiphon. A campaign from 558 to 561 in alliance with the first khan of the western Turks, Istämi (Sinǰībū), broke the power of the Hephthalites in the east, to whom the Iranians had paid tribute as late as the reign of Kawād. In the west, Xusrō had conquered Antioch in 540; the Iranian-Byzantine treaty of 561 stipulated free trade routes, but in 568 the Sasanians invaded the Yemen, ostensibly to protect Arab allies against the Greeks. The growing Sasanian navy now controlled the sea route to India and the Far East, temporarily crippling the Byzantine silk trade until an overland route north and then south through Turkish-controlled Sogd to China could be negotiated between Byzantium and the khan. Xusrō's grandiose foreign adventures, which may have served as a model for the expansionist policies of Xusrō II Abarwēz, overextended Sasanian forces and overtaxed the treasury, weakening the country socially and militarily without securing any long-range advantages.

According to Agathias, Xusrō had studied the works of Plato and Aristotle with a Syrian tutor, and when in 529 Justinian I closed the academy of Athens, Xusrō invited the philosophers to reside at Gundēshāpūr, near Susa, which had been devastated in the fourth century by Šābuhr II following a Christian uprising. The homesick Greek scholars were returned to Byzantium by the treaty of 561. But Xusrō's reign was truly the golden age of the native, Zoroastrian culture of Iran: the king called a conclave of sages for the final compilation of the twenty-one *nask*s (divisions) of the Avesta, and

many religious treatises in Pahlavi were probably set down in writing then. According to an imperial rescript quoted in the *Dēnkard* (Acts of the religion), Xusrō put down heresy and ordained that the Avesta and Zand (Interpretation) be studied zealously. Al-Mas͑ūdī (*d.* 956) wrote that Xusrō enforced Zoroastrian observance throughout Iran, prohibiting religious controversy and polemic.

The Pahlavi text *Xusrō ud rēdag* (Xusrō and his page) provides a vivid picture of the sumptuous and refined culture of court life, and a number of books of maxims (*andarz*) on religious and secular matters are attributed to the king and to his vizier, Wuzurgmihr. A number of Indian texts were translated into Pahlavi at Xusrō's order: his physician, Burzōi, procured a book of fables from the *Panchatantra*, which was rendered into Arabic by the eighth-century Persian scholar Ibn al-Muqaffa͑ as the *Kalīla wa-Dimna*. The Buddhist tale of Barlaam and Josaphat found its way to medieval Europe via Sasanian Iran, and Indian astronomical and astrological learning reached Arab science through Pahlavi translations in Xusrō's reign.

BIBLIOGRAPHY

Esin Atıl, *Kalila wa Dimna: Fables from a Fourteenth-century Arabic Manuscript* (1981); Edward G. Browne, *A Literary History of Persia*, I (1902); Arthur Christensen, "La légende du sage Buzurǰmihr," in *Acta orientalia*, 8 (1929/1930), and *L'Iran sous les Sassanides*, 2nd ed. (1944); Richard N. Frye, *The Heritage of Persia* (1963) and "The Political History of Iran Under the Sasanians," in *The Cambridge History of Iran*, III, pt. 1 (1983), 153–162; M. Grignaschi, "La riforma tributaria di Ḥosrō I e il feudalismo sassanide," in *La Persia nel medioevo* (Accademia Nazionale Dei Lincei, quaderno 160, 1971); Heinz H. Schöffler, *Die Akademie von Gondischapur: Aristoteles auf dem Wege in den Orient* (1979); Geo Widengren, "Xosrau Anōšurvān, les Hephtalites, et les peuples turcs," in *Orientalia suecana*, 1 (1952); R. C. Zaehner, *Zurvan: A Zoroastrian Dilemma* (1955).

JAMES R. RUSSELL

[See also **Agathias; Armenia: History of; Avesta; Ctesiphon; Gundēshāpūr; Hephthalites; Justinian I; Khan; Mas͑ūdī, al-; Mazdakites; Muqaffa͑, ͑Abd Allāh ibn al-; Pahlavi Literature; Šābuhr II; Sasanian Culture; Sasanian History; Zoroastrianism.**]

XUSRŌ II ABARWĒZ (Khusrau, Khosrau) (Pahlavi, "the Victorious"; Persian: *Parwīz*), Sasanian king (591–628). His father, Hormizd IV (r. 579–590), was deposed by Bahrām VI Čōbēn, a general of the Parthian Mihrān family, whose challenge to the throne utilized both the disaffection of some nobles with the Sasanians and millenarianist feeling among the Iranian people. Xusrō fled to Byzantium and was returned to the throne with the aid of the Byzantine emperor Maurice. According to al-Ṭabarī, Xusrō married the emperor's daughter Maria, but Byzantine sources know nothing of this marriage, which is probably a fiction supporting Xusrō's claim to a direct relationship with Maurice. He was undoubtedly married to at least one Christian woman, Šīrēn (Shirīn), who was Assyrian or Armenian and exerted considerable influence over him, according to contemporary sources. Using as a pretext the murder of Maurice by Phokas, Xusrō invaded Asia Minor, Syria, and Palestine: Antioch fell in 611; Jerusalem, in 614; and Alexandria, in 617. Xusrō had the Holy Cross taken from Jerusalem to Ctesiphon, and by 619 Sasanian Iran seemed to be at the apogee of its power, with the western quadrant including areas as remote as Egypt and the Yemen.

In 622 Heraklios counterattacked, reaching Media Atropatene, where, in revenge for the theft of the cross, the Byzantines sacked the fire temple of Ādur Gušnasp (modern Takhi-i Sulaiman), the second holiest shrine of the Sasanians. Iranian forces pursued the invader back to the very gates of Constantinople, but in 628 Heraklios returned to sack the royal palace of Xusrō at Dastagird. In the same year, Xusrō was murdered by Šērōy (later crowned Kawād II), whom he had passed over for the succession in favor of Mardānšāh, his son by Šīrēn.

The wealth and majesty of Xusrō's court were celebrated in contemporary and, later, Islamic, sources, and his practices were imitated by Muslim rulers. The royal crown was so heavy it had to be suspended on a chain from the ceiling of the throne room, according to Ibn Isḥāq (who describes the crown in connection with Xusrō I), al-Ṭabarī (who connects it to Xusrō II), and others. The throne itself was veiled from view. At Taq-i Bostan, Xusrō had carved a grotto in the form of a splendid *īwān* (*eyvān*) adorned with various scenes in bas-relief: an enthronement scene with Ohrmazd and Anāhitā; the king on horseback in battle; and the royal hunt. The complex is unique for the later Sasanian period, and the scene of the hunt is particularly striking. Whereas in most Sasanian depictions of the hunt the king is shown in individual combat on horseback with two or three beasts, here the hunt is a vast panorama of men and animals on a broad landscape, as though Xusrō were not merely a king in the old Iranian heroic mold, but ruler of all the world. Indeed, Xusrō may have intended by the capture of the Holy Cross to exalt the church of Persia above the Byzantine, and to make himself ruler of both the Christian and Zoroastrian worlds. Xusrō I had nurtured similar cosmic ambitions.

Even as Xusrō's religious policy provoked only a destructive crusade, the magnificence of his court and his military campaigns ruined the Iranian economy, and his haughty behavior alienated the Arab Lakhmids of al-Ḥira, whose forces had guarded the populous heartland of Sasanian Mesopotamia from Arab nomadic attack. Xusrō's marriage to at least one foreign Christian woman diluted the Sasanian line and alienated the nobility and the Zoroastrian priesthood. Financially exhausted, exposed on the west, and torn by internal political and religious disunity, Iran was to fall before the cohorts of Islam scarcely a generation after Xusrō's death.

BIBLIOGRAPHY

Sources. Frédéric Macler, trans., *Histoire d'Héraclius par l'évêque Sebeos* (1904); Theodor Nöldeke, trans., *Geschichte der Perser und Araber zur Zeit der Sasaniden: Aus der arabischen Chronik des Ṭabarī* (1879, repr. 1973).

Studies. The Cambridge History of Iran, III, pts. 1 and 2 (1983); Arthur Christensen, *L'Iran sous les Sassanides*, 2nd ed. (1944); Richard Ettinghausen, *From Byzantium to Sasanian Iran and the Islamic World* (1972); B. Faravashi, "Les causes de la chute des Sassanides," in *La Persia nel medioevo* (Accademia Nazionale dei Lincei, quaderno 164, 1971); Shinji Fukai and Kiyoharu Horiuchi, *Taq-i-Bustan*, 2 vols. (1969–1971); Paul Goubert, *Byzance avant l'Islam*, I: *Byzance et l'Orient* (1951); Ernst Herzfeld, "Der Thron des Khosrô," in *Jahrbuch der Preussischen Kunstsammlungen*, 41 (1920).

JAMES R. RUSSELL

[See also **Armenia: History of; Bahrām VI Čōbēn; Byzantine Empire: History; Ctesiphon; Eyvān; Heraklios; Ḥira, al-; Lakhmids; Maurice, Emperor; Parthians; Phokas; Sasanian Culture; Sasanian History; Ṭabarī, al-; Taq-i Bostan; Zoroastrianism.**]

XWADĀY NĀMAG (Khwadāy nāmag, "Book of kings"), a seventh-century chronicle of the Persian kings written in Pahlavi in the late Sasanian period. It was translated into Arabic in the eighth century, and although both the Pahlavi original and the Arabic translations are now lost, small fragments of the latter survive in the works of some Arab historians. Sources for the chronicle include legends, genealogies, Iranian epic tales, Zoroastrian wisdom literature, and the Alexander romance. *Xwadāy nāmag* was the direct source for early Arab historians writing on pre-Islamic Iran, and the indirect source for Firdawsī's *Shāhnāma*. The Zoroastrian element is greatly reduced in the Islamic texts deriving from this chronicle.

BIBLIOGRAPHY

Mary Boyce, "Middle Persian Literature," in Bertold Spuler, ed., *Handbuch der Orientalistik*, I:IV:2:1 (1968), 57–60; Theodor Nöldeke, *Das iranische Nationalepos*, 2nd ed. (1920), 12–19.

WILLIAM LIPPINCOTT HANAWAY, JR.

[See also **Pahlavi Literature; Sasanian History; Shāhnāma; Zoroastrianism.**]

YAḤYĀ IBN SAʿĪD. See **Yahya of Antioch.**

YAHYA OF ANTIOCH (Yaḥyā ibn Saʿīd), an Arab historian and physician and a Melchite Christian, lived from about 980 to 1066. He wrote a continuation of the work of Eutychios, a tenth-century historian. Yahya was born in Egypt and was very possibly a relative of Eutychios. He lived in Egypt until 1013 or 1014, when he emigrated to Antioch in the wake of the persecutions of Christians and Jews by the Fatimid caliph al-Ḥakim. His history, which begins in the 930's and ends either in 1034 or with his death, concentrates on events in Egypt, Syria, and the Byzantine Empire and employs both Christian and Muslim sources. It is an excellent reference for the history of the period, especially for the years when he lived and had firsthand knowledge of events. The history had two editions: one written before his move to Antioch and a second employing new sources that he found in that city.

BIBLIOGRAPHY

Alexander A. Vasiliev, *Byzance et les Arabes*, II, *La dynastie macédonienne* (1950).

LINDA C. ROSE

[See also **Eutychios the Melchite; Ḥakim bi-Amr Allāh, al-.**]

YĀM is a Mongol term for the relay stations that were situated at regular intervals along the principal roads of the Mongol Empire. Official messengers and foreign envoys received fresh mounts and hospitality at each station. Both the term and the relay system itself are probably of Chinese origin. Successors of the Mongols such as the Jalayirids and Timurids also maintained relay stations in villages and caravansaries. Sometimes the term *yām* was also applied to buildings where merchants displayed their wares. Thus, a building in Baghdad erected in 1359 is described in its inscription as a "*yām* with shops." It has a central vaulted hall surrounded by two stories of rooms and appears to have functioned as a market.

BIBLIOGRAPHY

ʿAlī Akbār Dehkhoda, *Loghat-nāma* (1975); Gerhard Doerfer, *Türkische und mongolische Elemente im Neupersischen*, IV (1975), 110–119; Friedrich Sarre and Ernst Herzfeld, *Archaeologische Reise im Euphrat- und Tigrisgebiet* (1911–1920), II, 187–196, III, plate 51.

PRISCILLA P. SOUCEK

[See also **Islamic Art and Architecture.**]

YAʿQŪB IBN LAYTH (*d*. 879), with his brother ʿAmr the founder of a vast but transient military empire in eastern and southern Iran and in Afghanistan, based on the province of Sīstān (now divided between Iran and Afghanistan), and having a significance beyond the brief period of its florescence (861–910), in that its creation marked the first great breach in the unity of the Abbasid caliphate. Whereas lines of provincial governors such as the Tahirids in eastern Iran and the Ikhshidids in Egypt acknowledged and to a considerable extent acted in accordance with their dependence on the caliphate in Baghdad, Yaʿqūb and his kinsmen were openly contemptuous of the Abbasids and their claim to universal authority in Islam, regarding the Abbasid empire as built on deceit and trickery. It is because of this disregard of the "caliphal fiction"—that all power emanated from the caliph himself—that Yaᶜqūb and his brother are treated with hostility in the orthodox Sunni sources, so that it is not easy to arrive at a dispassionate view of his achievement; fortunately, we have a corrective for this in the local history of Sīstān, which regards him as a local hero who made this obscure corner of the Iranian world famous for a short period.

Yaᶜqūb and ᶜAmr were of plebeian origin, and the former's trade as a coppersmith (ṣaffār) gave its name to the dynasty which they founded, that of the Saffarids. Yaᶜqūb seems to have begun in Sistan as a member of one of the bands of vigilantes formed to combat the Kharijite radical religious sectarians there. He pushed rivals aside, by 861 achieving the expulsion of the caliphal governor, and proclaimed himself the emir of Sistan. After thus strengthening his internal position, Yaᶜqūb embarked on a career of external conquest, subduing the Kharijites and incorporating many of them into his own army. He pushed into eastern Afghanistan and attacked the indigenous, pagan dynasties of the Zunbīls in Zabulistan and the Kābul-shāhs, capturing rich plunder that was forwarded to the caliph and that caused a sensation in Baghdad. When he turned westward, however, Yaᶜqūb was bound to clash with the established caliphal authority there. He took over Kirmān (Kermān) and Makrān (southern Baluchistan), and then in 875 mounted a large-scale invasion into the rich province of Fārs that carried him beyond the Iranian frontier into Iraq, where he was halted only fifty miles (80.5 km) from Baghdad (876). In eastern Iran, Yaᶜqūb had already in 873 expelled the last Tahirid governor of Khorāsān from his capital, Nishapur, and had penetrated as far as the Caspian provinces. In 879, however, he died at Jundīshāpūr in southern Iran, and his brother ᶜAmr, who had been concerned with the imposition of Saffarid authority on Khorāsān against various local contenders for power, succeeded him as emir, until he himself was defeated by the Samanids in 900, leading to the collapse shortly afterward of the vast empire that these two remarkable brothers had built up.

BIBLIOGRAPHY

Sources. See such general chronicles as that of Ibn al-Athīr, *al-Kāmil fiᵓl-taᵓrīkh,* 7 vols., C. J. Tornberg, ed. (1851–1876); but above all, see the anonymous *Taᵓrīkh-i Sistān,* M. S. Bahār, ed. (1935), trans. into English by Milton Gold (1976).

Studies. C. E. Bosworth, *Sīstān Under the Arabs: From the Islamic Conquest to the Rise of the Ṣaffārids* (1968), 109–123, and "The Ṭāhirids and Ṣaffārids," in *Cambridge History of Iran,* IV: *The Period from the Arab Invasion to the Saljuqs,* R. N. Frye, ed. (1975), esp. 106–116; Theodor Nöldeke, "Yakúb the Coppersmith and His Dynasty," in *Sketches from Eastern History* (1892), 176–206; Samuel M. Stern, "Yaᶜqūb the Coppersmith and Persian National Sentiment," in *Iran and Islam: In Memory of the Late Vladimir Minorsky,* C. E. Bosworth, ed. (1971), 535–555.

C. E. BOSWORTH

[See also **Afghanistan; Fārs; Ikhshidids; Iran, History: After 650; Saffarids; Tahirids.**]

YAᶜQŪBĪ, AL- (Abū 'l-ᶜAbbās Aḥmad ibn Abī Yaᶜqūb, *fl.* late ninth century), Arab historian and geographer. Born into a family of the secretarial class in Baghdad, he left the capital at a young age and went to Armenia. This was the beginning of a lifetime of travels, in which he visited the provinces of the East and served in the bureaucracy of the Tahirids of Khorāsān, journeyed to India, and then returned west to Egypt and North Africa. He was a professional governmental secretary with a passion for history and historical geography, and during his extensive travels he gathered a wide variety of data from local sources, took detailed notes of his observations, and queried other travelers for theirs. The last years of his life he spent in Egypt. His death is commonly placed in 897/898, but this is impossible since a later source quotes him concerning an event he witnessed in Egypt in 905, while elsewhere he refers in the past tense to the caliphate of al-Muᶜtaḍid (*r.* 892–902).

Al-Yaᶜqūbī's most important work is his *Taᵓrīkh* (History), the first half of which consists of a detailed synopsis of ancient history. Beginning with creation (this section has not survived), he covered as much of ancient history as was known to him from his studies and travels. His remarkably universal outlook included not only such customary topics as the prophets, Persian history, and pre-Islamic Arabia, but also Jesus and his apostles, the Assyrians and Babylonians, the Indians, Greeks, and Romans, the northern nations, Egyptians, Berbers, Abyssinians, the Zanj and other African peoples, Turks, and Chinese. His attitude toward the past is quite critical here. He complains of how little information is reliable for certain periods, and tries to present peoples and cultures in terms of their own literature. He seems to have used at least one Syriac source in translation, repeatedly cites both the Old and New Testaments, and quotes copiously from such classical scholars as Hippocrates, Galen, Socrates, Plato, Aristotle, and Ptolemy. He also discusses the Persian and Roman calendars, and provides some nomenclature of the Khazar kings that is found in no other source.

The second, larger part of the *Taʾrīkh* is a history of Islam to 872. His stated goal in this part is simply to provide an accurate summary account of events already known from earlier sources. Material is arranged according to the reigns of the caliphs, each section beginning with astrological data to show how the heavens affected the course of events. His compilations are generally accurate and evenhanded, though he does show particular favor for the Twelver Shīᶜa imams, a certain sympathy for the Muᶜtazila, marked antipathy toward the Umayyads, and a tendency to sycophancy in discussing the Abbasids. The *Taʾrīkh* becomes extremely sparse as al-Yaᶜqūbī approaches his own time. Overall, the work is a useful source for the Umayyads and early Abbasids, but is more of a cultural document than a history.

In Egypt in 891, al-Yaᶜqūbī wrote another work, the *Kitāb al-buldān* (Book of the regions). It begins with long, detailed descriptions of Baghdad and Samarra, then provides shorter accounts of cities and provinces in the East, and of the area comprising the lands of central Iraq and the pilgrimage route to the Hejaz and Yemen. Most of the section on Basra, eastern Arabia, the Byzantine Empire, India, and China, as well as part of the description of Syria, is lost. The work concludes with Egypt, Nubia, North Africa, and Spain. Historical details, statistics, and topographical observations abound in this work, in which the author obviously made use of the materials he had collected during his travels. Probably the first work in Arabic on historical geography, the *Kitāb al-buldān* is an intriguing book of considerable importance.

There has also survived a short essay of al-Yaᶜqūbī's entitled *Mushākalat al-nās li-zamānihim wa-mā yaghlibu ᶜalayhim fī kulli ᶜaṣrin* (The adaptation of men to their time and what characterizes them in every age). This work consists mostly of anecdotes illustrating how the deeds and innova-

tions of rulers are imitated by society at large. All of al-Yaᶜqūbī's other works are lost. These include a monograph on the Tahirids, a historical geography of the Byzantine Empire, a history of the conquest of North Africa, a geographical dictionary, and a history of ancient peoples (perhaps actually a part of his *Taʾrīkh*).

BIBLIOGRAPHY

Sources. Al-Yaᶜqūbī's *Taʾrīkh* was first published in M. T. Houtsma, ed., *Ibn-Wādhih qui dicitur al-Jaᶜqubī historiae*, 2 vols. (1883, repr. 1969), from which the several printings of Beirut and Najaf are derived. A new edition would be very useful. The *Kitāb al-buldān* appears in M. J. de Goeje, ed., *Bibliotheca geographorum arabicorum*, VII (1892); it has been translated into French, with a good essay on the author, in Gaston Wiet, ed. and trans., *Les pays* (1937). For an assessment and English translation of the short *Mushākalat al-nās li-zamānihim*, see William G. Millward, "The Adaptation of Men to Their Time: An Historical Essay by al-Yaᶜqūbī," in *Journal of the American Oriental Society*, **84** (1964).

Studies. The range of material on al-Yaᶜqubi includes: Carl Brockelmann, *Geschichte der arabischen Litteratur*, 2nd ed. (1943–1947), 226–227, 405; D. M. Donaldson, "Al-Yaᶜqūbī's Chapter About Jesus Christ," in *The MacDonald Presentation Volume* (1933, repr. 1968); ᶜAbd al-ᶜAzīz al-Dūrī, *Baḥth fī nashʾat ᶜilm al-taʾrīkh ᶜinda l-ᶜArab* (1960), which has been translated as *The Rise of Historical Writing Among the Arabs*, Lawrence I. Conrad, ed. and trans. (1983); R. Y. Ebied and L. R. Wickham, "Al-Yaᶜḳūbī's Account of the Israelite Prophets and Kings," in *Journal of Near Eastern Studies*, **29** (1970); M. J. de Goeje, "Über die Geschichte der Abbasiden von al-Jaᶜḳūbī," in *Travaux de la 3ème session du Congrès international des orientalists*, 2 (1879); T. M. Johnstone, "An Early Manuscript of Yaᶜḳūbī's 'Taʾrīh,'" in *Journal of Semitic Studies*, 2 (1957); Martin Klamroth, "Der Auszug aus den Evangelien bei dem arabischen Historiker Jaqubi," in *Festschrift zur Einweihung des Wilhelmsgymnasiums in Hamburg* (1885), and "Über die Auszüge aus griechischen Schriftstellern bei al-Jaᶜqūbī," in *Zeitschrift der Deutschen Morgenländischen Gesellschaft*, **40** (1886) and **45** (1887); David S. Margoliouth, *Lectures on Arabic Historians* (1930, repr. 1972); William G. Millward, "Al-Yaᶜqūbī's Sources and the Question of Shīᶜa Partiality," in *Abr-Nahrain*, **12** (1971–1972); André Miquel, *La géographie humaine du monde musulman jusqu'au milieu du 11e siècle*, I (1967), 102ff., 285ff.

LAWRENCE I. CONRAD

[See also **Abbasids; Geography and Cartography, Islamic; Historiography, Islamic; Tahirids; Umayyads; Zanj.**]

YARMUK, a river along the present Syrian-Jordanian frontier. Forming from smaller streams in the adjacent Hauran, it flows southwest through the rugged terrain of the Golan Heights, which it deeply cuts with steep ravines and gorges, and pours into the Jordan River 7 kilometers (4.4 miles) south of Lake Tiberias (the Sea of Galilee). The Yarmuk was the site of a major battle between Arab and Byzantine forces during the Islamic conquest of Syria, and it is to this event that the river owes its historical significance.

There are numerous accounts of the Yarmuk campaign in the Arabic, Syriac, and Greek sources, but in all cases the historiographical difficulties are such that no detailed account of the battle can be reconstructed with any degree of certainty. Despite these problems, however, it is still possible to obtain a fairly reliable general view of Yarmuk and its importance.

The date of the battle is disputed, but the strongest evidence places it in the late summer of 636. By this time it was clear to the Byzantine emperor Heraklios (*r.* 610–641) that the Arab forces that had penetrated the various provinces of geographic Syria were no mere raiders, and that the empire was in imminent danger of losing the entire region. A very large army was thus dispatched to deal with this threat; according to some accounts it contained significant contingents of local auxiliaries in addition to regular imperial troops. Reliable estimates of its size are not available, but even allowing for exaggeration (by both sides) it appears to have been an immense force, at least double the strength of the Arab army and perhaps even larger. Marching south through Syria, it compelled the Arab invaders to fall back and consolidate their ranks. This maneuvering finally ended at the Yarmuk River, with the two armies encamped in the same general vicinity for a considerable length of time before the final clash.

The battle itself was a disastrous and total defeat for the Byzantines. Various sources mention desertions and low morale among the emperor's forces, and infiltration by Arab horsemen behind the Byzantine lines before the battle. The Arabs do seem to have caught the Greek army by surprise, but Theophanes' explanation—that the Arabs attacked as a great dust storm was blowing into the faces of the Byzantine troops—is unlikely. The fighting was apparently desperate for a time, but the Greeks were finally put to flight with enormous losses: many accounts mention that large numbers of soldiers perished as they fled, falling down the steep ravines that plunge into the river.

There is no doubt that Yarmuk was the decisive battle in the contest for Syria, for it witnessed the destruction of a large army that could not be replaced. The immediate result of the utter disaster suffered by the Byzantines was that their ability to offer stiff resistance to the Arab advance collapsed almost entirely. With no standing army to impede them, the Arab forces split up after Yarmuk and spread across the countryside, meeting only isolated resistance from larger garrisoned towns. In short, Yarmuk assured the Arab occupation of Syria.

In another sense, the campaign was even more important. The great victory came at a time when the young Islamic regime based in Medina had by no means managed to win over, much less integrate under its authority, all the bedouin tribes of Arabia and the Syrian and Iraqi steppes. These tribes wielded great power in the unstable circumstances of the early years of Islam. The victory at Yarmuk, and hence in Syria in general, probably did much to enhance the prestige of the caliph ʿUmar ibn al-Khaṭṭāb (634–644) and to demonstrate to the tribes Islam's viability as an order capable of systematic expansion and permanent rule.

BIBLIOGRAPHY

The pioneering work on the conquest of Syria—and the role played by the Yarmuk campaign—was the product of early orientalist scholarship. See Leone Caetani, *Annali dell'Islām,* III (1909), 549–618; M. J. de Goeje, *Mémoire sur la conquête de la Syrie,* 2nd ed. (1900), 103–136; Theodor Nöldeke, "Zur Geschichte der Araber im 1. Jahrhundert d. H. aus syrischen Quellen," in *Zeitschrift der Deutschen Morgenländischen Gesellschaft,* **29** (1875); Julius Wellhausen, *Skizzen und Vorarbeiten,* VI: *Prolegomena zur ältesten Geschichte des Islams* (1899), 51–68. The presentation in John Bagot Glubb, *The Great Arab Conquests* (1963), 173–185, is valuable as the view of a professional soldier intimately familiar with the terrain, but it provides a picture far clearer than the state of the evidence can justify. All these works are now superseded by Fred M. Donner, *The Early Islamic Conquests* (1981), 128–148.

LAWRENCE I. CONRAD

[See also **Byzantine Empire: History (330–1025); Caliphate; Heraklios; Islam, Conquests of; Syria; ʿUmar I ibn al-Khaṭṭāb.**]

YAROSLAV THE WISE (*r.* 1019–1054), grand prince of Kievan Rus. The son of Grand Prince Vladimir, the "Christianizer of Russia," Yaroslav took the throne of Kiev in 1019 after a prolonged war against his half-brother Svyatopolk I. Svyatopolk had murdered three of his half-brothers after their father's death in 1015, among them the youths Boris and Gleb, considered saints by the Russian people for the equanimity with which they accepted their martyrdom. At first Yaroslav had to divide the Russian state with his half-brother Mstislav, but at Mstislav's death in 1036 Yaroslav reunited the country. Brave in battle, although lame since childhood, Yaroslav launched attacks against the Turkic peoples of the steppe, Baltic tribes, Finnic groups to the northwest and northeast, and the Poles, extending the country's borders in all directions, but most notably south into the steppe. In 1043 he even mounted a campaign against Constantinople to enforce Russian trading privileges with the Byzantines.

Yaroslav's reign was the golden age of medieval Russian culture. He beautified his capital of Kiev with marvelous monasteries and churches, including the famous cathedral of Hagia Sophia, and built new city walls and the renowned Golden Gate. Foreign visitors could compare Yaroslav's Kiev only with Constantinople. Literate himself and fluent in several languages, Yaroslav founded schools and libraries and supported professional translators to translate works into Slavic. He also authorized Russia's first law code. Active diplomatically, Yaroslav was eventually related by marriage to the royal families of Sweden, Norway, Poland, Hungary, Byzantium, and France. Metropolitan Ilarion (Hilarion), a Russian whom Yaroslav had appointed to head the Russian church, rightly stated that Yaroslav "had given the famous city of Kiev a crown of glory." At his death in 1054 he divided his realm among his sons.

BIBLIOGRAPHY

For a wealth of information on Yaroslav's reign, see *Povest vremennykh let,* Dmitriĭ S. Likhachev, ed., 2 vols. (1950); for an English translation of this work, the earliest version of which was probably written under Yaroslav, see *The Russian Primary Chronicle: Laurentian Text,* Samuel H. Cross and Olgerd P. Sherbowitz-Wetzor, eds. and trans. (1953).

Good treatments of the Kievan period include: Boris D. Grekov, *Kiev Rus,* Dennis Ogden, ed., Y. Sdobnikov, trans. (1959); Boris A. Rybakov, *Early Centuries of Russian History,* John Weir, trans. (1965); George Vernadsky, *A History of Russia,* II, *Kievan Russia* (1948, repr. 1980).

GEORGE P. MAJESKA

[See also **Hagia Sophia (Kiev); Ilarion; Kievan Rus; Russian Architecture; Russian Art; Russian Orthodox Church.**]

YAROSLAVL, a city on the Volga River north of Moscow, was founded in the early eleventh century and raided by the Mongols in 1238. It became incorporated into the principality of Moscow in 1463 and grew into an important trading center in the sixteenth and seventeenth centuries, when many foreigners passed into Russia from the White Sea (an inlet of the Barents Sea). During the seventeenth century, many churches were erected in the city by its prosperous merchants, and Western influence, specifically the illustrated Bible of Piscator, is evident in the frescoes of these churches.

BIBLIOGRAPHY

Robert O. Crummey, *The Formation of Muscovy: 1304 to 1613* (1987), 41 and *passim*; Konstantin D. Golovshchikov, *Istoriia goroda Iaroslavlia* (1889); George H. Hamilton, *The Art and Architecture of Russia,* 3rd ed. (1983), 135–137; Stanislav I. Maslenitsyn, *Yaroslavian Icon Painting,* K. M. Cook, trans. (1983).

ANN E. FARKAS

[See also **Mongol Empire; Muscovy, Rise of; Russia, Nomadic Invasions of; Russian Art and Architecture.**]

YAŠTS. The Yašts, which constitute a section of the Avesta, the ancient Zoroastrian scriptures, are twenty-one hymns of praise devoted to the *yazata*s, "beings worthy of worship." Although the language of the Yašts is Younger Avestan, in contrast to the Gathic Avestan employed by the prophet Zarathustra in his hymns (Gāthās), the content and metrical form of the Yašts suggest a kinship with the hymns of the *Rig Veda.* Together, the Yašts and Vedic hymns reflect an ancient Aryan tradition of composition by poet-priests.

Indeed, the most vivid and lengthiest Yašts are devoted to divinities that may well have been worshiped by Iranians before the time of Zarathustra: Ardvī Sūrā Anāhitā, the goddess of the waters;

Tishtrya, the star Sirius, a rain god; Mithra, the Indo-Iranian deity of covenants; the *fravashi*s, the souls of the righteous; Verethraghna, the god of victory; and Khvarenah, *yazata* of divine grace. Whether the inclusion of the Yašts in the Zoroastrian sacred canon represents a superficial Zoroastrianization of ancient traditions, a re-emergence of priestly (magian) influence after Zarathustra's reform, or a faithful expression of Zarathustra's own views are hypotheses still debated by scholars.

In addition to the light they shed on the history of Zoroastrianism, the Yašts are a valuable source for the study of the Iranian legendary tradition in that many of the heroes and villains of later Iranian literature, notably the *Shāhnāma,* the tenth-century Persian national epic composed by Firdawsī, put in an initial appearance in the Yašts. Particularly interesting in this respect are the Yašts devoted to Ardvī Sūrā Anāhitā (Yašt 5), the *fravashi*s (Yašt 13), and Khvarenah (Yašt 19).

BIBLIOGRAPHY

Arthur E. Christensen, *Les Kayanides* (1931); James Darmesteter, ed., *The Zend-Avesta*, II, *The Sirozahs, Yashts, and Nyayesh* (1883, repr. 1965); Herman Lommel, *Die Yästs des Awesta* (1927); Ilya Gershevitch, *The Avestan Hymn to Mithra* (1959, repr. 1967).

DALE L. BISHOP

[See also **Avesta; Gathas; Zoroastrianism.**]

YAZĪD I IBN MUᶜĀWIYA (*r.* 680–683), the second Umayyad caliph and the most controversial ruler of early Islamic times. Born about 646, he was Muᶜāwiya's son by his wife Maysūn from the Kalb tribe. As Yazīd grew up in Syria among the Kalb, his education was distinctly Arab—poetry, genealogy, and tribal lore—but also included the Koran and prophetic tradition. In later times Yazīd was ranked among early Syrian transmitters of *ḥadīth.* He was also an able military leader, and when Muᶜāwiya launched an unsuccessful expedition against Constantinople in 669, it was Yazīd who led the army. The sources report that his personal life was outlandish, and that he reveled in song, drink, and the company of boon companions and dancing girls.

Muᶜāwiya went to great lengths to ensure that his son should succeed him as caliph. Any other choice would have upset the delicate balance of tribal forces and loyalties that Muᶜāwiya through great tact and talent had established. In this respect, Yazīd's succession was a means to strengthen the Umayyad alliance with the Quḍāᶜa and other established tribal groups in the northern Hejaz and in Syria. This plan was naturally agreeable to the Kalb tribe and its allies. But other tribes stood to lose from the arrangement and opposed it; and in any case, swearing allegiance to a reigning caliph's son was a novel principle at which many Arab leaders balked. Nevertheless, Muᶜāwiya was able to obtain oaths of fealty from most of them, and upon his death in 680, his son, Yazīd, acceded to the throne without incident.

Difficulties arose almost immediately, however. In Medina, al-Ḥusayn ibn ᶜAlī and ᶜAbd Allāh ibn al-Zubayr maintained their earlier refusal to acknowledge Yazīd as caliph and fled to the sacred precincts of Mecca to avoid arrest. Several months later, al-Ḥusayn, encouraged by letters and optimistic reports of support in Kufa for his own claim to the caliphate, set out for Iraq to establish himself there. But his supporters in Kufa were quickly crushed by Umayyad forces, and al-Ḥusayn himself was trapped with a small retinue at Karbalāᵓ, some twenty-five miles (forty kilometers) northwest of the city. Though vastly outnumbered, he refused to surrender; in a final battle traditionally dated to 10 October 680, he and most of his party were killed. The death of this martyr of the Shīᶜa very soon became the clarion call for the Alid cause.

In Arabia the situation was becoming extremely dangerous, for after the death of al-Ḥusayn, Ibn al-Zubayr (*d.* 692) was the only viable rallying point for those who opposed Umayyad rule. Such forces were numerous. Tribes recently arrived in Syria sought to break up the Umayyad-Quḍāᶜa hegemony there; Khārijite groups resented strong central authority; provincial powers were jealous of Syria's privileged position; and Arabian leaders were alarmed by the rapidly declining influence of the Hejaz in general. Grievances of these groups were usually expressed in religious terms, but it is important to note that pious circles in the holy cities gave little credence to such pronouncements, and that the Alid family there, even after the Battle of Karbalāᵓ, remained neutral.

The final explosion came in 683, when a conflict over Umayyad land confiscations provoked a revolt in Medina. The deposition of Yazīd was proclaimed, and Umayyad elements were driven out of the city. At the same time, Ibn al-Zubayr was acclaimed as caliph in Mecca. But unlike him, the Medinans had no particular program and had far overestimated their own strength. Yazīd sent an expedition against them, and at the Battle of al-Ḥarra in the summer of 683, the Medinan army was practically annihilated. The Umayyad force plundered the city, then proceeded south to deal with Ibn al-Zubayr. Mecca was besieged, and during the fighting the Kaaba was burned. Ibn al-Zubayr's revolt probably would have been crushed had it not been for the sudden death of Yazīd (683, in Syria) two months into the siege. As the succession was uncertain, the Umayyad force quickly tried to come to terms with Ibn al-Zubayr; when this failed, it withdrew to Syria. Within a few months the regime's enemies had almost everywhere capitalized on the mounting confusion: Khārijites rebelled in Arabia and Persia; most of the provinces recognized Ibn al-Zubayr as caliph; and in Syria, opponents of the Umayyads and their allies massed to dislodge them from power.

There were also other difficulties during Yazīd's reign. Invading Arab forces in the east, though advancing in Transoxiana, suffered serious setbacks in Sistan and Zabulistan, in present-day Afghanistan. The Berbers revolted in North Africa, and with Byzantine aid the Christian mountain tribes of northern Syria forced the caliph to take additional defensive measures along the northern frontier.

Yazīd's short reign was thus one of disaster. Later historians stressed this and maligned him as a frivolous debaucher, the murderer of the Prophet's grandson al-Ḥusayn, and the violator of Islam's holy cities. Much of this is, of course, later polemic. Had Yazīd lived, he most likely would have defeated Ibn al-Zubayr and avoided civil war. Pious men of his own time were not as offended by his high-spirited way of life as later writers claimed, and in any case disapproved of rebellion against him. Some reports outside of the hostile Kufan tradition state that Yazīd was dismayed by the events at Karbalāʾ, and one Latin European source (the accuracy of which cannot be verified) even describes Yazīd in very positive terms. It is clear that he basically tried to continue his father's policies and had some of Muᶜāwiya's talent for dealing with the tribes. In Syria he enacted some administrative and fiscal reforms. Interested in agriculture, he expanded the irrigation system of the Damascene oasis and earned a reputation for his water projects. In the final analysis, however, it is unlikely that scholars will ever be able to settle the question of his personal responsibility for the turmoil of his reign and the legacy of Karbalāʾ.

BIBLIOGRAPHY

Marshall G. S. Hodgson, *The Venture of Islam: Conscience and History in a World Civilization*, 3 vols. (1974), I, 219–221; Syed Husain M. Jafri, *The Origins and Early Development of Shiᶜa Islam* (1978), 174–221, an assessment by a modern Muslim scholar; M. J. Kister, "The Battle of the Ḥarra: Some Socio-economic Aspects," in *Studies in Memory of Gaston Wiet*, Myriam Rosen-Ayalon, ed. (1977), 33–49, reprinted in M. J. Kister, ed., *Studies in Jāhiliyya and Early Islam* (1980), a very important study; Henri Lammens, *Études sur le règne du calife omaiyade Moᶜâwia Iᵉʳ* (1908), 281–448, valuable and very detailed, but often wrong and markedly hostile to Islam, and *Le califat de Yazîd Iᵉʳ* (1921). Still important are Julius Wellhausen's *Das arabische Reich und sein Sturz* (1902, repr. 1960), trans. by Margaret Graham Weir as *The Arab Kingdom and Its Fall* (1927), chap. 3, and his *Die religiös-politischen Oppositionsparteien im alten Islam* (1901), ed. and trans. by R. C. Ostle and S. M. Walzer as *The Religio-political Factions in Early Islam* (1975), pt. 2, chap. 2, 105–120.

LAWRENCE I. CONRAD

[See also ᶜAbd Allāh ibn al-Zubayr; Alids; Caliphate; Hejaz; Ḥusayn ibn ᶜAlī, al-; Islam, Conquests of; Kaaba; Kufa, al-; Mecca; Muᶜāwiya; Shiᶜa; Syria; Transoxiana; Umayyads.]

YEAR 1000, THE. "The terrors of the year 1000" is a term that has been used to refer to apocalyptic expectations associated with the advent of the millennium since the Incarnation. Jules Michelet, writing in the 1830's, was the most eloquent of those describing a world awaiting that year with both terror and hope. Toward the end of the nineteenth century, however, historians examined this depiction of the turn of the millennium and found little support for it. First of all, the eschatological millennium of the Book of Revelation dealt with a 1,000-year period after the Second Coming. More important, much of the evidence had nothing to do with the year 1000 itself. Finally, those who did mention the year 1000 spoke of beginnings rather than ends (Thietmar von Merseburg's "new dawn").

Michelet's imagery turned out to be a paraphrase of a most unreliable source, the gyrovague monk-historian Radulphus Glaber. Contrary to the impression one gets from his *Five Books of Histories*, however, the vast majority of the documents show no special interest in the year 1000. Indeed, most people at that time seemed to have had no chronological sense at all; the Christian calender was little used, and there was little agreement on which year A.D. it really was. The year 1000, medievalists agreed, had no special meaning to contemporaries; it passed like any other. The "apocalyptic fantasy" turned out to have originated in Caesar Baronius' *History of the Church* (12 vols., 1558–1607). This refutation of the "Romantic" vision of the year 1000 received rapid and widespread acceptance from historians, and by the turn of the nineteenth century it had few remaining supporters. In this century it is a given of medieval historiography that the "terrors of the year 1000" were a Romantic fiction.

The rejection of the Romantic vision, however, ignores important evidence. Once one looks more closely, and expands the horizon to include the generations on either side of the year in question (965–1035), thereby including other dates associated with the year 1000 (for example, 1033 as the millennium of the Passion), the evidence of apocalpytic concerns marks the period as exceptional, even in the eschatologically obsessed Middle Ages. Moreover, Augustine himself pointed the way to viewing the 1,000-year period since the Incarnation as the millennium spoken of in Revelation 20:7 (*City of God* 20. 7–9), thus making the year 1000 or 1033 a time for expecting the Antichrist and Last Judgment. Furthermore, Michelet and Glaber spoke of "terrors and hopes" and associated these apocalpytic expectations with positive developments like the Peace of God; their detractors spoke of apocalypticism only in terms of terrors. This larger perspective, which acknowledges the powerful ambiguity of apocalyptic expectation, suggests new approaches to a variety of early-eleventh-century religious and social phenomena, such as the appearance of popular heresy.

Moreover, knowledge (as opposed to use) of A.D. dating, far from unfamiliar or uncertain, was widespread, and variant dating systems often represented efforts either to confuse the issue (in 983 Abbo of Fleury, the great foe of apocalyptic expectations, corrected Bede's work by twenty-one years, thereby jumping straight to 1004), or to prolong the expectation (Glaber's mention of the switch from the millennium of the Incarnation to that of the Passion). Finally, the absence of explicit documents may in some cases reflect not indifference but an ecclesiastical reluctance to discuss so volatile an issue, an attitude which dated back to Augustine at least (Landes). The absence of apocalyptic invocations in Cluniac charters for the years around 1000 may have been part of a larger pattern (Focillon) rather than the product of chance (Lot). And Otto III's visit to Charlemagne's tomb may have represented a grand and anxious gesture by a non-Carolingian emperor trying to assert his legitimacy in an unquiet world by linking the emperor of A.D. 1000 with the emperor of 6000 *Annus Mundi.* (Duby, Verhelst, Landes) So much of the documentation suggests or permits apocalyptic interpretations that even the most cautious historians familiar with the evidence have concluded that the question deserves reopening (Hugenholtz, Verhelst).

BIBLIOGRAPHY

George L. Burr, "The Year 1000 and the Antecedents of the Crusades," in *American Historical Review,* 6 (1901); Georges Duby, *L'an mil* (1967); "Essays on the Peace of God: The Church and the People in Eleventh-century France," Thomas Head and Richard Landes, eds., special issue of *Historical Reflections,* 14 (1987); John France, *Historiarum libri quinque et Vita Willelmi Rudolfi Glabri* (1988). Henri Focillon, *The Year 1000,* Fred D. Wieck, trans. (1969); F. N. W. Hugenholtz, "Les terreurs de l'an mil: Enkele Hypothesen," in *Varia Historica aangeboden ann Professor Doctor A. W. Byvanck* (1954); R. B. C. Huygens, "Un témoin de la crainte de l'an 1000: La lettre sur les Hongrois," in *Latomus,* 15 (1956); Richard Landes, "Lest the Kingdom Come: Ecclesiastical Chronology and the Postponing of the Millennium from Barnabas to Charlemagne," in W. Verbeke, D. Verhelst, and A. Welkenhysen, eds. *The Use and Abuse of Eschatology in the Middle Ages* (1988); Ferdinand Lot, "Le mythe des terreurs de l'an mille," in *Recueil des travaux de Ferdinand Lot,* I (1968); Dom Plaine, "Les prétendues terreurs de l'an mille," in *Revue des questions historiques,* 13 (1873); Edmond Pognon, *L'an mille* (1947); D. Verhelst, "Adso van Montier-en-Der en de angst voor het jaar Duizend," in *Tijdschrift voor Geschiedenis,* 90 (1977).

RICHARD LANDES

[See also **Abbo of Fleury; Bede; Calendars and Reckoning of Time; Dionysus Exiguus; Heresy; Millennialism, Christian; Otto III Emperor; Peace of God, Truce of God; Radulphus Glaber; Thietmar von Merseburg.**]

YEMEN. In the early Islamic period, the Yemen was a geographical rather than a political unit that was ruled by a number of local dynasties organized around city-states. These local dynasties competed with a series of governors sent by the Abbasid caliphs in the seventh, eighth, and early ninth centuries. By the middle of the ninth century, however, the Abbasids had ceased to send governors, and the area experienced constant struggle between local dynasties until the Ayyubid conquest.

The history of the Yemen as a political entity began with its conquest in 1173/1174 by Turanshah, a brother of Saladin, the Ayyubid ruler of Egypt. The interest of the Ayyubids in the Yemen probably had to do with its importance in the Indian Ocean trade. The Fatimids had traditionally sent a fleet to safeguard Egyptian vessels there, and the Ayyubids undoubtedly shared their interest in preserving this vital link, particularly the port of Aden.

From the time Turanshah entered the northern Tihama in 1173 until 1229, much of the Yemen was part of the Ayyubid empire. The Ayyubids either destroyed or absorbed most of the petty dynasties. The one exception to this rule was the Zaydi imamate in the north, with its capital at Saᶜda, which provided continuous challenges to Ayyubid rule.

In the thirteenth century, the power of the Ayyubids was eclipsed by the rise of the Rasulids. This family had been neither influential nor an ally of the Ayyubids. They came to power over a period of time primarily through the succession of *iqṭāᶜ* grants by the Ayyubids to Rasulid family members. This process culminated in 1221, when the Ayyubid sultan al-Masᶜūd Yūsuf granted the city of Sanᶜa as an *iqṭāᶜ* to the Rasulid Badr al-Dīn Hasan. Almost immediately, Badr al-Din declared his independence.

For the next decade or so, the Yemen was the source of numerous internal problems that were exacerbated by the reluctance of Ayyubid emirs to accept this unpopular posting. During this period, the Rasulids consolidated their rule, and under the sultan al-Muẓaffar Yūsuf (1249–1294), when the kingdom stretched from the Hejaz to Ḥadramawt, the dynasty reached its highest point. Only the Zaydis in Saᶜda remained independent of the Rasulids.

In 1323, the Zaydis took Sanᶜa, ending Rasulid control in the north. The Rasulids remained powerful in the south, however, where they took a particular interest in fostering the agricultural activity that was the basis of the Yemen's economy.

Several important agricultural treatises were written by Rasulid rulers.

From the mid fifteenth century on, the situation of the Yemen as a whole was reflected in the struggles of the Tahirids and Zaydis for control of Sanᶜa and the gradual decline of the Rasulids' power in the south. In 1515, the Mamluks conquered the Yemen.

BIBLIOGRAPHY

Historical information is in Henry Cassels Kay, *Yaman: Its Early Mediaeval History* (1892), a translation of the chronicle of ᶜUmāra al-Yamani; Robert B. Serjeant and Ronald Lewcock, eds., *Ṣanᶜāʾ: An Arabian Islamic City* (1983); Gerald R. Smith, *The Ayyubids and the Early Rasulids in the Yemen (567–694/1173–1295)* (1978), II. See also D. Thomas Gochenour, "A Revised Bibliography of Medieval Yemeni History," in *Der Islam*, 63 (1986).

On the importance of agriculture, see Robert B. Serjeant, "The Cultivation of Cereals in Mediaeval Yemen," in *Arabian Studies*, I (1974), a translation of part of an agricultural treatise by the Rasulid sultan al-Malik al-Afdal (1370).

The importance of the port of Aden in the trade with India is treated in Solomon D. Goitein, *Letters of Medieval Jewish Traders* (1973) and "From Aden to India," in *Journal of the Economic and Social History of the Orient*, 23 (1980).

New light undoubtedly will be shed on the economic role of the Yemen in the Mamluk period when the documents discovered at Quseir al-Qadim on the Red Sea are examined. See D. Whitcomb and J. Johnson, "1982 Season of Excavations at Quseir al-Qadim," in *American Research Center in Egypt Newsletter*, no. 120 (1982).

PAULA SANDERS

[See also **Arabia, Islamic; Ayyubids; Iqṭāᶜ; Sanᶜa; Zaydis.**]

YESHIVA. See **Schools, Jewish.**

YEVELE, HENRY, English Late Gothic architect, designer ("devyser") of the king's works beginning in 1360. From his shop in London, Yevele directed construction of the nave at Canterbury, begun in 1379; continuation of the nave of Westminster Abbey, begun in 1362; and restoration of Westminster Hall (with the carpenter Hugh Herland), 1394–1400. Yevele was consultant to a number of projects and earned as much as £3,000 a year.

BIBLIOGRAPHY

John Harvey, *The Gothic World: 1100–1600* (1969).

CARL F. BARNES, JR.

YIDDISH, a European Jewish language from the Middle Ages that eventually became the Jewish language with the largest number of speakers.

The origins of Yiddish lie in the tenth-century migration of Jews from northern France to the Rhineland, where the Jews adopted the language of the local German-speaking population. From the Rhineland the Jews spread to other Middle High German speech areas. From the outset Yiddish differed from German: it contained a Romance element brought from France as well as a rich Semitic (Hebrew and Aramaic) element drawn from Jewish tradition. Moreover Yiddish, like all other Jewish languages, is written in the Hebrew alphabet.

The period of the earliest development of Yiddish lasted until the mid thirteenth century, which marked a turning point. It was then that Yiddish moved away from Germanic norms, as its speakers migrated eastward into a Slavic environment to such places as Bohemia and Poland. A number of Czech elements are the earliest surviving Slavic influences; other Slavic contributions to Yiddish came from Polish and later also from Belorussian and Ukrainian. The Yiddish-speaking territory eventually extended across much of Europe. The vastness of this region led to dialectical differentiation, resulting in three main groups: West Yiddish (Holland, Alsace-Lorraine, Switzerland, and most of Germany), East Yiddish (the Ukraine, Rumania, Galicia, Belorussia, Lithuania, Latvia, and Poland), and the transitional Central Yiddish (Bohemia, Moravia, western Slovakia, and western Hungary). Although there was no standard pronunciation, this period of Old Yiddish, which lasted from about 1250 to 1500, saw the rise of a relatively uniform literary language, known from a small surviving corpus of Bible translations, poetry, and official records kept by communal scribes.

Because of the paucity of texts from the early period and the relatively standardized nature of the literary language of many that are extant, it is difficult to study the historical development of Yiddish. Nevertheless, it can be said that as Yiddish developed, the three main elements—the Semitic, Slavic, and Germanic—did not remain separate

entities. Rather, there was a process of synthesis: morphological markers, semantics, systems of word formation, and affixes were freely shared. In addition there was spontaneous development in phonology and semantics and the rise of new forms, words, and constructions through analogy, isolation, shifts in syntactical connection, and other developments.

There are few surviving examples of medieval Yiddish literature. What little there is from the earliest stage of Yiddish includes Bible glosses and glossaries from the twelfth century. A Cairo genizah manuscript from 1382 contains versions of the stories of Abraham, Joseph, Moses, and the binding of Isaac. There are also fourteenth-century transcriptions of German works into Yiddish. Done for a Jewish audience, such works usually excised or changed Christian religious references found in the originals. In the fifteenth and sixteenth centuries biblical epics based on Samuel and Kings were composed. These works, which employed German poetic conventions, embellished the original biblical tale with talmudic and midrashic references. By the end of the fifteenth century, the Ashkenazic Jews in northern Italy were producing an original secular literature.

Yiddish as a spoken and literary language continued to develop beyond the Middle Ages. The years 1500–1700 are the period of Middle Yiddish. Modern Yiddish includes those forms of the language in use from 1700 to the present.

[See also **Arthurian Literature; Ashkenaz; German Language; Jews in Europe; Slavic Languages and Literature.**]

YNGLINGATAL, a late-ninth-century skaldic poem by the Norwegian poet Þjóðólfr ór Hvini. It was composed in honor of a local Norwegian "king" or chieftain, Rǫgnvaldr heiðumhárr (or heiðumhæri) of Vestfold. Nothing is known about this king except that he was the cousin of the first monarch to unify Norway, Harald Fairhair (*ca. 853–932*). *Ynglingatal* is a genealogical poem, the first of its kind in the Norse poetic tradition. It comprises ninety half stanzas in the meter *kviðu-*

háttr, enumerating twenty-seven generations of Rǫgnvaldr's ancestors, and tracing them back to the Swedish Yngling dynasty in Uppsala. Each king is commemorated in two to five stanzas that provide his name, information about his death, and usually a place-name designating the location of his burial.

Snorri Sturluson used *Ynglingatal* as the main source for his *Ynglinga saga,* the first section in his history of the Norwegian kings (*Heimskringla*). Snorri's version is likely to be complete because the same genealogical list, with minor variations, is recorded earlier in Ari Þorgilsson's *Íslendingabók* (*ca.* 1130) and the anonymous *Historia Norwegiae* (between 1170 and 1220). Snorri's account also provides information about the Yngling kings not found in *Ynglingatal,* suggesting that the poem was transmitted with an explanatory prose commentary, possibly derived from Swedish sources.

Structurally, *Ynglingatal* falls into three parts. The first covers eight Yngling kings, whose names are clearly rooted in myth and legend. The circumstances surrounding their deaths can be quite bizarre (drowning in a mead vat, for example). One king, Dómaldi, was reputedly sacrificed by the Swedes to ensure good crops. The ritualistic overtones of such deaths led earlier scholars to speculate about sacral kingship in ancient Sweden, but recent assessments are more skeptical.

The second part of *Ynglingatal* surveys fifteen kings with alliterating names (vowel alliteration). This alliterative pattern persisted among the historical kings of Uppsala. Two of the kings mentioned in this part of *Ynglingatal,* Óttarr and his son Aðils, are also mentioned in the Old English *Beowulf* (Ohtere and his son Eadgils), indicating that this part of the Swedish dynasty was deeply rooted in ancient east Scandinavian tradition.

The last part of *Ynglingatal* commemorates the alleged Norwegian branch of the Yngling dynasty (six kings, including Rǫgnvaldr). There is no reason to believe that the connection between the Swedish Yngling family and the Vestfold kings was Þjóðólfr's invention, but because the composition of *Ynglingatal* coincided with King Harald Fairhair's consolidation of Norway it is not unlikely that the poem was originally conceived as a political statement endorsing the official lineage of the Vestfold dynasty.

BIBLIOGRAPHY

Sources. Bjarni Aðalbjarnarson, ed., *Heimskringla,* I (1941); Finnur Jónsson, ed., *Den norsk-islandske skjaldedigtning,* **AI** and **BI** (1912–1915); Ernst A. Kock, *Den norsk-isländska skaldediktningen,* I (1946). A translation is Lee M. Hollander, trans., *Heimskringla: History of the Kings of Norway* (1964).

Studies. Walter Åkerlund, *Studier över Ynglingatal* (1939); Walter Baetke, *Yngvi und die Ynglingar: Eine quellenkritische Untersuchung über das nordische "Sakralkönigtum"* (1964); Siegfried Beyschlag, *Konungasögur: Untersuchungen zur Königssaga bis Snorri. Die älteren Übersichtswerke samt Ynglingasaga* (1950), esp. 21–111; Lars Lönnroth, "Dómaldi's Death and the Myth of Sacral Kingship," in *Structure and Meaning in Old Norse Literature: New Approaches to Textual Analysis and Literary Criticism,* John Lindow, Lars Lönnroth, and Gerd Wolfgang Weber, eds. (1986); Edith Marold, *Kenningkunst: Ein Beitrag zu einer Poetik der Skaldendichtung* (1983), esp. 114–153. Further references are in Lee M. Hollander, *A Bibliography of Skaldic Studies* (1958).

KARI ELLEN GADE

[See also **Kviðuháttr; Norway; Skaldic Poetry; Snorri Sturluson; Þjóðólfr ór Hvini.**]

YNGVARS SAGA VÍÐFÖRLA. Set in the first half of the eleventh century, the "Saga of Yngvarr the Far-traveled" describes a romantic search for the source of a great river. The title hero is a Christian warrior of royal descent whose father is said to have been the grandson of King Eiríkr sigrsæli (the Victorious), and who is said to have spent years in Russia after being banished from Sweden.

When King Ólafr of Sweden refuses to bestow on Yngvarr the title of king, Yngvarr takes a fleet of thirty ships across the Baltic and up the waterways of Russia, where he encounters not only a hostile population but also giants, dragons, and demons. Some of Yngvarr's men succumb to the temptations of women and gold, losing their lives as the result. Several of the landmarks on the way lie far beyond Russia (Sigeum, Heliopolis, Scythopolis) and are evidently borrowed from learned sources, such as Isidore of Seville's *Etymologies.* References to elephants, cyclopes, and the dragon Jaculus appear to have the same origin. Yngvarr tries to convert the beautiful Queen Silkisif of Heliopolis to Christianity and she offers him her kingdom and herself, but he will not give up his journey. After many tests of endurance he finally learns that the great Russian river has its source near the Red Sea. On his way back he is taken ill and dies, the survivors leaving the body with Queen Silkisif for burial and then making their way back to Sweden to tell the news.

Several years later Yngvarr's natural son, Sveinn, leads a second expedition to the east. After Queen Silkisif has embraced the faith and built a church dedicated to "Saint" Yngvarr, Sveinn marries her and becomes king of the realm. Eventually, however, he decides to go back to his homeland, reaching Sweden after many remarkable adventures.

Yngvars saga víðförla is an extraordinary combination of historical fact, foreign learning, popular fantasy, and literary motif. Yngvarr and the characters figuring in the first part of the story were real historical personages; according to the Icelandic Annals, Yngvarr died in 1041. In Sweden there are about thirty runic stones, all apparently dating from the eleventh century, commemorating the deaths of his companions on the way to the east.

In an interesting, if controversial, epilogue the saga is said to have been composed by "the learned monk Oddr [Snorrason]," who belonged to the Benedictine monastery of Þingeyrar in the north of Iceland and flourished in the latter part of the twelfth century. Oddr is said to have used three oral informants mentioned by name; their sources are also given. Although most scholars have rejected Oddr's authorship, no conclusive evidence has been put forward to disprove it.

The saga has obvious affinities with certain other works with a historical basis, including *Óláfs saga Tryggvasonar* and *Eymundar þáttr Hringssonar*. The earliest reference to it is in *Göngu-Hrólfs saga*, claiming that the river Dvina "is the third or fourth biggest in the world and it was to find its source that Yngvarr the Far-traveled set out, as told in his saga."

BIBLIOGRAPHY

F. Braun, "Hvem var Yngvarr enn viðforli? Ett bidrag till Sveriges historia under XI århundradets första hälft," and Otto von Friesen, "Hvem var Yngvarr enn viðforli?" in *Fornvännen*, 5 (1910); D. Hofmann, "Die Yngvars saga víðförla und Oddr munkr inn fróði," in *Speculum Norroenum*, U. Dronke *et al.*, eds. (1981), and "Zu Oddr Snorrasons Yngvars saga víðförla," in *Skandinavistik*, 14 (1984); Rudolf Meissner, "Das rote Meer," in *Zeitschrift für deutsches Altertum und deutsche Literatur*, 73 (1936); Emil Olson, ed., *Yngvars saga víðförla* (1912); Alf Thulin, "Ingvarståget—en ny datering?" in *Arkiv för nordisk filologi*, 90 (1975).

HERMANN PÁLSSON

[See also **Fornaldarsögur; Gongu-Hrólfs Saga; Isidore of Seville, St.; Oddr Snorrason; Óláfs Saga Tryggvasonar; Sweden.**]

YORK PLAYS. The York cycle of mystery plays is a sequence of short dramatic episodes telling the story of salvation history from Creation to the Last Judgment. The sequence was performed at York annually on Corpus Christi Day by the craft guilds of the city under the auspices of the city council. The first evidence for the existence of the cycle is for 1376, and the last known performance took place in 1569, before it was suppressed by the Elizabethan ecclesiastical commission. At that time, the text disappeared along with the two other religious plays performed in York, the Creed play and the Paternoster play. In the nineteenth century, the cycle was recognized among the manuscripts then in the library of the earl of Ashburnham. For many years the only scholarly edition was that of Lucy Toulmin Smith, titled *York Plays*. A new edition by Richard Beadle, called *The York Plays*, appeared in 1982.

The manuscript, now in the British Library (Add. MS 35290), is the master copy, or register, of episodes that were the property of the craft guilds. It was made for the corporation of York sometime after 1475. Marginal notations in the hands of later clerks, blank leaves, episodes entered during the sixteenth century, and other manuscript peculiarities indicate that what survives is a practical working script, not a polished literary text.

Nothing is known about the authorship of the plays. Earlier scholars argued for several layers of composition, one succeeding another in an evolving complexity of verse pattern, but arguments about layers of composition are not now regarded as reliable. Although the text contains a great variety of verse forms, there is a remarkable unity of thought patterns and imagery. The cycle, which forms a unified dramatic whole, both tells the Christian story and celebrates Christian salvation. Its statement is a positive one. Again and again the episodes offer members of the audience explicit models for leading a Christian life through the patriarchs, Mary, Joseph, and Christ and his disciples. As the cycle progresses the spectators are led to lament at the fall of Lucifer, rejoice at the birth of Christ, suffer with him through the Passion sequence, revel in the defeat of Satan at the Harrowing of Hell, and consider, finally, their individual salvation at the Last Judgment.

The manuscript contains forty-eight separate episodes (although episode 17 is, in large part, a repetition of 16) and a fragment of a sixteenth-century play on the coronation of the Virgin. Blank leaves have been left for the Vintners' play on the Marriage Feast at Cana and the Ironmongers' on the Washing of Christ's Feet. Assuming that 16 and 17 were never both performed in the same year, the register indicates that it is possible that forty-seven separate episodes may have been performed in one day.

Many civic and guild records survive concerning the play. The most important for an understanding of the text are the two lists of episodes and their sponsoring crafts in the civic memorandum book (York, City Archives, E 20). The first list, dated 1415, gives a description of forty-one episodes. The second, undated, list apparently contains fifty-seven episodes. The corrections, deletions, and marginal notations in the 1415 version indicate that it was the working master list, altered as the episodes themselves changed. From other evidence it is clear that a major revision was undertaken in the early 1420's. The final shape of the episodes on the death, assumption, and coronation of the Virgin was not determined until the 1480's. Further revisions took place in individual episodes after the register was made, but the detailed alterations were made only in the guild copies. Only one unaltered guild copy, that of the Scriveners' episode of Doubting Thomas, survives.

A craft guild or group of guilds was responsible for the production of each episode. The guilds owned, repaired, and made careful provision for storing special wagons called pageants that served as stage sets. Evidence from the Mercers' Guild and from descriptions of craft pageant wagons used in royal entries indicate that they were elaborate and sophisticated vehicles richly decorated and frequently fitted out with elevating devices or other mechanical contrivances. Costuming was frequently lavish, and divine or diabolical figures seem to have been masked. The standard of acting was controlled by a committee of the city council. The evidence indicates that both amateur actors and paid professionals were used. Individual actors were forbidden to perform in more than one episode during the day.

Until about 1467 the play was preceded by a separate civic event, the procession of Corpus Christi. From 1468 on, the procession took place the day after Corpus Christi, leaving the feast itself as the day for playmaking. The craft guilds were ordered to be ready with their pageants at 4:30 A.M. beside the south gate of the city. Each episode in the sequence was then performed first outside the gates of the priory of Holy Trinity and then again in order at each stop or "station" within the walls of the city appointed by the city council for the hearing of the play. The normal number of stations was twelve. Some modern scholars have challenged this reconstruction of the method of performance, claiming it is too cumbersome and time-consuming. The contemporary evidence is, however, irrefutable. What is not definitely known is whether the full cycle of a possible forty-seven episodes was ever performed in one year.

The York Plays were revived by E. Martin Browne for performance in York as part of the Festival of Britain in 1951. A shortened version of the text was prepared for that production by Canon John S. Purvis, who subsequently modernized the complete text. Similar versions of the cycle have been performed regularly in York since 1951 as part of the triennial York Festival. Other abridged versions have been presented. Two full-length experimental productions using pageant wagons and many separate groups acting as craft guilds—one at the University of Leeds in 1975 and one at the University of Toronto in 1977—have done much to clarify the original method of production and have led to a greater appreciation of the integrity of the text.

BIBLIOGRAPHY

The general field of medieval drama is served by Carl J. Stratman, ed., *Bibliography of Medieval Drama*, 2 vols., 2nd rev. ed. (1972). See also Richard Beadle, ed., *The York Plays* (1982); Richard J. Collier, *Poetry and Drama in the York Corpus Christi Play*, 1978; Clifford Davidson, *Creation to Doom* (1984); Stanley J. Kahrl, *Traditions of Medieval English Drama* (1975); Rosemary Woolf, *The English Mystery Plays*, (1972).

The external evidence concerning the plays at York has been collected and edited by Alexandra F. Johnston and Margaret Rogerson, eds., *York: Records of Early English Drama*, 2 vols. (1979). The first volume has a select bibliography containing all the books and articles relating to the external evidence concerning the play and the staging controversy. The Toronto production of the cycle was extensively reviewed by David Bevington *et al.*, "The York Cycle at Toronto," in *Research Opportunities in Renaissance Drama*, **20** (1977), and discussed by

Alexandra F. Johnston, "The York Cycle: 1977," in *University of Toronto Quarterly*, 48 (1978).

ALEXANDRA F. JOHNSTON

[See also **Chester Plays; Corpus Christi, Feast of; Drama, Liturgical; Guilds and Métiers; Guilds of Artists; Mystery Plays; N-Town Plays.**]

YORK RITE. The liturgical rite of pre-Reformation York was a local variant of the Roman rite which developed after 1066. Prior to the Conquest, liturgical practices in York reflected the influences of the Roman and Celtic churches. The extensive Norman reform of the eleventh century imposed Norman-French liturgical customs and rituals at York and elsewhere in the English church.

The York Mass rite is mainly the Gregorian Mass of the eighth century with many interpolations from a second source, most probably the church of Rouen. The earliest printed missal of the York rite was produced at Rouen in 1509. Subsequent editions of the York missal appeared at Rouen in 1516, 1517, and 1530. In 1533 an edition was also known at Paris.

Although the Mass rites of York and Sarum do not belong to the same group (the York rite belongs to the Gregorian, not the Sarum, group), the two are similar in many respects. As in the Sarum rite and the other English rites, the prayers at the foot of the altar were in a short form and Psalm 42 was recited by the celebrant on the way to the altar. At York the priest's blessing of the deacon and the deacon's response before the reading of the Gospel did not follow the Sarum pattern. Furthermore, the "secret" blessing at the end of the Gospel was unique to the York rite. During the offertory, the celebrant was instructed to wash his hands twice, once before touching the host and once after censing the altar. During the latter washing he recited the hymn *Veni Creator Spiritus.* The host and the chalice were offered simultaneously, and the choir responded to the "Orate fratres et sorores" by repeating the first three verses of Psalm 19 in a low voice. The canon was identical with that of the Roman rite, except for the mention of the king in the Memento. The formula for the kiss of peace at York is another unique feature. Instead of the usual "Pax tibi et ecclesiae" (Peace to you and to the church), the York formula was "Habete vinculum pacis et caritatis ut apti sitis sacrosanctis mysteriis

Dei" (Keep the bond of peace and love so that you may be fit for the sacred mysteries of God). At York the prayers that preceded Communion were different from those in the Sarum form and the formula for the priest's reception of the Sacrament was unique. The number of sequences included in the Mass propers in the York Missal exceeds those of the Sarum Missal.

The York Breviary contains many minor variations from both Sarum and Rome. The York Manual and remaining service books, while maintaining a close affinity to Sarum, do demonstrate some distinctive features, most notably the troth-plighting of the York marriage rite, which omits the words "with my body I thee worship." York had its own calendar and special feast, which Henderson includes in his edition of the Missal. Little is known of the color sequence at York, but it probably was not different from that of Sarum.

BIBLIOGRAPHY

Walter H. Frere, "The Newly-Found York Gradual," in *Journal of Theological Studies,* 2 (1901); W. G. Henderson, ed., *York Manual and Processional* (Surtees Society 63) (1875); W. G. Henderson, ed., *York Missal* (Surtees Society 59, 60) (1872); Archdale A. King, *Liturgies of the Past* (1959), 276–374; S. Lawley, ed., *York Breviary* (Surtees Society 71, 75) (1880, 1883); George O. Sayles, *The Medieval Foundations of England* (1961), 45–49; 249–269; Thomas F. Simmons, ed., *Lay Folks Mass Book* (Early English Text Society 71) (1879), xvii–lxxi, 90–117, 352–357.

CLEO LELAND BOYD

[See also **Celtic Church; Colors, Liturgical; Mass, Liturgy of; Rouen, Rite of; Sarum Rite.**]

YORK TRACTATES, a collection of extraordinary, anonymous texts in the unique codex Cambridge, Corpus Christi College, MS 415, a manuscript that belonged to Matthew Parker, archbishop of Canterbury, and passed into the library at Corpus shortly before his death in 1575. Although the tractates were cited in the seventeenth century by Bishop Joseph Hall in his work on married clergy, they were not really discovered in modern times until 1895, when Karl Hampe found them, and they were given to Heinrich Böhmer for partial publication in 1897 in the *Libelli de lite* series of the *Monumenta Germaniae historica*. Since that time scholars have devoted special attention to the extraordinary statements in the tractates regarding ecclesio-political relationships and clerical marriage and to the identity of the anonymous author or authors of the tractates. So similar are the positions taken on these two subjects to those of the early Anglican church in the sixteenth century —the supremacy of secular rulers over ecclesiastical, and approval of clerical marriage—that one of the tractates' keenest students, George Williams, once wondered aloud in his Harvard lectures if the manuscript were not a forgery of the sixteenth century—although since that time Bernhard Bischoff has dated the codex to about 1100 and not later than 1120.

The codex contains some thirty diverse writings generally referred to as tractates. In fact, some are only fragments, pedagogical pieces, sketches of arguments, first and second versions of a single tract, and loosely related pieces that attracted a later title either within the table of contents or in the body of the manuscript itself. And although scholars' attention has focused on the ecclesio-political matters and clerical marriage, the spectrum of subjects touched in the tractates is extremely wide: canon law, sacraments, liturgy, problems related to the ecclesiastical orders, biblical exegesis, freedom of metropolitans from primatial encroachment, the illegitimacy of papal exemption of monasteries from episcopal jurisdiction, support for the ordination of the sons of priests, a protestation against the abbey of Fécamp, the questionable primacy of Lyons over Rouen, and the relationship of Canterbury and York.

Although Bishop Hall had noted in 1621 that the anonymous author of the tractates had described himself as from Rouen in Normandy, Böhmer attributed the tractates to the Norman archbishop of York, Gerard, an attribution he later withdrew while nonetheless continuing to call the author the Anonymous of York. Since that time a number of scholars have supported this attribution to a Yorkish author, most notably and recently Norman Cantor. Other scholars have argued that the author may have written in both Normandy and England. A third group has seen several authors as responsible for the tractates. But the consensus of scholarly opinion now seems to follow the lead of George Williams and attributes the totality of tractates to one man who should be styled as the Norman Anonymous. Whether or not the Anonymous was William Bona Anima, as Williams powerfully argued, is still debated, but many signs point to this archdeacon and then archbishop of Rouen (1079–1110) as the person responsible for the tractates. The most significant research on the origins of the tractates since Williams' work has shown their close connection to liturgical, canonical, and patristic texts in circulation in Normandy at the time of the manuscript's compilation and their similarity to those issuing from the contemporary chapter school of Laon.

BIBLIOGRAPHY

Anne Barstow, *The Defense of Clerical Marriage in the Eleventh and Twelfth Centuries: The Norman Anonymous and His Contemporaries* (diss., Columbia Univ., 1979); Norman Cantor, *Church, Kingship, and Lay Investiture in England, 1089–1135* (1958); Wilfried Hartmann, "Beziehungen des Normannischen Anonymous zu frühscholastischen Bildungszentren," in *Deutsches Archiv für Erforschung des Mittelalters,* **31** (1975); Ruth Nineham, "The So-called Anonymous of York," in *Journal of Ecclesiastical History,* **14** (1963), and "K. Pellens' Edition of the Tracts of the Norman Anonymous," in *Transactions of the Cambridge Bibliographical Society,* **4,** pt. 4 (1967); Karl Pellens, "The Tracts of the Norman Anonymous: C.C.C. MS. 415," *ibid.,* **4,** pt. 2 (1965); Roger E. Reynolds, "The Unidentified Sources of the Norman Anonymous," *ibid.,* **5,** pt. 2 (1969), *The Ordinals of Christ from Their Origins to the Twelfth Century* (1978), and "Liturgical Scholarship at the Time of the Investiture Controversy: Past Research and Future Opportunities," in *Harvard Theological Review,* **71** (1978); George H. Williams, *The Norman Anonymous of 1100 A.D.* (1951); Kennerly M. Woody, "Marginalia on the Norman Anonymous," in *Harvard Theological Review,* **66** (1973).

ROGER E. REYNOLDS

[See also **Celibacy; Clergy; Ecclesiology.**]

YPRES, an important medieval town and center of cloth production, is located on the Iperleet, a tributary of the Yser River, and on a canal joining the Yser to the Lys River. The town of Ypres (Ieper in Flemish and Villa Yprensis in Latin), is situated about twenty-four kilometers (almost fifteen miles) north of Lille and a few kilometers east of the French border. Throughout the Middle Ages, Ypres was a part of the county of Flanders, which under a succession of strong counts became virtually an independent state, with few feudal and political ties to the French kings and Holy Roman emperors. Modern Ypres is a town of 35,000 inhabitants, about 7,000 more people than it had at the height of its economic prosperity during the middle of the thirteenth century.

Ypres owes its origin to the Viking raids of the ninth century. To defend the region that lay close to the North Sea, the counts of Flanders constructed castles at strategic points. At Ypres a *castrum* was erected on the islet of Iperleet, and it was here that the count's castellon had his headquarters, defending the castle and nearby region with a garrison and administering the financial and judicial affairs of the surrounding territory known as the castellany of Ypres. The castellan was a vassal of the counts and held in fief from them extensive lands in return for his services. Until the tenth century there was nothing at Ypres that could be considered a town with a community of merchants and craftsmen.

Thanks to the strategic location of Ypres on the Yser River and on the principal route between Bruges and towns such as Arras, Laon, and Paris, Ypres was one of the first Flemish sites to benefit from the economic revival of Western Europe. During the tenth century a community of merchants settled just across the Iperleet from the castle in a area known as a forum. Here arose the merchants' homes and commercial buildings, and here was located a market and eventually a hall that became the center for a thriving trade in wool cloth.

Until the twelfth century this growing community of merchants and craftsmen was under the governance of the feudal castellan. Although the inhabitants of the forum originally had no political power, they nevertheless did come to receive elementary privileges that gave them various legal, economic, and social liberties. Unlike the peasants in the countryside, the townspeople who lived in the forum became legally free.

As Ypres, Bruges, Ghent, and neighboring St. Omer and Arras grew in population and expanded their economic activities, they began to negotiate for and to demand concessions from the counts that would give them the privilege of local self-government. Such concessions came quite rapidly after the assassination of Count Charles the Good at Bruges on 2 March 1127. Because there were no heirs, civil war broke out among a number of contenders who, in order to obtain support from the growing towns, granted them charters that made them self-governing communes. Although the original charger for Ypres has not survived, that granted to St. Omer

has, and it is known that most such charters were almost identical in the privileges granted. The forum of Ypres was freed from most of the castellan's authority and thereby escaped from his feudal jurisdiction. Henceforth, the burghers of the forum were responsible for all urban affairs, such as finance, justice, fortifications, public works, security, and regulation of local commerce and the guilds.

Ypres was governed through the mechanism of a municipal magistracy, known as an *échevinage*. The individual magistrates, called *échevins*, were generally leading merchants. There were thirteen of them, and in the early years they were appointed for life. During the twelfth century it was the count who appointed, or at least nominated, the *échevins*. Early in the thirteenth century the *échevinage* was significantly reorganized. Under the charter of 1209 the *échevins* were no longer apointed for life. Instead, the term of office was set at one year, and the *échevins* were appointed or elected by the inhabitants of Ypres. From this time until the Burgundian dukes became rulers of Flanders in the late fourteenth century, the authority of the courts in Ypres was nominal at best; sometimes, when there was a weak count or there were political and military crises, the count's authority was non-existent.

Before the thirteenth century Ypres was the preeminent town in Flanders for the production of wool cloth. It was already importing some wool from England and merchants were coming from all over Western Europe to purchase its finished products. We know, for instance, of a group of Lombard merchants in Ypres in 1127. When news of the assassination of Count Charles reached them, they hurriedly departed.

By 1127 a strong stone wall had been erected around an area that embraced not only the forum but also the churches of St. Martin, St. Jacob, and St. Peter. In the first half of the thirteenth century the fortifications were extended around new suburbs (*faubourgs*). And by the late fourteenth century walls had been erected on the other side of the Iperleet. Long before, the castle had ceased to function as a fortress, and no longer did the castellan reside there. All was under the local authority of the *échevinage*.

The golden age of economic and political power for Ypres was in the thirteenth century. Along with Ghent and Bruges, Ypres virtually controlled the political and economic affairs of Flanders. They became known as "the three cities of Flanders" (*les trois villes de Flandre* or *de drie steden van Flaenderen*). Their *échevinages* forced the counts to grant them more privileges and to follow economic and political policies that benefited their interests.

The leading merchant families of Ypres came to dominate the political life of the town, developing aristocratic airs and tastes. They and their counterparts in the other towns came to be known as patricians. This coincided with a marked civic spirit that resulted in the construction of the famous cloth hall of Ypres, which was the largest and most magnificent in Flanders and in Western Europe. In addition, many churches were erected, public works supported, elementary schools organized for the instruction of the children of the bourgeoisie, hospitals founded, and all sorts of charitable works sustained.

Commerce in thirteenth-century Ypres included not only a wholesale trade in wool cloth but also a system of finance that extended credit to both producer and buyer. Records known as *lettres de foire* (fair letters) show that wool cloth was purchased on credit at Ypres and that the buyers would settle their accounts later, usually at one of the Champagne fairs. Along with Messines, Thourout, Lille, and Douai, Ypres was the site of a fair to which came merchants from Italy, France, and Germany. Ypres was also a member of the Hanse.

Toward the end of the thirteenth century the economic fortunes of Ypres began to deteriorate, mostly because of the bitter social and economic conflicts between the craftsmen and the merchant-entrepreneurs, who had exploited the former economically and had denied them any role in the political affairs of Ypres. As these tensions grew in the early fourteenth century, Ypres also suffered from the wars between France and Flanders, which caused heavy war taxes, widespread strife across Flanders, and the eventual loss of much Flemish territory near Ypres. These setbacks invariably hurt trade and industry. Then in 1316 came the great famine of northern Europe, which severely hurt Ypres. It has been estimated that Ypres lost 2,794 of its habitants to famine and attendant disease. Some thirty years later came the bubonic plague, which took a further toll. As a result the population of Ypres fell at one point to as low as 8,000.

When the county of Flanders came under the rule of the Burgundian duke Philip the Bold in 1384, the economic decline of Ypres was beyond repair. Already the cheaper wool cloth fabricated in England was sweeping Flemish cloth from the European markets. To help the cloth industry of Ypres the Burgundian dukes forbade the manufacture of wool cloth in the rural area around the town in neighboring small villages such as Poperinghe. But the decline continued, and early in the sixteenth century only 100 looms were still working. The area around Ypres had become a rural slum. In the centuries that followed, the troubles of Ypres were exacerbated by religious strife and by the wars of the Habsburgs and French kings. On the frontier between the territories of these two powers, Ypres became a prinicpal fort; vestiges of these fortifications survived into the twentieth century.

BIBLIOGRAPHY

Although somewhat dated, these studies by Guillaume Des Marez remain fundamental: *Étude sur la propriété foncière dans les villes du moyen âge et spécialement en Flandre* (1898, repr. 1978) and *La lettre de foire à Ypres au XIIIᵉ siècle* (1901). See also Guillaume Des Marez and E. de Sagher, *Comptes de la ville d'Ypres de 1267 à 1329*, 2 vols. (1909–1913); Napoléon de Pauw, *Ypre jeghen Poperinghe angaende den verbonden* (1899).

Other useful studies that deal with Ypres are Patrick Chorley, "The Cloth Exports of Flanders and Northern France During the Thirteenth Century: A Luxury Trade?" in *Economic History Review*, 2nd ser., 40 (1987); François L. Ganshof, *Étude sur le développement des villes entre Loire et Rhin au moyen âge* (1943); Henri Pirenne, *Histoire de Belgique*, I, 5th rev. ed. (1929), and II, 3rd rev. ed. (1922), and *Les villes et les institutions urbaines*, 2 vols. (1939); various articles of Hans van Werveke in his *Miscellanea Mediaevalia* (1968); and the new edition of the *Algemene Geschiedenis der Nederlanden*, I–II (1981–1982).

BRYCE LYON

[See also **Black Death; Bruges; Burgundy, Duchy of; Castellan; Commune; Échevin; Fairs; Famine in Western Europe; Flanders and the Low Countries; Ghent; Hanseatic League; Lille; Rouen; Textile Technology; Textile Workers; Trade; Urbanism; Wool.**]

YSENGRIMUS (Iron Mask), a Flemish animal epic written in Latin about 1150 by Magister Nivardus, according to a fourteenth-century Berlin florilegium. Consisting of 6,574 lines in unrhymed, elegiac distichs, it presents twelve episodes in seven books. Symmetrically structured in a partial frame, the episodes relate the decline and death of the wolf Ysengrim, whose mounting misfortunes are largely engineered by the fox Reinard, his malevolent and ever-present relative and adviser.

The manuscripts are the following: *A*, from St. Trond near Maastricht, Liège University Library, no. 668 (thirteenth century); *E*, from Huy on the Meuse, Liège University Library, no. 669 (fourteenth century); *C*, Brussels, Bibliothèque Royale Albert Ier, no. 2838 (fourteenth century); *D*, Pommersfelden, Schönborn Library, no. 2671 (fourteenth century); *B*, Paris, Bibliothèque Nationale, no. 8494 (fourteenth century). *Ysengrimus* also appears in florilegia: *f*, Ghent University Library, no. 267 (thirteenth/fourteenth century), 416 lines; *g*, Douai Town Library, no. 371 (thirteenth century), 182 lines; *h*, Berlin, Deutsche Staatsbibliothek, Berlin MS Diez B. Santen, 60 (fourteenth century), 104 lines; *i*, Berlin, cod. theol. fol. 381 (fifteenth century), 738 lines. Two lines each appear in *k*, Douai no. 292; *b*, Strassburg, cod. 105; and *m*, Wolfenbüttel, cod. Helmstadt 185. Albert von Stade's *Troilus* (thirteenth century) contains four lines.

The place of composition has been given as Ghent, Lille, and Liège. The action takes place on the Flemish-French language border; the terms *teutonicus* and *teutonice* are probably used to mean Dietsch (medieval Flemish), not German. Important time indexes mentioned in text are the Second Crusade (1148), lamented in 7.465ff.; and the attack on Bishop Anselm of Tournai (1146–1149) in 5.109ff.

The chronological sequence of episodes in the plot is 4, 5, 6, 7, 1, 2, 3, 8, 9, 10, 11, 12. Episode 7, the lion's sickness, serves as frame for 1, 2, and 3. The work opens with 4, the division of a ham, the wolf's only success in the poem: On the verge of devouring Reinard, Ysengrim releases the fox, who promises him a share in a ham that he will take from a passing peasant with Ysengrim's help. When Reinard returns after tricking the peasant, he finds the wolf has devoured the ham; only a string is left (1.1–528). Reinard takes revenge in 5, the fishing episode, in which he persuades the wolf to fish with his tail in freezing water. The immobilized wolf is attacked by peasants, who hack off his tail (1.529–2.158). In 6, Reinard makes Ysengrim act as surveyor for four rams who are dividing a plot. The wolf is gored as the rams simultaneously attack from four sides (2.159–688). In 7, Rufanus, the sick lion, is cured when he is wrapped in the flayed wolf's skin at Reinard's suggestion (3.1–1,198). At the celebration of his recovery, the boar reads

Bruno's poem, which chronicles the three episodes that took place before the division of the ham.

Episode 1 tells of Bertiliana the roe's pilgrimage, during which the fox restrains the wolf from attacking the animal pilgrims (4.1–810). A tale of fox and rooster (2) follows, in which fox tricks rooster but is outwitted by the bird (4.811–5.316). In 3, Ysengrim enters the monastery of Blandigny as a monk and antagonizes the brethren. While the monks thrash the wolf, Reinard visits his lair, dishonors his children, and violates his wife (5.317–1,130). Episode 8 tells of an altercation between stallion and stork (5.1,131–1,166). The horse is then approached by the wolf, who demands his skin and a buttock. The stallion persuades the wolf to examine his foot and kicks him in the face (5.1,167–1,322). In 9, Reinard persuades Ysengrim to eat Joseph the ram, who instead jumps into the wolf's jaws, injuring him severely (6.1–132). When a calf is divided between the lion, Ysengrim, and Reinard in episode 10, Ysengrim loses his skin once more, while Reinard divides the calf to the lion's satisfaction (6.133–348). Ysengrim attempts to gain a new skin from Carcophas the ass in episode 11, but instead loses a foot in a trap (6.349–550). When he encounters the sow Salaura and her companions in episode 12, the swine tear Ysengrim to pieces and devour him (7.1–708).

Structured like a classical epic (*Aeneid*), *Ysengrimus* emphasizes the dialogue form in its presentations. Short statements used for transition by the poet, frequently omitted from book 6.53 onward, introduce these altercations, which depict the triumph of intelligence over brute strength. The poet is a masterly stylist at home with literature (Boethius, Cato, Horace, Juvenal, Lucan, Sedulius, Statius); has a wealth of biblical quotations and folklore at his command; and shows an intense and thorough knowledge of Ovid, whose flowing elegance he successfully emulates. Relying on the extended metaphor of the wolf-monk, the *Ysengrimus* interlaces proverbs, exempla, metaphors, and sententiae; shows use of litotes in irony and sarcastic perversion of prayer and benediction formulas; and at times rises to rabid anticlerical invective that pillories regular and nonregular clergy as well as the pope.

Jokes that center on beatings or on parts of the body impart a farcical cartoon quality to an upside-down world in which the wolf is victimized by his usual prey. The sometimes drastic language sustains a ruthlessly tortured dialectic that turns dialogue into malevolently polished debates. Threats, greed, and bloodthirstiness unfold in edifying, sententious, ceremonial clauses; there is no wickedness for which the speakers do not have a mellifluous and persuasive argument. The poem becomes a vehicle for the expression of educated depravity and refined libertinism.

Ernst Voigt believed that beast-epic evolution was guided by a broadening force seeking variety and a vertical one seeking unity. Léonard Willems (1895) decided that the wolf predominated in the early beast epic and the fox in the later, with the *Ysengrimus* located at the point of balance. Nineteenth-century Aesopist and folklorist views led both Karl Voretzsch and Jan van Mierlo to assume that a folklore cycle centering on the layman fox fused in the *Ysengrimus* with material of monastic provenance based on the Aesopic fable, undergoing epic embellishment—perhaps in characteristic parody of the heroic epic. But as early as 1894 (and 1910) Gaston Paris had emphasized the antagonism between fox and wolf as a general characteristic of the beast epic. Hans Jauss denied the existence of separate cycles and claimed evolutionists had ignored the implications of the fox-wolf relationship because of its seeming constancy. For Jauss, this antagonism illustrated the universal conflict between wisdom and folly, subordinated in the *Ysengrimus* to the *fortuna* theme, which endowed discrete, comical episodes in the wolf's life with the inner cohesion of elegiac resignation. Magister Nivardus' *Fortuna* dispensed galling favors to the lucky and slowly wore out the miserable; the pitiless *fatum* of antiquity (see 3.1ff.), she is a rare phenomenon in the Middle Ages, according to Jauss.

Ysengrimus abbreviatus (Codex berolinensis lat. quart 2, fols. 32–41) is an excerpt of *Ysengrimus*, condensing dialogue and eliminating satire, emphasizing physical rather than moral power, and eliminating the idea of the wolf-monk. The abbreviator was probably a pious monk who lived around 1300 near Aachen.

BIBLIOGRAPHY

Sources. Texts include *Reinardus vulpes*, Franz Joseph Mone, ed., (1832), the original edition; *Reinhard Fuchs*, Jakob Grimm, ed. (1834), 1–24, the *Ysengrimus abbreviatus*; *Ysengrimus*, Ernst Voigt, ed. (1884, repr. 1974), the definitive edition, with an indispensable though dated introduction. Translations include *Magister Nivardus' Isengrimus*, Jan van Mierlo, trans. (1946), in Dutch;

Isengrimus: Das mittelalterliche Tierepos, Albert Schönfelder, trans. (1955), German prose; *Waltharius, Ruodlieb, Märchenepen: Lateinische Epik des Mittellalters mit deutschen Versen,* Karl Langosch, trans. (1956), 218–249, 387–379, *Ysengrimus* I, 1–528 in German verse, plus commentary; *Ysengrimus,* Jill Mann, ed. and trans. (1987), in English; *Ysengrimus by Master Nivardus,* F. J. Sypher and Eleanor Sypher, trans. (1980), in English; Elisabeth Charbonnier, *Recherches sur l'Ysengrimus. Traduction et étude littéraire* (1983).

Studies. L. van Acker, "De *Ysengrimus* in zijn dichter," in *Spiegel historiael,* 9 (1974); J. Bosch, *Reinaert-Perspectief* (1972), 44, an *Ysengrimus* bibliography; Elizabeth Charbonnier, "Recherches sur l'*Ysengrimus:* Traduction et étude littéraire," in *Perspectives médiévales,* 9 (1983), "Manger et boire dans l'*Ysengrimus,*" in *Manger et boire au moyen âge,* I: *Aliments et société* (1984), and "L'âne Charcophas dans l'*Ysengrimus:* Une figure de l'intellectuel en XIIᵉ siècle," in *Revue des langues romanes,* 90 (1986); T. Erb, "*Pauper et dives im Ysengrimus,*" in *Philologus: Zeitschrift für klasissches Altertum,* 115 (1971); John F. Flinn, *Le Roman de Renart dans la littérature française et dans les littératures étrangères au moyen âge* (1963), 27–34; Lucien Foulet, *Le Roman de Renard* (1914); W. T. H. Jackson, *The Literature of the Middle Ages* (1960), 332–340; Hans R. Jauss, *Untersuchungen zur mittelalterlichen Tierdichtung* (1959), 93–113; Fritz Peter Knapp, *Similtudo: Stil und Erzählfunktion von Vergleich und Exempel in der lateinischen, französischen und deutschen Grossepik des Hochmittelalters,* I, pt. 1 (1975), 372–408, "Materialistischer Utilitarismus in der Maske der Satire: Magister Nivards *Ysengrimus,*" in *Mittellateinisches Jahrbuch,* 10 (1976), and *Das lateinische Tierepos* (1979).

Jill Mann, "'Luditur Illusor': The Cartoon World of the *Ysengrimus,*" in *Neophilologus,* 61 (1977), and "Proverbial Wisdom in the *Ysengrimus,*" in *New Literary History,* 16 (1984); Jan van Mierlo, *Het vroegste dierenepos in de letterkunde der Nederlanden: Isengrimus van Magister Nivardus* (1943); Gaston Paris, *Mélanges de littérature française du moyen âge* (1912), 337–423; Karl Reissenberger, ed., *Reinhart Fuchs* (1886, 2nd ed. 1908), 1–16; Ute Schwab, "Gastmetaphorik und Hornarithmetik im *Ysengrimus,*" in *Studi medievali,* 10 (1969); Walther Suchier, *Tierepik und Volksüberlieferung* (1922); Léopold Sudre, *Les sources du Roman de Renard* (1892, repr. 1974), dated but with informative details; Kenneth Varty, "Le viol dans l'*Ysengrimus,* les branches II–Va et la branche I du *Roman de Renart* et dans le *Reinhart Fuchs* d'Heinrich von Glichezare," in Danielle Buschinger et al., eds., *Amour, mariage, et transgressions au moyen âge* (1984); Karl Voretzsch, "Jakob Grimms Thiersage und die moderne Forschung," in *Preussische Jahrbücher,* 80 (1895), and "Einleitung," in Georg Baesecke, ed., *Heinrichs des Glichezares Reinhart Fuchs*

(1925); Max Wehrli, "Vom Sinn des mittelalterlichen Tierepos," in *German Life and Letters,* n.s. **10** (1956–1957), reprinted in Wehrli's *Aufsätze* (1969); Léonard Willems, *Étude sur l'Ysengrinus* (1895).

Three collections of essays are particularly useful: E. Rombauts and E. Welkenhuysen, eds., *Aspects of the Medieval Animal Epic* (1975), which contains essays by W. Bershin, D. Lambrecht, and Rombauts; *Canadian Journal of Netherlandic Studies,* **4** (1983), a special issue entitled "Le Roman de Renart" that includes essays by Charbonnier, Mann, J. Scheidegger, and Varty on the translation and interpretation of *Ysengrimus;* and *Third International Beast Epic, Fable, and Fabliau Colloquium* (1981), which includes essays by L. Peeters and D. Yates.

FRANK RAINER JACOBY

[See also **Beast Epic; Ecbasis Captivi; Fables; Renard the Fox.**]

ZABARELLA, FRANCESCO (1360–1417), leading canonist and distinguished ecclesiastical statesman during the turbulent years of the Great Schism. He was born in Padua and died while participating in the Council of Constance. He began his studies in canon law under Johannes de Lignano at the University of Bologna, but went on in 1385 to the University of Florence, where he received the degree of *doctor utriusque iuris.* He taught there until about 1390, when he moved to the University of Padua, where he taught for the next twenty years. During those years he undertook diplomatic missions for the city and served as legal adviser to Popes Boniface IX and Innocent VI (Roman line) and John XXIII (Pisan line). Though he never received major orders, he was made archpriest of the cathedral of Padua in 1398. In 1411, John XXIII made him cardinal. Sent by that same pope as ambassador to Emperor Sigismund, he helped engineer the opening of the Council of Constance in November 1414. During the next three years he played a crucial role in the events leading up to the passage of the decree *Haec sancta synodus* (1415), the trial and deposition of John XXIII, the trial and execution of Jan Hus, and the decision by the council fathers to proceed to the election of a new pope. Zabarella's funeral oration was preached at Constance by the Italian humanist Poggio Bracciolini, and some felt that, had he lived longer, he might himself have been chosen pope.

One of Zabarella's students was Nicolaus de Tudeschis (Panormitanus), a leading canonist of the next generation. Zabarella wrote commentaries on both the decretals and the Clementines and left behind numerous *repetitiones* and *consilia.* His writings betray a wide acquaintance with philosophical and theological issues as well as a passionate concern with justice. Of upright character and charitable disposition, he emerged at the Council of Constance as an advocate not only of ecclesiastical reform, but also of the strict conciliar theory. His conciliarist views are expressed most forcefully in the *Tractatus de schismate,* a work that was later printed separately but that can also be found embedded in the form of a gloss in his great commentary on the decretals (10.1.6.6).

Drawing his arguments in that work from decretist and decretalist alike, Zabarella depicted the plenitude of power (*plenitudo potestatis*) as residing fundamentally in the whole church as in a corporate body and only derivatively in the pope as "the principal minister" of that corporation. And, in response to the "oligarchic" views long since current at the papal curia, he also portrayed the college of cardinals as sharing with the pope the exercise of the reduced plenitude of power allotted to him. Few conciliarist writings so clearly reveal the canonistic building blocks that Walter Ullmann and Brian Tierney have claimed to lie at the very foundation of conciliar theory.

BIBLIOGRAPHY

Zabarella's canonistic works are listed in Alphone van Hove, *Prolegomena,* 2nd ed. (1928, repr. 1945). The *Tractatus de schismate* is in Simon Schardius, *De jurisdictione, autoritate, et praeeminentia imperiali ac potestate ecclesiastica* (1566), 688–711. See also August Kneer, *Kardinal Zabarella* (1891); Brian Tierney, *Foundations of the Conciliar Theory* (1955); Walter Ullmann, *The Origins of the Great Schism* (1948); Gasparo Zonta, *Francesco Zabarella* (1915).

FRANCIS OAKLEY

[See also **Bologna, University of; Church, Latin; Conciliar Theory; Councils, Western; Decretals; Decretists; Hus, John (Jan); Nicolaus de Tudeschis; Plenitudo Potestatis; Schism, Great.**]

ZACHARIAS OF MYTILENE (*b. ca.* 465–*d.* after 536), church historian and bishop of Mytilene. Zacharias was a native of Gaza who studied rhetoric in Alexandria and law in Beirut between 485 and 491. He moved to Constantinople in 492 and began to practice law. He is consequently known as Zacharias Rhetor. Between 491 and 518, he wrote an ecclesiastical history covering the years 450 to 491 as well as a life of Severus, the Monophysite theologian. In 518 he became bishop of Mytilene on the island of Lesbos. His works were written in Greek but survive only in Syriac versions. The history, in twelve books, has come down to us only in a summary made by an anonymous Syriac compiler, and it has been suggested by some writers that the extant version represents a pseudo-Zacharias rather than a true summary. The work includes a description of Rome and is an important source for the period.

BIBLIOGRAPHY

Zacharias, *The Syriac Chronicle Known as That of Zachariah of Mytilene,* F. J. Hamilton and E. W. Brooks, trans. (1899).

LINDA C. ROSE

[See also **Byzantine Literature; Rhetoric, Byzantine; Syrian Christianity.**]

ZAHN, DER, a late-fourteenth-century Middle High German verse tale (*Märe*) of 104 lines preserved in one manuscript only. In it a rich but rather simple-minded man takes a beautiful wife whom he loves dearly, but she is full of falsehood and also has a lover. One day she makes her husband believe that he is ill and must not leave his bed, only to enjoy greater privacy with her paramour, who, growing suspicious at her profuse protestations of undying love, demands as proof that she bring him the best tooth from her husband's mouth. But when she produces the tooth, having tricked her spouse into parting with it out of love for her, her lover, shocked at such depravity, decides that she would be capable even of murder and leaves her. There are many such women, the author adds, and may the devil take them!

The probably Alemannic poet exhibits no particular talent or interest in developing the rather simple plot but spends nearly one-third of the poem (thirty-two lines) moralizing about wicked women who scheme and deceive their husbands.

Marital trickery and deceit is a favorite theme in medieval comic and didactic literature. The humor frequently derives from gullible men fooled and cuckolded by their clever and contentious wives

rebelling against their traditional role of submission. There are also numerous *Mären* in which the lesson is expounded by way of advice given, which then leads to counterproductive or disastrous results.

BIBLIOGRAPHY

Hanns Fischer, *Studien zur deutschen Märendichtung,* 2nd ed. (1983), 429; H. Niewöhner, "Der Zahn," in *Die deutsche Literatur des Mittelalters: Verfasserlexikon,* IV (1953); Hans-Joachim Ziegeler, *Erzählen im Mittelalter: Mären im Kontext von Minnereden, Bispelm und Romanen* (1985).

KLAUS WOLLENWEBER

[See also **Mären; Middle High German Literature.**]

ZAK^CARIDS, an important feudal house in Caucasia from the eleventh to the fourteenth century. Xosrov, the first historically visible member of this family, emigrated from southern Armenia to southern Georgia in the eleventh century, at the time of the Seljuk invasions. When the district of Lōři, where they had settled, was joined to Georgia in 1118, the Zak^carids became vassals of the Georgian king David (Dawit^c) II (IV) the Builder, and, from the 1120's on, were vassals of the new lords of Lōři, the Orbēlean family. It is believed that, at the time of their arrival, the Zak^carids were Nestorians with some relation to the Arcrunid family of Vaspurakan in southern Armenia, but that subsequently they adopted Armenian Apostolic Christianity. In 1161 the Georgian king Giorgi III (1156–1184) appointed Sargis ("the Great") Zak^carean as governor of the city of Ani—a position he held for only one year before that city was retaken by the Shaddadids. In 1177, when the Orbēlean family and other nobles rebelled against the crown, Sargis Zak^carean defended Giorgi against his enemies. Thereafter, the Zak^carids rose quickly in favor and authority: in 1185 Queen Tamar (1184–1212) appointed Sargis the *amirspasalar* (commander-in-chief) and gave him Lōři, property of the ousted Orbēleans. During the 1190's, Zak^carid power increased further when the brothers Zak^carē and Iwanē Mχargrzeli ("Long-hand") as *amirspasalar*s led the Armeno-Georgian armies. For some thirty years they waged war on the Seljuks and retook all of northeastern Armenia. This area comprised the Zak^carid principalities, of which there were two main branches.

Subject to Zakᶜarē and his descendants were lands in northwestern historical Armenia, with Ani as the center. Subject to Iwanē and his descendants were lands in eastern Armenia, with the cities of Dwin and later Bǰni as centers. Smaller branches of the Zakᶜarids ruled certain districts in Georgia. In the early thirteenth century, the Zakᶜarids also had influence in southern Armenia, where Iwanē's daughter Tᶜamtᶜa became the coruler of Xlatᶜ (ca. 1212–1231).

In 1203 Zakᶜarē was given the duties of keeper of the court seal and chief of the royal bodyguard (mandatortᶜuxucᶜēs). In 1191 Iwanē became the msaxurtᶜuxucᶜēs (great vizier of the court), and after Zakᶜarē's death in 1212/1213, he became atabeg and amirspasalar. Zakᶜarē's son Šāhan-Šāh was the msaxurtᶜuxucᶜēs, while Iwanē's son Awak was amirspasalar and atabeg. Down to Zaza (1345–1380), the titles of amirspasalar and atabeg appear within the main branches of the Zakᶜarid family.

At the time of the Mongol invasions (1236), the Zakᶜarids' power and control over Armenian and Georgian affairs was utilized by the invaders to maintain order. Soon, however, the Mongols began manipulating the natural rivalries that existed among the Caucasian lordly houses, elevating or reducing the influence of the Zakᶜarids, Arcrunids, and Orbēleans to suit their own interests. The decline of Zakᶜarid influence dates from the 1260's. The shift in international trade routes from northern to southern Armenia in the fourteenth century was also a factor in the demise of the Zakᶜarids. While there is little or no information on the fifteenth- and sixteenth-century Zakᶜarids, at the end of the eighteenth century the supposed descendants of the Zakᶜarids, the Argutinskiĭ-Dolgorukids, entered the ranks of the Russian nobility.

BIBLIOGRAPHY

Sources. The most important Georgian source is the anonymous Georgian Chronicle, which covers the years 1207–1318. See S. Quaxčišvili, ed., Kᶜartᶜlis Cᶜxovreba, II (1959). A French translation is Histoire de la Géorgie depuis l'antiquité jusqu'au XIXᵉ siècle, Marie Brosset [Marii Ivanovich Brosse], trans., 2 vols. (1849–1854).

Among the Armenian sources are Grigor Aknercᶜi, Kirakos Ganjakecᶜi, Mxitᶜar Ayrivanecᶜi, Samuēl of Ani, Stepᶜannos Orbēlean, Tᶜovma Arcruni's Continuator, Tᶜovma Mecopᶜecᶜi, and Vardan Arewelcᶜi, as well as numerous thirteenth- and fourteenth-century colophons and minor chronicles. On the editions and translations of these texts and for a study of the Zakᶜarids, see Robert Bedrosian, "The Turco-Mongol Invasions and the Lords

of Armenia in the 13th–14th Centuries" (diss., Columbia Univ., 1979), 1–248, 249–292.

Studies. Lewon H. Babayan, Soltsialno-ekonomicheskaia i politicheskaia istoria Armenii v XIII–XIV vekakh (1969); S. Eremyan, "The Zakᶜarids," in Haykakan Sovetakan Hanragitaran, III (1977), 676–677; Cyril Toumanoff, "Medieval Georgian Historical Literature (VII–XVth Centuries)," in Traditio, 1 (1943).

ROBERT BEDROSIAN

[See also Amirspasalar; Ani in Širak; Arcrunis; Armenia: History of; Atabeg; Dwin; Georgia: Political History; Giorgi III; Lōri; Šahan-Šāh; Seljuks; Shaddadids; Tamar; Xlatᶜ.]

ŽAMATUN. See Gawitᶜ.

ZAMZAM, the sacred well within the precincts of the Meccan sanctuary. According to Islamic tradition the water of Zamzam gushed forth at the heels of the infant Ismāᶜīl, saving him and his mother from dying of thirst. The water is brackish and exceedingly heavy to the taste, but it is held in great esteem throughout the Islamic world and looked upon as a panacea for all ills.

BIBLIOGRAPHY

Alfred Guillaume, The Life of Muhammad: A Translation of Ishāq's Sīrat rasūl Allāh (1955), 45–65.

GHAZI I. BISHEH

[See also Islam, Religion; Kaaba; Mecca; Mosque.]

ZANDANĪJĪ. Among the many designations for textiles in Islamic sources, such as mulḥam and dībāj, the term zandanījī is unique in that it can be securely linked to extant fabrics. The appellation zandanījī for woven silk textiles of the eighth and ninth centuries is based upon the identification of a textile, now in the collegiate church of Notre Dame in Huy, Belgium, that bears on its reverse an inscription in ink written in the Sogdian language, "long 61 spans Zandanījī . . . cloth(?)." The inscription is dated on epigraphic grounds about 700.

Zandanījī textiles were produced in the neighborhood of Zandanah (Zandane), a village suburb to the north of Bukhara, a city in Transoxiana (now

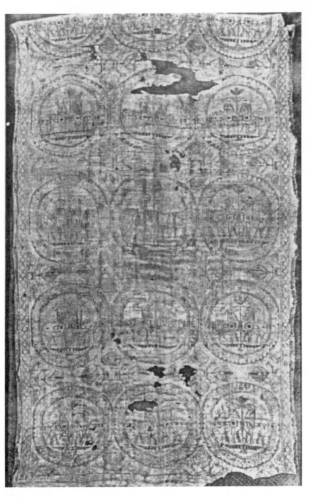

Zandanījī textile of *ca.* 700. COLLEGIATE CHURCH OF NOTRE DAME OF HUY, BRUSSELS

drawn from royal iconography was employed for commercial purposes, affecting their wide dissemination in all media.

Fragments of *zandanījī* textiles and closely related types have been excavated at tomb sites in Egypt, Central Asia, and China. Many were used to wrap the bones of saints and made their way as relics in the Middle Ages to European church treasuries, where they are still preserved. Patterned textiles of the Islamic world, including those identified as *zandanījī,* had a great impact on the art of the Middle Ages in Europe. Not only did the imports stimulate local production of patterned silk textiles, but their overall repeat patterns also influenced developments in all the decorative arts.

BIBLIOGRAPHY

Carol Manson Bier, "Textiles," in Prudence O. Harper, ed., *The Royal Hunter: Art of the Sasanian Empire* (1978), 119–140, esp. 139; Robert B. Serjeant, *Islamic Textiles: Material for a History Up to the Mongol Conquest* (1972), 46ff. and 99ff.; D. G. Shepherd and W. B. Henning, "Zandanījī Identified?" in *Aus der Welt der Islamischen Kunst: Festschrift für Ernst Kühnel zum 75. Geburtstag . . . ,* Richard Ettinghausen, ed. (1959), 15–41.

CAROL MANSON BIER

[See also **Bukhara; Dībāj; Iran, History of: After 650; Mulḥam; Sasanian Art; Silk; Taq-i Bostan; Textiles, Islamic.**]

in western Uzbek SSR). They were brilliant in colors now faded, woven with a compound weft-faced structure, and characterized by an overall repeat pattern with rows of roundels bearing pairs of highly stylized animals and a central tree or other vegetal motif. Denaturalized floral ornament is often placed between the roundels. The outlines of all forms are angular, probably resulting from commercialized weaving on a drawloom. These richly patterned textiles, produced in quantity for sale and export, are thus distinguished by the angularity of their style. The motifs derive from the time of pre-Islamic Iran, where similar designs appear on the garments worn by Sasanian kings and their attendants represented on carved rock reliefs at Taq-i Bostan in western Iran. After the fall of the Sasanian dynasty, this repertory of images

ZANJ (also called Zinj), the name of indigenous East Africans in medieval Arabic texts. Although knowledge of the Zanj in the Middle East predates Islam, the first recorded use of the word, invoking the image of a Zanj slave, refers to A.D. 680. The socially inferior position of the Zanj in Islamic society promoted an attitude of superiority on the part of Arabic writers and reinforced racial and cultural hostility reflected in literature and folklore. The Zanj were thought to be lazy, lecherous, dishonest, and stupid. Descriptions of the Zanj slaves invariably emphasize their blackness (perceived as a negative attribute), their "strange" physique, and their levity. They were also believed to possess special magical power.

Such an apprehensive or distrustful attitude toward the Zanj was reinforced for centuries by the great slave uprising that occurred between 868 and 883 in lower Iraq. The Zanj, a major body of the rebels, were joined by other slaves and free Arabs employed as navvies in the area of Shaṭṭ al-ʿArab, where they worked in large gangs of 500 or more to reclaim the salinated lands for agriculture. Kept alive on a meager diet of flour, semolina, and dates in the unhealthy conditions of the marshland, these slaves aspired to material and social as well as spiritual equality with their masters. Newly introduced to Islam, they dressed their proclamation of war in Islamic terms; their leader, referred to as "lord of the Zanj," was an ʿAlid pretender named ʿAlī ibn Muḥammad who later adopted Kharijite ideology. The movement also may have been influenced by Qarmatian Shiite propaganda.

The rebels aimed to establish a vaguely communistic society in which the property and women of their former masters would be shared, but they ended up owning slaves themselves. In the first phase of the war the Zanj successfully attacked Ubulla and ʿAbbādān, took southern Ahvāz, and sacked Basra, advancing with a fleet as far as Wāsiṭ in 877. In the second phase the initiative belonged to the Abbasid regent al-Muwaffaq, who in 882 after a prolonged siege took the rebel capital of Mukhtāra (south of Basra) and suppressed the rebellion.

Despite the resurrection of the old order, the memory of terror and destruction brought about by a social war waged by slaves apparently prevented further use of large concentrations of slave labor in Islamic countries, even though black slaves continued to be popular as soldiers and domestic servants.

Islamic scholars theorized that the Zanj were descendants of Ham through Kush and Canaan. The Zanj were distinguished from the other blacks (*sūdān*), including *Nūba* (Nubians), Ḥabasha (Ethiopians), and Barābara (Galla-Somali). All linguistic evidence points to Zanj identity as Bantu speakers. In a few instances the name "Zanj" was used by Muslim geographers as a translation of the Greek generic term "Aethiopes," usually rendered in Arabic by the ethnonym "Ḥabasha."

The information of Arabic sources about the Zanj in Africa is limited to coastal areas; it is nonetheless of great value as the only written evidence concerning East Africa from antiquity to the arrival of the Portuguese. The country of the Zanj is first mentioned in the eighth century by al-Fazārī; al-Masʿūdī (tenth century) gives its first traveler's description, while al-Idrīsī (twelfth century) provides the most extensive one. In the view of medieval Islamic geographers, the area formed the south

shore of the Indian Ocean; it bordered in the west on the land of Barābara and Ḥabasha and in the east on the land of Sofāla, where the Zanj also lived (Mozambique). This part of the coast was known to Hellenistic and Byzantine Greeks as Azania, Zingis, or Zingion—names probably derived from the earlier pronunciation "Zang" or "Zeng." "Zäng" is also the Persian form of the word; the name of Zanzibar Island is derived from the Persian Zäng-e bār (land of Zang). Like its Arabic equivalent, Arḍ al-Zanj, it initially applied to the East African coast.

The land of Zanj is described as having rivers, harbors, islands, mountains, and volcanoes. The sources of the ninth to fourteenth centuries mention a number of Zanj cities: among them can be identified Malindi, Mombasa, Kilwa, Maputu, Mkumbuu and Mtambwe at Pemba, and Unguja and Tumbatu at Zanzibar. The Zanj were divided into ethnic groups and kingdoms and were constantly at war; since they had no horses, their soldiers rode cattle. Their kings ruled according to custom, and if a ruler transgressed against justice, he was killed and his progeny banned from succession. The people were engaged in trade, farming, mining gold, fishing, and hunting, especially for leopards and elephants. They wore iron jewelry, filed their teeth, and loved music and dancing. They also had deep admiration for the Arabs and such an inordinate fondness for dates that children as well as adults could be easily kidnapped by slave merchants who came to the Zanj ports from as far away as the mysterious land of Wāq-Wāq (an unknown region that was believed to extend from the land of Sofāla to the far eastern islands).

Their pagan beliefs included worship of idols and other man-made objects that they smeared with grease and of nature (plants, stones, animals, stars). They knew a supreme being and had medicine men. The Zanj were illiterate but eloquent, and their religious leaders might address an assembly from dawn to dusk. The process of Islamization of the Zanj began from the north and for a long time remained limited to the coast: Islam among the Zanj is first noted by al-Masʿūdī in his description of Pemba. Later Ibn al-Mujāwir mentions competition between Kharijites and Shafiites, while Yāqūt (thirteenth century) makes reference to Muslim migrations from the Middle East to the Zanj coast. From this time the sources reflect conversion of the Zanj rulers to Islam by calling them "sheikhs" and "sultans" rather than "kings." In the fourteenth century, when Ibn Baṭṭūṭa visited Kilwa, the city's Muslims were engaged in a holy war against the heathen Zanj of the mainland.

Beginning in the fifteenth century, traditional Arabic geographic literature merely repeats earlier information on the Zanj, and Arabic nautical manuals, while describing the East African coast, contain little about the Zanj.

BIBLIOGRAPHY

L. Marcel Devic, *Le pays des Zendjs* (1883); Greville S. P. Freeman-Grenville, *The East African Coast: Select Documents from the First to the Earlier Nineteenth Century* (1962); M. J. de Goeje, ed., *Annales quos scripsit Abu Djafar Mohammed ibn Djarir at-Tabari*, 3rd ser. (1901, repr. 1964), 1,742–1,787, 1,835–2,103; ᶜAmr ibn Bahr al-Jāḥiẓ, "Kitāb fakhr al-sūdān ᶜalā 'l-bīḍān," in Gerholf van Vloten, ed., *Tria opuscula auctore: Abu Othman Amr ibn Bahr al-Djahiz Basrensi* (1903); Bernard Lewis, *Race and Color in Islam* (1971); L. Massignon, "Zandj," in *The Encyclopaedia of Islam*, IV, 1st ed. (1934); V. V. Matveyev, "*Muluk al-Zinj*, King of Zinjs According to Arabic Sources of the 9th–10th Centuries," in *International Congress of Anthropological and Ethnological Sciences, 7th, Moscow, 1964*, 9 (1970); Alexandre Popovic, *La révolte des esclaves en Iraq au IIIᵉ–IXᵉ siècle* (1976); Richard Reusch, *History of East Africa* (1954, repr. 1961); Gernot Rotter, *Die Stellung des Negers in der islamisch-arabischen Gesellschaft bis zum XVI. Jahrhundert* (1967); Chauncey H. Stigand, *The Land of Zinj* (1913, repr. 1966); Friedrich Storbeck, "Die Berichte der arabischen Geographen des Mittelalters über Ostafrika," in *Mitteilungen des Seminars für orientalische Sprachen*, 17 (1914); M. A. Tolmacheva, "Vostochnoe poberezhe Afriki v arabskoi geograficheskoi literature," in *Strany i narody Vostoka*, 9 (1969), "The Zanj Language," in *Kiswahili*, 45 (1975), and "Toward a Definition of the Term 'Zanj'," in *Azania*, 21 (1986); J. Spencer Trimingham, "The Arab Geographers and the East African Coast," in H. Neville Chittick and Robert I. Rotberg, eds., *East Africa and the Orient* (1975).

M. A. TOLMACHEVA

[See also **Blacks; Basra; Baṭṭūṭa, Ibn; Caliphate; Geography and Cartography, Islamic; Idrīsī, al-; Masᶜūdī, al-; Navigation: Indian Ocean, Red Sea; Nubia; Slavery, Islamic World; Slavery, Slave Trade; Wāq-Wāq Islands.**]

ZĀWĪYA (or *zāwiyya*; Arabic, "corner"), a building in the Arab and Turkish Mediterranean regions. The period in which these buildings began to appear is as yet uncertain. By the thirteenth century

Zāwīya, in foreground, attached to the mother convent of the Mawlawīya order at Konya. (The founder of the order, Rumi, is buried beneath the mausoleum.) SONIA HALLIDAY PHOTOGRAPHS

they are documented in Egypt and Palestine and Anatolia.

What this structure was is still a matter of some debate, since the building of *zāwīya*s did not seem to have been generally undertaken by princes or by central governments, although there were exceptions. It can tentatively be suggested that the funding and building of a *zāwīya* was the work of one of the many para-orthodox factions or groups that gathered around religious figures. The nature of the faction or group varied from place to place; but a *zāwīya* always contained a room or rooms set aside for travelers. Thus, in North Africa *zāwīya*s came to be ensembles comprising the tomb of a holy man and a number of rooms where pilgrims or local pious individuals could stay for private devotions or, more frequently, for association with other like-minded devotees. In Egypt a list of *zāwīya*s provided by a fifteenth-century description of Cairo seems to deal with the tombs of saintly but perhaps minor personages. In Jerusalem, textual and epigraphic evidence suggests that the *zāwīya*s were small private chapels with living quarters. In Anatolia, the association with funerary architecture is less clear, but it has been argued that the characteristic appearance in fourteenth-century Anatolian mosques of side rooms that seem isolated from the main prayer halls—for instance at the mosque of Umur Bey in Brusa (Bursa)—are in fact the addition of *zāwīya*s, in this case rooms reserved for the pious soldiers and colonizers who formed the spearhead of the Islamization of Anatolia. To call these *zāwīya*s convents, as has been done, is to exaggerate their importance or distort their character, for there is little evidence that they served more than a transient population. It is indeed likely, however, that in Anatolia and possibly elsewhere they were the physical setting of a whole range of internal associations, mystical or nonmystical, within the religious world of Islam about which Westerners are still ill-informed.

BIBLIOGRAPHY

For Anatolia, see Aptullah Kuran, *The Mosque in Early Ottoman Architecture* (1968). For the Arab world the best way to begin is through the many volumes of Max van Berchem, *Materiaux pour un corpus inscriptionum arabicarum* (1890–).

OLEG GRABAR

[See also **Brusa; Cairo; Islamic Art and Architecture.**]

ZAYDIS (**Zaydids, Zaydites**), the most moderate of the Shiite Islamic sects. The name originally referred to the supporters of Zayd ibn ʿAlī, who was killed leading a Shiite revolt in Kufa in 740. Zayd was a grandson of Ḥusayn, the martyr of the Shīʿa killed at Karbalāʾ, and a brother of Muḥammad al-Bāqir (*d. ca.* 735), who had been widely recognized among the more radical Shīʿa as their imam until his death some years before Zayd's rebellion. Zayd found support chiefly among the moderate Shīʿa, while the radicals, disappointed by his failure to condemn the three caliphs preceding ʿAlī unequivocally as apostates, turned to support his nephew Jaʿfar al-Ṣādiq (*d.* 765). The Zaydi movement survived the death of Zayd and continued to espouse the ideas of the moderate Shīʿa who backed the rights of the family of the Prophet to the caliphate but would not accuse the majority of Muslims of infidelity because of their failure to recognize these rights. In contrast to the political quietism adopted by the radical Twelver Shīʿa (Imāmīya), the Zaydis maintained the revolutionary spirit of the early Shīʿa and considered armed rebellion against the illegitimate rulers a religious obligation. They repudiated the basic Imāmīya belief in a continuous line of divinely appointed and guided imams descended from Ḥussayn and came to hold that any descendant of ʿAlī and Fatima, daughter of the Prophet, was entitled to the imamate and the armed backing of the faithful if he was both learned in religion and the law and claimed the imamate by rising against the illegitimate rulers. If there was more than one claimant, the candidate with the highest qualifications deserved the imamate.

Centered in Kufa, the early Zaydis supported numerous unsuccessful revolts of ʿAlids during the eighth and ninth centuries. Eventually they were able to set up two small states in regions remote from the centers of caliphal power and protected by mountain ranges. In 864 al-Ḥasan ibn Zayd founded a Zaydi state in Ṭabaristān, on the southern coast of the Caspian Sea and north of the Elburz Mountains, and in 897 al-Hādī ila'l-Ḥaqq Yaḥyā established the Zaydi imamate in the highlands of northern Yemen. Al-Hādī was also the founder of a doctrinal school in law and theology based on the earlier teaching of his grandfather al-Qāsim ibn Ibrāhīm Tabāṭabā al-Rassī. It was adopted by all Zaydis in the Yemen and by some in Ṭabaristān. The Caspian state was later shifted further west, to the lands east of the river Safīd Rud. There were the territories of the Daylamites and Gilites, who had been converted to Islam largely by the efforts of the Zaydi imam al-Nāṣir li l-Ḥaqq al-Uṭrūsh (or al-Kabīr, *d.* 917). Al-Nāṣir founded another legal and doctrinal school that predominated in the regions converted by him. Rivalry between the two schools often led to the establishment of separate ʿAlid reigns among the Caspian Zaydis. While religious learning flourished there in the tenth and eleventh centuries, the tiny Zaydi states were politically impotent. The Caspian Zaydi community survived, however, until the early sixteenth century, when it was absorbed by the Twelver Shīʿa. In the Yemen, where the Zaydi community has lasted into the late twentieth century, the political fortunes of ʿAlid rule varied greatly in time. In the early period, the imamate was mostly based in Saʿda, near the northern boundary of the country, later often in Sanʿa, the capital city. Rarely did the rule of the imams extend over all the country, especially the coastal regions. The Zaydi state lapsed completely at times, for prolonged periods. In other parts of the Muslim world, the Zaydi Shīʿa has never been significant.

The inherent instability of the Zaydi imamate was caused by several factors. The principle that the imamate belonged to the most excellent descendant of ʿAlī and Fatima with the highest qualification of religious and legal learning who rises to claim it generally militated against dynastic succession. Rival claims by other ʿAlids occurred frequently. The Zaydi ʿulamāʾ, as the custodians of religious knowledge, were in a powerful position to impugn the scholarship or conduct of a pretender or ruler. Lack of any claimant with the full qualifications of religious learning often resulted in the recognition of an ʿAlid ruler as a mere *dāʿī* (caller to God), below the rank of imam. Late Zaydi doctrine in the Yemen developed the theory of a lower-rank imamate with limited functions and rights.

Zaydi religiosity was generally marked by strong ethical and ascetic impulses. The obligation of *hijra* (hegira), emigration from the abode of the unjust if they could not be overcome, was often stressed. Zaydi doctrine does not permit the practice of precautionary dissimulation of religious beliefs permitted and, under certain circumstances, required by Imāmīya doctrine. Sufism was opposed for its mysticism and antinomian tendencies. The Zaydi imams were teachers of the law and theology, subject to human error, not infallible dispensers of an esoteric spiritual knowledge like the imams of the Twelver and Ismaili Shīʿa. They also lacked the power of the latter to intercede for the offenders of their community in the hereafter. Zaydi law generally deviated less from Sunni law than did Imāmīya law, though the legal doctrine of al-Naṣir li l-Haqq al-Uṭrūsh showed specific influences of the latter. Even more directly than the Twelver Shīʿa, the Zaydis came under the influence of the rationalist theological doctrine of the Muʿtazila. Much of the literature of the later Muʿtazilite school has been preserved only by the Zaydis after its suppression in Sunni Islam.

BIBLIOGRAPHY

Cornelis van Arendonk, *Les débuts de l'imāmate zaidite au Yémen,* Jacques Ryckmans, trans. (1960); Henri Laoust, *Les schismes dans l'Islam* (1965); Wilferd Madelung, *Der Imam al-Qāsim ibn Ibrāhīm und die Glaubenslehre der Zaiditen* (1965); R. B. Serjeant, "The Zaydis," in Arthur J. Arberry, ed., *Religion in the Middle East,* II (1969), 285–301.

WILFERD MADELUNG

[See also ʿAlī ibn Abī Ṭalib; Caliphate; Heresy, Islamic; Ḥusayn ibn ʿAlī, al-; Imam; Islam, Religion; Ismāʿīlīya; Kufa, al-; Muʿtazila, al-; Philosophy and Theology, Islamic; Sects, Islamic; Shīʿa; ʿUlamāʾ; Yemen.]

ZEALOTS, a term applied variously in episodes of Byzantine political and ecclesiastical strife, often to the conservative or monastic function in religious controversies. But it refers most specifically to a self-identified group of popular leaders in an epoch of fierce social turmoil in mid-fourteenth-century Thessaloniki.

Economic disruption had aggravated social inequities and had exasperated the always volatile character of the Thessalonian populace. Indignation was directed at the inordinate wealth and power of the great magnates, who were extending their domination of society through such representatives as Andronikos III's powerful minister, John Kantakouzenos. When, in 1341, the latter began a civil war to claim the Byzantine throne, popular risings in several provincial cities violently expelled his supporters. In Thessaloniki, leadership was assumed by a group identified as Zealots, who established a popular regime in their city and who allied themselves with the legitimist dictator of Constantinople, Alexios Apokavkos, supporter of John V Palaiologos, the legal Palaiologan dynast. When Alexios was assassinated in 1345, his son, John, who ruled in Thessaloniki alongside the Zealots, sought accommodation with Kantakouzenos, plotting with prominent Thessalonians to hand over the city to his forces. The Zealots organized a violent reaction that ended in the brutal massacre of John Apokavkos and some hundred of his supporters, and the expulsion or plundering of the city's elite. A renewed Zealot regime ruled the city for the next four years, refusing to receive the new metropolitan, Gregory Palamas, who was identified with Kantakouzenos, with the privileged classes, and with the hesychast doctrine, all abhorred by the Zealots. But popular support weakened under pressure from Kantakouzenos, now ruler in Constantinople, and an eleventh-hour attempt by the Zealot leaders at an alliance with Serbia further brought them into discredit. Kantakouzenos gained entry to Thessaloniki in 1350, to establish his rule and his friend Palamas firmly within it.

The Zealot movement has fascinated historians. It has been compared or related to contemporaneous popular upheavals in Western Europe, especially in Italian cities. As an expression of popular demand for social justice it has particularly attracted Marxist and socialist historians, who have stressed the "radical" character of the Zealots and have credited them with a conscious and visionary social program. Such speculation has been based upon a misreading of a treatise by Nikolaos Kavasilas (Cabasilas), once thought to be an attack upon Zealot ideas but now recognized as without direct bearing upon them. Our sources for the Zealot revolt are, in fact, pitifully limited and fragmentary, almost all written from a hostile and pro-Kantakouzenian perspective. Indeed, the Zealot movement is inseparable from its context of dynastic strife: two of its known leaders themselves used the dynastic family name of Palaiologos. On the other hand, the Zealots clearly gave expression to a desperate popular resentment of social and economic injustices. We can regard skeptically the descriptions of them by conservative enemies as demagogues seeking an utterly new and unknown political order. But whether the Zealots were true radicals with a clear plan for the transformation of their society, in terms comparable to latter-day radicalism, remains unproven speculation.

BIBLIOGRAPHY

John W. Barker, "The 'Monody' of Demetrios Kydones on the Zealot Rising of 1345 in Thessaloniki," in *Essays in Memory of Basil Laourdas* (1975); Peter Cha-
ranis, "Internal Strife in Byzantium during the Fourteenth Century," in *Byzantion*, 15 (1941), repr. in his *Social, Economic, and Political Life in the Byzantine Empire* (1973); Donald M. Nicol, *The Last Centuries of Byzantium, 1261–1453* (1972); Ihor Ševčenko, "Nicolas Cabasilas' 'Anti-Zealot' Discourse: A Reinterpretation," in *Dumbarton Oaks Papers*, 11 (1957), "The Author's Draft of Nicolas Cabasilas' 'Anti-Zealot' Discourse in *Parisinus Graecus 1276*," in *Dumbarton Oaks Papers*, 14 (1960), and "A Postscript on Nicolas Cabasilas' 'Anti-Zealot' Discourse," in *Dumbarton Oaks Papers*, 16 (1962); Oreste Tafrali, *Thessalonique au quatorzième siècle* (1913).

JOHN W. BARKER

[See also **Byzantine Empire: History (1204–1453)**; **Hesychasm**; **John V Palaiologos**; **John VI Kantakouzenos**; **Kantakouzenoi**; **Palaiologoi**; **Thessaloniki**.]

ZENO THE ISAURIAN (*d.* 491), Byzantine emperor. An Isaurian chieftain originally named Tarasicodissa, Zeno was summoned to the capital by the emperor Leo I to counteract the influence of Aspar the Alan and the Ostrogoths in Constantinople. He married Leo's eldest daughter, Ariadne, in 466, and when Leo died in 474 Zeno became co-emperor with his own son Leo II. When the child died in the same year, he became sole emperor. In 475 he was deposed by a conspiracy, but he regained the throne in 476 and ruled until 491. During his reign the final collapse of the Roman Empire in the West occurred, but the conquerer of Italy, Odoacer, recognized the suzerainty of Byzantium and, with the title *magister militum per Italiam*, governed there as the emperor's viceroy. Christological controversy continued, and Zeno attempted to solve it in 482 through the issuance of the pro-Monophysite *Henotikon*, or Edict of Union, which pleased the Eastern churches but was repudiated by the pope and led to a thirty-five-year schism between Constantinople and Rome.

BIBLIOGRAPHY

E. W. Brooks, "The Emperor Zenon and the Isaurians," in *English Historical Review*, 8 (1893); George Ostrogorsky, *History of the Byzantine State*, Joan Hussey, trans. (1957, rev. ed. 1969), 61–64.

LINDA C. ROSE

[See also **Byzantine Empire: History (330–1025)**; **Henotikon**; **Isaurians**; **Leo I, Emperor**; **Magister Militum**;

Monophysitism; Odoacer; Schisms, Eastern-Western Church; Syrian Christianity.]

ZINDĪQ. See **Manichaeans.**

ZIRIDS, the principal dynasty of Ifrīqiya from the departure of the Fatimids in 972 to the capture of Mahdia by the Normans in 1148. The eponymous founder, Zīrī ibn Manād, chief of the Talkāta Berbers of the mountains southwest of Algiers, from 935 onward ruled the western borders of Fatimid Ifrīqiya from his citadel of Ashīr on behalf of the Fatimid caliph. He played an important part in the defeat of the rebel Abū Yazīd between 946 and 947, and after the Fatimid conquest of Egypt in 969 became the favorite to become the Fatimid viceroy in the Maghrib. But in 971 he was killed by his chief rival, Jaᶜfar ibn ᶜAlī ibn Ḥamdūn, governor of Msila, and the Fatimid caliph Muᶜizz chose Zīrī's son Buluggīn instead. In 1972, with the title Sayf al-Dawla Abū 'l-Futūḥ Yūsuf, Buluggīn became Fatimid overlord of Ifrīqiya, including, in 979, Tripoli. But most of his time was spent on campaign against the Zanāta Berber allies of the Spanish Umayyads in the west, while the administration was left to a governor, ᶜAbd Allāh ibn Muḥammad al-Kātib, at the capital, Qayrawān. At Buluggīn's death in 984 he was succeeded by his son al-Manṣūr, but an attempt was made by the Fatimid caliph ᶜAzīz to change the arrangement by promoting ᶜAbd Allah al-Kātib to be the senior Fatimid officer in North Africa. ᶜAbd Allah, however, was slain by al-Manṣūr in 987, the fait accompli was accepted by Cairo, and the Zirids emerged as hereditary monarchs of Ifrīqiya in the name of the Fatimids, permanently resident in the palace of Ṣabra at Qayrawān.

As a dynasty, the Zirids were promptly beset by quarrels over the succession, whether it was to be by primogeniture or pass to a brother or an uncle. The family was large, and at the death of Manṣūr in 996, the candidates were numerous. In the struggle to succeed, the slave troops of the sultan preserved the throne for Manṣūr's son Bādīs, a boy of eleven, while the great-uncles of the young prince rebelled, and were driven from the central Maghrib only by his uncle Ḥammād. Ḥammād in consequence was entrusted, like his ancestor Zīrī, with the govern-

ment of the western regions of the Ifrīqiyan empire from 1005 onward. In 1008 Ḥammād moved from the westerly citadel of Ashīr to a new capital, which he had founded near Msīla. Called the Qalᶜa, or Castle, of the Banū Ḥammād, this became the seat of a second dynasty, the Hammadids, following Ḥammād's rebellion against Bādīs in 1015 and subsequent reconciliation with his son and successor al-Muᶜizz in 1017. The Zirids themselves then ruled principally in the region of Tunisia.

To the east, relations with Cairo remained cordial down to the reign of al-Muᶜizz, despite a brief attempt by the caliph Ḥākim between 1002 and 1003 to appoint a governor to Tripoli as well as Barca in Cyrenaica. But Barca was threatened by Arab Bedouin, and Tripoli by Zanāta Berbers who had fled from the tribal warfare of the western Maghrib. In 1012 the Arab Banū Qurra seized and held Barca, and in 1022 the Zanāta took Tripoli permanently from the Zirids. Al-Muᶜizz meanwhile, who came to the throne aged eight in 1016, grew up under the influence of Malikite teachers and scholars of Qayrawān, at a time when the Ismaili Fatimid connection of the dynasty was becoming increasingly unpopular; in 1017 Ismailis were massacred in all the main cities. In 1036 an important estrangement occurred when al-Muᶜizz tried to take over Muslim Sicily, but the Fatimids concluded a treaty with Byzantium in 1038 recognizing the Greek claim to the island. At that time, Berber tribal raiders from the south had begun to threaten Qayrawān, and the warrior Arab tribes of the Banū Hilāl were arriving from the east in Tripolitania. Political, religious, and tribal unrest had an economic background: the shift of trade away from Ifrīqiya following the departure of the Fatimids in Egypt. In 1048 al-Muᶜizz tried to regain the initiative by renouncing his allegiance to Cairo, and transferring it to the Abbasids in Baghdad.

His purpose was to win popularity at Qayrawān, and to create a militant anti-Fatimid alliance with Tripoli and Burca under his leadership. The scheme failed in 1052, mainly because al-Muᶜizz quarreled with the Zughba and Riyāḥ, Hilālī Arab tribes whom he had enlisted against the Berbers of southern Ifrīqiya. His army was routed by them at the Battle of Ḥaydarān south of Qayrawān. His authority thereupon collapsed. Encouraged by the Fatimids, who sent an envoy to Gabès between 1053 and 1054, most of the main cities abandoned him, and in 1057 he himself abandoned Qayrawān for Mahdia, where he returned to Fatimid allegiance.

Al-Mu^cizz's failure precipitated the political disintegration of Ifrīqiya, in preparation since the beginning of the eleventh century. At Mahdia, the Zirids became the rulers of one of several city-states. Mu^cizz's son, Tamīm (r. 1062–1108), recovered Sousse between 1063 and 1064 and Sfax in 1100, but the interior of the country fell largely into the hands of Arab tribes with which the Zirids were forced to ally. Abroad, Tamīm made a second attempt to take power in Sicily (1063–1069), but his sons were unable to unite the island, whose invasion by the Normans had begun. During the 1070's he probably assisted the emir of Castrogiovanni against the Normans, as well as attacking the coasts of Sicily and southern Italy with a large pirate fleet. But in 1087 Mahdia itself was surprised and sacked by a Pisan-Genoese expedition. Under Tamīm's successors, Yaḥyā (r. 1108–1116) and ^cAlī (r. 1116–1121), a more vigorous attempt was made to reconquer the whole of Tunisia, including Tunis, which briefly submitted, but this ended with the accession of the twelve-year-old al-Hasan (r. 1121–1167), whose reign was overshadowed by the ambitions of Roger II of Sicily. A first Norman attack was repulsed in 1123; this was followed by years of peace in which Mahdia became heavily dependent on Sicilian grain. But from the occupation of Jerba in 1135 onward, Roger conquered most of the cities along the Ifriqiyan coast, including Mahdia itself in 1148. Al-Ḥasan fled toward Morocco, and eventually returned with the Almohad caliph ^cAbd al-Mu^ɔmin, who recaptured Mahdia between 1159 and 1160. He remained as a resident until finally exiled to Morocco in 1171, where he died on arrival.

The Zirids of Granada (1010–1090) were founded by Zāwī ibn Zīrī, who fled to Andalus following the defeat of the family rebellion against the accession of Bādīs in 996. Taking service with the Umayyads, he became ruler of Elvira at the beginning of the civil wars in which the Umayyad caliphate disintegrated. His successors transferred their residence from Elvira to Granada, ruling a "party kingdom" in the Sierra Nevada until it was abolished by the Almoravids and its last rulers, the brothers ^cAbd Allah and Tamīm, were sent into exile at Aghmāt.

BIBLIOGRAPHY
Michael Brett, "The Zughba at Tripoli, 429H (A.D. 1037–38)," in *Society for Libyan Studies, Sixth Annual Report* (1974–1975), 41–45; *Cambridge History of Africa*, II (1978), 589–636; Hady Roger Idris, *La Berbérie orientale sous les Zīrīdes, X^e–XIIe siècles*, 2 vols. (1962).

MICHAEL BRETT

[See also **Abbasids; Almohads; Berbers; Fatimids; Ifrīqiya; Islam, Conquests of; Qayrawān, al-; Sicily, Islamic; Spain, Muslim Kingdoms of; Tripoli; Tunis; Umayyads of Córdoba.**]

ZIYADA, Arabic word meaning "addition" and used to refer to large tracts between a mosque and the surrounding city. *Ziyadas* characterized early (ninth-century) mosques (Cairo, Samarra) rather than later ones. The exact function of these spaces is unknown, but they form effective transitions between open and restricted areas.

OLEG GRABAR

[See also **Islamic Art and Architecture; Mosque.**]

ZOË THE MACEDONIAN (978/980–1050), Byzantine empress. After the death of her father, Constantine VIII, in 1028, Zoë perpetuated the Macedonian dynasty by a series of three marriages, to Romanos III Argyros (1028–1034), Michael IV the Paphlagonian (1034–1041), and Constantine IX Monomachos (1042–1055), and by the adoption of Michael IV's nephew, who became Michael V Kalaphates (1041–1042). Zoë ruled alone with her sister Theodora for three months in 1042.

BIBLIOGRAPHY
Sources. Georgius Cedrenus, *Historia,* Immanuele Bekker, ed., II (1839); *The Chronographia of Michael Psellus,* E. R. A. Sewter, trans. (1953).
Studies. Charles Diehl, *Byzantine Empresses* (1963); Nicholas Oikonomides, "The Mosaic Panel of Constantine IX and Zoe in Saint Sophia," in *Revue des études Byzantines,* 36 (1978).

ALICE-MARY M. TALBOT

[See also **Byzantine Empire: History; Constantine IX Monomachos; Macedonians.**]

ZONARAS, JOHN (*fl.* first half of the twelfth century), Byzantine writer, high-ranking official, and canonist who retired to a monastery, where he wrote the *Epitome historiarum,* a chronicle covering the period from the Creation to 1118. The first books are dedicated to ancient history and utilize some lost sources, such as Dio Cassius. In books XIII–XVIII Zonaras deals with Byzantine history from Constantine the Great, mostly reproducing extant sources; only the reign of Alexios I is treated independently. A representative of the civil bureaucracy, Zonaras treated Alexios inimically; he is reported to have transformed the empire into his private property, lavishly endowing his kinfolk, while the senate was held in disdain. Zonaras criticized previous historians, who had described only military deeds and sieges of cities. Zonaras' tendency to restrict imperial power was reflected in his commentaries on the canon law and in many additions to his sources inserted into the *Epitome*. Zonaras combined efforts at learned Atticizing with popular tales of natural catastrophes and curiosities. His work was translated into Slavic during the Middle Ages. The *Lexicon* known under his name does not belong to Zonaras.

BIBLIOGRAPHY

Sources. Theodor Büttner-Wobst, ed., *Joannis Zonarae Epitomae historiarum libri XVII* (1897), a critical edition of the Byzantine portion; Ludovic Dindorf, ed., *Ioannis Zonarae Epitome historiarum*, 6 vols. (1868–1875); Angelica Jacobs, ed., *Die byzantinische Geschichte bei Joannes Zonaras in slavischer Übersetzung* (1970).

Studies. M. Di Maio, "History and Myth in Zonaras' Epitome Historiarum," *Byzantine Studies / Études byzantines,* **10** (1983); Herbert Hunger, *Die hochsprachliche profane Literatur der Byzantiner,* I (1978), 416–419; A. P. Kazhdan, with Simon Franklin, *Studies on Byzantine Literature of the Eleventh and Twelfth Centuries* (1984), 59–63; Mikhail E. Krasnožen, *Tolkovateli kanoničeskago kodeksa vostočnoj cerkvi: Aristin, Zonara, i Val'samon* (1911); Franz H. Tinnefeld, *Kategorien der Kaiserkritik in der byzantinischen Historiographie von Prokop bis Niketas Choniates* (1971); K. Ziegler, "Zonaras Ioannes," in *Paulys Realenzyclopädie der klassischen Altertumswissenschaft,* 2nd ser., X(A) (1972), 718–732.

ALEXANDER P. KAZHDAN

[See also **Alexios I Komnenos; Byzantine Empire: History; Byzantine Literature; Constantine I, the Great; Historiography, Byzantine.**]

ZOROASTRIANISM, the most important religion of ancient Iran and one of the oldest living religious traditions, was preached by the prophet Zarathu-

stra, known in the West as Zoroaster. He lived probably between 1500 and 1200 B.C. among Iranian pastoralists on the southern Russian steppes. His faith spread slowly among Iranians and was adopted by Cyrus the Great of Persia before he founded the Achaemenian Empire in 550 B.C. This empire had Greeks and the Jews among its subjects, and Zarathustra's teachings have been seen as powerfully influencing early Ionian philosophy and Judaism. They also gained the admiration of Plato and his school. Alexander's conquest of the Persian Empire appears to have stimulated the growth of Zoroastrian apocalyptic literature, which gained currency in the Hellenistic world. From the second century B.C., Jews of the eastern diaspora came again under Iranian rule with the founding of the Parthian Empire, succeeded in the third century A.D. by the second Persian Empire of the Sasanians. Both had Zoroastrianism as their state religion. Zoroastrian influence has been seen strongly in Jewish writings of the intertestamentary period and in Christian eschatology and soteriology. Zoroastrianism flourished in Armenia until the fourth century A.D. and survived locally in Asia Minor until at least the sixth century. It was overthrown as the state religion of Iran by the Arabs in the seventh century, but continues as a minority religion there and as the religion of the Parsis ("Persians") of India. The conquering faith, Islam, which evolved into Shiite Islam, itself owes much to Zoroastrianism in doctrine and observance.

One reason why Zoroastrianism was so influential is that Zoroastrian rulers wielded imperial power in the Near East for about 1,000 years, and Persian administrators and colonists with their priests, the renowned magi, were present in all Achaemenian lands. Another reason is the faith's doctrinal strength. Zoroaster was a priest as well as prophet and gave his religion a profound and coherent theology. The pre-Zoroastrian Iranian faith had had a strong ethical element, linked with worship of the *ahura*s ("lords")—Mazda, lord of wisdom, and Mithra and Varuna, lords of loyalty and truth. Zoroaster, through a series of visions, saw Ahura Mazda as God himself, the one uncreated eternal being, wholly wise and beneficent, and author of all that is good. But, deeply conscious of cruelty and injustice, he also apprehended the existence of another uncreated being, Angra Mainyu ("hostile spirit"), by nature evil. To destroy him, Ahura Mazda created this world as a battleground between good and evil. He carried out the act of creation in seven stages through his holy spirit, Spenta Mainyu. He also called into being to aid him six Holy Immortals (Amesha Spentas), and through them many other divinities, called *yazata*s ("beings worthy of worship"), who included the beneficent gods of the pre-Zoroastrian faith. Angra Mainyu countered by creating evil beings, the *daēva*s. Ahura Mazda created the world first in an immaterial, ideal state, then gave it material form. Angra Mainyu invaded the material world, bringing moral and physical ills, including death. The good creation of Ahura Mazda strives against Angra Mainyu instinctively, helped by the divine powers; man should do so consciously, by deliberate choice. At death each individual faces judgment. If the good thoughts, words, and deeds outweigh the bad, the soul crosses a broad bridge and ascends to heaven. If not, the bridge contracts underfoot, and the soul falls into hell with its torments.

The aim of all virtuous striving is to bring about the salvation of the world. In the last days the world savior, the Saoshyant, will come in glory. There will be a great battle between *yazata*s and *daēva*s, good men and bad, ending in victory for the good. The bodies of those who have died earlier will be resurrected and united with their souls and the Last Judgment will take place. Metals in the mountains will melt and cover the earth in a fiery flood, which will destroy the wicked and purge hell. (By a later doctrine, first attested in the ninth century A.D., the wicked, purified by this ordeal, will survive to join the blessed.) The kingdom of Ahura Mazda will come on earth, and the blessed will rejoice everlastingly in his presence.

These doctrines appear to have been wholly new in their essentials when Zoroaster preached them, and equally revolutionary when introduced centuries later into the Near East. They are to be found, allusively, in the Gāthās (seventeen hymns composed by the prophet, and preserved in the Zoroastrian liturgy); in other texts of the Avesta (the sacred canon, closed apparently in all essentials by the end of the Achaemenian period); and in Pahlavi or Middle Persian books (Middle Persian being the language of the Sasanians). The Pahlavi literature includes translations with exegesis of Avestan texts, known collectively as the *Zand* (Interpretation). Middle Persian forms of Zoroastrian terms became widely known (for example, Ōhrmazd for Ahura Mazda and Ahriman for Angra Mainyu).

Zoroaster sought urgently to awake mankind to seek salvation. After his death the community's

hopes fixed on the coming of the Saoshyant, who is to be born of the prophet's seed, miraculously preserved, and a virgin mother. This expectation can be traced to before 550 B.C. Zoroastrians had the duty to pray five times daily before fire, symbol of righteousness. An icon cult of *yazata*s was introduced in the late fifth century B.C., but an iconoclastic movement that may have inspired Christian iconoclasm finally triumphed under the Sasanians. Traditional purity laws were extended on a dualistic basis and formed a rigid code that hindered the wider spread of the faith. The all-embracing nature of this code may have encouraged a parallel development of the Jewish one. The only major heresy, Zurvanism, developed under the Achaemenians. It was a monism, with a deity, Zurvān ("time"), postulated as the father of Ahura Mazda and Angra Mainyu; Ahura Mazda, however, was still worshiped as creator. This heresy, with a remote supreme being, a subordinate creator god, and the concept, shared with Zoroastrian orthodoxy, of three times (eternity past, present time in which good and evil are mingled, and eternity to come), was a major influence on various gnostic faiths.

During the Sasanian period Zoroastrianism came under pressure from proselytizing Buddhists, Christians and Manichaeans, and responded with intermittent persecutions. (The last against Christians was in the late fifth century.) At the time of the Arab conquest Zoroastrianism was a strong and immensely wealthy state religion, and at first it yielded only sporadically to Islam. In the ninth century Zoroastrians still formed a substantial part of Iran's population, but thereafter erosion of their numbers was more rapid. The main group of Parsis, having left in search of religious freedom, reached Gujarat, in western India, in 936; their descendants lived there in obscurity until the seventeenth century, when they began to prosper as merchants, attaining fame for their wealth, strict honesty, and general charity. In Iran their co-religionists suffered greatly during Turkish and Mongol invasions, and from the thirteenth century were reduced to a small, persecuted minority, living mostly in villages. Being impoverished and cut off from the outside world, their priests gradually lost their tradition of learning and in the end could do little but maintain essential beliefs and preserve manuscripts by copying. Rituals and daily prayers also served to inculcate beliefs. There was emphasis on strict observance of the purity laws, and standards of purity remained notably high.

BIBLIOGRAPHY

Matthew Black, "The Development of Judaism in the Greek and Roman Periods," in Matthew Black and H. H. Rowley, eds., *Peake's Commentary on the Bible* (1963); Mary Boyce, "Middle Persian Literature," in *Handbuch der Orientalistik*, IV, 2 (1968), "Iconoclasm Among the Zoroastrians," in Jacob Neusner, ed., *Studies in Judaism in Late Antiquity*, XII: *Christianity, Judaism, and Other Greco-Roman Cults*, pt. IV (1975), *A History of Zoroastrianism*, 2 vols. (1975–1982), and *Zoroastrians: Their Religious Beliefs and Practices* (1979, 3rd ed. 1987), 78–144; John R. Hinnells, "The Zoroastrian Doctrine of Salvation in the Roman World," in E. J. Sharpe and John R. Hinnells, eds., *Man and His Salvation: Studies in Memory of S. G. F. Brandon* (1973) and "Zoroastrian Influence on the Judeo-Christian Tradition," in *Journal of the K. R. Cama Oriental Institute*, 45 (1976); Werner W. Jaeger, *Aristotle: Fundamentals of the History of His Development*, Richard Robinson, tr., 2nd ed. (1948), 43, 132ff.; James H. Moulton, *Early Zoroastrianism* (1913, repr. 1972), 343–390; Jal Dastur Cursetji Pavry, *The Zoroastrian Doctrine of a Future Life from Death to the Individual Judgement*, 2nd ed. (1929, repr. 1965); Morton Smith, "II Isaiah and the Persians," in *Journal of the American Oriental Society*, 83 (1963); M. L. West, *Early Greek Philosophy and the Orient* (1971); David Winston, "The Iranian Component in the Bible, Apocrypha, and Qumran," in *History of Religions*, 5 (1966).

MARY BOYCE

[See also **Ardešir I; Avesta; Bundahishn; Dēnkard; Gāthās; Iranian Languages; Manichaeans; Pahlavi Literature; Parthians; Sasanian Culture; Sasanian History; Vidēvdād; Yašts; Zurvanism.**]

ZOSIMUS, a lawyer and *exadvocatus fisci* in Constantinople in the late fifth and early sixth centuries, and author of a strongly pagan *New History* in six books covering the years 295 to at least 410. Since Zosimus drew heavily on Eunapius and Olympiodorus, much of whose work has perished, he is an important witness to fourth- and fifth-century pagan historiography. The extent to which he copied out his sources is much disputed in detail, but in general he seems to have followed the earlier works closely. His work is also an important testimony regarding the question of Eastern attitudes to the fall of the Roman Empire in the West.

BIBLIOGRAPHY

Sources. Ludwig Mendelssohn, ed., *Zosimi: Historia nova* (1887, repr. 1963); François Paschoud, *Zosime: Histoire nouvelle*, 3 vols. (1971–1979).

Translation. Zosimus: Historia nova, James J. Buchanan and Harold T. Davis, trans. (1967).

Studies. R. C. Blockley, "Was the First Book of Zosimus' *New History* Based on More Than One Source?" in *Byzantion*, 50 (1980); Alan Cameron, "The Date of Zosimus' *New History*," in *Philologus*, 113 (1969); Walter Goffart, "Zosimus: The First Historian of Rome's Fall," in *The American Historical Review*, 76 (1971); Walter Emil Kaegi, Jr., *Byzantium and the Decline of Rome* (1968); François Paschoud, "Cinq études sur Zosime," in *Historia*, 20 (1971), repr. in his *Cinq études sur Zosime* (1975); R. T. Ridley, "Zosimus the Historian," in *Byzantinische Zeitschrift*, 65 (1972); Lellia Cracco Ruggini, "Zosimo: Ossia il rovesciamento delle 'Storie Ecclesiastiche,'" in *Augustianum*, 16 (1976), and "The Ecclesiastical Histories and the Pagan Historiography: Providence and Miracles," in *Athenaeum* (Univ. of Pavia), n.s. 55 (1977).

AVERIL CAMERON

[See also **Historiography, Byzantine.**]

ZUBAYR, AL-. See **Abd Allāh ibn al-Zubayr.**

ZURVANISM is variously defined as a heresy or a form of Zoroastrianism. Those scholars who regard it as a heresy point out that neither the Zoroastrian scriptures nor their accompanying commentaries call for worship of the god Zurvān (Zrvan, "time"). Advocates of this position further note that Zurvanism is opposed to orthodox Zoroastrianism in a number of ways; for instance, the Zurvanist tendency toward fatalism stands in sharp contrast to the orthodox Zoroastrian emphasis on free will and the responsibility of each believer to give form to his destiny by actively choosing between good and evil. Those scholars who consider Zurvanism to be a tendency within the broad range of acceptable Zoroastrian beliefs argue that it was a prominent form of Zoroastrianism for much of the period of Zoroastrian ascendancy in Iran, from the late Achaemenian period until the Arab conquest.

In the Zurvanite creation myth the eternal Zurvān desired a son and began the ritual sacrifice required for the safe birth of offspring. The rite was flawed, however, by Zurvān's doubt about the efficacy of sacrifice. As a result, Zurvān produced twins, Ahura Mazda (Ōhrmazd) and Angra Mainyu (Ahriman, the evil or hostile spirit). Angra

Mainyu, dark and foul-smelling, was the more aggressive of the two and forced his way out of the womb first. Honoring his vow to give the first-born rights of sovereignty, Zurvān granted Angra Mainyu dominion over the world, but limited his rule to a finite period of 9,000 years. After this time, Ahura Mazda, having vanquished evil within the temporal and material trap of the created world, would rule for unlimited time.

In contrast to the classical Zoroastrian dualism of the Avesta, a dualism between Spenta Mainyu, the beneficent spirit created by Ahura Mazda, and Angra Mainyu, the evil spirit, Zurvanism was essentially a monism superimposed upon an ethical dualism. By making Ahura Mazda and Angra Mainyu twin sons of Zurvān, the Zurvanists altered the original doctrine of Zarathustra that maintained that good and evil are completely separate in nature. They also lessened the importance of Ahura Mazda, the supreme being in the orthodox Zoroastrian pantheon.

It is difficult to assess the provenance or the significance of Zoroastrianism known to Christian writers of the period (to whom we owe our knowledge of the myth of Zurvān). Zurvanism provided the nomenclature for Iranian versions of the Manichaean cosmology and had an enormous influence on various gnostic traditions.

BIBLIOGRAPHY

The best summary of the controversy about Zurvanism is to be found in R. C. Zaehner, *Zurvan: A Zoroastrian Dilemma* (1955, repr. 1972), which contains translations of the relevant Zoroastrian and non-Zoroastrian texts. See also Mary Boyce, *A History of Zoroastrianism*, II (1982); and Gherardo Gnoli, "Zurvanism," in *The Encyclopedia of Religion*, XV (1987).

DALE L. BISHOP

[See also **Avesta; Manichaeans; Sasanian Culture; Sasanian History; Zoroastrianism.**]

ZWART^CNOC^C. The Armenian church of Zwart^cnoc^c (the angels) was erected near Erevan around 650/659 by the *kat^colikos* Nersēs III Išχanec^ci (Nersēs the Builder, 641–661), according to the Armenian historical accounts of Sebēos, Movsēs Dasχuranc^ci, the *kat^colikos* Yovhannēs, and a Greek inscription on one of the capitals. Constructed at the traditional site of the meeting between Trdat the Great and St. Gregory the Illu-

Reconstruction of the 7th-century church of Zwart^cnoc^c. REPRODUCED FROM JOSEF STRZYGOWSKI, *DIE BAUKUNST DER ARMENIER UND EUROPA* (1918)

minator during the period of the founding of the Armenian church in the fourth century, Zwart^cnoc^c is dedicated to the angels who appeared to St. Gregory in his vision, and by the tenth century it housed his relics.

Destroyed in the tenth century, the church was excavated in 1901–1907. Only the foundations, portions of the vaulting and walls, some capital bases, sections of piers and columns, and fragments of sculpture survive. These remains, the dimensions and load-bearing capability of the piers, and comparisons with a later Armenian copy in Ani, the church of St. Gregory (Grigor Lusaworic^c), built in the year 1000, have enabled scholars to describe the plan and propose reconstructions of the superstructure (T^coramanyan, 1905; Kuznecov, 1951; Marut^cyan, 1963; and Mnats^cakanyan, 1959 and 1971).

Erected on a stepped platform, the large, circular (*ca.* 36 m/118 ft), domed church built of tuff stone had an outer, continuous ambulatory that enclosed an inner quatrefoil defined by four huge piers. Each foil comprised six columns, except for the eastern hemicycle, which had a solid wall. A rectangular chamber on the east was annexed later. The massive central cupola set on pendentives with squinches was supported by arches that joined the four piers and were buttressed by the semidome vaults of the foils. The semidomes in turn were abutted by the ambulatory vaults. The complex system of supports attests the mastery of Armenian architects in the medium of stone construction.

According to reconstructions (T^coramanyan, Marut^cyan and Mnats^cakanyan), the exterior had a three-story elevation with cylinders of diminishing size. Each of the thirty-two sides of the first two levels and sixteen sides of the drum had windows. Round windows like those on the church model of St. Gregory at Ani appear on the first level. Much scholarly debate has centered on the type of elevation and form of the second level, if any.

Zwart^cnoc^c was lavishly decorated with blind arcades, relief sculpture, mosaics, and wall paintings. Sculptural fragments include nine exterior spandrel figures holding construction tools, a capital with the Greek monogram of Nersēs, and the magnificent eagle capitals of the piers, the only ones of this type in existence.

The origins of the church may be found in fifth- and sixth-century Syrian and northern Mesopotamian quatrefoils, but Zwart^cnoc^c is a unique monument in early medieval architecture because its dome was stone, not wood like its predecessors. In Armenia, its forms may be traced in seventh-century multi-apsed churches such as Zōravar and Irind.

Later Caucasian churches inspired by Zwart^cnoc^c include Išḥani (seventh century, erected by Nersēs), Liakit^c (seventh century), Bana (early tenth century), and St. Gregory at Ani.

BIBLIOGRAPHY

Architettura medievale armena, Roma, Palazzo Venezia, 10–30 giugno, 1968 (1968), 102; Sirarpie Der Nersessian, *The Armenians* (1969), 104–106, 110–136, and *Armenian Art,* Sheila Bourne and Angela O'Shea, trans. (1977–1978), 39–103; Step^can K. Mnats^cakanyan, *Zvartnoc, Pamjatnik armjanskogo zodčestva VI–VII BB.* (1971), with English summary; Joseph Strzygowski, *Die Baukunst der Armenier und Europa* (1918), I, 108–119, 421–427, II, 586–587, 682–687.

Lucy Der Manuelian

[See also **Ani, Monuments of; Armenia: History of; Armenian Art; Bana; Gregory the Illuminator, St.; Išḥani; Nersēs III Išχanec^ci; Trdat III/IV the Great, St.**]

The Wheel of Fortune, medieval symbol of mutability (see page 624). Miniature from Rouen, Bibliothèque Municipal, MS 1044, fol. 74. GIRAUDON/ART RESOURCE